A BIBLIOGRAPHY OF CANADIAN IMPRINTS, 1751–1800

A BIBLIOGRAPHY OF CANADIAN IMPRINTS

1751–1800

By

MARIE TREMAINE

UNIVERSITY OF TORONTO PRESS

Toronto Buffalo London

Toronto Buffalo London

First published in 1952 by University of Toronto Press.
Reprinted 1999

Printed in Canada

ISBN 0-8020-4219-8

Printed on acid-free paper

Canadian Cataloguing in Publication Data

Tremaine, Marie, 1902–1984
A bibliography of Canadian imprints, 1751–1800

Includes bibliographical references and index.
ISBN 0-8020-4219-8

1. Canada – Imprints. 2. Canada – Bibliography. I. Title.

Z1365.T7 1999 015.71 C98-932651-9

University of Toronto Press acknowledges the financial assistance to its publishing program of the Canada Council for the Arts and the Ontario Arts Council.

This reprint of Marie Tremaine's classic work of Canadian bibliographical scholarship is published as a companion to *Early Canadian Printing: A Supplement to Marie Tremaine's 'A Bibliography of Canadian Imprints, 1751–1800'* by Patricia Lockhart Fleming and Sandra Alston (Toronto: University of Toronto Press, 1999). Fully integrated with Tremaine's numerical sequence of imprints, *Early Canadian Printing* updates the entries in this volume with current library locations and references to microformat copies, and provides indexes to all of the imprints, other than newspapers and magazines (pp. 593–659). Also a sequel to Tremaine, *Early Canadian Printing* identifies and describes many previously unrecorded eighteenth-century Canadian imprints, from books and official documents to job printing such as handbills, licences, and commercial notices.

As *Early Canadian Printing* can only be understood in conjunction with Tremaine's original work, now long out of print, the University of Toronto Press is pleased to publish this photographic reprint of the original 1952 edition.

PREFACE

THIS work was begun in 1935 as a study of Canadian life and thought in the last decade of the eighteenth century. It was an attempt to digest and record the entire production of the printing press in a limited area for a limited time in the era when general communication of ideas depended on the *printed* word. In discovering what was published (even what was projected for, but failed of, publication), one might gain a useful view of the activities and preoccupations of a little society. The record of its sparse imprints, in contrast with the spate of print in our own time, might give instructive insight into both periods. As the work progressed the artificiality of the time span became apparent. That critical decade could not be isolated even bibliographically from its precedents. So the study was recast to begin with the setting up of printing presses in the various provinces which practically coincided with the beginning of effective British settlement in Nova Scotia, Quebec, New Brunswick, Island of Saint John, and Upper Canada. It was recast to bring out through the record of the imprints themselves something of the nature of the society which produced them. The material is arranged to show each year's output from all the provinces' presses.

This work includes books, pamphlets, leaflets, broadsides, handbills, and some pictorial publications recorded year by year, also newspapers and magazines, produced in the colonies now provinces of Canada, from 1751 through 1800. It includes works known to have been produced, whether they are known to survive or not. It includes works for which there was an authentic impulse for publication, that is, works projected by printers but in a sense rejected or unconfirmed by the community, and so not actually published in this country. Full bibliographical descriptions are given for items known to be extant, and any descriptive data available for items not known to survive. Information on technical production, prices, circumstances of publication, and subject matter is included as an essential part of the story that these titles tell of their time. It is my hope that *Canadian Imprints, 1751-1800* will be of interest to collectors of Canadiana and of use also to students of Canada's social background.

Mention should be made here of two microfilming projects under way as this volume goes to press. The copying programme of the Canadian Library Association's newspaper microfilming project is planned to include ultimately all newspapers listed in this bibliography. Many of the titles have already been filmed. Full particulars may be obtained from the Canadian Library Association, 46 Elgin Street, Ottawa, Ontario. The Canadian Bibliographic Centre hopes shortly to have microfilms of all books, pamphlets, broadsides, etc., included in this bibliography, of which copies are available for photographing. Over 500 titles have already been filmed. Further details may be obtained from the Canadian Bibliographic Centre, Public Archives of Canada, Ottawa, Canada.

This study was carried on during 1935-1937 under the direction of Dr. Andrew Keogh, then Librarian of Yale University, by means of two consecutive fellowship grants from the Carnegie Corporation of New York, tenable in the Department of General Studies, Graduate School, Yale University. Field work was continued for short periods each year (excepting 1940-1945) until 1947. Deep thanks are given to the Carnegie Corporation, to Dr. Keogh and his colleagues in the Sterling Memorial Library, particularly to Dr. Charles E. Rush, now Director of Libraries, University of North Carolina. I owe a special debt of gratitude to Dr. Lawrence C. Wroth for stimulus and counsel, and to his colleagues in the John Carter Brown Library; to the staff of the Public Archives of Canada who have aided me in its Manuscripts Room and Library over many years, and to Dr. W. Kaye Lamb, now Dominion Archivist, who has helped this book to, and through publication. Several obscure works sometimes only known copies, have been located mainly through the good offices and special skills of certain librarians and collectors: Dr. Allyn B. Forbes of the Massachusetts Historical Society; `Mr. Robert M. Hamilton, Assistant Librarian of Parliament, Ottawa; Mr. Gerald MacDonald of the New York Public Library; Mr. Fred G. Ketcheson, Thornhill, Ont.; Father A.-M. Morisset, o.m.i., Librarian of the University of Ottawa; Dr. James B. Childs of the Library of Congress. To the staff of the Rare Book Rooms of the Library of Congress and the New York Public Library, to the American Antiquarian Society and to Laval University, my warm thanks for their long-term hospitality. A particular word of thanks goes to my former colleagues, Florence Murray and Donalda Putnam, for reading and criticizing parts of the manuscript and to Jean Horwood for her infinite patience in the exacting task of typing it. Publication has been made possible by a grant-in-aid from the Canadian Social Science Research Council and by assistance from the Publications Fund of the University of Toronto Press. To the Council, to the Canadian Library Association and its executive secretary, Elizabeth Morton, to Dr. George Brown, editor of the University of Toronto Press, I express finally my deep gratitude.

M. T.

CONTENTS

Preface vii

List of Illustrations xi

Introduction xiii

Method of Bibliographical Description xxiii

Collections in Which Copies are Located xxvii

CANADIAN IMPRINTS, 1751-1800 1

NEWSPAPERS AND MAGAZINES 593

Printing-Offices and Biographical Notes on Printers 661

Authorities: MSS 671

Index 681

ILLUSTRATIONS

(following page 356)

I. Governor Hopson's Proclamation for forming Militia, 1753

II. Protestant Grantees of Lands of the Acadians, 1759

III. Nova Scotia House of Assembly Votes, 1762 and 1764

IV. Nova-Scotia Calendar for 1770

V. Governor Carleton's Proclamation to Succour Wounded Rebels, 1776

VI. General Burgoyne's Manifesto, 1777

VII. Montreal Citizens' Petition on Mesplet's behalf, 1778

VIII. "Every Able-bodied Seaman," 1779

IX. Notice to Refugee Loyalists, 1784

X. Scott's Brief View of the Religious Tenets, 1784

XI. St. John Island House of Assembly Journal, 1788
St. John Island Acts of the General Assemblies, 1789

XII. Samuel Neilson's Price List, 1789

XIII. Cochran's Sermon Preached at Falmouth, 1793
Viet's Sermon Preached at Sissaboo, 1799

XIV. Nova Scotia Chronicle, 1769

XV. Royal American Gazette, 1787

XVI. Courier de Québec, 1788

INTRODUCTION

THE craft of printing appeared very late upon the Canadian scene. A small press set up in Halifax in 1751 by Bartholomew Green, Jr., was, so far as we know, the first to be used anywhere in the vast area now comprising Canada. Nor was the development of the trade during the ensuing half century in the least spectacular. Between 1751 and 1800 only sixteen printing offices were opened in Nova Scotia, New Brunswick, Prince Edward Island, Quebec, and Ontario. They were located in Halifax, Shelburne, Saint John, Charlottetown, Quebec, Montreal, Newark, and York (now Toronto). In 1800, nine of them were still functioning in six of these towns.

The pages that follow do not record every item printed on these pioneer presses; time and chance have taken their inevitable toll. But so much has survived that the general picture is clear. Additional items may possibly come to light from time to time, but they are unlikely to change the picture in any significant way.

Every printer produced, or tried to produce, a newspaper. If he received a salary as official government printer, laws and legal notices filled much of his paper. If not, he probably published some official matter anyway, along with municipal regulations and notices. Advertisements were apt to be repeated without change, issue after issue. News of the outside world was copied in the main from American, British, or other Canadian papers. As local news and views were usually known before the paper appeared, they received relatively little space. Original essays, poems, and letters appeared occasionally, editorial statements rarely.

Almanacs were the colonial printer's staple. Published about the turn of the year, they included a calendar, lists of government officials, a variety of practical information, and anecdotes designed to amuse and instruct. Several variations on the standard English colonial almanac appeared in Canada. French and French-English almanacs were produced in Quebec; one in German was printed in Nova Scotia. "Sheet almanacs," with abridged data on a broadside for the wall, were popular. For many years an Indian calendar was printed in quantity for a devoted missionary to distribute among the Montagnais.

Only two magazines were published before 1800. They appeared about the same time, one in Halifax and the other in Quebec. Both contained mainly material reprinted from English and American books and periodicals. Practical articles on agriculture were a feature, for these magazines happened to appear in the era of "the Hungry Year," 1788-1789, when crop failure and immigration made future good harvests vital. Both were short-lived. Lack of subscribers and contributors (and, in Quebec, the printer's preoccupation with other work) led to their demise.

The eighteenth-century thriller was the "confession" or "true story" of a man about to be hanged, usually for theft or murder. Several sixpenny dreadfuls of the kind appeared in the larger towns at the time of executions. They invariably recorded the condemned man's repentance as well as his crime, and included a description of how his execution was carried out. That they were "best-sellers" is attested by the books of the Quebec printing firm of Brown & Gilmore, and by the fact that like the "Indian captivities" of the American colonial period, they were so literally read to pieces that very few examples survive. There is no record, incidentally, of an "Indian captivity" being produced in Canada, possibly because there was more friendly understanding between the French and the Indians than between the latter and the settlers of New England. Roman Catholic and Church of England prayers, and primers and calendars in Indian dialects were published, but no captivities.

Another regular (though non-profit-making) production of some of the offices was the "carrier's address." This consisted of verses on a broadside, which the newsboy presented to his customers at the New Year. Several examples survive from the *Quebec Gazette* and one or two other papers—enough, considering their ephemeral character, to suggest that this little compliment was a common custom of the newspaper printer. The verses are usually jingles, obviously of local origin, sometimes with a gay and plaintive charm, sometimes commenting wittily on current affairs. In view of the great dearth of spontaneous voices from that distant time these little verses, dull or sparkling, with their authentic ring, make us wish for more.

In glancing through the output of the early presses one is struck with the high proportion of legal and legislative material. In each colony the laws passed by the legislature were printed regularly after each session, usually once a year. In Nova Scotia, where enactments were passed as either "temporary" or "perpetual," they were published in two annual series. Except in New Brunswick, there were collected or revised editions of the statutes as well. Occasionally British statutes relating to the colonies were reprinted, notably the Stamp Act, the Quebec Act, and the Constitutional Act. A collected edition of such material appeared in Quebec in 1800. In Quebec, too, the mingling of two cultures after 1759 necessitated the publication of laws which were traditional to the French but unknown to the English, and of practices long customary to the English but new to French use. Cugnet's famous four-volume treatise of 1775 on the law of the *ancien régime,* and a French translation of Burns's handbook for justices of the peace, were two of the major printing efforts of the period.

The House of Assembly's *Journal* was published regularly after each session, and sometimes day by day during the session. Many proclamations, orders-in-council, and regulations were printed; those governing such matters as land grants, road building, road maintenance, post-road travel, inns, horses, and militia, give much information about the opening up of new country, and about living conditions both there and in long-settled areas.

The principal (and sometimes the sole) printer in each colony was the government or King's printer, and the printing of official publications was his duty and mainstay. He received a modest salary, which ranged upwards from the £40 a year allowed William A. Rind in Charlottetown. In Nova Scotia and Quebec the salary was £50 in 1765, and rose later to £100. In New Brunswick no salary seems to have been attached to Christopher Sower's commission as King's printer, and government work was given both to him and to a rival Saint John printer on a contract basis. King's printers sometimes held other salaried posts as well; Christopher Sower was deputy postmaster in New Brunswick, and William Rind served as clerk of the House of Assembly in the Island of St. John. In Upper Canada (Ontario) the printer's salary ranged from £80 to £100. In all the colonies the work covered by the salary included the routine printing in the *Gazette* of laws, proclamations, certain official speeches, notices, advertisements, and so on. Much additional printing, including forms of many kinds, and the laws and journals in book form, were ordered and paid for separately. Payment for still other assignments was more than occasionally in dispute.

Various factors tended to offset the advantage of a government salary. For one thing, the recipient could scarcely print material that was distasteful to the administration. In Quebec, the official printer suffered from the added handicap of having to print government material in both French and English. The firm of Brown & Gilmore complained upon both scores in 1768-1769, and although their salary was increased, accounts for extra-routine jobs continued to be a frequent matter of dispute. In 1789, Brown's nephew and successor in the business, Samuel Neilson, drew up a comprehensive price schedule for general printing and *Gazette* insertions, and this was adopted in lieu of salary. Anthony Henry of Halifax also suffered, though not in silence, under "restraint," low salary, and undetermined "duty" as government printer in Nova Scotia. His successive "Proposals," detailing the year's work for the year's salary, seem to have regularized his duties, as a royal commission as King's printer in 1788 did his status.

Surprisingly few of the items printed relate directly to the industries of the time. One is struck, for example, by the complete absence of books and pamphlets on the fur trade. The celebrated North West Company contributes no more than blank forms such as one headed *Instructions pour les voyageurs qui montent la Grande Rivière en canots.* Of all the merchant princes of Montreal, whose fur empire stretched almost to the northern and western seas, only one appears, and he is the subject of a funeral oration. The fishing industry and the grain trade are represented merely by handbills and newspaper advertisements. When, after the serious crop failure of 1788, the Government undertook to stimulate agriculture, handbills were issued and circulars were distributed through the clergy in Quebec. Agricultural societies were formed there, and also in Nova Scotia and New Brunswick. Extant publications of the societies in Quebec and Nova Scotia show that efforts were made to reprint the results of experiments and experience abroad. Other items were issued to encourage hemp production, and to suggest ways and means of eliminating the smut that was then threatening Canadian wheat.

Handbills record various trades and services, including bread and biscuit making, starch and tobacco manufacturing, watch making, the cleaning of clothes, Mrs. Ward's "scouring business," the dentist's "elegant artificial teeth," and the doctor's innoculation service. Playbills printed in Quebec by Brown and Neilson show that two or three local acting groups produced dozens of current and classic London successes in the 1780's and 1790's. One or two of the titles suggest a play of local origin or at least a local adaptation. Other facilities for entertainment and instruction are indicated: "jockey-bills" for "feats of horsemanship," handbills for the circus, the rope-dancer, a puppet ("l'automate, ou figure parlante surprenante"), concerts, lectures, etc. Although, in the nature of things, only a small fraction of the forms and handbills printed has been preserved, those that have survived have a significance for research workers and book collectors who seek printed records of ways of life and thought in the past, and who are baffled by their absence in more conventional format.

School books of an elementary sort were a staple of the colonial presses in Canada as elsewhere. Termed variously "alphabets" or primers, mainly in French or Latin in Quebec, where organized education under Catholic auspices provided a market, they were produced frequently and in quantity—and used to death, apparently, for only one or two examples from this period survive. In the later years of the century a few editions of standard European French and Latin manuals were published. In the main, however, books beyond the A-B-C level were imported. Their supply was affected by winds of war as well as weather, and their scarcity was a real hardship. In 1777 one of the seminaries wrote to a correspondent in Paris: "Si la Providence vous procure quelque circonstance favorable et que vous puissiez en profiter pour nous faire parvenir sept ou huit douzaines de livres français et autant de livres latins pour l'usage de nos classes, vous nous rendrez un service signalé."

The accomplishments of the higher French Catholic schools are impressive. They published several *palmares*, or honours lists at graduation, a couple of plays for closing exercises, and various theses defended by their students.

After the influx of Loyalists in the 1780's a province-wide school system, topped by an interdenominational college, was proposed. One of the Roman Catholic clergy connected with the Quebec Seminary wrote in support of the scheme, but it represented a minority view and only came to fruition later. English and Protestant schooling in Quebec continued to be carried on privately by clergymen and others. Small scattered schools of this sort provided no market sufficient to support the local production of textbooks, and those advertised in the newspapers were imported from England.

In Upper Canada a practising schoolmaster published, in 1795, a pamphlet calling for a liberal educational programme for children, and an examination to screen schoolmasters who scarce knew "a B from a bull's foot." The author, Richard Cockrel, printed a list of a score of mathematical books from England which he thought might be "useful to some few in this Province."

In Nova Scotia the beginnings of organized education appeared in 1789, when the Government sponsored a college (King's College) at Windsor, where an academy with English and Latin schools had been started the previous year under Church of England auspices. At the turn of the century an ineffective move towards a public school system on a provincial scale was made in the Nova Scotia Assembly. Its failure meant that school-book production on any scale was still in the future.

In sum, although the Quebec printer, serving French Canadians, did well by elementary school books, this seems not to have been true of printers elsewhere. The English settlers, fewer and newer, with less organized schooling, filled their needs from sources abroad, as did French-language schools for books that were used in relatively small quantities.

Religious works were published in a fairly wide range. Some were printed and sold in sufficient quantity to ensure a profit; others were subsidized by the Government or a religious institution. The first substantial volume produced in Quebec was a Roman Catholic catechism, published in 1765. Since no printing was done under the French régime, and since supplies from France had been cut off by war, the accumulated demand for the book was so great that a second edition was printed within a year. At least seven editions appeared before the end of the century, "Quebec Use" beginning with that of 1777. Fleury Mesplet, Montreal's first printer, who opened shop in 1776 in straitened circumstances and under close Government surveillance, worked almost entirely on devotional (and a few school) books, with the Séminaire de Saint Sulpice as sponsor. Most of the many prayer books and religious manuals published in Canada were naturally reprints of older European works, endeared by generations of use. One of Canadian origin, however, appeared in 1795. This was a collection of canticles compiled by a parish priest, Jean Baptiste Boucher-Belleville, from his own experience, as he said, especially with young people.

Protestant devotional books are conspicuously lacking in early printing in Quebec. With the exception of a few items prepared for use amongst the Indians, they were imported. In Nova Scotia, however, doctrinal disputes gave the printers almost as much work for a short time as did Roman Catholic devotional books in Quebec. Among the New Englanders who settled in Nova Scotia, Henry Alline's inspired evangelism roused enthusiasm and antipathy comparable to that caused by the New Lights in New England itself. Cutting across denominational lines, Alline's sermons and teachings drew not only converts but also doctrinal attacks from Congregationalist, Methodist, and Anglican. Long after his death, Bishop Inglis's persistent references to the evils of "enthusiasm" paid tribute to the effects of Alline's preaching.

Sermons that achieved publication usually marked some special occasion. They are remarkable for the range of denominations represented (Roman Catholic, Anglican, Congregational, Presbyterian, Methodist, and New Light), and, except in the case of the New Light sermons, for absence of doctrinal fervour and controversy. Few of them, with the exception of those from the pen of Andrew Brown, the Presbyterian, have that eloquent expression of common human experience and simple Christian ideals which gives value to such works beyond their time and occasion. The duller outpourings and more dated harangues probably better reflect in their thought and feeling the common attitudes and temper of the times: a quiet piety, occasionally rent by highly charged emotional evangelism; a preoccupation with small day-to-day affairs of home and community; loyalty and mutual helpfulness; a formal allegiance to the Crown. The sermons, charges, etc., of Charles Inglis, consecrated first Anglican Bishop of Nova Scotia in 1787, show a conscious responsibility and activity in temporal as well as spiritual affairs. With the outbreak of revolution in France, Bishop Inglis notably outspoke all other clergy except the Roman Catholic in denunciation, but when hostilities broke out between Britain and revolutionary France all churches preached holy war, even, albeit with some restraint, the dissenters in Nova Scotia.

Poetry, drama, and belles lettres appeared hardly at all from the earliest Canadian presses. Two poems, indeed, were printed in pamphlet form in Quebec, apparently in small editions for their authors, but both are remarkable rather for their then fashionable style than for poetic significance. Another, *Annapolis Royal*, a country clergyman's tribute to a beautiful valley, has an awkward gait, but expresses a feeling for the region that Canadians of a later generation recognize with sympathetic understanding.

Plans to publish collected editions of the poems of local amateurs and of a European best-seller, Robert Burns, alike failed for lack of support. The earliest days of the printing press were also the earliest days of settlement in each province except Quebec, and even there they coincided with the arrival of the first English-speaking settlers. Such practical matters as land clearing, road and home building, trade development and government were pressing and universal problems. The output of local printing offices closely reflected these pioneer activities. This is not to say that the early settlers were unlettered people. Printers and merchants frequently advertised books for sale in the newspapers, and occasionally their announcements expanded into extensive lists of the works that were available. These lists contain a higher proportion of "solid" reading matter than is usually found in a general bookseller's stock at the present day. For example, James Durward, apparently a Quebec merchant, advertised in August, 1780, as "just imported and to be sold," prayer books, psalm books, testaments, a *Biographia Britannica*, and Guthries' *History of the*

World; books on geography, divinity, philosophy, fortification, navigation, and arithmetic; the works of Savage, Churchill, Colman, Scott, Cibber, Armstrong, Ovid, Swift, Sterne, Rousseau, and others; and, finally, the *Spectator* and a collection of "Romances, Novels and Histories." A similar list of 150 works imported and advertised for sale in September, 1787, by William Brown, the Quebec printer, included, among others, the poetry of Thomson, Dodsley, Young, Goldsmith, Collins, Gray, Pope, Dryden, Milton, and Shakespeare; fiction by Fielding, Smollett, and Sterne; history and philosophy by Robertson, Cook, Wraxall, Young, Kalm, Hume, Swift, Chesterfield, Voltaire, Sully, Plutarch, Locke, Blair, Burke, and Montesquieu; works on astronomy, electricity, medicine, navigation, architecture, mathematics, and botany; grammars, dictionaries, ready reckoners, letter writers, *Every man a complete builder*, a volume entitled *Manner to secure buildings from fire*, and so on. The stock advertised by Robert Fletcher in Halifax through the 1770's and 1780's likewise contained a high proportion of current European publications, "popular" reading among the more limited reading public of that time, but now in many instances ranked as classics. It is noticeable that such advertisements increased from the time that the American Revolution caused troops and refugees to come to what is now Canada.

The number of book auctions in Quebec for which the Brown-Neilson printing office produced catalogues is impressive. As a rule they listed collections of old residents of the province, recently deceased; occasionally that of "a gentleman returned to Europe." None of these auction catalogues has survived; we know of them only through the Brown-Neilson office records. Similar collections, of which we have no record, were doubtless dispersed in Montreal and Halifax.

The first "public library" in what is now Canada was started in 1779 in Quebec. It was financed by subscription, but enjoyed the cordial support of Governor Haldimand, as is shown by his letter to a London agent dated March 2, 1779: "The Ignorance of the natives of this colony, having been in my apprehension, the principal cause of their mis-behaviour, and attachment to Interests evidently injurious to themselves, I have sought to encourage a Subscription for a public library, which more are come into, than would have been at first expected, a pretty good sum has already been raised and . . . I hope [the library] will greatly tend to promote a more perfect coalition of sentiment and union of Interests between the old and new subjects of the Crown than has hitherto subsisted."

The backing of the Roman Catholic clergy, on whose attitude the "sentiments" of the "new subjects" to some extent depended, was more tentative. A letter from M. Montgolfier, head of the Séminaire de Saint Sulpice in Montreal, to Bishop Briand, reads in part: "Je vous avoue, monseigneur, que si je contribue à cet établissement, ce ne serait, qu'à contrecœur et par un pur motif de politique chrétienne. Je suis intimement persuadé que dans tous les établissements de l'Imprimerie et de Bibliothèque publique, quoiqu'ils aient en eux-mêmes quelque chose de bon, il y a toujours plus de mauvais que de bon, et qu'ils font plus de mal que de bien, même dans les lieux où il y a une certaine police pour la conservation de la foi et des bonnes mœurs. J'espère, monseigneur, que Votre Grandeur voudra bien avoir la bonté de me donner sur cela un conseil prudent et salutaire." Bishop Briand, however, favoured the establishment of the library, gave it his own support, and influenced other French Canadians to do likewise. Its collection was developed and used, as its several published catalogues testify. By 1796 it contained 2,686 works, about equally divided between the English and French languages, and consisted mainly, like the stock of the booksellers, of recent European publications in the fields of history, philosophy, government, and belles letters.

The Quebec library was not an isolated phenomenon, for a similar enterprise functioned in Montreal in 1796 and 1797. Thomas Cary (author of *Abram's Plains*, the first Canadian poetical publication) started a circulating library and reading room in Quebec. For the other provinces there is less information available. In Nova Scotia a law library is known to have been started in Halifax, and also a library at King's College in Windsor. Collections of books were sent to Anglican clergymen by the Society for the Propagation of the Gospel. But we have no evidence of the existence of libraries for general readers in the less populous provinces until somewhat later than the period of this study.

From this rapid survey it is apparent that the staple products of the earliest Canadian presses, as of colonial presses elsewhere, were newspapers, almanacs, laws and legislative publications, handbills, printed forms, and those kinds of educational and religious publications for which there was a substantial market. Other works of various kinds, including institutional manuals, sermons, plays, and polemics, were produced in small editions for private organizations and individuals. Only rarely did the printer act as publisher in the modern sense; in that capacity he produced little more than a few "thrillers" and the complimentary carriers' addresses. He printed almost no creative works of imagination, thought, or research, either as original publications or in the form of reprints of titles published abroad. The small demand for such material was met by importing, mainly from Great Britain, current European favourites. Incidentally, the printer revealed the nature and extent of that demand by inserting advertisements in newspapers, and by occasionally producing a catalogue for a book auction or library. Nearly every printer required government work as a mainstay for his shop. Restrained by this business relationship with government, he produced almost no work relating to current political affairs that was not official in origin.

METHOD OF BIBLIOGRAPHICAL DESCRIPTION

CANADIAN publications 1751-1800 are grouped as (1) "imprints": monograph books, pamphlets, etc. (with individual issues of such periodical or serial publications as almanacs, legislative journals, and sessions laws treated as monographs) and broadsides; (2) newspapers and magazines. The "imprints" are arranged by year of the title-page imprint or colophon (excepting almanacs arranged by year of printing so far as it can be ascertained), and within each year alphabetically. Any discrepancy between date of imprint and year of actual printing is noted in the description of the item, and reference thither is made from the other year(s) concerned.

MONOGRAPHS

For books, pamphlets, leaflets,[1] and broadsheets[2] each entry is composed of heading, title, collation, contents, notes, and record of copies located. Title, collation, and contents of a perfect, normal copy are given, if possible.

The heading (in upper case) comprises the author's name, in full with dates if personal, in contemporary (eighteenth-century) official form if that of a corporate body; or, brief title. If the heading would be identical with the title (e.g. a short, supplied title) it is omitted. For convenience, almanacs are headed: Almanacs . . .; A-B-C's: Primers . . .; Carrier's addresses, by name of newspaper.

The title is transcribed in full from the title page with wording, spelling, and punctuation reproduced exactly. Line endings, case (but not font) of type, rules, ornaments, borders, etc., are indicated. Superior letters are represented superior, long s, as short s. If the work lacks title page, the bastard or caption title and colophon, if possible, are given in the same detail as title page. If the work has a title page with imprint, also a colophon, the latter is quoted at the end of the collation. If no copy of the item has been located, the title is quoted from a contemporary record (the printer's, author's, or a newspaper) if possible, and the source indicated in notes. This supplied title is enclosed in square brackets, no attempt being made to supply line endings. If no imprint appears, the place, printer's surname, and date are supplied at the end of the title within the square brackets in lower case italic. If brief imprint is supplied, or if printer's name, or place or date of printing does not appear on title page, these are given in italic in full, with authority indicated at end of collation in the form: *Printed at Quebec by Brown & Gilmore*, as recorded. . . .

Collation includes format (paper fold), register of signatures, pagination,[3] size of type-page (height by width including all marginal matter, headline,

[1]This term is used here for a single sheet (or half-sheet) folded once, forming four pages, and printed on one or more pages. It is to be distinguished from a "double broadside."

[2]A single sheet (or half-sheet) printed on both sides. In some cases important broadsheets have been given the fuller description usually limited to broadsides.

[3]For clarity, l. (for leaf) appears as *l.* when combined with numeral(s).

signature, catchword, etc.) in centimetres. In the register of signatures, unsigned sections are represented by the inferred symbol, e.g. [A] if following section is signed B, otherwise by an arbitrary symbol [*]; doubled and mixed alphabets are represented by a prefixed number and upper case, e.g. AA: 2A; Aaaa: 4A. The number of leaves in each section is represented by a superior number, e.g. A^4, $B\text{-}D^8$. In pagination, unpaged preliminary matter is specified as p.l. if the count of its pages is not continued in sequence by the paging of the text.

Contents of the recto and verso of every leaf (including blanks) in preliminary and appended matter is indicated with page, or if section is unpaged, with leaf, reference. Contents of the main divisions of the text are indicated (with inclusive pagination); their captions are given in the briefest form, not of necessity *verbatim, literatim, et punctuatim.* In sermons, the biblical text is shown.

Notes include information concerning the printing, subject matter, and author of the work, quoted, if possible, from contemporary records, although modern commentaries are occasionally cited. Details concerning the printer and his shop are repeated, if necessary to a full description of each item. If an author is entered more than once, however, general biographical information appears in one (the earliest, substantial) entry only; references to this and to other related entries are included in notes—in an attempt to make of the individual entries, an integrated record of Canadian publication during the eighteenth century. References are given to bibliographical and historical works which contain (1) information cited in this work, and (2) information on the item which does not appear in its entry here. References are not given to bibliographies, etc., which merely record the item or copies; references are given to other editions and particularly to modern reprints of the item. Works cited more than occasionally are represented by abbreviated reference and listed with detailed description in the Authorities cited at the end of the volume.

Broadsides

An attempt has been made to arrive at a form of bibliographical description which will suit both broadside and double broadside,[1] and which will accommodate in a single pattern the varying degrees of detail in which different items are described. Degrees of detail vary of necessity. Some items were examined in their original eighteenth-century broadside form. Of some, no copy of original broadside edition is available but the text has been read in eighteenth-century manuscripts or newspapers, or in a modern edition reprinted from eighteenth-century manuscript or newspaper. Of some, no copy or text could be found, but the fact of its printing is recorded beyond doubt. The description is an attempt to identify an eighteenth-century broadside in hand[2]; to indicate the

[1]The double broadside is a format indigenous to Quebec, a bilingual province. It is a two-page typographical unit on one side of a single sheet, inner margins narrow, outer margins wider, as in a book page. The text in English (usually on left) and French (usually on right) is in similar type, layout, and ornament, though sometimes the type size varies. The double broadside is usually printed on one side of a full-sheet folio or a half-sheet quarto. It is to be distinguished from a single broadside in which the text appears in English and/or French in a single type-page. Both sides of the double broadside are fully described.

[2]Cf. American Imprints Inventory, *Instructions for the Description of Broadsides.* Chicago, The Historical Records Survey, 1939. (17 *l.*) The Canadian broadsides are described on the same principle, though most of the work had been completed before the *Instructions* drawn up by the late Douglas C. McMurtrie appeared.

scope and significance of its subject matter, noting reprinted texts, also related primary or secondary material, and to locate copies of the 18th century original now extant. The broadside entry includes heading, title, colophon (if any), collation, content of text, notes and record of copies located.

Heading for official and unofficial publications is given in conventional form as for monographs.

Title or salutation is given from first word (or ornament) to the word "Greeting," (or "Proclamation") *verbatim, literatim, et punctuatim.* Upper and lower case, line endings, ornaments (but *not* ornamental capitals) are indicated. Part of title showing rank and offices of author may be omitted and indicated by . . .; title is enclosed in square brackets if not transcribed from original 18th-century-printed broadside, and line endings, etc. are omitted.

After the word *Proclamation*, the text is represented thus: <Text> but not quoted here. Then follows the closing paragraph usually beginning: Given (place, date, name of issuing official, translator, secretary; God Save the King) *verbatim, literatim, punctuatim*, line endings, upper and lower case. Unimportant words here may be omitted and indicated: . . .

Colophon (if any) is given in the fullest form like the title (i.e. upper and lower case, line endings) and introduced by the word *Colophon*.

Collation is indicated: Broadside, number of type lines, size of type-page (height by width) in centimetres. If no colophon appears, the printer's name, and the place and date of publication are given in italics. Any note on the production from printer's, or other, records is given here, unless this record has wider implications, and appears in the contents note after the text quotation.

Contents: The text is quoted to show salient points of subject matter, verbatim, using . . . or [etc.] for omitted words; if not quoted from the original broadside, the source is indicated. Notes on the subject matter are added, and reprinted editions or other pertinent references mentioned.

Copy located: If the copy would be difficult for the custodian to lay hand upon, the place where it was seen by the writer is indicated, e.g. in MSS. or newspaper file.

Though no special search has been made for works of graphic art, some wood cuts and engravings are included. Illustrations, portraits, published separately by Canadian printers are listed with any information available from the printer's accounts or advertisements, as part of the record of Canadian printing of the time.

Newspapers and Magazines

A half-century (particularly the first) in colonial printing is too short a period for more than the beginning of a newspaper bibliography. As all extant numbers of the papers were scanned for the broader purpose of this study however, it seemed worthwhile to make an informal record of the issues, noting the nature of the papers and details of their production—in the hope that even this limited record of holdings would be useful to students, and the material as a whole the basis of a more extensive work by another hand.

Most of the collections, public and private, in which copies are located, were searched between October 1, 1935 and September 30, 1937. A few were searched subsequently till 1947, and a few new locations added even while the work was in press. The collections are represented by symbols similar to those used in the Library of Congress Union Catalog, and a key to the symbols is given below.

This key does not include collections which were searched without finding eighteenth-century Canadian imprints at that time, however. Duplicate copies in a collection are noted: (2 cop.). No description of individual copies is given. Condition, mutilated or missing pages are noted only if sufficiently serious to impair the usefulness of that copy. Binding, MS annotations, marks of ownership, provenance, sales records, and prices of individual copies are noted only if significant for the use of the copy concerned. For a few items commonly found in collections of Canadiana and Americana, a note to that effect is substituted for the long record of copies.

COLLECTIONS IN WHICH COPIES ARE LOCATED OR RECORDED

Baxter	Hon. Mr. J. B. M. Baxter, Saint John, N.B. (*d.* 1946).
CSmH	Henry E. Huntington Library, San Marino, Cal.
CU	University of California, Berkeley, Cal.
CaB	British Columbia Provincial Library, Victoria, B.C.
CaN	New Brunswick Legislative Library, Fredericton, N.B.
CaNFS	York-Sunbury Historical Society, Fredericton, N.B.
CaNS	Free Public Library, Saint John, N.B.
CaNSA	New Brunswick Archives, Saint John, N.B.
CaNSC	Common Clerk's Office, City Hall, Saint John, N.B.
CaNSa	Mount Allison College Library, Sackville, N.B.
CaNU	University of New Brunswick, Fredericton, N.B.
CaNW	L. B. Fisher Memorial Library, Woodstock, N.B.
CaNs	Nova Scotia Legislative Library. Halifax, N.S.
CaNsB	Public Library, Bridgewater, N.S.
CaNsHA	Public Archives of Nova Scotia, Halifax, N.S.
CaNsHD	Dalhousie University, Halifax, N.S.
CaNsHK	University of King's College, Halifax, N.S.
CaNsWA	Acadia University, Wolfville, N.S.
CaO	Library of Parliament, Ottawa, Ont.
CaOKU	Queen's University, Kingston, Ont.
CaOLU	University of Western Ontario, London, Ont.
CaONHi	Niagara Historical Society, Niagara-on-the-Lake, Ont.
CaOOA	Public Archives of Canada, Ottawa, Ont.
CaOT	Public Library, Toronto, Ont.
CaOTA	Ontario Provincial Archives, Toronto, Ont.
CaOTL	Ontario Legislative Library, Toronto, Ont.
CaOTO	Osgoode Hall (Upper Canada Law Society and Law School), Toronto, Ont.
CaOTU	University of Toronto, Toronto, Ont.
CaP	Prince Edward Island Legislative and Public Library, Charlottetown, P.E.I.
CaQ	Quebec Provincial Legislative Library, Quebec, Que.
CaQM	Bibliothèque Civique, Montreal, Que.
CaQMA	Advocates' Library, Montreal, Que.
CaQMC	Collège de Montréal, Montreal, Que.
CaQMF	Fraser Institute, Montreal, Que.
CaQMJ	École Normale Jacques Cartier, Montreal, Que.
CaQMM	McGill University, Montreal, Que.
CaQMS	Bibliothèque de St. Sulpice, Montreal, Que.
CaQN	Seminaire de Nicolet, Nicolet, Que. (This collection was not examined by the writer, but copies of a few items are located here from references)
CaQQA	Quebec Provincial Archives, Quebec, Que.

CaQQAr	L'Archevêché, Quebec, Que.
CaQQB	Bar Association, Palais de Justice, Quebec, Que.
CaQQH	Literary and Historical Society of Quebec, Quebec, Que.
CaQQL	Laval University, Quebec, Que.
CtY	Yale University, New Haven, Conn.
DLC	Library of Congress, Washington, D.C.
Daviault	Mr. Geo.-A. Daviault, Berthier, Que.
GBLBM	British Museum, London. Copies located only in Haldimand papers (Brit. Mus. Add. Mss. 21661-21892)
GBLP	Public Record Office, London. Papers relating to Canada 1751-1800 have been searched for text of Canadian-printed enclosures.
Gordonsmith	Charles Gordonsmith, Esq., Montreal, Que. (Collection sold posthumously)
Hingston	Dr. Donald Hingston, Montreal, Que., *deceased.*
Hodgins	Collection of John George Hodgins, 1821-1912, Deputy Superintendent of Education in Ontario, sold by D. Sutherland, Toronto, Dec. 1901.
ICJ	John Crerar Library, Chicago, Ill.
Ketcheson	Fred G. Ketcheson, Esq., Thornhill, Ont.
Learmont	Collection of Joseph Bowles Learmont, 1839-1915, of Montreal, sold by Anderson Galleries, N.Y., Mar.-Apr. 1917 and Jan. 1918.
M	State Library of Massachusetts, Boston, Mass.
MB	Public Library, Boston, Mass.
MBAt	Boston Athenaeum, Boston, Mass.
MBF	Freemasons: Grand Lodge of Massachusetts, Boston, Mass.
MH	Harvard University, Cambridge, Mass.
MHi	Massachusetts Historical Society, Boston, Mass.
MWA	American Antiquarian Society, Worcester, Mass.
MiD	Detroit Public Library, Detroit, Mich.
MiD-B	Burton Historical Collection, Detroit Public Library, Detroit, Mich.
MiU	University of Michigan, Ann Arbor, Mich.
MiU-C	William L. Clements Library, University of Michigan, Ann Arbor, Mich.
Morin	Victor Morin, Esq., Montreal, Que. Since 1948 Dr. Morin has been dispersing his collection through the G. Ducharme Co., Montreal.
N	New York State Library, Albany, N.Y.
NBu	Buffalo Public Library, Buffalo, N.Y.
NBuG	Grosvenor Public Library, Buffalo, N.Y.
NN	New York Public Library, New York, N.Y.
NNB	Association of the Bar of the City of New York, New York, N.Y.
NNC	Columbia University, New York, N.Y.
NNHi	New York Historical Society, New York, N.Y.
NNHunt.	Huntington Free Library and Reading Room, New York, N.Y.
NhD	Dartmouth College, Hanover, N.H.
PHi	Pennsylvania Historical Society, Philadelphia, Penn.
PPL	Library Company of Philadelphia, Philadelphia, Penn.
RPB	Brown University Library, Providence, R.I.

RPJ	John Carter Brown Library, Providence, R.I.
WHi	State Historical Society of Wisconsin, Madison, Wis.
Webster	Dr. J. C. Webster, Shediac, N.B. Dr. Webster, who died in 1950, transferred his collection to the New Brunswick Archives, Saint John, N.B.
White	T. H. White, Esq., Shelburne, N.S.
Witton	W. P. Witton, Esq., Hamilton, Ont. Following Mr. Witton's death in 1947, his collection of Canadiana (with a few exceptions) was purchased by the Bibliothèque Civique, Montreal.

CANADIAN IMPRINTS, 1751-1800

CANADIAN IMPRINTS 1751-1800

1. HALIFAX GAZETTE

[Proposals for publishing the Halifax gazette.]

? Broadside or leaflet *printed at Halifax, N.S., at the Green > Bushell printing office, 1751-52.*

Bartholomew Green brought a printing office from Boston to Halifax in Aug., 1751. He died a few months later (in October?) and John Bushell, who had been his partner in Boston, came to Halifax in Jan., 1752, to take over the office. On Mar. 23, 1752, Bushell published the first number of the *Halifax gazette* and inserted this notice: "As many of the Subscribers to the Proposals for the publishing of this Paper, may be desirous of knowing the Cause why it hath been so long delayed, the Printer begs Leave to inform them, that the Gentleman who is possess'd of the original Subscriptions whenever desired will give them a satisfactory Account. And as the Letter-Press is now commodiously fixed for the Printing Business, all such Gentlemen Merchants, and others, as may have Occasion for anything in that Way, may depend upon being served in a reasonable and expeditious Manner by their Most Obedient, Humble Servant, John Bushell."

Bushell's enigmatic statement suggests that the *Proposals* were issued by Green or some one else, before he himself assumed the responsibility of the printing office. He published the *Halifax gazette*, 1752-61, when it was continued by Anthony Henry till 1766.

Copy located: None.

2. HALIFAX, N.S., *City*. CORONER

Halifax ss [i.e. place for seals] AN INQUISITION Indented, taken at Halifax within the said County of Halifax / the [blank] Day of [blank] in the [blank] Year of / the Reign of our Sovereign Lord GEORGE II . . . / . . . before / Samuel Shipton, Gent. Coronor [sic] . . . / . . . upon View of the Body of [blank] of [blank] aforesaid / then and there being dead, by the Oaths of [blank] / good and lawful Men of [blank] and of said [blank] within the County aforesaid; / who being charged and sworn to enquire for our said Lord the King, when, and by what / Means, and how the said [blank] came to [blank] Death: Upon their Oaths / do say, [blank] / In Witness whereof, as well I the coroner aforesaid, as the Jurors aforesaid, to this / Inquisition have interchangeably set our Hands and Seals, the Day and Year aforesaid.

Broadside: 13 lines; type-page: 20 × 23 cm. *Probably printed at Halifax, N.S., by John Bushell, 1752-60.*

A "printed blank," one of the earliest productions of the printing press in Canada.

Copy located: MHi.

3. NATHANS & HART

PRICE CURRENT. / Halifax, 175 [blank] / NEw England Rum [etc. 59 lines] / Your Humble Servants, / Nathans and Hart. / HALIFAX: Printed by John Bushell. 1752. /

fo. 2 *l.*; type-page: 31.2 × 17.5 cm. 63 lines (including the list, 59 lines, printed in 2 col. divided by ornamental rule). An identical impression of the printed matter appears on recto of each leaf; verso, blank.

This *Price current* contains a list of 99 commodities such as liquors, food stuffs, building materials, and "Produce of Halifax" (fish), with blank space for prices. It was published by a Jewish firm which advertised in the *Halifax gazette*, Apr. 13, 1752: "Just imported and to be sold by Nathans and Hart, at their Dwelling-House in Hollis Street opposite his Excellency's, for ready Money or short Credit, by Whole-sale or Retale at reasonable Rates, viz. [list of foodstuffs, etc.] and many other Articles too tedious to mention. N.B. Said Nathans and Hart buy Oyl, Blubber, &c." The firm soon ceased business, however, according to the notice: "Nathans & Hart—co-partnership is dissolved and all creditors desired to make speedy payment and avoid further trouble."—*Halifax gazette*, May 4, 1754.

Copy located: MHi.

4. NOVA SCOTIA. GOVERNOR, 1752-1756 (*Hopson*)

[Alteration of the chronological stile . . . correcting the Calendar now in use.]

Probably a broadside *printed at Halifax, N.S., by John Bushell, 1752*, and distributed by the government as resolved:

> "Resolved that the following advertisement [text not given] be printed and disposed thro the Province for the better information and Regulation of all Persons in regard to the alteration of the Chronological sile [i.e. stile] for regulating the Commencement of the Year and for correcting the Calendar now in use." —P.A.N.S., N.S. Legislative Council *Minutes*, Aug. 31, 1752.

This was Gov. Hopson's proclamation inaugurating in Nova Scotia, the use of the Gregorian calendar, which became legal in Great Britain by the Calendar (New Style) Act of 1750 (Sept. 3, 1752 to be accounted Sept. 14) and which, by another statute of the same year, was extended to the colonies. The revision of the Julian calendar conducted, 1572-82, by Pope Gregory XIII to adjust March 21 to the spring equinox and to set the beginning of the year on Jan. 1, was adopted slowly by non-Catholic countries, Great Britain being almost the last in western Europe.

Copy located: None.

5. NOVA SCOTIA. GOVERNOR, 1752-1756 (*Hopson*)

Caption title: A / CARTEL / For the Exchange of Deserters. /
French Caption: CARTEL / Pour l'Echange des Deserteurs. /

2 unsigned unpaged leaves in fo., outer pages blank, text on inner pages in 2 col. each, English and French; type-page: 29 × 20 cm. *Printed at Halifax, N.S., by John Bushell, 1752.*

Contents: p. [1-2], A Cartel, signed at end: "Given, published and signed at Halifax, this Eighth Day of November, 1752. P. T. Hopson. By His Excellency's Command, Wm. Cotterell, Secr."

The *Cartel* states (1) that English and French deserters shall be reciprocally returned, (2) that on neither side shall they be punished by death, (3) that Duquesne undertakes observance of the Cartel by other French governors in America, and Hopson enforces it within his own government, (4) that the Cartel is in force Nov. 8. 1752-Aug. 30, 1753, then becomes permanent with Duquesne's assent, or terminates on three months' notice.

The *Cartel* was drawn up and published by Hopson on the suggestion of Gov. Duquesne in a letter from Quebec, Sept. 30, 1752. Hopson answered from Halifax, Nov. 8, 1752: "Je me trouve infiniment honoré dans la confiance dont Votre Excellence me charge en me permettent seul de dresser le Cartel que vous me proposez. . . . [J'] envoye . . . quelque Copies imprimés du Cartel en Anglais et en François [etc.]."

Hopson also transmitted (from Halifax, Dec. 6, 1752) printed copies of the *Cartel*, with copies of the correspondence, to the Lords of Trade, London, for royal assent.

Copies located: GBLP (2 cop., in C.O. 217/13: No. H. 123; C.O. 217/40: No. 241).

6. NOVA SCOTIA. LAWS, STATUTES, *etc.*

Caption title: (1) / [royal arms] / At a Council holden at Halifax, on Wednes-/day the 6th of December 1752, It was enac-/ted as follows. / [ornamental rule] / AN / ACT / For the Relief of Debtors, with / Respect to the Imprisonment of their Persons. /

Colophon: [ornamental rule] / Halifax: Printed by J. Bushell, Printer to the Government. 1752. /

fo. A², [B]¹; 6 p.; type-page: 27.2 × 16 cm.

Contents: p. 1-6, An Act, etc.

This is a handsome piece, printed on crisp heavy paper with clean impression from good type. The text is laid out in formal style with marginal notes.

Copy located: CaNsWA.

7. NOVA SCOTIA. GOVERNOR, 1752-1756 (*Hopson*)

[royal arms] / PROCLAMATION for the forming of a MILITIA. / By His EXCELLENCY / PEREGRINE THOMAS HOPSON, Esq; / Captain General and Governour in Chief, in . . . Nova- / Scotia, . . . / . . . &c. / In COUNCIL. / <Text> / Done in the Council Chamber at Halifax, this Twenty-second Day of March . . . / . . . 1753 . . . / P. T. Hopson. / By His Excellency's Command, . . . / . . . / Wm. Cotterell, Secr. / God save the KING. / [ornamental rule] / HALIFAX: Printed by J. Bushell, Printer to the Government. 1753. /

Broadside: 37 lines; type-page: 34.5 × 23 cm.

Text: "Whereas I am directed by His Majesty's Royal Instructions to cause a Militia to be Established . . . I . . . issue this Proclamation . . . enjoyning all Planters, Inhabitants, and their Servants, between the Ages of Sixteen and Sixty, residing in . . . Halifax, . . . Dartmouth, and the Parts adjacent, (excepting the Foreign Settlers . . .) . . . [to] forthwith provide themselves and Servants with proper and sufficient Fire-Arms, Consisting of a Musket, Gun, Fuzil not less than three Foot long in the Barrel [etc.] . . . and appear with [firearms etc.] at such Rendezvous as shall be by Proclamation appointed . . . on or after the 22d Day of May next . . . And in Default . . . [the Planters etc.,] will be liable to the Penalty of Forty Shillings . . . [or] One Month's Imprisonment and hard Labour [etc.]."

A printed copy of the proclamation (located below) was enclosed in a letter from Gov. Hopson, Halifax, July 23, 1753, to the Lords of Trade; he states ". . . the enclosed Proclamation was Issued and it had indeed more effect than I at first expected, for on my appointing the Day [June 6], the Inhabitants did appear to the number of Six hundred and ninety two and there were but very few unfurnished with Arms and Ammunition as ordered by Proclamation. . . ."—Can.P.A., N.S."A" 52, p. 74.

The proclamation and a resolution "that an Act be forthwith prepared for the Regulation of the said Militia" appears in the Minutes of the Legislative Council, Mar. 22, 1753. It is reprinted in Akins: *Selections from public documents of Nova Scotia*, 693-94; also in J. Plimsoll Edwards: *The militia of Nova Scotia, 1749-1867*, in N.S. hist. soc. *Coll.* 17: 63-109, 1913, p. 68-69.

Copy located: GBLP (in C.O. 217 / 14: No. H. 194).

8. NOVA SCOTIA. LAWS, STATUTES, *etc.*

[An Act for establishing and regulating a Militia.]

? fo. leaflet about 4 p., *printed at Halifax, N.S., by John Bushell, 1753.*

This act was passed by the governor-in-council May 10, 1753, in 21 sections or clauses, and amended July 18, 1753. The publication was advertised by Bushell: "The Act of this Government for establishing and regulating a Militia, also an additional Act to the same, to be sold by the Printer hereof."—*Halifax gazette*, Aug. 4, 1753.

It was published apparently in a small edition, for Bushell reprinted the text of the Act of May 10, 1753, in the *Halifax gazette*, Jan. 5, 1754 (where it occupies all of the first page, and concludes on the first page of Jan. 12, 1754) with the introductory note: "The following Act of this Province for establishing and regulating a Militia, being in the Hands of but a few Persons: we thought the publishing it at this Time of Military Watches might not be unacceptable to our Readers."

Copy located: None.

9. NOVA SCOTIA. TREATIES

Caption title: [ornamental rule] / TREATY, / OR, / Articles of Peace and Friendship re-/newed, between / His EXCELLENCY / Peregrine Thomas Hopson, Esq; / Captain General and Governor in / Chief, in and over His Majesty's / Province of Nova-Scotia or Acca-/die, Vice Admiral of the same, / and Colonel of one of His Majes-/ty's Regiments of Foot, and His / Majesty's Council on Behalf of / His Majesty; / AND / Major Jean Baptiste Cope, / Chief Sachem of the /

Tribe of Mickmack Indians, inha-/biting the Eastern Coast of the / said Province, and Andrew Had-/ley Martin, Gabriel Martin, and / Francis Jeremiah, Members and / Delegates of the said Tribe, for / themselves and their said Tribe, / their Heirs, and the Heirs of their / Heirs forever; / Begun, made and / concluded in the Manner, Form / and Tenor following, Viz, /

Colophon: HALIFAX: Printed by JOHN BUSHELL, Printer to the / Government. 1753. /

fo. 4 p.; type-page: 27.7 × 16.6 cm. Printed in 2 col., English and French.

Contents: p. [1]-4, Treaty, etc. signed at end: "Halifax, this Twenty-Second Day of November, 1752, in the Twenty-Sixth Year of His Majesty's Reign. P. T. Hopson, Chas. Lawrence, Benj: Green, Jno. Salusbury, Willm. Steele, Jno. Collier. [signed also:] Jean X his Mark Baptiste Cope, Andree X his Mark Hadley Martin, François X his Mark Jeremie, Gabriel X his Mark Martin."

This work was published according to an order: "that the Treaty of Peace lately made with the Indians be printed."—P.A.N.S., N.S. Legislative Council *Minutes*, Dec. 22, 1752.

The text of the treaty and a resolution to issue a proclamation announcing the treaty and prohibiting acts of war against the Indians is recorded in N.S. Legislative Council *Minutes*, Nov. 22-24, 1752 and printed in Akins: *Selections from public documents of Nova Scotia*, 683-86.

Copies located: NN (Brinley no. 5492, Sabin no. 33004); NNHi (Rufus King collection).

10. NOVA SCOTIA. LIEUTENANT-GOVERNOR, 1753-1756 (*Lawrence*)

[royal arms / Charles Lawrence Esq., / Lieutenant Governor and Commander in Chief of His Majesty's / Province of Nova Scotia, or Acadie. / A Proclamation. / <Text> Given at Halifax, this 14th Day of May, 1756, . . . By His Excellency's Command, Chas. Lawrence. Wm. Cotterell Secr. God Save The King.

Colophon: Halifax: Printed by J. Bushell, Printer to the Government, 1756.]

Broadside: about 13″ × 5″, described and reprinted by James S. Macdonald, in *Memoir of Lieutenant-Governor Michael Francklin*, in N.S. hist. soc. *Coll.* 16: 7-40, 1912, p. 11-12, from which this entry is taken.

Text: "Whereas notwithstanding the gracious Offers of Friendship and protection made by us, in his Majesty's Name, to the Indians inhabiting this Province . . . the Indians have of late . . . carried away divers of his Majesty's Subjects. . .

"For these causes We . . . authorize and command all Officers, civil and military, and all His Majesty's Subjects, to annoy, distress, take and destroy the Indians inhabiting the different parts of this Province. . .

"And we do hereby promise . . . a Reward of Thirty Pounds for every male Indian Prisoner, above the Age of Sixteen Years, brought in alive; for a Scalp of such Male Indian Twenty-five Pounds and for every Indian Woman or Child brought in alive; [etc.]."

Copy located: None.

11. NOVA SCOTIA. EXECUTIVE COUNCIL

[Province of Nova Scotia. Council Chamber, Halifax 3d January, 1757 <Text: Resolutions of the Governor in Council respecting the calling of an Assembly in that Province, signed:> Chas. Lawrence, By His Excellency's Command with the Advice and Consent of His Majesty's Council. I. Duport, Secr. Conc.]

Broadside: text in 2 col.; paper page: 18″ × 14″. Probably *printed at Halifax, N.S., by John Bushell, Jan. 3-Mar. 12, 1757*, for one of the groups of complainants against Gov. Lawrence's delay in establishing a House of Assembly (the several groups are described by J. B. Brebner in *New England's outpost* (New York, 1927), 255 n.; and the governor's attitude set forth by D. C. Harvey in *Governor Lawrence's case against an assembly* in *Canadian historical review*, 13: 184, June, 1932.

These resolutions adopted a detailed plan for the election of a representative assembly, drawn up by the Executive Council during Dec., 1756. An elective assembly was an integral part of the system of government planned for Nova Scotia by the Board of Trade in 1751. Its inauguration, however, had been postponed repeatedly by Gov. Lawrence. Agitation, especially of recent settlers from New England, and pressure from the Board of Trade, induced the governor to execute these resolutions on May 20, 1758. The House of Assembly, duly elected, met for the first time in Oct., 1758.

Copy located: GBLP (in C.O. 217 / 16: No. I, 39, Jan. 3, 1757). This copy was enclosed in a letter to the Lords of Trade, dated at Halifax, Mar. 12, 1757, signed by Jonathan Belcher, Jno. Collier, Robt Grant, Charles Morris, members of the Executive Council. The letter states that though "the inclos'd printed preliminaries [measures the most expedient for summoning a House of Representatives] dated January 1757 were unanimously resolved the Governor still delays writs for election of members."

12. NOVA SCOTIA. LIEUTENANT-GOVERNOR, 1756-1760 (*Monckton*)

[Royal arms] / By the Honourable / ROBERT MONCKTON, / Lieutenant Governor and Commander in Chief of His Majesty's Province of Nova-/Scotia, or Accadie, &c. &c. &c. / A PROCLAMATION. / <Text> [ornamental rule] / HALIFAX: PRINTED by John Bushel [sic], Printer to the Government. /

Broadside: type-page: 33 × 22.2 cm.

The text states ". . . that the several Islands and Colonies belonging to the French in America, have in times of war been frequently supplied with provisions of various kinds, by means of trade carried on from His Majesty's islands & colonies to the colonies . . . [of] the Dutch and other neutral powers. . . . We do forthwith give immediate directions that an embargo be laid upon all ships & vessels clearing out with provisions except those . . . to any other of His Majesty's colonies [etc.]. Given at Halifax, this 26th Day of January, 1757, and in the 30th Year of His Majesty's Reign. Robt Moncton. By Command of the Lieut. Governor, Archd Hinshelwood, D.Sec. God Save the King."

Copy located: Henry Stevens Sons & Stiles, booksellers, London, who kindly supplied the description above, Dec. 3, 1937, and listed the item in their catalogue, *The sea, voyages, travel, etc.*, issued June, 1941, no. 341.

13. NOVA SCOTIA. GOVERNOR, 1756-1761 (*Lawrence*)

[royal arms] / By His EXCELLENCY / CHARLES LAWRENCE, Esq; / Captain-General and Governor in Chief in . . . / . . . Nova-Scotia. . . / . . . &c. / A PROCLAMATION. / <Text> / Given . . . at Halifax, this Twelfth Day of / October, 1758 . . . / Chas. Lawrence. / By His Excellency's Command . . . / . . . / Jno. Duport, Sec: Conc: / GOD save the KING. / A DESCRIPTION of the Lands [etc., in 15 lines] / [rule] / HALIFAX: Printed by J. BUSHELL, Printer to the Government. 1758. /

Broadside: 45 lines; type-page: 36.8 × 18.4 cm.

The text of the proclamation states that: "Whereas by the late Success of His Majesty's Arms in the Reduction of Cape-Breton . . . [and other French Settlements] . . . a favourable Opportunity now presents for the peopling and cultivating, as well the Lands vacated by the French, as every other Part of this valuable Province"; Lawrence is ready to receive proposals for settling the lands.

The *Description* describes 100,000 acres of plow-lands, 100,000 acres of grass lands, also wild timber lands. Appended is note: "Proposals will be received by Mr. Hancock at Boston, and by Messrs. Delancie and Watts at New York to be transmitted to the Governor . . . at Halifax."

By this proclamation the lands of the expelled Acadians were thrown open to settlers from New England and other colonies. This proclamation, description, and notice were published in Boston, in a proclamation of the governor of Massachusetts, Oct. 31, 1758, and reprinted widely in colonial newspapers of the day. They are also reprinted in W. O. Raymond: *Colonel Alexander McNutt and the pre-loyalist settlements of Nova Scotia*, in Royal Society of Canada. *Proceedings*, ser. 3, v. 5, sec. 2, p. 23-115, 1911, p. 104-05.

Copy located: GBLP (in C.O. 217 / 16: No. I, 87).

14. NOVA SCOTIA. GOVERNOR, 1756-1761 (*Lawrence*)

[By Charles Lawrence, Esq; . . . A Proclamation <Text> Given in the Council Chamber at Halifax, this fourteenth Day of November . . . 1758, . . Chas Lawrence. By His Excellency's Command, with the Advice of His Majesty's Council, Jno. Duport, Sec. Conc.]

Broadside: *Printed at Halifax, N.S., by John Bushell, 1758.*

The text states that in view of the great wages given to artificers and labourers, the extravagant prices of provisions, the scarcity of vegetables and milk for the army, on orders of General Amherst, officers are to permit and encourage men to work for the inhabitants, at a rate of not more than 18*d.* a day for artificers; 6*d.* a day for labourers. Gov. Lawrence hereby proclaims that he is "ready and zealous to give all countenance to a Design so laudable and calculated to promote . . . Agriculture . . . and Commerce."

Copy located: GBLP (in C.O. 217 / 16: No. I, 88, 14 Nov. 1758. This copy was enclosed in Gov. Lawrence's despatch to the Lords of Trade, dated Halifax, Nova Scotia Dec. 26, 1758, which states: "Your Lordships will perceive by the enclosed

Proclamation dated in November [14, 1758] that I have endeavour'd to Avail myself of . . . the Arrival of troops not quarter'd before in any part of this Province for reducing the enormous price of labour . . . the benefitt will be universally felt . . . particularly by such as I esteem the most valuable, those who engage in Agriculture and the fishery").

15. GREAT BRITAIN. ADJUTANT GENERAL'S OFFICE

[ornamental rule] / EXPLANATIONS / OF THE / Manual Exercise for the Foot; / WITH / Some General Field-Directions. / [ornamental rule] / HALIFAX: / Printed and Sold by J. Bushell, 1759. / [ornamental rule] /

4to. [A]-D^4, E 1 + ?; 34 + ? p. (p. 35 to end wanting in only copy seen); type-page: 15 × 11.5 cm.

Contents: p. [1], t.-p.; p. [2], blank; p. [3]-5 Exercise for the Foot, June, 1757; p. 6-23, The Manual Exercise; p. 24-26, Order of the 18th April, 1756; p. 27-34+? Directions.

Copy located: MWA (p. 35 to end wanting).

16. NOVA SCOTIA. GOVERNOR, 1756-1761 (*Lawrence*)

[Province of Nova Scotia. By His Excellency Charles Lawrence Esq; . . . A Proclamation <Text> Given in the Council-Chamber at Halifax, this third day of October 1759 . . . Chas. Lawrence. . . . J^{no} Duport, Sec. Conc: God Save the King.]

Broadside: *Printed at Halifax, N.S., by John Bushell, 1759.*

Text forbids exaction of money from persons applying for land grants.

Copy located: GBLP (in C.O. 217 / 16: No. I, 94, Oct. 3, 1759. Two copies apparently enclosed in Gov. Lawrence's despatch to Lords of Trade, dated Halifax, Sept. 20, 1759. This despatch includes a detailed account of the success of proclamations of Oct. 12, 1758, and Jan. 11, 1759, in attracting settlers from New England, but no reference to this enclosed proclamation of Oct. 3, 1759).

17. NOVA SCOTIA. HOUSE OF ASSEMBLY

[Votes of the House of Assembly of the Province of Nova-Scotia. ? *Printed at Halifax, N.S., by John Bushell, 1759.*]

The House of Assembly met in its first session, Oct. 2-Dec. 21, 1758, Feb. 1-Apr. 17, 1759, and apparently had its *Journal* printed seriatim, for on Mar. 5, 1759, the clerk of the Council brought down a message: "the Council are informed that the Printer delays printing the Laws that have been enacted, alledging that he is employed in printing the Journals of the House of Representatives. The council in consequence of two messages from the Assembly that their constituents were murmuring for want of publication of the Laws . . . passed the Revised Laws with expedition and they therefore desire that the Assembly will countermand their order to the Printer that there be no further reason for uneasiness among the Inhabitants." The House ordered the printer to postpone printing the *Votes* of the House of Assembly until he had printed the *Revised Laws*, unless he could print the former without obstructing the latter.—N.S., H. of As. *Journal*, Mar. 5, 1759, in Can.P.A., N.S. "D" 2.

The laws were published accordingly. But whether Bushell (who had the only printing office in the province) completed printing the *Journal*, or how it was issued in this and the following session, remains unknown. In the provincial government's official file of Assembly *Journals*, the first four sessions (1758-60) are in MS.

Copy located: None.

18. NOVA SCOTIA. LAWS, STATUTES, *etc.*

Caption title: (1) / [ornamental rule] / An Act for Quieting of Possessions to the Protestant Grantees / of the Lands formerly occupied by the French Inhabitants, / and for preventing vexatious Actions relating to the same. /

Colophon: [ornamental rule] / HALIFAX: Printed by JOHN BUSHELL, Printer to the / GOVERNMENT. 1759. / [ornamental rule] /

A single sheet printed on both sides, 2 p.; type-page: 27.5 × 15.5 cm.

Contents: p. 1-2, 33 Geo. II c.3, passed at Halifax, 1759. The preamble states that whereas grants of land in Nova Scotia made under the French administration are invalid; and whereas the French settlers who refused to take oath of allegiance to King George II were removed and their lands included in township grants made to many substantial and industrious farmers, protestants, from the neighbouring colonies; and whereas some doubts have arisen among persons intending to settle the lands, concerning the title of the former French inhabitants "Be it enacted by His Excellency the Governor, Council and Assembly . . . that no Action shall be retained in any of his Majesty's courts of Record in this Province for the Recovery of any of the Lands . . . by Virtue of any former Right . . . of the former French Inhabitants [etc.]."

Copy located: GBLP (in W.O. 34 / 11: 185-186).

19. NOVA SCOTIA. LAWS, STATUTES, *etc.*

Caption title: [ornaments] / At the GENERAL-ASSEMBLY of the / Province of Nova-Scotia, begun and / holden at Halifax, on Monday the / 2^{d} Day of October, 1758, and in / the 32^{d} Year of His Majesty's Reign. / [ornamental rule] /

fo. A-D^{2}, D-2F^{2}; 111 [i.e. 115] + [3]p. *Printed at Halifax, N. S., by John Bushell, 1759.*

Contents: p. [1]-111, 32 Geo. II c. I-XXXV, acts passed in the first session of the first assembly, Oct. 2-Dec. 21, 1758, Feb. 1-Apr. 17, 1759; p. 111 verso, blank; p. [1-3] at end, "Index to the Laws of Nova Scotia" (a contents table listing the acts passed in the order of their appearance in the preceding pages); p. [3] verso, blank.

After sig. D, p. 16, an extra section is inserted also with signature "D" and each of its four pages also numbered 16. This section contains "The Resolution or Act referred to, and confirmed in the foregoing Act" on original p. 16.

The sessions laws 1758-66 bore no chapter number till they appeared in a revised edition (No. 111 and No. 114). The copies located at Acadia University are those used by Chief Justice Belcher for the revision and show his MS. numbers, notes, etc. They were published in a single series for each session till 1766, then in two series, perpetual and temporary acts, continuing the distinction made in the revised edition.

Though without printer's name or date, this work was certainly printed at John Bushell's printing office in Halifax. But the fact that he is known to have been ill, together with the typographic style of the publication, suggest that the printing was actually done by Bushell's young assistant and successor, Anthony Henry. Though paged continuously, the text is broken by blank spaces following acts which end mid-page—the blank page-end embellished, in Henry's characteristic fashion, with rows of ornament in tasteless array. This work was apparently issued in parts, as soon as printed (hence the number of acts beginning on a new page), for its publication was awaited with impatience (*see* No. 17 *note*).

Copies located: CaNsWA (p. 3-4 wanting); GBLP (2 cop. in C.O. 219 / 6).

20. NOVA SCOTIA. LAWS, STATUTES, *etc.*

Caption title: (112) / [ornaments] / At the GENERAL-ASSEMBLY of the / Province of Nova-Scotia, begun / and holden at Halifax, on Mon-/day the 2^{d} Day of October, 1758, / in the 32^{d} Year of His Ma-/jesty's Reign, and there continued / by Prorogation untill Wednesday / the First Day of August 1759, in / the 33^{d} Year of His Majesty Reign. / [ornamental rule] /

fo. sig. 2F-2H^{2}; p. 112-122; paged in continuation of No. 19, even numbers on rectos. *Printed at Halifax, N.S., by John Bushell, 1759.*

Contents: p. 112-122, 33 Geo. II c. I-VII, acts passed in the second session of the first assembly, Aug. 1-13, 1759.

Copies located: CaNsWA; GBLP (in C.O. 219 / 6).

21. PONTBRIAND, HENRI MARIE DUBREUIL de, *bp. of Quebec*, 1708-1760

HENRI MARIE DUBREIL DE PONTBRILLANT. / Par la Miséricorde de Dieu et la Grace du Saint Siège, Evêque de Québec, Conseiller du Roi en tous ses / Conseils, au Clergé et aux Fidèles de notre Diocèse, Salut et Benediction en Notre Seigneur J.C. / [29 lines text] / Sera le présent Mandement lu et publié au Prône des Messes Paroissiales le / premier Dimanche après la réception d'icelui. Donné à Québec, sous notre Seing et / le Sceau de nos Armes et la souscription de notre Secretaire. / (Ainsi signé.) H.M. EV. DE QUEBEC. / Ces Prières publiques dureront jusqu'au premier Octobre. / Par MONSEIGNEUR, / HUBERT, PTRE. SEC. /

Broadside: 39 lines; type-page: 21.2 × 15 cm.

The text begins: "De tous cotés, nos trés-chers Frères, l'Ennemi fait des préparatifs immenses, ses forces au moins six fois supérieures aux notres se mettent déja en mouvement; nos préparations sont plus lentes, le Fleuve est à peine entièrement navigable, les semailles qui pressent . . . vous retiennent dans les Campagnes . . . Tout semble nous manquer à la fois et jamais la Colonie ne s'est trouvée dans un état si critique et si dangereux. . . . A ces causes, Nous avons ordonné [etc.]" then follow the bishop's directions for procession and prayers for divine assistance in defence of Quebec against the English.

Said to have been printed in Quebec by Bishop Pontbriand in 1759, this printed mandement is similar (with minor variations in wording and spelling) to Bishop Pontbriand's mandement dated at Quebec, Feb. 17, 1759, printed (from MS.) in Têtu and Gagnon: *Mandements de Québec,* 2: 133-34; also to his mandement of Apr. 18, 1759, translated in Wm. Smith's *History of Canada* (2 v., Quebec, 1815), 1: 277-80.

There is nothing in the text or appearance of this broadside and No. 22 to indicate that they were printed at the time the mandements were issued. The paper, a closely integrated wove, with some non-linen content (and the watermark EB in one copy of No. 22) was not in use in 1759. Wove paper, first produced for John Baskerville, the English printer, in small quantities from about 1757 and introduced into France in 1777, became generally used in England in the 1780's and began to appear occasionally in Canada in the 1790's.

Moreover no printing press was in the bishop's possession at the time of his death in 1760 (Fauteux: *Introduction of printing into Canada,* 69).

The words "(Ainsi signé)" before the bishop's signature in both No. 21 and 22 and the words "Et plus bas, par Monseigneur" before the secretary's, in No. 22 suggest that these broadsides were printed later by some churchman or antiquary interested in the appearance and authenticity of the documents rather than by the bishop, intent on saving the colony from the English. Both broadsides have the appearance, in paper and typography, of work produced after 1810.

They are recorded as the earliest Quebec (province) imprints, however, in Gagnon: *Essai de bibliographie canadienne,* I: no. 2780 (with facsim. illus.) and D. C. McMurtrie: *The first printing in the province of Quebec* (Chicago, 1928).

Copies located: CaQM; CaQQL.

22. PONTBRIAND, HENRI MARIE DUBREUIL DE, *bp. of Quebec,* 1708-1760

HENRI MARIE DUBREIL DE PONTBRILLANT, / Par la Miséricorde de Dieu et la Grace du Saint Siège, Evêque de Québec, Conseiller du Roi en tous ses / Conseils, au Clergé Séculair et Regulier et à tous les Fidèles de notre Diocèse, Salut et Bénédiction / en Notre Seigneur J.C. / <Text [43 lines]> / Ces Prières se continueront jusqu'au vingt et un de May, excepté le Temps de / Pâque . . . / . . . Donné à Montréal sous notre Seing, le Sceau de nos Armes et la sous- / cription de notre Secretaire, ce vingt huit Octobre 1759. / (Ainsi signé) H.M. EV. DE QUEBEC. / Et plus bas, par MONSEIGNEUR, / HUBERT Secretaire. /

Broadside: 54 lines; type-page: 28.4 × 15 cm.

The text begins: "Il n'est personne parmi vous, Nos très-chers Frères, qui ne ressente la triste situation de cette colonie [etc.]." It continues, pointing out the peril of New France, the sins of its inhabitants, then recommending reform and prayer and ordering the continuance of special prayers for New France also services and masses for Montcalm and others who died in defence of Quebec.

This mandement, issued after the fall of Quebec and before the capitulation of Montreal, is printed also in Têtu and Gagnon: *Mandements de Québec*, **2**: 141-42.

This broadside, said to have been printed at Montreal by Bishop Pontbriand in 1759, was probably printed in the early part of the 19th century (*see* No. 21 *note*). It is reproduced in D. C. McMurtrie: *The first printing in the province of Quebec* (Chicago, 1928).

Copies located: CaQM; CaQQL.

23. NOVA SCOTIA. HOUSE OF ASSEMBLY

[Votes of the House of Assembly of the Province of Nova-Scotia. *Printed at Halifax, N.S., by John Bushell, 1759-60.*]

The House met in the first session of the second assembly, Dec. 4, 1759-Mar. 29, 1760. On Dec. 11, 1759, it "resolved that the Minutes of the House be printed weekly, and that Mr. Salter, Burbridge and Deschamps be a committee to correct the said Minutes and report the same to the House every Monday morning during the sitting of the House."

The resolution was duly executed, and on Saturday, Dec. 15, 1759, "the Committee . . . reported the Minutes to December 8, which being read, were ordered to be printed."—N.S., H. of As. *Votes*, 1759.

Copy located: None.*

24. NOVA SCOTIA. HOUSE OF ASSEMBLY

[Votes of the House of Assembly of the Province of Nova-Scotia. *Printed at Halifax, N.S., by John Bushell, 1760.*]

The House met in its second session of the second assembly, Sept. 8-27, 1760, and may have had its *Votes* printed as in the previous session.

Copy located: None.*

25. NOVA SCOTIA. LAWS, STATUTES, *etc.*

Caption title: [At the General Assembly of the Province of Nova-Scotia . . . the 4th Day of December, 1759.]

Note: title above is not transcribed from copy.

fo. A-H^2, [I]^1; 33 p. *Printed at Halifax, N.S., by John Bushell, 1760.*

Contents: 33 Geo. II c. I-XXII, acts passed in the first session of the second assembly, Dec. 4, 1759-Mar. 29, 1760; p. 33 verso, blank.

Copy located: CaNsWA.

*The Nova Scotia Assembly's still extant file of its printed *Journal* included the *Votes* previous to 1761 in MS. only, when the file was indexed by Uniacke in 1789. So it seems not unlikely that the *Votes* for these sessions remained unprinted despite the order of the House to print.

26. NOVA SCOTIA. LAWS, STATUTES, *etc.*

Caption title: [At the General Assembly of the Province of Nova-Scotia . . . the 8th Day of September, 1760.]

Note: title above is not transcribed from copy.

fo. sig. K-P²; p. 35-56, 1 *l.*, paged in continuation of No. 25. *Printed at Halifax, N.S., by John Bushell, 1760.*

Contents: p. 35-56, 34 Geo. II c. I-XX, acts passed in the second session of the second assembly, Sept. 8-27, 1760; 1 *l.* at end, blank.

Copy located: CaNsWA.

27. NOVA SCOTIA. ADMINISTRATOR, 1760-1761 (*Belcher*)

[Account of Ceremonial at proclaiming H.M. George III, at Halifax, Feb. 11, 1761.]

? Broadside: *Printed at Halifax, N.S., by ? Anthony Henry, 1761.* (Henry succeeded to John Bushell's printing office on the latter's death, about Feb., 1761.)

This was prepared according to instructions from the Lords of Trade, London, Oct. 31, 1760, "to proclaim His Majesty . . . in the most solemn manner and most proper parts of the Province, and to return a Speedy Account of the Proceedings thereon."

The proclamation begins: "Whereas it hath pleased Almighty God to call to his mercy our late Sovereign Lord King George the Second . . . we therefore the President . . . and members of the Council . . . do hereby . . . publish & proclaim . . . George, Prince of Wales is now . . . become our only and lawful Sovereign [etc.]. Given in the Council Chamber at Halifax this 11th day of February 1761, in the First year of His Majesty's Reign. God Save the King."

The Account of Proceedings begins: "The President and Council being assisted by the officers Civil and Military and the Principal Inhabitants, on the 11th Instant, proceeded from the Court House in the following Order, vizt First a Company of Grenadiers . . . His Most Sacred Majesty was proclaimed amidst the acclamations of the People, at the five following Places vizt At the Court House Door [etc.]."

The MS. text of *Account of Ceremonial*, including notes of instruction to the printer concerning layout, etc., is in P.A.N.S., v. 219, no. 98-99 (*N.S. Miscellaneous papers, 1748-63*, v. 1). The MS. text of the proclamation, and related correspondence, and of the *Account* is in Can. P.A., N.S. "B" 10: 116-25.

Copy located: None.

28. NOVA SCOTIA. HOUSE OF ASSEMBLY

Caption title: [Votes of the House of Assembly for the Province of Nova-Scotia, etc.]

Note: title above is not transcribed from copy.

fo. A-L², [M]¹; 45 p.; type-page: 26 × 13.3 cm. *Printed at Halifax, N.S., by Anthony Henry, 1761.*

Contents: p. 1-45, Journal and votes of the first session of the third assembly, July 1-Aug. 15, 1761; p. 45 verso, blank.

This is the earliest printed *Journal* of the House of Assembly located in Canada, though there is evidence that previous sessions' records may have been printed.

Anthony Henry succeeded to John Bushell's printing office, the only one in Nova Scotia, about Feb., 1761.

Copies located: CaNs; CaNsHA; CaP (p. 1-20, 37-40, 45 wanting).

29. NOVA SCOTIA. LAWS, STATUTES, *etc.*

Caption title: (57) / [ornaments] / At the GENERAL ASSEMBLY of / the Province of Nova-Scotia, / Begun and holden at Halifax, on / Wednesday the First Day of July, / 1761, and in the First Year of / His Majesty's Reign. / [ornamental rule] /

fo. p. 57-92 + [7] p.; paged in continuation of No. 26. *Printed at Halifax, N.S., by Anthony Henry, 1761.*

Contents: p. 57-92, 1 Geo. III c. I-XIX, acts passed in the first session of the third assembly, July 1-Aug. 15, 1761; p. [1-7] at end, Index to the second session (this is a contents table of the printed publications of the laws, from the second session of the first assembly to the first session of the third assembly inclusive, Aug., 1759-61).

Copy located: CaNsWA.

30. NOVA SCOTIA. LAWS, STATUTES, *etc.*

Caption title: [At the General-Assembly of the Province of Nova-Scotia . . . the 17th Day of March, 1762.]

Note: title above is not transcribed from copy.

fo. p. 93-115; paged in continuation of No. 29. *Printed at Halifax, N.S., by Anthony Henry, 1762.*

Contents: p. 93-115, 2 Geo. III c. I-XI, acts passed in the second session of the third assembly, Mar. 17-Aug. 28, 1762; p. 115 verso, blank.

Copy located: CaNsWA.

31. NOVA SCOTIA. HOUSE OF ASSEMBLY

Caption title: [Votes of the House of Assembly of His Majesty's Province of Nova-Scotia.]

Note: title above is not transcribed from copy.

fo. [A]-S^2, T^1; 71 p. + [3] blank pages between p. 33-34; even numbers thereafter on rectos. *Printed at Halifax, N.S., by Anthony Henry, 1763.*

Contents: p. 1-71, Journal and votes of the second session of the third assembly, Mar. 17-Aug. 28, 1762.

The House "ordered that the Votes of the last [i.e. second] and of the present [i.e. third] session be printed."—*Journal and votes*, May 7, 1763. The following year it "voted that £41.0.0. be paid to Anthony Henry for printing the Votes of Assembly in 1762 and 1763."—N.S., H. of As. *Journal*, Apr. 9, 1764.

Copies located: CaNs; CaNsHA.

32. NOVA SCOTIA. HOUSE OF ASSEMBLY

Caption title: [Votes of the House of Assembly of the Province of Nova-Scotia.]

Note: title above is not transcribed from copy.

fo. A-F²; 24 p.; *Printed at Halifax, N.S., by Anthony Henry, 1763.*

Contents: p. 1-24, Journal and votes of the third session of the third assembly, Apr. 25-July 21, 1763.

Copies located: CaNs; CaNsHA.

33. NOVA SCOTIA. HOUSE OF ASSEMBLY

Caption title: [Votes of the House of Assembly of the Province of Nova-Scotia.]

Note: title above is not transcribed from copy.

fo. sig. G-[P², Q¹]; p. 25-61, 1 *l.* paged in continuation of No. 32. *Printed at Halifax, N.S., by Anthony Henry, 1763.*

Contents: p. 25-61, Journal and votes of the fourth session of the third assembly, Oct. 19-Nov. 26, 1763; p. 61 verso, blank; 1 *l.* at end, blank.

Copies located: CaNs; CaNsHA.

34. NOVA SCOTIA. LAWS, STATUTES, *etc.*

Caption title: [At the General Assembly of the Province of Nova-Scotia . . . the 25th Day of April 1763, etc.]

Note: title above is not transcribed from copy.

fo. A-[E², F¹]; p. 116-136, paged in continuation of No. 30. *Printed at Halifax, N.S., by Anthony Henry, 1763.*

Contents: p. 116-136, 3 Geo. III c. I-VI, acts passed in the third session of the third assembly, Apr. 25-July 21, 1763.

Copy located: CaNsWA.

35. NOVA SCOTIA. LAWS, STATUTES, *etc.*

Caption title: (1) / [ornamental rule] / At the GENERAL-ASSEMBLY of the / Province of Nova-Scotia, begun / and holden at Halifax, on Wed-/nesday the First Day of July 1761, / in the First Year of His Majesty's / Reign, and there continued by se/veral Prorogations until Wednesday / the 19th Day of October, 1763, in the / third Year of his Majesty's Reign. / [ornamental rule] /

fo. 32 p.; type-page: 25 × 13.2 cm. *Printed at Halifax, N.S., by Anthony Henry, 1763.*

Contents: p. 1-32, 3-4 Geo. III c. I-XV, acts passed in the fourth session of the third assembly, Oct. 19-Nov. 26, 1763.

Copies located: CaNSA (p. 5-8 wanting); CaNsWA.

36. BARKLY, GILBERT

[Representations to the Publick; *printed at Quebec, by Brown & Gilmore, 1764.*]

Brown & Gilmore's *Memorial A* records several Barkly-Hay publications in the *Quebec gazette*, 1764-65, also the following:

"Sept. 24, 1764.	200 Representations to the Publick with Copy's of Affadavids [sic] for Gilbert Barkly—£2.10.
Oct. 26, 1764.	200 Answers to Gilbert Barkly's Libel—£2.16.6.
Nov. 12, 1764.	200 Replys to John Hays answer to Gilb:t Barkly's representation to the Publick—£3.
Nov. 24, 1764.	200 Answers to Gilbert Barkly's reply of the 2d inst. [sic] £1.10.
Nov. 29, 1764.	150 of John Hays answers with Gilb:t Barkly's marginal notes—£1.10.
Nov. 3, 1765. [sic].	An addition to Barkly's Answer of 2:d of Nov. 1764—18/."

These are probably broadsides published in disputes which arose over the firm's records at the dissolution of the partnership of Barkly (or Barclay) & Hay, merchants, formerly of Philadelphia. Both parties published vindications of character, etc., in the *Quebec gazette*, Oct. 17-24, 1765. "About 1765" Barkly came to Quebec from Philadelphia, whither he returned in 1773, remaining there till the Revolution, when he retired to Scotland (*see* G. B. Keen: *The descendants of Jöran Kyn*, in *Pennsylvania magazine*, 5: 338, 1881).

Copy located: None.

37. HAY, JOHN

[Answers to Gilbert Barkly's libel; *printed at Quebec by Brown & Gilmore, 1764.*]

Hay's publications in the Barkly-Hay disputes, 1764-65, are listed in No. 36.

Copy located: None.

38. NOVA SCOTIA. HOUSE OF ASSEMBLY

Caption title: [Votes and Journals of the House of Assembly for the Province of Nova-Scotia.]

Note: title above is not transcribed from copy.

fo. [A-E^2]; 17 p., 1 *l.*; *Printed at Halifax, N.S., by Anthony Henry, 1764.*

Contents: p. 1-17, Journal and votes of the fifth session of the third assembly, Mar. 22-Apr. 9, 1764; p. 17 verso, blank; 1 *l.* at end, blank.

In the following session the House "voted that £26.11.0 be paid to Anthony Henry, printer, for payment of his account for printing the Votes of Assembly."*—N.S., H. of As. *Journal*, Nov. 3, 1764.

Copies located: CaNs; CaNsHA.

*Probably of the fifth session.

39. NOVA SCOTIA. HOUSE OF ASSEMBLY

A / JOURNAL / OF THE / VOTES / OF THE / Lower House of Assembly, / FOR THE / Province of NOVA-SCOTIA: / From Friday October 12th. 1764, to Saturday No-/vember 3d. 1764. / [royal arms] / [double rule] / HALIFAX, in NOVA-SCOTIA: / Printed by ANTONY [sic] HENRY, Printer to the Governor and Council. / [title within double rule frame]

fo. [A]-H²; 30, [2]p.; sig. A is folded around sig. B-H, to form p. l. and [2]p. at end.

Contents: p.[1], t.-p.; p.[2], blank; p. 3-30 and p.[1-2] at end, Journal and votes of the sixth session of the third assembly, Oct. 12-Nov. 3, 1764. The text continues without a break from p. 30 to p.[1-2] at end, apparently unnumbered through oversight. This is the first N.S., H. of As. *Journal* published with a title page.

In the following session the House ordered that £16 be paid to Henry for printing its votes.*—N.S., H. of As. *Journal*, June 17, 1765.

Copies located: CaNs; CaNsHA (p. 23-30 wanting).

40. NOVA SCOTIA. LAWS, STATUTES, *etc.*

Caption title: [At the General-Assembly of the Province of Nova-Scotia . . . the 22nd Day of March, 1764.]

Note: title above is not transcribed from copy.

fo. p.[33]-40; paged in continuation of No. 35. P.[33-39] are unpaged, the numbers 1-7 have been printed thereon, then erased; p. 40 has been corrected from 49. *Printed at Halifax, N.S., by Anthony Henry, 1764.*

Contents: p.[33]-40, 4 Geo. III c. I-VII, acts passed in the fifth session of the third assembly, Mar. 22-Apr. 9, 1764.

Copy located: CaNsWA.

41. NOVA SCOTIA. LAWS, STATUTES, *etc.*

Caption title: [At the General-Assembly of the Province of Nova Scotia . . . the 12th Day of October, 1764.]

Note: title above is not transcribed from copy.

fo. sig. U-[Y², Z¹]; p. 15-18 [sic], 45-54; paged in continuation of No. 40, p.[41-44] being mispaged: 15-18. *Printed at Halifax, N.S., by Anthony Henry, 1764.*

Contents: p. 15 [sic]-54, 4-5 Geo. III c. I-VII, acts passed in the sixth session of the third assembly, Oct. 12-Nov. 3, 1764.

Copy located: CaNsWA.

42. NOVA SCOTIA. SECRETARY'S OFFICE

[Advertisement Secretary's Office, Halifax August 13th, 1764 <Text, signed:> By His Excellency's Command, Rich: Bulkeley Sec:]

Broadside: *Printed at Halifax, N. S., by Anthony Henry, 1764-66.*

*Probably of the sixth session.

Text: "Whereas the Lands on the Road leading from Fort Sackville to Falmouth in King's County were granted and assigned on the conditions of clearing forthwith a certain space in front of the said Lands . . . the Intention . . . being to keep the Road dry . . ." notice that lands not so cleared within 30 days will be forfeited and reserved again by the government.

Copy located: GBLP (in C.O. 217/21 no. N 107, Aug. 13, 1764. This copy was enclosed in a letter to the Lords of Trade, dated at Halifax, Nova Scotia, 2ᵈ September 1766, from Michael Francklin then administrator of the province).

43. QUEBEC, *Province.* GOVERNOR, 1764-1768 (*Murray*)

[Advertisement for discovering the Assassination of Thomas Walker.]

Probably a small broadside, text in English and French. *Printed at Quebec by Brown & Gilmore,* as recorded:

"1764, Dec. 10. To printing 400 Advertisements French and English for discovering the Assassination of Thomas Walker. £1.10."—Brown & Gilmore's account, Nov. 20, 1765, in Can.P.A., "*S*" *Pub. accts, 1759-66.*

The text is probably similar to that of the advertisement "for discovering the Persons who assaulted Thomas Walker," published by the government in the *Quebec gazette,* Dec., 1764-Feb., 1765 (9 weeks for £3 6*s.* according to the printers' bill cited above). The price of the "400 Advertisements" suggests that they were printed from type already set for the *Gazette.*

Walker, an English merchant and justice of the peace in Montreal, was assaulted (badly beaten and deprived of one ear, not killed) by masked ruffians on Dec. 6, 1764. He was conspicuous in the quarrels between military and civilian English in Montreal, and soldiery were suspected of the attack. Gov. Murray and Attorney-General Maseres made persistent efforts to discover and convict Walker's assailants but were completely baffled (*see also* No. 103). "Few incidents of such a nature have been historically so important as this Walker outrage. It was the turning point of Murray's period of government in Canada. It threw the newly conquered province into a great turmoil and was responsible for the recall of its first governor."—A. L. Burt, *The mystery of Walker's ear,* in *Canadian historical review,* 3: 233-55, Sept., 1922.

Copy located: None.

44. QUEBEC, *Province.* GOVERNOR, 1764-1768 (*Murray*)

[By His Excellency, A Proclamation, Quebec L S* Whereas it is highly necessary & expedient for the well being and Good government of His Majesty's loving Subjects in this Province, that Commissions of the peace be issued without loss of time for hearing & determining petty Causes in a Summary way, . . . I . . . appoint Justices of the peace for the respective Districts of this Province, etc. Given . . . at the Castle of St. Louis in the City of Quebec this Twenty eight day of August 1764 (signed) Ja. Murray, etc.]

? Broadside: *Printed at Quebec by Brown & Gilmore, 1764.*

*i.e. *locus sigilli,* place for the seal.

This title is taken from Quebec Legislative Council Minutes, Aug. 28, 1764, in Can.P.A., *State* A, p. 18-20, where the proclamation is recorded with the note: "the same was ordered to be printed & published in the Weekly Gazette." It does not appear in the *Quebec gazette* but was issued separately as Brown & Gilmore's account of Nov. 20, 1765 (covering work July 5, 1764-Sept. 10, 1765) shows:

"1764, Aug. 31. To printing 36 Proclamations for appointing Justices of the Peace &c in English—£1.2.6.
To printing 60 in French for Ditto—£1.3.6."

—Can.P.A., "*S*" *Pub. accts, 1759-66.*

The proclamation records the first appointments made by the governor-in-council after the establishment of British civil government in the former French colony. The commissioners or justices of the peace were the popular magistrates who met in quarter and in special sessions holding courts to hear petty causes in the two districts, and to regulate government and order in the towns of Quebec and Montreal.

This proclamation is reprinted in Can.P.A., *Report, 1918.*

Copy located: None.

45. QUEBEC, *Province.* GOVERNOR, 1764-1768 (*Murray*)

[Par Son Excellence. Proclamation. Québec. Attendu qu'il est hautement nécessaire et expédient pour le bon gouvernement des féaux sujets de Sa Majesté en cette province, que les commissaires de la paix, soient émises sans perte de temps, pour entendre et juger les petites causes d'une façon sommaire . . . J'ai cru devoir . . . constituer et nominer des juges de paix dans de divers districts de cette province, etc. Donné . . . au Château St-Louis, en la ville de Québec, ce vingt-huitième jour d'Août, 1764 (Signé) Ja: Murray. Par ordre de Son Excellence (contre signé) J. Gray, Sec. adjoint. Vive le Roi.]

? Broadside: *Printed at Quebec by Brown & Gilmore, 1764,* in an edition of 60 copies as recorded in No. 44 *note.* This is a French translation of No. 44. It is reprinted in Can.P.A., *Rapport, 1918.*

Copy located: None.

46. QUEBEC, *Province.* LAWS, STATUTES, *etc.*

[double rule] / AN / ORDINANCE, / For regulating and establishing the CURRENCY of the / PROVINCE. / By His Excellency JAMES MURRAY, Esq; Captain-General and Go-/vernor in Chief, in and over the Province of QUEBEC, . . . / . . . / . . . / . . . In / Council, this 14th Day of September . . . / . . . 1764. /

fo. [2]p. (recto and verso of single leaf); type-page: 29 × 16.8 cm. *Printed at Quebec, by Brown & Gilmore,* as recorded in their bill to government dated Nov. 20, 1765:

"1764, Sept. 22. To printing 100 Ordinances for Regulating & Establishing the Currency F[rench] & E[nglish] 1 sheet folio.—**£3.**"

—Can.P.A., "*S*" *Pub. Accts, 1759-66.*

Contents: p.[1-2], An Ordinance, signed at end: "Quebec, the 14th of September . . . 1764 . . . Ja: Murray. By Order of His Excellency in Council, J. Gray. D.Sec."

This ordinance fixed the value of Spanish, French, and English coins current in the province at New England currency rate (6*s.* : $1.00), superseding York (8*s.* : $1.00) which obtained in Montreal and Trois Rivières, and Halifax (5*s.* : $1.00) which obtained in Quebec and the lower part of the province during the military régime. "Quebec currency" as it was called, thus established by Gov. Murray, was unpopular with merchants, and this ordinance was repealed in 1777 by 17 Geo. III, c. 9, in favour of Halifax currency.

The English and French text (*see* item following) of this ordinance were probably printed and issued together on a single folio sheet uncut (making [4]p.). They were also issued separately and sold by the printers at the rate of 2 copies for 7½*d.* In addition to the hundred printed for government, another hundred copies, or more, are recorded sold to private purchasers, in Can.P.A., Brown & Gilmore: *Memorial A*, Sept. 17, 1764, *et seq.*

This ordinance is reprinted in Can.P.A., *Report, 1913.*

Copy located: CaQQL.

47. QUEBEC, *Province.* LAWS, STATUTES, *etc.*

[Ordonnance pour régler et établir le Cour de Monnoies dans cette Province.]

fo. 2 p. *Printed at Quebec by Brown & Gilmore, 1764.*

Contents: p.[1-2], Ordonnance, signed at end: "à Québec, le 14me Jour de Septembre . . . 1764 . . . Ja: Murray. Par Ordre de Son Excellence au conseil, J. Gray, D.Sec."

This is a French translation of the item above, printed in an edition of 100 copies for government, also additional copies for sale by the printers. It is reprinted in Can.P.A., *Rapport, 1913*, from which this description is taken.

Copy located: None.

48. QUEBEC, *Province.* LAWS, STATUTES, *etc.*

[An Ordinance, For ratifying and confirming the Decrees of the several Courts of Justice established in the Districts of Quebec, Montreal and Trois-Rivieres, prior to the Establishment of Civil Government throughout this Province, upon the tenth Day of August, Seventeen hundred and Sixty-four . . . <text of ordinance> Given by His Excellency James Murray Esq; . . . In Council at Quebec, the 20th day of September, . . . 1764 . . . JA:MURRAY. By Order of His Excellency in Council. J. Gray, D.Sec.]

French side: [Ordonnance, Pour ratifier et confirmer les Décrets des différentes cours de Justice établiës dans les Districts de Québec,

Montréal et Trois Riviéres, antérieurement à l'Etablissement du Gouvernement Civil par toute la Province, le Dixième d'Août, 1764 . . . <text of ordinance> Donné par son Excellence Jacques Murray, Ecuyer, . . . Au Conseil à Québec, le 20me Jour de Septembre . . . 1764 . . . Ja: Murray etc. Ordre de Son Excellence au Conseil. J: Gray, D.Sec.]

Double broadside (or fo. [4]p.): *Printed at Quebec by Brown & Gilmore, 1764,* as recorded in the printers' bill to the government dated Nov. 20, 1765:

"1764, Oct. 8. To printing 150 Ordinances for ratifying and confirming the Decrees of Military Courts prior to Civil Government. 150 Copies F[rench] & E[nglish]—£3.10."—Can.P.A., *"S" Pub. accts, 1759-66.*

From capitulation in Sept., 1760 till Aug. 10, 1764, Quebec was under the jurisdiction of General Amherst, British commander-in-chief with headquarters in New York. It was governed by three district military governors, who erected courts of French-Canadian militia officers to administer local government and justice. The "laws" of the interim government or "Military Régime," confirmed by this ordinance, were printed for the first time in Can.P.A., *Report, 1918.*

This ordinance is reprinted in Can.P.A., *Report, 1913.*

Copy located: None.

49. QUEBEC, *Province.* LAWS, STATUTES, *etc.*

[An Ordinance for regulating and establishing the courts of judicature, etc.]

fo. ? 3 p. *Printed at Quebec by Brown & Gilmore, 1764,* 150 copies printed on Sept. 24, 1764, as recorded in No. 51 *note.*

Copy located: None.

50. QUEBEC, *Province.* LAWS, STATUTES, *etc.*

[An Ordinance for regulating and establishing the courts of judicature, etc.]

fo. ? 3 p. *Printed at Quebec by Brown & Gilmore, 1764.* Another edition printed, in 150 copies, on Sept. 29, 1764, as recorded in No. 51 *note.*

Copy located: None.

51. QUEBEC, *Province.* LAWS, STATUTES, *etc.*

Caption title: AN / ORDINANCE, / For regulating and establishing the Courts of JUDICATURE, / Justices of the PEACE, QUARTER-SESSIONS, BAILIFFS, / and other Matters relative to the Distribution of Justice / in this PROVINCE. / By His Excellency JAMES MURRAY, Esq; . . . / . . . / . . . / . . . / . . . In / Council, this 17th Day of September, in the Fourth Year of His Ma-/jesty's Reign, Annoque Domini, 1764. /

At head of title: A SUPPLEMENT to the QUEBEC GAZETTE, / dated October 4, 1764, N° XVI. / [rule] /

fo. [3]p.; type-page: 30 × 17 cm. *Printed at Quebec by Brown & Gilmore, 1764,* as recorded below. This is probably a reprint, with addition of the *Gazette* heading, from the types of the edition of Sept. 29.

Contents: p.[1-3] An Ordinance; p.[3] verso, blank.

Two editions (and a reprint) in English, and three editions (and a reprint) in French (in all, 950 copies) were printed by Brown & Gilmore at Quebec, as their bill to the government, Nov. 20, 1765, records:

"1764, Sept. 24. To printing 150 Ordinances for establishing courts of Justice, 1 sheet Folio in English—£1.10.

To printing 150 Ditto in French for Ditto—£3.10.

Sept. 25. To Reprinting the French (half [of the type] being distributed) 150 copies—£1.18

Sept. 29. To Reprinting the English the Whole [of the type] being distributed—£3.10.

To reprinting the French a third time, the whole [of the type] being distributed—£3.10.

Oct. 4. To printing 100 English as a Supplement to Gazette [no.] 16—16/8.
To Ditto 100 French as Ditto—16/8."

Note: the charge for the last two items indicates that the type was not reset for this printing.—

Can.P.A., "*S*" *Pub. accts, 1759-66.*

An extraordinarily large number of copies of this ordinance (400 in English, 550 in French) were distributed by the government; for though Brown & Gilmore advertised it for sale as usual (*Quebec gazette,* Sept. 27, 1764) they did not record copies sold.

The text was prepared on order of the governor-in-council, Aug. 13, 1764, by Chief-Justice William Gregory and Attorney-General George Suckling ("probably the attorney general, George Suckling did most of the work"—A. L. Burt: *Old province of Quebec,* Minneapolis, 1933, 88). It was designed to provide the judicial framework for the English civil administration of French Canada, inaugurated Aug. 10, 1764. It included, however, English practices, especially in property law and and court procedure, vehemently resented by the numerous French litigants and lawyers; it occasioned confusion in the courts, and controversy among judges and officers of government. It was amended in 1766 and 1770 (*see* No. 152) and superseded by the Quebec Act, 1774 (*see* No. 187) and provincial statutes 17 Geo. III c. 1, 2, 5 (in No. 268).

This ordinance is reprinted in Can.P.A., *Report, 1913.*

Copies located: CaOOA (bound in the printers' file of the *Quebec gazette,* following no. 16, Oct. 4, 1764, this copy bears MS. note: "Printing 16/8"); GBLP (in C.O. 42 / 2: 35; another copy in C.O. 42 / 25: 383-85).

2. QUEBEC, *Province.* LAWS, STATUTES, *etc.*

[Ordonnance, Pour régler et établir les Cours de Justice, etc.]

fo. ? 3 p. *Printed at Quebec by Brown & Gilmore, 1764,* 150 copies printed on Sept. 24, 1764, as recorded in No. 51 *note.*

Copy located: None.

53. QUEBEC, *Province.* LAWS, STATUTES, *etc.*

[Ordonnance, Pour régler et établir les Cours de Justice etc.]

fo. ? 3 p. *Printed at Quebec by Brown & Gilmore, 1764.* Another edition, partly reprinted from the type of the item above, published in 150 copies on Sept. 25, 1764, as recorded in No. 51 *note.*

Copy located: None.

54. QUEBEC, *Province.* LAWS, STATUTES, *etc.*

[Ordonnance, Pour régler et établir les Cours de Justice, etc.]

fo. ? 3 p. *Printed at Quebec by Brown & Gilmore, 1764.* Another edition printed in 150 copies on Sept. 29, 1764, as recorded in No. 51 *note.*

Copy located: None.

55. QUEBEC, *Province.* LAWS, STATUTES, *etc.*

[double rule] / ORDONNANCE, / Pour régler et établir les Cours de Justice, Juges de Paix, / Séance de Quartier, Baillis, et autres Matiéres touchant / la Distribution de la Justice dans cette Province. / Par Son Excellence JACQUES MURRAY, . . . / . . . / . . . / . . . / . . . Au Conseil, ce 17me Jour de / Septembre, en la Quatrième Année du Regne de Sa Majesté, Annoq; / Domini, 1764. /

fo. [3]p.; type-page: 29 × 17 cm. *Printed at Quebec by Brown & Gilmore, 1764,* as recorded in No. 51 *note,* this is probably a reprint from the type of the edition of Sept. 29.

Contents: p.[1-3], Ordonnance; p.[3] verso, blank.

The French text was published in the *Quebec gazette,* Oct. 4, 1764, also issued separately on the same date. It is reprinted in Can.P.A., *Rapport, 1913.*

Copy located: CaOOA (bound in the printers' file of *Quebec gazette,* following no. 16, Oct. 4, 1764, this copy bears MS. note at foot of p.[1]: "Printed 100—16/8").

56. QUEBEC GAZETTE

QUEBECK. / To the Publick. Au Public. / <Text, signed:> BROWN AND GILMORE. /

Broadside: printed in 2 col. English (81 lines) and French (88 lines). *Probably printed in Philadelphia in the printing office of Wm. Dunlap, 1763, and published in Quebec, 1763-64.*

This is a prospectus of the *Quebec gazette,* brought from Philadelphia to Quebec and distributed by Wm. Brown, while his partner, Thomas Gilmore, went to England to purchase equipment for their printing office. The text of the prospectus states:

"As every considerate Mind is solicitous to know the State of the World about him, and the Circumstances of the several Nations, joint Inhabitants of the Universe with him, so it must be an additional Satisfaction to be acquainted from Time to Time with the Events and important Transactions in the different Quarters of the

Globe: . . . This Principle can only be gratified in its most extensive Latitude by Means of the Press. . . .

". . . Our design is . . . early in the Spring to settle in this city in the Capacity of Printers and forthwith to Publish a Weekly News-Paper . . . in French and English: This Method will afford a Weekly Lesson for Improvement to every Inhabitant willing to attain a thorough facility in the Language of the Place, . . . different from that of his Mother Tongue, whether French or English. . . . But as our coming hither, and setting up a complete Printing-Office, will be attended with a much greater expence than our present Circumstances will admit of, we offer the following Proposals to the Inhabitants of this Place, their encouraging of which will determine our settling among them.

"1. that as soon as three hundred Subscriptions for the News-Paper, above proposed, can be procur'd, we will engage to set up a genteel Printing-Office, in some convenient Part of Quebeck, consisting of a good Assortment of new Types, a good Press, and all other Materials necessary for carrying on said Business in the most extensive Manner and with Expedition."

Proposals 2-5 set forth price (blank), terms of subscription and delivery of papers "even to the remotest parts of the Country."

The newspaper thus proposed was published in its first issue at Quebec, June 21, 1764, as the *Quebec gazette.* Brown & Gilmore's printing office was the second established in Canada.

Copy located: CaOOA (bound in the *Quebec gazette*, following no. 1, June 21, 1764).

57. ALMANACS. QUEBEC

[L'Almanac de Cabinet pour l'année commune 1765 pour la latitude de Québec. Fait exactement par Monsr. Maurice Simonin, ancien Capitaine de Navire. *Printed at Quebec by Brown & Gilmore, 1765.*]

This almanac was announced (in *Quebec gazette*, Jan. 17, 1765) for publication on Monday, Jan. 21, 1765, then advertised: "Les Imprimeurs viennent de publier L'Almanac de Cabinet pour l'année commune 1765, pour latitude de Québec. Fait exactement par Monsr. Maurice Simonin, ancien Capitaine de Navire. Comme il n'a point été publié d'Almanac de cette epéce en cette ville jusques à present, nous éspérons que le Succes de la Vente nous encouragera à en imprimer au commencement de chaque Nouvelle Année, en y ajoutant toujours quelque chose de nouveau.

"Le prix sera Neuf Sols. d'argent de cours de Québec chaque . . . Six chillins d'argent aussi de Québec, par Douzaine."—*Quebec gazette*, Jan. 24, 1765, *et seq.*

A broadside, this was a sheet almanac or wall calendar probably with contents similar to No. 170. Brown & Gilmore printed 300 copies and reckoned the cost as £4 8½*d.* (*Memorial A*, Dec. 28, 1765). They sold copies retail in Quebec at 9*d.* the copy, also 6*s.* the dozen, and sent a supply to merchants in Montreal (100 copies to John Thompson the postmaster, at £3 15*s.*) and Trois Rivières; but many of these were returned. Less than 100, they stated (*see* item following), were sold altogether.

The *Almanac de Cabinet* soon justified itself, however, for that for 1765 was the first of a series published annually (excepting 1766) through the 18th and into the 19th century. It became the best-seller of the Brown > Neilson printing office. Of the hundreds of copies sold each year (as their account books show) only a few sun-browned, fly-blown specimens survive, the earliest being that for 1774.

Copy located: None.

58. ALMANACS. QUEBEC

[L'Almanac de Cabinet pour l'année commune 1766.]

Proposed printing at Quebec by Brown & Gilmore 1765, was advertised in a long notice (in French only) published in the *Quebec gazette,* Oct. 3-31, 1765. The notice stated that the printers had published an *Almanac de Cabinet* in the preceding January, hoping to clear expenses, but less than 100 copies were sold and they lost considerably on the venture. Perhaps it had appeared too late for distribution through so large a province early in the year. However, for the next year's almanac the printers propose (1) that as soon as 400 copies are subscribed for, they will begin to print and have the almanac ready for distribution by the end of November. (2) The price will be one Spanish Piastre [6*s*. Quebec currency] per dozen, to be paid when the almanacs are delivered. (3) No subscription of less than six copies will be accepted. (4) The almanacs will be sent free of extra cost to subscribers in Montreal and Trois Rivières. (5) Subscriptions will be received by John Thompson, postmaster at Montreal, and by the printers at Quebec.

Not sufficiently subscribed at 6*s*. the dozen before Nov. 1, when the Stamp Act increased costs, this almanac was not printed.

59. CATHOLIC CHURCH. CATECHISMS. *French*

CATECHISME / DU DIOCESE / DE / SENS. / Par Monseigneur JEAN-JOSEPH / LANGUET, Archevêque de SENS. / [ornament] / A QUEBEC: / Chez BROWN & GILMORE, Imprimeurs de la Pro-/vince. M,DCC,LXV. /

12mo. A-X^4, Y^2; 177, [3]p.; type-page: 15 × 9 cm.

Contents: p. [1], t.-p.; p. [2], blank; p. [3]-12, Abrégé de la doctrine chrétienne; p. 13-131, Catéchisme; p. 132-77, Instruction, Prières; p. [1 (verso of p. 177)-3] at end, Table (contents).

Prepared by Jean-Joseph Languet de Gergy, 1677-1753, noted as an anti-Jansenist, later archbishop of Sens; and first published at Soissons, 1727, this catechism was used in the diocese of Quebec till 1777. It was the first work of book size and the first comparatively large edition printed by Brown & Gilmore as recorded:

> "1765. Nov. 21, Rec[d.] for general printing 2000 Catechisms of the Diocese of Sens printed and d[d.] [delivered] Germain in Sheets—£91.16."
>
> —Can.P.A., Brown & Gilmore: *Memorial A*.

This edition was exhausted and another printed within five months (*see* No. 76). The depressed condition of Quebec during the war, the hazard and finally the curtailment of communication with France had cut off the supply of books to French Canada, creating by 1765 a ready market for Catholic devotional works. These formed a considerable part of Brown & Gilmore's printing business, Louis Langois, dit Germain, a merchant in Quebec till his death in 1798, often acting as publisher, or as agent between printer and clergy.

Copies located: CaQM; CaQMS (4 cop.); CaQQL.

60. FREEMASONS

THE YOUNG / Free-Mason's Assistant. / BEING A / CHOICE COLLECTION / OF / MASON SONGS: / With a variety of / TOASTS AND SENTIMENTS. / TO WHICH ARE ADDED / A FEW OF THE MOST CELEBRATED / SONGS, / SCOTCH AND ENGLISH, / [double rule] / QUEBEC: / Printed by BROWN & GILMORE / M, DCC, LXV /

12mo. in 6's; 2 p. l., p. 5-6, VII-XXIII, 1-155; type-page: 13 × 7 cm.

Contents, supplied by Maggs bros., London, Feb. 13, 1937, from the only copy located: "Half title, The Young Free-Mason's Assistant; title; Advertisement (pp. 5 & 6); Index (pp. VII-XII; Toasts and Sentiments (pp. XIII-XXIII); text (pp. 1-155). With the exception of the title the book was printed and published at Aberdeen, Dec. 20, 1764 by W. Chalmers. Of this Scottish edition we are not able to locate a single copy but have been given to understand that one copy does exist. According to a note in the volume arrangements were made with Brown & Gilmore of Quebec to bring out an American edition. . . . The title is printed on a separate leaf evidently originally forming one of the front end-papers. It is of the same texture and bears the same watermark as the back end-paper. Accompanying the volume are two additional specimens of the title printed on what have evidently formed end-leaves from another contemporary volume. On the reverse of these titles are some contemporary manuscript notes with the date 1764 and the name Elizabeth Carpenter. We should imagine that these titles were the work of an apprentice employed by Messrs. Brown & Gilmore and were printed by way of practice in type-setting."

No local contemporary evidence could be found to authenticate the imprint, however, and the experienced eye of Mr. Carl P. Rollins proved it spurious. Maggs bros. then generously published notes on the anachronism:

"Brown & Gilmore's accounts, which are extant in great detail for this period, report no importation, printing or sale of this work; nor does it appear among books advertised for sale by the firm in the *Quebec gazette* during the eighteenth century. The Quebec imprint is in fact a twentieth century addition to an eighteenth century publication. I am indebted to Mr. Carl P. Rollins, Yale University Press, for identifying the types from photostats: 'Regarding the title-page of "The Young Free Mason's Assistant," apparently issued by Brown & Gilmore, Quebec, 1765, the type used for the title lines, including rules and date line at bottom, appear to me to be quite likely of the date of the book—1765. At least there is no anachronism apparent. The line QUEBEC is printed in Cheltenham Old Style Italic, designed by Bertram Grosvenor Goodhue, and first cut for the Mergenthaler Linotype Co. about 1905. The type used in this title-page is probably the foundry casting of the American Type Founders Co. of New York. The line Printed by BROWN & GILMORE appears to be set in a type face called "Della Robbia," designed by [Thomas Maitland Cleland about 1902] and first cut about the same time as the Cheltenham between 1900 and 1906. If not Della Robbia, it is some type face gotten out in imitation of it. (signed) Carl P. Rollins. New Haven, 12 July 1937.' "

Copy located: Maggs bros., London. MB has a copy of a work identical with that described by Maggs bros. in content, format, and title page, excepting the imprint which reads "Dumfries, Printed by Robert M'Lachlan, for W. Chambers bookseller, 1784."

61. GREAT BRITAIN. LAWS, STATUTES, *etc.*

[Abstracts from the Statutes of Great Britain.]

4to. 6 p.; 150 copies in English, *printed at Quebec by Brown & Gilmore, 1765*, as recorded:

> "1765, March 23. Printed for the Government of Quebec, Abstracts from the Statutes of Great Britain in French and English, the French making 6 in Pica, and English 6 pages on English [type] the 2 making 1½ sheets of Demy 4to, with Long Primer Notes, 150 copies of each—£7.4.
>
> [Same date:] Sold to the Government of Quebec, 3 Quires of Demy printing paper for covering the Abstracts from the Statutes. [@] 1/3—3/9."
>
> —Can.P.A., Brown & Gilmore: *Memorial A.*

Similar entries appear in the printers' bill to the government, Nov. 20, 1765 (in Can.P.A., "*S*" *Pub. accts, 1759-66*), no allusion to the subject matter of the abstracts occurring in either case.

Copy located: None.

62. GREAT BRITAIN. LAWS, STATUTES, *etc.*

[Extraits des Statuts de la Grande Bretagne.]

4to. 6 p. *Printed at Quebec by Brown & Gilmore 1765*, this is the French edition (150 copies) of the item above.

Copy located: None.

63. NOVA SCOTIA. HOUSE OF ASSEMBLY

A / JOURNAL / OF THE / VOTES / OF THE / Lower House of ASSEMBLY, / FOR THE / Province of NOVA-SCOTIA: / From Tuesday, May 28th, 1765, to Monday, / June 17th, 1765. / [royal arms] / [double rule] / HALIFAX, in NOVA-SCOTIA: / Printed by ANTHONY HENRY, Printer to the Government. / MDDCLXV [sic] / [title within double rule frame]

fo. 1 p l., 33 p.

Contents: p. l. recto, t.-p.; verso, blank; p. 1-33, Journal and votes of the first session of the fourth assembly, May 28-June 17, 1765; verso of p. 33, blank.

The House voted that the treasurer pay "To Anthony Henry, printer for printing the Votes of this House two sessions*—£42.10.0."—N.S., H. of As. *Journal*, Aug. 1, 1766.

Copies located: CaNs; CaNsHA.

64. NOVA SCOTIA. LAWS, STATUTES, *etc.*

Caption title: [At the General Assembly of the Province of Nova-Scotia . . . the 28th Day of May, 1765.]

Note: title above is not transcribed from copy.

*Probably the sessions of May-June, 1765 and June-Aug., 1766.

fo. p. 55-86; paged in continuation of No. 41. *Printed at Halifax, N.S., by Anthony Henry, 1765.*

Contents: p. 55-86, 5 Geo. III c. I-XII, acts passed in the first session of the fourth assembly, May 28-June 17, 1765.

Copy located: CaNsWA.

65. PRIMERS. QUEBEC. *French*

[Alphabet]

16mo. about 64 p. *Printed at Quebec by Brown & Gilmore, 1765.*

500 copies were printed and stitched at a cost of £8, and sold at 6*d.* the single copy, with discount for larger purchase. Numerous transactions concerning this item are recorded by the printers, e.g.:

"1765, July 1, Received for 48 Alphabets sold to the Jesuits School—16/9¼.
July 27, John Dean folded stitched and cut 512 Alphabets for us for £2.
Aug. 16, Sent John Thomson [Brown & Gilmore's agent at Montreal] to sell for us 24 Alphabets—12/.
Dec. 31 [balancing year's accounts] Alphabets owes General Printing for 500 Copies making 2 Sheets in sixteens—£6."

—Can.P.A., Brown & Gilmore: *Memorial A.*

It was advertised: "A Vendre, Par Jaques Jorand [i.e. Jordan], à la Ruë des Carrieres, près du Jardin du Chateau de St. Louis, Des Alphabets (ou A.B.C.) François complets, et ajustés avec une methode qui facilite beaucoup les Enfans à apprendre à lire—Ce sont les meilleurs A,B,C, qui ayent paru jusques à présent, suivant l'aveu des Connoisseurs. N.B. Il facilitera ceux qui en prendront une quantité considérable pour revendre."—*Quebec gazette,* July 4, 1765.

This *Alphabet* or primer was the first of many editions printed in thousands of copies by Brown & Gilmore and their successors in Quebec during the 18th century—as their office records and newspaper advertisements show. Its content was probably similar to that of the 1800 edition (No. 1194), the earliest copy located. French and Latin primers and other school books, found a ready market in Quebec at this time. For ten years the supply from France had been curtailed by the war and finally cut off by the peace, which severed connections between New and Old France.

The "Jesuits School," which bought 48 Alphabets on July 1, 1765, was the Collège des Jésuites, founded at Quebec in 1635. A secondary school (though it included a primary class, "le petit école") similar in organization and curricula to the Order's schools in Europe, the Collège remained the centre of classical education in French Canada till 1768, when it was closed by the English administration. cf. Amédée Gosselin: *L'Instruction au Canada sous le régime français, 1635-1670* (Quebec, 1911); also, Lionel A. Groulx: *L'Enseignement français au Canada,* v. I, *Dans le Québec* (Montréal, 1931).

Copy located: None.

66. QUEBEC, *Province.* COURT OF QUARTER SESSIONS OF THE PEACE (Quebec District)

Caption title: AT / THE FIRST COURT OF / QUARTER-SESSIONS / Of the PEACE, / HELD AT QUEBEC, IN October 1764. / [double rule] /

4to. A-B⁴; 16 p.; type-page: 18.8 × 15 cm.

Contents: p. [1]-2, His Worship the president's Charge to the Grand-jury; p. 2-4, Presentments of October Sessions, signed by James Johnston foreman and 21 others; p. 4-6, Protest against Roman Catholics serving on grand and petty juries and against army officers having judicial authority over civilians "Signed . . . by all the Protestant members then present, the 20th of October, 1764. James Johnston" and 13 others; p. 6-10, Stricture on the foregoing Presentments, by Samuel Gridley for the justices of the peace; p. 11-16, Remarks upon the strictures, signed by James Johnston and 13 other Protestant jurors; p. 16 at end, a letter dated Oct. 22, 1764, signed by Wm. Mackenzie and others including Wms. Conyngham and George Allsopp, thanking the grand jurors for their Presentments, on behalf of the merchants, traders, and principal inhabitants of Quebec.

Printed at Quebec by Brown & Gilmore 1765, as recorded:

> "1765, Mar. 29. Printed for James Johnston, The Grand Jury's Presentments, Justices Strictures, and G. Jury's Remarks thereon, 4½ Sheets in Quarto, French & English, 450 Copies, at £3 Halifax for the 1st 150, and 10/. for each 150 after, of each Sheet—21/12/0."
>
> —Can.P.A., Brown & Gilmore: *Memorial A*.

This was the first piece of political propaganda printed in Canada. It was "published" by James Johnston, foreman of the first grand jury of the court of general quarter sessions of the peace, and one of the leaders of a small group of English merchants in Quebec. It was part of an attack upon the privileges and powers of the French Catholics and the British military groups in the colony, also an attempt to promote the grand jury's claims to serve as a sort of legislative assembly for the province. (*See Canadian historical review*, 17: 349-50, 1936, for notes on related texts and facsimile illustration of p. [1] of the *Presentments*.)

This pamphlet is reproduced in the Massachusetts Historical Society *Photostat Americana*, ser. 2, no. 11 (Boston, 1936). It is reprinted in Shortt and Doughty: *Documents, 1759-1791*, 1: 213-16.

Copies located: CtY; MHi.

67. QUEBEC, *Province*. COURT OF QUARTER SESSIONS OF THE PEACE (Quebec District)

Caption title: [double rule] / A / LA PREMIER COUR DE / SEANCE DE QUARTIER / DE LA PAIX, / Tenuë à QUEBEC, en OCTOBRE, 1764. / [rule] / La CHARGE d'Instruction donnée par le RESPECTABLE PRESIDENT / aux GRAND-JURES, /

4to. A-E²; 19 p.; type-page: 18.8 × 15 cm. *Printed at Quebec by Brown & Gilmore, 1765,* in an edition of 450 copies. This work was probably issued separately, also with some copies of No. 66, of which it is a French translation.

Contents: p. [1]-2, la Charge; p. 2-5, "Representations de la Séance, [dated and signed at end:] le 20 d'October 1764 . . . James Johnston [and 21 others]"; p. 5-6 [Representation against Roman Catholics serving on juries, etc., Oct. 20, 1764, signed by James Johnston and 14 other English members]; p. 7-12, "Remarques sur les Representations," by the justices of the peace; p. 12-18," Observations sur les Remarques," signed by James Johnston and 11 other English members; p. 18-19, "Aux Grands Jures," a letter of thanks for *Representations* of Johnston, etc., signed by William Mackenzie and 45 other citizens, "A Quebec, le 22 de Octobre, 1764"; p. 19 verso, blank.

This pamphlet is reproduced (not in facsimile) in Bibliographical Society of Canada, *Reprint series* no. 2 (Toronto, 1949).

Copy located: CaQQL.

68. QUEBEC, *Province.* COURT OF QUARTER SESSIONS OF THE PEACE (Quebec District)

[Fares and Rates for the Carriage of Wood . . . and other Merchandizes] SUPPLEMENT à la GAZETTE de QUEBEC, N°. XLII. / A SUPPLEMENT to the QUEBEC GAZETTE, N°. XLII. /

A single sheet printed on both sides; recto, English text, type-page: 29.5 × 20.5 cm.; verso, French text, type-page: 35 × 20.5 cm. *Printed at Quebec by Brown & Gilmore, 1765*, as recorded:

"1765, Apr. 1. Jeremiah C. Russell D^r^ to General Printing For printing the Justices' Table of Rates and Fares for Carters 1 Sheet folio, 50 copies in 2 Languages—£1.16."—Can.P.A., Brown & Gilmore: *Memorial A*.

Contents: Rates I-XI, signed at end: "By Order of the Court of General-Quarter-Sessions of the Peace [Quebec] March 28, 1765. J. C. Russell, Clerk." These rates were established according to the ordinance of Nov. 6, 1764, which required that "the Justices in their several Sessions of the Peace, held for the Districts of Quebec, and Montreal, shall . . . in . . . March . . . and . . . September regulate the Fares and Rates of Carriage of Wood, Barrels, Hogsheads and other Merchandizes in the Towns of Quebec, Montreal and Trois Rivières, and their Suburbs [Trois Rivières was part of Montreal district, 1764-1790] and shall cause a table of the several rates . . . to be printed and posted up in the most publick Places about the said Towns [etc.]."

Justices of the peace in quarter or special sessions formed the local or municipal governing bodies in all the settled parts of Canada until well into the 19th century (excepting the City of Saint John, N.B., incorporated in 1785). Their regulations, orders, notices, etc., published in newspapers, also sometimes separately as broadsides and handbills, comprised a considerable part of the printers' work. With a few exceptions, however, such publications, often routine reprints slight in format, have not been recorded independently, year by year, in this work, the item described above serving as prototype of its numerous successors.

Copy located: CaOOA (filed in *Quebec gazette*, 1765).

69. QUEBEC, *Province.* CUSTOMS OFFICE

Headline: SUPPLEMENT to the Quebec-Gazette of JULY 18, 1765, N°. 57. / [rule] /

Caption: BY AUTHORITY. THE following is an Accompt of the Duties paid at Quebec on spirituous Liquors and Wines since the Conquest of this Province, except what was received by Mr. Alexander Mackenzie, in / 1760, [etc.]

A single sheet printed on both sides, text in 2 col., English only; type-page: 36 × 25.5 cm. *Printed at Quebec by Brown & Gilmore, 1765*, as recorded:

"1765, July 23. To pr. An Accompt of all the Spirituous Wines and Liquors imported and exported for 4 years—£8.0.0."—Brown & Gilmore's account [to the government] Nov. 20, 1765, in Can.P.A., "*S*" *Pub. accts, 1759-66*.

This is a record of monies collected 1761-64, in pursuance of a 6*d*.-a-gallon customs duty on liquors, levied by Gov. Murray, Nov. 22, 1760. It was the principal source of provincial revenue besides rent from the king's posts.

Copy located: CaOOA (bound in *Quebec gazette,* following issue of July 18, 1765).

70. QUEBEC, *Province.* EXECUTIVE COUNCIL

Headline: SUPPLEMENT to the QUEBEC-GAZETTE, July 4, 1765. / [List of fees for the different Officers in this Province, Quebec, June 20, 1765.]

A single sheet printed on both sides, text in 2-3 col. type-page: 34 × 20.5 cm. *Printed at Quebec by Brown & Gilmore, 1765*, as recorded:

"1765, July 9. To printing a list of all the Public Officers' fees—£5."—Brown & Gilmore's account [to Government] Nov. 20, 1765, in Can.P.A., "*S*" *Pub. accts, 1759-66*.

Contents: List of fees, with preamble at head of col. 1: "Council-Chamber, Quebec 20th June, 1765, Present, . . . James Murray Esq. Governor, &c. &c. and other Members of His Majesty's Council. Ordered, That the following list of fees for the different Officers in this Province be published in the next Week's Gazette; and that an exact Copy be affixed in each of the respective Offices that none may pretend Ignorance." The list includes fees to be charged for official duties by the governor, secretary, register, clerk of council, judges and justices, sheriffs, court cryers, jury, lawyers, clerks of courts, attorney-general, door keeper of council, public notary, coroner and naval officer. It is signed at end: "By Order of His Excellency in Council, Ja. Potts, D.C.C."

The list did not appear "in next Week's Gazette [June 27, 1765]," as ordered, but was published as a supplement the week following, probably issued with the *Gazette* and also distributed separately. The French text was published among advertisements and other matter in the *Quebec gazette supplement*, Aug. 29-Sept. 5, 1765 (for which the printers charged £5 15*s*) and was probably not distributed separately.

Copy located: CaOOA (bound in *Quebec gazette* following issue of July 4, 1765).

71. QUEBEC, *Province.* LAWS, STATUTES, *etc.*

A la CHAMBRE du CONSEIL à QUEBEC, Mercredi le 13me Jour de / NOVEMBRE, 1765. / PRESENS, / Son Excellence l'Honorable JAQUES MURRAY, Ecuyer, GOUVERNEUR, / ET / Un Nombre suffisant des MEMBRES du CONSEIL de Sa Majesté. / <Text of Resolution on "Publication," in 6 lines, signed:> / Par Ordre de Son EXCELLENCE, / JA: POTTS, D.C.C. / [rule] /

Following Resolution on "Publication" is:

ORDONNANCE / Pour régler et établir le Mésurage du Bois de Chauffage qu'on exposera en Vente / en cette Province. / <Text in

54 lines > Donné par Son Excellence . . . / . . . / . . . / . . . Au Conseil à Québec, le Treiziéme Jour de Novembre, Anno Domini, 1765, . . . / . . . / . . . / JA: MURRAY. / Par Ordre de Son Excellence au Conseil, / JA: POTTS, D.C.C. /

Broadside: 81 lines; type-page: 42 × 21.5 cm. *Printed at Quebec by Brown & Gilmore, 1765*, as recorded:

> "1765, Nov. 29. Printed the Government of Quebec, An Ordinance concerning Fire Wood in French—£2.5.
> ditto in English—£1.13."—Can.P.A., Brown & Gilmore: *Memorial A*.

Contents: Resolution of Council, Nov. 13, 1765, with text:

"Vu que la Méthode ordinaire de publier les Ordonnances, &c. etoit par le Moyen de La Gazette de Québec, et qu'on a actuellement cessé de publier la dite Gazette: Il a donc été Resolu, Que désormais la Publication des Ordonnances, Proclamations, &c. au Son du Tambour, dans les Villes de Québec, Montréal, et Trois Riviéres, et la Lecture d'icelles qui se fera par les Curés des différentes Paroisses de la Province, à leurs Congrégations, et l'Affichement des dites Ordonnances, Proclamations, &c. qui se fera ensuite aux Endroits les plus publics des dites Villes, et aux Portes des Eglises des dites Paroisses, seront censés en être, une Publication suffisante à toutes Fins et Intentions."

This *Resolution* suspended the ordinance of Oct. 3, 1764 "that the publick Reading of any Ordinance by the Provost-Marshall . . . in Quebec, Montreal and Trois Rivières after Notice by Beat of Drum and the publishing the same in the Quebec Gazette shall be deemed sufficient Publication thereof." The Catholic clergy became the principal "publishers" of laws, etc., as before the advent of printing in Quebec. The *Gazette* was suspended from Oct. 21, 1765 till May 29, 1766, owing, as the printers state in the latter issue, "to the impositions of the grievous Stamp: An Act more dreadful than the icy chains of our inhospitable Winter."

The *Ordinance* was designed to prevent fraud in the sale of fire wood. It (but not the *Resolution*) is reprinted in Can.P.A., *Rapport, 1913*.

Copy located: CaQQL; photostat in CaOOA (in *Quebec, Proclamations 1765-1775*, portfolio).

72. QUEBEC, *Province.* LAWS, STATUTES, *etc.*

[Resolution of Council concerning publication of Ordinances, 13 Nov. 1765; also An Ordinance, For regulating and establishing the Admeasurement of Fire-wood, exposed to Sale in this Province. <text &c.> Quebec the 13th Day of November Anno Domini 1765 . . . JA: MURRAY]

Broadside: *Printed at Quebec by Brown & Gilmore, 1765*, in an edition apparently much smaller than the French edition above (*see* note).

The *Ordinance* is reprinted (without the *Resolution*) in Can.P.A., *Report, 1913*.

Copy located: None.

73. QUEBEC, *Province.* LAWS, STATUTES, *etc.*

[An Ordinance, For the better and more regular providing Firewood for the Use of His Majesty's Forces in Garison in this Province, And for declaring that all Power and Authority of any Captain or other Officer of the Militia, established in this Province before the Conquest thereof, and afterwards continued until the Establishment of British Civil Government within the same, was thereby abolished and taken away <Text> Given by His Excellency the Honourable James Murray . . . In Council, at Quebec, the 27th Day of November . . . 1765 . . . Ja: Murray. By Command of His Excellency in Council, Ja: Potts, D:G.G.]

Broadside: *Printed at Quebec by Brown & Gilmore, 1765,* as recorded:

"1765, Dec. 19. Printed for the Government of Quebec in a Broadside An Ordinance for the better furnishing the garrisons with fire wood &c. in English 50 copies—£2.5.0.
An Ordinance for ditto in French 150 copies—£2.15.0."
—Can.P.A., Brown & Gilmore: *Memorial A.*

This ordinance is reprinted in Can.P.A., *Report, 1913,* from which the title as above is taken.

Copy located: None.

74. QUEBEC, *Province.* LAWS, STATUTES, *etc.*

[Ordonnance Pour faciliter et pour régler la Fourniture de Bois de Chauffage aux Troupes de sa Majesté en Garnison dans cette Province; et pour déclarer que tout Pouvoir et Autorité de quelque Capitaine ou autre Officier de Milice que ce soit établis en cette Province avant la Conquète d'icelle, et continués ensuite jusques à l'Epoque de l'Establissement du Gouvernement Civil Britannique, en icelle, ont été abolis et anéatis par l'Etablissement du dit Gouvernement <Text> Donné par son Excellence l'Honorable Jacques Murray . . . au Conseil à Québec, le 27me Jour de Novembre . . . 1765 . . . Ja: Murray. Par Ordre de Son Excellence au conseil, Ja: Potts, D:G:G.]

Broadside: *Printed at Quebec by Brown & Gilmore, 1765,* in an edition of 150 copies, as indicated in No. 73 *note.* It is reprinted in Can.P.A., *Rapport, 1913,* from which the title as above is taken.

Copy located: None.

75. ALMANACS. QUEBEC

[Kalendrier perpétuel à l'usage des Sauvages Montagnais, Mistassins, Papinachois, et autres des Postes du Roi, de Tadoussac, Chécoutimy, Rivière de l'Assomption, etc. *Printed at Quebec by Brown & Gilmore, 1766.*]

? Broadside. This calendar was advertised: "Les Imprimeurs [Brown & Gilmore] donnent avis aux Missionaires des diverses Nations Sauvages de ce continent, qu'ils impriment présentement un Kalendrier perpetuel à l'usage des Sauvages de Montagnais . . . de l'Assomption &c. Ce Kalendrier qui veut servir à tous les autres sauvages qui vont en chasse, ou qui passent un tems considerable loin du lieu de la Mission se trouve à l'Imprimerie."—*Quebec gazette*, Oct. 20, 1776, *et seq.*

This calendar was probably prepared by, and printed for the Jesuit father, Jean Baptiste de La Brosse, missionary among the Montagnais, who took 1,000 copies as recorded:

"1766, Oct. 25. Received on Acc^t^ of General Printing . . . 1000 Indian Kalendars for Pere La brosse—£4.10."

—Can.P.A., Brown & Gilmore: *Memorial A*.

Copy located: None.

76. CATHOLIC CHURCH. CATECHISMS

CATECHISME / DU / DIOCESE / DE / SENS. / Par Monseigneur JEAN-JOSEPH / LANGUET, Archevêque de SENS. / [printer's ornament] / A QUEBEC: / Chez BROWN & GILMORE, Imprimeurs de la Province. / [rule] / M,DCC,LXVI. /

12mo. A-T^4; 148, [3] p. type-page: 15 × 8.7 cm. small pica and bourgeois throughout.

Contents: p. [1], t.-p.; p. [2], blank; p. [3]-11, Abrégé de la doctrine Chrétienne; p. 12-102, Catéchisme; p. 103-148, Instruction, etc., Prières; [3] p. at end: Table; verso of p. [3], blank.

This is another edition of 2,000 (or, to be exact, 1,997) copies of the *Catéchisme* of 1765 (No. 59). The type has been reset throughout, *la Doctrine* and *le Catéchisme* in smaller type, *l'Instruction etc.* in the same size, as that of the 1765 edition. The text is unchanged, but the page numbers of entries in contents table are omitted.

The printer recorded this work:

"1766, April 16. Rec^d^ for General printing 2000 Catechisms of Sens of Mr Germain after allowing for 3 copies they fell short £91.12."

—Can.P.A., Brown & Gilmore: *Memorial A*.

Copies located: CaQMS; CaQQL.

77. CAWTHORNE, JOSEPH

[Considerations on the present languishing state of trade in Canada.]

Proposed printing at Quebec by Brown & Gilmore, 1766, was advertised:

"Proposals for Printing by Subscription. Considerations on the Present languishing State of Trade in Canada; with some Observations on the Duties lately imposed by Proclamation: Addressed to Thomas Ayl-n Esq; with some Encomiums on that Gentleman. By Joseph Cawthorne.

"As soon as 300 copies shall be subscribed for, [work] will be begun and finished in about 3 or 4 weeks. It will be contained in about 40 pages in 8vo. printed on entire new Type and suitable Paper. The Price to Subscribers, will be Half a Dollar for each Copy, to be paid on the Delivery of it. . . . It will be stitch'd, cut, and delivered at places of subscription. Subscriptions are taken in at the Printing Office, Quebec; by Mr. Jos. Standfield at Three Rivers; at the Post-Office in Montreal. No more Copies will be printed than subscribed for. Such as subscribe for Six, shall have a Seventh gratis."

The *Proposals* appeared only once in the *Quebec gazette*, and there is no evidence that this work was published as proposed.

78. GREAT BRITAIN. LAWS, STATUTES, *etc.*

ANNO REGNI / GEORGII III. / REGIS / Magnæ Britanniæ, Franciæ, & Hiberniæ. / QUINTO. / Au Parlement commencé et tenu à WESTMINSTER, le Dixneuviéme / Jour de Mai, Anno Domini 1761, dans la premiére Année du / Régne de notre Souverain Seigneur GEORGE III. par la Grace / de DIEU, de la Grande-Brétagne, de France et d'Irlande, ROI, / Défenseur de la Foi, &c. / Et continué depuis par plusieures Prorogations jusques au Dixiéme Jour de / Janvier, 1765, qui fait la Quatriéme Séance du Douziéme Parlement de la / Grande-Brétagne. / [rule] / [royal arms] / [rule] / A QUEBEC: / De l'Impression de BROWN & GILMORE, Imprimeurs. / [rule] / M,DCC,LXVI. /

[A]-H^2, $[I]^1$; 33 p.; type-page: 20 × 15.3 cm.

Contents: p. [1], t.-p.; p. [2], blank; p. 3-33, 5 Geo. III c. 12; p. 33 verso, blank.

Caption title p. 3: "Anno Quinto Georgii III Regis. Cap. XII. Un Acte pour accorder de certains Droits ou Impôts de Timbrages, et autre Impôts, dans les Colonies et Etablissemens Britanniques à l'Amérique, et pour les rendre applicables en outre à subvenir aux Frais de défendre, de proteger et d'assurer les dites Colonies et Etablissements."

Note at end of text, p. 33: "Du Bureau de Secretariat, de Québec le 10 Mars, 1766. L'Acte du Parlement ci dessus a été traduit par Ordre de Son Excellence le Gouverneur et conseil pour en informer tous les Sujets de sa Majesté, faisans residence en cette Province, et il est etroitement enjoint et prescrit aux Curés de rendre cet Acte public dans leurs Paroisses respectives en telle Maniere que Personne n'en puisse prétendre Cause d'ignorance. Par Son Excellence le Gouverneur J. Goldfrap D. Sec[ry]."

The printers recorded this work:

"1766, March 3. Recv[d] for general printing 400 copies of the Stamp Act making 4 [sic] Sheets in 4to with Brevier Notes for Mr. Drummond—£24."
—Can.P.A., Brown & Gilmore: *Memorial A*.

Stamped paper arrived in Quebec by the *Glory*, Sept. 27, 1765, to be distributed by "Mr. Drummond at his office in Jesuit College Quebec, and at the office of Jacques Jordon, Montreal." Little comment on the Act was printed by Brown & Gilmore, excepting occasional letters from British merchants, in the *Quebec gazette*, e.g., July 28, 1765. It went into force apparently without demonstration of protest. Gov. Murray wrote to the secretary of state, Feb. 14, 1766, that "the inhabitants of this province had not followed the example of the neighbouring colonies but had willingly submitted to the authority of the British legislature."—Can.P.A., "Q" 3: 26.

This was not substantiated by the report of Adam Mabane, to his fellow members of the Council, Mar. 27, 1766, on discontents in Montreal: ". . . It is likewise my my duty to report that the people in that part of the Province begin to murmur at the Stampt [sic] Act tho' by the firmness of the Magistrates it is Strictly obeyed, the Traders of Montreal are mostly natives of the other provinces [i.e. American colonies] or at least get their goods from them by which means they have constant correspondence with them and every post brings Letters from the other provinces telling them of the proceedings of the Sons of Liberty and their intention to oppose the Stampt [sic] act. 'Tho the Canadians are very tractable they express an Uneasiness at paying a Tax from which the other provinces are at present exempt, & any Relaxation on the part of the Magistrates would be followed with much opposition to that Law. . . "—Can.P.A., Que. Leg. Co. *Minutes A*, Mar. 27, 1766.

French notaries in the country districts, however, bought little stamped paper from Messrs. Drummond or Jordan during the winter of 1765-66. "On conserve encore dans nos greffes quelques actes écrits sur le papier timbré imposé en 1765. Après un examen minutieux des documents reçus entre le premier novembre 1765 et la nouvelle du rappel de l'acte dans l'été de 1766, nous devons dire, cependant, qu'à part les notaries anglais des villes, très peu de notaires des campagnes employèrent le papier timbré, et les autorités semblent n'avoir porté aucune attention à ces manquements à la loi."—J. E. Roy: *Histoire du notariat au Canada* (4 v., Levis, 1899-1902), 2: 31.

Brown & Gilmore announced a rise in the price of the *Gazette*, from $1.50 to $2.00 per annum from Nov. 1. "This may seem high for a Gazette of this size. But the printers must henceforth buy from one person only, paper at 36 shillings per ream which stood us formerly but 8 shillings." On Oct. 31, they discontinued the *Gazette* for lack of subscribers, but advertised: "There is no Stamp-Duty on Hand Bills." Only in the Resurrection number, May 29, 1766, did they comment on "the impositions of the grievous Stamp: An Act more dreadful than the icy chains of our inhospitable Winter; whose harmful Blasts spread Desolation over the Plains and stop the Source of Commerce, as the latter displays its sleaky Banners only half the Year, But the Former, less benign would have continued its desolating Ravages during the Whole . . . Now happily extricated (by the wisdom and Lenity of the British Parliament whose Goodness extends to the remotest parts of its extensive Empire) . . . we have recommenced publication of the *Quebec Gazette*, at its usual price."

The Quebec edition seems to be the only separate issue of the Stamp Act in Canada, none being recorded from the only other press, that of Anthony Henry in Halifax. The latter, however, with his apprentice, Isaiah Thomas, continued publishing his paper, the *Halifax gazette*, protesting with ingenuity and humour against the Stamp. *See* J. B. Brebner: *The neutral Yankees of Nova Scotia* (New York, 1937), 157-63, *also* W. B. Kerr: *The Stamp Act in Nova Scotia* in *The New England quarterly*, 6: 552-66, Sept., 1933.

Copies located: CaQMS; CaQQL. Facsim of t.-p. of CaQMS copy reproduced in Fauteux: *Introduction of printing into Canada*, 82.

79. GREAT BRITAIN. TREATIES

[Convention for the Liquidation of the Canada Paper Money, belonging to the Subjects of Great-Britain, between the King of Great-Britain, and the Most Christian King.]

? Broadside or leaflet, *printed at Quebec by Brown & Gilmore, 1766*, as recorded:

"1766, June 10. Printed for the Government of Quebec 40 Conventions for liquidating the Canada Paper Money—£2.10.
Ditto for Ditto 100 Ditto in French—£2.16."
—Can.P.A., Brown & Gilmore: *Memorial A.*

The English and French texts were printed in parallel columns (in brevier type) in the *Quebec gazette,* June 12, 1766. The English text, signed: "Done at London, this 29th day of March, 1766. (L.S.) H.S. Conway" is reprinted in Shortt: *Documents relating to Canadian currency, exchange, and finance,* 2: 1043-51 (from which the title above was taken) from *A collection of all the treaties of peace* [*etc.*] (London, J. Almon, 1772), 2: 296.

This treaty sets forth the conditions and rates at which the French government was to redeem paper money formerly issued by the French administration in Canada, and held in 1766 by persons in England, Canada, and France. Paper had long been a feature of currency in New France and as the colony prepared for its final war against the English, various types of paper were issued at Quebec in increasing quantities, to be converted later into notes of exchange payable in Paris. Quebec fell, however, and payment was ordered suspended, Oct. 15, 1759. Much of the unredeemed paper in the hands of Quebecois is said to have been bought up by British speculators. The Treaty of Paris, 1763, included a promise of redemption by the French and after considerable negotiation by the French the conditions and rates were settled by this Convention.

Copy located: None.

80. GREAT BRITAIN. TREATIES

[Convention pour liquider le Papier de Canada appartenant aux Sujets de la Grande-Bretagne, entre le Roi Très-Chrétien & le Roi de la Grande-Bretagne.]

? Broadside or leaflet, *printed at Quebec by Brown & Gilmore, 1766.* This is the French edition of the item above, printed in 100 copies.

The French text is signed: "Fait à Londres, ce vingt-neuvième jour de mars mil sept cent soixante-six. (L.S.) Signé Guerchy L.S. Signé H.S. Conway." It is reprinted in Shortt: *Documents relating to Canadian currency, exchange, and finance,* 2: 1042-50 (from which the title above was taken) from French official edition with imprint: *A Paris L'Imprimerie Royale. M.DCCLXVI.*

Copy located: None.

81. NOVA SCOTIA. HOUSE OF ASSEMBLY

Caption title: [Journal and Votes of the House of Assembly for the Province of Nova-Scotia.]

Note: title above is not transcribed from copy.

fo. [66] p. *Printed at Halifax, N.S., by Anthony Henry, 1766.*

Contents: p. [1-66] Journal and votes of the second session of the fourth assembly, June 3-Aug. 1, 1766 (including p. [16, 28, 32, 60 blank).

This *Journal* has the appearance of a rough proof, pulled and published seriatim during the session—unpaged, with blank pages (versos) and part pages following the end of a day's record. It is uncouth in style, with rows of crowns and other small ornaments amassed capriciously in blank spaces. A gesture of derision by Henry, perhaps, for, in disgrace since the Stamp Act fracas, he saw a new government printer arriving to replace him about this time. The *Journal* records a stormy session, the Assembly at deadlock with governor-in-council over control of salaries. The administration published its version of proceedings as soon as the new printer started work, in the *Nova-Scotia gazette*, Aug. 15, 1766. The Assembly in its next session ordered this misrepresentation corrected by a publication in the same *Gazette* and by reference to this *Journal*.

Copies located: CaNs; CaNsHA.

82. NOVA SCOTIA. HOUSE OF ASSEMBLY

Caption title: [Journal and Votes of the House of Assembly for the Province of Nova Scotia.]

Note: title above is not transcribed from copy.

fo. 50 [i.e. 48] p.; p. [4] blank, p. [5], numbered 4; 5, also 45-46 omitted in numbering. *Printed at Halifax, N.S., by Robert Fletcher, 1766.*

Contents: p. 1-50, Journal of the third session of the fourth assembly, Oct. 23-Nov. 22, 1766.

This is Fletcher's first edition of the Assembly *Journal*, for which (and stationery) he charged £18 16*s*. 4*d*. His typographic style is quite distinct from that of his predecessor (and successor), Anthony Henry. Fletcher eschewed ornament and black letter. He had a simple and consistent arrangement of headings, captions, etc., and a modest variation in type, with caps, small caps, occasional italics, and plain rules. His text was the same as Henry's roman (? Caslon old face in pica), but his orderly layout, neat composition, and restraint in ornament, give his production an entirely different appearance.

Copies located: CaNs; CaNsHA; GBLP (in C.O. 220/6).

83. NOVA SCOTIA. LAWS, STATUTES, *etc.*

Caption title: [At the General Assembly of the Province of Nova-Scotia . . . the 3rd day of June, 1766.]

Note: title above is not transcribed from copy.

fo. p. 87-110; paged in continuation of No. 64. *Printed at Halifax, N.S., by Anthony Henry, 1766.*

Contents: p. 87-110, 6 Geo. III c. I-XII, acts passed in the second session of the fourth assembly, June 3-Aug. 1, 1766.

Copy located: CaNsWA.

84. NOVA SCOTIA. LAWS, STATUTES, *etc.*

Caption title: [At the General Assembly of the Province of Nova-Scotia . . . the 23rd day of October 1766.]

Note: title above is not transcribed from copy.

fo. p. 111-[123?] paged in continuation of No. 83; the only copy located, containing 6 Geo. III c. 1-8, lacks p. 119 to end, but a MS. index records 6 Geo. III c. X (which occupies about one page in the revised edition) beginning on p. 122. *Printed at Halifax, N.S., by Robert Fletcher, 1766.*

Contents: p. 111-[123?], 6-7 Geo. III c. I-X, acts passed in the third session of the fourth assembly, Oct. 23-Nov. 22, 1766.

Copy located: CaNsWA (p. 119 to end wanting).

85. PRIMERS. QUEBEC

[Latin Alphabet, *Printed at Quebec by Brown & Gilmore, 1766.*]

The printers' records note occasional sales of Latin Alphabets, or primers, in 1766, but do not indicate the format, size of edition, nor date of printing, e.g.,

"1766, June 30. Rec.[d] for sundry Articles sold this week as per Cash viz.—
. . . Alphabets 48 Latin ones sold in Sheets—12/.
Aug. 23. Sold to Joseph Bargeas 4 Doz. Latin Alphabets @ 3/—12/.
Dec. 31. [balancing year's accounts] 300 Latin [alphabets] sold in Sheets —£3.15.
1767, June 11. Joseph Bargeas has brought home, stitched and cut, 182 Latin Alphabets, for which we agreed to give him a Sol a piece—9/1."
—Can.P.A., Brown & Gilmore: *Memorial A.*

Copies were sold at about half the price of the French Alphabet of 1765, and at about the same rate as the Latin edition of 1767. Joseph Bargeas, the book binder, repeatedly bought Alphabets in sheets during 1766, apparently to stitch and sell in retail. The following year he stitched for the printers' retail trade.

Copy located: None.

86A. QUEBEC, *Province.* COURT OF QUARTER SESSIONS OF THE PEACE (Quebec District)

[Rates for ferries]

Broadside. 50 copies, *printed at Quebec by Brown & Gilmore, 1766,* as recorded by the printers (*see* No. 86B).

Copy located: None.

86B. QUEBEC, *Province.* COURT OF QUARTER SESSIONS OF THE PEACE (Quebec District)

[Regulations for Ferries.]

? Broadside: *printed at Quebec by Brown & Gilmore, 1766,* as recorded:

"1766, Aug. 16. Printed for the Justices of the Peace of the District of Quebec, by Order of James Shepherd, who promised to see us paid. 50 Regulations for Ferries in a folio Page—£1.1.
50 Tables of Rates for D.[o] in a 4to Page—12/."
—Can.P.A., Brown & Gilmore: *Memorial A.*

Copy located: None

87. QUEBEC, *Province.* GOVERNOR, 1764-1768 (*Murray*)

[By His Excellency Proclamation. <Text> Given under my Hand and Seal at Arms at . . . Quebec, this twenty-fifth day of April . . . 1766. Ja. Murray. By His Excellency's Command, Ja: Potts, D.C.C.]

? Broadside: *Printed at Quebec by Brown & Gilmore, 1766.* This is the English edition of the item below, printed in 60 copies.

The text contains Gov. Murray's proclamation of disallowance by His Majesty-in-council [London] Nov. 22, 1765, of "Rules and Regulations made in [Quebec] . . . intituled as follows Viz^{t}:

"An Ordinance for the better discovering & Suppressing unlicensed houses, dated 3^{d} Novr 1764.

"An Ordinance for the better observance of the Lords Day dated the 6 Novemr. 1764.

"An Ordinance for billeting His Majesty's Troops . . . dated the 12 Novr 1764. Together with an additional ordinance published on the 29 of the same month in further explanation of it. [etc.]."

The proclamation is reprinted in Can.P.A., *Report, 1918,* from which this description is taken.

Copy located: None.

88. QUEBEC, *Province.* GOVERNOR, 1764-1768 (*Murray*)

QUEBEC, / à sçavoir. } / PAR SON EXCELLENCE, / PROCLAMATION. / <Text> / Donné . . . dans la Ville de Québec, ce 25me Jour d'Avril . . . / . . . 1766. / JA: MURRAY. / Par Son EXCELLENCE, / JA: POTTS, D.C.C. / VIVE le ROI. /

Broadside: 29 lines; type-page: 19.3 × 31.8 cm.; *Printed at Quebec by Brown & Gilmore, 1766,* as recorded:

"1766, May 9. Printed for the Government of Quebec a Proclamation in English repealing 4 Ordinances 60 Copies—£1.5.
Ditto for Ditto in French. 130 Copies—£1.10."
—Can.P.A., Brown & Gilmore: *Memorial A.*

The text begins: "Ayant reçu les Ordres Royaux de sa Majesté au Conseil, donnés à la Cour à St. James, le 22me de Novembre, 1765, . . . J'ai donc jugé à propos . . . de faire sortir cette Proclamation, faisont sçavoir . . . les Ordres Royaux . . . concernant les Ordonnances [etc.]."

This is Gov. Murray's proclamation of the disallowance by His Majesty-in-council, dated: "à la Cour à St. James, le 22me Novembre, 1765," of ordinances passed by the governor-in-council of Quebec, "[1] . . . pour supprimer les Maisons ou l'on débite des Boissons sans permis . . . 3me de Novembre, 1764; [2] . . . pour faire mieux observer le Dimanche . . . 6me de Novembre, 1764; [3] . . . pour faire loger les troupes . . . par billet . . . le 12me Novembre, 1764; [4] . . . 29me de même mois pour expliquer . . . la precedente."

The royal disallowance was ordered to be published by proclamation immediately—Can.P.A., Que. *State,* Apr. 19, 1766. This proclamation is reprinted in Can.P.A., *Rapport, 1918.*

Copy located: CaQQL; Photostat in CaOOA.

89. QUEBEC, *Province.* GOVERNOR, 1764-1768 (*Murray*)

[Proclamation concerning enregistering deeds, etc.]

? Broadside: *Printed at Quebec by Brown & Gilmore, 1766,* as recorded:

"1760, May 3. Printed for the Government of Quebec a Proclamation concerning enregistering Deeds &c. 60 cop.—£1.5.
Ditto for Ditto in French 130 copies—£1.10."
—Can. P.A., Brown & Gilmore: *Memorial A.*

This *Proclamation* probably contained the text, or concerned the terms, or extended the time limit of "An Ordinance for registering Grants, Conveyances and other Instruments in Writing, of or concerning, any Lands, Tenements or Hereditaments within this province." This law, passed at Quebec, Nov. 6, 1764, required deeds, etc., to lands granted under the French régime, to be registered with British authorities in Quebec, by June 24, 1765.

The ordinance is reprinted in Can.P.A., *Report, 1918.* But the Proclamation does not appear in the *Quebec gazette,* May-July, 1766, nor in modern reprint of 18th-century documents.

Copy located: None.

90. QUEBEC, *Province.* GOVERNOR, 1764-1768 (*Murray*)

[Proclamation pour l'enrégistrement des concessions etc.]

? Broadside: *Printed at Quebec by Brown & Gilmore, 1766.* French edition of the item above, published in 130 copies.

Copy located: None.

91. QUEBEC, *Province.* GOVERNOR, 1764-1768 (*Murray*)

[By His Excellency the Honble. James Murray, Esquire, Captain General and Governor in Chief of the Province of Quebec, . . . Proclamation. <Text> Given under my sign and seal . . . at Quebec, the 27th May, . . . One Thousand Seven hundred and sixty six. Long live the King. Ja. Murray. By Order of His Excellency J. Goldfrap D. Secretary.]

? Broadside: *Printed at Quebec by Brown & Gilmore, 1766,* in 40 copies, English edition of the item below. No example of the 18th century English version could be found; a modern translation from the French edition (No. 92) is printed in Can.P.A., *Report, 1918,* from which this entry is taken.

Text: "Whereas a convention to liquidate, and make a final settlement respecting the Canada paper money belonging to the subjects of Great Britain, has been signed in London, on March 29th last . . . I deem it proper . . . to notify all subjects of His Majesty, . . . who are proprietors or holders of Canada paper, that they must henceforth send this paper to London, in order that it may arrive there to be declared before the Commissioners . . . before the first day of October next. . . . The attention of His Majesty to the welfare of his subjects has engaged him in this matter, to provide for the just satisfaction of their demands at the French Court, it is however by no means the intention of His Majesty that persons other than true subjects of Great Britain may be benefitted . . . I enjoin and require strictly all those in this government . . . under no pretext whatever, to trade . . . or send to England, any paper money which may come from France, belonging to French subjects. [etc.]."

Copy located: None.

92. QUEBEC, *Province.* GOVERNOR, 1764-1768 (*Murray*)

Par Son Excellence l'Honorable JAQUES MURRAY, . . . / . . . / . . . / PROCLAMATION. / <Text> / Donné sous mon Seing . . . à Québec, le 27 de Mai, . . . / . . . Mil Sept Cens Soixante Six. / JA: MURRAY. / Par Ordre de Son EXCELLENCE, / J. GOLDFRAP, D. Secrétaire, / VIVE LE ROI. /

Broadside: 29 lines; type-page: 12 × 21 cm. *Printed at Quebec by Brown & Gilmore, 1766,* as recorded:

"1766, May 28. Printed for the Government of Quebec 40 Proclamations in English concerning Canada Paper Money—£1.5.
Ditto for Ditto 100 in French concerning Ditto—£1.10."
—Can.P.A., Brown & Gilmore: *Memorial A.*

Text: "Vu qu'une Convention pour liquider, et faire une Termination finale du Papier de Canada appartenant aux Sujets de la Grande-Brétagne, a été signée à Londres le Vingt-neuviéme Jour de Mars dernier, . . . je juge à propos de . . . faire sçavoir à tous les Sujets . . . qui sont propriétaires ou Dépositaires de Papier du Canada, qu'ils ayent à les envoyer dorénavant à Londres, à fin qu'il y arrive pour être déclaré par devant les Commissaires . . . avant le Premier Jour d'Octobre prochain, [etc.]."

This is Gov. Murray's proclamation notifying British subjects in Canada how to secure redemption of paper money issued by the former French administration. It is reprinted (facsim. illus.) in Shortt: *Documents relating to Canadian currency and exchange,* 2: 1056; also reprinted in Can.P.A., *Rapport, 1918.*

Copy located: CaQMS. Photostat in CaOOA (in Can.P.A., "*S*" *Quebec proclamations, 1765-1775*). ?Another copy not located is reproduced as facsim. illus. by Shortt, *Documents relating to Canadian currency and exchange.*

93. QUEBEC, *Province.* GOVERNOR, 1764-1768 (*Murray*)

[Proclamation concerning 2 Acts Parliament.]

? Broadside: *Printed at Quebec by Brown & Gilmore, 1766,* as recorded:

"1766, May 31. Printed for the Government of Quebec 40 English Proclamations concerning 2 Acts Parliament + ye Acts—£1.10.
Ditto for Ditto 100 in French—£1.16."
—Can.P.A., Brown & Gilmore: *Memorial A.*

This is probably Gov. Murray's proclamation, and the text, of 6 Geo. III c. 11. "An act to repeal . . . an act for granting and applying certain stamp duties . . . in the British colonies"; also 6 Geo. III, c. 12, "An act for the better securing the dependency of His Majesty's dominions in America on the crown and parliament of Great Britain" (the repeal of the Stamp act; also the Declaratory act). The text of the latter appeared in the *Quebec gazette,* June 5, 1766.

Copy located: None.

94. QUEBEC, *Province.* GOVERNOR, 1764-1768 (*Murray*)

[French edition of the item above.]

Printed at Quebec by Brown & Gilmore, 1766, in an edition of 100 copies.

Copy located: None.

95. QUEBEC, *Province.* LAWS, STATUTES, *etc.*

[An Ordinance, For repairing and amending the High-Ways in this province. <Text> Given by His Excellency the Honorable James Murray, Esq; Captain-General and Governor in Chief of the Province of Quebec, . . . In Council, at Quebec, the 27th Day of March, Anno Domini, 1766, . . . Ja:Murray. By Command of His Excellency in Council, Ja: Potts, D:G:G:]

? Broadside: *Printed at Quebec by Brown & Gilmore, 1766;* as recorded:

"1766, Apr. 5. Printed for the Government of Quebec, an Ordinance in English For Repairing the High Way's, 60 copies—£3.15.
Ditto in French, 130 copies—£3.15."
—Can.P.A., Brown & Gilmore: *Memorial A.*

This was a basic law for the construction and maintenance of main roads, bridges, and ferries, etc., in the districts of Quebec and Montreal. The work was to be done by the inhabitants under direction of a voyer or overseer for each district, the justices of the peace administering the terms of the ordinance.

It is reprinted in Can.P.A., *Report, 1913.*

Copy located: None.

96. QUEBEC, *Province.* LAWS, STATUTES, *etc.*

[Ordonnance pour faire reparer et raccommoder les Grands Chemins en cette Province.]

? Broadside: *Printed at Quebec by Brown & Gilmore, 1766,* in 130 copies. French edition of the item above.

It is reprinted in Can.P.A., *Rapport, 1913.*

Copy located: None.

97. QUEBEC, *Province.* LIEUTENANT-GOVERNOR, 1766-1768 (*Carleton*)

[By the Honorable Guy Carleton, Esq; Lieutenant-Governor and Commander in Chief of the Province of Quebec, Brigadier-General of His Majesty's Forces, &c. &c. A Proclamation <Text> Given under my Hand and Seal . . . Quebec, this 24th Day of September . . . One thousand and Seven Hundred and Sixty-six. Guy Carleton. By the Lieutenant-Governor's Command, J. Goldfrap, D.Secy. God Save the King.]

? Broadside: *Printed at Quebec by Brown & Gilmore, 1766,* as recorded:

"1766, Sept. 27. Printed for the Government of Quebec 2 Proclamations continuing all public Officers in their Employment, viz. 40 English—£1.3. 120 French—£1.10. [Total:] £2.13.0."

—Can.P.A., Brown & Gilmore: *Memorial A.*

Text: "Whereas His Majesty has been most graciously pleased, by His Commission . . . 7th Day of April, 1766, To Constitute and Appoint me Lieutenant-Governor and Commander in Chief in and over His Province of Quebec, . . . I . . . [order] that [all] Officers do continue in their several Employments, [etc.]."

This was the first official publication of Guy Carleton, later Lord Dorchester, who as lieutenant-governor, then governor, of Quebec, later governor of Lower Canada with jurisdiction also over the other provinces, had the most extended career of any English administrator in Canada during the 18th century.

This proclamation is reprinted in Ontario Archives, *Report, 1906;* also (more accurately) in Can.P.A., *Report, 1918,* from which the description above is taken.

Copy located: None.

98. QUEBEC, *Province.* LIEUTENANT-GOVERNOR, 1766-1768 (*Carleton*)

[Québec à Scavoir: Par l'Honorable Guy Carleton, Ecuier, Lieutenant-Gouverneur et Commandant en Chef de la Province de Québec, Brigadier-Général des Troupes, de sa Majesté, &c.&c. Proclamation <Text> Donné sous le seing et sceau de mes armes, au Chateau St.-Loüis, à Québec, le 24 jour de Septembre . . . 1766. Guy Carleton. Par Ordre du Lieutenant-Gouverneur, J. Goldfrap, D. Secretaire.]

Broadside: *Printed at Quebec by Brown & Gilmore, 1766,* in 120 copies, French edition of the item above.

Text: "Comme il a plû très gracieusement à sa Majesté, par sa Commission . . . datée à St. James le septiéme jour d'Avril, 1766, de me nommer et constituer Lieutenant-Gouverneur et Commandant en Chef de la Province de Québec . . . j'ai jugé à propos . . . [d'ordoner] que [tous les] officiers ayent à continuer dans leurs différens Emploix [etc.]."

This proclamation is reprinted in Can.P.A., *Rapport, 1918.*

Copy located: None.

99. QUEBEC, *Province.* LIEUTENANT-GOVERNOR, 1766-1768 (*Carleton*)

[Québec, à Sçavoir: Par l'Honorable Guy Carleton, Lieutenant-Gouverneur . . . <Text> Donné . . . à Québec, ce 22 Jour de Decembre . . . 1766. Guy Carleton. Par Ordre du Lieutenant-Gouverneur, J. Goldfrap, D. Secrétaire.]

? Broadside: *Printed at Quebec by Brown & Gilmore, 1766.* This proclamation, published in English and French in the *Quebec gazette,* Dec. 29, 1766-Jan. 5, 1767, was also printed separately in French only, for distribution by the government, as recorded:

"1766, Dec. 31. Printed for the Government of Quebec 140 Proclamations in French for discovering the Authors of Outrages on the Indians—£1.10.

1767, Jan. 10. Printed for the Government of Quebec 2 Weeks double [i.e. in English and French] A Proclamation for discovering [etc.] . . .N°. 105 [*Quebec gazette*]—£1.17."

—Can.P.A., Brown & Gilmore: *Memorial A*.

Text: "Vu que des avis ont été reçûs, Que plusieurs violences et meurtres ont été commis sans sujet sur les Sauvages . . . Son Excellence le Lieutenant Gouverneur en Conseil . . . enjoignent . . . à tous les habitants . . . d'éviter toute occasion d'offenser les Sauvages, et de traitor avec eux comme amis et frères. . . . Et à fin de decouvrir . . . les personnes coupables des susdites violences . . . le Lieutenant-Gouverneur et le Conseil avertissent . . . que la personne faisant pareille découverte, recevra . . . une recompense de Cinquante Livres."

This proclamation is reprinted in Can.P.A., *Rapport, 1918*, the English text (not printed in broadside form apparently) is in Can.P.A., *Report, 1918*.

Copy located: None.

100. REFLEXIONS SUR LE CANAIDEN GEMISSANT

[Reflexions sur le canaiden gemissant.]

? Broadside: *Printed at Quebec by Brown & Gilmore, 1766*, as recorded:

"1766, June 28. Rec[d] on Acc[t] of General Printing . . . for 100 Reflexions sur le Canaiden [sic] gemissant—£1.1."

—Can.P.A., Brown & Gilmore: *Memorial A*.

Neither author nor subject matter of *Reflexions* has been ascertained. The printers' record indicates it to have been slight in size and produced for a private customer. The title suggests a political theme.

Brown & Gilmore printed very little, either in the *Quebec gazette* or for private distribution, concerning the local disturbances of their time. That they did *some* work not "becoming Printers for the Government" appears in their petition of Aug. 27, 1768, for increase in salary: ". . . [the printers] have not only been unable to conduct [the *Gazette*] with so much Regularity and Caution as they could wish, but have also been obliged by their narrow Circumstances, in Order to get a Livelihood, to interfere in Things that otherwise they would be very glad to decline [etc.]."

—Can.P.A., "*S*" *Int. corres.* 17: 129.

Copy located: None.

101. ST. JOHN'S RIVER SOCIETY

WHEREAS it has been thought expedient, for the Information of the Proprietors of sundry Tracts of Land, situate in the Province / of Nova-Scotia, or Acadia, to make known the Tenor of the several Grants under which the said Lands are held, therefore the / following Extracts are printed. / [etc. 75 lines] / (QUEBEC: Printed by BROWN & GILMORE.)

fo. 2 *l.* without signature pagination; type-page: 32.7 × 21.2 cm. text in 79 lines on recto of *l.* [1]; *l.* [1] verso-*l.* [2], blank.

Contents: Extracts from text of four patents granted by Gov. Wilmot of Nova Scotia to Thomas Falconer and sixty others, on Oct. 18, 1765, for 50,000 acres in the township of Gage; Oct. 18, 100,000 acres in the township of Burton; Oct. 19, 30,000 acres in the township of Maugerville; and on Oct. 31, to Thomas Falconer and sixty-six others, about 125,000 acres in the township of Sunbury.

This leaflet was printed for one of the grantees, Jacob Jordan, of Montreal, as the printers' records show:

"1766, Oct. 23. Rec.[d] on Acc.[t] of General Printing for 200 Extracts from the Patents for granting Land in Nova Scotia and Paper, from Jacob Jordan —£3.3."—Can.P.A., Brown & Gilmore: *Memorial A*.

The land company which became known as the St. John's River Society (known also in Nova Scotia as the Canada Company, or the Quebec Company) was formed early in 1764 by a group of officers in the Royal American, the 44th Foot, and other regiments stationed in Montreal. It later comprised sixty-eight members, military officers, colonial officials, and merchants, in Montreal, Quebec, New York, Massachusetts, and Ireland. In 1764 Captain Beamsley Glazier was sent from Montreal to investigate the lands advertised in Nova Scotia (*see* No. 13) and to secure grants for the company. He obtained patents to five townships on the lower part of the St. John River, which were surveyed and, in 1768, divided among members of the company, each receiving about 5,000 acres. From 1766 the enterprise was directed from committee meetings in New York or Boston; all members paid £15 New York currency annual fee, and their representative and a member of the company (Glazier, then in 1767, James Simonds, a merchant who had settled at the mouth of the River) remained on the St. John to promote settlement of the lands according to the terms of the grant. Slight progress was made, the unsettled lands became liable to Escheat and were so declared by the governor of Nova Scotia in 1783 (*see also* No. 410). They were regranted in the land boom following the American Revolution to loyalists and others.

This leaflet is reprinted in W. O. Raymond: *Papers relating to the St. John's River Society*, in N.B. hist. soc. *Coll.* no. 6: 302-57, 1905, p. 302-06. *See also* W. O. Raymond: *At Portland Point* in *New Brunswick magazine*, 1: 186-201, 1898; and W. O. Raymond: *Glimpses of the past, history of the River St. John, A.D. 1604-1784* (Saint John, 1905).

Copies located: DLC; MHi (both lack *l.* [2] blank); NN (complete). Another copy, not located, is recorded in Chas. F. Heartman *Auction Sale Catalogue no. 138* (Metuchen, N.J., Apr. 24, 1922), item no. 26-31 ([2] *l.*, also a map and other MS. and printed pieces relating to the St. John's River Society).

102. ALMANACS. QUEBEC

[Almanac de Cabinet ou Kalendrier pour l'année de grace, 1767. *Printed at Quebec by Brown & Gilmore, 1767.*]

Broadside. This sheet almanac was announced: "Almanac de Cabinet on Kalendrier pour l'année de grace, 1767" (in *Quebec gazette*, Jan. 12, 1767) for publication on Thursday, Jan. 15, 1767, then advertised:

"Just published and to be sold at the Printing-Office at 18 coppers each or one dollar per dozen. A Sheet Almanac for the Year of our Lord 1767, fitted to the

Latitude of Quebec. And to encourage those who buy to sell again, the printers will take back, and return their money, any time before July 1st next, all copies not sold if they are not used or damaged."—*Quebec gazette,* Jan. 19, 1767, *et seq.*

The printers sold copies at 1*s.* each, 6*s.* the dozen from January till Aug., 1767, about 200 in all. They reckoned the cost of printing at £2 8*s.*

Copy located: None.

103. DISNEY, DANIEL, *defendant*

THE / TRIAL / OF / DANIEL DISNEY, Esq; / Captain of a Company in His Majesty's 44th Regiment of Foot, and Town-/Major of the Garrison of Montreal, at the Session of the Supreme-Court / of Judicature, holden at Montreal, on Saturday the 28th Day of February, / and thence continued by Adjournments to Wednesday the 11th Day of / March, 1767, before the Honourable WILLIAM HEY, Esq; Chief-/Justice of the Province of Quebec, upon an Indictment containing two / Charges, the one for a Burglary and Felony, in breaking and entering / Mr. Thomas Walker's House, at Montreal, on the Night of the 6th Day / of December, in the Year 1764, with an Intention to murder the said / Thomas Walker, the other for feloniously and of Malice aforethought cut-/ting off the Right Ear of the said Thomas Walker, with Intention thereby / to disfigure him, against the Form of the Statute of 22 and 23 Car.II. / Cap.i. in that Case made and provided. / [double rule] / QUEBEC: / Printed by BROWN & GILMORE. / [rule] / M,DCC,LXVII. /

4to. A-L², M¹: 46 p.; type-page: 19.7 × 14.2 cm.; p. 17-37 printed in 2 col.

Contents: p. [i], t.-p.; p. [ii], blank; p. iii, Introduction; p. [iv], blank; p. 5-46, Record of this proceeding, (including (p. 7-17) Attorney-General Maseres's speech opening the case, (p. 17-37) evidence for prosecution and defence, (p. 37-46) Maseres's reply and address to jury, and (p. 46) verdict and discharge of prisoners); p. 46 at foot, Oath of John Welles, Mar. 23, 1767, that text is an exact copy of his shorthand record taken in court, the French evidence being translated by Mr. Gallwey, sworn interpreter.

This is a record of the only trial pushed to a conclusion in the Walker case (*see* No. 43). After more than two years' investigation, thwarted by mutually antagonistic groups of French Canadians, English merchants, and army officers, and by the caprice of Walker himself, the government prosecuted Disney for the assault upon Walker. The crown's case was conducted by Attorney-General Francis Maseres, with McGovrack, one of the alleged assailants as king's evidence. Disney was acquitted, apparently with justification, the real culprits, members of the Twenty.eighth Regiment, having left the country. Gov. Murray was recalled to answer charges rising from colonial complaints in London. Walker fumed about the colony, in conztant |controversy, till 1776, when he returned to the United States with the America invaders in retreat.

Issued early in 1768, this word was advertised: "Just published and to be sold at the Printing office, stitched in blue paper for ready money only, Price one half a French dollar (taken down in Short hand at the time . . .) The Trial of Daniel

Disney. . . . It is printed on an entire new small type and good paper and contains 46 pages in large quarto."—*Quebec gazette*, Jan. 28, 1768. From Feb. 11, 1768, the advertisement read: "To be Sold by Joseph Bargeas the book binder, near the steps leading to the Lower-Town, stitched in blue paper. . . . The Trial of Daniel Disney [etc.]."

Printed by Brown & Gilmore, this work was apparently "published" by Joseph Bargeas, the book binder, to whom the printers credited the few copies they sold in Quebec, also the 82 copies sold in London by their agent, and to whom they transferred most of the edition, as recorded:

> "1768, Jan. 30. Sold J. Bargeas the following Articles ⅔ of the Amount payable the first of May next, the other ⅓ the 1st of July next, 278 Disney's Tryals at 80 Dollars for 300—£22.4.9½."
>
> —Can.P.A., Brown & Gilmore: *Memorial A*.

Bargeas had an interest in the case. For while he was in jail for debt and his wife carrying on his business, she had been arrested, one of many suspects, on the deposition of English merchants. She was kept in custody Dec. 8, 1764-Apr. 25, 1765, then dismissed. Bargeas published a lengthy vindication which suggests the wider implications of the case: "This piece is a true portrait of those Evil Disposed Persons who have torn the Reputation of my Spouse and destroyed my credit [etc.]." French text in the *Quebec gazette*, Mar. 9, 1767, English translation, *ibid.*, Mar. 23, 1767.

Facsim. illus. of t.-p. of this production, appears in Can.P.A., *Report, 1914-15*, no. 276; also in Fauteux: *Introduction of printing into Canada*, 66.

The work was reprinted: *The trial of Daniel Disney supposed to have been written by Francis Maseres*, New York, John Holt, 1768 (Evans, no. 10958; Sabin, no. 20265).

Copies located: CSmH; CaO; CaOOA (p. 45-46 wanting); CaQMS; CaQQL; MiU-C; RPJ.

104. LA BROSSE, JEAN BAPTISTE DE, 1724-1782

[Catalogue of the Indians at Tadousak; *printed at Quebec by Brown & Gilmore, 1767*.]

The printers recorded this work:

> "1767, July 13. Received of General Printing &c. of Pere La Brosse For . . . 200 Catalogues of the Indians at Tadousak. &c.—£1.16."
>
> —Can.P.A., Brown & Gilmore: *Memorial A*.

Copy located: None. *See also* Pilling: Algonquian, 282.

105. [LA BROSSE, JEAN BAPTISTE DE], 1724-1782

NEHIRO-IRINIUI / AIAMIHE / MASSINAHIGAN, / SHATSHEGUTSH, MITINEKAPITSH, / ISKUAMISKUTSH, NETSHEKATSH, / MISHT', ASSINITSH, SHEKUTIMITSH, / EKUANATSH, ASHUABMUSHU-ANITSH, / PIAKUAGAMITSH, / Gaie missi missi nehiro-iriniui Astshitsh / ka tatjits, ka kueiasku aiamihatjits ka utshi. / [ornamental rule] / [printer's ornament] / [ornamental rule] / UABISTIGUIATSH. / Massinahitsetuau, BROUN gaie GIRMOR. / [rule] / 1767. /

Colophon, p. 96: UABISTIGUIATSH, Tshi-tiskuetaets, BROUN gaie GIRMOR, 9, / usaku-pihissimutsh, 1767.

In some copies examined (CSmH, DLC one copy) colophon appears: . . . tshi-t-isk uetauets . . .

8vo. A-B^4, E^4, G-K^4, M-P^4, R^4; 96 p.; type-page: 14.3 × 8.8 cm.

Contents: p. [1], t.-p.; p. [2], blank; p. 3-5, approbation; p. [6], blank; p. 7-92, prayers, etc.; p. 93-96, index; p. 96, colophon, errata.

Printed at Quebec by Brown & Gilmore, 1767, this work was recorded by the printers:

"1767, Oct. 16. Received on account of General Printing for 2000 Indian Prayer books containing 6 Sheets in 8vo on English [type] in Algonkin Language, at 25 dollars per Sheet, from La Brosse, Jesuite missionaire —£45."—Can. P.A., Brown & Gilmore: *Memorial A.*

"The title page shows that this manual was prepared for the use of the Montagnais Indians [Nehiro-iriniui] of the missions on the Saguenay and about Lake St. John, at Shatshegu, Mitnekapi (now Lake Portneuf) Iskuami (Escoumains, Saguenay county) Netsheka (Lake Nitcheguan?) Mishtassini (Lake Mistassini) Shakutimi (Chicoutimi) Ekuan, Ashuabmushuan, and all Nehiro-iriniui places whatsoever, who rightly pray (i.e. are Christians)."—Trumbull, quoted by Pilling: *Algonquian,* 281.

The approbation by Jean Olivier Briand, bishop of Quebec, indicates that the work was prepared by Jean Bapist Tshitshisahigan (the brush), i.e. Jean Baptiste de La Brosse. The latter, a Jesuit, was missionary among the Montagnais between 1756 and 1782. This work, entirely in Montagnais, an Algonkian dialect, was the first and is still one of the few so printed. It contains prayers, catechisms, etc. of the Catholic church.

Daniel Claus, commending his Mohawk translation of Church of England prayers (No. 335), to the Society for the Propagation of the gospel, in a letter from Montreal, Oct. 9, 1782, commented upon La Brosse's work: "It grieved me much to see an Indian Mass Book printed at Quebec, by Father La Brosse, for the use of his Mission in the River Saguenay 40 leagues below Quebec, a port of Furr Trade frequented by a parcell of the most savage Nation in America, speaking the Misisaga Language. The trade of wch Port is enjoyed by some English gentlemen from Quebec at whose expence that popish Book was printed, principally one of the company who is no less than a privy Councillor & p:t: [pro tem?] chief judge [Adam Mabane?], professes to be a Member of the Church and undertook the direction of the work, the Jesuite attend[ed] the Press & dispersion of the books . . . a performance the Ind^{ns} are indifferent about."—Can.P.A., *Claus papers,* 3: 177.

La Brosse's work was widely used, however, for a second edition with errata corrected, was published at Quebec, 1817; and a third, Quebec, 1844. His translation is discussed by N. E. Dionne: *Les langues sauvages du Canada et l'oraison Dominicale,* in Congrès international des americanistes: XVe session tenue à Quebec en 1906. [Compte rendu] 2 v. 1907, 2: 211-15.

Facsim. illus. of t.-p. of this work appears in Pilling: *Algonquian,* 281, also in Toronto Public Library, *Bibliography of Canadiana,* no. 411.

Copies located: CSmH; CaO; CaOT; CaQM; CaQMS; CaQQAr (2 cop.); CaQQL; DLC (3 cop.); MH; MiU-C; NN; RPJ (2 cop.).

106. [LA BROSSE, JEAN BAPTISTE DE,] 1724-1782

[Primer in Montagnais dialect, beginning p. 1:] (1) / [ornamental rule] / ABEGHJIKMNOPRSTU. /

Colophon, p. 8: UABISTIGUIATSCH. / Massinahitsetuau, BROUN gaie GIRMOR. / [rule] / 1767. /

4to. A-B^2; 8p.; type-page: 20.5 × 14.5 cm. Without t.-p. or caption title, the text begins on p. 1, as above. Entirely in Montagnais, it contains alphabet and syllables, also prayers and other devotional matter in responsive form.

It was *printed at Quebec by Brown & Gilmore, 1767*, as recorded:

"1767, July 13. Received of General Printing &c of Father La Brosse, For 3000 Indian Alphabets making 1 sheet 4to.—£10.4.0."

"1767, Oct. 16. To make the Indian Alphabets in 4to at the Same Price with the above 8vo [i.e. folding and stitching? the Alphabets at the same rate as *Nehiro*]—£1.10."—Can.P.A., Brown & Gilmore: *Memorial A*.

Copy located: CaQQAr (bound in 19th-century red morocco and gilt (binder's title: *Mss Montagnais*) with three Montagnais MSS., notes, sermon and instructions, by F. de Crepieul, J. B. Maurice, and A. Silvie respectively). This copy is described by Pilling: *Algonquian*, 282, with illus. representing p. 1. cf. Alexandre Chambre: *Un grande apôtre du Canada, le R. P. J.-B. de la Brosse, né à Jauldes* (*Charente*) 363 p., pub. at Jauldes (Charente), France, by the author, about 1904.

107. NOVA SCOTIA. GOVERNOR, 1766-1773 (*Campbell*)

[Proclamation of Governor Campbell and an Advertisement concerning Coal Mines.]

? Broadside. *Printed at Quebec by Brown & Gilmore, 1767*, as recorded:

"1767, June 17. Printed for John Woolsey 50 Proclamations of Governor Campbell's and an Adv.^{t} concerning Coal Mines in English—12/
D^o for D^o in French—12/.
[Total:]—£1.4.0."—Can. P.A., Brown & Gilmore: *Memorial A*.

This publication was probably a hand-bill prepared for circulation in Quebec, advertising coal being mined and sold in Cape Breton by a group of Halifax merchants. Similar notice was published by Woolsey in the *Quebec gazette*, July 3, 1767, *et seq.*

John Woolsey, of the firm John & Robt. Woolsey, also Woolsey & Bryan, was a mercantile agent in Quebec, for whom Brown & Gilmore printed hand-bills, blanks, and advertisements till the firms were dissolved in 1772.

See J. B. Brebner: *The neutral Yankees of Nova Scotia* (New York, 1937), 136-38, on the coal-mining enterprise.

Copy located: None.

108. NOVA SCOTIA. GOVERNOR, 1766-1773 (*Campbell*)

[Proclamation]

? Broadside. French edition of No. 107, *printed at Quebec by Brown & Gilmore, 1767*, in an edition of 50 copies.

Copy located: None.

109. NOVA SCOTIA. HOUSE OF ASSEMBLY

Caption title: [Journal and Votes of the House of Assembly for the Province of Nova Scotia.]

Note: title above is not transcribed from copy.

fo. A-[N]^2; 52 p. *Printed at Halifax, N.S., by Robert Fletcher, 1767.*

Contents: p. 1-52, Journal of the fourth session of the fourth assembly, July 1-Aug. 1, 1767.

Copies located: CaNs; CaNsHA; GBLP (in C.O. 220/11: 1-52).

110. NOVA SCOTIA. HOUSE OF ASSEMBLY

Caption title: [Journal and Votes of the House of Assembly for the Province of Nova Scotia.]

Note: title above is not transcribed from copy.

fo. 4 p. *Printed at Halifax, N.S., by Robert Fletcher, 1767.*

Contents: p. 1-4, Journal of the fifth session of the fourth assembly, Oct. 17-19, 1767.

Copies located: CaNs; CaNsHA.

111. NOVA SCOTIA. LAWS, STATUTES, *etc.*

THE / PERPETUAL ACTS / OF THE / GENERAL ASSEMBLIES / OF / HIS MAJESTY'S PROVINCE OF / NOVA SCOTIA. / [double rule] / [royal arms] / [double rule] / HALIFAX, in NOVA SCOTIA: / Printed by ROBERT FLETCHER. / [rule] / M.DCC.LXVII. / [title within double rule frame]

In some copies the imprint appears: HALIFAX, in NOVA SCOTIA: / Printed and Sold by ROBERT FLETCHER. / [rule] / M.DCC.LXVII. /

fo. [*^{2}, A]-B^2, C^1,D-F^2, A-3F^2; 13 p. l., 206 p., 1 *l.* (Errata); type-page: 25.4 × 15.3 cm. In some copies the errata leaf follows p. l.13.

Contents: p.l. 1 recto, t-p.; verso, Authority for publication; p.l. 2 recto, Dedication; verso, blank; p.l. 3 recto-6 recto, Table of titles (chronological); p.l. 6 verso, blank; p.l. 7 recto-verso, Table of titles (alphabetical); p.l. 8 recto-9 recto, Table of English statutes enacted in Nova Scotia; p.l. 9 verso, blank; p.l. 10 recto-11 recto, Table of Nova Scotia acts based on English statutes; p.l. 11 verso, blank; p.l. 12 recto-13 verso, Table (subject index); p. 1-206, 32 Geo. II c. 1-6 Geo. III c. 4 (acts passed in Nova Scotia, 1758-66); 1 *l.* at end: recto, errata; verso, blank.

Authority for publication (t.-p. verso) states: "Halifax the 13th Day of May, 1767. This edition of the Laws of the Province as prepared and collated from the Records by John Duport, Esq; with the Revisal and Marginal References to Acts of Parliament and Authorities in Law, by Mr. Chief Justice Belcher, was begun by Order of the General Assembly on the Special Recommendation of . . . Governor Francklin and continued by Order of . . . Governor . . . Campbell, [signed:] Richard Bulkeley, Secretary of the Province."

This was the first revised edition of Nova Scotia statutes. It contains, session by session, 1758-Oct., 1766, the text of acts passed and still in force, with titles of acts passed but no longer in force. Laws of a temporary character formerly published among the permanent enactments of each session were excluded from this work and published in a separate revised edition (No. 114) a little later. This distinction between Perpetual and Temporary acts was continued in the sessional publications, the laws of each session being published thenceforward in two series, Perpetual and Temporary, paged in continuation of this work and No. 114 respectively. This revision was made following a resolution of the Council: "[1766, Sept. 9] On considering the want of a sufficient number of copies of the laws of the province and the great necessity of a correct and complete edition, Resolved that Mr. John Duport do prepare such edition which shall be printed in folio by Mr. Robert Fletcher he furnishing 200 copies for which he shall be paid £180.0.0."

—P.A.N.S., N.S. Legislative Council *Minutes*.

On July 31, 1767, the Council voted £60 to be paid to Mr. John Duport "as a further consideration for his services in preparing a new edition of the Laws and correcting press." But the House of Assembly cut the sum to £40.

—P.A.N.S., N.S. Council and Assembly *Papers*.

This work was sold by Fletcher for several years with supplemental sessions laws to date (several copies located are so bound), though after Fletcher relinquished the printing business (1770) these sessional supplements were actually printed by Anthony Henry. Fletcher advertised this work for sale with No. 112 for 12*s*. in sheets, 18*s*. bound, from Mar. 17, 1768.

Copies located: CaN; CaNs; CaNsHA; CaNsWA; CaO; CaOOA (2 cop., one defective); CaOTO; CaQQL; DLC; GBLP (2 cop. in C.O. 219/7); ICN; MB (highly defective); MH (2 cop.); NN; NNB; PHi.

112. NOVA SCOTIA. LAWS, STATUTES, *etc.*

Running title: [rule] / 1767. Anno Septimo Regis GEORGII III. CAP, I[-VIII]. / [rule] /

Caption title: At the GENERAL ASSEMBLY of the Province / of Nova Scotia, . . . / [8 lines] / . . . being the Fourth / Session of the Fourth GENERAL ASSEM-/BLY convened in the said Province. / [rule] /

fo. $3G^2$, $3H^1$; p. 207-212; type-page: 25 × 15.5 cm. paged in continuation of No. 111. *Printed at Halifax, N.S., by Robert Fletcher, 1767.*

Contents: p. 207-212, Cap. I-VIII, perpetual acts passed in the session July 1-Aug. 1, 1767.

Copies located: CaN; CaNs; CaNsHA; CaNsWA; CaO (2 cop.); CaOOA (3 cop.); DLC; GBLP (in C.O. 219/7); ICN; MB; MH (2 cop.); N; NNB.

113. NOVA SCOTIA. LAWS, STATUTES, *etc.*

Running title: [rule] / 1767. Anno Septimo Regis GEORGII III. CAP.I [-II]. / [rule] /

Caption title: At the GENERAL ASSEMBLY of the Province / of Nova Scotia, . . . / [8 lines] / . . . being the Fifth / Session of the

Fourth GENERAL ASSEM-/BLY convened in the said Province. / [rule] /

fo. sig. [3 H2], 3 I²; p. 213-217; type-page: 25 × 15.5 cm. paged in continuation of No. 112. This work was probably printed and issued with No. 112, for in some (at least) of the copies located, p. 211-12 of the latter and p. 213-14 of the former are printed upon the two leaves of an undivided sheet in folio. *Printed at Halifax, N.S., by Robert Fletcher, 1767.*

Contents: p. 213-17, Cap. I-II, perpetual acts passed in the session, Oct. 17-19, 1767; p. 217 verso, blank.

Copies located: CaN; CaNs; CaNsHA; CaNsWA; CaO (2 cop.); CaOOA (3 cop.); DLC; GBLP (in C.O. 219/7); ICN; MB; MH (2 cop.); N; NNB.

114. NOVA SCOTIA. LAW, STATUTES, *etc.*

THE / TEMPORARY ACTS / OF THE / GENERAL ASSEMBLIES / OF / HIS MAJESTY'S PROVINCE OF / NOVA SCOTIA. / [double rule] / [royal arms] / [double rule] / HALIFAX, in NOVA SCOTIA: / Printed and Sold by ROBERT FLETCHER. / [rule] / M.DCC.LXVII. / [title within double rule frame]

fo. [*]², A-R²; 2 p. l., 65 p., 1 *l.*; type-page: 24.8 × 15.6 cm.

Contents: p. l. 1 recto-verso, blank; p. l. 2 recto, t.-p.; verso, blank; p. 1-65, 32 Geo. II c. 1-7 Geo. III c. 1; verso of p. 65, blank; 1 *l.*, blank.

This is a revised edition of acts passed for a limited time or purpose by the Nova Scotia legislature, 1758-Oct., 1767. It gives title and marginal note of acts expired, repealed, etc. and text of those still in force. The revision was made by Judge Duport with notes by Chief Justice Belcher. It covers two later sessions than No. 111 (as the latter's indices indicate) and was published shortly afterwards as advertised:

"This Day are publish'd, Elegantly printed on a new Letter and Super fine Paper (in Two Volumes) the Perpetual and Temporary Laws of the Province of Nova Scotia from the first Session of the General Assembly to the Present time, carefully revised and digested after the best Method; illustrated with Marginal notes, Extracts, and References to all the British Acts of Parliament; as also many useful tables which never appeared before in any book of the kind. . . . The whole Temporary and Perpetual Acts complete will be sold for 13/ in Sheets [later 12/], or 18/ neatly bound. Those gentlemen who were Purchasers of the Perpetual Acts some time since and require the Temporary Laws to complete their set to the present time are requested to apply for them immediately as there are few copies remaining in Hand."—*Nova-Scotia gazette,* Mar. 17, 1768, *et seq.*

Like No. 111 this work was sold for several years following publication, with the temporary sessional laws to date, printed by Anthony Henry.

Copies located: CaNs; CaO (2 cop.); CaOOA; MH (2 cop.); NN; NNB; PHi.

115. PRIMERS. QUEBEC

[Latin Alphabet]

16mo. ?16 p. *Printed at Quebec by Brown & Gilmore, 1767.* The printers' records indicate two printings, each of 2,000 copies, from a single setting of type:

"1767, Sept. 25. Rec· on Acc[t] of General Printing for 2000 Latin Alphabets in Sheets making ½ sheet 16[s] on Demy for the Seminary of Montreal —£6.18.

Nov. 27. Printed for [Joseph Bargeas] and delivered at this Date payable [the last of February next] the following Alphabets, viz. 2000 Small ones containing 16 Pages from off a form composed for Montgolphier*—Halifax £4."

In the same entry appears: "Sold Joseph Bargeas, the following Alphabets payable the last of Feb[y] next. They were delivered him the 19th of October last—

272 in French stitched and cut @ 2[d] Halifax—£2.5.4.
340 in Latin in Sheets @ 2[d]—2.16.8.
177 in Do Stitched & cut @ 2½[d]—1.16.10¼ [sic]
[total in Halifax]—£10.18.10¼ [sic] difference in currency—2.3.9¼.
[total in Quebec currency] £13.2.7½."

—Can.P.A., Brown & Gilmore: *Memorial A*.

In this year, Primers (or Alphabets) were added to Brown & Gilmore's advertisement of printed blanks, etc., which had appeared almost from the first issue of their newspaper, e.g. "To be sold at the Printing-Office, Blank bonds, bills of lading, Powers of Attorney; Seamen's articles, Prentices indentures. Also English, French & Latin Primers."—*Quebec gazette*, May 14, 1767.

The 2,000 Latin Alphabets printed for the Seminary of Montreal were probably prepared for use in the Collège de St. Raphael, a school opened at Longue Point in 1767, which in 1773 was moved into Montreal and became the Collège de Montréal.

Copy located: None.

116. QUEBEC, *Province*. LAWS, STATUTES, *etc.*

ORDINANCES, / MADE FOR THE / PROVINCE / OF / QUEBEC, / BY THE / GOVERNOR AND COUNCIL / of the said PROVINCE, since the ESTABLISHMENT / of the CIVIL GOVERNMENT. / [rule] / [royal arms] / [double rule] / QUEBEC: / Printed by BROWN & GILMORE, near the Bishop's Palace. / [rule] / MDCCLXVII. /

French t.-p.:

ORDONNANCES, / FAITES POUR LA / PROVINCE / DE / QUEBEC, / PAR LE / GOUVERNEUR ET CONSEIL / de la dite PROVINCE, depuis l'ETABLISSEMENT / du GOUVERNEMENT CIVIL. / [rule] / [royal arms] / [double rule] / QUEBEC: / Imprimées par BROWN & GILMORE, proche du Palais épiscopal. / [rule] / MDCCLXVII. /

fo. A-X²; 81 p., 1 *l.*; type-page: 27.5 × 15.8 cm.

Contents: p. [1], English t.-p.; p. [2], French t.-p.; p. 3-81, text of 27 ordinances passed Sept. 14, 1764-Jan. 27, 1767 (English text of each ordinance followed by French translation); p. 81 verso, blank; 1 *l.*, blank.

Advertised: "Now in the Press and speedily will be published, in English and French, All the Ordinances of the Province of Quebec, since the establishment of Civil Government, as well those which have hitherto been printed in this paper,

*Superior of the Séminaire de Saint Sulpice, Montreal.

as those printed separately during its intermission [i.e. Nov. 1, 1765-May 29, 1766, during the enforcement of the Stamp Act]. Printed on this type and suitable paper [later advertised 'Superfine Imperial paper']. No more will be printed than are agreed for. Therefore gentlemen who chuse to take copies are desired to give their names in all this month, to the Printers . . . [and agents in Montreal and Trois Rivières] where copies will be delivered as soon as finished, covered with blue paper. . . . Two Spanish Dollars each."—*Quebec gazette*, Dec. 1, 1766.

Four hundred and fifty copies were printed, of which the Government took two hundred, the printers selling the remainder at 12*s*. the copy. They recorded numerous transactions, including:

"1767, Mar. 6. Sold the following Persons Ordinances payable on Demand . . . [20 copies @ 12/]—£12.

Mar. 12. Joseph Bargeas [book binder in Quebec] is to be credited . . . For cutting and stitching 101 Ordinances—£1.0.2.

Oct. 8. Rec[d] on Acc[t] of Ordinances for 200 copies in Sheets for the Government of Quebec, 25 on Writing paper, as per Agreement—£100.

Dec. 31, [balancing the year's accounts] Ordinances [owe General Printing] for printing 450 Copies containing 20½ Sheets folio—£50."

—Can.P.A., Brown & Gilmore: *Memorial A*.

This work, the first collected edition of the provincial statutes of Quebec, is reprinted in Can.P.A., *Report, 1913*.

Copies located: CaNsWA; CaO; CaOOA (2 cop.); CaOTO; CaQM; CaQMA; CaQMM; CaQQL; DLC; GBLP (in C.O. 42/28: 5-85); ICN; MH; MHi; MiD-B; MiU; N; NN; NNB; PHi.

117. QUEBEC, *Province.* LAWS, STATUTES, *etc.*

[Ordonnance Pour revoquer une Ordonnance de cette Province faite ci-devant; touchant la sommation des grands et petits Jurés. <Text> Donné par son Excellence l'honorable Guy Carleton . . . au Conseil . . . [à] Québec, Mardi le 27 Jour de Janvier . . . 1767. Guy Carleton. Par Ordre du Lieutenant-Gouverneur, Ja. Potts, D.C.C.]

? Broadside: *Printed at Quebec by Brown & Gilmore, 1767*, as recorded:

"1767, Feb. 4. Printed for the Government of Quebec, 120 Copies in French of an Ordinance to repeal an Ordinance concerning the Summoning Juries—£1.1.0."—Can.P.A., Brown & Gilmore: *Memorial A*.

This ordinance revoked one of Mar. 9, 1765, in order: (1) that jurors might be selected from local residents (not from the province at large) to serve in sessions of the supreme court held in Montreal; and (2) that the Thomas Walker case (*see* No. 43) might be investigated by the chief justice in Montreal with local jurors, according to an order of king-in-council of Nov. 22, 1765.

This ordinance is reprinted in Can.P.A., *Rapport, 1913*, from which the description above is taken.

The English text was not published separately for distribution like the French. It was printed in the *Quebec gazette*, Feb. 2, 1767 (at a charge of £1 4*s*. as the printers' records show).

Copy located: None.

118. WRIGHT, JOHN, *botanist, Quebec*

[Catalogue of seeds]

? Broadside or leaflet, *printed at Quebec by Brown & Gilmore, 1767*, as recorded: "1767, July 24. Printed for John Wright 300 Catalogues of Seeds &c. £2.14."
—Can.P.A., Brown & Gilmore: *Memorial A.*

This was probably the first botanical publication in Canada. The nature and scope of Wright's enterprise appears from his advertisement four years later:

"John Wright, Collector of seeds for a Society of noblemen and Gentlemen in Great Britain will have for sale, by the end of September the seeds of every tree, shrub and flower, that are Natives of Canada.—Such gentlemen, as may want a Collection, will be pleased to send their Orders as soon as possible—N.B. His Ship-Broker at London will convey with great care, any Parcels that may be ordered for any Part of France. Mount-Pleasant, near Quebec, 23d July, 1771."
—*Quebec gazette*, July 25, 1771.

Copy located: None.

119. ALMANACS. NOVA SCOTIA

[The Nova-Scotia Calender, or an almanac for the year of the Christian Æra, 1769. *Printed at Halifax, N.S., by Anthony Henry, 1768.*]

Advertised: "Just published and to be sold by A. Henry [the printer, and others]."—*Nova Scotia chronicle*, Jan. 3, 1769, this is the earliest number of the *Nova-Scotia calender* known to have been published.

Copy located: None.

120. ALMANACS. QUEBEC

[Almanac de Cabinet, ou Kalendrier, pour l'année de Grace 1768, calculé pour la latitude de Québec. *Printed at Quebec by Brown & Gilmore, 1768.*]

Broadside. This sheet almanac was advertised: "L'on vient de publier et l'on vend à l'Imprimerie a dix-huit sols la pièce, ou un piastre par Douzaine Un Almanac de Cabinet ou Kalendrier, pour l'année de Grace, 1768, calculé pour la latitude de Québec."—*Quebec gazette*, Jan. 28, 1768, *et seq.*

The printers sold copies at 1*s.* each, 6*s.* the dozen, from Jan. 22 through July, 1768—about 200 in all. They reckoned the cost of printing at £2 8*s.*

Copy located: None.

121. ALMANACS. QUEBEC

[Almanac de Cabinet, ou Kalendrier pour l'année 1769, pour la latitude de Québec. *Printed at Quebec by Brown & Gilmore, 1768.*]

Broadside. This sheet almanac was advertised: "On vient de publier de à vendre à l'Imprimerie et chez M. M. Thompson et Lilly à Montréal, à 15 sols la piece ou un Piastre par douzaine, Des Calendriers de Cabinet pour M.DCCLXIX, par latitude de Québec."—*Quebec gazette*, Dec. 29, 1768.

The printers produced the calendar a little earlier than usual this year, and sold copies ($4\frac{1}{2}d.$ cheaper) at $7\frac{1}{2}d.$ each, till as late as Oct., 1769. They reckoned their printing cost at £2.

Copy located: None.

122. ALMANACS. QUEBEC

[Indian Kalendar. *Printed at Quebec by Brown & Gilmore, 1768.*]

? Broadside or leaflet, probably prepared by Rev. Jean Baptiste de La Brosse, for Montagnais Indians, this almanac was recorded by the printers:

> "1768, May 7, Received on Acc[t] of General Printing for 199 Indian Kalendars for Labrosse—£2.6.0.
>
> Sept. 24. Received . . . Balance remaining on Labrosse's Indian Calendars from Md[me] Germain—14/."
>
> —Can.P.A., Brown & Gilmore: *Memorial A*.

Md[me] Germain was the wife of Louis Langlois dit Germain, a merchant in Quebec, who occasionally acted as agent between Father La Brosse and the printers.

Copy located: None.

123. NOVA SCOTIA. HOUSE OF ASSEMBLY/

Caption title: [Journal and Votes of the House of Assembly for the Province of Nova Scotia.]

Note: title above is not transcribed from copy.

fo. 39 p. *Printed at Halifax, N.S., by Robert Fletcher, 1768.*

Contents: p. 1-39, Journal of the sixth session of the fourth assembly, June 18-July 9, 1768; p. 39 verso, blank. This *Journal* was certainly printed from week to week during the session, for the lieutenant-governor sent a message to the House on July 4, concerning a "Resolution in their printed Votes of June 28."

Copies located: CaNsHA; GBLP (in C.O. 220/11: 55-94).

124. NOVA SCOTIA. LAWS, STATUTES, *etc.*

Running title: [rule] /1768. Anno Octavo Regis GEORGII III. CAP.I[-XII]. / [rule] /

Caption title: At the GENERAL ASSEMBLY of the Province / of Nova Scotia, . . . / [8 lines] / . . . being the Sixth / Session of the Fourth GENERAL ASSEMBLY / convened in the said Province. / [rule] /

fo. sig. $3K\text{-}3O^2$; p. 219-237; type-page: 25.5 × 15.3 cm. paged in continuation of No. 113. *Printed at Halifax, N.S., by Robert Fletcher, 1768.*

Contents: p. 219-237, Cap. I-XII, perpetual acts passed in the session June 18-July 9, 1768; p. 237 verso, blank.

Copies located: CaB; CaN; CaNs; CaNsHA; CaNsWA; CaO; CaOOA (2 cop.); DLC; MB (defective); MH; N; NNB.

125. NOVA SCOTIA. LAWS, STATUTES, *etc.*

Running title: [rule] / 1768. Anno Octavo Regis GEORGII III. CAP.I / [rule] /

Caption title: At the GENERAL ASSEMBLY of the Province / of Nova Scotia, . . . / [9 lines] / being the Sixth Session of the Fourth / GENERAL ASSEMBLY convened in the / said Province. / [rule] /

fo. sig. S[2]; p. 67-69; type-page: 25.8 × 15.3 cm. paged in continuation of No. 114. *Printed at Halifax, N.S., by Robert Fletcher, 1768.*

Contents: p. 67-69, Cap. I, temporary act passed in the session June 18-July 9, 1768; p. 69 verso, blank.

Copies located: CaNs; CaO (2 cop.); CaOOA; DLC; MH (2 cop.); NNB.

126A. RESTIF DE LA BRETONNE, NICOLAS EDME, 1734-1806

LUCILE, / OU / LES PROGRÈS / DE LA / VERTU. / Par un Mousquetaire. [in ornamental frame] / [ornament] / À QUÉBEC, / Et se trouve à PARIS, / Chez {DELALAIN, libraire, rue / Saint Jacques. / VALADE, libraire, rue de la / Parcheminerie, maison / de M. Grangé. / [double rule] / M. DCC. LXVIII. / [title in double frame of rules and ornaments]

12 mo. a, $\overline{\text{A,C,E,G,I,L,N,P}}^{8}$, $\overline{\text{B,D,F,H,K,M,O,Q}}^{4}$, R[3] (in DLC copy); xvi, 198p. type-page: 11.3 × 5.8 cm.

Contents: p. [i] half title; p. [ii] blank; p. [iii] t.-p.; p. [iv] blank; p. [v]-x, A Mademoiselle, signed: R.D.L.B.; p. xi-xiv, Preface; p. xv-xvi, Table des chapitres; p. [1]-198, Lucile.

First edition, apparently, of a romantic tale by a popular and prolific European-French author.

Despite the imprint this work was probably *not* printed or published in Quebec, 1768. The half-title, title, and letter of dedication, headings on p. xi and p. [1], and initial letters at beginning of chapters throughout, are in types not used in any productions from the only press then operating in Quebec, that of Brown & Gilmore. The firm's account books (kept in great detail at that period) record neither work done on, nor sales of, this publication. Nor does *Lucille* appear among works advertised for sale in the *Quebec gazette.*

On the other hand, the author is quoted by Paul Lacroix in his *Bibliographie et iconographie de tous les overages de Restif de la Bretonne par P. L. Jacob* (510 p., Paris 1875), p. 82: "Je fis *Lucile* en vingt jours . . . Je ne pus vendre ma *Lucile* que trois louis au juif Valade, qui en tira 1,500, au lieu de 1,000 (exemplaires) [etc.]."

Copies located: CSmH (this copy bears the words: "Par un Mousquetaire" in the small ornamental frame on t.p.); DLC (this copy lacks words in frame).

126B. ST. JOHN'S RIVER SOCIETY

[Description of the Harbour and River St. John's, in Nova Scotia, and of the Townships of Sunbury, Burton, Gage, and Conway, lying on the said River, as received from Charles Morris, Esq., Surveyor-General of Halifax, and contained in a Letter wrote to Capt. William Spry, one of the Proprietors of said Townships. Dated 25th, January, 1768.]

fo. 4 p.

Entry from Chas. F. Heartman: *Auction sale catalogue,* no. 138 (Metuchen, N.J., Apr. 24, 1922), no. 27, which includes note: "Canadian printing, 1768." This item *may* have been printed in Halifax, N.S., by Anthony Henry or Robert Fletcher, but was more probably produced in New York like Wm. Spry's [*Remonstrance*] *New York, April 11, 1768, to the Revd. Doctor Oglevie* (*see* N.B. hist. soc. *Coll.* 6: 339-43).

This *Description* describes the course of the river, mile by mile, noting the quality of the land, potential crops, timber, etc. Morris, like Spry "one of the proprietors," suggests establishing settlers at the Society's expense on some of the land, to raise the value and induce settlement of adjacent land—indicating the Society's failure hitherto to fulfil the settlement terms of their grants.

Copy located: None.

127. ALMANACS. NOVA SCOTIA

THE / Nova-Scotia CALENDER, / OR AN / ALMANACK / For the Year of the Christian Æra, 1770. / [5 lines] / Wherein is contained, / The Eclipses of the Luminaries . . . / [5 lines] / To which is added, / An Account of the City and Tower of Babylon, / [9 lines] / Calculated for the Meridian of HALIFAX, in Nova-Scotia, / . . . / . . . / . . . / [rule] / By A. LILIUS. / [rule] / HALIFAX: Printed and Sold by ANTHONY / HENRY, at the New-Printing-Office. / [title within ornamental frame.]

16mo. [25] p.; type-page: 13.3 × 8 cm.

Contents: p. [1], t.-p.; p. [2-3], Introduction by A. Lilius, verses; p. [4], Eclipses, vulgar notes; p. [5-7], "All covet, all loose, or the Retaliation"; observations on weather; p. [8], Recipes for diseases in cattle, etc.; p. [9-20], Calendar; p. [21-22], Tales, verses; p. [22-25], Government of Nova Scotia: lists governor, lieutenant-governor, members of Council and Assembly, judges, justices of peace, etc., court sessions, also a note that a complete list of militia officers is unobtainable, and so, is omitted; verso of p. 25, blank.

This almanac was advertised: "Just published and to be sold . . . 6*d.* single [copy], 4/6 per dozen."—*Nova Scotia chronicle,* Nov. 7, 1769, *et seq.*, also in *Nova-Scotia gazette,* Nov. 9, 1769, *et seq.*

Copy located: CaNsHD.

128. ALMANACS. QUEBEC

[Calendrier de Cabinet, pour l'année MDCCLXX. *Printed at Quebec by Brown & Gilmore, 1769.*]

Broadside. This sheet almanac was advertised:

"On vient de publier et à vendre a l'Imprimerie et chez M M Thomas et Lilly à Montréal à 15 sols la pièce ou à une Piastre par douzaine, Des Calendriers de Cabinet pour l'annee MDCCLXX."—*Quebec gazette,* Dec. 28, 1769.

The printers sold copies at 7½*d.* each and reckoned their printing cost for the entire edition [of about 200 copies?] at £2.

Copy located: None.

129. ALMANACS. QUEBEC

[Indian Calendar for 1769. *Printed at Quebec by Brown & Gilmore, 1769.*]

? Broadside or leaflet in Montagnais dialect, the first of four years' calendars [? for 1769-1772] printed for Rev. Jean Baptiste de La Brosse, recorded briefly by the printers:

"1769, Sept. 29. Rec[d] on Acc[t] of Printing Office for 4 Years Indian Calendars and 125 Bishops Mandates French and Indian from Labrosse—£7.10.0."
—Can.P.A., Brown & Gilmore: *Memorial A.*

Copy located: None.

130. ALMANACS. QUEBEC

[Indian Calendar for 1770. *Printed at Quebec by Brown & Gilmore, 1769.*]

? Broadside, or leaflet in Montagnais dialect, the second of four years' calendars recorded as in No. 129 *note.*

Copy located: None.

131. ALMANACS. QUEBEC

[Indian Calendar of 1771. *Printed at Quebec by Brown & Gilmore, 1769.*]

? Broadside or leaflet in Montagnais dialect, the third of four years' calendars recorded in No. 129 *note.*

Copy located: None.

132. ALMANACS. QUEBEC

[Indian Calendar for 1772. *Printed at Quebec by Brown & Gilmore, 1769.*]

? Broadside or leaflet in Montagnais dialect, the fourth of four years' calendars, recorded as in No. 129 *note.*

Copy located: None.

133. BRIAND, JEAN-OLIVIER, *bp. of Quebec,* 1715-1794

[Mandates in French and Indian]

Printed at Quebec by Brown & Gilmore, 1769, as recorded:

"1769, Sept. 29. Rec[d] on Acc[t] of Printing Office for 4 Years Indian Calendars [No. 129-32] and 125 Bishop's Mandates French and Indian from LaBrosse.—£7.10.0."

—Can.P.A., Brown & Gilmore: *Memorial A.*

Father La Brosse, a Jesuit, was missionary among the Montagnais Indians. The purport of this mandate, which he had printed, remains unknown. It was probably prepared by Bishop Briand whose diocese embraced all Catholic Canada.

Copy located: None.

134. BRITANNIA'S INTERCESSION FOR . . . JOHN WILKES

[Britannia's intercession for the deliverance of John Wilkes, Esq; from persecution and banishment to which is added A Political and Constitutional Sermon, and a Dedication to L*** B*** the seventh edition.]

Probably *printed at Halifax, N.S., by Anthony Henry, 1769,* who advertised in the *Nova Scotia chronicle,* June 13, 1769: "This day will be published and sold by Anthony Henry—Britannia's intercession [as above] . . . the seventh edition. Price Seven Pence. Halifax, June 13, 1769"; also advertised in subsequent issues of the same paper as "Just published and sold by Anthony Henry." This was apparently a Halifax reprint of a popular pamphlet published in London in at least nine editions during 1768. Anthony Henry, superseded as government printer during the years 1766-69, was operating an "opposition press" in Halifax, and reprinted several articles concerning the English agitator, Wilkes, in his newspaper, the *Nova Scotia chronicle.* This pamphlet had considerable attention in the colonies at this time (cf. Evans no. 11191).

Copy located: None.

135. CATHOLIC CHURCH. BOOK OF HOURS

[Heures de vie]

Printed at Quebec by Brown & Gilmore, 1769, as advertised:

"On vient d'achever d'imprimer à Québec (dans la même caractere que cet Advertisement) [i.e. small pica] des HEURES DE VIE, qui se vendent chez Joseph Bargeas, par douzaine et en détail, à un prix raisonable. On se propose de continuer l'impression de toute sorte de livres de dévotion."—*Quebec gazette,* Sept. 21, 1769, *et seq.*

This advertisement appeared occasionally for many months, but Brown & Gilmore's account books first show copies sold nearly a year later. The printers recorded several sales of this work (perhaps of a later printing from the same type) to various merchants in Quebec:

"1770, Sept. 12. Rec[d] on Acc[t] of Printing Office for 50 copies of Heures de Vie —£1.13.4.

Sept. 13. Sold Joseph Bargeas as per his Receipt dated the 12 Sept[r] last, 500 Heures de Vie in sheets—£16.13.4.

Oct. 31. Rec[d] . . . for 50 Euer [sic] de Vie—£1.13.4.

Nov. 1. Lessard Butcher 150 Copies Heures de Vie in sheets—£5.

Dec. 22. Lessard Butcher 222 ditto—£7.8."

—Can.P.A., Brown & Gilmore: *Memorial A*.

Copy located: None.

136. LATHAM, J.

[Regiments for children.]

? Broadside. *Printed at Quebec by Brown & Gilmore, 1769*, as recorded:

"1769, April 15. Printed for J. Latham 400 Regiments for Children—£1.
D[o] for D[o] 200 D[o] for adults translated from E[nglish]—15/."

—Can.P.A., Brown & Gilmore: *Memorial A*.

These were probably handbills with rules for health, perhaps with recommendations of treatment and care for persons inoculated against smallpox. Latham, an enterprising physician, for a time surgeon in the Eighth or the King's Regiment of Foot, was the first person known to practise inoculation in Canada. His fulsome advertisements appear at intervals in the *Quebec gazette* from Aug., 1768 till 1786 or later, announcing inoculation "by Mr. Sutton's Method," to be given in Quebec, Trois Rivières, and Montreal, including services to the poor free of charge. His advertisements recommended inoculation and gave directions for emergency measures during epidemic; latterly they denounced rival methods and their practitioners. Other advertisements for inoculation appeared in the *Nova-Scotia gazette* in Aug., 1775, during an outbreak of smallpox in Halifax.

Copy located: None.

137. NOVA SCOTIA. HOUSE OF ASSEMBLY

Caption title: [Journal and Votes of the House of Assembly for the Province of Nova-Scotia.]

Note: title above is not transcribed from copy.

fo. 48 p. *Printed at Halifax, N.S., by Robert Fletcher, 1769.*

Contents: p. 1-48, Journal of the seventh session of the fourth assembly, Oct. 22, 1768-Feb. 6, 1769.

Copies located: CaNsHA; GBLP (in C.O. 220/11: 95-142).

138. NOVA SCOTIA. HOUSE OF ASSEMBLY

Caption title: [Journal and Votes of the House of Assembly for the Province of Nova-Scotia.]

Note: title above is not transcribed from copy.

fo. 30 p. *Printed at Halifax, N.S., by Robert Fletcher, 1769.*

Contents: p. 1-30, Journal of the eighth session of the fourth assembly, Oct. 10-Nov. 9, 1769.

Copy located: GBLP (in C.O. 220/11: 143-73) transcribed in Can.P.A., N.S. "D."

139. NOVA SCOTIA. LAWS, STATUTES, *etc.*

Running title: [rule] / 1768. Anno Octavo Regis GEORGII III. CAP. I[-X]. / [rule] /

Caption title: At the GENERAL ASSEMBLY of the Province / of Nova Scotia, . . . / [9 lines] / being the Seventh Session of the Fourth / GENERAL ASSEMBLY convened in the / said Province. / [rule] /

fo. sig. 3P-3R[2]; p. 239-249; type-page: 25.5 × 15.3 cm. paged in continuation of No. 124. *Printed at Halifax, N.S., by Robert Fletcher, 1769.*

Contents: p. 237-249, Cap. I-X perpetual acts passed in the session Oct. 22, 1768-Feb. 6, 1769; p. 249 verso, blank.

Copies located: CaB; CaN; CaNs; CaNsHA; CaNsWA; CaO; CaOOA (2 cop.); DLC; MB (defective); MH; N; NNB.

140. NOVA SCOTIA. LAWS, STATUTES, *etc.*

Running title: [rule] / 1768. Anno Octavo Regis GEORGII III. CAP. I[-IX]. / [rule] /

Caption title: At the GENERAL ASSEMBLY of the Province / of Nova Scotia, . . . / [9 lines] / . . . being the Seventh Session of the / Fourth GENERAL ASSEMBLY convened / in the said Province. / [rules] /

fo. sig. T-2B[2]; p. 71-96, 1 *l.*; type-page: 25.8 × 15.3 cm. paged in continuation of No. 125. *Printed at Halifax, N.S., by Robert Fletcher, 1769.*

Contents: p. 71-96, Cap. I-IX temporary acts passed in the session Oct. 22, 1768-Feb. 6, 1769; 1 *l.* blank.

Copies located: CaNs; CaO (2 cop.); CaOOA; DLC; MH; NNB.

141. NOVA SCOTIA. LAWS, STATUTES, *etc.*

Running title: [rule] / 1769. Anno Nono Regis GEORGII III. CAP. I[-III]. / [rule] /

Caption title: At the GENERAL ASSEMBLY of the Province / of NOVA SCOTIA, . . . / [8 lines] / . . . being the Eighth Session of the Fourth GENERAL / ASSEMBLY convened in the said Pro-/vince. / [rule] /

fo. sig. 3S[2]; p. 251-253; type-page: 25.5 × 15.3 cm. paged in continuation of No. 139. *Printed at Halifax, N.S., by Robert Fletcher, 1769.*

Contents: p. 251-253, Cap. I-III perpetual acts passed in the session Oct. 10-Nov. 9, 1769; p. 253 verso, blank.

Copies located: CaB; CaN; CaNs; CaNsHA; CaNsWA; CaO; CaOOA; DLC; MB (defective); MH; N; NNB.

142. NOVA SCOTIA. LAWS, STATUTES, *etc.*

Running title: [rule] / 1769. / Anno Nono Regis GEORGII III. CAP. I[-IV]. / [rule] /

Caption title: At the GENERAL ASSEMBLY of the Province / of Nova Scotia . . . / [9 lines] / being the Eighth Session of the Fourth / GENERAL ASSEMBLY convened in the / said Province. / [rule] /

fo. sig. $2C^2$; p. 97-100; type-page: 25.8 × 15.3 cm. paged in continuation of of No. 140. *Printed at Halifax, N.S., by Robert Fletcher, 1769.*

Contents: p. 97-100, Cap. I-IV, temporary acts passed in the session Oct. 10-Nov. 9, 1769.

Copies located: CaNs; CaO (2 cop.); CaOOA; DLC; MH; NNB.

143. ALMANACS. NOVA SCOTIA

THE / Nova-Scotia Calender, / Or an / ALMANACK / For the Year of the Christian Æræ, 1771; . . . / [5 lines] / Wherein is contained / The Eclipses of the Luminaries, . . . / [5 lines] / To which is added, / Prognosticks, or Predictions, . . . / [8 lines] / Calculated for the Meridian of Halifax, . . . / . . . / . . . / . . . / By A. LILIUS. / [rule] / HALIFAX: Printed and SOLD by Anthony Henry / and Mr. Fletcher's on the Parade. / [title within ornamental rule] /

16mo. 32 p.; type-page: 13.3 × 8.3 cm.

Contents: p. [1], t.-p.; p. [2-3] Introduction, verses; p. [4], Eclipses, vulgar notes; p. [5-16], Calendar; p. [17-24], "Prognosticks, or Predictions on the days of the week . . . relating to weather, scarcity and plenty, diseases that will happen to people, also to cattle," etc.; p. [25-31], Province of Nova Scotia, administrative officers, legislature, courts, justices, etc.; p. [31-32], Verses.

Copy located: CaNsHD.

ALMANACS. QUEBEC

[Indian Calendar for 1770] *See* No. 130.

144. ALMANACS. QUEBEC

[Calendrier de Cabinet pour l'Année MDCCLXXI. Pour la latitude de Québec. *Printed at Quebec by Brown & Gilmore, 1770.*]

Broadside. This sheet almanac, probably published at the end of Dec., 1770, was advertised:

"On vient de publier, et à Vendre à l'Imprimerie et chez Pierre M'Clement à Montreal (pour argent comptant seulement) à 15 sols la pièce ou un Piastre par Douzaine, *Des Calendriers de Cabinet* pour l'Année MDCCLXXI. Pour la latitude de Quebec."—*Quebec gazette,* Jan. 3, 1771.

Copy located: None.

145. COLMAN, GEORGE, 1732-1794

[The Jealous Wife, a comedy in five acts.]

Pamphlet, *published at Halifax, N.S., by Robert Fletcher, 1770,* as advertised:

"To morrow morning will be publish'd and Sold by Robert Fletcher on the Parade, The Jealous Wife, a comedy in 5 Acts, written by George Colman, Esq. esteemed one of the best Comedies in the English language."

—*Nova Scotia chronicle,* Apr. 3, 1770.

"This day is published [etc. wording as above]."

—*Nova-Scotia gazette,* Apr. 5, 1770.

This piece may have been actually printed at Halifax by Fletcher, or it may have been printed in London, imported and issued in Halifax with Fletcher's imprint, for its advertisement in his paper, the *Gazette,* is followed by a list of works "just imported and to be sold" by Robert Fletcher.

The jealous wife was produced by Garrick at Covent Garden on Feb. 12, 1761. "Though not written with much genius, it was yet so well adapted to the stage and so well exhibited by the actors, that it was crowded for near twenty nights," wrote Dr. Johnson to Joseph Baretti, June 10, 1761. A comedy of manners after Fielding's *Tom Jones, The jealous wife* was one of the most popular plays of the 18th century; it was performed almost every year in London, the arbiter of colonial fashion, and appeared with corresponding frequency in Halifax and Quebec newspaper advertisements of entertainment by local thespians.

First published in London by Thomas Becket in Feb., 1761, the pamphlet is listed occasionally among works imported and sold in Quebec and Halifax, but the entry as above, seems to represent a local publication, if not a local printing.

Copy located: None.

146. DOYLE, WILLIAM, *b.* 1705?

THE / UNIVERSAL PRAYER, / To which is added, / The Form of anointing the Sick, / As prescribed / In KING EDWARD the VI's, and / QUEEN ELIZABETH's First Com-/mon Prayer Books; / AS ALSO / A Critical DISCOURSE / On that RITE. / By WILLIAM DOYLE, LLB. / [ornamental rule] / HALIFAX: Printed by ANTHONY HENRY. /

12mo. A-D^{8}, E-F^{4}, G^{2}; 84 p.; type-page: 13.5 × 7.3 cm.

Contents: p. [1], t.-p.; p. [2], blank; p. 3-7, Dedication to Frederic, Prince & Bishop of Osnabruck*; p. 8-18, Advertisement; p. 19-67, Prayer (a paraphrase of the Lord's prayer) and Remarks; p. 68-83, Form for anointing (extreme unction) and Remarks; p. 84, Subscribers (twelve persons, forty-six copies).

Probably printed in the autumn of 1770, as advertised in Anthony Henry's newspaper: "Proposals for printing by Subscription The Universal Prayer . . . by the Rev. Wm. Doyle. Printed for the Author, sold by R. Fletcher, [Halifax] . . . Richard Draper, Boston, Hugh Gaine, New York, Bradford & Son, Philadelphia. The work to contain 3 sheets letter press, elegantly printed. Price to Subscribers One Shilling . . . in half binding."—*Nova Scotia chronicle,* Aug. 21, 1770.

*The second son of King George III.

The author was probably William Doyle of Brambleston, County Kilkenny, a member of an Irish protestant family distinguished in public service, and a scholar of Trinity College, Dublin, (M.A. and LL.B. 1729) who became master-in-chancery of Ireland. His grandson, Sir Charles Hastings Doyle, was later lieutenant-governor of New Brunswick, 1866-67, and Nova Scotia, 1867-73. Wm. Doyle apparently visited America, for in 1770 he published *Some account of the British Dominions beyond the Atlantic* (London, 1770), and in the *Universal prayer* mentions conversations with Catholics of Quebec.

This book of devotions appears, from the author's *Remarks*, to have been prepared for Church of England clergymen to use with congregations of dissenting protestants (numerous in Nova Scotia) and·of His Majesty's Catholic subjects in Ireland and Quebec. An effort was being made at this time to proselytize Catholics in Quebec province. In his *Remarks*, etc., Doyle recommends that all persons under a British administration attend public services of the Established Church, as an acknowledgement of authority, whatever sectarian affiliations they also maintain. He suggests, too, means by which the Church of England may gain adherents among protestant dissenters and Catholics—among the latter, by administering extreme unction, and by adding the order of that rite to a French translation of the Church of England liturgy for use in Quebec.

Copy located: MWA; another copy, Brinley No. 122 (p. 83-84 wanting) has not been located.

147. LA BROSSE, JEAN BAPTISTE DE, 1724-1782

AKITAMI / KAKIKEMESUDI-ARENARAG' / AUIKHIGAN, / Messiui Arenâbak / Uâbanakéuiak uitsi / Pépâmkamigék éitsik, / Kisittunésa JAN BAPTIST NUDENANS, / MEKAZEUSSEUET / NEGE / U-d-Aresigâtegui PATRIHANSA. / [ornamental rule] / KEBEK-DARI, / ARENARAG' AUIKHIGEBANIK / BROUN, té GIRMORE. / 1770. /

8vo. [*][4]; [i] 7 p.; type-page: 14.4 × 8.5 cm.; paged with odd numbers on versos.

Contents: p. [i], t.-p.; p. 1-3, alphabet, syllables; p. 3-7, prayers, etc.

Printed at Quebec by Brown & Gilmore, 1770, as recorded:

"1770, Dec. 31. [From Nov. 10, 1770] J. B[te] La Brosse owes . . . 600 Indian Alphabets in Abenaquis Language making Half a Sheet 8vo. in English [type]—£3."
—Can. P.A., Brown & Gilmore: *Memorial A.*

A primer in the Abnaki dialect, the first and probably the only work printed in that dialect in the 18th century in Canada. The Abnaki in Canada dwelt along the St. John River (in the present New Brunswick); also south of the St. Lawrence on the St. Francis (near the present Pierreville), and on the Becancourt Rivers (opposite Trois Rivières). The St. Francis and Becancourt villages were built since about 1680 by bands moving west from territory in the present Maine and New Hampshire, and contained after the Seven Years' War about a thousand Abnaki. Missions were maintained there, also on the St. John, by the Jesuits, one of whom, Father C. G. Coquart, was said to have prepared a French-Abnaki dictionary and a grammar, before his death in 1765. La Brosse, whose name appears on the title page above in its Algonquian form Nudenans, was a protégé of Coquart. The former worked mainly among the Montagnais below Quebec, and he may have had this primer prepared for another associate of Father Coquart, Father Charles Germain, the last Jesuit missionary to the Abnaki, who died at St. Francis in 1779.

See Pilling: *Algonquian*, 282; also Alexandre Chambre: *Un grand apotre du Canada, le R. P. J.-B. de la Brosse, né à Jauldes* (*Charente*) 363 p., pub. at Jauldes (*Charente*) France by the author, about 1904; J. P. A. Maurault: *Histoire des Abenakis depuis 1605 jusqu'a nos jours* (Sorel, 1866); and *The Jesuit relations and allied documents* ed. by R. G. Thwaites (73 v., Cleveland, 1896-1901), 73: 62.

Copy located: CaQMS (t.-p. facsim. from this copy in Fauteux: *Introduction of printing into Canada*, 70).

148. NOVA SCOTIA. HOUSE OF ASSEMBLY

Caption title: [Journal and Votes of the House of Assembly for the Province of Nova-Scotia.]

Note: title above is not transcribed from copy.

fo. 36 p. *Printed at Halifax, N.S., by Robert Fletcher, 1770.*

Contents: p. 1-36, Journal and votes of the first session of the fifth assembly, June 6-July 2, 1770.

Copy located: GBLP (in C.O. 220/11: 175-210).

149. NOVA SCOTIA. LAWS, STATUTES, *etc.*

Running title: [rule] / 1770. Anno Decimo Regis GEORGII III. CAP. I[-X]. / [rule] /

Caption title: At the GENERAL ASSEMBLY of the Province / of Nova Scotia, . . . / [5 lines] / . . . being the First Session of the Fifth / GENERAL ASSEMBLY convened in the / said Province. / [rule] /

fo. sig. 3T-3X²; p. 255-265; type-page: 25.5 × 15.3 cm. paged (apparently) in continuation of No. 139. *Printed at Halifax, N.S., by Anthony Henry, 1770.*

Contents: p. 255-265, Cap. I-X, perpetual acts passed in the session June 6-July 2, 1770; p. 265 verso, blank.

Copies located: CaB; CaN; CaNs; CaNsHA; CaNsWA; CaO; CaOOA; DLC; MB (defective); MH; N; NNB.

150. NOVA SCOTIA. LAWS, STATUTES, *etc.*

Running title: [rule] / 1770. Anno Decimo Regis GEORGII III. CAP. I[-VI]. / [rule] /

Caption title: At the GENERAL ASSEMBLY of the Province / of Nova Scotia, . . . / [5 lines] / . . . being the First Session of the Fifth / GENERAL ASSEMBLY convened in the / said Province. /

fo. sig. 2D-2E², 2F¹; p. 101-110; type-page: 25.8 × 15.3 cm. paged (apparently) in continuation of No. 140. *Printed at Halifax, N.S., by Robert Fletcher, 1770.*

Contents: p. 101-110, Cap. I-IV, temporary acts passed in the session June 6-July 2, 1770.

Copies located: CaNs; CaO (2 cop.); CaOOA; DLC; MH; NNB.

151. QUEBEC, *City*. SEMINAIRE DE QUEBEC

QUOD FELIX, FAUSTUM QUE AD PERPE-/TUAM REI MEMORIAM: / EX liberalitate, et munificentiâ illustrissimi, at que Reverendissimi, / D. D. JOANNIS OLIVARII BRIAND, Quebecensis Epis-/copi, in Collegio Seminarii Quebecensis idib. Augusti Septuagesimo / Supra millesimum Septingentesimum Anno publica, et Solemnis prae-/miorum distributio. /

Broadside: 55 lines; type-page: 33 × 19.6 cm. *Printed at Quebec by Brown & Gilmore, 1770.*

This is a "Palmare" or Honours list, Aug., 1770, for the school year 1769-70, in the Petit Séminaire de Québec. It shows 15 students ranking for prizes and 24 receiving honourable mention in Schola humanitorum, Schola quarta, and Schola sexta.

The Séminaire de Québec was established in 1663 by Bishop Laval and supported by the Société des Missions étrangères of Paris, as a theological training school. Five years later le Petit Séminaire was instituted "pour françiser les sauvages" but it served as a preparatory school for French students of a religious vocation, who later entered the grand Séminaire. The Séminaire and Collège des Jésuites received each other's students in some classes, and when the latter was closed in 1768, the former extended its instruction along classical lines to prepare students for the liberal professions as well as the priesthood. After the English conquest the Séminaire severed connections with the Société des Missions étrangères of Paris and became an independent French-Canadian institution under the bishop of Quebec. It further extended its work to higher education in the 19th century, assuming administrative control of Laval University on its establishment in 1851, the schools of the Séminaire and its rich and ancient library becoming a part of Laval University. Le Petit Séminaire de Québec remains one of the largest preparatory schools in Canada, its members in student cap and green-girdled surcoat are still a familiar sight in the streets of Quebec. Cf. Amédée E. Gosselin: *L'Instruction au Canada sous la régime français 1635-1760* (Quebec, 1911), also E.-A. Taschereau: *Histoire du Séminaire des Missions étrangères de Québec*, chap. XXXI [1755-63] in *Le Canada français*, 20: 628-34, 1933.

Copy located: CaQQL.

152. QUEBEC, *Province*. LAWS, STATUTES, *etc.*

Heading: SUPPLEMENT to the QUEBEC-GAZETTE, N° 273. / SUPPLEMENT à la GAZETTE DE QUEBEC, N° 273. / MARCH 22, 1770. /

Caption title: An ORDINANCE, / For the more effectual Administration of Justice, and / for regulating the Courts of Law in this Province. /

French caption, col. 2: ORDONNANCE qui, pour rendre l'Administration de / la Justice plus prompte et plus efficace, Régle les Cours / de Judicature en cette Province. /

fo. 10 p.; Printed in 2 col. English and French, in long primer type with marginal notes in brevier. *Printed at Quebec by Brown & Gilmore, 1770,* in the usual *Quebec gazette* format and issued separately as recorded:

"1770, Oct. 5. Rec[d] of the Gov[t] of Quebec for half a year Salary [£55] due the 24th of June last and for printing 400 copies of an Ordinance relating to the Courts of Justice—£69.13.2."

—Can.P.A., Brown & Gilmore: *Memorial A.*

This ordinance was distributed by the government, also sold by the printer for a few years at 1*s.* the copy. Passed by governor-in-council, Quebec, Feb. 1, 1770, it is an amendment to the ordinance of Sept. 17, 1764 (No. 49-55) and transfers jurisdiction in civil suits from justices of the peace to the Court of Common Pleas. Popular with French litigants, it was hotly opposed by the English-speaking merchants.

This ordinance is reprinted with related documents in Shortt and Doughty: *Documents, 1759-1791,* 1: 401-16.

Copy located: CaO (bound with *Quebec gazette,* at end of 1769).

153. QUEBEC, *Province.* SUPERINTENDENT OF POST HOUSES

Ordres et Instructions pour [blank]

Broadside: 67 lines. type-page: 25.5 × 16.5 cm.

Contents: Ordres I-XI. Without signatures or date, the orders begin: "I° Vous devez garder un nombre suffisant de bons chevaux forts, et de bonnes voitures, et vous devez être prêt, ainsi que vos domestiques, à toutes heures du jour ou de la nuit, pour pourvoir des chevaux . . . pour le courier . . . de sa Majesté [etc.]."

This is instructions for maîtres de postes issued by Hugh Finlay as director or superintendent of post houses. It was certainly *printed at Quebec by Brown & Gilmore,* and is the same as, or similar to, the work recorded:

"1770, May 30. Printed for Hugh Finlay 150 Regulations for Post Riders between this and Montreal, in French—£2. [including paper] 3 Quires thick Post—6/."—Can.P.A., Brown & Gilmore: *Memorial A.*

Maîtres de postes, or keepers of post houses, were appointed and strictly regulated by the governor-in-council from the beginning of the English régime. For they provided horses and accommodation for post riders who, carrying letters, merchandise, and passengers, were the principal means of communication and transportation between settlements.

Hugh Finlay, 1732-1801, postmaster of Quebec, assumed supervision of maîtres de postes and post riders, for conveyance of mails and about 1773 was officially appointed director or superintendent of post houses by Gov. Carleton. After the conquest Quebec had become part of the colonial postal system directed by the postmaster general in London, with Benjamin Franklin and John Foxcroft joint deputies in America. Finlay succeeded Franklin as deputy in 1774, and after the Revolution was reappointed deputy postmaster general for the remaining British colonies. He continued to direct Canadian post offices under imperial regulations and to superintend post houses, etc., under provincial ordinances, extending both systems as settlement increased; in 1799, however, he was dismissed for defaultin; in post office returns to London. *See* Wm. Smith: *History of the post office in British North America, 1639-1870* (Cambridge, Eng., 1920); *also* Can.P.A., *Finlay papers.*

Copy located: CaOOA (filed with other printed blanks and signed "Hugues Finlay Directeur des Postes [1767-1779]" in Quebec Legislative Council papers, 1780, in Can.P.A., "S" series).

154. QUEBEC, *Province.* SUPERINTENDENT OF POST HOUSES

[Regulations for Post Riders]

Broadside. English edition of (or similar to) the item above. *Printed at Quebec by Brown & Gilmore, 1770,* as recorded:

"1770, June 11. Printed for H. Finlay 100 Regulations for Post in English —£1.5. [including paper] 2½ Quires thick Post. 5/."

—Can.P.A., Brown & Gilmore: *Memorial A*.

The printers' records show many editions of 50 to 500 copies, English and French, of regulations, attestations, and other forms, printed for Hugh Finlay as director of Post Houses, also as deputy postmaster, during the 18th century.

Copy located: None.

155. SECCOMBE, JOHN, 1708-1792

A / SERMON / Preached at HALIFAX, July 3d, 1770, / At the ORDINATION / OF THE / Rev. Bruin Romcas Comingoe. / To the Dutch Calvanistic [sic] Presby-/terian Congregation at Lunen-/burg, / By JOHN SECCOMBE, / of Chester, A.M. / Being the First preached in the Province of No-/va-Scotia, on such an Occasion. / To which is added / An APPENDIX. / [rule] / We find no Evil in this Man: but if a Spirit or an / Angel hath spoken to him, let us not fight / against GOD. Act. 23.9. / , have appear'd unto thee to make thee a Minister. / Act. 26.16 / Would GOD, that all the Lords People were pro-/phets, and that the Lord would put his Spirit / upon them. Num. 11, 29. / [ornamental rule] / Halifax: Printed by A. HENRY, 1770. / (Price One Shilling.) / [title within ornamental frame]

12mo. A-C[8], D[4]; 3 p. l., 31, 16 p. 1 *l.* (blank) at end; 1 *l.* (errata) inserted after t.-p.; type-page: 14.5 × 8.2 cm.

Contents: p. l. 1 recto, t.-p.; verso, blank; p. l. 2 recto-verso, Dedication; p. l. 3 recto, Preface; verso, blank; p. 1-31, "Ordination sermon, [text:] John 21.15.16. Jesus said to Simon Peter, Simon son of Jonas, lovest thou me more than these? [etc.]"; verso of p. 31 blank; p. 1-16, "An appendix . . . reasons of the Ordination of . . . Comingoe"; 1 *l.* blank.

The dedication to Malachy Salter pays tribute to the efforts of Salter and of persons in Boston, in establishing a fund to support dissenting ministers in Nova Scotia, and states this ordination to be the first "to promote the Protestant dissenting in this Province."

Anthony Henry, himself a German, announced: "It is with pleasure we can inform the Public, that this day the Rev. Messrs Secombe, Lyon, Phelps & Murdoch set a-part to the Office of the Holy Ministry, Mr. Bruin Rumkis Comingoe (known by the name of Brown) at the earnest request of more than Sixty Families of the Dutch Calvinist Presbyterian congregation at Lunenburgh."—*Nova Scotia chronicle,* July 3, 1770.

Later he advertised: "Just published and to be sold by Anthony Henry, A Sermon preached at Halifax, July 3, 1770 . . . Rev. Bruin Romcas Comingoe . . . (Price One Shilling)."—*ibid.*, Aug. 15, 1770.

Seccombe, born in Medford, Mass., graduated from Harvard in 1728. He published a poem on the college caretaker, *Father Abbey's Will,* 1731, considered a masterpiece of humour at the time. Seccombe served as minister in the village of Harvard, Mass., 1733-57, then he moved to Nova Scotia. He settled in Chester (like Lunenburg, a village on the south shore) served the Congregational church there till his death in 1702 and also "supplied" the Protestant dissenting church in Halifax. Seccombe was charged before the Executive Council, Dec. 23, 1776, "with preaching a Sermon . . . Sept. 1, 1776 tending to promote Sedition and rebellion among the people [of Chester]," but proved his innocence.

Several hundred German settlers arrived in Nova Scotia, 1750-52. Most of them, and some families of French Protestants, were moved in June, 1753, from Halifax, sixty miles down the coast to found the town of Lunenburg. They were some 1,453 in all, Lutheran, Reformed, Anabaptist, and Calvinist. Each sect strove to maintain its own worship. But, like other small dissenting groups, each had difficulty in securing a minister who taught its doctrines, in a province where the Church of England was established by law and its clergy subsidized by the Society for the Propagation of the Gospel. In 1769-70 the Lutherans built their church by local subscription, their first in Canada, and imported a minister from Germany.

The Dutch Reformed Calvinists were served by one of their own community, Bruin Romcas Comingoe. Born in Groningen, Holland, 1723, he came to Nova Scotia in 1752, took land a Lunenburg, and after the ordination described in the title above, ministered to his neighbours till 1818. He died at Lunenburg in 1820.

See M. B. Des Brisay: *History of the county of Lunenburg* (Toronto, 1895); also W. C. Murray: *History of St. Matthews Church, Halifax, N.S.* (with portrait of Comingoe) in N.S. hist. soc. *Coll.* 16: 137-70, 1912. Facsim. illus. of t.-p. appears in Toronto Public Library, *Bibliography of Canadiana,* no. 437.

Copies located: CaNsHA; CaNsHD; CaOT; CaQMS; CtY; Ketcheson; MBAt; NhD; NN; NNHi; RPJ (this copy has occasional MS. notes through text, and on blank leaf at end 2 pages of MS. written about 1772, giving an account of the German settlement, and of Church of England efforts to proselytize dissenters, at Lunenburg).

156. ALMANACS. NOVA SCOTIA

THE / Nova-Scotia Calender, / Or an / ALMANACK / For . . . 1772; . . . / [5 lines] / Wherein is contained / The Eclipses . . . / [5 lines] / To which is added, / Prognosticks, . . . / [13 lines] / Calculated for the Meridian of Halifax, . . . / . . . / . . . / . . . / . . . / By A. LILIUS. / [rule] / HALIFAX Printed and SOLD by Anthony Henry / and Mr. Fletcher's on the Parade. / [title within ornamental frame]

16mo. [16 + ?] p.; type-page: 15.2 × 8.8 cm.

Contents: The only copy located is highly defective, comprising: p. [1], t.-p.; p. [2], "Letter in answer to query of Mr. Carlus, 24 May, 1770, on the true time of his birthday"; p. [?], Ephemeris; verso, eclipses, vulgar notes; [12] p. Calendar. The contents listed on t.-p. show the missing pages to have contained prognosticks, aphorisms, articles on printing a poem, liberty of the press, etc., lists of officers of government, courts, etc., of Nova Scotia.

Copy located: CaNsHD (defective).

157. ALMANACS. QUEBEC

[Calendrier de Cabinet pour l'An MDCCLXXII, pour la Latitude de Québec. *Printed at Quebec by Brown & Gilmore, 1771.*]

Broadside. This sheet almanac was advertised: "L'on vient de publier et à Vendre à l'Imprimerie chez Malcolm Fraser, Ecuier, aux Trois Rivieres, et chez Mr. Patrick M'Clement à Montreal, à 15 sols chaque, ou une Piastre par Douzaine, pour de l'Argent comptant seulement. Un Calendrier de Cabinet pour l'An M.DCC. LXXII pour la Latitude de Québec plus exact et plus ample que celui des années précédentes."—*Quebec gazette*, Jan. 2, 1772.

The Calendar, more exact and fuller than those of preceding years, was announced in the *Quebec gazette*, Dec. 12, 1771, as then in the press, and as containing the moon's phases calculated from observations by S. Holland,* the time of rising and setting of the sun, the seasons, etc., royal festivals and holidays, religious festivals, observances etc., for the diocese of Quebec.

It was sold at 7½*d.* the copy, 5*s.* the dozen, with a noticeable increase in the sales recorded in Brown & Gilmore's account books.

Copy located: None.

ALMANACS. QUEBEC

[Indian Calendar for 1771] *See* No. 131.

158. NOVA SCOTIA. HOUSE OF ASSEMBLY

Caption title: [Journals and Votes of the House of Assembly for the Province of Nova-Scotia]

Note: title above is not transcribed from copy.

fo. 22p. *Printed at Halifax, N.S., by Anthony Henry, 1771.*

Contents: p. 1-22, Journal and votes of the second session of the fifth assembly, June 5-July 6, 1771.

Copy located: GBLP (in C.O. 220/11: 211-32); transcribed in Can.P.A., N.S."D."

159. NOVA SCOTIA. LAWS, STATUTES, *etc.*

Running title: [rules] / Anno undecimo Regis GEORGII III. CAP. I[-IX]. 1771. / [rule /

Caption title: At the GENERAL-ASSEMBLY of the Province of Nova-/Scotia, . . . / [7 lines] / being the Second Session of the Fifth GENERAL-/ASSEMBLY convened in the said Province. / [row of dots] /

fo. sig. 3Y-3Z²; p. 267-274; type-page: 25 × 15 cm. paged in continuation of No. 149. *Printed at Halifax, N.S., by Anthony Henry, 1771.* Similar in style to No. 160, the typography of this work indicates that the government's printer was no longer Robert Fletcher but Anthony Henry.

*Samuel Holland, surveyor-general of Quebec and the Northern District of America.

Contents: p. 267-274, Cap. I-IX, perpetual acts passed in the session June 5-July 6, 1771.

Copies located: CaB; CaN; CaNs; CaNsHA; CaNsWA; CaO; CaOOA; DLC; MB; MH; NNB.

160. NOVA SCOTIA. LAWS, STATUTES, *etc.*

Running title: [rule] / 1771. Anno undecimo Regis GEORGII III. CAP. I[-X, i.e. XIII]. / [rule] /

Caption title: At the GENERAL-ASSEMBLY of the Province of Nova-/Scotia, . . . / [7 lines] / being the Second Session of the Fifth GENERAL- / ASSEMBLY convened in the said Province. / [row of dots]

fo. sig. 2G-2I[2]; p. 110-116 [i.e. 121]; type-page: 25 × 15 cm. paged in continuation of No. 150, 110 being repeated in numbering; p. 113 mispaged: 123 and 118-121: 113-116. *Printed at Halifax, N.S., by Anthony Henry, 1771.* This work is printed from the same founts of type as the laws of preceding sessions, produced by Robert Fletcher, but in different typographic style. Henry took over Fletcher's printing business in Sept., 1770, and this work, spotted with black letters and inaccuracies, is typical of Henry's earlier work.

Contents: p. 110-116 [i.e. 121], Cap. I-XIII, temporary acts passed in the session June 5-July 6, 1771.

Copies located: CaNSA; CaNs; CaO; CaOOA; DLC; MH; NNB.

161. PRIMERS. QUEBEC

[ALPHABET]

Printed at Quebec by Brown & Gilmore, 1771, for Louis Langlois, dit Germain, as recorded:

"1771, Oct. 29, Received on Acc[t] of Printing for 900 Alphabets sold to Germain —£5.8.0." —Can.P.A., Brown & Gilmore: *Memorial A.*

Copy located: None.

162. WOOD, THOMAS, *d.* 1778

A / SERMON / Occasioned by / The DEATH of / The HONORABLE / Mrs. Abigail Belcher, / Consort of / JONATHAN BELCHER, Esq; / late / Lieutenant-Governor, and Commander in Chief, / and His Majesty's present Chief Justice of His / Province of Nova-Scotia; / Delivered / At St. PAUL'S Church at Halifax in Nova-Scotia, / October 13th, 1771, being the Sunday after / Her Funeral. / [rule] / By THOMAS WOOD, Vicar / of St. PAUL'S; and a Missionary, in the Ser-/vice of the Venerable Society, for the Propaga-/tion of the Gospel, in foreign Parts. / [rule] / HALIFAX, Nova-Scotia: Printed by / A. HENRY, 1771. / [title within double rule frame.]

8vo. A-C[4]; 1 p. l., 17, 5 p.; type-page: 16 × 10 cm.

Contents: p. l. recto, t.-p.; verso, blank; p. 1-17, "A funeral sermon, [text:] Corinthians I, chap. 15, verse 55: O Death! Where is thy sting." At end: p. 1-3,

"Extract from the *Nova-Scotia gazette*, No. 59, October 15, 1771 [account of funeral of Mrs. Belcher on Oct. 9, 1771.]"; p. 4-5, "Monumental threnody sacred to the Memory of Mrs. Belcher."

This pamphlet, handsomely printed on heavy paper (probably in a small edition for Chief Justice Belcher), is one of the best specimens of printing craft ever issued from Henry's office.

Thomas Wood, apparently a native of New Jersey, "bred to physick and surgery," was ordained in London, then returned as Society for the Propogation of the Gospel missionary to New Jersey. In 1751 he moved to Nova Scotia. For a time an itinerant missionary, he settled in 1764 at Annapolis Royal. Wood acquired some knowledge of Micmac, and in 1766 sent to the Society for the Propogation of the Gospel, London, MSS. containing a grammar, a dictionary, and prayers in that dialect. These were probably the work of Abbé Maillard, long a Catholic missionary among the Micmacs, states Dr. J. C. Webster of Shediac, N.B., who has Wood's MSS. They have never been published.

Copy located: DLC (bound with: *A Sermon occasioned by the death of theHonorable Abigail Belcher . . . delivered at Halifax . . . October 20, 1771, by John Seccombe . . . with an Epistle by Mather Byles, D.D. of Boston*, Boston, printed by Thomas and John Fleet, 1772).

163. ALMANACS. NOVA SCOTIA

THE / Nova-Scotia CALENDAR / Or an / ALMANACK / For . . . 1773 / . . . / . . . / . . . / . . . / . . . . / Wherein is contained, / The Eclipses . . . / . . . / . . . / . . . / . . . / To which is added, / Essays of Luther, &c. . . . / [12 lines] / Calculated for the Meridian of Halifax . . . / . . . / . . . / . . . / By A. LILIUS. / [rule] / HALIFAX: Printed and SOLD by ANTHONY HENRY, / at Mr. Robert Fletcher's STORE, and at Mr. Francis Boyd's. / [title within ornamental frame]

16mo. [30] p.; type-page: 15.1 × 8.8 cm.

Contents: p. [1], t.-p.; p. [2], Letter to reader by A.L., Courts of Nova Scotia etc.; p. [3], Eclipses; p. [4], Essays of Luther; p. [5-28], Calendar on rectos, on verso's: Of Zvinglius, Progress of Lutheranism, Of the Anabaptists, Rules and recipes for the care of live stock; Province of Nova Scotia officers of government, courts, customs, militia; recipes, distances from Halifax; p. [29], Verses; p. [30], advertisement of Francis Boyd, [stationery], recipes.

This *Calendar* was advertised: "This day is published *The Nova-Scotia Calendar* . . . 5/ per dozen 6*d*. single."—*Nova-Scotia gazette*, Dec. 1, 1772.

Copy located: CaNsHD.

164. ALMANACS. QUEBEC

[Calendrier de Cabinet pour l'an M,DCCLXXIII, pour la latitude de Québec. *Printed at Quebec by Brown & Gilmore, 1772*]

Broadside: this sheet almanac was advertised in the *Quebec gazette*, as in the preceding year, and sold by the printers at 7½*d*. the copy, 5*s*. the dozen, from Jan. 2, 1773.

Copy located: None.

ALMANACS. QUEBEC

[Indian Calendar for 1772] *See* No. 132.

165. CATHOLIC CHURCH. LITURGY AND RITUAL

NEUVAINE / A L'HONNEUR / DE S. FRANCOIS / XAVIER, / DE LA COMPAGNIE DE JESUS, / Apôtre des Indes et du Japon. / [printer's ornament] / [rule] / QUEBEC: / Imprimé par BROWN & GILMORE, / Et à vendre chez Joseph Bargeas. / [rule] / M,DCC,LXXII. /

18mo. A-M⁹; 215, [1] p.; type-page: 10.6 × 6 cm.

Contents: p. [1], t.-p.; p. [2], Prières; p. [3]-71, Neuvaine; p. [72], blank; p. [73]-129, Petit office; p. 130, Indulgence (Sept. 24, 1753); p. [131]-215, Les Sentimens; p. 215 at end of text: "Jean Olivier Briand, Evêque de Québec, &c.&c. permettons de vendre et debiter dans notre Diocèse, le present livre . . . n'aiant trouvé dans cette édition que ne fut conforme à l'ancienne. Donné à Québec . . . le 14 Octobre 1773 [sic]"; [1] p. at end (verso of p. 215), Table des Sentimens.

Though its printing probably started in 1772, this work was published in 1773, as the bishop's approbation and printers' records indicate:

"1773, Oct. 18. Bonds & Notes owe Printing Office for Lessards Note of Hand payable in May next given us for 500 Copies of the Neuvaine of St. Francis printed for J. Bargeas, making 6 Sheets Eighteens said Bargeas finding the Paper—£10.15.0."

—Can.P.A., Brown & Gilmore: *Memorial A.*

It was advertised:

"On vient d'achever l'Impression de la Neuvaine et de Sentiments de St. Francois de Xavier, faisant un volume de 215 pages, imprimé sur du très beau papier et de meme caractere que cet avertissement. Il se vendra chez Joseph Bargeas, libraire, rue Couillard à Quebec."—*Quebec gazette,* Nov. 11, 1773.

This is the last work with the imprint of Brown & Gilmore, for Gilmore died about Feb. 4, 1773, probably *after* the first sheets (including title page) of the book were printed, but *before* the work was completed and published.

Copies located: CaNsWA; CaQMM; CaQMS; Ketcheson.

166. NOVA SCOTIA. HOUSE OF ASSEMBLY

Caption title: [Journals and Votes of the House of Assembly for the Province of Nova Scotia.]

Note: title above is not transcribed from copy.

fo. 24 p. *Printed at Halifax, N.S., by Anthony Henry, 1772.*

Contents: p. 1-24, Journal and votes of the third session of the fifth assembly, June 9-July 8, 1772.

Copy located: GBLP (in C.O. 220/11: 233-57).

167. NOVA SCOTIA. LAWS, STATUTES, *etc.*

Running title: [rule] / 1772. Anno Duodecimo Regis GEORGII III. CAP. I[-VI]. / [rule] /

Caption title: At the GENERAL-ASSEMBLY of the Pro-/vince of Nova-Scotia, . . . / [8 lines] / . . . being / the Third Session of the Fifth GENERAL / ASSEMBLY convened in the said Province. / [ornamental rule] /

fo. sig. 4A², 4B¹; p. 275-280; type-page: 25.8 × 14.8 cm. paged in continuation of No. 159. *Printed at Halifax, N.S., by Anthony Henry, 1772.*

Contents: p. 275-280, Cap. I-VI, perpetual acts passed in the session June 9-July 8, 1772.

Copies located: CaB; CaN; CaNs; CaNsHA; CaNsWA (p. 279-80 wanting); CaOOA; DLC; MB; MH; NNB.

168. NOVA SCOTIA. LAWS, STATUTES, *etc.*

Running title: [rule] / 1772. Anno Duodecimo Regis GEORGII III. CAP. I[-III]. / [rule] /

Caption title: At the GENERAL-ASSEMBLY of the Pro-/vince of Nova-Scotia . . . / [8 lines] / . . . being / the Third Session of the Fifth GENERAL / ASSEMBLY convened in the said Province. / [ornamental rule]

fo. sig. 2K-2L², [2M]¹; p. 123-131; type-page: 25 × 15 cm. paged in continuation of No. 160. *Printed at Halifax, N.S., by Anthony Henry, 1772.*

Contents: p. 123-31, Cap. I-III, temporary acts passed in the session June 9-July 8, 1772; p. 131 verso, blank.

Copies located: CaNs; CaO; CaOOA; DLC; MH; NNB.

169. ALMANACS. NOVA SCOTIA

THE / Nova-Scotia CALENDAR / Or an / ALMANACK / For . . . 1774; . . . / [5 lines] / Wherein is contained, / The Eclipses . . . / [5 lines] / To which is added, / A Moral and Political Map of Europe . . . / [5 lines] / Calculated for the Meridian of Halifax . . . / [4 lines] / By A. LILIUS. / [rule] / HALIFAX: Printed and SOLD by A. HENRY, / by Mr. Robert Fletcher, and Mr. Francis Boyd. / [title within ornamental frame.]

16mo. [22 + ?] p.; type-page: 13.7 × 8 cm. Printed by Anthony Henry, sold by Henry, also by the merchants, Fletcher and Boyd.

Contents: The only copy located is highly defective, comprising: p. [1], t.-p.; p. [2], Eclipses; [12] p. Calendar; (pages missing here); [2] p. Chronology of events 1757-1771, aphorisms; [2] p., Moral and political map of Europe; [1] p. Anecdotes; [3] p. Province of Nova Scotia list of officers of government (incomplete).

This almanac was advertised: "This day is published The Nova-Scotia Calendar, [etc.]."—*Nova-Scotia gazette*, Dec. 14, 1773.

Copy located: CaNsHD (defective).

170. ALMANACS. QUEBEC

CALENDRIER pour l'Année 1774, pour Québec, qui est par les 306$^{d.}$ 30$^{m.}$ de Longitude, et 46$^{d.}$ 55$^{m.}$ de Latitude. / [ornamental rule] /

Broadside: type-page: 42.5 × 38 cm. with ornamental rule frame.

Contents: Signes du zodiaque, phases de la lune, nombres, fêtes mobiles, quartre tems, commencement des 4 saisons, eclipses de soleil (arranged in 7 col. of 4-5 lines, across the sheet beneath title); Calendrier (12 tables in 4 col. with ornamental rules). The calendar tables indicate fêtes (Catholic), moon's quarters, sun and moon's rising and setting. No provincial information, civil or military, is included however, till several years later.

Printed at Quebec by Wm. Brown, ?1773, the *Calendrier* was advertised: "L'on vient de publier et a Vendre à l'Imprimerie, chez Malcolm Fraser Ecuier, aux Troix Rivières et chez Mr. Jacques Perry sur la place de Marché à Montreal, a Quinze Sols chaque, ou un Piastre par Douzaine pour l'argent comptant seulement un Calendrier, [etc.]."—*Quebec gazette,* Jan. 13, 1774.

Published each year (except 1766) since 1765, this is the earliest *Calendrier* of which a copy has been located.

Copy located: CaO (bound in *Quebec gazette,* preceding 1774).

171. ALMANACS. QUEBEC

[Indian Calendar for 1773. *Quebec, Wm. Brown, 1773.*]

? Broadside or leaflet, in Montagnais dialect. This was the first of a series of six calendars for the year 1773 and each of the five succeeding years to 1778. They were probably prepared by Father Jean Baptise de La Brosse, Catholic missionary to the Montagnais and neighbouring Algonkian tribes in the Saguenay-Lake St. John district, and were all *printed at Quebec by Wm. Brown, 1773,* as recorded:

"1773, July 29. Printed for J. B^{te} Labrosse Indian Calendars for 1773, 4, 5, 6, 7, & 8, for each 127 copies and delivered them to Louis Germain his Agent 25/6 per Year.—£7.13."—Can.P.A., Brown & Gilmore, *Memorial A.*

"1774, Apr. 11. Received of J. B^{te} Labrosse by the Hands of Louis Germain for Indian Calendars—£7.13."—*ibid.*

Copy located: None.

172. ALMANACS. QUEBEC

[Indian Calendar for 1774. *Quebec, Wm. Brown, 1773.*]

? Broadside (a sheet almanac) or leaflet, in Montagnais dialect, prepared by Father La Brosse and *printed at Quebec by Wm. Brown, 1773* as recorded in the latter's accounts. *See* No. 171 *note.*

Copy located: None.

173. ALMANACS. QUEBEC

[Indian Calendar for 1775. *Quebec, Wm. Brown, 1773.*]

? Broadside (a sheet almanac) or leaflet, in Montagnais dialect, prepared by Father La Brosse and *printed at Quebec by Wm. Brown, 1773,* as recorded in the latter's accounts. *See* No. 171 *note.*

Copy located: None.

174. ALMANACS. QUEBEC

[Indian Calendar for 1776. *Quebec, Wm. Brown, 1773.*]

? Broadside (a sheet almanac) or leaflet in Montagnais dialect, prepared by Father La Brosse and *printed at Quebec by Wm. Brown, 1773,* as recorded in the latter's accounts. *See* No. 171 *note.*

Copy located: None.

175. ALMANACS. QUEBEC

[Indian Calendar for 1777. *Quebec, Wm. Brown, 1773.*]

? Broadside (a sheet almanac) or leaflet, in Montagnais dialect, prepared by Father La Brosse and *printed at Quebec by Wm. Brown, 1773,* as recorded in the latter's accounts. *See* No. 171 *note.*

Copy located: None.

176. ALMANACS. QUEBEC

[Indian Calendar for 1778. *Quebec, Wm. Brown, 1773.*]

? Broadside (a sheet almanac) or leaflet in Montagnais dialect, prepared by Father La Brosse and *printed at Quebec by Wm. Brown, 1773,* as recorded in the latter's accounts. *See* No. 171 *note.*

Copy located: None.

177. DELAROCHE, PETER, *d.*1795

THE / GOSPEL OF CHRIST / PREACHED to the POOR / BY / PETER DELAROCHE, Missionary. / [rule] / Repent ye therefore, and be converted, that your / Sins may be blotted out—St. Peter, in Acts 3.19. / [rule] / [printer's ornament] /LUNENBURG: / PRINTED: At the Author's Expence, / To be given and not to be Sold. / —Freely ye have received, freely give. / JESUS CHRIST, in Mat. 10.8. / MDCCLXXIII. /

12mo. [*][4], A-F[8], G[2]; viii, 99 p., 1 *l.* (Errata) inserted after p. viii; type-page: 15 × 9 cm.

Contents: p. [i], t.-p.; p. [ii], blank; p. [iii]-viii, Dedication; 1 *l.* (inserted) recto, Errata; verso, blank; p. [1]-3, Introduction; p. 4-14, Part I, Of gospel doctrine (text and exposition of the Creed); p. 15-54, Part II, Of religious duties (text and exposition of Commandments 1-4), Lord's prayer; p. 55-96, Part III, Of moral duties, duties towards your neighbour (Commandments 5-10), duties respecting ourselves: self denial, humility, sobriety, chastity, contentedness, patience, industry, vigilence, and persistence); p. 96-99, Conclusion; verso of p. 99, blank.

This was *probably printed at Halifax, N.S., by Anthony Henry,* for no press is known to have been in Lunenburg at this time. Also, this edition is in the same typographic style as the second (No. 511) and shows the same eccentric ornamentation, characteristic of the German, Henry—a heavy massing of small floral and other ornaments in frames and rules, and a combining of many sizes of type, roman and italic, in captions, running titles, etc. The imprint date, MDCCLXXIII, may be in error for MDCCLXXVII, for this edition was said by the author to have been printed ten years before the second, which is dated MDCCLXXXVII.

The dedication "To all the settlers and inhabitants of . . . Lunenburg in Nova-Scotia; and especially the poor, whether bound or free, [signed, p. viii] Your zealous pastor and faithful servant for Jesus sake, Peter Delaroche, Missionary," states "I know that being obliged to work hard you cannot spend much time in reading and study, therefore I have endeavoured to keep within a small compass, so that by reading a few pages every Sunday you may soon understand all the Christian doctrine . . . as far as it is necessary in your Station: for as you have neither so much leisure nor so much opportunity as the Rich to study Religion, it is not required that you should have so much knowledge . . . I have got this little book printed at very great expence to myself, which I am hardly able to bear: but notwithstanding I bear it with pleasure in hopes that it shall not be intirely bestowed in vain. . . . It is wrote for all Christians, whether Lutherans, Calvinists, or of our own church [of England]."

Delaroche presented this work to his congregation "one copy to every amily of which one member is capable of reading and explaining it to those who cannot understand or read the English language" in the course of a sermon. The latter is included as No. 18 (undated) in his "Sermons on various Subjects and Occasions preached at Lunenburg . . . MDCCLXXXI," a MS. of some 440 p. 4to., (containing sermons No. 1-20, 1771-81) now in Dalhousie University library, Halifax, N.S.

Delaroche, a French protestant, educated at Geneva, was ordained by the Bishop of London in 1771, and came as a Society for the Propagation of the Gospel missionary to Lunenburg through the influence of Moreau whom he succeeded there. Both Moreau and Delaroche are cited as Calvinist victims of Church of England proselytizing in a contemporary MS. (*see* No. 155, note to copy located at RPJ), but Delaroche is acknowledged "a serious good minister." He remained at Lunenburg till about 1786, preaching in French, German, and English; he also started a school for the French then continued as missionary at Manchester, N.S., and Guysboro, till his death in 1795.

Copy located: CaNsHD.

178. NOVA SCOTIA. HOUSE OF ASSEMBLY

Caption title: [Journals and Votes of the House of Assembly of the Province of Nova-Scotia.]

Note: title above is not transcribed from copy.

fo. 8 p. *Printed at Halifax, N.S., by Anthony Henry, 1773.*

Contents: p. 1-8, Journal and votes of the fourth session of the fifth assembly, Apr. 20-24, 1773.

Copy located: GBLP (in C.O. 220/11: 259-69).

179. NOVA SCOTIA. HOUSE OF ASSEMBLY

Caption title: [Journals and Votes of the House of Assembly for the Province of Nova-Scotia.]

Note: title above is not transcribed from copy.

fo. A-G^2, H^1; 29 p. *Printed at Halifax, N.S., by Anthony Henry, 1773.*

Contents: p. 1-29, Journal and votes of the fifth session of the fifth assembly, Oct. 12-Nov. 12, 1773; p. 29 verso, blank.

Copies located: CaNs; GBLP (in C.O. 220/11: 271-99).

180. NOVA SCOTIA. LAWS, STATUTES, *etc.*

Running title: [rule] / 1773. Anno Tertio Decimo Regis GEORGII III. CAP. I[-V]. / [rule] /

Caption title: At the GENERAL-ASSEMBLY of the Pro-/vince of Nova-Scotia, . . . / [8 lines] / . . . being / the Fourth Session of the Fifth / GENE-/RAL-ASSEMBLY convened in the said / Province. / [ornamental rule]

fo. p. 133-136 [i.e. 137]; type-page: 25.5 × 15 cm. paged in continuation of No. 168; p. [137] mispaged: 136. *Printed at Halifax, N.S., by Anthony Henry, 1773.*

Contents: p. 133-136 [i.e. 137], Cap. I-V, temporary acts passed in the session Apr. 20-24, 1773; p. 136 [i.e. 137] verso, blank.

These acts are the complete legislation of a short session, no perpetual acts being passed.

Copies located: CaNs; CaO; CaOOA; DLC; MH; NNB.

181. NOVA SCOTIA. LAWS, STATUTES, *etc.*

Running title: [rule] / 1773. Anno Tertio Decimo Regis GEORGII III. CAP. I[-IV]. / [rule] /

Caption title: At the GENERAL-ASSEMBLY of the Pro-/vince of Nova-Scotia, . . . / [9 lines] / . . . being the Fifth GENERAL-/ASSEMBLY convened in the said Pro-/vince. / [ornamental rule] /

fo. sig. 4B[1], 4C[2]; p. 280-285; type-page: 25 × 14.5 cm. paged in continuation of No. 167, 280 being repeated in numbering; even numbers on rectos. *Printed at Halifax, N.S., by Anthony Henry, 1773.*

Contents: p. 280-285, Cap. I-IV, perpetual acts passed in the fifth session of the fifth assembly, Oct. 12-Nov. 12, 1773. No perpetual acts were passed in the fourth session, Apr. 20-24, 1773.

Copies located: CaB; CaNs; CaNsHA; CaNsWA; CaOOA; DLC; MB (defective); MH; N; NNB.

182. NOVA SCOTIA. LAWS, STATUTES, *etc.*

Running title: [rule] / 1773. Anno Quarto Decimo Regis GEORGII III. CAP. I[-IX]. / [rule] /

Caption title: At the GENERAL-ASSEMBLY of the Pro-/vince of Nova-Scotia, . . . / [9 lines] / . . . being the Fifth GENERAL-/ASSEMBLY convened in the said Pro-/vince. / [ornamental rule] /

fo. p. 138-149; type-page: 24.5 × 14. 5cm. paged in continuation of No. 180. *Printed at Halifax, N.S., by Anthony Henry, 1773.*

Contents: p. 138-149, Cap. I-IX, temporary acts passed in the fifth session of the fifth assembly, Oct. 12-Nov. 12, 1773.

Copies located: CaNs; CaO; CaOOA; DLC; MH; N; NNB.

183. QUEBEC, *City*. SEMINAIRE DE QUEBEC

[List of Scholars excelling and getting Prizes.]

Probably a broadside, text in Latin, similar to the "Palmare" or honours list of 1770 (No. 151) and of 1775 (No. 215). *Printed at Quebec by Wm. Brown, 1773,* as recorded:

"1773, Aug. 11. Rec^{d} on Acc^{t} Printing Office for 100 Lists of Scholars excelling and getting Prizes—10/."—Can.P.A., Brown & Gilmore: *Memorial A.*

Copy located: None.

184. ALMANACS. NOVA SCOTIA

[The Nova-Scotia Calender or an Almanack for 1775. *Printed at Halifax, N.S., by Anthony Henry, 1774.*]

Advertised: "Thursday next [i.e. Dec. 1, 1774] will be published and sold by Anthony Henry . . . in octavo, on large demy-paper, at 8*d.* a single copy, or 6 shillings a dozen, The Nova-Scotia Almanack, For the Year . . . 1775, Wherein is contained, The Eclipses . . . To which is added, Drinking to excess corrected, A Chinese anecdote, A table of the beginning of each reign from the Conquest, etc., Navy list of Great Britain, New ships building in England, Admirals of the Royal Navy, Sundry useful recipes, Table of Postage rates, Receipts, History of Cidal Achmet, The Art of getting Riches, Jests, the names of the Governor . . . and other officers of government."—*Nova-Scotia gazette,* Nov. 29, 1774.

Copy located: None.

185. ALMANACS. QUEBEC

CALENDRIER pour l'Année 1775, pour Québec, qui est par les 306$^{d.}$ 30$^{m.}$ de Longitude, et 46$^{d.}$ 55$^{m.}$ de Latitude. / [ornamental rule] /

Broadside: type-page: 42.5 × 38 cm. with ornamental rule frame.

Contents: Signes du zodiaque, phases de la lune, nombres, fêtes mobiles, quatre tems, commencement de 4 saisons, eclipses de soleil, (arranged in 7 col. across the sheet beneath title); Calendrier (12 tables in 4 col. with ornamental rules).

Advertised: "L'on vient de publier un Calendrier . . . se vend à l'Imprimerie, chez Mr. Malcolm Fraser aux Trois Rivieres et chez Mr. Jacques Perry sur la place du Marché à Montréal à Quinze Sols chaques ou Un Piastre par Douzaine."
—*Quebec gazette,* Dec. 29, 1774.

Copy located: CaO (bound in *Quebec gazette* at end of 1774).

ALMANACS. QUEBEC.

[Indian Calendar for 1774] *See* No. 172.

186. CATHOLIC CHURCH. PSALTERS

[Le Pseautier de David avec les Cantiques à l'usage des Ecoles.]

Pamphlet or small book, *printed at Quebec by Wm. Brown, 1774,* as advertised: "L'on vient d'Imprimer "Le Pseautier de David, avec les Cantiques à l'usage des Ecoles" sur bon Papier et beau Caractère, bien relié en Basane, qui se vendra à l'Imprimerie en Gros et en Detail, et chez Joseph Bargeas, en Detail."

—*Quebec gazette*, Sept. 8, 1774.

From Sept. 17, 1774, Brown recorded numerous sales of *Le Pseautier* at 1*s.* 8*d.* the single copy, 15*s.* the dozen, and on Nov. 14, 1776, 100 copies to Dufau at £5. He also recorded on Dec. 7, 1776, "Paid on Acc[t] Joseph Bargeas to George Hips for 37 sheep skins to bind Pseautiers in, for which I gave my note the 20th Oct. 1774, to see them paid—£1.16.0."—Can.P.A., *Neilson papers*, v. 46.

Commonly used in schools in France and in New France this little book was put into the children's hands when they had mastered the ABC or primer, and were ready for words of two or three syllables. P. G. Roy: *Les premiers manuels scolaires canadien*, in *Bulletin des recherches historiques*, 52: 291-303, Oct., 1946.

Copy located: None.

187. ESSAY ON THE PRESENT STATE OF . . . NOVA-SCOTIA

AN / ESSAY / On THE / Present State Of THE / PROVINCE / OF / NOVA-SCOTIA, / With some Strictures on the Measures / pursued by Government from its / first Settlement by the English in / the Year, 1749. /

8vo. [*-3*][4]; 24 p.; type-page: 18.5 × 10.5 cm. The typographic style, use of small ornaments, etc., suggests that this work was *probably printed at Halifax, N.S., by Anthony Henry, 1774-75.* The t.-p. of one of the copies located bears the date 1774, in MS.

Contents: p.[1], t-p.; p. [2], quotations from Lampreade, Algernon Sydney, etc.; p. 3-24, Essay, signed at end: "A Member of Assembly." This was probably prepared by John Day, a merchant in Halifax and leader of the popular party in the Nova Scotia Assembly, or by one of the members of his committee, appointed to draw up an *Address* to the King, dated June 24, 1775 (No. 205). *See* J. B. Brebner: *The neutral Yankees of Nova Scotia* (New York, 1937), 229-67.

Copies located: RPJ (2 cop.); photostat in CaNsHA.

188. GREAT BRITAIN. LAWS, STATUTES, *etc.*

ANNO REGNI / GEORGII III. / REGIS / Magnæ Britanniæ, Franciæ, & Hiberniæ, / DECIMO QUARTO. / At the Parliament begun and holden at Westminster, the Tenth Day of May, / Anno Domini, 1768, in the Eighth Year of the Reign of our Sovereign Lord / GEORGE the Third, by the Grace of God, of Great Britain, France and / Ireland, King, Defender of the Faith, &c. / And from thence continued, by several Prorogations, to the Thirteenth Day of January, / 1774; being the Seventh Session of the Thirteenth Parliament of Great Britain. / [rule] / [royal arms] / [double rule] / QUEBEC: / Printed by WILLIAM BROWN, Printer for the Province. / [rule] / M,DCC,LXXIV. /

French t.-p.:

DANS LA / Quartorze Année du Regne / DE / GEORGE III. / ROI de la Grande Bretagne, de France, et d'Irlande. / Au Parlement commencé et tenu à Westminster, le Dixieme jour de Mai, de l'année / de notre Seigneur mil sept cens soixante-huit, dans la Huitieme année du Regne / de notre Souverain Seigneur GEORGE Trois, par le Grace de Dieu, Roi de / la Grande Bretagne, de France, et d'Irlande, Defenseur de la Foi, &c. / Et depuis coutinué [sic] par differentes Remises au Treizieme jour de Janvier, mil sept cens / soixante-quatorze; etant le Septieme Sçeance de Treizieme Parlement de la Grande Bretagne. / [rule] / [royal arms] / [double rule] / A QUEBEC: / Chez GUILLAUME BROWN, Imprimeur de la Province, / [rule] / 1774. /

4to. A-D[4]; 29 p., 1 *l.*; type-page: 15.5 × 12 cm. Text in English and French on opposite pages.

Contents: p. [1], English t.-p.; p. [2], blank; p. [3], French t.-p.; p. 4-5, Proclamation of publication of the acts, signed at Quebec, Dec. 3, 1774, by Guy Carleton; p. 6-21, 14 Geo. III c. 83 (Quebec Act); p. 20-29, 14 Geo. III c. 88 (Quebec Revenue Act); p. 29 verso, blank; 1 *l.* blank.

Passed by the Parliament of Great Britain in June, 1774, transmitted to Quebec, read by the governor-in-council on Oct. 11, 1774, translated into French, re-read and ordered printed, Nov. 25, these acts were published in the *Quebec gazette,* Dec. 8, 1774, also separately from different types in the edition described above.

Brown's account was passed Jan. 6-9, 1775: "Printing and bindg. up 300 of ye Quebec Acts for the officers of government, etc.—£40 [sterling, i.e. £44.9. Quebec currency]."—Can.P.A., Que. Leg. Co. *Minutes A.*

Brown's records show sales of this edition at his shop for 1*s.* 3*d.* the copy, from 1775 till 1782.

Long in preparation, the Quebec Act was designed by the British administration to provide a constitution for a colony of peculiar difficulty. It covered boundaries, religion, laws, and government. From its inception to the present day the Quebec Act has been one of the most discussed measures in the history of Canada, and is frequently cited as a factor in determining American and Canadian attitudes to revolution in 1775. The Revenue or Enabling Act provided a provincial income from duties on imported liquors, etc., licences to public houses, and feudal dues continued from the French régime.

Both acts have been reprinted frequently, e.g. in Kennedy: *Statutes;* Shortt and Doughty: *Documents, 1759-91,* 1: 533-80 (with memoranda, preliminary draughts, and extensive references to related materials); see also: R. Coupland: *The Quebec Act* (Oxford, 1925); and A. L. Burt: *The old province of Quebec* (Minneapolis, 1933), chap. 9.

Copies located: (blank leaf at end occasionally missing) CaO (bound in *Brochures canadiennes, 1774-1809*); CaQM; CaQMJ; CaQMS; CaQQL (2 cop.).

189. NOVA SCOTIA. HOUSE OF ASSEMBLY

Caption title: (1) / [ornamental rule] / JOURNALS / AND / VOTES / OF THE / HOUSE of ASSEMBLY, / For the Province of Nova-Scotia. / [ornamental rule] /

fo. 53 p. type-page: 25.5 × 14 cm. *Printed at Halifax, N.S., by Anthony Henry, 1774.*

Contents: p. 1-46, Journal and votes of the sixth session of the fifth assembly, Oct. 6-Nov. 12, continued, p. 47-53, Dec. 5-13, 1774.

Copies located: CaNSA (p. 5 to end wanting); GBLP (in C.O. 220/11: 301-47, continued p. 351-58) transcribed in Can.P.A., N.S. "D" 10.

190. NOVA SCOTIA. LAWS, STATUTES, *etc.*

Running title: [rule] / 1774. Anno Quinto Decimo Regis GEORGII III. CAP. I[-X]. / [rule] /

Caption title: At the GENERAL-ASSEMBLY of the Pro-/vince of Nova-Scotia, . . . / [9 lines] / . . . being the Fifth GENERAL-/AS-SEMBLY convened in the said Pro-/vince. / [ornamental rule] /

fo. sig. 5D-5G[2]; p. 286-300; type-page: 25.5 × 14.5 cm. paged in continuation of No. 181, even numbers on rectos. *Printed at Halifax, N.S., by Anthony Henry, 1774.*

Contents: p. 286-300, Cap. I-X, perpetual acts passed in the sixth session of the fifth assembly, Oct. 6-Nov. 12, Dec. 5-13, 1774; p. 300 verso, blank.

Copies located: CaB; CaN; CaNs; CaNsHA; CaNsWA; CaOOA; DLC; MB (defective); MH; NNB (p. 180-87 wanting and supplied in photostat).

191. NOVA SCOTIA. LAWS, STATUTES, *etc.*

Running title: [rule] / 1774. Anno Quinto Decimo Regis GEORGII III. CAP. I[-VI]. / [rule]

Caption title: At the GENERAL-ASSEMBLY of the Pro-/vince of Nova-Scotia . . . / [9 lines] / . . . being the Fifth GENERAL- / AS-SEMBLY convened in the said Pro-/vince. / [ornamental rule] /

fo. p. 286 [i.e. 150]-164; type-page: 25 × 14.5 cm. paged in continuation of No. 182. p. [150-153] mispaged: 286-289. *Printed at Halifax, N.S., by Anthony Henry, 1774?*

Contents: p. 286 [i.e. 150]-164, Cap. I-VI temporary acts passed in the sixth session of the fifth assembly, Oct. 6-Nov. 12, Dec. 5-13, 1774; p. 164 verso, blank.

Copies located: CaNs; CaO; CaOOA; MH; NNB.

192. PRIMERS. QUEBEC. *French*

[**ALPHABET** en Francaise.]

Pamphlet; *printed at Quebec by Wm. Brown, 1774,* as recorded:

"1774, Nov. 3 [Credit] To Printing Office 100 Alphabets—£1.
Nov. 11, Ditto, 2 Doz. Primers in Sheets—5/
Nov. 17, Ditto 100 Alphabets from Dufau—£1
1774, Nov. 2 [-Nov. 18. Debit] By Printing Office for Stitching [500] Alphabets —£1.0.8."—Can.P.A., *Neilson papers,* v. 45.

This work was advertised: "On y vend [à l'imprimerie] . . . des Alphabets Doubles en Français en Gros et en Detail."—*Quebec gazette,* Nov. 13, 1774.

Copy located: None.

193. [ACCOUNT OF THE BATTLE AT MONTREAL]

Broadside? in English and French? *printed at Quebec by Wm. Brown, 1775,* as recorded:

"1775, Sept. 30. Printed for the Gov[t] of Quebec, 400 Accounts of the Battle at Montreal—£1.10."—Can.P.A., *Neilson papers,* v. 46.

This item is also recorded in the public accounts:

"1775, Sept. 30. To printing 400 Relations of the Battle at Montreal—£2." —Wm. Brown's bill for printing Sept. 9, 1775-Aug. 10, 1776, Can.P.A., *"S" Pub. accts., 1774-76.*

The *Account* or *Relation* is probably a report of the skirmish near Long Point, Sept. 25, the Americans' first sortie on Montreal, in which Ethan Allen was captured. It has probably the same text as the report in the *Quebec gazette,* Oct. 5, 1775 (in English and French, about 250 words each): ". . . the rebels who had posted themselves very advantageously behind some houses in the neighbourhood of Mr. Christie's farm . . . were at length dislodged and totally defeated. . . . the melancholy Supineness of the Province cannot but be lamented, and more especially when it is known to be in the power of the Inhabitants, by a moment's Exertion, to drive off those Vagabonds, who come with no other View but that of Plunder and Pillage [etc.]."

Copy located: None.

194. [ADRESSE AUX CANADIENS DE LA PART DE LEURS COMPATRIOTES]

Broadside? *printed at Quebec by Wm. Brown, 1775,* as recorded:

"1775, Oct. 16. Printed for Government of Quebec 200 [sic] Addresses to Canadians—£2.10."—Can.P.A., *Neilson papers,* v. 46.

"1775, Oct. 14. To printing 400 [sic] Addresses to Canadians—£2." —Wm. Brown's bill for printing Sept. 9, 1775-Aug. 10, 1776, Can.P.A., *"S" Pub. accts., 1774-76.*

A separate issue or another edition of *Adresse aux Canadiens de la part de leurs Compatriotes* signed: "Canadiens," which appeared in the *Quebec gazette,* Oct. 12, 1775. The text in the *Quebec gazette* is set solid in pica, type-page 32.2 × 10 cm. (about 600 words). It begins: "Peuple infortuné du Canada, ne fera-ce pas avec juste droit, que le Roi pourra vous dire les paroles que disoit autrefois notre Seigneur au peuple d'Israël—Popule meus, quid fecit tibi? aut in quo contristavi te? [etc.]."

Probably written by one of the Catholic clergy in Quebec, *Adresse* is strong pulpit oratory on the benefits of British rule to French Canadians: free exercise of their religion, their old civil laws, peaceable possession of their property, few taxes, etc.; it exhorts them to spurn rebellion and rally to the royal banner. Another address in the same style entitled *Mea Culpa,* signed: "Civis Canadensis," appeared in the *Gazette,* Oct. 5, 1775. Both are examples of the Church's effort to whip up French-Canadian support of the established government at the time of the Americans' invasion.

Copy located: None.

195. ALMANACS. NOVA SCOTIA

[The Nova-Scotia Calender or an Almanack for 1776. *Printed at Halifax, N.S., by Anthony Henry, 1775.*]

16mo. [16 + ?] p., 1 plate; type-page: 14 × 8.2 cm.

Contents: The only copy located lacks t.-p., is highly defective but contains: [12] p. Calendar for 1776; [2] p. Recipes; [2] p. Province of Nova Scotia list of officers of government (incomplete); plate: wood-cut illustration of Halifax Harbour, showing in foreground, four ships with full sail, in background promontory with lighthouse and buildings, a church, tents, another building (Province House?), Union Jack on staff, cannon; verso, blank.

This is apparently the first Canadian printed book with illustration.

Copy located: CaNsHD (defective).

ALMANACS. QUEBEC

[Indian Calendar for 1775] *See* No. 173.

196. BEDARD, THOMAS LAURENT, 1747-1795, *praeses*

THÈSES / DE / MATHÉMATIQUE, / QUI SERONT SOUTENUES / AU / SÉMINAIRE DE QUÉBEC, / VENDREDI, 26 MAI, depuis neuf heures jusqu'à Midi. / Par M.M. { [names in 3 line column:] BERNARD CLAUDE PANET, / CHARLES PERRAULT, / CHARLES CHAUVEAUX, / ÉTUDIANS en PHYSIQUE, / SOUS / Mr. THOMAS BEDARD DIACRE, / Professeur de PHILOSOPHIE. / [rule] / A QUEBEC: / Chez GUILLAUME BROWN, derriere l'Eglise Cathédrale. / [rule] / M,DCC,LXXV. /

4to. A-C^2; 1 p. l., 9 p.; type-page: 15.8 × 12.1 cm.

Contents: p. l. recto, t.-p.; verso, blank; p. 1-9 Thèses; p. 9 verso, blank.

"1775, May 19. [Debtor to Printing office] To 200 Mathematical theses from Gravé [second assistant in the Séminaire] £3.15."

—Can.P.A., *Neilson papers,* v. 45.

The theses cover arithmetic, algebra, proportions, geometry, and trigonometry. According to the mediaeval university custom, notice was given: "On Friday the 26th Instant, at the Seminary in Quebec; a Mathematical Thesis will be maintained by Messrs. Bern. Panet, Ch. Perrault, and Ch. Chevaux [sic] Students in Natural Philosophy. They offer to demonstrate such Theorems, and resolve such Problems in Algebra and Geometry as may be proposed to them."—*Quebec gazette,* May 18, 1775. In addition to the theorems and problems thus proposed and printed in this work, the students received through the *Quebec gazette*, propositions from "Philomathus" in Montreal, which were duly solved. "But the printer having no algebraical sorts for diagrams, the manuscript solutions [were] left for Philomathus in Montreal where the Gazettes are delivered."—*Quebec gazette*, Aug. 10, 1775.

Thomas Laurent Bédard, born at Charlesbourg near Quebec, was educated in the Séminaire de Québec, and ordained priest Sept. 27, 1775. He taught in the Séminaire from that year till his death, and was twice chosen its superior (1781-87, 1793-95). Quebecois born and bred, he gave strong expression to the French-Canadian viewpoint in controversies on education and land tenure which arose later.

Copies located: CaQ, CaQM, CaQMS, CaQQL, Ketcheson, NN, RPJ.

197. CUGNET, FRANÇOIS JOSEPH, 1720-1789

TRAITÉ / DE LA / LOI DES FIEFS. / Qui a toujours été suivie en Canada depuis son éta-/blissement, tirée de celle contenuë en la Coûtume de / la Prevôté et Vicomté de Paris, à laquelle les Fiefs / et Seigneuries de cette Province sont assujettis, en / vertu de leurs titres primitifs de Concession, et des / Edits, Reglemens, Ordonances et Declarations de sa / Majesté très Chrétienne, rendus en consequence; et / des diferens Jugemens d'Intendans rendus à cet / égard, en vertu de la Loi des Fiefs, et des dits E-/dits, Reglemens, Ordonances et Declarations. / Traité utile à tous les Seigneurs de cette Province, tant nouveaux / qu'anciens Sujets, aux Juges et au Receveur-général des Droits / de sa Majesté. / [rule] / Par FRANÇOIS JOSEPH CUGNET, Ecuier, Seigneur de St. / Etienne, &c. &c. / [rule] / In magnis voluisse sat est. / [double rule] / QUEBEC: / Chez GUILLAUME BROWN, / MDCCLXXV. /

4to. [A^2], B-L^4; 2 p. l., p. ix-xiv, 71 p., 1 *l.*; type page: 15.3 × 10 cm.

Contents: p. l. 1 recto, half title; verso, blank; p. l. 2 recto, t.-p.; verso, Table [of contents]; p. ix-x, Dedication to Governor Carleton, signed by F. J. Cugnet, 10 Novembre, 1774; p. xi-xii, Preface; p. xiii-xiv, Introduction; p. 1-71, Traité; p. 71 verso, blank; 1 *l.* blank.

This and the three following publications were announced in the *Quebec gazette*, Nov. 24, 1774: "It has been decided to print the ancient laws customs and usages of Canada, for the advancement of both old [English] and new [French] subjects, since these are in force by Act of Parliament [etc.]." It was proposed to print three treatises prepared by F. J. Cugnet: "Les loix des fiefs et celui de la Police," to be published at the middle of February; "Les loix municipales," on May 1, and "Extrait des Edits [etc.]" on June 15, 1775. One hundred subscribers were required at one guinea the set, unbound.

The set was actually printed for the government, four works, four hundred copies of each, finished a month betimes, an indication of Brown's zeal and equipment. His difficulties, however, are intimated:

"1775, Feb. 28, [Debit] By Profit and Loss given Tom for exerting himself on the Loix des Fiefs et Police—7/6.

March 31, Printing Office owes Stationery for 5 Reams superfine Propatria for Cugnet's Canadian Laws—£5. 5*s*.

Dec. 10, Bonds and Notes owes Printing Office for J. Williams [Governor Carleton's secretary] two Notes payable the 1st and 2nd of Sept[r] next for having printed Cugnet's Works which by verbal Agreement were to have been paid the 13th of May last when finish'd. So much for publick faith—£116. 5*s*.

1776, Nov. 7, Received . . . from J. Williams for printing 400 copies of Cugnet's Canadian Laws payable 13th May, 1775—£116.13.4."

—Can.P.A., *Neilson papers*, v. 46.

The three treatises were prepared by Cugnet, 1771-73, to set forth the basic principles of the civil law of the French régime, still in force in the Province of Quebec. A thorough reorganization of the legal and administrative system had been planned by the British government since 1767, and various schemes drawn up by interested groups. To inform the English legislators on the French laws of Quebec, Carleton ordered digests to be prepared by F. J. Cugnet, Duchenaux, and two priests of the Séminaire de Québec, MM. Jacrau and Pressard. These digests, known in Quebec at the time as "Extraits des Messieurs," were published: *An abstract of the Loix de Police* (London, 1772); *An abstract of several royal edicts* (London, 1772); *An abstract of the custom of Paris* (London, 1772); *The sequel of the abstract of the custom of Paris* (London, 1773).

Cugnet writing to Blackstone from Quebec, July 24, 1773, complained bitterly of the English parliamentarians' lack of insight into French law, owing, he surmised, to the limitations of the *Abstracts*, prepared in haste and dealing only with form and procedure, not with fundamental principles. To supply this lack he sent Blackstone among other documents, a handsome MS. copy (now in McGill University library) of "Lois Municipales de Québec divisées en trois Traités" comprising: "Traité de la loy des Fiefs, Quebec, 1771"; "Traité des anciennes loix de propriété, Quebec, 1772"; and, "Traité de la Police, Québec, 1773." These, with a volume of supporting documents, *Extraits des Edits*, were published in Quebec, 1775, as described here. Cugnet's case for French civil law, opposed notably by Attorney-General Francis Maseres, probably aided its retention in the Quebec Act, passed in June, 1774.

A modern historian has expressed the French-Canadian view of Cugnet: "C'était un Canadien qui avait pris la plume pour défendre nos coutumes et nos lois françaises, et réclamer des droits que nos défaites n'avaient pu supprimer. Ce champion national était né à Québec . . ."—Sir J. A. T. Chapais: *Cours d'histoire du Canada, 1760-1867* (8 v., Québec, 1919-34), 1: 126.

Cugnet, the most brilliant Canadian jurist of his time, was trained in Quebec, partly in the classes of Guillaume Verrier, procureur général de la Cour Supérieur, who conducted the first law "school" in Canada 1733-58. With the English occupation, Cugnet was appointed to a succession of posts in which he was able to present the French-Canadian viewpoint to authority. On Feb. 24, 1768, he was made French secretary to the governor and council explicitly "to assist [them] when they will require information or explanation of . . . usages in force during the French régime" (*Quebec gazette*, May 12, 1768), a service which he rendered till his death in 1789.

Copies located: A valued reference work, many copies have been preserved and are available in most large public, university, legislative, and law libraries in Canada and the United States. Especially to be noted is Maseres's copy with MS. notes, in Harvard College library. With the Quebec *Ordinances* (No. 942) and *A collection of the acts* (No. 1169), Cugnet's *Traités* and *Extraits* are the commonest of 18th-century Canadian imprints. Though apparently published in only 400 copies, they still appear on the market with surprising frequency.

198. CUGNET, FRANÇOIS JOSEPH, 1720-1789

TRAITÉ / Abregé des ancienes Loix, Coutumes et usages de la / Colonie du Canada, aujourd'huy Province de Qué-/bec, tiré de la coutume de la prevôté et vicomté de / Paris, à laquelle la dite Colonie était assujétie, en / consequence de l'Edit de l'établissement du Conseil / Souverain du mois d'Avril 1663; avec l'explica-/tion de chaque titre et de chaque article, puisée / dans les meilleurs autheurs qui ont écrit et co-/menté la dite coutume. / Necessaire à toutes les personnes qui voudront avoir / une teinture des dites ancienes loix, coutumes et / usages, et qui pourra les faciliter dans l'étude qu'ils / seront obligés d'en faire, tant comme Juges, que / comme Avocats ou Procureurs. / [rule] / Par FRANÇOIS JOSEPH CUGNET Ecuier, Seigneur de St. / Etienne, &c. &c. / [rule] / O Judices! diligite justitiam, nàm qui justificat impium, et qui condem-/nat justum, abominabilis est uterque apud Deum. / Lib. sap. et Proverb. ch. 17. v. 16 / [double rule] / QUEBEC: / Chez GUILLAUME BROWN / MDCCLXXV. /

4to. [*][2], N-Z[4], Aa-Mm[4], Nn[2]; 1 p. l., 188 p., 1 *l.*; type-page: 15.3 × 10 cm.

Contents: p. l. recto, half title; verso, blank; p. [i] t.-p.; p. [ii]. Table (des chapitres); p. iii-iv, Preface; p. 5-188, Traité; 1 *l.* recto, Avertissement (i.e. Errata in *Traité de la loi des fiefs*); verso, "Liste des livres seulement necessaires à l'intelligence entiere des lois Municipales de cette Province."

Printed in an edition of 400 copies (*see* No. 197 *notes*) this work was advertised: "L'impression du Traité des Loix Municipales (faisant 192 pages d'imprimé) avertie pour le premier du prochain, fut achevée Mardi dernier."—*Quebec gazette*, Apr. 13, 1775.

Copies located: Like No. 197, with which it is often found bound, this work has been preserved in many reference libraries; some thirty copies have been seen by the writer.

199. CUGNET, FRANÇOIS JOSEPH, 1720-1789

TRAITÉ / DE LA / POLICE. / Qui a toujours été suivie en Canada, aujourdhui / Province de Québec, depuis son établissement jusqu'à / la conquête, tiré des diférens réglemens, jugemens / et ordonnances d'Intendans, à qui par leurs com-/missions, cette partie du gouvernement était totale-/ment atribuée, à l'exclusion de tous autres juges, / qui n'en pouvaient connaitre qu'en qualité de leurs / subdélégués. / Traité qui pourrait être de quelqu'utilité aux Grands / Voyers, et aux juges de Police en cette province. / [rule] / Par FRANÇOIS JOSEPH CUGNET, Ecuier, Seigneur de St. / Etienne, &c. &c. / [rule] / Cura rerum publicarum. / [double rule] / QUEBEC: / Chez GUILLAUME BROWN, / MDCCLXXV. /

4to. [*A]-*C[4], *D[2]; 2 p. l., p. iii, 5-25, [1] p.; type-page: 15.5 × 10 cm.

Contents: p. l. 1 recto, half title; verso, blank; p. l. 2 recto, t.-p.; verso, blank; p. iii, Preface; verso, blank; p. 5-25, Traité; [1] p. (verso of p. 25) Table des chapitres.

"J'ay cru qu'aïant rédigé mes deux traités de la loy des Fiefs, et des loix de propriété de cette province, je devais pour completer mon ouvrage, et rendre en entier les loix Municipales, en composer un troisieme concernant la Police; cette partie si necessaire au maintien du bon ordre, étant totalement negligée."—Preface.

Copies located: Like No. 197-198, this work has been preserved in many reference libraries; some thirty copies have been seen by the writer.

200. CUGNET, FRANÇOIS JOSEPH, 1720-1789

EXTRAITS / Des Edits, Declarations, Ordon-/nances et Reglemens, de sa Ma-/jesté Très Chretienne. / Des Reglemens et Jugemens des / Gouverneurs Generaux et Inten-/dans concernans la justice; et des / Reglemens et Ordonnances de Po-/lice rendues par les Intendans, / Faisans partie de la legislature en / force en la Colonie du Canada, / aujourd'hui Province de Québec. / Tirés des Regîtres du Conseil Supe-/rieur et de ceux d'Intendance. / [rule] / Par FRANÇOIS JOSEPH CUGNET Ecuier, Seigneur de St. / Etienne, &c. &c. / [double rule] / QUEBEC: / Chez GUILLAUME BROWN, / MDCCLXXV. /

4to. [$_*$D] 3-4, $_*$E-$*$R[4]; 2 p. l., 3-106 p.; type-page: 15.3 × 10 cm.

Contents: p. l. 1 recto, half title; verso, blank; p. l. 2 recto, t.-p.; verso, Table (des chapitres), Avertissement; p. 3-106, Extrait des édits, etc.

"Je ne donne ces extraits . . . qu'au soutien des citations que j'ai faites dans mes diferens traités, des Edits [etc.] de Sa Majesté T-C. . . . Et aussi pour detromper les personnes, à qui des esprits mal intentionnés, ont voulu persuader que j'étais le plus ignorant des Canadiens, et que j'écrivais à tort et à travers ce qui me venait dans la tête [etc.]."—Avertissement.

Copies located: Like No. 197-199, this work has been preserved in many reference libraries; some thirty copies have been seen by the writer.

201. NAPIER, *Capt.*

[Hand-bill for enlisting Sailors in the King's service.]

Broadside, text in English and French; *printed at Quebec by Wm. Brown, 1775,* as recorded:

"1775, Sept. 22. Printed for Cap.t Naper [sic] 75 double hand-bills for enlisting Sailors in the King's service—12/6.
Do. for Do. 75 more on Acc.t his mistake—12/6.
Paid Oct. 11 '77."—Can.P.A., *Neilson papers,* v. 46.

The state of the garrison on Nov. 30, 1775, showed about 450 masters, mates, and seamen from ships in port enlisted for defence of Quebec.—[Hugh Finlay's] *Journal of the siege and blockade of Quebec, 1775-1776,* in Lit. and hist. soc. of Quebec: *Manuscripts relating to Canada,* ser. 4, *Historical documents* [etc.] (Quebec, 1875).

"Capt Naper," who ordered this handbill to be printed, was probably Captain Napier who commanded the snow (or armed brigantine) *Fell*, and brought Gov. Carleton into Quebec on Nov. 19, 1775, after his flight from Montreal. He seems to be identified with Hon. Charles Napier, 1731-1807, member of a family distinguished in British naval service.

Copy located: None.

202. NOVA SCOTIA. COMMISSIONERS APPOINTED TO COLLECT TAX FOR MILITIA

[Hand Bill for assessors raising money for the Militia.]

Broadside; *printed at Halifax, N.S., by Anthony Henry, 1775*, as recorded:

"1775, Dec. 7. To Hand Bills for assessors raising money for the militia—5*s*." —Anthony Henry's "Bill for Sundry Extra work for Government, 1775 & 1776," P.A.N.S. v. 301.

The handbill was probably prepared for the sixty commissioners appointed by the Executive Council, Dec. 5, 1775, to assess all adult males, and to levy and collect a tax of not less than 5*s*. and not more than £5 per head, according to 16 Geo. III c. 1, "An Act for raising a tax . . . [for] supporting the Militia, [etc.]." This was an emergency measure passed by the Nova Scotia legislature Nov. 17, 1775, in apprehension of attack from New England. Vigorously protested through the province, the levy was deferred on Jan. 8, 1776, then allowed to drop.

Copy located: None.

203. NOVA SCOTIA. GOVERNOR, 1773-1782 (*Legge*)

[By His Excellency Francis Legge Esquire, Captain General & Governor in Chief &c. &c. &c. A Proclamation <Text> Given at Halifax October 16, 1775, (Sign'd) Francis Legge. . . . God Save the King.]

Broadside; *printed at Halifax, N.S., by Anthony Henry, 1775*, as recorded:

"1775, Oct. 17. To printing a proclamation for people taking shelter in this province from the Continent & for continuing [i.e. in *Nova-Scotia gazette* Oct. 17-Nov. 14 (or later) 1775]—£2.10.
[same date] To printing the same in full face—£2.10."—Anthony Henry's "Bill for Sundry Extra work for Government, 1775 & 1776," P.A.N.S. v. 301.

Text (from N.S. Executive Council *Minutes*, Oct. 16, 1775, in Can.P.A., N.S. "B" 16, p. 196-99) begins: "Whereas by letter bearing date the 1st July last, from the Right Honorable the Earl of Dartmouth, his Majesty's principal Secretary of State for the Colonies, it is signified therein, that His Majesty having been most Graciously pleased, to take into his Royal Consideration that the Rebellion in North America has compell'd many of his subjects to the necessity of abandoning their country.

"And his Majesty extending his tender regard to all such persons in their sufferings, wishing to afford them every possible Assistance and having consider'd that . . . Nova Scotia may become an happy Asylum to many unfortunate families, and may . . . afford those supplies to the West India Islands which they can no longer receive from other Colonies [etc.]." Accordingly Gov. Legge will grant to refugees land, free and exempt from quit rent for ten years; licences to cut and export timber to West Indies, with promise of bounty thereon; victuals to the value of 6*d*. sterling per day, per person.

On Oct. 17, 1775, Gov. Legge wrote Dartmouth that he had issued a proclamation (as above) "setting forth the particulars which I shall endeavour to spread on the continent [i.e. of America] . . . the Scarcity of Provisions in this Town . . . is such that none at present is to be purchased but I shall pay all due attention to His Majesty's Orders as soon as any shall arrive."—Can.P.A., N.S. "A" 94, p. 222.

Copy located: None.

204. NOVA SCOTIA. GOVERNOR, 1773-1782 (*Legge*)

[By His Excellency Francis Legge, Esquire, Captain General & Governor in Chief &c. &c. &c. A Proclamation <Text> Given at Halifax, December 8, 1775.]

Broadside; *printed at Halifax, N.S., by Anthony Henry, 1775,* as recorded:

"1775, Dec. 8th. To a Proclamation in full face for persons coming into this province to give their Names, and findg. paper—£2.10."—Anthony Henry's "Bill for Sundry Extra work for Government, 1775 & 1776," P.A.N.S. v. 301.

The text as published has not been seen by the writer, but it is recorded in the *Journal* of the Executive Council, Dec. 8, 1775: "The Governor propos'd to the Council that a Proclamation be publish'd requiring all Persons not settled inhabitants, who since the last of September have, or shall come into this Town to give notice, (to two magistrates who shall be appointed for that purpose) on pain of their being treated as Spies; Also requiring all Inn Keepers and publick House Keepers to give notice of the arrival of Strangers under like penalty of neglect; Also forbidding all vessels to enter the North West Arm without special licence from Capt. Hammond of H. M. Ship *Roebuck*." The Council agreed.—Can.P.A., N.S. "B" 16, p. 219-20 (also in P.A.N.S. v. 212).

Copy located: None.

205. NOVA SCOTIA. HOUSE OF ASSEMBLY

[To the King's Most Excellent Majesty, the Lords Spiritual and Temporal, and the Commons of Great Britain, in Parliament Assembled. The Address, Petition and Memorial of the Representatives of the freeholders of the Province of Nova Scotia, in General Assembly. Halifax, June 24, 1775.]

8vo. *Printed at Halifax, N.S., ? by Anthony Henry, 1775?* Of the only copy recorded, it was stated: "it bear[s] no imprint or publisher's name, but it gives us the impression that it was printed at Halifax, N.S."—Henry Stevens, Sons & Stiles: *Rare Americana, a catalogue,* no. 4 (London, 1928), item no. 372.

The address was drawn up by a committee of the Assembly (John Day, Halifax, chairman) which ordered it transmitted to London where it was presented to the king by Sept. 16, 1775.

"The address was a triple affair providing, as it did, suggested remedies for the revolutionary situation in North America, for avoidance of clashes in which Nova

Scotian governors, councils and assemblies had been almost continuously involved since 1758, and for specific administrative reform of the colony, [etc.]."—*See* J. B. Brebner: *Nova Scotia's remedy for the American Revolution*, in *Canadian historical review*, 15: 171-81, 1934.

It was reprinted as *Extract from the votes of the House of Assembly of the Province of Nova-Scotia, containing an address, petition and memorial, etc.* (13 p. 8 vo., Boston, Draper, 1775) (copy in MHi). It was reprinted also in Wm. Cobbett and Wright: *A parliamentary history of England* (36 v., London, 1806-20), 18: 699-705; also in J. B. Brebner, *Nova Scotia's remedy for the American Revolution*, in *Canadian historical review*, 15: 171-81, 1734.

Copy known: A copy was offered for sale by Henry Stevens, Sons & Stiles, 1928, as cited above; but it has not been located.

206. NOVA SCOTIA. HOUSE OF ASSEMBLY

Caption title: [Journals and Votes of the House of Assembly for the Province of Nova-Scotia.]

Note: title above is not transcribed from copy.

fo. 58 p. *Printed at Halifax, N.S., by Anthony Henry, 1775.*

Contents: p. 1-58, Journal and votes of the seventh session of the fifth assembly, June 12-July 20, 1775.

Copy located: GBLP (in C.O. 220/11:359-416) transcribed in Can.P.A., N.S. "D."

207. NOVA SCOTIA. HOUSE OF ASSEMBLY

Caption title: [Journals and Votes of the House of Assembly for the Province of Nova-Scotia.]

Note: title above is not transcribed from copy.

fo. 22 p. *Printed at Halifax, N.S., by Anthony Henry, 1775.*

Contents: p. 1-22, Journal and votes of the eighth session of the fifth assembly, Oct. 20-Nov. 18, 1775.

Copies located: CaNs; GBLP (in C.O. 220/1: 789-811. Another copy not located, recorded in Henry Stevens, Sons & Stiles: *Americana*, n.s. no. 7 (London, [1931?]), item no. 400.

208. NOVA SCOTIA. LAWS, STATUTES, *etc.*

Running title: [rule] / 1775. Anno Quinto Decimo Regis GEORGII III. CAP. I. / [rule] /

Caption title: At the GENERAL-ASSEMBLY of the Pro-/vince of Nova-Scotia, . . . / [9 lines] / . . . being the Fifth GENERAL-/ASSEMBLY convened in the said Pro-/vince. / [ornamental rule] /

p. 301 only in broadside; type-page: 25 × 14.5 cm. paged in continuation of No. 190. *Printed at Halifax, N.S., by Anthony Henry, 1775.*

Contents: p. 301, Cap. I, perpetual act passed in the seventh session of the fifth assembly, June 12-July 20, 1775; p. 301 verso, blank.

Copies located: CaN; CaNs; CaNsHA; CaNsWA; CaOOA; DLC; MB; MH; NNB.

209. NOVA SCOTIA. LAWS, STATUTES, *etc.*

Running title: [rule] / Anno Quinto Decimo Regis GEORGII III. CAP. I[-III]. / [ruleI /

Caption title: At the GENERAL-ASSEMBLY of the Pro-/vince of Nova-Scotia . . . / [9 lines] / . . . being the Fifth GENERAL-/ASSEMBLY convened in the said Pro-/vince. / [ornamental rule] /

fo. p. 166-169; type-page: 24.5 × 15.5 cm. paged in continuation of No. 191. *Printed at Halifax, N.S., by Anthony Henry, 1775.*

Contents: p. 166-169, Cap. I-III temporary acts passed in the seventh session of the fifth assembly, June 12-July 20, 1775.

Copies located: CaNs; CaO; CaOOA; MH; NNB.

210. NOVA SCOTIA. LAWS, STATUTES, *etc.*

Running title: [rule] / 1775. Anno Sexto Decimo Regis GEORGII III. CAP. I[-VI]. / rule] /

Caption title: At the GENERAL-ASSEMBLY of the Pro-/vince of Nova-Scotia, . . . / [9 lines] / . . . being the Fifth GENERAL-/ASSEMBLY convened in the said Pro-/vince. / [ornamental rule] /

fo. sig. 5I-5L²; p. 303-314; type-page: 25 × 14.5 cm. paged in continuation of No. 208. *Printed at Halifax, N.S., by Anthony Henry, 1775.*

Contents: p. 303-314, Cap. I-VI perpetual acts passed in the eighth session of the fifth assembly, Oct. 20-Nov. 18, 1775.

Copies located: CaB; CaN; CaNs; CaNsHA; CaNaWA; CaOOA; DLC; MB (defective); MH; N; NNB.

211. NOVA SCOTIA. LAWS, STATUTES, *etc.*

Running title: [rule] / 1775. Anno Sexto Decimo Regis GEORGII III. CAP. I[-VI]. / [rule] /

Caption title: At the GENERAL-ASSEMBLY of the Pro-/vince of Nova-Scotia, . . . / [9 lines] / . . . being the Fifth GENERAL-/ASSEMBLY convened in the said Pro-/vince. / [ornamental rule] /

fo. p. 170-178; type-page: 24 × 14.5 cm paged in continuation of No. 209. *Printed at Halifax, N.S., by Anthony Henry, 1775.*

Contents: p. 170-178, Cap. I-VI, temporary acts passed in the eighth session of the fifth assembly, Oct. 20-Nov. 18, 1775; p. 178 verso, blank.

Copies located: CaNs; CaO; CaOOA; MH; NNB.

212. PHELPS, BENAJAH, 1737-1817

DEATH: / The Way to the Believer's / compleat Happiness. / ILLUSTRATED and IMPROVED, / In a SERMON, occasioned / BY the / DEATH / OF / Mrs. JANE CHIPMAN, / Consort to Handley Chipman, Esq; / And delivered, the Sabbath She was enter'd, / April 9th, 1775. /

[rule] / By BENAJAH PHELPS, A.B. / Minister of the Gospel, and late Pastor of the / Church in CORNWALLIS. / [rule] / HALIFAX: Printed by A. HENRY. / [title within mourning border of double rules]

12mo. [*][8]; 15p.; type-page: 15.7 × 9.2 cm.

Contents: p. [1], t.-p.; p. [2], blank; p. [3], prefatory note; p. [4], blank; p. 5-15, Sermon, text: John, 20th chap., 23d verse, "And Thomas said unto him, My lord and my God"; p. 15 verso, blank.

The sermon is an elaborate development (in four sections with numbered subsections) of the theme expressed in the title, with an address to the mourners, and an "application of the whole to the congregation in general."

Phelps, born at Hebron, Conn., graduated from Yale college in 1761. He was ordained at Hartford in 1765 and sent to minister to New England Congregationalists at Cornwallis and Horton, Nova Scotia. He proved an unpopular appointee, however, possibly because of his political views. Disputes arose over financial arrange ments at Cornwallis—Phelps was to receive £80 annual salary. He appears to have left his charge about the time of this publication and returned to New England in Aug., 1778, later settling near Hartford, Conn.—F. B. Dexter: *Biographical sketches of the graduates of Yale college, 1701-1815,* (16 v., New York, 1885-1912), 2: 713-14; and A. W. H. Eaton: *The history of King's county, Nova Scotia* (Salem, Mass., 1910).

Copy located: DLC.

213. PRIMERS. QUEBEC

[Alphabet or Primer, *printed at Quebec by Wm. Brown, 1775?*]

The following entry in Brown's account book is interesting principally in speculation of the use of the *Alphabets* (*see also* No. 264 and 561). Gov. Carleton's own children were aged two years, one year, and two months respectively, at this time.

"1775, Sept. 11. printed for Gen. Carleton some time ago a broadside containing the Alphabets, Spelling, &c.—15*s*.
Ditto the Alphabet in Capitals Rom. & Ital. on 2 cards @ 2/6—5*s*.
D° D° D° Small D° in a Demy folio—10*s*.
D° this day D° D° D° on 9 different cards @ 2/6.—£1.2.6. [total £2.12.6]
pd. Feb. 15 '78."—Can.P.A., *Neilson papers*, v. 46.

214. QUEBEC, *City.* SEMINAIRE DE QUEBEC

LE / MONDE DEMASQUÉ: / COMEDIE FRANCOISE. / EN TROIS ACTES. / Qui sera Representée dans la Cour du Séminaire à QUEBEC, par les / ECOLIERS du Séminaire, Mercredi neuf Aoust, à onze heures du matin. / [14 lines] / [ornamental rule] / LE / CONCERT RIDICULE: / FARCE. / [15 lines] / La Distribution solemnelle des Prix, donnés par Son Excellence GUY CARLETON, / Major-général et Commandant en Chef de la Province de Québec, termina le Spectacle. /

Broadside, 41 lines; type-page: 31.5 × 19.3 cm.; *printed at Quebec by Wm. Brown, 1775,* in 800 copies, as recorded:

"1775, Aug. 5. Printed for C. F. Bailly 700 coarse and 100 on fine Paper, Play Bills making a folio page—£1.15."—Can.P.A., *Neilson papers*, v. 46.

Prepared for commencement exercises for the school year 1774-75, in the Séminaire de Québec, the programme lists the characters in the plays and the students in the roles. The prize list was published separately (*see* No. 215). Bailly de Messein was professor of rhetoric in the Séminaire, 1771-76, and became tutor to Gov. Carleton's children. Both were interested in a plan for higher education in Quebec (*see* No. 635).

Copies located: CaO (bound with *Quebec gazette*, Aug. 3-10, 1775); CaQQL.

215. QUEBEC, *City*. SEMINAIRE DE QUEBEC

PALMARE / Quod felix, faustum, fortunatum que sit omnibus Collegii Seminarii Quebecensis / alumnis ex Dono et Munificentiâ ILLUSTRISSIMI et EXCELLENTISSIMI / D.D. GUIDONIS CARLETON, pro Regis / in Provincia Quebecensi et Agonothetæ. / In Solemni Præmiorum Distributione facta VII° Idus Augusti, Septuagesimo quinto supra Mille- / simûm Septingentesimum anno. / [ornamental rule] / <Text>

Broadside, 74 lines; type-page: 39 × 21.5 cm. *printed at Quebec by Wm. Brown, 1775*, as recorded:

> "1775, Aug. 12. Printed for C. F. Bailly [*see* No. 635 note] 150 Lists of Premiums—£1.15."—Can.P.A., *Neilson papers*, v. 46.

The *text*, entirely in Latin, is the honours list for the school year 1774-75, in the Séminaire de Québec. In Schola rhetoricus, Tertia schola, Quinta schola and Sexta schola, it records thirteen first prizes, nine second prizes, and forty "honourable mentions" of thirty-seven scholars.

Copies located: CaO (bound with *Quebec gazette*, Aug. 3-10, 1775); CaQQL.

216. QUEBEC, *Province*. GOVERNOR, 1768-1778 (*Carleton*)

Heading: THE / QUEBEC / GAZETTE / [ornamental rule] / THURSDAY, APRIL 27, 1775. / [ornamental rule] / [heading to col. 1, as above; in centre of leaf: royal arms; heading to col. 2:] NOMB. 537.. / LA / GAZETTE / DE / QUEBEC / [ornamental rule] / JEUDI, le 27 AVRIL, 1775. / [ornamental rule] /

Caption, col. 1: By His Excellency / GUY CARLETON, / . . . / . . . / . . . / . . . / . . . / A PROCLAMATION. /

Caption, col. 2: Par SON EXCELLENCE / GUY CARLETON, / . . . / . . . / . . . / . . . / PROCLAMATION. /

Colophon: QUEBEC: Printed by W^{M} BROWN, behind the Cathedral Church. [ornament] A QUEBEC: chez G. BROWN, derriere l'Eglise Cathedrale. /

Broadside, printed in 2 col. English and French; type-page: 34.5 × 21 cm.; verso, blank; a separate issue of p. [1] of *Quebec gazette*, no. 537.

The proclamation, dated Quebec, Apr. 26, 1775, and signed by Guy Carleton, concerned the temporary administration of justice pending reorganization under the

Quebec Act. By it Gov. Carleton appointed commissioners of the peace (gardiens ou conservateurs de la paix) to take charge of the administration of justice from May 1, 1775. On this date the Quebec Act came into effect, rendering void all previous commissions, etc., but the governor's instructions for the reorganization arrived in Quebec only in April. By Aug. 17, the new Legislative Council was appointed; but martial law had been proclaimed in June, the Americans invaded the province in Sept., 1775, and the new civil constitution remained in abeyance till 1777.

Copy located: CaOOA.

217. QUEBEC, *Province.* GOVERNOR, 1768-1778 (*Carleton*)

BY HIS EXCELLENCY / GUY CARLETON, / Captain-general and Governor in Chief, in and over the Province of / Quebec, . . . / . . . / . . . / A PROCLAMATION. / <Text> / GIVEN under my Hand and Seal of Arms at Montreal, this Ninth Day of June, One Thousand Seven Hundred and Seventy-five . . . / . . . / . . . / GUY CARLETON. / By His EXCELLENCY'S Command, / H. T. CRAMAHÉ. / GOD save the KING. /

French on right:

PAR SON EXCELLENCE / GUY CARLETON, / Capitaine-général et Gouverneur en Chef dans toute la Province de Quebec / . . . / . . . / . . . / PROCLAMATION. / <Text> / Donné sous mon Seing et le Sceau de mes Armes, à Montréal, ce Neuvieme jour de Juin, Mil sept cens / soixante et quinze . . . / . . . / . . . / GUY CARLETON. / Par Son EXCELLENCE, / H. T. CRAMAHÉ. / VIVE LE ROI. /

Double broadside; English on left, 40 lines, type-page: 24.5 × 19.8 cm.; French on right, 43 lines, type-page: 25 × 19.8 cm.; verso, blank. *Printed at Quebec by Wm. Brown, 1775.*

Text: "Whereas a Rebellion prevails in many of His Majesty's Colonies in America, . . . I shall . . . execute Martial Law . . . throughout this Province, and to that End I shall order the Militia within the same to be forthwith raised [etc.]."

French text: "L'Esprit de Rebellion s'etant manifesté dans plusieurs des Colonies de sa Majesté en Amérique; . . . j'ai résolu d'emploïer le secours des Lois Militaires . . . dans toute l'étendue de cette province, et d'ordonner en consequence qu'on mette incessamment sur pieds les Milices de la dite Province [etc.]."

The text is reprinted in Canada, Department of Militia: *History,* 2: 53-54 from [F. Maseres] *Additional papers concerning the province of Quebeck* (London, 1776); also reprinted in Can.P.A., *Report, 1918.*

Copies located: CaQQL (2 cop., English side wanting in one copy).

218. QUEBEC, *Province.* GOVERNOR, 1768-1778 (*Carleton*)

[Par Son Excellence Guy Carleton, Capitaine-général et Gouverneur en Chef dans toute la Province de Québec, et Territoires en Dépendans en Amérique, Vice-amiral d'icelle, Marêchal des Camps et

Armées de sa Majesté, Commandant le Département Septentrionale, Ec. Ec. Ec. A tous les Capitaines et autres Officiers commandans les Milices dans la Province de Québec, &c. <Text> Donné à Montréal, le 14 Octobre, 1775. GUY CARLETON.]

Broadside? *printed at Quebec by Wm. Brown, 1775,* in 200 copies, as recorded:

"1775, Oct. 18. Printed for the Gov.t 200 Orders to the habitans by the Governor —£1.10."—Can.P.A., *Neilson papers,* v. 46.

Text (from *Quebec gazette,* Oct. 19, 1775): "Vue qu'on nombre considérables fidèles sujets de sa Majesté qui se sont rendus près de Nous, (pour donner des preuves de leur zèle et fidelité envers sa dite Majesté) ont laissé beaucoup de travaux imparfaits chez eux; et qu'il ne seront pas juste que de tels sujets souffrissent pour s'être distingués; . . . A ces Causes, Nous vous ordonnons de faire faire . . . par les habitans qui sont restés chez eux, . . . tous les ouvrages et travaux que les dits habitans . . . qui servent près de Nous, . . . ne peuvent faire; comme faucher les foins, couper les avoines ou autres grains, serrer et engranger le tout bien conditionné, faire les guérets et labours, réparer et mettre les bâtimens en état d'hivernement. . . .

"Nous vous mandons . . . de faire immediatement publier tant à la porte des Eglises . . . que par-tout ailleurs où besoin sera notre dit présent ordre [etc.]."

This order with its unusual display of Carleton's prestige and its confident tone, commanding habitants who remain at home to tend the crops of those who enlist, was a subtle encouragement, to stiffen resistance to the American invaders and to induce habitants to quit the farm for military service. It appeared with unusual prominence, conspicuous in type and layout, in the *Quebec gazette,* Oct. 19-Nov. 9, 1775; and was reprinted in Verreau: *Invasion du Canada,* 57-58, and in Canada, Department of Militia; *History,* 2: 105-06.

Copy located: None.

219. QUEBEC, *Province.* GOVERNOR, 1768-1778 (*Carleton*)

BY HIS EXCELLENCY / GUY CARLETON, / Captain-general and Governor in Chief in and over the Province of / QUEBEC, . . . / . . . / . . . / A PROCLAMATION. / <Text> / GIVEN . . . at . . . QUEBEC, / this Twenty-second Day of November, One Thousand Seven Hundred and Seventy-five . . . / . . . / . . . / GUY CARLETON. / . . . / . . . / . . . /

French on right:

PAR SON EXCELLENCE / GUY CARLETON, / Capitaine-general et Gouverneur en Chef dans toute la Province / de Quebec, . . . / . . . / . . . / PROCLAMATION. / <Text> / Donné . . . dans la ville de QUEBEC, / le vingt-deuxieme jour de Novembre, mil sept cens soixante quinze . . . / . . . / . . . / (Signé) GUY CARLETON. / Par Ordre de son Excellence, / (Signé) H. T. CRAMAHE. / Traduit par ordre de Son Excellence. / F. J. CUGNET, S.F. / VIVE LE ROI. /

Double broadside; English on left, 45 lines, type-page: 24 × 19 cm.; French on right, 48 lines, type-page: 25 × 19 cm.; verso, blank. *Printed at Quebec by Wm. Brown, 1775,* as recorded:

"1775, Nov. 22. Printed for the Gov[t] of Quebec 150 Proclamations ordering Persons out of Town, &c.—£1.15."—Can.P.A., *Neilson papers*, v. 46.

Text: "WHEREAS it has been found expedient to raise . . . a Militia within this City, . . . to assist His Majesty's Troops . . . in the Preservation of the City . . . against certain Rebellious Persons who have invaded this Province, a number of whom have lately appeared in Arms before the Walls of this Town . . . in Order to rid the Town of all useless, disloyal, and treacherous Persons, . . . I do hereby strictly order . . . Persons . . . who have refused . . . to enroll their Names in the Militia Lists . . . to quit the Town in four Days from the Date hereof, together with their Wives and Children, . . . to deliver in forthwith to the Hon. GEORGE ALLSOPP, Esquire, Comissary, a true Inventory or List of their Provisions and Stores, in order that they may be fairly and justly valued and the full price paid to the respective Proprietors before their Departure."

French text: "COMM'IL a été trouvé necessaire de lever et incorporer la milice dans cette ville . . . j'ordonne . . . à tous et chacuns sujets quelconques . . . qui ont refusé ou évité de faire inscrire leurs noms dans les listes de la Milice, et de prendre les armes . . . de vuider la ville . . . dans quatre jours de la date des presentes [etc.]."

Reprinted in Canada, Department of Militia: *History*, 2: 134-35, also in Can.P.A., *Report, 1918*, and discussed in Verreau: *Invasion du Canada*, 110-11.

Copy located: CaQQL.

220. QUEBEC, *Province.* LIEUTENANT-GOVERNOR, 1771-1782 (*Cramahé*)

[By the Honourable Hector Theophilus Cramahé, Esq., Lieutenant-Governor of the Province of Quebec, &c[a].,&c[a]., A Proclamation. <Text> Given . . . at Quebec this Sixteenth day of September, . . . 1775. In the Absence and by the Order of His Excellency the Governor. H. T. Cramahé. God Save the King.]

French part:

[Par l'honorable Hector Théophile Cramahé, Ecuier, Lieutenant-Gouverneur de la Province de Québec, &c. &c. Proclamation. <Text> Donné . . . à Québec ce seizième jour de Septembre, . . . 1775. Dans l'absence et par l'ordre de son Excellence le Gouverneur. (Signé) H. T. Cramahé. Traduit par ordre du Lieutenant Gouverneur. Vive le Roi.]

Double broadside. *Printed at Quebec by Wm. Brown, 1775*, as recorded below.

English text (from Can.P.A., *Report, 1918*): "Whereas great Mischiefs and Inconveniences may . . . ensue from permitting Strangers, who may be in the Interest of the Rebels to resort to the Town of Quebec . . . I do hereby strictly Order . . . all Persons not Settled Inhabitants of this Place who since the Thirty first Day of August last have . . . come into the Town of Quebec . . . to signify to one of the Conservators of the Peace . . . their Names and place of abode . . . upon pain of being . . . treated as Spies . . . And I do likewise Order . . . all Tavern-keepers . . . to Report the Name . . . within two hours after the coming of such . . . Strangers, [etc.]."

French text (from Canada, Department of Militia: *History*, 2: 77): "Comme il peut arriver de grands malheurs et inconvéniens, et qu'il en est probablement arrivé de permettre à des étrangers, qui peuvent être dans les interêts des Rebels, de Venir dans la ville de Québec . . . J'ordonne et je commande vigoureusement, par ces présentes, à toutes personnes qui ne sont point censés être habitans de cette place, qui sont arrivées dans la ville de Québec, depuis le trente-unième jour du mois d'août dernier . . . de paraitre immédiatement en personnes, ou de déclarer devant un des conservateurs de la paix . . . leurs noms, le lieu de leurs demeures, et les raisons pour lesquelles elles sont venues en cette ville, sous peine d'être regardées et traitées comme Espions . . . Et j'ordonne . . . à tous hoteliers . . . de donner les noms . . . de tous tels étrangers . . . dans deux heures de l'arrivés de tels étrangers [etc.]."

The printer recorded this work:

"1775, Sept. 19. Printed for the Gov.[t] of Quebec 200 Double Proclamations for preventing Spies in Quebec &c. (on Sunday)—£1.15.

[About the same time other emergency measures were printed:]

1775, Sept. 9. Printed for the Gov.[t] by Order of Mr. Finlay [deputy postmaster and superintendent of maitres des postes] 100 double Orders to Keepers of Post houses forbidding them to carry persons without a pass—15*s*.

Sept. 19. 50 Orders for preventing Persons travelling without a Pass (on Sunday)—7/6.

Do. 50 Ditto with additions of Tonancour [Lt. Col. L. J. Tonnancour, militia officer]—7/6."—Can.P.A., *Neilson papers*, v. 46.

Reprinted in Canada, Department of Militia: *History*, 2: 76-77; also in Can. P.A., *Report, 1918*.

Copy located: None.

221. QUEBEC, *Province*. LIEUTENANT-GOVERNOR, 1771-1782 (*Cramahé*)

BY THE HONORABLE / HECTOR THEOPHILUS CRAMAHE, Esq; / Lieutenant-governor of the Province of QUEBEC, &c.[a] &c.[a] / A PROCLAMATION. / <Text> / GIVEN . . . at Quebec, this 28th Day of September . . . / . . . 1775. / In the Absence, and by Order of His Excellency the GOVERNOR, / H. T. CRAMAHE. / GOD Save the KING. /

French on right:

PAR l'HONORABLE / HECTOR THEOPHILE CRAMAHE, Ecuier, / Lieutenant-gouverneur de la Province de Québec, Ec. Ec. / PROCLAMATION. / <Text> / Donné . . . à Québec, ce vingt-huitieme jour de Septembre, . . . 1775. / Dans l'absence et par ordre de son Excellence le GOUVERNEUR, / H. T. CRAMAHE. / Traduit par ordre du Lieutenant-Gouverneur. / F. J. CUGNET, S.F. / VIVE LE ROI. /

Double broadside; English on left, 17 lines, type-page: 16.5 × 18.3 cm.; French on right, 20 lines, type-page: 18 × 18.3 cm.; verso blank. *Printed at Quebec by Wm. Brown, 1775*, as recorded:

"1775, Sept. 29. Printed for the Gov.[t] of Quebec 200 Proclamations laying an Embargo on Shipping—£1.15."—Can.P.A., *Neilson papers*, v. 46.

English text: "It being absolutely necessary in the present Disorders, to provide in the most effectual Manner for the Defense of the Town and Province of Quebec: And whereas great Assistance may be derived from the Sailors on Board the Ships and Vessels in the different Parts of the Province, It is hereby Ordered that no Ship . . . do proceed in her Voyage . . . before the Twentieth Day of October next; [etc.]."

French Text: "Etant absolument nécessaire dans les troubles présens, de pourvoir . . . à la défense de la ville et de la Province de Québec: Et comm'on peut retirer un grands secours des matelots . . . Il est par ces presentes ordonné, qu'aucuns bâtimens . . . ne partiront . . . avant le vingtiéme jour d'Octobre prochain; [etc.]."

Reprinted in Canada, Department of Militia: *History,* 2: 83-84; also in Can. P.A., *Report, 1918.*

Copy located: CaQQL.

222. QUEBEC, *Province.* LIEUTENANT-GOVERNOR, 1771-1782 (*Cramahé*)

BY THE HONORABLE / HECTOR THEOPHILUS CRAMAHE, Esq; / Lieutenant-governor of the Province of QUEBEC, &c. &c. / A PROCLAMATION. / <Text> / GIVEN . . . at Quebec, this Twentieth Day of October, . . . / . . . 1775. / In the Absence, and by Order of His Excellency the GOVERNOR, / H. T. CRAMAHE. / GOD Save the KING. /

French on right:

PAR l'HONORABLE / HECTOR THEOPHILE CRAMAHE, Ecuier, / Lieutenant-gouverneur de la Province de Québec, Ec. Ec. / PROCLAMATION. / <Text> / Donné . . . à Québec, ce vingtieme jour d'Octobre . . . / . . . 1775. / Dans l'absence et par ordre de son Excellence le GOUVERNEUR, / H. T. CRAMAHE. / Traduit par ordre du Lieutenant-Gouverneur. / F. J. CUGNET, S. F. / [VIVE LE ROI.] /

Double broadside; English on left, 16 lines, type-page: 16 × 18 cm.; French on right, 19 lines, type-page: 16.2 × 18 cm. (cropped); verso, blank. *Printed at Quebec by Wm. Brown, 1775* (*see also* No. 223).

"1775. Oct. 20. Printed for the Gov^{t} of Quebec 200 Proclamations extending an Embargo—£1.10."—Can.P.A., *Neilson papers,* v. 46.

English text: "Whereas by a Proclamation dated the 28th Day of September last, an Embargo was laid on all the Shipping . . . it is hereby Ordered that the Embargo shall be extended to the Fourth of November next [etc.]."

French text: "Comme par une Proclamation en date du 28$^{me.}$ jour du mois de Septembre dernier, il a été defendu à tous les vaisseaux . . . d'en sortir . . . Il est par ces presentes ordonné, qu'elle continuera jusqu'au quatriéme jour de Novembre prochain [etc.]."

Reprinted in Can.P.A., *Report, 1918.*

Copies located: CaOOA (Photostat of cropped copy filed in Can.P.A., "*S,*" *Proclamations, Quebec, 1765-1775*); CaQQL (cropped).

223. QUEBEC, *Province.* LIEUTENANT-GOVERNOR, 1771-1782 (*Cramahé*)

Another edition of No. 222, *printed at Quebec by Wm. Brown, 1775,* as recorded: "1775. Oct. 24. Reprinted for Gov.t 200 Proclamations extending the Embargo —£1.10."—Can.P.A., *Neilson papers,* v. 46.

As no distinction between the two printings is indicated by the printer, the description and copies located under No. 222 may apply to either edition.

224. ALMANACS. NOVA SCOTIA

THE / Nova-Scotia CALENDER / OR, / AN ALMANACK, / For the Year . . . 1777 . . . / [5 lines] / Wherein is contained, / The Feasts and Fasts of the Church . . . / [5 lines] / Calculated for the Meridian of Halifax, . . . / [4 lines] / By METONICUS. / [ornamental rule] / HALIFAX: Printed and sold by A. HENRY. / [title within ornamental frame]

16 mo. [18 + ?] p.

Contents: The only copy located is defective, comprising: p. [1], t.-p.; p. [2], Vulgar notes, etc. p. [3-14], Calendar. p. [15-16] Royal family, British naval list; p. [17?] Zodiac; p. [18-20?] Province of Nova Scotia list of officers of government (incomplete).

This (or possibly a *Nova-Scotia Calender for 1776*) was the first calculated by Metonicus, whose identity remains unknown. The Metonicus calendars are, on the whole, more sedate and scientific than their predecessors. Instead of the homely if innocuous advice of the A. Lilius calendars, Metonicus's calendar tables are headed by moon's phases; instruction upon methods of avoiding colds or quenching thirst replace the earlier calendars' bawdy tales and, in keeping with this informative policy, the section upon the Nova Scotia government is expanded.

Copy located: CaNsHD (defective).

ALMANACS. QUEBEC

[Indian Calendar for 1776] *See* No. 174.

225. ALMANACS. QUEBEC

ALMANACH / ENCYCLOPÉDIQUE, / OU / CHRONOLOGIE / Des Faits les plus remarkables de / l'Histoire Universelle, / depuis JE / SUS-CHRIST; / Avec des Anecdotes curieuses, utiles / et interessantes. / [rule] / Mil sept cent soixante dix-sept. / [rule] / [ornament] / A MONTREAL; / Chez FLEURY MESPLET & CHAR- / LES BERGER, Imprim. Lib. / [rule] / 1777. / [title within ornamental frame] /

18mo. 60 p.; type-page: 11.2 × 5.6 cm. Text in French. p. [1], t.-p.; p. [2], Avertissement; p. [3], Comput ecclésiastique, fêtes mobiles, eclipses; p. [4-27], Calendrier; p. 28-54, Chronologie des faits le plus remarquables, etc.; p. 55-60, Anecdotes.

In *Avertissement* p. [2], the printers announce that the reception of this number will determine them whether to continue the series. If encouraged, it will form an abridgement of ancient and modern history, useful for young people's instruction. Following this announcement is a list of books for sale by the printers: viz., *Calendrier* (No. 228), *Cantiques de Marseilles* (No. 232), *Journée de chrétien, Le gout de bien des gens,* (Fauteux: *Mesplet,* p. 175, no. 2), *Jonathan et David* (No. 229), *Heures de vie.*

This list suggests that *Almanach Encyclopédique* was issued before their publications of 1777. It is said to be the first almanac published in Montreal and probably the first in French published in America. In Mesplet's *Almanach,* religious events and ecclesiastical information (Catholic) predominate over secular and local affairs. Indeed in this first number, no Canadian and little North American data are included —even in the *Chronologie des faits.*

In the copy examined by the writer, the t.-p. (with *Avertissement* etc., on verso) was not the original t.-p., but a reprint in modern types on modern paper, of the t.-p., etc., of a copy owned by Abbé N. Dubois, Montreal. For another description, see Fauteux: *Mesplet,* no. 13.

Copies located: CaQMS; CaQQL (t.-p. wanting and supplied in modern reprint).

226. ALMANACS. QUEBEC

CALENDRIER pour l'Année 1776, pour Québec, qui est par les $306^{d.}$ $30^{m.}$ de Longitude, et $46^{d.}$ $55^{m.}$ de Latitude. / [ornamental rule] /

Broadside: type-page: 42.5 × 38.5 cm. with ornamental rule frame.

Contents: Signes du zodiaque, Calendrier (as in No. 170).

This sheet almanac was *printed at Quebec by Wm. Brown, probably early in 1776.* His printing office suspended operations from the beginning of Dec., 1775, till ?Mar., 1776, owing to the siege and attack on the city, Dec., 1775, by the American invaders. The *Calendrier* was advertised for sale in the first number of the *Quebec gazette* published after printing was resumed Mar. 14, 1776.

Copy located: CaO (bound in *Quebec gazette,* at end of 1775).

227. ALMANACS. QUEBEC

CALENDRIER pour l'Année 1777, pour Québec, qui est par les $306^{d.}$ $30^{m.}$ de Longitude, et $46^{d.}$ $55^{m.}$ de Latitude. / [ornamental rule] / *Quebec, Wm. Brown, 1776.*

Broadside: type-page: 43.5 × 38 cm. with ornamental rule frame.

Contents: Les Signes du zodiaque, Calendrier, (the content, layout, and type are like those of No. 170).

This sheet almanac was *printed at Quebec by Wm. Brown, 1776,* sold at 7½*d.* the copy, 5*s.* the dozen, from Dec. 2, and advertised for sale at Quebec, Trois Rivières, and Montreal, as usual, in the *Quebec gazette* from Dec. 5, 1776.

Copy located: CaO (bound in *Quebec gazette* at end of 1776).

228. ALMANACS. QUEBEC

[Calendrier pour Montréal . . . pour l'année 1777. *Montreal, Mesplet & Berger, 1776.*

This publication, the first sheet almanac issued in Montreal, was printed by Fleury Mesplet and Charles Berger, 1776, and listed among their books for sale in the *Almanach* for 1777 (No. 225) p. [2] as "Calendrier sur une feuille volante."

Copy located: None.

229. [BRUMOY, PIERRE], 1688-1742

JONATHAS / ET / DAVID, / OU / LE TRIOMPHE / DE L'AMITIÉ. / [rule] / TRAGÉDIE / En Trois Actes. / Représenté par les Ecoliers de Montréal. / [printer's ornament] / A MONTREAL; / Chez FLEURY MESPLET & CH. BERGER, / Imprimeurs & Libraires. 1776. / [title within ornamental frame]

12mo.; [*][2], A-E[4]; 2 p. l.; 40 p.; type-page: 15.5 × 8 cm.

Contents: p. l. 1 recto, t-p.; verso, Personnages; p. l. 2 recto-verso, Prologue; p. 1-40, Jonathas et David.

Personnages lists the roles and the names and addresses of twenty-three schoolboys who played them. The text, in rhyming pentameter couplets, is based, according to a note following the *Prologue,* on Kings, chap. 17-28, ". . . L'amitié mutuelle de Jonathas & de David, leurs malheurs, leur séparation, leurs adieux, [etc.]."

The author is said to have been Pierre Brumoy, s.j., and the work to have been published in his *Recueil de divers ouvrages en prose et en vers* (Paris, 1741), in v. 4 (Fauteux: *Mesplet,* 178). Brumoy, who was born at Rouen in 1688 and died in Paris, 1742, was a distinguished Jesuit teacher and litterateur. He published numerous critical works on rhetoric, poetry and drama, translations of the classics, also original verses and plays. Among the latter, especially prepared for use in schools, was *Jonathas et David.* This edition was probably printed for a performance by students at the closing exercises of the Collège de Montréal, in Aug., 1776.

The Collège de Montréal was first established at Longue Pointe (as the Collège de Saint-Raphael) by Abbé J.-B. Curateau de la Blaiserie, a Sulpician, in 1767; then six years later it was moved into Montreal. A secondary school of the classical type, for boys, the Collège continued under Sulpician auspices, gradually extending the scope of its teaching. It is now affiliated with the faculty of arts in the Université de Montréal. (*See* Henri Gauthier: *Supitiana* (Montreal, 1926); also J. B. Meilleur: *Memorial de l'éducation de Bas-Canada, 1615-1855* (Montreal, 1860).)

For t.-p. facsim. see Fauteux: *Introduction of printing into Canada,* 92.

Copies located: CaQM; CaQMS.

230. CONFRERIE DE L'ADORATION PERPETUELLE DU SAINT SACREMENT ET DE LA BONNE MORT. *Montreal*

REGLEMENT / DE LA CONFRERIE. / DE L'ADORATION PERPETUELLE / DU / S. SACREMENT / ET / DE LA BONNE MORT. / Erigée dans l'Eglise Paroissiale de Vil-/le-Marie, en l'Isle de Montreal, / en Canada. /

12mo. A-C^6, D^2; 40 p.; type-page: 11 × 5.8 cm.; p. 37 mispaged: 73.

Contents: p. [1], t.-p.; p. [2, form of entrant's vow]; p. 3-5, Fin de l'Association; p. 6-13, Pratiques; p. 13-40, Prières.

Long thought to have been printed in Philadelphia, 1775-76, (*see* McLachlan: *Mesplet*) this work is considered now to have been printed after Mesplet's arrival in Montreal, 1776 (*see* Fauteux: *Mesplet*, 169). It was produced for the Séminaire de St. Sulpice, and sets forth the purpose, organization, and rules of a lay association directed by a priest of the Séminaire. This association, or brotherhood, was a mutual benefit society, into which the members paid an entrance fee and annual dues of 20 to 30 sols (half-pennies approximately). Elected officers supervised the temporal relief of needy members and the Sulpician director, their spiritual welfare.

Copies located: CaQMS (2 cop.); RPJ.

231. CONFRERIE DE L'ADORATION PERPETUELLE DU SAINT SACREMENT ET DE LA BONNE MORT. *Montreal*

RÉGLEMENT / DE LA CONFRERIE / DE L'ADORATION PERPÉTU-ELLE / DU / S. SACREMENT, / ET / DE LA BONNE MORT. / Erigée dans l'Eglise Paroissialle de Ville-Ma-/rie, en l'Isle de Montréal, en Canada. / Nouvelle Edition revue, corrigée & augmentée. / [printer's ornament] / A MONTREAL. / Chez F. MESPLET & C. BERGER, Impri-/ meurs & Libraires; près le Marché. 1776. /

16mo. A-B^8, C^4; 40 p.; type-page: 10.4 × 6 cm.

Contents: p. [1], t-p.; p. [2, form of entrant's vow]; p. 3-5, Fin de l'association; p. 5-12, Pratiques; p. 13-40, Prières.

Second edition of the item above, with the type entirely reset and the text augmented by two additional short prayers.

Copies located: Most libraries and private collectors of Canadiana have copies of this "Nouvelle édition revue." Some twenty have been seen by the writer and others recorded. They include several copies in mint condition, bound in light boards covered with old but fresh damask wall paper. Most (but not all) of such copies appear to have been released from some cache early in the present century.

232. DURAND, LAURENT, 1629-1708

CANTIQUES / DE L'AME DÉVOTE. / DIVISÉS EN XII. LIVRES. / Où l'on représente d'une maniere nette & facile / les principaux mysteres de la Foi, & les prin-/cipales vertus de la Religion Chrétienne. / Accommodés à des Airs vulgaires. / AVEC UNE AUG-MENTATION NOTABLE: / Le tout mis dans un ordre particulier. / NOUVELLE ÉDITION, Imprimée sur celle / de Marseille, avec son ancienne Appro-/bation. / PREMIERE PARTIE. / Par M. LAURENS DURAND, Prétre / du Diocèse de Toulon. / Implemini Spiritu Sancto, loquentes vobismet ipsis / In Psalmis & Hymnis & Canticis spirituali-bus / cantantes, & psallentes in cordibus vestris Domino. / Eph. ch. 6.

v. 18 & 19. / [printer's ornament] / A QUEBEC: / Chez FLEURY MESPLET & CHARLES / BERGER, Imprimeurs & Libraires, 1776. /

12mo. a^6, A-Bb^{12}, Cc^6; 6 p. l., 610 p., 1 *l.*; type-page: 14.3 × 7 cm.

Contents: p. l. 1 recto, t-p.; verso, blank; p. l. 2 recto-verso, "Epitre de l'Editeur, [signed:] Fleury Mesplet"; p. l. 3 recto-verso, "Au lecteur chretien"; also, "Approbation, [signed:] A Paris ce 15 Novembre 1723, J. Grancolas"; p. l. 4 recto-6 recto, Table; p. l. 6 verso, Avis au public; p. 1-328, Cantiques, première partie; p. 329-610, seconde partie; 1 *l.* blank.

Without music; tunes indicated by title.

Despite the imprint, this item was probably *printed and actually published in Montreal*, where Mesplet established his press in May, 1776. There is no evidence that he was in the town of Quebec at this time. Conceivably the imprint and "Quebec" in his "Avis," p. l. 6, signifies Province of Quebec. It is noticeable that another of Mesplet's 1776 productions (No. 230) bears *no* place of printing.

A popular devotional work, first printed in 1678 and generally known as "Cantiques de Marseilles," this edition was published for the Catholics of French Canada, according to the policy outlined by the first French printer in Canada: "Le Sr. F. Mesplet à Quebec, présente ses respects au Public, & prend la liberté de le prévenir qu'il imprime & vend, au meilleur prix possible, les Livres à la usage de l'Eglise Romaine, & qu'il continuera à travaillera sans relâche, pour pouvoir se former en peu de tems, une Collection complette de ce qui concerne Notre Sainte Religion, des autres bons Livres d'Histoire, Belles-Lettres, &c. Il ose se flatter d'être bientôt en état de satisfaire les personnes qui voudront bien lui faire leurs demandes & l'employer dans son Art."—Avis au public, p. l. 6 verso.

This work was advertised occasionally for several years by Mesplet in Montreal, and by Wm. Brown, the printer, in Quebec, who recorded sales at 5*s.* the copy. When Mesplet's stock was sold at auction Nov. 21, 1785, the sale included: "cinquante livres cantiques de Marseilles, adjugés à trois livres [i.e. about three shillings] pièce—150."—McLachlan: *Mesplet*, 269.

Copies located: CaQ; CaQM; CaQMS (2 cop.); CaQQL; DLC; Ketcheson; NN; Witton.

233. [FOR THE 31st OF DECEMBER, AN ODE]

fo. 2 p.; *printed at Quebec by Wm. Brown, 1776*, as recorded:

"1776, Dec. 28. Printed for the Managers of the Ball, 300 Odes for 31st Inst. 2 folio pages Demy—£1.10."—Can.P.A., *Neilson papers*, v. 46.

Tuesday, Dec. 31, 1776, the Quebec militia in commemoration "of the signal Victory obtained over the Rebel Army in their Assualt on this City [Dec. 31, 1775] march'd in Procession to the several Churches where Sermons were preached suitable to the Occasion. . . In the Evening a most elegant Supper and Ball were given by the Militia, at which were present near 300 Ladies and Gentlemen. An excellent Band of Musick was provided on this glorious Occasion and the whole Entertainment was conducted with the greatest Regularity and Elegance. . . . At Seven, an Ode written on the Occasion was perform'd, after which Dancing commenced, etc."—*Quebec gazette*, Jan. 2, 1777.

In the same issue of the paper the text of the *Ode* (70 lines in 4 stanzas with title as above) appeared in the Poet's Corner, beginning:

"When wide extended o'er each Frost-bound Plain,
Winter, Grim Pow'r! usurp'd his Sullen Reign:—
When gath'ring Snow-Storms blacken'd in the Sky:—
Then, all-resolv'd to conquer or to die.
Montgom'ry with his Rebel Band,
Invaders of this Peaceful Land,
Wrapt in the Shade of Night's impervious Gloom,
Intent to bury in one common Tomb
Our Laws—our Freedom—came prepar'd;
Whilst with indignant Scorn
And Patriot Zeal elate,
We hail'd the welcome Morn,
That hasten'd on their Fate
And saw Rebellion meet its just Reward.
For soon th' Almighty's piercing Eyes,
Which look thro' all things at a single View
Saw, and dispers'd the Gloom—the Shades withdrew—
The Rebel starts appal'd, and in a Moment dies."

For several years the repulse of the Americans' attack on Quebec under Montgomery and Arnold, Dec. 31, 1775, was celebrated by public and private entertainment, duly reported in the *Gazette*. The *Ode* was reprinted in the *The Times*, Quebec, Dec. 29, 1794.

Copy located: None.

234. GREAT BRITAIN. KING, 1760-1820 (*George III*)

[Royal arms] / By the KING, / A PROCLAMATION, / For suppressing Rebellion and Sedition. / GEORGE R. / <Text> / Given at Our Court of St. James's, the Twenty-third Day of August, One thousand / seven hundred and seventy-five, in the Fifteenth Year of Our Reign. / God save the King. /

French side (from Can.P.A., *Rapport, 1918*):

[Par le Roi. Proclamation. Pour Eteindre la Rebellion et Arreter la Sedition. George R. <Text> Donné à notre Cour, à St. James, ce vingt troisième jour d'Aoust, mil sept cent, soixante quinze, dans la quinzième année de notre Regne. Vive le Roi.]

Double broadside: English side (as above): 35 lines; type-page: 32 × 21 cm. French side: no copy located. Though difficult to identify with certainty, the English broadside described above is probably the English side of a double broadside *printed at Quebec by Wm. Brown, 1776* and recorded:

"1776, Aug. 10. To printing 130 King's Proclamations double for suppressing Rebellion and Sedition—£2.10."—Wm. Brown's Account for printing for Government [Sept. 9, 1775-Oct. 10, 1776], in Can.P.A., "*S*" *Pub. accts., 1774-76.*

English text (from original broadside): "Whereas many of Our Subjects in divers parts of Our Colonies and Plantations in North America . . . proceeded to an open and avowed rebellion . . . We do strictly charge and command all Our Officers . . . and loyal subjects . . . to disclose . . . all Treasons and traitrous Conspiracies which they shall know to be against Us, [etc.]."

French text (from Can.P.A., *Rapport, 1918*): "Comme un grand numbre de nos sujets en divers endroits de nos colonies et plantations en l'Amerique Septentrionale, . . . sont enfin venus au point de se rebeller publiquement et ouvertement, . . . Nous commandons et ordonnons rigoureusement à tous nos officiers . . . et à tous autres nos fidèles et obéissans sujets . . . pour découvrir et donner connoissance de toutes trahisons et perfides conspirations qu'ils sçauroient être trameés ou machinées, contre Nous, [etc.]."

This proclamation was printed (English only) in London, by Charles Eyre and Wm. Strahan, 1775, also in Boston by John Howe, 1775 (Evans no. 14077). It was printed in English and French as recorded above, also in the *Quebec gazette*, Aug. 8, 1776, and from there reprinted in Can.P.A., *Report, 1918*.

Copy located: CaOOA (English only in "Proclamations" portfolio in the Library); photograph of CaOOA copy is in CaNW.

235. NOVA SCOTIA. GOVERNOR, 1773-1782 (*Legge*)

[Proclamation concerning His Majesty's Loyal Regiment of Nova Scotia Volunteers. *Halifax, N.S., Anthony Henry, 1776.*]

Several unidentified proclamations or notices concerning this regiment were *printed at Halifax, N.S., by Anthony Henry, 1776*, as the records show:

"1776, Feb. 29. To Cash Paid Anthony Henry. Printing Hand bills and attestations—£6. 8. 10."—Account of Contingent expenses for H.M. Loyal Regiment of Nova Scotia Volunteers, Dec. 25, 1775-May 6, 1776, in Can.P.A., N.S. "A" 95, p. 333.

"1776, Mar. 3[d]. To a Proclamation concerning Governor Legg's Regiment —£2. 5."—Anthony Henry's Account for sundry extra printing [for Government] 1775-76, in P.A.N.S., *N.S. Miscellaneous papers, 1777*.

Gov. Legge undertook in Dec., 1775, to enlist residents of Nova Scotia in a regiment under his own command for defence of the province. Lack of provisions, a non-belligerent attitude in Nova Scotians, and the governor's political enemies combined to frustrate his persistent efforts. The returns of the regiment, Dec. 25, 1775-May 24, 1776, showed 130 officers and men enrolled, and costs, £3245. 9*s*. 11½*d*. —Can.P.A., N.S. "A" 95: 346-47. *See* J. B. Brebner: *The neutral Yankees of Nova Scotia* (New York, 1937), 282.

Copy located: None.

236. NOVA SCOTIA. GOVERNOR, 1773-1782 (*Legge*)

[Proclamation for regulating the Price of provisions, Halifax, April 2? 1776.]

Broadside? *Printed at Halifax, N.S., by Anthony Henry, 1776*, as recorded:

"1776, Apr. 9th. To a Proclamation for Regulating the Price of Provisions —15*s*."—Anthony Henry's Account for sundry extra printing [for Government] 1775-76, in P.A.N.S., *N.S. Miscellaneous papers, 1777*.

This proclamation is recorded in the Nova Scotia Executive Council *Minutes*, Apr. 2, 1776: "Resolved that a Proclamation be issued for fixing the Price of Beef,

Veal, Lamb, Mutton and Fresh Pork at one Shilling *per* pound Halifax currency, Milk at sixpence [per] quart . . . and Fresh Butter at one Shilling and Sixpence [per] pound. . . And that All Persons transgressing this Regulation shall be deem'd Extortioners [etc.]." The resolution was passed on the report of a committee appointed Apr. 1, to devise means of regulating prices of provisions, following an announcement of the arrival of 3,200 troops and civilians evacuating Boston.

On Aug. 13, 1776, it was further "Resolved that a proclamation be issued to reduce the price of provisions, vizt. Beef etc., to nine pence [per] pound, Butter one shilling [per] pound."—P.A.N.S., v. 212; also Can.P.A., N.S. "B" 17.

Copy located: None.

237. NOVA SCOTIA. HOUSE OF ASSEMBLY

Caption title: [Journals and Votes of the House of Assembly for the Province of Nova-Scotia.]

Note: title above is not transcribed from copy.

fo. A-[D², E¹]; 18 p. *Printed at Halifax, N.S., by Anthony Henry, 1776.*

Contents: p. 1-18, Journal and votes of the ninth session of the fifth assembly, June 15-29, 1776.

Copies located: CaNs; GBLP (2 cop. in C.O. 220/1: 813-31; *ibid.*, 833-51).

238. NOVA SCOTIA. LAWS, STATUTES, *etc.*

Running title: [rule] / 1776. Anno Sexto Decimo Regis GEORGII III. CAP. I [-V]. / [rule] /

Caption title: At the GENERAL-ASSEMBLY of the Pro-/vince of Nova-Scotia, . . . / [9 lines] / . . . being the Fifth GENERAL- / ASSEMBLY convened in the said Pro-/vince. / [ornamental rule] /

fo. sig. 5M², [*]¹; p. 215-220 [i.e. 315-320]; type-page: 24.5 × 14.5 cm. paged in continuation of No. 210; p. [315-320] mispaged: 215, 116-117, 218-220. *Printed at Halifax, N.S., by Anthony Henry, 1776.*

Contents: p. 215-220 [i.e. 315-320], Cap. I-IV, perpetual acts passed in the ninth session of the fifth assembly, June 15-29, 1776.

Copies located: CaN; CaNs; CaNsHA; CaNsWA; CaOOA; DLC; MB (defective); MH; N; NNB.

239. NOVA SCOTIA. LAWS, STATUTES, *etc.*

Running title: [rule] / 1776. Anno Sexto Decimo Regis GEORGII III. CAP. I[-IV]. / [rule] /

Caption title: At the GENERAL-ASSEMBLY of the Pro-/vince of Nova-Scotia . . . / [9 lines] / . . . being the Fifth GENERAL- / ASSEMBLY convened in the said Pro-/vince. / [ornamental rule] /

fo. sig. D², [*]¹; p. 181-186; type-page: 24.5 × 14.5 cm. paged in continuation of No. 211. *Printed at Halifax, N.S., by Anthony Henry, 1776.*

Contents: p. 181-186, Cap. I-IV, temporary acts passed in the ninth session of the fifth assembly, June 15-29, 1776.

Copies located: CaNs; CaO; CaOOA; DLC; MH; NNB.

240. NOVA SCOTIA. JUSTICES OF THE PEACE. SPECIAL SESSIONS (Halifax County)

[Handbills, *printed at Halifax, N.S., by Anthony Henry, 1776.*]

Regulations made by the justices of the peace in their quarter and special sessions were published in the local newspaper, also sometimes in a broadside edition or reprint. The broadsides have rarely survived, but occasionally a record of their printing does. The *Handbills* noted here, are typical of numerous publications from most of the early Canadian printing offices, publications as important to the printer's business as to the life of his community. Henry's work is recorded:

"1776, May 2. To printing Hand Bills for regulating the Assize of Bread—7*s*.
To Ditto—D° for truckage, in follio & finding paper—18*s*.
To inserting the above two advert. in the [Nova-Scotia] Gazette & continuing—£1. 15.
May 14. To 1 advert: Gazette for regulating the prise [sic] of provisions and continuing—£2.
To Hand Bills of the same in follio—18*s*."—Anthony Henry's Account for printing, certified by the clerk of the peace, June 14, 1776, in P.A.N.S., v. 301.

These regulations were passed by the justices in the special sessions held by order of the governor-in-council, to enforce laws, to prevent forestalling, regrating and extorting (in foodstuffs, house rents, etc.) after the arrival in Halifaxof roopsm evacuating Boston.

Copy located: None.

241. QUEBEC, *Province.* COURT OF QUARTER SESSIONS OF THE PEACE (Montreal District)

A UNE COUR / DE SÉANCE GÉNÉRALE / DE QUARTIER DE LA PAIX, / Tenue en la Chambre d'Audience à Montréal, Mardi le 10 Septembre 1776. / Presens. { GABL. ELEZD. TACHEREAU [sic., and nine others] Equiers Commissaires. / <Text> / Par Ordre de la COUR. / J. BURKE, Greffier de la Paix. /

Broadside: 34 lines. *Probably printed at Montreal by Fleury Mesplet & Charles Berger (or possibly at Quebec by Wm. Brown), 1776.*

Text: "Vu que plusieurs Etrangers sont derniérement arrivés & arrivent journellement dans cette Province, dont plusieurs pourroient entretenir des correspondences avec les Rebelles, & corrompre les fideles Sujets de Sa Majesté, etc." The text conveys orders for all persons entering the province after June 17, 1776, to report to the commissioners of the peace. The orders were issued to prevent agents of the rebel Americans from communicating with Montréalais and from corrupting loyal subjects of King George.

Commissioners, or conservators, of the peace for the districts of Quebec and Montreal, were appointed by Gov. Carleton in Apr., 1775, to serve temporary officers of local government until the administrative system to be established by the Quebec Act on May 1, 1775, should become operative—actually till 1777.

Copy located: CaQQL. A modern MS. copy simulating the style of the original printed broadside, is bound with *Quebec gazette*, Sept. 12, 1776, in CaOOA.

242. QUEBEC, *Province.* COURT OF QUARTER SESSIONS OF THE PEACE (Montreal District)

A UNE SEANCE GENERALE / DE QUARTIER, / Des Commissaires de Sa Majesté pour la Paix, tenue à Montréal, Mardi / le 1 Octobre, 1776. / Presens. {GABL. ELEZD. TASCHEREAU [and 4 others]} / Ecuyers Commiss. / <Text> / Par Ordre de la Cour, / J. BURKE, Greffier de la Paix. /

Broadside: 27 lines; type-page: 25 × 17 cm *Probably printed at Montreal by Fleury Mesplet & Charles Berger (or possibly at Quebec by Wm. Brown), 1776.*

The text conveys the commissioners' orders for all present retail liquor sellers to turn in their licences by Oct. 15; and for applicants for new licences to present certificates of good conduct. These certificates must be signed by a notable and two magistrates in the city, or by the curé and militia officer in the country. Applications from Trois Rivières must be signed by Joseph Godfrey de Tonnancour, commissioner of the peace, and forwarded to Montreal.

Copy located: CaQQL. A modern MS. copy simulating the style of the original broadside, is bound in *Quebec gazette*, Oct. 3, 1776, in CaOOA.

243. QUEBEC, *Province.* GOVERNOR, 1768-1778 (*Carleton*)

BY HIS EXCELLENCY / GUY CARLETON, / Captain-general and Governor in Chief of the Province of QUE-/BEC, . . . / . . . / . . . / . . . / A PROCLAMATION. / <Text> / GIVEN . . . at . . . QUE- / BEC, this Tenth Day of May, One Thousand Seven Hundred and Seventy-six . . . / . . . / . . . / GUY CARLETON. / By His EXCELLENCY'S Command, H. T. CRAMAHE. / GOD Save the KING. /

French on right:

PAR SON EXCELLENCE / GUY CARLETON, / Capitaine-general et Gouverneur en Chef de la Province de Quebec, . . . / . . . / . . . / . . . / PROCLAMATION. / <Text> / Donné . . . dans la ville de QUEBEC, / le dixieme jour de Mai, mil sept cens soixante-seize, . . . / . . . / . . . / (Signé) GUY CARLETON. / Par Ordre de son Excellence, / (Signé) H. T. CRAMAHE. / Traduit par ordre de son Excellence. / F. J. CUGNET, S. F. / VIVE LE ROI. /

Double broadside: English on left, 28 lines, type-page: 22.1 × 17.3 cm., French on right: 30 lines, type-page: 23 × 17.3 cm.; verso, blank. *Printed at Quebec by Wm. Brown, 1776.*

English text: "Whereas I am informed that many of His Majesty's deluded subjects of the neighbouring Provinces labouring under Wounds and diverse disorders are dispersed in the adjacent Woods and Parishes, and in great Danger of perishing for want of proper Assistance; All Captains and other officers of Militia are hereby commanded to make diligent search for such distressed Persons, . . . and convey them to the General Hospital, [etc.]."

French text: "Comme je suis informé que beaucoup des sujets abusés de sa Majesté des Provinces, qui souffrent de leurs blessures . . . sont dispersés dans les bois et paroisses voisines, . . . Il est ordonné . . . à tous Capitaines et Officiers de Milice, de faire une prompte recherche de toutes telles personnes malades . . . de les faire conduire à l'Hôpital-general, où on en aura grand soin, [etc.]."

As publication of the *Quebec gazette* was suspended Mar. 21-Aug. 8, 1776, this proclamation was distributed in broadside only. It was published immediately, for a printed copy was enclosed in Gov. Carleton's despatch no. 2, May 14, 1776, now in the Public Record Office, London.

This proclamation is reprinted in Can.P.A., *Report, 1918,* also in Canada, Department of Militia: *History,* 2: 155-56.

Copies located: CaQQL (French only); GBLP (in C.O. 42/35: 52-53 English and French).

244. QUEBEC, *Province.* GOVERNOR, 1768-1778 (*Carleton*)

BY HIS EXCELLENCY / GUY CARLETON, / Captain-general and Governor in Chief in and over the Province of QUE- / BEC, . . . / . . . / . . . / A PROCLAMATION. / < Text > / GIVEN . . . at . . . QUE- / BEC, this Twelfth Day of May, One Thousand Seven Hundred and Seventy-six, . . . / . . . / . . . / GUY CARLETON. / . . . / . . . / GOD SAVE THE KING. /

French on right:

PAR SON EXCELLENCE / GUY CARLETON, / Capitaine-general et Gouverneur en Chef dans toute la Province de / Quebec, . . . / . . . / . . . / PROCLAMATION. / <Text> / Donné dans la ville de QUEBEC / le douzieme jour de Mai, mil sept cens soixante-seize . . . / . . . / . . . / (Signé) GUY CARLTON. / Par Ordre . . . / . . . H. T. CRAMAHE / Traduit par ordre de son Excellence. / F. J. CUGNET, S.F. / VIVE LE ROI. /

Double broadside: English on left, 28 lines, type-page: 22 × 17.5 cm.; French on right: 30 lines, type-page: 23.3 × 17.5 cm.; verso, blank. As publication of the *Quebec gazette* was suspended Mar. 21-Aug. 8, 1776, this proclamation was published in broadside only. It was undoubtedly *printed at Quebec by Wm. Brown, Aug. 12-14, 1776,* for a printed copy was enclosed in Gov. Carleton's despatch no. 2, May 14, 1776, now in the Public Record Office, London.

English text: "Whereas I found it necessary, by a Proclamation dated the twenty-second Day of November, . . . to order . . . Persons . . . who had refused . . . to take up Arms . . . to quit the Town . . . I do now hereby order that no Person . . . who quitted the City . . . nor any Person . . . who . . . deserted . . . shall presume to enter the said City again without a Permission in writing under my Hand, or under the Hand of the Lieutenant-governor of this Province [etc.]."

French text: "Comme j'ai trouvé necessaire d'ordonner . . . par une Proclamation en date du Vingt-deuxième jour de Novembre . . . à toutes . . . personnes . . . qui ont refusé . . . de prendre les armes . . . de vuider la ville . . . J'ordonne presentement . . . Que toutes telles Personnes . . . ainsi que toutes celles qui ont deserté . . .

ne pretendent point entrer encor . . . sans une Permission par écrit donné sous mon seing [etc.]."

This proclamation is reprinted in Can.P.A., *Report, 1918;* also in Canada, Department of Militia: *History,* 1: 154-55.

Copies located: CaOOA (French only); CaQMS; CaQQL; GBLP (in C.O. 42/35: 56-57).

245. QUEBEC, *Province.* GOVERNOR, 1768-1778 (*Carleton*)

Messire GUY CARLETON, Chevalier du Bain, / Capitaine-général et Gouverneur en Chef de la Province de / Québec . . . / . . . / . . . / <Text> / Donné . . . / —[à] QUEBEC, ce douzième jour de Décembre, . . . / . . . / . . . 1776. / GUY CARLETON. / Par Ordre de Son Excellence, / GEO. ALLSOPP. /

Broadside: 30 lines; type-page: 24.5 × 16 cm., *printed at Quebec by Wm. Brown, 1776,* as recorded:

"1776, Dec. 28. Printed for the Govt. of Quebec by Order of Mr. Allsopp, 200 Orders for repairing Roads—£1. 7. 6.
75 D° reprinted on Acct of a Mistake not the Printer's—7/6.
Dec. 31. Printed for the Govt. of Quebec in No. 591 [*Quebec gazette* Dec. 26, 1776] . . . An Order for repairing the Highways.—£1."—Can.P.A., *Neilson papers,* v. 46.

Text: "Comm'il est indispensablement nécessaire pour le service du Roy, et la commodité du Public, que tous les chemins Royaux, ainsi que ceux qui y communiquent, soient en Hiver battus et entretenus doubles, ou assés larges pour qu'ils puissent y passer . . . deux voitures de front. . . . J'ordonne à tous les Capitaines et autres officiers de Milice . . . d'obliger . . . tous les Habitans et Propriétaires de terres . . . de battre chacun incessament un chemin de huit pieds de largeur, sur la devanture de leurs terres . . . de l'entretenir tout l'Hiver en bon ordre, et de poser des balises de sept à huit pieds de hauteur en têtes de sapin ou de cèdre, distantes de vingt-quatre pieds en vingt-quatre pieds, aux deux côtés du dit chemin; et . . . les voiageurs seront tenus d'en prendre toujours la droite [etc.]."

Apparently published in French only, the broadside conveys orders for habitants and land owners to keep open throughout the winter, a road 8 feet wide with windbreaks on each side, and for travellers to keep to the right along the road.

This order is reprinted in Canada, Department of Militia: *History,* 2: 197-98.

Copy located: CaOOA.

246. UNITED STATES. *Continental Congress*

[Extracts from the Boston & New Hampshire Papers, *Halifax, N.S., Mills & Hicks, 1776.*]

This item is recorded in Nova Scotia Executive Council *Minutes,* July 12, 1776: "The Lieutenant-Governor [Arbuthnot] call'd on the Council to give their advice in respect of a Public News Paper lately publish'd in this Town without the name of the Printer, entitled, 'Extracts from the Boston & New Hampshire News Papers, being an Account of proceedings, of the people of Rhode Island & Boston,' in which are contain'd expressions of the most insolent and outrageous nature, against the King and his Government, and the most open and avow'd declarations of Rebellion. The Publication . . . Directly tending to inflame the minds of the King's subjects in this Province and to Seduce them from their Duty and Allegiance by asserting the most malignant falsehoods and misrepresentations." The printer (not named) summoned, said he had been solicited to print the paper by several of the gentlemen who had lately come from Boston with the army and had received the papers from Mr. Hutchinson, lately one of the judges of the courts of law of Massachusetts Bay. Hutchinson summoned, said he wanted "to show how the people of Rhode Island and Boston had openly avowed Rebellion despite their former protestations to the contrary." He was excused and the printer was reprimanded and dismissed with instructions to collect and destroy all copies. The Council then "Ordered that a Proclamation be Issued against reprinting or Publishing treasonable papers."—Can.P.A., N.S. "B" 17, p. 60-62.

This item is also recorded in a letter to Gov. Legge, then in London, written by Captain R. Gibbons, Halifax, N.S., July 13, 1776: "I yesterday saw a Paper Printed here by Mills and Hicks and published the day before, containing what were called Extracts, from some Continental Papers, some of which are most audacious and traiterous Proceedings, carrying on by the Rebels. I have used every measure in my power to procure one to transmit to your Excellency but my endeavours are hitherto fruitless, altho' I have offered to give a Dollar apiece . . . Mr. Hutchinson, a Judge and Brother to the Governor [of Massachusetts], by whose advice it is said the Printer made the Publication . . . excused himself by saying the Printers had made a mistake in Printing those Extracts without some Notes or Introduction which he intended making to them. . . . The Papers contain a Resolution of the General Congress for the total and perpetual independence of the Colonies and Separation from Great Britain, and an Instrument called an Act of the Colony of Rhode Island absolving the People from their allegiance to the King and forever renouncing him and his Authority (in Terms too highly criminal for me even to repeat) [etc.]. P.S. 7 o'clock P.M. 13th July 1776 . . . [Anthony] Henry . . . says he was applied to, to print [the Papers] by Doct[r] Gardner, One of the Boston Refugees and Professional Friends to the Government, but declined doing it and then it was put into the hands of Mills and Hicks . . . there were about Eight hundred copies struck off tho' none now to be found."—Can.P.A., *Dartmouth*, portfolio II. 1. 2., 1032e. *See also* J. B. Brebner: *The neutral Yankees of Nova Scotia* (New York, 1937), 340.

Copy located: None.

247. ALMANACS. NOVA SCOTIA

THE / Nova-Scotia CALENDER / OR, / AN ALMANACK, / For the Year of the Christian Æra, 1778; . . . / [5 lines] Wherein is contained, / The Lunations and Eclipses . . . / [5 lines] Calculated for the Meridian of Halifax, . . . / . . . / . . . / . . . / . . . / By METONICUS. / [ornamental rule] / HALIFAX: Printed and sold by A. HENRY. / [title within ornamental frame] /

16mo. [32] p., fold. table; type-page: 14.5 × 7.7 cm.

Contents: p. [1], t.-p.; p. [2-3], Rules to judge weather, vulgar notes; p. [4] Eclipses; fold. table: Coin values; p. [5-16] Calendar?; p. [17-24], Table of expenses or wages; weather and prognosticks of winter, spring, summer & autumnal quarters; Zodiac etc.; p. [25-32], Kings and queens of England, weights and values of coins, Province of Nova Scotia civil list: administration, Assembly, judges, justices, courts; tides, etc.; Thoughts on several subjects.

Copy located: CaNsHD (p. [5-16] calendar? wanting).

248. ALMANACS. QUEBEC

ALMANACH / CURIEUX / ET INTERESSANT; / Contenant la Liste des Prêtres & / Religieux Desservants les Eglises / de Canada; la connoissance des / monnoies courantes; des Poids & / Mesures, &c. Anecdotes, Fables, / Curiosités naturelles, &c. / [rule] / Mil sept cent soizante dix-huit. / [rule] / [printer's ornament] / A MONTREAL; / Chez FLEURY MESPLET & CHAR-/LES BERGER, Imprim. Lib. / [rule] / 1778. / [ornamental frame]/

24mo. A^6, B-D^8; 60 p.; type-page: 10.8 × 6 cm. Text in French.

Contents: p. [1], t.-p.; p. [2], Comput ecclésiastique etc.; p. [3], Eclipses; p. [4-27], Calendrier; p. 28-33, Catalogue du clergé; p. 34-41, Monnaies, poids et mésures; p. 42-52, Anecdotes etc.; p. 53-60, fables.

In this number the printers began including local information, viz., an extended list of the clergy, regular and secular, throughout the diocese, also tables of Quebec and Halifax currency. Though the imprint bears the date 1778, this work was printed in 1777, for Wm. Brown, the printer in Quebec, received 18 copies of the *Almanach* by carrier, on Dec. 30, 1777, and sold them at 1*s*. 3*d*. the copy.

A well preserved copy (in CaQM) shows that the *Almanach* was issued, stitched in wall paper covers of a cheerful clover-blossom pattern. This copy includes the printers' advertisement printed upon the back-cover lining, listing ten books (mainly devotional works printed by Mesplet & Berger) and articles of stationery for sale at the printing office.

Copies located: CaQM (includes printers' advertisement, 1 p., on cover lining); CaQMS (includes printers' advertisement); CaQQL (no printers' advertisement).

249. ALMANACS. QUEBEC

CALENDRIER pour l'Année 1778, pour Québec, par les $306^{d.}$ $30^{m.}$ de Longitude, et $46^{d.}$ $55^{m.}$ de Latitude. / [ornamental rule] /

Colophon: A QUÉBEC: chez WM. BROWN, derriere l'Eglise Cathédrale. /

Broadside: type-page: 45.5 × 38.5 cm.

Contents: Les Signes du zodiaque, Phases de la lune, Nombres, Fetes mobiles, Quatre tems, Commencement des quartre Saisons, Eclipses.

The content, layout, and type are like those of No. 185 with the addition of a note at the end of the text: "N.B. l'an dernier l'on crût que l'annonce de l'Eclipse de soleil était fausse, parce qu'on n'avait pû l'observer . . . l'on donne ici une manière de l'observer, [etc.]."

This sheet almanac was sold by Brown at 7½*d.* the copy, 5*s.* the dozen from Dec. 1, and advertised for sale at Quebec, Trois Rivières, and Montreal as usual in the *Quebec gazette* from Dec. 4, 1777. About 350 *Calendrier*'s (at least) were issued a year at this time, for Brown's *Cash Book* for 1778 includes the entry:

"1778, Dec. 31. [Credit] to Printing Office Almanacks for 77 & 78.—£17. 10."
—Can.P.A., *Neilson papers*, v. 46.

Copy located: CaO (bound in *Quebec gazette*, at end of 1777).

250. ALMANACS. QUEBEC

Calendrier / pour Montréal . . . pour l'année 1778. /

Broadside: paper-page: 52 × 38 cm. This is a sheet-almanac, *printed at Montreal by Fleury Mesplet & Charles Berger, 1777.*

Copy located: CaQMS (described in Fauteux: *Mesplet*, no. 21, from which this entry is taken).

ALMANACS. QUEBEC

[Indian Calendar for 1777] *See* No. 175.

251. [BONNEFONS, AMABLE], 1600-1653

Le petit / Livre de vie, / qui apprend / à bien vivre / et / bien prier Dieu. / A l'usage du Diocèse de Québec / [vignette] / A Montréal; / chez Fleury Mesplet & Char-/les Berger, Imprim. & Libr. / M.DCC.LXXVII. /

2 p. l., [xxii], 456, [4] p., front., illus.; paper-page: 15.5 × 9.25 cm.

Contents: p. l. 1, front.; p. l. 2 recto, t-p.; verso, blank; p. [i-xxii], Calendars, emblems, etc.; p. 1-456, text; p. [1-4] at end, table (contents).

This is apparently the second Canadian printed book to be illustrated. The frontispiece (representing Christ on the cross) and a dozen emblematic figures in the text, though crudely executed, bear no evidence as to where, or by whom, they were made.

This description is taken from Fauteux: *Mesplet*, no. 18.

Copy located: CaQMS.

252. BRIAND, JEAN OLIVER, *bp. of Quebec*, 1715-1794

LETTRE CIRCULAIRE de Monseigneur l'Evêque, au / Clergé du Diocèse de Quebec. /

fo. 2 *l.*; type-page: 24.6 × 14 cm.

Contents: l. 1 recto, Lettre, 42 lines; verso, blank; *l.* 2, blank.

A circular letter prepared to accompany copies of *Missa in festo* (No. 256) and *Officium in honorem D.N.J.C.* (No. 257) distributed by the Bishop among the clergy of Quebec. The text begins: "Je vous envoie ci-joint un exemplaire de l'Office & de la Messe de Sacerdoce de Notre Seigneur Jésus-Christ . . . Je ne doute pas que vous faissez un plaisir & un devoir d'entrer dans l'esprit de cette Fête," and ends: "A Quebec, le [blank] 1777." The copies located are signed and dated in MS.: "J: Ol: Evêque de Québec. Juin 15."

This *Lettre* is reprinted in Têtu and Gagnon: *Mandements de Québec,* 2:291-92.

Copies located: CaO; CaOOA; CaQQL.

253. BURGOYNE, JOHN, 1722-1792

BY JOHN BURGOYNE ESQ; / Lieutenant General of his Majesty's Armies in America, Colonel of the Queen's Regiment of Light Dragoons, Governor of Fort / William in North-Britain, one of the Representatives of the Commons of Great-Britain in Parliament, and commanding an / Army and Fleet employed on an Expedition from Canada, &c. &c. &c. / <Text> / Camp at [blank] 1777. / J. BURGOYNE, [to left of signature:] By Order of His EXCELLENCY / the Lt GENERAL / ROB^t KINGSTON, Secretary. / [? *Quebec, Wm. Brown, 1777.*]

Broadside: 46 lines; type-page: 38.8 × 27.5 cm.

Text: "The forces entrusted to my command are designed to act in concert, and upon a common principle, with the numerous Armies and Fleets which already display, in every quarter of America, the power, the justice, and when properly sought, the mercy of the King. . . To the eyes and ears of the temperate part of the public, and to the breasts of Suffering Thousands in the provinces, be the melancholy appeal whether the present unnatural rebellion has not made the foundation of the compleatest system of Tyranny that ever God in his displeasure suffered for a time over a froward and stubborn generation. . . Arbitrary imprisonments, confiscation of property, persecution and torture, . . . are inflicted by assemblies and committees . . . for the sole crime . . . of allegiance [to the Crown]. . . Animated by these considerations; at the head of troops in the full powers of health, discipline and valour; determined to strike where necessary, and anxious to spare where possible, I by these presents invite and exhort all persons, in all places where the progress of this army may point—and by the blessing of God I will extend it far—to maintain such a conduct as may justify me in protecting their lands, habitations, and family [sic]. . . The domestick, the industrious, the infirm, and even the timid inhabitants I am desirous to protect provided they remain quietly at their houses, that they do not suffer their cattle to be removed, nor their corn or forage to be secreted or destroyed; that they do not break up their bridges or roads; nor . . . endeavour to obstruct the operations of the King's troops, or supply or assist those of the Enemy . . . Let not people be led to disregard it [this invitation] . . . I have but to give stretch to the Indian forces under my direction, and they amount to thousands, to overtake the hardened Enemies of Great-Britain. . . The messengers of justice and of wrath await them in the field; and devastation, famine, and every concomitant horror that a reluctant but indispensible prosecution of military duty must occasion, will bar the way to their return."

The "manifesto" as its author termed this work, was prepared for distribution among Americans during Burgoyne's campaign of 1777. Burgoyne came from

England to Quebec where he stayed May 6-14, 1777, thence to Montreal where he remained May 19-June 13. He then proceeded with full force into New York, distributing the "manifesto" when he reached Lake Champlain ten days later. The campaign closed with Burgoyne's surrender at Saratoga, Oct. 17, 1777. The "manifesto" was possibly *printed in Quebec by Wm. Brown, and / or in Montreal by Fleury Mesplet, 1777,* in one or two broadside editions (*see also* No. 254). It was also printed (later and from another setting of type) in the *Quebec gazette,* July 31, 1777, in English and French, with the text dated: "Putnam-creek, June 29, 1777." Its style as well as the subject matter roused considerable resentment among the Americans, who retorted with a counter-manifesto (by Washington) also with burlesques, etc. It is discussed, with bibliographical references in J. Winsor: *Narrative and critical history of America* (8 v., Boston, 1884-89), 6: 349.

Copies located: NNHi (in Gates papers, box 6, no. 221. This copy is dated in MS. (following the words "Camp at"): "near Ticonderoga July 2"); GBLP (in C.O. 42/36 p. 369. This copy, inscribed (following the words "Camp at"): "the River Bouquet," was enclosed in Burgoyne's letter to Lord Germain, dated: "Camp upon the River Bouquet near Lake Champlain, June 22, 1777"). Another copy (dated in MS.: "The River Bouquet, June 23$^{d.}$") was recorded in the Anderson Galleries' *Catalogue, no. 1797* (New York, Jan. 21-22, 1924), item no. 107 (with facsim.); it has not been located by the writer.

254. BURGOYNE, JOHN, 1722-1792

By JOHN BURGOYNE, ESQ; &c. &c. / Lieut. General of his Majesty's Forces in America, / Colonel of the Queen's Regiment of Light Dra-/goons, Governor of Fort-William, in North-/Britain, one of the Representatives of the Com-/mons of Great-Britain in Parliament, and com-/manding an Army and Fleet in an Expedition / from Canada. &c. &c. &c. / <Text> / J. BURGOYNE. / Camp at the River BONGRETT [sic], } / June 23d, 1777. / By Order of his Excellency the Lieutenant General, / ROBERT KINGSTON, Sec'ry. /

Broadside: 99 lines, 2 col.; type-page: 15 × 13.5 cm.

The *text* is the same as that of No. 253, excepting for several slight differences in spelling, punctuation, etc. This is another edition of No. 253, printed from different (apparently newspaper) type. The place and date of issue (of the "manifesto," *not* of this broadside), "Camp at the River Bongrett [i.e. Bouquet] June 23d, 1777," appear in print not MS.—suggesting that this edition was produced after Burgoyne left Canada, that it was reprinted from a copy of No. 253, possibly in Quebec or Montreal, or on some loyalist press in the American colonies.

This edition is reprinted in Massachusetts Historical Society, *Proceedings,* 12: 189-90, Jan., 1872.

Copy located: MHi.

255. CATHOLIC CHURCH. CATECHISMS. *French*

CATÉCHISME / A L'USAGE / DU DIOCESE / DE QUEBEC. / Imprimé par l'Ordre de Monseigneur JEAN / OLIVIER BRIAND, Evêque de / Quebec. / [rule] / PREMIERE PARTIE, / CONTENANT / LE PETIT

CATECHISME / ou Abrégé de la / DOCTRINE CHRETIENNE / [printer's ornament] / A MONTREAL; / Chez FLEURY MESPLET & CHARLES BERGER, / Imprimeurs & Libraires, 1777. /

12mo. [*][6], A-Bb[4], Cc[2]; 6 p. l., 7-59, [i] p., 1 *l.*, 61-205, [3] p.; type-page: 15 × 8.5 cm.

Contents: p. l. 1 recto, blank; verso, Mesplet's advertisement of books for sale; p. l. 2 recto, t-p.; verso, blank; p. l. 3-4, Mandement, dated and signed: "Donné à Québec . . . le 7 Mars, 1777, J. Ol. Evêque de Québec"; p. l. 5, Avertissement; p. l. 6, Introduction; p. 7-59, Le petit catéchisme; p. [60], Table de matières; 1 *l.* blank; p. 61-205 Le grand catéchisme; p. [1-3] at end, Table du grand catéchisme.

This work, the third edition of the Catholic catechism printed in Canada, and the first edition of the Quebec use, has the text of the *Catéchisme . . . de Sens,* as hitherto used (*see* No. 59 and 76) with slight changes. Montgolfier, superior of the Séminaire de St. Sulpice, writing from Montreal, Jan. 19, 1777, to Bishop Briand, stated that Mesplet proposed printing the catechism and Montgolfier suggested that the Sens text be retained and that certain sections dispensible for less educated members of the Church be printed in italic. He suggested also that Bishop Briand issue a mandement to encourage the use of the catechism, of which two thousand copies, he thought, should be printed, and of which he undertook to send the bishop a prospectus and a model.—Gosselin: *L'Eglise après la conquête,* 1: 384-85.

Le Petit Catéchisme was apparently issued first, separately (advertised in the *Quebec gazette,* Aug. 14, 1777). Wm. Brown, printer and bookseller, sold the double catechism retail in Quebec from Oct., 1777, at 1*s.* 6*d.* the copy, and himself printed the next edition in 1782. This text remained the catechism authorized in Quebec long past the end of the 18th century, and was reprinted several times with the mandement of Mar. 7, 1777. The mandement, printed from MS., appears in Têtu and Gagnon: *Mandements de Québec,* 2: 285-87.

Copies located: C.O. (p. 205 to end wanting); CaOOA; CaQMS.

256. CATHOLIC CHURCH. LITURGY AND RITUAL. BREVIARIES

[Group of type ornaments] / MISSA / IN FESTO DIVINI SACERDOTII / DOMINI NOSTRI J.C. / ET OMNIUM SANCTORUM / SACERDOTUM ET LEVITARUM. /

4to. A[2]; 4 p.; type-page: 19.5 × 12.5 cm. printed in latin, 2 col.

Probably printed at Montreal by Fleury Mesplet, 1777, for the Séminaire de St. Sulpice, and issued by Bishop Briand from Quebec with *Officium* (*see* No. 257).

Copy located: CaQQL.

257. CATHOLIC CHURCH. LITURGY AND RITUAL. BREVIARIES

OFFICIUM / IN HONOREM / DOMINI NOSTRI J.C. / SUMMI SACERDOTIS / ET / OMNIUM SANCTORUM / SACERDOTUM / AC LEVITARUM. / [printer's ornament] / MONTI-REGALI; / Apud FLURIUM MESPLET, Typographum & Bibliop. / [rule] / M. DCC. LXXVII. / [title within ornamental frame]

12mo. A-B[4]; 1 p. l., 11 p., 1 *l.*; type-page: 14 × 9.2 cm. Printed in 2 col. with rules and marginal guides, each page within a single rule frame.

Contents: p. l. recto, t-p.; verso, blank; p. 1-11, Officium; verso of p. 11, blank; 1 *l.* at end: recto, Consecratio Jesu et Mariæ; verso, blank.

Caption, p. 1: "Feria V. quæ prima occurrit post diem 29 Augusti festem Divini Sacerdoti D.N.J.C. et omnium ss. sacerdotum et levitarum." This office, celebrated in Quebec the first Thursday after Aug. 29, is said to have been unpopular in the diocese and to have been abolished by Bishop Plessis in 1822.—Gagnon 1: no. 2581.

Officium and *Missa* (No. 256) were prepared in the Séminaire de St. Sulpice, Montreal, according to a plan arranged during Bishop Briand's visit there in 1773-74, and printed for the Superior, Montgolfier. The latter wrote from Montreal, Jan. 19, 1777, to Bishop Briand ". . . J'ai fait imprimeur l'office de Sacerdoce à six cent exemplaires. Je n'attends plus qu'une occasion favorable pour vous en envoyer des paquets."—Gosselin: *L'Eglise après la conquête,* 1: 386.

Officium and *Missa* were distributed by the bishop with a circular letter, June 15, 1777 (*see* No. 252). A mandement was prepared to accompany these works but was apparently not issued. It is printed from MS. in Têtu and Gagnon, *Mandements de Québec,* 2: 284-85.

Copies located: CaO; CaOT (2 cop.); CaQM; CaQMM; CaQMS; CaQQL; NN; RPJ.

258. CATHOLIC CHURCH. PRAYER BOOK. *French*

FORMULAIRE / DE PRIERES, / A L'USAGE / DES PENSIONNAIRES / DES / RELIGIEUSES URSULINES. / NOUVELLE EDITION, / Revue, corrigée & augmentée de l'Office de la / sainte Vierge, sans renvoi, & de Prières / pour offrir son intention en communiant les / Fêtes principales de l'année. / [printer's ornament] / A MONTREAL; / Chez FLEURY MESPLET & CHARLES / BERGER, Imprimeurs & Libraires. / [rule] / M.DCC.LXXVII. /

12mo. [*][4], A-T[12], V[8]; 4 p. l., 467, [5] p.; type-page: 14 × 7 cm.

Contents: p. l. 1-2, blank; p. l. 3 recto, t.-p.; verso, blank; p. l. 4 recto, Table des fêtes mobiles; verso, Meditation; p. 1-340, Formulaire etc.; p. 341-467, L'Office etc.; at end: p. [1-5], Table; p. [5], "Approbation . . . Formulaire des prières . . . une nouvelle édition. A Paris, ce Juin 1755. P. Germain."

The *Formulaire* used by the Ursuline sisters in Paris was published for members of that teaching order in Canada. Their convent in Quebec had been established by Mère Marie de l'Incarnation in 1639 and from the beginning, their work included the teaching of Indians and later of French girls. A second convent with school and hospital was opened at Trois Rivières in 1697.

Copy located: CaNsWA (defective, nearly half the pages are wanting).

259. DE LISLE DE LA CAILLETERIE, JEAN GUILLAUME.

[Un livre qui traite de l'administration des œuvres de fabrique en Canada. ? *Montreal, Mesplet, 1777.*]

De Lisle, who was a notary at Montreal, 1768-87, and clerk of the fabrique of

Montreal, is said to have published "vers 1777, un livre qui traite de l'administration des oeuvres de fabrique en Canada. C'était un érudit, très éstimé pour son caractère et ses vastes connaissances, principalement en physique."—J.-E. Roy: *Histoire du notariat au Canada* (4 v., Levis, 1899-1902), 2: 44-45. No other record of this work or its publication has been found, however.

Copy located: None.

260. [DU MONCEAU, ALEXIS]

EXERCICE / TRE'S-DEVOT / ENVERS / S. ANTOINE / DE PADOUE / LE THAUMATURGE, / De l'Ordre Séraphique / DE S. FRANÇOIS. / Avec un petit recueil de quelques princi-/paux Miracles. / [printer's ornament] / A MONTREAL; / Chez F. MESPLET & C. BERGER. / Imprimeurs & Libraires. 1777. /

18mo. a^6, B-H^6; [viii], 88 p.; type-page: 11 × 5.7 cm.

Contents: p. [i], t-p.; p. [ii], blank; p. [iii-iv] "A S. Antoine, [dedication signed:] F. A. D."; p. [v-viii], Préface; p. 1-73, Le petit office; p. 74-88, Les saintes correspondences du Bernard Colnago, Jesuite; p. 88 at foot: "Vidi 20 Novembris 1696. Fr. Desqueux, Pastor S. Stephani Decan. Christianitatis Insulensis."

This work is said to have been prepared by a Franciscan, Frère Alexis du Monceau, and to have been printed for the first time in 1692 (Fauteux: *Mesplet*, 179).

Copies located: CaO; CaQMS (2 cop.); Ketcheson.

261. NOVA SCOTIA. HOUSE OF ASSEMBLY

Caption title: [Journals and Votes of the House of Assembly for the Province of Nova-Scotia.]

Note: title above is not transcribed from copy.

fo. $[A-E]^2$; 19 p. *Printed at Halifax, N.S., by Anthony Henry, 1777.*

Contents: p. 1-19, Journal and votes of the tenth session of the fifth assembly, June 6-25, 1777; p. 19 verso, blank.

Copies located: CaNs (2 cop.); CaNsHA; GBLP (2 cop. in C.O. 220/1: 853-72; *ibid.*, 873-92).

262. NOVA SCOTIA. LAWS, STATUTES, *etc.*

Running title: [rule] / 1777. Anno Septimo Decimo Regis GEORGII III. CAP. I[-VI]. / [rule] /

Caption title: At the GENERAL-ASSEMBLY of the Province / of Nova Scotia, . . . / [8 lines] / . . . being the Fifth / General Assembly convened in the said Pro-/vince. / [rule] /

fo. sig. 5 O^2; p. 221-224 [i.e. 321-324]; type-page: 26.5 × 15.5 cm. paged in continuation of No. 238; p. [321-324] mispaged: 221-224. *Printed at Halifax, N.S., by Anthony Henry, 1777.*

Contents: p. 221-224 [i.e. 321-324], Cap. I-VI, perpetual acts passed in the tenth session of the fifth assembly, June 6-25, 1777.

Copies located: CaNs; CaNsHA; CaNsWA; CaOOA; DLC; MH; NNB.

263. NOVA SCOTIA. LAWS, STATUTES, *etc.*

Running title: [rule] / 1777. Anno Septimo Decimo Regis GEORGII III. CAP. I[-VII]. / [rule] /

Caption title: At the GENERAL-ASSEMBLY of the Province / of Nova Scotia, . . . / [8 lines] / . . . being the Fifth / General Assembly convened in the said Pro-/vince. / [rule] /

fo. p. 187-92; type-page: 26 × 15.5 cm. paged in continuation of No. 239. *Printed at Halifax, N.S., by Anthony Henry, 1777.*

Contents: p. 187-92, Cap. I-VII, temporary acts passed in the tenth session of the fifth assembly, June 6-25, 1777.

Copies located: CaNs; CaO; CaOOA; MH; NNB.

264. PRIMERS, QUEBEC

[Alphabet, *printed at Quebec by Wm. Brown, 1777.*]

Several transactions in *Alphabets* (primers) are recorded by Brown during 1777:

"1777, May 31. Sold Picard [i.e. Pierre Picard, book binder and stationer in Quebec] 450 French Alphabets in Sheets payable 31st October next @ 20/ a hundred—£4. 10. gave his note.

"July 10. [Credit] To Printing Office 100 Alphabets sold Germain [i.e. Louis Langlois dit Germain, merchant in Quebec]—£5.

"Sept. 13. Printed for Gen[l]. Carleton by Order of the Preceptor 50 Alphabets with figures and Syllables—10/ pd. Feb[y]. 15, '78."

The Printer also recorded occasional sales of *Alphabets* in single copies or small lots, without specifying whether French, Latin, or English, at prices ranging from 6*d.* to 1*s.* 8*d.* the copy.—Can.P.A., *Neilson papers*, v. 45-46.

Copy located: None.

265. PRIMERS. QUEBEC. *Mohawk*

IONTRI8AIESTSK8A / IONSKANEKS / N'AIEIENTERIHAG GAIATONSERA / TE GARI8TORARAGON / Ong8e on8e Ga8ennontakon. / [printer's ornament] / TEIOTIAGI; / 8ESKLET, Tsi Thonons8te, ok / niore Tsi Iontkerontak8a. / [rule] / 1777. /

8vo. [*][8]; 16 p.; type-page: 13 × 7 cm. *Printed at Montreal* (*Teiotiagi*), *by Fleury Mesplet, 1777.*

Contents: p. [1], t-p.; p. [2], blank; p. 3-16, text, p. 13-16 being prayers.

A primer with Catholic prayers, etc., printed entirely in the Mohawk dialect from MS. of Father Bruyas—R. W. McLachlan: *The first Mohawk primer*, in *Canadian antiquarian and numismatic journal*, ser. 3, v. 5, p. 51-63, 1908. *See also* Pilling: *Iroquoian*, 90; *also*, Antoine Roy: *Les Lettres, les sciences et les arts au Canada sous le régime français* (Paris, 1930), 38-40.

This work is recorded in the inventory of Mesplet's estate, 1794: "Dix livres de prières en sauvage 6.00 livres" (approximately shillings); also in the sale of his effects: "Seize brochures de prières sauvages, le tout pour 10 sols," (approximately half-pennies).—McLachlan: *Mesplet*, 285, 298.

Copy located: WHi.

266. QUEBEC, *Province.* GOVERNOR, 1768-1778 (*Carleton*)

[Aveu et Dénombrement of Seigniories.]

Broadside? printed at *Quebec by Wm. Brown, 1777,* as recorded:

"1777, Aug. 23. Printed for J. Cugnet* or Gov[t]. 400 Aveu et Dénombrement of Seigniories making 2½ Sheets of a Large Demy Broadside with Rules, requiring 3 pulls at the Press—£12. 10."—Can.P.A., *Neilson papers,* v. 46.

This substantial order represents printed forms with blanks for recording lands held from the crown, granted during the French régime. This record was to be prepared from land rolls, and title deeds submitted in pursuance of Gov. Carleton's proclamation of Aug. 28, 1777. The latter required seigneurs to render "Fealty and Homage which they owe to His Majesty according to the ancient laws . . . [and] to give in their respective Terrars or Land-Rolls" within forty days of Dec. 1, 1778.† The record was designed to show rents, duties, etc., owing to the crown. The proclamation, however, was regarded rather in the breach than in the observance. Its period was extended repeatedly (*see* No. 298) but the seigneurs' submission of land rolls, and the government's compilation of *Aveu et Dénombrement,* etc., remained incomplete.

Copy located: None.

267. QUEBEC, *Province.* GOVERNOR, 1768-1778 (*Carleton*)

[By Sir Guy Carleton, Knight of the most honorable order of the Bath, Captain General and Governor in chief of the province of Quebec, etc. A Proclamation <Text> Given . . . at the castle of St. Lewis in the city of Quebec the third day of May one thousand seven hundred and seventy seven . . . Guy Carleton. By His Excellency's command, J. Williams, C.C. God Save the King.]

French side:

[Par Messire Guy Carleton, Chevalier du très honorable ordre du Bain, Capitaine-general et Gouverneur en Chef de la Province de Québec, etc. Proclamation. <Text> Donné . . . au Château St. Loüis, dans la ville de Québec, le troisième jour de Mai . . . (Signé) Guy Carleton. Par Ordre de son Excellence. (Signé) J. Williams. Traduit par Ordre de son Excellence, F. J. Cugnet, S.F. Vive le Roi.]

English text: "Whereas it is inexpedient, and might prove dangerous, at this time, and in the present circumstances of the province, to allow of a free exportation of the provisions thereof, I have thought fit, . . . to issue this proclamation, . . . prohibiting all catle [sic] or other live stock, during the course of the present year . . . to be exported . . . except such as shall have been purchased for the use of his Majesty's forces under my command, or that shall be necessary for the sustenance . . . [of persons] belonging to his Majesty's ships, or other vessels departing [from this province]. . . And I do order and direct that no corn, flour, or biscuit be exported except for the use . . . above mentioned, [etc.]."

*Probably F.-J. Cugnet, French secretary to the governor-in-council.
†Can.P.A., *Report, 1918.*

French text: "N'étant pas à propos et pouvant être dangereux, actuellement, et dans les circonstances présentes de la Province, de permettre une sortie libre des provisions d'icelle, j'ai jugé à propos . . . de faire publier cette Proclamation, pour faire très expresses inhibitions et défenses de sortir ou d'exporter d'icelle, pendant le cours de cette présente annee . . . toutes les bêtes à corne et autres animaux vivans, excepté ceux qui auront été achetés pour le service des armées de sa Majesté . . . et j'ordonne et commande qu'il ne soit exporté ou envoié de la Province, aucun bled, farine ou biscuit, excepté pour l'usage et l'effet ci-dessus mentionés, [etc.]."

Double broadside, *printed at Quebec by Wm. Brown, 1777.* This was probably an off-print from the *Quebec gazette*, May 8, 1777. The proclamation was proposed in "Privy Council" (Gov. Carleton's confidential but unconstitutional group of advisors within the Legislative Council) on May 3, 1777, ordered to be published in the *Quebec gazette* . . . "also that fifty printed copies be struck off and distributed throughout the Province."—Can.P.A., Que. *State* E.

This embargo on the export of food stuffs was partially, then completely, lifted by proclamation, July 25, Oct. 11, 1777; then reproclaimed Nov. 7, 1778, etc. It probably complicated commissariat routine, for Wm. Brown recorded:

"1777, Aug. 27. Printed for Henry Caldwell 500 Instruments for victualling the King's Ships making 2 pages in pica on a folio copy—£2. 10."

—Can.P.A., *Neilson papers*, v. 46.

This proclamation is reprinted in Can.P.A., *Report, 1918*, from which the title and text are taken.

Copy located: None.

268. QUEBEC, *Province.* LAWS, STATUTES, *etc.*

ORDINANCES / MADE AND PASSED / BY THE / GOVERNOR / AND / LEGISLATIVE COUNCIL / OF THE / PROVINCE / OF / QUEBEC. / [rule] / [royal arms] / [double rule] / QUEBEC: / Printed by WILLIAM BROWN, behind the Cathadral [sic] Church. / [rule] / M,DDC, LXXVII. /

French t.-p.:

ORDONNANCES / FAITES ET PASSÉES / PAR LE/ GOUVERNEUR / ET LE / CONSEIL LÉGISLATIF / DE LA / PROVINCE / DE / QUÉBEC. / [rule] / [royal arms] / [double rule] / A QUEBEC: / Chez GUILLAUME BROWN, derriere l'Eglise Cathédrale. / [rule] / M, DCC, LXXVII. /

fo. [*]², A-[Ll]²; 1 p. l., [i], 134 p., 1 *l.*; type-page: 23.5 × 13 cm.; odd numbers on verso, even numbers on recto; text in English and French on opposite pages.

Contents: p. l. recto, English t-p.; verso, blank; p. [i], French t-p.; p. 1 (i.e. verso of p. [i])-134, Ordinances, 17 Geo. III, c. I-XVI; p. 134 verso, blank; 1 *l.* blank, this leaf occasionally at end, or occasionally preceding t-p., is more frequently missing from copies extant.

These ordinances were the first passed by the legislative authority established under the Quebec Act of 1774. They appeared *seriatim* in the *Quebec gazette* early in 1777, and were reprinted from another setting of type in the edition described above—an edition of two hundred copies, for which the printer apparently received an allowance from the government:

"1777, July 21. [Credit] To Printing Office an allowance for Ordinances —£55. 11. 1."—Can.P.A., *Neilson papers*, v. 45.

From the middle of May, 1777, Brown sold single copies in blue paper wrappers at 7*s*. 6*d*., also (probably bound) at 10*s*. The government, however, probably took most of the edition, though "300 Gazettes with Ordinances in them" had been delivered previously to the clerk of the Legislative Council.

These ordinances are reprinted in Can.P.A., *Report, 1914-15;* t-p. facsim. in Toronto Public Library, *Bibliography of Canadiana*, no. 510.

Copies located: CaO; CaOOA (2 cop.); CaOT; CaOTO (2 cop.); CaQ; CaQM; CaQMA; CaQQL; GBLP (in C.O. 44/3); Ketcheson; M; MH; MWA; NN; NNB; PHi; RPJ; WHi.

269. QUEBEC GAZETTE. CARRIER'S ADDRESS

ETRENNES / Du GARÇON qui porte la GAZETTE de / QUEBEC aux Pratiques. / Le I JANVIER, 1778. /

Broadside: 36 lines; type-page: 21 × 10.5 cm. with ornamental frame. *Printed at Quebec by Wm. Brown, 1777.*

Contents: Etrennes, 4 stanzas of 7 lines each, the second paying tribute to Guy Carleton who resigned as Governor of Quebec in 1777:

"En finissant
Je la trouve plus belle encore
En finissant,
Qu'elle n'etoit en commençant
CARLETON, l'appui de son Prince,
Met a l'abri notre Province
En finissant."

Copy located: CaO (bound in *Quebec gazette*, at end of 1777).

270. ALMANACS. QUEBEC

Almanach / Curieux / et intéressant; / contenant l'idée des Etats, Royau-/mes & Républiques de l'Europe / avec les naissances des Princes & / Princesses; la liste des Prêtres / & Religieux desservants les Egli- / ses de Canada; la Connaissance des Monnoies courantes, & la distance / marquée d'une Poste à un autre, / depuis Québec jusqu' à Montréal. / Mil sept cent soixante dix-neuf. / A Montréal. / Chez Fleury Mesplet, Impri-/meur et Libraire. / MDCC.LXXIX /

62 p.; paper-page: 11.5 × 8 cm. Though dated 1779 in the imprint, this, like the *Almanach* for 1778 was probably printed at the end of the preceding year.

Contents: p. [1], t.-p.; p. [2] blank; p. [3]-62, text.

Copy located: CaQMS (described in Fauteux: *Mesplet*, no. 30, from which this description is taken. The copy ascribed by Fauteux to Laval University was not seen there by the writer).

271. ALMANACS. QUEBEC

Calendrier / pour Montréal pour l'année 1779 /

Broadside: paper-page: 53 × 38 cm. This is a sheet almanac *printed at Montreal by Fleury Mesplet, 1778.*

Copy located: CaQMS (described in Fauteux: *Mesplet*, no. 31, from which this entry is taken).

ALMANACS. NOVA SCOTIA

No copy of the *Nova-Scotia Calender* for 1777 has been recorded, nor has any reference to its publication been noted in newspapers or elsewhere. The *Calender* may have been printed this year as usual, however, for its printer, Anthony Henry did not habitually advertise his publications.

272. ALMANACS. QUEBEC

CALENDRIER pour l'Année 1779, pour Québec, par les 306$^{d.}$ 30$^{m.}$ de Longitude, et 46$^{d.}$ 55$^{m.}$ de Latitude. / [ornamental rule] /.

Colophon: A QUEBEC: chez WM. BROWN, derrière l'Eglise Cathédrale. /

Broadside type-page: 49 × 38 cm. (*Calendrier:* 42.5 × 38 cm. in ornamental frame).

Contents: Calendrier, Les signes du zodiaque, Phases de la lune, Nombres, Fêtes mobiles, Quatres tems, Commencement des quatre Saisons, calendar. Officiers civils de la province de Québec (in 6 col. across the sheet beneath the *Calendrier*, listing) Gouverneur, Commissaires de la paix, juges, greffiers, etc., poids et cours de l'or suivant l'Ordonnance de 29 mars, 1777.

The content, layout, and type of the calendar section are like those of No. 170. The list of officials and other provincial information appeared for the first time on *Calendrier de Québec* in this edition.

This sheet almanac was sold at 7½*d.* the copy, 5*s.* the dozen, from Dec. 10, and advertised for sale at Quebec, Trois Rivières, and Montreal as usual in the *Quebec gazette,* from Dec. 10, 1778.

Copy located: CaO (bound in *Quebec gazette,* at end of 1778).

ALMANACS. QUEBEC

[Indian Calender for 1778] *See* No. 176.

273. ALMANACS. QUEBEC

[Indian Almanack for 1779. *Quebec, Wm. Brown, 1778.*]

? Broadside (a sheet almanac), or leaflet in Montagnais dialect. This was the first of a series of seven almanacs, probably for the year 1779 and each of the six succeeding years to 1785. A similar series for the years 1773-78 had been printed in 1773 (No. 171-76). These, like their predecessors, were prepared by Father La Brosse, and *printed at Quebec by Wm. Brown, 1778,* as recorded:

"1778, June 5. Printed for the Rev[d] J. Bt[e] Labrosse, Jesuite Missionary Indian Almanacks for 7 years to come, 500 copies for each year making in the whole 350 [sic] @ 1¼—£18. 4. 7. [scored out] giv'n in 16. 16. 6. [sic] paid Nov[r] 30 '78."—Can.P.A., *Neilson papers*, v. 46.

Copy located: None.

274. ALMANACS. QUEBEC

[Indian Almanack for 1780. *Quebec, Wm. Brown, 1778.*]

? Broadside (a sheet almanac), or leaflet, in Montagnais dialect, prepared by Father La Brosse and *printed at Quebec by Wm. Brown, 1778,* as recorded in the latter's accounts. *See* No. 273 *note*.

Copy located: None.

275. ALMANACS. QUEBEC

[Indian Almanack for 1781. *Quebec, Wm. Brown, 1778.*]

? Broadside (a sheet almanac), or leaflet, in Montagnais dialect, prepared by Father La Brosse and *printed at Quebec by Wm. Brown, 1778,* as recorded in the latter's accounts. *See* No. 273 *note*.

Copy located: None.

276. ALMANACS. QUEBEC

[Indian Almanack for 1782. *Quebec, Wm. Brown, 1778.*]

? Broadside (a sheet almanac), or leaflet, in Montagnais dialect, prepared by Father La Brosse and *printed at Quebec by Wm. Brown, 1778,* as recorded in the latter's accounts. *See* No. 273 *note*.

Copy located: None.

277. ALMANACS. QUEBEC

[Indian Almanack for 1783. *Quebec, Wm. Brown, 1778.*]

? Broadside (a sheet almanac), or leaflet in Montagnais dialect, prepared by Father La Brosse and *printed at Quebec by Wm. Brown, 1778,* as recorded in the latter's accounts. *See* No. 273 *note*.

Copy located: None.

278. ALMANACS. QUEBEC

[Indian Almanack for 1784. *Quebec, Wm. Brown, 1778.*]

? Broadside (a sheet almanac), or leaflet, in Montagnais dialect, prepared by Father La Brosse and *printed at Quebec by Wm. Brown, 1778,* as recorded in the latter's accounts. See No. 273 *note*.

Copy located: None.

279. ALMANACS. QUEBEC

[Indian Almanack for 1785. *Quebec, Wm. Brown, 1778.*]

? Broadside (a sheet almanac), or leaflet, in Montagnais dialect, prepared by Father La Brosse and *printed at Quebec by Wm. Brown, 1778,* as recorded in the latter's accounts. *See* No. 273 *note.*

Copy located: None.

280. CATHOLIC CHURCH. CATECHISMS. *English*

AN / ABSTRACT / OF THE / DOUAY CATECHISM. / [ornamental rule] / Published with PERMISSION of the LORD / BISHOP of QUEBEC. / [double rule] / Suffer little Children to come unto me: For / the Kingdom of God is for such. / ST. MARK X. 14. / [ornamental rule] / QUEBEC: Printed by Wm. BROWN, MDCCLXXVIII. /

18mo. A-F^6, G^2; 75 p.; type-page: 10.6 × 6.5 cm.

Contents: p. [1], t-p.; p. [2], the A B C; p. [3]-75, Catechism; p. 75 verso, blank.

The printer recorded the cost of this work but not the customer for whom they were printed:

"1778, July 25. [Credit] To Printing Office for 1000 Douay Catechisms—£18. 10.
To D°. for 1000 Catholic's Companions—£15. 8. 4."

—Can.P.A., *Neilson papers,* v. 45.

The two works were apparently issued together, all copies located are so bound (in old bindings). They were reprinted at Quebec in 1800.

The "Douay catechism" was prepared by Henry Turberville, a priest at Douai, where a school and refuge was long maintained for English Roman Catholics, and it was first published there in 1649. A smaller simplified edition was produced: *An abstract of the Douai catechism for the use of children and ignorant people* (London, 1688), of which this Quebec edition is one of the many reprints.

Copies located: CaOOA; CaQMS (2 cop.).

281. CATHOLIC CHURCH. LITURGY AND RITUAL

THE SINCERE / Catholick's Companion. / [double rule] / Published with PERMISSION, / Of my LORD JOHN OLIVER BRIAND, / Bishop of QUEBEC. / [double rule] / [ornamental rule] / QUEBEC: / Printed by WM. BROWN, MDCCLXXVIII. /

18mo. A-E^6; 60 p.; type-page: 11 × 6.5 cm.

Contents: p. [1], t,-p.; p. [2], blank; p. [3-7], A calendar of feasts and fasts; p. [8-9], Necessary rules; p. [10], blank; p. [11]-57 Prayers; p. 57-60, "Profession of the Catholic Faith extracted out of the Council of Trent by Pope Pius IV. [signed at end:] J. McK."

Printed in 1,000 copies, like the *Abstract of the Douay catechism* with which it was issued (*see* No. 280), a devotional work for English-speaking Catholics. These two publications are said (by P.-G. Roy in *Les premierrs manuels scolaires canadiens* in *Bulletin des recherches historiques,* 52: 291-303, Oct., 1946) to have been produced at the expense of the bishop of Quebec for the use of some hundreds of Irish Catholic families in Quebec at that time.

Copies located: CaOOA; CaQMS (2 cop.).

282. CATHOLIC CHURCH. LITURGY AND RITUAL. HOLY WEEK OFFICES

L'OFFICE / DE LA / SEMAINE / SAINTE, / SELON LE MESSEL / & Breviaire Romain; / Avec l'explication des sacrés Mysteres représentés / par les cérémonies de cet Office. L'Ordinaire de / la Messe, les Sept Pseaumes de la Pénitence, les / Litanies des Saints, & les Prieres pour la Con-/fession & Communion, tirées de l'Ecriture Sainte. / [rule] / Imprimée sur la meilleure Edition de Paris. / [rule] / [printer's ornament] / A MONTREAL; / Chez FLEURY MESPLET & CHARLES / BERGER, Imprimeurs & Libraires. / [rule] / M.DCC.LXXVIII. /

12mo. A-Mm[6]; 420 p.; type-page: 14 × 7 cm.

Contents: p. [1], t.-p.; p. [2], blank; p. 3-16, Ordinaire de la messe; p. 17-420, Offices, etc.

This is said to have been the last work printed by Mesplet with Berger in partnership. Announced in the *Almanack* for 1778 it was probably published in Feb., 1778.—Fauteux: *Mesplet,* 181, no. 22.

Copies located: CaQMM; CaQMS (2 cop.); Ketcheson; NN.

283. CATHOLIC CHURCH. LITURGY AND RITUAL. NOVENAS

NEUVAINE / A L'HONNEUR / DE / SAINT FRANÇOIS / XAVIER, / DE LA COMPAGNIE / de JESUS, / Apôtre des Indes & du Japon. / [printer's ornament (Jesuit device)] / A MONTREAL, / Chez FLEURY MESPLET, Imprimeur & / Libraire, près le Marché. 1778. / [title within ornamental frame]

16mo. A-I[8], K[2]; 147 p.; type-page: 12 × 6.7 cm. p. 81 unnumbered in some copies.

Contents: p. [1], t.-p.; p. [2], Prières; p. 3-55, Instruction, etc.; p. 56-85, Petit office; p. 86-147, Sentiments; p. 147 verso, blank.

Copies located: CaOT; CaQMM; CaQMS (2 cop.); CaQN; CaQQL; Hingston; RPJ.

284. DU CALVET, PIERRE, *d.*1786

Caption title, p. 1: (1) / [ornamental rule] / COUR / DES PLAIDOYERS COMMUNS. / BROOK WATSON & ROBERT RASHLEIGH, Négociants de Londres; / stipulant pour eux, Pierre Panet, Ecuyer, fondé de leur Procu-/ration, Demandeurs; / CONTRE / PIERRE DUCALVET, de Montréal, Ecuyer, Défendeur. / DEFENSES. / FAIT. /

Marginal note: Province de / Québec, / District de / Montréal. /

Colophon, p. 4: [rule] / Chez FLEURY MESPLET, Imprimeur & Libraire, près de la Marché. /

4to. 4 p.; type-page: 19 × 13 cm.

Contents: p. 1-4, "Défenses, [signed:] Pierre Ducalvet, Montréal, le 24 Septembre, 1778."

In the case of Watson & Rashleigh, general merchants, London, *versus* Du Calvet in the Court of Common Pleas, Montreal, to collect £1,034 7*s.* 4*d.*, Quebec currency, the defendant claimed that he made his remittances in grain, 1773-75 which had not been credited to his account. Du Calvet presented his *Défenses*, as above. Pierre Panet, acting for the plaintiffs, filed Répliques (not printed) which Du Calvet countered with his *Dupliques*, Oct. 22, 1778, as below. Panet published *Réponses au dupliques* (No. 295) which Du Calvet refuted in a *Mémoire*, Jan. 11, 1779 (No. 313). Du Calvet eventually lost the case. Having been long involved in acrimonious controversy with local judges, and suspected of treason by the provincial authorities, he transferred the case to his brother-in-law in London, Oct., 1781, for appeal to the Privy Council.

Du Calvet, a French Protestant, came to Canada in 1758, settled at Montreal and engaged in the fur and importing trade. Under the English administration he became a justice of the peace and transacted occasional business with the government. Du Calvet, however, had numerous law suits arising from commercial affairs, which he frequently lost in Montreal and Quebec courts, and he published his grievances against the judges in *Gazette littéraire*, Montreal, Mar.-Apr., 1779. He became suspected of promoting American interests in Montreal after the invasion of 1776, and from Sept., 1780 till 1783, was kept in custody in Quebec. Upon his release Du Calvet instituted proceedings for redress against Gov. Haldimand in London, publishing thereon his *Appel à la justice de l'état, etc.* (320 p., Londres, 1784); translated as: *The case of Peter Du Calvet, Esq. of Montreal* (284 p., London, 1784). (*See* Toronto Public Library, *Bibliography of Canadiana*, no. 569-70.) He died, however, in 1786 before the case was settled.

Copy located: CaQM. Another copy, formerly in possession of the late Cyrille Tessier, Quebec (Fauteux: *Mesplet*, 182, no. 27) not located.

285. DU CALVET, PIERRE, *d.*1786

Caption title, p. 1: (1) / [ornamental rule] / District de / MONTREAL. / PROVINCE DE QUEBEC. / COUR / DES PLAIDOYERS COMMUNS. /BROOK WATSON & ROBERT RASHLEIGH, Défendeur [i.e. Démandeur]; / CONTRE PIERRE DUCALVET, Ecuyer Défendeur. / DUPLIQUES. /

Colophon, p. 12: [rule] / A MONTREAL, Chez FLEURY MESPLET, Imprimeur & Libraire. /

4to. A-C²; 12 p.; type-page: 19-19.7 × 13 cm.

Contents: p. 1-12, "Dupliques, [signed:] Pierre Ducalvet."

The text beginning "La Replique du Procureur fondé des Demandeurs est un tissu du mensonges," is the defendant's vigorous refutation, paragraph by paragraph, of a *Réplique*, filed in court but not printed apparently, which had been prepared by Panet, lawyer for the plaintiffs, in answer to Du Calvet's *Défenses* of Sept. 24, 1778 (*see* No. 284 *note*).

Copy located: CaQM (subscribed in MS. below printed signature of Ducalvet: "à Montreal le 22e. 8bre 1778 [etc.]").

286. GAZETTE DU COMMERCE ET LITTERAIRE. *Montreal*

AUX CITOYENS / DE LA VILLE ET DISTRICT DE MONTREAL. / MESSIEURS, / L'ETABLISSEMENT d'un PAPIER PERIODIQUE <Text, signed:> FLEURY MESPLET, Imprimeur. /

Broadside: 47 lines; type-page: 24.5 × 13 cm. *Printed at Montreal by Fleury Mesplet, 1778.*

This is a separate issue of the French side of the item below.

Copy located: GBLBM (in *Haldimand papers,* 185: 58. Add. MSS. 21845: 58).

287. GAZETTE DU COMMERCE ET LITTERAIRE. *Montreal*

Caption title: TO THE CITIZENS / OF THE TOWN AND DISTRICT OF MONTREAL. / GENTLEMEN, / THE ESTABLISHMENT of a PERIODICAL PAPER,

[2] p. text in English on recto, French on verso of a single leaf; type-page: 19 × 13 cm. *Printed at Montreal by Fleury Mesplet, 1778.*

The text, undated and signed: "F. Mesplet, Printer," begins:

"Gentlemen, The Establishment of a Periodical Paper . . . by which means trade and Commerce will be carried on with a greater facility, correspondence with a greater ease, and a noble emulation will naturally ensue to the great advantage of the publick, the Citizen will with more speed and in a conciser manner communicate his ideas: hence the progress of Arts and Sciences in general and the necessary introduction to concord and union amongst individuals, from which flows several advantages to Society. . . The facility of giving notice to the Publick at any time of the sale ot Goods . . . Mouvables [sic], Houses, Lands, besides the conveniency of advertising for lost effects, Slaves deserted from their Masters, the want of clerks . . . [I] will print Publick advertisements and other affairs . . . also a Collection of facts both entertaining and instructive . . . a choice collection of the newest pieces; and I don't doubt but this will stir up the genius of many who have remain'd in a state of inaction, or could not communicate their productions without the help of the Press. I will insert, everything that one or more Gentlemen will be pleased to communicate to me provided always no mention is made of Religion, Government or News concerning present affairs unless I am authoriz'd by the Government for so doing."

The subscription, he continued, was to be 2½ Spanish dollars per annum, single copies 10 coppers; advertisements 1 Spanish dollar for 3 weeks to subscribers, 1½ Spanish dollars to non-subscribers. The paper, printed on a quarto sheet, was to be published weekly on Wednesdays beginning June 3, 1778.

This is a prospectus of *Gazette du commerce et littéraire,* printed at Montreal by Fleury Mesplet, June 3, 1778-June 2, 1779. The French text was also issued separately, and is reprinted in McLachlan: *Mesplet,* 236-37.

Copy located: CaQM.

288. LA CORNE, SAINTE-LUC DE, 1712-1784

JOURNAL / DU / VOYAGE / DE M. SAINT-LUC / DE LA CORNE, Ecuyer, / Dans le Navire l'Auguste, en l'an 1761. / [printer's ornament] / A MONTREAL; / Chez FLEURY MESPLET, Imprimeur & / Libraire. / [rule] / M.DCC.LXXVIII. /

A-D^4, E^3; 1 p. l., 38 [i.e. 36] p.; type-page: 12.5 × 6.5 cm. 7-8 omitted in paging.

Contents: p. l. recto t.-p.; verso, blank; p. 1-38 [i.e. 36), Journal.

The ship *Auguste* left Montreal, Sept. 27, 1761, and sailed from Quebec on Oct. 15, carrying French officers and soldiers, also a few civilians who purposed returning to France under terms of the capitulation of Montreal. The ship was wrecked off Cape Breton on Nov. 15; of the seven survivors La Corne alone made his way to Fort Cumberland, Nova Scotia, thence overland to Quebec where he arrived Feb. 24, 1762. He reported to the British authorities, Gov. Murray at Quebec, General Gage in Montreal, also apparently, by letter to Amherst in New York. For tipped to the last page of some copies of this edition of the *Journal* is a printed letter, dated at the head: "A la Nouvelle-York, le 28 Mars, 1762," signed and addressed at the end: "Jeff Amherst. A Mr de Saint Luc la Corne A Montreal."

This letter acknowledges the receipt of La Corne's letter of Mar. 3, 1762, and of his journal, and expresses sorrow for the tragedy of the ship *Auguste*. Amherst's letter was apparently printed ([2] p. type-page: 13.5 × 7 cm.) about the same time as the *Journal* though on paper of different texture.

Saint-Luc de La Corne subsequently settled in Quebec and became a British subject. The tale of his adventure was retold by Philippe Aubert de Gaspé in *Les anciens canadiens* (Quebec, 1863). This work was reprinted: *Journal du voyage de M. Saint-Luc de La Corne, ecr., dans le navire l'Auguste, en l'an 1761* (seconde édition, 28 p., Québec, A Coté et cie, 1863), 27-28 containing Amherst's letter described above.

Copies located: CaQM; CaQMS (2 cop.); CaQQL. Amherst's letter, described above, appears in one copy at CaQMS and in CaQQL copy.

289. [LANAUDIÈRE, CHARLES LOUIS DE], 1743-1811

[A Consultation of 2 Lawyers of the Parlement of Paris.]

8vo. 16 p.; 25 copies *printed at Quebec by Wm. Brown, 1778,* as recorded:

"1778, Aug. 31. Printed for Chas. L. De Lanaudiere A Consultation of 2 Lawyers of the Parlement of Paris, making 16 pages large 8vos. in small Pica, 25 copies, 8 Guineas by Agreemens [sic]—£9. 6. 8. [Quebec Currency]." —Can.P.A., *Neilson papers*, v. 46.

"1779, May 3. [Credit to] Printing Office from Mr. Lanaudiere for a Consultation 16 Pages 8vo—£9. 6. 8." —Can.P.A., *Neilson papers*, v. 45.

Brown's customer was probably Charles Louis de Lanaudière, a French-Canadian seigneur and aide to Gov. Carleton; but the purpose of this publication, its subject matter, and the authorship remain a mystery.

Copy located: None.

290. LIVRE POUR APPRENDRE A BIEN LIRE EN FRANCAIS

LIVRE / POUR APPRENDRE / à bien lire en Français, / ET POUR APPRENDRE / en même-temps / LES PRINCIPES / DE LA LANGUE / ET DE L'ORTHOGRAPHE. / Il pourra être utile aux personnes avancées qui / voudront s'assurer qu'elles parlent & écrivent / correctement, / [rule] / On ne peut lire ni écrire correctement, si l'on ne / sçait conjuguer les Verbes. / [rule] / [printer's ornament] / A MONTREAL; / Chez FLEURY MESPLET, Imprimeur & Libraire, / près le Marché. 1778. /

16mo. A-F^8 + ?; 92 + ? p.; type-page: 10.3 × 7 cm.

Contents: p. [1], t.-p.; p. [2], blank; p. 3-4, Aux Maîtres & Maitresses d'école; p. 5-92 + ?, Lettres, etc. In the only copy located, the last section, "Explication de quelques mots," p. 83-92 + (containing a list of about 150 words arranged alphabetically, A-R) is incomplete; nor is there any indication if other sections followed. This is an elementary school book, the text comprising the alphabet, syllables, Catholic prayers; then sections on the noun, verb, the use of accents, and of certain difficult or confusing words.

Copy located: CaOOA (p. 13-14, 93 to end wanting).

291. MONTREAL, *City.* CITIZENS

A SON EXCELLENCE / GUY CARLETON, / Chevalier du Très-Honorable Ordre du Bain, Capitaine-Général & Gouver-/neur en Chef de la Province de Quebec, Général & Commandant en Chef / des Forces de Sa Majesté dans ladite Province & Frontieres d'icelle, &c. / <Text>

fo. 2 *l.*; 27 lines on recto of *l.* 1; type-page: 19.2 × 16.5 cm. *Printed at Montreal by Fleury Mesplet, 1778.*

The text states: "Nous Soussignés, Citoyens de Montréal, représentons humblement à Votre Excellence, la mortification que nuos [sic] cause le départ du sieur Fleury Mesplet, Imprimeur en cette Ville; l'Ordre à lui donné verbalement par le Général P * * * de vuider la Province sous trois mois, nous a surpris: la conduite qu'il a tenu depuis son arrivée en ce pays, la régularité de ses mœurs, paroissoit nous assurer de le conserver plus long temps, & devoir le mettre à l'abri d'une telle disgrace . . . il est notre Concitoyen, continuellement sous nos yeux . . . & nous ne scaurions lui faire aucun reproche; son zèle pour procurer de l'Instruction & de l'Amusement, en donnant un Papier Périodique, nous marque un bon Patriote. Le Loi qu'il s'est imposé, de ne traiter que des matieres que ne regardent, ni l'Etat, ni la Religion, nous prouve sa délicatesse; . . . nous supplions Votre Excellence d'avoir égard à notre très-humble Représentation, [etc.]"

This representation against the order for deportation of Fleury Mesplet bears witness to his straight-forward character, the innocence of his newspaper, and the advantage of a printing press to citizens of Montreal.

The only copy located is signed in MS. on recto and verso of *l.* 1 by 46 French signatories; *l.* 2 blank, is endorsed in contemporary hand: "Memorial of Sundry french Gentlemen of Montreal in favor of F. Mesplet the Printer—Augt 1778."

Mesplet had brought a printing office from Philadelphia to Montreal in 1776, as part of the American plan to engage French Canada in the Revolution. After the withdrawal of the American invaders, Mesplet remained to settle in Montreal. Though he printed mainly Catholic devotional and school books and since June, 1778 the *Gazette du commerce et littéraire*, he was suspected by military authorities of rebel sympathies, and by religious authorities of "Voltairianisme." This order to leave the province within three months was suspended by Gov. Carleton, and Mesplet actually spent the rest of his life there.

This representation and related documents are reprinted in McLachlan: *Mesplet*, 238.

Copy located: GBLBM (in *Haldimand papers*, Add. MSS. 21845: 59-60).

292. NOVA SCOTIA. HOUSE OF ASSEMBLY

Caption title: [Journals and Votes of the House of Assembly for the Province of Nova Scotia.]

Note: title above is not transcribed from copy.

fo. A-[F]^2; 33 [i.e. 23] p.; p. [23] mispaged: 33. *Printed at Halifax, N.S., by Anthony Henry, 1778.*

Contents: p. 1-33 [i.e. 23], Journal and votes of the eleventh session of the fifth assembly, June 6-25, 1778; p. 33 [i.e. 23], verso, blank.

Copies located: CaNs (2 cop.); CaNsHA; GBLP (2 cop. in C.O. 220/1: 893-916; *ibid.*, p. 917-39).

293. NOVA SCOTIA. LAWS, STATUTES, *etc.*

Running title: [rule] / 1778. Anno Octavo Decimo Regis GEORGE [sic] III. CAP. I[-VI]. / [rule] /

Caption title: At the GENERAL-ASSEMBLY of the Pro-/vince of Nova-Scotia, . . . / [9 lines] / being the Fifth GENERAL ASSEM-/BLY convened in the said Province. / [ornamental rule] /

fo. p. 325-332; paged in continuation of No. 262. *Printed at Halifax, N.S., by Anthony Henry, 1778.*

Contents: p. 325-332, Cap. I-VI perpetual acts passed in the eleventh session of the fifth assembly, June 6-25, 1778.

Copy located: MH; DLC (photo.)

294. NOVA SCOTIA. LAWS, STATUTES, *etc.*

Running title: [1778. Anno Octavo Decimo Regis, Georgii III. Cap. I-V.]

Caption title: [At the General Assembly of the Province of Nova Scotia . . . the Fifth General Assembly convened in the said Province.]

Note: titles above are not transcribed from copy.

fo. p. 193-200; paged in continuation of No. 263. *Printed at Halifax, N.S., by Anthony Henry,* 1778.

Contents: p. 193-200, Cap. I-V temporary acts passed in the eleventh session of the fifth assembly, June 6-25, 1778.

Copies located: CaNs; NNB.

295. PANET, PIERRE MÉRU, 1731-1804

[Réponse aux Dupliques de Pierre Du Calvet, Ecuyer, par Pierre Panet, procureur fondé de Watson & Rashleigh. *Montreal, Mesplet, 1778.*]

Probably *printed in Montreal by Fleury Mesplet, Oct.-Nov. 1778,* this work is mentioned by Du Calvet in his *Mémoire* (No. 313), p. 4-5. He stated there that Judge Sanguinet made a motion in court on Nov. 19, 1778 that Du Calvet, defendant in the case of Watson & Rashleigh *versus* Du Calvet, retract certain statements in his *Dupliques* (No. 285). The latter refused, saying that Panet, lawyer for the plaintiffs, had already replied to the statements in a printed document which Du Calvet offered to produce in court. "Dans le même temps que Me Sanguinet, pour le procureur fondé, faisait cette motion, il avait en liasse plusieurs exemplaires d'un libelle imprimé, composé par Me Panet et dont le Sieur Du Calvet avait dans le même moment dans sa poche une copie."

In the same *Mémoire,* Panet's *Réponses* is refuted paragraph by paragraph so that its argument, of personalities, fact and law, and indeed its style, may be reconstructed from its complement (*see also* Fauteux: *Mesplet,* 183, no. 32).

Panet, born in Paris, came to Canada in 1746. He was a barrister and notary at Montreal and held official posts under both French and English régimes.

Copy located: None.

296. QUEBEC, *Province.* ADJUTANT GENERAL'S OFFICE

(Circulaire.) A Québec, le 31 Janvier, 1778. / Messieurs, / J'ai l'honneur d'être chargé de la part de Son Excellence Monsieur / le Gouverneur Général . . . / . . . de Vous assurer, qu'il compte beaucoup sur votre Zéle à servir / votre Prince, et votre Patrie, en cas que les Rebelles vinssent à tenter / une nouvelle Invasion de cette Province. [etc.]

A single sheet printed on both sides: type-page: 26.5 × 15.7 cm. *Probably printed at Quebec by Wm. Brown, 1778.*

Contents: recto-verso, "Circulaire [ending] Votre très humble et très obeissant Serviteur, [blank] A M. le Capitaine les Officiers et Miliciens de la Paroisse de [blank]." This is a circular letter probably prepared for François Le Maistre, adjutant general of militia, to send to local militia officers through the province. It gives orders for militia to keep ready to march in case the Americans invade Quebec again, to arrest strangers without passports, to keep roads passable and wheeled vehicles in repair. It includes a scale of cash awards and clothing ready for distribution to those who served in 1776-77, and gives instructions where to apply for the same in each district.

Copies located: CaQMS (2 cop.); CaQQL.

297. QUEBEC, *Province.* GOVERNOR, 1778-1786 (*Haldimand*)

[By His Excellency Frederick Haldimand, Captain General, and Governor in Chief in and over the Province of Quebec. . . A Proclamation. <Text> Given . . . in the City of Quebec this Seventh day of November . . . one thousand seven hundred and seventy eight. Fred: Haldimand . . . God save the King.]

French side:

[Par Son Excellence Frederic Haldimand, Capitaine-general et Gouverneur en chef dans toute la province de Quebec. . . Proclamation. <Text> Donné . . . dans la ville de Québec, le septieme jour de Novembre . . . Mil sept cens soixante dix-huit. (Signé) Fred. Haldimand. . . . Vive le Roi.]

Double broadside, *Printed at Quebec by Wm. Brown, 1778,* as recorded:

"1778, Nov. 29. Printed for Gov^{t}. of Quebec 75 double Proclamations prohibiting the Exportation of flour &c.—£1. 15."

—Can.P.A., *Neilson papers,* v. 46.

English text: "Whereas great prejudice at this time may arise to His Majesty's Service, and distress to this Province, from a free exportation of Wheat, Flower and Biscuit. I have therefore thought fit . . . to Issue this Proclamation," etc., prohibiting the export of wheat, etc., without permit till Dec. 1, 1778, and from Dec. 1, 1778 till Aug. 1, 1779 unconditionally.

French text: "La libre exportation du bled, Farine et biscuit pouvant être actuellement très préjudiciable au service de sa Majesté, et occasioner le malheur de cette Province, J'ai, à ces causes jugé à propos . . . de faire publier cette Proclamation, par laquelle il est défendu à toutes personnes quelconques de . . . exporter hors de cette Province, de ce jour et après . . . aucuns Bled, Farine ou Biscuit, [etc.]."

This proclamation is reprinted in Can.P.A., *Report, 1918,* from which title and text above are taken.

Copy located: None.

298. QUEBEC, *Province.* GOVERNOR, 1778-1786 (*Haldimand*)

By His EXCELLENCY / FREDERICK HALDIMAND, / Captain-General and Governor in Chief in and over the Province of / QUEBEC, . . . / . . . / . . . / . . . / A PROCLAMATION. / <Text> / GIVEN . . . at the Castle of St. Louis, [Quebec, 30 November, 1778] . . . / . . . / . . . / Fred: Haldimand. / By Order [etc. 3 lines]

French on right:

Par Son EXCELLENCE / FREDERIC HALDIMAND, / Capitaine-general et Gouverneur en Chef dans . . . Qué-/bec . . . / . . . / . . . / PROCLAMATION. / <Text> / Donné au Château St. Loüis, dans la ville / de Québec, [30 Novembre, 1778] . . . / . . . / (Signé) Fred: Haldimand. / Par Ordre [etc. 5 lines]

Double broadside: English on left, 39 lines, type-page: 23 × 18.7 cm.; French on right, 39 lines, type-page: 23 × 18.7 cm. *Printed at Quebec by Wm. Brown, 1778,* as recorded:

"1778, Dec. 5. Printed for Government of Quebec by Order of Secretary 200 double Proclamations postponing the time of making foy et hommage. —£2. 5."—Can.P.A., *Neilson papers,* v. 46.

English text: "Whereas Sir Guy Carleton, . . . [on Aug. 28, 1777] issued a Proclamation therein requiring all proprietors of Signiories [sic] . . . before [Dec. 1, 1778] to make Fealty and Hommage . . . to render their respective Terrars or Land Rolls . . . to Exhibit their Title Deeds, and make a declaration of the several Estates, they hold under His Majesty, and the Rents and duties they owe thereupon. I have thought fit . . . [to] extend the time thereby allowed unto . . . [Dec. 31, 1779, etc.]."

French text: "Messire Guy Carleton, . . . aiant fait publier [le 23me aout, 1777] . . . une Proclamation, qui ordonne à tous propriétaires de Fiefs et Seigneuries . . . [de] rendre et porter Foi et Hommages à Sa Majesté, au Chateau St. Louis . . . avant [le 1re décembre, 1778] . . . J'ai jugé à propos . . . [d'accorder] un tems plus long, et l'étens jusqu'au [le 31me décembre, 1779, etc.]."

This proclamation is reprinted in Can.P.A., *Report, 1918*. *See also* No. 266.

Copy located: CaQQL.

299. QUEBEC GAZETTE. CARRIER'S ADDRESS

ETRENNES / Du Garçon qui porte la GAZETTE / de QUEBEC aux Pratiques. / Le I JANVIER, 1779. / *Quebec, Wm. Brown, 1778.*

Broadside: 34 lines; type-page: 19.5 × 10.5 cm. with ornamental frame.

Contents: "Etrennes," 3 stanzas, 10 lines each, of pleasant platitudes, with a tribute to Gov. Carleton, "Solomon of the North," at the end. Stanza III:

"Joignons tous nos prières
Nos vœux les plus sinceres
Pour notre Gouverneur
Et de bouche et de coeur
Chantons tous d'un accord
Qu'il est la vraie image
De nom et de courage
Que l'univers entier
Célèbre en ce guerrier,
LE SALOMON DU NORD."

Copy located: CaO (bound in *Quebec gazette* at end of 1778).

300. RESTAUT, PIERRE, 1696-1764

ABRÉGÉ / DES REGLES / DE LA / VERSIFICATION / FRANÇAISE [sic] / [rule] / Par Mr. RESTAUT, Avocat au Parlement, & ap-/prouvé de l'Académie des Sciences à Paris. / [rule] / [printer's ornament] / A MONTREAL; / Chez FLEURY MESPLET, Imprimeur & / Libraire. / [rule] / M.DCC.LXXVIII. /

8vo. A-K[4]; 80 p.; type-page: 13 × 7.5 cm. p. 67 mispaged: 77.

Contents: p. [1], t.-p.; p. [2], blank; p. 3-80, Abrégé des règles.

This is an abridgement of Restaut's *Traité de la versification* prepared in 1732 to accompany the author's *Grammaire française*, 1730, long the only elementary work on the French language.

The post mortem inventory of Mesplet's effects recorded: "Quarante-six Versifications françaises—15. 00 [livres, about 15*s*]."—McLachlan: *Mesplet*, 285. This was possibly the remainder of the 1778 edition.

Copies located: CaQMS; CAQQL (2 cop.).

301. SECCOMBE, JOHN, 1708-1792

A / SERMON, / Occasioned by the DEATH of / Mrs. MARGARET GREEN; / Consort of the late Honourable / BENJAMIN GREEN, Esq; / Delivered at HALIFAX, / In the Province of NOVA-SCOTIA, / February 1st, 1778. / By John Seccombe, / of CHESTER, A.M. / [rule] / The Saints are the excellent in the Earth. Ps. 16.3. / A Woman that feareth the LORD she shall be praised. / Prov. 31.30. / The Righteous have Hope in his Death. Prov. 14.32. / They shall be in everlasting Remembrance. Ps. 112.6. / [double rule] / HALIFAX. Printed: By A. HENRY. / [Title within a double rule frame]

4to A-C[4]; 21 p., 1 *l.*; type-page: 17.5 × 11.2 cm.

Contents: p. [1], t.-p.; p. [2], blank; p. 3-21, Sermon, text: 1 Corinthians 15: 56, 57, The sting of death is sin, and the strength of sin is the law. But thanks be to God who giveth us the Victory through our Lord Jesus Christ; p. 21 verso, blank; 1 *l.* blank.

The late Mrs. Green is characterized by the Congregationalist minister as a young woman who "had the highest Esteem and Relish for Doctrines of Grace . . . that system of evangelical truths which is commonly called Calvinistical . . . Books of meer Amusement (Plays, Romances, Novels &c.) she seldom looked into, esteeming Time too precious to be trifled away in Vanity." She was the widow of Benjamin Green, 1713-72, long a councillor and the provincial treasurer of Nova Scotia.

Copies located: CaNsHD; MHi.

302. ALMANACS. NOVA SCOTIA

THE / Nova-Scotia CALENDER, / OR AN / ALMANACK, / For the Year of the Christian Æra, 1780; . . . / [5 lines] / Wherein is contained, / The Eclipses . . . / [5 lines] / [rule] / [verse] / [ornamental rule] / Calculated for the Meridian of HALIFAX . . . / [4 lines] / By METONICUS. / [ornamental rule] / HALIFAX: Printed and Sold by A. HENRY. / [title within ornamental frame] /

16mo. 71 p.; type-page: 14 × 7.5 cm. p. 45 mispaged: 35; 46: 64.

Contents: p. [1], t.-p.; p. [2], blank; p. 3-4, Table of areas of countries, eclipses; p. 5-6, Value of coins, vulgar notes, etc.; p. [7-18], Calendar; p. 19-21, Nova Scotia administration, assembly, judges, customs and tax collectors, etc.; p. 22-25, Tables of currencies; p. 26-29, Royal families; p. 29-36, British officials, ministers, judges, etc.; p. 36-69 British army list and navy list, etc., staffs in America, garrisons, rates of pay, etc.; p. 70-71, Exchange value of coins at rate $1: 4*s.* 8*d.*; verso of p. 71 blank.

This almanac was advertised: "Just published (price 2/6 sewed in marble paper and Writing paper between each month) And to be sold by Anthony Henry, A Register with an Almanack for the year 1780, containing the Eclipses etc., the Nova Scotia Administration . . . the British Administration . . . Army, Navy, Staff in America and location of regiments there, [etc.]."—*Nova-Scotia gazette,* Nov. 2, 1779. Also: "Just published and to be sold by Anthony Henry, the Nova Scotia Almanack for 1780. 1/ single [copy]; allowance given to those who sell again."—*Nova-Scotia gazette,* Nov. 30, 1779.

Thus it appears that the *Nova-Scotia calender* for 1780 (also 1781) was published in its customary format (about 32 p., comprising probably p. [1]-29, 70-71 as above), also in an enlarged edition (71 p.) which included a register of British and colonial information for the English soldiery and American loyalists recently arrived in Nova Scotia. The enlarged edition appears to have been printed throughout by Henry, though the "register" (especially in the 1781 edition) *may* have been imported in sheets from the United States. Henry advertised copies for sale of *Mills & Hicks' British American Register . . . for 1780* (printed in New York, 112 p.) in his *Nova-Scotia gazette*, June 6, 1780.

Copies located: CaNsHD (p. 19-22 wanting); CaNsWA (p. 65 to end wanting); CaOOA (all before p. [15] and after p. 28 wanting).

303. ALMANACS. QUEBEC

CALENDRIER pour l'Année Bissextile 1780, pour Québec, par les 306$^{d.}$ 30$^{m.}$ de Longitude, et 46$^{d.}$ 55$^{m.}$ de Latitude / [ornamental rule] /

Colophon: A QUEBEC: chez WM. BROWN, derriere l'Eglise Cathédrale. /

Broadside: type-page: 40 × 38.5 cm. (*Calendrier:* 42.5 × 38.5 in ornamental frame).

Contents: Les signes du zodiaque, Calendrier, Officiers civils. The content, layout, and type are like those of No. 272.

This sheet almanac was sold at 7½*d.* the copy, 5*s.* the dozen, from Dec. 7, and advertised for sale at Quebec, Trois Rivières, Berthier, and Montreal, as usual, in the *Quebec gazette*, from Dec. 2, 1779. Brown's account book shows that he had supplied his agents in these towns with sixty-two dozen copies by Feb. 7, 1780.

Copy located: CaO (bound in *Quebec gazette*. at end of 1779).

304. ALMANACS. QUEBEC

[Indian Almanack for 1779, or 1780? *Quebec, Wm. Brown, 1779.*]

? Broadside (a sheet almanac), or leaflet, in Montagnais dialect. This was the first of a series of seven almanacs, probably for the years 1779 (or 1780?) and each of the six succeeding years to 1785 (or 1786?). A similar series for seven years had been printed and delivered in 1778 (*see* No. 273-79). Whether the 1779 editions replaced those of 1778, owing to error, accident, or loss of the latter, or whether the "Indian Almanacks" printed in 1779 were in a different dialect for use by different tribes, is unknown. Like the earlier editions, these were prepared by Father La Brosse and *printed at Quebec by Wm. Brown, 1779,* as recorded:

> "1779, May 31. Printed for John Baptist Labrosse, Jesuite, Missioner, at Tadoussak, 7 Years Indian Almanacks making together 2000 copies, and sent him the four first Years the 28th inst. by Francis Valiere as per his receipt, and sent him the remaining three years to Louis Germain this day by Sandy.*—£14." —Can.P.A., *Neilson papers*, v. 47.
>
> "1779, Oct. 29. Credit to Printing Office from P^{re} Labrosse Indian Almanacks. —£14."—*ibid.*, v. 45.

Copy located: None.

*Brown's printer's devil.

305. ALMANACS. QUEBEC

[Indian Almanack for 1781. *Quebec, Wm. Brown, 1779.*]

? Broadside (a sheet almanac), or leaflet, in Montagnais dialect, prepared by Father La Brosse and *printed at Quebec by Wm. Brown, 1779,* as recorded in the latter's accounts. *See* No. 304 *note.*

Copy located: None.

306. ALMANACS. QUEBEC

[Indian Almanack for 1782. *Quebec, Wm. Brown, 1779.*]

? Broadside (a sheet almanac), or leaflet, in Montagnais dialect, prepared by Father La Brosse and *printed at Quebec by Wm. Brown, 1779,* as recorded in the latter's accounts. *See* No. 304 *note.*

Copy located: None.

307. ALMANACS. QUEBEC

[Indian Almanack for 1783. *Quebec, Wm. Brown, 1779.*]

? Broadside (a sheet almanac), or leaflet, in Montagnais dialect, prepared by Father La Brosse and *printed at Quebec by Wm. Brown, 1779,* as recorded in the latter's accounts. *See* No. 304 *note.*

Copy located: None.

308. ALMANACS. QUEBEC

[Indian Almanack for 1784. *Quebec, Wm. Brown, 1779.*]

? Broadside (a sheet almanac), or leaflet, in Montagnais dialect, prepared by Father La Brosse and *printed at Quebec by Wm. Brown, 1779,* as recorded in the latter's accounts. *See* No. 304 *note.*

Copy located: None.

309. ALMANACS. QUEBEC

[Indian Almanack for 1785. *Quebec, Wm. Brown, 1779.*]

? Broadside (a sheet almanac), or leaflet, in Montagnais dialect, prepared by Father La Brosse and *printed at Quebec by Wm. Brown, 1779,* as recorded in the latter's accounts. *See* No. 304 *note.*

Copy located: None.

310. ALMANACS. QUEBEC

[Indian Almanac for 1786? *Quebec, Wm. Brown, 1779.*]

? Broadside (a sheet almanac), or leaflet, in Montagnais dialect, prepared by Father La Brosse and *printed at Quebec by Wm. Brown, 1779,* as recorded in the latter's accounts. *See* No. 304 *note.*

311. LEMAITRE DUEME, FRANÇOIS, *defendant*

[District de Montréal—Province de Québec—Cour des Plaidoyers communs. Les Dames Ursulines des Trois-Rivières, Demandresses, contre François Lemaitre Duème, Défendeur.—Duplique. ? *Montreal, F. Mesplet, 1778-79.*]

This work was probably printed at Montreal by Fleury Mesplet before Apr., 1779, for François Lemaitre Duème, or Duhaime. The latter was defendant in the case of the Ursuline Sisters of Trois Rivières *versus* Lemaitre Duème, a complicated suit over land, in the Court of Common Pleas, Montreal.

No copy of this publication is known, but its existence is established by the publication following (No. 312, which has been examined by Mr. Aegidius Fauteux, from whose *Mesplet*, 184, no. 34-35, this note is translated). In his defence to the *Mémoire* of Mézière, lawyer for the Ursulines, Lemaitre Duème states expressly that the Ursulines, having furnished the court with a replication to his plea, he himself replied with a printed rejoinder, but that on communicating this rejoinder (*Duplique*) to the ladies' lawyer, the latter consented to withdraw his replication provided that Duème's printed rejoinder did not appear. Lemaitre Duème should have sustained his rejoinder, for he specifically reproached Mézière in the work following (No. 312) for having broken his word by producing in court a *Mémoire* which he said himself was an *addition* to the withdrawn replication. Mézière himself in this *addition* which is printed in No. 312 mentions a printed defence by Lemaitre Duème and attributes it to the defendant's vanity.

The suit was won by the defendant in the Court of Common Pleas, also on its appeal, in the Court of Appeal, Quebec, and before the Privy Council in London, to which the Ursulines had final recourse. *See: Les Ursulines des Trois-Rivières depuis leur établissement jusqu'à nos jours* (4 v., Trois Rivières, 1888-1911), I: 415.

Copy located: None.

312. LEMAITRE DUEME, FRANÇOIS, *defendant*

District de / Montréal / Province de Québec / Cour des Plaidoyers Communs /

Caption at head of col. 1: Les Dames Religieuses / Ursulines des Trois-Rivières / Demandresses, / Contre / François-Lemaitre Duème / Défendeur. / Moyens subsidiaires employés par les / Demandresses devant les Honorables Juges / de la Cour, pour servir l'addition aux Ré-/pliques à défense précédement fournis. /

Caption at head of col. 2: Réponse / de François-Lemaitre Duème / à l'écrit diffamatoire fourni par Mr Mézière, avocat des Dames / Religieuses des Trois-Rivières. /

Colophon at end: A Montréal, chez Fleury Mesplet, Imprimeur & Libraire. /

4to. 20 p.; paper-page: 25.5 × 19.25 cm.; p. 1-19 printed in 2 col., text in French.

Contents: Col. 1, ". . . l'addition aux Répliques [signed:] Mézière," is the plaintiffs' lawyer's *addition* or supplement to his replication to the defence (*see*

No. 311). Col. 2, containing the defendant's response to the arguments in col. 1, is signed: "Fr. Lemaitre Duème, Montréal, le 15 avril, 1779."

This work was advertised: "A vendre chez l'Imprimeur, vendredi, le 16 du courant, Mémoire signé Pierre Mézière comme avocat des Dames Religieuses Ursulines des Trois Rivières et la Réponse de François-Lemaitre Duème. Ces ouvrages [i.e. col. 1 and col. 2 as described above] serviront à faire distinguer le bon du mauvais."—*Gazette littéraire*, Montreal, Apr. 14, 1779.

The title and description of this work are taken from Fauteux: *Mesplet*, 184, no. 35.

Copy located: CaQMS.

313. DU CALVET, PIERRE, *d.* 1786

Caption title, p. 1: (1) / [rule] / [printer's ornaments] / [rule] / MÉMOIRE / EN REPONSE A L'ECRIT PUBLIC, / DE Me PANET, fondé de Procuration de WATSON / & RASHLEIGH de Londres, Demandeurs. / CONTRE / PIERRE DUCALVET de Montréal, Ecuyer, Défendeur. / STUPETE GENTES /

Colophon, p. 25: [rule] / A MONTREAL, Chez FLEURY MESPLET, Imprimeur & Libraire. /

4to A-F^{2}, [G^{1}]; 25 p.; type-page: 19.5 × 12.8 cm.

Contents: p. 1-25, "Mémoire, [signed:] Pierre Ducalvet, Montréal, le 11 Janvier 1779"; p. 25 verso, blank.

This is Du Calvet's refutation of Pierre Panet's *Réponse* (No. 295) and his third defence tract printed for the case Watson & Rashleigh *versus* Du Calvet, Montreal, 1778-79.

Copy located: CaQM; Daviault (photostat in CaOOA).

314. MACLEAN, ALLAN, 1725-1784?

By ALLAN MACLEAN, Esq; / Brigadier-general and Lieutenant-colonel Commandant of / His Majesty's 84th Regiment of Foot. / To all Gentlemen VOLUNTEERS and LOYALISTS, willing to / serve His Majesty in the 84th Regiment of Foot: /

Broadside: 32 lines, type-page: 23.5 × 15.5 m. *Printed at Quebec by Wm. Brown, 1779*, as recorded:

"1779, Sept. 13. Printed for Col. Maclean 400 Recruiting terms—£1. 15.
D^{o}. 200 D^{o}. in French—£1. 7. 6."—Can.P.A., *Neilson papers*, v. 47.

The text, undated, is signed: "Allan MacLean, Brigadier-general in Canada." It states that the subscriber is ordered to add twenty men to each company of the regiment, and sets forth the terms of enlistment. These include an offer to volunteers for the continuance of the Rebellion, of two hundred acres of land (with fifty additional for wife and each child) in any province of North America; the land to be free of quit rents and all fees, "conditions which no other regiment . . . have in their power to grant."

The Royal Highland Emigrants, or 84th Regiment, was raised by Maclean in America during the American Revolutionary War, and the terms of enlistment made by royal command. The "conditions" of this offer of land were later sought by members of other regiments who received grants and settled in Canada after the war. *See* No. 664. *See also* Norman Macdonald: *Canada 1763-1841, immigration and settlement* (London, 1939), chap. 2.

Copy located: CaOOA (filed in Can.P.A., "S" 17, *Int. Corresp.*, and dated in MS. 1779).

315. MACLEAN, ALLAN, 1725-1784?

[French edition of No. 314, *printed at Quebec by Wm. Brown, 1779.*]

Copy located: None.

316. NOVA SCOTIA. HOUSE OF ASSEMBLY

Caption title: (1) / [4 rules] / JOURNAL and VOTES / OF THE / HOUSE of ASSEMBLY, / For the Province of Nova-Scotia. / [rule] / Monday June 7th, 1779. /

fo. A-F²; 23 p. *Printed at Halifax, N.S., by Anthony Henry, 1779.*

Contents: p. 1-23, Journal and votes of the twelfth session of the fifth assembly, June 7-28, 1779; p. 23 verso, blank.

Copies located: CaNs (2 cop.); GBLP (2 cop. in C.O. 220/1: 941-63; *ibid.*, p. 965-87); MH.

317. NOVA SCOTIA. LAWS, STATUTES, *etc.*

Running title: [rule] / 1779. Anno Domini nono [sic] Regis GEORGII III. CAP. I[-X]. / [rule] /

Caption title: At the GENERAL-ASSEMBLY of the / Province of Nova-Scotia, . . . / [nine lines] / being the Sixth [sic] GENERAL-ASSEM-/BLY convened in the said Province. / [rule] /

fo. sig. 5Q², 5Q² [sic], [$_*$¹]; p. 333-342 paged in continuation of No. 293. *Printed at Halifax, N.S., by Anthony Henry, 1779.*

Contents: p. 333-342, Cap. I-X, perpetual acts passed in the twelfth session of the fifth assembly, June 7-28, 1779.

Copies located: MH; DLC.

318. NOVA SCOTIA. LAWS, STATUTES, *etc.*

Running title: [rule] / 1779. Anno Decimo Decimo nono Regis, Georgii III. CAP. I[-VII]. / [rule] /

Caption title: At the GENERAL-ASSEMBLY of the Province of Nova-Scotia, . . . / [9 lines] / being the Sixth [sic] GENERAL-ASSEM-/BLY convened in the said Province. / [rule] /

fo. sig. A-C²; p. 201-212; paged in continuation of No. 294. *Printed at Halifax, N.S., by Anthony Henry, 1779.*

Contents: p. 201-212, Cap. I-VII, temporary acts passed in the twelfth session of the fifth assembly, June 7-28, 1779.

Copies located: CaNs; MH; NNB.

319. PRIMERS. QUEBEC. *French*

[French Alphabet, *printed at Quebec by Wm. Brown, 1779.*]

?16mo. 64 p. No detail of format is recorded but this work approximated, probably, the size of the Latin Alphabet of three months earlier (No. 320) according to the price rate set by the printer:

"1779, Sept. 30. Printed for Louis Germain 1500 French alphabets @ $2\frac{1}{2}$ [d.] —£15. 12. 6. (paid Jany 8. 80)."—Can.P.A., *Neilson papers*, v. 47.

320. PRIMERS. QUEBEC. *Latin*

[Latin Alphabet, *printed at Quebec by Wm. Brown, 1779.*]

Probably 16mo. 64 p., as the printer recorded:

"1779, June 30. Printed for Louis Germain 2000 Latin Alphabets making 2 Sheets Crown Sixteens on English [type] @ $2\frac{1}{2}$ d.—£20. 16. 8. (paid Jany 8. 80)."—Can.P.A., *Neilson papers*, v. 47.

321. QUEBEC, *Province*

INSTRUCTIONS pour les VOYAGEURS / qui montent la Grande Rivière en Canots. /

2 *l.* Text, 24 lines, type-page: 13. 7 × 12. 7 cm., on recto of *l.* 1; *l.* 1 verso-*l.* 2, blank *Printed at Quebec by Wm. Brown, 1779.*

Instructions (dated at end: "Donné à [blank] le [blank] 1779") concern (1) permits for fur-traders' canoes, going up the Ottawa River, to Michilimackinac and beyond; (2) procedure at posts in the Upper Country; (3) registration with Sheriff Gray at Montreal of *engagés* employed in trading expeditions there.

This entry is included as an example of numerous printed blanks of various kinds, prepared by Wm. Brown in Quebec, and probably also by Mesplet in Montreal, for the government. The latter's regulation of fur traders, especially of the movement westward of men and supplies, became stringent during the war period. *See also* W. E. Stevens: *The northwest fur trade, 1763-1800* (Urbana, Ill., 1928); *also* G. L. Nute: *The voyageur* (New York, 1931).

Copy located: GBLBM (in *Haldimand papers*, Add. MSS. 21880, fo. 189-90).

322. QUEBEC, *Province.* GOVERNOR, 1778-1786 (*Haldimand*)

By His EXCELLENCY / FREDERICK HALDIMAND, / Captain-General and Governor in Chief in . . . / QUEBEC . . . / . . . / . . . / . . . / PROCLAMATION. / <Text> / GIVEN. . . [at Quebec, 17 May, 1779] / . . . / . . . / . . . / FRED: HALDIMAND. / [3 lines]

French on right:

Par Son EXCELLENCE / FREDERIC HALDIMAND, / Capitaine-general et Gouverneur en Chef dans . . . / Québec . . . / . . . / . . . / PROCLAMATION. / <Text> / Donné . . . [dans Québec 17 Mai, 1779] / . . . / . . . / (Signé) FRED: HALDIMAND. / [5 lines] /

Double broadside: English on left, 38 lines, type-page: 24.2 × 18.5 cm. French on right, 40 lines, type-page: 24.5 × 18.5 cm. *Printed at Quebec by Wm. Brown, 1779,* as recorded:

"1779, May 22. Printed for the Gov^t by Order of the Secretary 175 Double Proclamations prohibiting the Exportation of Grain &c—£2. 7. 6."

—Can.P.A., *Neilson papers,* v. 47.

English text: "Whereas His Majesty's service in the month of November last, did require a temporary prohibition upon the exportation of Wheat, Flower, and Biscuit, out of this Province . . . AND WHEREAS by the artful management of rapacious and designing Men, Wheat and Flower, at a time of great plenty, have been advanced to an exorbitent [sic] price; to the great prejudice, the oppression of His Majesty's Subjects in this Province in general; and of the Poor in particular. His Majesty's service, the comfort and happiness of His Subjects make it necessary, further to extend the prohibition . . . [to Jan. 1, 1780] . . . And the more effectually to prevent such acts of public Oppression and distress, by the just punishment of those, whom the love of Gain, or more insidious motives have induced to violate the Laws; to commit actions which must bring inevitable Calamity and distress upon all His Majesty's Subjects, in this Province, the Commissioners of the Peace . . . are hereby enjoined . . . to be diligent in discovering the Persons who have offended . . . in Forestalling, Regrating, and Engrossing."

French text: "Le Service de Sa Majesté aiant requis de faire dans le mois de Novembre une défense, pour un tems, de sortir de cette Province des Bleds, Farines et Biscuits, . . . Et comme la conduite artificieuse de gens avides et mal-intentionnés qui a fait monter à un prix exhorbitant les Bleds et Farines dans un tems d'abondance au grand préjudice et détriment de tous les Sujets de Sa Majesté en cette Province, et particulierement des Pauvres, demande, tant pour le service de Sa Majesté que pour le soulagement et le bonheur de ses Sujets, de prolonger la défense . . . [jusqu'à jan. 1, 1780]. . ."

This proclamation extends the terms of No. 297 to Jan. 1, 1780, and urges the search for black marketeers. It is reprinted in Can.P.A., *Report, 1918.*

Copy located: CaQQL.

323. QUEBEC, *Province.* GOVERNOR, 1778-1786 (*Haldimand*)

[Instructions For the Captains of Militia when His Majesty's Forces are upon the March or go into Quarters in the different Parishes <Text> Given under my Hand at Quebec, this 9th of January 1779. Fred: Haldimand.]

French side: Instructions Pour les Capitaines de Milices envers les Troupes de sa Majesté quant celles-cy sont en Marche, ou en Quartiers dans les differentes Paroisses <Text> Donné à Québec ce neuf de Janvier 1779. Fred: Haldimand. Au Capitaine de la Paroisse de [blank] Gouvernement de [blank].

Double broadside: English on left, type-page: 29.5 × 16.5 cm.; French on right, type-page: 29.8 × 16.5 cm.

Printed at Quebec by Wm. Brown, 1779 as recorded:

"1779, Jan. 30. Printed for the Govt. by Order of Lieutenant Governor, 300 Military Instructions—£3. 7. 6.
250 Circular letters to Captains of Militia—£2. 7. 6."
—Can.P.A., *Neilson papers*, v. 47.

Contents: Instructions, no. 1-15. They are reprinted in Canada, Department of Militia, *History*, 3: 86-87.

The "Circular letters" in the printer's record remain unidentified. Several printed blanks and circulars, doubtless prepared in Brown's shop at this period, are preserved in the Haldimand papers, British Museum Add. MSS. 21880, fo. 174-93.

Copy located: GBLBM (in *Haldimand papers*, Add. MSS. 21,831, fo. 19-20).

324. QUEBEC, *Province.* GOVERNOR, 1778-1786 (*Haldimand*)

By His EXCELLENCY / FREDERICK HALDIMAND, / Captain-General and Governor in Chief in and over His Majesty's Province of / QUEBEC, . . . / . . . / . . . / PROCLAMATION. / <Text> / GIVEN . . . at . . . QUEBEC, / . . . [14 June, 1779] . . . / . . . / FRED: HALDIMAND. / . . . / . . . / . . . /

French on right:

PAR SON EXCELLENCE / FREDERIC HALDIMAND, / Capitaine-general et Gouverneur en Chef dans toute la Province de Québec . . . / . . . / . . . / . . . / PROCLAMATION. / <Text> / Donné . . . dans la ville de Québec, . . . / [14 juin, 1779] . . . / . . . / (Signé) FRED: HALDIMAND. / [5 lines] /

Double broadside: English on left, 67 lines, type-page: 38.8 × 22 cm. French on right, 67 lines, type-page: 38.8 × 22 cm. *Printed at Quebec by Wm. Brown, 1779,* as recorded:

"1779, June 24, Printed for the Gov[t]. A Double Proclamation 1 week [in the *Quebec gazette*, June 17, 1779] making known the Law against Forestalling &c 10 [i.e. Space units]—£3. 17. 6.
D[o] For 300 on English [type] a sheet Demy for the Country—£3. 17. 6."
Can. P.A., *Neilson papers*, v. 47.

English text: "Whereas upon an Enquiry made by the Magistrates for the District of Quebec, into the causes of the great price of Wheat and Flower, at a time of plenty; It hath been represented to Me, that the several Persons who had been induced to violate the Laws, and commit the Offences and Crimes of Forestalling, Regrating and Ingrossing, had become offenders from an ignorance of the Statutes and Laws of England, . . . I have THEREFORE THOUGHT FIT, . . . to make known to all his Majesty's Subjects in this Province, what are the Laws against Forestalling, Regrating and Ingrossing. [etc.]."

French text: "Aiant été faite une Enquête par les Magistrats du District du Québec pour connaitre les causes qui ont occasionné le prix exhorbitant des bleds et farines dans un tems d'abondance, Il m'a été représenté que plusieurs particuliers qui ont violé les Loix à cet égard, et y ont contrevenus en les enlevant, les revendant et s'en rendant maitres, n'ont été coupables que par l'ignorance dans laquelle ils sont des Statuts et Loix d'Angleterre, . . . A CES CAUSES, J'ai jugé à propos de . . .

donner connaissance aux Sujets de sa Majesté en cette Province, quelles sont les Loix contre ceux qui enlevent, revendent et se rendent maitres des Denrées nécessaires à la vie. [etc.]."

Then follow sections numbered I-VI setting forth the statute, 5-6 Edward VI, c. 14, against forestallers, etc.; also measures of enforcement thereof by magistrates in the British colony, Quebec. It is the English law of 1552 against cornering food supplies and forcing up prices, applied in French Canada during the war crisis. The proclamation is reprinted in Can.P.A., *Report, 1918.*

Copies located: CaOOA (in "Proclamations" portfolio in the Library); CaQQL (cropped).

325. QUEBEC, *Province.* GOVERNOR, 1778-1786 (*Haldimand*)

Caption title, col. 1: A TRANSLATION of His Excellency / General HALDIMAND's Speech / to the ONEIDA Indians in the Rebel / Interest, as delivered to them in the / Iroquois Language.

Caption, col. 2: GORAGH ASHAREGOWA / Raoweana tekawena-dennion Tyogh-/tyaky nonwe yeghsagodadigh ONEA-/YOTRONON. /

fo. [2] p. 1 *l.*, type-page: 33 × 20 cm. text in 2 col. English and "Indian" (presumably the Oneida dialect) on p. [1-2]; 1 *l.* blank. *Printed at Quebec by Wm. Brown*, as recorded:

> "1779, Apr. 10. Printed for the Gov[r]. by Order of Col. Claus 102 Speeches to the Oneida Indians, in Indian & English making 2 folio pages on superfine thick folio post with a blank ½ Sheet.—£2. 17. 6."
>
> —Can.P.A., *Neilson papers*, v. 47.

The text begins: "Brothers, Be very attentive, to what I Asharegowa the Great King of England's Representative in Canada am going to say.

"By this string of Wampum I shake you by the head to rouse you, that you may seriously reflect upon my Words. *A String of Wampum.*

"Brothers, It is now about four Years ago, since the Bostonians began to rise and rebel against their Father the King of England, since which Time you have taken a different part from the rest of the five Nations your confederates, and have likewise deserted the King's Cause, thro' the deceitful Machinations and Snares of the rebels, who intimidated you with their numerous Armies, by which Means you became bewildered, and forgot all your Engagements with, and former care and favors from the Great King of England your Father," etc. Haldimand reminds the Oneidas of the untrustworthiness of the American colonists, now rebels, warns them that he can send pro-British Indians against them, reiterates the advantages of the King's Bounty, invokes the name of Sir William Johnson, and closes:

"These are the Facts, Brothers, that unless you are lost to every Sense of Feeling cannot but create in you a most hearty Repentance, and deep Remorse, for your past vile Actions. *The Belt.*"

The Oneidas alone of the six Iroquois nations declared against the Confederacy joining the King's side in the American Revolution. The other five assisted the British independently and sporadically, but as some of the tribes were divided within themselves on war policy, disaffection from the British interest was stimulated effectively by the Oneidas. Gov. Haldimand wrote to Lt.-Col. Hamilton from Quebec, Apr. 8, 1770: "Finding that the perfidy of the Rebel Oneida Nation is come to that pitch that they even presume to debauch and invite the Five Nations to be of their

Sentiments . . . I judged it for the good of His Majesty's Ind[n] Interest to send them a Speech, thereby to make them sensible of their daring & traiterous Behaviour, A Copy of which I hereby enclose to you." Then follow instructions for Campbell to despatch to Oneida, or Canaghsaragy, a deputation of trustworthy Indians, to be designated by Mr. Brant, "the bearer of this letter." The deputation is to deliver the speech and is to be accompanied by "a sober and faithful Interpreter" who will report its effect. Haldimand wrote Hamilton again Apr. 30, 1779: ". . . I am pleased to hear my letter to the Oneida Indians met with such general approbation" and gave further instructions for its distribution.—Can.P.A., "B" 113, p. 13-18.

Copies located: GBLBM (2 cop. in *Haldimand papers:* Add. MSS. 21779, fo. 187; Add. MSS. 21880, fo. 195).

326. QUEBEC, *Province.* LAWS, STATUTES, *etc.*

Caption title: (2) / [ornamental rule] / ANNO DECIMO NONO / GEORGII III. REGIS. / [rule] / CHAP. II. / An ORDINANCE / For continuing an Ordinance made the twenty-/ninth day of March, in the seventeenth year / of His Majesty's Reign, Intituled, "An Or-/"dinance for regulating the Militia of the / "Province of QUEBEC, and rendering it of / "more general utility towards the preserva-/"tion and security thereof." /

French caption: (3) [ornamental rule] / ANNO DECIMO NONO / GEORGII III. REGIS / [rule] / CHAP. II / ORDONNANCE / Qui continue une Ordonnance passée le vingt-neu-/vieme jour de Mars, dans la dix-septieme année / du Régne de sa Majesté, intitulée, "Ordonnance / "Qui régle les Milices de la Province de Québec, / "et qui les rend d'une plus grande utilité pour / "la conservation et la sureté d'icelle." /

fo. [A]-D²; 15 p. type-page: 23.3 × 12.8 cm. Text in English and French on opposite pages. ***Printed at Quebec by Wm. Brown, 1779***, as recorded:

> "1779, Feb. 6. Printed for the Gov[t] by Order of the Lieutenant-Governor, 250 Copies of an Ordinance for regulating the Militia together with that continuing it, making 4 Sheets on pot [i.e. pott paper, a small sheet about 14″ × 12″ in size] in English [type] with Brevier notes @ 55/—£11.
>
> Paid Stitching the above—10/." —Can.P.A., *Neilson papers*, v. 47.

Contents: p. [1] blank; p. 2-3, 19 Geo. III c. 2, with title as above; p. 4-15, 17 Geo. III c. 8 with title: "Anno Decimo Georgii III. Regis Chap. VIII. An Ordinance For regulating the Militia, [etc.]"; p. 15 verso, blank.

19 Geo. III c. 2, enacted Jan. 16, 1779, extended till 1781 the terms of 17 Geo. III c. 8. The latter, enacted Mar. 29, 1777, and extended periodically thereafter, regulated military service in Quebec till superseded by 27 Geo. III c. 2.

All these ordinances are reprinted in Can.P.A., *Report, 1914.*

Copy located: GBLBM (in *Haldimand papers* Add. MSS. 21885, fo. 60-67).

327. QUEBEC, *Province.* PROVINCIAL NAVY

QUEBEC, February 3, 1779. / EVERY able-bodied Seaman [etc.] *French side:* QUEBEC, ce 3 Fevrier, 1779. / TOUS bon Matelots [etc.]

Double broadside: English on left, 16 lines, type-page: 16.3 × 13.4 cm. French on right, 19 lines, type-page: 19.2 × 13.4 cm. *Probably printed at Quebec by Wm. Brown, 1779.*

The text states: "Every able-bodied Seaman who will enter for His Majesty's Naval Service in the Province of Quebec, to serve on the High Seas or on the Lakes shall receive Forty Shillings Sterling per month, . . . and shall be protected from being Press'd on board any of His Majesty's Ships . . . [apply] to Captain John Schanks at the Coffee-House, or at Captain Bouchette's House in Chamberlain Street, . . . and receive one month's Wages in Slops or Bedding."

French text: "Tous bons Matelots voulant prendre partis pour le Service Naval de Sa Majesté en la Province de Québec, pour servir sur Mer ou sur les Lacs, recevront Quarante Shellings Sterling par mois . . . et seront exemple d'être pressés pour servir sur aucun autre Vaisseau armé de Sa Majesté" etc.

Jean-Baptiste Bouchette, 1736-1804, who was born in Quebec, served in the French militia during the Seven Years' War, later entered the British service in Canada, and became commandant of the Provincial Marine fleet.

The Provincial Navy or Provincial Marine Department (of which the Royal Canadian Navy of today is a lineal descendant) comprised ship and shore establishments on the Great Lakes, the St. Lawrence River, and Lake Champlain. It was transferred from control of the British quartermaster general in New York to that of the governor of Quebec (Haldimand) about 1778. Besides defence duties it had to prevent Canadian trade with the American rebels. (*See* G. A. Cuthbertson: *Freshwater,* Toronto, 1931, chap. 7, based on *Provincial marine papers,* Can.P.A. "C" 722A-742, also "B" 141-45.)

Copy located: GBLBM (in *Haldimand papers,* Add. MSS. 21880, fo. 185-86).

328. QUEBEC, *Province.* PROVINCIAL NAVY

[Hand-bill for Seamen; *printed at Quebec by Wm. Brown, 1779.*]

Broadside. This publication, probably for enlisting sailors in the Provincial Marine Fleet like the item above, was recorded by the printer:

"1779, Aug. 24. Printed for Capt Robinson of the Guadaloupe, 75 folio hand-bills for Seamen—10/

For pasting them up—2/6." —Can.P.A., *Neilson papers,* v. 47.

Copy located: None.

329. QUEBEC GAZETTE. CARRIER'S ADDRESS

ETRENNES / Du GARÇON qui porte la GAZETTE / de QUEBEC aux Pratiques. / Le I JANVIER, 1780. / [*Quebec, Wm. Brown, 1779.*]

Broadside: 28 lines; type-page: 18.8 × 11.7 cm. with ornamental frame.

Contents: "Etrennes," 6 stanzas of 4 lines each, light verse without local or political allusion.

Copy located: CaO (bound in *Quebec gazette* at end of 1779).

330. ALMANACS. NOVA SCOTIA

[The British American Register . . . an Almanack for the year . . . 1781. *Halifax, N.S., A. Henry, 1780.*]

This almanac was advertised: "Just published and to be sold by A. Henry the British American Register containing 106 pages with an Almanack for . . . 1781, with contents as follows—the Eclipses, the Nova Scotia court sessions, the British Administration, Army, Navy, [etc.]."—*Nova-Scotia gazette,* Nov. 28, 1780. The contents listed in the advertisement appear similar to those in the *Nova-Scotia Calender for 1780* (No. 302), though they occupy 35 additional pages. This work was, perhaps, a combination of *The British American Register,* formerly published in New York by Mills & Hicks (now loyalist refugees) and *The Nova-Scotia Calender* regularly published at Halifax by Anthony Henry.

Copy located: None.

331. ALMANACS. QUEBEC

Almanach / curieux / et interessant / pour l'année / mil sept cent quatre-vingt-un / [printer's ornament] / A Montréal, / Chez Fleury Mesplet, Impri-/meur & Libraire, / M.DCC.LXXXI. /

48 p.; paper-page: 12 × 8 cm. Though the imprint bears the date of the title, this almanac, like No. 248, was probably printed at the end of the preceding year. This and No. 351 were probably produced by Mesplet's wife and some assistant in the printing office, for Mesplet was in jail in Quebec from June, 1779 till Sept., 1782.

Contents: p. [1], t.-p.; p. [2], blank; p. [3]-48, text.

Copy located: CaQMS (described in Fauteux: *Mesplet,* no. 36, from which this description is taken).

332. ALMANACS. QUEBEC

ALMANACH / DE / QUEBEC, / POUR / L'Année Bissextile / M,DCC,LXXX. / [double rule] / [printer's ornament] / [double rule] / A QUEBEC: / Chez GUILLAUME BROWN, à la Haute-ville / derriere l'Eglise Cathédrale. /

12mo. 60 p.; type-page: 10.5 × 6 cm.

Contents: p. [1], t.-p.; p. [2-4], Epoques, fêtes, eclipses, etc.; p. [5-16], Calendrier; p. 17-25, Explication du Systême solaire; p. 26-31, Instructions pour les capitaines de milices; p. 32-36, Officiers civiles de Québec; p. 37, Poids de la monnaie (suivant l'ordonnance, 29 mars, 1777); p. 38-45, Souverains de l'Europe; p. 45, Douane; p. 46, la Poste de Québec à Montréal; p. 47-51, Catalogue du clergé; p. 51-53, Seigneurs primitifs de Québec; p. 54-57, Remèdes choisis; p. 57-59, Bons mots; p. 60, Masons in Canada.

This number is almost entirely in French, the militia instructions alone appear in both languages, and the list of Freemasons' lodges (of which Brown was a member) in English only.

It was announced as a forthcoming publication in Brown's newspaper, the *Quebec gazette,* Dec. 30, 1779, and advertised for sale on Feb. 3, 1780. For several

days thereafter nearly half the transactions in Brown's shop were almanac sales at 1*s*. 6*d*. the copy, 2*s*. interleaved. In the first week he sent fifteen dozen to his agent in Montreal (where Mesplet's *Almanack* was temporarily suspended) and five dozen to other agents, at 15*s*. the dozen, also to each agent "one interleaved copy for self."
—Can.P.A., *Neilson papers*, v. 47.

Published on Feb. 3, 1780, this was the first of a series which appeared yearly with few exceptions, till 1841. From the beginning the little volumes were tastefully designed, well printed, and competently edited. For the first decade, the *Almanach de Québec* was prepared in the style of colonial almanacs, familiar, no doubt, to Brown in his Philadelphia apprenticeship twenty-five years earlier—though adapted to a French Catholic community. By his successors (e.g. Samuel Neilson in 1791), however, its scope and detail were extended greatly and it became the most informative on local affairs of all early Canadian almanacs.

Copies located: CaOOA (photostat copy); CaQQL.

333. ALMANACS. QUEBEC

CALENDRIER pour l'Année 1781, pour Québec, par les 306$^{d.}$ 30$^{m.}$ de Longitude, et 46$^{d.}$ 55$^{m.}$ de Latitude. / [ornamental rule] /

Colophon: A QUEBEC: chez WM. BROWN, au milieu de la Grande Côte. /

Broadside: type-page: 53 × 41 cm.

Contents: Calendrier (in ornamental rule frame, 44 × 38.5 cm.); Poste entre Québec et Montréal; Maisons de Poste depuis Montréal jusqu'à St. Jean, et de là à Sorel, établies en Juillet, 1780; Auberges etc. entre Québec et Montréal; Abstraits de l'Ordonnance, du 9 Mars, 1780, concernant la Poste. Par Ordre, Hugh Finlay D.D.G.P. (to right of Calendar printed in 5 columns along length of sheet). This is the first time that the distances, and prices, post houses, and regulations for travelling on the post road between Quebec and Montreal, appeared on the *Calendrier*.

This sheet almanac was sold at 7½*d*. the copy, 5*s*. the dozen from Dec. 18, and advertised for sale at Quebec, Trois Rivières, Berthier, and Montreal, as usual, in the *Quebec gazette*, from Dec. 21, 1780.

Copy located: CaO (bound in *Quebec gazette* at beginning of 1781).

ALMANACS. QUEBEC

[Indian almanack or calendar for 1781] *See* No. 275 and No. 305.

334. CALDWELL

A Mohawk SONG and DANCE. / SEGO Sawerohaddy / Skawiyodiro Skahiyodaddy / [rule] / A TUNE to an Indian DRUM. / Tsi héh danniyo hoya-né / Yané hoh whi. / [text complete as above, within an ornamental frame] Printed for little Master CALDWELL, 1780 /

Broadside: type-page: 10.2 × 8 cm. *Probably printed at Quebec by Wm. Brown, 1780*, for the five-year-old son of Lt.-Col. Henry Caldwell, Seigneur of Lauzon. The child, later Sir John Caldwell (1775-1842), succeeded his father as receiver-general of Lower Canada in 1810.

Copy located: GBLBM (in *Haldimand papers*, Add. MSS. 21885, fo. 121).

335. CHURCH OF ENGLAND. LITURGY AND RITUAL. PRAYER BOOK, *Mohawk*

THE ORDER / For MORNING and EVENING PRAYER, / And ADMINISTRATION of the / SACRAMENTS, / AND SOME OTHER / OFFICES OF THE CHURCH / OF ENGLAND, / Together with / A Collection of Prayers, and some Sentences of the Holy / Scriptures, necessary for Knowledge and Practice. / NE YAKAWEA. / Niyadewighniserage Yondereanayendakhkwa Orhoenkéne, / neoni Yogarask-ha Oghseragwegouh; [etc. eight lines in Mohawk] / [rule] / THE THIRD EDITION, / Formerly collected and translated into the Mohawk or Iroquois Lan-/ guage, under the direction of the Missionaries from the Venerable / Society for the Propagation of the Gospel in foreign Parts, to the / Mohawk Indians. / PUBLISHED / By Order of His Excellency FREDERICK HALDIMAND, / Captain-general and Commander in Chief of all his Majesty's / Forces in the Province of Quebec, and its Dependencies, and / Governor of the same, &c. &c. &c. / Revised with CORRECTIONS and ADDITIONS by / DANIEL CLAUS, Esq; P.T. Agent / For the six Nation Indians in the Province of Quebec. / [rule] / Printed in the Year, M,DCC,LXXX. /

8vo. [*]^4, A-Cc^4; 3 p. l., 208 p., 1 *l.*; type-page: 16 × 9 cm. Text in Mohawk, with English and Mohawk caption titles.

Contents: p. l. 1 recto, t.-p.; verso, blank; p. l. 2 recto-verso, Advertisement; p. l. 3 recto, Contents; verso, blank; p. 1-195, Prayers, etc.; p. 196-208, Psalms, hymns (no music); 1 *l.*, blank.

Printed at Quebec by Wm. Brown, 1780, as recorded:

"1780, Aug. 21. Printed for Daniel Claus Esqr. for Govt. 1000 Copies of an Indian prayer book making 204 pages in 8vo by Agreement—£90.

D°. an Addition of 10 pages taken from manuscript, in proportion to the rest of ye book—£4. 7. 6.

Postage of sundry letters from Montreal with corrected Copy and Prooves —£1. 2. 6. [Total:] £95. 10.

1780, Nov. 18. Paid on Acc^{t} of Daniel Claus Esqr. to P. Picard for binding 100 Mohawk prayer books @ 1/3, as per Picard's receipt filed—£6. 5."

—Can.P.A., *Neilson papers*, v. 47.

Brown's account for £95 10*s*. was paid by the governor's warrant from "monies for contingent and extraordinary expences of His Majesty's Forces," Aug. 30, 1780.

Church of England prayers had been twice translated into Mohawk and three times printed previously in the American colonies (*see* Pilling: *Iroquoian*, 44-46, 126). This publication was prepared for the Mohawks, previously living in upper New York, who had moved into Canada during the Revolution and who, as Claus said, "feared lest Divine worship among them must become obsolete and their posterity fall into heathen darkness again." With Claus's primer (*see* No. 355) it was to strengthen English influence among the Indians but was apparently less successful than the primer. Claus wrote to Morice, secretary of the Society for the Propagation of the Gospel, London, from Montreal, Oct. 9, 1782: "Since ye public^{n} of ye Books there have been delivered out upwards of 250 Prayer Books and as many primers . . . the French R^{n} C^{c} Indians having seen the Book of Prayers &c with ye Mohks in this Neighborhood are very anxious to have them, and demanded some of both kinds from me wch I granted. But their Missionaries have forbid them by pain of Excomm^{n} to ask for any more, they found a primer among them wch they publicly burnt. There are about 600 copies of the prayer Books unbound in the Library at Quebec. I thought if they were interspersed with prints of the different Offices as usual in common prayer Books with a Frontispiece representing His Majesty delivering the Book to an Ind^{n} kneeling &c it would please an ignorant set of people much. This I leave to [your] better judgement . . . I have not 50 of the Primers left and I apprehend there will be a demand for a Second edition. In which I propose some amendments or alter & add anything the Society may think necessary."—Can.P.A., *Claus papers*, 3: 177-79.

When the Society published its edition of the prayer book in 1787, however, it printed a new translation by Joseph Brant.

Copies located: CSmH; CaQM; DLC; Ketcheson; MB; N; NNHi; RPJ.

336. FARGUES, PETER, *d.* 1780

[CATALOGUE FOR SALE OF PETER FARGUES' BOOKS AND FURNITURE, QUEBEC, APRIL 26, 1780.]

Printed at Quebec by Wm. Brown, 1780, as recorded:

"1780, April 15. Printed for Melvin & Wills [auctioneers and brokers, Quebec] 300 Catalogues for Sale P. Fargues books & Furniture on Demy—£2.7.6." —Can.P.A., *Neilson papers*, v. 47.

Peter Fargues, a merchant in Quebec, died Jan. 20, 1780. The sale was advertised: "[To be sold on Apr. 26, 1780] at the late Mr. Peter Fargues House—Lower Town, . . . a large parcel of elegant Household furniture, wines, &c., &c. Also, A choice collection of Books, French and English, by the most reputed Authors. Catalogues of which may be had by applying to Melvin & Wills, auctioneers and brokers. N.B. There are many sets of valuable books broke, which cannot be sold unless those wanting are returned previous to the time of the Sale, [etc.]"—*Quebec gazette*, Apr. 13, 1780.

This item, the earliest book catalogue actually recorded in Canada, represents a type of printing job, as well as a feature of social life, becoming more frequent as settlement increased in Quebec, Montreal, and Halifax.

Copy located: None.

337. HENRY, GEORGE, 1710?-1795

BROTHERLY LOVE / EXPLAINED AND RECOMMENDED, / IN A / SERMON, / PREACHED BEFORE THE / ANCIENT AND HONOURABLE / SOCIETY / OF / FREE AND ACCEPTED / MASONS, / AT QUEBEC, / ON MONDAY the 27th of DECEMBER, 1779. / BY THE / REV. GEORGE HENRY, M.A. / [rule] / PUBLISHED at the REQUEST of the SOCIETY. / [rule] / QUEBEC: / PRINTED by WILLIAM BROWN, / M,DCC, LXXX. /

8vo. [*]^{2} A-B^{4}; 19 p.; type-page: 15 × 9 cm.

Contents: p. [1], t.-p.; p. [2], blank; p. [3], "To the Right Worshipful . . . John Collins Esq; grand master of this province [etc.] . . . This Discourse delivered and published at their Request, is inscribed"; p. [4], blank; p. [5]-19, "A Sermon &c. Let brotherly Love continue. Heb. xiii, I"; p. 19 verso, blank.

Printed in an edition of three hundred copies, issued stitched in gray [blue?] paper covers distributed by the Freemasons at 1*s.* the copy, as the printer's records and newspaper advertisements indicate:

"1780, Feb. 4. Printed for Tho[s]. Aylwin 300 Sermons explaining and recommending Brotherly Love, by G. Henry. By Ag[t]. [Agreement] 34 Spanish Dollars. delivered in Sheets.—£8.10. Paid 7th."

—Can.P.A., *Neilson papers*, v. 47.

"1780, Feb. 17. [Credit] To Printing Office for 300 Sermons on Brotherly love, 1¼ Sheet 8vo. on pica—£8.10." —*ibid.*, v. 45.

Advertised: "This Day is Published. Price One Shilling in Octavo Stitched, Best type and Paper. A Sermon . . . by the Rev. M[r]. Henry. To be had of Mr. John Franks and Messrs Brown & Gibbon at Quebec, Mr. T. M. Murray at Montreal and Mr. M'Pherson at Three Rivers."—*Quebec gazette*, Feb. 17, 1780.

Rev. Mr. Henry, ordained in the Church of Scotland, came to America as a military chaplain, and was appointed minister to the Presbyterian church in Quebec, when a congregation was organized there about 1765. His obituary stated that he "died, in his eighty-sixth year [on July 6, 1795] . . . thirty years minister of the Presbyterian church at Quebec. An able divine . . . an useful teacher of Christianity and an ornament to Society."—*Quebec gazette*, July 9, 1795.

Copy located: CaQMS.

338. NOVA SCOTIA. HOUSE OF ASSEMBLY

Caption title: (1) / [ornamental rule] / JOURNAL and VOTES / OF THE / HOUSE of ASSEMBLY, / For the Province of Nova-Scotia. / [rule] / Monday October 9th, 1780. /

fo. A-E²; 20 p.; type-page: 27.5 × 16 cm. *Printed at Halifax, N.S., by Anthony Henry, 1780.*

Contents: Journal and votes of the thirteenth session of the fifth assembly Oct. 9-Nov. 3, 1780.

Copies located: CaNSA; CaNs (2 cop.); CaNsHA; GBLP (in C.O. 217/55: 125-44; another copy p. 1-4, 9-12 only, in C.O. 217/28: 151-58).

339. NOVA SCOTIA. LAWS, STATUTES, *etc.*

Running title: [rule] / 1780. Anno Vicessimo Regis GEORGII III. CAP. I[-III]. / [rule] /

Caption title: At the GENERAL-ASSEMBLY of the Province / of Nova-Scotia . . . / [8 lines] / . . . being the Seventh [sic] / GENERAL ASSEMBLY convened in the said / Province. / [double rule] /

fo. R² p. 343-345 paged in continuation of No. 317. *Printed at Halifax, N.S., by Anthony Henry, 1780.*

Contents: p. 343-345, Cap. I-III, perpetual acts passed in the thirteenth session of the fifth assembly, Oct. 9-Nov. 3, 1780; p. 345 verso, blank.

Copy located: DLC.

340. NOVA SCOTIA. LAWS, STATUTES, *etc.*

Running title: [rule] / 1780. Anno Vicessimo Regis, GEORGII III. CAP. I[-VII] / [rule] /

Caption title: At the GENERAL-ASSEMBLY of the Province / of Nova-Scotia, . . . / [8 lines] / . . . being the Seventh [sic] GENERAL ASSEMBLY convened in the said / Province. / [double rule] /

fo. p. 213-218; paged in continuation of No. 318. [*Printed at Halifax, N.S., by Anthony Henry, 1780.*]

Contents: p. 213-218, Cap. I-VII, temporary acts passed in the thirteenth session of the fifth assembly.

Copies located: MH; NNB.

341. QUEBEC, *Province.* COURT OF QUARTER SESSIONS OF THE PEACE (Quebec District)

[District of Quebec . . . Regulations for Carters, etc. *Quebec, Wm. Brown, 1780.*]

Probably fo. [2] p., text in 2 col., English and French, reprinted from *Quebec gazette,* May 11, 1780. Brown recorded the printing:

"1780, May 31. Printed for Gov^{t} by Order of D. Lynd. 150 Double [i.e. English and French] regulations of Police, also in Gazette—£5.10."

—Can.P.A., *Neilson papers,* v. 47.

Contents: Preamble, quoting ordinance authorizing commissioners of the peace to regulate police; Record of a meeting of the court, Apr. 11-22, 1780; Regulations for carters, I-XVIII; Regulations for police, I-XIX; Regulations for public ferries; Signed: "For the Court, David Lynd, C.P."

This entry represents a type of publication frequently produced from the early Canadian printing offices. The commissioners', or justices', of the peace regulations appeared regularly in the local *Gazette,* sometimes for several weeks after their enactment. Sometimes offprints were issued separately (as above). Occasionally a separate edition was printed from larger types. These regulations were published also with the *Ordinances* of 1780 (No. 343).

Copy located: None.

342. QUEBEC, *Province.* GOVERNOR, 1778-1786 (*Haldimand*)

Heading: BY / FREDERICK HALDIMAND, / Captain-General and Governor in Chief of the Province of / QUEBEC and Territories depending thereon, &c.&c.&c. / General and Commander in Chief of His Majesty's Forces in said Province / and Frontiers thereof &c.&c.&c. /

fo. text, [2] p. on recto and verso of *l.* 1; *l.* 2, blank. *Printed at Quebec by Wm. Brown, 1780,* as recorded:

"1780, Sept. 2. Printed for Milit^{y} Sec^{y} 100 Declarations to the oppress'd Inhabitants on the frontiers and two intercepted Letters on a Sheet of fine foolscap on both sides—£2.17.6." —Can.P.A., *Neilson papers,* v. 70.

Contents: p. [1]: Declaration, with heading as above and text: "Being informed of the distressed Situation in which the Inhabitants of the back Settlements bordering on Canada are, and being well assured that very many of them, wearied out with the Oppression and Tyranny under which they have groaned for some Time, are desirous of returning to their Allegiance, . . . I therefore promise to such of them (without Exception) as will surrender themselves to the Commanding Officers of His Majesty's Garrisons . . . on the Frontiers, a safe and commodious Retreat, in the interiour Parts of Canada, . . . until such Time, as Peace being restored . . . they may . . . return to their Habitations . . . ; but on the contrary, if under a Pretence of retiring from the oppression of the Congress, they continue their Encroachments upon the Indian Country . . . reserved, by Treaty, for the Indians, all [such] persons . . . must be considered as Abettors of the Rebellion [etc.]. Given under my Hand at Quebec in the Year of our Lord 1780."

p. [2]: "The following Letters, which were lately intercepted on the Ohio, are published to shew the distressed Situation of the revolted Provinces, and to undeceive the unhappy People who have so long been the Victims of the ambitious and interested Views of their Leaders." Then follow texts of two letters, the first, dated at Williamsburg, Mar. 19, 1780 is signed: "Th: Jefferson" and is addressed "To Col. Todd." It announces the withdrawal "of troops in the Illinois . . . to the South side of the Ohio where our paper money is current." It also treats of Congress's lack of cash and credit at home and abroad and gives Todd instructions concerning bills. The second letter, dated at Williamsburg, Mar. 19, 1780 and signed "Th. Jefferson," is addressed "To Col. Clarke." It touches the same topics as the first letter and includes instruction that Clarke abandon attack on Detroit, that he consider a campaign against hostile Indians, and that he aid militia in crushing an insurrection of Tories.

This publication was probably never issued, for the only copy located (in Gov. Haldimand's papers in the British Museum) bears MS. note on verso of the blank leaf: "Proclamation intended to have been issued upon the Ohio." A MS. transcript of the entire work is in Can.P.A., "B" 220 p. 173-80 (calendared in Can.P.A., *Report, 1889*, 103). The text of the intercepted letters is abstracted in Can.P.A., *Report, 1888*, 777-78.

Copy located: GBLBM (in *Haldimand papers*, Add. MSS. 21880, fo. 195-96).

343. QUEBEC, *Province*. LAWS, STATUTES, *etc.*

ORDINANCES / MADE AND PASSED / BY THE / GOVERNOR / AND / LEGISLATIVE COUNCIL / OF THE / PROVINCE / OF / QUEBEC. / [rule] / [royal arms] / [double rule] / QUEBEC: / Printed by WILLIAM BROWN, in Mountain-Street. / [rule] / M,DCC,LXXX. /

French t.-p.:

ORDONNANCES / FAITES ET PASSÉES / PAR LE / GOUVERNEUR / ET LE / CONSEIL LEGISLATIF / DE LA / PROVINCE / DE / QUÉBEC. / [rule] / [royal arms] / [double rule] / A QUEBEC: / Chez GUILLAUME BROWN, au milieu de la Grande Côte. / [rule] / M,DCC,LXXX. /

fo. [*][2], A-[X][2]; 1 p. l., [i], 86 p., 1 *l.*; type-page: 23.3 × 13 cm.; odd numbers on verso, even numbers on recto; text in English and French on opposite pages.

Contents: p. l. recto, English t.-p.; verso, blank; p. [i] (recto of p. 1), French t.-p.; p. 1-2, Proclamation announcing royal disallowance of 17 Geo. III c. XVI, An ordinance concerning the estates . . . of persons leaving the province without paying their debts; p. 3-8, Ordinances, 19 Geo. III c. 1-3; p. 9-70, Ordinances, 20 Geo. III c. 1-4; p. 71-86, District of Quebec, Court of quarter sessions of the peace, Quebec, Apr. 11-22, 1780: Regulations for carters, police, public ferries; verso of p. 86, blank; 1 *l.* at end, blank (in some copies folded around back to precede t.-p.; frequently lacking altogether).

The printer, Wm. Brown, recorded this work:

"1780, Aug. 21, Printed for Govt. by Order of Mr. Williams [secretary to Governor] and dd [delivered] Picard [book binder] 200 Copies of the Ordinances made in 1779 & 1780, making a volume of 22½ Sheets on folio pott @ 60—£67.10." —Can.P.A., *Neilson papers*, v. 47.

Brown sold the volume retail at 17*s.* 6*d.* the copy, from the beginning of August. All of the text had appeared previously, from time to time, in the *Gazette*, and the *Regulations* were also issued separately, printed from the *Gazette* types. The ordinances are reprinted in Can.P.A., *Report, 1914-15.*

Copies located: CaO; CaOOA; CaOT; CaOTO (2 cop.); CaQM; CaQMA (defective); CaQQL (2 cop.); GBLP (2 cop.: in C.O. 42/40 p. 471-559; C.O. 44/3); M; MH; NN; NNB (2 cop.); PHi; RPJ; WHi.

344. QUEBEC, *Province.* LAWS, STATUTES, *etc.*

[Anno Vicesimo Georgii III. Regis. Chap. 3. An Ordinance for regulating all such persons as keep horses and carriages to let and hire, for the accomodation of travellers, commonly called and known by the name of maîtres de poste.]

French side:

[Anno Vicesimo Georgii III. Regis. Chap. 4. Ordonnance qui régle tous les particuliers qui tiendront des chevaux et voitures de louage, pour la commodité des voiageurs, vulgairement appellés et connus sous le nom de maîtres de poste.]

? Double broadside. *Printed at Quebec by Wm. Brown, 1780,* as recorded:

"1780, Sept. 12. Printed for the Govt. or Hugh Finlay by his Order 48 Copies of the Road Ordinance.—17/6." —Can.P.A., *Neilson papers*, v. 47.

20 Geo. III c. 4, passed Mar. 9, 1780, this ordinance contains schedules of distances, prices, and conditions of service for post horses, carriages, ferries, etc., in the province. Hugh Finlay, deputy postmaster-general for Canada and superintendent of maîtres de poste, had tried repeatedly to have the transportation system regulated by ordinance. He drew up the heads of a bill in Mar., 1777 and prepared memoranda from time to time for the governor-in-council (Can.P.A., *Finlay papers*, 1777 *et seq.*). The ordinance, finally passed in 1780 for two years, was renewed by 35 Geo. III c. 7, sec. 1. It is reprinted in Can.P.A., *Report, 1914-15* (from which this entry is taken).

Copy located: None.

345. QUEBEC GAZETTE. CARRIER'S ADDRESS

NEW-YEAR'S / VERSES / Of the PRINTER'S BOY, who carries about the / Quebec Gazette to the CUSTOMERS. / JANUARY 1, 1781. / [*Quebec, Wm. Brown, 1780.*]

Broadside: 37 lines; type-page: 21.5 × 13 cm. in ornamental frame.

Contents: 8 stanzas of 4 lines each without local or political reference.

"Serious and solemn be the song
Which hails this still-returning day;
Let measure guide the rhyme along,
And gratitude inspire the lay.
[Etc.]"

Copy located: CaO (bound in *Quebec gazette* at beginning of 1781).

346. ROGERS, ROBERT, 1731-1795

[Petition for Discovering the North West Passage.]

Printed at Quebec by Wm. Brown, 1780, as recorded:*

"1780, Feb. 16. Printed for R. Rogers 250 Petitions for Discovering the North West Passage. 8½ g^{s} [guineas] per Ag^{t}.—£9.18.4."

—Can.P.A., *Neilson papers*, v. 47.

"Rogers the Ranger," a New-Englander, bred to bush life was in more or less continuous colonial military service from 1755. A loyalist in the Revolution, he recruited for the British, notably the Queen's Rangers, but throughout his varied and adventurous career he seldom held the confidence of administrative officials except as an Indian fighter. On Aug. 12, 1765, and again in Feb., 1772, he presented memorials in London begging permission and support to explore for the "North West Passage"—without success (*see* Allan Nevin's *Introduction* in Rogers' *Ponteach*, Chicago, 1914). Wintering riotously in Quebec, 1779-80, Rogers apparently revived his scheme and prepared this printed petition to carry to England in Apr., 1780. No evidence has appeared to show that the petition was approved or even presented (Rogers material, scattered through several series in the Public Record Office, London, has been searched for reference to this 1780 petition, without result), and Rogers returned to America no more.

Copy located: None.

347. ACCOUNT . . . OF . . . RELIGION . . . IN . . . NISQUEUNIA

[An account of the matter, form and manner of a new and strange Religion taught and propagated by a number of Europeans living in a place called NISQUEUNIA in the state of New York. *Halifax, N.S., Anthony Henry, 1781.*]

The price for printing suggests a work of some difficulty, or of some size—perhaps a pamphlet of sixteen pages or so, judging by the price of printing No. 337.

*Brown recorded several other transactions with Lieut-Col. Robert Rogers in Feb., 1780, mainly in printed blanks "for enlisting Rangers."

This work was advertised in a single issue only of Henry's newspaper:

"Just published and sold at Mr. Henry's Printing Office, An Account of the matter[etc., title as cited above] (Price 8*d*.)."—*Nova-Scotia gazette*, **July 31, 1781**.

It was probably a pamphlet published (or imported?) by the German-born printer, Anthony Henry, for distribution among members of the Dutch Reformed Church—mainly in the German settlement at Lunenburg, Nova Scotia. It probably related to a revival movement in the Dutch Reformed Church at Niskayuna, a settlement on the Mohawk River near Schenectady, N.Y.

Copy located: None.

348. ALLINE, HENRY, 1748-1784

TWO MITES / ON / Some of the MOST IMPORTANT and / much disputed POINTS of / DIVINITY, / Cast into the TREASURY for the Welfare / of the Poor and Needy, and committed / to the Perusal of the unprejudiced and / impartial READER, / BY HENRY ALLINE, / Servant of the LORD to his / CHURCHES. / [ornamental rule] / HALIFAX: Printed by A. HENRY. / [rule] / MDCCLXXXI. / [title within ornamental frame]

16mo. A-X[8]; [vii], 342 p., 1 *l*.; type-page: 12.6 × 6.8 cm. odd numbers on verso, even numbers on recto.

Contents: p. [i], t.-p.; p. [ii], blank; p. [iii-vii], Preface; p. 1-342, Two mites, etc.; p. 342 verso, blank; 1 *l*. at end, blank.

Henry Alline, born in Newport, R.I., in 1748, came to Nova Scotia with his parents in 1760, settling at Falmouth, where in 1775 he experienced a profound religious conversion. Bred (and ordained) a Congregationalist, strongly influenced by the New Light movement in New England, and having intense conviction and a lively eloquence, Alline became the prophet of a religious awakening in Nova Scotia. From 1776 till 1783 he travelled from settlement to settlement preaching continuously. (Several of his sermons were published, as were his *Hymns and Spiritual Songs*, Boston, 1786.) Alline's message of individual salvation, with his naive sincerity and dramatic style, had a moving appeal to some members of all denominations, and his activity disrupted congregations wherever they had been organized. John Wesley warned Benjamin Chappell in the Island of St. John, against Alline in a letter from London, Nov. 27, 1783: ". . . But I doubt whether Henry Alline be not the person . . . who has wrote and published a book* which is full of broad ranting Anti-nominianism . . . He is a wild absurd man, wiser in his own eyes than seven men that can render a reason; and he has done much mischief among the serious persons there, setting every man's sword against his brother . . . Have a care of him, for he will do more harm among you than ever he can do good."—*Letters of John Wesley* (ed. by J. Telford, 8 v., London, 1931), 7: 200. So spoke most of the clergy in Nova Scotia, but Alline held them in controversy (*see* No. 442) and part at least of their congregations in a religious enthusiasm, till he succumbed to tuberculosis in 1784. His converts did not cohere as an organized sect and, after his death, drifted eventually into the dissenting churches, especially the Baptist, strengthening the evangelical element therein. *See The life and journal of the Rev. Mr. Henry Alline* (180 p., Boston, 1806); also Ian F. MacKinnon: *Settlements and churches in Nova*

*Probably *The Anti-traditionalist*, No. 386.

Scotia, 1749-1776 (Halifax, 1930), with further bibliographical references; also Samuel D. Clark: *Church and sect in Canada* (Toronto, 1949), chaps. I, IV.

This work was reprinted: *Two mites cast into the offering of God for the benefit of mankind, by Henry Alline . . . with some amendments by Bejamin Randle, minister of the Gospel at New Durham, New Hampshire* (iv, 250 p., Dover, N.H., 1804).

Copies located: CaNsHD; CaNsWA.

349. ALMANACS. NOVA SCOTIA

[Astronomical diary, or Almanack, calculated for the Meridian of Halifax in Nova Scotia, for the year 1782. *Halifax, John Howe, 1781.*]

The only record of this publication occurs in a long article devoted to it, occupying the entire first page of the *Nova-Scotia gazette*, Mar. 19, 1782. The article gives detailed criticism of the astronomical information in "Astronomical Diary or Almanac, said in its title page to be calculated for the Meridian of Halifax in Nova Scotia for this year 1782." The writer shows its errors in calculation of latitude, longitude, moon and sun age, and time, etc., and ends, saying that he sends this criticism so that "my own poor labours in this same line, are not corrected by the anonymous performance alluded to . . . an imposition upon both printer and public, and a base insult to the noble science of Astronomy. [signed:] Your humble servant, Metonicus, Halifax, 24th Jan. 1782."

Metonicus prepared the calculations for Anthony Henry's *Nova-Scotia Calender* from about 1776 till at least the end of the century. His article suggests that a rival almanac, the *Astronomical Diary*, was produced in Halifax probably by the recent arrival, John Howe, or alternatively, that Henry and Howe together produced an almanac for 1782, using another astronomer's calculations.

Copy located: None.

350. ALMANACS. NOVA SCOTIA

[The Nova-Scotia Calender, or an Almanack for . . . 1782 . . . Calculated for the meridian of Halifax . . . by Metonicus. *Halifax, N.S., Anthony Henry, 1781.*]

The only evidence of publication of the *Nova-Scotia Calender* for this year is its otherwise unbroken continuity from 1768 till the end of the century, and the inference drawn from Metonicus's criticism of rival calculations, which he wrote as a defence of his own (*see* No. 349).

Copy located: None.

351. ALMANACS. QUEBEC

Almanach / curieux / et intéressant / pour l'année / mil sept cent quatre-vingt-deux. / [printer's ornament] / A Montréal / chez Fleury Mesplet, Impri-/meur & Libraire. / M.DCC.LXXXII. /

48 p.; paper-page: 12 × 8 cm.

Contents: p. [1], t.-p.; p. [2], blank; p. [3]-48, text. This work, like No. 331, was probably produced by Madame Mesplet and some assistant in the printing office.

Wm. Brown, the printer in Quebec, received a copy of this "Montreal Pocket Almanack" from his Montreal agent, E. Edwards, Feb. 20, 1782, and paid a shilling for it.

Copy located: CaQMS (described in Fauteux: *Mesplet*, no. 38, from which this description is taken).

352. ALMANACS. QUEBEC

ALMANACH / DE / QUEBEC, / POUR / L'ANNEE / M,DCC,LXXXII. / [double rule] / [printer's ornament] / [double rule] / A QUEBEC: / Chez GUILLAUME BROWN, sur la / Grande Côte. /

12mo. A-D^6; 48 p.; type-page: 10.5 × 6 cm.

Contents: p. [1], t.-p.; p. [2-4], Epoques, fêtes, eclipses; p. [5-16], Calendrier, p. 17-24, Officiers civils de Québec; p. 25-29, la Poste, Québec à Montréal; p. 30-35, Instructions pour les capitaines de milices; p. 36, Poids de la monnaie; p. 37-41, Catalogue du clergé; p. 41-44, Historie la plus moderne des barres électriques à detourner à foudre; p. 44-48, Anecdotes etc. The text is entirely in French except the militia instructions which appear also in English.

This was the second number of the *Almanach de Québec*, as none was published for 1781. It was issued on Dec. 20, 1781, and sold at 1*s*. 8*d*. the copy (2*s*. interleaved), and at 15*s*. the dozen. In Montreal, it was to be sold "at the Montreal price" [i.e the same price as Mesplet's *Almanach*], Brown instructed his agent, Edward Edwards, sending him 150 copies at the year's end and possibly others later, all of which were sold in Montreal excepting 14 copies, returned to Brown in Sept., 1782.

Copies located: CaOOA; CaQQL.

353. ALMANACS. QUEBEC

CALENDRIER pour l'Année 1782, pour Québec, par les 306$^{d.}$ 30$^{m.}$ de Longitude, et 46$^{d.}$ 55$^{m.}$ de Latitude. / [ornamental rule] /

Colophon: A QUEBEC: chez WM. BROWN, au milieu de la Grande Côte. /

Broadside: type-page: 52 × 39 cm.

Contents: Calendrier (in ornamental rule frame 44.5 × 38.5 cm.); Officiers civils, (beneath *Calendrier*); Note on arrangement of *Calendrier* (printed lengthwise of the sheet in right margin).

This sheet almanac was advertised (in the *Quebec gazette* from Nov. 19, 1781) as for sale in Quebec, Trois Rivières, Berthier, and Montreal. It was sold (from Dec. 3) at 1*s*. the copy (a rise in price, above that of former editions, of 4½*d*.) and at 7*s*. 6*d*. the dozen.

Brown sent instructions to his agents to meet the price of Mesplet's *Calendrier pour Montréal* (which was 10*d*.) but he continued to sell his *Calendrier* in Quebec at a shilling the copy. Of the thirty-four dozen *Calendriers* which he sent Edwards in Dec., 1781, to sell in Montreal itself, only seventeen copies were returned unsold in Sept., 1782.

Copy located: CaO (bound in the *Quebec gazette* at end of 1781).

354. ALMANACS. QUEBEC

Calendrier / pour Montréal qui est par les 71 degrés 49m. 45″ de Longitude ouest, méridien de Londres & 45 degrés 30m. de Latitude septentrionale pour l'année 1782 /

Colophon: A Montréal, chez Fleury Mesplet, Imprimeur Libraire où se trouve l'Almanach de poche, 1782.

Broadside: paper-page: 52 × 38.5 cm.

Edward Edwards, a merchant-stationer in Montreal, sent a copy of Mesplet's *Calendrier, 1782* to Wm. Brown the printer in Quebec, and charged him 10*d*.

Copy located: CaQMS (described in Fauteux: *Mesplet*, no. 40, from which this description is taken).

ALMANACS. QUEBEC

[Indian calendar or almanack for 1782] *See* No. 276, 306.

355. CLAUS, DANIEL, 1727-1787

A / PRIMER / FOR THE / USE OF THE MOHAWK CHILDREN, / To acquire the Spelling and Reading / of their own: As well as to get ac-/quainted with the English Tongue, / which for that purpose is put on the / opposite Page. / WAERIGHWAGHSAWE IKSA-/ONGOENWA Tsiwaondad-derigh-/ honny Kaghyadoghsera; Nayondewe-/yestaghk ayeweanaghnòdon ayeghyà-/dow Kaniyenkehàga Kaweanondagh-/ kouh; Dyorheas-hàga oni tsinihadiwea-/notea. / [rule] / Montreal, Printed at Fleury Mesplets, / 1781. /

16mo. A⁸, B¹, C-G⁸, [H]²; 18, [1], 19-97 p.; type-page: 12.3 × 7 cm. In the second signature, the first leaf (p. 17-18) is signed: B, the second and fourth leaf: C, C3; recto of second leaf is blank and omitted in pagination, verso paged: 19; thence to the end, odd page numbers appear on verso. After [C7] an unsigned leaf is inserted with recto paged 32, verso blank, and pasted to blank recto of p. 33 (D1). Text in English and Mohawk.

Contents: p. [i], t.-p.; p. 2-18, Alphabet, syllabics, etc.; [1] (recto of p. 19), blank; p. 19-93, Catechisms, prayers, scriptural readings; p. 93-97, Numerals.

Though this work bears Mesplet's imprint, it was printed without benefit of his skill, as its uncouth imposition and press work testify. For Mesplet was smouldering in the jail at Quebec from June, 1779 till Sept., 1782, suspect of revolutionary activities in Montreal. It was probably printed in Mesplet's shop, however, with whatever assistance the latter's wife could muster. About three hundred copies were struck off (*see* No. 335 *note*). The text, which appears accurate enough, was closely supervised by Daniel Claus, a son-in-law of Sir Wm. Johnson, and deputy superintendent of Indians in Canada, 1760-87. This was the second Mohawk primer published in Montreal and differs slightly in linguistics and in text from that prepared under French Catholic auspices (No. 265).

It proved extremely useful among the pro-British Mohawks settling in Canada at this time. Claus wrote to Gov. Haldimand from Montreal, Sept. 27, 1781: ". . . I have nominated a Clerk to read prayers on Sunday and a Schoolmaster to teach the Children to read and write, and to facilitate the latter's teaching, have composed in my Leisure hours a primer in Mohawk and English (the first they ever had [!]) which may make those of some genius acquainted with the reading of English & be a help to become good Interpreters. They are fond of the little Book, both old & young & I have already from the Mohawks at Niagara rec[d] Messages to send some there. I shall send your Excellency a specimen of it by the first opportunity." —Can.P.A., "B" 114: 200.

Reproduced in Massachusetts historical society, *Photostat Americana*, second ser., no. 114, 1940.

A second edition, with a frontispiece by James Peachey depicting a class of Mohawk children, was printed for the Society for the Propagation of the Gospel, in London, 1786 (*see* Toronto Public Library, *Bibliography of Canadiana*, no. 543).

Copies located: GBLBM; NN (t.-p. facsim. in Pilling: *Iroquoian*, 138); Museum of the American Indian, Huntington Free Library, 8 Westchester Sq., The Bronx, N.Y.

356. MELVIN & WILLS, *Auctioneers & brokers, Quebec*

[Catalogue of furs saved out of the ship *General Haldimand*, to be sold, June 20, 1781, at auction.]

Printed at Quebec, by Wm. Brown, 1781; whose charge would suggest the work to be a pamphlet of about eight pages, or more.

> "1781, June 13. Print d for Melvin & Wills 300 Catalogues for sale of furs sav'd out of the General Haldimand—£6.10."
>
> —Can.P.A., *Neilson papers*, v. 47.

The sale was advertised: "To be sold by Public Auction at the British Coffee House [Quebec] on 20th June next, at ten o clock forenoon, for the benefit of the under writers and others concerned—A large quantity of furs & peltries of all sorts sav'd out of the ship General Haldimand stranded below Bic. The Furs may be seen at Messrs Johnson & Purss Store . . . and Catalogues may be had from Melvin & Wills."—*Quebec gazette*, May 31, 1781.

Copy located: None.

357. NOVA SCOTIA. HOUSE OF ASSEMBLY

Caption title: [Journal and Votes of the House of Assembly for the Province of Nova-Scotia]

Note: title above is not transcribed from copy.

fo. A-G^2; 28 p. *Printed at Halifax, N.S., by Anthony Henry, 1781.*

Contents: sig. A-G^2; p. 1-28, Journal and votes of the fourteenth session of the fifth assembly, June 11-July 5, 1781.

Copies located: CaNs (2 cop.); CaNsHA (p. 1-4 wanting); MH (p. 1-8, 21-24 wanting); GBLP (in C.O. 220/1: 991-1018).

358. NOVA SCOTIA. LAWS, STATUTES, *etc.*

Running title: [rule] / 1781. Anno Vicessimo Primo GEORGII III. [sic] CAP. I[-VI]. / [rule] /

Caption title: At the GENERAL-ASSEMBLY of the Pro-/vince of Nova-Scotia, . . . / [9 lines] / being the Seventh [sic] GENERAL-AS-/ SEMBLY convened in the said Pro-/vince. / [ornamental rule] /

fo. sig. 5 P^2 [*]^1; p. 347-351; paged in continuation of No. 339. *Printed at Halifax, N.S., by Anthony Henry, 1781.*

Contents: p. 347-351, Cap. I-VI, perpetual acts passed in the fourteenth session of the fifth assembly, June 11-July 5, 1781; p. 351 verso, blank.

Copy located: DLC; MH.

359. NOVA SCOTIA. LAWS, STATUTES, *etc.*

Running title: [rule] / 1781. Anno Vicessimo Primo GEORGII III. [sic] CAP. I[-V]. / [rule] /

Caption title: At the GENERAL-ASSEMBLY of the Pro-/vince of Nova-Scotia, . . . / [9 lines] / being the Seventh [sic] GENERAL-AS- / SEMBLY convened in the said Province. / [ornamental rule] /

fo. p. 219-223; paged in continuation of No. 340. *Printed at Halifax, N.S., by Anthony Henry, 1781.*

Contents: p. 219-223, Cap. I-V, temporary acts passed in the fourteenth session of the fifth assembly, June 11-July 5, 1781; p. 223 verso, blank.

Copies located: MH; NNB.

360. QUEBEC, *Province.* GOVERNOR, 1778-1786 (*Haldimand*)

By His EXCELLENCY / FREDERICK HALDIMAND, / Captain-general and Governor in Chief of . . . / . . . QUEBEC, . . . / . . . / . . . / . . . / PROCLAMATION. / <Text> / Given . . . at the Castle of St. Lewis . . . / [15 Jan. 1781] . . . / . . . / FRED: HALDIMAND. / [3 lines]

French on right:

Par Son EXCELLENCE / FREDERIC HALDIMAND, / Capitaine-general et Gouverneur en Chef . . . en la / Province de Québec . . . / . . . / . . . / . . . / PROCLAMATION. / <Text> / Donné . . . au Château St. Louis, . . . / [15 jan. 1781] . . . / . . . / (Signé) FRED: HALDIMAND. / [5 lines] /

Double broadside: English on left, 42 lines, type-page: 24 × 17.5 cm.; French on right, 43 lines, type-page: 24 × 17.5 cm. *Printed at Quebec by Wm. Brown, 1781,* as recorded:

"1781, Jan. 13. Printed for the Government by Order of the Sec^y 300 Proclamations ordering the inhabitants to give in an account of their corn and cattle—£3.10."—Can.P.A., *Neilson papers*, v. 47.

English text: "Whereas the safety of the property of his Majesty's liege Subjects, and the necessary defence of this province, may speedily require that all Grain, Cattle and Provisions, which might . . . afford succour to an Invasion in this province by the King's subjects in Rebellion, should be deposited in places of security, [etc. 22 lines, giving orders for subjects to thresh and prepare grain, ready for removal if necessary, and for militia captains to take count of cattle, grain and flour, reporting results to district headquarters]."

French text: "La sureté des propriétés apartenans aux Fidels Sujets de sa Majesté et la défense de cette Province, pouvant éxiger que tous les Grains, Bestiaux et Denrées . . . qui pouraient . . . aider les sujets Rebels de sa Majesté dans l'invasion de cette Province, soient deposés en lieux surs . . . [etc. 21 lines]."

Lieut.-Gov. Cramahé objected to this measure as "equally improper and impolitic; What end could it answer but to alarm the People, encourage Cabals, and give time to the Enemies of Government to concert Measures for distressing it effectively [etc.]." He recommended that the supplies be purchased with cash indirectly for the government, but Haldimand objected that this plan was too slow for the existing emergency.—Can.P.A., "B" 95; 94-100.

The proclamation was distributed for publication by the parish clergy, accompanied by a confidential circular from the bishop of Quebec "pour diriger votre conduite et vous faire connaitre ce que notre Gouverneur attend de votre religion et de votre attachement au gouvernement."

The proclamation is reprinted in Can.P.A., *Report, 1918*, also (English side only) in Ont. Archives, *Report, 1906*. It was reproclaimed in 1782 and 1783 (*see* No. 379, 404).

Copies located: CaOOA (cropped); CaQQL.

361. QUEBEC, *Province.* LAWS, STATUTES, *etc.*

[Anno vicesimo primo Georgii III Regis. Chap. I. An Ordinance for further continuing . . . "An Ordinance to regulate the proceedings in the Courts of Civil Judicature in the Province of Quebec."

. . . . Chap. II. An Ordinance for further continuing . . . "An Ordinance for regulating the Militia, etc."

. . . . Chap. III. An Ordinance for further continuing . . . "An Ordinance to empower the Commissioners of the Peace to regulate the Police of the Towns of Quebec and Montreal for a limited time."]

French side:

[Anno vicesimo primo Georgii III regis. Chap. I. Une ordonnance pour continuer . . . "Une ordonnance pour réglementer les procédures dans la cour de judicature civile de la province de Québec."

. . . . Chap. II. Une ordonnance pour continuer . . . "Une ordonnance pour réglementer la milice de la province de Québec."

. . . . Chap. III. Une ordonnance pour continuer . . . "Une ordonnance pour autoriser les commissaires de la paix à réglementer la police dans les villes de Québec et de Montréal durant une période limitée."]

Double broadside? Text in English and French. *Printed at Quebec by Wm. Brown, 1781,* as recorded:

"1781, Jan. 26. Printed for Gov[t] by Order of Mr. Williams [i.e. Jenkin Williams, clerk of the Legislative Council] 200 Copies of three Ordinances—£4.17.6."
—Can.P.A., *Neilson papers,* v. 47.

These ordinances were passed Jan. 20, 1781, to continue for two years laws previously enacted for a limited period. They were printed also (from another setting of type, at a charge of £4 6*s.* 3*d.*) in the *Quebec gazette,* Jan. 25, 1781, and reprinted in Can.P.A., *Report, 1914-15* (from which this entry is taken in an abbreviated form).

Copy located: None.

362. QUEBEC GAZETTE. CARRIER'S ADDRESS

NEW-YEAR'S / VERSES / Of the PRINTER'S LAD, who carries about the / QUEBEC GAZETTE / to the CUSTOMERS. / JANUARY 1, 1782. /

Broadside: 30 lines; type-page: 22 × 13 cm. with ornamental rule frame. *Probably printed at Quebec by Wm. Brown, 1781.*

Contents: 6 stanzas, of 4 lines each, without local or political allusion.

Stanza I: "Once more my days their circling race
With winged speed have run:
Once more my life an equal pace
Hath travell'd with the Sun.
[Etc.]"

Copy located: CaO (bound in *Quebec gazette,* at end of 1781).

363. VIALAR, ANTHONY

[Catalogue of books to be sold at auction, Quebec, August 19, 1781.]

Probably a leaflet in fo., *printed at Quebec by Wm. Brown, 1781,* as recorded:

"1781, Aug. 11. Printed for Cha[s]. Stewart [auctioneer] 100 Catalogues of Vialar's books, making a pott folio on pica—£1.12.6."
—Can.P.A., *Neilson papers,* v. 47.

The sale was advertised: "By Public Auction will be sold on August 19, at the late Mr. Anthony Vialar's House in Lower Town at 10 o'clock, A parcel of Household furniture, Wearing apparel, Wines, etc., also a Collection of books, Catalogues [to be had of Mr. Charles Stewart, auctioneer, etc.]."—*Quebec gazette,* Aug. 9, 1781.

Copy located: None.

364. ALLINE, HENRY, 1748-1784

A / SERMON / PREACHED TO, and at the Request, / OF A RELIGIOUS SOCIETY OF / YOUNG MEN / UNITED AND ENGAGED FOR THE MAINTAINING AND / ENJOYING OF / RELIGIOUS WORSHIP / IN LIVERPOOL, / On the 19th November, 1782. / By HENRY ALLINE. / [rule] / HALIFAX: Printed by A. HENRY. /

12mo. A-D[4], [E][2]; 36 p.; type-page: 14 × 7.8 cm. There are numerous typographical errors throughout.

Contents: p. [1], t.-p.; p [2], blank; p. 3-4, Preface; p. 4-33, Sermon, text: Mark 16: 5, And entering into the sepulchre they saw a young man sitting on the right side, clothed in a long white garment; p. 34-36, The young man's song (verse).

The sermon is a prophetic interpretation of the religious symbolism of the young man clothed in a long white garment. It is an inspired appeal to the young men of Liverpool to give up their worldly goods and lose themselves in God.

Copies located: CaNsWA; NNHi.

365. ALLINE, HENRY, 1748-1784

A / SERMON / On a Day of THANKSGIVING / PREACHED at LIVERPOOL, / By HENRY ALLINE. / On the 21st, of November 1782. / [ornamental rule] / HALIFAX. Printed by A. HENRY. /

12mo. A-E[4]; 40 p.; type-page: 14 × 7.8 cm.

Contents: p. [1], t.-p.; p. [2], blank; p. 3, Preface; p. 4-39, Sermon, text: Psalm 107: 31. Oh that Men would praise the Lord for his Goodness, and for his wonderful works to the Children of men; p. 39-40, A Song of praise to a good God.

The sermon is Alline's passionate exhortation to his hearers to love God and to repent of their sins.

Copies located: CSmH; CaNsWA; RPJ.

366. ALMANACS. NOVA SCOTIA

THE / NOVA-SCOTIA CALENDER, / OR AN / ALMANACK, / For the Year of the Christian Æra, 1783; and from the Crea-/tion of the World, according to Chronology 5732, being the / third after Leap Year; and in the Twenty Third Year of / the Reign of His Majesty King GEORGE the Third, / . . . / Wherein is Contained, / The Eclipses of the Luminaries, . . . / [4 lines] / [rule] / Calculated for the Meridian of HALIFAX . . . / . . . / . . . / . . . / By METONICUS. / [rule] / "On their own Axis as the Planets run, / [etc., 5 lines] / Pope. / [rule] / HALIFAX, PRINTED and Sold by A. HENRY and / J. HOWE. / [title and each page within double rule frame]

12mo. A-D[4], [32] p.; type-page: 16 × 9.5 cm.

Contents: p. [1], t.-p.; p. [2-19], Calendar, etc.; p. [19-21], Stage-fares, distances, sheriffs; p. [21-24], Tales; p. [25-32], Army, militia, Nova Scotia administration, legislature, courts, [etc.].

This almanac was advertised: "Just published and to be sold by A. Henry and J. Howe, the Nova-Scotia Calender, or an Almanack for 1783 . . . by Metonicus [etc.]."—*Nova-Scotia gazette,* Dec. 10, 1782. It looks like the other *Nova-Scotia Calender's,* products of Henry's printing house, with crowded title-page and the frequent, apparently haphazard, change of type font and size, characteristic of Henry's composition. The imprint, however, includes the name of John Howe, a loyalist from Boston, who established a printing shop in Barrington Street, Halifax. This was their only joint venture in almanac publishing. Henry continued the *Nova-Scotia Calender* and Howe who apparently produced an *Astronomical diary or Almanack,* in 1781, resumed his own *Almanack* in 1790.

Copy located: MH.

367. ALMANACS. QUEBEC

ALMANACH / CURIEUX / ET INTERESSANT / POUR L'ANNÉE / [rule] / Mil sept cent quatre-vingt-trois. / [rule] / [printer's ornament] / A MONTREAL; / Chez FLEURY MESPLET, Impri-/meur & Libraire. / [rule] / M.DCC.LXXXIII. / [title within ornamental frame]

12mo. $A^8B^4C^8D^4$; 48 p.; paper-page: 11.75 × 7.5 cm. Text in French.

Contents: p. [1], t.-p.; p. [2-3], Comput ecclésiastique etc., Eclipses; p. [4-27], Calendrier; p. 28-33, Catalogue du Clergé; p. 31-46, Princes et Princesses de l'Europe; p. 46-48, Liste & valeurs des Monnoies.

Copies located: CaQMS; CaQQL.

368. ALMANACS. QUEBEC

ALMANACH / DE / QUEBEC, / POUR / L'ANNÉE / M,DCC,LXXXIII. / [double rule] / [ornament] / [double rule] / A QUEBEC: / Chez GUILLAUME BROWN, sur la / Grande Côte. /

A-F^6; 72 p.; type-page: 10.5 × 6 cm.

Contents: p. [1], t.-p.; p. [2-4], Epoques, eclipses; p. [5-16], [Calendrier]; p. 17-29, Officiers civils de la Province de Québec; p. 30-35, Instructions pour les capitaines de Milice; p. 36-41, Poids et cours de monnaie, etc., catalogue du clergé; p. 42-54, Reglemens pour les charetiers; p. 54-71, Reglemens pour la police; p. 70-71, Mesure Angloise et françoise; p. 72, Verses.

The text is entirely in French, excepting the militia instructions, regulations for carters, police regulations, and tables of linear measure, which appear also in English.

Issued on Dec. 21, 1782, l'*Almanach portatif* or the *Pocket Almanac,* as it was termed, was sold at 1*s.* 8*d.* the copy (2*s.* interleaved), or 15*s.* the dozen (18*s.* interleaved), in Quebec, 1*s.* 6*d.* up the River where it was sold in competition with Mesplet's *Almanach.*

Copy located: None. CaOOA has a photostat, however, of a copy not located. The original was possibly the copy formerly in possession of Abbé Dubois at the École Normale Jacques Cartier, Montreal

369. ALMANACS. QUEBEC

CALENDRIER pour l'Année 1783, pour Québec, par les 306$^{d.}$ 30$^{m.}$ de Longitude, et 46$^{d.}$ 55$^{m.}$ de Latitude. / [ornamental rule] /

Colophon: A QUEBEC: chez WM. BROWN, au milieu de la Grande Côte. /

Broadside: type-page: 51 × 39 cm.

Contents: Calendrier in ornamental rule frame, 44 × 38.5 cm. has note on arrangement running lengthwise alongside. A list of *Officiers civils* appears below *Calendrier.*

This sheet almanac was sold at 1*s.* the copy, 7*s.* 6*d.* the dozen from Dec. 5, and advertised for sale at Quebec, Trois Rivières, Berthier, and Montreal as usual, in the *Quebec gazette* from Dec. 5, 1782.

Copy located: CaO (bound in the *Quebec gazette* at end of 1782).

370. ALMANACS. QUEBEC

Calendrier / pour Montréal . . . pour l'année 1783.

Colophon: A Montréal, chez Fleury Mesplet . . . 1783.

Broadside: paper-page: 51 × 38.5 cm.

Copy located: CaQMS (described in Fauteux: *Mesplet*, no. 43, from which this description is taken).

ALMANACS. QUEBEC

[Indian calendar or almanack for 1783] *See* No. 277, 307.

371. AMICABLE SOCIETY, *Quebec city*

[List of the Members and Subscribers of the Amicable Society.]

Broadside: Text in 8 col. *Printed at Quebec by Wm. Brown, 1782*, as recorded:

"1782, July 26. Printed for the Amicable Society by order J. Rowe 500 Lists of the Members and Subscribers on a large Broadside Demy in 8 Columns Small Pica—£6. 15."—Can.P.A., *Neilson papers*, v. 47.

The "Amicable Society for Extinguishing Fires" was organized in Quebec during, or before, 1775, when its notices began appearing in the *Gazette*, "gratis" as the printer noted in his accounts. He recorded also the printing of "1200 Letters for convening [the Society], 800 in English, 400 in French, £1.5.," on Feb. 21, 1777, suggesting that the membership was largely English, in a city preponderantly French. The members were engaged to assist each other, and "in case of fire, paid-up subscribers must be protected first." The Society's financial statement for 1782-83 indicated that "From the bountiful Subscriptions of 1780, the Society expected to maintain a liberal establishment, but payments have been backward [etc.]," a situation which did not improve; for the following year "Of four fire engines, one is broken up, three in need of repair, and a new one ordered from London has just arrived but the Society has not funds to pay the charges [etc.]."—*Quebec gazette*, May 6, 1784, Aug. 11, 1785. About 1789 the Amicable Society disappeared and the Fire Society of Quebec appeared in the local news.

That the fire hazard was always high in Quebec is shown by government regulations under the French régime (*see* P. G. Roy: *La protection contre le feu à Québec sous le régime Français*, in *Bulletin des recherches historiques*, 30: 129-40, 1924) and by the repeated ordinances of the English administration for the cleaning and inspection of chimneys.

Copy located: None.

372. AMICABLE SOCIETY, *Quebec city*

[Rules and Regulations of the Amicable Society.]

Broadside: Text in English and French. *Printed at Quebec by Wm. Brown, 1782*, as recorded:

"1782, Aug. 10. Printed for the Amicable Society by Order Mr. Rowe Their Rules and Regulations 2 languages on a broadside Demy 400 Copies 400 —£6.10."—Can.P.A., *Neilson papers*, v. 47.

Copy located: None.

373A. CATHOLIC CHURCH. CATECHISMS. *French*

CATECHISME / A / L'USAGE / DU / DIOCESE / DE / QUEBEC. / Imprimé par l'Ordre de MONSEIGNEUR JEAN / OLIVIER BRIAND, Evêque de Québec. / [rule] / A QUEBEC. / Chez GUILLAUME BROWN, / IMPRIMEUR de la Province. / [rule] / MDCCLXXXII. /

12mo. A-Q[6], R-T[4]; 5 p. l., 7-59, [1] p.; 1 *l.*, 61-205, [3] p., 1 *l.*; type-page: 15 × 8.5 (varies).

Contents: p. l. 1 recto, t.-p.; verso, blank; p. l. 2-3, Mandement, "[dated and signed:] 7 Mars 1777, J. Ol. évêque de Québec"; p. l. 4, Avertissement; p. l. 5, Introduction; p. 7-59, Le Petit Catéchisme; [1] p. (verso of p. 59), Table du Petit Catéchisme; 1 *l.*, blank; p. 61-205, Le Grand Catéchisme; p. [1-3] at end, Table du Grand Catéchisme; 1 *l.*, blank.

Second edition of the Catholic Catechism, Quebec use, reprinted without change from that of 1777, for Michel Dubord. *Le Petit Catéchisme* was also issued separately —as recorded by the printer:

"1782, Oct. 10. Sold Michel Dubord & deliver'd the last yesterday for which he promised to pay £100 by the Sailing of the Fleet, and the Remainder before the 1st of May next,
1278 Single Catechisms @ 6*d.*—£31.19.
2624 Double D°. @ 1/1—£142.2.8. [Total:] £174.1.8."
—Can.P.A., *Neilson papers*, v. 47.

The work was advertised: "Nouvelle édition du Catéchisme de Québec, elle est entièrement conformé à la précédente, qui se trouve, épuisse depuis quelques années. Elle est faite à Québec avec l'approbation de Monseigneur l'Evêque après les voeux d'une infinité de familles qui la demandoient. Elle se vend chez Dubord à Québec, au pied de la Côte de Basse Ville, et à Montreal chez Franchere, on y trouve en nombre le petit Catéchisme séparé du Grand, et qui se vendra si l'on veut séparement."—*Quebec gazette*, Nov. 7, 1782, *et seq.* Single copies of *Le Petit Catéchisme* were sold by Wm. Brown at 1*s.* the copy.

This work, "published under the auspices of Bishop Briant, printed by the late Mr. William Brown, King's Printer," was cited as evidence that the Catholic clergy were proselytizing in Quebec, contrary to the Quebec Act, in a letter to the bishop of London, signed: "John Ball Junr.," Berthier, Jan. 25, 1790, and printed in the *Quebec Herald*, Feb. 1, 1790.

Copies located: CaQMF; CaQMS; CaQQA; CaQQL.

373B. CATHOLIC CHURCH. CATECHISMS. *French*

[Le Petit Catéchisme. *Quebec, Wm. Brown, 1782.*]

12mo. 5 p. l., 7-59 [1] p.; type-page: 15 × 8.5 cm.

This was a separate issue of the first part of *Catéchisme à l'usage du diocèse de Québec . . . seconde édition.* It was printed at Quebec by Wm. Brown, 1782, and 1,278 copies sold to the publisher, Michel Dubord, by Oct. 10, 1782. Brown himself sold single copies retail at 1*s.* *See* No. 373A *notes.*

Copy located: None.

374. CATHOLIC CHURCH. LITURGY AND RITUAL. PSALTER

PSEAUTIER / DE DAVID, / AVEC / LES CANTIQUES / à l'usage des Ecoles. / [ornament] / A MONTREAL, / Chez FLEURY MESPLET; Imprimeur / & Libraire. / [rule] / M.DCC. LXXXII. /

16mo. [*][8], A-T[8]; xvi, 304 p.; type-page: 10 × 6.8 cm; illus.: woodcut medallion at foot of p. 299.

Contents: p. [i], t.-p.; p. [ii], Prière; p. iii-xvi, Prières; p. 1-296, Le Pseautier de David; p. 297-99, Les Repons de la messe; p. 300-304, Prières pour renouvelle les promesses du Baptême.

The "illustration" at the foot of p. 299 is a wood-cut medallion about 1½" × 1" in size. The roughly cut lines represent a female head and shoulders in religious habit, presumably the Virgin Mary. This single ornament was probably cut by a local "artist," now unknown. It is the third decoration outside of type-metal ornaments known to appear in a Canadian-printed book (cf. No. 195 and No. 251).

Copies located: CaOLU; CaQMS; RPJ.

375. NOVA SCOTIA. HOUSE OF ASSEMBLY

Caption title: (1) / [ornamental rule] / JOURNAL and VOTES / OF THE / HOUSE of ASSEMBLY, / For the Province of Nova-Scotia. / [rule] / Tuesday June 11th, 1782. /

fo. [A-H][2]; 29, [2] p. *Printed at Halifax, N.S., by Anthony Henry, 1782.*

Contents: p. 1-29, Journal and votes of the fifteenth session of the fifth assembly, June 11-July 4, 1782; p. 29 verso, blank; p. [1-2] at end, Report of Committee on Treasurer's Accounts, June 17, 1782.

Copies located: CaNs (2 cop.; p. [1-2] at end wanting in cop. 2); MH (p. 17 to end wanting).

376. NOVA SCOTIA. LAWS, STATUTES, *etc.*

Running title: [rule] / 1782. Anno Vicessimo Secunda Regis GEORGII III. CAP. I[-V]. / [rule] /

Caption title: At the GENERAL ASSEMBLY of the Province / of Nova-Scotia, . . . / [8 lines] / . . . being the Fifth GEN-/ERAL-ASSEMBLY convened in the / said Province. / [ornamental rule] /

fo. p. 353-358; paged in continuation of No. 358. *Printed at Halifax, N.S., by Anthony Henry, 1782.*

Contents: p. 353-358, Cap. I-V, perpetual acts passed in the fifteenth session of the fifth assembly, June 11-July 4, 1782.

Copies located: CaNSA (p. 357-58 wanting); DLC; MH.

377. NOVA SCOTIA. LAWS, STATUTES, *etc.*

Running title: [rule] / 1782. Anno Vicessimo Secundo Regis, GEORGII III. CAP. I[-VI]. /

Caption title: At the GENERAL-ASSEMBLY of the Province / of Nova-Scotia, . . . / [8 lines] / . . . being the Fifth GENERAL-ASSEMBLY convened in / the said Province. / [ornamental rule] /

fo. p. 225-234; paged in continuation of No. 359. *Printed at Halifax, N.S., by Anthony Henry, 1782.*

Contents: p. 225-234, Cap. I-VI, temporary acts passed in the fifteenth session of the fifth assembly, June 11-July 4, 1782.

Copies located: MH (p. 233-34 wanting); NNB.

378. PRIMERS, QUEBEC. *French?*

[Grand Alphabet, *printed at Quebec by Wm. Brown, 1782.*]

Collation: 16mo., about 72 p. recorded by the printer:

"1782, Oct. 30. This day agreed with Michel Dubord at the Post Office in presence of Labadie,* to print for him 3000 of the Grand Alphabets for £33, the price understood to be paid on delivery, but no time fixed for its being finished.

"1782, Dec. 31. Printed for M. Dubord 3000 Grand Alphabets making $2\frac{1}{4}$ Sheets 16° on Crown by Agt.—£33."—Can.P.A., *Neilson papers*, v. 47.

Copy located: None.

379. QUEBEC, *Province.* GOVERNOR, 1778-1786 (*Haldimand*)

[By His Excellency Frederick Haldimand, Captain-General and Governor in Chief of . . . Quebec . . . Proclamation. <Text> Given . . . at the Castle of St. Lewis . . . 2nd February, 1782 . . . Fred: Haldimand. By His Excellency's Command, Geo: Pownall, Secy. God Save the King.]

French side:

[Par Son Excellence Frederic Haldimand, Capitaine-general et Gouverneur en chef . . . en la Province de Québec . . . Proclamation <Text> Donné au Château St. Louis . . . 2me. fevrier, 1782 (Signé) Fred: Haldimand. Par Ordre de Son Excellence, (Signé) Geo: Pownall, Secre. Traduit par Ordre de Son Excellence, F. J. Cugnet, S.F. Vive le Roi.]

*Dubord and Labadie were couriers who carried parcels of the *Gazette* for subscribers outside Quebec.

Double broadside: text in English and French. *Printed at Quebec by Wm. Brown, 1782*, as recorded:

"1782, Feb. 4. Printed for gov[t] by Order of Sec[y] 360 D[ble] Proclamations requiring an Acc[t] of Corn & Cattle—£3.17.6."

—Can.P.A., *Neilson papers*, v. 47.

English text: "Whereas the safety of the property of His Majesty's liege Subjects [etc.]" repeats the terms of the proclamation of Jan. 15, 1781 (No. 360); gives orders to faithful subjects to thresh all grain, ready for transfer to a place of safety if the rebel Americans should invade the province again; also orders to militia officers to record local supplies of grain and cattle and report them to the district colonels who are named.

French text: "La Sureté des propriété apartenans aux Fidels Sujets de Sa Majesté [etc.]."

The proclamation is reprinted in Can.P.A., *Report, 1918* (from which this entry is taken), also (English side only) in Ont. Archives, *Report, 1906*.

Copy located: None.

380. QUEBEC, *Province*. GOVERNOR, 1778-1786 (*Haldimand*)

[By His Excellency Frederick Haldimand, Captain General and Governor in Chief . . . PROCLAMATION <Text> Given . . . Quebec, 3 Oct. 1782 . . . FRED HALDIMAND. etc. By His Excellency's Command, Geo: Pownall, Secy.]

French side:

[Par Son Excellence Frederic Haldimand, Capitaine-general et Gouverneur en Chef . . . Proclamation. <Text> Donné . . . à Québec . . . 3 oct., 1782. (Signé) Fred: Haldimand. Par Ordre de son Excellency. (Signé) Geo: Pownall Secre, Traduit par Ordre de son Excellence, F. J. Cugnet, S.F. Vive le Roi.]

Double broadside: text in English and French. *Printed at Quebec by Wm. Brown, 1782*, as recorded:

"1782, Oct. 4. Printed by Order of the Secretary 100 D[ble] proclamations repling [sic] the Forestalling Ordinance.—£2.7.6."

—Can.P.A., *Neilson papers*, v. 47.

English text: "Whereas His Majesty in His most honourable privy Council at St. James's on May 18, 1781, . . . hath been pleased to Signify His Royal disallowance of . . . An Ordinance [on] . . . Forestallers . . . I do Therefore notify all judges, Magistrates and others . . . that the said Ordinance . . . is . . . repealed [etc.]."

French text: "Aiant plû à sa Majesté dans son Très Honorable Conseil Privé, tenu à St. Jacques, 18 mai, 1781 . . . de signifier sa Roiale désapprobation . . . [d'] Ordonnance qui désigne les personnes qui seront réputées Forestallers . . . j'avertis publiquement tous Jugés, Magistrats ou autres . . . qui la dite Ordonnance . . . est . . . invalide [etc.]."

This proclamation, repealed 20 Geo. III c. 2, passed at Quebec, Apr. 12, 1780, "An Ordinance describing the persons who shall be deemed Forestallers . . . and inflicting punishments upon those who shall be found guilty [etc.]." The text of the ordinance (18 articles) was published in *Ordinances, 1780* (No. 343), p. 19-34. It was passed for two years and then was continued by 22 Geo. III c. 2 (No. 382) passed on Feb. 11, 1782, then was repealed by this proclamation on Oct. 3, 1782, of the disallowance signified in London nearly a year and a half before. This proclamation is reprinted in Can.P.A., *Report, 1918,* from which this entry is taken.

Copy located: None.

381. QUEBEC, *Province.* LAWS, STATUTES, *etc.*

[Anno Vicesimo Secundi Georgii III. Regis. Chap. V. An Ordinance for Altering, fixing and establishing the Age of Majority. <Text> Fred. Haldimand. Ordained and enacted . . . Quebec . . . 16 Feb. 1782. By His Excellency's command, J. Williams, C.L.C.]

French side:

[Anno Vicesimo Secundi Georgii III. Regis. Chap. V. Ordonnance Qui change, fixe et établit l'age de majorité. <Text> (Signé) Fred. Haldimand. Statué et Ordonné . . . à Quebec, 16me fevrier, 1782. Par ordre de Son Excellence (Signé) J. Williams, G.C.L. Traduit par Ordre de Son Excellence, F. J. Cugnet, S.F.]

Broadside: text in English and French, *printed at Quebec by Wm. Brown, 1782,* as recorded:

"1782, Feb. 22. Printed for Gov^t^. by Order of Mr. Williams 200 Copies of Ordinances fixing the Age of Majority—£3.10."

—Can.P.A., *Neilson papers,* v. 47.

This brief law, effective from Jan. 1, 1783, changed the legal age of majority from 25 to 21 years. It is reprinted in Can.P.A., *Report, 1914-15,* from which this entry is taken.

Copy located: None.

382. QUEBEC, *Province.* LAWS, STATUTES, *etc.*

[Anno vicesimo secundi Georgii III. Regis. Chap. I. An Ordinance for continuing . . . "An Ordinance to prohibit for a limited time, the exportation of wheat . . . also of horned cattle, etc."

. . . Chap. II, An Ordinance For continuing . . . "An Ordinance describing . . . Forestallers, etc."

. . . Chap. III. An Ordinance For continuing . . . "An Ordinance for the regulation and establishment of fees."

. . . Chap. IV. An Ordinance For continuing . . . "An Ordinance for regulating . . . Maîtres de Poste."]

French side:

[Anno Vicesimo Secundo Georgii III. Regis. Chap. I. Ordonnance Qui continue . . . "Ordonnance qui défend pour un tems limité, l'exportation des Blés, Pois, Avoine, Biscuits, Fleur et Farines quelconques ainsi que des Bêtes à cornes."

. . . Chap. II. Ordonnance Qui continue . . . "Ordonnance qui désigne les personnes qui seront réputées Forestallers, etc."

. . . Chap. III. Ordonnance Qui continue . . . "Ordonnance qui établit les Honoraires."

. . . Chap. IV. Ordonnance Qui continue . . . "Ordonnance qui régle tous les particuliers . . . connus sous le nom de Maîtres de Poste." Quebec, 11 fev. 1782.]

Broadside? text in English and French? *Printed at Quebec by Wm. Brown, 1782*, as recorded:

> "1782, Feb. 16. Printed for Gov[t] by Order of Mr. Williams 200 Copies of 4 Ordinances on a larger type than published in Gazette—£5.15."
>
> —Can.P.A., *Neilson papers*, v. 47.

These four short ordinances were passed Feb. 11, 1782, and renewed, for a further two-year period, four laws passed in 1780. They were printed in the *Quebec gazette*, Feb. 14, 1783, in English and French in parallel columns at a charge of £4 10*s*. They are reprinted in Can.P.A., *Report, 1914-15*, from which this entry is taken in an abbreviated form.

Copy located: None.

383. SCOTT, THOMAS CHARLES HESLOP, *d.* 1813

[Handbill on claims for appointment as Church of England clergyman to the parish of Sorel. ? *Printed at Montreal by Fleury Mesplet, 1782.*]

Scott was deputy (and acting) chaplain to the 34th Regiment stationed at Sorel. When it was ordered disbanded, Scott petitioned Gov. Haldimand to be appointed clergyman to the parish of Sorel, with some local support to his petition. He had been embroiled with the military authorities, however, and his claims were discredited by General Riedesel, who wrote Haldimand from Sorel, Jan. 3, 1782: "Mr Scott seems to be a man of such a turbulent disposition and improper conduct I think him a dangerous person to be left at such a place as Sorel, especially after the connections he has formed there . . ." Scott defended his claims, apparently, with a vigorous offensive, which included the publication of the *Handbill* of which Riedesel again wrote Haldimand from Isle aux Noix Aug. 31, 1782: ". . . Before I left Sorel [about Aug. 29] the Rev[d] Mr. Scot had the confidence to dispense a number of Hand bills, which being of a very extraordinary nature I beg leave to enclose one."

Scott remained at Sorel till 1784 or later, then went to Quebec, where, opening a school, he spent the rest of his life (*see* H. C. Stuart: *Church of England in Canada, 1759-1793*, Montreal, 1893; also Can.P.A., "B", 75: 201, Scott's statement of the case; also *ibid.*, 137: 1, 246).

Copy located: None.

384. SKETCHLEY & FREEMAN, *Brokers & auctioneers, Quebec*

[Catalogue of Books for Sale.]

Leaflet of 1 to 4 p. *Printed at Quebec by Wm. Brown, 1782,* as recorded:

"1782, Nov. 23. Printed for Sketchley & Freeman 500 Catalogues of Books on a folio Demy—£4."

Another printing (on smaller paper, this also folded in folio making a leaflet of 1 to 4 p.) is recorded:

"Nov. 30. Printed for Sketchley & Freeman on a pott folio 500 Handbills for sale Books—£1.8.6." —Can.P.A., *Neilson papers,* v. 47.

Copy located: None.

385. TOOL, JOHN, *d.* 1782, *and* WALLACE, ROBERT, *d.* 1782

[Dying Speech and Confession of John Tool and Robert Wallace. *Printed at Quebec by Wm. Brown, 1782.*]

Probably a broadside or small pamphlet, this work was one of the few Canadian publications known, of a genre extremely popular in the 18th century. The event it celebrated is recorded:

"Quebec, November 21. On Monday last [Nov. 18, 1782] were executed on the Heights of Abraham pursuant to the sentence pass'd on them last Saturday, John Tool and Robert Wallace, for the wilful Murder and Robbery of Capt. William Steed in the month of December, 1779, near the top of the Hill leading from the Upper to the lower Town [Quebec]. They behaved decently and seemingly very penitent before a numerous concourse of Spectators. Their Dying Speech and Confession &c. to be had at the Printers on Saturday." —*Quebec gazette,* Nov. 21, 1782.

On publication day, Nov. 23, 1782, and thereafter for a time, their *Dying Speech* sold more rapidly (at a shilling the copy) than anything else noted on Brown's account books at that time.

Copy located: None.

386. ALLINE, HENRY, 1748-1784

[ornamental rule] / THE / ANTI-TRADITIONIST. / THE AUTHOR / HENRY ALLINE. / [ornamental rule] / [? *Halifax, N.S., Anthony Henry, 1783.*]

12mo. [A]-I⁴, 70 p., 1 *l.*; type-page: 14 × 8 cm. Errata leaf without signature or pagination inserted after Sig. A1, in the only copy located.

Contents: p. [1], t.-p.; p. [2], blank; errata leaf with Errata on recto, verso, blank; p. 3-5, A court for the trial of Anti-traditionist; p. 6-70, First thought, etc.; 1 *l.* at end, blank.

Though without printer's name, place, or date of printing, this work was probably printed at Halifax in the shop of Anthony Henry, and published by the author, about 1783 (before Jonathan Scott's reply, No. 442, at any rate). It has the appearance of pamphlets which slipped occasionally from Henry's shop, as if in a rough proof. The typography is as unorthodox as the author's doctrines; errors abound. A sympathetic compositor was inspired to emphasize Alline's exposition with the hand and other signs, ornaments, rules, and a liberal use of the upper case. The text comprises

"Six thoughts," Alline's intuitive conception of the fundamentals of Christianity. It is a most comprehensive, though unorganized, statement of his belief and a desperately earnest evangelical message—characterized by John Wesley as "broad and ranting anti-nomianism" (*see* No. 348 *note*). *See also* Long: *Nova Scotia authors* (on Alline).

Copy located: MH (in Divinity School Library).

387. ALLINE, HENRY, 1748-1784

A / SERMON / PREACHED ON THE 19th OF FEB. 1783. / At FORT-MIDWAY, / BY / HENRY ALLINE. / [ornamental rule] / HALIFAX. Printed by A. HENRY. /

12mo. A-E[4], F[2]; 1 p. l. 3-44 p.; type-page: 13.7 × 9 cm.

Contents: p. l. recto, t.-p.; verso, blank; p. 3-4, Preface; p. 4-44, Sermon, text: Genesis, 37: 16, I seek my brethren.

The preface states "Since the happy moment (never to be forgotten) when Jesus deigned to pluck me from the Jaws of Hell, and manifest his Everlasting love to my soul by his Spirit, I have not only vowed . . . to be for him only but . . . [to] make his Name my theme for Time and Eternity." The sermon bears eloquent testimony to the love and charity of Christ, describes in vivid and generous detail, the sins of man, and pleads with the sinners to come to Christ.

Port Medway (Fort-Midway in the title) was a small outport of New England fishermen on the southeast coast of Nova Scotia near Liverpool.

This work was reprinted: *A Sermon preached at Fort-Midway on the 19th of February, 1783, by Henry Alline* [*etc.*] (39 p., 8vo., Dover, N.H., 1797).

Copies located: CaNsHA; MHi; RPJ.

388. ALMANACS. NOVA SCOTIA

THE / NOVA-SCOTIA CALENDER, / OR AN / ALMANACK, / For the Year of the Christian Æra, 1784; . . . / . . . / . . . / . . . / . . . / Wherein is Contained, / The Eclipses of the Luminaries . . . / . . . / . . . / . . . Sittings of the several Courts / and Sessions in this Province, &c. &c. / [rule] /. Calculated for the Meridian of HALIFAX, in NOVA-SCOTIA. / . . . / . . . / . . . / By METONICUS. / [rule] / When the Tubb'd Cynick went to Hell, and there / Found the pale Ghost of goldon [sic] Cræsas [sic] bare, / He Stops, and geering till he Shugges again, / Says, O thou Richest King of Kings, what Gains / Have all they [sic] large heaps brought the [sic], since I Spy / Thee here alone, and poorer now than I? / For, all I had, I with me bring: But thou / Of all thy Wealth, hath not one Farthing Now / EPIGR. ON DIOGENES. / [rule] / HALIFAX, PRINTED, and Sold by A. HENRY. / [title and each page within double rule frame.] /

12mo. [A-C][4]; [24] p.; type-page: 16.3 × 9.3 cm.

Contents: p. [1], t.-p.; p. [2-4], Eclipses, etc., verses; p. [5-16], Calendar; p. [17-24], Nova Scotia administration, legislature, courts, army, customs, hospital, etc., Halifax-Annapolis distances and inns, tides, recipes. Note (p. [4] at foot): "The Verses at the Head of each Monthly Page, in this Almanack, are the favor of a virtuous, Worthy, and well deserving Friend. M."

This almanac was advertised as "Just published and to be sold by A. Henry, The Nova-Scotia Calender . . . for . . . 1784 [etc.]."—*Nova-Scotia gazette*, Dec. 9, 1783.

Copies located: CaNS (badly worn); CaNsWA (p. [1-6, 17] to end, wanting); CSmH.

ALMANACS. QUEBEC. *See also* No. 367.

389. ALMANACS. QUEBEC

ALMANACH / CURIEUX / ET INTERESSANT / POUR L'ANNÉE / [rule] / Mil sept cent quatre-vingt-quatre. / [rule] / [printer's ornament] / A MONTREAL; / Chez FLEURY MESPLET, Impri-/meur & Libraire. / [rule] / M.DCC.LXXXIV. /

The only copy seen, incomplete, has collation: A[5], B-D,[6] E[5]; [29], 30-58 [i.e. 56] p., fold *l.*; type-page: 11 × 5.5 cm. The fold *l.* mispaged: (37), is inserted after p. 44; 45-46, omitted in numbering. Text in French.

Contents: p. [1-2], blank but fo· border of type ornaments; p. [3], t.-p.; p. [4-5] Comput ecclésiastique etc., eclipses; p. [6-29], Calendrier; p. 30-35 Catalogue du Clergé; p. 36-51, Reglements de police de Montréal, 8 Avril, 1783, etc.; p. 52-58 Valeur de monnaies; fold *l.*, Passage des Rivieres.

Copies located: CaQMS (described in Fauteux: *Mesplet*, no. 47); CaQQL (described above, incomplete, back cover and 1 or 2 *l.* wanting).

390. ALMANACS. QUEBEC

ALMANACH / DE / QUEBEC, / POUR / L'ANNÉE / M,DCC,LXXXIV. / [double rule] / [printer's ornament] / [double rule] / A QUEBEC: / Chez GUILLAUME BROWN, sur la / Grande Côte. /

12mo. A-D[6]; 48 p.; type-page: 10.8 × 6 cm. Text in French.

Contents: p. [1], t.-p.; p. [2-3], Epoques, etc.; p. [4], Eclipses; p. [5-16], Calendar; p. 17-38, Officiers civils, etc., clergé seculaire; p. 39-47, Discours, anecdotes, verses; p. 48, Poids et cours de la monnoie.

Discours (p. 39-40) is a treatise on Cow-pox (la Picotte) by Rev. Auguste-David Hubert, curé of Quebec (*see* index for other works by Hubert).

Published on Dec. 25, 1783, the "pocket almanac" was sold at 1*s*. 8*d*. the copy in Quebec, 1*s*. 6*d*. in Trois Rivières, Berthier, and Montreal.

Copy located: CaQM (p. 47-48, wanting). Another copy formerly in possession of Abbé Dubois at École Normale Jacques Cartier, Montreal, not located. Photostat of complete copy in CaOOA.

391. ALMANACS. QUEBEC

Calendrier perpétuel calculé suivant la correction grégorienne ou Nouveau style. Qui indique le lever & / coucher du soleil, pour Québec & Montréal, les Lunaisons, Fêtes mobiles, etc. /

Colophon: A Montréal, chez Fleury Mesplet, 1783.

Broadside: Paper-page: 70 × 36 cm.

Copy located: CaQMS (described in Fauteux: *Mesplet*, no. 42, from which this description is taken).

392. ALMANACS. QUEBEC

CALENDRIER pour l'Année Bissextile 1784, pour Québec, par les $306^{d.}$ $30^{m.}$ de Longitude, et $46^{d.}$ $55^{m.}$ de Latitude; / [ornamental rule] /

Colophon: A QUEBEC: chez WM. BROWN, au milieu de la Grande Côte. /

Broadside: type-page: 51 × 39 cm.

Contents: Calendrier in ornamental rule frame: 44.3 × 38.5 cm. Note on arrangement; Officiers civils etc., as in previous years.

This sheet almanac was sold at 1*s.* the copy, from Nov. 20, 1783, when it was advertised (in the *Quebec gazette*) for sale in Quebec, Trois Rivières, Berthier, and Montreal, and on the same day, 20 dozen copies were sent to Montreal by Wm. Brown.

Copy located: CaO (bound in *Quebec gazette*, at beginning of 1784).

393. ALMANACS. QUEBEC

Calendrier / pour Montréal . . . pour l'année 1784. /

Broadside: paper-page: 51.25 × 40 cm. This is a sheet almanac *printed at Montreal by Fleury Mesplet, 1783*, whose imprint, however, does not appear on the broadside.

Copy located: CaQMS (described in Fauteux: *Mesplet*, no. 48, from which this description is taken).

ALMANACS. QUEBEC

[Indian calendar or almanack for 1784] *See* No. 278, 308.

394. CATHOLIC CHURCH. LITURGY AND RITUAL

LA / DEVOTION / AUX / SS. ANGES / GARDIENS. / [printer's ornament] / A MONTREAL; / Chez FLEURY MESPLET, Impri-/meur & Libraire, 1783. /

16mo. A-E^8; 77 p., 1 *l.*; type-page: 9.5 × 5.8 cm.

Contents: p. [1], t.-p.; p. [2], blank; p. [3-7], Avis au lecteur; p. [8] verso, blank; p. 9-42, L'association des anges gardiens; p. 43-77, L'office, etc., p. 77 verso, blank; 1 *l.* at end: list of books for sale by Mesplet.

This is an anonymous devotional work, the first part of the text (p. 9-42) showing the qualifications, duties, and rewards of those who would associate themselves with a guardian angel, the latter part (p. 43-77) containing prayers and devotions in which the good Catholic effects a spiritual union with, and enjoys the protection of, his guardian angel.

Copies located: CaQMS: CaQQL.

395. COCKBURN, JAMES, *defendant*

[Sentence of a General Court Martial held at the Horse Guards, Monday the 12th of May 1783, and continued by adjournment for Several Days, on Lieutenant Colonel James Cockburn, Commander of His Majesty's Forces in the Island of St. Eustatius when captured by the French on the 26th of November, 1781.]

Probably a broadside or leaflet. *Printed at Quebec by Wm. Brown, 1783*, as recorded:

"1783, Nov. 20. Printed for Major Lernoult [Adjutant General of Quebec] 100 Sentences of Gen[l]. Court Martial on Lieutenant Colonel Cockburn —£1.2.6."—Can.P.A., *Neilson papers*, v. 47.

Issued by command, this is the Canadian publication of an event of no little notoriety in social and military circles of the day. St. Eustatius, a small island in the Dutch West Indies, temporarily in British hands, was captured by a small French force under Marquis de Bouille, Nov. 26, 1781. "It was an instance [of surprise] perhaps without parallel by daylight. The Island [and two million livres of spoils] was lost in a few minutes and without the expense of a man to the enemy . . . It has not often happened that English troops have met with so signal a disgrace,"—*Annual register, 1782*, p. *194-95. Cockburn, who was thought to have been bribed, was court martialed, found guilty of culpable neglect and cashiered. The record of his trial was ordered to be circulated to every corps in His Majesty's Service. The text appeared in General Orders by General Haldimand (in Can.P.A., "B" 84: 34-35) from which the title above is taken.

Copy located: None.

396. DELAROCHE, PETER, *d.* 1795

[A Doctrinal and Practical Commentary on the New Testament to which is prefixed: A Harmony in one, of the four Gospels; the whole intended for the use of the unlearned especially.]

Proposals to print "A Doctrinal and Practical Commentary on the New Testament, to which is prefixed: A Harmony in one, of the four Gospels; the whole intended for the use of the unlearned especially," appeared intermittently with specimens of the text, etc., in the *Nova-Scotia gazette*, July 8, 1783-Sept., 1784, or later. The work, of which the *Harmony* was ready for the press and the *Commentary* in preparation, was projected in three volumes, octavo, of forty sheets (about 640 pages) each, in type similar to Stanhope's *Paraphrase &c on the Epistles of the Gospels*,

1761 edition, "because it is easy reading even for the weakest eyes." The price was to be 5*s.* each volume, bound in sheep; 3*s.* 6*d.* covered with blue paper. Two thousand copies must be subscribed before printing could begin. On July 29, 1783, the conditions were changed "because the printer could not formerly get a sufficient idea of the work itself": one thousand copies at 7*s.* the volume, sewed in blue paper, must be subscribed before publication would be feasible. On Dec. 28, 1785, Gov. Parr in council sent to the assembly a recommendation that some assistance be given Delaroche "to enable him to print his Commentary of the Four Gospels which appears to be an ingenious work and worthy of encouragement" (P.A.N.S., *Miscellaneous Assembly papers, 1785*). But there is no evidence that the Assembly granted a subsidy or that this work was ever published, though M. B. Des Brisay so states in *History of the county of Lunenburg* (2nd ed., Toronto, 1895). A previous work, *A practical commentary on the New Testament* (not in harmony) had been prepared by Delaroche and part of it, covering the first half of Matthew, published serially in thirty-seven numbers of the *Nova-Scotia gazette* beginning in July, 1777. A MS. *Doctrinal and practical commentary on the New Testament intended for the use of the unlearned especially,* v. 2-3, dated at Lunenburg, N.S., 1782, is said to be in the library of King's College, Halifax, N.S.

397. FINLAY, HUGH, 1732-1801

[Song]

Probably a small broadside, *printed at Quebec by Wm. Brown, 1783,* as recorded: "1783, Apr. 30. Printed for H. Finlay [deputy postmaster general for Canada] 30 Songs.—10*s.*" —Can.P.A., *Neilson papers*, v. 47.

The text of the song and the occasion which it celebrated, remain unknown.

Copy located: None.

398. GREAT BRITAIN. SOVEREIGNS, *etc.*, 1760-1820 (*George III*)

[royal arms] / BY THE KING. / A PROCLAMATION, / Declaring the Cessation of Arms, as well by Sea as Land, agreed upon / between His Majesty, the Most Christian King, the King of Spain, / the States General of the United Provinces, and the United States of / America, and enjoining the Observance thereof. / <Text> / Given at Our Court at St. James's, . . . / . . . [Feb. 14, 1783] / GOD SAVE THE KING. / [double rule] / LONDON: Printed by CHARLES EYRE and WILLIAM STRAHAN, Printers to the KING'S Most Excellent MAJESTY. 1783. / [rule] / QUEBEC: Re-printed by WILLIAM BROWN, Printer to the KING'S Most Excellent MAJESTY. 1783. /

French on right:

[royal arms] / DE PAR LE ROI. / PROCLAMATION, / Publiant la Cessation d'Armes par Terre et par Mer, dont sa Majesté, / le Roi Très Chrêtien, le Roi d'Espagne, les Etats Généraux des Pro-/vinces Unies, et les Etats Unis de l'Amérique, sont convenus, et qui / enjoint au sujets de sa Majesté de s'y conformer. / <Text> / Donné à Notre Cour à St. James, . . . / . . . [14 fev. 1783] / VIVE LE ROI. / [double rule] / LONDRES: Imprimé par CHARLES EYRE et GUILLAUME STRAHAN, Imprimeurs de sa Très Excellente MAJESTÉ, 1783. / [rule] / QUEBEC: Re-imprimé par GUILLAUME BROWN, Imprimeur de sa Très Excellente MAJESTÉ. 1783. /

Double broadside: English on left, 48 lines, type-page: 37 × 19.7 cm.; French on right, 46 lines, type-page: 30.3 × 19.7 cm.

This proclamation, issued in London after ratification of the preliminary articles of peace signed at Versailles, Jan. 20, 1783, closed the war phase of the American Revolution. It was published in Quebec, not in the *Quebec gazette*, then the only newspaper in the province. but in a broadside edition of 200 copies (described above) as recorded by Wm. Brown:

"1783, Apr. 26. Printed for the Milit[y] Sec[y]. 200 King's Proclamations for Cessation of Hostilities. 2 Impressions—£3.17.6."

—Can.P.A., *Neilson papers*, v. 47.

Copies located: CaOOA (in "Proclamations" portfolio in the Library); MiU-C.

399. GREAT BRITAIN. TREATIES

COPIES / AUTHENTIQUES / DES ARTICLES / PRELIMINAIRES / DE LA PAIX, / ENTRE / S. M. BRITANNIQUE, / S. M. TRES-CHRETIENNE, / S. M. TRES-CATHOLIQUE / ET / LES ETATS UNIS / de l'Amérique. / Signés à Versailles, le 20 Janvier 1783. / [double rule] / A MONTREAL, / Chez FLEURY MESPLET, M.DCC.LXXXIII. /

4to. A-[C][4], [*][2]; p. l., 25 p., type-page: 14 × 7.5 cm.

Contents: p. l. ([*2] folded around back to precede t.-p.) blank; p. [1], t.-p.; p. [2], blank; p. 3-11, "Traduction des articles . . . entre Sa Majesté Britannique & le Roi très chrétienne, 20 Jan. 1783"; p. 12-17, "Traduction des articles . . . entre S.M. Britannique et S.M. Catholique, 20 Jan. 1783"; p. 18-25, "Articles convenus par & entre Richard Oswald Ecuyer, Envoyé de S.M. Britannique . . . & Jean Adams, Benjamin Franklin, Jean Jay & Henry Laurens, quatre Députés des dits Etats"; p. 25 verso, blank.

Canadian-printed edition of the treaty proclaimed in Canada by No. 398. The definitive treaty, signed at Paris Sept. 3, 1783, was published in English and French in the *Quebec gazette*, Oct. 21, 1784.

Copies located: CaQMS (2 cop.).

400. JOHNSTON & PURSS, *Merchants*, *Quebec*

[Directions for brewing Spruce.]

Probably a small double broadside, text in English and French, *printed at Quebec by Wm. Brown, 1783*, as recorded:

"1783, Jan. 24. Printed for Johnston & Purss 10,000 Double Directions for brewing Spruce by Ag[t].—£7.10."—Can.P.A., *Neilson papers*, v. 47.

A recipe for spruce beer, a staple if heady beverage still "home-brewed" in eastern Canada. It was issued no doubt by the enterprising merchants, to purchasers of the essential molasses.

Copy located: None.

401. MESPLET, FLEURY, 1735?-1794

To the Honorable the President and Members of the Congress of the / United-States. / THE MEMORIAL of FLEURY MESPLET of Montreal, in / the Province of Quebec. / SHEWETH, /

fo. 2 *l.*; type-page: 17.5 × 15.3 cm.; type: english.

Contents: l. [1] recto, text (26 lines); verso, blank; *l.* [2], blank. The text begins: "That your Memorialist was a Citizen of Philadelphia; and in the Year 1776, was happily Established in his business of a Printer in that City: [etc.]." It continues stating that on instructions from Congress, Mesplet moved his press from Philadelphia to Montreal, supported American interests there till the evacuation; remaining in Montreal he was imprisoned for three years and three months, to his then and subsequent deprivation. It concludes begging "such relief as [his case] may seem to merit."

This *Memorial* is reprinted with facsimile illustration in D. C. McMurtrie: *A memorial printed by Fleury Mesplet* (Chicago, 1929). Another edition was prepared by Mesplet in 1784 (No. 422).

Copy located: DLC (filed in MSS. *Papers of Continental Congress*, no. 41, v. VI, fo. 305; this copy is signed in MS.: "Fleury Mesplet, Montréal, 1er Août 1783"; it bears MS. note on *l.* [2] verso: "No. 49 Mun[r]. Fleury Mesplet, Read 30 Sept. 1783. Referred to—Mr. Holden [etc.], discharged Nov. 1, 1783."

402. MONTREAL, *District.* MANAGERS OF A LOTTERY TO BUILD A PRISON, 1783

[Plan for a lottery for building a Prison, for the Town and District of Montreal . . . Lotterie pour bâtir une Prison pour la ville et le district de Montréal, . . . le plan.]

Probably a broadside, *printed at Montreal by Fleury Mesplet, 1783.*

The records of the managers include a bill "from the Government of Quebec to the Managers of the lottery," dated Mar. 18, 1784, which contains the items:

"[undated] Paid Fleury Mesplet for printing the Scheme and Tickets per Account—£21.15.

"[undated] Paid Wm. Brown for printing the Scheme in two languages 28 Weeks in the [Quebec] Gazette and Postage. £13.14.1."

—Can.P.A., "S" *Int. corres. 1784.*

The Plan for a Lottery to raise funds to build a gaol in Montreal signed and dated: La Corne St. Luc, Edwd Wm Gray, James McGill, Pre Guy, Jacob Jordon, Managers, Montreal, Apr. 29, 1783, appeared in the *Quebec gazette* during 1783-84. But as no newspaper was published in Montreal at this time, Mesplet's edition of the Plan was probably printed as a broadside or leaflet in English and French. The *Plan* or "Scheme" as set forth in the *Quebec gazette* comprised the issue of 13,000 tickets at 46*s.* 8*d.* to raise £30,333. 6*s.* 8*d.* The tickets were to be drawn on Feb. 3, 1784, for prizes ranging from the first, of £850, to 4,025 prizes of 4*s.* each.

The lottery was arranged on the authority of an ordinance (23 Geo. III c. 5) passed by the governor-in-council on Feb. 5, 1783, enacting the presentment of the grand jury of the Montreal district. The latter outlined the enterprise to build a gaol and included a plan for a lottery. The gaol built with the proceeds of this lottery on the site of the present "old" court house in St. James Street, Montreal, was burned down in 1803. Lottery tickets are preserved in the Public Archives of Canada (with *Quebec gazette* Nov. 20, 1783, in *Miscellaneous newspaper clippings 1812-1837* portfolio) and are reproduced as illustration in J. D. Borthwick: *From darkness to light, history of the eight prisons . . . in Montreal . . . 1760-1907* (Montreal, 1907), p. 10-11.

Copy located: None.

403. NOVA SCOTIA. HOUSE OF ASSEMBLY

Caption title: [Journal and Votes of the House of Assembly for the Province of Nova Scotia.]

Note: title above is not transcribed from copy.

fo. A-O², [*]¹; 56 p. 1 fold. *l. Printed at Halifax, N.S., by Anthony Henry, 1783.*

Contents: p. 1-56, Journal and votes of the sixteenth session of the fifth assembly, Oct. 6-Dec. 2, 1783; fold. *l.*, An Account of impost and excise for the District of [blank].

Copies located: CaNs (2 cop.); GBLP (2 cop. in C.O. 220/14: 591-654; C.O. 217/59: 421-76).

NOVA SCOTIA. LAWS, STATUTES, *etc.*

Acts passed in the 1783 session of the Nova Scotia legislature were printed in 1784 (No. 430, 431).

404. QUEBEC, *Province.* GOVERNOR, 1778-1786 (*Haldimand*)

[By His Excellency Frederick Haldimand, Captain General and Governor in Chief of . . . Quebec . . . Proclamation. <Text> Given . . . at the Castle of St. Lewis . . . 17 Jan. 1783 . . . By His Excellency's Command. God Save the King.]

French side:

[Par Son Excellence Frederic Haldimand, Capitaine Général et Gouverneur en Chef . . . en la Province de Québec . . . Proclamation <Text> Donné au Chateau St. Louis . . . 17 jan. 1783, etc.]

Double broadside, *printed at Quebec by Wm. Brown, 1783,* as recorded:

"1783, Jan. 21. Printed for Gov^t. by Order G. Pownall, 380 D^ble Proclamations for an Acc^t Corn &c.—£3.17.6." —Can.P.A., *Neilson papers*, v. 47.

English text: Whereas the safety of the property of His Majesty's liege Subjects [etc.].

French text: La Sureté des propriété apartenans aux Fidels Sujets de Sa Majesté [etc.].

This Proclamation repeats the terms of that of Jan. 15, 1781 and of Feb. 2, 1782 (*see* No. 360, 379). It is reprinted without the governor's signature, in Can. P.A., *Report, 1918* (from which this entry is taken), also (English side only) in Ont. Archives, *Report, 1906*.

Copy located: None.

405. QUEBEC, *Province.* LAWS, STATUTES, *etc.*

[Anno Vicesimo tertio Georgii III. Regis. Chap. I. An Ordinance For Further continuing . . . "An Ordinance to regulate the proceedings in the courts of civil judicature . . ." and in amendment of the same.

. . . Chap. II. An Ordinance For further continuing an Ordinance . . . for regulating the Militia, etc.

. . .Chap. III. An Ordinance For further continuing an Ordinance . . . to empower the Commissioners of the peace to regulate the Police of the Towns of Quebec and Montreal, etc.

. . . Chap. IV. An Ordinance For raising a sum of money by Lottery, for building a gaol in the Town of Montreal.]

French side:

[Anno vicesimo tertio Georgii III. Regis. Chapitre I. Ordonnance Pour continuer encore une Ordonnance . . . qui régle les formes de procéder dans les Cours Civiles de Judicature . . . Et la Correction d'icelle.

. . . Chapitre II. Ordonnance Pour continuer encor une Ordonnance . . . qui régle les Milices, etc.

. . . Chapitre III. Ordonnance Qui continue encor une Ordonnance . . . qui autorise les Commissaires de Paix à régler la Police dans les villes de Québec et de Montréal, etc.

. . . Chapitre IV. Ordonnance Pour lever une somme d'argent par Lotterie pour bâtir des Prisons dans la ville de Montréal.]

Double broadside? Text in English and French. *Printed at Quebec by Wm. Brown, 1783*, as recorded:

"1783, Feb. 12. Printed for Gov[t] 4 Ordinances 200 Copies by Order Mr. Williams [i.e. Jenkin Williams, clerk of the Legislative Council].—£8.15."
—Can.P.A., *Neilson papers*, v. 47.

These ordinances were passed by governor-in-council Feb. 5, 1783, chap. I-III continuing for two years 17 Geo. III c. 2, 8, 15 respectively. They were printed (in English and French, from another setting of type, at a charge of £7 10*s.*) in the *Quebec gazette*, Feb. 6, 1783, and reprinted in Can.P.A., *Report, 1914-15* (from which this entry is taken).

Copy located: None.

406. QUEBEC LIBRARY

[Catalogue of books in the Quebec Library.]

Printed at Quebec by Wm. Brown, 1783, as recorded:

"1783, Oct. 20. The Gov[t] of Quebec, Dr. To printing 200 Catalogues of books —£3.7.6."—Can.P.A., *Neilson papers*, v. 48.

"Dec. 4. The Quebec Library, Backing 200 Catalogues books—15/."
—*ibid.*, v. 47.

This publication was announced: "In consequence of a meeting of the trustees, the Public is advertised that the Catalogue of the Books which belong to the Quebec Library has been printed, and that each subscriber may have a copy by applying for it at the Secretary's [i.e. Governor's Secretary's] Office. The French books tho' commissioned have not been sent on account of the difficulties occasioned by the War. [etc.] N.B. the English Books have cost £374 Sterling."—*Quebec gazette,* Nov. 6, 1783.

Copy located: None.

407. QUEBEC LIBRARY

[Les Régles et les Loix de la Bibliothèque de Québec.]

4to. 4?p. *Printed at Quebec by Wm. Brown, 1783,* as recorded:

"1783, Dec. 29. Printed for Quebec Library (by Order Mr. Lymburner) 100 Rules in French. ½ Sheet 4to—£1.10."

—Can.P.A., *Neilson papers,* v. 47.

French edition of No. 408.

Copy located: None.

408. QUEBEC LIBRARY

[Rules and Laws for the Quebec Library.]

Printed at Quebec by Wm. Brown, 1783, as recorded:

"1783, Dec. 9. Printed for Quebec Library by Order Mr. Lymburner 175 Rules & Laws for Quebec Library—£1.17.6."

—Can.P.A., *Neilson papers,* v. 47.

The Quebec Library, maintained and used from 1779 by subscribers only, was opened in 1783 to the public at large. A new set of rules and conditions requisite to the arrangement of the trust, and for the preservation of books given to the public, was prepared by the trustees and approved by the subscribers. The library, it was announced, would be open on Tuesdays and Fridays from ten till two o'clock, and would have "near two thousand useful and entertaining books before the end of the ensuing year."—*Quebec gazette,* Dec. 4, 1783.

Copy located: None.

The Quebec Library was organized during the winter of 1778-79 on the impetus of Gov. Haldimand, as a means of stimulating and guiding popular opinion. The governor secured the support of the somewhat reluctant Catholic clergy (*see* Gosselin: *L'église du Canada après la conquête,* I: 387) and the enterprise was announced:

"A Subscription has been commenced for the establishment of a Public Library for the City and District of Quebec. It has met with the Approbation of His Excellency the Governor and of the Bishop, and it is hoped that an Institution so peculiarly useful to the Country will be generally encouraged. A list of those who have already subscribed is lodged at the Secretary's Office, where those who chuse may have an opportunity to add their names. The Subscribers are requested to attend at the Bishop's Palace at 12 o'clock the 15th Instant in order to chuse Trustees [etc.]."

—*Quebec gazette,* Jan. 7, 1779.

The trustees (three English and two French, including Bishop Briand's secretary and three government officials) set the fees (£5 entrance, and £2 annual) and proceeded to draw up rules and a list of books for purchase, announcing that "The Public may be assured that particular attention will be given that no Books contrary to Religion or good Morals will be permitted."—*ibid.*, Jan. 21, 1779. The list, Gov. Haldimand forwarded in a letter dated at Quebec, Mar. 2, 1779, to Richard Cumberland, a playwright who acted as agent for the province in London, describing his purpose: "The ignorance of the natives of this colony having been in my apprehension the principal cause of their misbehaviour and attachment to interests evidently injurious to themselves, I have sought to encourage a Subscription for a public Library, which now more are come into than could have been at first expected; A pretty good sum has already been raised and I hope . . . [the Scheme] will greatly tend to promote a more perfect coalition of sentiment and union of Interests between the old [English] and new [French] subjects of the Crown than has hitherto subsisted [etc.]." He asked Cumberland to purchase the books listed and to recommend others suitable for the purpose.—Can.P.A., "B", 66: 107.

The Quebec Library developed spasmodically, and, despite recurrent hard times and the competition of other subscription libraries, it lived for eighty-five years. Its occasional catalogues and the book stock still extant, indicate its early release from government control. The collection, equally English and French, of wide range in subject and opinion, contained by the end of the 18th century, the best-sellers of London and Paris, including the works of the philosophical radicals, but little of American, and nothing of local, origin. The Library remained for some time in its original quarters in the Bishop's Palace; finally after an eventful life, it was absorbed in 1866, by the Literary and Historical Society of Quebec, on whose shelves its books now stand.

409. QUEBEC THEATRE

[Play Bills, *printed at Quebec by Wm. Brown, 1783.*]

From March of this year Brown recorded occasional printing for the Quebec Theatre, an acting company giving private performances for subscribers, of popular London plays, also public performances once or twice a month. The latter were advertised regularly in the *Quebec gazette*, sometimes "with decorations, music and dancing," or "for benefit of a distressed family," or "at the particular desire ofseveral ladies." Brown printed tickets and playbills, usually about three hundred of the former, and fifty to seventy of the latter for 10*s.* or 12*s.* 6*d.* In 1783 he recorded the printing of several unidentified play-bills, also those for *The tragedy of George Barnwell*, Mar. 27; *High life below stairs*, July 21; *A bold stroke for a wife*, Sept. 4.—Can. P.A., *Neilson papers*, v. 47.

Copy located: None.

410. SAINT JOHN'S RIVER SOCIETY

Caption title: [The following Description, with Extracts of Letters Patent, and Proceedings of Committees for dividing and settling the Townships of Gage, Burton, Conway, Sunbury, and other Tracts on St. John's River in the Province of Nova Scotia, now Collected by the Proprietors in Canada; and published for the General information of all persons concerned or desirous to make settlements in that Country.]

After caption: [The Remonstrance of Capt. William Spry, one of the Proprietors of the Townships, dated New York, April 11, 1768; [followed by:—] A Resolution of fifteen proprietors recommended at the meeting of the same, held in Montreal June 2nd, 1783.]

4to. 14 p.

? *Probably printed in Montreal by Fleury Mesplet after October, 1783,* and published by the Montreal and Quebec proprietors in a last-minute effort to establish settlers on their lands on the St. John River and so avert impending escheat (*see* No. 101 *note*).

Spry's *Remonstrance* contained the plan on which the Society's lands were allotted to the proprietors in 1768. The *Resolution of . . . June 2nd 1783* was "for the more effectual settlement of these lands and the [appointment] of an Agent for that purpose." On the proprietors' petition, June 9, to Gov. Haldimand, himself a proprietor, the agent, Capt. John Munro, and three attendants, were granted four months' leave and provisions, "considering the liberal and public motives . . . in this undertaking" to inspect and report upon their lands.—Can. P.A., "B" 108: 155.

The following Description is probably the report, or excerpts therefrom, prepared by Munro, of his journey, July 7-Oct., 1783 from Quebec to Halifax and Parr (now the city of Saint John, N.B.) thence, Sept. 26, up the St. John River. He described briefly the land between Halifax and Parr, then, in detail, that of the St. John valley, noting quality of soil, timber, extent of settlement, and those sections already escheated. His report is printed in Can.P.A., *Report, 1891,* 25-31, from MS. in the Haldimand Papers. Its text, describing the lower St. John valley, closely resembles in substance and wording Edward Winslow's *Sketch of the province of Nova Scotia, 1783,* printed in the N.B. hist. soc. *Coll.* 4: 142-53, 1899, p. 147-53.

The proprietors in Canada included Col. Guy Johnson, Lt.-Col. Campbell, Jacob Jordan, Major Heyes, Hugh Finlay, Major Samuel Holland, Col. Daniel Claus, Gov. Haldimand "and other gentlemen"—officers, government officials, loyalists from New York and other colonies. John Munro, 1731-1800, whose *Report* appears in this publication came to America in 1756, settled in Vermont, secured large land grants there, in New York, and in Nova Scotia. A loyalist in the Revolution, he served in the King's Royal American Regiment of New York, lost his old properties and settled again in Upper Canada.—Ryerson: *Loyalists,* 2: 261; Raymond: *Winslow papers,* 360-61.

Copy located: A copy, not located, was sold at auction by C. F. Heartman, Metuchen, N.J., Apr. 24, 1922. It is described in Heartman's *Sale Catalogue,* no. 138, item no. 28 from which the title above is taken.

411. ALMANACS. NOVA SCOTIA

THE / NOVA-SCOTIA CALENDER, / OR AN / ALMANACK, / For the Year . . . 1785 . . . / [4 lines] / Wherein is Contained, / The Eclipses . . . / [4 lines] / [rule] / Calculated for the Meridian of HALIFAX, . . . / [3 lines] / By METONICUS. / [rule] / Awake! / [verse] . . . / [5 lines] / [rule] / Halifax, Printed and Sold by A. HENRY. / [title with double rule frame] /

12mo. A-C?[4]; [24?] p.; type-page: 16.5 × 9.5 cm.

Contents: The only copy seen was incomplete, comprising: p. [1], t.-p.; p. [2-4], Vulgar notes, zodiac, verses, etc.; p. [5-16], Calendar. Probably a final section (p. 17-24) set forth the Nova Scotia administrative officers, the legislature, military establishment, court sittings, etc., as listed upon the title-page.

This almanac was advertised as "Just published and for sale by A. Henry, The Nova-Scotia Calender . . . for . . . 1785 [etc.]."

—*Nova-Scotia gazette*, Nov. 30, 1784.

Copy located: CaNsHA.

412. ALMANACS. QUEBEC

ALMANACH / DE / QUEBEC, / POUR / L'ANNÉE / M,DCC,LXXXV. / [double rule] / [ornament] / [double rule] / A QUEBEC: / Chez GUILLAUME BROWN, sur la / Grande Côte. /

12mo. A-E^4; 48 p.; type-page: 10.5 × 6 cm.

Contents: p. [1], t.-p.; p. [2-4], Epoques, eclipses; p. [5-16], Calendar; p. 17-38, Officiers civils (the text seen, wants p. 17-22, probably containing lists of provincial and district officials, p. 23-38, has lists, in French, of notaries, customs officers, post-house keepers, rates and routes, Catholic and Church of England clergy); p. 39-47, Sur les principes de l'agriculture (in French and English on opposite pages); p. 46-48, Verses, etc.

This almanac was published on Dec. 16, 1784, and sold at 1*s*. 3*d*. the copy (1*s*. 6*d*. interleaved), 12*s*. the dozen, prices somewhat lower than previous years.

Copy located: Copy formerly in possession of Abbé Dubois at École Normale Jacques Cartier, Montreal, not located. Photostat in CaOOA.

413. ALMANACS. QUEBEC

CALENDRIER pour l'Année 1785, pour Québec, par les 306$^{d.}$ 30$^{m.}$ de Longitude, et 46$^{d.}$ 55$^{m.}$ de Latitude. / [ornamental rule] /

Colophon: A QUEBEC: chez WM. BROWN, au milieu de la Grande Côte. /

Broadside: type-page: 51.5 × 39 cm.

Contents: Calendrier (in ornamental rule frame: 44 × 38.5 cm. with note below on arrangement), Officiers civils (as in previous years).

This sheet almanac was sold at 9*d*. the copy, 6*s*. the dozen (a price lower than previous years) from Nov. 27, 1784. It was advertised for sale in Quebec, Trois Rivières, Berthier, and Montreal, as usual in the *Quebec gazette* from Dec. 2, 1784.

Copy located: CaO (bound in *Quebec gazette* at end of 1784).

ALMANACS. QUEBEC

[Indian calendar or almanac for 1785] *See* No. 279, 309.

414. CALCOTT, WELLINS

[A Candid disquisition of the principles and practice of the most ancient and honourable Society of Free and accepted Masons, together with some strictures on the origin, nature and design of that institution, dedicated by permission to the most noble and most worshipful Henry Duke of Beaufort, &c.,&c., Grand Master, by Wellins Calcott, P.M. Ab ipso Ducit Opes animumque febro—Hor. Od.]

? Printed at Saint John, N.B., by Lewis & Ryan, 1784. This work was advertised: "Just published and to be sold by the printers hereof, A Candid disquisition [etc., as above]."—*Royal Saint John's gazette,* Sept. 9, 1784. It seems unlikely that Lewis and Ryan could have undertaken to print so large a work at that time, when living and working conditions were so difficult, supplies and cash so scarce, in the new settlement, Saint John. More likely they were advertising their sale of copies imported. This work had been published in London, 1769, and reprinted in Boston, 1772, in 256 p., 8vo. The latter edition had been circulated in Nova Scotia, for "Animadversions on [its] list of subscribers" signed "Yorker," had been published in the *Nova-Scotia gazette,* Jan. 12, 1773.

Copy located: None.

415. [DEBONNE, PIERRE AMABLE], 1758-1816

Caption title: A MES COMPATRIOTES / CANADIENS, / Qui se sont trouvés à l'Assemblée convoquée dans le Couvent / des R.R.P.P. Recolets, le 30 du mois de Novembre / dernier, & autres, / [*Montréal, Chez Fleury Mesplet, 1784.*]

4to. [4] p.; type-page: 18-19 × 12.5 cm.

Contents: p. [1-4], letter with heading as in caption title, signed: "DeBonne, Montréal, le 7 decembre, 1784." It was prepared probably by Pierre Amable DeBonne, for the French-Canadian group which elected him to the Comité canadien at Recollet House, Montreal, Nov. 30, 1784, and it protests against his exclusion from the Comité through the influence of James McGill and Frobisher. Appended to the letter is a certification of DeBonne's election, signed by Le Gras Pierreville and fourteen other French Canadians, also a guarded endorsement thereof signed: "F. Mesplet, Montréal, 7 decembre 1784." *See also* No. 441.

This leaflet was *probably printed at Montreal by Fleury Mesplet* (who signed the endorsement) *1784,* as a copy was enclosed in a letter by Hugh Finlay, deputy postmaster-general in Canada, from Quebec, Jan. 10, 1785, to Evan Nepean, London, with the comment that he had received it from Montreal.—Can.P.A., "C.O. 42," 17: 184.

Copies located: CaQM; CaQMS; GBLP (2 cop., in C.O. 42/17: 7 Dec. 1784; C.O. 42/63: 237-40).

416. L'ÉCU DE SIX FRANCS

L'ÉCU / DE SIX FRANCS. / [printer's ornament] / A PARIS; / Réimprimé à MONTREAL / Chez FLEURY MESPLET, Imprimeur / & Libraire. / [rule] / 1784. /

12mo. A-C^6; 35 p.; type-page: 11-11.5 × 6.5 cm.

Contents: p. [1], t.-p.; p. [2], blank; p. [3]-35, L'écu; p. 35 verso, blank.

The life story of a crown piece minted in Paris in 1774, this work, written in a light and charming style with no indication of authorship, is a satire on society in France. It shows the dishonesty of the merchant, ignorance of the doctor, extravagance of the rich, misery of the poor, the villainy of the tax-collector, and the frivolity and cynicism of all types—excepting, however, in royalty and the Church.

The title and text of this piece as well as the imprint, has the appearance of Mesplet's work, the ornament, however, is new in Canadian typography. It is the liberty cap on a pole in the midst of military standards, enclosed by a chaplet of bay leaves—more common in Parisian printing of the period.

Copies located: CaQM; CaQMS.

417. FRERES & COMPATRIOTES

Caption title: FRERES & COMPATRIOTES. / [*Montreal, Fleury Mesplet, 1784.*]

4to. [*]^2; [3] p.; type-page: 19.5 × 12.5 cm.

Contents: p. [1-3], Text, signed: "Vos Vrais Amis Canadiens"; p. [3] verso, blank.

Probably printed at Montreal by Fleury Mesplet, 1784. Hugh Finlay, the deputy postmaster-general, enclosed a copy in a letter from Quebec, Jan. 10, 1785, to Evan Nepean, London, saying that he had received it from Montreal.

—Can.P.A., "C.O. 42," 17: 184.

Written in a clerical style with a tone of mingled authority and counsel, this leaflet attacks the petition of the "Reform Committee" of which the true object, it states, is the repeal of the Quebec Act, the extinction of Catholic freedom and of French municipal law in Quebec. It warns the habitants against the tyranny and taxation of government by popular assembly; advises that they look to their seigneurs and clergy for leadership, not to the British. It finally suggests that if a representative government be introduced in Quebec, it be on the basis of three equal estates "le Clergé, la Noblesse et la Bourgeoisie."

This work is described in Shortt and Doughty: *Documents, 1759-1791*, 2: 762, *note.*

Copies located: CaQQL; GBLP (in C.O. 49/17, Jan. 10, 1785).

418. FRIENDLY FIRE CLUB, *Shelburne, N.S.*

[Rules and Orders of the Friendly Fire Club. *Shelburne, N.S., A. Robertson, 1784.*]

This work is said to have been printed at Shelburne, N.S., by Alexander Robertson following the organization of the Friendly Fire Club on Aug. 5, 1784.—Thos. Robertson: *A history of the county of Shelburne, N.S.*, an unpublished MS. of 1871, in Akins historical prize essays, in King's College, Halifax, N.S.

Copy located: None.

419. GREAT BRITAIN. SURVEYOR-GENERAL OF H.M. WOODS IN AMERICA, 1783-1820 (*Sir John Wentworth*)

Extract from the Statutes for the Preservation of his Majesty's / Timber in America, published by Order of the Surveyor / General of his Majesty's Woods in America for public / Information / . . . [23 lines] / HALIFAX, NOVA-SCOTIA, January 12th, 1784. /

Broadside: 28 lines; type-page: 27 × 14 cm. *Probably printed at Halifax, N.S., by Anthony Henry, 1784*, though in style and materials this broadside is superior to Henry's usual work.

Quoted from 8 Geo. I c. 12 and 2 Geo. II c. 35, these extracts comprise regulations against cutting down of white pine within the colonies. After the American Revolution, the Canadian provinces, especially New Brunswick, became increasingly important as a source of mast pines for the British Navy, and the crown timber reserves more highly regarded. Crown timber rights in America were regulated by Wentworth for half a century. He had been surveyor-general of woods from 1766, and lieutenant-governor of New Hampshire, till the Revolution. A loyalist, he was recommissioned surveyor-general in 1783 and settled in Halifax, N.S. He later became lieutenant-governor of Nova-Scotia, 1792-1808, and a baronet in 1795. Both before and after the Revolution, Wentworth introduced some ameliorations of the timber restrictions, but his enforcement of them met with general, and frequently successful opposition. (*See* R. G. Albion: *Forests and sea power, the timber problem of the British Navy, 1652-1862,* Cambridge, Mass., 1926, 249, 290, 350, *et seq.*).

Copy located: MWA.

420. [LA ROCHE DU MAINE, JEAN PIERRE LOUIS DE, *Marquis de Luchet*], 1740-1792

PARIS / EN / MINIATURE, / D'apres les Dessins / D'UN NOUVEL ARGUS. / [printer's ornament] / A LONDRES; / Et se trouve à PARIS, / Chez PICHARD, Libraire, Quai & / près des Théatins. / [rule] / M.DCC.LXXXIV. /

Colophon: p. 104: Réimprimé A MONTREAL / le 24 Août 1784, / Chez FLEURY MESPLET, Imprimeur-Libr. /

12mo. A-N[4]; 104 p.; type-page: 13.3 × 7 cm.

Contents: p. [1], t.-p.; p. [2], blank; p. 3-104, Paris, en miniature.

It is significant that Mesplet kept his name from the title page of this publication. Whether he actually reprinted it or simply reissued the imported sheets, he apparently hesitated to sponsor too conspicuously a work of "Voltairianisme."

Published in several editions at Amsterdam, Geneva, and London in 1784, this is an *exposé* of contemporary Parisian society. It describes the debauchery and parasitism of the arts and professions and the materialism and decadence of the upper classes. The author, a French *littérateur* and protégé of Voltaire, was at this time in the service of the elector of Hesse-Cassel.

Copy located: CaQQL.

421. [MELVILLE, DAVID]

[An Accurate History of the Settlement of His Majesty's exiled loyalists on the north side of the Bay of Fundy formerly called Arcadia on the River St. John—observations on the air, climate and soil —on the first settlement by the French—on the second by a few straggling settlers from New-England . . . by a person of information who lived on the spot and is possessed of authentic documents.]

Proposal to print, at Parr-Town, N.B., by Lewis & Ryan, 1784,* was advertised in the *Royal St. John's gazette,* Sept. 9, 1784. The prospectus indicated that the work was to include "[I] History [as above] II, Some strictures on the peace between the United States of America and Great Britain . . . III, Investigations of the many disputes between the inhabitants and their agents, so-called, concerning . . . distribution of lands . . . The probability of this settlement being brought under the subjection of the United States if the leaders are not closely watched [etc.]." The introduction to the *History,* also printed in the *Gazette, supra,* is a bitter complaint of the unjust treatment of loyalist settlers on the St. John River.

It was proposed to publish the work in three volumes octavo, of about one hundred pages each, on fine paper and good type. The price, 7*s.* 6*d.*, was to be paid half in advance, and the book put to press when one thousand subscriptions had been received by the printers and Mr. David Melville, Parr-Town.

There is no evidence that this work was published.

422. MESPLET, FLEURY, 1735?-1794

To the Honourable the President and Members of the Congress / of the UNITED-STATES. / THE Memorial of Fleury Mesplet of Montreal, in the / Province of Quebec; Sheweth. /

French on right:

A l'Honorable Président, & Respectables Membres du / Congrès des ETATS-UNIS de l'Amérique. / Représentation du Sr. Fleury Mesplet, actuellement à Montréal, dans la Province de Quebec, en Canada. /

Double broadside: English on left, 40 lines, type-page: 21 × 13 cm., type: english with long primer footnote; French on right, 39 lines, type-page: 20 × 13 cm., type: pica with long primer footnote. This is another edition of Mesplet's Memorial of Aug. 1, 1783 (No. 401); the English text with wording unchanged, is entirely reset and a footnote added. Also a French version of the text is added, with a translation of the footnote.

English text begins: "That your Memorialist was a Citizen of Philadelphia [etc.]." The footnote states that in 1776 Mesplet sold stock for specie which he exchanged at par for American paper money of which he still holds some $5,000—worthless.

French version: "Le Représentant prend la liberté de rapeler dans la mémoire de vos Seigneuries, qu'ayant été établi à Philadelphie en l'année 1776, [etc.]."

*Now Saint John.

This Memorial was read in Congress May 14, 1784, and tabled on July 26. Another copy was presented Mar. 11, 1785 with Mesplet's claim for $9,189. Of this, Congress resolved, May 27, 1785, that Mesplet be paid $426 45/90 for transporting his press from Philadelphia to Montreal.—U.S. Continental Congress: *Journals, 1774-1789,* (34 v., Washington, 1904-37), v. 27-28.

Copies located: DLC (2 cop., signed in MS.: "Montreal 27the [sic] March 1784 fleury Mesplet," filed in MSS. *Papers of Continental Congress,* no. 41, v. VI, fo. 336-37, 362-63, respectively).

423. NEW BRUNSWICK. GOVERNOR, 1784-1786 (*Carleton*)

[By His Excellency Thomas Carleton Esqr Captain General and Governor in Chief of the Province of New Brunswick and Territories thereon depending, Chancellor and Vice Admiral of the Same &c &c &c. A Proclamation. <Text> Given under my hand and seal in the Council chamber, in Parr-Town . . . 22 Nov. 1784. (Signed) Thomas Carleton. By His Excellency's Command. (Signed) Jonathan Odell. God Save the King.]

Text: "His Majesty having been pleased by His Royal Commission this day published, to constitute and appoint me Captain General of New Brunswick, bounded on the Westward by the mouth of the River St. Croix . . . ; I do therefore, by and with the advice of His Majesty's Council, publish this Proclamation, hereby requiring and commanding all officers, civil and military, within this province, to continue in the execution of their respective offices; And I do strictly charge and command all persons to yield them due obedience [etc.]."

Broadside: *Printed at Parr-Town,* N.B., by Lewis & Ryan, 1784.*

Lewis and Ryan's first bill to the provincial government of New Brunswick, for printing, etc., during 1784-85, begins with the following items:

"1784, [Nov.] 24th. To printing 500 Proclamations on broadside—£4.
[Nov.] 25th D^o. 500 D^o. on D^o.—£4.
[Nov.] 25th D^o. 500 D^o. on D^o.—£4.
[1785, Jan.] 17th. [D^o 500 Regulations on D^o.—£4."

This bill, receipted on verso, Jan. 24, 1786, is indecipherable in spots but is substantiated by a rough draft in "Contingent Accounts" which includes the note:
"Printing 3 sets of Proclamations—£12.
D^o Regulations—£4." —N.B. Ex. co. *Papers.*

These entries probably refer to the proclamation above and to No. 424, 425, and 461, respectively. Carleton, appointed governor of the newly organized province of New Brunswick, arrived at Parr-Town Nov. 21, 1784, and on Nov. 22 held the first meeting of his Council. At this and the two succeeding meetings, Nov. 24-25, these proclamations were passed and ordered published, according to Carleton's despatch to Lord Sydney, no. 1-3, Nov. 24-25, 1784.—N.B. *Carleton;* also in Can.P.A., N.B. "A," 1: 83, *et seq.*, with transcript of the proclamation, from which this entry is taken.

Copy located: None.

*Now Saint John.

424. NEW BRUNSWICK. GOVERNOR, 1784-1786 (*Carleton*)

[royal arms] / By His EXCELLENCY / THOMAS CARLETON, ESQ; / Captain General and Governor in Chief of the Province of New-Brunswick . . . / . . . / A PROCLAMATION. / <Text> / GIVEN . . . at . . . / . . . Parr-Town, this Twenty-fourth Day of November, . . . / . . . / . . . One Thousand Seven Hundred and Eighty-four. / THOMAS CARLETON. / By his Excellency's Command, / JONATHAN ODELL, / God save the King. /

Broadside: 23 lines; type-page: 33 × 23.5 cm. *Printed at Parr-Town,* N.B., by Lewis & Ryan, 1784,* in an edition of 500 copies (*see* No. 423 *note*).

Text: "Whereas the late Accession of His Majesty's Loyal Subjects, from the United States of America to this Province has been productive of a mutual inter-course, under color of which many persons have carried on an irregular trade contrary to the Act of Navigation, . . . I . . . publish this Proclamation, forbidding all persons, Subjects or Foreigners, to enter the Ports of this Province for the purpose of such illicit trade . . . under the penalty of forfeiture of such Vessel and Cargo [etc.]."

Copy located: GBLP (in Adm. 1/491, Nov. 24, 1794).

425. NEW BRUNSWICK. GOVERNOR, 1784-1786 (*Carleton*)

[By His Excellency Thomas Carleton, Esqr, Captain General and Governor in Chief of the Province of New Brunswick, etc. A Proclamation. <Text> Given under my Hand and Seal at the Council Chamber in Parr-Town, . . . 25 Nov. 1784. (Signed) Thos Carleton. By His Excellency's Command, (Signed) Jonathan Odell. God save the King.]

Broadside; *Printed at Parr-Town,* N.B., by Lewis & Ryan, 1784,* in an edition of 500 copies (*see* No. 423 *note*).

Text: "His Majesty having been pleased by Letters patent under the Seal of Great Britain, to constitute and establish a separate government in this Province of New Brunswick, which was heretofore a part of the Province of Nova Scotia, . . . I . . . publish this Proclamation, requiring all persons . . . to exhibit and register all such grants of land within this Province as they may respectively hold under the government of Nova Scotia . . . at Parr-Town, within the term of three months from the date hereof." This entry is taken from Can.P.A., N.B. "A", 1: 90-91.

Copy located: None.

426. NOVA SCOTIA. AGENTS TO REFUGEES ON THE RIVER ST. JOHN

[An Address from the Agents to the Loyal Refugees on the River St. John's, containing An accurate Account of all their Proceedings from the first commencement of the Agency to the present time.]

*Now Saint John.

Printed at Parr-Town, N.B., by Lewis & Ryan, 1784,* this publication was advertised: "Next Saturday [Jan. 31, 1784] will be published Price eight coppers An Address from the Agents to the Loyal Refugees on the River St. John's, containing An accurate Account of all their Proceedings from the first commencement of the Agency to the present time."—*Royal St. John's gazette,* Jan. 29, 1784.

Over 14,000 "loyal refugees" had arrived from New York at the mouth of the St. John River by Oct., 1783. To these the government of Nova Scotia (which included, till May, 1784, the present province of New Brunswick) made grants of land and distributed building materials and provisions through its agents. The latter were Rev. John Sayre, Wm. Tyng, George Leonard, John Coffin, James Peters, and Gilfred Studholme. Climate and lack of accommodation caused great hardship during the winter, the absence of local administrative organization delayed relief, producing controversy and resentment against the agents. The early numbers of the *Royal St. John's gazette,* contain frequent and bitter protests by the new settlers, and occasionally a "vindication" by the agents (*see* W. O. Raymond: *A sketch of the life and administration of General Thomas Carleton, first governor of New Brunswick,* in N.B. hist. soc. *Coll.,* no. 6, 1905, p. 439-80).

Copy located: None.

427. NOVA SCOTIA. HOUSE OF ASSEMBLY

Caption title: [ornamental rule] / JOURNALS / AND / VOTES / OF THE / HOUSE of ASSEMBLY / Of the Province of NOVA-SCOTIA. / [rule] / Monday, 1st November, 1784. /

fo. A-L²; 41 p., 1 *l. Printed at Halifax, N.S., by Anthony Henry, 1784.*

Contents: p. 1-41, Journal and votes of the seventeenth session of the fifth assembly, Nov. 1-Dec. 8, 1784; p. 41 verso, blank; 1 *l.* at end, blank.

Copies located: CaNs; GBLP (in C.O. 217/58: 128-68); MH (p. 29-32 wanting).

428. NOVA SCOTIA. LAWS, STATUTES, *etc.*

THE / PERPETUAL ACTS / OF THE / GENERAL ASSEMBLIES / OF / HIS MAJESTY'S PROVINCE / OF / NOVA SCOTIA. / AS REVISED, / In the YEAR 1783. / [double rule] / G. III [Royal arms] R / [double rule] / HALIFAX, in NOVA SCOTIA: / Printed and Sold by ANTHONY HENRY. / [rule] / M.DCC.LXXXIV. / [title within ornamental frame] /

fo. [*]², a-g², h¹, A-2P², 2P², 2P², 2Q-3L² [*]¹; 17 p. l., 229 p.; type-page: 25.1 × 15.3 cm.; p. 149a-152a, 149b-152b inserted after p. 152.

Contents: p. l. 1 recto, t.-p.; verso, blank; p. l. 2 recto, House of Assembly committee report; verso, blank; p. l. 3 recto-p. l. 6 recto, Table of titles of acts, 1758-1782; verso, blank; p. l. 7 recto-17 verso, [Subject index]; p. l. 17 recto at foot, Errata; p. 1-228, 32 Geo. III c. 1-22 Geo. III c. 2, 1758-1782; p. 229, 18 Geo. III c. 5, 1778 (which should appear on p. 218); verso, blank.

This revised edition gives text of acts passed, session by session, and still in force. The chapters are renumbered where necessary, for acts passed, but no longer in force, are not recorded by title in this revision.

*Now Saint John.

The report (p. l. 2) reads: "House of Assembly 11th October, 1783. The Gommittee [sic] of His Majesty's Council and House of Assembly appointed to examine the Laws of this Province, which have been revised by Isaac Deschamps and James Brenton Esq; having considered and examined the same, Report that they find them done with great Judgment and Accuracy, and that it would be right and proper to have the same put into Force accordingly. [signed:] Henry Newton [etc.]."

This work was advertised:

"Just published and to be sold by the Printer The Perpetual Laws as revised and corrected by Order of the House of Assembly . . . neatly bound in 1 folio volume with a compleat Alphabet and Index. Price of this edition as regulated by the House of Assembly—£1.10.1." —*Nova-Scotia gazette*, Feb. 17, 1784.

The House of Assembly itself included in its estimates passed Nov. 22, 1783, the sum of £125 to be paid to "Mr. Henry for one hundred copies (to be bound) of the revised perpetual acts."—N.S., H. of As. *Journal*. The following year they included £260 "to be paid to Deschamps and Brenton for revising the Province Laws." —*ibid.*, Nov. 25, 1784.

Copies located: CaNW; CaNsHA; CaNsWA (2 cop., errata leaf wanting in 1 cop.), CaO (2 cop.); CaOTO; MH (3 cop.); N; NN; RPJ.

429. NOVA SCOTIA. LAWS, STATUTES, *etc.*

THE / TEMPORARY ACTS / OF THE / GENERAL ASSEMBLIES / OF / HIS MAJESTY's PROVINCE OF / NOVA SCOTIA. / As REVISED IN THE Year 1783. / [double rule] / G. III [royal arms] R / [double rule] / HALIFAX, in NOVA SCOTIA: / Printed and Sold by ANTHONY HENRY. / rule] / M.DCC.LXXXIV. / [title within ornamental frame.]

fo. [*², **¹], A-P², Q¹ (incomplete); 3 p. l., 62 p. (incomplete); type-page: 25.5 × 15 cm.; p. 34 mispaged: 48; p. [60] not paged.

Contents: p. l. 1 recto, t.-p.; verso, blank; p. l. 2 recto-verso, Contents table (chronological); p. l. 3 recto-verso, Subject index; p. 1-62, Temporary acts revised, 5 Geo. III c. 1—15 Geo. III c. 2.

Note: In all copies located, the text stops with 15 Geo. III c. 2, p. 62, but the chronological contents table indicates that 22 Geo. III c. 6 followed; the subject index (in Harvard copy) includes entries for 23 Geo. III c. 1, 5, on p. 63, 69, respectively. These acts appear in No. 431, on p. 235-37, 241-42, respectively.

Copies located: CaO (p. l. 3, p. 63 to end, wanting); CaNsHA (p. l. 3, p. 63 to end, wanting); MH (p. 63 to end, wanting).

430. NOVA SCOTIA. LAWS, STATUTES, *etc.*

Running title: [rule] / 1783. Anno Vicessimo Tertio Regis, GEORGII III. CAP. I[-XI]. / [rule] /

Caption title: At the GENERAL ASSEMBLY of the Province / of Nova-Scotia, . . . / [8 lines] / . . . being the Thirteenth [sic] Session of the / Fifth General Assembly convened in the said / Province. / [rule]

fo. sig. 3M-3P²; p. 231-241 [i.e. 245]; type-page: 25.5 × 15 cm.; p. [242] mis-paged: 142; 239-241 repeated on p. [243-245]; paged in continuation of No. 428. *Printed at Halifax, N.S., by Anthony Henry, 1784.*

Contents: p. 231-241 [i.e. 245], Cap. I-XI, perpetual acts passed in the sixteenth session of the fifth assembly, Oct. 6-Dec. 2, 1783; p. 241 [i.e. 245] verso, blank.

The 1783 Session's laws were printed after the revised edition of perpetual acts 1758-1782, sold with copies of the latter, and are now usually so found.

Copies located: CaNW; CaNsHA; CaNsWA; CaO (2 cop.); CaOTO; MH; N; NN.

431. NOVA SCOTIA. LAWS, STATUTES, *etc.*

Running title: [rule] / 1783. Anno Vicessimo Tertio Regis, GEORGII III. CAP. I[-VII]. / [rule] /

Caption title: At the GENERAL ASSEMBLY of the Province / of Nova-Scotia, . . . / [8 lines] / . . . being the Thirteenth [sic] Session of the / Fifth General Assembly convened in the said / Province. / [rule] /

fo. p. 235-44; type-page: 25.5 × 15.3 cm.; paged in continuation of No. 377. *Printed at Halifax, N.S., by Anthony Henry, 1784?*

Contents: p. 235-44, Cap. I-VII, temporary acts passed in the sixteenth session of the fifth assembly, Oct. 6-Dec. 2, 1783.

Copies located: CaNsHA; CaO; MH; N; NNB.

432. NOVA SCOTIA. LAWS, STATUTES, *etc.*

Running title: [rule] / 1784. Anno Vicessimo Quarto Regis, GEORGII III. CAP. I[-VI]. / [rule] /

Caption title: At the GENERAL ASSEMBLY of this Province / of Nova-Scotia, . . . / [8 lines] / . . . being the Thirteenth [sic] Session of the Fifth General Assembly convened in the said / Province. / [rule] /

fo. sig. 3Q-3R², 3S¹; p. 243-251; type-page: 25.5 × 15.3 cm. paged in continuation of No. 430. *Printed at Halifax, N.S., by Anthony Henry, 1784?*

Contents: p. 243-251, Cap. I-VI, perpetual acts passed in the seventeenth session of the fifth assembly, Nov. 1-Dec. 8, 1784; p. 251 verso, blank.

Copies located: CaO; DLC; MH.

433. NOVA SCOTIA. LAWS, STATUTES, *etc.*

Running title: [rule] / 1784. / Anno Vicessimo Quarto Regis, GEORGII III. CAP. I[-V]. / rule] /

Caption title: At the GENERAL ASSEMBLY of this Province / of Nova-Scotia, . . . / [8 lines] / . . . being the Thirteenth [sic] Session of the / Fifth General Assembly convened in the said / Province. / [rule] /

fo. sig. U-Z²; 2A¹; p. 245-264 [i.e. 266]; type-page: 25.5 × 15.3 cm. paged in continuation of No. 431; p. 250-51 numbers interchanged; p. [253] *et seq.* mispaged: 252 *et seq.;* 263 repeated. *Printed at Halifax, N.S., by Anthony Henry, 1784.*

Contents: p. 245-264 [i.e. 266], Cap. I-V, temporary acts passed in the seventeenth session of the fifth assembly Nov. 1-Dec. 8, 1784.

Copies located: CaNsHA; CaO; MH; NNB.

434. QUEBEC, *Province.* CITIZENS

Caption title: (1) / OBJECTIONS / AUX DEMANDES FAITES, / A NOTRE AUGUSTE SOUVERAIN; / Par l'Adresse lue dans une Assemblée tenue chez les R.R. / P.P. Recolets, le 30 Novembre 1784. /

4 p.; type-page: 18.8 × 12.4 cm.

Printed at Montreal by Fleury Mesplet, 1784, as appears from a MS. note in Mesplet's hand, appended to the text of a copy of the leaflet enclosed in a letter from Gov. Dorchester, Quebec, Jan. 10, 1789, to Lord Sydney (now in the Public Record Office, London, in C.O. 42, v. 63): "Je certifie que dans le courant du mois de Décembre de l'année 1784 j'ai imprimé aux environ de Deux cens exemplaires des objections ci-dessus & environ le même nombre d'une adresse à Sa Majesté* en Opposition à la Chambre d'Assemblée (dans le meme epace de temps) Montréal 29 Xbre 1788 fl. Mesplet, imprimeur."

Objections comprises a brief statement of requests set forth in a prologue; then articles I-XIV of the Reform Committee's petition with categorical objections to each article (*see* No. 453). *Objections* was formulated following a meeting at Recollet House, Montreal, Nov. 30, 1784, arranged by French-Canadian seigneurs and clergy, also English officials and others whose interests conflicted with those of the British mercantile group. The former prepared also a counter petition (*see* No. 435). *Objections* is reprinted and translated in Great Britain: Parliament, House of Commons: *Papers relative to the province of Quebec* [*1759-1789*] *ordered to be printed, 21st April, 1791* (205 p., London, 1791), 76-83; also in Shortt and Doughty: *Documents, 1759-91,* 2: 754-62.

Copies located: GBLP (3 cop. in C.O. 42/17: 187-90; C.O. 42/47: 133-36; C.O. 42/63: 257-60—this copy bears Mesplet's MS. note).

435. QUEBEC, *Province.* CITIZENS

LA Très-humble ADRESSE des Citoyens & Habitants Catholiques Romains de différents Etats, dans la Province de / Quebec en Canada. / AU ROI. / SIRE, / <Text> / SIRE, / DE VOTRE MAJESTÉ, / Les très-humbles, très obeissants, / Fideles & Loyaux Sujets. /

Broadside: 53 lines; type-page: 37.4 × 29 cm. *Printed at Montreal by Fleury Mesplet, 1784,* in an edition of about 200 copies—as appears from a MS. note by Mesplet (*see* No. 434).

The text begins: "Les Bontés dont votre Coeur Royal & Généreux, a pris plaisir à combler vos fideles & Loyaux Sujets Canadiens; Les démarches actuelles & prématurées de vos anciens Sujets, résidents dans notre Province, & le petit nombre de

*No. 435.

nouveaux qui se sont joint à eux, nous sont espérer que Votre très-gracieuse MAJESTE', nous permettra de nous prosterner de rechef au pied de son Trône, pour implorer Sa Bienfaisance & sa Justice."

The petitioners beg (1) that Catholic priests and teachers be permitted to come to Canada from Europe, (2) that the number of Catholic [French] Canadians in the Legislative Council be increased in proportion to their population in the province. The petitioners dissociate themselves from the requests made in the name of old [British] and new [French-Canadian] subjects by the so-called Reform Committee, particularly from the request for a House of Assembly (*see* No. 453). The real needs of the new subjects are clergy from Europe, free exercise of religion and the municipal and civil laws of their forefathers.

This address was prepared by the so-called Comité canadien appointed at a public meeting held at Recollet House in Montreal, Nov. 30, 1784. It opposes before the king, the viewpoint of British merchants in Quebec with that of French-Canadian seigneurs and clergy.

It is reprinted with an English translation, in Shortt and Doughty: *Documents, 1759-1791*, 2: 762-66. A similar petition is printed with English translation in Great Britain: Parliament, House of Commons: *Papers relative to the province of Quebec* [*1759-1789*] *ordered to be printed, 21st April, 1791* (205 p., London, 1791), 68-72.

Copy located: GBLP (in C.O. 42/47: 137).

436. QUEBEC, *Province*. COURT OF QUARTER SESSIONS OF THE PEACE (Quebec District)

[Prohibitions to sell liquor on Sunday]

? Broadside, *printed at Quebec by Wm. Brown, 1784*, as recorded:

"1784, May 15. Printed for the Govt. by order Mr. Lind, 100 Prohibitions to sell liquor on Sunday &c.—£1.2.6."

—Can.P.A., *Neilson papers*, v. 47.

"Mr. Lind" was probably David Lynd, clerk of the Court of quarter sessions of the peace, which issued police regulations for the district of Quebec.

Copy located: None.

437. QUEBEC, *Province*. LAWS, STATUTES, *etc*.

[Anno Vicesimo quarto Georgii III. Regis. Chap. I. An Ordinance For continuing an Ordinance . . . for regulating . . . Maîtres de Poste.

. . . Chap. II. An Ordinance For continuing an Ordinance . . . for the regulation . . . of Fees.]

French side:

[Anno Vicesimo quarto Georgii III. Regis. Chapitre I. Ordonnance Pour continuer une Ordonnance . . . qui régle . . . Maîtres de Poste.

. . . Chapitre II. Ordonnance Pour continuer une Ordonnance . . . qui établit les Honoraires.]

Broadside? Text in English and French? *Printed at Quebec by Wm. Brown, 1784*, as recorded:

"1784, May 13. Printed for the Gov^{t}. by Order Mr. Gray 200 Copies of 2 Ordinances continuing others.—£1.17 6."

—Can.P.A., *Neilson papers*, v. 47.

Passed at Quebec, Apr. 14, 1784, these ordinances continue for two years, 20 Geo. III c. 4 (*see* No. 344) and 20 Geo. III c. 3, respectively. They are reprinted in Can.P.A., *Report, 1914-15*, from which this entry is taken.

Copy located: None.

438. QUEBEC, *Province*. LAWS, STATUTES, *etc.*

[Anno Vicesimo quarto Georgii III. Regis. Chap. III. An Ordinance for securing the Liberty of the Subject, and for prevention of Imprisonment out of this Province.]

French side (if any):

[Anno Vicesimo quarto Georgii III. Regis. Chapitre III. Ordonnance Pour la Sureté de la Liberté du Sujet dans la Province de Québec, et pour empêcher les Emprisonemens hors de cette Province.]

Printed at Quebec by Wm. Brown, 1784, as recorded:

"1784, May 13. Printed for the Gov^{t}. by Order Mr. Gray 500 [Copies] of the Habeas Corpus Ordinance—£5.17.6."

—Can.P.A., *Neilson papers*, v. 47.

Passed at Quebec, Apr. 29, 1784, this ordinance was published in the *Quebec gazette*, May 13, 1784 (comprising the entire number, [4]. p. fo., text in 2 col., English and French) at a charge of £12 2*s*. 6*d*. The work recorded above by Brown may have been an offprint from the *Gazette* types, of the *Ordinance* in both languages. Or it may have been a separate edition printed from a new setting of type in one language only—thus reducing the cost as recorded. The ordinance is reprinted in Can.P.A., *Report, 1914-15*, from which this entry is taken.

Copy located: None.

439. QUEBEC, *Province*. MILITARY SECRETARY'S OFFICE

QUEBEC, 25th February, 1784. / THIS is to give notice . . . / . . . [to] Refugée Loyalists and disbanded Troops [etc., text, signed:] By His Excellency's Command, / R. MATHEWS. /

2 *l*. Notice, 23 lines on recto of *l*. 1; verso and *l*. 2, blank.

The text states: "This is to give notice that His Excellency the Governor, in order to fulfill His Majesty's gracious Intentions for the Welfare of the Refugée Loyalists and Disbanded Troops, . . . has caused . . . Lands to be examined by the Surveyor-General . . . to establish advantageous settlement, [etc.]." It orders those who want grants between Pointe au Baudet and Cataraqui, to repair to Lachine, those for Chaleur Bay, to report at Sorel or Quebec, by Apr. 2, 1784; and warns that provisions will be issued after Apr. 10, at Quebec, Sorel, and Lachine only.

Printed at Quebec by Wm. Brown, 1784, this was one of many government leaflets and forms concerning the settlement of loyalists and soldiers in Canada, which provided work in Brown's printing-office, e.g.:

"1784, May 8. Printed for Milit^y Sec^y 1500 Grants of Land to Loyalists on a Sheet Propatria—£12.5.0.

D^o for D^o 1500 Permits to settle Lands on a half Sheet thick 4to—£8.10.0.

Oct. 5. Printed for Capt Wood 100 Single pott 4to Hand bills notifying Loyalists to embark for Louisbourg—7/6.

Oct. 13. Printed for J. Craigie (per Order Mr Chapman) 2½ Reams provisions Receipts in 2 editions 1st, 30th ult.—£10.15.0.

1 R^m D^o for Royalists with a Return—£6.0.0.

Dec. 22. Printed for Capt Wood 77 Rules & Directions on a Royal Broadside—£5." —Can.P.A., *Neilson papers*, v. 47.

Copy located: GBLBM (in *Haldimand papers*, Add. Mss. 21880, fo. 187-88).

440. QUEBEC GAZETTE. CARRIER'S ADDRESS

NEW-YEAR'S / VERSES / Of the PRINTER'S LAD who carries about the / QUEBEC GAZETTE / TO THE CUSTOMERS. / JANUARY 1, 1785. / [*Quebec, Wm. Brown, 1784.*]

Broadside: 48 lines; type-page: 32 × 19 cm. in ornamental rule frame.

Contents: This year the *Verses* describe, realistically enough, the *Quebec gazette* itself:

"So wondrous intelligent, it tells all the news,
Of Nabobs and Rajahs and both the Tippoos.
With the Russias and Porte it very familiar is,
But almost forgets what a doing in England is. . . .

Of news more domestic, what's worse, 'tis quite dry,
Unless when some great man bids us goodbye. . . .

Where attempting some flowers poetic to pluck,
By Canada's frosts they find them all struck.
And sometimes by Chance tells a wonderful tale
Of erring-saints, hurricanes or a strong gale,
With bankrupts by scores and false ribs ran away,—
Whilst lawyers and auctioneers are in full pay
Then goods new imported, of seven years long standing
With shop-dust ingrain'd, and worn thread-bare by handling."

Copy located: CaO (bound in *Quebec gazette*, at end of 1784).

441. ST. OURS, CHARLES LOUIS ROCH DE, 1753-1834

Caption title: (1) / [double rule] / AU PUBLIC. / DEFENSES de Mr. de Saint-Ours, adressées au / Comité opposé à la chambre d'Assemblée, tenue chez / les R.R.P.P. Recolets, le 30 Novembre 1784. /

4to. 4 p.; type-page: 18.7 × 12.2 cm.

Probably printed at Montreal by Fleury Mesplet, between Dec. 25, 1784 and Jan 10, 1785. Following the text is the author's note that he learned of criticism against him only on Dec. 24 [1784] and, thinking that the printer would not work over Christmas, he was issuing his *Défenses* as early as possible. A printed copy was enclosed in a letter from Hugh Finlay, Quebec, Jan. 10, 1785, to Evan Nepean, London, with the comment that it had come from Montreal.

Contents: p. 1-4, "Défenses, [signed at end:] Charles St. Ours le Jeune."

St. Ours, a wealthy young seigneur, was one of those who met at Recollet House, Montreal, Nov. 30, 1784, to launch a campaign against the petition of the Reform Committee of Quebec (*see* No. 453). Like De Bonne, St. Ours was of the faction which split off from the main body of anti-Reform opinion represented by the Comité canadien. Further dissension arose in the De Bonne-St. Ours group. In his *Défenses*, St. Ours explains the reasons for disagreement in the minority group and for dissent from *La très-humble adresse* of the Comité canadien.

Copies located: CaQMS; CaQQL; GBLP (in C.O. 42/17: Jan. 10, 1785).

442. SCOTT, JONATHAN, 1744-1819

A / BRIEF VIEW / OF THE / Religious TENETS and SENTIMENTS, / Lately published and spread in the Province of NOVA- / SCOTIA; which are contained in a Book, entitled / "TWO MITES, on some of the most / important and much disputed Points / of Divinity, &c." / AND / "In a SERMON preached at Liverpool, / November 19, 1782;" / AND, IN A PAMPHLET, ENTITLED / "THE ANTITRADITIONIST:" / ALL BEING PUBLICATIONS OF / Mr. HENRY ALLINE. / WITH / Some brief Reflections and Observations: / ALSO, / A VIEW of the Ordination of the Author / of these Books: / TOGETHER WITH / A DISCOURSE on external Order. / [rule] / By JONATHAN SCOTT, / Pastor of a Church in YARMOUTH. / [rule] / JUDE, verse 3. Beloved, when I gave all Diligence to write unto you / of the common Salvation: It was needful for me to write unto you, / and exhort you that ye should earnestly contend for the Faith which / was once delivered unto the Saints. / [double rule] / HALIFAX: / Printed by JOHN HOWE, in BARRINGTON-STREET. / [rule] / MDCCLXXXIV. /

8vo. A^4,B-X^8; viii, 334 p., 1 *l.*; type-page: 18.5 × 9.6 cm.

Contents: p. [i], t.-p.; verso, blank; p. [iii]-iv, Contents; p. v-viii, Preface; p. 1-14, Introduction; p. 15-334, A brief view, I-XVII; 1 *l.* at end, blank with errata slip pasted on recto.

Scott, born at Lunenburg, Massachusetts, in 1744, was bred a shoemaker. He settled at Yarmouth, N.S., in 1765, fishing in the summers and making, as he stated, "swift progress in sin." He served as lay preacher at Congregationalist meetings however (his library consisting of two books on divinity and the bible); then in 1772 he went to Massachusetts to be ordained. Returning, he preached steadily in and around Yarmouth, making a scanty living for his large family from barren soil and gifts from neighbours. He left Nova Scotia in 1792. Scott, like many others, was deeply disturbed by the evangelical preaching of Henry Alline. This work probably represents an attitude not peculiar to Scott and its publication must have been supported by sympathizers.

Scott's journal, Oct., 1764-Nov. 23, 1777, was published in a modern newspaper, *The Yarmouth* [*N.S.*] *light*, from which clippings were deposited in Massachusetts Historical Society in 1922.

Copies located: CaNsHA; CaNsHD; CaQM; NN; RPJ.

443. SKETCHLEY & FREEMAN, *Auctioneers, Quebec*

[Catalogue of Books and Jewellery.]

fo. 2 p., text in 2 col. *Printed at Quebec by Wm. Brown, 1784*, as recorded:

"1784, June 21. Printed for Sketchley & Freeman, 200 Catalogues Books & Jewellery 2 folio pages Demy, 2 cols.—£2.17.6."

—Can.P.A., *Neilson papers*, v. 47.

Copy located: None.

444. WILLCOCKS, *Miss*

[Poem on Miss Willcocks]

? Broadside *printed at Quebec by Wm. Brown*, as recorded:

"1784, May 26. Printed for Dr. Bowman 50 Poems on Miss Willcocks—10/ *gratis*." —Can.P.A., *Neilson papers*, v. 47.

This is perhaps an offprint of the verses which appeared in the *Quebec gazette* with the notice:

"On Wednesday the 19th Instant, died Miss Willcocks. Having received the following poem from an unknown hand prevents our attempting to pay that tribute due to the merits of so amiable a young lady. EXTEMPORE, on the Death of Miss WILLCOCKS, By her Friend MARIA.

"What obdurate heart, will not grieve,
At this shock, which we feel so severe!
Sure none, that her smiles did receive;
In our Sorrows, that will not share. . . ."

—*Quebec gazette*, May 27, 1784.

This poem has 32 lines in 8 stanzas, set in long primer leaded making a type area 14.5 × 10 cm.

Dr. James Bowman was a physician and surgeon in Quebec from about 1760 till his death in 1787.

Copy located: None.

445. ADDRESS TO THE PUBLIC ON THE PRESENT STATE . . . OF NOVA-SCOTIA

ADDRESS / TO THE / PUBLIC, / ON THE / PRESENT STATE / OF THE / PROVINCE / OF / NOVA-SCOTIA; / [rule] / HALIFAX: / Printed by JOHN HOWE, at his PRINTING-OFFICE, / in BARRINGTON STREET, Corner of / SACKVILLE STREET. / MDCCLXXXV /

8vo. [*][8]; 13 p., 1 *l.*; type-page: 16 × 8.5 cm.

Contents: p. [1], t.-p.; p. [2], blank; p. [3]-13, Address; p. 13 verso, blank; 1 *l.* blank.

This address was written by one "long a Resident, and deeply interested in the welfare of this Province"—p. [3], possibly Richard Bulkeley, provincial secretary. The author attacks a recent law on the confiscation of estates of insolvent debtors, stating the case for the resident land-owner. He also "furnishes a few useful hints to promote the general good," describing how capital and settlers may be attracted, the export trade and agriculture developed, and the natural resources utilized. He suggests the formation of agricultural and other societies to assist schemes of commerce, public utility, and charitable purpose.

The first half of *Address to the public* was printed without comment on author or subject matter, in the *Port Roseway gazetteer*, June 9, 1785, with note: "To be continued" (later issues not seen).

Copy located: CaNsHD; another copy, sold at auction by Charles Heartman, Metuchen, N.J., Oct. 10, 1934 (described in his *Catalogue*, no. 261, item no. 2) not located. This item was also listed by Lathrop C. Harper, in *Catalogue of Americana*, New York, pt. 1, Apr., 1941, no. 1551.

446. ALMANACS. NEW BRUNSWICK

AN ASTRONOMICAL / DIARY / OR / ALMANACK, / For the Year of our LORD CHRIST / 1786, / Being the Second after Bissextile, or Leap Year, / WHEREIN ARE CONTAINED, / The Eclipses of the Luminaries, Moon's Place / and Age, Sun and Moon's Rising and Setting, / Moon's Apogee and Perigee, Equation of Time, / Feasts and Fasts of the Church, Time of High / Water, &c.&c. / AND A VARIETY OF OTHER MATTER, / Useful and Intertaining. / Calculated for the Meridian of the City of SAINT / JOHN, in the Province of NEW BRUNSWICK; / but will serve without sensible Error, for any / Part of said Province. / [rule] / By JULIUS SCALIGER, Jun. / [rule] / CITY OF ST. JOHN: / Printed by CHRISTOPHER SOWER, / Printer to His MAJESTY. / [title within ornamental frame] /

12mo. [A]-D[4], [E][2]; [36] p.; type-page (within rule frame): 14 × 7.5 cm.

Contents: p. [1], t.-p.; p. [2], "To the Public, [signed:] The Printer"; p. [3], Zodiac; p. [4], Eclipses; p. [5-16], Calendar; p. [17], Province of New Brunswick: administration, courts, customs; p. [18], City of Saint John, magistrates; p. [18-21], County magistrates; p. [22], Supreme court terms, army staff, St. John River falls; p. [23-29], Tables of coins, interest; p. [30-31], Pot and pearl ashes, etc.; p. [32-33], Remarkable events, N.B. Assembly members; p. [34], Recipes for consumption, the itch, etc.; p. [35], Select anecdotes; p. [36], High water, distances.

The introduction (p. [2]) states: "The Printer on his arrival in this province, being informed that an Astronomical Diary or Almanack for . . . 1786, was in great request, and altho' late in the season and very sensible that such a calculation would at this time be attended with great expense—yet he ventured . . . The calculations agree, he believes, with the situation of the City of St. John, but he invites correction. He intends, if this first attempt meets encouragement, to print another for 1787, and asks for information on exact latitude, longitude, tides, moon's phases, also harbour information for all harbours in New Brunswick [etc.]."

This almanac was advertised, from Nov. 22, 1785, as "in the press," then: "Just published and to be sold at His Majesty's Printing Office . . . Price 12/ per dozen, An Astronomical diary or Almanack for 1786 etc."—*Royal gazette*, Saint John, N.B., Jan. 3, 1786.

Copy located: CaNS (t.-p. and p. [35-36], stained and torn); CaOOA (p. [1-36], stained and crumbling, backed with gauze).

447. ALMANACS. NOVA SCOTIA

THE / NOVA-SCOTIA CALENDER, / OR AN / ALMANACK, / For the Year of the Christian Æra, 1786; . . . / [4 lines] / Wherein is Contained, / The Eclipses . . . / [4 lines] / [rule] / Calculated for the Meridian of HALIFAX, . . . / [3 lines] / By METONICUS, / [rule] / [verse, 8 lines by] / POPE, / [rule] / HALIFAX, Printed and Sold by A. HENRY. / [title and each page within double rule frame]

12mo. [A-C][4]; [24] p.; type-page: 16.3 × 9.8 cm.

Contents: p. [1], t.-p.; p. [2], Verses; p. [3-4], Vulgar notes, eclipses, verse; p. [5-16], Calendar; p. [17-21], Nova Scotia administration, legislature, courts, justices, sheriffs, judges, customs, army, fairs and markets, tides, etc.; p. [22-24], inferior courts and sessions, distances, buoys, treatment of cancer.

This almanac was advertised "Just published and for sale The Nova-Scotia Calender, etc."—*Nova-Scotia gazette*, Dec. 13, 1785.

Copy located: CSmH; CaNsHA (several pages wanting from last section).

448. ALMANACS. QUEBEC

[Almanach de Québec pour l'année 1786. *à Québec, chez Guillaume Brown, sur la Grande Côté.*]

Published on Dec. 19, 1785, and sold, as Brown's account books show, at 1*s*. 3*d*. the copy, 2*s*. the dozen, this almanac was advertised:

"On vient de publier l'Almanach portatif de Québec, pour l'année 1786 . . . à vendre à l'Imprimerie de Quebec, chez Mr. Adam Scott . . . Montréal, chez Mr. Louis Aimé à Berthier, et chez Mr. Samuel Sills à Trois Rivières."

—*Quebec gazette*, Dec. 22, 1785.

Copy located: None.

449. ALMANACS. QUEBEC

[Almanach . . . pour l'année 1786. *Montréal, Chez Fleury Mesplet, 1785.*]

This almanac was advertised: "Le Calendrier pour Montréal [No. 451] et l'Almanach, à vendre. On les trouves chez Mr. Sarreau, Marchand, rue Notre Dame et chez l'Imprimeur."—*Montreal gazette*, Dec. 1, 1785, *et seq.*

Copy located: None.

450. ALMANACS. QUEBEC

Calendrier pour l'Année 1786, pour Québec, par les 306$^{d.}$ 30$^{m.}$ de Longitude, et 46$^{d.}$ 55$^{m.}$ de Latitude. / [ornamental rule] /

Colophon: QUEBEC: chez WM. BROWN, au milieu de la Grande Côte. /

Broadside: type-page: 51 × 39 cm.

Contents: Calendrier in ornamental rule frame: 44.5 × 32.5 cm., note on arrangement, officiers civils, as in previous years.

This sheet almanac was sold at 9*d.* the copy, 5*s.* the dozen from Nov. 5, 1784, and advertised for sale as in previous years, in the *Quebec gazette* from Nov. 17, 1785.

Copy located: CaO (bound in *Quebec gazette,* at the end of 1785).

451. ALMANACS. QUEBEC

[Calendrier pour Montréal, pour l'année 1786.]

Broadside: This sheet almanac, like the *Calendrier pour Montréal,* of preceding years, was undoubtedly *printed at Montreal by Fleury Mesplet, 1785.* It was advertised: "Le Calendrier pour Montréal et l'Almanach à vendre. On les trouve chez Mr. Sarreau, marchand, rue Notre Dame et chez l'Imprimeur."—*Montreal gazette,* Dec. 1, 1785, *et seq.*

Copy located: None.

ALMANACS. QUEBEC

[Indian almanac for 1786.] *See* No. 310.

452. ALMANACS. QUEBEC

[Perpetual chronological Tables, adapted to the Gregorian or New Stile, by E. W. Philomath.]

? Broadside, *possibly printed at Montreal by Fleury Mesplet, 1785,* who advertised in his newspaper: "For Sale at the Printing office . . . Perpetual chronological Tables, adapted to the Gregorian or New Stile, by E. W. Philomath."—*Montreal gazette,* Sept. 1, 1785.

This may refer to an English edition of No. 391, or it may be simply an English advertisement of the latter.

The identity of E. W. Philomath is unknown, but some clue thereto may appear in the following: "The Students in Natural Philosophy at the Quebec Seminary who supported a Mathematical Thesis the 26th of May last* received a Letter from Montreal, dated the 30th ult. in English, from a Person unknown, signed: Philomathus, in which he proposed to them the solution of two [mathematical] problems, etc."—*Quebec gazette,* Aug. 10, 1775.

Copy listed: None.

**See* No. 196.

453. AUX CITOYENS . . . DE QUEBEC

Caption title, p. 1: AUX / CITOYENS et HABITANTS / DES VILLES ET DES CAMPAGNES / DE LA PROVINCE DE / QUÉBEC. / [rule] /

4to.* [A]-D²; 15 p.; type-page: 19 × 13 cm. *Printed at Quebec by Wm. Brown, 1785*, as recorded:

> "1785. Feb. 25. Printed for the Commttee of Reform by Order of German [i.e. Louis Germain], Perrault, and Duniere an Address to Canadians and Petition to the King 1000 Copies 2 Sheets 4to on Crown by Agt. [i.e. agreement] 10 Guineas—11.13.4."—Can.P.A., *Neilson papers*, v. 47.

Contents: p. [1]-2, Introductory note addressed to "Messieurs et Compatriotes"; p. 2-15, "A la Très Excellente Majesté du Roi, L'Humble Adresse des anciens et nouveaux Sujets, Habitants de la Province de Québec. [dated and signed, p. 14:] Fevrier, 1785. A Montreal. James McGill [and 15 others]"; p. 15: "A Quebec, Juchereau Duchesnay [and 18 others, including James Johnston, Adam Lymburner, etc.]"; p. 15 at foot, Errata; p. 15 verso, blank.

Drawn up by the so-called Reform Committee, mainly English merchants in Quebec, and circulated from Nov. 24, 1784, this petition with some 2,300 signatures was presented to Gov. Dorchester, in Jan., 1785. Purporting to represent the views of old (English), and new (French) subjects, it prayed for reform of the Quebec Act of 1774, under fourteen heads—entailing a fundamental reorganization of the government and laws of Quebec to strengthen the position of the old [i.e. English] subjects. This included the introduction of government by popular elective assembly with powers to appoint sheriffs, levy taxes, and grant subsidies to trade. When the Quebec Act was finally revised this petition was published again (No. 653, cf. No. 709-710). It is reprinted (in English, with editorial notes) in Shortt and Doughty: *Documents, 1759-1791*, 2: 742-54.

Copies located: CSmH; CaOOA (p. 9-15, supplied in MS.); CaQM; CaQMJ (p. 13-15 wanting); CaQMS (2 cop.); CaQQL; GLBP (2 cop. in C.O. 42/63: 63-78; C.O. 42/63: 241-55); Ketcheson; RPJ.

454. [BADELARD, PHILLIPE LOUIS FRANCOIS], 1728-1802

[Direction pour la guerison du Mal de la Baie St. Paul. *Quebec, Wm, Brown, 1785.*]

fo. 2 to 4 p., or possibly a broadside: text in French. *Printed at Quebec by Wm. Brown, 1785*, as recorded:

> "1785, Apr. 9. Printed for Gov^{t}. by Order Dr. Bowman 2000 Directions &c for curing the Mal de la Baie St. Paul, on a folio Demy—£8.10."
> —Can.P.A., *Neilson papers*, v. 47.

This "Printed paper of Directions &c," to which occasional reference occurs in contemporary MS. records of government, was prepared for distribution among the clergy, seigneurs, and others, in Dr. Bowman's campaign against Mal de la Baie. It was probably the first edition of the work attributed to Dr. Badelard (No. 455).

Copy located: None.

*Some copies at least are in folio, the laid lines of the paper running lengthwise with the page, printed on 4 sheets fo. on pott (about $11\frac{1}{4} \times 15\frac{1}{2}''$) instead of 2 sheets 4to on crown (about $15\frac{1}{2} \times 18\frac{1}{2}''$).

455. [BADELARD, PHILLIPE LOUIS FRANCOIS], 1728-1802

DIRECTION / POUR LA / GUERISON / DU / MAL / DE LA / BAIE St. PAUL. / [double rule] / A QUEBEC: / CHEZ GUILLAUME BROWN, / AU MILIEU DE LA GRANDE COTE. / [rule] / M,DCC,LXXXV. /

8vo. A-B^4; 16 p.; type-page: 10.8 × 5.5 cm. Text in French. ? Second edition of No. 454.

Contents: p. [1], t.-p.; p. [2], blank; p. [3]-15, Direction; p. 16, Notice of free treatment by government and request for co-operation of those with disease, to eradicate it from the province (notice has no heading, signature, or date). Brown recorded the production of this work:

"1785, Apr. 27. Printed for [Gov^t.] by Order Dr. Bowman, 250 Directions for Cure of Mal de la Baie making 16 pages 8vo on Superfine pot—£3.
Picard for Stitching D^o @ 1½—£1.11.3.
22 Q^{rs} Superfine pott to interleave them £1.2.
2½ D^o Magazine blue to cover them—7/6.
[total] £6.0.9."—Can.P.A., *Neilson papers*, v. 47.

This work is generally attributed to Badelard, who came to Canada in 1757 as surgeon-major in the de Bery Regiment. Remaining here after the English conquest, he was appointed to the staff of the Military Hospital, Quebec.

Mal de la Baie, or St. Paul's Bay disease, as it was commonly called, though various place names were attached to it, seems to have been syphilis, and was apparently common through the St. Lawrence valley in the latter part of the 18th century, almost epidemic in the 1780's. From 1775 Gov. Carleton and his successor, Haldimand occasionally sent army doctors to country settlements to give free treatment, notably Badelard. He studied the disease and prepared a method of treatment. This was published in the *Quebec gazette*, July 29-Aug. 19, and again on Oct. 28, 1784, at the charge of the government: *Observations sur la Maladie de la Baie par Mons. Badelar* [sic] *Chirurgeon du Roi*.

About Mar. 7, 1785, Lieut.-Gov. Hamilton appointed Dr. James Bowman to take special measures in the country districts. Bowman was a British army surgeon who had come to Quebec soon after the conquest and served on the staff of the Military Hospital and of Hôtel Dieu, Quebec, till his death in 1787. During 1785 he conducted an elaborate campaign against Mal de la Baie, which included several little publications (also many thousand pill-box labels) printed by Wm. Brown. Then he presented the government with a bill for £2353 12*s*. 4*d*.

The Hamilton-Bowman enterprise was discredited in some quarters and during a long investigation of Bowman's accounts, most of the medical men in the colony gave evidence, stressing the importance of Badelard's cure, also mentioning Jones's work (No. 484).—Can.P.A., Que. *State*, Mar. 7, 1785, Aug. 15, 1791.

See W. A. Cochran: *Notes on measures adopted by government between 1775 and 1786 to check the St. Paul's Bay disease*, in Lit. and hist. soc. of Quebec, *Trans*. 4, no. 2: 139-52, 1854. J. J. Heagerty: *Four centuries of medical history in Canada* (2 v., Toronto, 1928), 1: 131-60; also 2: 324-26, a bibliography of primary and secondary material.

T.-p. facsim. (from CaQQL copy) appears in New York Academy of Medicine: *Catalogue of an exhibition of early and later medical Americana, Nov. 18, 1926* (New York, 1927), no. 4, pl. XII.

Copies located: CaQM (interleaved with blank pages bearing MS. notes, observations of symptoms, treatment, etc.); CaQMS (2 cop.); CaQQL.

456. CATHOLIC CHURCH. LITURGY and RITUAL. *Psalter*

PSEAUTIER / DE / DAVID, / AVEC LES CANTIQUES / A l'usage des ECOLES. / [rule] / [printer's ornament] / [double rule] / A QUEBEC: / Chez GUILLAUME BROWN, / Au Milieu de la Grande Côte. / [rule] / M,DCC,LXXXV. /

12mo. A-Ff^4; 231 p.; type-page: 12.7 × 6.6 cm.

Contents: p. [1], t.-p.; p. [2]-12, Prières; p. 13-203, Le Pseautier etc.; p. 203-18, Cantiques; p. 219-31, Litanies etc.; p. 231, verso, blank.

The printer's records are rather casual from Sept., 1785 to Dec., 1786 and indicate no details of the cost of printing, size of edition, or actual publisher of the *Pseautier*. Brown sold a few copies retail at 2*s*. the copy and fifty copies wholesale at 1*s*. 6*d*. the copy, in Jan., 1786. Part of the edition at least was bound at the printing office, as recorded:

"1785, Dec. 24. Bought of Wm. Laing the 6th Inst. 13 yds. Buckram for covering the Psalters—£1.1.8.

1786, Jan. 6. Printing Office owes Pierre Picard for loan of binding tools—10*s*."

—Can.P.A., *Neilson papers*, v. 84.

Copy located: CaQQL.

457. ESGLIS, LOUIS PHILIPPE MARIAUCHAU D', *bp. of Quebec*, 1710-1788

Caption title: LETTRE CIRCULAIRE A MESSIEURS LES CURÉS. / [rule] /

4to. [*]^2; [3] p.; type-page: 18 × 14 cm. *Printed at Quebec by Wm. Brown, 1785*, as recorded:

"1785, Apr. 13. Printed for Gov^t. 200 Circular Letters, making 3 pages on Small Pica, on 4to Post. by Order Mr. Gravé.—£2.17.6."

—Can.P.A., *Neilson papers*, v. 47.

Contents: p. [1-3], Lettre, signed: "L.Ph. Evêque de Québec. A St. Pierre, Isle d'Orleans, 12 Avril, 1785"; p. [3] verso, blank.

Prepared to accompany Badelard's *Directions* (No. 454-455) and printed at government expense for the bishop's secretary, Abbé Gravé, this letter instructs curés to assist the government in combatting St. Paul's Bay disease, also to register baptisms, marriages, and deaths according to the ordinance of Apr. 9, 1736, again in force following the Quebec Act.

Bishop Esglis, or Esgly, was coadjutor from 1770, and bishop of Quebec from 1784 till 1788. His papers are calendared in Quebec Province, Archives, *Rapport, 1930-31*, 185-98. This *Lettre* is reprinted in Têtu and Gagnon: *Mandements de Québec*, 2: 317-20.

Copies located: CaO; CaOOA.

458. GREAT BRITAIN. LAWS, STATUTES, *etc.*

[An Act for appointing commissioners further to enquire into the Losses and services of all such persons who have suffered in their rights, properties, and professions, during the late unhappy dissentions in America, in consequence of their loyalty to His Majesty and attachment to the British government. *Saint John, N.B., Christopher Sower, 1785.*]

? fo. 10 p. (2½ sheets); *Printed at Saint John, N.B., by Christopher Sower, 1785,* this work was advertised:

"Just published and to be sold by the Printer of this paper, An Act of the 25th of George the Third entitled: an Act for appointing commissioners [etc.]. This act is comprised in two sheets and a half and very interesting to every loyalist whose claim has not yet been investigated or entered."

—*Royal gazette,* Saint John, N.B., Dec. 6, 1785.

This act, 25 Geo. III c. 26, renewed for two years the appointment of commissioners made under 23 Geo. III c. 80. Two of the commissioners (Thomas Dundas and Jeremy Pemberton) came to Canada to investigate claims, 1785-89.

Copy located: None.

459. MAHIR, EDWARD, *d.* 1785

[Confession.]

fo. 2 p.; *Printed at Quebec by Wm. Brown, 1785,* as recorded:

"1785, June 17. Printed for J. Hill, Edward Mahir's Confession, making 2 folio pages pott in pica, [blank] copies by Ag[t]. [i.e. Agreement]—£2."

—Can.P.A., *Neilson papers,* v. 84.

Mahir was hanged for theft at Quebec, June 15, 1785, according to a notice in the *Gazette:*

"Quebec, June 16, [1785], Edward Mahir, for stealing out of a Shop, and Charles Shondorst, for a Burglary and Robbery, were executed yesterday at a Gallows on the Heights of Abraham pursuant to their Sentence."—*Quebec gazette* [*Supplement*], June 16, 1785.

Copy located: None.

460. MONTREAL GAZETTE

Caption, col. 1: THE / MONTREAL GAZETTE. /

Caption, col. 2: GAZETE / DE / MONTREAL. /

fo. [4] p. printed in 2 col. English and French. *Printed at Montreal by Fleury Mesplet, 1785.*

This is a prospectus, or preliminary number, of the *Montreal gazette.* It was published in Aug., 1785, and has the same format and general appearance as the regular numbers of the newspaper. It contains: "Proposal for the Establishment of a new Gazette, Englesh [sic] and Frencsh [sic] under the Title of the Montreal Gazette, Printed by F. Mesplet"; also a few pieces of light verse and prose and an advertisement of books and stationery for sale by Mesplet—no other advertisement or news appears in this preliminary number.

The *Proposal* states "There is scarce a Dominion in Europe that has not its Gazette, why should not this extensive Country have its own. The periodical Paper of 1778* had already place. The subscriptions would have been much more numerous the year following without the catastrophe which it is useless to mention [Mesplet's imprisonment] . . . The tranquility which this Province enjoys gives a fresh En-

*Mesplet's *Gazette du commerce et littéraire.*

couragement [etc.]." In the *Montreal gazette,* Mesplet states, he will publish monthly foreign news from Europe and the United States "quite different and in greater quantity . . . and literary News shall have a place . . . In all that shall be inserted in this Gazette, I shall inviolably observe to have the Sacred Image of Truth in view and not fall into Licentiousness. I shall endeavour to render the style, plain and correct, but likewise my Readers will observe we do not write so well on the sides of the River St. Lawrence as they do on the Banks of the Seine [etc.]." Mesplet continues, announcing that the first gazette will appear Thursday, Aug. 25, 1785. The subscription is 3 Spanish dollars a year (15*s.*), productions, instructing or entertaining, will be inserted gratis, advertisements in French and English will be 1 Spanish dollar; 2 or 3 insertions will be 1½ or 2 Spanish dollars respectively.

The newspaper thus announced was published on Aug. 25, 1785, and, with some changes, continues to appear.

Copy located: CaQQL (bound in file of the *Montreal gazette*).

461. NEW BRUNSWICK. GOVERNOR, 1784-1786 (*Carleton*)

REGULATIONS, by Order of His Excellency the / GOVERNOR in COUNCIL, to be observed for the orderly and / expeditious settlement of the Province of NEW-BRUNSWICK / by the several persons entitled to or petitioning for Farms, and by / all others concerned therein. / <Text> / By Command of his Excellency the Governor, / in Council, the 14th of January, 1785. / JONATHAN ODELL, Secretary. /

Broadside: 54 lines; type-page: 34 × 17.7 cm. *Printed at Parr-Town, N.B., by Lewis and Ryan, 1784,* in an edition of 500 copies (*see* No. 423 *note*).

The text comprises regulations 1-10, describing the form and routine for the petition, allotment, survey, and recording of grants, etc., and the methods to be pursued by groups disbanded from regiments. Regulation no. 4 states that the applicant must publish the substance of his petition three times in a newspaper, also in a notice posted in the nearest settlement to his prospective grant, "for the whole of which publication the Printers have agreed to take five shillings and no more."

Copy located: CaN (filed in bundle of MS. documents, mainly proclamations 1784-96, in vault).

462. NOVA SCOTIA. HOUSE OF ASSEMBLY

Caption title: [Journal and Proceedings of the General Assembly, of the Province of Nova-Scotia.]

Note: title above is not transcribed from copy.

fo. A-I²; 35 p. *Printed at Halifax, N.S., by Anthony Henry, 1785.*

Contents: p. 1-35, Journal and proceedings of the first session of the sixth assembly, Dec. 5-28, 1785; p. 35 verso, blank.

Though "Proceedings" was substituted for "Votes" in wording of title, this session and henceforward (also "General Assembly" for "House of Assembly," in editions of 1785-87), the content of the record remained unchanged. The *Journal* was printed regularly during the session and issued *seriatim* to members of government. The late date of prorogation suggests that general publication of this *Journal* may have taken place in 1786, like that of the sessions' laws.

Copies located: CaNs; GBLP (in C.O. 217/58: 213-47).

463. PRIMERS. QUEBEC

[ALPHABET. *Printed at Quebec by Wm. Brown, 1785.*]

Brown recorded the sale (wholesale) of 2,600 Alphabets or Primers, some at least in a French edition:

"1785, Feb. 10. Sold Louis Germain payable on Demand, 1600 Alphabets in French @ 2*d.*—£13.6.8.

"Mar. 5. I owe P. Picard for stitching 500 Alphabets @ 2/9 [per hundred]—13/9.

"Apr. 19. Pierre Beaufre owes for 1000 Alphabets as per note payable in all Septr. next—£10/2."

—Can.P.A., *Neilson papers*, v. 47.

Copy located: None.

464. QUEBEC, *Province.* LIEUTENANT-GOVERNOR, 1785-1789 (*Hope*)

[By the Honorable Henry Hope, Esq. Lieutenant Governor and Commander in Chief in and over the Province of Quebec . . . Proclamation. <Text> Given . . . at . . . Quebec, 2 November 1785. Henry Hope, etc.]

French side:

[Par l'Honorable Henry Hope, Ecuier, Lieutenant-Gouverneur et Commandant en Chef de la Province de Québec . . . Proclamation. <Text> Donné . . . à . . . Québec, 2 novembre, 1785. Henry Hope etc.]

Double broadside: text in English and French; *printed at Quebec by Wm. Brown, 1785*, as recorded:

"1785, Nov. 3. Printed for the Gov^{t}. by Order Mr. Pownall 50 D^{ble} Proclamations notifying Genl. Hope's taking the Civil Government.—£1.10."

—Can.P.A., *Neilson papers*, v. 47.

English text: "Whereas it has pleased His Most Gracious Majesty to appoint me, Lieutenant Governor . . . And Whereas during the absence of His Excellency Frederick Haldimand, Captain General and Governor in Chief . . . the trust . . . devolves on the Lieutenant Governor . . . therefore I . . . require all officers of His Majesty's Government . . . to take notice [etc.]."

French text: "Aiant plû à sa Très Gracieuse Majesté de me nommer Lieutenant-Gouverneur . . . Et en absence de Son Excellence Frederic Haldimand, Capitaine General et Gouverneur en Chef . . . la conduite du Gouvernement . . . étant confiée au Lieutenant-Gouverneur . . . J'ordonne . . . à tous les Officiers de Sa Majesté . . . d'en prendre connaissance [etc.]."

This proclamation is reprinted in Can.P.A., *Report, 1918*, from which this entry is taken.

Copy located: None.

465. QUEBEC GAZETTE. CARRIER'S ADDRESS

NEW-YEARS / VERSES / Of the PRINTER's BOY who carries about the / QUEBEC GAZETTE / TO THE CUSTOMERS. / JANUARY 1, 1786. / [*Quebec, Wm. Brown, 1785.*]

Broadside: 75 lines; type-page: 32.5 × 21 cm. in ornamental rule frame.

Contents: 6 stanzas in 2 col. beginning:

"Since Time, the old bald-pate, leads in a New-Year,
Your purse to lay siege to, again I appear;
Tho' a young Imp, no [sic] otherwise given to pilfer,
Than, once a year, glance at a little odd silver."

Copy located: CaO (bound in *Quebec gazette* at end of 1785).

466. QUEBEC LIBRARY

CATALOGUE / OF / ENGLISH AND FRENCH / BOOKS / IN THE / QUEBEC LIBRARY. / [rule] / M,DCC,LXXXV. /

8vo. 1 p. l., 23 p., 3 *l.*; type-page: 16 × 10 cm.

Contents: p. l. recto, t.-p.; verso, blank; p. 1-11, English books; p. [12], blank; p. 13-23, Livres françois etc.; p. 23 verso, blank; 3 *l.* (same paper as text) blank.

This work was *printed at Quebec by Wm. Brown, 1785*, in two parts, English and French, both parts issued (together) in 100 fine paper copies and 100 common or printing paper copies, as recorded:

"1784, Dec. 27. Printed for the Quebec Library by Order Mr. Monk 200 Catalogues in English [English books] making a Sheet of Demy in 8vo. half on fine paper—£4.15.

"1785, Jan. 14. Printed for the Quebec Library, 200 Catalogues of French books, half on superfine Demy and half on printing D°—£4.15."

—Can.P.A., *Neilson papers*, v. 47.

This *Catalogue* is analysed in Fauteux: *Les bibliothèques canadiennes.*

Copy located: CaQMS (fine paper copy).

467. SAINT JOHN, N.B., *City.* CHARTER

THE / CHARTER / OF THE / CITY OF SAINT JOHN, / IN THE / PROVINCE of NEW-BRUNSWICK. / [rule] / "O! FORTUNATI QUORUM JAM MOENIA SURGUNT." / [rule] / [rule] / NEW-BRUNSWICK: / PRINTED BY LEWIS AND RYAN, AT THEIR / PRINTING-OFFICE, No. 59, PRINCE WILLIAM-STREET. /

fo. [*[1] A] -K[2]; 42 p.; type-page: 23.5 × 15.4 cm.

Contents: p. [1], t.-p.; p. [2], blank; p. [3]-42, Charter, signed at end: "18th of May 1785, Thomas Carleton"; p. 42 at foot, Errata.

The Saint John corporation accounts show that Lewis & Ryan were paid £62 10*s.* for printing the charter but the number of copies printed does not appear.

Trading stations and a settlement of a few families had been around the mouth of the St. John River for twenty years, when in 1783-84, the arrival of about twelve thousand loyalists from the United States, produced a large town in a few months.

Townsites were laid out on both sides of the harbour, government supplies granted for buildings, and permission given for the incorporation of Carleton and Parr-Town, as the two sides were called, as the city of Saint John. It long remained the only municipal corporation in Canada. Halifax was refused a charter in 1785 and waited till 1842 for incorporation; York, till 1834 as Toronto; and Montreal (temporarily incorporated 1833-36), till 1840. (*See* W. O. Raymond's numerous articles on the settlement of Saint John in N.B. hist. soc. *Coll.*, also in his scrap books in the Saint John, N.B., Free Public library.)

Copies located: CaNS; CaNsHA; CaNsHD; GBLP (in C.O. 188/3: 403-44); MWA; NNHi.

468. SHELBURNE, N.S., *Town.* GENERAL QUARTER SESSIONS OF THE PEACE

[Handbill forbidding Negro Dances and Negro Frolicks in this Town of Shelburne.]

Broadside; *printed at Shelburne, N.S., by ? James Robertson Sr., 1785.*

"1785, May 12. It is ordered that 50 Handbills be immediately printed forbidding Negro Dances and Negro Frolicks in this Town of Shelburne."
—Shelburne, N.S., Quarter sessions, *Records.*

The printing was probably done by James Robertson, Sr., who was one of the justices of the peace. He was the surviving partner of the J. & A. Robertson printing firm, his brother Alexander, having died at Shelburne, N.S., Nov. 8, 1784.

The negro settlers apparently remained a recurrent source of disturbance, for the Quarter Sessions records of Aug. 9, 1786, include: "Ordered that a publication be made, restricting the assembling of Negroes for the purpose of Gaming, Frolicking and Dancing to the Prejudice of the inhabitants in the back part of the Town . . . in consequence of a memorial signed by a number of Inhabitants."

Shelburne, or Port Roseway, a coast town 160 miles south-west of Halifax, formerly settled as Port Razoir by the French, latterly as Jerusalem by Alexander McNutt, was resettled by loyalists. About 10,000 arrived between 1783 and 1785, many accompanied by negro "servants," and in a brief period they built one of the largest towns on the continent. The spot was unsuitable, however, and most of the new settlers, including three families of printers, the Robertsons, the Swords, and James Humphreys, moved elsewhere in a few years. The negro community there is still known as Burchtown. *See* T. W. Smith: *The loyalists at Shelburne*, in N.S. hist. soc. *Coll.* 6: 53-89, 1888; W. O. Raymond: *The founding of Shelburne*, in N.B. hist. soc. *Coll.* 8: 204-97, 1909; and J. P. Edwards: *The Shelburne that was and is not*, and *Vicissitudes of a loyalist city*, in *Dalhousie review*, 2: 179-97, 313-28, July-Oct., 1922.

Copy located: None.

469. SHELBURNE, N.S., *Town.* GENERAL QUARTER SESSIONS OF THE PEACE

[Handbill forbidding no meat, fish, vegetables or other articles of provisions be henceforth exposed to public sale on any Shambles, or in any street, lane or on the Strand or shore of this town, other than in the markets or places established by order of Sessions as Markets in King Street and at the Cove.]

Broadside: *printed at Shelburne, N.S., by ? James Robertson, 1785*, as recorded:

"1785, May 12. It is ordered that 50 handbills be immediately printed forbidding no meat, fish, vegetables or other articles of provisions be henceforth exposed to public sale [etc., as quoted above]."

—Shelburne, N.S., Quarter sessions, *Records*.

Copy located: None.

470. VONDENVELDEN, WILLIAM, *d.* 1809

[Proposals for printing the Canadian Surveyor.]

Printed at Quebec by Wm. Brown, 1785, as recorded:

"1785, Jan. 15. Printed for Wm. Vonden Velden [sic] 300 Proposals for printing the Canadian Surveyor.—£1.5." —Can.P.A., *Neilson papers*, v. 47.

The proposed publication was advertised:

"The Surveyor-General of the Province having recommended to the Subscriber (being himself otherwise employed) to compile the Principles of Surveying in a succinct manner and upon a plan which might become useful to the Surveyors of this Province; and the said Treatise having been examined and approved of by the Surveyor-General above mentioned, it will be published if a sufficient number of Subscribers can be obtained. The Canadian Surveyor, or a Treatise on Surveying of Lands, in 8° at Five Shillings per Copy. To which is prefixed a List of the Subscribers who may encourage the Publication thereof. Subscriptions will be received at the Printing Office, Quebec [etc., signed:] William Vondenvelden, Provincial Surveyor."*—*Quebec gazette*, Jan. 20, 1785.

There is no evidence that the proposed work was ever published, Voldenvelden, who surveyed intermittently for the government and later established his own printing business, was employed at this time as French translator in Wm. Brown's printing shop.

Copy located: None.

471. WEEKS, JOSHUA WINGATE, 1738?-1804

A / SERMON / PREACHED / AT ST. PAUL'S CHURCH IN HALIFAX, / ON FRIDAY JUNE 24, 1785, / BEING / THE FESTIVAL OF ST. JOHN THE BAPTIST, / BEFORE / THE GRAND LODGE, / AND THE / OTHER LODGES, / OF THE / ANCIENT AND HONORABLE SOCIETY / OF / FREE and ACCEPTED MASONS, / IN HALIFAX, NOVA-SCOTIA. / [rule] / By the Rev. JOSHUA WINGATE WEEKS, A.M. / [rule] / [rule] / HALIFAX: / PRINTED BY JOHN HOWE, AT HIS PRINTING-OFFICE, IN / BARRINGTON-STREET, CORNER OF SACKVILLE-STREET, / MDCCLXXXV. /

12mo. A-C[4], D[2]; 25 p., 1 *l.*; type-page: 16.5 × 8.5 cm.

*Appended is the text of Surveyor-General Holland's approbation.

Contents: p. [1], t.-p.; p. [2], blank; p. [3], recto, "Resolution of Grand Lodge, Halifax, N.S., June 29, 1785, signed: Joseph Peters, Grand Secretary," thanking Weeks and requesting copy of the sermon to print; p. [4], blank; p. [5], Dedication to John George Pyke, provincial grand master; p. [6], blank; p. [7]-25, Sermon, text: The rich and poor meet together; the Lord is maker of them all.—Prov. xxii, 2.; recto of *l.* at end, Officers of Grand lodge of Nova Scotia; verso, Lodges under its jurisdiction.

Weeks was born at Hampton, N.H., and graduated from Harvard College in 1758. Ordained in the Church of England, 1761, he became rector at Marblehead, Mass., but left there, a loyalist, in 1778, settling in Halifax, N.S. Apparently a popular character, Weeks held various minor posts, as chaplain of the garrison and of the House of Assembly, etc. and was suggested in 1790 as rector of St. Paul's. But Bishop Inglis objected: ". . . Poor Weeks is a mere Cypher, without authority or influence, or indeed any judgement to manage the affairs of the parish, and his dependent situation deprives him of the power of exertion . . . yet because he is a Free mason every other consideration is thrown aside."

—Can.P.A., *Inglis papers*, 1: 245.

Copies located: CaNsHD; MBF.

472. ALMANACS. NOVA SCOTIA

THE / NOVA-SCOTIA CALENDER, / OR AN ALMANACK, / For the Year . . . 1787 . . . / [4 lines] / Wherein is Contained. / The Eclipses . . . / [4 lines] / [rule] / Calculated for the Meridian of HALIFAX, . . . / [3 lines] / By METONICUS. / [rule] / [verse: 12 lines] / [double rule] / HALIFAX, PRINTED and Sold by A. HENRY. / [title within double rule frame] /

12mo. [A-C]^4; [24] p.; type-page: 16.5 × 10 cm.

Contents: p. [1], t.-p.; p. [2], Vulgar notes, eclipses; p. [3-4], Rules to judge change of the weather; p. [5-16], Calendar; p. [17-24], Nova Scotia administration, legislature, courts, army, customs, post fares and distances, tides, etc.

This almanac was advertised: "Just published and for sale by the printer hereof, The Nova-Scotia Calender, [etc.]."—*Nova-Scotia gazette*, Dec. 5, 1786.

Copy located: CaNsHA (p. [17-18] wanting).

473. ALMANACS. QUEBEC

ALMANACH / DE / QUEBEC, / POUR / L'ANNÉE / 1787. / [double rule] / [printer's ornament] / [double rule] / A QUEBEC: / Chez GUILLAUME BROWN, sur la / Grande Côté. /

12mo. A-D^6; [16], 17-48 p.; type-page: 10.5 × 6 cm. Text in French or English.

Contents: p. [1], t.-p.; p. [2-4], Epoques, eclipses; p. [5-16], Calendrier; p. 17, Table des marées; p. 18-33, Officiers civils, etc.; p. 34-43, Contes; p. 44-45, Remarkable events; p. 46-48, Interest and currency tables.

The tide table (Table des marées) is a new feature in the almanac this year but the usual list of Catholic clergy does not appear. The almanac was published on

Dec. 21, 1786, and sold at 1*s*. 3*d*. the copy (1*s*. 6*d*. interleaved) and 12*s*. the dozen in Quebec, Montreal, Berthier, and Trois Rivières.

Copy located: CaOOA (photostat copy); CaQQL. Another copy not located was formerly in possession of Abbé Dubois at École Normale Jacques Cartier, Montreal. Another copy at MHi, not available in Mar., 1936.

474. ALMANACS. QUEBEC

CALENDRIER pour l'Année 1787, pour Québec, par les 306^{d} 30^{m} de Longitude, et 46^{d} 55^{m} de Latitude. / [ornamental rule] /

Colophon: A QUEBEC: chez WM. BROWN, au milieu de la Grande Côté. /

Broadside: type-page: 51.5 × 38.5 cm. printed on heavy writing paper.

Contents: Calendrier (in ornamental frame: 44 × 38.5 cm. as in No. 353, but explanatory note formerly alongside, is now beneath the date tables, and within frame of Calendrier); *Du Calendrier* (a history of time computation and calendars printed in 4 col. below Calendrier, is a special feature of the sheet almanac for this year).

It was published Nov. 16, 1786, at 9*d*. the copy, 5*s*. the dozen, and advertised as usual in Brown's newspaper, the *Quebec gazette* from Nov. 23, 1786.

Copy located: CaO (bound in *Quebec gazette* at the end of 1786).

475. ALMANACS. QUEBEC

[Calendrier pour Montréal, pour l'année 1787.]

Broadside. This sheet almanac, like the *Calendrier pour Montréal* of preceding years, was undoubtedly *printed at Montreal by Fleury Mesplet, this in 1786*, though the date of imprint may appear the same as in title. It was advertised in his newspaper succinctly: "A vendre le Calendrier pour l'année 1787."—*Montreal gazette*, Jan. 4, 1787.

Copy located: None.

476. BUCHAN, WILLIAM, 1729-1805

[Domestic Medicine: or, A Treatise on the prevention and cure of diseases, by Regimen and simple Medicines; with An Appendix containing a Dispensatory (or directions for the ordering every ingredient, as to the quality and manner of making up every physical composition) for the use of private practitioners. By William Buchan, M.D., Fellow of the Royal College of Physicians, Edinburgh.]

Proposed printing at Quebec by Wm. Brown, 1786, was advertised: "Proposals for printing by subscription a new edition of Domestic Medicine . . . by Wm. Buchan . . . This Work now offered is the compleatest and most useful of its kind that has ever yet appeared in the English language. As there is scarcely a disease incident to the human body but that is treated of, and their various causes explained and different cures laid down . . . Even those of meanest capacity by following his prescriptions may, in most cases with safety and success, become their own physicians [etc.]." The work was to be printed on fine paper and good type (specimen appended) and was to be issued in ten numbers of 56 pages, 8vo., delivered to subscribers once a month, covered and stitched, at 1*s*. a number. Subscriptions were taken by "Henry Galbraith, the publisher, at Thomas Grahame's, tailor, near the Post Office, and by Wm. Brown, the Printer, Quebec, [etc.]."—*Quebec gazette*, June 1, 1786.

Buchan's *Domestic medicine*, the English prototype of "Every man his own doctor" was published in Edinburgh and London in at least seventeen editions between its first appearance in 1769 and 1800; and it sold there at 6*s*. the copy. Wm. Brown's account books record the sale of occasional copies (at 12*s*.) through several years. There is no evidence, however, that this work was printed in Quebec as proposed, in 1786.

477. COPE, FORBES, *d.* 1786, *and* HENEY, THOMAS, *d.* 1786

[Two letters addressed to the Public and written by Forbes Cope and Thomas Heney, the two malefactors who were executed on Friday last, near the City; printed at their request. *Printed at Saint John, N.B., by Christopher Sower, 1786.*]

This publication was advertised: "Just published and to be sold at the Printing Office in Dock Street—Price three-pence—Two letters addressed to the Public and written by Forbes Cope and Thomas Heney, the two malefactors who were executed on Friday last, near the City; printed at their request."—*Royal gazette*, Saint John, N.B., Oct. 17, 1786.

In the same issue of this paper, appeared the notice: "On Friday last [Oct. 13, 1786] were executed near this city, pursuant to sentence, Forbes Cope [in previous issue spelled: James Coap] and Thomas Heney [or George Heany], for a burglary committed on the house of George Sproule, Esq. At the place of execution they behaved with propriety, and left letters with Mr. M'Clean who attended them, addressed to the public, containing matters of confession."

Copy located: None.

478. DOTY, JOHN, 1745-1841

[A / Sermon / Preached at the opening / of / Christ's Church at Sorel / in the Province of Quebec / on Sunday the 25th of December 1785: / By / The Reverend John Doty, a Presbyter of the Church of / England; and Missionary from the Incorporated Society for / Propagation of the Gospel / in Foreign Parts. / Hitherto hath the Lord helped us. I. Sam. 7-12. / When I came to Troas to preach Christ's Gospel, a door was / opened into me of the Lord. 2 Cor. 2-12. / Montreal; / Printed by Fleury Mesplet. M.DCC.LXXXVI.]

12mo. [*-**][2]; 14 p. 1 *l*.; type-page: 15 × 8 cm.

Contents (incomplete): t.-p. as above is recorded in Fauteux: *Mesplet*, no. 56; p. 5-14, Sermon, text: Psalm XLIII, 3, O send out thy Light and thy Truth; 1 *l*., blank.

In his sermon, Doty drew attention to the lack of religious organizations in Canada, to the work here of the Society for the Propagation of the Gospel in Foreign

Parts, and to the need for churches. That just opened at Sorel, he stated, was established in a house built six years previously by James Grant, merchant taylor, of the best squared timber, 32 by 28 feet in size, purchased by Doty for £15. "It will admit a gallery on three sides and is now below very neatly pewed off so as to accommodate above one hundred and twenty persons . . . a modest building unpolluted by the meretricious ornaments of Superstition."—*Sermon*, p. 9.

Doty, born and educated in New York, came to Canada, a loyalist, in 1777. In 1784 he started a mission at Sorel (renamed William Henry in 1788) for "a mixed Society consisting of Dissenters, Lutherans and Churchmen," seventy families in all. The following year he opened the first Church of England church in Canada, west of the Maritimes. The opening was celebrated in this sermon (*see* C. F. Pascoe: *Two hundred years of the S.P.G. . . . 1701-1900*, London, 1901).

Copy located: CaQMJ copy, described in Fauteux: *Mesplet*, no. 56, not available in Mar., 1937; NNHi (all before p. 5, wanting).

479. ESGLIS, LOUIS PHILIPPE MARIAUCHAU D', *bp. of Quebec*, 1710-1788

Caption title: (CIRCULAIRE.)

fo. 2 *l.*; paper-page: 22.7 × 18.5 cm. 200 copies, *printed at Quebec by Wm. Brown, 1786* (*see* No. 496 *note*).

Contents: l. [1] recto, Circulaire [in 8 lines, beginning:] "Monsieur, Cette Lettre accompagne les Ordres du Gouvernement au sujet de la Maladie de la Baïe Saint-Paul [etc. signed:] L. Ph. Evêque de Quebec. A St. Pierre, Ile d'Orleans le 2 Mars, 1786." *l.* [1] verso blank; *l.* [2], blank.

This *Circulaire* is reprinted in Têtu and Gagnon: *Mandements de Québec*, 2: 320

Copy located: CaO.

480. FREEMASONS. NOVA SCOTIA. GRAND LODGE

CHARGES AND REGULATIONS, / OF THE / ANCIENT AND HONOURABLE SOCIETY / OF FREE AND ACCEPTED / MASONS, / EXTRACTED FROM / AHIMAN REZON, &c. / TOGETHER WITH / A concise Account of the Rise and Progress of / FREE MASONRY in NOVA-SCOTIA, from the first / Settlement of it to this Time; / AND / A CHARGE given by the Revd. Brother WEEKS, / at the Installation of His Excellency JOHN / PARR, Esq; GRAND MASTER. / DESIGNED / For the Use of the Brethren, and published by the / Consent and Direction of the GRAND LODGE of / this PROVINCE. / [rule] / HALIFAX: / Printed by JOHN HOWE, at his Printing Office, in / BARRINGTON-STREET, Corner of SACKVILLE-STREET. / [rule] / MDCCLXXXVI. /

8vo. [$*^4$, A]-C^4, D^8, E-H^4; xv, 64 p.; type-page: 16.5 × 9 cm.

Contents: p. [i], t.-p.; p. [ii], blank; p. [iii], recommendation to print, dated at Halifax, Dec. 7, 1785; signed J. Peters, G.S.; p. [iv], blank; p. [v], Dedication to Gov. Parr; p. [vi], blank; p. [vii]-x, An account of freemasonry in Nova Scotia; p. [xi], blank; p. [xii]-xv, A charge, etc.; p. xv, verso, blank; p. [1]-38, Ahiman rezon;

p. [39]-50, Rules and orders; p. [51]-62, Masons' songs; p. [63], List of officers of the Provincial Grand Lodge of Nova Scotia, 5786; p. 64, List of lodges in Nova Scotia.

This work was prepared for publication by Wm. Campbell, Rev. Joshua Wingate Weeks, Jonathan Deblois, and Fife. It includes the first Canadian printing (abridged) of Lawrence Dermott's *Ahiman rezon* published in London, 1756. An early lodge of Freemasons had been organized at Halifax, N.S., in 1750, under the Provincial Grand Lodge of Massachusetts. With the English occupation, in Nova Scotia as in Quebec, numerous regimental and other lodges became established, especially following the settlement of the Loyalists. At the time of the Revolution, connection with American lodges practically ceased; and most lodges established in the Maritime Provinces derived their authority from the Provincial Grand Lodge of Nova Scotia, or directly from England.

Copies located: DLC; GBLBM; MB; MBF.

481. FREEMASONS' POCKET COMPANION

[The Elements of Free-Masonry delineated; or, The Free-mason's Pocket Companion.]

Proposed printing at Quebec by Wm. Brown, 1786, was advertised:

"A new work will be published on the 27th [Dec. 1786] (St. John's Day) if there are 40 Subscribers by the 20th Instant. The Elements of Free-Masonry delineated; or The Free-mason's Pocket Companion. This work was published in England by a subscription of 1000 and in Jamaica, by a subscription of 300. It is esteemed a publication of great utility, as it not only serves for an instructor to young masons, but is also a useful monitor to the perfect mason. [etc.]." The work was to be printed "in a neat pocket volume, stitched in marble paper, price to subscribers one dollar each book . . . Subscribers' names will be received by Bro. Moore at his house in Mountain Street." The contents of the work were to comprise an answer to objections to freemasonry; charges, addresses, prayers for ceremonies of initiation, etc.; regulations for government of the lodge; anthems, songs, etc.—*Quebec gazette,* Dec. 7-21, 1786.

"Bro. Moore" was probably William Moore who later started a printing office of his own and produced the *Quebec herald.* He appears in Wm. Brown's printing office records occasionally from 1786 onwards, as setting the type for small items in which he had an interest. Probably the proposed production of *The elements of Free-Masonry* was to be a joint undertaking of Moore and Brown (also a freemason) in the latter's printing office.

The Free-mason's pocket companion was published anonymously in several editions in Edinburgh, London, etc., from 1763. Brown advertised it with his imported stock, and sold occasional copies through several years. There is no evidence, however, that this work was printed in Quebec as proposed in 1786.

482. GREAT BRITAIN. LAWS, STATUTES, *etc.*

[An Act of Parliament Passed in the last session, for the further Increase & Encouragement of Shipping and Navigation. ? Shelburne, N.S., J. Humphreys, 1786.]

Probably a pamphlet, *printed at Shelburne, N.S., by James Humphreys, 1786,* who advertised it in his newspaper:

"Just published and to be sold by the Printer hereof (Price One Shilling and Sixpence) An Act of Parliament of Great Britain Passed in the last session for the further increase of Shipping and Navigation. It is certainly necessary for every person concerned in vessels of fifteen tons and upwards to have this act by them."
—*Nova-Scotia packet*, Shelburne, N.S., Dec. 7, 1786, *et seq.*

This is probably the British statute, 26 Geo. III. c. 60, "An Act for the further Increase and Encouragement of Shipping and Navigation," passed in the session of Jan., 1786. The text begins: "Whereas the Wealth and Strength of this Kingdom and the Prosperity and Safety of every part of the British Empire, greatly depend on the Encouragement given to Shipping and Navigation: And whereas it is proper that the Advantages hitherto given by the Legislature to Ships owned and navigated by His Majesty's Subjects should from henceforth be confined to Ships wholly built and fitted out in His Majesty's Dominions etc." It enacts that from Aug. 1, 1786, no foreign-built ships, though owned by British subjects, may be entitled to privileges of British-built vessels; and in 44 clauses it defines "British-built vessels," regulates their registration, etc. *The statutes at large, of England and of Great Britain*, ed. by Sir T. E. Tomlins, John Raithby (10 v., London, 1811), 8: 600-11.

Copy located: None.

483. HALIFAX MARINE SOCIETY

LAWS / OF THE / MARINE SOCIETY; / INSTITUTED at HALIFAX, / February 13th, 1786. / [double rule] / HALIFAX: / Printed by JOHN HOWE, at his Printing-Office, in Bar-/rington-Street, Corner of Sackville-Street. / [rule] / MDCCLXXXVI. /

8vo. [*-**]^4; 14 p., 1 *l.*; type-page: 14.3 × 8.3 cm.

Contents: p. [1], t.-p.; p. [2], blank; p. [3]-11, Rules; p. 11-14, List of subscribers, officers for 1786, committee of charity; 1 *l.*, blank.

The Halifax Marine Society was established as a mutual benefit association of upper class seamen, as the fees (£1 on admittance, 5*s.* quarterly) and the list of thirty-two original members indicate. Its purpose was to improve marine knowledge, members being required to communicate information to that end, and "to relieve the distressed, indigent or superannuated masters and mates of vessels, their wives and orphan children . . . and such other seafaring persons as stand in need of Assistance."—Rule I. The Society met quarterly, and otherwise as occasion arose, at one of the taverns in Halifax, N.S., and became a strong organization in the social life of that maritime town.

Copy located: RPJ.

484. JONES, ROBERT

REMARKS / ON / The DISTEMPER / Generally known by the Name of the / MOLBAY DISEASE, / Including a Description of its Symptoms and Method of / Cure chiefly intended for the Use / Of the clerical and other GENTLEMEN residing in the / Country. / By / [rule] / ROBERT JONES, SURGEON. / [rule] / [printer's ornament] / MONTREAL. / Printed by FLEURY MESPLET, M.DCC.LXXXVI. /

8vo. A-B^4, C^2; 19 p.; type-page: 14.5 × 8.5 cm.; p. 7 mispaged: 1.

Contents: p. [1], t.-p.; p. [2], blank; p. [3], recto, "To . . . Lord Dorchester Dedication, [signed:] The Author, Montreal, 25 November, 1786"; p. [4], Errata; p. [5-6], Advertisement; p. 1 [i.e. 7]-19, Description of the Molbay disease, [etc.]; p. 19 verso, blank.

The *Advertisement* states that the author is moved to publish remarks from notes collected during some years' observation of the disease in this country. In the text he describes its symptoms adducing evidence that Molbay (or Mal de la Baie) is not a venereal disease; suggests remedies and methods of cure to be dispensed by seigneurs and clergy among their tenants and parishioners. The author was listed as a licensed "chirurgeon apothecaire et accoucheur" in the Montreal district until 1792 (or later) in the *Quebec almanac*. *See also* No. 455 and No. 517.

This work was advertised: "Lately published and to be sold at the Printing Office [of Fleury Mesplet], Price 30 Sols [i.e. half-pennies], *Remarks on the Distemper* [etc.]."—*Montreal gazette*, Dec. 21, 1786.

Copy located: CaOOA.

485. MINCHIN, PAUL

BY / PAUL MINCHIN, ESQUIRE, / Commander of his MAJESTY'S Ship RESOURCE, / &c.&c.&c. / <Text> / GIVEN under my Hand on board of his Majesty's Ship RESOURCE, in the / Harbour of Quebec, this Thirtieth Day of September, One Thousand Seven / Hundred and Eighty-six. / P. MINCHIN. /

French side:

PAR / PAUL MINCHIN, ECUYER, / Commandant du Navire de sa Majesté la Resource, / &c.&c.&c. / <Text> / Donne sous mon Seing, à bord du Navire de sa Majesté la RESOURCE, dans le / Havre de Quebec, ce trentieme jour de Septembre, mil sept cens quatre-vingt-/six. / P. MINCHIN. /

Double broadside: English on left, 29 lines, type-page: 19.5 × 15.8 cm.; French on right, 29 lines, type-page: 19.5 × 15.8 cm. *Probably printed at Quebec by Wm. Brown, 1786.*

The text, beginning: "Whereas it appears that a tract of land, [etc.]," warns unauthorized persons, especially those from the United States, against encroaching on the trading and fishing rights of the present lessees of lands in the islands and posts of Mingan, Napeu Shipu, Ourraman, and Anticosti, along the north shore of the St. Lawrence from Cape Cormorant (nine leagues below Seven Islands) to the River Ourraman.

Copy located: CaNsHA.

486. NEW BRUNSWICK. HOUSE OF ASSEMBLY

JOURNAL / OF THE / VOTES and PROCEEDINGS / OF THE / HOUSE OF ASSEMBLY / OF THE / PROVINCE of NEW-BRUNSWICK: / From Tuesday the 3d of JANUARY, to Wednesday the 15th of /

MARCH, 1786. / [ornamental rule] / [royal arms] / [ornamental rule] / ST. JOHN: / Printed by CHRISTOPHER SOWER, Printer to the / KING'S MOST EXCELLENT MAJESTY. 1786. / [t.-p. within frame of flower pieces.]

fo. [*][1], A-[S][2]; 73 p.; type-page: 24.5 × 13.5 cm.

Contents: p. [1], t.-p.; p. [2], blank. p. [3]-73, Journal of first session of first assembly; verso of p. 73, blank. Note at end of text: "House of Assembly, the 15th March, 1780. I do allow and order that Mr. Christopher Sower, Printer to the King's Most excellent Majesty, do print the Journal and Votes of the House of Assembly, and that no other person do presume to print the same. [signed:] Amos Botsford, Speaker."

The printing of its proceedings was one of the first matters which engaged the attention of the Assembly, for on Jan. 4, after arranging for a reply to the lieutenant-governor's opening address and for its rules of order, it directed that "Mr. Christopher Sower . . . print from time to time, the Journals and Votes of this House, and that no other person do presume to print the same."

An edition of 100 copies was printed, as Sower's bill to the Assembly indicates (*see* No. 487, *note*).

Copies located: CaN (t.-p. wanting); CaNU; CaOOA.

487. NEW BRUNSWICK. LAWS, STATUTES, *etc.*

ACTS / OF THE / GENERAL ASSEMBLY, / OF / His MAJESTY'S PROVINCE / OF / NEW-BRUNSWICK, / PASSED IN THE YEAR 1786. / [rule] / [royal arms] / [rule] / ST. JOHN: / Printed by CHRISTOPHER SOWER, PRINTER to the / KING'S MOST EXCELLENT MAJESTY. / [rule] / MDCCLXXXVI. / [title within ornamental frame]

fo. [*-**][2], A-2H[2]; 4 p. l., [3]-126 p.; type-page: 24.5 × 13.5 cm.

Contents: p. l. 1 recto, t.-p.; verso, blank; p. l. 2 recto, half-title; verso, blank; p. l. 3 recto-4 verso, Table of titles; p. [3]-126, 26 Geo. III c. 1-61, laws passed in the first session of the provincial legislature, Jan. 3-Mar. 15, 1786.

On Mar. 14, 1786, the House of Assembly "ordered that the Printer be directed to print one hundred and seventy copies of the Laws passed this sessions, to be distributed in the following manner, viz. [then follows the list of provincial, city and county officials, and number of copies allocated to each]." A few extra copies were struck off apparently, for Sower advertised copies for sale at his shop, in the *Royal gazette*, Aug. 1, 1786, and again June 17, 1788. These were exhausted in time, however, for Lieut. Gov. Carleton, answering the Duke of Portland's request for copies, wrote Oct. 11, 1798, ". . . the acts passed in the first and one or two subsequent Sessions of Assembly are out of print . . . besides the printed copies sent after every session, a complete collection to the year 1792 inclusive, was sent to Mr. Dundas, June 2, 1792 [and suggests that these copies be sought in the Colonial Office before Carleton orders a reprint]."

The printer presented a substantial account:

"To Printing 100 Copies of the Journal of the Hon[ble] House of Assembly —£51.1.3.

To Printing 170 Copies of the Laws of the Province £165.0.0.

To Covering & binding 170 Copies of Ditto @ 6*d*. each Copy—£4.5.0.
[Total:] £220.6.3.
St. John, July 24th 1786. Errors Excepted, Christ[r] Sower."
—N.B.As.*Papers, 1786*.

Of this sum Sower was allowed £173, when the accounts for 1786 were passed by the Assembly in its 1787 session. Circumstances of the second sessions' printing arrangement suggest that other differences had arisen also between Sower and government in 1786 (*see* No. 520 *note*).

Copies located: Baxter; CaNFS; CaOOA (4 p. l. wanting); GBLP (in C.O. 190/1); MH (4 p. l. wanting); MWA; NNB; NNHi; RPJ (p. l. 3-4, wanting).

488. NOVA SCOTIA. HOUSE OF ASSEMBLY

Caption title: [ornamental rule] / JOURNAL, / AND / PROCEEDINGS / OF THE / GENERAL ASSEMBLY, / Of the PROVINCE of NOVA-SCOTIA. / [rule] / Thursday, 8th, June 1786. /

fo. A-I², [K]¹; 37 p. *Printed at Halifax, N.S., by Anthony Henry, 1786.*

Contents: p. 1-37, Journal and proceedings of the second session of the sixth assembly, June 8-July 11, 1786; p. 37 verso, blank.

Extracts from the *Journal*, June 10 *et seq.*, were reprinted (from the *Halifax journal?*) in the *Nova-Scotia packet*, July 6, 20, 1786.

Copies located: CaNs; GBLP (in C.O. 217/58: 357-93); MH.

489. NOVA SCOTIA. LAWS, STATUTES, *etc.*

Running title: [rule] / 1785. Anno Vicessimo Sexco [sic] Regis, GEORGII III. CAP. I[-II]. / [rule] /

Caption title: At the GENERAL ASSEMBLY of the Pro-/vince of Nova-Scotia, . . . / [5 lines] / . . . Being the first Session of the / Sixth General Assembly convened in the / said Province. / [rule] /

fo. p. 253-254; type-page: 24.5 × 15 cm. paged in continuation of No. 432. *Printed at Halifax, N.S., by Anthony Henry, 1786?*

Contents: p. 253-254, Cap. I-II, perpetual acts passed in the session, Dec. 5-28, 1785.

These acts, given Gov. Parr's assent on Dec. 28, 1785, were probably printed early in 1786.

Copies located: CaO; DLC; MH.

490. NOVA SCOTIA. LAWS, STATUTES, *etc.*

Running title: [rule] / 1785. Anno Vicessimo Sexco [sic] Regis, GEORGII III. CAP. I[-VI, i.e. IV]. /

Caption title: At the GENERAL ASSEMBLY of the Pro-/vince of Nova-Scotia, . . . / [5 lines] / . . . Being the first Session of the / Sixth General Assembly convened in the / said Province. / [rule] /

fo. sig. A-B²; p. 265-271; type-page: 25 × 15.3 cm. paged in continuation of No. 433. *Printed at Halifax, N.S., by Anthony Henry, 1786?*

Contents: p. 265-271, Cap. I-IV, temporary acts passed in the session Dec. 5-28, 1785; p. 271 verso, blank.

These acts, given Gov. Parr's assent on Dec. 28, 1785, were probably printed early in 1786.

Copies located: CaNsHA; CaO; MH; N; NNB.

491. NOVA SCOTIA. LAWS, STATUTES, *etc.*

Running title: [rule] / 1786. Anno Vicessimo Sexto Regis, GEORGII III. CAP. I[-II]. / [rule] /

Caption title: At the GENERAL ASSEMBLY of the Pro-/vince of Nova-Scotia, . . . / [8 lines] / . . . being the Second Session of the Sixth General Assem-/bly convened in the said Province. / [rule] /

fo. sig. 2U[1]; p. 255-256; type-page: 25.5 × 15 cm. paged in continuation of No. 489. *Printed at Halifax, N.S., Anthony Henry, 1786.*

Contents: p. 255-256, Cap. I-II, perpetual acts passed in the session June 8-July 11, 1786.

Copies located: CaO; MH.

492. NOVA SCOTIA. LAWS, STATUTES, *etc.*

Running title: [rule] / Anno Vicessimo Sexto Regis, GORGII [sic] III. CAP. I[-VII]. 1786. / [rule] /

Caption title: At the GENERAL ASSEMBLY of the Pro-/vince of Nova-Scotia, . . . / [8 lines] / . . . being the / Second Session of the Sixth General Assem-/bly convened in the said Province. / [rule] /

fo. sig. C-E[2], F[1]; p. 273-286; type-page: 26 × 15.3 cm. paged in continuation of No. 490. Running title p. 274-86, corrected to read: ". . . Georgii [etc.]." *Printed at Halifax, N.S., by Anthony Henry, 1786.*

Contents: p. 273-86, Cap. I-VII, temporary acts passed in the session June 8-July 11, 1786.

Copies located: CaNsHA; CaO; MH; N; NNB.

493. QUEBEC, *Province.* GOVERNOR, 1786-1791 (*Dorchester*)

G. [royal arms] R. / By His EXCELLENCY the RIGHT HONORABLE / GUY LORD DORCHESTER, / GENERAL, and COMMANDER in CHIEF, &c.&c.&c. / RULES AND DIRECTIONS, / For the good Government, and Preservation of His Majesty's Barracks in Canada, and for procuring and issuing Fuel to the Troops / quartered therein. / <Text> / (Signed) DORCHESTER. / HEAD-QUARTERS, QUEBEC, 23d. December, 1786. / By His EXCELLENCY'S Command, / (Signed) FRANs. LEMAISTRE, M.S. [i.e. Military Secretary] /

Broadside: Text in 3 col. 63-68 lines each; type-page: 51 × 37.6 cm. *Printed at Quebec by Wm. Brown, 1786*, as recorded:

> "1786, Dec. 30. Printed for Store Keeper General, Rules and Directions for the Barracks in Canada, on a Royal* Broadside—£4.17.6."
>
> —Can.P.A., *Neilson papers*, v. 84.

Copy located: CaNSA (filed in *Winslow papers*, v. 3).

*Royal was a sheet of paper about 24 × 20 inches.

494. QUEBEC, *Province.* LAWS, STATUTES, *etc.*

[Anno vicesimo sexto Georgii III. Chap. I. An Ordinance for further continuing an Ordinance . . . for regulating the Militia, etc.

. . . Chap. II. An Ordinance for further continuing an Ordinance . . . for the regulation and establishment of fees.

. . . Chap. III. An Ordinance for further continuing an Ordinance . . . for regulating . . . Maîtres de Poste.]

French side:

[Anno vicesimo sexto Georgii III. Regis. Chap. I, Ordonance Qui continue une ordonance . . . qui régle les milices, etc.

. . . Chap. II. Ordonance Qui continue une ordonance . . . qui établit les Honoraires.

. . . Chap. III. Ordonance Qui continue une ordonance . . . qui régle . . . Maîtres de Poste.]

Broadside? text in English and French? *Printed at Quebec by Wm. Brown, 1786,* as recorded:

> "1786, Feb. 25. Printed for Gov[t]. by Order of Mr. W[ms] [i.e. Jenkin Williams, clerk of the Legislative Council] 50 Copies of three Ordinances.—£1.7.6."
> —Can.P.A., *Neilson papers,* v. 84.

As these ordinances were printed in the *Quebec gazette,* Feb. 23, 1786, at a charge of £3, the price for the 50 copy edition suggests that the latter was simply a separate issue printed from *Gazette* types similar to No. 531-35. Passed at Quebec, Feb. 20, 1786, 26 Geo. III c. 1-3 continued 17 Geo. III c. 8, 20 Geo. III c. 3-4, respectively, till Apr. 30, 1787. The text is reprinted (from No. 495) in Can.P.A., *Report, 1914-15,* from which this entry is taken.

Copy located: None.

495. QUEBEC, *Province.* LAWS, STATUTES, *etc.*

ORDINANCES / MADE AND PASSED / BY THE / GOVERNOR / AND / LEGISLATIVE COUNCIL / OF THE / PROVINCE / OF / QUEBEC. / [rule] / [royal arms] / [double rule] / QUEBEC: / Printed by WILLIM [sic] BROWN, in Mountain-Street, / [rule] / M,DCC.LXXXVI. /

French t.-p.:

ORDONNANCES / FAITES ET PASSÉES / PAR LE / GOUVERNEUR / ET LE / CONSEIL LEGISLATIF / DE LA / PROVINCE / DE / QUEBEC. / [rule] / [royal arms] / [double rule] / A QUEBEC: / Chez GUILLAUME BROWN, au milieu de la Grande Côte. / [rule] / M,DCC,XXXVI [sic].

fo. [*][2], A-2B[2]; 1 p. l., [i], 100 p.; type-page: 23 × 13 cm. odd numbers on verso, even on recto; p. 63 mispaged: 62; text in English and French on opposite pages.

Contents: p. l. recto, English t.-p.; verso, blank; p. [i], French t.-p.; p. 1 (verso of p. [i])-100, thirteen ordinances, 22 Geo. III c. 5-26 Geo. III c. 3, passed 1782-86, under Gov. Haldimand and Lieut.-Gov. Hamilton; p. 100 verso, blank.

The printer records this publication:

"1786, July 7. Printed for Gov[t] by Order Mr. Williams and deliver'd him this day, 200 Copies of the Ordinances made since the year 1780, making 26 Sheets on folio Pott in English and Brevier marginal notes at 60/ per Sheet.—£78.

"Aug. 5. Government owes . . . binding and furniture for Ordinances, Binding 20 books in Sheep and 3 in Calf @ 4/—£4.12.
Folding, stitching & covering in blue and marble 177 @ 9*d.*—£6.12.9."
—Can.P.A., *Neilson papers*, v. 84.

Brown also records the sale of a few copies at 6*s.* wholesale, 7*s.* 6*d.* retail.—*ibid.*

Copies located: CaO; CaOOA; CaOT; CaOTO (2 cop.); CaQM; CaQQL (3 cop.); GBLP (in C.O. 44/3: 1786); M; MH; MiD-B; NN; NNB; RPJ.

496. QUEBEC, *Province.* LIEUTENANT-GOVERNOR, 1785-1789 (*Hope*)

(CIRCULAIRE.) / QUEBEC, le 2 de Mars, 1786. /

fo. 2 *l.* without signature or pagination, text in French recto and verso of *l.* 1.; type-page: 29 × 15 cm. *Printed at Quebec by Wm. Brown, 1786*, as recorded:

"1786, Mar. 8. Printed for Gov[t] 200 Circular letters to Curés, with a Specimen of a Certificate from the Priests, relating to the Disease of St. Paul's Bay, on propatria* both sides.—£3.10.
D[o] 200 Circular letters from Bishop to the Curés on D[o]—£1.7.6."
—Can.P.A., *Neilson papers*, v. 84.

Contents: p. [1], letter addressed, with blank for name and place, to curé of parish, asking co-operation with Mr. Bowman authorized to treat Mal de la Baie St. Paul in the parishes; p. [2], Certificate "Etat de Guérison pour la maladie de la Baie St. Paul, paroisse de [blank]" names, dates, observations etc. to be filled in by curé as basis for payment of Dr. Bowman by the government; 1 *l.*, blank.

This circular is reprinted in Têtu and Gagnon: *Mandements de Québec,* 2: 320-24.

Copies located: CaOOA (filed in Can.P.A., "*S*" *St. Paul's Bay disease*); CaQQL. Both copies located are signed in MS. by Henry Hope.

497. QUEBEC, *Province.* LIEUTENANT-GOVERNOR, 1785-1789 (*Hope*)

[By The Honorable Henry Hope, Esq; Lieutenant-Governor and Commander in Chief in and over the Province of Quebec . . . A Proclamation. <Text> Given . . . at Quebec, 23 September, 1786. Henry Hope . . . God Save the King.]

French side:

[Par l'honorable Henry Hope, Ecuyer, Lieutenant-Gouverneur et Commandant en Chef dans toute la Province de Québec . . . Proclamation. <Text> Donné . . . à Québec, 23 septembre, 1786. Henry Hope . . . Vive le Roi.]

*Paper about $15\frac{1}{2} \times 12\frac{1}{2}$ inches in size.

Double broadside: text in English and French. *Printed at Quebec by Wm. Brown, 1786*, as recorded:

"1786, Sept. 25. Printed for Gov^{t} (by Order Mr. Pownall) 500 D^{ble} Proclamations forbidding obtruding on the King's Posts.—£3.17.6."

—Can.P.A., *Neilson papers*, v. 84.

English text: "Whereas the Lease under which His Majesty's Domain Lands and Posts, commonly called . . . the King's Posts and the Fisheries belonging to the same are held by . . . Alexander Davison, George Davison and Francis Baby . . . [for a term of ten years, etc.] I have thought fit to issue this Proclamation . . . forbidding all manner of Persons . . . from going to trade with the Indians . . . or molesting the said New Lessees . . . in their Exclusive right of trade [etc.]."

French text: "Le Bail accordé à . . . Alexandre Davison, Georges Davison et Francois-Baby, Ecuyers, . . . [des] Postes et Pêches pour l' . . . espace de dix années [etc.]. A ces Causes . . . j'ai jugé à propos de faire publier cette Proclamation, par laquelle il est rigoureusement prohibé et défendu à qui puisse être . . . d'aller traiter avec les Sauvages . . . comme aussi empêcher troubler et molester les dits nouveaux Fermiers . . . dans leur droit Exclusif d'y traiter [etc.]."

The proclamation is reprinted in Can.P.A., *Report, 1918* from which this entry is taken.

Copy located: None.

498. QUEBEC GAZETTE. CARRIER'S ADDRESS

ETRENNES / Du GARCON qui porte la Gazette de Québec / Aux PRATIQUES. / Le 1er. Janvier, 1787. / [*Quebec, Wm. Brown, 1786.*]

Broadside: 44 lines; type-page: 24.5 × 17 cm. in ornamental frame.

Contents: Etrennes in 3 stanzas, light verse without local or political allusion.

Copy located: CaO (bound in *Quebec gazette* at end of 1786).

499. QUEBEC THEATRE

[PLAY BILLS]

Broadsides: *Printed at Quebec by Wm. Brown, 1786.*

Performances by the Quebec Theatre, also by the Juvenile Theatre, were advertised frequently during 1784 and occasionally during 1785 in the *Quebec gazette*, but Brown recorded no printing of play bills after 1783 till 1786. In the latter year numerous entries were made in his accounts (Can.P.A., *Neilson papers*, v. 84) usually for editions of 300 play bills, at 15*s.* to 17*s.* 6*d.* charged to the Quebec Theatre or the Juvenile Theatre, e.g.:

1786, Mar. 23, The Irish Widow; July 18, printed for theatre 300 play bills folio page crown (Mr. Moore set it).* Notifying The Countess of Salisbury—17*s.* 6*d.* July 22, The Recruiting Officer; July 25, The Earl of Essex; July 26, The Busy Body; July 30, Romeo & Julliet, etc.; Aug. 3, The West Indian, etc.; Aug. 5, School for Scandal; Aug. 10, Richard 3^{d}; Aug. 14, Merchant of Venice; Aug. 17, Henry 4th; Aug. 21, Love in a Village; Aug. 24, The Orphanage; Sept. 12, Beaux Stratagem; Sept. 14, Jane Shore; Sept. 18, Love Makes the Man, etc.; Sept. 21,

*This is the earliest reference to Wm. Moore in Quebec, where he later established his own printing office and published the *Quebec Herald*.

Douglas; Sept. 23, The Rivals; Sept. 25, The Rivals; Sept. 28, Deaf Lover, etc.; Sept. 30, The Rivals; Oct. 5, Hamlet, etc.; Oct. 11, Revenge; Oct. 14, The Revenge; Oct. 17, A Bold Stroke for a Wife; Oct. 19, Siege of Quebec; Oct. 21, Country Lasses etc.; Oct. 28, The Countess of Salisbury; Oct. 30, A Dramatic fête; Oct. 31, Busy Body; Nov. 3, The Gamesters, etc.; Nov. 11, The School for Guardians; Nov. 17, The Fatal Falsehood; Nov. 20, Henry 4th; Nov. 23, The School for Guardians; Nov. 25, The Gamesters; Nov. 29, The Merry Wives of Windsor; Dec. 14, A Bold Stroke for a Wife; Dec. 19, La Fol Raisonable; Dec. 20, The School for Scandal; Dec. 23, The Wonder a Woman Keeps a Secret; Dec. 28, Recruiting Officer.

Copy located: None.

500. WESLEY, JOHN, 1703-1791

A / SERMON / PREACHED / On Occasion of the DEATH of the / Rev. Mr. JOHN FLETCHER, / Vicar of MADELY, SHROPSHIRE. / [rule] / by JOHN WESLEY, M.A. / [rule] / [rule] / LONDON: / Printed by J. PARAMORE, at the Foundry, 1785. / HALIFAX: / Re-printed by J. HOWE, in Barrington-Street, 1786. / <PRICE SIX-PENCE> /

8vo. A-C[4]; 22 p., 1 *l.*; type-page: 18.3 × 9.8 cm.

Contents: p. [1], t.-p.; p. [2], Introduction, signed John Wesley, London, Nov. 9, 1785; p. [3]-22, Sermon, text: Psalm xxxvii: 37, Mark the perfect man, and behold the upright; for the end of that man is peace; p. 22, Epitaph; 1 *l.* blank.

In this sermon Wesley has "hastily put together some memorials of this great man intending if God permit . . . to write a fuller Account of his life."—Introd. He describes Fletcher's life and his social-religious work in England and Wales, paying affectionate tribute to one termed (by Luke Tyerman) "Wesley's designated successor." On the publication of the Halifax edition, *see* No. 501 *note.*

Copies located: CaNsHA; CaNsHD (2 cop.); CaNsWA; NN (t.-p. is photographic copy).

501. WESLEY, JOHN, 1703-1791

A SHORT / HISTORY / OF THE / PEOPLE called METHODISTS. / [rule] / By the Reverend JOHN WESLEY, A.M. / Late Fellow of LINCOLN COLLEGE, Oxford. / [rule] / [rule] / "Come and hear, all ye that fear God, and I will declare what he hath done / for my Soul." PSALM lxvi. 10. / "Not unto us, O Lord, not unto us, but unto thy Name, give Glory," &c, / PSALM cxv. 1. / [rule] / [double rule] / LONDON: / Printed by J. PARAMORE, at the Foundery, Moorfield. / HALIFAX: / Re-printed by J. HOWE, at his Printing-Office, Sackville-Street. /

8vo. A-L[4]; 88 p.; type-page: 18.5 × 9.5 cm., type: pica.

Contents: p. [1], t.-p.; p. [2], blank; p. [3]-88, A short history, etc.

Even in an age prolific in pamphlets, the early Methodists were conspicuous for their system of publishing and distributing cheap, readable tracts prepared by leaders of the movement. All publications required Wesley's sanction and profits therefrom were deposited in "the common stock" (*Minutes of the Methodist conferences from . . . 1744*, London, 1862, 1: 151). In colonial America also, publication was controlled from the first conference in 1773 and centralized in Philadelphia, later in New York. After the American Revolution the increasing Methodist enterprise in Nova Scotia, though still closely connected with the American organization, was hampered by dependence on supplies imported from England. Freeborn Garrettson, the itinerant American preacher who was proselytizing in Nova Scotia 1785-87, wrote Wesley of the need for literature: " '*The Saint's Rest* and hymn-books are wanted; the small select hymn-book would sell; some pieces displaying the nature, manner and doctrine of the Methodists; your [Wesley's] journal and sermons; and Mr. Walsh's Life. Dear Mr. Fletcher's works have been a blessing in Cornwallis and Horton'." In Mar., 1787 he informed Wesley that he had received no books since his arrival in Nova Scotia. " 'We thought it expedient,' he added, 'to have about fifty pounds worth printed, as the printer was at leisure this winter. He printed several tracts very reasonably'." To which Wesley replied: "I do not blame you for printing the tracts." Among the latter were Wesley's *Short history* (printed at a cost of some £22) and his *Sermon preached on . . . Fletcher*, both on large type and roughly finished paper, remarkable rather for utility and economy than for elegance. *See* Thomas Watson Smith: *History of the Methodist church . . . of eastern British America* (2 v., Halifax, N.S., 1877-90), 1: 186 *et seq.*

Copies located: CaNsHA; CaNsHD; CaNsHK.

502. ALMANACS. NEW BRUNSWICK

[An Astronomical diary, or Almanack, for the Year . . . 1788 . . . Calculated for the Meridian of the City of St. John. *Saint John, N.B., C. Sower, 1787.*]

This almanac was advertised: "Now in the press and speedily will be published, A Diary or Almanack for the year 1788 [etc.]" in Christopher Sower's paper, *Royal gazette*, from Nov. 20 to Dec. 14, 1787, when the extant file stops. In the next issue seen, June 17, 1788, an advertisement still appears: "Just published and to be sold at the Printing Office, may also be had of Mr. S. Bent in this City, Israel Perley, Esq., Maugerville, and Mr. Richard Williams, Fredericton, A Diary or Almanack for . . . 1788 [etc.]."

Copy located: None.

503. ALMANACS. NOVA SCOTIA

Wood block title-page: Der / Neuschottländische / Calender, / Auf das Jahr CHristi / 1788. / Welches ein Schaltjahr von 366 / Tagen ist. / [double rule] / Halifax, gedruckt bey Anth. Heinrich. / [Title in German-letter type, set in a medallion within a wide border of wood cut figures printed, apparently, from a well-worn block.]

Title-page in type:

Der / Hochdeutsche / Neu-Schottländische / Calender, / Auf das Jahr, nach der heilbringenden Geburt / unsers HErrn JEsu Christi, /

1788. / Welches ein Schaltjahr von 366 Tagen ist. / Darinnen, nebst richtiger Festrechnung, die Sonn- und Monds- Finsternisse, / des Monds Gestalt und Viertel, Monds-Auf-und Niedergang, Monds-Zeichen, Aspecten / der Planeten und Witterung, Sonnen Auf-und Untergang, Des Siebengestirns / Aufgang, Südplatz und Untergang, der Venus Auf-und Untergang, / das hohe Wasser zu Halifax, Courten und andere zu einem / Calender gehörige Sachen; zu finden sind. / Imgleichen verschiedene, zum angenehmen Zeitvertreibe eingerichtete / Erzählungen, &c. / Mit sonderbarem Fleisz nach dem Horizont und Nordhöhe zu Halifax, / und andern Theilen der Provinz Neu-Schottland, berechnet. / [rule] / Zum Erstenmal herausgeben. /[double rule] / HALIFAX, / Gedruckt und zu haben bey Anthon Henrich, in der Sackville-Strasse. /

4to. [*]^2, A-E^4; [44] p.; type-page: 17.5 × 14 cm. Sig. [*]^2 forms p. [1-2, 43-44]. Most of the text is printed in 2 col., German letter throughout. p. [1], wood cut t.-p.; p. [2], Vorerinnerung; p. [3], t.-p.; p. [4-6], das hohe königliche Groszbritannische Hause, etc.; p. [6-9], Die Provinz Nova Scotia; p. [9, Chronology table of historic dates & events]; p. [10-33], Monthly calendar on verso's, on recto's: moon's phases, court days and tales running from page to page; p. [34-38] Hülf und Hausmittel; p. [39-41] Lieder, etc.; p. [42], Von Aderlassen und Schropfen [i.e. bloodletting & cupping]; p. [43], Erklärung der Zeichen, etc.; p. [44], Buoys in den Hafen zu Halifax, Entfernung Halifax—Annapolis, etc. [Abstract of act against copper coins & regulating weight gold & silver coins, etc., in Nova Scotia; also of act regulating sittings of Court common pleas in Nova Scotia.]

Among the historic events, Henry records the arrival of the first German families in Nova Scotia in 1750, their founding of Malagasch, or Lunenburg, in 1752, the repeal of the Stamp act, 1766, etc.

Printed at Halifax, N.S., by Anthony Henry, 1787, this is probably the earliest German language publication produced in Canada. It is certainly the first German-letter pamphlet—for the type (acquired since Aug. 14, 1787) appeared previously, only in an announcement, in the *Nova-Scotia gazette*, Oct. 23, 1787, of a meeting of the High German Society. It is a picturesque work. The type, in a modest range of sizes, is well composed, the ornaments and zodiac signs, relatively profuse and tastefully arranged. The composition was probably done by the journeyman, Henry Stirner, but the publication was apparently a labour of love for the German-born printer, Henry, as his introduction (translated from p. [2]) suggests.

"The great number of German almanacs which are brought yearly into this province from the state of Pennsylvania and bought by the inhabitants of this country, has induced me to make use of my recently obtained new German letters, first of all, in such a Calendar, which, according to my recently given promise, appears herewith for the first time in this Province. In all things it is adapted to this country and provided with appropriate historical matter. Hence I believe that if it be compared with the Pennsylvania almanac, it closely approaches the latter, although it is furnished outwardly with poor apparel. This is not my fault, for if I had known that such things [wood-cuts?] could not be properly made [here] then I should have had them imported with the new types. In general I must inform the German public that I have not yet obtained from the type founder all the letter founts requisite to a

German printing business, and on that account I am obliged to make a virtue of necessity in a few matters in this Calender. But I promise here most solemnly that I will publish the 1789 edition (if God gives me life and health) furnished with a brand new fine wood-cut according to the facilities and German craftsmanship in this country. The rest of the German types I expect daily, and if I am supported by the German people who live in this province, (as I doubt not) and can be recompensed thereby for my great expences, then will I use my greatest endeavour to keep our mother tongue current through this press—[a language] of which no real German either in this country or the United States, will be ashamed—although many of the young people declare an aversion for it, out of a wonderful conceit.

"To this end, I will publish every week on Fridays, a German newspaper under the title Die Welt und die Neuschottländische Correspondenz and, as the title indicates, [it] will incorporate therein all noteworthy occurrences in the four quarters of the world as they come to my ears through imported English papers generally, as also in particular, interesting matters of this province. The first will be published on the 4th of January 1788. I have already a number of subscribers and I am flattered that more are still coming in—Then, indeed, they will be convinced that I am fulfilling my promise.—Anth. Henrich."

Despite Henry's solemn promise, subsequent editions of *Der Neuschottlandische Calender* had titles printed from the same block, with the final figures of the title date and the lines thereafter reset. When Henry first used it, the block was already worn and cracked as imperfections of the title-page reveal. It was not necessarily old, however, for the year date figures, 178, appear to have been cut in the block with the final 8 only added in type. In the subsequent editions seen, the first (wood-cut) title-page showed more, then still more, imperfections.

This almanac was advertised (German text in roman letter) as published and ready for sale, in the *Nova-Scotia gazette*, Dec. 4, 1787, *et seq.*

Copy located: CaO.

504. ALMANACS. NOVA SCOTIA

THE / NOVA-SCOTIA CALENDER, / OR AN / ALMANACK, / For the Year . . . 1788; . . . / . . . / . . . / . . . / WHEREIN IS CONTAINED, / The Eclipses . . . / . . . / . . . / . . . / . . . / [rule] / Calculated for the Meridian of HALIFAX, . . . / . . . / . . . / . . . / By METONICUS. / [rule] / [verse, 14 lines] / [double rule] / HALIFAX, Printed and Sold by A. HENRY. / [title and each page within ornamental frame]

12mo. [A]-C[4]; [24] p.; type-page: 16 × 9.6 cm.

Contents: p. [1], t.-p.; p. [2], Vulgar notes, eclipses; p. [3-14], Calendar; p. [15-22], Nova Scotia administration, legislature, judges, justices, sheriffs, customs, army, courts; p. [22-24], Buoys, directions for fruit trees.

Copies located: CaNsHA (p. [15-18] wanting); CaNsWA; CSmH; MH; MWA.

505. ALMANACS. QUEBEC

ALMANACH / DE / QUEBEC, / POUR / l'ANNÉE / 1788. / [double rule] / [group of type ornaments framing masonic date: A.M. 5788] / [rule] / A QUEBEC: / Chez GUILLAUME BROWN, sur la / Grande Côte. /

12mo. A-E[6]; 60 p., fold table; type-page: 10.8 × 6 cm.

Contents: p. [1], t.-p.; p. [2-4], Epoques, éclipses, table des marées; p. [5-16], Calendrier; p. 17-30, Officiers civils, etc.; p. 31, Currency tables; p. 32-95, 27 Geo. III c. 3 Ordinance for quartering troops passed Apr. 23, 1787 (in English and French); p. 46-47, Ordres de quartier-général; p. 47-55, Militia, etc.; p. 55-56, Connétables, pilotes; p. 57-60, Fabliaux, interest tables, etc. The fold table is "Table de Tarif pour le Paiement des Habitans sur les Corvées. . . ." (Règlements de 9 janv., 2 fev., 1779).

The text is in French, excepting the ordinance, in English and French, and the interest table in English only. This almanac is considerably augmented by the text of the new militia law, etc. The schedule of payments for road work is a new feature.

The almanac was published Dec. 13, 1787, and sold at 1*s*. 2*d*. the copy, 13*s*. to 15*s*. the dozen. Nearly 400 copies were sold during the year apparently, for the printer recorded:

"1788, Dec. 31. Stationery owes Printing Office for Almks. sold this year and carried to its credit—£20." —Can.P.A., *Neilson papers*, v. 84.

Copies located: CaOOA; CaQQA; CaQQL.

506. ALMANACS. QUEBEC

CALENDRIER pour l'Année 1788, pour Québec, par les 306[d.] 30[m.] de Longitude, et 46[d.] 55[m.] de Latitude. / [line of dots] /

Colophon: A QUEBEC: chez WM. BROWN, au milieu de la Grande Côte. /

Broadside: type-page: 51.5 × 38.5 cm.

Contents: Calendrier (with foot note on arrangement, in ornamental rule frame: 43.5 × 38.5 cm.); Officiers civils (as in previous years).

From Nov. 15, 1787, this sheet almanac was sold at 9*d*. the copy, 6*s*. the dozen (5*s*. up the River where Mesplet's *Calendrier pour Montréal* created a lower price standard). It was advertised for sale at Quebec, Trois Rivières, Berthier, and Montreal, as usual in the *Quebec gazette* from Nov. 22, 1787.

Copy located: CaO (bound in *Quebec gazette* at end of 1787).

507. ALMANACS. QUEBEC

[Calendrier pour Montréal pour l'année 1788.]

Broadside. This sheet almanac like the *Calendrier pour Montréal* of preceding years, was undoubtedly *printed at Montreal by Fleury Mesplet*, this in 1787 (though the date of imprint may appear the same as in title). The printer advertised it: "Calendrier Pour l'année 1788, A Vendre à l'Imprimerie de Montréal."—*Montreal gazette*, Dec. 6, 1787.

Copy located: None.

508. BISSET, GEORGE, *d.* 1788

The Pleasure and Advantage of BROTHER-/LY UNITY. / [rule] / A / SERMON, / PREACHED BEFORE / THE WORSHIPFUL MASTER, / WARDENS AND BRETHREN, / OF THE / 54th REGIMENTAL LODGE

OF FREE AND / ACCEPTED MASONS, / IN THE PARISH CHURCH OF ST. JOHN. / ON DECEMBER 27th, 1786. / [double rule] / BY GEORGE BISSET, M.A. / RECTOR OF ST. JOHN, AND MISSIONARY FROM THE SOCIETY, / FOR THE PROPAGATION OF THE GOSPEL IN FOREIGN PARTS. / [ornamental rule] / ST. JOHN: / PRINTED BY CHRISTOPHER SOWER, PRINTER TO HIS MAJESTY. /

fo. A-C²; 12 p.; type-page: 19.5 × 13.2 cm. This work has a somewhat eccentric appearance in the only copy located, with type-page as for quarto format on a paper-page 23 × 18 cm., a folio in 2's.

Contents: p. [1], t.-p.; p. [2], blank; p. [3], Dedication, dated at Saint John, Dec. 28, 1786; p. [4], blank; p. 5-12, Sermon, text: Psalm CXXXIII, 1. Behold how good and how pleasant it is for brethren to dwell together in unity.

The sermon sets forth the social and spiritual benefits of the brethren's association in freemasonry. It was advertised: "Now in the press and will be published on Saturday next [Jan. 13, 1787] the Pleasure and advantage of brotherly unity, [etc., no price given]."—*Royal gazette*, Saint John, N.B., Jan. 9, 1787.

Bissett, assistant, then rector, of Christ's Church in Newport, R.I., 1767-79, was a loyalist who returned to England with the British army evacuating New York, then came to New Brunswick as rector of Saint John, 1786. He served in this post till his death, Mar. 3, 1788, much lamented by the congregation. "Lines on the death of Rev. George Bissett" published in the *Royal gazette*, Mar. 11, 1788, and attributed to Hon. Jonathan Odell (in *Acadiensis*, 6: 171, 1906) begin:

"A man most excellent, also replete
With Nature's gifts and grace's richer stores,
Thou Bissett wast [etc.]."

Copy located: MWA.

509. BOWMAN, JAMES, *d.* 1787

[Catalogue of Dr. Bowman's books]

Broadside: *printed at Quebec by Wm. Brown, 1787*, as recorded:

"1787, June 30. Printed for Phillips & Lane [auctioneers] 100 Catalogues of Dr. Bowman's books, 2 columns on a folio Demy—£1.12.6."

—Can.P.A., *Neilson papers*, v. 84.

Bowman, a British army surgeon, was noted for his work in connection with St. Paul's Bay disease (*see* No. 455 *note*).

Copy located: None.

510. CONFRERIE DE LA SAINTE FAMILLE

LA SOLIDE / DÉVOTION / A LA / TRES-SAINTE / FAMILLE, / DE JESUS, MARIE & JOSEPH. / [printer's ornament] / A MONTREAL; Chez F. MESPLET, Imprimeur & Libraire. / M.DCC.LXXXVII. / [rule] / Avec Approbation & Permission. /

16mo. A-G⁴; 56 p.; type-page: 12 × 6.5 cm.

Contents: p. [1], t.-p.; p. [2], blank; p. 3-5, Aux ames dévotes; p. 6-16, Patente, 14 mars, 1665; Bulles, jan. 28, jan. 22, 1665; p. 17-54, Règlements; p. 54-56, Instruction sur l'etablissement de la Sainte Famille en Canada, 1650.

First proposed in 1650 by Father Pijart, a Jesuit in Montreal, the Confrérie de la Sainte Famille was instituted as an association for lay women and girls by Mme. d'Ailleboust and Father Chaumonot, a Jesuit, in 1663. The group at Montreal under direction of the Séminaire de St. Sulpice, and that at Quebec, were formally constituted under papal bulls and Bishop Laval's patent in 1665. The latter had regulations for the Confrérie drawn up by Abbé Demezeret, superior of the Séminaire de Québec, and printed: *La solide devotion de la très Sainte Famille de Jesus, Marie et Joseph* . . . Paris, Chez Florentin Lambert, M.DC.LXXV. 12mo. 192, [4] p. (copy at CaQQL).

This work was reprinted (with omission of the catechism on p. 59-192 of the Paris edition, and addition of an historical note, p. 54-56, Montreal edition) as recorded above. The regulations set forth principles for guidance of the members of the Confrérie in their domestic relations, and their social and religious duties—modelled upon the conduct of the Holy Family. They include also rules for procedure, collection of funds, conditions of membership, order of prayers, etc.

Copies located: CaO; CaQMS; CaQQL.

511. DELAROCHE, PETER, *d.* 1795

THE / GOSPEL OF CHRIST / PREACHED / To the POOR / By / PETER DELAROCHE, / Missionary. / [rule] / Repent ye therefore, and be converted, that your Sins may be / blotted out.—St. Peter, in Acts. III, 19. / [rule] / SECOND EDITION. / [printer's ornament] / HALIFAX, / Printed and Sold by ANTHONY HENRY, / MDCCLXXXVII. /

12mo. A-F^{8}; 96 p.; type-page: 15 × 8.6 cm.

Contents: p. [1], t.-p.; p. [2], [Preface to second edition]; p. [3]-8, [Dedication] To all the settlers . . . Lunenburg; p. [9]-11, Introduction; p. 12-21, Part I; p. 22-57, Part II; p. 58-95, Part III; p. 95-96, Conclusion.

This is a reprint of the edition of ?1773, with the addition of a preface. The text has been reset in smaller types, with errata corrected, but no other change. The preface, p. [2], states: "The first edition of this little work was privately printed ten years ago for the use of the Author's Flock; but this second edition is intended for the general good of all in this province, who are not above receiving religious instruction, and yet can afford neither much Time for reading nor much Money for the Purchase of good Books. . . To them this little Work is recommended as containing as much Admonition as the Poor are capable of receiving [etc.]."

Copies located: CaNsHA; CaNsHD.

512. [DELISLE, DAVID CHABRAND], 1730?-1794

[ornamental rule] / SERMON / FUNÉBRE / Prononcé à l'occasion de la Mort de / Mr. BENJAMIN FROBISHER. / [ornamental rule] /

Colophon, p. 15: A MONTREAL: / Chez F. MESPLET, Imprimeur. 1787. /

12mo. [*]^{2}, A-B^{4}; 2 p. l., 15 p.; type-page: 13.3 × 7 cm.

Contents: p. l. 1 recto, t.-p.; verso, blank; p. l. 2 recto-verso, "A Messieurs Frobisher, négociants [signed:] D^{d} C^{d} Delisle"; p. 1-15, Sermon, text: Gen. 3: 19, Tu es poudre, & tu retourneras en poudre; p. 15 verso, blank.

A proper funeral oration, enunciating the appropriate religious attitudes: "Quel triste & humiliant spectacle présente l'homme. Il commence la vie par le sentiment de la doleur [etc.]. Bien heureux sont ceux, dit St. Jean, qui meurent au Seigneur [etc.]." It expresses society's tribute to any mortal remains: "A la piété, à la charité . . . il joignoit les qualités & les vertus propres à tout les états de sa vie."

Frobisher, one of the early merchant princes of Montreal, came to Canada from England in 1769. He pursued an adventurous and profitable career in the fur trade and, with his brother Joseph, was an original partner in the North West Company.

Delisle, a Swiss who became a Church of England clergyman, was sent by the British government in 1766 to encourage protestantism in French Canada. He was rector of the parish of Montreal, also chaplain to the garrison till his death.

This work was reprinted in English: *A Sermon preached at the funeral of Mr. Benjamin Frobisher, at Montreal in Canada, on Sunday, April 16, 1787. Translated from the French by Abraham Skelton of Leeds*, York [England] printed by Benjamin Frobisher Blanchard, 1796.

Copies located: CaQMS (3 cop.); CaQQL.

513. DOTY, JOHN, 1745-1841

[An Address on the subject of His Majesty's Royal Proclamation for the encouragement of piety and virtue and for preventing and punishing of Vice, Profaneness, and Immorality. Delivered in Christ's Church at Sorel, in the Province of Canada, on Sunday, the 4th of November, 1787. By John Doty, Presbyter of the Church of England; missionary from the Incorporated Society for the propagation of the Gospel in foreign parts; and one of His Majesty's Justices of the peace for the District of Montreal. Who hath ears to hear, let him hear. Mat. 13.9.]

? Probably printed at Montreal by Fleury Mesplet, 1787, this work was advertised:

"Just published and to be sold at the Store of E. Edwards, Bookseller, Montreal, Price—One Shilling. An Address [etc. as above]."—*Montreal gazette*, Dec. 6, 1787.

Copy located: None.

514. GREAT BRITAIN. ADJUTANT-GENERAL'S OFFICE

[The Manual Exercise with Explanations as ordered by His Majesty.]

Probably printed at Montreal by Fleury Mesplet, 1787, this work was advertised:

"In press and to be sold the 30th Inst., at the Printing-office [of Fleury Mesplet] in Montreal, the Manual Exercise [etc.]."—*Montreal gazette*, Aug. 23, 1787.

"Just published and to be sold at the Printing-office in Montreal, The Manual Exercise [etc.]."—*Montreal gazette*, Aug. 30-Sept. 6, 1787.

This pamphlet was also published in a "second edition" by Mesplet seven months later (No. 553).

Copy located: None.

515. HUBERT, JEAN FRANCOIS, *bp. of Quebec*, 1739-1797

Caption title: Lettre Circulaire à Messieurs les Curés de Campagne. / [rule] /

4 to. 2 *l.* without signature or pagination, text in French on recto of *l.* 1; type-page: 18.5 × 13.8 cm. *Printed at Quebec by Wm. Brown, 1787* (*see* below).

Contents: l. [1] recto, Lettre, 21 lines; verso, blank; *l.* [2] blank. The letter, beginning: "Monsieur, Pour entrer dans les vues du Gouvernement qui a sagement fait annoncer dans la Gazette de Québec [etc.]" is signed: "Jean Franc[s] Ev. d'Almire, Coadj[tr] de Québec. Québec, 16 Mars, 1787."

It states that according to an announcement in the *Quebec gazette*, Mar. 15, 1787, applicants for licences to sell liquor must have a letter of recommendation from the parish priest or captain of militia, and instructs priests to recommend very few, persons of known probity, likely to maintain orderly establishments. It was issued by the coadjutor, Bishop Hubert, titular bishop of Almira, acting for Bishop Esglis, whom he succeeded to the see of Quebec in 1788. But the provincial government was responsible for the publication, as the printer's record indicates:

"1787, Mar. 16. Printed for Gov[t] (by Order of the Coadjutor Bishop) 120 Circular letters to the Priests respecting licences. £1.2.6."

—Can.P.A., *Neilson Papers*, v. 84.

Lettre is reprinted in Têtu and Gagnon: *Mandements de Québec*, 2: 326.

Copies located: CaO; CaOOA (2 cop.); CaQQL.

516. INGLIS, CHARLES, *bp. of Nova Scotia*, 1734-1816

A / SERMON / PREACHED / BEFORE HIS EXCELLENCY / THE LIEUTENANT GOVERNOR, / HIS MAJESTY'S COUNCIL, / AND / THE HOUSE OF ASSEMBLY, / OF THE PROVINCE / OF NOVA-SCOTIA, / IN / ST. PAUL'S CHURCH AT HALIFAX, / ON SUNDAY, NOVEMBER 25, 1787. / [rule] / BY THE RIGHT REVEREND / CHARLES INGLIS, D.D. / BISHOP OF NOVA-SCOTIA. / [double rule] / HALIFAX: / PRINTED BY ANTHONY HENRY, MDCCLXXXVII. /

4to. A-H^2, X^2; 32, [4]p.; type-page: 17 × 11 cm.

Contents: p. [1], half title; p. [2], letter to Inglis dated at Halifax, N.S., November 27, 1787, and signed by Richard Bulkeley, conveying the House of Assembly's thanks for the sermon and request that it be printed; p. [3], t.-p.; p. [4], Dedication; p. 5-32, Sermon, text: Proverbs XIV, 34, Righteousness exhalteth a nation, but sin is a reproach to any people; p. [1-4] at end: Appendix, being extracts from the Assembly *Journal*, Nov. 13-22, the Legislative Council's address to Lieut.-Gov. Parr, Nov. 26, and the latter's message to the Assembly, Dec. 6, 1787—all concerning measures to establish an academy at Windsor and a school; p. [4] at foot: Inglis's note on the matter, and errata.

This impressive discourse treats, with episcopal authority, of spiritual and temporal matters affecting Nova Scotia; of divine favour and prosperity for the righteous nation (presumably the British Empire) and the inevitable decline of the vicious (presumably the United States), the necessity of an established church, of education (especially a free school in Nova Scotia), etc. It ends in praise of the christian rule of George III, the Navigation Act, the colonial bishopric, etc.

In both Nova Scotia and Quebec, Bishop Inglis exerted considerable influence on government to found colleges and schools. At the session during which this sermon was preached, the Nova Scotia legislature voted £400 to open an academy at Windsor. Of this the bishop wrote at length to the archbishop of Canterbury, Dec. 26, 1787, and reported: ". . . the Governor, Council and Assembly requested me to preach before them; and I received a hint that it would be agreeable if I officiated in my Episcopal habit . . . the Sermon, at the desire of the Legislature, is now printed with the design of being distributed through the Province. Mr. Houseill, [i.e. Houseal] Missionary to the Germans at Halifax, is translating it into German, that it may be circulated among the Germans who do not understand English [etc.]."

—Can.P.A., *Inglis papers*, v. 1.

There is no record of the publication of a German version of this sermon, mentioned by Bishop Inglis.

Copies located: CaNsHD; NNHi; RPJ.

517. JONES, ROBERT

REMARQUES / SUR / LA MALADIE CONTAGIEUSE / DE / LA BAIE SAINT PAUL, / Avec la Description de ses Symptômes, & la Méthode / d'en faire la Cure; / A l'usage du CLERGÉ, & autres MESSIEURS résidants / à la Campagne. / PAR / [rule] / ROBERT JONES, CHIRURGIEN, / [rule] / Non ignara mali, miseris succerrere disco. / VIRG. Liv. I. / Mes malheurs m'ont rendu l'Ami des Malheureux, / [printer's ornament] / A MONTREAL, / Chez FLEURY MESPLET, Imprimeur-Libraire. 1787. /

8vo. [A]-C[4]; 22, [2] p.; type-page: 14 × 8.3 cm. This work is a French translation, by an unknown hand, of No. 484.

Contents: p. [1], t.-p.; p. [2], blank; p. [3], Dedication; p. [4], blank; p. [5], "A l'Auteur [tribute to *Les Remarques*, signed:] La Traducteur"; p. [6], blank; p. [7-8], Avertissement; p. 9-22, Description, etc.; [2] p. at end, Liste de MM les Souscripteurs.

Thirty-three subscribers (for 126 copies) are listed, six French twenty-seven British, mainly merchants in Montreal. Alexander Henry, Sr. took 12 copies, Jacob Jordon, James McGill, Benjamin and Joseph Frobisher, 6 copies each, Dr. Jobert, alone of Jones's own profession, and Rev. Mr. Doty alone of the clergy, took 4 copies each. No government official appears to have encouraged the publication by a subscription.

Copies located: CaQ (4 p. l. wanting); CaQMS.

518. MASCALL, EDWARD JAMES, *d.* 1823

[Tables of the net duties payable, and of drawbacks allowed, on certain Goods, Wares, and Merchandise, Imported, Exported, and Carried Coastwise, together with A List of the Bounties published under the inspection of Mr. Edward James Mascall of the Custom-House, London. To which are added A Table of the duties . . . in the Excise; . . . Licences. . . Stamp duties . . . The whole agreeable to the consolidation Act of 27 Geo. III; and prefaced with a most elegant and beautiful Speech of the Rt. Hon. Wm. Pitt . . . 27th Feb. 1787.]

Proposed printing at Shelburne, N.S., by James Humphreys, 1787, was advertised: "Proposals for printing by subscription the following new and useful work (just arrived from London) viz. *Tables of the net duties* [etc.]." The work was to be printed on good demy paper in large octavo the same as the London edition, and stitched in a paper cover. It was to go to press as soon as a hundred subscribers had encouraged the printer. The price to subscribers was to be $1.00, half payable on subscribing; to non-subscribers $1.50. Subscriptions would be received by the printer, James Humphreys, at Shelburne, and by John Howe, printer, Halifax.—*Nova-Scotia packet*, Oct. 25-Dec. 20, 1787 (later issues not seen).

This work was published in London: *The consolidation of the customs and other duties. Tables of the net duties* [etc.] (107 p., 8vo., London, Lowndes, 1787). There is no evidence, however, that it was ever printed at Shelburne, N.S.

519. NEW BRUNSWICK. EXECUTIVE COUNCIL

[Handbills forbidding the Entrance with Creepers into the Council Chamber. *Printed at Saint John, N.B., by Christopher Sower, ? 1787.*]

Sower's account for printing for government, Nov. 15, 1785-Feb. 27, 1787, included the item: "Handbills forbidding the Entrance with Creepers into the Council Chamber—7/6" (Can.P.A., N.B. Ex. co. *Minutes*, Mar. 2, 1787). It was probably a notice posted in the winter months requesting the councillors and their visitors to raise their creepers—spiked boot guards, an excellent precaution against slipping upon ice and snow, still used.

Copy listed: None.

520. NEW BRUNSWICK. HOUSE OF ASSEMBLY

JOURNAL / OF THE / VOTES AND PROCEEDINGS / OF THE / HOUSE / OF / ASSEMBLY. / OF THE / PROVINCE of NEW-BRUNSWICK: / From Tuesday FEBRUARY the 13th, to Thursday MARCH the 8th, 1787. / [rule] / ST. JOHN: / Printed by JOHN RYAN, at his PRINTING-OFFICE, No. 58, / PRINCE WILLIAM STREET. /

fo. A-G[2]; 1 p. l., [75]-100 p.; type-page: 24.2 × 14 cm. paged in continuation of No. 486. One leaf of sig. G is folded around sig. A-F to form p. l. bearing t.-p.

Contents: p. l. recto, t.-p.; verso, blank; p. [75]-100, Journal of the second session of first assembly. Note at end of text: "House of Assembly, March the 8th, 1787. I do allow and order that Mr. John Ryan do print the Journal and Votes of the House of Assembly, and that no other person do presume to print the same. [signed:] Amos Botsford, Speaker."

Though Christopher Sower was commissioned king's printer of New Brunswick, he and John Ryan, were both asked to submit tenders for the printing of the Assembly *Journal* and *Acts* of 1787. Sower stated his terms, Mar., 1787:

> "In compliance with request of yesterday, I beg leave to propose printing the Journals and Laws of this Session both together, for £2, the first 100 of every Sheet and 26 Shillings & 8d. for every 100 above the first, or in that proportion for any larger number.
>
> "But when I make this proposal, I beg it to be understood that when I have once begun the work, I must from time to time be furnished with the manuscript copy when called for; nor must I be kept waiting for a Proof Sheet any longer time than is necessary to read it. I shall also expect a reasonable time to do the work in, as at this price myself and apprentice alone must perform it. The money of course is expected to be paid on delivery of the work.
>
> "You will, I know, excuse me making it a condition not to be kept out of copy, when you reflect that last year when the Laws were copying to be sent to England I have been wanting it for days together at my great cost and expence."

Sower withdrew his condition of payment upon delivery, the following day. But Ryan's tender was couched in more pleasing style:

> ". . . I beg leave to inform you that I conceive £100 in ready money to be as near as possible the Current price and what I should be content to receive for [printing work equal in extent and quality to Sower's edition of the Laws of 1786] or in case I waited any time for the money that it should be made Guineas instead of Pounds."—N.B. *Papers*, 1787.

On Mar. 7, Ryan was offered the work on the terms of Sower's tender—£2 a sheet for the first 100 copies, £1 6*s*. 8*d*. for each additional 100, payment next session—which Ryan accepted. And the following day the House "ordered that the Printer be directed to print 200 copies of the Votes and Journals of . . . Assembly and 200 copies of the Laws. [and] Resolved that John Ryan print the Journals and Votes and no other person do presume to print the same."

—N.B. As. *Journal 1787*.

Ryan's bill

"To printing 200 copies of the Laws containing 8½ Sheets @ £3.6.8. per sheet —£28.6.8.

To ditto 200 Copies of the Journals containing 7 Sheets @ £3.6.8. per sheet —£23.6.8.

To Sewing &c 400 copies of Laws & Journals @½*d*. each—£3.6.8. [Total:] £55." was duly passed for payment in Aug., 1788, but only paid in part for a small "ballance [of £5] due him" was included in the accounts passed in Oct., 1789.—N.B. As. *Papers, 1788-89*.

Copies located: CaN (t.-p. wanting); CaNSA; CaNU; CaNsWA; CaOOA (2 cop.); MWA; RPJ.

521. NEW BRUNSWICK. LAWS, STATUTES, *etc.*

ACTS / OF THE / GENERAL / ASSEMBLY, / OF / His MAJESTY'S PROVINCE / OF / NEW-BRUNSWICK, / PASSED IN THE YEAR 1787. / [double rule] / ST. JOHN: / Printed by JOHN RYAN, at his PRINTING-OFFICE, No. 58, / PRINCE WILLIAM STREET. / [rule] / MDCCLXXXVII. /

fo. [*[1], **[2]], A-[G][2]; 3 p. l., [129]-155 p.; type-page: 24.5 × 14 cm. paged in continuation of No. 487; p. 130-31 mispaged: 4-5. On p. 131 running title 27 G. III appears as 26 G. III. In some copies the errors in pagination and running title are corrected by tiny cancel slips and in others by resetting of type.

Contents: p. l. 1 recto, t.-p.; verso, blank; p. l. 2 recto, half title; verso, blank; p. l. 3 recto, Table of titles; verso, blank; p. [129]-155, 27 Geo. III, c. 1-12, acts of the second session of the first assembly; verso of p. 155, blank.

An edition of 200 copies was printed on order of the Assembly (according to terms recorded in No. 520 *note*) and distributed by government.

Copies located: Baxter; CaOOA; MH; MWA; NNB; NNHi.

522. NOVA SCOTIA. HOUSE OF ASSEMBLY

Caption title: (1) / [ornamental rule] / JOURNAL, / AND / PROCEEDINGS / OF THE / GENERAL ASSEMBLY, / Of the PROVINCE of NOVA-SCOTIA. / [rule] / Thursday 25th October, 1787. /

fo. A-L[2]; 44 p. *Printed at Halifax, N.S., by Anthony Henry, 1787.*

Contents: p. 1-44, Journal and proceedings of the third session of the sixth assembly, Oct. 25-Dec. 12, 1787.

Though the session extended late in the year, this *Journal* was printed in 1787, for the copy transmitted to the secretary of state bears MS. note: "Halifax, Decem^{r} 14th 1787. The foregoing forty four pages contain the printed Journals of the House of Assembly of the Province of Nova Scotia. Attest. S. S. Blowers, Speaker."

Copies located: CaNs; GBLP (in C.O. 217/60: 147-90); MH.

523. NOVA SCOTIA. LAWS, STATUTES, *etc.*

Running title: [rule] / 1787. Anno Vicessimo Octavo Regis, GEORGII III. CAP. I[-XII]. / [rule] /

Caption title: At the GENERAL ASSEMBLY of the Province / of Nova-Scotia, . . . / [8 lines] / . . . being the Third / Session of the Sixth General Assembly, con-/vened in the said Province. /

fo. sig. 2X-3A²; p. 257-272; type-page: 25.5 × 15 cm. paged in continuation of No. 491. *Printed at Halifax, N.S., by Anthony Henry, 1787?*

Contents: p. 257-272, Cap. I-XII, perpetual acts passed in the session Oct. 25 Dec. 12, 1787.

Copies located: CaO; DLC; MH (2 cop.).

524. NOVA SCOTIA. LAWS, STATUTES, *etc.*

Running title: [rule] / 1787. Anno Vicessimo Octavo Regis, GEORGII III. CAP. I[-IV]. / [rule] /

Caption title: At the GENERAL ASSEMBLY of the Province / of Nova-Scotia . . . / [8 lines] / . . . being the Third / Session of the Sixth General Assembly, con-/vened in the said Province. / [rule] /

fo. sig. A-E²; p. 287-305; type-page: 25.5 × 15 cm. paged in continuation of No. 492. *Printed at Halifax, N.S., by Anthony Henry, 1787?*

Contents: p. 287-305, Cap. I-IV, temporary acts passed in the session, Oct. 25-Dec. 12, 1787; p. 305 verso, blank.

Copies located: CaNsHA; CaO; GBLP (p. 299-302 only in C.O. 217/107: 467-70); MH; N; NNB.

525. PARTRIDGE, J.

[Feats of horsemanship.]

Double broadside: text in English and French, *printed at Quebec by Wm. Brown, 1787*, as recorded:

"1787, Sept. 13. Printed for J. Partridge, Horse jockey, 200 D^{ble} handbills notifying Feats of Horsemanship. 2 folio pages pott.—£1.17.6."

Brown recorded other items, recording at the same time the social interests of his time:

"1787, Sept. 15. Printed for J. Partridge 100 single hand-bills postponing his feats of Horsemanship—7/6.

"Sept. 20. Printed for J. Partridge 200 D^{ble} Jocey [sic]-bills—£1.

"Oct. 1. Printed for J. Partridge 200 Single Jocey [sic]-bills (compos'd by Moore. 1 half sheet folio pott.—10/."

—Can.P.A., *Neilson papers*, v. 84.

Copy located: None.

526. PHILLIPS & LANE, *Auctioneers & brokers, Quebec*

[Catalogue of books]

Broadside, *printed at Quebec by Wm. Brown, 1787*, as recorded:

"1787, Mar. 3. Printed for Phillips & Lane, 150 Catalogues of Books—a large Broadside on Demy with Rules—£2.17.6."

—Can.P.A., *Neilson papers*, v. 84.

This sale at Mr. Prenties Rooms, Upper Town, Quebec, Mar. 27, 1787, of "A choice and large collection of books being the libraries of several gentlemen who have gone to Europe, Printed Catalogue with particulars [etc.]" was advertised in the *Quebec gazette*, Feb.-Mar., 1787.

Copy located: None.

527. QUEBEC, *Province.* COURT OF QUARTER SESSIONS OF THE PEACE (Quebec District)

[Royal arms] / *English caption:* At a Court of General-Quarter-Sessions of the Peace / held in the city of Quebec, on Tuesday the tenth day of / July, 1787, and continued . . . to the / fourteenth day of August following . . . / . . . / It is Ordered and Directed as follows: / <Text>

French caption: Dans Une Cour de Quartier-General de Sessions de la / Paix, tenue en la ville de Québec, Mardi le 10 de Juillet 1787, . . . au 14 / d'Aoust suivant, par les Commissionaires . . . / Il est Ordonné et Statué ainsi qu'il suit: / <Text>

Broadside: text in 2 col. English and French; type-page: 35 × 21 cm. *Printed at Quebec by Wm. Brown, 1787.*

The text is signed by D. Lynd, C.P. [i.e commissioner of the peace]. It contains orders 1-6, regulating the sale of fire-wood; stray goats in the streets; the playing of ninepins or skittles; hawkers; boys playing with coppers in the streets; unloading of gunpowder from ships; carrying of gunpowder in the streets.

Copy located: CaO (bound in *Quebec gazette*, following no. 1142, July 5, 1787).

528. QUEBEC, *Province.* COURT OF QUARTER SESSIONS OF THE PEACE (Quebec District)

[royal arms] / *English caption:* Extract from BURN'S JUSTICE. / The Power of a constable as a conservator of / the peace. / <Text>

French caption: EXTRAIT de BURN, / Touchant le pouvoir des conétables, comme conservateurs de la paix. / <Text>

Broadside: Text in 2 col. English and French; type-page: 33.5 × 21.5 cm. *Printed at Quebec by Wm. Brown, 1787.*

The text is signed: "A true Extract. David Lynd C.P., Quebec, 13 August, 1787." Lynd was clerk of the court, i.e. the commissioners (or justices) of the peace, in general quarter sessions, July 10-Aug. 14, 1787.

Copy located: CaO (bound in *Quebec gazette* following no. 1147, Aug. 9, 1787).

529. QUEBEC, *Province.* GOVERNOR, 1786-1791 (*Dorchester*)

GUY LORD DORCHESTER, / . . . / . . . / To THOMAS AINSLIE, Esq. / Collector, and THOMAS / SCOTT, Esq. Comptroller, and others, OFFICERS of / the CUSTOMS of the Province of QUEBEC. /

Broadside: printed in 2 col. type-page: 32.8 × 22.2 cm. *Printed at Quebec by Wm. Brown, 1787,* as recorded:

"1787, May 23. Printed for Lieu[t]. Governor's Sec[y] (by Order Tho[s] Ainslie) 400 Regulations for Trade with American States.—£2.17.6."

—Can.P.A., *Neilson papers,* v. 84.

Contents: col. 1 sets forth orders to permit free importation by Lake Champlain, of lumber, naval stores, grain, livestock "and whatsoever else is of the growth of the United States," free exportation of produce and manufacture of Quebec (except furs) and to exclude rum and non-British goods from overseas; dated at Quebec, Apr. 18, 1787; col. 2: 27 Geo. III chap. VIII, "An Act or Ordinance for the free importation of Tobacco, pot and pearl ashes, into this province, by the inland communication by Lake Champlain and Sorel . . . enacted, Quebec, 30 April 1787."

Copy located: CaOOA (filed in Can.P.A. "S" *Ordinances, P. of Q. 1787* with drafts etc., of legislation on opening trade with Vermont).

530. QUEBEC, *Province.* LAWS, STATUTES, *etc.*

ORDINANCES / MADE AND PASSED / BY THE / GOVERNOR / AND / LEGISLATIVE COUNCIL / OF THE / PROVINCE / OF / QUEBEC. / [rule] / [royal arms] / [double rule] / Quebec: / Printed by WILLIAM BROWN, in Mountain-Street. / [rule] / M,DCC,LXXXVII. /

French t.-p.:

ORDINANCES / FAITES ET PASSÉES / PAR LE / GOUVERNEUR / ET LE / CONSEIL LEGISLATIF / DE LA / PROVINCE / DE / QUEBEC. / [rule] / [royal arms] / [double rule] / A QUEBEC: / Chez GUILLAUME BROWN, au milieu de la Grande Côte. / [rule] / M,DCC,LXXXVII. /

fo. A-T[2]; 1 p. l., [1], 1-72 p.; type-page: 23 × 12.5 cm. Even numbers on recto, odd numbers on verso. Text in English and French on opposite pages.

Contents: p. l. recto, English t.-p.; verso, blank; p. [1] (recto of p. 1), French t.-p.; p. 1-72, 27 Geo. III, c. I-XII (enacted Feb. 27-Apr. 30, 1787); verso of p. 72, blank.

Brown records the printing of this work:

"1787, July 31. Printed for Government by Order of Mr. Williams [i.e. Jenkin Williams then Clerk of the Council] 300 Copies of the Ordinances of L[egislative].C[ouncil]. making 19 Sheets on folio pot in English & Brevier notes at 3£ per Sheet.—£57.

"Sept. 27. Gov[t]. owes Printing Office for furnishing guards and covering and paying stitching &c 300 books Ordinances of 1787 @ 4½*d.*—£5.12.6."

—Can.P.A., *Neilson papers,* v. 84.

From Aug. 4, 1787, Brown also recorded the sale of single copies at 5*s.*—*ibid.*

Copies located: CaQM; CaQQL (3 cop.); MiD-B; NN; NNB.

531. QUEBEC, *Province.* LAWS, STATUTES, *etc.*

NUM. 1124. / THE / QUEBEC / GAZETTE / [rule] / THURSDAY, MARCH 1, 1787. / [rule] / [in centre: royal arms] / [on right:] LA / GAZETTE / DE / QUEBEC. / [rule] / JEUDI, le 1 MARS, 1787. / [rule] /

English caption: Anno Vicesimo Septimo Georgii III Regis. Chap. I An Ordinance To regulate proceedings in certain cases in the Court of King's bench, and to give the subject the benefit of Appeal from Large Fines. [signed at end by Dorchester, Quebec, Feb. 27, 1787.]

French caption: . . . Chap. I. Ordonance qui régle les formes de procéder, dans de certains cas, en la Cour du Banc du Roi, et qui donne au sujet le bénéfice d'apel de fortes amendes.

Broadside: text in 2 col., English and French. *Printed at Quebec by Wm. Brown, 1787.*

This, and the four items following, were reprinted from *Gazette* types on *Gazette* paper. They contain the customary *Gazette* heading, the ordinance and the customary *Gazette* colophon, but no other printed matter. The printing was regularly recorded on Brown's books—e.g.:

"1787, Mar. 3. Printed for Gov[t]. by Order Mr. Williams 150 copies of Ordinance Chap. I—£1.7.6.

"Printed for Gov[t] 1 week D[ble] [i.e. in English and French] in N°. 1124 [*Quebec gazette*] Chap. I of Ordinances,—£3.10."

—Can.P.A., *Neilson papers*, v. 84.

The printing in the *Gazette* constituted legal publication of laws and it was covered by the government's contract with Brown, for which he received at this time a semi-annual allowance, or salary, of £55 11*s*. 1*d*., Quebec currency. The separate issues were "extra work" however, and their printing is so charged in Brown's semi-annual account to Jenkin Williams, clerk of the council, e.g. that of Apr. 10-Oct. 10, 1787, includes:

"Apr. 26. To printing 250 copies Ordinances Chap. 2, on a whole Sheet —£2.10.

"D°, 250 copies Ordinances Chap. 3, on a whole Sheet—£2.10.

"May 5. D° 150 copies Ordinances Chap. 4, 5, 6, on a Sheet—£2.5.

"May 14. D° 150 copies Ordinances Chap. 7, 8, 9, 10, 11, 12, on a Sheet —£2.5."

Appended to the bill is Brown's oath sworn before notary, May 8, 1788, that the articles listed were done and delivered by Williams's order and are "charged no higher than the usual prices hitherto charg'd and paid by Individuals for the like."

—Can.P.A., "S" *Pub. Accts, 1788.*

The ordinances in this and the four items following, were also printed together from another setting of type in July, 1787 (No. 530). They are reprinted in Can. P.A., *Report, 1914-15.*

Copies located: CaOOA (in portfolio "*Quebec gazette*, Mar. 1, 1787"); CaQMA.

532. QUEBEC, *Province.* LAWS, STATUTES, *etc.*

NUM. 1132 / THE / QUEBEC / GAZETTE / [rule] / THURSDAY, APRIL 26, 1787. / [rule] / [in centre: royal arms] / [on right:] LA /

GAZETTE / DE / QUEBEC. / [rule] / JEUDI, le 26 AVRIL, 1787. / [rule] /

English caption: Anno Vicesimo Septimo Georgii III. Regis. Chap. II. An Ordinance for better regulating the Militia of this Province and rendering it of more general utility towards the Preservation and Security thereof. [signed at end by Dorchester, Quebec, Apr. 23, 1787]

French caption: . . . Chap. II. Ordonance. Qui régle plus solidement les milices de cette Province et qui les rend d'une plus grande utilité pour la conservation et sureté d'icelle.

fo. [*][2]; [3] p. Text in 2 col., English and French on p. [1-3]; p. [3] verso, blank. *Printed at Quebec by Wm. Brown, 1787,* in an edition of 250 copies (*see* No. 531 ***note***).

This ordinance (in this edition?) was advertised by Montreal merchants: "A vendre, chez Mrs. Franchere & Jean Bouthillier. Ordonance qui régle plus solidement les milices [etc.]."—*Montreal gazette,* Aug. 16, 1787.

Copies located: CaOOA (bound in *Quebec gazette,* 1787); CaQMA.

533. QUEBEC, *Province.* LAWS, STATUTES, *etc.*

SUPPLEMENT to the QUEBEC GAZETTE, N° 1132. / SUPPLEMENT à la GAZETTE de QUEBEC, N° 1132. / [double rule] /

English caption: Anno Vicesimo Septimo Georgii III Regis, Chap. III. An Ordinance for quartering the troops upon certain occasions in the country parishes, and providing for conveyance of effects belonging to the government. [signed at end by Dorchester, Quebec, Apr. 23, 1787]

French caption: . . . Chap. II. [sic] Ordonance, Pour loger les troupes dans certaines ocasions chés les habitans des campagnes et qui pourvoit aux transports des effets du gouvernement.

fo. [*]; [3] p. Text in 2 col. English and French on p. [1-3]; p. 3 verso, blank. *Printed at Quebec by Wm. Brown, 1787,* in an edition of 250 copies (*see* No. 531 ***note***).

Copies located: CaOOA (in portfolio "*Quebec gazette,* Mar. 1, 1787"); CaQMA.

534. QUEBEC, *Province.* LAWS, STATUTES, *etc.*

NUM. 1133. / THE / QUEBEC / GAZETTE / [rule] / THURSDAY, MAY 3, 1787. / [rule] / [in centre: royal arms] / [on right:] LA / GAZETTE / DE / QUEBEC. / [rule] / JEUDI, le 3, MAI, 1787. / [rule] /

English caption: Anno Vicesimo Septimo Georgii III. Chap. IV. An Ordinance to continue . . . "an Ordinance to regulate the form of proceedings in the courts of civil judicature."

French caption: . . . Chap. IV. Ordonance, Qui continue . . . "Ordonance qui régle les formes de procéder dans les cours civiles de judicature [etc.]"

Printed at Quebec by Wm. Brown, 1787, in an edition of 150 copies (*see* No. 531 *note*).

fo. [*][2] [3] p. Text in 2 col. English and French, contains 27 Geo. III c. 4-6, each ordinance signed by Dorchester, Quebec, Apr. 30, 1787; p. [3] verso, blank.

Copy located: CaOOA (in portfolio "*Quebec gazette*, Mar. 1, 1787").

535. QUEBEC, *Province.* LAWS, STATUTES, *etc.*

NUM. 1134 / THE / QUEBEC / GAZETTE / [rule] / THURSDAY, MAY 10, 1787. / [rule] / [in centre: royal arms] / [on right:] LA / GAZETTE / DE / QUEBEC. / [rule] / JEUDI, le 10 MAI, 1787. / [rule] /

English caption: Anno Vicesimo Septimo Georgii III, Regis. Chap. VII. An Act or Ordinance further to continue . . . the ordinance for the regulation of fees.

French caption: . . . Chap. VII. Ordonance, Qui continue encor, . . . "Ordonance qui etablit les honoraires."

Printed at Quebec, by Wm. Brown, 1787, in an edition of 150 copies (*see* No. 531 *note*).

fo. [*][2]; [4] p. Text in 2 col. English and French, contains 27 Geo. III c. 7-12, each ordinance signed by Dorchester, Quebec, Apr. 30, 1787.

Copies located: CaOOA (in portfolio "*Quebec gazette*, Mar. 1, 1787"); CaQMA.

536. QUEBEC, *Province.* LEGISLATIVE COUNCIL

DRAUGHT / OF AN / ACT OR ORDINANCE / For the better ADMINISTRATION of JUSTICE, / and to Regulate the PRACTICE of the LAW, / IN THE / PROVINCE OF QUEBEC: / Now laying on the TABLE of the / HONORABLE LEGISLATIVE COUNCIL. /

4to. A-C[4]; 12 p.; type-page: 18.5 × 12.5 cm. *Printed at Quebec by Wm. Brown, 1787,* as recorded:

"1787, Mar. 12. Printed for R. Lister &c. A Draught of an Ordinance, 200 Copies in English, 1½ Sheet Crown 4to—£5.5.
300 Copies in French 1½ Sheet Crown 4to—£5.5. at 3 Guineas a Sheet by Agreement."—Can.P.A., *Neilson papers*, v. 84.

Contents: p. [1], t.-p.; p. [2], Introduction, dated at Quebec, Mar. 12, 1787; p. [3]-12, Draught of an act.

This *Draught of an act*, drawn up by Chief-Justice Smith, "was procured by some Gentlemen of Quebec and Montreal, and is printed at their own expence to prevent mistakes and to set those to right who may have erroneously conceived that it [was] . . . unfavourable to His Majesty's [French] Canadian Subjects, affecting either their property or civil rights."—*Introd.*, p. [2].

Wm. Smith, formerly chief-justice of New York, a loyalist, came to Canada in 1786 as chief-justice of Quebec. At the first legislative session of the council he introduced several measures to implement a reorganization of government. This bill relating to the civil courts, proposed the customary biennial renewal of 17 Geo. III c. 2 with certain amendments. The latter were designed to eliminate delays and inefficiencies in the existing procedure, also to establish English common law in the Court of Common Pleas for litigants of British origin, and to erect judicial districts in areas of recent loyalist settlement. British settlers and traders who objected to the French civil law had increased in numbers through immigration of American loyalists and English law actually obtained in some courts. A rival bill standardizing the French system in a renewal of 17 Geo. III c. 2, was introduced in Council by Paul Roch de St. Ours. In the storm of nationalist controversy which followed, both bills were lost, and another, a compromise, measure was passed—27 Geo. III c. 4. Following the session a general investigation into the administration of justice in Quebec was ordered by Gov. Dorchester, but the judicial system was only reorganized in 1794 (*see* No. 889).

Smith's *Draught of an act*, with related documents, is reprinted in Shortt and Doughty: *Documents, 1759-1791*, 2: 847-54.

Copies located: GBLP (3 cop. in C.O. 42/19, 106-117; C.O. 42/51: 559-70; C.O. 42/87: 675-86, respectively).

537. QUEBEC, *Province.* LEGISLATIVE COUNCIL

[ornamental rule] / PROJET / D'ACTE OU ORDONNANCE / Pour la meilleure ADMINISTRATION de la JUSTICE, et / qui regle la PRATIQUE de la LOI / DANS LA / PROVINCE DE QUEBEC: / MAINTENANT SUR LA TABLE POUR LA CONSIDERATION DE / L'HONORABLE CONSEIL LEGISLATIF. / [ornamental rule] /

4to. A-C²; 12 p.; type-page: 18.5 × 12.5 cm. *Printed at Quebec by Wm. Brown, 1787*, a French edition, in 300 copies, of No. 536.

Contents: p. [1], t.-p.; p. [2], Introduction, dated at end: "A Quebec, 12me Mars, 1787"; p. 3-12, Projet.

Copies located: CaOOA (photostat of a copy not located); GBLP (in C.O. 42/51, p. 571-82).

538. QUEBEC, *Province.* LIEUTENANT-GOVERNOR, 1785-1789 (*Hope*)

(Copie) / QUEBEC, le 3 de Mars, 1787. / MONSIEUR, / J'AI la satisfaction de vous transmettre les Ordres du Quartier General de ce jour / [etc.].

fo. 2 *l.*, type-page: 24 × 15.3 cm. *Printed at Quebec by Wm. Brown, 1787*, as recorded:

"1787, Mar. 8. Printed for Genl Hope (by Order Mr. Craigie) 180 Genl Orders &c respecting the Canadian Companies. 2 folio pages on foolscap. —£2.17.6."—Can.P.A., *Neilson papers*, v. 84.

Contents: *l.* 1 recto with caption as above, is signed: "Henry Hope," and addressed: "A Monsieur le Lieutenant-Colonel Baby, Adjutant-Général des Milices, à Québec." It contains orders that grants of land and rations of food are to be given to militia under Capt. Boucherville, Rouville, and Desaunier Beaubien, in same proportion as other companies; schedule of rations appended; verso, blank.

l. 2 recto has caption: (COPIE) / ORDRES DU QUARTIER-GENERAL, QUEBEC, le 3 Mars, 1787. / It contains order for, and schedule of land grants to the 3 Canadian companies and list of Canadian officers whose provincial rank and half pay have been confirmed; signed: "Fras. Le Maistre, S.M. [secretaire militaire]"; verso, blank.

Copy located: CaQQL.

539. QUEBEC GAZETTE. CARRIER'S ADDRESS

ETRENNES / DU GARÇON, qui porte la / GAZETTE DE QUEBEC / AUX PRATIQUES / Le I Janvier, 1788. / [*Quebec, Wm. Brown, 1787.*]

Broadside: 37 lines; type-page: 23.5 × 15.5 cm. in ornamental rule frame.

Contents: Etrennes, 32 lines of light verse.

Copy located: CaO (bound in *Quebec gazette* at end of 1787).

540. QUEBEC THEATRE

[PLAY BILL]

Broadside, *Printed at Quebec by Wm. Brown, 1787.*

The following playbills were printed by Brown during 1787. In his account books they were usually recorded: "[date] Printed for Theatre 300 Play-bills on Demy notifying [title]—15/." For "Theatre," the name "Ashton," "Ashton & Potts," or "Wm. Moore," occasionally appears.

1787, Jan. 15, The Country Lasses, etc.; Jan. 19, The Natural Son; Jan. 25, The London Merchant; Jan. 27, Follies of a Day; Feb. 1, The London Merch[t].; Feb. 3, Fashionable Lover, etc.; Feb. 10, Fair Canadian; June 26, Busy-body, etc.; July 10, Humours, etc.; July 14, Mirror, etc.; July 10, Solomangunda, etc.; July 23, Court of Melpomene, etc.; July 25, The Muse in Good Humour, etc.; July 30, The Bargain, etc.; Aug. 28, King Henry IV, etc.; Aug. 30, She Stoops to Conquer; Sept. 5, The Devil on 2 Sticks; Sept. 10, Moore's Benefit; Sept. 15, The Duenna (postponed); Sept. 27, Mrs. Allen's Benefit; Sept. 28, The Mayor of Garratt, etc.; Oct. 4, The Tempest, Devil to Pay, etc.—Can.P.A., *Neilson papers*, v. 84.

Copy located: None.

541. SPARK, ALEXANDER, 1762-1819

AN / ORATION / DELIVERED AT THE DEDICATION OF / FREE-MASON's HALL / IN THE / CITY OF QUEBEC, / BY ALEX[R]: SPARK, A.M. / [rule] / PUBLISHED AT THE REQUEST OF THE SOCIETY. / [rule] / Sapienta ædificavit Donum suam; excidit Columnas suas septem. / Solomon. / [rule] / QUEBEC: / PRINTED BY WILLIAM BROWN, / [rule] / M,DCC,LXXXVII. /

12mo. A-B[4]; 16 p.; type-page: 13 × 8.5 cm.

Contents: p. [1], t.-p.; p. [2], blank. p. [3], Resolution of thanks and request to print the oration, dated at Quebec, Nov. 3, 1787; p. [4], Spark's reply to "Officers of the Provincial Grand Lodge and the Society of free and accepted masons of the city of Quebec," dated at Belmont, Nov. 12, 1787; p. [5]-16, An oration.

Brown, himself a freemason, recorded the printing and his brotherly charge for his work and materials:

"1787, Nov. 30. Printed for the Free Masons, 259 copies of Rev[d] A. Sparks Oration at the dedication of Free Mason's Hall. 25 of the copies on fine demy, with Stitching and covering and alter'd by order of Rev. Mr. Sparks—£5."—Can.P.A., *Neilson papers*, v. 84.

The work was advertised for sale (no price stated) in Quebec and Montreal "the produce of the Sale to be applied after defraying the charge of printing, to the Fund of Charity."—*Quebec gazette*, Dec. 6, 1787; also *Montreal gazette*, Dec. 13, 1787.

The oration is a panegyric on the ancient and modern glories of "Masonry, whose task is to lighten and to adorn—behold the Heaven-born Virgin appear, bearing in her hand the Lamp of Science, the Mirror of Truth with the various Ensigns of Art, Joy smiling in her Countenance, the fair Semblance of Virtue and internal Peace [etc.]."—p. 9.

The event, the first, or one of the first, of its kind in Canada, was duly described: "On Saturday 3rd [Nov., 1787] the house lately Mrs. Prenties' (now Free Masons Hall) purchased by the Society of Free & Accepted Masons in this City, was solemnly dedicated to Masonry, Virtue, Charity & Universal Benevolence. The Ceremony was honored with the presence of His Excellency the Rt. Hon. Lord Dorchester, Lady Dorchester, General Hope, and a numerous Company of Ladies and Gentlemen, who expressed great satisfaction at the regularity and decorum with which it was conducted. The Reverend Brother Spark delivered an Oration [etc.]."

—*Quebec gazette*, Nov. 15, 1787.

Spark came to Canada from Scotland in 1780 as a school teacher and was long one of the best classical tutors in Canada. Ordained in the Church of Scotland in 1784, he served the Presbyterian congregation in Quebec until his death and was its appointed minister from 1795. Spark had a close connection with Brown's printing-office after the latter's death. For he was guardian of its young owner, Brown's nephew, John Neilson, 1793-97; he superintended publication of the *Gazette* for a time, and edited the *Quebec magazine*, 1792-94.

Copies located: CaQMS; CtY.

542. ALMANACS. NOVA SCOTIA

Wood-block t.-p.: Der / Neuschottländische / Calender, / Auf das Jahr Christi / 1789. / Welches ein Gemeines Jahr von 365 / Tagen ist. / [double rule] / Halifax, gedruckt bey Anth. Heinrich. / [title in German letter type, set in a medallion within a wide border of wood-cut figures, printed from the same block as No. 503]

t.-p. in type:

Der / Neu-Schottländische / Calender, / Auf das Jahr, nach der heilbringenden Geburt / Unsers HErrn JEsu Christi, / 1789. / Welches ein Gemeines Jahr von 365 Tagen ist. / Darinnen, . . . [etc., contents listed in 10 lines, the same as on t.-p. of No. 503] / [rule] / Zum Zweytenmal heraus-gegeben. / [double rule] / HALIFAX, / Gedruckt und zu haben bey Anthon Henrich, in der Sackville-Strasse. /

4to. A-E[4]; [40] p.; type-page: 17.5 × 14.2 cm.; most of the text is printed in 2 col., German letter throughout.

Contents: p. [1], wood-cut, t.-p.; p. [2], verse; p. [3], t.-p.; p. [4-40], Calendar (in matter and arrangement similar to No. 503).

Copy located: CaOOA.

543. ALMANACS. NOVA SCOTIA

THE / NOVA-SCOTIA CALENDER, / OR AN / ALMANACK, / For the Year . . . 1789; . . . / [4 lines] / WHEREIN IS CONTAINED, / The Eclipses . . . / [3 lines] / [rule] / Calculated for the Meridian of HALIFAX, . . . / [3 lines] / By METONICUS. / [rule] / [verse: 10 lines] / [double rule] / HALIFAX, Printed and Sold by A. HENRY. / [title and each page within ornamental frame]

8vo. [28] p.; type-page: 18 × 10.5 cm.

Contents: p. [1], t.-p.; p. [2], Vulgar notes; p. [3-4], Eclipses, verses; p. [5-16], Calendar; p. [17], Ephemeris; p. [18-23], Nova Scotia administration, legislature, judges, justices, sheriffs, customs, army officers; p. [24-27], Court sessions, post fares and distances, buoys, naval yard officers, postage rates; p. [27-28], Recipes for insects on fruit trees, for cancer, for sage wine, errata.

This almanac was advertised: "Just published and to be sold by Anthony Henry, the Nova-Scotia Calender [etc.]."—*Nova-Scotia gazette,* Dec. 9, 1788.

Copies located: CaNsHA (p. [17-24] wanting); CaQMS; DLC.

544. ALMANACS. QUEBEC

ALMANACH / DE / QUEBEC, / POUR / l'ANNÉE / 1789. / [rule] / [group of type ornaments incorporating the masonic date: 5789] / [double rule] / A QUEBEC: / Chez Guillaume Brown, / AU MILIEU DE LA GRANDE-COTE. /

12mo. A-E[6]; 60 p.; type-page: 11 × 6 cm.

Contents: p. [1] t.-p.; p. [2-3], Epoques, eclipses; p. [4], Table des Marées; p. [5-16], Calendrier; p. 17-29, Officiers civils; p. 30-34, "Ordonnance qui change la presente méthode de fixer les ménoires aux . . . traines et carioles" (28 Geo. III c. 9); p. 34-37, 28 Geo. III c. 4, Act to allow the import of Rum etc. into Quebec; p. 38-42, British army officers in Canada; p. 43-53, Officiers des milices; p. 53-55, Clergé, connétables, pilotes, currency rules; p. 56, Experiences curieuses sur les probabilité de la vie; p. 57-58, Enigmes; p. 59-60, Interest tables, etc.

The army and militia lists are new features in this almanac, as are the life expectancy tables for men and women (in French). The almanac was published Dec. 26, 1788, and sold at 1*s.* 6*d.* the copy (2*s.* interleaved) for a fine paper copy, 1*s.* 2*d.* for a "coarse" or "common" paper copy. This was the beginning of the Brown-Neilson practice of issuing the *Quebec almanac* on two paper stocks, and it is the last almanac published by Wm. Brown, who died on Mar. 22, 1789.

Copies located: CaOOA; CaQQAr.

545. ALMANACS. QUEBEC

Calendrier de l'année 1789 pour Montréal.
Colophon: A Montréal, chez Fleury Mesplet.

Broadside: paper-page: 38.5 × 30.5 cm. This sheet almanac was printed in 1788; it was advertised: "Le Calendrier de Montréal pour l'Année 1789, A Vendre Chez François Sareau, rue Notre Dame et chez l'Imprimeur."—*Montreal gazette*, Jan. 1, 1789, *et seq.*

Copy located: CaQMS (described in Fauteux: *Mesplet*, no. 62, from which this entry is taken).

546. ALMANACS. QUEBEC

CALENDRIER pour l'Année 1789, pour Québec, par es $306^{d.}$ 30^{m} de Longitude, et $46^{d.}$ $55^{m.}$ de Latitude / [row of dots] /
Colophon: A QUEBEC: chez WM. BROWN, au milieu de la Grande Côte. /

Broadside: 52 × 38.5 cm. Printed like the *Calendrier pour . . . 1786*, on heavy writing paper stock.

Contents: Calendrier (and footnote on arrangement, in ornamental rule frame: 44.5 × 38.5 cm.); officiers civils (as in previous years).

This sheet almanac was sold at 9*d.* the copy, 5*s.* the dozen, from Nov. 24, 1788, and advertised as usual in the *Quebec gazette*, from Nov. 20, 1788.

Copy located: CaO (bound in *Quebec gazette*, at the end of 1788).

547. ALMANACS. QUEBEC

[Moore's English Sheet Almanack for the Year of our Lord MDCCLXXXIX. *Quebec, Wm. Moore, 1788.*]

Broadside: *printed at Quebec by Wm. Moore, 1788*, who announced its publication for Nov. 17, 1788, in the *Prospectus*, and advertised it in the first number of his newspaper: "Just published Moore's English Sheet Almanack for the year of our Lord MDCCXXXIX. Price Nine Pence."—*Quebec herald*, Nov. 24, 1788.

This was the first sheet almanac for the English in Quebec. The French-speaking inhabitants were well supplied by Wm. Brown's *Calendrier de Québec* since 1765 and Mesplet's *Calendrier de Montréal* since 1776.

Copy located: None.

548. ALMANACS QUEBEC

Moore s Pocket Almanack and General Pocket Register, for the Year of our Lord 1789.]

8vo. 50 p. *Printed at Quebec by Wm. Moore, 1788*, this almanac was announced from Oct. 25, 1788, as a forthcoming publication to appear on Dec. 30, 1788, then advertised:

"For Sale, Moore's Pocket Almanack and General Register, for the year of our Lord 1789, Being the first after Bissextile, or Leap Year, calculated for the Latitude and Longitude of the centre of this Province, containing the Lunations, Eclipses Rising and Setting of the Sun . . . Time of high water at Quebec . . . Feasts and Fasts, a Table showing the bearing [and] distance . . . of most cities . . . from London; Tables of interest at six per cent; Stages from Halifax via Quebec to Albany; the Royal Family, British ministers, etc. the Quebec Provincial calendar [the administration, judiciary, army and militia etc.] doctors, post offices, chronology &c. The Public may rely on the above lists being correct, the Printer being favoured with them from their respective offices.

"Printed in foolscap 8vo. containing 50 pages. Prices two shillings stitched; Two and two-pence, in a blue cover; Two and four-pence in marble; Two and six-pence in marble interleaved with writing paper for memorandums [sic]. Quebec, Printed and Sold at the Herald Printing Office, opposite Freemason's Hall; and [at the places and agents enumerated in No. 558]."—*Quebec herald*, Jan. 5, 1789.

Copy located: None.

549. BURN, RICHARD, 1709-1785

[Souscription pour la Traduction du traité de Burn sur l'Office des Juges à Paix &c.]

8 p. *Printed at Montreal by Fleury Mesplet, 1788?* This is a prospectus of Burn's *Le juge à paix*, published by Mesplet in 1789 (No. 583).

Copy known but not located: Sold by G. Ducharme, Montreal, as listed in his *Catalogue no. 35*, item no. 17322, fév., 1930.

550. CHURCH OF ENGLAND. DIOCESE OF NOVA SCOTIA

[Address of the clergy of the diocese of Nova Scotia to Bishop Inglis, Halifax, June, 1788, and Bishop Inglis' Answer thereto.]

Probably printed in Halifax, N.S., by Anthony Henry, 1788, in leaflet form, or in the *Nova-Scotia gazette.* This publication originated in the earliest diocesan meeting of the Church of England, in Canada, held at Halifax, June 18-22, 1788. Of it Bishop Inglis wrote from Halifax, July 7, 1788, to the archbishop of Canterbury: ". . . the number of clergy which met . . . was eleven, the greatest that ever assembled here at one time, all indeed . . . in the Province met, except two, one of whom was prevented by bad weather, the other, by poverty. Mr. Peters, formerly a missionary in Connecticutt, now resident in England [i.e. Samuel Peters, author of *A general history of Connecticut*, London, 1781, and himself an aspirant to the bishopric of Nova Scotia] wrote to many of the clergy here, exhorting them to have no connection with me. [At the meeting, however] the Clergy presented an address to me, of which I knew nothing till that time. The address and my answer thereto are printed . . . [My Charge to the Clergy] I shall probably prepare for the press after my return from New Brunswick" (*see* No. 594).—Can.P.A., *Inglis papers*, 8:16, 174.

Copy located: None.

551. COURIER DE QUEBEC

QUEBEC, JANV. I. 1788. / AVEC PERMISSION DE SON EXCELLENCE LE TRE'S-HONORABLE / GUY LORD DORCHESTER. / [rule] /

Sera publié livré aux Souscripteurs et autres, Lundi le Martin dans chaque / Semaine, a commencer dans le Mois de Juin prochain, / UNE GAZETTE EN FRANCOIS INTITULE'E/COURIER DE QUEBEC. / Omne Tulit punctum qui miscuit utile dulci—Hor. / <Text>

Broadside: 40 lines; type-page: 26.5 × 17 cm. *Printed at Quebec by Wm. Moore, 1788.*

The text sets forth the conditions of publication and proposed contents of a newspaper to be edited by Mr. Tanswell, a school master in Quebec, and printed by Wm. Moore. It was to be issued weekly on Monday mornings, in French, 4 p. 4to., containing occurrences of the province, moral and instructive essays, anecdotes and advertisements. The subscription was to be half a guinea or 40 francs a year, single copies 10 sous. Advertisements were solicited at 3*s.* 6*d.* for 10 lines, 6*d.* each line after, also news items, articles, essays, poetry, etc., postpaid.

The newspaper, thus announced, actually appeared on Nov. 24, 1788, and ran for three weeks as *Courier de Québec, ou Heraut François.*

Copy located: CaQQL.

552. DONEGANE, *Rope-dancer*

[Hand-bill, notifying Feats of activity]

Broadside or leaflet, *printed at Quebec by Wm. Brown, 1788,* as recorded:

"1788, Sept. 22. Printed for Donegane, Rope-dancer, 200 Hand-bills notifying Feats of activity &c. 1 folio page on Crown. 10/

"Sept. 27, Oct. 3, 11, 18, 23, 27 [Further entries as above]."

—Can.P.A., *Neilson papers,* v. 84.

Copy located: None.

553. GREAT BRITAIN. ADJUTANT-GENERAL'S OFFICE

THE / MANUAL EXERCISE, / WITH / EXPLANATIONS, / As Ordered by / His MAJESTY./The Second Edition./[2 ornamental rules] /MONTREAL; / Printed by FLEURY MESPLET, MDCC.LXXXVII. /

12mo. A⁴, C-E⁴; 32 p.; type-page: 12 × 7.5 cm.

Contents: p. [1], t.-p.; p. [2], blank; p. [3]-32, Manual Exercise (text entirely in English, in 2 col.: left col. containing words of command, right col., explanations).

Probably a reprint of the work published by Mesplet in 1787 (*see* No. 514), this pamphlet was advertised:

"Just published and to be sold at the Printing Office, Montreal, The Manual Exercise [etc.] A Book which every Militia man should have who is not proficient in Exercises; to be had at the moderate price of One Shilling."—*Montreal gazette,* Mar. 27, 1788.

T.-p. facsim. is in Fauteux: *Introduction of printing into Canada,* p. 104.

Copy located: CaQMS.

554. GREAT BRITAIN. COMMISSION APPOINTED TO ENQUIRE INTO THE LOSSES OF AMERICAN LOYALISTS, 1783-1789

OFFICE OF AMERICAN CLAIMS, / MONTREAL, 14th April, 1788. / <Text> / JAMES BETTS, SECY. / to the COMMISSIONERS. /

Broadside: 28 lines, type-page: 10.5 × 9 cm. Text in English (above) and French (below). *Probably printed at Montreal by Fleury Mesplet, 1788,* and issued with the *Montreal gazette,* Apr. 17, 1788, this notice was also published in the *Montreal gazette,* Apr. 24-May 29, 1788. The text notifies claimants under 23 Geo. III c. 80, and 25 Geo. III c. 26 (*see* No. 458) to appear before the commissioners sitting in Montreal till June 1, 1788. The latter, Jeremy Pemberton and Col. Thomas Dundas, took evidence on claims at Halifax, N.S., Saint John, N.B., Quebec, Montreal, Carleton Island and Niagara, 1785-89. Their proceedings are printed in the Ontario Archives, *Report, 1904.*

Copy located: CaOT (bound with *Montreal gazette,* Apr. 17, 1788).

555. HALIFAX, N.S., *City.* ST. PAUL'S CHURCH

An Hymn, / To be sung in St. Paul's Church, on Sunday, / December 7th, 1788. / When a SERMON will be preached for the Benefit of the SUN-/DAY SCHOOLS, and of the Poor in Halifax. /

Broadside: 35 lines within frame; type-page: 25.5 × 15.5 cm. *Probably printed at Halifax, N.S., by Anthony Henry, 1788.*

Anonymous, though probably composed by, or for, Bishop Inglis, the hymn, in six verses, begins:

"Who made the Earth, to Earth came down,
And quitting his celestial crown,
Shone forth in Mercy's gentle Rays;
He opened wide the heav'nly Door,
Bade Wealth relieve the helpless Poor,
And all their bounteous Saviour praise."

Two Sunday schools were opened in Halifax, N.S., by Bishop Inglis, Apr. 20, 1788. He wrote to the archbishop of Canterbury, Dec. 18, 1788: "My two Sunday Schools are in a promising way . . . thirty-one children, I lately preached a charity sermon for their benefit. I pay £10 a year to Master and Mistress, and there is no money that I disburse with more cheerfulness. The Schools began in April and some of the children who were thus taught the alphabet, can now read tolerably. This winter I propose to print my Charge to the Clergy and . . . add in appendix the Regulations I have established in the Schools to make them known and induce others to adopt them" (*see* No. 594). Sunday classes, giving secular as well as religious instruction were an essential part of Inglis's diocesan policy. "These Schools [he wrote] are peculiarly necessary to this country, not indeed for the industrious who are employed all the week, for we have but few of such, but for the poor who cannot afford the expense of a School, and for the ignorant, careless and idle, who run wild all the week and spend Sunday like the other days" (*see* R. V. Harris: *Charles Inglis, missionary, loyalist, bishop, 1734-1816,* Toronto, 1937, p. 124-25).

Copy located: CaNsHD.

556. HUBERT, JEAN FRANCOIS, *bp. of Quebec*, 1739-1797

Caption title: [ornamental rule] / SOLI DEO GLORIA. [within frame] / [ornamental rule] / MANDEMENT / DE MONSEIGNEUR / L'EVEQUE DE QUEBEC, / Touchant la jurisdiction des Prêtres de son Diocèse. / [rule] / JEAN FRANCOIS HUBERT / . . . / . . . Evêque de Québec, &c.&c.&c. A tous les Curés, / Vicaires, Missionaires, Prêtres Séculaires et Reguliers de notre / Diocèse, Salut et Bénédiction. /

4to. A[4]; 8 p., type-page: 19 × 14 cm. *Printed at Quebec by Wm. Brown, 1788*, as recorded:

"1788, Dec. 16. [Credit] to Printing Office for 400 Mandements of Bishop's Secretary—£4.10."—Can.P.A., *Neilson papers*, v. 49.

Contents: p. [1]-8, Mandement, dated at end: "Donné à Québec . . . le dix Décembre, de l'an mil-sept-cent-quatre-vingt-huit. Jean François, Evêque de Québec." The mandement was issued apparently by the bishop's secretary, Rev. J. O. Plessis, whose MS. signature appears on the copies located.

It was superseded by that of Oct. 28, 1793 (No. 875). It is reprinted in Têtu and Gagnon: *Mandements de Québec*, 2: 353-60.

Copies located: CaO; CaQQL; Ketcheson; RPJ.

557. MACGREGOR, JAMES, 1759-1830

[row of ornaments] / A / LETTER / TO / A CLERGYMAN / Urging him to set free a BLACK GIRL he held in / SLAVERY. / [row of ornaments] /

4to. [*[4], **[2]]; 11 p.; type-page: 16.8 × 10.8 cm.

Contents: p. [1], t.-p.; p. [2], blank; p. [3]-11, Letter; p. 11 verso, blank.

Probably printed at Halifax, N.S., by Anthony Henry, 1788. The typographic style, especially the heavy rows of floral ornaments on the title page, are peculiar to Henry's work in Canadian printing of the period.

The *Letter* is a violent harangue, setting forth the current social and religious arguments against slave-owning—well seasoned with personal abuse. MacGregor, ordained an Anti-Burgher Presbyterian, came to Pictou, N.S., in 1787. A conscientious abolitionist, he attacked the neighbouring Burgher presbytery of Truro, whose minister, Daniel Cock, owned two slaves. In 1788 he sent a letter to Cock "received with a sort of bewildered surprise," then he published it, as above. *See* Geo. Patterson*: *Memoir of the Rev. James MacGregor, D.D., . . . and of the social and religious condition of the early settlers* (533 p., Philadelphia, etc., 1859), also Patterson's *A few remains of the Rev. James MacGregor, D.D.* (Philadelphia, etc., 1859). The latter contains the text of the *Letter* (lacking the last few sentences) and of twelve other works by MacGregor in English or Gaelic.

Copy located: CaNsHD.

*MacGregor's grandson.

558. MOORE, WILLIAM

Heading p. [1]: QUEBEC, OCTOBER 25th, 1788. / [royal arms] / TO THE PUBLIC, / [rule] / WILLIAM MOORE, PRINTER, /

Imprint, p. [1] at foot: QUEBEC: PRINTED and SOLD at the HERALD PRINTING-OFFICE, opposite / FREE-MASON'S HALL; and the following PLACES, viz. Mr. HOWE'S PRINT-/ING-OFFICE, Halifax; Mr. ROBERTSON'S PRINTING-OFFICE, Island St. / John's; Mr. SILL'S Trois Rivieres; Mr. AMIE'S Berthier; Mr. SAWYER'S Will- / iam Henry; Mr. DAVID DAVID'S Montreal; Mr. GILL'S TAVERN St. John's; / JACKSON HOYLE'S wholesale and retail store at new Johnstown, in the township / of Cornwall, in the district of Lunenburg and at Oswegatchie, in Augusta; Mr. / CLARK'S Kingston, (late Cataraqui) and at the Bay of Quenty; Mr. EDWARD'S / Niagara; and at Mr. HAND'S Detroit. /

fo. [4] p.; type-page: 28.5 × 15.2 cm.

Contents: p. [1], Announcement of Moore's printing office "now open for Type printing in general, and consists of a more extensive variety of types than ever before imported into this province"; also "Moore's English Sheet Almanack for MDCCLXXXIX," to be published Nov. 17; p. [2], Announcement of "Moore's English Almanack and General Pocket Register for 1789," to be published Nov. 17; p. [2-3], Announcement of "The Quebec Herald and Universal Miscellany," to be published weekly from Monday, Nov. 24; p. [4], Advertisement soliciting the printing of blanks for public offices and of advertisements with illustrations (specimens appended); also Notice: "Wanted, as an apprentice, a youth that writes French and English."

This leaflet announced the opening of the second printing office in Quebec city.

Copy located: CaOOA (bound with *Courier de Québec*).

559. NEW BRUNSWICK. HOUSE OF ASSEMBLY

JOURNAL / OF THE / VOTES AND PROCEEDINGS / OF THE / HOUSE / OF / ASSEMBLY, / OF THE / PROVINCE OF NEW-BRUNSWICK. / From Tuesday JULY the 15th, to Saturday AUGUST 2d, 1788. / [rule] / ST. JOHN: / PRINTED BY JOHN RYAN, AT HIS PRINTING-OFFICE, / N°. 58, PRINCE WILLIAM STREET. /

fo. A-E^2, F^1, G-[L]^2; 1 p. l., [102]-141 p.; type-page: 24.5 × 14. 3cm. Even numbers on recto, odd numbers on verso; paged in continuation of No. 520. One leaf of sig. L is folded around sig. A-G, to form p. l., bearing t.-p.

Contents: p. l. recto, t.p.; verso, blank; p. [102]-141, Journal of the third session of the first assembly.

As in 1787, both printers in Saint John were invited to submit tenders for the session's printing. Sower, still aggrieved at his slight of the previous year, wrote Amos Botsford, speaker of the House, July 5, 1788:

"I have enclosed to you a copy of my commission as King's printer and agreeable to your request of yesterday I now propose to print the Laws and Votes of the

Hon[ble] House of Assembly of this province for the same price and on the same terms they were printed last year [by Ryan, on Sower's terms!] and if any proposals for printing them cheaper should be made I will print them on as good paper and at as low a price as any other printer whatever.

"I beg leave, Sir, to submit to your superior judgement whether the printing of the Laws does not appertain to the Office of King's printer—the Laws of England as you will recollect are always printed by him and the Journals by M[r] Harris the Printer to the House of Commons [etc.]."

The commission which Sower enclosed, signed by Lord Sidney for King George III at St. James, Apr. 8, 1785, appointed him "our Printer within . . . New Brunswick . . . for the printing of all such Books, Statues [sic], Proclamations and other acts of government, the Printing whereof appertains to the office of our Printer within Great Britain, to have, to hold, execute and enjoy the said Office . . . with all the Profits, Perquisites, Advantages and Emoluments thereunto belonging [etc.]."
—N.B.As. *Papers, 1788.*

The fine royal words availed nought, however, for the House awarded its printing to Ryan on precisely the same terms as the year before. The *Journal,* though undated in imprint, was published within two to three months, for Lieut.-Gov. Carleton sent a copy of both *Acts* and *Journal* to the Lords of Trade and the colonial secretary on Oct. 23, 1789. Ryan petitioned on Jan. 2, 1789, "for payment of £53.6.8. for printing Acts passed in the last Session, also Journals."

[i.e. 200 copies of the Acts 4½ Sheets @ £3.6.8.—£15.
200 copies of the Journal, 10½ Sheets @ £3.6.8.—£35.
Sewing &c 400 Acts & Journals @ ½*d.* *3.6.8.*
Total:] £53.6.8.—N.B. Ex. co. *Papers.*

Copies located: CaN (t.-p. wanting); CaNU; CaNsWA (p. 140-41 wanting); CaOOA (2 cop.); GBLP (in C.O. 188/3: 831-72, p. 140-41 wanting); RPJ.

560. NEW BRUNSWICK. LAWS, STATUTES, *etc.*

ACTS / OF THE / GENERAL ASSEMBLY, / OF / HIS MAJESTY'S PROVINCE / OF / NEW-BRUNSWICK, / PASSED IN THE YEAR 1788. / [double rule] / ST. JOHN: / PRINTED BY JOHN RYAN, at his PRINTING-OFFICE, No. 58, / PRINCE WILLIAM STREET. / [rule] / M,DCC,-LXXXVIII. /

fo. [*[1], **[2], [A]-C[2]]; 3 p.l., [163]-78 p.; type-page: 24.2 × 14.3 cm. paged in continuation of No. 521.

Contents: p. l. 1 recto, t.-p.; verso, blank; p. l. 2 recto, half title; verso, blank; p. l. 3 recto, Table of titles; verso, blank; p. [163]-74, 28 Geo. III c. I-X, acts passed in the third session of the first assembly.

An edition of 200 copies was printed Aug.-Oct., 1788, as indicated in No. 559 *note.* While at least 135 copies were distributed in the province by the government, Ryan kept a few for sale, for he advertised that copies "may be had of the printer" in *Saint John gazette,* May 1, 1789.

Copies located: Baxter; CaOOA; GBLP (in B.T. 6/56: 57-74); MH; NNB; NNHi.

561. PRIMERS. QUEBEC

[An Alphabet or primer, presumably for private distribution, or for use in the Governor's household, was *printed at Quebec by Wm. Brown, 1788*, as recorded:]

"1788, Apr. 3. Printed for Lord Dorchester (by order of My Lady) 3 pages of Sylables [sic] in 4to on superfine demy, 18 copies—15/."

—Can.P.A., *Neilson papers*, v. 84.

Copy located: None (*see also* No. 213).

562. PRIMERS. QUEBEC. *French*

[An Alphabet or primer in French *printed at Quebec by Wm. Brown in 1788 or earlier*, is recorded:]

"1788, Sept. 22. Young La france stitched 288 French Alphabets @ ½[d] apiece—12/

"Dec. 19. F. Saro [Montreal] bo't 4 Doz. French Alphabets @ 3/4 —13/4."—Can.P.A., *Neilson papers*, v. 84.

Copy located: None.

563. PRIMERS. QUEBEC. *Latin*

[An Alphabet or primer in Latin, *printed at Quebec by Wm. Brown, 1788 or earlier*, is recorded:]

"1788, Dec. 9. F. Saro Montreal bo't 1 Doz. Latin Alph[ts]—3/6.

"Dec. 10. F. Saro bo't 5 doz. Latin Alphabets @ 3/4—16/8."

—Can.P.A., *Neilson papers*, v. 84.

Copy located: None.

564. QUEBEC, *Province*. LAWS, STATUTES, *etc.*

NUM. 1183 / THE / QUEBEC GAZETTE / [rule] / THURSDAY, APRIL 17, / 1788. /

English caption: Anno Vicesimo Octavo Georgii III. Kegis [sic]. Chap. I. An Act or Ordinance Further to regulate the inland Commerce of this Province, and to extend the same.

French caption: . . . Chap. I. Acte ou Ordonance, Qui régle plus amplement, et étend d'avantage le Commerce intérieur de cette Province.

fo. 11 p.; text in 2 col. English and French, *printed at Quebec by Wm. Brown, 1788*.

Contents: 28 Geo. IIIc. 1-9, passed at Quebec, Apr. 13, 1788, reprinted (with continuous pagination added) from the *Quebec gazette*, Apr. 17-24, May 8-15, 1788. Brown entered against the government in his account book a total of £34 8*s*. 6*d*. for printing the ordinances in the *Gazette* (Can.P.A., *Neilson papers*, v. 84, Apr. 30-May 31, 1788). For the reprint he billed the government:

"Printed for Gov[t] (by order of, and agreement with J. Williams, Esq[r]) 100 Copies of the Ordinances of last session upon the types of the Gazette before distributed, making 3 Sheets @ 45/.—£6.15.0 [endorsed by Williams, Oct. 10, 1788]." —Can.P.A., "S" *Pub. accts*, 1788.

Brown sold single copies of this reprint at 1*s.* 8*d.*

Copies located: GBLP (3 cop., filed respectively in: C.O. 42/59, p. 445-55; C.O. 42/60, p. 327-37; C.O. 42/61, p. 385-95).

565. QUEBEC GAZETTE. CARRIER'S ADDRESS

ETRENNES / DU GARÇON qui porte la / GAZETTE DE QUEBEC / AUX PRATIQUES. / Le 1er Janvier, 1789. / [*Quebec, Wm. Brown, 1788*]

Broadside: 49 lines; type-page: 27 × 15 cm. in ornamental triple rule frame.

Contents: Etrennes, 44 lines of light verse beginning:

"Bon jour, bon an, me voici
Très bien portant, Dieu merci. . . ."

Copy located: CaO (bound in *Quebec gazette*, at end of 1787).

566. QUEBEC HERALD AND UNIVERSAL MISCELLANY

[Specimen of the Quebec Herald.]

Broadside: *printed at Quebec by Wm. Brown*, as recorded:

"1788, May 31. Printed for Wm Moore Printer, 300 Quarto demy Handbills Specimen of his Quebec Herald (he composing it)—7/6."
—Can.P.A., *Neilson papers*, v. 84.

This seems to be a preliminary announcement of the second newspaper to be published in Quebec City. Wm. Moore, its printer, set his notice in type in the *Quebec gazette* office before his own equipment had arrived and Wm. Brown, who had produced the *Gazette* since 1764, printed the specimen of its prospective rival. The *Quebec herald* itself appeared on Nov. 24, 1788, and ran till Feb., 1793.

Copy located: None.

567. QUEBEC THEATRE

[Play-bill: Too civil by half.]

Broadside: *Printed at Quebec by Wm. Brown, 1788*, as recorded:

"1788, Apr. 28. Printed for Mechtler, 300 Play-bills on pott, notifying Too civil by half &c.—15/." —Can.P.A., *Neilson papers*, v. 84.

Copy located: None.

568. SAINT JOHN, N.B., *City*. AUCTION SALE

[TO BE S]OLD, / [AT] AUCTION, / [?] on Friday, the 12th day of July next, [etc.]

[TO BE S]OLD / [AT] AUCTION / [?] on Friday the 1st of August next, [etc.]

Broadside, *probably printed at Saint John, N.B., by John Ryan, 1788.*

The first sale is apparently of land "at Bass River or five Islands near to Partridge Island" suitable for fishery or saw mills. Partridge Island lies in the mouth of the St. John River. The second sale advertises: "the following Premises . . . [broadside mutilated] with two excellent Stills of 1000 Gallons each . . . Cistern with Worm Tubbs, Worms, Pumps . . . also a Rum House [etc.]." The sales probably took place in the year 1788, when the dates mentioned fell upon Friday, the day mentioned.

Copy located: CaNSA (a highly defective copy, bearing on blank verso, MS. notes of Edward Winslow's powers of attorney mainly from members of loyalist regiments who had taken land grants; it is filed in *Winslow papers*, 2: 198).

569. ST. JOHN, ISLAND OF. HOUSE OF ASSEMBLY

JOURNAL / AND / VOTES / OF THE / HOUSE OF ASSEMBLY, / FOR HIS MAJESTY'S ISLAND / SAINT JOHN. / Begun and held at CHARLOTTE-TOWN, the Twenty-second / Day of JANUARY, in the Year of our LORD one Thous-/and, seven Hundred and Eighty-eight. / 28th GEORGE III. / [rule] / CHARLOTTE-TOWN: / PRINTED by JAMES ROBERTSON, M,DCC,LXXXVIII. /

fo. 1 p. l., 51, [2] p.; paper-page: 30.5 × 19 cm.

Contents: p. l. recto, t.-p.; p. 1-51, Journal; [2] p. at end, Appendix.

This is the *Journal* of the first (and only) session of the fifth assembly of the Island of St. John, Jan. 22-Feb. 21, 1788. Appended to the text is a letter and two documents. The letter is headed: "Charlotte Town 8th of April, 1788." It is signed by Edmund Fanning and directed: "To James Robertson, Esq; Printer to the Government of the Island of St. John." In it Lieut.-Gov. Fanning requests Robertson to annex at the end of the *Journal* attested copies of records expunged from *Journal*, viz. "Number I, A Resolution made on the 7th and expunged [from] the Journals on the 13th February, 1788, Number II An Address presented and rejected on the 13th February, 1788." Then follow the text of the Resolution and Address, certified by A. Richardson, clerk of the House of Assembly, Charlottetown, Apr. 7, 1788. Both addresses congratulate Fanning on his efforts to restore peace and harmony in the government, and were expunged, apparently by influence of friends of his predecessor in office.

This is the first *Journal* of Assembly which was printed in the Island of St. John.

Copies located: GBLP (2 cop. in C.O. 226/12: 297-352; C.O. 229/1: 507-560).

570. STERNS, JONATHAN, *d.* 1798, and TAYLOR, WILLIAM

[ornamental rule] / COLLECTION / OF ALL THE / Publications relating to the Impeachment / OF THE / JUDGES / OF HIS MAJESTY'S SUPREME COURT / OF THE / Province of Nova-Scotia. / [ornamental rule] /

4to. A-E^4, [F]^1; vii, 34 p.; type-page: 17 × 11.2 cm.

Contents: p. [i] recto, t.-p.; p. [ii], blank; p. [iii]-vii," To the public," signed by J. Sterns and W. Taylor; p. vii verso, blank; p. [1]-29, Extracts from proceedings of H.M. Council, Feb. 21, 28, 1788, also, letters signed by Sterns and Taylor, reprinted from the *Halifax journal*, and replies thereto signed by "Plain Truth," and by S. S. Blowers, attorney-general, reprinted from the *Nova-Scotia gazette*, Mar. 5-Apr. 2?, 1788; p. [30], blank; p. 31-34, Letters from *Halifax journal*, signed by "Common Sense," and by Sterns and Taylor, Apr. 20, 1788.

Probably printed at Halifax, N.S., by John Howe, 1788, for in this controversy Howe and his *Journal* worked for the Assembly, Anthony Henry and his *Gazette* for the governor and Council. The date of printing of the body of this work is suggested by the content, also by a contemporary endorsement on the Public Record Office copy: "A Printed paper delivered by Messers Sterns & Taylor, May 17, 1788, [this copy was] enclosed in an anonymous letter [to Lord Sydney, dated:] Halifax Apr. 19, 1788." The letters on p. 31-34 and/or the t.-p. and preliminary matter may have been added later.

In Dec., 1787, on evidence submitted by Jonathan Sterns and Wm. Taylor, both recently established as lawyers in Halifax, N.S., the House of Assembly begged an investigation into the conduct of Isaac Deschamps and James Brenton, judges in the Supreme Court. Dissatisfaction with the administration of justice became one of the issues rising from antagonism between loyalist immigrant and pre-revolutionary settlers (*see* B. Murdoch: *A history of Nova-Scotia or Acadie*, 3 v., Halifax, 1865-67, 3: chap. 5-8). In this case, which was carried to the Privy Council, the administration supported the judges. *See also* No. 621 and No. 646.

Copies located: CaNsWA; GBLP (p. [1]-29 only, in C.O. 217/60, 377-405); DLC (p. [1]-29 only).

571. [VIETS, ROGER], 1738-1811

Caption title: [ornament] / Annapolis-Royal / [rule] / [? *Halifax, N.S., Anthony Henry, 1788.*]

8vo. X^4; 7 p.; type-page: 16 × 9.3 cm.; ornamental head-piece on each page, and tail-piece on p. 7.

Contents: p. 1-7, Annapolis-Royal; p. 7 verso, blank. The poem, thirteen verses in rhyming pentameter couplets, begins:

"The King of Rivers, solemn, calm and slow,
Flows tow'rd the Sea, yet scarce is seen to flow;
On each fair Bank, the verdant Lands are seen,
In gayest Cloathing of perpetual Green:"

Attributed to Roger Viets (in F. H. Viets: *A genealogy of the Viets family*, Hartford, Conn., 1902, 34) this work was *possibly printed in Halifax, N.S., by Anthony Henry, 1788*, or, like some of Roger Viets's other writings, it may have been published for his old friends in Connecticut. It appeared also, printed from a different setting of type, in the *Nova-Scotia gazette*, Aug. 12, 1788.

Viets graduated from Yale College in 1758, was ordained in the Church of England and served as a missionary of the Society for the Propagation of the Gospel at Simsbury, Conn., 1763-83. A loyalist, he was transferred by the Society to Nova Scotia. In 1787 he established a mission at Digby (near Annapolis Royal) from which he served southwestern Nova Scotia till his death.

Copy located: MB; photostat in MHi.

572. WINDSOR ACADEMY

[Account of the opening of the Academy at Windsor.]

Probably printed at Halifax, N.S., by Anthony Henry, in November, 1788, this work is mentioned by Bishop Inglis: "The first day of November being fixed for the opening of the Academy I repaired to Windsor, where I proceeded as the printed account will inform your Grace."—Bishop Inglis to the archbishop of Canterbury, Halifax, Nov. 20, 1788. Inglis also wrote to Gov. Dorchester, Halifax, Dec. 26, 1788: ". . . Our Academy has been opened. Inclosed is an account of it which was printed by the Governors for the information of the public. It has cost me a good deal of trouble . . . Seventeen students were admitted the first day, their number is now upwards of twenty. Next Summer they will probably amount to forty [etc.]."

—Can.P.A., *Inglis papers,* 1: 112, 127.

The Academy was established on an annual grant of £400 from provincial funds, following a report from the House of Assembly Committee on schools, Nov. 22, 1787: "[It is] indispensably necessary that a Public School be established . . . that an exemplary clergyman of the established church, well skilled in Classical learning, Divinity, Moral Philosophy and Belles Lettres be head of the school at a salary of not less than £200 per annum, that a professor of mathematics and natural philosophy be likewise provided, at £100 per annum [etc.]."

The Academy comprised an English school and a Latin school for boys of eight years and upwards, and was closely affiliated with King's College from the time of the latter's establishment. The first principal of the Academy, Archibald Peane Inglis, nephew of Bishop Inglis, was succeeded in 1789 by William Cochran, who served also as president of the College. The Academy is known now as King's Collegiate School.

Copy located: None.

573. AGRICULTURAL SOCIETY IN CANADA

Endorsed title on verso of l. 2: Projet d'Institution d'une / Societé pour l'encourage-/ment de l'agriculture dans / le Province de Quebec, / 1789. / [*Quebec, Wm. Moore, 1789.*]

fo. 2 *l.*; type-page: 25 × 16.5 cm. Text 33 lines on recto of *l.* 1: "Société d'agriculture établie en Canada, . . . [lists patrons, directors, terms of membership, etc.]" *l.* 1 verso-2 recto, blank; *l.* 2 verso, endorsed title printed as above.

This leaflet was *printed at Quebec by Wm. Moore, 1789,* as the Society's records show:

> "1789, Apr. 16. To Wm. Moore for printing a Prospectus of the Society, Advertisements in the [Quebec] Gazette &c., p. account—£6.5*s*."
>
> —Ag. soc. *Accounts, 1789-95,* published in *Quebec gazette,* Sept. 24, 1795.

The Agricultural Society was organized at Quebec under government auspices, Feb. 22, 1789, during a severe food shortage caused by crop failure from smut in 1788. Gov. Dorchester was president, and Hugh Finlay, deputy postmaster-general and chairman of the Land Board, was treasurer. A board of sixteen directors, English and French, governed the Quebec branch; Montreal, and later other centres, had local boards of directors; the members paid an annual fee of one guinea and met quarterly. They were mainly government officials, large landowners and merchants, and included few, if any, of the French-Canadian habitants who tilled most of the cultivated soil in the province. The organization was used by the government as a means of distributing seed, guiding and stimulating production (especially of hemp for use in the navy), and encouraging agricultural experiments. The Society had ceased to function, however, before 1817, when a new and more popular "Quebec Agricultural Society" was organized.

The Society published a collection of papers in 1790 (No. 623). Its proceedings, advertisements, and reports appeared in the *Quebec gazette, Quebec herald,* and *Montreal gazette.* The MS. minutes and letter books of the Quebec branch are preserved in the Literary and Historical Society of Quebec.

Copy located: CaQQL.

574. ALMANACS. NEW BRUNSWICK

[An Astronomical Diary, or Almanack for . . . 1790 . . . calculated for the Meridian of . . . Saint John, etc. *Saint John, N.B., printed by Christopher Sower.*]

12mo. [18 + ?] p.; type-page (within rule frame): 15.5 × 9.6 cm. published some time after Oct. 27, 1789 and before Mar. 9, 1790.

Contents: The only copy located is a fragment of eighteen unnumbered pages, containing New Brunswick administration, legislature, courts, City of Saint John magistrates, county magistrates, army and naval officers, [8] p.; Principal cities of the world (arranged alphabetically, all before Petersburg torn away in only copy located) chronology of remarkable occurrences, tables of measurement for land, interest, time, currency, [10] p. The work probably included about eighteen additional pages containing matter indicated in the advertisement below.

This almanac was advertised: "Just published and to be sold <Price 7½d each or 6/ per dozen> *An astronomical diary or Almanack,* for the year of our Lord Christ 1790, being the Second after Bissextile or Leap year; wherein are contained the Eclipses of the luminaries, Moon's place and age, Sun's and Moon's Rising and Setting, Moon's Apogee and Perigee, Equation of time, Feasts and fasts of the Church, Time of high water, &c.&c. And a Variety of other matters useful and entertaining. Calculated for the Meridian of the City of Saint John, in the province of New Brunswick; but will serve without sensible error for any part of the said province. May also be had in this City of James M'Pherson, at Maugerville of Israel Perley Esq; at Fredericton of James Sutter, at Digby of William M'Donald, Esq. at Annapolis of Mr. John Burkit [etc.]."

—*Royal gazette,* Saint John, N.B., Mar. 9, 1790.

Copy located: CaNSA (incomplete).

575. ALMANACS. NOVA SCOTIA

AN / ALMANACK, / For the Year of Our LORD, 1790; / . . . / CALCULATED FOR THE MERIDIAN OF / HALIFAX, IN NOVA-SCOTIA: / . . . / CONTAINING, / THE ECLIPSES, [etc. 6 lines in 2 col. separated by double rule] / WITH EVERY OTHER MATTER USEFUL OR NECES-

SARY. / [rule] / BY THEOPHRASTUS. / [rule] / —PARENT or NATURE, WHOSE UNCEASING HAND, / ROLLS ROUND THE SEASONS OF THE CHANGING YEAR, / [etc. 4 lines] / THOMPSON [sic]. / [rule] / HALIFAX: / Printed and sold by JOHN HOWE, at his Printing-Office, Corner of / BARRINGTON and SACKVILLE-STREETS. / [title and each page in double rule frame]

12mo. [A^4, B^2, C^4]; [24] p. type-page: 15.8 × 9.7 cm.

Contents: p. [1], t.-p.; p. [2-3], The Anatomy of Man's body (signs of the Zodiac), To the Public (autobiographical note signed "Theophrastus"), Ephemeris; p. [4], Eclipses, vulgar notes; p. [5-16], Calendar; p. [17-24], Nova Scotia administration, legislature, judges, justices, sheriffs, customs officers, court sittings, Navy, Army, distances Halifax-Annapolis, buoys.

The autobiographical note states in a fanciful style that this is "Theophrastus' " first and youthful attempt at almanac-making. His calculation was disputed by "Metonicus" (who calculated the *Nova-Scotia calendar*) in an article published in the *Royal gazette*, Halifax, N.S., May 4, 1790; in which "Metonicus" alludes to an error on the first page of the calendar. "Theophrastus" calculated subsequent editions of John Howe's *Almanack*.

Copy located: CSmH (complete copy in excellent condition, bound in original marbled paper covers, interleaved with blank pages bearing MS. notes in contemporary hand, on weather (daily), ship arrivals and departures, business, apparently written by Townsend, Halifax, N.S.).

576. ALMANACS. NOVA SCOTIA

[Der Neuschottländische Calender Auf das Jahr Christi 1790 . . . *Halifax, N.S., gedruckt bey Anth. Henrich.*]

Advertised in Anthony Henry's newspaper as "Just published and ready for sale, The High German Almanack for the year of our Lord 1790."—*Royal gazette*, Halifax, N.S., Nov. 24, 1789. This was probably no. 3, similar in format and content to *Der Neuschottländische Calender* no. 1-2, and no. 4, published in 1787-88 and in 1790 respectively (No. 503, 542, 628).

Copy located: None.

577. ALMANACS. NOVA SCOTIA

THE / Nova-Scotia Calender, / OR AN / ALMANACK, / For the Year . . . 1790, . . . / [4 lines] / WHEREIN IS CONTAINED, / The E-clipses . . . / [4 lines] / [rule] / Calculated for the Meridian of HALIFAX, . . . / [3 lines] / By METONICUS. / [double rule] / HALIFAX, Printed and Sold by A. HENRY. / [ornamental rule frame]

16mo. 60 p.; type-page: 12.3 × 7.3 cm.

Contents: p. [1], t.-p.; p. [2], verse; p. [3], Vulgar notes; p. [4], Aspects; p. [5], Eclipses, verse; p. [7-9], Royal family, etc.; p. [10-15], British government in America & West Indies; p. [16-17], Ephemeris; p. [18-19], verses; p. [20-43], Calendar; p. [44-55], Nova Scotia administration, legislature, county officials, judges, courts, army, navy, fire company, buoys; p. [56-60], postal rates, distances.

This almanac was advertised: "Just published and to be sold by A. Henry, An Almanack [etc.]."—*Royal gazette*, Halifax, N.S., Nov. 24, 1789.

Copies located: CaNs (p. [1-2, 15-18] wanting); CaNsHA (p. [43-44] wanting). The copy recorded in Learmont sale, Cat. no. 1284, item no. 6, is actually the copy of Howe's *Almanack* (No. 575) now in Henry E. Huntington Library.

578A. ALMANACS. QUEBEC

Almanach de Québec pour l'année 1789 was never published owing to a fire in Samuel Neilson's printing office, Dec. 25, 1789. The printer advertised:

"The public are informed that the publication of the Quebec pocket almanac has been unavoidably retarded by the late fire, but that every effort will be made to repair the damage and publish it as soon as possible. Notice will be given in the Gazette when finished, Jan. 6, 1790."—*Quebec gazette*, Jan. 7, 1790.

The notice never appeared, however, nor do the printer's account books record any almanac for 1790.

578B. ALMANACS. QUEBEC

[The British Gentleman's Pocket Almanack, and General Register —For the year of our Lord M.DCC.XC. *Quebec, Wm. Moore, 1789.*]

8vo. 56 p. *Printed at Quebec by Wm. Moore, 1789,* this almanac was advertised: "Just published the British Gentleman's Pocket Almanack and General Register for the Year of our Lord M.DCC.XC. Containing a Calendar, the Eclipses, tide table [etc.] a Provincial Register: the Commander in Chief, Members of the Council, Civil officers, Magistrates of Quebec, Montreal, St. John's, Mecklenburgh, Lunenburgh, Nassau, Hesse & Gaspé, Barristers [in same municipalities], the Peace officers of Quebec, Constables of Montreal, Clergy and Vestry of Quebec, the Presbyterian clergy, and school masters in Quebec, Montreal and Three Rivers, the English Protestant congregation in Montreal, Agricultural society officers, Fire Society, Patentees of the Dorchester Bridge and rates of passage, Customs, Pilots; Post road rates & Post house keepers, from Halifax to Quebec, Montreal and Albany; the ferry from Quebec to Montreal. The staff of Quebec and Montreal regiments; Royal artillery, Hospital, Engineering and British militia officers; Dept. of Commissary and Superintendents of Inland revenue. Also British lists, the Royal family, Privy council [etc.].

"Printed in small 8vo on fine paper with new types, 56 pages. Price stitched plain 2/; in marble [paper covers] and interleaved with writing paper 2/6.

"The Public are respectfully informed that the Gentleman's Register has considerable provincial additions."—*Quebec herald*, Dec. 15, 1789.

It was announced later that "the printer having lost considerably last year by printing too large a quantity, he only printed half that quantity this year and distributed them equally in the Country and in Quebec and the Vicinity [etc. and from time to time Moore requested unused copies of the *English Sheet Almanac, Gentleman's Pocket almanac* and *Lady's Diary*, to be returned to his Printing Office as none were left] except the Ladyses [sic] Diaries." —*Quebec herald*, Jan. 18-Apr. 19, 1790.

Copy located: None.

579. ALMANACS. QUEBEC

[British Lady's Diary and Pocket Almanack for the Year of our Lord M.DCC.XC. *Quebec, Wm. Moore, 1789.*]

8vo. 25 p. *Printed at Quebec by Wm. Moore, 1789,* who announced, from Sept. 21, 1789, its forthcoming publication in December, then advertised in his newspaper:

"This day is published The British Lady's Diary and Pocket Almanack for the year of our Lord M.DCC.XC. Containing a Calendar, several useful recipes in cooking, pickling, preserving &c. Enigmatical questions, Rebuses, Poetry, Songs &c.

"Small 8vo. containing 25 p. price stitched in marble & interleaved with writing paper, 1 shilling 9 pence.

"It is intended by the publisher to furnish the ladies useful subjects, whatever is interesting and congenial to improve the fair sex, will be particularly considered; the Selections will be made from authors most eligible for stile and purity of morals. If from such a conduct any entertainment or instruction should accrue to the publication, through the medium of which the Editor exposes himself to the female world, the warmest wish of his heart will be abundantly gratified, and his sole endeavour crowned with Success."—*Quebec herald,* Jan. 4, 1790.

Copy located: None.

580. ALMANACS. QUEBEC

CALENDRIER pour l'Année 1790, pour Québec, par les 306$^{d.}$ 30$^{m.}$ de Longitude, et 46$^{d.}$ 55$^{m.}$ de Latitude. / [rule] /

Colophon: A QUEBEC: chez SAMUEL NEILSON, au milieu de la Grande Côte. /

Broadside: 52.5 × 38.5 cm.

Contents: Calendrier (in ornamental rule frame: 42 × 38.5 cm. the note on arrangement is omitted this year); below *Calendrier* printed in 4 col. is "De l'Origine de la Mésure du Temps et de sa première Determination chez les Anciens"—a special feature in the sheet almanac for this year, the first under Samuel Neilson's direction.

It was sold as usual at 9*d.* the copy, 5*s.* the dozen, from Dec. 8, 1789.

Copy located: CaO (bound in *Quebec gazette,* at end of 1789).

581. ALMANACS. QUEBEC

[Calendrier pour Montréal, pour l'année 1790. *Montreal, F. Mesplet, 1789.*]

Broadside. This sheet almanac, like the *Calendrier pour Montréal* of preceding years, was undoubtedly *printed at Montreal by Fleury Mesplet,* this in 1789 (though the date of imprint may appear the same as in title). It was advertised: "Le Calendrier de Montréal pour l'année 1790, à vendre chez François Sarreau, rue Notre Dame, et chez l'Imprimerie [de F. Mesplet]."—*Montreal gazette,* Dec. 31, 1789, *et seq.*

Copy located: None.

582. ALMANACS. QUEBEC

[Moore's English Sheet Almanack for the Year of our Lord, 1790. *Quebec, Wm. Moore, 1789.*]

Broadside: *printed at Quebec by Wm. Moore, 1789,* who on Sept. 25, 1789, announced publication for December, then advertised in his newspaper: "Ready for Sale, Moore's English Sheet Almanack in English [sic] on an enlarged plan. Price Nine Pence."—*Quebec herald,* Dec. 7, 1789.

Samuel Neilson also advertised: "This day is published, The Quebec English Sheet Almanack or Cabinet Calendar, for the year 1790. Sold at Montreal by Mr. Francis Saro, at Berthier by Mr. Louis Aimé, at Three Rivers and at the Printing Office [of S. Neilson] Mountain Street, Quebec."—*Quebec gazette,* Dec. 3-31, 1789. This is the first English sheet almanac advertised by the Brown-Neilson printing house, which had been issuing a French *Calendrier* annually since 1765. It was probably Moore's publication, at least there is no evidence as yet that Neilson actually *printed* an English sheet almanac in 1789. But he *sold* it widely with his own French sheet almanacs through the distributing depots of the *Quebec gazette,* as his records show:

"1789, Dec. 8. Sent to Montreal per Dubord & Labadie [carriers]:
Sold Francois Sarrault of Montreal 30 Doz. French Calendars @ 5/—£7.10
6 Doz. English Ditto @ 6/—1.16
12 Doz. French & English ditto to sell in Quebec @ 6/—3.12
N.B. Agreed to take back such as may remain unsold of the above Calendats."—Can.P.A., *Neilson papers,* v. 70.

Copy located: None.

583. BURN, RICHARD, 1709-1785

LE / JUGE A PAIX, / ET / OFFICIER DE PAROISSE, / Pour la Province de Quebec. / EXTRAIT de RICHARD BURN, Chancellier / du Diocèse de Charlisle, & un des Juges à Paix / de Sa Majesté, pour les Comtés de Westmorland / & Cumberland. / [rule] / TRADUIT Par Jos. F. PERRAULT. / [rule] / [printer's ornament] / A MONTREAL; / Chez FLEURY MESPLET, Imprimeur, rue Notre-Dame, / près les R.R.P.P. Recollets. / [rule] / M.DCC.LXXXIX. /

8vo. [a]-c[4], A-3B[4], 3D-4A[4]; 576 p.; type-page: 17.5 × 8.5 cm. p. 168 mispaged: 368; 228: 128; 476:479; p. [562-576] unpaged.

Contents: p. [i], t.-p.; p. [ii], blank; p. [iii-iv], "A Son Excellence . . . Lord Dorchester [signed:] Jos. Fr. Perrault"; p. v-vi, Avant propos; p. vii-xxi, Introduction; p. 22-561, Des juges à paix; p. [562-575] Table (index); p. [576], Errata.

Issued monthly in 18 parts of 32 pages each, Mar. ? 1789-Oct. ? 1790, at 1*s.* a part, this publication was announced in the *Montreal gazette,* Dec. 25, 1788, also in a separate prospectus (*see* No. 549). The former states that the introduction of English criminal law into Quebec, the establishment of the various new offices of justice of the peace, sheriff, coroner, constable, etc., and the admission of French Canadians to these offices necessitates some guide for the latter to these duties, or they must depend upon the advice of their English fellow citizens. This publication is a translation (omitting the sections on police regulations and local laws, not applicable to Quebec) of the standard English work by Burn: *The justice of the peace and parish officer* [*etc.*] (2 v., London, 1755), frequently reprinted.

Joseph François Perrault, 1753-1844, born in Quebec, and bred to business, was at this time studying law. He became clerk of the peace at Quebec in 1795, prothonotary in 1802, and was occupied till his death in duties described in his *Le juge à paix.*

Copies located: CSmH; CaNsWA; CaO (2 cop.); CaOLU; CaOT; CaQ; CaQM; CaQMA; CaQMM; CaQMS; CaQQA; CaQQB; CaQQL (bound with original paper covers of parts no. II and IV giving short title and lists of subscribers); DLC; Ketcheson; MH; N; NN; RPJ; Witton. A few other copies have been noted in sale catalogues but not located.

584. BURNS, ROBERT, 1759-1796

[Poems]

Proposed printing at Charlottetown, Island of St. John, by James Robertson, 1789, was advertised:

"Charlottetown, May 4, 1789. Proposals for printing by subscription, the Poems of that celebrated Scots ploughman Robert Burns. To be printed in one neat pocket volume, three to four hundred pages, on fine writing paper and a good type. Price to Subscribers, six shillings . . . Subscriptions are received by Mr. James Robertson (the Publisher) at his Printing Office in the Island of St. John and at the Printing Office . . . Quebec.

"The fame of this author is spreading rapidly and the merit of his works is acknowledged by all who have had an opportunity of seeing them. The Demand is so great that the first edition (published last May) is already exhausted and a second edition is now being printed in London. Price 6 Shillings in boards."

—*Quebec gazette,* June 18, 1789.

It was advertised again:

"In the Press and Speedily will be published Burns' Poems. Such persons as are desirous to procure these valuable and surprising productions of Rustic Genius are requested to leave their Names at the Printing Office, Mountain Street, Quebec."

—*Quebec gazette supplement,* Aug. 13, 1789.

A similar advertisement of Burns's *Poems* "to be printed by James Robertson on the Island of St. John" appeared in the *Royal gazette,* Saint John, N.B., Mar. 9, Oct. 27, 1790.

There is no evidence, however, that this work was ever printed as advertised. Robertson left Charlottetown about June, 1789, ostensibly to visit Quebec, and he does not seem to have resumed printing in Charlottetown thereafter. Copies of Burns's *Poems, chiefly in the Scottish dialect,* actually sold in Quebec, were probably imported from Britain. *See also* Anna M. Painter: *American editions of the poems of Burns before 1800,* in *Library,* ser. 4, v. 12, p. 434-56, Mar., 1932.

585. CARY, THOMAS, 1751-1823

ABRAM'S PLAINS: / A / POEM. / [rule] / Haec studia adolescentia alunt, senectutem oblectant, secundas res ornant, / adversis solatium et perfugium præbent; delectant domi, non impe-/diunt foris; pernoctant nobiscum, peregrinantur, rusticantur. / TULL. / [rule] / [double rule] / By THOMAS CARY, Gent. / [double rule] / QUEBEC: / PRINTED FOR THE AUTHOR. / [rule] / M,DCC,LXXXIX. /

4to. [A]-E [i.e. F]²; 2 p. l., 20 p.; type-page: 20 × 13 cm.

Contents: p. l. 1 recto, t.-p.; verso, blank; p. l. 2 recto-verso, Preface, dated Jan. 24, 1789; p. [1]-20, Abram's Plains.

Printed at Quebec by Wm. Brown, 1789, as recorded eight days before his death:

"1789, Mar. 14. Printed for Thomas Cary, Abram's Plains a poem, making 3 Sheets on Quarto Demy 30/ pr. Sheet—£4.10.

"Sold Ditto 4½ Quires blue Demy to cover D°—5/

"Paid postage of letter to Saro [Montreal agent] concerning D° & to Courier 2/6—3/3. [total] £4.18.3." —Can.P.A., *Neilson papers*, v. 84.

The work was advertised "to be published by subscription, price two shillings [the copy] . . . with a large and elegant type," in *Quebec gazette*, Jan. 8, 1789, and later, "to be sold at 2/6 (for cash only) [by the printer and agents] and by the Author at Mme. Bellonie's, Quebec."

The poem, about 600 lines in rhyming pentameters, was patterned, according to the preface, after "the Harmonious Thompson* so strikingly unparalleled and inimitable are the beauties of his numbers," also after Pope's *Windsor Forest* and Goldsmith's *Deserted Village*. It begins:

"Thy Plains, O Abram! and thy pleasing views
Where hid in shades I sit and court the muse
Grateful I sing, For there from care and noise,
Oft have I fled to taste thy silent joys."

Replete with classical references, apothegms, and patriotic trumpetings, Cary's poem treats of the various features of Canadian life: the St. Lawrence waterway, civilization of the Indians, the Loyalists, masts for the British navy, etc. He expresses a current English-Canadian attitude to the French Canadians:

"Be thankful, swains, Britannia's conquering sword
Releas'd you from your ancient sov'reign lord . . .

Then the poor pittance of the scanty soil
Hard earn'd became the prowling tyrant's spoil . . .

Hence smiling peace and laughing plenty reign
And gay content, festive, delights the plain.
Grateful, ye peasants, own your mended state
And bless, beneath a George, your better fate."

This was written in 1789, long known from the crop failure and general distress, as the "Hungry Year"!

Cary, who came to Quebec from England before 1787, was working, when this poem was published, as a clerk in one of the government offices at £40 a year, with occasional extra work at 5*s*. a day "for writing." In 1797 he became secretary to Gov. Prescott and in the same year established a subscription library in Quebec.

Cary continued his literary and political interests in the *Quebec mercury*, a newspaper which he founded in 1805, and which remained the organ of English conservative opinion in Quebec till 1905. His descendants operated a printing-publishing business there through the 19th century.

Copy located: CaQM.

*James Thomson, author of *The Seasons*, 1730.

586. CHURCH OF ENGLAND. LITURGY AND RITUAL

[A Form of Prayer and Thanksgiving to Almighty God; to be used at morning and evening service, . . . throughout the cities of London and Westminster . . . on Sunday, the first day of March, 1789; and in all churches and chapels throughout England and Wales as soon as the minister thereof receives the same.]

Broadside? *printed at Quebec by Wm. Moore, 1789.* This was a prayer of about 300 words on the recovery of George III, prepared by the archbishop of Canterbury. Printed copies were despatched by Lord Sydney from London, Mar. 4, 1789, to the provincial governments in Canada. Arriving in Halifax, on Apr. 22, the text was published by Anthony Henry in a *Royal gazette extra*, Friday, Apr. 24, 1789. Nearly a month later it reached Quebec and was advertised by Moore: ". . . The Form of prayer will be neatly printed and ready . . . Tuesday morning [May 19]. Price Three pence."—*Quebec herald*, May 18, 1789. The Prayer itself appeared in the same paper the following week, from which the title, as above, is taken.

Copy located: None.

587. CHURCH OF ENGLAND. LITURGY AND RITUAL

[A Form of Prayer and Thanksgiving to Almighty God, etc.]

Broadside? Another edition of the item above, *Printed at Charlottetown, Island of St. John, by James Robertson, 1789.* On receipt of Lord Sydney's despatch of Mar. 4, 1789, in the Island of St. John, Lieut.-Gov. Fanning-in-Council ordered a day of public thanksgiving to be proclaimed for May 27, 1789, "And Mr. Robertson is ordered to print One Hundred Copies of the Form of Prayer before mentioned." —Executive Council Minutes, May 18, 1789, in Can.P.A., P.E.I. "B".

Copy located: None.

588. CHURCH OF ENGLAND. LITURGY AND RITUAL

[A Form of Prayer and Thanksgiving to Almighty God, etc.]

Broadside? Two editions of No. 586 (or, as the price suggests, two impressions from the same setting of type) were *printed at Quebec by Samuel Neilson, 1789*, as recorded:

"1789, June 13. Printed for Civil Secretary 100 Copies of the Prayer of Thanks for the King's Recovery—£1.0.10.

"June 15. Printed for Civil Secretary, 68 Prayers for the King.—7/6."

—Can.P.A., *Neilson papers*, v. 70.

Copy located: None.

589. [A COLLECTION OF ORIGINAL POEMS]

[A COLLECTION OF ORIGINAL POEMS.]

Proposed printing at Quebec by Wm. Moore, 1789, was advertised:

"To the Ladies and Lovers of elegant Poetry. Proposals for printing by subscription a Collection of original poems, written in elegant stile by various ingenious

Ladies and Gentlemen, who favoured a friend of the Printer with copies; which copies for the benefit of the community he has favoured the Printer with.

"Conditions: to be printed in quarto on Demy paper with large new types to form a neat volume. Subscription 7/6 payable on delivery of the book. Miss Seward's *Monody on the death of Major André* and a list of the subscribers will be given . . . (gratis). Work will not be begun till there are a sufficient number of subscribers to defray the expence, then it will be completed in one month."

—*Quebec herald*, Dec. 8-29, 1788.

There is no evidence, however, that this work was ever published as proposed by Moore.

590. COURIER DE QUEBEC OU HERAUT FRANCOIS

PROSPECTUS / D'UNE / Gazette Française. / [rule] /

A single sheet printed on both sides, *Printed at Quebec by Wm. Moore, ? 1789.*

The text, undated and in unidiomatic French, states that William Moore "editeur de la gazette anglaise intitulée Heraut de Québec offre aux Messieurs Canadiens d'en imprimeur une en Français [etc.]."

The proposed paper, *Courier de Québec ou Heraut François*, was to be entirely in French, as complaints had been received that the *Quebec herald* (entirely in English) refused to publish French answers to its English correspondents. Also the British ministry was interested in the establishment of an organ of French opinion in Canada. All citizens have a right to write upon matters of government, Moore states, and he solicits such contributions to the *Courier de Québec.*

This paper was to be published weekly on Thursdays, in 4to, 4 p. each number. The subscription, ½ guinea a year, and the advertisement rates, 3*s.* 6*d.* for 15 lines, were the same as those of the Monday edition of *Courier de Québec*, which appeared in three issues only, Nov. 24-Dec. 8, 1788. This prospectus of a Thursday edition was probably published in 1789 when Moore was advertising for subscriptions to a *Courier de Québec* (cf. *Quebec herald*, Apr. 13, 1789) and was planning a Thursday edition of the *Herald* (cf. No. 618). There is no evidence, however, that *Courier de Québec ou Heraut François* was published in a Thursday edition as proposed in this prospectus.

Copy located: CaQQL.

591. GREAT BRITAIN. PARLIAMENT. HOUSE OF LORDS

His Majesty's Recovery, /

Broadside, printed in 2 col. of 52, 53 lines respectively; type-page: 20.5 × 10.8 cm. *Probably printed at Quebec by Wm. Moore, 1789.*

Contents: Col. 1 begins: "Arrived last night [May 15, 1789] the Achilles, Capt. Pile, in 49 days from Liverpool, by the assistance of friends, we are happy to confirm His Majesty's recovery, by the following address of the Lords to his Majesty and his Majesty's gracious answer." Then follows the text of the Address, dated Mar. 11, 1789, and of the royal reply.

Copy located: CaOOA (bound in *Quebec herald* following v. 1, no. 25, May 4-11, 1789).

592. HUBERT, JEAN FRANCOIS, *bp. of Quebec*, 1739-1797

LETTRE CIRCULAIRE A MESSIEURS LES CURÉS. / <Text> / JEAN FRANC[s] Evêque de Québec. / BON POUR COPIE. /

4to. 2 *l.*; type-page: 18.5 × 13.5 cm. *Printed at Quebec by Wm. Brown, 1789,* as recorded:

"1789, Jan. 29. Printed for the Bishop's Secretary (24th [inst]) 120 Circular letters to the Curés, 1 on a Sheet superfine thick 4to post plain—£1."
—Can.P.A., *Neilson papers,* v. 84.

Contents: The text, in French on recto of *l.* 1, is a circular letter exhorting the parish clergy to obtain for the needy poor a certain amount of seed grain for spring sowing, to be distributed by the government. In the copies seen, the letter is dated and signed in MS.: "Québec 25 Janvr. 1789, Plessis, P[tre] Sec[r] du Diocèse." *l.* [1] verso-*l.* [2], blank.

This letter is reprinted in Têtu and Gagnon: *Mandements de Québec,* 2: 360.

Copies located: CaO; CaQQL.

593. HUBERT, JEAN FRANCOIS, *bp. of Quebec*, 1739-1797

Lettre Circulaire à Messieurs les Curés. / MONSIEUR. / <Text> / JEAN FRANC[s] EVEQUE DE QUEBEC. / QUEBEC, 9 DECEMBRE, / 1789. } / BON POUR COPIE /

4to. 2 *l.*; type-page: 15 × 13.6 cm. *Printed at Quebec by Samuel Neilson, 1789,* as recorded:

"1789, Dec. 16. Printed for the Government 200 Circular letters from the Bishop to the Curates, 1 on a Sheet 4to Post—£1.6 8."
—Can.P.A., *Neilson papers,* v. 70.

Contents: The text, in French on *l.* 1 recto, is a circular letter, bearing instructions to curés to take census of their parishes, according to wish of Gov. Dorchester, on forms to be obtained from vicar-general of each district before February first of each year; *l.* 1 verso-*l.* 2, blank.

This letter is reprinted in Têtu and Gagnon: *Mandements de Québec,* 2: 396.

Copies located: CaO; CaOOA; CaQQL.

594. INGLIS, CHARLES, *bp. of Nova Scotia*, 1734-1816

A / CHARGE / DELIVERED TO THE / CLERGY / OF THE / DIOCESE OF NOVA SCOTIA, / AT THE / PRIMARY VISITATION / HOLDEN IN THE TOWN OF HALIFAX, / IN THE MONTH OF JUNE 1788. / [rule] / BY / THE RIGHT REVEREND CHARLES, / BISHOP OF NOVA SCOTIA. / [double rule] / HALIFAX: Printed by ANTHONY HENRY; Printer To The King's / MOST EXCELLENT MAJESTY. / MDCCLXXXIX. /

8vo. A-F^4, G^2, H-I^4, [K]^1; vi, 64 p.; type-page: 16 × 8.7 cm.

Contents: p. [1], recto, t.-p.; p. [ii], blank; p. iii-vi, Address, signed: "Charles Nova Scotia, Halifax, December 30, 1788"; p. 1-42, Charge; p. 43-46, Appendix; Address of the clergy, June 18, 1788, to the Bishop, and the latter's reply; p. 47-58,

Sunday Schools; p. 59-60 form of testimonial; p. 60-64, Academy near Windsor, p. 64 at foot, Errata.

The Address of the clergy, p. 43-46, had been published previously (*see* No. 550). The Sunday Schools regulations, etc., p. 47-58, is the publication promised by Bishop Inglis the year previously (in No. 555). Appendix no. IV on the Academy near Windsor is introduced by the note: "The Printer having two or three blank pages and signifying a wish that they might be filled, it was judged proper to insert the following account of the Opening and first Visitation of our Academy." This account contains the address to the bishop by the magistrates and gentlemen of the county of Hants and the bishop's reply, on the importance of the Academy and the community to each other, both addresses delivered at the opening ceremonies, Windsor, Nov. 1, 1788. The report on the first visitation, dated Halifax, Feb. 20, 1789, describes curricula and examinations in the Latin and English schools and states that the Academy has 25 students including 10 boarders.

Copies located: CaNsHA (p. 63-64 wanting); CaNsWA; CaQM; RPJ (p. 63-64 wanting).

595. INGLIS, CHARLES, *bp. of Nova Scotia*, 1734-1816

[Injunctions to the Clergy of the province of Quebec.]

Probably printed at Quebec by Wm. Moore, 1789. The careful records of the semi-official Quebec printer, Samuel Neilson, include no reference to this work, nor does it appear in the newspapers of the day. So it was probably printed as a broadside or pamphlet by the other local printer, Wm. Moore. For Bishop Inglis noted in his Diary [Quebec] Aug. 6, 1789: ". . . prepared a set of injunctions for the Clergy," ". . . Agreed to have my injunctions printed."—And again on Aug. 8: "This day my injunctions were printed."—Can.P.A., *Inglis papers*, v. 5.

"These injunctions dealt with such matters as the behaviour of the clergy . . . sermons . . . baptism and catechising of children . . . annual financial statements . . . fees . . . election of wardens . . . These injunctions are the origin and basis of church polity in Quebec even to the present day."—R. V. Harris: *Charles Inglis, missionary, loyalist, bishop* (Toronto, 1937), 105. They were prepared during Bishop Inglis's first visitation in Quebec, over which he had "jurisdiction spiritual and ecclesiastical" by a special patent of Aug. 13, 1787, until the Diocese of Quebec was established with its own bishop in 1793.

Copy located: None.

596. LA POTERIE, DE, *Catholic priest*

Le Jeudi 3 Septembre dernier, Fete du Sacerdoce; d'anciens / et respectables Citoyens de la Ville de Québec, ont presentés / la Requête Suivante: A NOS SEIGNEURS, / NOS SEIGNEURS Illustrissimes et Révérendissimes, Pères en Dieu, / Les EVEQUES de QUEBEC, / Et le VENERABLE CLERGÉ de ce Diocèse, /

4to. 2 *l.*; text in French in 2 col. on recto of *l.* 1; type-page: 24 × 21 cm. Probably printed for La Poterie at one of the two printing offices in Quebec, either Wm. Moore's or Samuel Neilson's, in 1789.

Contents: l. [1] recto, A petition signed by Pierre Dufau and 27 others, dated Quebec, Sept. 3, 1789, begging reinstatement of the priest, M. de La Poterie, into his pastoral work; appended is La Poterie's letter of Sept. 5, 1789, to the bishop of Quebec, begging reinstatement; and finally an advertisement for teaching reading, writing, French, Latin, Italian "et former l'esprit et le cœur de ses éleves tant aux Sciences, [signed:] De La Poterie." *l.* 1 verso-*l.* 2, blank.

Copy located: CaQQL.

597. MELVIN & BURNS, *Auctioneers, Quebec*

[Catalogue of books, Medicine and Wines to be sold at Auction Quebec, Dec. 28-29, 1789]

Printed at Quebec by Wm. Moore or Samuel Neilson, 1789, for the sale which was advertised:

"By Public Auction Dec. 28-29, 1789, at Melvin & Burns Auction Rooms, A large parcel of Valuable Books, chest of Medicine, choice Wines, etc. Printed Catalogues will be distributed previous to the Sale."—*Quebec gazette*, Dec. 24, 1789.

Copy located: None.

598. MONTREAL, *City*

Tableau des rues et Faubourgs de Montréal.

Broadside: paper-page: 20 × 29 cm. *Printed at Montreal by Fleury Mesplet, 1789.* This work was advertised by Mesplet: "A Vendre à l'Imprimerie, Le Tableau des Rues et Fauxbourgs de Montréal. [no price]."—*Montreal gazette*, June 4-11, 1789. It was included in the post mortem inventory of his stock, Feb. 17-20, 1794: "Un paquet de Tableau des Rues—£1.10."—McLachlan: *Mesplet*, 285.

The only copy known, is described (as above) by Fauteux in *Mesplet*, no. 70. He states: "Cet ancêtre du Directory de Montréal doit dater de 1788 d'après certains indices. Il ne porte pas de nom d'imprimeur, mais il a été certainement imprimé par Mesplet."

Copy known: CaQMS.

599. NOVA SCOTIA. HOUSE OF ASSEMBLY

Caption title: [Journal and Proceedings of the House of Assembly of the Province of Nova Scotia.]

Note: title above is not transcribed from copy.

fo. A-N^2; 52 p. *Printed at Halifax, N.S., by Anthony Henry, 1789.*

Contents: Journal and proceedings of the fourth session of the sixth assembly, Mar. 5-Apr. 9, 1789 (no session having been held in 1788).

Copies located: CaNs; GBLP (in C.O. 217/61: 166-217).

600. NOVA SCOTIA. LAWS, STATUTES, *etc.*

Running title: [rule] / 1789. Anno Vicessimo Nono Regis, GEORGII III. CAP. I[-XII]. / rule] /

Caption title: At the GENERAL ASSEMBLY of this Province / of Nova-Scotia, . . . / [8 lines] / . . . being the Fourth Session / of the Sixth General Assembly, convened / in the said Province. / [rule] /

fo. sig. 3B-3E[2]; p. 273-287; type-page: 25.5 × 15 cm. paged in continuation of No. 523 (no session having been held in 1788). *Printed at Halifax, N.S., by Anthony Henry, 1789.*

Contents: p. 273-287, Cap. I-XII, perpetual acts passed in the session, Mar. 5-Apr. 9, 1789; p. 287 verso, blank.

Copies located: CaNsHA; CaO; DLC; MH (2 cop.)

601 NOVA SCOTIA. LAWS, STATUTES, *etc.*

Running title: [rule] / 1789. Anno Vicessimo Nono Regis, GEORGII III. CAP. I[-V]. / [rule] /

Caption title: At the GENERAL ASSEMBLY of this Province / of Nova-Scotia, . . . / [8 lines] / . . . being the Fourth Session / of the Sixth General Assembly, convened / in the said Province. / [rule] /

fo. sig. F-H[2], I; p. 307-320; type-page: 25.5 × 15 cm. paged in continuation of No. 524 (no session having been held in 1788); *Printed at Halifax, N.S., by Anthony Henry, 1789.*

Contents: p. 307-320, Cap. I-V, temporary acts passed in the session Mar. 5-Apr. 9, 1789.

Copies located: CaO; MH; NNB.

602. NOVA SCOTIA. LAWS, STATUTES, *etc.*

[An Act in amendment of an act, made in the third year of his present Majesty's reign, entitled, an Act to prevent Frauds in the selling of flour and biscuit, or ship bread in casks.]

Broadside, *probably printed at Shelburne, N.S., by James Humphreys, 1789,* according to an order of the justices of the peace:

"Sessions Court, July 16, 1789. Ordered that the Act respecting the selling of flour, Indian meal &c. be published on hand Bills and put up in the different parts of the town."—Shelburne, N.S. Quarter sessions *Records.*

This order probably referred to the provincial act, 29 Geo. III c. 10, with title as above, passed at Halifax, in Mar., 1789, in amendment of 3 Geo. III c. 3, requiring meal or flour to be sold by weight only.

Copy located: None.

603. QUEBEC, *Province.* LAWS, STATUTES, *etc.*

English caption: [three rules] / An ACT or ORDINANCE, / To continue the Ordinances regulating the Practice of the Law, and to provide / more effectually for the dispensation of Justice, and especially in the new Districts. /

French caption: ACTE ou ORDONNANCE, / Qui continue les Ordonnances qui réglent la Pratique de la Loi, et qui pourvoient / plus efficacement à la dispensation de la Justice, et spécialement dans les / nouveaux Districts. /

Colophon: [rule] / QUEBEC: Printed by WM. BROWN, in Mountain-street.—A QUEBEC: chez G. BROWN, au milieu de la Grande Côte / [rule] /

A single sheet printed on both sides in 2 col., English and French; type-page: 32.7 × 20.7 cm.

Contents: p. [1-2]: Articles I-IX, a preliminary draft of 29 Geo. III. c. 3 (articles I-VI, VIII). This draft was amended to exclude its article VII (confirming notarial acts transacted by unauthorized notaries) and to add 3 articles (IX-XI in Ordinance) on jurisdiction of civil courts and limitation of actions in district of Hesse; and proofs admissible in the new districts—to be those admissible by ancient or present laws of the province and of England, as the districts "probably will be chiefly inhabited by persons born within the ancient dominions of the crown of Great Britain." The ordinance was passed at Quebec, Apr. 30, 1789.

This draft was ordered printed and distributed in not less than twelve copies to each member of the Legislative council.—Can.P.A., Que. *State* Feb. 17, 1789. Brown recorded the printing:

"1789, Feb. 28. Printed for Government (by Order of J. Williams) 500 Copies of Drafts of an Ordinance regulating the practice of the Law. ½ Sheet Crown in brevier—£3.5." —Can.P.A., *Neilson papers*, v. 84.

Copies located: CaOOA (2 cop. bearing MS. emendations, filed in Can.P.A., "S" *Legislative Council papers 1789*).

604. QUEBEC, *Province.* LAWS, STATUTES, *etc.*

EXTRAORDINARY. / [rule] / NUM. 1235. / THE / QUEBEC / GAZETTE. / [rule] / MONDAY, APRIL 13, 1789. /

English caption: Anno Vicesimo Nono Georgii Tertii Regis. Chap. I. An Act or Ordinance, for the Relief of the Poor, in the Loan of Seeds for Corn and other Necessaries.

French caption: Anno Vicesimo Nono Georgii Tertii Regis. Chap. I. Acte ou Ordonance, Qui aide le Pauvre dans le Prêt des Semences de Bled et autres Grains nécessaires.

Broadside, text in 2 col., English and French. *Printed at Quebec by Samuel Neilson, 1789,* as recorded:

"1789, Apr. 30. Printed for Government (by Order of J. Williams, 300 Copies of Ordinance. Chap. I—£1.2.6.

"D° 100 copies D° Chap. II [*See* No. 605]—7/6."

—Can.P.A., *Neilson papers*, v. 84.

This is a separate issue of the ordinance reprinted from types set for the *Quebec gazette*. This ordinance and the one following were both passed on Apr. 11, and occupied part of the first page of the *Gazette Extra*, Apr. 13, and the *Gazette*, Apr. 16, 1789, respectively.

The text is reprinted in Can.P.A., *Report, 1914-15*.

Copy located: CaQMA.

605. QUEBEC, *Province.* LAWS, STATUTES, *etc.*

NUM. 1236. THE / QUEBEC / GAZETTE. / [rule] / THURSDAY, APRIL 16, 1789. / [rule] /

English caption: Anno Vicesimo Nono Georgii Tertii Regis. Chap. II. An Act or Ordinance to strengthen certain Deeds and Writings in the District of Hesse.

French caption: Anno Vicesimo Nono. Georgii Tertii Regis. Acte ou Ordonance, Pour valider certains Actes et Contrats dans le District de Hesse.

Broadside, text in 2 col., English and French. 100 copies *printed at Quebec by S. Neilson, 1789,* from *Quebec gazette* types (*see* No. 604 *note*).

Copy located: CaQMA.

606. QUEBEC, *Province.* LAWS, STATUTES, *etc.*

NUM. 1239 / THE / QUEBEC / GAZETTE. / [rule] / THURSDAY, MAY 7, 1789. / [rule] / [in centre: royal arms] / on right: LA / GAZETTE / DE / QUEBEC. / [rule] / JEUDI, le 7 MAI, 1789. / [rule] /

English caption: Anno vicesimo [sic] Georgii Tertii Regis. Chap. III. An Act, to continue the Ordinances regulating the Practice of the Law, and to provide more effectually for the dispensation of Justice, and especially in the New Districts.

French caption: Anno vicesimo [sic] Georgii Tertii Regis. Chap. III. Acte, Qui continue les Ordonances qui reglent les formes de procéder, et qui pourvoient plus efficacement à l'administration de la Justice, et spécialement dans les Nouveaux Districts.

Colophon: QUEBEC: Printed by SAMUEL NEILSON, in Mountain-street.—A QUEBEC: par SAMUEL NEILSON, au milieu de la Grande Côte.

fo. [4] p. text in 2 col. English and French.

Contents: p. [1-3], 29 Geo. III c. 3; p. [3-4], 29 Geo. III c. 4. An Act or Ordinance, to explain and amend an Act, intitled "An Act or Ordinance for better regulating the Militia of this Province [etc.]."

This is a separate issue of the ordinances printed from the types set for the *Quebec gazette.* In this separate issue, however, "NUM. 1239" appears in centre (not right hand side) of heading; the captions on p. [1] are in larger type with the word "Nono" omitted, and p. [4] is blank below end of the ordinance and colophon.

Copies located: CaOOA (2 cop. bound in *Quebec gazette,* 1789); CaQMA.

607. QUEBEC, *Province.* LAWS, STATUTES, *etc.*

NUM. 1240 / THE / QUEBEC / GAZETTE. / [rule] / THURSDAY, MAY 14, 1789. / [rule] / [in centre: royal arms] / on right: LA / GAZETTE / DE / QUEBEC. / [rule] / JEUDI le 14 MAI, 1789. / [rule] /

English caption: Anno Vicesimo Nono Georgii Tertii Regis. Chap. V. An Ordinance to continue the Ordinance empowering the Commissioners of the Peace to regulate the Police of the Towns of Quebec and Montreal for a limited time.

French caption: Anno Vicesimo Nono Georgii III. Regis. Chap. V. Ordonnance, Qui continue l'Ordonnance qui autorise les Commissionaires de Paix à Regler la Police des Villes de Québec et de Montréal, pour un tems limité.

Broadside: text in 2 col. English and French. *Printed at Quebec by Samue Neilson, 1789.*

Contents: 29 Geo. III c. V-VII, passed Apr. 30, 1789, and signed by Dorchester. This is a separate issue of the ordinances as they appeared on the first page of the *Quebec gazette*, May 14, 1789.

Copy located: CaQMA.

608. QUEBEC, *Province.* LAWS, STATUTES, *etc.*

[Anno Vicesimo Nono Georgii Tertii Regis. Chap. I. An Act or Ordinance for the Relief of the Poor in the Loan of Seeds for Corn and other Necessaries.

. . . Chap. II. An Act or Ordinance to strengthen certain Deeds and Writings in the District of Hesse.]

French side: [. . . Chap. I. Acte ou Ordonance, Qui aide le Pauvre dans le Prêt des Semences de Bled et autres Grains nécessaires.

. . . Chap. II. Acte ou Ordonance, Pour valider certains Actes et Contrats dans le District de Hesse.]

Broadside or a single sheet printed on both sides; text probably in 2 col. English and French. This appears to be a reprint of No. 604 and 605. *Printed at Quebec by Samuel Neilson, 1789,* as recorded:

"1789, Aug. 4. Printed for the Government (by order of J. Williams) 250 Copies of Ordinances, Chap. 1 & 2, on ½ Sheet—£1.12.6."

—Can.P.A., *Neilson papers,* v. 70.

Neilson sold "Ordinances [passed] in Session 1789" at 2*s.* the copy.—*ibid.*

Copy located: None.

609. QUEBEC, *Province.* LAWS, STATUTES, *etc.*

English caption: [double rule] / A BILL / (Not yet Passed,) / [rule] / To explain and amend the Act intitled, "An Act or / "Ordinance for promoting the Inland Navigation." / [rule] /

French caption: [double rule] / BILL / (Qui n'est point encor Passé,) / [rule] / Pour expliquer et amender l'Acte intitulé, "Acte ou / Ordonnance qui encourage la Navigation Intérieure." / [rule] /

Colophon, p. 4: QUEBEC: Printed by SAMUEL NEILSON, in Mountain-street.—A QUEBEC: Par SAMUEL NEILSON, au milieu de la Grande Côte. / [rule] /

fo. 4 p.; Text in 2 col., English and French; type-page: 34 × 20 cm.

Contents: p. [1]-4, "A Bill . . . inland navigation"; p. 4, "A Bill (not yet passed) to amend an Act intitled, An Act or Ordinance for regulating the Fisheries in the River of Saint Lawrence [etc., 28 Geo. III c. 6]." At end of p. 4, endorsed titles in English and French within a frame, printed lengthwise on page: "A Bill (Not yet passed) [etc. as above]."

These bills were ordered printed in Apr., 1789, and tabled till the next session. The navigation bill was amended and finally passed Apr. 11, 1791, as 31 Geo. III c. 1. The second bill penalizing the export of salmon without customs inspection, was protested by fishermen and dropped. Neilson recorded the printing:

"1789, June 29. Printed for the Government (by Order of J. Williams) 250 Copies of the Inland Navigation & Fishery bills, making 1 Sheet folio Crown.—£3.5."—Can.P.A., *Neilson papers*, v. 70.

Copies located: CaOOA (2 cop. filed (1) with MS. memoranda in Can.P.A., *"S" Ordinances P. of Q. 1789;* (2) in *Miscellaneous newspaper clippings, 1812-1837,* portfolio).

610. QUEBEC, *Province.* LAWS, STATUTES, *etc.*

[A Bill, not yet passed, for securing more effectually a. toll of the bridge over the River St. Charles, near Quebec. *also:* A Bill, not yet passed, to discourage desertion, and for regulating seamen in the merchant-service.]

French side:

[Bill, qui n'est point encor passé, qui assure plus efficacement le droit de Pontage du Pont sur la Rivière St. Charles, près Québec. *aussi:* Bill, qui n'est point encor passé, qui empêche la désertion des Matelots du Service Marchand.]

2 p. Text probably in 2 col. English and French, *Printed at Quebec by Samuel Neilson, 1789, as recorded:*

"1789, Sept. 20. Printed for Government (by Order of J. Williams) 250 Copies of 2 Bills not yet passed. 1 for the Toll of the Bridge over the River St. Charles. the Other for preventing desertion and regulating Seamen. making 2 pages on ½ Sheet on Crown. Long Primer with endorsement. —£1.12.6."—Can.P.A. *Neilson papers*, v. 70.

These bills, introduced in the 1789 session, were tabled and passed (with amendments?) Apr. 12, 1790, as 30 Geo. III c. 3 and c. 6 respectively.

Copy located: None.

611. QUEBEC, *Province.* LEGISLATIVE COUNCIL

English caption: [double rule] / A BILL / (Not yet Passed,) / [rule] / To prohibit the Use of Small Stills. / [rule] /

French caption: [double rule] / BILL / (Qui n'est point encor Passé,) / [rule] / Qui défend l'usage des petits Alambics. / [rule] /

Colophon, p. 2: [double rule] / QUEBEC: PRINTED BY SAMUEL NEILSON, IN MOUNTAIN-STREET A QUEBEC: IMPRIMÉ PAR SAMUEL NEILSON, RUE DE LA MONTAGNE / [double rule] /

fo. [2] p. Text in 2 col. English and French; type-page: 34.5 × 20.5 cm.

Contents: p. [1]: "A bill . . . small stills"; p. [1-2]: "A Bill (Not yet passed,) For securing and improving Correspondence throughout the Province, and to facilitate Intercourse by Post between the Western Districts and Montreal. [*French caption:*] Bill (Qui n'est point encor passé,) Qui assure et étend la Correspondence par toute la Province et qui la facilite par Poste entre les Districts du Ouest et Montréal"; p. [2] at foot, endorsed titles in English and French printed lengthwise on page within a frame: "A Bill (Not yet Passed,) [etc.]."

These bills, known as "The Small Stills bill" and "The Post Office bill" were ordered printed by the Legislative Council in Apr., 1789, and tabled. They were committed to committees, Mar. 25, 1791, but were not enacted as ordinances of the province of Quebec. Neilson recorded the printing:

> "1789, July 16. Printed for Government (by Order J. Williams) 250 Copies of 2 Ordinances not passed for preventing small stills and for facilitating Communication throughout the Province, making ½ Sheet Crown in Long Primer with Brevier notes and endorsed.—£1.15."
>
> —Can.P.A., *Neilson papers,* v. 70.

Copies located: CaOOA (2 cop. filed in *Miscellaneous newspaper clippings 1812-1837* portfolio).

612. QUEBEC, *Province.* LEGISLATIVE COUNCIL

English caption: [double rule] / EXTRACT from a Report of the Proceedings / of a Committee of the whole Legislative Coun-/cil, upon a Bill (not yet passed) respecting / the High Roads and Bridges in the central / Districts of Quebec and Montreal. / [rule] /

French caption: [double rule] / EXTRAIT d'un Rapport des procédés d'un / Comité de tout le Conseil Législatif sur un / Bill (qui n'est pas encore passé) concer-/nant les Chemins Public et Ponts dans les Districts centraux de Québec et de Montréal. / [rule] /

Colophon, p. 11: [double rule] / QUEBEC: PRINTED BY SAMUEL NEILSON, IN MOUNTAIN-STREET. A QUEBEC: IMPRIME' PAR SAMUEL NEILSON, RUE LA MONTAGNE. / [double rule] /

fo. [*-3*]²; 11 p., Text in 2 col. English and French; type-page: 35 × 20.5 cm.

Contents: p. [1]-6, Extract (as in caption above) from Legislative Council *Minutes,* Apr. 11-19, 1789; This comprised the text of the "privy council's" bill, clause I-XXI, with the legislative council's amendment thereto. The bill was drawn up by a committee of Hugh Finlay and four others, appointed to report upon a

Memorial by Charles-Louis de Lanaudière, the latter, as grand voyer (overseer of roads) having presented a comprehensive criticism of existing legislation; p. 6-11, "Extract from the Proceedings had on the New Bill which related to the High Roads and Bridges in the central Districts of Quebec and Montreal" extracted from Legislative Council *Minutes*, Apr. 21 *et seq*, 1789, comprising "selections from the whole [as in p. 1-6] devising . . . such provisions as seem to be necessary for immediate relief" with amendments thereto; verso of p. 11, endorsed titles in English and French (within a frame): "Extract from a Report [etc.]."

The Legislative Council recommended that the first part be printed for further consideration, and it passed the new bill, Apr. 30, 1789. The governor, however, withheld assent, had 250 copies of the two bills (as above) printed, and referred back to the Council, Mar. 16, 1790. The matter was postponed till the 1791 session, then disappeared. The general revision of the road and bridge legislation only took place in 1796, long after the reorganization of the province (*see* No. 999-1000).

Neilson recorded this publication:

"1789, Sept. 7. Printed for Government (by Order J. Williams) 250 Copies of a Bill not yet passed concerning the high Roads & Bridges in the District of Quebec and Montreal, making 3 Sheets in long Primer with Brevier Notes, including indorsement, by Ag^{t} @ £2.10 for first hundred and 10/ each after—£9.15.0.

Paid Bookbinder for folding and stitching Ditto ½d each—10/5. [total] £10.5.5."—Can.P.A., *Neilson papers*, v. 70.

Copy located: CaOOA (in portfolio *Miscellaneous newspaper clippings, 1812-1837*); Another copy, Hodgins, no. 103, not located.

613. QUEBEC, *Province.* LEGISLATIVE COUNCIL

**Caption title:* Council-Chamber, Quebec, 17th February, 1789, Rules and Regulations for the Conduct of the Land-Office Department.

? *Colophon:* Printed by William Brown, Mountain St Quebec.

[2] p. text in English and French in 2 col. on recto and verso of a single leaf; paper-page: 32.5 × 27 cm.

This is a revision of the land granting regulations, prepared by a special committee of the Council (appointed Dec. 29, 1788), passed by the governor-in-council and ordered printed, Feb. 17, 1789. Following Gov. Dorchester's visit to the western districts, July-Sept., 1788, during which representation had been made of the delay and expense to new settlers of securing their land allotments from the Council in Quebec, land boards were appointed in the six districts between Gaspé and Detroit, Dec. 29, 1788 to Apr. 12, 1789. The Regulations were revised, as above, to describe the process and conditions of the grant and to define the duties of the local boards to both grantee and the Council—Can. P.A., Que. *Land A*, pt. 2. *See also* G. C. Paterson: *Land settlement in Upper Canada*, 29.

This publication is recorded in the bill of the late Wm. Brown Estate to the Government of Quebec:

"1789, Mar. 5. Printing 500 Rules and Regulations for the Land Office Department, English & French—£3.10."—Can.P.A., "*S*" *Pub. Accts*, 1789.

It is reprinted in Ontario Archives, *Report, 1905*.

Copy located: GBLP (in C.O. 42/67, p. 383-84). *Copies recorded but not located:* Hodgins, no. 61-66, 97.

*Wording *only* of title transcribed from copy.

614. QUEBEC, *Province.* LEGISLATIVE COUNCIL

English caption: [double rule] / COUNCIL-CHAMBER, QUEBEC, 25th. August, 1789. / [rule] / Additional RULES and REGULATIONS / For the Conduct of the Land-Office Department. / [rule] /

French caption: [double rule] / CHAMBRE DU CONSEIL, QUEBEC 25 Août, 1789. / [rule] / Ajouté RE'GLEMENS / Pour la Conduite de l'Office du Département des Terres. / [rule] /

Colophon: QUEBEC: Printed by SAMUEL NEILSON, in Mountain-street.—A QUEBEC: par SAMUEL NEILSON, au milieu de la Grande Côte. /

2 *l.* (without signature or pagination) in fo.; Text in 2 col. English and French on recto and verso of *l.* 1., type-page: 33 × 20.5 cm., *l.* 2 blank.

Contents: l. 1, recto-verso, Additional rules, no. 1-10; *l.* 2, blank. This is a supplement to *Rules and regulations* of Feb. 17, 1789, transferring from surveyors to the district land boards, all discretionary powers relating to "town-scites," roads, etc. It was passed by the governor-in-council, Aug. 26, 1789, ordered to be printed and copies transmitted to the land boards and surveyor-general's department.

—Can.P.A., *Que. Land A*, pt. 2.

This publication is recorded by Neilson:

"1789, Sept. 7. Printed for Government (by Order of J. Williams) 500 Additional Rules & Regulations for the Conduct of Land Office, 1 on a Sheet—Long Primer—£2.17.6." —Can.P.A., *Neilson papers*, v. 70.

Copies located: CaOOA (2 cop. filed in (1) Can.P.A., *"S" Int. Corres., L.C.Land sundries, 1789-90;* (2) *Miscellaneous newspaper clippings 1812-1837* portfolio); CaOT; GBLP (in C.O. 42/67: 385-86).

615. QUEBEC, *Province.* LEGISLATIVE COUNCIL

Caption title: [double rule] / At the Council Chamber at Quebec, / [rule] / Monday 9th. November 1789. / [rule] / PRESENT, / His Excellency . . . LORD DORCHESTER. / [etc.]

Colophon: QUEBEC: / PRINTED BY / S. NEILSON. / [within ornamental frame]

4to. 2 p., 1 *l.;* type-page: 17 × 12 cm.

Contents: p. [1]-2, Order-in-council for (1) land boards to preserve a registry of names of persons "who had adhered to the Unity of Empire and joined the Royal Standard before the Treaty of separation in 1783, . . . that their posterity may be discriminated from future Settlers . . . as proper Objects . . . for Benefits and Privileges." (2) Land boards to provide for sons of Loyalists "on full age" and for daughters on full age or marriage, lots of 200 acres each: 1 *l.*, blank.

Neilson recorded the printing:

"1789, Nov. 21. Printed for Council Office, 500 Orders in Council 2 pages, 4to. Crown, Pica, for Locations to Sons and daughters of Loyalists—£2.1. Folding and cutting—5/
[Total:] £2.6."—Can.P.A., *Neilson papers*, v. 70.

Copy located: CaOOA (in portfolio *Miscellaneous newspaper clippings, 1812-1837);* another copy, Hodgins, no. 61-4, not located.

616. QUEBEC BENEVOLENT SOCIETY

Rules and Regulations / OF THE / Quebec Provident, Benevolent, / and Friendly / SOCIETY. / [rule] / ESTABLISHED THE FIRST WEDNESDAY IN / MAY, M.DCC.LXXXIX. / HELD AT THE MERCHANT'S COFFEE-HOUSE. / [double rule] / QUEBEC: Printed by W. Moore, / AT THE / HERALD PRINTING-OFFICE. /

12mo. A-C[4]; 24 p.; type-page: 14 × 6.8 cm.

Contents: p. [1], t.-p.; p. [2], blank; p. [3]-20, Rules, 1-28; p. 21-22, Pledge, dated Quebec, May 1, 1789, and signed by 22 members (all English); p. 22, Officers chosen; p. 23-24, List of payments, forfeitures, and benefactions.

Printed for members at 1*s.* 3*d.* a copy by William Moore, who was a steward in the society, and ready for distribution June 24, 1789 (*Quebec herald,* June 22, 1789) these rules set forth the purpose, fees, procedure at meetings, etc. The organization was a mutual benefit society, establishing a fund for the support of infirm members, their widows and children, administered by the officers. In 1789 it was limited to fifty members, who paid an entrance fee of £1 3*s.* 4*d.* and monthly dues of 2*s.* 6*d.*, and who could draw benefits only after a year's membership. The convivial character of its monthly meetings (with a sixpenny fee for expenses) is suggested by rule no. 17:

"Upon the misbehaviour of any member, or members on a meeting night, by challenging to fight, or game, by offering wagers, party disputes, obscene discourse, oaths or drunkenness, for every such offence, [the offender(s)] shall be fined 1*s.* and not being silent when three times demanded by the President . . . he or they so misbehaving, shall forfeit 2/6 each, and upon any further misbehaviour the same evening, the said member or members shall quit the room at the request of the President or forfeit 10/."

The Society, incorporated in 1807 by provincial act 47 Geo. III c. 17, frequently revised and reprinted its *Rules* during its long life. The latest edition (1875) seen by the writer, included a list of 121 members.

Copies located: CaQM; CaQMS.

617. QUEBEC GAZETTE. CARRIER'S ADDRESS

ETRENNES / Du Garçon qui porte la / GAZETTE DE QUEBEC / AUX PRATIQUES. / Le 1er Janvier, 1790. / [*Quebec, S. Neilson, 1789.*]

Broadside: 51 lines; type-page: 27 × 12.5 cm. in ornamental rule frame.

Contents: Etrennes, 5 stanzas of 8 lines each, light verse, in simple and pleasing rhythm:

"Je viens ici gaillardement
Selon l'antique usage
Vous faire un petit compliment,
Vous rendre mon hommage
[Etc.]"

Copy located: CaO (bound in *Quebec gazette*, at end of 1789).

618. QUEBEC HERALD

QUEBEC, September 21, 1789. / THE FRIENDS OF THE PRINTER AND READERS IN GENERAL OF THE / QUEBEC HERALD, /

A single sheet printed on both sides; type-page: 31 × 18.3 cm. *Printed at Quebec by Wm. Moore, 1789.*

Contents: p. [1-2], Notice of forthcoming publications by Moore, viz., announcement that the *Quebec herald* will finish v. I with no. 52, on Nov. 16, 1789, and that "on the 23d [Nov.] a title page and copious index will be given to form the volume. On Monday November 23d, will be published number I, of the second volume to be continued regularly from Monday to Monday . . . And on Thursday November 26, will be published number I, of the first volume of the Thursday paper, to be regularly continued from Thursday to Thursday. Forming two distinct volumes annually [etc.]. In the month of December next, will be published the Lady's Diary, and Pocket Almanack: for the Year . . . M.DCC.XC [etc.]. In the same month will be published the Gentleman's Pocket Almanack and General Register: for the year . . . M.DCC.XC. [etc.]. In the same month will be likewise published Moore's English Sheet Almanack for the year . . . 1790; On an enlarged plan. Price Nine Pence."

The same notice was printed (from smaller type) in the *Quebec herald*, Oct. 12, 1789.

Copy located: CaOOA (bound with *Quebec herald*, Sept. 21-28, 1789).

619. ST. JOHN, ISLAND OF. LAWS, STATUTES, *etc.*

ACTS / OF THE / GENERAL ASSEMBLIES / OF HIS MAJESTY'S / ISLAND OF SAINT JOHN, / AS CORRECTED AND REVISED, PURSUANT TO APPOINTMENT, AT THEIR LAST SESSION, IN THE / YEAR, ONE THOUSAND SEVEN HUNDRED AND EIGHTY EIGHT, / BY PHILLIPS CALLBECK, AND JOSEPH APLIN, ESQUIRES. / [rule] / [royal arms] / [rule] / [double rule] / CHARLOTTE-TOWN: PRINTED BY JAMES ROBERTSON, / 1789. /

4to. [*][1], A-3R[2], 1 p. l., 250 [i.e. 254] p.; type-page: 21 × 15 cm.; four pages without signature or pagination inserted between p. [138-39]; p. [248]-50, even no. on recto; p. 249-50 has running title: 1786 Anno Vicesimo Octavo Regis Georgii III, in error for 1788 etc.

Contents: p. l. recto, t.-p.; verso, blank; p. [1]-137, 13 Geo. III c. 1-21 Geo. III c. 17, 1773-1781; p. [138], blank; [4] p. 21 Geo. III c. 13, An act for enforcing payment of quit rent due (this act was reserved for royal assent and does not appear in its proper order at foot of p. 129); p. [139]-246, 25 Geo. III c. 1-26 Geo. III c. 16, 1785-Apr. 1786; p. [247], 26 Geo. III c. 1, Nov. 1786; verso of p. [247], blank; p. [248]-250, 28 Geo. III c. 1, 1788; verso of p. 250, blank.

This was the first printed publication of the laws of the Island of St. John, passed after its separation from Nova Scotia, 1769, and the establishment of its House of Assembly, 1773. In the session of 1788. following Lieut.-Gov. Fanning's opening address to the Assembly, Jan. 22, 1788, in which he made a suggestion "of the publick expediency of a revision and printing of the Laws of this Island," James Robertson laid before the House, Feb. 2, his estimate of the project:

"To the Honorable Speaker and House of Representatives of the Island of St. John. Gentlemen. Agreeable to your Order I have looked over the several Acts of Assembly put into my possession. Some of them I am told have expired and others yet remain in the hands of Individuals—Add to these circumstances their being wrote in different Hands renders it difficult to ascertain with exactness the number of pages—But I suppose the whole may be comprised in One hundred and twenty (or thirty) Sheets (Foolscap Folio) I have therefore to propose that I will print Five hundred Copies (on a new Type if possible) of the Acts and Journals for Fifty Shillings per Sheet exclusive of paper, receipts for which I shall lay before your Honorable House to make appear that I charge no profit on that article. [signed:] James Robertson."

On Feb. 21, 1788, the Assembly begged the lieutenant-governor "to order Mr. Robertson to print five hundred copies [of the Laws] as soon as possible" postponing consideration of payment till its next session. But there is little evidence of the number of copies and cost of the work actually published. The government's casual records indicate a total of £294 8*s*. 9*d*. paid Robertson and his journeyman, William Rind, Dec. 15, 1788 to Sept. 17, 1790, for salary and for unspecified printing work. Attorney-General Callbeck received £40 for services and expenses, and Solicitor-General Aplin, £30 for services in revising these laws.—St. John Is., As. *Journal.* Probably started early in 1788, the printing of the *Acts* was completed by Dec. 23, 1789, when Lieut.-Gov. Fanning sent a copy to Stephen Cottrell, London.

Copies located: GBLP (in B.T. 6/56: 835-1087); NNHi.

620. ST. JOHN, ISLAND OF. LIEUTENANT-GOVERNOR, 1786-1804 (*Fanning*)

G [royal arms] R / BY HIS EXCELLENCY / EDMUND FANNING, LL.D. / Lieutenant-Governor and Commander in Chief in and over his Majesty's Island / ST. JOHN, and the Territories adjacent thereunto, Chancellor of the same, / &c.&c.&c. / A Proclamation. / <Text> / GIVEN . . . at Charlotte-Town, Island of / St. John . . . this 24th Day of JULY . . . 1789, / . . . / EDMUND FANNING. / BY HIS EXCELLENCY'S COMMAND, / THOMAS DESBRISAY, Secretary. / GOD SAVE THE KING. /

Broadside: 31 lines; type-page: 50.4 × 31 cm. *Printed at Charlottetown, Island of St. John, by James Robertson, 1789.*

Text: "Whereas it is apprehended from the short harvests of the last year, that Persons, Inhabitants of this Island, employed in the Fisheries upon this coast, may suffer great Distress for want of Bread, Flour and Indian corn: I have therefore thought fit, in this Case of public Emergency . . . to issue this Proclamation, hereby allowing the Importation . . . from the Countries belonging to the United States of America, of Bread, Flour and Indian Corn . . . by British Subjects, in British Ships owned by his Majesty's Subjects" etc. by licence, from Sept. 1, 1789 till Jan. 1, 1790.

Copy located: GBLP (in C.O. 226/12: 415).

621. STERNS, JONATHAN, *d.* 1798, *and* TAYLOR, WILLIAM

[double rule] / THE / REPLY / OF / Messrs. STERNS & TAYLOR, / TO THE / ANSWERS / GIVEN BY THE / JUDGES of the SUPREME COURT of NOVA SCOTIA, / TO / THE FACTS BY THEM RELATED, / WHEN SUMMONED / Before the HOUSE of ASSEMBLY of that PROVINCE, in Committee, / FOR THE PURPOSE OF / Investigating the Official Conduct of the said Judges. / [double rule] / [? *London or Halifax, N.S., 1789.*]

4to. A-P[2]; 59 p.; type-page: 20 × 13.5 cm.

Contents: p. [1], t.-p.; p. [2], blank; p. [3]-36, Reply, etc., signed by J. Sterns; p. 37-54, Mr. Taylor's Reply, signed by W. Taylor, No. 38 Frith Street, Soho, Sept. 25, 1789; p. 55-59, Appendix of supporting documents; p. 59, verso, blank.

Without place or date of publication, this work was printed either in Halifax, by John Howe, or, more likely, in London, in 1789, where the text was prepared. A copy (in the Public Record Office, London) was enclosed in a letter to Lord Grenville from Sterns and Taylor, dated London, Sept. 23, 1789.

Copies located: GBLP (in C.O. 217/61: 263-320); MBAt.

622. WARD, *Sergeant*

[Handbill for Mrs. Ward's Scouring Business]

This slight but significant entry appears in Neilson's accounts:

"1789, Aug. 7. Printed for Sergeant Ward of 24th Regt. 200 Handbills for his Wife's setting up the Scouring Business. by Agreement 6/."

—Can.P.A., *Neilson papers*, v. 70.

Copy located: None.

623. AGRICULTURAL SOCIETY IN CANADA. QUEBEC BRANCH

PAPERS / AND / LETTERS / ON / AGRICULTURE, / Recommended to the Attention of the Canadian Farmers, / BY / The Agricultural Society in Canada. / [double rule] / [printer's ornament] / [double rule] / QUEBEC: / Printed by SAMUEL NEILSON, N° 3 Mountain-street. M.DCC.XC / [title within double rule frame.]

French t.-p.: PAPIERS / ET / LETTRES / SUR / L'AGRICULTURE, / Recommandés à l'Attention des Cultivateurs Canadiens. / PAR / La Société d'Agriculture en Canada. / [double rules] / [printer's ornament] / [double rule] / A QUEBEC: / Chez SAMUEL NEILSON, N° 3 Rue la Montagne. M. DCC. XC. / [title within double rule frame.]

8vo. [A][8], B-[E][4], G-K[4]; 2 p. l., ii [i.e. iv], 34 [i.e. 68] p.; type-page: 17.3 × 10.3 cm. Text in English and French on opposite pages numbered in duplicate.

Contents: p. l. 1 recto, English t.-p.; verso, blank; p. l. 2 recto, French t.-p.; verso, blank; recto of p. i (English), blank; p. i-ii, Introduction; verso of p. ii,

(French) blank; recto of p. 1 (English), blank; p. 1, Original plan for establishing an agricultural society, Quebec, Feb. 22, 1789; p. 2-4, Circular, lists of subscribers, resolves of Quebec branch, Apr. 6, 1789; p. 4-34, Papers, correspondence, etc., on wheat, gypsum as fertilizer, hemp culture; verso of p. 34 (French), blank.

Neilson recorded the cost of this publication:

"1790, July 23. Printed for the Agricultural Society 1200 copies being vol. I for 1789 of Papers and Letters on Agriculture, making 5 sheets of Demy in Long Primer Type at 40/ for the first hundred, and 10/ for each subsequent hundred per Sheet— £37.10.
Binding or stitching ditto @ 2½*d*.— £12.10.
Binding 6 ditto in morocco gilt @ 8/8— £ 2.13.4.
Transcribing from the Minutes and translating ditto—£ 5.10.
[Total]— £58. 3.4."

—Can.P.A., *Neilson papers*, v. 70.

The section on gypsum (p. 9-17) was reprinted in *On the effects of gypsum or plaster of paris as a manure chiefly extracted from Papers . . . by the Agricultural society in Canada* (19 p., 8vo., London, 1791). The entire work was reprinted in French only: *Papiers et lettres sur l'agriculture recommandés à l'attention des cultivateurs canadiens par la Société d'agriculture en Canada, imprimés en 1789* (56 p., 8vo., [Quebec], 1882).

T.-p. facsim. in Toronto Public Library, *Bibliography of Canadiana:* no. 616.

Copies located: CaOOA (all before p. 3 wanting); CaOT; CaQM; CaQMJ; CaQMS; CaQQH; CaQQL (this copy has engraved front entitled "Method recommended for preparing Hemp in Canada"); Ketcheson; MBAt; NN; RPJ; Witton.

624. [AGRICULTURAL SOCIETY OF NEW BRUNSWICK]

[Plan of an institution for the encouragement and improvement of agriculture in the province of New Brunswick.]

? Broadside. ? *Printed at Saint John, N.B., 1790.* An account of the organization of an agricultural society in New Brunswick, dated Saint John, Aug. 3, [1790], appeared in the *Quebec herald,* Thurs., Sept. 16, 1790. It contained *Plan of an institution* [etc. as above] the constitution, list of subscribers, Lieut.-Gov. Carleton's letter of approbation, dated May 24, 1790, and a minute of the first meeting, June 2, 1790. The latter included a resolution "that 200 copies of the Plan together with His Excellency the Lieutenant Governor's letter approving the same, be printed and circulated throughout the province; that Hon. G. G. Ludlow, Robert Parker and Elias Hardy, Esquires, be requested to superintend such publication and circulation, also to prefix to the said Plan, an introductory letter." Whether the *Plan* [etc.] was actually printed as resolved does not appear.

Copy located: None.

625. ALMANACS. NEW BRUNSWICK

[An Almanac for 1791. ? *Printed at Saint John, N.B., by Christopher Sower, or by Christopher Sower & John Ryan.*]

12mo. The only copy located is incomplete, comprising: sig. A_{2-4}, B-D^4, i.e. p. [3-32]; type-page: 15.1 × 8.7 cm. in single rule frame. In this fragment there is no title or imprint but the calendar includes the daily time of high water at the city of Saint John, N.B., and its tables closely resemble in typography and information those in *An Astronomical diary or almanack for . . . 1786*, printed at Saint John, N.B., by Christopher Sower.

This fragment contains: p. [3-4], Zodiac, eclipses; p. [5], Table of the periods of the planets; p. [6-7], Computation of the number of people in the world; p. [8-31], Calendar for 1791; p. [32], An astronomical chart.

Copy located: CaOOA (bound with John Ryan's *British almanack for 1790*, and Sower and Ryan's *British American almanack for 1792*, each piece labelled: The Delancy-Robinson Collection).

626. ALMANACS. NEW BRUNSWICK

THE / BRITISH AMERICAN / ALMANACK, / AND / Astronomical Ephemeris, / [rule] / For the Year of our LORD CHRIST 1790. / Being the Second after BESSEXTILE [sic] or LEAP YEAR. / [rule] / Containing the Common Notes, Fasts, Feasts of the Church, the / Rising and Setting of the Sun, Moon and Principal fixed Stars, the / Moon's Place, Moon's Age, time of High Water, besides more / Calculations and other Matter never published in an Almanack. / [rule] / BY ABRAHAM ZAGUSTUS, A.P. / [rule] / JOVE saw the Heavens, fram'd in a little Glass; / [11 lines of verse] / [double rule] / St. JOHN. / Printed by JOHN RYAN, at his Printing Office, No. 58, Prince / William Street. MDCCXC. / [title and each page within ornamental frame.]

12mo. [36] p. type-page: 15.5 × 9.5 cm.

Contents: p. [1], t.-p.; p. [2], Zodiac; p. [3-4], Eclipses, etc.; p. [5-16], Calendar; p. [17-18], Table of distances from Saint John, N.B.; p. [19-21], Remarkable occurrences, 449-1782 A.D.; p. [22-24], Table of interest, coin weights, etc.; p. [25-26], Province of New Brunswick, officers of government; p. [26-27], City of Saint John officials; p. [27-31], County boundaries and magistrates; p. [31-32], Army and Navy list; p. [33-36], Tables of time, currency, expences, coin values.

Copy located: CaOOA (p. [11-14] wanting).

627. ALMANACS. NOVA SCOTIA

AN / ALMANACK, / For the Year of our LORD, 1791; / . . . / CALCULATED FOR THE MERIDIAN OF / HALIFAX, IN NOVA SCOTIA / . . . / CONTAINING / THE ECLIPSES [etc, 7 lines in 1 col.] / LIST of PROVINCIAL OFFICERS [etc., 7 lines in 2 parallel col.] / WITH EVERY OTHER MATTER USEFUL OR NECESSARY. / [rule] / BY THEOPHRASTUS. / [rule] / The Sun, still running round his yearly race, / shews all the seasons turn'd by constant cause, / By certain order rul'd, and steady laws. / Lucretius. / [rule] / HALIFAX: / Printed and Sold by JOHN HOWE, at his Printing-Office, Corner of / BARRINGTON and SACKVILLE-STREETS. / [title within double rule frame].

12mo. [16 + ?] p.; type-page: 16 × 9.2 cm.

Contents: The only copy located is a fragment of sixteen pages comprising: p. [1], t.-p.; p. [2-3], Zodiac, Directions to farmers, Ephemeris; p. [4], Eclipses; p. [5-16], Calendar. The contents listed upon the t.-p. indicate that this almanac included also: "Sittings of the courts, list of provincial officers, officers of the navy on this station, officers of the army under General Ogilvie, officers of the navy yard and hospital [etc.]."

This almanac was advertised: "This day is published and to be sold by John Howe, An Almanack for . . . 1791," a brief notice in Anthony Henry's newspaper the *Royal gazette*, Halifax, N.S., Nov. 16, 1790, *et seq.*, following a detailed description of the *Nova-Scotia calender* published by Henry.

Copy located: CaNsHA (incomplete).

628. ALMANACS. NOVA SCOTIA

Wood block t.-p.: Der / Neuschottländische / Calender, / Auf das Jahr Christi / 1791. / Welches ein Gemeines Jahr von 365 / Tagen ist / [double rule] / Halifax, gedruckt bey Anth. Henrich. / [title in German letter type set in a medallion within a wide border of woodcut figures, printed from the same block as No. 503.]

t.-p. in type:

Der / Neu-Schottländische / CALENDER, / Auf das Jahr, nach der heilbringenden Geburt / unsers HErrn JEsu Cdristi [sic], / 1791. / Welches ein Gemeines Jahr von 365 Tagen ist. / Darinnen [etc., contents listed in 8 lines, practically the same as in No. 503] / [rule] / Zum Viertenmahl herausgegeben. / [double rule] / HALIFAX, / Gedruckt und zu haben bey Anthon Henrich, in der Sackville-Strasse. /

4to. A-E[4]; [40] p.; type-page: 18.3 × 14.1 cm. Most of the text is printed in 2 col., German letter throughout.

Contents: p. [1], Wood-cut t.-p.; p. [2], Notable events [etc.]; p. [3], t.-p.; p. [4-6], Royal families in Europe; p. [7], Key to signs of zodiac, etc.; p. [8-32], Monthly calendar on versos, moon's phases, court sessions, tales and recipes on rectos; p. [32-34], Recipe and verse; p. [34-37], Nova Scotia civil list, etc.; p. [38], Zodiac; p. [39-40], Verse, etc., distances to farms, etc., between Halifax and Annapolis, buoys in Halifax harbour.

This almanac was advertised in Anthony Henry's newspaper: "Just published and to be had of the printer, The German Almanack for the Year of our Lord, 1791."
—*Royal gazette*, Halifax, N.S., Nov. 30, 1790.

Copy located: DLC.

629. ALMANACS. NOVA SCOTIA

THE / NOVA-SCOTIA CALENDER, / OR AN / ALMANACK. / FOR THE YEAR OF THE CHRISTIAN ÆRA / 1791. / . . . / . . . / . . . / . . . / WHEREIN IS CONTAINED / The Eclipses . . . / . . . / . . . / . . . / [rule] / Calculated for the Meridian of HALIFAX . . . / . . . / . . . / . . . /

By METONICUS. / [rule] / [verse, 10 lines, signed:] / METON. / [ornamental rule] / HALIFAX: / Printed and Sold by ANTHONY HENRY, at his Printing-Office in / Sackville Street, corner of Grafton Street. / [title within double rule frame.]

8vo. [32] p.; type-page: 17 × 10 cm.

Contents: p. [1], t.-p.; p. [2], Zodiac; p. [3], Vulgar notes; p. [4], Eclipses; p. [5-16], Calendar; p. [17], Ephemeris; p. [18-23], Nova Scotia administration, legislature, courts [etc.]; p. [23-24], Naval and army officers in Nova Scotia; p. [25], Fire company of Halifax, etc.; p. [26-28], Tables of measures; p. [29-30], Chronology; p. [31], Coin tables; p. [32], Recipes, distances, etc.

This almanac was advertised: "Just published and to be sold by Anthony Henry, The Nova-Scotia Almanack [etc.]."—*Royal gazette*, Halifax, N.S., Nov. 16, 1790.

Copies located: CaNsHA; CaNsWA.

630. ALMANACS. QUEBEC

ALMANACH / DE / QUEBEC, / POUR / l'ANNEE / 1791. / [double rule / [printer's ornament] / [double rule] / A QUEBEC: / CHEZ SAMUEL NEILSON, / N° 3 RUE LA MONTAGNE. /

English t.-p.:

THE / QUEBEC / ALMANACK / FOR / The Year 1791. / [rule] / [printer's ornament] / [double rule] / QUEBEC: / Printed by Samuel Neilson, / N° 3 MOUNTAIN STREET. / [ornamental frame]

12mo. A-H^6; 1 p. l., [2]-94 p., fold map; type-page: 10.8 × 6 cm. even numbers on rectos.

Contents: p. l., recto, blank; verso, English t.-p.; p. [2], French t.-p.; p. [3-32], Epochs, etc., Calendrier; p. 33-74, Liste civile, les milices, l'état écclésiastique, la poste, les arpenteurs, notaires, docteurs; p. 75-82, Du chanvre; p. 82-85, Société d'agriculture, Société de feu; p. 86-90, Extrait des lettres patentes 19 Fev. 1788; p. 90-94, Connétables etc.; p. 94 verso, blank.

This almanac is mainly in French, the epochs and calendar are in both languages, the English militia, clergy and schools, in English only. The paper on hemp culture (p. 75-82) and regulations on fees (p. 86-90) are special features in this year's almanac.

The map, 23 × 39 cm., folded and inserted preceding t.-p., bears title: "A new map of Canada or Province of Quebec—Nouvelle Carte du Canada ou Province de Québec"; this title is framed in the legend: "For the Quebec Pocket Almanack for the Year 1791. M. Létourneau Sculpt. J. Baillargé Red^t." The map shows rivers, lakes, and towns; locates and names Indian tribes from Detroit eastward; the hills, lakes, and coastline are shaded. This seems to be the first map drawn and engraved in Canada. Neilson paid Michel Létourneau £6 10*s.* on Jan. 10, 1791, "for the amount of his account of work till this day." One François Letourneaux, engraver, 18 Buade St. appears in MacKay's *Directory for Quebec 1790* (No. 650).

The almanac was published Dec. 30, 1790 with, also without, the map, printed on common, also on fine, paper, to sell at 1*s.* 8*d.*, 2*s.*, or 2*s.* 6*d.* the copy. It was advertised in the *Quebec gazette* from Jan. 6, 1791.

Copies located (with map): CaQQAr. *Copies located (without map)*: CaNsWA; CaOOA; CaQMC; CaQMS; CaQN; CaQQA (p. 92-94 wanting).

631. ALMANACS. QUEBEC

[The British Gentleman's Pocket Almanack and General Register for the Year of our Lord M.DCC.XCI. *Quebec, Wm. Moore, 1790.*]

8vo. 56 p. *Printed at Quebec by Wm. Moore, 1789,* this almanac was announced from time to time, in a lively sales campaign in his newspaper:

"The British Gentleman's Pocket almanac and General Register for the Year of our Lord M.DCC.XCI. Containing the Calendar [etc., detailed contents given as in No. 578B], Provincial Register [etc.], British Lists, [etc.]. Printed in small 8vo. on a fine paper with new types, 56 pages. Price, stitched plain 2/; in marble, interleaved with writing paper, 2/6 . . . With considerable Provincial additions."

—*Quebec herald,* Nov. 25, 1790.

"The British Gentleman's Pocket Almanack [etc. as above]. The disposition of the Register will be entirely new arranged and the useful offices and officers in their proper district or circle. The lists are considerably enlarged and carefully collected from the various offices . . . Will be published December 27, [etc.]."

—*ibid.,* Dec. 9, 1790.

This advertisement, appearing in each issue of the *Herald,* was soon amended: "The Military list is taken from the list of the army to Feb. 1790 . . . [the Almanack is] to be ready January 4 at noon." On Dec. 30, 1790—"Publication [is] deferred a few days." Finally on Jan. 6, 1791, with appropriate prominence, the British Gentleman's Pocket Almanac was announced "Ready for Sale."

Copy located: None.

632. ALMANACS. QUEBEC

CALENDRIER pour l'Année 1791, pour Québec, par les $306^{d.}$ $30^{m.}$ de Longitude, et $46^{d.}$ $55^{m.}$ de Latitude. / [double rule] /

Colophon: QUEBEC: chez SAMUEL NEILSON, N° 3 Rue la Montagne. /

Broadside: type-page: 53.8 × 39 cm.

Contents: Calendrier in ornamental rule frame: 41 × 39 cm.; below Calendrier printed in 4 col.: Idées sur l'astronomie et la mesure du temps.

This sheet almanac was advertised as "just published" in the *Quebec gazette,* Nov. 28, 1790. On Dec. 1 Neilson sent 62 dozen copies up the River, including 40 dozen to his agent Sarreau, in Montreal, at 5*s.* the dozen; single copies were sold at 9*d.*

Copy located: CaO (bound in *Quebec gazette* at end of 1790); CaOOA (bound in *Quebec gazette,* at beginning of 1791, cropped below calendar tables).

633. ALMANACS. QUEBEC

[Calendrier pour Montréal pour l'Année 1791.]

Broadside: This sheet almanac like *Calendrier pour Montréal* of preceding years, was undoubtedly *printed at Montreal by Fleury Mesplet,* this one in 1790 (though the date of imprint may appear the same as in title). It was advertised: "Le Calendrier de Montréal pour l'Année 1791, à vendre chez François Sareau, rue Notre Dame, et chez l'Imprimeur."—*Montreal gazette,* Dec. 16, 1790.

The *Calendrier . . . 1791*, was cited in a letter to the bishop of Quebec, signed by "Agricola," Montreal, Dec. 19, 1790, and published in the *Montreal gazette*, Dec. 23, 1790. Agricola pointed out the excessive number of religious fêtes to be observed in Quebec, according to the *Calendrier* and respectfully suggested that, as these were a source of brigandage and horrors in the country districts of the diocese, the bishop revise the list and abolish some of the fêtes (cf. No. 707).

Copy located: None.

634. ALMANACS. QUEBEC

[Moore's English Sheet Almanack for the year 1791. *Quebec, Wm. Moore, 1790.*]

Broadside: *printed at Quebec by Wm. Moore, 1790,* who announced publication for Dec. 18, then advertised in his newspaper: "For Sale, Different parts of the Country will be Supplied by this Post, Moore's English Sheet Almanack, with the Planets and several useful Lists and Tables. Price 9d."

—*Quebec herald*, Dec. 23, 1790.

Copy located: None.

635. BAILLY DE MESSEIN, CHARLES FRANCOIS, *bp. of Capsa*, 1740-1794

[double rule] / COPY of the LETTER / OF / The Bishop of Capsa, Coadjutor of Quebec, &c. / To / The President of the Committee on Education, &c. / [rule] / Doctrinam magis, quam aurum eligite. / [rule] / Prefer Knowledge to choice Gold—Prov. Chap. VIII. / [double rule] / COPIE de la LETTRE / DE / L'Evêque de Capsa Coadjuteur de Québec, &c. / AU / Président du Comité sur l'Education, &c. / [rule] / Doctrinam magis, quam aurum eligite. / [rule] / Préferez la Doctrine à l'Or.—Proverbe de Saloman, Chap. VIII. / [double rule] /

4to. A-C^4; 1 p. l., 10. [i.e. 20] p.; type-page: 15.4 × 9.2 cm. Text in English and French on opposite pages numbered in duplicate. *Printed at Quebec, by Samuel Neilson, 1790*, as recorded:

"1790, Oct. 8. Printed for C. F. De Lanaudiere, 300 copies of the Bishop of Capsa's Letter to the Committee on Education, he to pay for the 1st

hundred (by agreement)—	£5.
the remaining 2 hundred @ £2. 10—	£5.
Binding 300 @ 1d.—	£1. 5. 0
Total:	£11. 5. 0

Agreed to sell the above on my own account."

—Can.P.A., *Neilson papers*, v. 70.

Cancel slips (blank) appear in *some* of the copies located, pasted over a footnote on p. 6. The footnote thus cancelled, reads: "Bishop Briand alone has received upwards of sixty thousand Livres and continues to receive annually five thousand Livres from His Majesty [also in French]."

Contents: p. l. recto, t.-p.; verso, blank; recto of p. [1] (English), blank; p. [1]-10, Letter, signed: "Charles François de Capse, Coadjutor of Quebec, Pointe aux Trembles, 5th April, 1790; verso of p. 10 (French), blank."

This letter supports the government's project to establish a non-denominational college in the province and controverts Bishop Hubert's objections thereto in the Catholic interest (*see* No. 669). The educational project came to nought, and Bailly de Messein's advocacy of it increased the antagonism between bishop and coadjutor bishop.

Born in Montreal and educated in Paris, Bailly de Messein was ordained priest at Montreal, Mar. 10, 1767. He served as missionary to the Acadians, as professor of rhetoric at the Séminaire de Québec, and, 1778-82, as tutor to Gov. Carleton's children. Yielding in 1788 to Bishop Hubert's request for a coadjutor *cum futura successione*, Carleton, then Lord Dorchester, suggested Bailly de Messein, as the appointee. In the spring of 1790, the coadjutor began attacking the bishop's ecclesiastical policies in the *Quebec gazette;* the clergy, however, rallied behind the bishop. The latter reported later that Bailly de Messein repented his insubordination and repudiated the activities of 1790, on his death bed in June, 1794, for he did not live to succeed to the episcopacy.

Advertised as "just published" in the *Quebec gazette*, Oct. 14, 1790, this work was sold briskly by the printer at 1*s*. 3*d*. the copy.

The text of this letter (in French only) is in Têtu and Gagnon: *Mandements de Québec*, 2: 398-409 with related documents. Other MSS. on the subject in Archives de l'Archevêché de Québec, are calendared in Quebec, Provincial Archives, *Inventaire de la correspondence de Mgr J.-F. Hubert . . . et de M C. F. Bailly de Messein* in *Rapport de l'Archiviste de la province de Québec pour 1930-1931*, 199-351 (*see* p. 222 *et seq.*).

T.-p. facsim. in Gagnon: *Essai de bibliographie canadienne* 1: no. 988.

Copies located: CaO (2 cop.); CaOOA; CaOT; CaQ (p. 4-6 supplied in MS.); CaQM; CaQMJ; CaQMS; CaQQL; GBLP (in C.O. 42/21, Apr. 5, 1790); MBAt; MHi.

636. CHURCH OF SCOTLAND. CATECHISMS

[The Shorter Catechism, composed by the Reverend Assembly of Divines.]

Printed at Quebec by Wm. Moore, 1790, this work, was advertised: "In the Press, and will be published in the course of a month, The Shorter Catechism, composed by the Reverend Assembly of Divines [i.e. the Westminster Assembly]. The above work is printing from the true copy as now used in Scotland. Those who may chuse to be supplied, may have them, single at 9d., a dozen at 7/6, by fifties at 28/, by the hundred at 50/. Orders taken by . . . Mr. Mathews [at] William Henry, (at whose desire they are published) [etc.]."—*Quebec herald*, Aug. 16, 1790.

Subsequent advertisements in the *Herald* indicate that this work was issued by Moore on Aug. 31, 1790.

Copy located: None.

637. FITZGERALD, WILLIAM MOONEY, 1763-1789, and CLARK, JOHN, *ca.* 1763-1789

[The Last words, dying Speech and Confession, Birth, Parentage and Education, Life, Character and Behaviour of Wm. Mooney Fitzgerald and John Clark, who were executed on Friday the 18th Day of December, 1789.]

8vo. 28 p. *Printed at Saint John, N.B., by Christopher Sower, 1790?* This work was advertised:

"Just published and may be had of the Printer hereof [Christopher Sower], The Last words, dying Speech and Confession, Birth, Parentage and Education, Life, Character and Behaviour of Wm. Mooney Fitzgerald and John Clark, who were executed on Friday the 18th Day of December, 1789, for feloniously and burglariously breaking into the house of Mr. William Knutton, of the City of Saint John in the Province of New Brunswick, in the night between the 18th and 19th of October, 1789. Being a plain narrative faithfully taken from the Mouths of the said William Mooney Fitzgerald and John Clark, while under Sentence of Death in the Cells of condemned Prisoners in the Jail of Saint John. Comprised in 28 Pages, Octavo. May also be had at Maugerville of Israel Perley, Esq. [etc.]."—*Royal gazette*, Saint John, N.B., Mar. 9, 1790 (earliest copy seen, after date of the execution).

The editor of *The Last words* "faithfully taken from the Mouths of" the condemned men, was probably Charles William Milton, who wrote: *Narrative of the gracious dealings of God in the conversion of W. Mooney Fitzgerald and John Clark two malefactors, who were executed on Friday, Dec. 18, 1789, at St. John's, New Brunswick, Nova Scotia, for burglary; in a letter from the Reverend Mr. Milton to the Right Honourable the Countess Dowager of Huntingdon* (22 p., 12mo., London, 1790). *See* Toronto Public Library, *Bibliography of Canadiana*, no. 619.

Copy located: None.

638. GREAT BRITAIN. POST OFFICE

GENERAL / INSTRUCTIONS / FOR / Deputy Post Masters. / [rule] / [royal arms] / [rule] / QUEBEC: / PRINTED BY WILLIAM MOORE, / AT THE HERALD PRINTING OFFICE. /

8vo. [*-2*][4]; 16 p.; type-page: 16 × 9 cm.

Contents: p. [i], t.-p.; p. [ii], blank; p. [iii]-iv, General instructions, form of oath; p. 5-16, Detailed directions concerning custody, receiving, despatching, delivering, and franking mail, also quotations from 9 Anne, c. 10, 7 Geo. III, c. 25, etc., on penalties for infringement of British postal regulations.

Postal service in Canada at this time was a branch, not of the provincial governments, but of the Post Master General's department in London. This work was probably printed for Hugh Finlay, deputy postmaster-general in Canada, sometime between 1788 and 1793. The only copy located bears MS. inscription "1790?"

Copy located: CaQMS.

639. HUBERT, JEAN FRANCOIS, *bp. of Quebec*, 1739-1797

LETTRE CIRCULAIRE A MESSIEURES LES CURÉS. / <Text> / QUEBEC, 25 Mars, 1790. /

Broadside, 16 lines, type-page: 12 × 12 cm. 130 copies *printed at Quebec by Samuel Neilson, 1790.* (*See* No. 660 *note*, quotation from Neilson's records.)

The text (signed in MS. by Bishop Hubert) instructs parish clergy to assist the government in collecting information for use in a map of the province. It is reprinted in Têtu and Gagnon: *Mandements de Québec*, 2: 398.

Copy located: CaQQL.

640. HUBERT, JEAN FRANCOIS, *bp. of Quebec*, 1739-1797

[Lettre Circulaire à Messieurs les Curés <Text> Jean François, Evêque de Québec. Québec, 7 août, 1790.]

Broadside? *Printed at Quebec by Samuel Neilson, 1790,* as recorded:

"1790, Aug. 9. Printed for Lord Dorchester's Secretary's office, 150 Circular Letters to the curates, on quarto post gilt—£1."

—Can.P.A., *Neilson papers*, v. 70.

The text recommends the clergy to support the government's effort to raise militia for local defence. It was written by Bishop Hubert and printed for the government to circulate with its General Orders of July 22, 1790 (No. 652). It is reprinted in Têtu and Gagnon: *Mandements de Québec*, 2: 432.

Copy located: None.

641. INGLIS, CHARLES, *bp. of Nova Scotia*, 1734-1816

A / CHARGE / DELIVERED TO THE / CLERGY / OF THE / Province of QUEBEC, / AT THE / PRIMARY VISITATION / HOLDEN IN THE CITY OF QUEBEC, / IN THE MONTH OF AUGUST 1789. / [rule] / BY / THE RIGHT REVEREND CHARLES, / BISHOP of NOVA SCOTIA. / [double rule] / HALIFAX: / Printed by ANTHONY HENRY; Printer to the King' [sic] / Most Excellent Majesty. / MDCCLXC [sic]. /

8vo. A-L[4]; 87 p.; type-page: 15.5 × 9 cm. Also issued in large paper copies, printed from the same type in 4to format.

Contents: p. [1], t.-p.; p. [2], blank; p. 3-4, Letter "To the reverend clergy of Quebec," dated Halifax, Dec. 30, 1789; p. 5-39, Charge; p. 40-58, Appendix No. I-II, addressed to Bishop Inglis and his replies etc., on visits to Charlottetown (Island of St. John), Montreal and Quebec, May 23-Aug. 10, 1789; p. 59-85, No. III, List of books for a clergyman's library; p. 86-87, No. IV, Academy near Windsor, Feb. 2, 1790; p. 87, Errata; verso of p. 87, blank.

Inglis, the loyalist rector of Trinity church, New York, 1777-83, was consecrated, Aug. 12, 1787, bishop of Nova Scotia, the first colonial bishopric. By a separate patent, Aug. 13, 1787, he was given jurisdiction over Quebec, New Brunswick, and Newfoundland. In this, his first visitation, he travelled some thousand miles, he states, and his clergy, who had known no bishop nearer than London, came, some of them 400 miles, to hear his charge. He recommended the exemplary clerical life: devotion to duty, close conformity to traditional liturgy, the study of theology and avoidance of atheistic attitudes such as Hobbes's, Shaftesbury's, Hume's, and Gibbon's. He advised simple sermons, pointing a clear moral, attention to youth and assiduous visiting of parishioners.

The list of 139 essential books for young clergymen is a revelation of the intellectual interests of the loyalist clergy. It explicitly excludes all writers tainted with infidelity (atheism), enthusiasm (evangelism), and democracy. Bishop Inglis's list contains few names which still live in the history of 18th-century thought.

Copies located: CaNsHD, 8vo.; CaOT, 8vo.; RPJ, 4to.

642. LEBRUN DE DUPLESSIS, JEAN BAPTISTE, 1739?-1807

Caption title: (1) / [double ornamental rule] / MÉMOIRE / ABRÉGÉ / OU Exposition justificative du cas de JEAN-BAPTISTE / LEBRUN, de la Paroisse de St. Sulpice, dans le / District de Montréal. / Vera redit facies; assimulata perit. / PETR. SATYR. Cap. 80. /

Colophon p. [16]: [ornamental rule] / A MONTRÉAL; / Chez FLEURY MESPLET, Imprimeur. / [rule] / 1790. /

8vo. [*]-**[4]; 16 p.; type-page: 17.5 × 8.3 cm.

Contents: p. 1-16, Mémoire, signed at end by J. B. Lebrun. This purports to refute calumnious gossip that Le Brun had stolen money from Sieur Jean Ducondud, chirurgeon, in Sept., 1789, and had abused his notarial office in 1768-69 by misappropriating funds. It includes certifications of his character by Francis Maseres, attorney-general in Quebec, 1766-69, and by others.

Le Brun came to Canada with the French army before 1760, and acted as attorney and notary under French and English régimes. In 1769, however, his notarial commission was withdrawn by Gov. Carleton. A fiery controversialist in a small provincial society alive with feuds, Le Brun distinguished himself by his use of the press to confound personal and legal enemies. His eloquent vilification of Jean Claude Panet in the *Quebec gazette*, 1767-69, enlivens the columns of that circumspect journal. This *Mémoire* is more restrained in style and somewhat obscure in its allusions. Two of the author's grandchildren established literary reputations in Canada during the 19th century—Julia Beckwith Hart in fiction, and Abbé Ferland in historical writings. *See* J. E. Roy: *Histoire du notariat au Canada* (4 v., Levis, 1895-1902), 2: 22-26.

Copies located: CaOOA; CaQQL (2 cop.).

643. [McMURRAY, WILLIAM]

[Two Poems, First poem entitled: Labrador; Second Poem entitled: Advice to a New Married Lady.]

4to. 16 p. *Printed at Quebec by Wm. Moore, 1790,* this work was advertised: "Proposals for printing by subscription two poems written at Labrador, by Mr. William McMurray, Mariner, who was unfortunately drowned, and has left a widow and two children. 1st Poem entitled LABRADOR. Being a descriptive daily instructor how to dispose of time to the best advantage in the various businesses on that coast during the year; it is well wrote and the language would not discredit any of our most celebrated Poets, being chaste and harmonious. It contains as many lines as there are days in the year. SPECIMEN:

"The Winter o'er, the birds their voices tune,
To welcome in the genial month of June;
Love crowds with feather'd tribes each barren isle
On all creation nature seems to smile.

"2d. Poem entitled ADVICE TO A NEW MARRIED LADY, by the same Author. SPECIMEN:

"Be frugal plenty round you seen,
And always keep the golden mean,
Be always clean but seldom fine
Plain in your neatness always shine;
If once fair decency be fled
Love soon departs the nuptial bed."

To be printed in quarto demy, on large new types, 16 pages stitched. Price to subscribers 1*s.* 6*d.* To be put to press as soon as one hundred copies are subscribed. "The public are entreated to favour this publication it being meant to assist the widow and fatherless [etc.]."—*Quebec herald,* Apr. 12, 1789.

And again: "This day is published and for Sale [by Wm. Moore] Two Poems [etc.]."—*ibid.*, May 10, 1790.

Copy located: None.

644. NEW BRUNSWICK. HOUSE OF ASSEMBLY

JOURNAL / OF THE / VOTES and PROCEEDINGS / OF THE / HOUSE OF ASSEMBLY / OF THE / PROVINCE of NEW-BRUNSWICK: / From Tuesday the 6th to Saturday the 24th of OCTOBER 1789. / [ornamental rule] / [royal arms] / [ornamental rule] / ST. JOHN: / Printed by CHRISTOPHER SOWER, Printer to the / KING'S MOST EXCELLENT MAJESTY. / [title within a frame of flower pieces.]

fo. [*[1], A]-F[2]; 1 p. l., [144]-66 p., fold table; type-page: 24 × 14 cm. Even numbers on recto, odd numbers on verso, paged in continuation of No. 559.

Contents: p. l. recto, t.-p.; verso, blank; p. [144]-66, Journal of fourth session of first assembly; p. 166 verso, blank; fold. table inserted correctly between p. 155-56; Summary of duties, from July 1, 1788 to Sept. 30, 1789.

Two hundred copies of the *Journal* and of the *Acts* (No. 645) of this session were ordered printed. And at the same time it was resolved that the governor be asked to pay the printer's bill when presented, the House guaranteeing the sum in next year's supplies—N.B. As. *Journal,* Oct. 24, 1789. This relieved the printer of the real hardship of waiting for his money till the House had met again, perhaps a year later, and passed his account.

This was the first session's printing done by Sower since 1786. A warrant for his payment was issued June 19, 1790: "To pay to Christopher Sower, Esq., the Sum of £31.17.8, for printing the Acts and Journals of the House of Assembly in the last session."—N.B. As. *Papers, 1794.* The charge was distinctly lower than that of previous sessions, and, as the government's free distribution list (and hence the size of edition) was not decreased, Sower apparently cut his rate to get the Assembly's work again.

Copies located: CaN (t.-p. wanting); CaNU; CaOOA; GBLP (in C.O. 188/4: 139-63); RPJ.

645. NEW BRUNSWICK. LAWS, STATUTES, *etc.*

ACTS / OF THE / GENERAL ASSEMBLY, / OF / His MAJESTY'S PROVINCE / OF / NEW-BRUNSWICK, / PASSED IN THE YEAR 1789. / [ornamental rule] / [royal arms] / [ornamental rule] / ST. JOHN: / Printed by CHRISTOPHER SOWER, PRINTER to the / KING'S MOST EXCELLENT MAJESTY. / [rule] / MDCCXC. / [title within frame of flower pieces]

fo. [*^{2}, A-E^2]; 3 p. l., 180-196 p.; type-page: 25 × 14 cm. Even numbers on recto, odd numbers on verso; paged in continuation of No. 560; p. 180 mispaged: 280 in some copies.

Contents: p. l. 1 recto, t.-p.; verso, blank; p. l. 2 recto, half title; verso, blank; p. l. 3 recto, Titles of the acts; verso, blank; p. 180-196, 29 Geo. III c. I-IX acts passed in the fourth session of the first assembly; p. 196 verso, blank.

Probably printed in an edition of 200 copies, most of which were distributed by the government within the province.

Copies located: Baxter; CaOOA; GBLP (in B.T. 6/56: 227-49); MH; NNB; NNHi.

646. NOVA SCOTIA. HOUSE OF ASSEMBLY

[double rule] / THE / HUMBLE PETITION / OF THE / HOUSE OF REPRESENTATIVES / OF THE / Province of NOVA SCOTIA, of the Session of the / General Assembly of Year 1790, / TO THE KING'S MOST EXCELLENT MAJESTY; / TOGETHER WITH / The ARTICLES of IMPEACHMENT exhibited by the HOUSE, / against ISAAC DESCHAMPS and JAMES BRENTON, / Esquires, Justices of his Majesty's Supreme Court for the said Province. / [double rule] / [*?London, or Halifax, N.S., 1790-1792.*]

4to. [*]^1, A-D^2; 2 p. l., [3]-16 p.; type-page: 19 × 13.5 cm.

Contents: p. l. 1 recto, t.-p.; verso, blank; p. l. 2 recto-verso, Introduction by Wm. Taylor; p. [3]-4, The humble petition, dated House of Assembly, Apr. 8, 1790; p. 5-15, Articles exhibited against Deschamps and Brenton, signed: "Rich. John Uniacke, Speaker"; p. 16, Summary of proceedings (apparently by Wm. Taylor), signed: "Richd J^{no} Uniacke, Speaker."

Without indication of place or date of printing, and similar in appearance to Sterns's and Taylor's *Reply* (No. 621), this work *may have been published in Halifax, N.S., by John Howe in 1790; or in London, 1791-92* for circulation among English officials. The Assembly's charges of Dec. 1, 1787 being dismissed by Lieut.-Gov. Parr, Mar. 12, 1789, the House formally impeached the judges in Mar., 1790. The matter was referred to the Privy Council for hearing in London, 1791, whither Major Barclay, Jonathan Sterns and Foster Hutchinson were sent to represent the Assembly's interest. The Privy Council dismissed the case before June 6, 1792.

Copy located: MBAt.

647. NOVA SCOTIA. HOUSE OF ASSEMBLY

Caption title: [Journal and Proceedings of the House of Assembly, of the Province of Nova-Scotia.]

Note: title above is not transcribed from copy.

fo. A-W²; 88 p. *Printed at Halifax, N.S., by Anthony Henry, 1790.*

Contents: Journal and proceedings of the fifth session of the sixth assembly, Feb. 25-Apr. 21, 1790.

The "Journals and Proceedings of the House of Assembly . . . now sitting" was published week by week in Henry's newspaper, the *Royal gazette*, Mar. 9, *et seq.* This was exceptional, however, for of preceding and succeeding sessions, only formal opening (and closing) speeches and the acts passed, were published in the newspapers.

Copies located: CaNs; GBLP (in C.O. 217/62: 193-280).

648. NOVA SCOTIA. LAWS, STATUTES, *etc.*

Running title: [rule] / 1790. Anno Tricessimo Regis GEORGII III. CAP. I[-X]. / [rule] /

Caption title: At the GENERAL ASSEMBLY of this Province / of Nova-Scotia, . . . / [8 lines] / . . . being the Fourth [sic] Session / of the Sixth General Assembly, convened / in the said Province. / [rule] /

fo. sig. 3B-3C², 3D¹; p. 273-282 [!]; type-page: 25 × 15 cm. paged in continuation of No. 523, repeating the pagination of No. 600. *Printed at Halifax, N.S., by Anthony Henry, 1790.*

Contents: p. 273-282 [!], Cap. I-X, perpetual acts passed in the fifth session of the sixth assembly, Feb. 25-Apr. 21, 1790.

Copies located: CaO; DLC; MH.

649. NOVA SCOTIA. LAWS, STATUTES, *etc.*

Running title: [rule] / 1790. Anno Tricessimo Regis, GEORGII III. CAP. I[-V]. / [rule] /

Caption title: At the GENERAL ASSEMBLY of this Province / of Nova-Scotia, . . . / [8 lines] / . . . being the Fourth [sic] Session / of the Sixth General Assembly, convened / in the said Province. / [rule] /

fo. sig. 3F-3H², I¹; p. 289-302; type-page: 25.5 × 15 cm. paged in continuation of No. 600, in error for No. 601, this work repeats (approximately) the pagination of No. 524. The erroneous sequence was continued in the two following years, then corrected in No. 847. *Printed at Halifax, N.S., by Anthony Henry, 1790.*

Contents: p. 289-302, Cap. I-V, temporary acts passed in the fifth session of the sixth assembly, Feb. 25-Apr. 21, 1790.

Copies located: CaNsHA; CaO; MH; NNB.

650. QUEBEC, *City*. DIRECTORY

THE / DIRECTORY / FOR THE / City and Suburbs of Quebec. / CONTAINING, / [col. 1:] The names of the house / keepers, / Their various avocations, / whether in civil or mi-/litary stations. / Streets of residence, / Number, / Proprietors, / [in col. 2:] Members of the Honble. / Legislative Council, / Magistrates, / Subscribers to the Fire Society, / Officers of British Mili-/tia, / Constables, &c.&c. / [rule] / TO WHICH ARE ADDED THE / FIRE ENGINES WITH THEIR HOUSES OF DEPOSITE [sic], / ALSO THE / PRESENT COMMITTEE. / [rule] / Collected by HUGH MACKAY, A.O.S. / TO BE CONTINUED ANNUALLY. / [rule] / HERALD PRINTING-OFFICE: 1790. /

8vo. A-G[4]; vi, [3]-52 p.; type-page: 13 × 6.5 cm. One leaf of sig. A is folded around sig. B-G to become p. [51]-52; p. [51] mispaged: 52.

Contents: p. [i], t.-p.; p. [ii], blank; p. [iii]-v, Dedication, etc.; p. vi, Explanations; p. [3]-50, Directory; p. 50-52, Fire engines, Errata.

The preliminary matter (excepting t.-p.) is printed in English then French. The directory lists householders, A-Y, with name and address in English or French, occupation in both languages, and membership in Council, etc., indicated by an ingenious system of symbols. The dedication by MacKay to the "Justices of the Peace for the City & District of Quebec [states:] The public office I have the pleasure to be in, I am indebted to you for: In methodizing that business I was led into the thought of compiling the following pages, which I believe to be of great utility." —p. [iii].

MacKay, who held a succession of minor official posts under municipal and provincial governments of Quebec, was employed to make "a roll of all male inhabitants in the Parish of Quebec from 16 to 19, and from 19 years upwards," as part of the Legislative Council's census project of 1790. And "having acquired sufficient knowledge of the Inhabitants in the City and Suburbs of Quebec" he compiled this "Director" as he termed it. It was published by subscription at 1*s*. (fine paper) or 9*d*. (coarse paper) the copy, and issued Sept. 22, 1790, according to advertisements in *Quebec herald*, Aug. 16-Oct. 11, 1790. The printer, Wm. Moore, incidentally, was the compiler's son-in-law, having married "the amiable Miss Agnes M'Kay" on Mar. 11, 1790.

Though an incomplete guide to Quebecois of 1790, the *Directory* affords an interesting view of their occupations. It includes several periwig-makers, a perfumer, a painter of likenesses, shop-keepers, and numerous day-labourers; connected with the printing trade are two printers, two journeymen printers, a "taylor & book-binder," an engraver, and a translator.

The *Directory* was revised and reprinted in 1791 (No. 718).

Copies located: CaQMS (p. [51]-52 mutilated and partly supplied in MS.); CaQQL (p. 47-48 supplied in MS., p. 49-52 in photostat). Another copy? not located.

651. QUEBEC, *City*. SEMINAIRE DE QUEBEC

THÈSES / DE / MATHÉMATIQUE / ET DE / PHYSIQUE, / QUI SERONT SOUTENUES / AU / SÉMINAIRE DE QUÉBEC, / MARDI 5

Octobre, depuis 9 heures du matin, / jusqu'à 3 après midi. / [rule] / Par M.M.—[6 names in 1 col.:] MICHEL BRUNET, JEROME RAIZENNE, AUGUSTIN CHABOILLEZ, DENYS DENECHAU, LOUIS BEDARD, EUSTACHE DUMONT, } [3 words in 1 col:] ETUDIANS EN PHYSIQUE, / [rule] / SOUS / Mr. EDMUND BURKE, PRETRE, / Professeur de PHILOSPHIE. /

Colophon, within frame on verso of t.-p.: CHEZ / S. NEILSON, / Rue la Montagne /

8vo. [A]-C^2; 1 p. l., 10 p.; type-page: 16 × 12.3 cm.

Contents: p. l. recto, t.-p.; verso, colophon; p. [1]-10, Thèses, comprising propositions 1-112, under headings: La géometrie, La trigonometrie, etc., Le calcul, La mécanique, etc., L'optique, L'astronomie, sustained Oct. 5.*

Rev. Edmund Burke, 1753-1820, born in Ireland and educated at the University of Paris, came to Canada in 1786 to teach at the Séminaire de Québec. He completed his second course of instruction in philosophy, mathematics, and astronomy in 1790, with the production of the present *Thèses*. Shortly afterwards he left Quebec, going to the Upper Country as a missionary, later to Nova Scotia to organize Catholic educational and religious work there.

The printer apparently used odds and ends of paper stock for this little pamphlet. For, though the type-page is set in quarto proportions, it is printed in two of the copies located, in 8vo., the paper having chain lines running vertically and the water mark at the top of the inner margin. Another copy has folio post paper, the chain marks vertical and the water mark central upon the page.

Copies located: CaQM; CaQMS; CaQQL (2 cop. dated in MS. 1790). Another? copy not located, but recorded in Gerald E. Hart sale, Boston, Apr. 15-19, 1890, item no. 2162 "richly bound in full morocco mosaic inlay gilt edges by Lemieux [of Quebec]."

652. QUEBEC, *Province.* ADJUTANT-GENERAL'S OFFICE

GENERAL ORDERS / for the Militia of the / Province of Quebec. / [rule] / —22D. JULY, 1790.— / [rule] / ORDRE du Quartier-/General de Quebec pour la / Milice de la Province. / [endorsed title, printed lengthwise with the page and enclosed in ornamental frame on recto of *l.*]1

fo. 2 *l.* text in English and French. *Printed at Quebec by Samuel Neilson, 1790,* as recorded:

> "1790, Aug. 9. Printed for Lord Dorchester's Secretary's Office 300 General Orders for militia. 1 Sheet Superfine foolscap.—£2.10."
>
> —Can.P.A., *Neilson papers*, v. 70.

Contents: l. 1 recto, title (as above); verso, English text; *l.* 2 recto, French text; verso, blank. The text, signed: "By His Excellency's Command, Fra. Le Maitre, F. Baby, A.G. [Adjutant general]" contains orders for provincial defence by local militia, in case the regular forces are withdrawn from Quebec for war with Spain. Armed conflict was apprehended at this time, in a dispute resulting from Spanish

*1790, when Oct. 5 fell on a Tuesday.

seizure in 1789, of British trading vessels in Nootka Sound—settled by the Nootka Convention, Oct. 28, 1790.

General Orders is reprinted with Bishop Hubert's circular prepared to accompany it, in Têtu and Gagnon: *Mandements de Québec,* 2: 432-35.

Copies located: CaQQL; GBLP (in C.O. 42/67: 25-27).

653. QUEBEC, *Province.* CITIZENS

[L'Humble Adresse des Anciens et Nouveaux Sujets, Habitans de la Province de Québec, au Roi sa Tres Excellente Majesté, aux Lords et Communes de la Grande-Bretagne etc.]

Broadside: paper-page: 30 × 53 cm. *Probably printed at Quebec by Wm. Moore about 1790.*

Contents: Adresse, or petition, with heading as above, a preamble, and fourteen points in prayer of petition, and summary dated: "Québec, 24 Novembre, 1784." Appended are printed names of numerous signatories.

This is another edition of the so-called Reform Committee's petition in No. 453, q.v. It was probably reprinted at this time to impress English-Canadian mercantile opinion upon British authorities engaged in preparation of the Canada or Constitutional Act. References to the petition in the *Quebec herald* in 1790 suggest that the *Herald's* printer, Wm. Moore, may have printed this edition of *L'Humble adresse.*

Copy located: GBLP (C.O. 42/70: 255. This copy was enclosed in Gov. Dorchester's despatch No. 61, from Quebec, Oct. 24, 1790, to Lord Grenville in London).

654. QUEBEC, *Province.* COURT OF QUARTER SESSIONS OF THE PEACE (Montreal District)

[Des Réglemens de Police pour la ville de Montréal.]

? *Printed at Quebec by Samuel Neilson, 1790.* This title is included in a list of books advertised as "Printed and for sale at the Printing Office of the Quebec Gazette." No English edition is mentioned, the title appearing only in the French section of the list, which bears the caption: "also for sale by Mr. Saro, Montreal." —*Quebec gazette,* Nov.-Dec., 1790. "Mr. Saro" was François Sarreau, Neilson's agent in Montreal. This work was not advertised in the *Montreal gazette* during 1790. Its content was probably similar to police regulations published from time to time for the Quebec district. Commissioners or justices of the peace were empowered by provincial ordinance to make and enforce police regulations in the districts of Quebec, Montreal, and later of Trois Rivières.

Copy located: None.

655. QUEBEC, *Province.* LAWS, STATUTES, *etc.*

[A Bill (Not yet Passed) Proposed as an addition to the Act, intitled, "an Act or Ordinance Further to regulate the Inland Commerce of this Province, and to extend the same," passed in the twenty-eighth year of His Majesty's Reign.

French title at head of col. 2: Bill (non encor passé) Proposé comme un ajoute à l'Acte intitulé, "Acte ou Ordonnance qui regle plus amplement le Commerce Intérieur de cette Province et qui l'etend" passé dans la vingt-huitieme année de Regne de sa Majesté.]*

Broadside: Text in 2 col. English and French. *Printed at Quebec by Samuel Neilson, 1790* (between Feb. 22, when it was ordered printed and Mar. 16, when a printed copy was submitted in Council).

This bill provided for free importation from Vermont of pig and bar iron and blocks of lead, and for extension to inland customs of regulations for the sea port customs. It was prepared following a Council committee's report, Feb. 22, 1790, upon a memorial of Stephen Keyes and Jabez Gale Fitch, Vermont traders. The memorial states that similar conditions in Quebec and Vermont, their isolation "covered with deep snow and almost insufferable Frost six months of the year," demanded an exchange of commodities; and that if products of Vermont were admitted to Quebec, "British manufactures sent to Vermont through Quebec would render the inhabitants entire consumers of British manufactures and thereby increase the Commerce of this Province."—Can.P.A., Que. *State*, Feb. 22, 1790.

Hotly contested in Council, this bill was passed with amendment and a suspending clause, to become 30 Geo. III c. 2.

Copy located: GBLP (in C.O. 42/12: 607).

656. QUEBEC, *Province.* LAWS, STATUTES, *etc.*

[Draught of a Bill for the Creation of a District and Courts of Justice at Three Rivers, and to provide for the better arrangement of the Sittings of the Court of Common Pleas there and at Quebec and Montreal.]

In English and French, *probably printed at Quebec by Samuel Neilson, 1790*, this draught of a bill was ordered "printed in both Languages," Feb. 22, 1790. The "Bill printed" was included in addenda to documents before the Legislative Council on Mar. 16, 1790. It became a statute as 30 Geo. III c. 5.—Can.P.A., Que. *State*, 1790.

Copy located: None.

657. QUEBEC, *Province.* LAWS, STATUTES, *etc.*

[Anno tricesimo Georgii tertii Regis. Chap. I An Act or Ordinance, to amend the Ordinance entitled "An Ordinance for regulating the Pilotage in the River St. Lawrence, and for preventing abuses in the Port of Quebec."

French side:

. . . Chap. I Acte ou Ordonnance, Qui amende l'Ordonnance intitulée, "Ordonnance qui régle le Pilotage dans le Fleuve St. Laurent et qui empêche les abus dans le Port de Québec."]

*Title taken from the transcript in Can.P.A. "Q" of the only printed copy located.

4to. 2 *l.*? Text in English and French. *Printed at Quebec by Samuel Neilson, 1790*, as recorded:

"1790, Apr. 29. Printed for Council Office (by Order of Mr. Williams) 500 Copies of Ordinance Chap. I @ 5/ [per] 100, making ½ Sheet Crown—£1.5. Folding Ditto—5/."

—Can.P.A., *Neilson papers*, v. 70.

This ordinance is reprinted in Can.P.A., *Report, 1914-15*.

Copy located: None.

658. QUEBEC, *Province.* LAWS, STATUTES, *etc.*

[Anno tricesimo Georgii tertii Regis. Chap. II. An Act or Ordinance in Addition to an Act intitled "An Act or Ordinance further to regulate the Inland Commerce of this Province" etc.

French side:

. . . Chap. II. Acte ou Ordonnance, Qui ajoute à l'Acte intitulée, "Acte ou Ordonnance qui regle plus amplement le Commerce Intérieur de cette Province, et qui l'Étend" etc.]

4to. 2 *l.*? Text in English and French. *Printed at Quebec by Samuel Neilson, 1790*, as recorded:

"1790, Apr. 29. Printed for Council Office (by Order of Mr. Williams) 500 Copies of Ordinance chap. 2, 3, & 4, making ½ Sheet Crown, @ 5/ per 100—£1.5.
Folding Ditto—5/."

—Can.P.A., *Neilson papers*, v. 70.

Contents: 30 Geo. III c. 2 (as above); 30 Geo. III c. 3, An Act . . . for securing more effectually the toll of the bridge over the River St. Charles near Quebec; (also in French); 30 Geo. III c. 4. An Act for preventing cattle going at large; (also in French).

These ordinances are reprinted in Can.P.A., *Report, 1914-15*.

Copy located: None.

659. QUEBEC, *Province.* LAWS, STATUTES, *etc.*

[Anno tricesimo Georgii tertii Regis. Chap. v. An Act or Ordinance to form a new district between the Districts of Quebec and Montreal and to regulate the said Districts.

French side:

. . . Chap. v. Acte ou Ordonnance Qui érige un nouveau District entre les Districts de Québec et de Montréal, et qui regle les dits Districts.]

4to. 20 p.? Text in English and French. *Printed at Quebec by Samuel Neilson, 1790*, as recorded:

"1790. Apr. 29. Printed for the Council Office (by Order of Mr. Williams) 500 Copies of Ordinance Chap. 5, 6, 7, 8 & 9, making 2½ Sheets Crown —£3.15.

Folding Ditto—5/."

—Can.P.A., *Neilson papers*, v. 70.

Contents: 30 Geo. III c. 5 (as above); 30 Geo. III c. 6. An act to prevent the desertion of seamen from the merchant service; (also in French); 30 Geo. III c. 7. An Act to amend an act for preventing accidents by fire, etc.; (also in French); 30 Geo. III c. 8. An Act for the better preservation of the ancient French records; (also in French); 30 Geo. III c. 9. An Act to prevent for a limited time the exportation of biscuit, flour, wheat, etc. (also in French).

These ordinances are reprinted in Can.P.A., *Report, 1914-15*.

Copy located: None.

660. QUEBEC, *Province.* LAWS, STATUTES, *etc.*

[double rule] / Au Château Saint-Louis, dans la Ville de Quebec. / [rule] / PRESENT, / SON EXCELLENCE LE TRÉS HONORABLE / GUY LORD DORCHESTER, / EN CONSEIL,—22me Février, 1790. /

4to. [*]², [4] p.; type-page: 15.6 × 12 cm. *Printed at Quebec by Samuel Neilson, 1790.*

Contents: p. [1-2], Text, an order-in-council for the preparation by the surveyor-general, of a map of the province of Quebec (scale "six milles au pouce") and maps of the various districts of the province (scale "deux milles au pouce,") signed J. Williams; p. [3], blank; p. [4], endorsed title in a frame: Ordre de renvoi, de Son Excellence le Lord Dorchester, en conseil, le 22me Fevrier, 1790.

To assist in the preparation of these maps, a committee was appointed in Council, Feb. 22, 1790 (Hugh Finlay, chairman) to report a list of parishes, seigneuries, and land grants therein, also returns of all males in the province, 16 to 19 years, and of 19 years and over. The committee issued printed circulars and blanks with this order-in-council, to seigneurs, clergy, and militia officers, and from their (incomplete) returns, compiled the report presented to the governor-in-council, July 16, 1790.

—Can.P.A., Que. *State*, 1790.

There is no evidence that the maps were printed then or later (a MS. copy of the general map, scale: six miles to inch, is in Can.P.A. Map Collection). Some of the data collected therefor were used, however, in *Plan of a part of the province of Lower Canada from Montmorency . . . to St. Regis*, by Samuel Gale and John B. Duberger, 1794-95, printed in Doughty and McArthur: *Documents, 1791-1818*.

Neilson recorded the papers printed for the map project:

"1790, Mar. 31. Printed for Council Office (by order of Mr. Finlay, Chairman of a Committee of Council)

530 Copies of an Order of Reference of—22ᵈ February, 1790, 1 on a sheet 4to post gilt— 2 8 4

130 Copies of a circular Letter to the Curés by the Chairman (indorsed) 1 on a sheet of 4to post. 1 5

400 Copies of a Circular Letter to the Seigniors by the Chairman 1 on a sh. d° 2 6

130 formules de Rôles 1 on a sheet of superfine foolscap (indorsed) 1 15
130 Blank Rôles 1 on a sheet of superfine foolscap. 1 12 6
130 Circular Letters of Bishop to the Clergy—on quarto Post. 1 5
250 Circular Letters of the Adjutant General of Militia to the Officers of Militia, 1 on a sheet Sup. 4to post. 1 10

Extra Expences

11 quires Superfine foolscap to accompany the blank Rolls. 13 9
Folding and stitching do to the Rolls. 5
Cash paid A. Gosselin for folding and addressing Circular Letters to the Officers of Militia in the District of Montreal. 7 6
1 box Wafers, quills, &c. 1 9
[Total:] 13 4 4"

—Can.P.A., *Neilson papers*, v. 70.

Copies located (of Order-in-council only): CaOT; CaQMS.

661. QUEBEC, *Province.* LAWS, STATUTES, *etc.*

ORDINANCES / OF THE / PROVINCE OF QUEBEC: / Being a Selection of all the Laws and Regulations concerning / Pilots and the Navigation of the River St. Lawrence below / Montreal, or expressive of the Duties of Masters of Vessels / in the Ports of Quebec and Montreal. / [rule] / Extract of Ordinance Chap. I passed 12th. April, 1790. / "And that he (Captain of the Port) do deliver the same printed or in / "writing, and signed by him, to every such Master on his arrival in / "Port, if he be desirous thereof; for which the Master of the Port, or / "person so appointed may lawfully take and receive from every Ship- / "master, THE SUM OF FIVE SHILLINGS AND NO MORE." / [double rule] / [royal arms] / [double rule] / QUEBEC: / Printed by SAMUEL NEILSON, N° 3. Mountain-street. M.DCC.XC. / [title within double rule frame]

French t.-p.:

ORDONNANCES / DE LA / PROVINCE DE QUEBEC, / Contenant toutes les Loix et Réglemens concernant les Pilotes, / et la Navigation du Fleuve St. Laurent au-dessous de / Montréal, et les devoirs des Maitres de Vaisseaux dans les / Ports de Québec et de Montréal. / [rule] / Extrait de l'Ordonnance Chap. I. passée le 12 Avril, 1790. / "Et que le Capitaine de Port . . . / . . . / . . . / . . . / . . . / [double rule] / [ornament] / A QUEBEC: / Chez SAMUEL NEILSON, N° 3 Rue la Montagne. M.DCC.XC. /

8vo. A-C[4] D[2]; 2 p. l., 11[i.e. 22] p., 1 *l.*; type-page: 17.7 × 10 cm. Text in English and French on opposite pages numbered in duplicate.

Contents: p. l. 1 recto, English t.-p.; verso, blank; p. l. 2 recto, French t.-p., verso, blank; recto of p. [1] (English), blank; p. [1]-6, Pilotage: 28 Geo. III c. V; Art. I-XVI, 30 Geo. III c. I (section relating to pilotage); p. 6-10, Regulations for the port of Quebec: 17 Geo. III c. XIV, Art VIII, 28 Geo. III c. V, Art. XVII-XXIV, 30 Geo. III c. I (section relating to port of Quebec); p. 11, 30 Geo. III c. VI, An act to prevent the desertion of seamen from the merchant service; verso of p. 11 (French), blank; 1 *l.*, blank.

Neilson recorded the printing of this work:

"1790, June 30. Printed for James Frost, Capt. of the Port, 150 Copies of Ordinances concerning the Pilotage of the River St. Lawrence and the Port of Quebec, making 28 pages 8vo on fine Demy—£5.2.6.
Folding and Stitching ditto in boue paper—12/6
[Total] £5.15." —Can.P.A., *Neilson papers*, v. 70.

Copies located: CaQMS; PHi.

662. QUEBEC, *Province.* LAWS, STATUTES, *etc.*

ORDINANCES / OF THE / PROVINCE OF QUEBEC: / CONCERNING / THE MILITIA, QUARTERING TROOPS, AND TRANS-/PORT SERVICE. &c.&c.&c. / [double rule] / [royal arms] / [double rule] / QUEBEC: / Printed by SAMUEL NEILSON, N° 3. Mountain street. M.DCC.XC. /

French t.-p.:

ORDONNANCES / DE LA / PROVINCE DE QUEBEC, / CONCERNANT / LES MILICES, LE LOGEMENT DES TROUPES, ET / LES CORVE'ES. / [double rule] / [royal arms] / [double rule] / A QUEBEC: / Chez SAMUEL NEILSON, N° 3. Rue la Montagne. M.DCC.XC. / [double rule frame]

4to. A-I⁴, K²; 2 p. l., 35 [i.e. 70] p.; type-page: 15.3 × 12.3 cm. Text in English and French on opposite pages numbered in duplicate.

Contents: p. l. recto, English t.-p.; verso, blank; p. l. 2 recto, French t.-p.; verso, blank; recto of p. 1 (English), blank; p. 1-17, 27 Geo. III c. 2; p. 18-30, 27 Geo. III c. 3; p. 31-35, 29 Geo. III c. 4; verso of p. 35 (French), blank.

Neilson recorded the printing of this work:

"1790. July 23. Printed for Lord Dorchester's Secretary's Office 500 Copies of the Ordinances respecting the Militia, Quartering troops and the Transport Service on 4to Pott English type, with Brevier Notes, making 9½ Sheets at 27/6 [per] Sheet for the 1st hundred and 7/6 each subsequent 100—£27.6.3.
Folding stitching & covering ditto in blue paper £2.1.8.
[Total:] £29.7.11."
—Can.P.A., *Neilson papers*, v. 70.

Neilson also sold single copies at 1*s.* 3*d.*

The text of all three ordinances is reprinted in Can.P.A., *Report, 1914-15.*

Copies located: CaQMS; Ketcheson.

663. QUEBEC, *Province.* LEGISLATIVE COUNCIL

Caption title: [Second Addition to the Rules and Regulations for the Conduct of the Land Office Department.]

4to. 2 *l.* text in English and French; paper-page: 30.5 × 21.5 cm. *Printed at Quebec by Samuel Neilson, 1790.*

Contents: Preamble and rules 1-6, passed by the Council, Jan. 20, 1790. This is a supplement to *Rules and regulations* of Feb. 17, 1789, ordering a certain routine to be followed by district land boards in recording their transactions: in keeping a journal, petitions and minutes thereon, surveyors' returns, etc., in filing, storing and indexing the same, and transmitting duplicates to the governor-in-council.

Neilson recorded the printing of this and the two following publications:
"1790, Jan 30. Printed for the Council Office (by order of J. Williams)
500 Copies of 3[d] Addition to the Rules and Regulations of Land Office ½ Sheet Long P.—£2.5.0.
Cutting and folding ditto—5/
500 Copies of 2[d] Addition to the same ½ Sheet Crown Long Primer—£2.5.0.
Cutting and folding ditto—5/
500 Copies of the Report of the Committee on . . . Location &c.—£2.5.0.
Cutting and folding ditto—5/
[Total]—£7.10.0."—Can.P.A., *Neilson papers*, v. 70.

Second addition [*etc.*] is reprinted in Ontario Archives, *Report, 1905*.

Copy located: GBLP (in C.O. 42/67: 389).

Copies recorded but not located: Hodgins, no. 61, 98.

664. QUEBEC, *Province.* LEGISLATIVE COUNCIL

Caption title: [Third addition to the Rules and Regulations for the Conduct of the Land Office Department.]

Colophon: [Quebec: Printed by Samuel Neilson, N° 3 Mountain-street.]

4to. 2 *l.*; text in English and French; paper-page: 33 × 24 cm.

Contents: Preamble and regulations 1-7, passed by the Council Jan. 20, 1790. They authorized district land boards to execute the order of the governor-in-council of Oct. 22, 1788, for putting certain reduced officers upon an equal footing with those of the 84th Regiment. This order extended generally to officers, veterans of the American revolutionary war, settling in Quebec, who had improved those lands already granted them by royal instructions of 1783, 1787, or otherwise, grants of land on the scale promised as King's bounty, Apr. 3, 1775, to officers serving in Royal Highland Emigrants (84th) Regiment; i.e. to field officers 5,000 acres; captains 3,000; lieutenants 2,000 acres.

This publication was printed in an edition of 500 copies, Jan. 30, 1790. *See* No. 663 *note*.

It was reprinted in Ontario Archives, *Report, 1905*.

Copy located: GBLP (in C.O. 42/67: 391-92).

Copies recorded but not located: Hodgins, no. 61, 97.

665. QUEBEC, *Province.* LEGISLATIVE COUNCIL

Caption title: [Extract from a Report respecting Locations in Lunenburg &c.]

Colophon: [Quebec: Printed by S. Neilson.]

4to. [2] *l.*; text in English and French; paper-page: 30.5 × 23 cm. *Printed at Quebec, by Samuel Neilson, 1790,* in an edition of 500 copies as recorded in No. 663 *note.*

Contents: An extract from the Legislative Council minutes of Jan. 20, 1790, signed at end: "J. Williams, C.C." It includes preamble, supporting documents and committee's recommendations (signed: Jan. 12, 1790, Wm. Smith, chairman) on policy and procedures in granting lands north of Lake Ontario to Loyalists.

Copy located: GBLP (in C.O. 42/67: 393).

666. QUEBEC, *Province.* LEGISLATIVE COUNCIL

[A Bill, not yet passed, to have wind and screen Cribbles in Grist Mills for the cleaning of wheat.]

4to. 2 *l.*? Text in English and French. *Printed at Quebec by Samuel Neilson, 1790,* as recorded:

"1790, July 23. Printed for Council Office, 500 Copies of a Bill not yet passed concerning Cribbles, 1 on a ½ Sheet Crown at 21/ for the first hundred and 5/ for each subsequent hundred—£2.1.
Cutting and Folding ditto—5/."

—Can.P.A., *Neilson papers,* v. 70.

This bill was tabled in the 1790 and 1791 session of the Legislative Council, then disappeared.

Copy located: None.

667. QUEBEC, *Province.* LEGISLATIVE COUNCIL

EXTRACT / OF THE PROCEEDINGS / Of a Committee of the whole Council. / [rule] / Under the following Order of Reference relative to a Conversion / of the present Tenures in the Province of Quebec into that of / FREE AND COMMON SOCCAGE: Printed by Order of His Ex-/cellency the Governor in Council of the 20th. October, 1790, / for the Use of the Members of the Legislative Council. / [double rule] / [printer's ornament] / [double rule] / QUEBEC: / PRINTED BY SAMUEL NEILSON, N° 3 MOUNTAIN-STREET, M.DCC.XC. / [title within a double rule frame]

French t.-p.:

EXTRAIT / DES / Procédés d'un Commité de tout le Conseil, / En Vertu de l'Ordre de Référence qui suit, quant à un Changement / des présentes Tenures dans la Province de Québec, en FRANC ET / COMMUN SOCCAGE, Imprimé par l'Ordre de Son Excellence le Gou-/

verneur en Conseil, en date du 20 Octobre, 1790, pour l'Usage des / Membres du Conseil Législatif. / [double rule] / [printer's ornament] / [double rule] / A QUEBEC: / CHEZ SAMUEL NEILSON, N° 3 RUE LA MONTAGNE, M.DCC.XC. / [double rule frame]

4to. A-I[4], [*][1]; 2 p. l., 34[i.e. 68] p.; type-page: 16.1 × 12.3 cm. Text in English and French on opposite pages, numbered in duplicate.

Contents: p. l. 1 recto, English t.-p.; verso, blank; p. l. 2 recto, French t.-p.; verso, blank; recto of p. [1] (English), blank; p. [1]-34, Extract of the proceedings, etc.; verso of p. 34 (French), blank.

Neilson recorded the printing of this work:

"1790, Nov. 16. Printed for Council Office (by Order of J. Williams) 300 Copies of the Proceedings of a Committee . . . soccage. Making 9¼ Sheets 4to Crown in Pica Type at 32/6 for 1st hundred and 10/ each after per Sheet—£24.5.7½.
Binding ditto @ 2d. per Sheet—£2.10.0.
Cutting ditto—6 [shillings] [Total:] £27.1.7½."

—Can.P.A., *Neilson papers*, v. 70.

The printer sold copies retail from Nov. 11 [sic] at 2*s*. each.—*ibid*.

The Council was ordered Aug. 25, 1790, to investigate the relative advantages and disadvantages of the French seigniorial system of land tenure as used in Quebec, and the English freehold system; also to draft measures to implement a change to the latter if desirable. This *Extract* includes the surveyor- and solicitor-general's reports on lands granted and revenue collected under the seigniorial system; evidence of Charles de Lanaudière, a seigneur who favoured change to freehold; a bill framed by Chief-Justice Smith to effect change to freehold and Adam Mabane's dissent from the last.

Freehold tenure was urged by the English group to attract settlers (especially pro-British Americans) to new lands and to throw open old lands held en fief. General French-Canadian disapproval persuaded the Council to drop Smith's bill. Its essentials had been incorporated by Smith in a preliminary draft of the Constitutional Act in 1789. The final act, 31 Geo. III c. 31, provided for freehold tenure for future grants only. Lands held en fief in Quebec at this time remained so until the Seigniorial Act of 1854.

The French point of view was expressed by T. L. Bédard in his *Observations* (No. 699). The documents in this *Extract* are reprinted in: Canada, Governor-General, 1847-1854 (Elgin). *Titles and documents relative to seigniorial tenure, required by an Address of the Legislative assembly* [*Aug. 29*,] *1851* (216 p., 8vo., Quebec, 1851), 25-44.

Copies located: CaO (2 cop.); CaOOA (2 cop.); CaOT; CaQM; CaQMJ; CaQMS (2 cop.); CaQQL (2 cop.); GBLP (in C.O. 42/21 Oct. 20, 1790); Ketcheson; MH; PPL.

668. QUEBEC, *Province*. LEGISLATIVE COUNCIL. COMMITTEE APPOINTED TO REPORT LIST OF PARISHES, *etc*.

Formule, / Que Monsieur le Curé aura la bonté de suivre en composant le Rôle des Paroissiens / dans sa Paroisse, en conformité à l'Ordre de Renvoi de son Excellence le Lord Dorchester, en Conseil, le 22me. Février 1790, ci-joint. / [double rule] / Supposans la Paroisse de Beauport. / [double rule] / <Text>

fo. 2 *l.*; type-page: 25 × 15.3 cm. *Printed at Quebec by Samuel Neilson, 1790* (*see* No. 660 ***note***, fifth item in Neilson's record).

Contents: *l.* 1 recto, text in 33 lines, an example (based on the parish of Beauport and prepared for Finlay's committee by M. de Salabery, seigneur, and by the curé of Beauport) of the form to be followed in taking census of members of a parish; *l.* 1 verso,—*l.* 2 recto, blank; verso of *l.* 2, endorsed title in a frame: "Formule Que Monsieur le Curé aura la bonté de suivre en composant le Rôle des Paroissiens dans sa Paroisse. Cette Formule fait voir comment remplir les Blanc dans le Rôle qu'on vous a envoyé."

Copy located: CaOT.

669. QUEBEC, *Province.* LEGISLATIVE COUNCIL. COMMITTEE ON EDUCATION

REPORT / OF A / COMMITEE OF THE COUNCIL / ON THE SUBJECT OF / PROMOTING / The Means of Education. / [rule] / [printer's ornament] / [rule] / QUEBEC: / Printed by SAMUEL NEILSON, N° 3 in Mountain-Street. M.DCC.XC. / [title within double rule frame]

French t.-p..

RAPPORT / DU / COMMITE' DU CONSEIL, / SUR L'OBJET / D'AUGMENTER / Les Moiens d'Education. / [rule] / [printer's ornament] / [rule] / A QUEBEC: / Chez SAMUEL NEILSON, N° 3 Rue la Montagne. M.DCC.XC. / [title within double rule frame]

4to. A^4, B-C^2, D-H^4, $[I]^2$; 2 p. l., 26 [i.e. 52] p., 1 *l.*; type-page: 15.5-17 × 12.2 cm. Text in English and French on opposite pages numbered in duplicate. Through error in imposition of signature H, p. 22-24 appear in the following order (in Massachusetts Historical Society's copy): 22 (English), 23 (French), 24 (English), 22 (French), 23 (English), 24 (French). In most of the copies located p. 22 (French) is mispaged: 24; p. 24 (English): 22.

Contents: p. l. 1 recto, English t.-p.; verso, blank; p. l. 2 recto, French t.-p.; verso, covering letter, signed: "Quebec . . . 26th November, 1789, William Smith, Chairman"; recto of p. [1] (English), covering letter in French; p. [1]-26, Journal of a committee, etc.; p. 26, Order to print and distribute the report; verso of p. 26 (French), blank; 1 *l.* blank.

This *Report* was ordered by the Council "to be printed in both languages . . . and forwarded to all sheriffs" for distribution among magistrates and parish clergy, Dec. 24, 1789—p. 26.

The committee was appointed May 31, 1787, with Chief-Justice Wm. Smith as chairman, to ascertain the best method of improving educational facilities, the cost, and means of raising funds. The *Report* includes a questionnaire, with the bishop of Quebec's letter in answer (Nov. 18, 1789), and a plan prepared by Smith which the committee passed almost without change. Smith's plan recommended the establishment of free parish, or village, schools for elementary instruction, county schools for intermediate, and a non-denominational college at Quebec for students of liberal arts and sciences. The modest cost was to be defrayed from the Jesuits' estates which the government had appropriated but had devoted as yet, to no purpose. In answering the questionnaire the bishop of Quebec analysed and commended Catholic educational facilities of elementary and intermediate types. He opposed Smith's plan for a non-denominational college, proposing instead the establishment of a third classical college (supplementing the Séminaire de Québec in Quebec city, and the Séminaire de Saint-Sulpice in Montreal) to replace the disestablished Collège des Jésuites. He also suggested that funds from the Jesuit estates be devoted to the existing educational institutions under Catholic direction. Smith's plan, ostensibly designed to reconcile the viewpoints of English and French Canadians in their youth, never materialized.

Bishop Hubert's arguments were controverted by his coadjutor (*see* No. 635). The bishop's letter to the committee, with related material, is reprinted in Têtu and Gagnon: *Mandements de Québec*, 2: 385 *et seq.*

The publication of this *Report* is cited in the obituary of Simon Sanguinet as having induced him to bequeath funds to establish a university (*see* No. 737 *note*).
—*Quebec gazette*, Mar. 25, 1790.

Neilson recorded the printing of this work:

"1790, Feb. 27. Printed for government (by order of J. Williams) 600 Copies of a Report of Committee on . . . Education making 7 Sheets ½ Crown 4to in Pica at 32/6 for first 100 and 10/ ea. subsequent 100—£30.18.9.
Difference in price of Paper on 50 copies printed on fine paper—£1.
Binding at 2*d* each—£5. Cutting—10/
[Total:] £37.8.9."—Can.P.A., *Neilson papers*, v. 70.

Copies located: CaNsWA; CaO; CaOLU; CaOOA; CaQ; CaQM; CaQMS (2 cop.); CaQQL (2 cop.); Ketcheson; MBAt; MHi; MWA; RPJ (pagination correct).

670. QUEBEC, *Province*. LEGISLATIVE COUNCIL. COMMITTEE ON FINES

[double rule] / Committee-Chamber, Bishop's Palace, Quebec, 6th November 1790. / Sir, / <Text>

Broadside 36 lines; type-page: 23.5 × 19 cm. *Printed at Quebec, by Samuel Neilson, 1790,* as recorded:

"1790, Nov. 16. Printed for the Council Office, 150 letters from the President of a Committee on Fines, &c. One on a Sheet superfine folio Post —£1.17.6."—Can.P.A., *Neilson papers*, v. 70.

This letter was directed (name in MS.) to magistrates and notaries public and signed (in MS.) by Edward Harrison, chairman of the committee. The text states that by order-in-council of July 22, 1788, magistrates, etc., and notaries public were ordered to report fines, etc., collected in the last ten years, also *quints, lodes et ventes*, etc., during tenure; to pay the same to the receiver-general by Oct. 1, 1788, and to continue to do so half yearly. By this letter the committee, appointed May 17, 1790, "to make inquiry how far the said Order of the 22d of July 1788 has been complied with by the different Officers . . . required to furnish Estreats and Reports of the

Sums accrued to His Majesty, . . . calls upon You for the Reason why the said Order has not been complied with on your Part"; and orders answers to be sent to Jenkin Williams, clerk of council.

Like No. 266, this item represents the government's effort to encourage payment of seigniorial dues under laws not strictly enforced. *See* A. L. Burt: *Old province of Quebec* (Minneapolis, 1933), 471 *et seq.*

Copy located: CaOOA (in *Askin papers*, v. 31).

671. QUEBEC GAZETTE. CARRIER'S ADDRESS

VERSES / of the Printer's Boy / WHO CARRIES THE QUEBEC GAZETTE / To the Customers. / [rule] / JANUARY 1, 1791. /

French side:

ETRENNES / du Garçon qui porte la / GAZETTE DE QUEBEC / AUX PRATIQUES. / [rule] / Le 1er JANVIER, 1791. / [*Quebec, S. Neilson, 1790.*]

Broadside: type-page: 26 × 32 cm. English verse on left, 44 lines; French on right in 2 col. of 31 lines each. The English and French texts are quite different in content, the former more spirited, the latter following closely the conventional pattern of *Étrennes*. They begin:

"Since its freedom the press triumphant maintains,
And it quite the *ton* is, that all squeeze their brains;
Where, as in bad cheese, maggots swell into birth,
Which glow worms crawl out t'enlighten the earth."

French side:
"Pour me conformer à l'usage
Etabli depuis si longtemps
Je viens vous rendre mon hommage
Tel qu'on vous le rend tous les ans."

Carrier's addresses in English *or* French have been located for several previous years. Possibly they were published in both languages *separately* each year. But this is the first bilingual example of the genre located. Like the *Quebec almanack* for 1792, it shows Samuel Neilson's policy of equalizing the two languages, of presenting *both*, instead of only his own, French *or* English, to whoever could read in Quebec.

Copy located: CaO (bound in *Quebec gazette*, at end of 1790).

672. QUEBEC LIBRARY

[Additions to the Quebec library.]

? Broadside: *Printed at Quebec, by Samuel Neilson, 1790*, as recorded:

"1790, Oct. 8. Printed for the Quebec Library 25 Copies of the additions to ditto.—10/."

—Can.P.A., *Neilson papers*, v. 70.

This was, apparently, a supplement to the Library's printed catalogue of 1785.

Copy located: None.

673. ST. JOHN, ISLAND OF. HOUSE OF ASSEMBLY

[Address of the General Assembly to Lieutenant-Governor Fanning, 24 March, 1790.]

Broadside, paper-page: 30.5 × 20 cm. *Printed at Charlotte Town, by Wm. A. Rind, 1790.*

Copies located: GBLP (2 cop. in C.O. 226/13: 214; B.T. 6/50: 1102).

674. ST. JOHN, ISLAND OF. HOUSE OF ASSEMBLY

[Journal of the House of Assembly of His Majesty's Island of Saint John, Begun and Holden at Charlotte-Town, The Twenty-second Day of March, in the year of Our Lord, One Thousand Seven Hundred and Ninety. XXX George III. *Charlotte-Town: Printed by James Robertson, 1790.*]

4to. 1 p. l. 44p., 1 fold. table (accounts); paper-page: 25 × 20 cm.

Contents: p. l. recto, t.-p.; verso, blank; p. 1-44, Journal of the first session of the sixth Assembly, Mar. 22-Apr. 5, 1790.

Though it bears the imprint of Robertson, the work on this publication was evidently done by his journeyman and successor, William Alexander Rind. The latter presented a petition to the Council, Apr. 20, 1790, "praying some Compensation for his Extraordinary Trouble in printing the Journal of the Assembly *de die in diem* by order of the House, to be delivered to the Governor, Council and Members of the Assembly—the Board advise the sum of Five Pounds to be paid to Mr. Rind for his Trouble in the above Business."—Can.P.A., P.E.I. "B"8.

Copies located: GBLP (2 cop. in C.O. 226/13: 249-294; B.T. 6/56: 1121-1167).

675. ST. JOHN, ISLAND OF. HOUSE OF ASSEMBLY

[Journal of the House of Assembly of His Majesty's Island of Saint John. Begun and Holden at Charlotte Town, On the Tenth Day of November, 1790 Being the Second Session of the Sixth General Assembly convened in the said Island. Thirty First George the Third. *Charlotte Town: Printed by William A. Rind, 1790.*]

fo. 27 p.

Contents: t.-p.; Journal, Nov. 10-20, 1790.

Copies located: GBLP (2 cop. in C.O. 226/13: 521-547; B.T. 1/2 In-Letters).

676. ST. JOHN, ISLAND OF. LAWS, STATUTES, *etc.*

ACTS / PASSED AT THE / GENERAL ASSEMBLY / OF HIS MAJESTY'S / ISLAND OF SAINT JOHN, / BEGUN AND HOLDEN AT CHARLOTTE-TOWN, ON THE TWENTY SECOND DAY OF MARCH, ONE / THOUSAND SEVEN HUNDRED AND NINETY. / THIRTIETH GEORGE THE THIRD. / [rule] / [royal arms] / [rule] / [double rule] / CHARLOTTE-TOWN: PRINTED BY JAMES ROBERTSON, / 1790. /

4to. B-E^2; 1 p. l., 14 p.; type-page: 22 × 14.8 cm. One leaf of sig. E is folded around sig. B-D to form t.-p.

Contents: p. l. recto, t.-p.; verso, blank; p. [1]-14, 30 Geo. III c. 1-10, acts passed in the first session of the sixth Assembly, Mar. 22-Apr. 5, 1790.

Though bearing the imprint of Robertson, the *Acts*, like the Assembly *Journal* of the same session, were probably the work of William A. Rind. They were printed promptly after assent at the end of session, for Lieut.-Gov. Fanning transmitted a printed copy to the secretary of state, in his despatch of Apr. 21, 1790.

Copies located: GBLP (2 cop. in C.O. 226/13: 295-310; B.T. 6/56: 1105-1120); NNHi.

677. ST. JOHN, ISLAND OF. LIEUTENANT-GOVERNOR, 1786-1804 (*Fanning*)

[Speech of Lieutenant-Governor Fanning to both Houses of Assembly, 22 March, 1790.]

fo. 2 p. paper-page: 30.5 × 20 cm. *Printed at Charlotte Town, by Wm. A. Rind, 1790.*

This is the lieutenant-governor's address opening the first session of the sixth Assembly.

Copies located: GBLP (2 cop. in C.O. 226/13: 211; B.T. 6/56: 1099-1100).

678. ST. JOHN, ISLAND OF. LIEUTENANT-GOVERNOR, 1786-1804 (*Fanning*)

[His Excellency Lieutenant-Governor Fanning's Reply to the Address of the General Assembly, March 24, 1790.]

Broadside, paper-page: 30.5 × 20 cm. *Printed at Charlotte Town, by Wm. A. Rind, 1790.*

Copies located: GBLP (2 cop. in C.O. 226/13: 215; B.T. 6/56: 1103).

679. [TAYLOR, THOMAS]

Caption title: (1) / FOR PUBLIC INFORMATION. /

8vo. [*-2*]^4, 15 p.; type-page: 17.5 × 8 cm. *Printed at Montreal, by Fleury Mesplet, 1790.*

Contents: p. 1-15, Memorial of Thomas Taylor with supporting documents, dated at end of text: "Montreal, 4th September, 1790"; verso of p. 15, blank.

This publication closely resembles in its typography and arrangement, Lebrun's *Memoire*, bearing Mesplet's imprint. It was probably reprinted from the *Montreal gazette*, where the English text appeared, followed by a French translation (not included in the pamphlet), Sept. 16-Oct. 28, 1790.

The *Memorial* states: "If my case was the first instance of abuse experienced of Judges belonging to the courts of this Province, my impatience would be increased . . . I am suffering without a shadow of reason given to justify the sentence under which I am deprived of my liberty and refused the benefit of the Habeas Corpus Act [etc.]."

Thomas Taylor, a merchant, was arrested Aug. 14, 1790, for contempt in connection with a case of his brother, William, before the Court of Common Pleas in Montreal. His memorial and complaints against Judges John Fraser and Hertel de Rouville were presented to the governor-in-council, Nov. 15, 1790. They indicate the enmity between Montreal business men and these judges, also the absence of commonly accepted laws and procedure in courts throughout the province.

Copy located: CaQQL.

680. WALTER, JOHN, *et al.*

A / DEFENCE / PREPARED AND INTENDED TO BE DELIVERED AT THE / BAR / OF THE / Court of King's Bench, / HELD IN THE / CITY OF QUEBEC; / In the Month of November, 1790; on a prosecution for a / LIBEL. / AT THE INSTANCE OF / Henry Caldwell, Esquire, / WITH AN / INTRODUCTION, POETICAL ADDRESS, AND / APPENDIX. / [rule] / 'The worthy Colonel's passing worth, / 'The manner how he sallied forth, / 'The Major's virtues and his own / 'Are in the following pages shewn.' / HUDIBRAS. / [rule] / QUEBEC: / PRINTED BY WILLIAM MOORE: / AT THE / HERALD PRINTING-OFFICE. /

8vo. A-C^4, C-D^4, [E]^2; viii, 36 p.; type-page: 16.7 × 10.5 cm.

Contents: p. [i], t.-p.; p. [ii], blank; p. [iii]-vi, Introduction, signed at end: "John Walter, Geo. Irwin, John Jones, Quebec, 6th Dec. 1790"; p. vi, Indictment [explanation for omission of]; p. [vii]-viii, An Address to the Public; p. [1]-21, Defence, etc.; p. [22], blank; p. [23]-36, Appendix [supporting documents] No. I-XI; p. 36 at foot: Erratum.

Published Dec. 20, 1790, at 1*s*. 6*d*. the copy (*Quebec herald*, Nov. 18-Dec. 23, 1790), this pamphlet shows the flare up after the militia act of 1787, of the long standing antagonism between English civilians and the army in Quebec. John Walter, George Irwin, and John Jones, merchants, who had settled in Quebec since 1775, and who were refused commissions in the two new militia regiments of 1789, evaded duty in the ranks. Caldwell, attempting to enforce regulations through the courts, was lampooned in a series of derisive letters in the *Quebec herald*, July 8-Aug. 23, 1790. He instituted a suit for libel against the merchants and Wm. Moore, the printer, but the case did not come to trial as the jury refused to return a true bill. The prospective defendants, however, published their *Defense* anyway, as an exposure of the military attempting to exert unauthorized power over civilians.

Caldwell, born in Ireland in 1738, held a commission in the British army, 1757-73, served under Wolfe at Louisburg and Quebec 1758-59, and settled in Canada after its cession. He became commander of militia and later receiver-general of Lower Canada and was one of the largest landowners in the country. (*See* J. E. Roy: *Histoire de la Seigneurie de Lauzon*, 5 v., Levis, 1897-1904, 3: 261-66, on the Walter case).

Copies located: CaO (all before p. 5 defective, bound in *Brochures Canadiennes*, v. 105); MWA; Ketcheson.

681. WILLIAMS, EDWARD

THE / Ready Reckoner, / FOR THE / Province of Quebec, Nova-Scotia, / and the States of America: / Containing Easy Rules for converting the different / Currencies of Sterling, Army, Quebec or Halifax, / and the States of America into each other. / [rule] / CALCULATED BY / Major WILLIAMS, of the Royal Artillery. / [rule] / TO WHICH ARE ADDED A / A [sic] TABLE OF THE WEIGHT OF GOLD / COIN, / With its VALUE in Quebec or Halifax, reduced to / Dollars, Livres & Sous. / AND AN EASY / TABLE OF GRAINS FROM 1 TO 1000, / With their Sum in Quebec Currency. / [double rule] / Quebec: Printed by WM. MOORE, / AT THE / HERALD PRINTING-OFFICE, 1790. /

12mo. $[A]^2$, B-E^4; 33, [1] p., 1 *l.*; type-page: 13.5 × 8.5 cm. One leaf of sig. [A] is folded around sig. B-E to form blank leaf at end.

Contents: p. [1], t.-p.; p. [2], blank; p. [3]-33, Easy Rules, etc. [covering ten currencies]; p. [1] (verso of p. 33), Contents table; 1 *l.*, blank.

Advertised "Speedily will be published, price 9*d*." in the *Quebec herald* from Aug. 16, 1790, this work was issued Nov. 1-8, price 1*s*. Though the *Ready reckoner* had long been stock in trade of printers and merchants advertising books for sale, this appears to have been the first actually published in Canada. It was an essential aid in business as [New] York currency (8*s*. to the Spanish dollar) was the favoured medium of exchange in Montreal and westward, Halifax, N.S., currency (5*s*.) was used in Quebec, while Sterling and Army figured of necessity in government and military offices. Quebec currency (6*s*.) had been superseded as the provincial standard by Halifax in 1777. English, Spanish, and French coins circulated, at weights and ratings established by the provincial ordinance, 17 Geo. III c. 9.

Edward Williams was major from 1786 in the Royal Regiment of Artillery, of which the different battalions relieved each other in Canada from year to year. But it is not clear if, or when, Williams was stationed in Quebec.

Copy located: CaQMS.

682. [LES ACTES DES APOTRES]

[Two Treatises on Government. *Printed at Quebec by Samuel Neilson, 1791.*]

This is a reprint of articles (text in English and French): "Scheme of a Constitution," in *Quebec gazette*, Feb. 3-10, 1791, *Sup.*; and "Scheme of a Constitution displayed" in *Quebec gazette*, Feb. 10-24, 1791, *Sup.* The first article has a note at the head: "The following two Essays on Government are extracted from a late French publication entitled 'Les Actes des Apotres' " and also a note at the end: "To be continued in this Supplement to form a succession independent of the *gazette*." The "succession" was issued as a separate publication, for Neilson recorded:

> "1791, May 6. Sold to Lord Dorchester's Secretary's Office 2 Treatises on Government, 6 Copies @ 6*d* [per] copy—3/."
>
> —Can.P.A., *Neilson papers*, v. 70.

Copy located: None.

683. [ADDRESS TO THE HUSBANDMEN OF CANADA]

[Address to the Husbandmen of Canada. *Printed at Quebec by Samuel Neilson, 1791.*]

This is probably a reprint of an unsigned article of this title in the *Quebec gazette,* June 9, 1791, *Sup.* p. [1-5]. The latter, written in an easy style, apparently by an English protestant, resident in Quebec, is a defence of the Legislative Council's report recommending the adoption of freehold land tenure (*See* No. 667). It exposes the evils and hardship in Quebec resulting from the traditional French system of tenure *en fief,* and of the payment of tithes to the Catholic church. The reprint of this article was issued between June 9, 1791 and May 3, 1792, for it was advertised with "Provincial publications for sale at the Printing Office . . . on the Feudal Tenures."—*Quebec gazette,* May 3, 1792.

Copy located: None.

684. [ADVERTISEMENT FOR CLEANING CLOTHING]

ADVERTISEMENT. AVERTISSEMENT. / <Text> / Montreal, 19th July 1791. Montréal, 19 Juillet, 1791. /

Broadside: 16-17 lines, text in 2 col., English and French; type-page: 7.8 × 19 cm. *Probably printed at Montreal by Fleury Mesplet, 1791.*

English text: "A person lately arrived at Montreal, who has conducted the under-mentioned Business to the entire satisfaction of the Ladies and Gentlemen in Quebec undertakes to Clean LADIES RIDING DRESSES, and GENTLEMEN'S WEARING APPAREL in the most compleat manner, let the stains be of what nature soever.

"For the Direction of Strangers, the Advertiser has erected a sign of the Cross Keys by the Marsh almost opposite to the Flagstaff, . . . Any orders communicated . . . at that place, will be obeyed with the utmost Punctuality, and at the shortest Notice: Montreal, 19th July, 1791."

Copy located: CaOT (bound in *Montreal gazette,* Aug. 11, 1791).

685. AGRICULTURAL SOCIETY IN CANADA. *Montreal branch*

[Circulaire concernant la Culture de Chanvre, et L'Abandon des Animaux. 26 Juillet, 1791.]

fo. [3] p. Text in French, *probably printed at Montreal, by Fleury Mesplet, 1791.*

Contents: p. [1], a covering letter (signed: "John M'Kindlay, Séc. A Montréal, 26 Juillet, 1791"; addressed: "A Monsieur Monsieur [sic] [blank] Curé de la Paroisse de [blank],") begging co-operation of the clergy; p. [2], order-in-council to encourage hemp culture, dated: "2 Mars, 1790"; notice of free distribution of seed for hemp, signed: "Henry Motz, Québec, 14 Fevrier 1791" (same text as No. 721); p. [3], a covering letter, signed: "Pour les Directeurs, John M'Kindlay, Séc. A Montréal, le [blank filled in MS.: 26] Juillet 1791." This is a covering letter for "l'Abandon" as it was termed colloquially, i.e. "An ordinance to prevent cattle going at large," 30 Geo. III c. 2, copies of which were sent to the parish clergy for distribution.

The curé of the parish was the most effective means of disseminating information among habitants. But such notices as these were usually communicated through a *Lettre circulaire* by the bishop, occasionally by the governor, but rarely as here were the notices sent directly by an officer of a lay organization.

Copy located: CaQQL.

686. AGRICULTURAL SOCIETY IN CANADA. *Quebec branch*

[Circular letter respecting the Abandon.]

Broadside: text in French. *Printed at Quebec, by Samuel Neilson, 1791*, as recorded:

"1791, July 9, Printed for Agricultural Society 60 Circular Letters respecting the abandon. 1 on a Sheet, large quarto post.—£1.0.0
100 Circular letters respecting Hempseed together with Order in Council and Notice on a sheet superf. propatria, 2 pages—£1.12.6."
—Can.P.A. *Neilson papers*, v. 70.

Contents: The contents were probably a covering letter by the secretary of the Quebec branch of the Society, Hugh Finlay, similar to that on p. [3], of the circular issued by the Montreal branch (No. 685).

Copy located: None.

687. AGRICULTURAL SOCIETY IN CANADA. *Quebec branch*

[Circular letter respecting Hemp Seed.]

fo. [2] p., text in French. *Printed at Quebec, by Samuel Neilson, 1791*, in an edition of 100 copies as recorded in No. 686 *note*.

This was probably similar to the circular letter, etc., in the *Quebec gazette*, sup. July 14, 1791, *et seq.*, "Circulaire a M. M. les Curés des Paroisses de Campagne." It is a notice that the government's free hemp seed is ready for distribution at John Lee's in Quebec, to habitants recommended by the curés, and a request for curés to transmit to the Society a list of habitants who want to sow hemp and in what quantity, signed: "Hugh Finlay, Sécr. Par Ordre. A Québec, [blank] Juillet, 1791"; also order-in-council of Mar. 3, 1790, for encouragement of hemp culture, and "Culture du Chanvre," announcing free distribution of hemp seed in May, 1791, signed: "Henry Motz, Quebec. 14 Fevrier, 1791."

Copy located: None.

688. ALMANACS. NEW BRUNSWICK

THE / BRITISH AMERICAN / ALMANACK, / Of the Motions of the Luminaries, / For the Year of our Lord Christ 1792. / BEING BISSEXTILE, OR LEAP YEAR. / [rule] / Containing / THE UNIVERSAL CALENDAR . . . / . . . / . . . / . . . / . . . / . . . / ALSO, A VARIETY of other Matter Useful and Entertaining. / Apud quos Temporum . . . / . . . / TATIANUS. / [BY W]illiam Green, / SCHOOL MASTER at Campo-Bello. / [double rule] / NEW-BRUNSWICK: / PRINTED by C. SOWER and J. RYAN. / [title within single rule frame]

12mo. [A]-C^{6}, [D-E]^{4}; [52] p.; type-page in single rule frame: 14.2 × 7.5 cm. The latter part of the work, in 4's, has a shorter page: 13.9 × 7.5 cm. Possibly a part was printed in the office of each printer, then both in Saint John, N.B.

Contents. p. [1], t.-p.; p. [2-4], Royal family, eclipses, p. [5-6], Of time; p. [7-18], Calendar; p. [19-26], Geographical description of the world, remarkable events, receipts, anecdotes; p. [27-36], Tables: bearing and distance of cities from Saint John, N.B., dry measure, interest, wages, coinage, mileage, currency; p. [37-40], New Brunswick administration, legislature, courts; p. [41], City of Saint John magistrates; p. [42-45], County magistrates; p. [46-52], Army, navy, clergy, Agricultural society, etc., postal rates, distances.

The joint production of the two printers of New Brunswick, this almanac is greatly superior, both in local information and in entertainment features, to the almanacs previously produced independently by either Sower or Ryan. Edward Winslow, in response to a request for information on duties, fees, etc. of officials in New Brunswick, sent a copy on Apr. 6, 1792, to Lieut.-Gov. Simcoe then organizing the administration of Upper Canada, with the message: "In the inclos'd Almanack for this year, you will find a correct list of Posts and Offices in this Government" (N.B., *Winslow papers*, 6: 109). This suggests the importance as well as the accuracy of the provincial information in these early almanacs.

Copies located: CaNS (p. [1-4, 35-36] wanting); CaNW; CaOOA (p. [1-6, 19-36, 51-52] wanting).

689. ALMANACS. NOVA SCOTIA

AN / ALMANACK, / For the Year of our LORD, 1792; / . . . / CALCULATED FOR THE MERIDIAN OF / HALIFAX, . . . / . . . / CONTAINING / The ECLIPSES [etc., 7 lines in 1 col.] / LIST OF PROVINCIAL OFFICERS [etc. 7 lines in 2 parallel col.] / . . . / [rule] / BY THEOPHRASTUS. / [rule] / HALIFAX: / Printed and sold by JOHN HOWE, at his Printing-Office, Corner of / BARRINGTON and SACKVILLE-STREETS. / [title within double rule frame]

12mo. [24] p.; type-page: 16 × 10.2 cm.

Contents: p. [1], t.-p.; p. [2], Ephemeris; p. [3], Zodiac, eclipses; p. [4-15], Calendar; p. [16], Nova Scotia provincial officials; p. [17-18], Courts; p. [19-21], Naval officers; army officers, stationed in Nova Scotia; p. [22], Postal rates, Halifax to Michilimackinac; p. [23], Distances from Halifax, etc.; p. [24], Halifax, New England and New York currency tables.

Copy located: CaNsHA.

690. ALMANACS. NOVA SCOTIA

[Der Neuschottländische Calender Auf das Jahr Christi 1792 . . . *Halifax, gedruckt bey Anth. Henrich, 1791.*]

The advertisement in Anthony Henry's newspaper suggests that *Der Neuschottländische Calendar* published for 1788-91, continued to appear: "Just published and to be sold by Anthony Henry, the Nova-Scotia Calendar for 1792, also the German Almanack for 1792."—*Royal gazette*, Halifax, N.S., Nov. 29, 1791.

Copy located: None.

691. ALMANACS. NOVA SCOTIA

THE / NOVA-SCOTIA CALENDER / OR AN / ALMANACK, / For . . . / 1792. / [4 lines] / WHEREIN IS CONTAINED. / THE ECLIPSES . . . / [7 lines] / CALCULATED FOR THE MERIDIAN OF / HALIFAX, . . . / [3 lines] / [double rule] / BY METONICUS. / [double rule] / HALIFAX: / Printed and sold by ANTHONY HENRY, at his Printing-/ Office, in Sackville-Street, Corner of Grafton-Street. /

12mo. [*-3*^{6}, 4*^{2}]; [40] p.; type-page: 14.9 × 8.5 cm.

Contents: p. [1], t.-p.; p. [2], Vulgar notes; p. [3], Eclipses; p. [4-27], Calendar, etc.; p. [28-29], Ephemeris; p. [30-33], Nova Scotia administration, courts, etc.; p. [34], Old and New Testament numerology; p. [35-38], Postal rates, etc.; p. [39-40], Interest rates, buoys, distances in Nova Scotia.

This almanac was advertised: "Just published and to be sold by Anthony Henry The Nova-Scotia Calender [etc.]" . . . *Royal gazette*, Halifax, N.S., Nov. 8, 1791. It was superseded in Jan., 1792, by "the second edition . . . with alterations and corrections" (No. 750).

Copies located: CaNsWA (p. [1-2] wanting, p. [3-4] mutilated); White.

692. ALMANACS. QUEBEC

CALENDRIER pour l'Année Bissextile 1792, pour Québec, par les 306$^{d.}$ 30$^{m.}$ de Longitude, et 46$^{d.}$ 55$^{m.}$ de Latitude. / [double rule] /

Colophon: A QUEBEC: chez SAMUEL NEILSON, Imprimeur et Libraire, N° 3 Rue la Montagne. /

Broadside: type-page: 56.5 × 39.5 cm.

Contents: Calendrier, in triple rule frame with corner ornaments: 41.5 × 39.5 cm.; below *Calendrier*, printed in 4 col.: "De la Terre—Arithmétique, politique," etc.

This sheet almanac was sold from Nov. 28, 1791, at the prices constant for several years now, viz. 6*s*. the dozen, (5*s*. to the Montreal dealer) and 9*d*. the single copy.

Copy located: CaO (bound in *Quebec gazette* at end of 1791).

693. ALMANACS. QUEBEC

[Calendrier pour Montréal pour l'Année 1792.]

Broadside. This sheet almanac like *Calendrier pour Montréal* of preceding years, was undoubtedly *printed at Montreal by Fleury Mesplet*, this one in 1791 (though the date of imprint may appear the same as in title). It was advertised: "Le Calendrier de Montréal Pour l'Année 1792, A Vendre chez François Sareau, rue Notre Dame et chez l'Imprimeur."—*Montreal gazette*, Dec. 1, 1791.

Copy located: None.

694. ALMANACS. QUEBEC

MOORE'S / POCKET ALMANACK, / CALCULATED / For the Year of our Lord, / MDCCXCII. / [rule] / TO WHICH IS ADDED A / General Companion, / OR / REGISTER, / OF THE PROVINCES OF / UPPER

AND LOWER CANADA, / AS AT PRESENT DIVIDED INTO / DISTRICTS and CIRCLES. / CONTAINING THE / Officers of Government, § Judges and Magistrates, / Public Offices and Officers, § Sittings of Courts. / All useful information possible, and Officers in every / department. / [rule] / UT NUNC EST. / [rule] / [ornaments] / [rule] / QUEBEC (City:) / PRINTED BY WILLIAM MOORE: / AT THE / HERALD PRINTING-OFFICE. / [t.-p. within ornamental rule frame] /

12mo. [A]², B⁶, B-F⁶; 76 p.; type-page: 13.5 × 7 cm.

Contents: p. [1], t.-p.; p. [2], Provincial chronology since 1760; p. [3], Eclipses, etc.; p. [4], Zodiac, etc.; p. [5-16], Calendar; p. [17]-74, General register; p. [75]-76, Contents table.

The *General register* includes local information under the headings listed in No. 548, a mass of factual information on the provincial and municipal administrations, social, religious and educational institutions, transportation facilities, also certain fees and rates of charges. Data upon Upper Canada (in process of organization) are few, excepting in the militia and courts sections. Lower Canada, however, is fully recorded, in some sections more fully than in Neilson's *Quebec almanack*.

Copy located: CaQMS.

695. ALMANACS. QUEBEC

THE / QUEBEC / ALMANACK / FOR / The Year 1792 / [double rule] / [printer's ornament] / [double rule] / QUEBEC: / Printed by Samuel Neilson, / N° 3. MOUNTAIN STREET. / [title within ornamental frame]

French t.-p: ALMANACH / DE / QUEBEC, / POUR / l'ANNEE / 1792. / [double rule] / [printer's ornament] / [double rule] / A QUEBEC: / CHEZ SAMUEL NEILSON, / N° 3 RUE LA MONTAGNE. / [title within ornamental frame]

12mo. A-H⁶, [*-4*]⁶, O-P⁶; 168 p., front.; type-page: 10.8 × 6 cm., p. 38-65, opposite pages numbered in duplicate; 67-94 omitted in numbering.

Contents: p. [1], English t.-p.; p. [2], blank; p. [3], French t.-p.; p. [4-33], Calendar, etc.; p. [34-37], Almanac 1791 [introduction by the printer]; p. 38-53, Œconomy of the universe; p. 53-55, Rules in trade; p. 56-58, Aphorisms; p. 58-60, Explanation of frontispiece; p. 60, Du Chanvre; p. 61-64, Indian nations in North America; p. 64-66, Currency rules, tables; p. [95]-135, Civil and military register for Lower and Upper Canada; p. 136-46, Clergy; p. 147-55, Post office, customs, notaries; p. 155-59, Doctors; p. 160-66, Societies, constables, pilots, surveyors, coin values; p. 167-68, Index.

In "Almanac 1791," Samuel Neilson states the principles on which the *Quebec almanack* is compiled: It contains five sections: the calendar; astronomical information; short sketches of political, moral or scientific truths, or "mere amusement"; a civil register of public functionaries for all communities and religious denominations to which the almanac will go; finally information on local affairs. The *Quebec almanack*, Neilson continues, will try to follow the mode of compilation of the most approved almanacs of Europe. "However, it is rather to be considered as an unexperienced attempt which if sanctioned by the Public approbation will afford a new motive of improvement in the succeeding years. . . . [This year it is printed throughout in English and French] excepting only the names of Public officers. The additional expense of such an arrangement we hope will be considered as a sufficient excuse for the necessary augmentation in price; and we trust the enlightened friends of literature will lend their influence in encouraging the productions of the PRESS; the great expediency of which is highly evident in every civilized country, and must ever be regarded to bear the same relation to the culture of the mind as the plow bears to that of the earth."—p. [34-37].

The frontispiece, an engraved illustration of the printing press, signed: "I. G. Hochstetter, Sculpt.," is "a print copied from a European Almanac, executed in Quebec."—p. 58.

This almanac was sold from Jan. 3, 1792, printed on common or fine paper, plain or interleaved, stitched or bound, at prices ranging from 2*s.* 6*d.* to 4*s.* 6*d.* retail. It was advertised: "Just published, Quebec Pocket Almanack for 1792, on a new and more extensive plan than ever before printed in this country, containing about 170 pages in 12mo, in the French and English languages, on fine paper and a good type with a neatly engraved frontispiece—being a most valuable collection of useful knowledge and a compleat Civil & Military Register for the Provinces of U. & L. Canada . . ."—*Quebec gazette*, Jan. 12, 1792.

Copies located: CaQM (this copy recorded as *Quebec almanack for 1791* by Gagnon, 1: 96, is really that for 1792, with a 29-day February; p. [1-12], 157-58, 165-68 wanting); CaQMC; CaQMS; CaQQAr; MHi. Photostat copy in CaOOA.

696. BEDARD, THOMAS LAURENT, 1747-1795

[double rule] / OBSERVATIONS / ON THE / REPORT / Respecting a Change in the Tenures of this Province. / [double rule] / OBSERVATIONS / SUR LE / PROJET / Du Changement des Tenures dans cette Province. / [double rule] / QUEBEC: / Printed by SAMUEL NEILSON, N° 3, Mountain-street. / [rule] / M.DCC.XCI. /

8vo. A-C[4]; 11[i.e. 21] p., 1 *l.*; type-page: 18 × 10.2 cm. Text in English and French on opposite pages numbered in duplicate.

Contents: p. [1], t.-p.; p. [2]-11, Observations, signed at end: "Quebec, 16th Feb. 1791. Thomas Bedard" (French text signed: "Thomas Bedard, Ptre."); verso of p. 11 (French), blank; 1 *l.* at end, blank.

This is a spirited defence of the seigniorial system of land tenure, with a detailed refutation of the Legislative Council's report recommending change to freehold. The author's arguments resemble closely those of Adam Mabane's dissent from the report (No. 667). Bédard sent his MS. *Observations* to Gov. Dorchester, who communicated it to the Council, Feb. 21, 1791 (now in Can.P.A., "S" *Land Sundries, 1791*). It was printed in English and French in the *Quebec gazette*, Mar. 24-Apr. 7, 1791, *Sup.* This pamphlet is a reprint from the *Gazette* type, on smaller paper. It was issued separately and sold by the printer at 7½*d.* the copy (Can.P.A., *Neilson papers*, v. 70, May 6, 1791).

Bédard, born at Charlesbourg, near Quebec, Oct. 14, 1747, and ordained in 1775, was professor of philosophy at the Séminaire de Québec, 1775-95, and its superior, 1781-87, 1793-95.

Copies located: GBLP (in C.O. 42/82: 385-405); MHi.

697. BOUTELIER, GEORGE FREDERICK, *defendant, d.* 1791

THE / TRIALS / OF / GEORGE FREDERICK BOUTELIER / AND / JOHN BOUTELIER, / FOR THE / MURDER / OF / FREDERICK EMINAUD, / BEFORE / A special Court of Oyer and Terminer and general Goal Delivery, / HELD AT / LUNENBURG, / IN AND FOR THE / COUNTY OF LUNENBURG, / IN THE / PROVINCE OF NOVA-SCOTIA, / AT THE / COURT-HOUSE IN THE TOWN OF LUNENBURG, / ON / Wednesday the 4th of May, 1791. / [rule] / BY JAMES STEWART, ESQUIRE, / OF COUNCIL FOR THE PROSECUTION. / [rule] / HALIFAX: / PRINTED BY JOHN HOWE, IN BARRINGTON-STREET. / M.DCC.XCI. /

8vo. A-E[4] 1 p. l., ii, 40 [i.e. 36] p., fold. *l.*; type-page: 19 × 9.8 cm. 5-8 is omitted in numbering and the hiatus is not supplied.

Contents: p. l. recto, t.-p.; verso, blank; p. [i]-ii, Introduction; p. [1]-36, Proceedings; p. 36-40, Conclusion. The folded leaf, 40.5 × 27.5 cm., is a rough illustration of the coast and islands near Lunenburg, indicating the movements of the Boutelier brothers at the time of the murder. It bears the legend: "Engraved By T. Hamman, Halifax," also "References," an explanation of symbols on the chart.

The brothers Boutelier beat to death Eminaud, a farmer living on the sea coast near Lunenburg, also his wife and grand-daughter, on Mar. 19, 1791; they stole about £10 and fired his house. Their trial took place at Lunenburg, May 3-5, 1791, before Chief Justice Thomas Andrew Strange. This work gives the evidence *verbatim* and a résumé of the proceedings of the court, also the condemned men's confession and an account of the execution on May 9, 1791.

Copies located: CaNsHA (fold. *l.* wanting); CaNsWA (fold. *l.* wanting); CaO; NNHi (fold. *l.* wanting).

698. BROWN, ANDREW, *d.* 1834

A / DISCOURSE / DELIVERED BEFORE THE / North-British Society, / IN / HALIFAX, NOVA-SCOTIA, / AT THEIR / ANNIVERSARY MEETING / ON THE / 30th of November, 1790. / [rule] / BY ANDREW BROWN, D.D. / [rule] / HALIFAX: / PRINTED BY JOHN HOWE, IN BARRINGTON STREET. / M.DCC.XCI. /

8vo. A-B[4], C[2]; 20 p.; type-page: 18.2 × 9 cm.

Contents: p. [1], t.-p.; p. [2], blank; p. [3], North British Society's vote of thanks, etc., to Brown, Dec. 4, 1790; p. [4], Dedication; p. [5]-20, A Discourse, text: Psalm cxxxvii, 5, 6. If I forget thee, O Jerusalem, let my right hand forget her cunning. If I do not remember thee, let my tongue cleave to the roof of my mouth.

The author treats of the origin of St. Andrew's day and of the North British Society founded in 1768; he justifies the convivial and humanitarian purposes of the Society, also the perpetuation of national divisions in a small pioneer community, by such organizations as the North British, High German, and Charitable Irish societies in Halifax. He also points out a few improvements towards a more effective and economical distribution of Society funds.

Brown, born in Biggar, Lanarkshire, graduated from the University of Edinburgh. He came to Nova Scotia in 1787, as Church of Scotland minister to St. Matthew's church, Halifax (a congregation of New England congregationalists and some Scottish presbyterians). His sermons, of which three were printed are conspicuous among the Canadian productions of this period, for an eloquence of style and for a humanitarianism and tolerance in view point. Bishop Inglis wrote to the archbishop of Canterbury, Halifax, Oct. 3, 1791: "Brown is an ingenious young man from Scotland of amiable manners and peaceable disposition. He was sent here by Drs. Robertson, Blaire [sic] and Hamilton of Edinburgh." Brown, he stated, was going to England to try to get a salary grant from the Lords of the Treasury, adding that he wished the young man could get a salary, but from some other source.
—Can.P.A., *Inglis papers*, 1: 272.

In 1795 Brown returned to Scotland and six years later succeeded Blair as professor of rhetoric and belles lettres at the University of Edinburgh. His MSS., including materials for a history of Nova Scotia, are in the British Museum (Add. MSS. 19069-19076), transcripts in the Provincial Archives of Nova Scotia (*see Canadian historical review*, 17: 172, 1936). A portrait of Brown appears in *History of St. Matthew's church, Halifax, N.S.*, by W. C. Murray, in N.S. hist. soc. *Coll.*, 16: 137-70, 1912, on p. 154.

Copy located: MH.

699. CATHOLIC CHURCH. CATECHISMS. *French*

CATECHISME / A / L'USAGE / DU / DIOCESE / DE / QUEBEC. / [rule] / Imprimé par l'Ordre de Monseigneur JEAN / OLIVIER BRIAND, Evêque de Québec. / [rule] / Se Vend chez Mr. L. GERMAIN, N° 5 Rue de la Fabrique. / [rule] / [printer's ornament] / [rule] / TROISIEME EDITION. / [rule] / A QUEBEC. / Chez SAMUEL NEILSON Imprimeur & Libraire, / N° 3. RUE DE LA MONTAGNE. / MDCCXCI. / [title in dotted line frame with star at corners]

12mo. A-S^6; 4 p. l., 7-210, [3] p.; type-page: 14.6 × 8.5 cm.

Contents: p. l. 1 recto, t.-p.; verso, blank; p. l. 2 recto-3 verso, Mandement, dated and signed "le 7 Mars, 1777, signé J. Ol. Evêque de Québec," etc.; p. l .4 recto, Avertissement; verso, Introduction; p. 7-58, Le Petit Catéchisme; p. [59], Table (contents of Le Petit Catéchisme); p. [60], blank; p. 61-210, Le Grand Catéchisme; p [1-3], Table (contents of Le Grand Catéchisme); verso of p. [3], blank.

The preliminary matter and text of this edition are the same as that of 1777, 1782, and of the other 1791 edition (No. 699). This edition differs from the latter typographically, in the frame of the title-page (dots), in the rules at the head of p. 7 (two rules), and in its continuous signatures and pagination. The type of both *Petit* and *Grand Catéchisme* is pica with long primer, badly worn. The paper in this edition has a rough surface; it is not "le meilleur papier."

Copies located: CaQQL (Ex. "A"); Ketcheson.

700. CATHOLIC CHURCH. CATECHISMS. *French*

CATECHISME / A / L'USAGE / DU / DIOCESE / DE / QUEBEC. / Imprimé par l'Ordre de Monseigneur JEAN / OLIVIER BRIAND, Evêque de Québec. / [rule] / Se Vend chez Mr. L. GERMAIN, N° 5 Rue de la Fabrique. / [rule] / [printer's ornament] / [rule] / TROISIEME EDITION. / [rule] / A QUEBEC. / Chez SAMUEL NEILSON Imprimeur & Libraire, / N° 3. RUE DE LA MONTAGNE. / MDCCXCI. / [title within a single rule frame, star at each corner]

12mo. A-E[6], F[1]; A-L[6]; 4 p. l., 7-58 p., 1 *l.*, 129, [3] p.; type-page: 15 × 8.5 cm.

Contents: p. l. 1 recto, t.-p.; verso, blank; p. l. 2 recto-3 verso, Mandement, dated and signed, "le 7 Mars 1777, signé J. Ol. Evêque de Québec"; p. l. 4 recto, Avertissement; verso, Introduction; p. 7-58, Le Petit Catéchisme; *l.* recto, Table (contents of Le Petit Catéchisme); verso, blank; p. 1-129, le Grand Catéchisme; p. [1-3], at end, Table (contents of Le Grand Catéchisme); verso of p. [3], blank.

This is another edition of No. 699 with the same content, printed from newer type on better paper. It is to be distinguished from No. 699 by the frame on its title-page (rule); also by the rules (three) at the head of p. 7. In this edition the *Petit* and *Grand Catéchisme* have separate signature sequences and pagination; *Le Petit Catéchisme* is printed from pica with long primer (like No. 699); *Le Grand Catéchisme* from small pica with brevier, smaller types than No. 699.

The printer recorded his work:

"1791, Aug. 4. Delivered Louis Langlois dit Germain [a merchant in Quebec]
6000 Double Catechismes of the Diocese of Quebec. @ 10*d.*—£250."
—Can.P.A., *Neilson papers*, v. 70.

It was advertised: "Le Catéchisme . . . de Québec, dont on vient d'imprimer tout recemment une troisième édition, sur le meilleur papier avec plus de beaux caractères que les deux premières, se vend in gros et en detail chez Mr. Louis Germain [etc.]."
—*Quebec Gazette*, Apr. 5, 1792 *et seq.*

Copies located: CaQQL (Ex. "B"); MBAt.

701. CATHOLIC CHURCH. CATECHISMS. *French*

[Le Petit Catéchisme]

Printed at Quebec, by Samuel Neilson, 1791, as recorded:

"1791, Feb. 26. Sent Louis Germain 3000 Petit Catechismes at 5*d.* by agreement.—£62.10."
—Can.P.A., *Neilson papers*, v. 70.

This was probably a separate issue of the first part of No. 699 or No. 700.

Copy located: None

702. [DESTRUCTION OF THE FEUDAL MONSTER IN FRANCE]

[Destruction of the Feudal Monster in France, in the Sessions of the National Assembly of the 4 & 5 Aug. 1789. *Printed at Quebec by Samuel Neilson, 1791.*]

This is probably a reprint of an article published in the *Quebec gazette*, Jan. 20-27, 1791, *sup.*, with title as above, and sub-titles: "Speeches that produced the abolition

of the Feudal System as well as Tythes"; "Decree by the National Assembly; or The Great Charter that abolishes in France every Species of Servitude. And the first hommage rendered the Eternal by Free Frenchmen." In the *Gazette,* the article of about 3,000 words was printed in English and French in parallel columns in brevier type, occupying 3 pages. This item was issued and sold separately at 6*d*. the copy.
—Can.P.A., *Neilson papers*, v. 70, May 6, 1791.

Copy located: None

703. GREAT BRITAIN. LAWS, STATUTES, *etc.*

[30 Geo. III c. 27. An Act for encouraging New Settlers in His Majesty's Colonies and Planations in America.]

Broadside? Text in English and French? *Printed at Quebec, by Samuel Neilson, 1791*, as recorded:

"1791, July 30. Printed for Lord Dorchester's Secretary's Office 400 Copies of an Act of Parliament for encouraging New Settlers in His Majesty's American Dominions—£1.5."—Can.P A., *Neilson papers*, v. 70.

This act was passed by the Parliament of Great Britain, and printed in English and French in the *Quebec gazette*, Oct. 7-14, 1790, also July 21, 1791. It sets forth regulations for importing household and other property, including slaves, by any subject of the United States desirous of settling in Bahama, Bermuda, etc., or in Quebec, Nova Scotia, etc., and requires such persons to take an oath of allegiance and of intention to reside in British territory.

Copy located: None.

704. GREAT BRITAIN. LAWS, STATUTES, *etc.*

ANNO REGNI / GEORGII III. / REGIS / Magnæ Britanniæ, Franciæ & Hiberniæ, / TRICESIMO PRIMO. / At the Parliament begun and holden at Westminster, the / Twenty-fifth Day of November, Anno Domini 1790, / in the Thirty-first Year of the Reign of our Sovereign / Lord GEORGE the Third, by the Grace of God, of / Great-Britain, France, and Ireland, King, Defender of / the Faith &c. / Being the first Session of the Seventeenth Parliament of Great-Britain. / [rule] / NUMBER II. / [rule] / [royal arms] / [rule] / QUEBEC: / Printed by WILLIAM MOORE, at the Herald-Printing / Office, 1791. / (PRICE ONE SHILLING) /

8vo. G-[K][4]; 1 p. l., [51]-78 [i.e. 79], [1] p.; type-page: 17.5 × 10.5 cm. One leaf of sig. [K] is folded around sig. G-I to form t.-p. In paging, 74 is repeated and numbering thereafter diminished by 1. Paged in continuation of Lymburner's *Paper*, this is the second and last of the series of documentary publications projected by Moore (*see* No. 709 *note*).

Contents: p. l. recto, t.-p.; verso, blank; p. [51]-75, 31 Geo. III c. 31 (the Canada or Constitutional Act); p. [76]-78, Proclamation of Lieut.-Gov. Alured Clarke, Quebec, Nov. 18, 1791; [1] p., at end (verso of p. 78), printer's advertisement of his publications.

Copies located: CaQMS; CaQQL (2 cop.); MHi.

705. GREAT BRITAIN. LAWS, STATUTES, *etc.*

THE / QUEBEC / GAZETTE. / [ornamental rule] / THURSDAY, DECEMBER 1, 1791 / [ornamental rule] / Num. 1378. / [royal arms] / LA / GAZETTE / DE / QUEBEC. / [ornamental rule] / JEUDI, I DECEMBRE, 1791. / [ornamental rule] /

Colophon, p. 11: QUEBEC: PRINTED BY SAMUEL NEILSON, No. 3 MOUNTAIN STREET.—A QUEBEC: CHEZ SAMUEL NEILSON, N° 3, RUE LA MONTAGNE.

fo. 11 p. type-page: 35 × 21 cm. Text in 2 col. English and French. p. 5 has heading: "Quebec gazette, Thursday, December 8, 1791 / Conclusion of the Act of Parliament, 31 Geo. III ch. XXXI, began in our last", also in French.

Contents: p. [1], Proclamation by Lieut.-Gov. Alured Clark, Quebec, Nov. 18, 1791, declaring when 31 Geo. III c. 31 shall have effect, and giving text of the order-in-council, London, Aug. 24, 1791, authorizing the division of the province of Quebec into Lower and Upper Canada; p. 2-11, 31 Geo. III c. 31, the "Canada Act," or "Constitutional Act" passed by the British Parliament, June 10, 1791, providing a constitutional frame work for the governments of Lower and Upper Canada; p. 11, "Erratas dans l'impression de la traduction de l'Acte [etc.]"; Colophon; verso of p. 11, blank.

The official and the first Canadian-printed publication of this proclamation and statute was that in the *Quebec gazette*, Dec. 1-8, 1791 (for which the printer charged £33 10*s*.). In some copies, apparently, of this regular *Gazette* issue, the proclamation is repeated on the last page. Of this edition a separate issue was struck off for the government, as the printer recorded:

"1791, Dec. 26. Printed for Council Office [per] order of Mr. Williams, 1000 Copies of the Act of Parl. of last sess. chap. 31, making 3 Sheets folio on Gazette types. 3 Sheets [@] 10s. [per] 100 each Sheet—£15.
Stitching, folding &c. of Ditto, each copy, £2.1.8.
[Total:] £17.1.8."—Can.P.A., *Neilson Papers*, v. 70.

These documents were frequently reprinted—in the 18th century and subsequently. For a modern edition, with related documents, *see* Doughty and McArthur: *Documents, 1791-1818*, also Shortt and Doughty: *Documents, 1759-1791*.

Copies located: CaOOA (2 cop.); CaOTL (bound with *Upper Canada gazette*, May 2, 1801); CaQM; CaQQL; MHi; NNB (Proclamation only, on recto of one leaf, verso, blank).

706. GREAT BRITAIN. LAWS, STATUTES, *etc.*

Caption title: (1) / [double rule] / ANNO REGNI DECIMO QUARTO, / GEORGII III. REGIS / [ornamental rule] / CHAP. LXXXIII. / An Act for making more effectual Provision for the / Government of the Province of Quebec in North / America. / [row of dots] /

French caption: [double rule] / ANNO REGNI DECIMO QUARTO, / GEORGII III. REGIS / [ornamental rule] / CHAP. LXXXIII. / Acte qui régle plus solidement le Gouvernement de la / Province de Québec, dans l'Amerique Septentri-/onale. / [row of dots] /

fo. 5 p. type-page: 35 × 21 cm. Text in 2 col. English and French. *Printed at Quebec, by Samuel Neilson, 1791.*

Contents. p. 1-3, Quebec Act, 14 Geo. III c. 83; p. 4-5, Quebec Revenue Act, 14 Geo. III c. 88. verso of p. 5, blank.

These acts, passed by the Parliament of Great Britain in 1774, were republished seriatim in the *Quebec gazette*, Dec. 15-22, 1791, with a note stating that as they were out of print and few copies extant in the province "we thought it would be essentially serving the Public [to] reprint the same . . . to be bound up with the Act [i.e. 31 Geo. III c. 31] given in our last." A separate issue was then struck off the *Gazette* types for the government, as recorded by Neilson:

"1791, Dec. 24. Printed for Council Office (by order Mr. Coffin) 600 Copies Chap. 83 & 88 Acts of Parl.—£7.10.
Folding, stitching, &c. of Do.—£1.5.
[Total:] £8.15."—Can.P.A., *Neilson papers*, v. 70.

Copies located: CaOOA (2 cop. filed in: Can.P.A. "S" *Proclamations, L.C.* (2); *Proclamations portfolio* in Library; CaQQL; MHi (with *Quebec gazette*, 1791).

707. HUBERT, JEAN FRANCOIS, *bp. of Quebec*, 1739-1797

Caption title: (9) / [ornamental rule] / SOLI DEO GLORIA. [within ornamental frame] / [ornamental rule] / MANDEMENT / DE MONSEIGNEUR / L'EVEQUE DE QUEBEC, / Qui permet de travailler à certains jours de Fêtes. / [rule] /

4to. B4; p. 9-15; type-page: 18.8 × 13.8 cm.; apparently paged in continuation of No. 556. *Printed at Quebec, by Samuel Neilson, 1791*, as recorded:

"1791, Apr. 17. Printed for the Bishop of Quebec, Un Mandement qui permet de travailler—£4 "
—Can.P.A., *Neilson papers*, v. 70.

Contents: p. 9-14, Mandement, dated and signed: "Donné à Québec sous notre seign . . . le quinze d'Avril, mil-sept-cent-quatre-vingt-onze, Jean François, Evêque de Québec, Par Monseigneur. Plessis, Prêtre, Secretaire"; p. 14-15, Liste des solemnités remises au Dimanche; note at end (in type:) "Collationné à la minute restée aux Archives de l'Evêché"; (in MS.:) "Plessis, ptre secr."; verso of p. 15, blank.

In response to certain suggestions (cf. No. 633), Bishop Hubert discontinued observances of some of the numerous feast days in his diocese by this mandement. It was superseded by that of Oct. 28, 1793 (No. 875) and is reprinted in Têtu and Gagnon: *Mandements de Québec*, 2: 437-43.

Copies located: CaO; CaOOA (2 cop.); CaQQL; Ketcheson; RPJ.

708. [LANAUDIERE, CHARLES LOUIS DE], 1743-1811

[To Mr. Bédard, Director of the Seminary of Quebec. A Monsieur Bédard, Directeur du Seminaire de Québec.]

A separate issue of *Supplement to the Quebec gazette*, no. 1344, Apr. 28, 1791, with colophon: *Quebec: Printed by Samuel Neilson, Mountain-Street.* The letter, about 4,000 words with captions as above, and signed by Lanaudière, occupies the entire *Supplement*, [4] p. fo. where it is printed in 2 col., English and French, in brevier type. The separate issue (possibly printed without the *Gazette* heading in single col. on smaller paper, about 16 p. 8vo. like No. 696) was sold by the printer at 6*d.* the copy from May 6, 1791.—Can.P.A., *Neilson papers*, v. 70.

This letter is a refutation of Bédard's *Observations* and a vindication of the evidence given by Lanaudière before the Legislative Council committee on tenures.

Lanaudière, born and educated in Quebec, fought against the British in 1759, but later (1770) became attached to the English administration as aide to Gov. Carleton, and from 1786 he held the lucrative post of grand voyer (overseer of roads). Though himself the owner of five seigniories, Lanaudière was conspicuous among the French-Canadian gentry for his advocacy of freehold tenure.

709. LYMBURNER, ADAM, 1746-1836

THE / PAPER / READ AT·THE / Bar of the House of Commons, / By MR. LYMBURNER; / Agent for the Subscribers to the Petitions from the / Province of Quebec. / Bearing date the 24th of Nov. 1784. / As Read the 23d of March, 1791. / [rule] / NUMBER I. / [rule] / QUEBEC: / PRINTED BY WILLIAM MOORE, / AT THE / HERALD PRINTING-OFFICE, 1791. / (PRICE ONE SHILLING ONLY.) /

8vo. [*][2], A-F[4]; 1 p. l., 47 p., 1 *l.*; type-page: 12 × 10 cm. The two leaves of sig. [*] are folded around sig. A-F, to form t.-p., and leaf at end.

Contents. p. l. recto, t.-p.; verso, blank; p. [1]-47, Paper read by Mr. Lymburner; verso of p. 47, blank; 1 *l.* at end, recto blank; verso, Printer's announcement.

This is the second edition, published about June 13, 1791, of a work previously printed in London (with title as above, but no imprint or colophon, 32 p. 1 *l.* in fo.) It presents the arguments of the English minority in Quebec against most of the clauses of the "Canada Bill," then before the House of Commons and soon to become the Constitutional Act, 31 Geo. III c. 31. Lymburner inveighs against division of the province and sets forth the case for English laws and institutions of government in Quebec, for the ultimate anglicization of the French Catholic majority, and for the advancement of mercantile over agricultural interests. Lymburner was a prosperous Scottish merchant, resident in Quebec since 1776.

The printer's announcement, dated at Quebec, June 8, 1791, states that he "Intends . . . to Print in the same Form as this Pamphlet, the Debates of Parliament relative to this Province, as minuted in Mr. Woodfall's Diary; the new Constitution as it may be enacted in the British Parliament and all the Laws that shall hereafter be confirmed by the House of Assembly and the Council in this Province or Provinces . . . Quebec, June 8th, 1791." Of this projected series, only No. II appeared (No. 704).

The Paper was reprinted in *Canadian review and magazine*, v. 2, no. 4, p. 399-434, Montreal, Feb. 1826.

Copies located: CaOOA; CaQMS; CaQQL; MHi; MWA; NN.

710. LYMBURNER, ADAM, 1746-1836

Caption title: [double rule] / PAPIER lu à la Barre de la Chambre des Communes par / MR. LYMBURNER, Agent pour les Souscrivants aux Pé-/titions de la Province de Québec en date du 24 Nov. 1784. / [double rule] / 23 MARS, 1791. / [double rule] /

Colophon, p. 31: [double rule] / A QUEBC [sic]: CHEZ SAMUEL NEILSON, N° 3. RUE LA MONTAGNE. / [double rule] /

8vo. [A]-D⁴; 31 p.; type-page: 17 × 10.1 cm.

Contents: p. [1]-31, Papier; verso of p. 31, blank. This is a French translation of No. 709. It was announced: "Actuellement sous presse, On va publier sous peu une traduction en François du Discourse de Mr. Lymburner, contenant des remarques très intéressantes sur le Bill de Constitution publié dans cette Gazette [May 26, 1791]."—*Quebec gazette*, June 16, 1791. Also: "On vient de publier, prix 9d., Une traduction [etc.]."—*ibid.*, July 14, 1791.

Copies located: CaQ; CaQM; CaQMJ; CaQMS (2 cop.); CaQQL.

711. [The Manners and Customs in British America and the West India Islands.]

Proposed printing at Quebec, by Wm. Moore, 1791, was advertised:

"Proposals for printing by Subscription, The Manners and Customs in British America and the West India Islands. In particular giving an Impartial account of the Soil, Cultivation, Produce, Commerce and inhabitants of all ranks and colours—with the method of cultivating . . . sugar, coffee . . . the treatment of slaves and the Slave trade—Also an impartial view at the present time, of their governors—and all others in Public Offices, Merchants, Planters, their Emoluments, &c.

" 'Here take a view and with impartial eyes
Consider and examine all who rise
Here see their actions, and their treacherous ends
How greatness grows, and by what steps ascends.
What murders, treasons, perjuries and deceits
How many crush'd to make some vile men great.'

From experience by a Traveller."

This work, about 250 pages, demy 8vo. was to go to press as soon as 150 subscriptions at $1.00 had been received, and was to be printed by Wm. Moore, Quebec. —*Quebec herald*, June 13, 1791. There is no evidence, however, that it was ever published.

712. NEW BRUNSWICK. HOUSE OF ASSEMBLY

JOURNAL / OF THE / VOTES and PROCEEDINGS / OF THE / HOUSE OF ASSEMBLY / OF THE / PROVINCE of NEW-BRUNSWICK: / From Thursday the 3d of FEBRUARY to Saturday the 5th of / MARCH, 1791. / [ornamental rule] / [royal arms] / [ornamental rule] / ST. JOHN: / Printed by CHRISTOPHER SOWER, PRINTER to the / KING'S MOST EXCELLENT MAJESTY. 1791. / [title within a frame of flower pieces]

fo. [*]¹, A-O², 1 p. l., [170]-224 p., fold table; type-page: 24 × 14 cm. Even numbers on recto, odd numbers on verso; paged in continuation of No. 644.

Contents: p. l. recto, t.-p.; verso, blank; p. [170]-224, Journal of the fifth session of the first assembly, no session being held in 1790; verso of p. 224, blank;

fold. table, correctly inserted between p. 217-18, is ". . . Account of goods imported into the Port of Saint John . . . subject to a Duty, at the Treasury office [Oct. 10, 1789-Jan. 17, 1791]."

Two hundred copies of the *Acts* (No. 713) and of the *Journal* of this session were ordered to be printed, and Sower was given the exclusive right of printing.—N.B. As. *Journal*, Feb. 5, Mar. 4, 1791. Sower's bill "for printing Acts and Journals of the last session—£58.0.4., certified by Committee of the House," was ordered, Oct. 7, 1791, to be paid by warrant on the treasury.—C.A., N.B.Ex.co. *Minutes*.

Copies located: CaN (t.-p. wanting); CaNU; CaNsWA; CaOOA; GBLP (in B.T.6/56: 355-413).

713. NEW BRUNSWICK. LAWS, STATUTES, *etc.*

ACTS / OF THE / GENERAL ASSEMBLY, / OF / His MAJESTY'S PROVINCE / OF / NEW-BRUNSWICK, / PASSED IN THE YEAR 1791. / [ornamental rule] / [royal arms] / [ornamental rule] / ST. JOHN: / Printed by CHRISTOPHER SOWER, PRINTER to the / KING'S MOST EXCELLENT MAJESTY. / [rule] / MDCCXCI. / [title within frame of flower pieces.]

fo. [$*^1 2*^2$, A]-G^2, H^1; 3 p. l., p. 204-33; type-page: 24.5 × 14 cm. Even numbers on recto, odd numbers on verso; paged in continuation of No. 645.

Contents: p. l. 1, t.-p.; verso, blank; p. l. 2, half title; verso, blank; p. l. 3 recto-verso, Titles of the acts; p. 204-233, 31 Geo. III c. I-XVI, acts passed in fifth session of the first assembly. An edition of 200 copies was printed, and distributed almost entirely by the government to officials and municipalities within the province.

Copies located: Baxter; CaNSA; CaOOA (p. 230-33 wanting); MH; NNB; NNHi.

714. NOVA SCOTIA. HOUSE OF ASSEMBLY

Caption title: (89) / [ornamental rule] / JOURNAL, / AND / PROCEEDINGS / OF THE / HOUSE OF ASSEMBLY, / Of the Province of NOVA-SCOTIA / [rule] / Monday 6th June, 1791. /

fo. sig. X-$2G^2$; p. 89-127; paged in continuation of No. 647. *Printed at Halifax, N.S., by Anthony Henry, 1791.*

Contents: p. 89-127, Journal and proceedings of the sixth session of the sixth assembly, June 6-July 5, 1791; verso of p. 127, blank.

Copies located: CaNs; GBLP (in C.O. 217/63: 146-84); MH (p. 109-120 wanting).

715. NOVA SCOTIA. LAWS, STATUTES, *etc.*

Running title: [rule] / 1791. Anno Tricessimo Primo Regis, GEORGII III. CAP. I[-XII]. / [rule] /

Caption title: At the GENERAL ASSEMBLY of this Province / of Nova-Scotia, . . . / [8 lines] / . . . being the Sixth Session of the Sixth General Assembly, convened / in the said Province. / [rule] /

fo. sig. 3E-3H[2]; p. 283 [!]-298; type-page: 25.5 × 15 cm. paged in continuation of No. 648 and repeating (p. 283-287) the pagination of No. 600. *Printed at Halifax, N.S., by Anthony Henry, 1791.*

Contents: p. 283 [!]-298, Cap. I-XII, perpetual acts passed in the session, June 6-July 5, 1791.

Copies located: CaO; DLC; MH (2 cop.).

716. NOVA SCOTIA. LAWS, STATUTES, *etc.*

Running title: [rule] / 1791. Anno Tricessimo Primo Regis, GEORGII III. CAP. I[-V]. / [rule] /

Caption title: At the GENERAL ASSEMBLY of this Province / of Nova-Scotia . . . / [8 lines] / . . . being the Sixth Session / of the Sixth General Assembly, convened / in the said Province. / [rule] /

fo. sig. 3K-3M[2], 3N[1]; p. 303-316; type-page: 25.5 × 15 cm. paged in continuation of No. 649. *Printed at Halifax, N.S., by Anthony Henry, 1791.*

Contents: p. 303-316, Cap. I-V, temporary acts passed in the session, June 6-July 5, 1791.

Copies located: CaO; MH; N; NNB.

717. OLIVER, WILLIAM SANDFORD, 1751?-1813

A COLLECTION / OF / PAPERS / AND / FACTS, / RELATIVE TO THE / DISMISSION OF / WILLIAM SANDFORD OLIVER, ESQ. / FROM THE / OFFICE OF SHERIFF OF THE CITY AND COUN-/TY OF ST. JOHN, IN THE PROVINCE / OF NEW BRUNSWICK. / Audi Alteram Partem. / PRINTED IN THE YEAR 1791. /

8vo. A-C[4]; 24 p.; type-page: 16 × 8 cm.

Contents: p. [1], t.-p.; p. [2], blank; p. [3], Advertisement, signed W.S.O.; p. [4], blank; p. [5]-24, A collection of papers and facts. The collection comprises an introduction and conclusion by Oliver and the text of thirteen letters by Al. Black, foreman of the grand jury of Saint John, N.B., W. S. Oliver, sheriff, Elias Hardy, clerk of the court of sessions and Jonathan Odell, secretary to the lieutenant-governor. It concerns an altercation between Oliver and the grand jury, following the latter's surprise visit to inspect the common gaol under Oliver's charge, and vindicates his conduct as sheriff.

Oliver, a native of Massachusetts, and son of its former lieutenant-governor, came to Halifax, a loyalist, with the British army from Boston, in 1776. He settled in Saint John and became its first sheriff, 1785. From this municipal post he was dismissed in 1791, during the dispute reviewed in this pamphlet. But the following year he was appointed marshall of the Court of Vice-admiralty of New Brunswick, reappointed sheriff in 1797, and made provincial treasurer in 1798, posts which he held till his death.

This pamphlet may have been printed at Saint John, N.B., by John Ryan, or possibly by Christopher Sower, but it has rather the appearance of a London publication, prepared for circulation among English officials (cf. MacFarlane: *New Brunswick Bibliography*).

Copy located: CaOT.

718. QUEBEC, *City*. DIRECTORY

NUMBER II / OF THE / DIRECTORY / FOR THE / City and Suburbs of Quebec: / CONTAINING / The names of the housekeepers, [etc. 6 lines in double col.] / [rule] / TO WHICH ARE ADDED THE / FIRE ENGINES WITH THEIR HOUSES OF / DEPOSITE, / ALSO THE / PRESENT COMMITTEE / [rule] / The whole Alphabetically arranged. / [rule] / Collected by HUGH MACKAY, A.O.S. / With considerable alterations and additions. / [rule] / QUEBEC: PRINTED BY WILLIAM MOORE, / AT THE / HERALD PRINTING OFFICE: 1791. / [rule] / TO BE CONTINUED ANNUALLY. /

12mo. A^2, B-C^6, D^4; 1 p. l., iv-v, [9]-40 p.; type-page: 14.5 × 8.5 cm.

Contents: p. l. recto, t.-p.; p. l. verso-p. v, Dedication, abbreviations; p. [9]-39, Directory; p. 39-40, Fire engines, etc. Similar in scope and arrangement to the *Directory* of 1790, *Number II* records 1,347 householders including 604 "proprietors." This was the last number published. For MacKay announced that though he had collected "every necessary information" he was "forced to discontinue it longer as the past two years did not pay for the paper."—*Quebec gazette*, July 19, 1792, *Sup.*

Copies located: CaQMS; CaQQL.

719. QUEBEC, *Province*. CITIZENS

[To his Excellency Lord Dorchester. The Memorial and Petition of the Subscribing Seigniors, Citizens and Inhabitants of the Province of Quebec. *Printed at Quebec, by Samuel Neilson, 1791.*]

? Broadside: text in 2 col. English and French, or possibly a leaflet of about 4 pages, issued in a style similar to, though smaller than No. 696.

The petition is dated Quebec, Mar. 10, 1791, and signed by Le Séminaire de Québec and 58 other French signatories. It protests against the change from seigniorial tenure to that of free and common soccage as recommended in the Legislative Council, 1790.

This *Memorial* was published in the *Quebec gazette*, Mar. 24, 1791 (where it occupies one full page, printed in 2 col., English and French) with the introductory note: "The following petition lately presented to his Excellency Lord Dorchester is published By Authority." It was also issued separately and sold by the printer at 6*d*. the copy.—Can.P.A., *Neilson papers*, v. 70, May 6, 1791.

Copy located: None

720. QUEBEC, *Province*. CITIZENS

Caption title: AU ROI / SA TRES EXCELLENTE MAJESTÉ / PLACET des très soumis et loyaux sujets de Votre Majesté / habitans soussignés de la Ville de Québec en Amerique / Septentrionale. /

Colophon: [double rule] / QUEBEC: / PRINTED BY SAMUEL BEILSON [sic], MOUNTAIN-STREET. / [double rule] / A QUEBEC: CHEZ SAMUEL NEILSON, N° 3 RUE LA MONTAGNE. / [double rule]

A single sheet printed on both sides in 2 col.; type-page: 33 × 21 cm.

Contents: Placet (a petition begging remission of arrears of lodes et ventes, collected from Québecois) dated: "Québec, 10 Fevrier, 1786 [sic]" and signed by Jean Denis Laloy and 87 others (in French only); p. [1, at foot,-2], Agriculture: On the history, culture and qualities of the potato recommended to the farmers of Canada (in English and French).

This piece was published between Mar., 1789 and Jan., 1793, the limits of Samuel Neilson's period as printer in Quebec. It was *probably* issued by some interested party in 1791, as evidence of the objections to French seigniorial tenure, and of the advantages of the English freehold system and government patronage of agriculture.

Copy located: CaO (bound in *Quebec gazette* following No. 1344, Apr. 28, 1791, which contains Lanaudière's letter to Bédard on tenures).

721. QUEBEC, *Province.* GOVERNOR, 1791-1796 (*Dorchester*)

[2 ornamental rules] / CULTURE OF HEMP. / [double rule] / <Text> [By Order of] His Excellency LORD DORCHESTER, / HENRY MOTZ. / [QUEBEC 14 Februar] y, 1791. /

French side: [2 ornamental rules] / CULTURE DU CHANVRE. / [double rule] / <Text> Par Ordre de Son Excellence le LORD DORCHESTER, / HENRY MOTZ. / QUEBEC, 14 Fevrier, 1791. /

Double broadside: 38 lines, type-page: 21 × 14 cm. (each side). Text in English (left) and French (right). *Probably printed at Quebec, by Samuel Neilson, or possibly by Wm. Moore, 1791.*

The text gives notice that 2,000 bushels of hemp seed, sent by the King, will be distributed free before May 15, or if its arrival is delayed, in time for next year's sowing. It also gives directions for applications for the seed to be made to officers of the Quebec and Montreal branches of the Agricultural Society.

Copy located: CaOOA (mutilated copy in the *Askin papers*, v. 31).

722. QUEBEC, *Province.* LAWS, STATUTES, *etc.*

[A Bill (not yet passed) to explain and amend the Act entitled an Act or Ordinance for promoting the Inland Navigation and to promote the Trade to the Western Country.]

Probably a single leaf text in 2 col., English and French, on recto, endorsed title on verso. *Printed at Quebec, by Samuel Neilson, 1791,* as recorded;

"1791, Jan. 17. Printed for the Council Office (by order of J. Williams) 300 bills not yet passed for the Inland Navigation ½ Sheet Crown long Primer with indorsement—£1.15.

Folding ditto—5/. [Total:] £2."

—Can.P.A., *Neilson papers*, v. 70.

Ordered printed in both languages for use of the Council, Jan. 4, 1791, this bill removed restrictions on transport, licensing of fur traders, sale of rum to Indians, etc., and forbade sale of liquor to canoemen en route. It was passed with some amendment to become 31 Geo. III c. 1. In reporting the bill, the committee (of which the chairman was Wm. Grant, proprietor of two of the four rum distilleries in Quebec at that time) stated: "When this Committee contemplates the inexplicable hazards of life, health and fortune, to which the followers of the internal commerce [i.e. the fur trade] are exposed, it cannot but recommend to its protector, the Noble Lord at the head of the Government [Gov. Dorchester] that it be freed of every Obstacle, every charge, every real or imaginary Evil with which it is encumbered. Left to itself it will flourish and expand—Touch it, it decays or dies."—Can.P.A., Que. Leg. co. *Minutes*. Jan. 4, 1791.

Copy located: None.

723. QUEBEC, *Province*. LAWS, STATUTES, *etc.*

A Bill (not yet passed) to continue the Acts or Ordinances therein me[ntioned respecting the practice of law in civil causes.]

Text in English and French. *Printed at Quebec, by Samuel Neilson, 1791.* This short bill, ordered printed for the Legislative Council, Feb. 2, 1791, was passed with minor amendments to become 31 Geo. III c. 2.

Copy located: None.

724. QUEBEC, *Province*. LAWS, STATUTES, *etc.*

[A Bill (not yet passed) to continue and amend an Act passed in the seventeenth year of His Majesty's reign, intitled, "An Act to impower the Commissioners of peace to regulate the police of the Towns of Quebec and Montreal for a limited time".]

Text in English and French. *Printed at Quebec, by Samuel Neilson, 1791*, as recorded:

"1791, Feb. 4. Printed for Council Office (by order Mr. Williams) 250 Copies of a bill not passed concerning the Police 1 on ½ Sheet, long primer, —£1.12.6.

Folding ditto—5/. [Total:] £1.17.6."

—Can.P.A., *Neilson papers*, v. 70.

This bill was passed to become 31 Geo. III c. 3.

Copy located: None.

725. QUEBEC, *Province*. LAWS, STATUTES, *etc.*

[A Bill (not yet passed) to continue an Act intitled An Ordinance for regulating all such persons as keep horses and carriages to let and hire for the accomodation of travellers commonly called and known by the name of Maîtres de poste.]

Text in English and French. *Printed at Quebec, by Samuel Neilson, 1791.* This short bill, ordered printed for the Legislative Council, Feb. 2, 1791, for use of Council, was passed to become 31 Geo. III c. 4.

Copy located: None.

726. QUEBEC, *Province.* LAWS, STATUTES, *etc.*

[A Bill (not yet passed) for promulgating the laws and usages in force in this province respecting the building and repairing of churches and parsonage houses.]

Probably a single leaf text in English and French on recto, endorsed title on verso. *Printed at Quebec, by Samuel Neilson, 1791,* as recorded:

"1791, Apr. 9. Printed for Council Office (by Order Mr. Williams) 250 bills not passed concerning parsonage houses, 1 on a ½ Sheet Crown & indorsed —£1.12.6.

Folding ditto—5/. [Total:] £1.17.6."

—Can.P.A., *Neilson papers,* v. 70.

This bill was reported in Council by a committee appointed to consider: (1) a memorial from the [Catholic] bishop of Quebec, praying that parishes be authorized to assess themselves to build and repair churches etc., as under the French régime; (2) a petition from the Church of England at Kingston, praying for government aid or endowment, to build a church. The committee recommended that the latter petition be refused, and that the former be granted, in effect, by this bill. The publication of this draft produced controversial correspondence in the *Quebec herald,* Apr. 21, 1791, but the bill was passed to become 31 Geo. III c. 6.

Copy located: None.

727. QUEBEC, *Province.* LAWS, STATUTES, *etc.*

[A Bill (not yet passed) etc.]

Probably a single leaf, text in English and French on recto, endorsed title on verso. *Printed at Quebec by Samuel Neilson, 1791,* as recorded:

"1791, Feb. 14. Printed for Council Office (on order Mr. Williams) 250 Copies of 2 bills not passed 1 on ½ Sheet of Crown in long primer indorsed —£1.2.6.

Folding ditto—5/. [Total] £1.17.6."

—Can.P.A., *Neilson papers,* v. 70.

The "two bills" are probably preliminary drafts of 31 Geo. III c. 5, an act to prevent obstructions to the inland commerce by death of a superintendant; and of 31 Geo. III c. 7, an act to reward Samuel Hopkins and Angus Macdonell for methods of making pot and pearl ashes.

Copy located: None.

728. QUEBEC, *Province.* LAWS, STATUTES, *etc.*

[Anno Tricesimo Primo Georgii Tertii Regis. Chap. I. An Act To explain and amend the Act . . . for promoting the Inland Navigation, etc.

French side:

Anno tricesimo primo Georgii tertii Regis. Chap. I. Acte qui explique et amend l'Acte . . . qui encourage la Navigation Intérieure, etc.]

fo. [4] p. text in 2 col., English and French. *Printed at Quebec, by Samuel Neilson 1791.*

Contents: 31 Geo. III c. 1 (as above); 31 Geo. III c. 2, an act to continue or amend the acts respecting the law in civil causes; 31 Geo. III c. 3, an act to continue and amend an act to empower commissioners of peace to regulate the police, etc.; French translation in col. 2.

This was a separate issue of the text of these three acts together as they appeared in the *Quebec gazette*, Apr. 14, 1791. It was probably reprinted with the usual *Gazette* heading and colophon but without the correspondence, etc., which appears after the text in the *Gazette* issue. Neilson recorded this reprint:

"1791, Apr. 29. Printed for Council Office (by order Mr. Williams) on the Gazette types, 500 Ordinances, chap. I, II, III, respecting Inland Navigation, Practice of law, and the Police, making 1 sheet Crown 10/ per Hundred.—£2.10.

Folding Ditto—10/. [Total] £3."

—Can.P.A., *Neilson papers*, v. 70.

There was also issued previously, reprints of each of these ordinances separately, recorded by the printer:

"1791, Apr. 15. Printed for the Council office . . .
500 Ordinances Chap. I . . . 10/ per hun[d] — £2.10.
500 Ordinances Chap. II . . . £2.10.
500 Ordinances Chap. III . . . £2.10.
Folding the above 1500 Ordinances—10/
[Total:] £8."

—*ibid.*, v. 70.

These ordinances are reprinted in Can.P.A., *Report, 1914-15*, from which the titles as above are taken.

Copy located: None.

729. QUEBEC, *Province.* LAWS, STATUTES, *etc.*

[Anno Tricesimo Primo Georgii Tertii Regis. Chap. IV. An Act to continue an Act . . . for regulating . . . Maîtres de Poste.

French side:

Anno tricesimo primo Georgii tertii Regis. Chap. IV. Acte Qui Continue un Acte . . . Maîtres de Poste.]

Text in 2 col. English and French, *Printed at Quebec, by Samuel Neilson, 1791.*

Contents: 31 Geo. III c. 4 (as above); 31 Geo. III c. 5, an act to prevent obstructions to the inland commerce by the death of a superintendent; 31 Geo. III c. 6, an act concerning the building and repairing of churches; French translation in col. 2.

Like No. 728, this publication was reprinted from the *Quebec gazette*, May 5, 1791, as recorded by the Printer:

"1791 May 6. Printed for Council Office (by order Mr. Williams) 500 Copies of Ordinances chap. IV, V & VI on the Gazette types @ 5/ per hundred, ½ Sheet Crown long primer—£1.5."

—Can P.A., *Neilson papers*, v. 70.

These ordinances are reprinted in Can.P.A., *Report, 1914-15*, from which the titles as above are taken.

Copy located: None.

730. QUEBEC, *Province.* LAWS, STATUTES, *etc.*

[*Marginal note within circular frame:*] PASSED / 30th April, 1791: / [rule] / J. WILLIAMS, / C.L.C. / [*Caption title:* double rule] / Anno Tricesimo Primo GEORGII Tertii REGIS. / CHAP. VI. / [rule] / AN ACT, / OR Ordinance concerning the building and / repairing of Churches, Parsonage Houses, / and Church-yards. /

French side:

[*Marginal note within circular frame:*] PASSÉ / Le 30 Avril 1791: / [rule] / J. WILLIAMS, G.C.L. [sic] / [*Caption title:*] [double rule] / Anno Tricesimo Primo GEORGII Tertii REGIS. / Chap. VI. / [rule] / ACTE, / ou Ordonnance qui concerne la Con-/struction et la réparation des Eglises, / Presbiteres, et Cimetieres. /

Endorsed title: La présente Ordonnance étant la Loi qu'il faudra suivre / désormais dans les cas de construction et de réparation des / Eglises, &c: Monseig[r] l'Eveque en fait adresser des copies / à tous les Curés du Diocèse, tant pour leur usage propre / que pour celui de leurs Paroisses respectives. / QUEBEC, 6 MAI, 1791:

1 *l.*; recto, 31 Geo. III c. 6, text in 2 col. English and French, type-page: 34 × 21.1 cm.; verso, endorsed title, also address: "A Monsieur [blank, etc.]."

Like No. 728-729, this is a separate issue of the ordinance reprinted from the types of the *Quebec gazette*, May 5, 1791. It was *printed at Quebec, by Samuel Neilson*, as recorded:

> "1791, May 6. Printed for the Bishop of Quebec 150 Ordinances respecting the building of churches—17/6."
>
> —Can.P.A., *Neilson papers*, v. 70.

This ordinance is reprinted in Can.P.A., *Report, 1914-15.*

Copy located: CaO.

731. QUEBEC, *Province.* LAWS, STATUTES, *etc.*

[Anno Tricesimo Primo Georgii Tertii Regis. Chap. VII. An Act or Ordinance to reward Samuel Hopkins, and Angus Macdonell and others, for their Inventions of two new and improved Methods of making Pot and Pearl Ashes.

French side:

Anno Tricesimo Primo Georgii Tertii Regis. Chap. VII. Un Acte. Une Ordonnance pour récompenser Samuel Hopkins et Angus Macdonell et autres pour leur découverte de deux nouvelles méthodes améliorées au sujet de la fabrication de la potasse et de la perlasse.]

Text in 2 col. English and French, reprinted from the *Quebec gazette*, June 23, 1791 (in the *Gazette*, Hopkins's and Macdonell's attestations and specifications follow the ordinance). *Printed at Quebec, by Samuel Neilson, 1791*, as recorded:

"June 24, 1791. Printed for Council Office (by order Mr. Williams) 500 Copies of Ordinance Chap. VII on the Gazette types, ½ Sheet Crown. 5/ [per] h[d] —£1.5."

—Can.P.A., *Neilson papers*, v. 70.

This ordinance is reprinted in Can.P.A., *Report, 1914-15*, from which the titles above are taken.

Copy located: None.

732. QUEBEC, *Province.* LEGISLATIVE COUNCIL

Caption title: [double rule] / A BILL / (Not yet assented to,) / [double rule] / For repealing certain Clauses in an Ordinance, intitled, "An Ordinance con-/"cerning Advocates, Attornies, Solicitors, and Notaries, and for the more / "easy collection of His Majesty's Revenues", passed in the 25th. Year of / His Majesty's Reign; and also, the Ordinance passed in the 27th Year of / His Majesty's Reign to amend the same. / [rule] /

Colophon: [rule] / QUEBEC: PRINTED BY SAMUEL NEILSON, N° 3 MOUNTAIN-STREET. /

French caption: [Double rule] / BILL / (Non encor statué) / [double rule] / Pour révoquer certaines Clauses dans l'Ordonnance Intitulée "Ordonnance con-/"cernant les Avocats, Solliciteurs, Procureurs et Notaires—et qui pourvoit plus / "efficacement aux Revenus de Sa Majesté," et aussi l'Ordonnance passée / dans la vingt-septieme année du Régne de Sa Majesté pour amender icelle. / [rule] /

Colophon: A QUEBEC: CHEZ SAMUEL NEILSON, N° 3 RUE LA MONTAGNE. / [rule] /

1 *l.*; text in 2 col. English and French, on recto; type-page: 25.7 × 21 cm.; verso, endorsed title within a frame: "A Bill (not yet assented to) [etc.], Bill (Non encor statué) [etc.]."

This bill confirmed the requirement of a licence from the governor for advocates [etc.], and required further, an examination by the attorney-general to ascertain the character, loyalty, and competency of the candidate. It was passed by the Council, but did not receive the governor's assent. Neilson recorded its printing:

"1791, June 21. Printed for Council Office 250 Copies of a bill not assented to concerning Lawyers and Notaries ½ Sheet, Long Primer, indorsed. £1.12.6. Folding ditto—5/ [Total:] £1.17.6."

—Can.P.A., *Neilson papers*, v. 70.

Copy located: CaOOA (filed with memorials in Can.P.A., Que. "S" *Leg.co.papers*, 1781 [sic]).

733. QUEBEC, *Province.* LEGISLATIVE COUNCIL

[A Bill (not yet passed) to explain and amend the Ordinances now in force relative to the Militia of the Province of Quebec.]

Probably 1 *l.*, text in 2 col., English and French on recto, endorsed title on verso. *Printed at Quebec, by Samuel Neilson, 1791,* as recorded:

"1791, Apr. 17. Printed for the Council Office (by order of Mr. Williams) 250 Bills not yet passed to explain and amend Ordinances now in force relative to the Militia of the Province. in half sheet Crown with indorsement —£1.12.6.

Folding ditto—5/ [Total:] £1.17.6."

—Can.P.A., *Neilson papers*, v. 70.

A committee of the Council, appointed Aug. 25, 1790, to revise militia laws, presented a report, Mar. 10, 1791, and draft of a bill (by François Baby, adjutant-general of militia). This bill with considerable amendment, especially by Col. Henry Caldwell, was ordered printed in both languages for use of Council, Apr. 7, 1791, but it was not passed by the end of the session, the last of the Legislative Council of the old province of Quebec.

Copy located: None.

734. QUEBEC, *Province.* LEGISLATIVE COUNCIL

[double rule] / ANCIENT / FRENCH ARCHIVES / OR / EXTRACTS / From the Minutes of Council / Relating to the Records of Canada / While under the Government of France. / [double rule] / [printer's ornament] / [double rule] / [double rule] / QUEBEC . . . . PRINTED BY SAMUEL NEILSON, ... M.DCC.XCI. / [double rule] /

French t.-p.:

[double rule] / ANCIENNES / Archives Françaises, / OU / EXTRAIT / Des Minutes du Conseil / Qui concernent les Regîtres du Canada / lorsqu'il étoit sous le gouvernement de France. / [double rule] / [ornament] / [double rule] / [double rule] / A QUEBEC . . . . CHEZ SAMUEL NEILSON, ... M.DCC.XCI. / [double rule] /

4to. A-N[4]; 2 p. l., [i], 49 [i.e. 98] p.; type-page: 14.2 × 10.5 cm. Text in English and French on opposite pages numbered in duplicate. One *l.* of sig. N is folded around sig. A-N3 to precede t.-p. After sig. L (and following p. 43 English) there is a leaf without signature, its recto (paged) bearing the text of p. 43 (French) and its blank verso pasted to the blank recto of p. 44 (English), the first leaf of sig. M. Sig. M and N (p. 44-49) were printed later than sig. A-L, but issued with them apparently.

Contents: p. l. [1], blank; p. l. [2] recto, English t.-p.; verso blank; p. [i] i.e. recto of p. [1] (English), French t.-p.; p. [1]-2, Ancient French archives, etc., minutes of Council, Dec. 27, 1787-Jan. 28, 1791, relating to investigation of archives and to publication of this work; p. 2-32, Report of the [investigating] committee for the district of Quebec (including an inventory of records) signed by Thomas Dunn, Quebec, Mar. 17, 1790; p. 33-43, Report of the [investigating] committee for the district of Montreal (including an inventory of records) signed by Picotte'e de Belestre, Montreal, Nov. 10, 1790; p. 44-49, Minutes of Council, July 23, 1791, with report of the [publication] committee, signed by Wm. Smith, chairman, Quebec, July 8, 1791; verso of p. 49, (French), blank.

This work was printed in 700 copies, of which 435 were distributed by the sheriffs among the judges, magistrates, and principal inhabitants, 80 copies among Catholic clergy and 6 to each legislative councillor. It was prepared in pursuance of the provincial ordinance, 30 Geo. III c. 8, an act for the better preservation and distribution of the ancient French archives. This states: "Whereas there are several hundred volumes of papers, manuscripts and records, very interesting to such of the inhabitants of this province as hold property under titles acquired prior to the conquest, which ought to be disposed of as to give cheap and easy access to them . . . the ancient records of the District of Montreal require speedy attention to preserve them from danger and ruin . . . the erection of Three Rivers as a separate district renders necessary the segregation of papers concerning that District. Therefore it may be lawful for the Governor-in-council to make orders touching the arrangement, removal, digesting, printing, publishing, distributing, preserving and disposing of the same papers, manuscripts and records. Every person possessed of records of any public office prior to the conquest may be ordered to surrender the same to the office."

The printing of this work was recorded:

"1791, Apr. 29. Printed for the Council Office (by Order Mr. Williams) 700 Copies (50 on fine paper) of Report of Committee . . . Records . . . containing 11 Sheets of Pott on Brevier types in 4to each Sheet at 37/6 for 1st hundred and 7/6 for each subsequent hundred (making about 1/3½ each copy).—£45.7.6.

Aug. 25. Printed for the Council Office (by order of Mr. Williams) 700 Copies of the last two sheets of the Reports on French Records (50 on fine paper) at 37/6 per sheet for the 1st hundred and 7/6 per sheet for each subsequent hundred—£8.5.

Binding covering stitching & cutting the above 700 copies @ 2d.—£5.16.8. [Total: £59.9.2.]"—Can.P.A., *Neilson papers*, v. 70.

Facsim. illus. of English t.-p. is in Gagnon: *Essai de bibliographie canadienne*, 1: no. 116; of French t.-p., in Can.P.A., *Report, 1914-15*, App. D, following p. 80.

The full text (of which this work was extracts only) of proceedings on ancient French archives, with additional papers on archives, 1791-99, is printed in Can.P.A., *Report, 1904*, [81]-189.

Copies located: CaO; CaOOA; CaOT (2 cop., cop. 2 imperfect); CaOTO; CaQ (2 cop.); CaQM; CaQMS (2 cop.); CaQQH (2 cop.); CaQQL; DLC; Ketcheson; MH (2 cop.); MHi; MWA; MiD-B (2 cop.); NN; RPJ; Witton.

735. QUEBEC, *Province.* LIEUTENANT-GOVERNOR, 1790-1791 (*Clarke*)

BY HIS EXCELLENCY, / ALURED CLARKE, ESQUIRE, / . . . / . . . / . . . / A PROCLAMATION. / <Text> / Given . . . / . . . [at] Quebec, . . . / . . . / [25th August, 1791] . . . / . . . / ALURED CLARKE. / By His EXCELLENCY'S Command, / HUGH FINLAY, Acting Secretary. /

French on right:

PAR SON EXCELLENCE / ALURED CLARKE, ECUIER. / . . . / . . . / . . . / . . . / PROCLAMATION. / <Text> / Donné . . . au /

Château St. Louis dans la Ville de Quebec, . . . / . . . / . . . / . . . [25e Aout, 1791] / ALURED CLARKE. / Par Ordre de SON EXCELLENCE, / HUGH FINLAY, A.S. / Traduit par Ordre de Son EXCELLENCE, / P.A. DE BONNE, A.S et T.F. /

Double broadside: English on left, 27 lines, type-page: 22.7 × 15.8 cm.; French on right, 32 lines, type-page: 24.5 × 15.8 cm. verso, blank. This is a handsome production set in types somewhat larger than usual. The English text is in english type well leaded, the French text in great primer; the headlines are uniform on both sides. It was *printed at Quebec, by Samuel Neilson, 1791*, as recorded:

> "1791, Aug. 25. Printed for Council Office (by Order Mr. Williams) 300 Proclamations on Gen. Clarke's taking command of the province. French & English on 4to Demy—£1.7.6.
>
> Pasting up same in Quebec.—5/6."
>
> —Can.P.A., *Neilson papers*, v. 70.

Text: "Whereas His Most Gracious Majesty has been pleased to grant His Royal Leave of Absence to . . . Guy Lord Dorchester, . . . in consequence of whose departure, the command of the said Province devolves upon me [etc., Clarke authorizes all officers of the crown to continue in their several offices]."

French text: "Ayant plu à sa très Gracieuse Majesté d'accorder son Congé Royal d'Absence à . . . Guy Lord Dorchester . . . en consequence de son départ le Commandement de la dite Province m'étant devolu, [etc.]."

This proclamation is reprinted in Can.P.A., *Report, 1918.*

Copy located: CaOOA (filed in Can.P.A., "*S*" *Proclamations, L.C., 1771-1791*).

736. QUEBEC GAZETTE. CARRIER'S ADDRESS

Verses of the Printer's Boy / WHO CARRIES THE QUEBEC GAZETTE / To the Customers / [rule] / JANUARY 1, 1792. /

French side:

Etrennes du Garcon / QUE PORTE LA GAZETTE / Aux Pratiques. / [rule] / Le 1er. JANVIER, 1792. / Sur l'air, Quand je vous ai donné mon Coeur, j'avois le votre engage. / ou sur celui de Joconde. /

Broadside: type-page: 34.5 × 27 cm. in double rule frame. *Printed at Quebec, by Samuel Neilson, 1791.* English verse on left, 64 lines; French on right, about 72 lines, partly in 2 col.

Copy located: CaO (bound in *Quebec gazette* at end of 1791).

737. PERRAULT, JOSEPH-FRANCOIS, 1753-1844

[ornamental rule] / MÉMOIRE / EN CASSATION / DU TESTAMENT / De Mr. SIMON SANGUINET, Ecuyer, Seigneur de / la Salle, &c. Précédé du TESTAMENT. / [ornamental rule] /

Colophon, p. 19: Ghez [sic] FLEURY MESPLET, Imprimeur & Libraire, rue Notre-Dame N° 44. /

4to. [*[2], 2-3*[4]]; 19 p.; type-page: 19.3 × 13 cm.

Contents: p. [1], t.-p.; p. [2], blank; p. 3-8, Copie du testament; p. 9-19, Mémoire, signed at end: "Montréal, 10 Janvier 1791. J. F. Perrault, Practicien des rives du Mississipi"; verso of p. 19, blank.

The will of Simon Sanguinet, judge in the Court of Common Pleas, Montreal district, who died Mar. 16, 1790, was contested by his heirs, whose case Perrault presented in this *Mémoire*. The will included in clause 10, the bequest described in Sanguinet's obituary:

". . . a liberal donation to the establishment of a university. The estate is said to be above £15,000 [Halifax] currency and that part bequeathed to a university, believed to be about £11,000, consists of an extensive seigneurie in the Montreal district and a house in the town of Montreal. It is reported that at the time of the making of his will, a copy of the printed report of the Committee on education was found on his bed—a striking instance of the utility of publication."—*Quebec gazette*, Mar. 25, 1790.

Copy located: CaOOA has photostat of a copy formerly owned by M. Cyrille Tessier of Quebec city, and later by M. Daviault, Berthier, Quebec.

738. ST. JOHN, ISLAND OF. LAWS, STATUTES, *etc.*

ACTS / PASSED AT THE / GENERAL ASSEMBLY / OF HIS MAJESTY'S / ISLAND OF SAINT JOHN, / BEGUN AND HOLDEN AT CHARLOTTE TOWN, ON THE TWENTY SECOND DAY OF MARCH, ONE THOUSAND / SEVEN HUNDRED AND NINETY, AND THENCE CONTINUED BY PROROGATION TO / THE FOURTH [sic] DAY OF NOVEMBER, IN THE YEAR AFORESAID. / ANNO TRICESSIMO PRIMO REGIS GEORGII III. / [rule] / [royal arms] / [rule] / [double rule] / CHARLOTTE TOWN, ISLAND OF SAINT JOHN: / PRINTED BY WILLIAM A. RIND,/ PRINTER TO THE KING'S MOST EXCELLENTY MAJESTY./ 1791. /

fo. [*[1], A]-D[2]; 1 p. l., 16 p.; type-page: 21.4 × 14.6 cm.

Contents: p. l. recto, t.-p.; verso, blank; p. 1-16, 31 Geo. III c. 1-8, acts passed in the second session of the sixth Assembly Nov. 10-20, 1790.

Copies located: GBLP (2 cop. in C.O. 226/13: 575-592; B.T. 1/2 In-Letters); NNHi.

739. [SILLS, JONATHAN]

LA / BASTILLE SEPTENTRIONALE, / OU / LES TROIS SUJETS / BRITANNIQUES OPPRIMES / Quod nequeo monstrare & sentio tantum. / [rule] / Prix 40 Sous. / [rule] / [printer's ornament] / Se Vend / A MONTREAL, / Chez FLEURY MESPLET, Imprimeur, / A QUEBEC, Chez Mr. BOUTHILLIER, au / Bureau de la Poste, / Aux Trois Rivières, chez Me. MELLISH; à Varennes, chez Mr. / ALEXIS LAHAYE; à Berthier, chez Mr. L. Labadie; / & à l'Assomption, chez Mr. FARIBAUT, Notaire. /

8vo. *-4*[4]; 32 p.; type-page: 16 × 8.5 cm.

Contents: p. [1], t.-p. p. [2], blank; p. [3-4], Préface de l'Auteur; p. 5-32, La Bastille Septentrionale etc. (including supporting documents, p. 26-32).

This work was probably written by Jonathan Sills and published between Nov., 1791 and Feb., 1792 (advertised "lately published" in the *Montreal gazette*, Feb. 23, 1792). It was occasioned by the prosecution, Aug., 1790-May, 1791, of Jonathan and Joseph Sills and Malcolm Fraser, sons of English settlers at Trois Rivières, who refused to perform militia duties under the local French officers. The preface is a protest against the infringement of the liberty of the subject by unequal and arbitrary administration of laws, especially the militia laws—passed when the two provinces [i.e. Lower and Upper Canada] groaned beneath "une Constitution éphémere." It concludes with an admonition to legislators under the new constitution: "Des bonnes loix forment de bons sujets."

The body of the work sets forth the circumstances of the Sills's and Fraser's arrest, imprisonment, trial, fine, appeal, etc., Aug., 1790-May, 1791. This was a *cause célèbre*, which, with other militia cases (*see* No. 680), inspired considerable correspondence in the Montreal and Quebec papers, 1790-92. His trial long since over, Sills may have published this statement of his grievance—in French—in connection with his suit for damages just instituted (he stated, p. 32 *note*) in the Court of Common Pleas—"Malheur aux Tyrans. Malheur sur-tout aux hommes injustes qui les favoriseoient." It is to be noted that shortly after this episode, Gov. Dorchester issued instructions for the organization in separate companies of French and English militia, under their own officers.

The text is reprinted with a discussion of the case by Benjamin Sulte: *Chevalier de Niverville*, in Roy. Soc. of Can., *Trans.*, 1909, ser. 3, v. 3, sec. 1, p. 43-72.

Copies located: CaQ; CaQMG; CaQMS (2 cop); CaQQL; Gordonsmith. Another copy, formerly owned by the late M. Cyrille Tessier, Quebec city, has not been seen by the writer, but it is believed to have passed into possession of M. Daviault, Berthier, Quebec.

740. SOCIETY FOR PROMOTING AGRICULTURE IN NOVA SCOTIA

LETTERS AND PAPERS / ON / AGRICULTURE: / EXTRACTED FROM THE CORRESPONDENCE / OF A / SOCIETY INSTITUTED AT HALIFAX, / FOR / Promoting Agriculture / IN THE / PROVINCE OF NOVA-SCOTIA. / TO WHICH IS ADDED / A SELECTION OF PAPERS ON VARIOUS BRANCHES / OF / HUSBANDRY / FROM SOME OF THE BEST PUBLICATIONS ON THE SUBJECT / IN / EUROPE AND AMERICA. / [rule] / VOL. I. / [rule] / Virum bonum cum laudabant majores, ita laudabant—"Bonum Agrico-/"lam, Bonum Colonum,"—amplissimè laudari existamabatur, qui ita lauda-/batur. / CATO DE RE RUSTICA. / When our ancestors would praise any person as a good man, they thought it / the amplest attestation of his merit to say— "HE WAS A GOOD FARMER, A / "GOOD HUSBANDMAN." / ANON. / [rule] / HALIFAX: / PRINTED BY JOHN HOWE, IN BARRINGTON-STREET. / M.DCC.XCI. /

8vo. A-S^4; 139, ii p., 1 *l.*; illus. (diagrs.), p. 105, 113; type-page: 18.5 × 9 cm.

Contents: p. [1], t.-p.; p. [2], blank; p. [3]-11, To the farmers and land holders in Nova-Scotia; p. 12-14, Plan of a society instituted at Halifax Dec. 10, 1789; p. 14-139, Minutes, proceedings, letters, and papers; verso of p. 139, blank; p. [i]-ii, contents: 1 *l.* blank.

This publication was advertised for sale at 1*s.* 3*d.* the copy, in Howe's newspaper, the *Halifax journal*, Mar. 29, 1792.

The Society for promoting agriculture in Nova-Scotia (like the Agricultural Society in Canada [i.e. Quebec] was instituted by members of the official and professional groups in Halifax. Lieut.-Gov. Parr was patron, Richard Bulkeley, the provincial secretary, and Rev. Wm. Cochran (head of the College and Academy at Windsor, N.S.) were active promoters. It encouraged the founding of local societies throughout the province and maintained close relations with similar organizations in Quebec, New Brunswick, the United States, and Great Britain, reprinting papers from journals from the latter two. It published agricultural news and advice in Halifax newspapers, offered medals and cash for clearing land, etc. Letters on the society and its interests appeared in the *Nova-Scotia magazine* of which Cochran was editor. This volume of *Letters and papers* apparently had no successor, although the secretary of the Society inserted a note in the *Royal gazette*, Halifax, N.S., Feb. 25, 1794, that "useful information . . . will be published in the next volume of the Society's *Papers*." Few of the papers in the first volume were written by members of the Society. So a silver medal was offered to encourage local talent in that direction. The semi-official introductory letter, p. 3-14, points out the value of scientific knowledge to the pioneer farmer, the necessity for local experimentation, and the superior importance of agriculture to fishing and other trades in promoting prosperity for Nova Scotia.

Copies located: CaNs; CaNsHD; CaQQL; MH; MWA.

741. TANSWELL, JAMES

[Grammar and Syntax of the English Language. Also, A Treatise of Arithmetic, in French.]

Proposed publication was suggested in a postscript to Tanswell's announcement of opening of his evening school at Quebec for the session, Oct. 31, 1791-May 1, 1792:

"In order to facilitate to the Canadians the knowledge of the English language, a thing so essentially necessary in this Country, he [Tanswell] offers to publish a grammar and Syntax with a set of Exercises all explained in French, by such an easy method, that anyone who can read, may make himself Master of the Language, with little or no assistance; and so concise, that the whole will form a small pocket Volume.

"ALSO a Treatise of Arithmetic in French calculated for the use of this country, and so clearly laid down, that any one may acquire the whole science, without the help of a Master.

"As he has only been led to the above arduous undertaking by an ardent desire of advancing the Cause of Learning, which is promoting the happiness of mankind, without the least view of profit, or any other Gratification, except that of the pleasure of being useful to Society: he will get them ready for of [sic] the Press as soon as any system, by subscription or otherwise, can be adopted, for defraying the necessary expences." —*Quebec gazette*, sup. Oct. 20, 1791, *et seq.*

There is no evidence that Tanswell published the school books thus proposed, though for many years he gave lessons in writing, arithmetic, bookkeeping, etc., also "the French and English languages . . . Geography and . . . the Copernican System, together with such Chronological Institutions as are necessary to understand history, the most useful study in Life."

Copy located: None.

742. WILLIAMS, EDWARD

[The Second Edition of the Ready Reckoner for the Province of Quebec, Nova Scotia and the States of America, containing Easy Rules for converting the different Currencies of Sterling, Army, Quebec or Halifax, and the States of America into each other. Calculated by Major Williams of the Royal Artillery. To which are added the following tables, viz. An easy table of grams from 1 to 1000; the weight of gold coin, with its value in Quebec or Halifax. With three additional tables not published in the first edition. *Printed at Quebec, by Wm. Moore, 1791.*]

This publication was advertised in Moore's newspaper, the *Quebec herald*, from Feb. 21, 1791: "In a few days will be published and ready, Price one shilling, The Second Edition of the Ready Reckoner [etc. as above]." It was issued about Apr. 4, "Price 1/6 in marble [paper covers]." The later advertisements indicate that the "three additional tables not published in the first [1790] edition [were:] Expences and income by the week or year from one penny to twenty shillings by the day; Foreign measures in English inches and decimals; The value of one hundred weight of goods at any price from one farthing to eighteen pence per pound."

—*Quebec herald*, Feb. 21-Apr. 4, 1791.

Copy located: None.

743. ZIMMERMANN, EBERHARDT AUGUST WILHELM VON, 1743-1815

[A Political Survey of the State of Europe, just prior to the present wars, in sixteen tables; illustrated with Observations on the Wealth and Commerce, the Government, Finances, Military State and Religion of the several countries. By E. A. W. Zimmerman, Professor of Natural History at Brunswick and member of several scientific societies.]

Proposed printing at Quebec, by Wm. Moore, 1790-91, was advertised in the *Quebec herald*, Sept. 27, 1790-May 16, 1791. The work was to be printed in demy 8vo. in "good sized letter" and issued in ten numbers of forty pages each, fortnightly on Saturdays, at 1*s.* each number. It was to go to press as soon as two hundred copies had been subscribed. "The present disturbances in Europe render this publication of universal utility. By it every reader may become a political geographer, as it is calculated to refresh the informed and at the same time adapted to instruct the weakest intellect."

Zimmermann's *Political survey* was first published in London, 1787, where, Moore stated, "It has gone through three editions of 4000 each and continues [1791] to have a rapid sale. [Also] It has been reprinted in the United States with great advantage to the publisher, James Rivington." There is no evidence, however, that it was printed in Quebec.

744. AGRICULTURAL SOCIETY IN CANADA. QUEBEC BRANCH

[double rule] / MOYENS / DE SE / PRESERVER / DU / BLED NOIR / [double rule] /

8vo. L-M^4, N^2; [35]-53 p. type-page: 16.5 × 10.2 cm. *printed at Quebec, by Samuel Neilson, 1792.*

Contents: p. [35], t.-p.; p. [36]-37, De la Gazette de Québec; p. 37-53, Mémoire sur les experiences faites dans la Paroisse de Surcy; p. 53 verso, blank.

The excerpt from the *Quebec gazette* (p. [36]-37) comprises a letter to Samuel Neilson stating: ". . . les Directeurs de la Société d'Agriculture vous prient de publier dans votre prochaine la lettre ci-joint adressée au President avec la Traité . . . lequel indique la cause du Bled noir et le moyens de prévenir. [signed:] Hugh Finlay Sécr." Appended is another letter signed: "Un Cultivateur des Côtes de la Rivière Chambly." This letter describes the Canadian farmer's experiences in planting and harvesting a crop according to advices published in the Agricultural Society's *Papers, 1790,* and recommends a *Mémoire* by M. Gonfreville, of Andelsey. The *Mémoire* (p. 37-53) describes experiments in the prevention of smut in wheat made by the author on his farm in Surcy parish [Andelsey, France].

This work is the French text of the item following (No. 745). The pagination suggests that both were issued in continuation of the Agricultural Society's *Papers and letters* of 1790 (No. 623). The production was recorded by Samuel Neilson:

"1792, May 7. Agricultural Society owes Printing Office for 300 Copies of the Pamphlet on means of preserving grain from Smut.—£7.12.6.
Stitching D^o in blue paper & pasting printed labels on 140 $\frac{1}{2}$d. each—12/6.
[Total:] £8.5.0 "—Can.P.A., *Neilson papers,* v. 70.

The printer's charge (£71 12*s.* 6*d.* for 300 copies of a work making 2$\frac{1}{2}$ sheets in 8vo., a rate approximately the same as that of No. 623) suggests that French and English text, No. 744 and No. 745, together formed the complete "pamphlet." It was issued, probably, the two sections together also separate.

Copy located: CaQMS (p. [35]-53 only, as described above. This fragment, now in a modern pamphlet cover, shows traces of two earlier binders' stitchings).

745. AGRICULTURAL SOCIETY IN CANADA. QUEBEC BRANCH

[double rule] / METHOD / OF / PRESERVING / Grain / FROM SMUT. / [double rule] /

Colophon, p. 67: Quebec: Printed by SAMUEL NEILSON, N° 3, Mountain-Street. /

8vo. [*^{1}, 2-3*^{4}]; p. l., 52-67 p.; type-page: 16.5 × 10.2 cm.

Contents: p. l. recto, t.-p.; verso, Excerpt from the *Quebec gazette*, containing a covering letter by Hugh Finlay, secretary of the Agricultural Society, and a letter signed: "A Farmer on the Banks of the River Chambly and a Member of the Agricultural Society." The latter describes his own experience and introduces "a Treatise wrote by Mr. Gonfreville of Andelsey in France, that fully shews the cause of smut in grain"; p. 52-67, An account of experiments made in Andelsey. Note at end: "Translated from the French."

This is an English translation of No. 744 with which it was issued, apparently, in continuation of No. 623 (*see* note in No. 744).

Copy located: MBAt (p. l., 52-67 p. only, as described above, bound in a volume of 18th-century pamphlets following a copy of the Agricultural Society's *Papers and letters, 1790*).

746. ALMANACS. LOWER CANADA

[Calendrier de Montréal pour l'Année 1793.]

Broadside. This sheet almanac like *Calendrier de Montréal* of preceding years, was undoubtedly *printed at Montreal, by Fleury Mesplet*, this in 1792 (though the date of imprint may appear the same as in title). It was advertised: "Le Calendrier de Montréal pour l'Année 1793, A Vendre chez François Sareau, rue Notre Dame, No. 29, et chez l'Imprimeur, No. 44."—*Montreal gazette*, Jan. 3, 1793.

Copy located: None.

747. ALMANACS. LOWER CANADA

CALENDRIER pour l'Année 1793, pour Quebec, par les $306^{d.}$ $30^{m.}$ de Longitude, et $46^{d.}$ $55^{m.}$ de Latitude. / [double rule] /

Colophon: A QUEBEC: chez SAMUEL NEILSON, Imprimeur et Libraire, N° 3 Rue la Montagne. /

Broadside: type-page: 56 × 40 cm.

Contents: Calendrier, in ornamental frame: 42 × 40 cm.; below *Calendrier*: "Histoire physique du corps de l'homme—Natural history of the human body" (text in 4 col. in French only).

This sheet almanac was advertised as "just published" in the *Quebec gazette*, Dec. 20, 1792.

Copy located: CaO (bound in *Quebec gazette* at end of 1792).

748. ALMANACS. LOWER CANADA

[The Quebec Almanack for 1793] was projected but not published. The printer advertised for copy:

"The Printer, ever studious to render his labours as useful as possible, intreats the Amateurs of the Respublica to favor him with the communication of any papers of public instruction or utility . . . by the middle of next month at the farthest [i.e. Nov. 15, 1792]. Last year several papers came too late for insertion in the Quebec Almanack."—*Quebec gazette*, Oct. 25, 1792.

The printer, Samuel Neilson, probably never completed the work of compiling and editing material for this almanac, for he died of tuberculosis, Jan. 12, 1793. Neither the Brown-Neilson printing office records nor the *Quebec gazette* contain any reference to a Quebec almanac for 1793, which would suggest that it was actually published.

749. ALMANACS. NOVA SCOTIA

[Der Neuschottländische Calendar Auf das Jahr Christi 1793 . . . ? *Halifax, N.S., gedruckt Anth. Henrich, 1792.*]

The advertisement in Anthony Henry's newspaper suggests that *Der Neuschottländische Calender*, published for 1788-91, continued to appear:

"Just published . . . the Nova Scotia Calender for 1793, [etc.] Likewise just published and ready for sale The German Almanack for 1793."—*Royal gazette*, Halifax, N.S., Nov. 20. 1793.

Copy located: None.

750. ALMANACS. NOVA SCOTIA

[The Nova-Scotia Calender or an Almanack for . . . 1792. second edition. *Halifax, N.S., A. Henry, 1792.*]

This almanac was advertised on Jan. 10, 1792: "In a few days will be published [etc.]" and on Jan. 17, 1792: "[Published and] To be sold by the Printer, the Second Edition of the Nova-Scotia Calender, or an Almanack . . . with alterations and additions."—*Royal gazette*, Halifax, N.S., Jan. 10-17, 1792. This "second edition" was probably a reissue of the sheets of No. 691 with a cancel leaf (or leaves, p. [29-30 or 32]) recording changes in the Nova Scotia administration due to the death of Lieut.-Gov. Parr, Nov. 25, 1791. Possibly it included also as additional matter, some eulogy or account of the obsequies, similar to that in the special mourning number of the *Royal gazette*, Halifax, N.S., Nov. 29. 1791.

Copy located: None.

751. ALMANACS. NOVA SCOTIA

THE / NOVA-SCOTIA CALENDER / OR AN / ALMANACK, / FOR THE YEAR . . . / 1793. / . . . / . . . / . . . / WHEREIN IS CONTAINED. / THE ECLIPSES . . . / [6 lines]/ The View of HALIFAX, was taken from FOSTER'S, on the Eastern side of / the Harbour. / [rule] / Calculated for the Meridian of / HALIFAX, . . . / . . . / . . . / [rule] / By METONICUS. / [rule] / [verse, 4 lines] / [rule] / HALIFAX: / Printed and Sold by ANTHONY HENRY, at his Printing Office in Sackville-/ Street, Corner of Grafton-Street. / [title within single rule frame]

12mo. [36] p. (incl. illus.), fold table; type-page: 16 × 9.7 cm.

Contents: p. [1], View of Halifax; p. [2], Explanation of calendar; p. [3], t.-p.; p. [4], Vulgar notes; p. [5], Zodiac; p. [6], Court sittings, etc.; p. [7-18], Calendar; p. [19], Ephemeris; p. [20-24], Short description of New-England; p. [25-31], Nova

Scotia administration, legislature, judges, justices, naval and army officers; p. [32], Clergy, Halifax fire company, buoys; fold table: 15.2 × 20.5 cm., Postal rates; verso, blank; p. [33-35], Postal rates; p. [36], Distances, etc.

This almanac was advertised: "Just published and to be sold by Anthony Henry, The Nova Scotia Calender . . . for . . . 1793 [etc.]."—*Royal gazette*, Halifax, N.S., Nov. 13, 1792.

Copy located: CaNsWA (p. [33-36] mut).

752. [BAILLARGÉ, PIERRE FLORENT]

ELEGIE: / [rule] / Sur l'air du "Couronnement du Roi."

Broadside: 40 lines, text in French, 2 col., type-page: 21 × 15 cm. *Probably printed at Quebec, by Samuel Neilson, 1792.*

Contents: Stanzas I-VIII, eight lines each, beginning:

"Pleure ville infortunée
Le plus chéri des pasteurs,
Sa mort trop primaturée
Doit attendrir tous les coeurs;"

The elegy laments the death of Auguste David Hubert, nephew of Bishop Hubert. Born at Quebec Feb. 15, 1751, he was educated and ordained there (in 1774) and from 1775 he served as curé of Quebec, greatly loved by his parishioners and widely respected. He was drowned off Ile d'Orléans, May 21, 1792. This elegy is attributed (by Pierre Georges Roy) to Pierre Florent Baillargé. It has been perpetuated locally as a popular ballad. The text is reprinted in P. G. Roy, *L'Ile d'Orléans* (Quebec, 1928), 396-97.

Copies located: CaQM; CaQQL.

753. BIRNIE, S., & JONES, J. *Merchants, Montreal*

S. BIRNIE & J. JONES beg leave to inform the Public . . . that they have taken the House and Premises occupied by late Mr. Levy Solomons where they mean to conduct the business of Bread and Biscuit baking, Hair Powder, Starch and Tobacco manufactories, &c . . . Montreal, 23d August, 1792.

Broadside, 25 lines; text in English & French. type-page: 12.5 × 10 cm. Distributed as a handbill with the *Montreal gazette*, Aug. 23, 1792 (for lack of space in that issue), this advertisement appeared (in the same type) in the issue of Aug. 30.

Copy located: CaOT (with *Montreal gazette*, Aug. 23, 1792).

754. BROWN, JOSEPH, *Dentist, Montreal*

[Directions.]

Broadside: Text in French and English, *printed at Quebec, by Samuel Neilson, 1792*, as recorded:

"1792, Oct. 20. Printed for Jo^{s} Brown, Dentist, 100 Directions French & English, 1 page folio roman—£1."—Can.P.A., *Neilson papers*, v. 70.

Brown had started business in Montreal, with the announcement: "Brown, Dentist, lately arrived from Halifax . . . takes this method of informing Ladies and Gentlemen that he makes and fastens in artificial teeth in so elegant a manner as to be but little inferior to natural, either in use or beauty [etc.]. Montreal, 22d November, 1791." He advertised his services, also drugs, medicines, herbs, etc., almost continuously in the *Montreal gazette*, in which from July 25, 1793, appeared the notice: "Joseph Brown . . . will sell on the most reasonable terms at his medical store, No 8 St. Joseph Street opposite the Hôtel-Dieu, for Cash or Country produce, or on short credit with approved security. For private families, Captains of ships and Indian traders may be had at the same store Medicine Chests, ready put up with printed directions how to use each articles [sic] from two guineas and upwards [etc.]."

The "printed directions" were probably those, or similar to those, printed by Neilson.

Copy located: None.

755. BURNS & WOOLSEY, *Auctioneers, Quebec*

[Catalogue of a considerable parcel of Books, Wines, Jewellry, Groceries, Dry goods, etc., to be sold at Auction, Apr. 11, 1792.]

? Broadside: *Printed at Quebec, by Samuel Neilson, 1792,* as recorded:

"1792 Apr. 5. Printd for Burns & Woolsey 150 folio Demy Catalogues of books &c.—£1.7.6."

—Can.P.A., *Neilson papers*, v. 70.

The sale was advertised:

"By Auction will be sold on Wednesday, 11th April [1792] and following evenings at Burns & Woolsey's Auction Rooms, a considerable parcel of Books, some choice Wines, Jewellry, Groceries, Dry goods, anniseed, lime juice, &c &c. Any persons desirous to have goods disposed of at the said sale, send a list to Burns & Woolsey by 31st March, that they may be inserted in the printed Catalogue."

—*Quebec gazette*, Mar. 15, 1792.

Copy located: None.

756. CHURCH OF ENGLAND. DIOCESE OF NOVA SCOTIA

[Address from the Clergy of New Brunswick to the Bishop of Nova Scotia and the latter's Answer.]

? *Printed at Halifax, N.S., by Anthony Henry, 1792.* A small pamphlet or perhaps merely a section of a Halifax or Saint John newspaper, published after Bishop Inglis's trip to New Brunswick, 1792. It was mentioned in the latter's letter to the Archbishop of Canterbury [Halifax, N.S.], Nov. 26, 1792: ". . . I take the liberty of inclosing a printed paper which contains an address from the Clergy of New Brunswick, with my answer; as they shew the good understanding and harmony that subsists among us; for I was perfectly sincere in what I said and I believe the clergy were equally so."—Can.P.A., *Inglis papers*, v. 2.

Copy located: None.

757. DUNIERE, L., *Grain agent, Quebec*

QUEBEC, [blank] JANVIER, 1792. / MONSIEUR, / PERMETTEZ-MOI de vous offrir mes services comme Facteur de Grains / . . . /

Ayant des Quais et Hangards spacieux, j'offre aux propriétaires de toutes especes de Grains, de les reçevoir, de barquer et soigner à raison de deux sols du Minot et un sol par mois de Magasinage, [etc., signed:] L. Duniere.

Broadside; type-page: 17.5 × 14 cm. *Probably printed at Quebec, by Samuel Neilson or by Wm. Moore, 1792.*

Copy located: CaQQL (the blank in the headline is dated in MS.: "25").

758. FRANCE. CONSTITUTION

[The New Constitution of France, as established by the Representatives of the French People.]

Printed at Quebec, by Samuel Neilson, 1792, this work was advertised among "Provincial [i.e. Lower Canada] publications for sale at the Printing Office, Quebec," in the *Quebec gazette,* May 3, 1792. This publication was probably reprinted from *Gazette* types, for *The New Constitution,* articles I-XVIII, appeared in the *Quebec gazette,* Dec. 29, 1791. with the note: "To be continued." Subsequent issues included minutes and decrees of the National Assembly of France, correspondence of Louis XVI, and news items, but no further articles of the constitution appeared in copies of the *Gazette* examined.

Copy located: None.

759. INGLIS, CHARLES, *bp. of Nova Scotia,* 1734-1816

A / CHARGE / DELIVERED TO THE / CLERGY of NOVA-SCOTIA, / AT THE / TRIENNIAL VISITATION / HOLDEN IN THE TOWN OF HALIFAX, / In the Month of June 1791. / [rule] / BY / THE RIGHT REVEREND CHARLES, / BISHOP OF NOVA-SCOTIA. / [double rule] / HALIFAX: / Printed by ANTHONY HENRY, Printer to the / King's Most Excellent Majesty. / M.DCC.CXII [sic]. /

4to. A-H^4, I^2; 68 p.; type-page: 15.6 × 8.5 cm.

Contents: p. [1], t.-p.; p. [2], blank; p. 3-5, Letter to the clergy; p. 6-68, Charge; p. 68 at end, Errata, also the bishop's announcement of his intention to publish separately, an appendix to this Charge, containing a corrected edition of his "Catalogue of books for a theological library" (*see* No. 641) and other matter.

A cancel slip bearing errata as on p. 68, is pasted over a cancelled errata slip (with same information in different arrangement) pasted on p. [2].

In the *Letter* (not delivered at the visitation) Bishop Inglis reviews the state of the province since his arrival in 1789, commenting on the erection of churches, the Grammar School at Halifax, and the Academy at Windsor, and finally upon peace with Spain and the excellent government of King George III. Then he criticises fiercely "Enthusiasm" and the activity in Nova Scotia, of the New Lights, an evangelical sect connected with Congregationalists in New England, and continuing the work of Henry Alline in Nova Scotia. His *Charge* resembles that delivered to the clergy of Quebec in 1787. Here, however, he delivers a thrust at the doctrines of Catholics and of Protestant dissenters and stresses the importance of the Established Church in a well organized society.

Copies located: CaNsHD; CaOT; NNHi; RPJ.

PROCLAMATION for the forming of a MILITIA.

By His EXCELLENCY

PEREGRINE THOMAS HOPSON, Esq;

Captain General and Governour in Chief, in and over His Majesty's Province of *Nova-Scotia*, or *Accadie* in *America*, Vice Admiral of the same, and Colonel of one of His Majesty's Regiments of Foot, &c.

In COUNCIL.

WHEREAS I am directed, by His Majesty's Royal Instructions, to cause a MILITIA *to be established, as well for the Defence of the Lives and Properties of His Majesty's Subjects, as the Honour and Security of this His Province;*

I HAVE thought fit, by and with the Advice and Consent of His Majesty's Council, to issue this Proclamation, hereby strictly requiring and enjoyning all *Planters*, *Inhabitants*, and their *Servants*, between the Ages of *Sixteen* and *Sixty*, residing in and belonging to the Town, Suburbs, or the Peninsula of *Halifax*, the Town and Suburbs of *Dartmouth*, and the Parts adjacent, (excepting the Foreign Settlers as it is intended that they shall be formed at their Out-Settlement) that the said *Planters* and *Inhabitants* do forthwith provide themselves and *Servants* with proper and sufficient Fire-Arms, consisting of a Musket, Gun, or Fuzil, not less than three Foot long in the Barrel, two spare Flints, and twelve Charges of Powder and Ball suitable to their respective Fire-Arms; which said Arms and Ammunition the said Planters, Inhabitants, and their Servants, are to have and appear with, at such Rendezvous as shall be by Proclamation appointed, at any Time on or after the 22*d* Day of *May* next, in the Year of our Lord 1753, at which Time the said Planters and Inhabitants are to be accountable for themselves and Servants. And in Default of such Appearance and Provision aforesaid, they will be liable to the Penalty of *Forty Shillings*, to be levied on the Goods and Chattles of such Offender or Offenders, by Warrant of Distress and Sale, under the Hand and Seal of one or more of His Majesty's Justices of the Peace for the Town and County of *Halifax*; and for want of sufficient Distress, such Offender or Offenders to suffer One Month's Imprisonment and hard Labour. Such Warrant to be granted upon Information of such Officer or Officers as shall be appointed to muster the Persons so required to appear as aforesaid.

Done in the Council Chamber at Halifax, *this* Twenty-second *Day of* March, *in the Year of our Lord* 1753, *in the* Twenty-sixth *Year of his Majesty's Reign.*

P. T. Hopson.

By His Excellency's Command, by and with the Advice and Consent of His Majesty's Council,
Wm. Cotterell, Secr.

God save the KING.

HALIFAX: Printed by *J. Bushell*, Printer to the Government. 1753.

I. No. 7.

An Act for Quieting of Possessions to the *Protestant Grantees*, of the Lands formerly occupied by the *French* Inhabitants, and for preventing vexatious Actions relating to the same.

'WHEREAS this Province of *Nova-Scotia* or *Accadie*, and the Property thereof, did always of Right belong to the Crown of *England*, both by Priority of Discovery and ancient Possession, and that no Grant of Property to any of the Lands or Territories belonging thereto, is of any Validity, or can give the Possessor thereof any legal Right or Title to any Part thereof, unless derived from thence.

' And, *whereas* by a Treaty of Peace concluded at *Utrecht*, in the Year of our Lord, *One Thousand, Seven Hundred and Thirteen*, between her most Sacred Majesty *Ann of Glorious Memory*, Queen of *Great-Britain*, &c. and His most Christian Majesty, it was concluded and agreed on, that all *Nova-Scotia* or *Accadie*, with it's ancient Boundaries, and all other Things in those Parts which depend on the said Lands, together with the Dominion, Property, and Possession of the said Lands and Places, and all Right whatsoever by Treaties or any other Way attained, which the most Christian King, the Crown of *France*, or any other the Subjects thereof, had to the Lands and Places, and to the Inhabitants of the same, are yielded and made over to the *Queen of Great-Britain*, and to her Crown for ever.

' And *whereas* at the Time of that Cession, many of the *French* King's Subjects did reside and dwell within this His Majesty's Province of *Nova-Scotia*, and did not remove from the same, within the Space of *Twelve Months*, according to the Limitation of that Treaty, whereby they and their Posterity became Subjects of the Crown of *Great-Britain* in every Respect; notwithstanding which, contrary to their Allegiance, they began from that Time, and continued at all Times to aid, assist, and support and join with His Majesty's Enemies; and altho' His Majesty, notwithstanding their manifest Treasons and Rebellion, in order to extend His Indulgence towards them, and if possible to reclaim and reduce them to His Obedience, was most graciously pleased, by His Royal Instructions to the Governors of this Province, to declare that the said *French* Inhabitants should have the peaceable Possession of such Lands as were under their Cultivation, *Provided*, That they the said Inhabitants should within *Three Months* from such Time as should be thought proper by the Governor, take the Oath of Allegiance appointed to be taken by the Laws of *Great-Britain*, and likewise behave themselves as become good Subjects: And altho' several Proclamations had hitherto been issued by His Majesty's Governors of this Province, requiring their Oath of Allegiance, yet so far were they from obeying the same, that by a general Deputation of their principal Men, before His Majesty's Governor and Council, they absolutely refused to take the said Oaths so required of them, but on the contrary did still continue to aid, assist, and join with His Majesty's Enemies, and *Five Hundred* of them were found in Arms, within the Fort of *Beausejour* when the same was surrendered, and many of them, in Company with the Indian Savages, did frequently commit many horrid and barbarous Murders on His Majesty's Protestant liege Subjects, who were endeavouring to settle themselves on the Lands within this Province, whereby the Progress of the Settlement of this Province, with His Majesty's Protestant Subjects was

A true Copy, Examined by Ar Rippert Secr Cor.

' was retarded, and the Crown put to an excessive great Expence, to defend and protect them; and also by such their treacherous Practices, His Majesty's most gracious Designs, as well towards them, as also towards His said Protestant Subjects, were frustrated; and had they not been timely removed by the Prudence and Vigilancy of His Excellency the present Governor, from the said Lands and Territories, into other His Majesty's Dominions, this invaluble Province, during the Course of this War, must inevitably have fallen into the Hands of His Majesty's Enemies the *French*.

' And *whereas* since the Removal of the said *French* Inhabitants, His Excellency the Governor, in order to make an effectual Settlement in this Province, and to strengthen the same, has been pleased to make Grants of Townships to many substantial and industrious Farmers, Protestants, His Majesty's Subjects of the Neighbouring Colonies, in which Townships are contained some of the Lands formerly occupied by the said *French* Inhabitants; and as many other substantial and industrious Farmers Protestants, are daily applying for Grants of Townships, wherein such Lands will be comprehended: And as some Doubts have arisen among the said Persons intending to settle the said Lands, concerning the Title of the said *French* Inhabitants to any of the said Lands, that may fall within their Townships: And altho' the said *French* Inhabitants have not, nor ever had, any legal Right or Title to the said Lands, derived from the Crown of *Great-Britain*, yet in order to remove such Doubts, and to prevent any troublesome or vexatious Suits of Law that may hereafter be brought for the Maintenance of any such Right or pretended Right to any of the Lands within this Province, formerly possessed or occupied by the said *French* Inhabitants;

Be it enacted by His Excellency the Governor, Council and Assembly, and by the Authority of the same it is hereby enacted. That no Action shall be retained in any of His Majesty's Courts of Record in this Province, for the Recovery of any of the Lands, within the same, by Virtue of any former Right, Title, Claim, Interest, or Possession, of any of the former *French* Inhabitants, or by Virtue of any Right, Title, Claim, or Interest, holden under or derived from them, by Grant, Deed, Will, or any other manner whatsoever.

And be it further enacted, That when any Action shall be brought for the Recovery of any Lands within this Province, and it shall appear upon Evidence, that the Grounds of such Action is founded upon any such Right, Title or Possession of the said *French* Inhabitants, or derived from them as aforesaid, that then this Act may be pleaded in Bar to all such Actions: And all His Majesty's Judges and Justices of the said Courts, are hereby required and enjoined, upon such Plea and Proof thereof, to dismiss such Action, and award Costs for the Defendants.

HALIFAX:

Printed by JOHN BUSHELL, Printer to the GOVERNMENT. 1759.

II. No. 18.

(22)

Thursday *April* 15*th*, 1762.

Bill relating to the Duties of Excise / Committed / Reported / Agreed to — Agreable to the Order of Yesterday, the Bill for altering and amending several Acts of this Province, relating to the Duties of Excise on Wines, &c. was consider'd in a Committee of the whole House, and reported by *Archibald Hinshelwood*, Esqr; agreed to with Amendments.

Sent up with the Bill agreed to Yesterday — *Order'd*, That it be sent to His Majesty's Council with the Bill agreed to Yesterday.

Bill sent down for regulating the Indian Trade. — The Council sent down a Bill, intitled, *an Act for the Regulation of the Indian Trade*, which was read; *order'd*, that it be taken into Consideration to morrow Morning.

Then adjourn'd till to morrow Morning 10 o'Clock.

Friday *April* 16*th*, 1762.

Bill for regulating the Indian Trade. / Committed / And agreed to with Amendments / Sent up — The Bill for the Regulation of the Indian Trade, was read a 2d Time, and committed to the Consideration of a Committee of the whole House, and reported, agreed to with some Amendments, and the Bill with said Amendments was sent up to the Council.

Motion relating to the Act for suppressing unlicensed Houses — Upon a Motion that the Act for suppressing unlicensed Houses, and for granting to His Majesty a Duty on Persons hereafter to be licensed, required some Amendments, in Order to render said Act more effectual to answer the Purposes thereby intended; and that it is also necessary to continue the said Act for a further space of time.

Order thereon — Resolved and *Order'd*, That a Bill in Addition to and Amendment of, and to further prolong the said Act be prepared by to morrow Morning.

Then adjourn'd till to morrow Morning 10 'oClock.

Saturday

No. 31.

A

JOURNAL

OF THE

VOTES

OF THE

Lower House of ASSEMBLY,

FOR THE

Province of NOVA-SCOTIA:

From *Friday October* 12*th*. 1764, to *Saturday November* 3*d*. 1764.

HALIFAX, *in* NOVA-SCOTIA:

Printed by ANTONY HENRY, Printer to the *Governor and Council*.

No. 39.

THE
Nova-Scotia CALENDER,
OR AN
ALMANACK
For the Year of the Christian Era, 1770.

And from the Creation of the World according to Chronology, 5719:

Being the Second after Bissextile or Leap-Year, and in the Tenth Year of the Reign of His Majesty King GEORGE the Third, consisting of 365 Days;

Wherein is contained,

The Eclipses of the Luminaries, Sun & Moon's Rising and Setting; Moon's Place, Time of High Water; Lunations, Aspects, Spring Tides, Judgment of the Weather; Feasts and Fasts of the Church; the Sittings of the several Courts and Sessions in the Province of *Nova-Scotia*, &c.

To which is added,

An Account of the City and Tower of Babylon, with Reflection thereon; *All Covet all loose*; or *the* Retaliation. *A Foll's Bolt is soon shot*; or the Apple-Pye broke loose. The Names of the Governor, Lieut. Governor, Members of His Majesty's Council, and House of Assembly, and other principal Officers of Government, &c. Curious Observations on the Weather. An Account of a Mermaid. Jests. Remedies for Diseases in Cows, Oxen, Calves, &c. to cure, &c.

Calculated for the Meridian of HALIFAX, in *Nova-Scotia*, Latitude 44d. 44m. North; and 4 Hours 13 Minutes and 20 Seconds West Longitude from *London*, but will serve without sensible Error, for any Part of *Nova-Scotia*.

By A. LILIUS.

HALIFAX: Printed and Sold by ANTHONY HENRY, at the *New-Printing-Office*.

IV. No. 127.

By His EXCELLENCY

GUY CARLETON,

Captain-general and Governor in Chief of the Province of QUEBEC, *and the Territories depending thereon; Vice-admiral of the same, Major-general and Commander in Chief of His Majesty's Forces, in the Province of* QUEBEC *and the Frontiers thereof,* &c. &c. &c.

A PROCLAMATION.

WHEREAS I am informed that many of His Majesty's deluded Subjects of the neighbouring Provinces labouring under Wounds and diverse disorders are dispersed in the adjacent Woods and Parishes, and in great Danger of perishing for Want of proper Assistance; All Captains and other Officers of Militia are hereby commanded to make diligent search for all such distressed Persons, and afford them all necessary Relief, and convey them to the General Hospital, where proper care shall be taken of them: All reasonable Expences which may be occurred in complying with this Order shall be repaid by the Receiver-general.

And least a Consciousness of past offences should deter such miserable Wretches from receiving that Assistance which their distressed situation may require; I HEREBY MAKE KNOWN to them, that as soon as their Health is restored, they shall have free Liberty to return to their respective Provinces.

GIVEN under my Hand and Seal of Arms at the Castle of St. Lewis, *in the City of* QUEBEC, *this Tenth Day of* May, *One Thousand Seven Hundred and Seventy-six, in the Sixteenth Year of the Reign of our Sovereign Lord* GEORGE *the Third by the Grace of* GOD, *of* Great-Britain, France, *and* Ireland, *King, Defender of the Faith, and so forth.*

GUY CARLETON.

By His EXCELLENCY'S *Command,*
H. T. CRAMAHE.

GOD Save the KING,

PAR SON EXCELLENCE

GUY CARLETON,

Capitaine-general et Gouverneur en Chef de la Province de Quebec, *et territoires en dépendans; Vice-amiral d'icelle, Marechal des Camps et Commandant en Chef des Armées de sa Majesté, dans la Province de* Québec *et frontieres d'icelle,* &c. &c. &c.

PROCLAMATION.

COMME je suis informé que beaucoup des sujets abusés de sa Majesté des Provinces voisines, qui souffrent de leurs blessures et d'autres maladies, sont dispersés dans les bois et paroisses voisines, et qu'ils courent grand risque de périr faute de secours nécessaires: Il est ordonné par ces presentes à tous Capitaines et Officiers de Milice, de faire une prompte recherche de toutes telles personnes malades, de leur procurer les secours necessaires, et de les faire conduire à l'Hôpital-general, où on en aura grand soin: toutes les depenses raisonables qui auront été faites en obéissance à cet Ordre, seront remboursées par le Receveur-general.

Et de peur que la crainte du châtiment de leurs crimes passés, n'empêche [illegible] ces malheureux de recevoir les secours que leur miserable situation peut exiger, Je leur donne à connaitre par ces presentes, qu'aussitôt que leur santé sera rétablie, ils auront l'entiere liberté de retourner dans leurs diferentes Provinces.

Donné sous mon seing et le sceau de mes armes, au chateau St. Louis, *dans la ville de* QUEBEC, *le dixieme jour de* Mai, *mil sept cens soixante-seize, dans la seizième année du Regne de Nôtre Souverain Seigneur* GEORGE *Trois, par la Grace de Dieu, Roy de la* Grande-Bretagne, *de* France *et* d'Irlande, *Defenseur de la Foy,* &c. &c. &c.

(Signé) GUY CARLETON

Par Ordre de son Excellence,
(Signé) H. T. CRAMAHE.
Traduit par ordre de son Excellence.
F. J. CUGNET, *S. F.*

VIVE LE *ROI.*

V. No. 243.

BY JOHN BURGOYNE ESQ;

Lieutenant General of his Majesty's Armies in America, Colonel of the Queen's Regiment of Light Dragoons, Governor of Fort William in North-Britain, one of the Representatives of the Commons of Great-Britain in Parliament, and commanding an Army and Fleet employed on an Expedition from Canada. &c. &c. &c.

THE forces entrusted to my command are designed to act in concert, and upon a common principle, with the numerous Armies and Fleets which already display in every quarter of America, the power, the justice, and when properly sought, the mercy of the King.

The cause in which the British Arms are thus exerted applies to the most affecting interests of the human heart: and the military servants of the Crown, at first called forth for the sole purpose of restoring the rights of the Constitution, now combine with love of their Country, and duty to their Sovereign, the other extensive incitements which spring from a due sense of the general privileges of Mankind. To the eyes and ears of the temperate part of the public, and to the breasts of Suffering Thousands in the provinces, be the melancholy appeal whether the present unnatural rebellion has not been made a foundation for the compleatest system of Tyranny that ever God in his displeasure suffered for a time to be exercised over a froward and stubborn generation.

Arbitrary imprisonment, confiscation of property, persecution and torture, unprecedented in the inquisitions of the Romish church are among the palpable enormities that verify the affirmative. These are inflicted, by assemblies and committees who dare to profess themselves friends to Liberty, upon the most quiet subjects, without distinction of age or sex, for the sole crime, often for the sole suspicion, of having adhered in principle to the Government under which they were born, and to which by every tye divine and human they owe allegiance. To consummate these shocking proceedings the profanation of religion is added to the most profligate prostitution of common reason; the consciences of men are set at nought; and multitudes are compelled not only to bear arms, but also to swear subjection to an usurpation they abhor.

Animated by these considerations; at the head of troops in the full powers of health, discipline, and valour; determined to strike where necessary, and anxious to spare where possible, I by these presents invite and exhort all persons, in all places where the progress of this army may point---and by the blessing of God I will extend it far---to maintain such a conduct as may justify me in protecting their lands, habitations, and familys. The intention of this address is to hold forth security not depredation to the country.

To those whom spirit and principle may induce to partake the glorious task of redeeming their Countrymen from dungeons, and reestablishing the blessings of legal government I offer encouragement and employment; and upon the first intellengence of their associations I will find means to assist their undertakings. The domestick, the industrious, the infirm, and even the timid inhabitants I am desirous to protect provided they remain quietly at their houses, that they do not suffer their cattle to be removed, nor their corn or forage to be secreted or destroyed; that they do not break up their bridges or roads; nor by any other acts directly or indirectly endeavour to obstruct the operations of the King's troops, or supply or assist those of the Enemy.

Every species of provision brought to my camp will be paid for at an equitable rate and in solid Coin.

In consciousness of Cristianity, my Royal Master's clemency, and the honour of soldiership, I have dwelt upon this invitation and wished for more persuasive terms to give it impression: And let not people be led to disregard it by considering their distance from the immediate situation of my camp -----I have but to give stretch to the Indian forces under my direction, and they amount to thousands, to overtake the hardened enemies of Great-Britain and America, I consider them the same, whereever they may lurk.

If notwithstanding these endeavours, and sincere inclinations to effect them, the phrensy of hostility should remain, I trust I shall stand acquitted in the eyes of God and men in denouncing and executing the vengeance of the State against the wilful outcasts--- The messengers of justice and of wrath await them in the field; and devastation, famine, and every concomitant horror that a reluctant but indispensible prosecution of military duty must occasion, will bar the way to their return.

Camp near Ticonderoga July 2nd 1777.

J. BURGOYNE,

By Order of His EXCELLENCY
the Lt. GENERAL
ROBt. KINGSTON, Secretary.

VI. No. 253.

A SON EXCELLENCE
GUY CARLETON,

Chevalier du Très-Honorable Ordre du Bain, Capitaine-Général & Gouverneur en Chef de la Province de Quebec, Général & Commandant en Chef des Forces de Sa Majeſté dans ladite Province & Frontieres d'icelle, &c.

NOUS Souſſignés, Citoyens de Montréal, repréſentons humblement à VOTRE EXCELLENCE, la mortification que nuos cauſe le départ du ſieur Fleury Meſplet, Imprimeur en cette Ville; l'Ordre à lui donné verbalement par le Général P*** de vuider la Province ſous trois mois, nous a ſurpris : la conduite qu'il a tenu depuis ſon arrivée en ce pays, la régularité de ſes mœurs, paroiſſoit nous aſſurer de le conſerver plus long temps, & devoir le mettre à l'abri d'une telle diſgrace. S'il eſt des raiſons d'Etat qui ne ſoient pas parvenus à notre connoiſſance, nous ne diſons rien; mais il eſt notre Concitoyen, continuellement ſous nos yeux, nous ſommes témoins de toutes ſes démarches, & nous ne ſçaurions lui faire aucun reproche; ſon zèle pour procurer de l'Inſtruction & de l'Amuſement, en donnant un Papier Périodique, nous marque un bon Patriote. La Loi qu'il s'eſt impoſé de ne traiter que des matieres qui ne regardent, ni l'Etat, ni la Religion, nous prouve ſa délicateſſe; nous n'y voyons que des Inſtructions pour les Jeunes Gens, & du plaiſir pour tous.

Nous ſupplions VOTRE EXCELLENCE d'avoir égard à notre très-humble Repréſentation, & d'être perſuadé que ſi Fleury Meſplet eut, à notre connoiſſance, donné lieu à ce traitement, nous regretterions à la vérité un homme auſſi utile; mais n'enviſageant pas l'utilité & l'agrément que peut nous procurer la Preſſe, nous nous tairions. Que n'aurions-nous pas à nous reprocher, ſi un de nos Concitoyens ſouffroit une exportation onéreuſe, faute par Nous de ne pas rendre hommage à la Vérité?

VII. No. 291.

QUEBEC, *February* 3, 1779.

EVERY able-bodied Seaman who will enter for His Majeſty's Naval Service in the Province of *Quebec*, to ſerve on the High Seas or on the Lakes ſhall receive FORTY SHILLINGS Sterling per month, and be entitled to every encouragement given to Seamen who ſerve in His Majeſty's Ships, and ſhall be protected from being Preſs'd on board any other of His Majeſty's Ships or Veſſels of war; all ſuch who are willing to enter, by applying to Captain JOHN SCHANKS at the Coffee-houſe, or at Captain BOUCHETTE's Houſe in *Chamberlain* Street, ſhall enter into preſent Pay, be conducted to their proper Ships and receive one month's Wages in Slops or Bedding.

QUEBEC, *ce* 3 *Fevrier*, 1779.

TOUS bons Matelots voulant prendre partis pour le Service Naval de Sa Majeſté en la Province de *Québec*, pour ſervir ſur Mer ou ſur les Lacs, recevront QUARANTE SHELLINGS Sterling par mois, et pourront prétendre aux mêmes encouragemens qui ſont accordés aux Matelots ſervant à bord les Vaiſſeaux du Roi, et ſeront exempts d'être preſſés pour ſervir ſur aucun autre Vaiſſeau armé de Sa Majeſté.

Tous ceux qui voudront prendre ce partis s'adreſſeront au Capitaine JEAN SCHANKS dans la maiſon du Caffé, ou au Capitaine BOUCHETTE, en ſa maiſon, ruë *Chamberland*; leur Paie commencera à courir du jour de leur engagement, et ſeront envoiés au Batiment pour lequel ils ſont deſtinés, et recevront un mois de Paie d'avance en Hardes et Lits, s'ils en ont beſoin.

VIII. No. 327.

QUEBEC, *25th February*, 1784.

THIS is to give notice that His Excellency the Governor, in order to fulfill His Majesty's gracious Intentions for the Welfare of the Refugée Loyalists and disbanded Troops residing in this Province, has caused such Lands to be examin'd by the Surveyor-General and his Deputies, as He thinks best calculated to establish advantageous Settlements for them: Such, therefore, of the Loyalists and disbanded Troops who are now dispersed thro'out the Province (Sorel excepted) and who wish to have Concessions of Land from the *Pointe au Baudet* (where the last settlements are) to Cataraqui and its Vicinity, are required to repair to La Chine (where Quarters will be allotted to them) by the 2d day of April next, and where proper Persons will be appointed to muster them, in order that the quantity of Land that will be wanted may be ascertained, and that Seigneuries may be marked out and granted by the Governor and Council according to His Majesty's Orders.

The Loyalists and disbanded Troops who are at present quartered in the upper part of the Province, and who wish to have Lands at the Bay of Chaleurs, will repair to Sorel by the 2d day of April next, where they will be mustered as above-mentioned.

Those who are at present at Quebec, and who wish to go to Chaleurs Bay, will give in their Names, by the said 2d day of April, at my Office.

All Issues of Provisions to the Refugée Loyalists and disbanded Troops will cease on the 10th day of April next, except at Quebec, Sorel, and the Quarters at La Chine.

By His Excellency's Command,

R. MATHEWS.

IX. No. 439.

A
BRIEF VIEW
OF THE
Religious TENETS and SENTIMENTS,

Lately publiſhed and ſpread in the Province of NOVA-SCOTIA; which are contained in a Book, entitled
"TWO MITES, on ſome of the moſt important and much diſputed Points of Divinity, &c."

AND

"In a SERMON preached at Liverpool, November 19, 1782;"

AND, IN A PAMPHLET, ENTITLED
"The ANTITRADITIONIST:"
ALL BEING PUBLICATIONS OF
Mr. HENRY ALLINE.

WITH
Some brief Reflections and Obſervations:

ALSO,
A VIEW of the Ordination of the Author of theſe Books:

TOGETHER WITH
A DISCOURSE on external Order.

By JONATHAN SCOTT,
Paſtor of a Church in YARMOUTH.

JUDE, verſe 3. *Beloved, when I gave all Diligence to write unto you of the common Salvation: It was needful for me to write unto you, and exhort you that ye ſhould earneſtly contend for the Faith which was once delivered unto the Saints.*

HALIFAX:
Printed by JOHN HOWE, in BARRINGTON-STREET,
MDCCLXXXIV.

X. No. 442.

JOURNAL

AND

VOTES

OF THE

HOUSE OF ASSEMBLY,

FOR HIS MAJESTY'S ISLAND

SAINT JOHN.

Begun and held at CHARLOTTE-TOWN, the Twenty-fecond Day of JANUARY, in the Year of our LORD one Thoufand, feven Hundred and Eighty-eight.

28th GEORGE III.

CHARLOTTE-TOWN:
PRINTED by *JAMES ROBERTSON*, M,DCC,LXXXVIII.

No. 569.

ACTS

OF THE

GENERAL ASSEMBLIES

OF HIS MAJESTY'S

ISLAND OF SAINT JOHN,

AS CORRECTED AND REVISED, PURSUANT TO APPOINTMENT, AT THEIR LAST SESSION, IN THE YEAR, ONE THOUSAND SEVEN HUNDRED AND EIGHTY EIGHT,

BY PHILLIPS CALLBECK, AND JOSEPH APLIN, ESQUIRES.

CHARLOTTE-TOWN: PRINTED BY JAMES ROBERTSON,
1789.

No. 619.

XI

Schedule of the Prices of Printing in Whole Sheets, from Folio Pott to Demy Paper
And
The Prices of Publications in the Quebec Gazette.

For printing	One Sheet on Pott paper		Double Pica Type	1st hundred	£1. 2. 6	and 7/6 for every additional hundred [illegible] inclosed denomination of Types, the Work and Paper being the same for each.
	One Sheet	same paper	Great Primer Type	1st hundred	1. 5. 0	
	One Sheet	same paper	English Type	1st hundred	1. 7. 6	
[Note]	One Sheet	same paper	Pica Type (Ordin.e Books)	1st hundred	1. 10. 0	
	One Sheet	same paper	Small Pica Type	1st hundred	1. 12. 6	
	One Sheet	same paper	Long Primer Type	1st hundred	1. 15. 0	
	One Sheet	same paper	Brevier Type	1st hundred	1. 17. 6	
For printing	One Sheet on Foolscap paper		Double Pica Type	1st hundred	1. 5. 0	and 2/6 for every additional hundred [illegible] the reasons above assigned.
	One Sheet	same paper	Great Primer Type	1st hundred	1. 7. 6	
	One Sheet	same paper	English Type	1st hundred	1. 10. 0	
	One Sheet	same paper	Pica Type	1st hundred	1. 12. 6	
	One Sheet	same paper	Small Pica Type	1st hundred	1. 15. 0	
	One Sheet	same paper	Long Primer Type	1st hundred	1. 17. 6	
	One Sheet	same paper	Brevier Type	1st hundred	2. 0. 0	
For printing	One Sheet on Crown paper		Double Pica Type	1st hundred	1. 10. 0	and 10/ for every additional hundred [illegible]
	One Sheet	same paper	Great Primer	1st hundred	1. 14. 0	
	One Sheet	same paper	English Type	1st hundred	1. 18. 0	
	One Sheet	same paper	Pica Type	1st hundred	2. 2. 0	
	One Sheet	same paper	Small Pica	1st hundred	2. 6. 0	
	One Sheet	same paper	Long Primer	1st hundred	2. 10. 0	
	One Sheet	same paper	Brevier Type	1st hundred	2. 14. 0	
For printing	One Sheet on Demy Paper		Double Pica Type	1st hundred	1. 15. 0	and 12/6 for every additional hundred [illegible]
	One Sheet	same Paper	Great Primer Type	1st hundred	2. 0. 0	
	One Sheet	same Paper	English Type	1st hundred	2. 5. 0	
	One Sheet	same Paper	Pica Type	1st hundred	2. 10. 0	
	One Sheet	same Paper	Small Pica	1st hundred	2. 15. 0	
	One Sheet	same Paper	Long Primer	1st hundred	3. 0. 0	
	One Sheet	same Paper	Brevier Type	1st hundred	3. 5. 0	

~~Crown paper~~

For printing in the Quebec Gazette Ordinances of the Province, Acts of Parliament, Proclamations, Letters [illegible] &c. &c. a Diminution of One fifth of the Prices hitherto paid by Government, that is to say: for every 10 lines English [illegible] every 10 lines French, or 20 lines together formerly 7/6. &6. now 6/- for the 1st insertion; and if continued 2/6 for the same [illegible] subsequent insertion. — N.B. It is understood that for common Advertisements, or such Matter as may not exceed 20 [illegible] in English & 20 lines French Government do pay as much as the Public in general.

Matters published only in English, instead of 5/ for every 10 lines formerly paid by Government, every 10 lines to be c[illegible] 3 Shillings only for the first week, and 1 shilling each subsequent insertion; Advertisements, &c under 20 lines excep[illegible] above.

A Diminution of one fourth has also been made on Advertisements of Seizures made by the Sheriffs of Quebec [illegible] Montreal.

The greatest part of Printing done for Government may be deduced from the above forms and prices; however should any [illegible] unprovided for in the present, separate they will be charged no more than in proportion to those above specified.

Quebec, 10th October, 1789.

Samuel Neilson

[Note] The paper and Type herein referred to, are those on which the Ordinances of the Province have always been print[illegible] last impression was in 1787, when Government paid for 300 Copies at the rate of £3. per sheet — whereas by the present [illegible] the same number would be at the rate of only £2. 2. 6 per sheet. All the other forms of Work are charged in similar Propo[illegible] Pott, Foolscap & Crown Paper are the sizes generally used — Demy is the largest, and very seldom made use of.

XII. S. Neilson Price List, 1789.

SERMON

PREACHED IN THE

Church at Falmouth, Nova-Scotia,

On FRIDAY, *the* 10*th of* MAY, 1793.

BEING THE DAY APPOINTED BY PROCLAMATION

FOR A

GENERAL FAST

AND

Humiliation before Almighty GOD.

BY THE REVEREND WILLIAM COCHRAN,
PRESIDENT OF KING'S COLLEGE, WINDSOR.

HALIFAX:
Printed by JOHN HOWE, at his Printing-Office, opposite the PARADE.

M DCC XCIII.

No. 828.

A
SERMON,

PREACHED AT

SISSABOO,

NOW CALLED

WEYMOUTH,

IN

NOVA-SCOTIA,

On the 15*th October,* 1797.

BY ROGER VIETS,
RECTOR OF DIGBY, AND MISSIONARY FROM THE VENERABLE SOCIETY FOR THE PROPAGATION OF THE GOSPEL IN FOREIGN PARTS.

SAINT JOHN:
PRINTED BY JOHN RYAN, FOR THE AUTHOR.
—1799.—

No. 1153.

XIII

[January, M.DCC.LXIX.] (1) [Numb. 1]

THE NOVA SCOTIA CHRONICLE, And WEEKLY ADVERTISER;

Containing the freſheſt Advices, both Foreign and Domeſtic; with a Variety of other Matter, uſeful, inſtructive, and entertaining.

TUESDAY January 3, 1769. (No. 1, of Vol. I.)

From the GAZETTEER, *Aug.* 13, 1768.

I Think as well of, and wiſh as well to our fellow ſubjects in America, as I do to any of thoſe in England; and would wiſh the ſame privileges and immunities which are enjoyed by Yorkſhiremen, to be equally enjoyed alſo by Boſton and New-England men; ſo far, I mean, as the diſtance they are removed to will admit of, and allow as practicable.

But I am one of thoſe, who from general and looſe notions of Liberty, can deſire to ſee the Britiſh Empire ſplit into a number of ſeperate independant ſtates, without any common coerſive authority of parliament to [illegible] and give force and energy to the whole Our enemies cannot wiſh for a more effectual method of diſarming us, and rendering all parts of the empire ſubject to the impreſſions of every Invader.

Upon this account it is, that I believe the whole period of Engliſh hiſtory does not furniſh an inſtance of ſuch open and deſperate wickedneſs as that which by the laſt accounts is now practiſing at Boſton; a ſet of men, many of them of bad characters & deſperate fortunes, have been working up the populace to ſuch a frenzy of rage, as to induce them in the proceedings of their town meetings, openly to arraign the whole legiſlature of Great Britain, and to accuſe the King, Lords, and Commons of this realm, with having violated their fundamental rights. For this they tell us that they are a juſtly incenſed people, and have dared to inſult the Majeſty of the Britiſh empire; to brave to us the combat; and to tell us that they are not ſo baſe as to give up their pretenſions without ſtruckle. That though to contend with their parent ſtate be the moſt ſhocking and dreadful extremity, yet that they are determined to come to it, rather than relinquiſh their pretenſions; and are unalterable reſolved to defend their rights, at the utmoſt hazard of their lives and fortunes. Such is the language of the town of Boſton, to the King, Lords, and Commons of this realm: They could not ſend over a herald to deliver this meſſage, becauſe they knew that he muſt be hanged as ſoon as he had delivered it. But, that we might not think that there was any degree of preſumption too great for them; they have drawn up their two papers, which they call a Petition and Inſtructions, in direct menacing terms of a declaration of war.

That no one may ſuſpect this to be aſſertion without proof, I here ſend you an extract of the principal parts of the declaration of war with Spain 1739, and the town of Boſton's declaration in the year 1768. The Topics of argument, and the motives and injuries alledged, do not lie exactly in the ſame order, but the reader will ſee ſo near a reſemblance, as to leave no room to doubt but that theſe high and migthy ſtates of Boſton mean to render themſelves as independent of the Engliſh nation, as the Crown of England is of that of Spain. Not to add, that this nation is treated by them in terms of ſtronger menace and inſult than Sovereign Princes ever uſe to each other, the reader ſees them both, and will judge for himſelf, upon the compariſon, which of them ſpeaks in the higher tone

GEORGE R.

Whereas many unjuſt ſeizures have been made, and depredations carried on for ſeveral years, in the Weſt-Indies, by Spaniſh guarda coſtas, and other ſhips acting under the commiſion of the King of Spain, or his governors; contrary to the treaties ſubſiſting between us and the Crown of Spain, and to the laws of nations; to the great prejudice of the lawful trade and commerce of our ſubjects; and great cruelties and barbarities have been exercised on divers perſons of our ſubjects whoſe veſſels have been ſo ſeized. And whereas the evils abovementioned have been principally occaſioned by an unwarrantable claim and pretention, ſet up on the part of Spain, that the guarda coſtas, and other ſhips authoriſed by the King of Spain, may ſtop detain, and ſearch the ſhips and veſſels of our ſubjects navigating in the American Seas. And whereas, beſides the notorious grounds of complaint abovementioned, many other infractions have been made on the part of Spain, of the ſeveral treaties and conventions ſubſiſting between us and that Crown; and particularly of that concluded in the year 1767; as well by the exorbitant duties and impoſitions laid upon the trade and commerce of our ſubjects, as by the breach of antient and eſtabliſhed privileges, ſtipulated for them by the ſaid treaties; for the redreſs of which grievances, the ſtrongeſt inſtances have been from time to time, made by our ſeveral miniſters reſiding in Spain, without any effect. And whereas a convention had been concluded between us and the King of Spain from which his Majeſty doubtleſs hoped, that all grievances and cauſes of complaint would from that time ceaſe; becauſe the convention, he ſays, was made for that purpoſe. But, (doubtleſs through the ſame evil diſpoſition of the King of Spain) his Majeſty tells us, the convention was violated and broken, and the means *of obtaining* future ſecurity for the trade and navigation of our ſubjects are contrary to good faith fruſtrated and defeated. We have therefore taken into our royal conſideration, theſe injuries which have been offered to us and our ſubjects, notwithſtanding the repeated inſtances we have given of our deſire to cultivate a good underſtanding with Spain; and for vindicating our undoubted rights, and ſecuring to our loving ſubjects the privileges of navigation and commerce, to which they are juſtly intitled, we have thought fit to declare war, againſt the King of Spain, relying upon the help of Almighty GOD, who knows the uprightneſs of our intentions

AFTER the Repeal of the late American Stamp Act, we were happy in the pleaſing proſpect of a reſtoration of that tranquility and unanimity among ourſelves, and that harmony and affection between our parent country, and us, which had generally ſubſiſted before that deteſtable act. But with the utmoſt grief and concern, we find that we have flattered ourſelves too ſoon, and the root of biterneſs is yet alive. The principle on which that act was founded, continues in full force; and a revenue is ſtill demanded from America.

We have the mortification to obſerve one act of parliament paſſed after another, for the expreſs purpoſe of raiſing a revenue from us. In open violation of the fundamental rights of Britons, laws and taxes are [illegible]

XIV. *See* p. 602.

SATURDAY September 15, 1787. THE [Number I.—Volume I.]

ROYAL AMERICAN GAZETTE,

AND

WEEKLY INTELLIGENCER OF THE ISLAND OF SAINT JOHN.

CHARLOTTE-TOWN: Printed by JAMES ROBERTSON.

To the PUBLIC.

A Long Dessertation upon the Importance of a PRINTING-OFFICE would be futile, as its Utility is perfectly understood; and, it will be readily granted, that the Cultivation of this Island, for want of such an Establishment, has been much retarded.

Interested Men in the neighbouring Provinces, gave such an unfavourable Representation of this, that the baneful Effects have been severely felt, not only by the Inhabitants, who had not the Means to contradict the injurious Reports, but by a vast Number of Loyalists, who, putting implicit Confidence in an almost general though uncandid Description of this Island, have settled upon sterile Lands, the Production of which can never compensate for the Expence of Cultivation.-----Had the real Value of this Soil, at the Termination of the late War, been universally known, the numerous Accession of Inhabitants, which constitute the Riches of a Country, would have accelerated the Zenith of this.

Impress'd with an Idea that former Prejudices are not unconquerable, and that, like a well tuned Instrument, every Part of this Community will act in Unison, the Editor has ventured to issue this Specimen of

THE ROYAL AMERICAN GAZETTE,

which for a Series of Years has been favourably received by the Public.-----If it is fortunate enough to meet the Approbation of the respectable Inhabitants of this Island, no Exertions shall be wanting to render it useful and entertaining.

CONDITIONS.

I. It will be published every Saturday and delivered at the Printing-Office, where Subscriptions, at Twelve Shillings per Annum, will be thankfully received.

II. One Half of the Subscription Money to be paid on subscribing, and the Residue at the Expiration of the Year.

III. The ingenuous Productions of literary Gentlemen who wish to communicate Improvements upon Agriculture or any Sience, or whose Study is to amuse and instruct, will be gratefully received and inserted gratis.

IV Advertisements not exceeding Fifteen Lines will be inserted at Five Shillings the First Time, and Two Shillings for each Reinsertion-----Those of a greater Length will be charged in Proportion.

V. If a sufficient Number of Subscriptions are obtained, before Saturday the 29th Instant, to pay the Expence, the GAZETTE will be published, and continued agreeable to the first Condition; but, if not, the Money will then be returned.

From the Situation of this Island it is evident that the Inhabitants will receive earlier Intelligence from Europe, the West Indies, &c. than those of the Capital of His Majesty's North-American Dominions; and during the Time this Coast is inaccessible, some of the important Debates in the British Senate, which, from their Length, cannot be inserted as received, Extracts from the Magazines and other late European Publications, together with domestic Occurrences and Essays, will be a never failing Source of literary Amusement.

In populous Towns the Veichles of Intelligence are crowded with Advertisements which amply defray the Expence of each Impression; and, though the Paper is large, seldom more than one Page, often less, contribute to the Entertainment of the Reader. It is obvious that the Publisher can, at present, reap but a small Emolument from Advertisements, he therefore hopes that the Inhabitants, as the Price is small, will not class Two or Three under one Signature and thereby defeat the Intention (through an ill-timed Parsimony) of gratifying themselves and fellow Subjects with a Weekly Production which ALL are anxious to see established.

HANOVER, April 29.

THE dreadful fire which happened at Grosshunzeldorf, about two miles from this city, has unfortunately reduced to ashes one hundred and sixty buildings, and plunged four hundred and eighty-two individuals in the greatest misery.

CONSTANTINOPLE, April 16, Government have at last published some accounts of our affairs in Egypt, which by letters dated from Alexandria, the 26th of February, confirm the agreeable news of a complete victory obtained by the Ottoman troops over the Rebels, of which the following are the particulars:—On the 16th of February the Ottoman troops, commanded by Hassan Bey and Ismael Kiaja, attacked the Rebel camp near Girge, where they made a stout resistance, and repulsed our troops three times; but at the fourth attack, which was a bloody one, and lasted upwards of six hours, the enemy were obliged to abandon their camp, and all it contained, after loosing most of their troops. Among the dead were found Kasim, Osman, and Aly, three of the Beys of the Rebels, together with several other principal officers, whose heads were all sent to Cairo. We do not know what is become of Ibrahim Bey, and with regard to Murat Bey we learn, that after his defeat, he fled, with about sixty of his men, towards the mountains of Ethiopia. Hassan is in pursuit of him with five hundred Mameluks.

POLAND, April 19, We learn from Constantinople, that the winter has been severer there than was ever remembered; that the snow has lain a foot deep in some parts of the country; the length and coldness of the winter have, however, had this advantage, that the plague has not appeared any where.

LEYDEN, June 6. The Council of the town of Leyden have passed a resolution to charge the Deputies to the States of Holland, to vote for the absolute suspension of William V. from his offices OF WHICH HE HAD PROVED HIMSELF TO BE SO UNWORTHY; to retain all his appointments, and not to contribute any finance whatsoever to the generality. The other towns, which form the majority of the States of Holland, have already passed, or are just about to pass, similar resolutions.-----So that we soon expect to see Holland obliged to dissolve the Union, and form an independent Republic, if William V. persists in destroying civil liberty.

These are the few particulars which this day's mail brings. The minds of the patriots, as they call themselves, are now exasperated beyond all bounds against the Stadtholder, to whom they impute all the mischiefs that have happened.---And it is to be observed, that in most of their letters and papers they term him only William V. but never the Stadtholder.

HAGUE, June 7, Tuesday last the Council of State presented to their High Mightinesses a plan of mediation, the purport of which was to put a stop to all hostilities, to march back the troops of both parties from Utrecht, the one towards Holland, and the other towards the province of Guelderland. Several petitions or addresses were presented yesterday to the States; one from the town of the Brielle, signed by 360 burgesses and inhabitants; one from Oud Beverland and Hyneroort, signed by 400 inhabitants; one from Soetermeer and Zegwaart, signed by 149; one from Rhynzoterwoude, Alphen, Boskoop, Wardinaveem, and Aalsmeer, signed by 443; one from Scheveringen, signed by 400; one from Pynacker, signed by upwards of 160; one from Benthuizen, signed by 39; one from Terheide, signed by 67; one from Loorduinez, signed by 113; one from Monster and Poeldyk, signed by 119; and one from Moer Cappel, signed by 56 inhabitants; the purport of all which was to restore his Highness the Stadtholder to his dignities, power, and privilege.

AMSTERDAM, May 31. The Burghers of this city, who are not used to commit excesses without a cause, were yesterday unfortunately drove to acts of violence, on the following occasion: A few days since, a petition was left to sign, at a house in a street called the Reguliers-Grach, in favour of the Stadtholder, tending to re-establish that Prince in all the Privileges he enjoyed in 1766, and to annul every thing that has been done to the contrary since, and a vast number signed it; however, from the violence of party on

XV. See p. 646.

COURIER DE QUEBEC: OU Heraut François.

NOMBRE 2. TOM I.

DEPUIS LUNDI, 24 NOVEMBRE, JUSQU' A LUNDI 1er. DECEMBRE, 1788.

1-4 MONTREAL, 24 *Nov.* 1788.

LE SOUSIGNE' à *son Magazin ou il Vend en gros et en Detail à très bon marchè*, à *l'enseigne du* Phœnix d'Or, et de la Ruche, *dans la rue de St. Paul (ou demeuroit autrefois Monsr. Vienne,) prend la liberte' d'informer ses amis, les Messieurs de l'Arme'e et le Public en general, qu'il a reçu par les derniers batimens de Londres un assortiment complet de Marchandises seches; parmi lesquelles il y a*

DES *Stroudes*, *Couvertes de Laines de toute espece*, *Moltons*, *Draps fins*, *Indiennes*, *Toiles d'Irelande*, *Souliers et Bas Militaires*, *Devans de Veste elegans*, *Soies et Brocards*, *Des ceintures elegant de Devonshire & de Herbert ganies*, *Etoffes d'hiver pour les Dames; lesquelles sont de la derniere et plus nouvelle mode, puisqu' il a reçu tous ces Articles par le Navire le Maxwell.*

IL A AUSSI A VENDRE,

De vieux Esprits de Jamaique de cinq ans, *Vin de Madere*, *de Bourgogne*, *et de Teneriffe*; *que l'on peut avoir, en quelle quantite' que ce [illegible] au-dessus de trois Gallons, et qui sera [illegible] sans aucune Depense chez l'acheteur.*

[illegible] ayant acquis la Maison & le Magazin de feu Messieurs Ben. & Jos. Frobisher *au [illegible] du Courant* (*que l'on appelle* Swift [illegible]) *à dessein de recevoir du Grain de [illegible] espèce, des Boissons & des Marchandises [illegible] pour Vendre á commission: aussi[illegible] a reçu quelq'un des susdits articles il [illegible] à celui, qui les lui aura con[illegible] une Lettre de change sur lui [illegible] montant de la Consignation [illegible] interêt, en donnant ordre de vendre [illegible] prix courant du marchè.*

N. B. Il [illegible] pourroit [illegible] cet Avertissement, sans rendre la plus [illegible] justice à sa sensibilité, lorsqu' il fait mention du nom du feu possesseur, de la [illegible] magazin connu a present sous le nom de [illegible] Place *feu Monsr.* Benj. Frobisher [illegible] *de qui le soussigne' durant six anne'es [illegible] a demeure' a Montreal, a reçu toutes les politesses, amities, & attentions, qu'une personne auroit jamais pû temoigner à une autre [illegible] il croit doivent [illegible] ement, que la reconnoissance [illegible] dans [illegible] qu'il rende ce [illegible] á la memoire [illegible], son ami & concitoyen [illegible] est plus, mais dont le nom ne sera [illegible] effacè de la memoire des citoyens de Montreal, & des Canadiens employe's à conduire les Bateaux & Canots dans les pays [illegible] haut. L'unique ambition du soussigne' [illegible] il espere être digne de louange) est de [illegible] agir de maniere, que de meriter tant [illegible] peu le caractere public, que son ami [illegible] qui est mort s'etoit aquis de negociant & de [illegible]-Homme.*

ROSSETER [illegible]OYLE.

1-3 QUEBEC, [illegible] Nov. 1788.

BUREAU GENERAL DE POSTE

Pour les Provinces de Sa [illegible] dans l'Amérique Septentrionale.

UNE *Malle pour Angleterre sera close à ce Bureau Lundi le 8 Decembre à 4 heures après midi; et sera acheminée de Montréal Jeudi le [illegible] dit mois, pour être mise abord du Paquebot de Sa Majesté qui partira de la Nouvelle-Yore pour Falmouth, Mécredi le 7 de Janvier prochain.*

Le Portage du Paquebot ne peut être reçu en Amérique; mais celui d'ici à la Nouvelle-York doit être payé au Bureau où les lettres seront mises.

*** *Les lettres pour chaque partie du Continent de l'Europe doivent être envoyées sous enveloppe á un correspondant, à Londres sans quoi elles ne seront point acheminées:*

HUGH FINLAY, *Deputé Directeur Général de la Poste.*

Adresse de l'EDITEUR, aux CANADIENS.

C'EST *avec une entiere satisfaction, que je m'adresse á un peuple, qui est aujourd'hui le plus [illegible] eux qu'il y ait dans l'Univers, & qui, j'ose le dire, est le plus digne de l'etre. Un peuple, qui par un noble caractere d'Esprit, des Moeurs pures, une conduite sage, vertueuse & chretienne, & sur tout, par son attachement & sa Fidelite au Gouvernement, s'est attiré sans doute, les avantages & les prosperités dont il jouit. Un peuple commandé par un Gouverneur en Chef, qui possede dans un si haut dégré toutes les vertus civiles & militaires, & dont la douceur & l'affabilité feront reconreconoitre en lui la vraie image de cet Auguste Souverain, qu'il a l'Honneur de representer; qualités qui á jamais rendront sa memoire precieuse, et son nom cher á tous les Canadiens. Un peuple qui voit avec une joie inexprimable l'heureux Retour de son Lieutenant Gouverneur, General aussi brave, et experimenté, que politique habile, le protecteur des anciennes loix et coutumes, qui ont toujours fait le bonheur de ce même peuple, en un mot,*

XVI. *See* p. 620.

760. JOUVE, *Sieur, Musician, Quebec*

CONCERT / VOCAL ET INSTRUMENTAL, / Au Benefice du Sieur JOUVE, Musicien de Son Altesse, / Royale, DEMAIN (Mardi 21 Fevrier) dans la Nouvelle / Salle des Spectacles. / [rule] / <Text> / Le Concert commencera à sept heures—On trouvera des Billets à la porte; depuis / Quatre Heures à trois Chelins les premiers et un chelin et demi les seconds. /

Broadside: 28 lines; type-page: 19.5 × 16 cm. *Probably printed at Quebec, by Samuel Neilson, 1792.*

Copy located: CaQQL (bound with *Quebec gazette*, Feb. 23, 1792).

LOWER CANADA. ELECTIONS, 1792

Following the establishment of a Legislative Assembly as a branch of government, by 31 Geo. III c. 31, the "Constitutional Act," Lieut.-Gov. Clarke issued proclamation for election writs, May 14, 1792. Fifty representatives were to be returned by twenty-one counties, two cities, and two towns, June 11-27, 1792. One returning officer was appointed to each constituency, who fixed the times and places of voting throughout the constituency, and who could close a poll when no vote had been registered for one hour. Registration of votes was open. A candidate could run in more than one constituency but could represent only one, which he selected if returned by more than one.

The newspapers published formal "election cards" announcing candidacy and qualifications, but not other advertisement, of those soliciting votes. Electioneering matter was published separately in handbills and pamphlets. These stated the candidate's general attitude on public matters, usually on French and English rights; and in the Quebec city and county constituencies at least, they attacked the personal and public character of other candidates. After the election, there appeared notices of resignation by members elected in more than one constituency; also at least one pamphlet, No. 761, criticizing the conduct of the poll.

The MS. journal of Samuel Neilson, Quebec, the principal printer in the province, records a score of handbills, etc., amounting to 2,190 copies printed May 14-21, 1792, and subsequent orders for handbills, letters, "labels for hats, cocades," etc. (Can.P.A., *Neilson papers*, v. 70). Similar material was produced, no doubt, by Wm. Moore at Quebec, and Fleury Mesplet in Montreal, of which record is lost. Those publications of which definite information exists, are described *seriatim* below. They are entered individually under the name of the author or of the candidate in whose interest they were published, or of the person who defrayed the cost of printing; if none of these is apparent, the publication is listed by title. The text of the publications is in the language of the title unless otherwise specified.

See also E. F. Surveyer: *The first parliamentary elections in Lower Canada*, in McGill University *Publications*, ser. 6, no. 15, Montreal, 1927; also: J. Desjardins: *Guide parlementaire historique de la province de Québec, 1792 à 1902* (xxiv, 395p., Quebec, 1902); F. J. Audet and E. F. Surveyer: *Les députés au premier parlement du Bas-Canada, 1792-1796*. v. 1 (316 p., Montreal, 1946).

761. BERTHELOT D'ARTIGNY, MICHEL-AMABLE, 1738-1815

Caption title: [double rule] / CONVERSATION / Au sujet de l' Election de Charlesbourg. /

Colophon: A QUEBEC: de l'Imprimerie, Rue la Montagne, N°. 3./

12mo. A^6; 10 p., 1 *l.*; type-page: 13.5 × 7.7 cm. *Printed at Quebec, by Samuel Neilson*, probably between June 1792 and Feb. 1793, for Berthelot d'Artigny.

Contents: p. 1-10, Conversation; 1 *l.*, blank.

This is a discussion between two electors, on the new Canadian constitution, that of Great Britain, and of the former French régime in Canada. They also discuss the recent election, especially the Charlesbourg poll where some votes were bought and others not registered. The pamphlet appears to concern the election at Charlesbourg in the County of Quebec, where a riot occurred between the supporters of Louis de Salaberry and David Lynd, and those of Berthelot d'Artigny, a French-Canadian lawyer. The poll was closed hastily before all the votes were registered, Berthelot claimed, in an *Address to electors* published in the *Quebec gazette*, July 12-19, 1792. De Salaberry, who headed the poll, was also returned for Dorchester County. He resigned his Quebec County seat which Berthelot won by acclamation on Feb. 15, 1793.

Copy located: Ketcheson.

762. [BLACKWOOD, JOHN, & CO.], *Merchants, Quebec*

[Election circular. *Printed at Quebec, by Samuel Neilson, 1792.*]

Neilson included in his record of election printing a "Hand-bill" produced for John Blackwood & Co., Quebec. Neither the candidate nor his platform is indicated in the record.

Copy located: None.

763. [DEBONNE, PIERRE-AMABLE], 1758-1816

AUX CANADIENS. /

Broadside: type-page: 14 × 10 cm. *Printed at Quebec, by Samuel Neilson, 1792,* for ? P.-A. DeBonne.

The text, unsigned, states: "L'Intention et les vues de l'auteur de *l'avis aux Canadiens* [No. 764] sont trop bien connues pour qu'il fasse attention à un écrit signé *probus* qui n'est qu'un tissu d'injures et de sophismes, [etc.]." It is followed by: "Chanson, sur la Profession de foi de Probus, Air: A la façon de barbari, mon ami." The chanson contains eight ten-line stanzas ridiculing "Probus," and lauding the provincial administration.

Neilson's *Journal* records "200 chansons contre Probus" printed for P.-A. DeBonne (assistant French secretary to the governor-in-council, and a candidate for election).

Copy located: CaQQL.

764. [DEBONNE, PIERRE-AMABLE], 1758-1816

Avis Aux Canadiens.

Broadside: type-page: 21.5 × 17 cm. *Printed at Quebec, by Samuel Neilson, 1792* (publication announced in *Quebec gazette*, May 17, 1792, *Sup.*).

The text, unsigned, warns electors against efforts of English merchants to obtain control of the Assembly and urges them to support the French-Canadian candidates, A. Juchereau Duchesnay and Louis de Salaberry, for the County of Quebec, John Lees and Jean Baillargé, père, for Lower Town (Quebec city), and G. E. Taschereau and Berthelot Dartigny [sic] for Upper Town (Quebec city). De Salaberry later issued a handbill repudiating this publication. *Avis* states that the English merchants, by canvassing jointly, are making a coalition against French Canadians; if English members are returned, French Canadians will derive no advantage and their fundamental laws may be injured; the English have no real stake in Canada and on the first reverse, they will leave the country; it suggests that English merchants have no common interest with the French-Canadian agriculturalists.

Neilson's *Journal* records "350 Avis aux Canadiens & proposing members, 4to Demy," printed for P.-A. DeBonne.

Copies located: CaQMS; CaQQL.

765. [DEBONNE, PIERRE-AMABLE], 1758-1816

Avis important aux Electeurs Canadiens.

Broadside: type-page: 17 × 17 cm. *Printed at Quebec, by Samuel Neilson, 1792*, in 200 copies, for Louis Deschenaux, candidate for County of Quebec. This is an election circular dated: "Québec, 15 Mai, 1792," signed: "Un Citoyen de Québec," and apparently written by P.-A. DeBonne. It urges Canadians not to be deceived by fair words and promises, but to vote for a compatriot known for his merit and his zeal for public interest and "propriétés réelles."

Copies located: CaQMS; CaQQL.

766. DESCHENAUX, LOUIS

Aux libres Electeurs du Comté de Québec.

Broadside: type-page: 24 × 17 cm. *Printed at Quebec, by Samuel Neilson, 1792.* This is an election circular, dated: "Québec, le 15 Mai, 1792," signed by L. Deschenaux, fils; begging votes and undertaking to uphold interests of French Canadians, their laws, civil liberties, and their religion.

Copy located: CaQQL.

767. DIALOGUE SUR L'INTERET DU JOUR

Caption title: DIALOGUE / Sur l'Interêt du Jour, entre plusieurs Candidats et un Electeur libre et independent / de la Cité de Québec; / Destiné pour être prononcé au / Club Constitutionel Extraordinaire / Tenu le Samedi 19 Mai, 1792, par un Membre du dit Club, mais / qu'un accident imprevue a empechéz d'être lû. / Publié par une

SOCIETE D'AMIS DE LA PATRIE ET DE LA CONSTITUTION, adressée / à ses FRERES, Habitants et Compatriots /

Colophon: Se vendent à l'Imprimerie du HERALD à Quebec, prix un Sheling. /

4to. [3] p.; type-page: 23.5 × 19 cm. Text in 2 col. *Printed at Quebec, by Wm. Moore, 1792.*

Contents: p. [1-3], Dialogue between (in succession) le Seigneur, le Negociant, l'Avocat, le Mecanique, le Laboureur, and le Candidat; verso of p. [3], blank.

Copy located: CaQMS.

768. DUMAS, ALEXANDRE, 1726?-1802

[Speech.]

4to. 3 p. *Printed at Quebec, by Samuel Neilson, 1792.*

Neilson's *Journal* records 900 copies of A. Dumas's Speech, making 3 p. 4to demy, printed for the Constitutional Club, June 2, 1792. Dumas, resident in Quebec since the French régime, a merchant and lawyer, delivered this speech on the constitution before the Constitutional Club,* Quebec, May 30, 1792—J. E. Roy: *Histoire de la Seigneurie de Lauzon* (5 v., Levis, 1897-1904), 3: 288.

Copy located: None.

769. [FINLAY, HUGH], 1732-1801

[Election circular. *Printed at Quebec, by Samuel Neilson, 1792.*]

Copy located: None.

770. [GRANT, WILLIAM], 1741-1805

Commentaire sur le discours de l'ho-/norable Chas. Delanaudière / (qui a paru hier) / [rule] /

Broadside: 37 lines, type-page: 22.5 × 16.7 cm. Probably *printed at Quebec, by Wm. Moore, 1792.* This election circular, dated at end: "Québec, 21 Mai 1792," was prepared by, or on behalf of, Wm. Grant, candidate in Upper Town, Quebec city.

Copy located: CaQMS.

*The Constitutional Club was organized Jan. 14, 1792, by 60 of the 165 citizens who had celebrated the New Constitution, Dec. 16, 1791. The purpose of the Club was to acquire and diffuse a knowledge of the British constitution in Canada, and to promote commercial and agricultural industry. It was a convivial debating society which met fortnightly on Saturdays at Franks' Tavern, Quebec. The membership was predominantly British and mercantile; the presiding officers (Wm. Grant and Charles de Lanaudière were the first) nominated their successors. The Club's rules, twenty-five in number (including No. XVI: "No subject whatever relating to Religion, or the late Revolution in France, can be debated in this Club") were printed in the *Quebec gazette*, Jan. 26, 1792.

771. [LANAUDIERE, CHARLES LOUIS DE], 1743-1811

[Chanson. *Printed at Quebec, by Samuel Neilson, 1792.*]

Neilson's *Journal* records a total of 500 copies in English and French editions, of "Lanaudière's Song with an engraved caricature" printed for M. and J. MacNider (merchants in Quebec), during the election campaign of 1792.

Copy located: None.

772A. LANAUDIERE, CHARLES LOUIS DE, 1743-1811

Le Discours suivant, destiné par l'honorable Charles de Lanaudière, pour être Prononcé à la dernière Assemblée du Club Constitutionel; N'a pu l'être, parce que plusieurs rapports du Comité permanent ont paru devant le Club pour avoir Sa Décision. <Text>

Broadside: type-page: 25 × 18 cm. *Printed at Quebec, by ? Wm. Moore, 1792.*

This election circular commends Messrs. Lester & Young as candidates for Lower Town, and Wm. Grant, president of the Club, for Upper Town, Quebec city.

Copy located: CaQQL.

772B. [LANAUDIERE, CHARLES LOUIS DE], 1743-1811

[A Hand-bill against M. Deschenaux.]

? Broadside: 200 copies were *printed at Quebec, by Samuel Neilson, 1792,* for Lanaudière.

Copy located: None.

772C. [LANAUDIERE, CHARLES LOUIS DE], 1743-1811

[Speech to Habitants of Ste. Anne.]

? Broadside: text probably in French. 400 copies *printed at Quebec, by Samuel Neilson, 1792,* for Lanaudière.

Copy located: None.

773. LEES, JOHN, 1740-1807

Aux Electeurs de la Basse Ville de Quebec

Broadside; type-page: 21.5 × 17 cm. *Printed at Quebec, by Samuel Neilson, 1792.* This election circular is dated: "Aux Trois Rivières, le 8 [i.e. 18?] Juin, 1792," and signed by John Lees. The author begs to withdraw as representative of Quebec Lower Town "ayant eu l'honneur d'être élu un des Representans pour les Trois Rivières."

Copy located: CaQQL.

774. [LYMBURNER, ADAM], 1746-1836

[Hand-bills. *Printed at Quebec, by Samuel Neilson, 1792.*]

Broadside: Neilson's *Journal* records "300 Hand-bills in French & English proposing Mr. Lymburner a Representative for the Lower Town."

Copy located: None.

775. MACNIDER, MATTHEW, *Merchant*, *Quebec*, 1725-1800

Aux libres Electeurs du Comté de Hampshire, paroisses St. Augustin, Pointe aux Trembles, Ecureuils, Cap Santé, Déchambault, Grondines et Ste. Anne.

Broadside: type-page: 19.5 × 17 cm. *Printed at Quebec, by Samuel Neilson, 1792.* This election circular is dated: "Québec, 16 Mai, 1792"; and signed by Mathieu MacNider. The author begs votes, and states that he has retired from business to live among these electors and will sustain rights and privileges common to them and himself.

Copy located: CaQQL.

776. PANET, PIERRE-LOUIS, 1761-1812

To the Electors of the County of Quebec.

Broadside: type-page: 17 × 17 cm. *Printed at Quebec, by Samuel Neilson, 1792.* This election circular is dated: "Quebec, 19th May 1792," and signed by P.-L. Panet, who announces that if elected by electors his "acknowledgements will equal my patriotism and good intentions."

Copy located: CaQQL.

777. PROBUS, *pseud.*

Aux Electeurs du Bas Canada, / Et à ceux du Comté et des Villes de Quebec en particulier. /

A single sheet printed on both sides, type-page: 31 × 16.7 cm. *Printed at Quebec, by Samuel Neilson, 1792* (500 copies for John Jones, 200 copies for Wm. Roxburgh, French or English edition not specified).

The text, signed: "Probus, Quebec, 21 Mai, 1792," is a categorical refutation of *Avis aux Canadiens* (No. 764). It shows the English merchant to be the benefactor and ally of the French Canadian—providing work for wages, stimulating agriculture, increasing property values, and circulating wealth. It depicts the seigneur as ever the despot over his compatriots.

Copies located: CaQMM (bound with *Quebec gazette*, May 24, 1792); CaQQA (bound with *Quebec gazette*, May 24, 1792); CaQQL.

778. PROBUS, *pseud.*

To the Electors of Lower Canada, / and those of the County and Towns of Quebec in particular. /

A single sheet printed on both sides, type-page: 31 × 16.7 cm. *Printed at Quebec, by Samuel Neilson, 1792.* English edition of the item above. The text is signed: "Probus, May 21, 1792."

Copies located: CaQQA (bound with *Quebec gazette*, May 24, 1792); CaQQL.

779. SALABERRY, IGNACE-MICHEL-LOUIS-ANTOINE D' IRUMBERRY DE, 1752-1828

Au Public.

Broadside: type-page: 19 × 17 cm. *Printed at Quebec, by Samuel Neilson, 1792.*

This election circular is dated: "A Québec, le 19 Mai 1792"; and signed by de Salaberry. The author disclaims any connection with a writing entitled *Avis aux Canadiens*.

Copy located: CaQQL.

780. SALABERRY, IGNACE-MICHEL-LOUIS-ANTOINE D' IRUMBERRY DE, 1752-1828

Messieurs et Citoyens.

Broadside: type-page: 21 × 17.5 cm. *Probably printed at Quebec, by Samuel Neilson, 1792.*

This election circular is dated: "Québec, le 19 Juin, 1792"; and signed by de Salaberry. The author announces that he was elected yesterday to represent county of Dorchester; but is still a candidate for county of Quebec, and begs his supporters there to continue to be so.

Copy located: CaQQL.

781. SMITH, WILLIAM, 1769-1847

[Election circular. *Printed at Quebec, by Samuel Neilson, 1792.*]

Neilson included in his records of election printing, a "Hand-bill" for Wm. Smith. The latter was probably Wm. Smith, Jr., 1769-1847, then clerk of the Legislative Council, or possibly his father, Wm. Smith, 1728-93, the chief justice. The argument or the candidate advertised in the handbill does not appear in the printer's records.

Copy located: None.

782. LOWER CANADA. LAWS, STATUTES, *etc.*

NUM. 1391. / THE / QUEBEC / GAZETTE. / [rule] / THURSDAY, MARCH 1, 1792. / [rule] / [in centre: royal arms] / [on right:] LA / GAZETTE / DE / QUEBEC. / [rule] / JEUDI. I MARS, 1792. / [rule] /

English caption: Anno Tricesimo Secundo Georgii Tertii Regis. Chap. I. An Ordinance, Relating to Causes in Appeal to the Court of the Governor and Executive Council.

French caption: . . . Chap. I. Ordonnance, Concernant les Causes en Appel à la Cour du Gouverneur et Conseil Exécutif.

A single sheet printed on both sides, text in 2 col., English and French. *Printed at Quebec, by Samuel Neilson, 1792,* as recorded:

"1792, Mar. 5. Printed for Council Office, 50 [sic] Copies of Ordinances, Chap. 1 and 2 in ½ Sheet Crown, on Gazette Types 5/ [per] 100—£1.5."

—Can.P.A., *Neilson papers*, v. 70.

Contents: p. [1], 32 Geo. III c. 1 (as above); p. [2], 32 Geo. III c. 2, "An Ordinance to facilitate the production of parol proof in civil causes. Ordonnance pour faciliter la production des preuves verbales dans les causes civiles." Passed Feb. 24, 1792, and signed by Alured Clarke, these ordinances were published in the *Quebec gazette,* Mar. 1, 1792 (at a charge of £4. 14*s*. 2*d*.) and reprinted from the same type with *Gazette* heading and colophon.

Copies located: CaOOA (2 cop. in portfolio "Quebec gazette, Mar. 1, 1787").

783. LOWER CANADA. LAWS, STATUTES, *etc.*

[Anno tricesimo secundo Georgii tertii, Regis. Chap. III. An Ordinance for suspending the sessions of the Court of King's Bench at Montreal, and to facilitate the proceedings in Appeal Causes.

French side: . . . Chap. III Ordonnance pour suspendre les sessions de la Cour du banc du Roi à Montréal et pour faciliter les procédures dans les Causes en apel]

? Broadside: text in 2 col , English and French. *Printed at Quebec, by Samuel Neilson, 1792,* as recorded:

"1792, Nov. 15. Printed for Council Office (omitted August 31) 500 Copies on Gazette types [i.e. from *Quebec gazette,* Aug. 16, 1792] of an Ordinance respecting King's bench Court &c. $\frac{1}{2}$ Sheet Crown 10/ 1st 100 & 5/ after —£1.5. [i.e. £1.10.]."—Can.P.A., *Neilson papers,* v. 70.

This was the last ordinance passed in the Legislative Council of the old province of Quebec.

Copy located: None.

784. LOWER CANADA. LIEUTENANT-GOVERNOR, 1791-1795 (*Clarke*)

A PROCLAMATION, / To such as are desirous to settle on the Lands of the Crown in the Province / of Lower Canada: / By His Excellency ALURED CLARKE, Esquire, / . . . / . . . / <Text> / GIVEN . . . [at] Quebec, / . . . / . . . [Feb. 7, 1792] / ALURED CLARKE. / By His EXCELLENCY'S Command, / HUGH FINLAY, Acting Secretary. /

Broadside: 73 lines; type-page: 32.5 × 17 cm. *Text:* "Be it known to all concerned . . . the Terms of Grant and Settlement [etc.]," states terms 1-10, of grant and settlement of crown lands in Lower Canada.

This broadside was *printed at Quebec, by Samuel Neilson, 1792,* as recorded:

"1792, Feb. 17. Printed for Council Office [per] order of Mr. Williams, 1000 English Proclamations for settling the Lands of the Crown. half sheet Crown pica type. 21/ 1st 100, & 5/ each after—£3.6.

500 French D^{o}—£2.1.

[Total:] £5.7."—Can.P.A., *Neilson papers,* v. 70.

It is reprinted in Can.P.A., *Report, 1921.*

Copies located: CaOOA (15 copies filed in Can.P.A., "S" Proclamations, L.C., 1777-91; another copy in Proclamations portfolio in the Library); GBLP (in C.O. 42/109: 687).

785. LOWER CANADA. LIEUTENANT-GOVERNOR, 1791-1795 (*Clarke*)

[Proclamation, Pour telles Personnes qui désirent s'établir sur les Terres de la Couronne dans la Province du Bas Canada. Par Son Excellence Alured Clarke, Ecuier, . . . <Text> Donné . . . au Château St. Louis dans la ville de Québec . . . Fev. 7, 1792 . . . (Signé) Alured Clarke. Par Ordre de son Excellence, Hugh Finlay, faisant fonction de Sécrétaire. Traduit par Ordre de Son Excellence, P.A. DeBonne, AS. & TF.]

Broadside. French edition of No. 784, 500 copies *printed at Quebec, by Samuel Neilson, 1792.*

It is reprinted in Can.P.A., *Rapport, 1921.*

Copy located: None.

786. LOWER CANADA. LIEUTENANT-GOVERNOR, 1791-1795 (*Clarke*)

NUM. 1400 / THE / QUEBEC / GAZETTE. / [rule] / THURSDAY MAY 24, 1792. / [rule] / [in centre: royal arms] / [on right:] LA / GAZETTE / OF / QUEBEC. / [rule] / JEUDI, LE 24 MAI, 1792. / [rule] /

English side begins: "Alured Clarke. George the Third by the Grace of God of Great Britain France and Ireland, King, . . . To all Our loving Subjects whom these presents may concern."

French side begins: "Alured Clarke. George Trois, par la Grace de Dieu Roi de la Grande Bretagne, de France et d'Irlande, . . . A tous nos affectionés sujets que ces présentes peuvent intéresser."

fo. [3] p. text in 2 col. English and French; p. [1-3], Letter patent "to divide the said Province of Lower Canada into Districts, Counties, Circles or Towns and Townships . . . and to declare and appoint the number of Representatives to be chosen by each to serve in the Assembly," dated at Quebec, May 7, 1792; p. [3] at foot, Lieut.-Gov. Clarke's letter patent announcing the issue of "Writs in due form for calling together the Legislative Council and Assembly of Our said Province which Writs are to bear Teste on the Twenty-fourth day of May Instant, and to be returnable on the Tenth day of July following," dated at Quebec, May 14, 1792; verso of p. [3], blank.

This is the first "edition" of two documents, frequently republished, which defined the electoral districts and ordered the election of the first legislature under the new constitution.

This item is an offprint, with the regular newspaper heading but no other matter, from the *Quebec gazette.* It was *printed at Quebec, by Samuel Neilson, 1792,* as recorded:

"1792, May 26. 500 Copies of the Letters patent dividing the Province into Counties—on the Gazette types [i.e. from *Quebec gazette,* May 24, 1792] making 1 Sheet Crown at 10/ [per] 100—£2.10.0."

—Can.P.A., *Neilson papers,* v. 70.

Copy located: NNB.

787. MABANE, ADAM, 1734-1792, *and* GRAY, ALEXANDER, *d.* 1791

CATALOGUE / [English and French follow side by side:] Of the LIBRARIES of the late Ho-/norable ADAM MABANE, and ALEX-/ANDER GRAY, Esquires, to be Sold by / AUCTION on Tuesday the 24th. / Instant, and following Evenings, at / the MERCHANT'S Coffee-House, St. / Peter's Street, Lower Town. /

French side: Des Bibliotheques des Défunts l'hono-/rable ADAM MABANE, et ALEXAN-/DER GRAY, Ecuyer, à vendre par / encan Mardi le 24 du Courant, & / soirées suivantes, au Cassé de MAR-/CHANDS, ruè St. Pierre, à la Basse / ville. /

<Text (book titles) in 4 col.> / The SALE to begin each Evening at Seven o'Clock, and to continue till the / whole is sold off. CHA[s]. STEWART, Notr. Pub. / QUEBEC, 16th April, 1792. /

Broadside: 87 lines; type-page: 42 × 23 cm. *Printed at Quebec, by Samuel Neilson, 1792,* as recorded:

"1792, Apr. 18. Printed for Charles Stewart 200 Catalogues of Adam Mabane & A. Gray library on a half sheet demy paper—£1.15.
Distributing the same through the town—2/6.
[Total:] £1.17.6."—Can.P.A., *Neilson papers,* v. 70.

About 250 titles are listed in four groups: folio, quarto, octavo, and duodecimo, comprising British and colonial statutes, legal and historical works, 18th-century publications in English poetry and French philosophy. The sets of Voltaire and Rousseau lack several volumes, probably borrowed from the late owners. Frequent advertisements in local papers for the return of such volumes suggest their interest to Quebecois. The only works relating to Canada (except possibly some unspecified "pamphlets") in the libraries of Judge Mabane and Attorney-General Gray were Oldmixon's *History* and Maseres's *Canadian freeholder, Quebec papers,* etc. *Some account* of Mabane's life and a portrait were published in *Quebec magazine,* Dec., 1793, p. 294-99.

Copy located: CaQQL (bound in *Quebec gazette,* Mar. 29, 1792).

788. MENSFORTH, *Sergeant, 7th Regiment*

(AVEC PERMISSION.) AUX CURIEUX ET SPECULATIFS. / ON exhibera les Mardis, Jeudis et Samedis, entre / 11 et 3 heures, au Caffé des Marchands de Mr. / FERGUSON, à la Basse Ville. / L'AUTOMATE / ou Figure Parlante Surprenante. / [*A Québec, Chez Samuel Neilson, 1792.*]

Broadside: text in French, 21 lines; type-page: 22.5 × 16 cm. This diverting exhibit is described in the text: "Cette Figure est Femelle, et si bien faite d'après Nature qu'on n'y peut à peine remarquer aucune différence. Elle a 3 pieds de long, et sera suspendue du plafond avec un ruban. Cette invention est uniquement de l'exhibiteur . . . Ce remarquable AUTOMATE repondra à toutes les questions qui lui seront proposées soit en François ou en Anglois [etc.]."

The ingenious inventor of the "Automate," or automaton, was Sergeant Mensforth of the 7th Regiment, for whom Samuel Neilson printed 500 handbills in French and English, and 200 tickets on Feb. 11, and 250 more handbills on Feb. 20, 1792. —Can.P.A., *Neilson papers*, v. 70.

Copy located: CaQQL (bound with *Quebec gazette*, Jan. 5, 1792).

789. NEW BRUNSWICK. CUSTOMS OFFICE

CUSTOM-HOUSE, ST. JOHN, 1792. / TWENTY GUINEAS REWARD. / WHEREAS MR. RICHARD BATCHELLOR, sur-/veyor and searcher of His Majesty's Customs for the Port of SAINT / JOHN [etc.]

Broadside: 18 lines; type-page: 16.7 × 15.5 cm. *Probably printed at Saint John, N.B., by Christopher Sower* or *John Ryan, 1792.* This is the announcement of a reward offered for discovery of persons who on night of July 28, 1792, stole from the schooner *Sally* at Sackville, a quantity of geneva [gin], shoes, scythes, and wool-cards of the manufactory of the United States, small fur, cariboo and seal skins—goods which had been seized by Batchellor, declared forfeit and shipped on board the *Sally* to be delivered to the collector of customs at Saint John, N.B.

The enforcement of the imperial navigation laws was notoriously difficult, and smuggling a major enterprise along the Nova Scotia-New Brunswick coast—as the not infrequent newspaper notices similar to this broadside indicate.

Copy located: CaN (in [lieutenant-governor's] *Correspondence with officers of customs, 1790-95*, MSS. This copy is filed with a letter of Aug. 22, 1792, from Wanton & Withoff, merchants, begging the lieutenant-governor to offer a reward for the smugglers. The letter is endorsed: "Ans^d^ 31st authorizing advertisement."

790. NEW BRUNSWICK. HOUSE OF ASSEMBLY

JOURNAL / OF THE / VOTES and PROCEEDINGS / OF THE / HOUSE OF ASSEMBLY / OF THE / PROVINCE of NEW-BRUNSWICK: / From TUESDAY the 14th of FEBRUARY, to WEDNESDAY / the 7th MARCH, 1792. / [ornamental rule] / [royal arms] / [ornamental rule] / FREDERICTON: / Printed by CHRISTOPHER SOWER, Printer to the / KING'S MOST EXCELLENT MAJESTY. 1792. / [title in a frame of flower pieces]

fo. [*]^{1}A-M^2,N^1; 1 p. l., [228]-277 p., fold. table; type-page: 24 × 13. cm. Even numbers on recto, odd numbers on verso; paged in continuation of No. 712.

Contents: p. l. recto, t.-p.; verso, blank; p. [228]-277, Journal of the sixth and last session of the first assembly. The fold. table, properly inserted at p. 270-71, is ". . . Account of goods imported into the Port of Saint John . . . [Feb. 13, 1791-Feb. 4, 1792] subject to a Duty at the Treasury office."

It was ordered by the House, Feb. 15, 1792, "that Christopher Sower, Esquire, print the Journals of this House, and that the Clerk furnish him daily with copies of the same for that purpose." Also on Mar. 6, 1792, it was "Ordered that 300 Copies of the Acts and 200 Copies of the Journals be printed." At the same time the government's distribution list was revised, increasing the number of copies given the governor (to six), the supreme court and assembly members (to two) etc., so that two-thirds of the edition was absorbed before publication.

This and No. 791 are the first works published with the imprint of Fredericton, N.B. This town, 60 miles up the St. John River, had been selected as the provincial capital in 1785 and thither soon moved the offices of government. The mercantile community, however, remained at the mouth of the River in the City of Saint John where the government printing was regularly done. In 1792 Sower was persuaded to move his printing office to the seat of government for the session—probably to expedite the transmittal of copy and proof, a tedious business between Fredericton and Saint John in the winter months, and one which had caused trouble between king's printer and government in 1786-87. *See* No. 520 *note*. These, and provincial documents of 1795-98, remained the only Fredericton imprints till 1806 when another temporary press was established there.

The provincial accounts for 1792 included the following items:

"To Christopher Sower for bringing up his printing press and types and staying at Fredericton to print the Journal of the House—£12.

To Christopher Sower in satisfaction of his account [probably for printing the *Journal* and *Acts* of 1792]—£57.17.0."

—N.B.As. *Papers, 1793*; also 32 Geo. III c. XI.

Copies located: CaN (t.-p. wanting); CaNS; CaNU; CaNsWA; CaOOA; GBLP (in B.T. 6/56: 537-90); RPJ.

791. NEW BRUNSWICK. LAWS, STATUTES, *etc.*

ACTS / OF THE / GENERAL ASSEMBLY / OF / His MAJESTY'S PROVINCE / OF / NEW-BRUNSWICK, / PASSED IN THE YEAR 1792. / [ornamental rule] / [royal arms] / [ornamental rule] / FREDERICTON: / Printed by CHRISTOPHER SOWER, Printer to the / KING'S MOST EXCELLENT MAJESTY, 1792. / [title within frame of flower pieces]

fo. [*^{1}2*]^2, A-E^2, F^1; 3 p. l., 240-261 p.; type-page: 23.5 × 13 cm. Even numbers on recto, odd numbers on verso; paged in continuation of No. 713. One leaf of sig. F is folded around sig. A-E to form a p. l.

Contents: p. l. 1 recto, t.-p.; verso, blank; p. l. 2 recto, half title; verso, blank; p. l. 3 recto, Titles of the acts; verso, blank; p. 240-61, 32 Geo. III c. I-XI acts passed in the sixth session of the first assembly. This work was published in an edition of 300 copies. *See* No. 790 *note*.

Copies located: Baxter; CaOOA; GBLP (in B.T. 6/56: 505-32); NNB; NNHi.

792. NEW BRUNSWICK. TREASURY OFFICE

A GENERAL ACCOUNT of GOODS imported into the Port of SAINT JOHN, (NEW-BRUNSWICK) [Feb. 13, 1791-Feb. 4, 1792] subject / to a Duty at the TREASURY OFFICE. / <Text, signed:> February 24th, 1792. / RICHARD SEAMAN, / P. TREASURER. /

Broadside: type-page: 29.5 × 20.5 cm. *Printed at Fredericton, N.B., by Christopher Sower, 1792.* This is probably a separate issue of the fold. table in No. 790. The treasurer's *Account* appeared regularly in this form in the Assembly *Journal*.

Copy located: GBLP (in C.O. 188/4: 591).

793. NOVA SCOTIA. HOUSE OF ASSEMBLY

Caption title: (129) / [ornamental rule] / JOURNAL, / AND / PROCEEDINGS / OF THE / HOUSE OF ASSEMBLY, / Of the Province of NOVA-SCOTIA. / [rule] / Wednesday June 6th, 1792. /

fo. sig. 2H-2U²; p. 129-190 [i.e. 180]; paged in continuation of No. 714; p. 180 mispaged: 190. *Printed at Halifax, N.S., by Anthony Henry, 1792.*

Contents: p. 129-190 [!], Journal and proceedings of the seventh session of the sixth assembly, June 6-July 11, 1792.

Copies located: CaNs; CaNsHA; GBLP (in C.O. 217/64: 124-175); MH.

794. NOVA SCOTIA. LAWS, STATUTES, *etc.*

Running title: [rule] / 1792. Anno Tricessimo Secundo Regis, GEORGII III. CAP. I[-X]. / [rule] /

Caption title: At the GENERAL ASSEMBLY of this Province / of Nova-Scotia, . . . / [8 lines] / . . . being the Seventh Session of the / Sixth General Assembly, convened in the / said Province. / [rule] /

fo. sig. 3I-3L², 3M¹; p. 299-312; type-page: 25.5 × 15 cm. paged in continuation of No. 715. *Printed at Halifax, N.S., by Anthony Henry, 1792.*

Contents: p. 299-312, Cap. I-X, perpetual acts passed in the session, June 6-July 11, 1792.

Copies located: CaO; DLC; MH (2 cop.).

795. NOVA SCOTIA. LAWS, STATUTES, *etc.*

Running title: [rule] / 1792. Anno Tricessimo Secundo Regis, GEORGII III. CAP. I[-V]. / [rule] /

Caption title: At the GENERAL ASSEMBLY of this Province / of Nova-Scotia, . . . / [8 lines] / . . . being the Seventh Session of the / Sixth General Assembly, convened in the / said Province. / [rule] /

fo. sig. 3O-3S², [3T]¹; p. 317-337; type-page: 25.5 × 15 cm. paged in continuation of No. 716. *Printed at Halifax, N.S., by Anthony Henry, 1792.*

Contents: p. 317-337, Cap. I-V, temporary acts passed in the session, June 6-July 11, 1792; verso of p. 337, blank.

Copies located: CaO; MH; N; NNB.

796. QUEBEC, *City*. SEMINAIRE DE QUEBEC

EXERCICE / SUR LA / RHETORIQUE / [rule] / QUI SE FERA / DANS LA / SALLE DU / PETIT SEMINAIRE / DE QUEBEC / LE 13 AOUT 1792. / [rule] / PAR LES CANDIDATS / ANT. BEDARD JOS. BEDARD. / CHAR. DELERY FRAN. RANVOYZE / GAB. TACHERAUX J. B^{te}. NOEL / JOS. DEGUIRE JEAN FOURNEL / JAC^{es} PERRAS MED.

PETRIMOUX / OL. GERMAIN [rule]) ETUDIANS EN RHETORIQUE / SOUS / Mr JOSEPH BOISSONAULT, / PRETRE. /

4to. 3 *l.* without signature or pagination. type-page: 15 × 12 cm.

Contents: *l.* 1 recto, t.-p.; verso, blank; *l.* 2 recto-3 recto, Exercice; *l.* 3, verso, blank.

This little pamphlet was *printed at Quebec, by Samuel Neilson, 1792*, as recorded: "1792, Aug. 12. Printed for M^r^. Boissonault, Pretre, Un Exercise de Rhetorique —17/6.
Binding D^o^—7/6."—Can.P.A., *Neilson papers*, v. 70.

Copies located: CaQMS, CaQQL (2 cop.).

797. QUEBEC, *City*. SEMINAIRE DE QUEBEC

THÈSES / DE / MATHEMATIQUE / ET DE / PHYSIQUE, / [rule] / QUI SERONT SOUTENUES / AU / SÉMINAIRE DE QUÉBEC, / LUNDI 30 Avril, depuis 10 heures du matin, / jusqu'à 3 après midi. / [rule] / P.M.M.{[in col. 1:] FRERE FELIX BOSSU, / J. B. BEDARD, / JEAN DUPRAS, / PRISQUE FERLAND, / JOSEPH BORGIA.} [in col. 2:] ETUDIANS / EN / PHYSIQUE. / Depuis huit mois. / [rule] / sous / Mr. ROBERT PRETRE / Du Seminaire, Professeur de PHILOSOPHIE. /

4to. [$*^1$, 2-3$*^2$]; 1 p. l., 7 p.; type-page: 15.4 × 12 cm.

Contents: p. l. recto, t.-p.; verso, blank; p. [1]-7, Thèses; verso of p. 7, blank.

This pamphlet was *printed at Quebec, by Samuel Neilson, 1792*, as recorded: "1792, Apr. 25. Printed for Quebec Seminary, 150 Copies of the Mathematical Theses on Superfine folio post—£3.
Binding D^o^ in blue & embossed paper @ 1d. each 12/6."
—Can.P.A., *Neilson papers*, v. 70.

Copies located: CaQMS; CaQQL (2 cop.).

798. QUEBEC GAZETTE. CARRIER'S ADDRESS

VERSES / of the Printer's Boy / WHO CARRIES THE QUEBEC GAZETTE / To the Customers. / [rule] / JANUARY 1st, 1793. /

French side:

ETRENNES / DU GARCON qui porte la / GAZETTE DE QUEBEC / AUX PRATIQUES. / Le Ier Janvier, 1793. / [*Quebec, S. Neilson, 1791.*]

Broadside: type-page: 38.5 × 26.5 cm. in ornamental rule frame. English verse on left, 60 lines; French on right, 79 lines.

The addresses this year are not pleasant platitudes, but messages inspired by revolution in France.

"Imprimis—news foreign, eventful, I've brought ye;
Which, wisdom political, much may have taught ye;
From the whole in strong language, this lesson you learn,
That good sense must ever, at all extremes spurn;
'Gainst all kinds of tyrants the free heart must throb,
Be't the bad despot crown'd, or worse despot Mob."

French side:

"Un païs autrefois soumis au despotisme,
D'un spectacle imposant etonne l'Univers,
Et de la tyrannie ayant brise les fers,
S'achemine hardiment au republicanisme.
Les despots voisins, unissant leurs efforts,
D'un monarque déchu embrassant la défense,
Déploient en sa faveur les funestes ressorts,
De leur dangéreuse puissance."

Copy located: CaO (bound in *Quebec gazette*, at beginning of 1793).

799. QUEBEC LIBRARY

CATALOGUE / OF / ENGLISH AND FRENCH / BOOKS / IN THE / QUEBEC LIBRARY. / [rule] / QUEBEC: / Printed by SAMUEL NEILSON, Mountain-Street, / [rule] / M.DCC. XCII. /

8vo. 1 p. l., viii, 29 p.; type-page: 17.5 × 10.3 cm. p. [i]-viii, odd numbers on verso, even numbers on recto; text in English and French on opposite pages. Neilson recorded the printing:

"1792, Sept. 26. Printed for Quebec Library 100 Catalogues of the books with the Rules.—£10.10.
Binding D° in marble paper 2d. each—16/8.
[Total:] £11.6.8."—Can.P.A., *Neilson papers*, v. 70.

Contents: p. l., recto, t.-p.; verso, blank; recto of p. [i], blank; p. [i]-viii, Introduction; verso of p. viii, blank; p. 1-15, Catalogue (in English); verso of p. 15, blank; p. 17-29, Catalogue (in French); verso of p. 29, blank.

The introduction states . . . "The arrangement of Catalogues is an arbitrary matter, as the variety of plans in use sufficiently evince. They ought, however, to be systematical and conformable to the natural order of the subjects contained in the Library. Some compilers have followed the dates or order of time in which the books were printed, others the size of the volumes, some the alphabetical succession of authors, but the majority the subject matters. A good Catalogue should shew the subjects, the author, the edition, the language of each work and the size and number of the volumes.

"Books are generally divided into five principal classes, Theology, Jurisprudence, Arts and Sciences, Belles Lettres and History, which are again divided and subdivided. And this mode, apparently the most simple, has been followed with little variation in the present Catalogue. . . . And separate classes have been formed for Poetry, Plays and Novels—History, Biography and Travels—and miscellaneous works. . . . The date of the edition, the size and number of volumes and generally the names of the authors are inserted." The introduction gives also a sketch of the development, constitution and rules of the Library "which may become of greater advantage should it fortunately attract the attention of the Legislature and become a provincial institution."

The collection comprised (in 1792) 2,443 volumes (1,211 English, 1,209 French, 23 Greek and Latin) and "a pair of eighteen inch globes, mounted in the new manner." It was still housed in the Bishop's Palace and Mr. Brassard was "issuer of the Books."

Copies located: CaQMS; NhD.

800. THE QUEBEC MAGAZINE

[Proposals for publishing the Quebec Magazine.]

Broadside or leaflet, *printed at Quebec by Samuel Neilson, 1792.* Neilson's announcement of the *Quebec magazine,* published in the newspapers, stated that "Proposals containing a fuller account of the plan are to be had at Samuel Neilson's, Quebec, E. Edwards in Montreal, Peter Clarke in Kingston, George Leith in Detroit, John Howe in Halifax, and Christopher Sower in Saint John."

—*Montreal gazette,* Feb. 16, 1792.

Copy located: None.

801. RITCHIE, DAVID

A / DISCOURSE, / DELIVERED ON THE / DEATH / OF / JOHN FILLIS, ESQ. / ON / Sunday, July 22, 1792, / IN THE / PROTESTANT DISSENTING CHURCH, / HALIFAX. / AND / Published at the Request of his Friends. / [rule] / BY THE REVEREND DAVID RITCHIE. / [rule] / HALIFAX: / PRINTED BY JOHN HOWE, AT THE CORNER OF GEORGE AND BAR-/RINGTON STREETS, OPPOSITE THE PARADE. / [rule] / M.DCC.XCII. /

8vo. A-B[4]; 14 p.; 1 *l.*; type-page: 17.5 × 9 cm. Printed on wove paper, an early example of its use in Canada.

Contents: p. [1], t.-p.; p. [2], blank; p. [3]-14, A discourse, text: Rev. xiv, 13, Blessed are the dead which die in the Lord; 1 *l.*, blank.

Fillis, a merchant in Halifax, died July 16, 1792, in his sixty-eighth year. He was a member of the Legislative Assembly from its institution in Nova Scotia, 1758. He was also a prominent member in a protestant dissenting group (probably Congregationalist or Presbyterian) for he was referred to as "Deacon Fillis," and for a time at least helped administer funds raised in England to aid dissenting clergy in Nova Scotia.

Copies located: CaNsHD; MBAt.

802. ST. JOHN, ISLAND OF. CITIZENS

Caption title: The Necessity of the Circulation of Paper Money, explained, and / the ruinous Practice of taking Orders exposed; in a few / friendly Cautions, recommended to the immediate Consideration / of every Well-wisher of this Island. /

4to. 2 *l.* without signature or pagination; type-page: 22 × 11.7 cm. *Probably printed at Charlottetown by Wm. A. Rind, 1792.*

Contents: *l.* 1 recto-*l.* 2 recto, The necessity, etc.; verso of *l.* 2, blank;

The text is a declaration (with blank space at end for signatures) of the citizens of the Island of St. John, attesting to the necessity of encouragement to trade by the circulation of paper money; applauding the act "of last session" (provincial act,

31 Geo. III c.8) which directed the emission of £500 in paper currency; undertaking themselves to accept and make payments in that currency and to discountenance the giving and taking of "Orders." The declaration continues with an attack on merchants who prefer "Orders." The entire order must be taken out in goods at one time, from one merchant. The merchants, it states, set their own prices, and give *credit* for local produce, not *cash*, so that all the specie in the Island falls into the hands of the merchants who send it away.

The declaration was probably prepared for presentation to the Assembly. At its opening, Nov. 6, 1792, Lieut.-Gov. Fanning recommended that the late act, 31 Geo. III c. 8, not having "proved that efficient substitute for the want of a circulating currency . . . a [new] means be devised of satisfying demands of public creditors. The want of specie, . . . [he stated, is] a vast obstacle to trade, discouragement to industry, embarrassment and distress to individuals with sufficient property to satisfy demands of creditors but inability to convert their effects into money."

—Island of St. John, Assembly *Journal*, 1792).

Copy located: NNHi (bound with Island of St. John, *Acts*, 1790).

803. ST. JOHN, ISLAND OF. CITIZENS

Caption title: To His Excellency, Edmund Fanning . . . [Address of citizens of Cherry Valley and Vernon River, and Lieutenant-Governor Fanning's Answer.]

A single sheet printed on both sides; *probably printed at Charlottetown, Island of St. John, by Wm. A. Rind, 1791-92,* in a few copies for Lieut.-Gov. Fanning.

Contents: Address "May it please your Excellency, We the Subscribers, being the Inhabitants of the two Settlements of Cherry Valley and Vernon River, beg leave to express . . . our extreme Regret at hearing certain Complaints to have been exhibited against you and three other officers to . . . [the] Privy Council . . . representing your . . . administration to have been factious and arbitrary and . . . the administration of Justice since the Restoration of the Chief Justice [Peter Stewart . . . to have] been partial and subservient to . . . this pretended faction of Your Excellency [etc., undated, signed by] Joseph Beers, J.P. [and 13 others]." Appended is: "The Lieutenant Governor's Answer: Gentlemen, the Address . . . this day presented to me affords me a very singular pleasure. [etc., signed:] Edm. Fanning, Charlotte Town, 18th Nov. 1791."

This, and the publication following, were published by Lieut.-Gov. Fanning (probably after Jan. 1, and before Apr. 5, 1792) as part of his defence submitted to the Privy Council, London, 1792. The defence was an answer to charges preferred against Fanning and three officials by the proprietors—absentee landowners, who controlled most of the Island. *See* A. B. Warburton: *A history of Prince Edward Island* (Saint John, N.B., 1923), 260 *et seq.* where the Cherry Valley Address is reprinted. Can.P.A., P.E.I. "A" series includes transcripts (from C.O. 226/14) of the documents submitted by Fanning. The Public Archives of Canada has also a group of MS. and printed papers on the case, formerly in possession of Lord Sydney.

Copy located: GBLP (in C.O. 226/14: 499, enclosed in Lieut.-Gov. Fanning's letter to the Privy Council dated: "Charlotte Town, 5th April, 1792").

804. ST. JOHN, ISLAND OF. CITIZENS

Caption title: To His Excellency, Edmund Fanning . . . [Address of Citizens of Prince Town and County, and Lieutenant-Governor Fanning's Answer]

A single sheet printed on both sides; *probably printed at Charlottetown, Island of St. John, by Wm. A. Rind, 1791-92,* in a few copies for Lieut.-Gov. Fanning.

Contents: Address "May it please your Excellency, We, his Majesty's dutiful and loyal Subjects, the Inhabitants of Prince Town and County, having been informed that certain charges, of a Criminal Import, have been exhibited by Mr. John Hill, and Messrs Cambridge and Bowley, merchants of this Island, against your Excellency . . . [assure you of our approbation of your administration, of the administration of Justice and method of representation in Assembly, and of our dissatisfaction with failure of proprietors in settling their lands etc., undated, signed by] William Hunter [and 95 others, with note:] With many others, that could not be conveniently inserted in this sheet." Appended is: "The Lieutenant Governor's Answer. Gentlemen. This Address . . . cannot be otherwise than highly acceptable to me . . . [signed:] Edm. Fanning, Charlotte Town, 28th November, 1791." *See* No. 803 *note*

Copy located: GBLP (in C.O. 226/14: 501-502, enclosed like No. 803).

805. ST. JOHN, ISLAND OF. CITIZENS

Caption title: To His Excellency, Edmund Fanning . . . [Address of citizens of Hillsborough River, etc., and Lieutenant-Governor Fanning's Answer]

A single sheet printed on both sides; *probably printed at Charlottetown, Island of St. John, by Wm. A. Rind, 1791-92,* in a few copies for Lieut.-Gov. Fanning.

Contents: Address "May it please Your Excellency, We the Inhabitants of the several Settlements of Hillsborough River, Bedford Bay, Savage Harbour, and Saint Peters, beg leave to express . . . our extreme Regret at hearing Certain Complaints to have been exhibited against you and three other officers to . . . [the] Privy Council, . . . representing your . . . administration to have been factious and arbitrary [etc., text similar to that of address from Cherry Valley, undated, signed by:] John McDonald [and 137 others with note:] With one Hundred and thirty others." Appended is: "The Lieutenant Governor's Answer. Gentlemen, I return to you my sincere and grateful acknowledgements for your very obliging Address [etc. signed:] Edm: Fanning, Charlottetown, 30th December, 1791." *See* No. 803 *note*.

Copy located: GBLP (in C.O. 226/14: 503-504, enclosed like No. 803).

806. ST. JOHN, ISLAND OF. GRAND JURY

Caption title: To His Excellency . . . [Address of the Grand Jury, and Lieutenant-Governor Fanning's Answer]

fo. [2] p. *Probably printed at Charlottetown, Island of St. John, by Wm. A. Rind, 1792,* in a few copies for Lieut.-Gov. Fanning.

Contents: Address "May it please Your Excellency, We the Grand Jury of this his Majesty's Island of Saint John for this present Session, . . . Understanding that the Government of the Province of Nova Scotia by his Majesty's Royal Instructions has devolved upon your Excellency by the Death of Governor Parr, . . . express our sincere Sorrow at the Prospect of being deprived of a Governor, the whole Tenour of whose conduct . . . has been marked by the Greatest Moderation and Impartiality, . . . The Complaints exhibited to his Majesty's Ministers . . . we trust will prove ill-founded . . . and redound to your Excellency's Honour . . . [signed by:] S. Hayden, Foreman, [and 15 others including Wm. A. Rind, the printer, dated:] Charlotte Town, February 24th, 1792." Appended is: "His Excellency's Answer. Mr. Foreman, and Gentlemen of the Grand Jury. I return you my sincere and unfeigned Thanks for your very civil and obliging Address . . . [signed:] Edm. Fanning. Charlotte Town, 24th February, 1792."

Fanning made no reference in his *Answer* to the suggestion of his promotion to Nova Scotia. He remained, in fact, lieutenant-governor of the Island till 1804. *See* No. 803 *note*.

Copy located: GBLP (in C.O. 226/14: 505-506, enclosed like No. 803).

807. ST. JOHN, ISLAND OF. HOUSE OF ASSEMBLY

[Journal of the House of Assembly of His Majesty's Island of Saint John. Anno tricessimo tertio Georgii III. Third Session of the Sixth General Assembly. *Charlotte Town, Island of Saint John, Printed by William Alexander Rind* . . . 1792.]

4to. 28 p.

Contents: Journal, Nov. 6-17, 1792, the first meeting of the House since Nov., 1790.

Copy located: GBLP (in C.O. 226/14: 241-68).

808. ST. JOHN, ISLAND OF. LAWS, STATUTES, *etc.*

ACTS / PASSED / AT THE GENERAL ASSEMBLY / OF HIS MAJESTY'S / ISLAND OF SAINT-JOHN, / ANNO TRICESSIMO TERTO [sic] / REGIS GEORGII III. / [rule] / THIRD SESSION OF THE SIXTH GENERAL ASSEMBLY. / [rule] / [rule] / [royal arms] / [double rule] / CHARLOTTE TOWN, ISLAND OF SAINT JOHN: / [rule] / PRINTED BY WILLIAM ALEXANDER RIND, / PRINTER TO THE KING'S MOST EXCELLENT MAJESTY. / [double rule] / 1792. /

4to. Sig. [1]-3^2; 12 p.; type-page: 22.5 × 16 cm. One leaf of sig. 3 is folded around sig. [1]-2 to form t.-p. This is the first use of numerical signatures noted in Canadian printing.

Contents: p. [1], t.-p.; p.[2], blank; p. [3]-12, 33 Geo. III c. I-IV, acts passed during the session Nov. 6-17, 1792.

Copy located: NNHi.

809. SAINT JOHN, N.B., *City.* ORDINANCES, *etc.*

[Law for levying Anchorage Money.]

Broadside. *Printed at Saint John, N.B., probably by Christopher Sower, 1792,* as recorded:

"1792, Jan. 27. Ordered that Mr. Gilbert be desired to get Forty copies of the Law for leveying [sic] Anchorage Money printed and that copies be put at proper places (So as to prevent any person pleading ignorance of the same) and deduct the charges of the same out of the proceeds of the Tax."
—Saint John, N.B., Common Council, *Minute book,* v. 2.

The charges were probably included in Christopher Sower's unitemized bill for £3 11*s.* passed by the Council, May 16, 1792.—*ibid*

Copy located: None.

810. [SARREAU, FRANCOIS]

ELEGIE, / [rule] / Sur le funeste Evênement arrivé le 21 de Mai 1792 / sur le fleuve vis à vis la Pointe Levi. / Sur l'Air du Couronnement du Roi." / [rule]

Broadside, 37 lines, text in 2 col.; type-page: 22.3 × 16.5 cm. *Printed at Quebec, by Samuel Neilson, 1792.*

Contents: Seven stanzas on the shipwreck and death of Auguste David Hubert, curé of Quebec (*see* No. 752 *note*) beginning:

"Non loin de notre rivage,
A la vue de nos remparts,
Hélas! un fatal Naufrage
Fixe nos tristes regards,
Les Infortunées Victimes
Font retentir de leur cris
Le rivage des abimes
Où elles vont être englouties."

This item and No. 811 may have been written by Sarreau, who was Neilson's agent in Montreal, or simply published by him. The printer recorded both items:

"1792, Sept. 26. Printed for F. Saro [i.e. François Sarreau] 100 Elegies on the Curé—12/5.
100 Continuation of D°—12/6.
[Total:] £1.5."—Can.P.A., *Neilson papers,* v. 70.

Neilson also published (and sold numerously) "Price 6d . . . an elegant portrait and striking likeness of David Augustin Hubert, Curé of Quebec."—*Quebec gazette,* Apr. 18, 1793.

Copy located: CaQQL.

811. [SARREAU, FRANCOIS]

SUITE de l'Elégie du naufrage de Mr. Hubert Curé de Québec, sur la / consolation les Paroissiens ont eu de retrouver son Corps et de l'inhu-/mer dans l'endroit où il avoit lui même désigné. / [rule] /

Broadside, 62 lines, text in 2 col.; type-page: 30 × 17 cm. *Printed at Quebec, by Samuel Neilson, 1792,* as recorded in No. 810 *note.*

Contents: Twelve stanzas in continuation of No. 810 beginning:

"L'eau perd sur moi son empire,
Consolez vous, mon troupeau,
Dieu seul par qui tout respire,
Veut me rendre à mon hameau,
Mon corps livide et sans vie,
N'attend que votre secours,
Saurez le pour la patrie,
Dont il a reçu le jour."

Stanzas 8-10 form an acrostic: Augustin David Hubert.
Copy located: CaQQL.

812. [SEWELL, JONATHAN], 1766-1839, *comp.*

An ABSTRACT / From Precedents of Proceeding / IN THE / British House of Commons. / [rule] / EXTRAIT / Des Exemples de Procédés / DANS LA / Chambre des Communes / DE LA GRANDE BRETAGNE. / [rule] / [royal arms] / [double rule] / QUEBEC: PRINTED BY SAMUEL NEILSON, N° 3. Mountn. [sic] street. / M.DCC.XCII. / A QUEBEC: CHEZ SAMUEL NEILSON, IMPRIMEUR & LIBRAIRE. / [double rule] /

12mo. [*]^4, A-M^6; 4 p. l., 143 p.; type-page: 13.5 × 8 cm. text in English and French on opposite pages, p. [38]-143.

Contents: p. l. 1, blank; p. l. 2 recto, t.-p.; verso, blank; p. l. 3 recto, Dedication: "To the . . . Members of the Houses of Assembly in . . . Upper and Lower Canada"; verso, blank; p. l. 4 recto-verso, Preface, dated at Quebec, Oct. 25, 1792; p. [i], blank; p. [ii]-xxxvii, Introduction; p. [38]-143, Rules; verso of p. 143, blank.

The preface states: "The following sheets are a compilation of Rules and Orders of the British House of Commons relating to Parliamentary Proceedings in general, extracted from the Journals of the House, Lex Parliamentaria, and principally that collection of cases made by Mr. Hatsell. The origin of this Publication was the apparent utility of such a work at the present period, for it was conceived that nothing could be offered more appropriate to the proceedings of Legislatures founded on the British constitutions than the present practice of the British House of Commons [etc.]."

The *Abstract* was compiled by Jonathan Sewell (a loyalist from Massachusetts via New Brunswick, licensed as attorney in Quebec, 1789, and in 1793 appointed solicitor- and inspector-general and later chief justice, of Lower Canada). Sewell charged Neilson £11 13*s.* 4*d.* for his work.—Can.P.A., *Neilson papers*, v. 71, July 8, 1793.

It was published by Neilson "agreeable to the following Conditions, viz: that the Lt. Govenor [sic] should pay the late Samuel Neilson [d. Jan. 12, 1793] £50 and if he (the said Neilson) sold as many copies of the said work as would amount to more than £14, the overplus should be deducted from the said £50; but not having sold to the amount of £14, therefore [the Lieutenant-Governor owes S. Neilson estate:] £50."—*ibid.*, v. 71, Mar. 18, 1793.

The work was published between Nov. 22-29, 1792 (*Quebec gazette*) and sold at 3*s.* 6*d.* the copy.

Copies located: CaO; CaQMS (2 cop.); CaQQL (2 cop.); Witton.

813. SOLON, *pseud.*

[The New Constitution, explained by Solon. *Printed at Quebec by Samuel Neilson, 1792.*]

This work was advertised among "Provincial publications for sale at the Printing Office, Quebec," in the *Quebec gazette,* May 3, 1792. It was probably a reprint of an article published serially in the *Quebec gazette,* Feb. 23-Mar. 15, 1792 (in all, about 7 p. fo., text in 2 col., English and French). The article is headed: "To accompany the New Constitution," and the preamble, signed: "Solon," states that the Constitutional Club, "organized to diffuse a proper knowledge of our new Government and of the English Constitution," begins by publishing an explanation, clause by clause, of 31 Geo. III, c. 31.

This work may be "Mr. Dumas Explanation of the Constit^{n}" of which Neilson sold 50 copies to Charles Delanaudière, on June 6, 1792 (Can.P.A., *Neilson papers,* v. 70). "Mr. Dumas" was probably Alexandre Dumas, 1726?-1802, French-Canadian lawyer and merchant of Quebec, and a prominent member of the Constitutional Club.

Copy located: None.

814. TOOSEY, PHILIP, *d.* 1797

A CATALOGUE, / Of the valuable Household Furniture, / LIVE AND DEAD STOCK, Hay, Corn, Carriages, and / Implements of Husbandry of the Revd Philip Toosey. / To be SOLD by AUCTION, by John Jones, Auc. & Broker, / AT SANS-BRUIT FARM, on MONDAY, April 16th, . . . / . . . Conditions of Sale as usual. /

French side: CATALOGUE, Des Meubles precieux de Menage, / BESTIAUX, USTENCILES ET INSTRUMENS / D'AGRICULTURE, Foin, Grains, Voitures, appertenans au Rev^{d} / PHILIP TOOSEY, à vendre par Encan, par John Jones, Enc^{r} / A la METAIRIE de SANS-BRUIT, LUNDI le 16 D'AVRIL . . . / . . . Les Conditions de vente comme à l'Ordinaire. /

Double broadside; 90 lines; text in English and French; type-page: 36 × 21.5 cm. (each side). *Printed at Quebec, by Samuel Neilson, 1792,* as recorded:

"1792, Mar. 30. Printed for Philip Toosey 300 Catalogues in French & English —£1.15.

Folding and distributing 200 D^{o} through towns—2/.

[Total:] £1.17."—Can.P.A., *Neilson papers,* v. 70.

The catalogue lists 211 lots, describing the contents of each room in some detail, and showing the appointments of a modest gentleman's country establishment in 18th-century Quebec.

Toosey, a Church of England clergyman, was sent to Canada by the British government in 1785 with a salary of £200 per annum, a substantial sum, for the Society for the Propagation of the Gospel missionaries received but £50 to £100. He held no fixed charge, but ministered to Anglicans resident in Quebec city, and from 1789 till his death in 1797 acted as "Ecclesiastical Commissionary for the eastern district of Canada."

Copy located: CaQQL (bound in *Quebec gazette,* Mar. 29, 1792).

815. UPPER CANADA. LIEUTENANT-GOVERNOR, 1791-1799 (*Simcoe*)*

A PROCLAMATION, / To such as are desirous to settle on the Lands of the Crown in the Province / of Upper Canada: / By His Excellency JOHN GRAVES SIMCOE, Esquire, / Lieutenant Governor and Commander in Chief of the said Province, and Colonel Commanding His / Majesty's Forces, &c.&c.&c. / <Text> / GIVEN under my Hand and Seal in the City of Quebec, the Seventh Day of February, in the / Thirty-second Year of His Majesty's Reign, and in the Year of Our Lord One thousand / seven hundred and ninety-two. / JOHN GRAVES SIMCOE. / By His EXCELLENCY'S Command, / THO[s] TALBOT, Acting Secretary. /

Broadside: 73 lines; type-page: 32.3 × 17 cm. *Printed at Quebec, by Samuel Neilson, 1792,* as recorded:

> "1792, Feb. 17. Printed for Lieutenant governor Simcoe the same articles as the preceding entry for the Council Office [i.e. 1000 English Proclamations for settling lands of the Crown, 500 French Ditto]—£5.7."
>
> —Can.P.A., *Neilson papers*, v. 70.

Text is the same as that of No. 784, for this is Simcoe's proclamation for Upper Canada of the terms for granting land also proclaimed in Lower Canada by Lieut.-Gov. Clarke. It was published again by Simcoe in 1795 (*see* No. 968), and remained in force till 1796. *See also* Paterson: *Land settlement in Upper Canada.* This proclamation is reprinted in Ontario Archives, *Report, 1906*, also in Can.P.A., *Report, 1921.*

Copies located: CaOTU; GBLP (in C.O. 42/316: 111). Copy recorded but not located: Hodgins, no. 54.

816. UPPER CANADA. LIEUTENANT-GOVERNOR, 1791-1799 (*Simcoe*)

PROCLAMATION, / Pour telles Personnes qui désirent s'établir sur les Terres de la Couronne dans la Province du Haut Canada, / Par Son Excellence JOHN GRAVES SIMCOE, ECUYER, / Lieutenant Gouverneur et Commandant en Chef de la dite Province, et Colonel Commandant les Forces / de Sa Majesté, &c.&c.&c. / <Text: preamble and terms 1-10> / Donné sous mon seing et sceau dans la ville de Québec, le septième jour de Février . . . / . . . mil sept cent quatre-/ vingt douze (Signé) / JOHN GRAVES SIMCOE. / Par Ordre de son

*Simcoe was actually head of the administration in Upper Canada from 1792 (he took oath of office on July 8 at Kingston, U.C.) to 1796. His work however began even before his appointment (by royal commission, Sept. 21, 1791) and practically ceased when he appointed Peter Russell administrator, and left Canada in July, 1796. *In absentia* he remained nominally lieutenant-governor till the royal commission was rescinded Apr. 10, 1799.

Excellence, / THOMAS TALBOT, faisant fonction de Sécrétaire. / Traduit par Ordre de son Excellence, / P.A. DE BONNE, A.S & T.F. /

Broadside: 77 lines; type-page: 33.2 × 17 cm. *Printed at Quebec, by Samuel Neilson, 1792.*

A French translation of the item above, this proclamation is reprinted in Can. P.A., *Rapport, 1921.* It was published again in 1795 (No. 969).

Copy located: GBLP (in C.O. 42/316: 113).

817. UPPER CANADA. LIEUTENANT-GOVERNOR, 1791-1799 (*Simcoe*)

J. GRAVES SIMCOE. / PROCLAMATION. / GEORGE THE THIRD by the Grace of God of Great-Britain, France, and Ireland, KING / . . . / To all our loving Subjects to whom these Presents shall come or may concern, / GREETING, WHEREAS, we have thought fit, . . . / to divide our late Province of Quebec, into . . . Upper / Canada, and Lower Canada; . . . / [etc. 10 lines of preamble] / . . . KNOW / YE that . . . / . . . we do hereby continue, all, and every our Judges, Justices, and / all other our Civil Officers as aforesaid [i.e. as of 26 Dec. 1791] in their respective Offices and Employments within . . . / . . . Upper Canada. And further, that until some more convenient and general / means of publishing these presents, and all future public Acts, can be adopted, the same . . . / . . . / . . . / shall be communicated to the Clerks of the Peace . . . / . . . to be by them affixed in some open and public part of their / several offices, and that such publication shall be held and taken as a due and legal promulga-/tion thereof, of which all our loving Subjects, and all others whom it may concern, are to take / notice and govern themselves accordingly. IN TESTIMONY whereof we have caused these / our Letters to be made Patent, and the great Seal of our said Province to be thereunto / affixed; WITNESS our Trusty and well beloved JOHN GRAVES SIMCOE Esqr. . . . / . . . / . . . At our Government House in the Town of Kingston . . . / . . . / . . . [9 July, 1792] / J.G.S. / WM. JARVIS, Secretary. / [ornamental rule] / MONTREAL, Printed by FLEURY MESPLET. /

Broadside: 41 lines; type-page: 36.8 × 22.2 cm.

This is Simcoe's first proclamation made from Kingston, the first seat of government in Upper Canada. Its style, that of a royal letter patent, is unusually formal, and the typography of corresponding dignity. Printed from english type (14 point), widely leaded, on heavy crisp paper, this publication has a spacious and splendid appearance uncommon in Mesplet's work.

The text is reprinted in Ontario Archives, *Report, 1906.*

Copy located: CaOOA (in "Proclamations" portfolio in the Library); another copy, not located, Hodgins no. 56.

818. UPPER CANADA. LIEUTENANT-GOVERNOR, 1791-1799 (*Simcoe*)

J. GRAVES SIMCOE. / PROCLAMATION. / GEORGE THE THIRD by the Grace of GOD of Great Britain, / France and Ireland King . . . &. / To all our loving Subjects, whom these presents may concern, / WHEREAS in pursuance of an Act of Parliament, lately made . . . / . . . our late Province / of Quebec is become divided into the two Provinces, of Upper Canada and Lower Canada; . . . / [etc. 6 lines] / KNOW YE Therefore, that our trusty and well beloved JOHN GRAVES SIMCOE, Esq: / Lieutenant Governor . . . / . . . doth divide, the said Province of Upper Canada into / Counties; and hath and doth declare and appoint the Number of Representatives of them, and / each of them, to be as herein after limited, named, declared and appointed . . . / [etc. names and boundaries of 19 counties and number of members to be sent from each to the House of Assembly] / IN TESTIMONY where-of we have caused these Letters to be made Patent, and the great Seal / of our said Province of Upper Canada to be hereunto affixed. / WITNESS our Trusty and well beloved JOHN GRAVES SIMCOE Esqr. . . . / . . . / . . . At our Government House, in the Town of Kingston, . . . / . . . / . . . [16 July, 1792.] / J.G.S. / WM. JARVIS, Secretary. / [ornamental rule] / MONTREAL, Printed by FLEURY MESPLET. /

Broadside: 117 lines (including text in 2 col. of 113 lines each); type-page: 52.5 × 36.2 cm.

Reprinted (with omission of occasional words and typographical variations) in Ontario Archives, *Report, 1906*.

Copy located: CaOOA (in "Proclamations" portfolio in the Library).

819. UPPER CANADA. LIEUTENANT-GOVERNOR, 1791-1799 (*Simcoe*)

J. GRAVES SIMCOE. / PROCLAMATION. / GEORGE TROIS par la Grace de Dieu, Roi de la Grande-Bretagne, / France & Irlande, . . . &. / A tous nos affectionnés Sujets qu'il appartiendra, / COMME en conformité à un Acte du Parlement, derniérement fait & pourvu, . . . / . . . notre / Province anciénement de Quebec doit être divisée en deux Provinces, du Haut Canada & du Bas / Canada; . . . / [etc., 5 lines] / SACHEZ donc, que notre fidele & bien aimé JOHN GRAVES SIMCOE, Ecuyer, Lieu-/tenant Gouverneur . . . / . . . divise la dite Province du Haut Canada / en Comtés, & a déclaré & fixé, & déclare & fixe, que la nombre des Représentans d'iceux / & de chacun d'eux sera comme ci après limité, nommé, déclaré & fixé . . . / [etc. names

& boundaries of 19 counties & number of members to be sent from each to House of Assembly] EN FOI de quoi nous avons ordonné ces Lettres Patentes & d'y apposer le grand Sceau de notre / dite Province du haut Canada. / TE'MOIN notre fidele & bien aimé JOHN GRAVES SIMCOE, Ecuyer, . . . / . . . / —A notre Maison du Gouvernement, dans la ville de Kingston, . . . / . . . [16 Juillet 1792]. / J.G.S. / WM. JARVIS, Sécrétaire. / [ornamental rule] / MONTREAL, Imprimé par FLEURY MESPLET. /

Broadside: 115 lines (including text in 2 col. of 111 lines each); type-page: 50 × 36.5 cm. This is the French edition of No. 818.

Copy located: CaOOA (in "Proclamations" portfolio in the Library).

820. ALMANACS. LOWER CANADA

[Calendrier de Montréal pour l'Année 1794.]

Broadside. This sheet almanac, like *Calendrier de Montréal* of preceding years, was undoubtedly *printed at Montreal by Fleury Mesplet,* this in 1793 (though the date of imprint may be the same as in title). This was the last of a series which began in 1776, for Mesplet died on Jan. 28, 1794. It was advertised: "Le Calendrier de Montréal pour l'Année 1794, A Vendre chez Mr. François Sareau [sic] et chez l'Imprimeur."—*Montreal gazette,* Dec. 26, 1793.

Copy located: .None.

821. ALMANACS. LOWER CANADA

CALENDRIER pour l'Année 1794, pour Québec, par les $306^{d.}$ $30^{m.}$ de Longitude, et $46^{d.}$ $55^{m.}$ de Latitude. / [double rule] /

Colophon: [? *A Québec: chez Jean Neilson*] (in the only copy seen, cropped at foot, the colophon was wanting).

Broadside: type-page: 52 + ? × 39 cm.

Contents: Calendrier, in ornamental rule frame, 42.5 × 39 cm.; below *Calendrier:* "A Table of Reduction: Table de Reduction" (livres, guineas, £. Sterling & European coins in Halifax currency; tables and explanation in English and French) also Eclipses, in English (4 col. in all).

This is the first time that the Brown-Neilson *Calendrier* included information in English. It was published on Dec. 15, 1793 (*Quebec gazette,* Dec. 12-19, 1793) copies being sold wholesale at 6*s*. the dozen from Dec. 12, 1793.

Copy located: CaO (cropped at foot, bound in *Quebec gazette,* at end of 1793).

822. ALMANACS. LOWER CANADA

[Indian Calendar. *Quebec, J. Neilson, 1793.*]

? Broadside (a sheet almanac), or leaflet, in an unknown dialect by an unknown compiler, but *printed at Quebec, in John Neilson's shop, 1793,* as recorded:

"1793, Apr. 28. Printing Office received from Mr. Roy for printing 150 Indian Calendars—£2.6.8."

—Can.P.A., *Neilson papers,* v. 71.

"Mr. Roy" was perhaps Rev. Jean Joseph Roy, 1757-1824, who was director of the Séminaire de Québec in 1793. As curé at Tadoussac, 1785-90, and at Chicoutimi, etc., 1795 *et seq.*, he served as missionary to Algonkian bands below Quebec. Like his predecessor in that field, Father La Brosse, q.v., Roy, conceivably, had calendars printed in the Montagnais dialect for use among his Indian "parishioners."

Copy located: None.

823. ALMANACS. NOVA SCOTIA

AN / ALMANACK, / FOR THE / YEAR . . . 1794; / . . . / CALCULATED FOR THE MERIDIAN OF / HALIFAX, . . . / . . . / CONTAINING / The ECLIPSES [etc. 8 lines in col. 1] / SITTINGS of the COURTS [etc. 8 lines in col. 2] / WITH EVERY OTHER MATTER USEFUL OR NECESSARY. / [rule] / BY THEOPHRASTUS. / [rule] / HALIFAX: / Printed and Sold by JOHN HOWE, at his Printing-Office, Corner / of GEORGE and BARRINGTON STREETS, opposite the / PARADE. / [title within double rule frame]

12mo. A-C[6]; [36] p.; type-page: 14.7 × 8.3 cm.

Contents: p. [1], t.-p.; p. [2], Ephemeris; p. [3-4], Zodiac, eclipses; p. [5-16], Calendar; p. [17-20], Nova Scotia provincial officers, judges, justices, etc., customs, p. [21-22], Court sittings, naval officers, holidays, Halifax fire co.; p. [23-27], Army; militia; p. [28-30], Postal rates, etc.; p. [31-34], Clergy, anecdote, distances, sheriffs, statement of land area of United States, signed: "Thomas Hutchins, Geographer to U.S."; p. [35-36], Tables of days, expenses, etc.

Copies located: CaNsHA (p. [13-36] wanting); CaNsWA.

824. ALMANACS. NOVA SCOTIA

[Der Neuschottländische Calender auf das Jahr Christi 1794. ? *Halifax, N.S., gedruckt bey Anthon. Henrich, 1793.*]

The advertisement in Anthony Henry's newspaper suggests that *Der Neuschottländische Calender*, published for the years 1788-91, continued to appear: "Just published and to be sold, the Nova-Scotia Calender for 1794 [etc.], Just published and ready for sale, the German Almanack for the year 1794."—*Royal gazette*, Halifax, N.S., Dec. 3, 1793.

Copy located: None.

825. ALMANACS. NOVA SCOTIA

THE / NOVA-SCOTIA CALENDER / OR AN / ALMANACK, / FOR THE / Year . . . 1794. / . . . / . . . / . . . / . . . / WHEREIN IS CONTAINED / The ECLIPSES . . . / [6 lines] / The View of HALIFAX, was taken from FOSTER'S on the Eastern side of / the Harbour. / CALCULATED FOR THE MERIDIAN OF / HALIFAX . . . / . . . / . . . / . . . / [rule] / BY METONICUS. / [rule] / Time ever passing on, admits no stay. / But bears down King's and Kingdoms in it's Way. / So likewise doth the Wars, sweep off Mankind / And leaves the Marks of bloody Scenes behind! / [rule] / HALIFAX: / Printed and sold by ANTHONY HENRY, at his Printing-Office, in Sack-/ville-Street, Corner of Grafton-Street. / [title within a single rule frame]

12mo. [32 + ?] p.; illus.; type-page: 16 × 9.9 cm.

Contents: Both copies located appear to be incomplete, but complementary. Both have p. [1], t.-p.; p. [2], Vulgar notes; p. [3-14], Calendar; p. [15], Ephemeris; RPJ copy has six pages, listing Nova Scotia administration, legislature, judges, justices, courts. CaNsHA copy wants these pages but has sixteen pages listing Nova Scotia clergy, army, half-pay rates, postal rates, buoys, distances. Neither copy includes the "View of Halifax," which is probably the same as that in No. 751.

This almanac was advertised: "Just published and to be sold by Anthony Henry, The Nova-Scotia Calender [etc.]."—*Royal gazette*, Halifax, N.S., Nov. 19, 1793.

Copies located: CaNsHA (incomplete copy of [32] p.); RPJ (incomplete copy of [22] p.).

826. BROWN, ANDREW, *d.* 1834

A / SERMON / ON THE / DANGERS AND DUTIES / OF THE / SEAFARING LIFE; / PREACHED BEFORE THE / Protestant Dissenting Congregation, / AT HALIFAX, / AND PUBLISHED AT THE DESIRE OF THE / MARINE SOCIETY, / IN THAT PLACE. / [double rule] / BY ANDREW BROWN, D.D. / Minister of the Protestant Dissenting Congregation. / [double rule] / HALIFAX: / Printed by John Howe, at his Printing-Office, opposite the Parade. / [rule] / MDCCXCIII. /

8vo. A-C[4]; 23 p.; type-page: 17 × 8.8 cm.

Contents: p. [1], t.-p.; p. [2], blank; p. [3], Advertisement; p. [4], Resolution of Halifax Marine Society, Nov. 22, 1792, signed by John Allen, secretary; p. [5]-23, Sermon (text: Psalm cvii, v. 23-33, They that go down to the sea in ships); verso of p. 23, blank

In the Advertisement the author states that "the following sermon [was] hastily prepared at sea while the feelings it describes and the train of thought to which they led were fresh on the mind." He gives a vivid word picture of the beauty and variety in appearance of the sea "that magazine of moisture"; and shows how the seafaring man's work depends on trust in a constant natural law which the author identifies as a divine design of the universe and divine interest in man. The dangers of seafaring life enjoin the sailor to trust God, eschew sin, especially "the sin of profane swearing," to be temperate, sober, moderate, and frugal, for his wages are small and his life short, "there are but few grey headed sailors, and [those] can give but a sorrowful account of the companions of [their] youth and voyages."

The Halifax Marine Society was founded on Feb. 13, 1786, to relieve distress among seamen and their families, according to a notice in the *Nova-Scotia gazette*, Feb. 28, 1786.

This work was also printed in Boston, 1793 (Evans no. 25230), with contents the same as, and type somewhat larger than, the Halifax edition.

Copies located: MB; MBAt.

827. CHURCH OF ENGLAND. LITURGY AND RITUAL

A / FORM / OF / PRAYER, / TO BE USED / In all Churches, Chapels and Places of Public Worship, according to the usage / of the Church of England, throughout His Majesty's Province of Nova-Scotia, / on Friday the Tenth Day of May 1793; being the day appointed by Proclamation, / for a general FAST and Humiliation before Almighty God, to be observed in most / devout and solemn manner, by sending up our Prayers and Supplications to the Divine / Majesty: / FOR Obtaining pardon of our Sins, and for averting those heavy Judgements which our / manifold Provocations have deserved; and for imploring his assistance and blessing / on the Arms of his Majesty by Sea and Land, and for restoring and perpetuating / Peace, and Safety and prosperity to himself, and to his Dominions. / [rule] / By special desire of his Excellency, the LIEUTENANT GOVERNOR / [rule] / HALIFAX: / Printed by ANTHONY HENRY, Printer to the King's Most Excellent Majesty. / [title within double rule frame]

4to. 4 leaves without signature; 6 p., 1 *l.*; type-page: 19 × 15 cm.

Contents: p. [1], t.-p.; p. [2], blank; p. 3-4, The order for morning prayer; p. 4-5, The communion service; p. 5-6, The order for evening prayer, dated at end: "Halifax, [N.S.], April 23, 1793"; 1 *l.* (probably blank).

This is probably the work recorded in Henry's *Account for extra printing* [*for Government*] *1792-94*:

"To printing 300 prayers for a general fast—£2.5
To 13 Quires Demy for [ditto]—19/6."

—P.A.N.S. *Miscellaneous Assembly papers, 1794.*

Copy located: NNHi (lacks leaf at end).

828. COCHRAN, WILLIAM, 1757-1833

A / SERMON / PREACHED IN THE / Church at Falmouth, Nova-Scotia, / On FRIDAY, the 10th of MAY, 1793. / BEING THE DAY APPOINTED BY PROCLAMATION / FOR A / GENERAL FAST / AND / Humiliation before Almighty GOD. / [rule] / BY THE REVEREND WILLIAM COCHRAN, / PRESIDENT OF KING'S COLLEGE, WINDSOR. / [rule] / HALIFAX: / Printed by JOHN HOWE, at his Printing-Office, opposite the / PARADE. / [rule] / M DCC XCIII. /

8vo. A-B^4; 15 p.; type-page: 17 × 9 cm.

Contents: p. [1], t.-p.; p. [2], blank; p. [3], Dedication "to the Right Reverend father in God, Charles, by divine permission Bishop of Nova-Scotia, . . . [dated] Windsor, Nova-Scotia, June 4, 1793"; p. [4], Advertisement; p. [5]-15, Sermon (text: Jeremiah 5:9, Shall I not visit for these things? saith the Lord: and shall not my soul be avenged on such a nation as this?); verso of p. 15, blank.

The sermon shows how nations prosper only while they are virtuous; how France —where religion was corrupt in doctrine and practice, and government an arbitrary monarchy abhorred by Englishmen and disapproved by God—has come to misery and desolation. It admonishes magistrates to honour religion, and citizens to eschew idleness, drunkenness, and profanity. It discredits the false rumours being spread in Nova Scotia, as formerly in the American colonies, that the Church of England plans to introduce tithes. The sermon ends praising the British constitution.

Bishop Inglis (to whom this publication is dedicated) wrote to the archbishop of Canterbury, from Halifax, Oct. 17, 1791: "[Since] Mr. Cochran of the Academy was admitted to Priests orders last summer . . . [he] has preached regularly at Newport and Falmouth. He is prodigiously liked by the people,—and has . . . given a new turn to the Church [of England in the district under influence of the New Light movement]. I expected Mr. Cochran's Sermons would be sensible and rational and in this I was not disappointed, but contrary to my expectations he turns out to be a very animated preacher, which makes him popular."—Can.P.A., *Inglis papers*, 1:276.

Cochran, born in Ireland and graduated from Trinity College, Dublin, was professor of classics at Columbia College, New York, from 1784 till he went to Nova Scotia in 1788. He was principal of the Academy at Windsor from 1789, and president of King's College from its establishment in 1790 till 1802 (when the new constitution required an Oxford or Cambridge University graduate as president), then vice-president till 1831. *The Nova-Scotia magazine* was edited by Cochran during its first year, July, 1789-1700. *See* H. Y. Hind: *The University of King's College, Windsor, Nova Scotia, 1790-1890* (New York, 1890), 24 *note*.

Copy located: CaNsWA.

829. GREAT BRITAIN. ADJUTANT-GENERAL'S OFFICE

By His Majesty's Command. / [double rule] / Adjutant General's Office, / June 1, 1792. / RULES AND REGULATIONS / FOR THE / FORMATIONS, FIELD-EXERCISE, / AND MOVEMENTS, / OF / HIS MAJESTY'S FORCES. / [rule] / MONTREAL; / Printed by FLEURY MESPLET, Notre-Dame / Street N° 40. 1793. /

8vo. A-L^8; xx, 100, 54 p., 1 *l.*; type-page: 13.5 × 6.3 cm.

Contents: p. [i], half title; p. [ii], blank; p. [iii], t.-p.; p. [iv], blank; p. [v]-vi, Preface, dated Adjutant General's office, June 1, 1792, signed by William Fawcett, adjutant-general; p. [vii]-xx, Introduction; p. [1]-54, Part I—Instruction of the recruit; p. 55-100, Part II—Of the platoon or company; p. [1]-54 at end, Formation of the company; [1] *l.* at end, recto: list of the Adjutant-general's office publications, dated June 1, 1792; verso, blank.

This was ***probably printed in London and issued in Montreal with Mesplet's imprint***, for the typography of the latter differs from that of the rest of the work. The book as a whole has rather the appearance of the official and semi-official publications printed in London and distributed in Canada in the 18th century. These have usually a subtly different air, produced perhaps by a clearness of impression, cleanness of letter, and neatness in style, less common in Canadian productions of the period—especially those of Anthony Henry and Fleury Mesplet.

This publication was advertised "For sale at the Printing Office [of Fleury Mesplet]" in the *Montreal gazette*, Oct. 24, 1793.

Copy located: CaQMS.

830. [HUBERT, AUGUSTE DAVID], 1751-1792

[Portrait]

Probably a wood engraving, possibly drawn by J. G. Hochstetter, who executed engravings (including a portrait of Adam Mabane) published in the *Quebec magazine* during 1793; and certainly *printed at Quebec, by John Neilson, 1793,* as recorded:

"Just published, Price Sixpence and to be sold at the Printing Office, An elegant portrait and striking likeness of David Augustin Hubert, late curé of Quebec."—*Quebec gazette,* Apr. 18, 1793, *Sup.*

Copy located: None.

831. HUBERT, JEAN FRANCOIS, *bp. of Quebec,* 1739-1797

Caption title: (Circulaire à M. Mrs. Les Curés,) /

fo. 2 *l.* without signature or pagination, text on recto and verso of *l.* 1, *l.* 2 blank; type-page: 23 × 13.5 cm. *Probably printed at Quebec, by John Neilson, 1793.*

Contents: 1 1, Circulaire, signed: "Jean François, Evêque de Québec. Québec, Novembre, [9 inserted in MS. in all copies seen] 1793."

The circular states that, following rumour of a French fleet off the coast of the United States, having designs on Lower Canada, and in accord with wishes of Lord Dorchester, the bishop is reminding the parish priest that all bonds with France were broken in 1763, that oaths of fealty, social interest, and religion enjoin loyalty to the British government.

This *Circulaire* is reprinted in Têtu and Gagnon: *Mandements de Québec,* 2: 471-73. On efforts of the administration and clergy to counteract propaganda from French agents in the United States, *see* Sir J. A. T. Chapais: *Cours d'histoire du Canada* [*1760-1867*] (8v., Quebec, 1919-34), 2: 111 *et seq.*

Copies located: CaO; CaOOA (2 cop.); CaQQL.

832. INGLIS, CHARLES, *bp. of Nova Scotia,* 1734-1816

Steadfastness in Religion and Loyalty / RECOMMENDED, IN A / SERMON / Preached before the / LEGISLATURE / OF / His Majesty's Province of Nova-Scotia; / IN THE / Parish Church of ST. PAUL at HALIFAX, / On SUNDAY, April 7, 1793. / [double rule] / BY THE RIGHT REVEREND CHARLES, / BISHOP OF NOVA-SCOTIA. / [double rule] / HALIFAX: / Printed by JOHN HOWE, at his Printing-Office, opposite the / Parade. / [rule] / M DCC XCIII. /

8vo. A-D^4, E^2; 34 p., 1 *l.*; type-page: 17 × 9 cm. Some copies were printed (from the same types) on larger paper in 4to format.

Contents: p. [1], half-title; p. [2], Resolution of House of Assembly of Nova Scotia, Apr. 13, 1793, appointing a committee to request Bishop Inglis to furnish a copy of the sermon for printing; p. [3], t.-p.; p. [4], Dedication to the speaker and members of Assembly; p. [5]-34, Sermon, text: Proverbs xxiv: 21, My son fear thou the Lord and the King; and meddle not with them that are given to change; end of p. 34, Erratum; 1 *l.*, blank.

In this sermon preached at the request of the Legislature, Inglis made a vigorous attack on the principles of the French Revolution. He repudiated the existence of the so-called state of nature and recommended a society based on ordered government and religion, a constitutional monarch and the church established. Pointing to the disastrous results of subversion of king and clergy in France, the Bishop warned Nova Scotians against the dissemination of "enthusiasm" in their province by evangelical dissenters. A foot-note, p. 31, states that news of war between Great Britain and France arrived at Halifax, N.S., between the preaching and the printing of this sermon.

Bishop Inglis sent several copies to dignitaries of the Church in England.—Can. P.A., *Inglis papers*, 2: 48 *et seq*. The sermon was reprinted with title as above and imprint: *Halifax, printed: London re-printed for John Stockdale, 1793.* 32 p.

Copies located: CaNsWA (also London reprint); CaOT (London reprint only); MBAt; MWA; MiU-C; NN; NNC; NNHi (4to); WPJ (4to).

833. LA MARCHE, JEAN FRANCOIS DE, *bp. of St. Pol de Léon*, 1729-1806

LETTRE / DE / M. L'Evêque de LEON / AUX / ECCLESISATIQUES [sic] FRANÇAIS / Réfugiés en Angleterre. / [printer's ornament] / [double rule] / A QUEBEC: / DE L'IMPRIMERIE DE JEAN NEILSON, / N°. 3 Rue la Montagne. / [rule] / M.DCC.XCIII. /

12mo. A^6, B^4; 18 p., 1 *l.*; type-page: 13.2 × 7 cm.

Contents: p. [1], t.-p.; p. [2], blank; p. [3]-18, Lettre, signed: "30 Dec. 1792. J.Fr. Evêque de Leon"; 1 *l.* at end, blank.

Published in English and French editions in London, 1793, this work appeared in Quebec "printed in elegant new characters on Demy 12mo and sold at the Printing Office, Quebec and at M. Saro Montreal. price 12 sols [i.e. sixpence]."—*Quebec gazette*, Aug. 8, 1793.

La Marche, a Breton, bred to the army, took holy orders and became bishop in 1772. Twenty years later he moved to England when French revolutionary authorities disrupted the Church. This work, written to celebrate English succour of French refugees, lauds English character and institutions, and commends to French Catholic clergy, England's hospitality in the New World. The bishop urges emigration to Lower Canada where new lands, their own former countrymen and customs, also ecclesiastical preferments await French catholic clergy.

Lettre was also printed (from another setting of type) in *The Quebec magazine*, 3: 20-26, Aug., 1793. *See also* N. E. Dionne: *Les Ecclesiastiques et les royalistes français refugiés au Canada . . . 1791-1802* (Quebec, 1905).

Copies located: CaOT (2 cop.); CaQ; CaQM; CaQMS (5 cop.); CaQQL; Ketcheson; MB. *Note:* The work described as *Lettre addressé à ses Quailles par Mgr. J. Evêque de Léon* (Quebec, J. Neilson, 1792), listed as "No. 469, Canada Imprint" in Gerald E. Hart sale, *Catalogue*, Boston, Apr. 15-19, 1890, is actually the *Lettre aux Ecclesiastiques* described above. The Hart copy, t.-p. wanting, is one of those in CaOT.

834. LOWER CANADA. GOVERNOR, 1791-1796 (*Dorchester*)

[royal arms] / BY HIS EXCELLENCY THE RIGHT HONORABLE / GUY LORD DORCHESTER, / . . . / . . . / . . . / . . . / . . . / A PROCLAMATION. / Dorchester, Govr. / <Text> / GIVEN . . . [at] Quebec . . . / . . . / . . . / . . . [26 Nov. 1793] / D. Gr. / BY HIS EXCELLENCY'S COMMAND, / GEO: POWNALL, Secy. / GOD Save the KING. /

French side: [royal arms] / PAR SON EXCELLENCE LE TRES HONORABLE / GUY LORD DORCHESTER. / . . . / . . . / . . . / . . . /. . . / PROCLAMATION, / Dorchester Gouverneur, / <Text> / Donné . . . [à] Québec . . . / . . . / . . . / . . . [Nov. 26, 1793] / D.G. / PAR ORDRE . . . / GEO. POWNALL, Secr. / Traduit par ordre de Son Excellence / J. F. CUGNET, S. & T. F. / VIVE LE ROI. /

Double broadside: English on left, 43 lines, type-page: 31 × 19 cm.; French on right, 46 lines, type-page: 31.7 × 19 cm. verso, blank. *Probably printed at Quebec, by John Neilson, 1793.*

English text: "WHEREAS divers evil disposed Persons, have lately manifested seditious and wicked Attempts, to alienate the Affections of His Majesty's Loyal Subjects, by false Representations of the Cause and Conduct of the Persons at present exercising the supreme Authority in France; [etc. 21 lines, orders to seize all persons, especially foreigners, spreading sedition in Lower Canada]"

French text: "DIVERSES Personnes mal intentionées, aiant depuis peu manifesté des tentatives séditieuses et méchantes, pour aliéner l'affection des Loiaux Sujets de Sa Majesté, par de fausses Représentations de la cause et de la conduite des Personnes qui éxercent actuellement l'autorité suprême en France, [etc. 22 lines]"

This was part of the administration's effort to combat French revolutionary propaganda directed by agents in the United States.

On Nov. 22, 1793, Gov. Dorchester "laid before the [Council] board sundry French publications which His Excellency submitted . . . for report thereon and recommended the Board consider the best means of preventing ill-intentioned persons coming into the Province." On Nov. 26, the proclamation (as above) was read, passed, and "ordered published for three successive weeks in the *Quebec gazette* in both languages; also five hundred copies printed in each language, to be affixed against church doors and other parts of the Towns and Suburbs of Quebec, Montreal and Three Rivers and distributed in the different parishes of the Province."—Can.P.A., L.C.*State* A, 1793. Gov. Dorchester, writing to Home Secretary Dundas, from Quebec, Jan. 20, 1794, enclosed a copy of the proclamation "which [he stated] seems to have had a good effect. It was my wish still further to strengthen the hands of government by the introduction of an Alien Bill" (*see* No. 886).—Can.P.A., "Q" 67: 60.

Substantially the same proclamation was issued by Lieut.-Gov. Prescott, Quebec, Oct. 31, 1796.

This proclamation is reprinted in Can.P.A., *Report, 1921.*

Copies located: CaOOA (2 cop., one filed with MS. drafts in Can.P.A. "S" *Proclamations, L.C. 1771-1791;* another in *Proclamations* portfolio in the Library); GBLP (in C.O. 42/98: 134-35).

835. LOWER CANADA. HOUSE OF ASSEMBLY

JOURNAL / OF THE / HOUSE OF ASSEMBLY, / LOWER-CANADA. / [royal arms] / [ornamental rule] / QUEBEC: / PRINTED AND SOLD BY JOHN NEILSON. / [rule] / M.DCC.XCIII. /

French t.-p.:

JOURNAL / DE LA / CHAMBRE D'ASSEMBLÉE / DU BAS CANADA. / [royal arms] / [ornamental rule] / A QUEBEC: / IMPRIMÉ ET A VENDRE PAR JOHN NEILSON. / [rule] / M.DCC.XCIII. /

4to. A-X^4, Z^4, 2A-$4T^4$, $[4U]^1$; 691, [5] p.; type-page: 18.2 × 12.2 cm. Text in English and French on opposite pages. Through error in imposition, some copies have the pages of sig. N in the following order: 97, 102, 103, 100, 101, 98, 99, 104.

Contents: p. [1], English t.-p.; p. [2], blank; p. [3], French t.-p.; p. [4]-691, Journal of the first session of the first assembly, Dec. 17, 1792-May 9, 1793; verso of p. 691, blank; p. [1-2] at end, Errata (English); p. [3-5], Errata (French); verso of p. [5], blank.

A plan for the printing of its *Journal* was introduced in the House soon after the first session opened, with a motion, Dec. 22, 1793 "that the Votes of this House be printed, being first perused by the Speaker, and that he do approve the printing thereof and that no person but such as shall be appointed, do presume to print the same." Consideration was postponed till March, when a committee was appointed to get information on the printer's terms, etc. The committee reported in due course and on Apr. 18 its recommendations were approved by the House, viz.

"(1) That . . . John Neilson have the exclusive printing and disposing of the proceedings and votes of the House of Assembly, for one year, on condition that for this exclusive right he shall not be intitled to any pay for printing as aforesaid from the House of Assembly; (2) that . . . the said John Neilson, shall at the next Session of the Assembly lay before the House, a state of the expences for printing, and the money collected by him from the sale of the same and should it be found that [he] has incurred any loss thereby, that then the House will take the same into consideration; (3) that the paper and types . . . be left to Mr. Neilson, that he may use such as he shall judge the most saleable; (4) that a number not exceeding 100 copies be paid for by the House, to the end that the Governor, Lieutenant governor, the members of both Councils and of the Assembly, may each have a copy; (5) that the votes and proceedings be printed in the English and French languages, under the direction of the Speaker."

Three months later Neilson advertised:

"In the press and will be finished by October next, the Journals of the First Session of the House of Assembly, printed in English and French on fine Crown paper, good sizeable type. It will make 2 handsome volumes of about 400 pages each. Price of the 2 volumes in sheets—4 dollars. Purchasers may have 30 sheets now ready; and about 40 pages weekly till finished."—*Quebec gazette*, July 18-Nov. 7, 1793.

Actually about a hundred pages less than the printer predicted, the *Journal* was issued in one volume sewn in blue printer's paper covers, at 12*s*. 6*d*., and bound to order—e.g. 3 copies were bound for a purchaser in rough calf with slip cover at 15*s*. 6*d*. each on Nov. 27, 1793.

Neilson supplied the House of Assembly with 100 copies of the *Journal*, for which he was paid £100. He was also allowed a further sum of £50 "as an indemnity towards defraying the expence he has been at in printing the Journals."

—L. C. As. *Journal*, May 28, 1794.

An index was issued with caption title: "Index to the First Volume"; collation: 4to. A-E^4, F^2, A-E^4, F^3; [89] p., type-page: 16.5 × 12 cm. Text in English p. [1-44] and French p. [45-89]. Though undated it was printed ten or more years later than the *Journal*, for the copies seen are printed upon, or covered with, paper bearing the date 1802 in the watermark. The index is found as issued, sewn separately in blue printer's paper covers, also bound with some copies of the *Journal*.

Copies located: CaNsWA; CaO; CaOOA; CaOT (also *Index*); CaOTL; CaQM; CaQMA; CaQMM; CaQQL; CaQQLH; DLC; GBLP (in C.O. 42/103; another copy p. 1-275 only, in C.O. 42/94: 649-923); MH (2 cop.); N (also *Index*); NN; RPJ; WHi (also *Index*).

836. LOWER CANADA. HOUSE OF ASSEMBLY

RULES / AND / Regulations / OF THE / HOUSE of ASSEMBLY, / LOWER-CANADA. / [royal arms] / QUEBEC: / PRINTED FOR JOHN NEILSON, / [double rule] / M.DCC.XCIII. /

French t.-p.:

REGLES / ET / Reglements / DE LA / CHAMBRE D'ASSEMBLÉE / DU / BAS CANADA / [royal arms] / QUEBEC: / De l'Imprimerie de JOHN NEILSON / [double rule] / M.DCC.XCIII. /

This work was published in two issues of 100 copies each, both printed from the same types, excepting that the later issue had an additional section.

Earlier issue A: 12mo. A-G^6; 2 p. l., 73 p., 3 *l.*

Later issue B: 12mo. A-H^6; 2 p. l., 73 p., 3 *l.*, p. 74-83.

In both issues, type-page: 13.2 × 6.8 cm. Text in English and French opposite pages.

Contents: p. l. 1 recto, English t.-p.; verso, blank; p. l. 2 recto, French t.-p.; verso of p. l. 2 - p. 73, Rules, dated at end: "Passed 7th March, 1793"; verso of p. 73, blank; recto-verso of *l.* 1, Index in English and French; (Note at foot of recto: "Selected classed and published by order of the House of Assembly of Lower Canada of the 7th March, 1793. S. Phillips, Clk."); *l.* 2-3, blank; recto of p. 74, blank; p. 74-83, Rules relative to the introduction of private Bills, passed in the House Apr. 19, 1793; verso of p. 83, blank.

On Dec. 22, 1792, the House appointed a committee of nine (James McGill, chairman) to prepare rules of procedure, which the House considered item by item, Jan. 11-Feb. 27, 1793, and, on Mar. 7, ordered printed for use of members. A standing committee reported 9 further rules on Apr. 19, which were approved and (though the vote to print was negatived on Apr. 19.—L.C. As. *Journal, 1792-93*) printed and issued later with a reprint of 100 copies of the original *Rules*—as the printer's records show:

"1793, Apr. 9. For printing the Rules of the Assembly, making 3½ Sheets Demy—£7.17.6.
Stitching & Covering D^o—7/

Binding [six] copies in calf interleaved with fine paper 3/9—£1.2.6.
[Total:] £9.7.0.

June 5, For printing 100 Additional Rules of the House being 3½ Sheets on Demy paper—£2.15.
For 1 additional Sheet—£2.5.
Stitching folding and covering—19/
[Total:] £5.19.0."—Can.P.A., *Neilson papers*, v. 71.

Copies located of earlier issue A (*Rules of Mar. 7, 1793 only, 73 p.*): CaQMS (2 cop.); CaQQL (4 leaves appended bearing in MS.: *Suite de Régles*, no. 1-9); RPJ.

Copies located of later issue B (*Rules of Mar. 7, also of Apr. 19, 1793, 84 p.*): CaOOA; GBLP (in C.O. 42/95).

837. LOWER CANADA. LAWS, STATUTES, *etc.*

LAWS / OF / LOWER CANADA, / UNDER THE / CONSTITUTION erected 26th December Anno Domini 1791, / PURSUANT TO / ACT OF PARLIAMENT. / [double rule] / [ornament: seal] / [double rule] / QUEBEC: / PUBLISHED ACCORDING TO THE ORDER OF THE GOVERNMENT, / BY JOHN NEILSON, PRINTER TO THE KING'S MOST EXCELLENT MAJESTY, / FOR THE PROVINCE OF LOWER CANADA; / Printing-Office Mountain-Street, Anno Dom. / M.DCC.XCIII. /

French t.-p :

LOIX / DU / BAS CANADA, / SOUS / LA CONSTITUTION érigée le 26 Décembre Anno Domini 1791, / EN CONSEQUENCE / D'UN ACTE DU PARLEMENT. / [double rule] / [ornament: seal] / [double rule] / QUEBEC: / PUBLIÉ PAR ORDRE DU GOUVERNEMENT, / PAR JOHN NEILSON, IMPRIMEUR DU ROI / POUR LA PROVINCE DU BAS CANADA; / Rue la Montagne, / M.DCC.XCIII. /

This work was published in two issues, paged and unpaged, on different paper, but with t.-p. and text printed from the same setting of type.

ISSUE A: fo. [A]-F²; [12] *l.* type-page: 31 × 17 cm. Text in English and French on opposite pages.

Contents: *l.* 1 recto, t.-p.; verso, blank; *l.* 2 recto, French t.-p.; verso, English contents; *l.* 3 recto, French contents; *l.* 3 verso-*l.* 12 recto, Laws [33 Geo. III c. 1-8]; verso of *l.* 12, blank.

Printed on fine heavy paper (laid paper with chain lines running the length of the page, the watermark showing: G.R., a posthorn crowned, and counter mark: Budgen.) with clean impression of a deep and brilliant black, this is a handsome piece, due typographical tribute to the enactments of the first "popular" legislature in French Canada.

ISSUE B: fo. [A]-F²; 2 p. l., [i], 18 p.; type-page: 31 × 17 cm. Odd numbers on verso, even numbers on recto; text in English and French on opposite pages.

Contents: p. l. 1 recto, English t.-p.; verso, blank; p. l. 2 recto, French t.-p.; p. l. 2 verso, English contents; p. [i] (recto of p. 1) French contents; p. 1-18, Laws; verso of p. 18, blank. At end of text are pasted slips, on p. 17: "The Acts of the first

Session were all assented to on the 9th of May, 1793"; on p. 18, "Les Actes de la première Session ont tous été sanctionées le 9 Mai, 1793."

Unremarkable in appearance, this issue is printed on half sheets of lighter, coarser stock (laid paper with the chain lines running horizontal to the length of the page) cut to crown folio size.

The printer recorded this work but contrary to custom omitted to note difference in paper stock:

"1794, Sept. 17, [Debit] Governor's Office (omitted in June 1793) For printing in English and French the Acts of the 1st Session of the Legislature of Lower Canada (sanctioned 9th May, 1793) contained in 8 Chapters making 6 Sheets of folio Crown on English type at £1.18. per sheet for the first 100 of 500 copies and 10/ per sheet for each of the 400 subsequent—£23.8.0."—Can.P.A., *Neilson papers*, v. 71.

The government's accounts for Apr.-Oct. 1793, however, record but 300 copies printed:

"[To John Neilson] "For printing 300 Copies of the Laws of Lower Canada, passed during the last Session—£15.6."

—Can.P.A., L.C. *State* A, Dec. 11, 1793.

The ornament on the title pages shows the seal of the former province of Quebec. Reduced to two inches in diameter it depicts Cartier? pointing to a map, and bears the legend: "SIGNUM PROVINCIÆ NOSTRÆ. QUEBECENSIS. IN AMERICA. EXTENSÆ GAUDENT AGNOSCERE METÆ."

Copies located of Issue A: CaO; CaOOA; CaQQL ("Ex.B" [i.e. Copy 2]).

Copy located of Issue B: CaQQL ("Ex.A" [i.e. Copy 1]).

Another copy not located: Hodgins no. 102, "24 p. large fo., 8 pages slightly damaged."

838. LOWER CANADA. LAWS, STATUTES, *etc.*

PLAN / OF / A BILL, / PROPOSED TO THE / LEGISLATIVE COUNCIL, / And, now in COMMITTEE of the whole HOUSE, to be / taken into Consideration on the 10th. Day of March / next. / [royal arms] / [double rule] / QUEBEC: [3 dots] PRINTED FOR JOHN NEILSON, [3 dots] M.DCC.XCIII. / [double rule] /

French t.-p.:

PLAN / D'UN / BILL / PROPOSÉ AU / CONSEIL LEGISLATIF, / Et maintenant en COMITE' de tout la CHAMBRE, pour / être pris en Considération le 10me Jour de Mars / prochain. / [royal arms] / [double rule] / QUEBEC: [3 dots] POUR JOHN NEILSON, [3 dots] M.DCC.XCIII. / [double rule] /

4to. A-C[4]; D[1]; 25 p.; type-page: 14.5 × 10.5 cm. Text in English and French on opposite pages.

Contents: p. [1], t.-p.; p. [2], blank; p [3], French t.-p.; p. [4]-25, An act for the better division of the Province of Lower Canada, for altering the constitution of certain courts of justice within the said Province, for amending the judicature thereof, and for repealing certain laws herein mentioned; verso of p. 25, blank.

This is a preliminary draft of No. 839-840. It was reported by a Committee of the Council, Feb. 4, 1793, ordered printed for members, amended, finally passed by the Council Apr. 8, 1793.—Can.P.A., C.O. 42, v. 22, p. 211-19, with MS. text of amendments passed and rejected.

The printing is recorded:

"1793, Feb. 25. Council Office Dr to Printing Office, 400 Copies of a bill not passed making 3¼ Sheets on Long Primer at £1.15. for the 1st hundred and 7/6 for each additional hundred—£9.6.10½.
Fold. Stitch. & covering D° with blue paper @ ½d.—16/8.
[Total:] £10.3.6½."—Can.P.A., *Neilson papers*, v. 71.

This and No. 839-840 are the earliest productions of the Brown-Neilson printing house with John Neilson's name in the imprint. John succeeded to the business at the age of seventeen, after the death of his brother Samuel, on Jan. 12, 1793, Rev. Alexander Spark, Presbyterian minister in Quebec, serving as guardian and editor during young Neilson's minority.

Copies located: CaOOA; CaQ; CaQMS (2 cop.); GBLP (3 cop., of which 2 cop. are in C.O. 42/22; and another in C.O. 42/96: 37-61); Ketcheson.

839. LOWER CANADA. LAWS, STATUTES, *etc.*

PLAN / D'UN / BILL, / ENVOYE' A L'ASSEMBLE'E PAR / LE CONSEIL LE'GISLATIF, / LUNDI, 8me Avril, 1793. / [royal arms] / [double rule] / QUEBEC: [3 dots] IMPRIME' POUR JOHN NEILSON, [3 dots] M.DCC. XCIII. / [double rule] /

4to. A^4 $[*]^2$; 11 p.; type-page: 14.5 × 10.3 cm.

Contents: p. [1], t.-p.; p. [2], Order to print, dated: Chambre d'Assemblée, Lundi, 15me Avril, 1793"; p. [3]-11, Acte qui divise plus convenablement la Province du Bas Canada, qui amende la judicature d'icelle et qui rapelle certaines loix y mentionées; verso of p. 11, blank.

This is the French text of No. 840, with which it was printed in an edition of 300 copies, though issued separately.

Copies located: CaOOA (2 cop.); CaQMJ (mutilated and p. 9-11 wanting); CaQMS; CaQQL; GBLP (in C.O. 42/96: 75-85).

840. LOWER CANADA. LAWS, STATUTES, *etc.*

PLAN / OF / A BILL, / For altering the Courts of Justice, / SENT BY THE / LEGISLATIVE COUNCIL, / TO THE ASSEMBLY, / MONDAY, 8th April. 1793: / [royal arms] / [double rule] / QUEBEC: [3 dots] PRINTED FOR JOHN NEILSON, [3 dots] M.DCC. XCIII. /

4to. A^4, $[*]^2$; 11 p.; type-page: 14.5 × 10.3 cm.

Contents: p. [1], t.-p.; p. [2], Order to print, dated: "House of Assembly, Monday, 15th April, 1793"; p. [3]-11, An act for the better division of the Province of Lower Canada, for amending the judicature thereof and for repealing certain laws herein-mentioned; verso of p. 11, blank.

This *Plan* is reprinted in Doughty and McArthur: *Documents, 1791-1818*, p. 111-18, with the note:

"From the copy of the Bill as printed for John Neilson Quebec, MDCCXCIII. The plan for a judicial establishment proposed by Mr. Dundas was referred by Lieutenant Governor Clarke to the Chief Justice, Mr. Smith and to the Attorney General, Mr. Monk, who separately prepared drafts of bills. A third bill was proposed by a committee of the Legislative Council [No. 838]. All three were then considered by the Council and formed the basis of the bill here given. This bill was sent to the Assembly on April 8th, 1793, and was ordered to be printed for public distribution, but owing to the lateness of the season its consideration was deferred until the following season. [etc.]" It was passed in 1794 to become 35 Geo. III c. VI (*see* No. 889).

This work and its French translation (No. 839) were printed together (the two items of 11 p. each, "making 3 Sheets" folded in 4to) and perhaps issued separately, as the printer's charge for covering [600? pamphlets] suggests (cf. his charge for covering 400 pamphlets in No. 838). Nearly all the copies located have English and French editions bound together—though *not* in 18th-century binding.

"1793. June 15. [Debit] House of Assembly for printing 300 copies of Plan of a bill for altering the Courts of Justice, making 3 Sheets on Pott Paper, long primer type@ 35/ per Sheet for the 1st hundred 27/6 for every subsequent hundred—£7.10.
For Folding, Stitching & covering the same in blue paper—£1.17.4.
[Total:] £9.7.4."—Can.P.A., *Neilson papers*, v. 71.

The printer also sold copies for the retail trade at 6*s*. the dozen.—*Ibid*., Aug. 8, 1793.

Copies located: CaOOA; CaQMJ (p. [3]-11 mutilated); CaQMS; CaQQL; GBLP (in C.O. 42/96: 63-73).

841. LOWER CANADA. LIEUTENANT-GOVERNOR, 1791-1795 (*Clarke*)

[By His Excellency Alured Clarke, Esquire, Lieutenant Governor and Commander in Chief of the Province of Lower Canada . . . A Proclamation <Text> Given . . . at the Castle of Saint Louis Quebec, 24th April, 1793 . . . Alured Clarke. By His Excellency's Command, Geo. Pownall, Sec'y. God Save the King.

French side:

Par son Excellence Alured Clarke Ecuyer, Lieutenant Gouverneur et Commandant en chef de la Province du Bas Canada . . . Proclamation. <Text> Donné sous mon seing et sceau au Château de Saint Louis Québec 24 Avril, 1793 . . . Alured Clarke. Par ordre de son Excellence Signé Geo: Pownall Secr. Traduit par ordre . . . J. F. Cugnet, S. & T.F. Vive le Roi.]

Broadside: text in English and French. *Printed at Quebec, by (or for) John Neilson, 1793*, as recorded:

"1793. Apr. 26 [Debit] Lieutenant governor—For printing 100 copies of Proclamation announcing Declaration of war . . . in France, on English types, pott paper—£1."—Can.P.A., *Neilson papers*, v. 71.

Text: "Being informed . . . that the Persons at present exercising the supreme Authority in France have declared War against His Majesty on the First Day of February last; and being commanded to cause the same to be instantly made as public as possible in this Province, All His Majesty's Subjects within the same are hereby notified thereof, to the intent that care may be taken . . . to prevent any mischief which otherwise may happen from the present conduct of the French, and . . . to distress and annoy them by making capture of their ships and distroying [sic] their Commerce. [etc., information on granting of Letters of Marque, or commissions of privateurs, also on distribution of prize money, and benefit of convoy]."

French text: "Etant informé . . . que les Personnes qui exercent actuellement l'autorité suprême en France, ont declaré la guerre contre Sa Majesté, le premier jour de Février dernier, et étant commandé de la faire immediatement publier autant que possible dans la Province, tous les sujets de sa Majesté dans la dite Province en sont par ces presentes notifiés, à l'effet d'avoir soin, d'un côté, d'empêcher aucun malheur qui pourroit autrement arriver de la conduite presente des Français [etc.]."

This proclamation is reprinted in Can.P.A., *Report, 1921*, from which this description is taken. A similar proclamation was published on royal command, by Lieut.-Gov. Carleton of New Brunswick, May 3, 1793.—Can.P.A., N.B. Ex.co. *Minutes*, May 3, 1793. But no evidence of its publication otherwise than in the *Royal gazette* (Saint John, N.B.) has come to light.

Copy located: None.

842. MORT TRAGIQUE DU ROI DE FRANCE

MORT TRAGIQUE DU ROI DE FRANCE /

Broadside: text about 125 lines, printed in 3 col., type-page: 49 × 36 cm. engraved illus. at head of col. 2 (plate: 16 × 9.7 cm.). *Printed at Quebec, by John Neilson, 1793.*

The text includes: Decret de la Convention nationale, 15-20 Jan. 1793; Details sur les derniers moments de Louis XVI; Anecdotes; Testament de Louis XVI, 21 Dec. 1792.

The engraved illustration, entitled: "Vue de la Guillotine, ou Machine nouvellement inventée en France pour d'écapiter tout accusé condamné à perdre la vie," shows the guillotine in operation. It was also published as "Death of Louis XVI," in the *Quebec magazine*, 2: 166, Apr., 1793.

The printer recorded (though it is not clear whether he refers to the broadside or a separate issue of the engraving alone):

"1793, May 23, George Pownall [secretary to the governor] D^r^. to Printing Office for 150 Vues de la Guillotine—£5."

—Can.P.A., *Neilson papers*, v. 71.

The printer sold single copies at 1*s*. from May 28, 1793.—*ibid.*, v. 71.

Copy located: CaQQL.

843. NEW BRUNSWICK. HOUSE OF ASSEMBLY

JOURNAL / OF THE / VOTES and PROCEEDINGS / OF THE / HOUSE OF ASSEMBLY / OF THE / PROVINCE of NEW-BRUNSWICK: / From TUESDAY the 12th of FEBRUARY, to THURSDAY / the 14th MARCH, 1793. / [ornamental rule] / [royal arms] / [ornamental rule] / BROOKVILLE: / Printed by CHRISTOPHER SOWER, Printer to the / KING'S MOST EXCELLENT MAJESTY. 1793. / [title within a frame of flower pieces]

fo. A-[Q]²; 1 p. l., [280]-340 p., fold. table; type-page: 24 × 13.5 cm. Even numbers on recto, odd numbers on verso; paged in continuation of No. 790. One leaf of sig. [Q] is folded around sig. A-P, to form t.-p.

Contents: p. l. recto, t.-p.; verso, blank; p. [280]-340, Journal of the first session of the second assembly; verso of p. 340, blank; Fold. table correctly inserted between p. 315-316, is "... Account of Merchandize imported into the Port of Saint John ... [Feb. 25, 1792-Feb. 14, 1793] subject to Duty at the Treasury Office."

This and No. 844 are the earliest Brookville imprints located. This tiny settlement is about a dozen miles out of Saint John on the road to French Village. Here in 1792 Sower established his home and printing office, on a farm, or a group of farming lots, some 1,400 acres, which he had bought in the Hammond River intervale.

Three hundred copies of the *Acts* and two hundred copies of the *Journal* of this session were ordered by the House to be printed—N.B. As. *Journal*, Mar. 3, 1793. For printing the *Acts* (No. 844) and *Journal* of Assembly, 1793, Sower charged £62 17*s*. 8*d*.—as appears in the Supply bill of the next year—N.B. As. *Journal*, Feb. 21, 1794.

Copies located: CaN (t.-p. wanting); CaNU; CaNsWA; CaOOA; GBLP (in B.T. 6/56: 735-799); RPJ.

844. NEW BRUNSWICK. LAWS, STATUTES, *etc.*

ACTS / OF THE / GENERAL ASSEMBLY / OF / His MAJESTY'S PROVINCE / OF / NEW-BRUNSWICK, / PASSED IN THE YEAR 1793. / [ornamental rule] / [royal arms] / [ornamental rule] / BROOKVILLE: / Printed by CHRISTOPHER SOWER, Printer to the / KING'S MOST EXCELLENT MAJESTY. 1793. / [title within a frame of flower pieces.]

fo. [*¹, **]², A-E²; 3 p. l., 268-87 p.; type-page: 23.3 × 13.4 cm. Even numbers on recto, odd numbers on verso; paged in continuation of No. 791.

Contents: p. l. 1 recto, t.-p.; verso, blank; p. l. 2 recto, half title; verso, blank; p. l. 3 recto, Titles of the acts; verso, blank; p. 268-87, 33 Geo. III c. 1-X acts passed in the first session of the second assembly. This work was printed in an edition of 300 copies (*see* No. 843 *note*), 200 of which were distributed to officials, etc. in the province.

Copies located: Baxter; CaNsWA; CaOOA; DLC; GBLP (in B.T. 6/56: 677-702); MH; NNB.

845. NOVA SCOTIA. HOUSE OF ASSEMBLY

[rule] / JOURNAL / AND / PROCEEDINGS / OF THE / HOUSE OF ASSEMBLY. / [rule] /

fo. A-L², L-Q², R¹; 1 p. l., 68 p. *Printed at Halifax, N.S., by Anthony Henry, 1793.*

Contents: p. l. recto, t.-p.; verso, Proclamation; p. 1-68, Journal of the first session of the seventh assembly, Mar. 20-Apr. 27, 1793.

Henceforward the *Journal* was published in more formal style, with a preliminary leaf bearing (on recto) a bastard title, and (on verso) the lieutenant-governor's proclamation summoning the Assembly. Though printed regularly by the government (or king's) printer, it still had no imprint.

Copies located: CaNs (p. 63-68 wanting); CaNsHA (p. 67-68 wanting); GBLP (in C.O. 217/65: 108-176); MH.

846. NOVA SCOTIA. LAWS, STATUTES, *etc.*

Running title: [rule] / 1793. Anno Tricessimo Tertio Regis, GEORGII III. CAP. I[-XII]. / rules /

Caption title: At the GENERAL ASSEMBLY of the Province / of Nova-Scotia, . . . / [5 lines] / being the first Session of the Seventh Ge-/neral Assembly, convened in the said Pro-/vince. / [rule] /

fo. sig. 3E-3K²; p. 335-358; paged in continuation of No. 794 with 313-334 omitted in numbering. *Printed at Halifax, N.S., by Anthony Henry, 1792.*

Contents: p. 335-358, Cap. I-XII perpetual acts passed in the session, Mar. 20-Apr. 13, 1793.

Copies located: DLC; MH (2 cop.).

847. NOVA SCOTIA. LAWS, STATUTES, *etc.*

Running title: [rule] / 1793. Anno Tricessimo Tertio Regis, GEORGII III. CAP. I[-VII], / [rule] /

Caption title: At the GENERAL ASSEMBLY of the Province / of Nova-Scotia, . . . / [5 lines] / being the first Session of the Seventh Ge-/neral Assembly, convened in the said Pro-/vince. / [rule] /

fo. sig. 3U-3Y², 3Z¹; p. 371-388; type-page: 25.5 × 15 cm. paged in continuation of No. 795, with 338-370 omitted in numbering in compensation apparently for erroneous pagination of No. 649, 716, 795, the *Temporary Acts* of 1790, 1791 and 1792. *Printed at Halifax, N.S., by Anthony Henry, 1793.*

Contents: p. 371-388, Cap. I-VII temporary acts passed in the session Mar. 20-Apr. 27, 1793.

Copies located: CaO (2 cop.); MH (2 cop.); NNB.

848. NOVA SCOTIA. LIEUTENANT-GOVERNOR, 1792-1808 (*Wentworth*)

Caption title: [royal arms] / L.S.* [in ornamental frame] BY HIS EXCELLENCY / JOHN WENTWORTH, / . . . / . . . / . . . / A PROCLAMATION /

4to. 2 leaves without signature or pagination; type-page: 24 × 19 cm. *Printed at Halifax, N.S., by Anthony Henry, 1793,* as recorded:

"[1793?] To printing proclamation for prayers to be used in churches, Broadside on Demy—£1.7.6.

To 4 Quires Medium paper for prayers—16/."

—Henry's *Account for extra printing [for government], 1792-94,* in P.A.N.S., *Miscellaneous Assembly papers,* 1794.

Contents: l. [1] recto, Proclamation, dated at Halifax, Jan. 8, 1793, ordering use by clergy of the Established Church, of prayers for lieutenant-governor and Council, also for the Legislature when in session. The prayers were prepared by the Right Reverend Father in God, the bishop of Nova Scotia, who represented that their regular use "will have a tendency to impress the minds of the people with due sentiments of Reverence for the Civil Authority . . ."; and that such sentiments, by exciting a spirit of willing obedience for conscience sake, will contribute much to the peace and order of the community. verso of *l.* [1], blank; *l.* [2] recto, A prayer for the lieutenant-governor [etc.]; verso of *l.* 2, blank.

Bishop Inglis, who by special patent had ecclesiastical jurisdiction over the other provinces also, sent the text of the prayers and a request for their use, to New Brunswick. There "the said collects having been read and approved, His Excellency [Lieut.-Gov. Carleton] with the advice of the Council [was] pleased to declare his assent. Ordered a Proclamation to issue for this purpose and to be communicated to the Rev. Mr. Cooke, the Ecclesiastical Commissary."—Can.P.A., N.B. Ex.co. *Minutes,* Sept. 7, 1792 [sic]. No further evidence on publication of the New Brunswick proclamation has come to light.

Bishop Inglis also sent copies of the prayers to the lieutenant-governors of the Island of St. John, and of Lower and Upper Canada, with a memorial requesting their authorization there, and copies of Lieut.-Gov. Wentworth's *Proclamation.* The prayers were proclaimed in Upper Canada by Lieut.-Gov. Simcoe, Apr. 18, 1793. In Lower Canada the matter was referred to the Legislative Council in committee, which reported "that such alterations in service are declared by the King in privy council, and when introduced into churches in this province, the Royal pleasure is communicated . . . by special instructions to the Governor. And therefore greatly as they [the Council] applaud the piety of the Right Reverend Bishop of Nova Scotia . . . they find much difficulty on the subject of changes which by law belong to the Royal Supremacy, nor . . . ever delegated to any of its Representatives in the remote dependencies of the Empire [etc.]."—Can.P.A., L.C. *State* A, p. 377-81.

Copy located: CaOOA (endorsed: "in the Bishop of Nova Scotia's, 13 Mar. '93," and filed in Can.P.A., "S" 41, *Int. Corresp.,* L.C., 1793).

*I.e. *locus sigilli,* place for the seal.

849. NOVA SCOTIA. LIEUTENANT-GOVERNOR, 1792-1808 (*Wentworth*)

[A Proclamation by His Excellency. John Wentworth, LL.D., Lieutenant Governor . . . of Nova Scotia . . . <Text> Halifax, 13 April 1793.]

Broadside, *Printed at Halifax, N.S., by Anthony Henry, 1793,* as recorded:

"[1793] To printing Broadside on Demy for Reprisals of French ships—£1.5.

To 4 Quires Demy for printing proclamations for Reprisals [etc.] 6/."
—Henry's *Account for extra printing* [*for government*] *1792-1794,* in P.A.N.S., *Miscellaneous Assembly papers, 1794.*

Text: "Whereas the Persons exercising Supreme Authority in France having declared War against His Majesty on the first day of February last . . . His Majesty's subjects . . . may take care to prevent any mischief . . . from the French, . . . and may do their utmost to distress and annoy them . . . by destroying their Commerce . . . Letters of Marque or Commissions of Privateers [etc. will be granted in the usual manner and Prize Money is assured]."

A rough MS. draft of this proclamation is in P.A.N.S., Legislative Council papers 1760-1790, doc. 35. The proclamation was also printed in the *Royal gazette,* Halifax, N.S., Apr. 16-May 21, 1793, from which this entry was taken.

Copy located: None.

850. NOVA SCOTIA. LIEUTENANT-GOVERNOR, 1792-1808 (*Wentworth*)

[A Proclamation by His Excellency John Wentworth, LL.D., Lieutenant Governor of Nova Scotia . . . Whereas His Majesty . . . did by Proclamation . . . the first day of March 1793 . . . command a Publick Fast and Humiliation, I . . . extend the effect of the said Proclamation within this Province . . . Friday the tenth day May 1793 imploring blessing on His Majesty's Arms . . . Halifax, April 25, 1793.]

Broadside: *Printed at Halifax, N.S., by Anthony Henry, 1793,* as recorded:

"[1793] To printing proclamations for a general fast Broadside on Demy paper —£1.10.

To 8 Quires Demy for printing proclamations @ 1/6—19/6 [sic]."—Henry's *Account for extra printing* [*for government*] *1792-94,* in P.A.N.S., *Miscellaneous Assembly papers,* 1794.

Lieut.-Gov. Wentworth's proclamation was also published in the *Royal gazette,* Halifax, N.S., Apr. 3-May 7, 1793.

A similar proclamation by Lieut.-Gov. Carleton of New Brunswick, May 17, 1793, appointing June 3, 1793, a fast day, was ordered published—N.B. Ex.co. *Minutes,* May 17, 1793. But no evidence of its appearance otherwise than in the *Royal gazette,* Saint John, N.B., has come to light.

Copy located: None.

851. NOVA SCOTIA. LIEUTENANT-GOVERNOR, 1792-1808 (*Wentworth*)

[Proclamation by His Excellency, John Wentworth, LL.D., Lieutenant-Governor . . . of Nova Scotia <Text> Halifax, 3 September, 1793.]

Broadside, *Printed at Halifax, N.S., by Anthony Henry, 1793,* as recorded:

"[1793] To printing proclamations Broadside, for punishing Rogues & Vagabonds—£1.5.

To 4 Quires Demy for printing [same] @ 1/6—6/."—Henry's *Account for extra printing [for government] 1792-94,* in P.A.N.S., *Miscellaneous Assembly papers,* 1794.

Text: "Whereas by laws of this Province passed in the fourteenth year of His Majesty's Reign, entitled An Act for punishing Rogues, Vagabonds and other able and disorderly Persons . . . I call upon all Magistrates and well-disposed Citizens to . . . secure such persons and if they cannot exculpate themselves from suspicion of being Deserters from His Majesty's Army or Navy, send them back to the Regiment, or Ship, or place where they must belong [etc.]."

This proclamation was also published in the *Royal gazette,* Halifax, N.S., Sept. 10, 1793, *et seq.,* from which this entry was taken.

Copy located: None.

852. NOVA SCOTIA. LIEUTENANT-GOVERNOR, 1792-1808 (*Wentworth*)

[Proclamation By His Excellency, John Wentworth, LL.D., Lieutenant Governor . . . of Nova Scotia. <Text> Halifax, 9 October, 1793.]

Broadside, *Printed at Halifax, N.S., by Anthony Henry, 1793,* as recorded:

"[1793] To printing Proclamations for preventing Contagious Distempers, &c. —£1.5.

To 4 Quires Demy for printing [same]—6/."—Henry's *Account for extra printing [for government] 1792-94,* in P.A.N.S., *Miscellaneous Assembly papers,* 1794.

Text: "Whereas by an Act passed in the first year of His Majesty's Reign, entitled An Act to prevent the spreading of Contagious Distempers . . . and Whereas the City of Philadelphia is now infected with infectious distemper. I strictly forbid . . . all vessels coming from Philadelphia . . . to approach nearer to Halifax than Midway [i.e. Port Medway, about 60 miles south-west of Halifax]."

This proclamation was also published in the *Royal gazette,* Halifax, N.S., Oct. 15, 1793, *et seq.,* from which this entry was taken.

Copy located: None.

853. QUEBEC BENEVOLENT SOCIETY

RULES AND REGULATIONS / OF THE / QUEBEC BENEVOLENT SOCIETY, / ESTABLISHED THE FIRST WEDNESDAY IN MAY, /

M.DCC.LXXXIX. / [rule] / Printed for the Members information before being past. / [rule] / [printer's ornament] / [double rule] / QUEBEC: / PRINTED BY JOHN NEILSON, M.DCC.XCIII. / [rule] /

French t.-p.:

REGLES ET REGLEMENS / DE LA / SOCIETE' BIENVEILLANTE. / DE QUÉBEC, / ETABLIE LE PREMIER MECREDI [sic] DE MAI, / M.DCC.LXXXLX. [sic] / [rule] / Imprimis pour l'Instruction de ses Membres avant / de passer. / [rule] / [ornament] / [double rule] / A QUÉBEC: / DE L'IMPRIMERIE DE JOHN NEILSON, / M.DCC.XCIII. / [rule] /

12mo. A-C[6], D[2]; 39 p.; type-page: 13 × 7 cm. Text in English and French on opposite pages.

Contents: p. [1], English t.-p.; p. [2], blank; p. [3], French t.-p.; p. [4]-39, Rules (i.e., p. [4-5], preamble; p. [6]-39, rules no. 1-21); verso of p. 39, blank. This work was printed in sixty copies as a preliminary edition of the *Rules* published in 1794 (No. 906).

Copies located: CaO; CaQM.

854. QUEBEC GAZETTE. CARRIER'S ADDRESS

Verses of the Printer's Boy who carries the Quebec Gazette to the Customers. January 1, 1794.

French side:

Etrennes du Garçon qui porte la Gazette de Québec aux Practiques. Le Ier Janvier 1794. *Quebec, J. Neilson, 1793.*

Broadside, in English and French; contents not examined.

Copy located: CaQMS.

855. SAINT JOHN, N.B., *City.* ORDINANCES

[Fishery law.]

? Broadside. *Printed at Saint John, N.B., by John Ryan, 1793,* as recorded:

"Ordered that M[r] Ryan be paid one guinea for publishing the Fishery Law provided he be not appointed to print the Acts and Journals of the Assembly."—Saint John, N.B. *Minutes,* Mar. 31, 1793.

This order may refer to publication as a broadside and/or in the *Saint John gazette.*

Copy located: None.

856. SAINT JOHN, N.B., *City.* ORDINANCES

[Ordinance to prevent bringing in and spreading of infectious distempers in the City of Saint John.]

Printed at Saint John, N.B., by John Ryan and/or Christopher Sower, 1793, as recorded:

"Read and passed into law, an Ordinance to prevent bringing in and spreading of infectious distempers in the City of Saint John. Ordered that the same be printed in the newspapers and that One hundred Newspapers be printed by the Clark [sic]."—Saint John, N.B. *Minutes*, Oct. 3, 1793.

The "One hundred Newspapers" were probably a separate broadside issue of the ordinance printed from the newspaper types, as was the custom in Quebec. A similar decree closing Halifax to ships from Philadelphia, where an epidemic of yellow fever existed at that time, was issued by proclamation of the lieutenant-governor of Nova Scotia. See also: John J. Heagerty: *Four centuries of medical history in Canada and . . . Newfoundland* (2 v., Toronto, 1928), 1: 102.

Copy located: None.

857. SCHIEFFELIN, JACOB, *Merchant, Montreal*

MONTREAL, 10 July 1793. JACOB SCHIEFFELIN has received by the Ship Commerce Captain Christr. Backhouse from Liverpool, an extensive and general assortment of Earthern, China and Glass ware . . . at his Stores N^{O}. 114 and 127 St. Paul's Street . . . Also an assortment of Strouds and Cloths to the amount of 2000£ sterling . . . N.B. A clerk or an Apprentice wanted [etc.]

Broadside: 40 lines; type-page: 14.5 × 10 cm. Text in English (above) and French (below). *Probably printed at Montreal, by Fleury Mesplet, 1793.*

Copy located: CaOT (bound in *Montreal gazette*, July 11, 1793).

858. STACKHOUSE, THOMAS, 1677-1752

TWO SERMONS: / COLLECTED CHIEFLY FROM / STACKHOUSE'S BODY OF DIVINITY; / AND / PRINTED FOR THE USE / OF / PRIVATE FAMILIES / IN THE / ISLAND OF CAPE-BRETON. / [rule] / HALIFAX: / PRINTED BY JOHN HOWE, AT THE CORNER OF GEORGE / AND BARRINGTON-STREETS. / [rule] / M.DCC.XCIII. /

8vo. A-D^4, E^2; v, 31 p.; type-page: 17 × 9 cm. Even numbers on recto, odd numbers on verso in text.

Contents: p. [1], t.-p.; p. [ii], blank; p. [iii]-v, Advertisement; p. [1]-15, Sermon I, 1 John v. 7: There are three that bear record in Heaven; the Father, the Word, and the Holy Ghost; and these three are one; p. 16-31, Sermon II, Psalm xxxiv.15: The eyes of the Lord are over the Righteous, and his Ears are open unto their Prayers; Erratum at foot of p. 31.

The advertisement (p. [iii]-v) states: "the following Sermons were written by a Layman of eminent rank and character," who waives credit for his work, attributing them to Stackhouse. The latter was chiefly known for his *New history of the Holy Bible* (3 v., London, 1737); but his *Complete body of divinity . . . from the best ancient and modern writers*, first published in London 1729 (later editions 1734 and 1766) was a staple of devotional literature through the 18th century.

The two sermons published here. are pleasantly reasoned discourses. The first treats of the inevitable truth of biblical prophecy, and the necessity of faith on the part of man. The second sermon justifies the ten commandments *seriatim* and points out the rewards of obedience. It ends, however, on a different note: "Let us unite then, in imploring the Almighty that the harvest and fisheries of this infant colony may be plenteous and successful and that the aid of the mother country may be extended towards this island and foster it to maturity."

Cape Breton, after the French régime, was administered as part of Nova Scotia, excepting from 1784 till 1820, when it had separate colonial status under the crown, with its own lieutenant-governor and council. Its settlement was discouraged, however, to prevent development of its coal mines in competition with those in Britain. Population was small, even after the immigration of American loyalists, and here, as in Nova Scotia, Presbyterians and Congregationalists, lacking the state aid afforded the established church, had difficulty in securing ordained ministers. The little congregations held their own services, occasionally appointing a lay preacher. Such congregations had special need of acceptable sermons.

Copy located: MBAt.

859. THE TIMES, *Quebec*

[Preparatory address announcing the proposed publication of a newspaper.]

? Leaflet, *printed at Quebec, by John Neilson, 1793.* This, the first announcement of the *Times* is mentioned in its Prospectus, Quebec, June 23, 1794: ". . . Anxious to accelerate our publication as announced in our preparatory address of December last, we now present prospectus and specimen."

This *Preparatory address* is probably the work recorded by Neilson a little later:

"1794, Feb. 6. [Debit] Wm. Vondenvelden for printing 300 Proposals on Demy Quarto in English—12/6."—Can.P.A., *Neilson papers*, v. 71.

Copy located: None.

860. UPPER CANADA. EXECUTIVE COUNCIL

[double rule] / UPPER CANADA. / [rule] / COUNCIL-CHAMBER, / NAVY HALL, FEBRUARY 2, 1793. / [rule] / PRESENT / His Excellency JOHN GRAVES SIMCOE, Esquire; / Lieutenant-Governor, &c.&c.&c. —IN COUNCIL. / [rule] / <Text> / Extracted from the Minutes. / E. B. LITTLEHALES, / Acting Clerk of the Council. /

Broadside: 40 lines; type-page: 22.5 × 14.7 cm. *Probably printed at Newark, U.C., by Louis Roy, 1793.*

Previous publications by Simcoe had been printed at Quebec by Neilson, or at Montreal by Mesplet. This, however, appears to have been printed at Newark. Louis Roy, Neilson's journeyman whom Simcoe had engaged to print for the government in Upper Canada, was reported to have begun work at Newark in Jan., 1793. Mrs. Wm. Jarvis, wife of the secretary of Upper Canada, wrote from Newark, Jan. 15, 1793, to her father Dr. Samuel Peters in London: ". . . Our printer has got his press up and commenced printing, but nothing public as yet. A paper is expected to be weekly printed, and is likely to begin after the 18th [etc.]."*—In Jarvis papers

*The paper, the *Upper Canada gazette*, actually appeared Apr. 18, 1793.

in the collection of the late Æmilius Jarvis, Esq., Toronto, according to information kindly supplied by Mr. Jarvis in Sept., 1937.

Text: "His Excellency acquainted the Board, that He wished to call their attention to the Situation of the several Persons occupying Lands or claiming to be entitled thereto under various Authorities since the first Settlement of the Province, and to consult on the most effectual means of carrying his Majesty's gracious Intentions into Execution by making out regular grants of Allotments of Land to such Persons as are respectively entitled thereto," etc. Resolved that notice be given (1) to persons claiming allotments in the Home District to present their certificate, ticket of occupation, or warrant to the attorney-general, so that the lieut.-governor-in-council may make out regular grant according to *Rules and regulations of the Land Office Department;* (2) to persons in other districts later.

Copy located: CaOT.

861. UPPER CANADA. LAWS, STATUTES, *etc.*

Caption title: [double rule] / Acts of the Legislature / OF HIS MAJESTY'S PROVINCE OF / Upper Canada, / [rule] / Passed in the First Session, / and in the Thirty Second Year of the Reign of / OUR SOVEREIGN LORD / GEORGE THE THIRD. / [rule] /

Colophon, p. [8]: [ornamental rule] / NEWARK: Printed by LOUIS ROY, 1793. / [ornamental rule] /

8vo. A^4; 8 p.; type-page: 18 × 11.7 cm.

Contents: p. [1]-8, Acts, 32 Geo. III c. I-VIII, passed in the first session of the first assembly, Newark, U.C., Sept. 17-Oct. 15, 1792.

These acts are reprinted in Can.P.A., *Report, 1921. See also:* Eakins: *Bibliography of Canadian statute law.*

Copies located: CaOTL (imperfect); CaQMS; photostat in CaOOA and CaOTL.

862. UPPER CANADA. LAWS, STATUTES, *etc.*

Caption title: [double rule] / Acts of the Legislature / OF HIS MAJESTY'S PROVINCE OF / UPPER CANADA, / [rule] / Passed in the Second Session / and in the Thirty-Third Year of the Reign of / OUR SOVEREIGN LORD / GEORGE THE THIRD. / [rule] /

Colophon, p. [46]: [double rule] / UPPER CANADA: Printed by LOUIS ROY. / [triple rule]. /

8vo. B-E^4, F^3; p. [9]-46; type-page: 18 × 11.7 cm. Paged in continuation of No. 861. *Printed at Newark, U.C., by Louis Roy in ?1793.*

Contents: p. [9]-46, Acts, 33 Geo. III c. I-XIII, passed in the second session of the first assembly, Newark, U.C., May 31-July 9, 1793.

These acts are reprinted in Can.P.A., *Report, 1921.*

Copies located: CaQMS; photostat in CaOOA and in CaOTL.

863. UPPER CANADA. LIEUTENANT-GOVERNOR, 1791-1799 (*Simcoe*)

SPEECH / OF / HIS EXCELLENCY / JOHN GRAVES SIMCOE, ESQ; / LIEUTENANT GOVERNOR / of the Province of Upper Canada, &c.&c.&c. / UPON OPENING THE FIRST SESSION / of the Legislature of the said Province. / [rule] / WITH / The respective Addresses of both Houses thereupon. / [rule] / AND / HIS EXCELLENCY'S ANSWERS / [rule] / LIKEWISE / HIS EXCELLENCY'S SPEECH, / Upon Proroguing the said Session of the Legislature. / [double rule] / [royal arms] / [rule] / BY AUTHORITY. / [double rule] / UPPER CANADA: / Printed by LOUIS ROY, M,DCC,XCIII. / [title within double rule frame]

4to. [*][4]; 8 p.; type-page: 14.7 × 9.5 cm. *Probably printed at Newark, U.C., by Louis Roy, 1793. See* Sabin 81138, 98064; *see also* W. S. Wallace: *The earliest example of printing in Upper Canada,* in *Canadian historical review,* 10: 333-35, 1929.

Contents: p. [1], t.-p.; p. [2], blank; p. [3]-4, Speech of Simcoe upon opening the first session of the Legislature Sept. 18, 1792; p. 4-5, Address of the Legislative Council Sept. 19, 1792; p. 6, Simcoe's answer thereto; p. 6-7, Address of the House of Assembly Sept. 19, 1792; p. 7, Simcoe's answer thereto; p. 7-8, Speech of . . . Simcoe upon proroguing the Legislative Council and Assembly, Monday, Oct. 15, 1792.

Copies located: CaOT; CaOTU; DLC.

864. UPPER CANADA. LIEUTENANT-GOVERNOR, 1791-1799 (*Simcoe*)

JOHN GRAVES SIMCOE. / PROCLAMATION / GEORGE the Third by the Grace of God, of Great Britain, France / and Ireland, King, Defender of the Faith, &c.&c.&c. / To Our Beloved and Faithful Legislative Councillors of Our Province of / Upper-Canada, and Our Faithful Knigths [sic], Citizens and Burgesses of / Our said Province to the Assembly at Our Town of Newark, on the / Eight [sic] Day of this present Month of February, to be commenced and / held called and elected and to every of You, / GREETING; / <[royal arms] Text> / . . . At Our Government / House Navy Hall, this seventh Day of February, in the year of Our / Lord One thousand seven hundred and ninety-three, and in the / Thirty third of Our Reign. / J.G.S. / WM. JARVIS, Secretary.

Broadside: 39 lines; type-page: 32.7 × 18.7 cm. *Probably printed at Newark, U.C., by Louis Roy, 1793.*

The text announces the postponement of the second session of the first legislature from Feb. 8 to Mar. 18, 1793. The session actually opened at Newark, May 31, 1793.

Facsim. illus. in Toronto Public Library, *Bibliography of Canadiana,* 160.

Copy located: CaOT.

865. VIETS, ROGER, 1738-1811

A / SERMON / PREACHED TO THE / ANCIENT AND WORSHIPFUL SOCIETY / OF / FREE AND ACCEPTED MASONS, / AT THEIR / ANNIVERSARY FESTIVAL / OF THE / Blessed Evangelist St. JOHN, 1792, / IN / Trinity Church, Digby, Nova-Scotia. / [rule] / BY THE / REVEREND BROTHER VIETS, RECTOR and MISSIONARY. / [rule] / —Is thine Heart right, as my Heart is with thy Heart? / —If it be, give me thine Hand. / II KINGS, X. 15. / [rule] / HALIFAX: Printed by JOHN HOWE, at his Printing-Office, opposite the / PARADE. / [rule] / M DCC XCIII. /

8vo. A-B^4; 14 p., 1 *l.*; type-page: 17 × 9 cm.

Contents: p. [1], t.-p.; p. [2], blank; p. [3]-9, Sermon, text: II Corin. VI, 8-9. By Honour and Dishonour; by evil Report and good Report; as Deceivers, and yet true; as unknown and yet as well known —; p. [10], blank; p. [11]-14, A charge delivered to the lodge, no. 6, at Digby, in Nova Scotia on the anniversary of St. John the Evangelist, 5792 by the worshipful John Hill, master, dated at end: "Lodge Room at the House of Brothers Rutherford and Nash in Digby. 27th March, 5792." 1 *l.* at end, blank.

The sermon is a discourse in defence and praise of freemasonry—calumniated, says Viets, just as Christianity and its ministers are. The craft, imposing secrecy, prompts groundless criticism and handicaps its vindicators. The preacher, however, testifies freely to the virtue and benevolence of its members. "No profaneness, intoxication, nor obscene discourse, no slander, no political nor party matters, no religious disputes, nor controversies, are on any occasion or pretence, allowed in the Lodge." Treason, disloyalty, and religious schism receive no encouragement from freemasons. Viets thanks those of Digby for their support of church and state and commends them to Heaven. Digby was in a district where Henry Alline's New Light beliefs were widely held.

Viets, a native of Simsbury, Conn. and a missionary of the Society for the Propagation of the Gospel at that place, 1763-83, removed from the United States when the Society withdrew its support of missions there. He served as its missionary in Digby, N.S., from 1786 till his death.

Hill, addressing his brethren for the third time as master, admonishes them to attend church, provide for their families, "deal . . . on the square with all men . . . avoid . . . tipling and tavernhaunting. Flee from lawsuits as . . . from pestilence . . . maintain in your minds, a temper of contentment in your stations and circumstances . . . enter into no silly and fruitless chat respecting the Craft."

Copies located: MBAt; RPJ.

866. WALTER, JOHN, *Merchant, Quebec*

Answer to Mr. Barclay's Insertion in the Quebec Gazette of the 18th Instant. / [ornamental rule]. <Text> [signed:] John Walter, Quebec, April 20, 1793.

Broadside: 107 lines. text in 2 col.; type-page: 38 × 21.3 cm. *Probably printed at Quebec, by John Neilson, 1793.*

This is a sequel, published separately, to a series of recriminating communications between Walter, a merchant settled in Quebec, and David Barclay (also in Quebec then) of Schoolbred & Barclay, merchants with headquarters in London. Walter attacked Barclay in the *Quebec gazette*, Apr. 11, 1793, for tampering with his credits in London to compensate the firm's alleged losses through Wm. H. McNeill of Montreal. The latter was brother-in-law to Walter, also to Schoolbred, and an agent of Schoolbred and Barclay. Barclay retorted to Walter at great length in the *Quebec gazette* of Apr. 18, 1793, wherewith the editor declared its columns closed to further correspondence. Walter published his *Answer* separately as above, and McNeill also answered Barclay on his own behalf, in the *Montreal gazette*, May 2, 1793. The correspondence is violent in tone, suggesting a dispute of wider implications. The complicated family and mercantile antipathies reveal an intricate pattern of colonial trade—and its highly restricted personnel.

Copies located: CaNsWA (bound in *Quebec gazette*, 1793); CaO (bound in *Quebec gazette*, Apr. 18, 1793); CaOOA (bound in *Quebec gazette*, Apr. 25, 1793).

867. ALMANACS. LOWER CANADA

[Calendar for the year, 1795. *Quebec, New Printing office, 1794.*]

Broadside, probably similar in appearance and content to that issued by the same printer, Wm. Vondenvelden, in succeeding years. This almanac was advertised:

> "For sale at Mr. Louis Germain, Jun., Fabric-Street, No. 5, The Sheet Almanack only, for the year 1795, Printed at the New Printing Office, Quebec."
>
> —*The Times*, Quebec, Nov. 10, 1794, *et. seq.*

Copy located: None.

868. ALMANACS. LOWER CANADA

CALENDRIER pour l'Année 1795, pour Québec, par les 306$^{d.}$ 30$^{m.}$ de Longitude, et 46$^{d.}$ 55$^{m.}$ de Latitude. [double rule] /

Colophon: A QUEBEC: chez JOHN NEILSON, Imprimeur et Libraire, N° 3 Rue laMontagne. /

Broadside: type-page: 52.5 × 39 cm.

Contents: Calendrier in ornamental rule frame: 42 × 39 cm. below *Calendrier:* Table d'l'or en cour d'Halifax; Table de reduction; Du systeme planetaire; . . . Mesures courantes; Etendue et population des états de l'Europe (5 col., in French).

This sheet almanac was advertised.

"Just published [Dec. 7, 1794] Le Calendrier de Québec pour l'année, 1795 . . . at the bottom of the sheet are added [1], Useful tables reducing English and French currencies to Halifax; 2. The weight value of gold coins; 3. Population of the Kingdoms and states of Europe; 4. The Planetary systems; 5. An account of the comets; 6. Tables of the different measures in use."—*Quebec gazette*, Dec. 11, 1794.

It was sold at Neilson's printing office from Dec. 8, 1794, at 5*s*. the dozen, 7½*d*. the copy—a slight drop in price from the years immediately preceding.

Copy located: CaO (bound in *Quebec gazette* at the end of 1794).

869. ALMANACS. LOWER CANADA

THE / QUEBEC / ALMANACK / FOR / The Year 1794. / [double rule] / 46D. 55 M. N.LAT.—71D. 12M.W. LONG. / [double rule] / [printer's ornament] / [double rule] / Hail sacred Science! by thy friendly aid, / Are Nature's mysteries to man display'd; / . . . / . . . / . . . / . . . / [double rule] / QUEBEC: / Printed by JOHN NEILSON, / No. 3. MOUNTAIN STREET. / [title within ornamental rule frame]

French t.-p.: ALMANAC / DE / QUEBEC, / POUR / L'ANNEÉ 1794. / [double rule] / 46D. 55M. N.LAT—71D. 12M. W.LONG. / [double rule] / [printer's ornament] / double rule] / Ici l'on voit réduite à de courtes leçons, / La Science qui régle et fixe les saisons, / . . . / . . . / . . . / . . . / [double rule] / A QUEBEC: / CHEZ JEAN NEILSON, / N° 3 RUE LA MONTAGNE. / [title within ornamental rule frame]

12mo. A-L[6]; 132 p., front.; type-page: 10.8 × 6 cm.

Contents: p. [1], English t.-p.; p. [2], blank; p. [3], French t.-p.; p. [4-33], Epochs, eclipses, tide tables, calendar; p. 34-45, Latest discoveries in the solar system; p. 44-53, Maxims; p. 54-55, Currency rules and interest table; p. 56-58, Indian nations; p. [59]-131, Civil and military register, clergy, [etc.]; p. 131-132, Index.

The frontispiece is an engraving numbered: "I," entitled: "Etat primitif de l'homme—Primitive State of Society"; and signed by G. Hochstetter Sculpt. It depicts three nude figures, man, woman, and child, before a cave in a forest, the man armed with club, plucking fruit.

The content of this almanac is similar to *The Quebec almanac for . . . 1792*, excepting the special articles. This one includes the announcement of the division of the old province of Quebec into Upper and Lower Canada, Dec., 1791, and the new list of counties therein, also the personnel of the land granting departments of both provinces. This is the first almanac published by (or for) young John Neilson. It was issued on Feb. 3, 1794, and advertised in the *Quebec gazette*, Feb. 6, 1794, *et seq.*

Copies located: CaOOA; CaQ; CaQM; CaQMS; CaQQAr; CaQQL.

870. ALMANACS. NOVA SCOTIA

[An Almanack for the year of our Lord, 1795, calculated for the meridian of Halifax in Nova Scotia by Theophrastus. *Halifax, N.S., Printed and Sold by John Howe & M'Kinstry.*]

This almanac was advertised (following an announcement of the *Nova-Scotia Calendar for 1795*):

> ". . . likewise will be published on Thursday next [Nov. 19, 1794] Price 5/ per dozen, 7½*d* single, by Howe & M'Kinstry, An Almanack for . . . 1795 [etc.]."
>
> —*Royal gazette*, Halifax, N.S., Nov. 18, 1794.

In subsequent issues of the same paper it was advertised as "Just published and for sale [etc.]."

Copy located: None.

871. ALMANACS. NOVA SCOTIA

THE / NOVA-SCOTIA CALENDER / OR AN / ALMANACK, / FOR THE / Year . . . 1795. / . . . / . . . / . . . / . . . / WHEREIN IS CONTAINED / The ECLIPSES . . . / [six lines] The View of HALIFAX, was taken from FOSTER's on the Eastern side of / the Harbour. / CALCULATED FOR THE MERIDIAN OF / HALIFAX, IN NOVA-SCOTIA, / . . . / . . . / . . . / [rule] / BY METONICUS. / [rule] / Sir ISAAC NEWTON's Epitaph by Mr. POPE. / "Nature and Nature's Laws lay hid in Night, / "God said LET NEWTON BE, and all was Light." / [rule] / HALIFAX: / Printed and sold by ANTHONY HENRY, at his Printing-Office, in Sack-/ville-Street, Corner of Grafton-Street. / [title and each page within a single rule frame.]

12mo. [A-C^4, D^2, E^4]; [36] p. type-page: 15.8 × 9.8 cm.

Contents: p. [1], View of Halifax (wood cut 14.8 × 9.2 cm.); p. [2], blank; p. [3], t.-p.; p. [4-19], Eclipses, etc., Calendar; ephemeris; p. [20-36], Nova Scotia administration, legislature, judges, justices, militia, naval and army officers, clergy, postal rates, distances [etc.].

This almanac was advertised;

> "On Thursday next [Nov. 19, 1794] will be published, Price 5/ per dozen, 7½*d.* single, The Nova-Scotia Calender [etc.]"—*Royal gazette*, Halifax, N.S., Nov. 18, 1794.

Copies located: CaNsHA (p. [20] to end wanting); DLC.

872. CHURCH OF ENGLAND. DIOCESE OF NOVA SCOTIA

[Form of Prayer for a general fast on Friday, April 25, 1794.]

4to. 4 *l. Printed at Halifax, N.S., by Anthony Henry, 1794,* as recorded:

"[1794] To printing 300 Prayers in 4to Demy for the general Fast—£2.5.
To 13 Quires Demy for [ditto] 10/."—Henry's *Account for extra printing [for government] 1792-1794,* in P.A.N.S., *Miscellaneous Assembly Papers,* 1794.

Bishop Inglis noted this piece in his abstract of a letter, dated Halifax, May 3, 1794, to the Archbishop of Canterbury: ". . . that on my application to Governor Wentworth, April 25th was appointed for a General Fast—that I preached that day . . . and the Sermon was to be printed—that I had prepared a Form of Prayer, being chiefly that which was used in England last year—sent copies of the Form to the Governors of New Brunswick, Cape Breton, and Island of St. John."

—Can.P.A., *Inglis papers,* v. 2.

Copy located: None.

873. DEBONNE, PIERRE-AMABLE, 1758-1816

PRE'CIS / OU / ABRE'GE' / D'UN ACTE, / Qui pourvoit à la plus grande sureté du / BAS-CANADA, / Passé le 30me MAY, dans la trente-quatriéme année du règne / de Sa Majesté. / Par l'Hon. P. A. DEBONNE, / [rule] / QUEBEC: PRINTED AT THE NEW PRINTING OFFICE. / [rule] /

8vo. a-c[4], [d][1]; 25 p.; type-page: 17 × 12 cm. Due to error in imposition in some copies sig. b appears in the following order: p. 15, 16, 13, 14, 11, 12, 9, 10. This work was *printed at Quebec, by Wm. Vondenvelden, 1794,* between the time when he set up press in June, and October, when it was recorded

"[Credit] Wm. Vondenvelden . . . Printing 700 copies Précis of the Militia Bill, Circular letters & Certificates respecting Aliens. by Order of Attorney General.—£28.9.6 cy."—*Minutes,* Jan. 2, 1795, of Committee on accounts for Apr.-Oct., 1794, in Can.P.A., L.C. *State* B.

Contents: p. [1], t.-p.; p. [2], blank; p. [3], Dedication, "A Son Excellence, le Très Honorable Guy, Lord Dorchester . . . [signed:] P A. De Bonne, Colonel d'une division de Milices du Nord, dans le district de Quebec"; p. [4], blank; p. [5]-25, Précis ou Abre'ge d'un acte; verso of p. 25, blank.

This work is a digest, entirely in French, of the Militia Act, 34 Geo. III c. 4 (No. 884, 885). It arranges in five chapters the terms concerning the duties and powers of (1) the governor, (2) district commanders, (3) other officers, (4) militia (this is DeBonne's commen ary upon the method of raising militia by lot in Lower Canada), (5) justices of the peace, etc.

DeBonne, a lawyer and judge, was member for the county of York, L.C., in the Assembly which passed this act. He was also assistant French secretary and translator to the governor-in-council, and from 1794, a member of the Executive Council of Lower Canada.

Copies located: CaQ; CaQM; CaQMS (2 cop.); CaQQA; CaQQL; NN.

874. [DIALOGUE BETWEEN ANDRE AND BRIGITE]

[DIALOGUE BETWEEN ANDRE AND BRIGITE]

8vo. about 40 p. *Printed at Quebec, by John Neilson, 1794,* as recorded;

"1794, July 4. [Debit] Governor's Office 500 of 2 Sheets and a ½ 8vo Pott (Dialogue between Andre & Brigite) Eng. type.—£7.3.9.

Sept. 17 [belated entry] Gov. Office for folding and stitching 500 cop. of Dialogues between Andre & B. @ 1[d].—£2.1.8. [Total: £9.5.5]."

—Can.P.A., *Neilson Papers,* v. 71.

No further information on this publication has appeared. Circumstances suggest that it was issued by the government to confirm French Canadians in their allegiance to the British administration. It may have been a conversation—in French—bearing witness to the sufferings of church and crown in the French Revolution, the evil purposes of "the persons at present exercising supreme authority in France," or simply to the advantages of peace and of life under British institutions of government. This, however, is merely conjecture.

Copy located: None.

875. HUBERT, JEAN FRANCOIS, *bp. of Quebec,* 1739-1797

MANDEMENT / DU 28 OCTOBRE, / M.DCC.XCIII. /

Caption title, p. [1]: [triple rule] / MANDEMENT / DE MONSEIGNEUR / L'EVEQUE DE QUEBEC, / Qui révoque certaines dispositions de deux / Mandemens précédens et pourvoit à quel-/ques autres objets. / [rule] / JEAN FRANCOIS HUBERT, / . . . Evêque de Qué-/bec

&c.&c. A tous les Curés, Vicaires Missionaires, Prêtres / Séculaires et Réguliers de notre Diocèse, Salut et Benediction . . . / . . . /

4to. A-D²; 1 p. l., 13 p.; type-page: 18.8 × 14 cm. One leaf of sig. D is folded around sig. A-C, to form t.-p. *Probably printed at Quebec, by John Neilson, 1794*, for this appears to be the only *Mandement* prepared by the bishop near this date to which the following record could refer:

"1794, May 31. [Debit] Plessis Curé, 400 Mandements making 4 Half Sheets Crown 4to, English type—£6.15."—Can.P.A., *Neilson Papers*, v. 71.

Contents: p. l. recto, t.-p.; verso, blank; p. [1]-12, Mandement, signed: "Donné à Québec sous notre seing, . . . le vingt-huit Octobre, mil-sept-cent quatre-vingt-treize. Jean François, Evêque de Québec. Par Monseigneur J. O. Plessis Prêtre, Secrétaire"; p. 13, Liste des solemnites remises au dimanche; verso of p. 13, blank.

This mandement supersedes that of Dec. 10, 1788, on the jurisdiction of priests (No. 556) and that of Apr. 15, 1791, on the suppression of certain feast days (No. 707). Both these measures had evoked protests from Bishop Hubert's coadjutor, Bailly de Messein, Bishop of Capsa. Hubert submitted the disputed mandements to the pope, who suggested a few changes. The latter were incorporated into the mandements and the amended text is published here, with an introduction by Bishop Hubert and quotations from the communications from the Holy See. The work was reprinted with controversial letters which appeared in the *Quebec gazette*, 1790-93, in Têtu and Gagnon: *Mandements de Quebéc*, 2: 459-70.

Copies located: CaO; CaOOA (2 cop.); CaQQL; Ketcheson; RPJ.

876. INGLIS, CHARLES, *bp. of Nova Scotia*, 1734-1816

[Questions sent to the clergy of Nova Scotia preliminary to the Triennial visitation at Halifax, June, 1794.]

Probably printed at Halifax, N.S., by Anthony Henry, 1794, in a small edition for private circulation, this work was mentioned by Bishop Inglis in his letter (dated: Halifax, June 28, 1794) to Dr. Morice, secretary of the Society for the Propagation of the Gospel, "Triennial visitation just ended. Twelve clergymen attended, . . . [the business included] answers to my printed questions sent of the clergy [before the Visitation] also a scheme for the relief of widows and orphans of clergymen. The plan adopted in New York is too complicated. We avoid this. The fundamental rules of our Scheme are agreed to. The Governor has promised a charter of incorporation. The Rules and Charter (if obtained) will probably be printed with the Charge I delivered. [etc.]."—Can.P.A., *Inglis papers*, v. 2.

Excepting other references in Inglis's correspondence in 1794, (he sent the archbishop of Canterbury a copy of his *Questions*, on June 28, 1794) no further evidence of publication has appeared.

Copy located: None.

877. INGLIS, CHARLES, *bp. of Nova Scotia*, 1734-1816

A / SERMON / PREACHED IN THE / Parish Church of ST. PAUL at HALIFAX, / On FRIDAY, April 25, 1794: / Being the day appointed by PROCLAMATION / FOR / A GENERAL FAST and HUMILIATION / IN / His Majesty's Province of NOVA-SCOTIA. / [double rule] / BY THE

RIGHT REVEREND CHARLES, / Bishop of Nova-Scotia. / [double rule] / Published by desire of his Excellency the LIEUTENANT / GOVERNOR, of the Honourable Members of His Majesty's / COUNCIL, and of others. / [rule] / HALIFAX: / Printed by ANTHONY HENRY, Printer to the King's Most / Excellent Majesty, 1794 /

4to. A-E[4]; 38 p., 1 *l.*; type-page: 15.5 × 8.3 cm.

Contents: p. [1], t.-p.; p. 2, Advertisement, dated at Halifax, May 1, 1794; p. 3-34, Sermon, Hosea VI: 1. Come let us return unto the Lord; for he hath torn, and he will heal us, he hath smitten, and he will bind us up; p. 35-38, Appendix (announcement of arrival of Prince Edward at Halifax, while the Sermon was in the press; Bishop Inglis's address of welcome, May 26, 1794; the prince's answer, etc.); 1 *l.*, blank. *See also* No. 872.

This work was advertised: "Just published and to be sold by the Printer, Price 6*d.*, A Sermon preached . . . on Friday, April 25, 1794 [etc.]."

—*Royal gazette*, Halifax, N.S., July 1, 1794.

Copies located: NNHi; CaOT; RPJ.

878. LOWER CANADA. EXECUTIVE COUNCIL

Executive Council Office, Quebec, 10th October, 1794. / <Text> / By Command of His Excellency in Council, J. WILLIAMS. /

French side: BUREAU du CONSEIL EXECUTIF, Québec, 10 Octobre, 1794. / <Text> / Par Ordre de Son Excellence en Conseil, J. WILLIAMS.

Broadside: text in English (50 lines) and French (49 lines) in parallel col. type-page: 17.5 × 21 cm.

Text: "Whereas several Warrants of Survey of the ungranted Lands of the Crown, have been directed to be made out on behalf of divers Persons who have applied for the same and their Associates: And whereas it is expedient that prior to the issuing of any Grant of Land, enquiry should be made into the Principles and Character of such Persons as may be desirous of becoming Settlers in this Province, before they be admitted to take the Oaths and subscribe the Declaration by His Majesty's Instructions required; Public Notice is hereby given: [etc.]."

French text: "Attendu qu'il a été ordonné de faire plusieurs Warrants ou ordres de mesurage des terres non-concédées de la Couronne, en faveur de diverses personnes qui les ont demandés, ainsi qu'en faveur de leurs associés, et comme il est expédient, avant d'émaner aucune concession de terre, de s'informer des principes et du caractere de ceux qui pourront désirer s'établir en cette Province, et avant qu'ils soient admis à prêter les sermens et à souscrire les déclarations ordonnés d'être requis par les instructions de Sa Majesté, Avis Public [etc.]."

The public notice announces the names of fourteen land commissioners appointed by Gov. Dorchester, at Quebec, Three Rivers, William Henry, Montreal, St. Johns, Chambly, and Missiskoui Bay; also the particulars of information required of persons holding or applying for warrants of survey (a list of all associate and prospective settlers in the grant, their names, former places of abode, etc.); it describes procedure in application; and states penalty for non-compliance to be exclusion from His Majesty's Bounty and from grants of land.

This order was passed by the Council sitting as land board, Oct. 10, 1794, and ordered to "be published in English and French for three weeks in the *Quebec gazette*, and 500 copies by way of Hand bills [to] be struck off."—Can.P.A., L.C. *Land* C, pt. 3, p. 388-89. The printer recorded it:

"1794, Oct. 18. To Executive Council Office 500 Hand bills announcing the appointment of Commissioners for granting lands—£2.10."

—Can.P.A., *Neilson papers*, v. 54, p. 8.

It was designed to prevent persons of democratic tendencies, or otherwise undesirable as settlers and British subjects, from obtaining land as anonymous associates or settlers in township grants. With its amendment of Oct. 20 (No. 879), it was frequently cited and reprinted, e.g., in the *Quebec almanac, 1797*.

Copies located: CaOOA (filed in portfolio: *Miscellaneous newspaper clippings, 1812-1837*); GBLP (2 cop. filed (1) in C.O. 42/109: 717; (2) in C.O. 42/111: 462-63).

879. LOWER CANADA. EXECUTIVE COUNCIL

Executive Council Office, Quebec, 20th October, 1794. / <Text> / By Order of His Excellency the Governor in Council. / J. WILLIAMS. /

French side: Bureau du Conseil Exécutif, Québec, 20 Octobre, 1794. / <Text> / Par Ordre de Son Excellence le Gouverneur en Conseil, / J. WILLIAMS. /

Broadside: English (30 lines) and French (29 lines) in parallel col. type-page: 10.3 × 21 cm.

Text: "Whereas by an advertisement, bearing date the 10th instant inserted in the Quebec gazette of the 16th (No. 1529) Public Notice was given, that all Persons having obtained a Warrant of Survey should give in . . . a list containing . . . particulars [etc.] . . . In Order to obviate . . . [much expence and delay] Public Notice is hereby given that it will be deemed sufficient that the list . . . do contain the name and place of abode of the Leaders and their Associates respectively and the Township, or place in which they propose to settle, only, [etc.]."

French text: "Attendu que par un Avertissement, en date du 10 courant, inséré dans la Gazette de Québec du 16 No. (1529) avis a été donné au Public, que tous ceux qui ont obtenu un Warrant ou ordre de mesurage . . . donnent une Liste contenant les particularités suivantes . . . A fin d'y obvier [beaucoup de frais, et de delai du constatement] Avis Public est donné qu'il sera estimé suffisante que la Liste . . . contiennent seulement le nom et le lieu de residence des conducteurs et les Associés respectivement, et la jurisdiction ou place dans laquelle ils se proposent de s'etablir [etc.]."

Like the order-in-council which it amended, this, too, was ordered published in the *Quebec gazette* (where it appeared Oct. 23, 1794, *et seq.*), and 500 copies struck off by way of hand bills.—Can.P.A., L.C. *Land*, C, pt. 3, p. 390-91. It was recorded by the printer:

"1794, Oct. 21. To Executive Council, To printing 500 Hand bills, English & French respecting grants of land—£1.5."

—Can.P.A., *Neilson papers*, v. 54, p. 9.

Copies located: CaOOA (in portfolio, *Miscellaneous newspaper clippings, 1812-1837*); GBLP (2 cop. filed (1) in C.O. 42/109: 719; (2) in C.O. 42/111: 466-67).

880. LOWER CANADA. GOVERNOR, 1791-1796 (*Dorchester*)

[By His Excellency the Right Honorable Guy Lord Dorchester, Captain General and Governor in Chief in . . . Lower Canada, &c.&c. &c. Proclamation <Text> Given . . . Quebec, 11th December, 1794. Dorchester, By His Excellency's Command Geo. Pownall, Secy. God Save the King.

French side: Par Son Excellence le Très Honorable Guy Lord Dorchester, Capitaine Général et Gouverneur en Chef . . . du Bas-Canada, &c.&c.&c. Proclamation <Text> Donné . . . Québec 11me Décembre 1794. Dorchester. Par Ordre de Son Excellence Geo. Pownall, Sec. Pour vraie Traduction, X. Lanaudiere, AS & T.F.]

Broadside: text in English and French. *Printed at Quebec, by John Neilson,* as recorded:

"1794, Dec. 11. [Debit] Governor's Office for printing 100 copies of a Proclamation for putting in force the Judicature Bill—£1.5."
—Can.P.A., *Neilson papers,* v. 54.

Text: "Whereas in the last Session of the Legislature of this Province, a certain Bill intituled, 'An Act for the division of the Province of Lower Canada, for amending the Judicature thereof, and for repealing certain laws therein mentioned,' was passed . . . and was reserved by Me the Governor . . . for the signification of His Majesty's Pleasure thereon. And Whereas . . . His Majesty in Council hath been graciously pleased to grant His Assent to the same; I have therefore thought fit to declare that the said Bill has thereby become an Act of the Legislature of this Province [etc.] . . . hath full force and legal effect from the Day of Date hereof, and I do require that all Persons govern themselves accordingly."

French text: "Vu que dans la derniere Session de la Legislation de cette Province, un certain Bill intitulé 'Acte qui divise la Province du Bas-Canada, qui amende la judicature d'icelle, et qui rapelle certaines Loix y mentionnées,' a été passé . . . a été réservé par Moi Gouverneur . . . pour la signification du bon plaisir de Sa Majesté sur icelui. Et vû . . . qu'il a plû gracieusement à Sa Majesté en Conseil, de donner Son approbation à icelui, j'ai en conséquence trouvé convenable de déclarer que le dit Bill est devenu par ce moyen un Acte de la Législation de cette Province . . . est en pleine force, et a un effet legal du jour de la date de la présente; et je requiert toutes personnes de s'y conformer en conséquence."

34 Geo. III c. 6, An Act for amending the judicature, passed with other acts of the second session of the legislature of Lower Canada, May 31, 1794, was reserved for royal assent. The formal assent of the king-in-council was despatched to Quebec in the August packet, 1794. The packet was captured and the mail sunk, but Gov. Dorchester, advised in duplicate despatches that assent had been granted, directed, in council, the attorney-general to draw up a proclamation, Nov. 21, 1794. The proclamation, amended Dec. 2 and dated Dec. 11, was ordered published in English and French for three weeks in the *Quebec gazette,* where it appeared Dec. 11-25, 1794. —Can.P.A., L.C. *State* B, Nov. 21-Dec. 2, 1794.

It was also published separately as the printer's record indicates, and is reprinted in Can.P.A., *Report, 1921,* from which the titles and text above are taken.

Copy located: None.

881. LOWER CANADA. HOUSE OF ASSEMBLY

JOURNAL / OF THE / HOUSE OF ASSEMBLY, / OF / LOWER-CANADA. / From the 11th November, 1793, to the 31st May, 1794, / both days inclusive. / IN THE THIRTY-FOURTH YEAR OF THE REIGN OF / KING GEORGE THE THIRD. / [royal arms] / [double rule] / QUEBEC: / PRINTED, BY ORDER OF THE HOUSE OF ASSEMBLY, AND SOLD BY / JOHN NEILSON. / M.DCC.XCIV. /

French t.-p.:

JOURNAL / DE LA / CHAMBRE D'ASSEMBLEE / DU / BAS-CANADA. / Du 11me Novembre 1793, au 31me Mai 1794, / Inclusivement. / DANS LA TRENTE QUATRIEME ANNE'E DU REGNE DE / SA MAJESTE GEORGE TROIS. / [royal arms] / [double rule] / A QUEBEC: / IMPRIME PAR ORDRE DE LA CHAMBRE D'ASSEMBLEE ET A VENDRE / PAR JOHN NEILSON. / M.DCC.XCIV. /

4to. A-2R^4, 2S^2; 323 p., 1 *l.* (errata) inserted at end; type-page: 18 × 12.3 cm. Several sections (in some copies at least) have the chain lines of the paper running vertically as in a large 8vo. Text in English and French on opposite pages.

Contents: p. [1], English t.-p.; p. [2], blank; p. [3], French t.-p.; p. [4]-323, Journal of the second session of the first assembly, Nov. 11, 1793-May 31, 1794; verso of p. 323, blank; recto of *l.* at end, errors to correct; verso, Fautes à corriger.

The House "ordered that 100 copies of the *Journals* . . . for this Session be printed in the English and French languages for the use of the Members of this House under the direction of Samuel Phillips Esq., Clerk of this House . . . [also] that the said Journals be Printed by such person as shall be licensed by Mr. Speaker; and that no other person do presume to Print the same."—L.C. As. *Journal,* May 30, 1794.

Similar resolutions were passed in each succeeding session. The House regularly contributed toward the production at the rate of £125 for a book of 318 pages. The printer sold retail at about 10*s.* the copy, *Journals* printed over and above the hundred ordered by the House. He had the right of remuneration for a net loss on the publication, but does not appear to have required it for any *Journal* after that of the first session.

Copies located: CaO; CaOOA; CaOT (2 cop.); CaOTL; CaQM; CaQMA; CaQMM; CaQQL; CaQQLH; DLC; GBLP (in C.O. 42/103); N; NN; RPJ (all after p. 288, May 16, 1794, wanting); WHi. Errata leaf wanting in CaOOA, CaOT (one copy), DLC, GBLP copies.

882. LOWER CANADA. HOUSE OF ASSEMBLY. SERGEANT-AT-ARMS

[Paper for preventing people from going below in the House of Assembly.]

Broadside, probably in English and French, *printed at Quebec, by John Neilson, 1794,* as recorded:

"1794, April 11. [Debit] Hugh McKay for printing 20 copies of a paper for preventing people from going below in the House of Assembly—7/6."

—Can.P.A., *Neilson papers,* v. 71.

Hugh MacKay, compiler of *The Directory for Quebec, 1790-1791*, was at this time sergeant-at-arms in the House, at a half yearly salary of £37 10*s*. The significance of his prohibitory notice is not clear from this record.

Copy located: None.

883. LOWER CANADA. LAWS, STATUTES, *etc.*

[A Bill to provide for the greater security of this Province by better regulation of the Militia thereof, and for repealing certain Acts or Ordinances relating to the same.

French title: Bill qui pourvoit à la plus grande sûreté de cette Province, par une meilleure organization de la Milice, et qui rappelle certains Actes ou Ordonnances relatifs à icelle.]

4to. about 20 p.; text in English and French. *Printed at Quebec, by John Neilson, 1794*, as recorded:

> "1794, Apr. 4. [Debit] House of Assembly for printing 50 Copies of a Militia Bill, 2½ Sheets pott paper 4to size long primer type—£4.2.6."
>
> —Can.P.A., *Neilson papers*, v. 71.

This bill was drawn up by a committee of the Assembly appointed following the recommendation in Gov. Dorchester's speech opening the legislature on Nov. 11, 1793. It was ordered at its second reading to "be printed with the greatest diligence, and that whatever part thereof may be printed on Saturday next, be delivered to the Members of this House then in town, and the remainder by sheets, as soon as possible."—L.C. As. *Journal*, Tuesday, Apr. 1, 1794 (from which the title above is taken). The bill was hotly debated for seven weeks, finally passing the House with considerable amendment on May 19, 1794, to become 34 Geo. III c. 4.

Copy located: None.

884. LOWER CANADA. LAWS, STATUTES, *etc.*

GEORGE THE THIRD, / KING OF GREAT-BRITAIN, FRANCE AND IRELAND, &c. / AN ACT / Passed in the SECOND SESSIONS [sic] of the LEGISLATURE of / LOWER-CANADA. / IN THE TRIRTY [sic]-FOURTH YEAR OF HIS MAJESTY'S REIGN, / [rule] / To Provide for the Greater Security of this PROVINCE by / Regulating the MILITIA thereof, &c. <31st May 1794.> / [royal arms] / QUEBEC: / PRINTED BY ORDER OF GOVERNMENT, BY JOHN NEILSON, PRINTER TO THE / KING'S MOST EXCELLENT MAJESTY FOR THE PROVINCE OF / LOWER-CANADA; N° 3 Mountain-Street. / [double rule] / 1794. /

French t.-p.:

GEORGE TROIS, / ROI DE LA GRANDE-BRETAGNE DE FRANCE ET D'IRLANDE, &c. / ACTE / Passé dans la SECONDE SESSION de la LEGISLATURE du / BAS-CANADA. / DANS LA TRENTE QUATRIEME ANNEE DU REGNE DE SA / MAJESTE', / Qui pourvoit pour la meilleure surêté de cette PROVINCE par / des réglements concernant la MILICE d'icelle, &c. / <31 May, 1794.> / [royal arms] / A QUEBEC: / IMPRIME' PAR ORDRE DU GOUVERNEMENT, PAR JOHN NEILSON, IMPRIMEUR / A LA TRES EXCELLENTE MAJESTE DU ROI, POUR LA PROVINCE / DU BAS-CANADA.—N° 3, Rue la Montagne. / [double rule] / 1794. /

4to. A-K^{4}; 77 p., 1 *l.*; type-page: 15 × 11.5 cm. Text in English and French on opposite pages.

Contents: p. [1], English t.-p.; p. [2], blank; p. [3], French t.-p.; p. [4]-77, An act, etc.; verso of p. 77, blank; 1 *l.* at end, blank?

The printer recorded this work:

"1794, Aug. 1. [Debit] Governor's Office, 700 Copies of the Militia Ordinance, making 10 Sheets pot quarto size English type in French and English —£36.5.

Sept. 17, [belated entry] for folding and stitching 700 Copies of Militia Act @ 1½*d.*—£4.7.6.

[Total: £40.12.6.]."—Can.P.A., *Neilson papers*, v. 71.

Copies located (*l.* at end wanting in all): CaQ; CaQMS (2 cop.); CaQQL; Ketcheson (p 73-74 mutilated, p. 75 to end wanting).

885. LOWER CANADA. LAWS, STATUTES, *etc.*

[George the third, King of Great Britain, France and Ireland &c. An Act passed in the second session of the Legislature of Lower-Canada, in the thirty-fourth year of His Majesty's reign. To provide for the greater security of this Province by regulating the Militia thereof &c. 31st May 1794.

French title:

George trois, Roi de la Grande Bretagne de France et d'Irlande, &c. Acte passé dans la seconde session de la Legislature du Bas-Canada, dans la trente quatrième année du regne de Sa Majesté Qui pourvoit pour la meilleure surêté de cette Province par des réglements concernant la Milice d'icelle, &c, &c. 31 May 1794.]

fo. about 28 p. Text in English and French. *Printed at Quebec, by John Neilson, 1794*, as recorded:

"1794, Sept. 18. [Debit] Governor's Office for printing 600 copies of the Militia Bill, making 7 sheets crown folio English type @ £1.18. for the 1st hundred and 10/ for every subsequent hundred amount to £34.6."

—Can.P.A., *Neilson papers*, v. 54.

Probably another edition of No. 884, printed on larger paper, from another setting of the same size type.

Of Neilson's charge of £34 6*s.* currency (i.e. £31 17*s.* 5*d.* sterling) for printing this edition, £3 3*s.* sterling was disallowed by the Council for a reason not stated. —Can.P.A., L.C. *State* B, "Demands and allowances, 11 Apr.-10 Oct. 1794."

Copy located: None.

886. LOWER CANADA. LAWS, STATUTES, *etc.*

GEORGE THE THIRD, / KING OF GREAT-BRITAIN, FRANCE AND IRELAND, &c. / AN ACT / Passed in the SECOND SESSIONS [sic] of the LEGISLATURE of / LOWER-CANADA../ IN THE THIRTY-FOURTH YEAR OF HIS MAJESTY's REIGN, / [rule] / For Establishing Regulations respecting ALIENS, and certain Subjects of His / Majesty who have resided in France, coming into this Province, or residing there-/in. And for impowering His Majesty to secure and detain persons charged with or suspected of HIGH TREASON. / And for the Arrest and Commitment of / all Persons who may by SEDITIOUS PRACTICES, attempt to disturb the / Government of this Province. <31st May, 1794.> / [royal arms] / [double rule] / QUEBEC: / PRINTED BY ORDER OF GOVERNMENT, BY JOHN NEILSON, PRINTER TO THE / KING'S MOST EXCELLENT MAJESTY, FOR THE PROVINCE OF / LOWER-CANADA; N° 3, Mountain Street. / [double rule] / M.DCC.XCIV. /

French t.-p.:

GEORGE TROIS, / ROI DE LA GRANDE-BRETAGNE . . . / ACTE / Passé dans la SECONDE SESSION de la LEGISLATURE du / BAS-CANADA. / . . . / [rule] / Qui établit des Réglemens concernant des ETRANGERS, et certain Sujets de Sa / Majesté qui ont résidé en France, . . . / . . . / . . . / . . . / . . . (31 May 1794.) / [royal arms] / [double rule] / A QUEBEC: / IMPRIME' PAR ORDRE DU GGUVERNEMENT [sic] PAR JOHN NEILSON, IMPRIMEUR / . . . / . . . / [double rule] / M.DCC.XCIV. /

4to. A-G⁴; 53 p., 1 *l.*; type-page: 15 × 11.5 cm. Text in English and French on opposite pages. In some copies sig. B wrongly imposed, has pages in the order: 15, 16, 13, 14, 11, 12, 9, 10.

Contents: p. [1], t.-p.; p. [2], blank; p. [3], French t.-p.; p. [4]-53, An act (34 Geo. III c. 5); verso of p. 53, blank; 1 *l.*, blank?

The printer recorded this work:

"1794, Aug. 1. [To printing] 500 Copies of the Alien Act making 7 Sheets Pott 4to size English type in French & English—£18.13.6.

Sept. 17 [belated entry] For folding & stitching 500 Copies of Alien Act @ 1d —£2.1.8.

[Total: £20.15.2]."—Can.P.A., *Neilson papers*, v. 71.

Copies located: CaQMS (3 cop.); CaQQL.

887. LOWER CANADA. LAWS, STATUTES, *etc.*

ABSTRACT of An ACT of the LEGISLATURE of the Province of Lower Canada, / Intituled, "An ACT for establishing REGULATIONS respecting ALIENS and cer-/"tain Subjects of His MAJESTY who have resided in France, coming into this Province or residing / "therein;

and for empowering His MAJESTY to secure and detain Persons charged with or suspected / "of High Treason, and for the arrest and commitment of all Persons who may individually by Seditious / "Practices attempt to disturb the Government of this Province."—PASSED the 31 day of MAY 1794. / [rule] / <Text>

Colophon: [double rule] / QUEBEC: PRINTED BY JOHN NEILSON. M.DCC.XCIV. /

French side:

PRECIS d'un ACTE de la LEGISLATURE de la Province du Bas Canada, intitulé, / "ACTE qui établit des REGLEMENTS touchant les ETRANGERS, et certains Sujets / "du ROI qui ayant résidé en France viennent dans cette Province, ou y resident, et pour autoriser Sa / "MAJESTE' d'arrêter et détenir les gens accusés ou soupconnés de Haute Trahison, et d'arrêter et em- / "prisonner toutes Personnes qui pourront individuellement, par des pratiques Séditieuses, tenter de / "troubler le Gouvernement de cette Province."—PASSEE' le 31 MAI 1794. / [rule] / <Text>

Colophon: [double rule] / A QUEBEC: CHEZ JOHN NEILSON. M.DCC.XCIV. /

Broadside: 139 lines, type-page: 59 × 41 cm. English and French in parallel columns with double rule dividing line.

The text comprises an abstract (1) of the object of the bill (34 Geo. III c. 5) "To prevent the danger which . . . may arise to the Public Tranquility from the Resort and Residence of Persons . . . not being . . . Subjects of His Majesty"; and (2) of its articles, I-XXXIV.

The printer recorded this work:

"1794, Sept. 18, [belated entry] Printing 836 Abstracts of the Alien Act on double Crown, pica Type, at 42/ for 1st hundred and 10/ for each subseqt. hundred, (June 26th)—£5.16."—Can.P.A., *Neilson papers*, v. 54.

Copies located: CaOOA (in portfolio: *Miscellaneous newspaper clippings, 1812-1837*); GBLP (in C.O. 42/99: 453).

Note: Two editions of a covering letter for this publication were *printed at Quebec, by John Neilson, in 1794:*

"1794, June 20. [Debit] Governor's Office 6 Quires Letters to be folded up with the Abstract of the Alien Bill—£1.5.

July 4. 40 additional Copies of a Circular letter on foolscap to cover the Abstract of the Alien Bill—8/4."—Can.P.A., *Neilson papers*, v. 71.

But no further information nor any copy of the covering letter has been found.

888. LOWER CANADA. LAWS, STATUTES, *etc.*

LAWS / OF / LOWER-CANADA, / UNDER THE / CONSTITUTION, erected 26th December, Anno Domini 1791, / PURSUANT TO / ACT OF PARLIAMENT, / IN THE SECOND YEAR OF THE FIRST LEGIS-

LATURE. / [double rule] / [royal arms] / [double rule] / QUEBEC: / PUBLISHED ACCORDING TO THE ORDER OF THE GOVERNMENT, / BY WILLIAM VONDENVELDEN, PRINTER, AT THE NEW-PRINTING-OFFICE, / Mountain-Street, Anno Dom. / M.DCC.XCIV. /

French t.-p.:

LOIX / DU / BAS-CANADA, / SOUS / LA CONSTITUTION érigée le 26 Décembre Anno Domini 1791. / EN CONSEQUENCE D'UN / ACTE DE PARLEMENT, / DANS LA SECONDE ANNE'E DE LA PREMIE'RE LEGISLATION [sic]. / [double rule] / [royal arms] / [double rule] / QUEBEC: / PUBLIE' CONFORMEMENT AUX ORDRES DU GOUVERNEMENT, / Par GUILLAUME VONDENVELDEN, IMPRIMEUR A LA NOUVELLE IMPRIMERIE, / Rue de la Montagne, Anno Dom. / M.DCC.XCIV. /

fo. [A]-L², [*]², M-P²; 2 p. l., [1], 19-72 p.; type-page: 31.3 × 17.6 cm. Apparently paged in continuation of No. 837 Issue B. Odd numbers on verso, even numbers on recto, text in English and French on opposite pages.

Contents: p. l. [1] recto, English t.-p.; verso, blank; p. l. [2] recto, French t.-p.; verso, Contents; p. [1] (recto of p. 19), Table des matières; p. 19-72, Laws (34 Geo. III c. 1-5); verso of p. 72, blank.

The text was apparently printed in sections: 34 Geo. III c. 1-3 are printed without a break on p. 19-28 (sig. B 1 verso-D 2 recto), chap. 3 ending in the middle of p. 28 followed by a printer's ornament. The verso of p. 28 (sig. D 2 verso) is blank and pasted to recto of p. 29 (sig. E1 recto) also blank. Chap. 4 occupies p. 29-54 (sig. E 1 verso-L 2 recto) ending near head of page; the verso of p. 54 (sig. L 2 verso) blank, is pasted to recto of p. 55 (sig. [*] 1 recto) also blank, an unsigned section [* 1-2] being inserted between sig. L and M. Chap. 5 occupies p. 55-72 (sig. [*] 1 verso-P 2 recto). In the pagination the printer allowed for combining the three separately printed sections, and in the signatures he allowed for joining the second and third only. On p. 55-72 the numbering appears somewhat out of position, with a previous numbering 51-68, in the customary position, scratched out. In the contents tables also, a new page number 55-56 replaces a scratched number 51-52 in the entry for chap. V. In some copies seen, however, the original pagination, 51-68, remains unchanged.

This work was printed between June (when Vondenvelden began operating his press) and Oct., 1794, at a cost of £116 10*s.* 10*d.* currency.—Accounts, Apr.-Oct. 1794, in Can.P.A., L.C. *State* B, Jan. 15, 1795. It is a continuation of the first edition of the *Provincial statutes of Lower Canada*, 1792-93, and comprises the laws passed in the second session of the first legislature excepting chapter 6, the Judicature Act, passed with a suspending clause and published later (No. 889). It includes as chapter 1, the act providing for the separate publication of the provincial statutes in *book* form, as distinct from their publication in the *Quebec gazette*.

After this printing of the laws of this session, however, Vondenvelden abandoned the folio format. In 1795 he began printing the provincial statutes from the first session in quarto, using a smaller type and better paper. The quarto series continued with some changes till the provincial legislature of Lower Canada was discontinued in 1838.

It is to be noted that in this work, in place of the imprint of the Brown-Neilson printing house, which had appeared on all official publications since 1764, there appears that of Wm. Vondenvelden. The latter was actually commissioned law printer later, on Aug. 25, 1795.

Copies located: CaO (p. 51-68 numbering unchanged); CaOOA (2 cop., p. 51-68 numbering unchanged in one copy); CaQQL (2 cop.); MH; NN; NNB; RPJ.

889. LOWER CANADA. LAWS, STATUTES, *etc.*

ANNO REGNI / GEORGII III. / REGIS / MAGNÆ BRITANNIÆ, FRANCIÆ ET / HIBERNIÆ / TRICESIMO QUINTO. / At the General Assembly, begun and holden at Que-/bec, the eleventh day of November, Anno Domini 1793, / in the Thirty-third Year of the Reign of our Sovereign / LORD GEORGE THE THIRD, by the Grace of GOD of / Great Britain, France and Ireland KING, Defender of the / faith. &c. / And from thence continued by several Prorogations / to the Thirtieth [sic] Day of May, 1794, being the second / Session of the first General Assembly of / LOWER-CANADA, / [double rule] / [royal arms] / [double rule] / QUEBEC: PUBLISHED ACCORDING TO THE ORDER OF THE GOVERNMENT, / BY WILLIAM VONDENVELDEN, PRINTER AT THE NEW / PRINTING-OFFICE, Mountain-street, Anno Dom. / M.DCC.XCIV. /

French t.-p.:

ANNO REGNI / GEORGII III / REGIS / MAGNÆ BRITANNIÆ, FRANCIÆ ET / HIBERNIÆ / TRICESIMO QUINTO. / A l'Assemblée Général commencée et tenue à Québec, / le Onzieme jour de Novembre, Anno Domini 1793, dans / la Trente-troisieme Année du Regne de Notre Souverain / Seigneur GEORGE TROIS, par la Grace de DIEU, Roi / de la Grande Bretagne, de France et d'Irlande, Défenseur / de la foi &c. / Et de là continuée par plusieurs Prorogations jusqu'au / Trentieme [sic] Jour de Mai, 1794, dans la seconde Session / de la premiere Assemblée Générale du / BAS-CANADA, / [double rule] / [royal arms] / [double rule] / QUEBEC: / PUBLIE' CONFORMEMENT AUX ORDRES DU GOUVERNEMENT, / Par GUILM. VONDENVELDEN, / IMPRIMEUR A LA NOUVELLE IMPRIMERIE, / Rue de la Montagne, Anno Dom: / M. DCC. XCIV. /

fo. [Q]-U^2, [*]^2, V-Y^2, Z^1. 2 p. l., 73-104 p.; type-page: 30-30.5 × 17 cm. Paged in continuation of No. 888. Odd numbers on verso, even numbers on recto, text in English and French on opposite pages. The paper used in this publication varies: some copies are printed on fine white writing paper throughout, others entirely, or in part, on coarse, straw-coloured, or on gray, paper. In the English t.-p. "thirtieth" appears in error for thirty-first "Day of May." In the French t.-p. "trentieme" appears in error for trente unième "Jour de Mai."

Contents: p. l. 1 recto, t.-p.; verso, blank; p. l. 2 recto, French t.-p.; verso, blank; p. [1] (recto of p. 73), blank; p. 73-104, 35 Geo. III Chap. VI, an act for the division of the province of Lower Canada, for amending the judicature thereof, and for repealing certain laws therein mentioned; verso of p. 104, blank.

This is the latter part of the provincial statutes of 1794, issued separately and later than No. 888, and it is the final part of the first (folio) edition of the laws of Lower Canada. Drawn up in the first and passed in the second session of the legislature, this act, with a clause suspending operation till royal pleasure was known, was assented to by Gov. Dorchester, May 31, 1794. Later it received approval of the home government and went into force Dec. 11, 1794.

This act abrogated the legal system based upon the Quebec Act of 1774 and subsequent ordinances, which had produced for years confusion in the courts and occasionally serious dissension in the administration (*see* No. 536 *note*). It provided the first organization of the entire judicial system, dividing the province into judicial districts, laying down organization, personnel, jurisdiction, and sessions of the king's bench, circuit and justices of the peace courts, for civil suits, criminal cases, and preservation of order. It also regulated appeals to governor-in-council and to the king. This system obtained substantially, till the province itself was reorganized after the rebellion of 1837.

Copies located: CaO (fine paper except sig. T on coarse gray stock, 2 p.l. wanting); CaOOA (fine paper throughout, 2 p.l. wanting); CaQM; CaQQL (straw-coloured paper); NN; PHi.

890. LOWER CANADA. LAWS, STATUTES, *etc.*

Caption title: [ornamental rule] / ABSTRACT of the Judicature Bill, to which His Majesty / has granted the Royal Assent, as declared by His Excel-/lency the Governor's Proclamation, on the 11th Dec. 1794. / rule] /

fo. 6 p., 1 fold. table; type-page: 25.5 × 15.5 cm. p. 5 mispaged: 6.

Contents: p. [1]-6, Abstract; fold. table at end: 36 × 48 cm. "Table of Court days to be held annually by the several Courts established under this Act."

Probably printed at Quebec, by Wm. Vondenvelden, 1794, this work, which has format and typography similar to those of No. 888-889, was advertised:

"Just published and for sale at this [Vondenvelden's] office the Judicature Bill [No. 889] also a concise Abstract thereof with a table exhibiting in a ready manner the days of the commencement and continuance of the Terms of the Several Courts, Circuits and general Sessions of the Peace."—*The Times*, Quebec, Dec. 15, 1794. *The Times* of Dec. 22 contains the announcement that the abstract and table of judicature are issued "annexed to this day's paper as an appendage to the Times, to our Subscribers."

No information has been found concerning a French edition of the Abstract.

Copies located: CaO (bound with No. 888, 889); CaOOA (bound with No. 888-889); CaQMM (bound with No. 943).

891. LOWER CANADA. LAWS, STATUTES, *etc.*

[Ordinances relating to the Pilotage in the River St. Lawrence]

8vo. about 16 p. *Printed at Quebec, by John Neilson, 1794,* as recorded:

"1794, May 10. [Debit] Captain Frost, 150 Copies of the Ordinances relating to the Pilotage in the River St. Lawrence, making 2 half Sheets Octavo Demy, in English only, on English type.—£2.10."

—Can.P.A., *Neilson papers*, v. 71.

This is probably another edition of No. 657, printed from larger type, French text omitted. Frost was captain of the port of Quebec.

Copy located: None.

892. LOYAL ASSOCIATION. *Montreal*

ASSOCIATION. [royal arms] ASSOCIATION. / [2 rules] / MONTREAL. / [rule] / <Text and signatures>

Broadside: heading and text in 2 col., English (45 lines) and French (48 lines), subscribers' signatures in 8 col.; type-page (including printed signatures): 49.5 × 34.5 cm.

Text: "It is with infinite concern, we, whose names, are hereunto subscribed have perceived the efforts practised by the enemies of our Parent state, to disseminate the seeds of discontent [in Lower Canada, etc., as in No. 895]. And do declare, that we, the inhabitants of the city and district of Montreal, are firmly attached to our present government [etc.]"; signatures (in 8 col. of type) of J. Fraser, J. Walker, James McGill, and 332 others. This declaration was probably circulated in the town of Montreal soon after its appearance in Quebec (June 30, 1794) then published with, also without, local signatures, and circulated in Montreal district. *See* No. 895 *note*.

Printed from well worn type, somewhat erratically spaced, especially on the French side, with "&" consistently used for "and," all issues of the Montreal edition have a spotty and uncouth appearance. No. 892-894 are printed from the same setting of type, which differs from that of the Quebec edition, No. 895, in details of spelling, punctuation, spacing, etc. They *may have been printed at Quebec, by Wm. Vondenvelden,* like No. 895 or *at Montreal, by Edward Edwards, 1794.* For note on subject matter, *see* No. 895.

Edwards, a stationer-bookseller and postmaster in Montreal acquired type and paper at the auction of the late Fleury Mesplet's stock, Feb. 24-27, 1794. He apparently bought Mesplet's press also, from Sheriff Edward Wm. Gray, and began printing, for he advertised later:

"The Subscriber having purchased the Printing Office which belonged to the late Fleury Mesplet, and since his death has carried on the Printing business, purposes immediately to revive the *Montreal gazette* [etc., signed:] Edward Edwards."

—*Quebec gazette,* July 16, 1795.

Copies located: CaOOA (in Can.P.A., "S" 44, this copy has MS. appendix headed: "Paroisse de Chambly", comprising MS. signatures, marks, etc., dated: "Chambly, 2 Septembre, 1794"; another copy in Can.P.A., "S" 45, endorsed in MS. "Vaudreuil & Soulanges").

893. LOYAL ASSOCIATION. *Montreal*

ASSOCIATION. [royal arms] ASSOCIATION. / [3 rules] /

Broadside: ?*Printed at Montreal, by Edward Edwards, 1794.* Another issue of the Montreal edition of this broadside, printed from the same type and on paper of same size and texture as No. 892 but with Montreal in heading omitted (though retained in the Declaration) and printed signatures omitted. Type-page: 30.6 × 34.5 cm.

Copies located: CaOOA (in Can.P.A., "S" 43-44, are twelve copies with MS. additions. Each is inscribed with the name of a different parish in Lower Canada, and with subscribers' signatures or marks; some are dated July, Aug., or Sept., 1794; some, e.g. Caldwell Manor, bear note: "I do certify that the names and marks or both were done Voluntarily in my presence [signed:] Brunion." The copy from the Parish of Argenteuil, bears notes and signatures on verso: "We the Subscribers, Inhabitants of the Township of Hawkesbury in the County of Glengarry . . . Upper Canada, adhere to the Association of the Inhabitants of the City and District of Montreal Jno Daly Senr").

894. LOYAL ASSOCIATION. *Montreal*

ASSOCIATION. [royal arms] ASSOCIATION. / [3 rules] /

Broadside: ? *Printed at Montreal, by Edward Edwards, 1794.* type-page: 30.5 × 34.5 cm. Another issue of the Montreal edition printed from the same type as No. 892-893, but on heavy writing paper, with "Montreal" omitted from the heading and line 1-3 of the declaration reset to read: ". . . We, the Inhabitants of [blank] in the district of Montreal, [etc.]." Printed signatures are omitted from this issue also.

Copies located: CaOOA (in Can.P.A., "S" 44-45, five copies with blank filled in MS.: "Paroisse de Pointe Claire," "Rivière des Prairies," "Sault aux Recollets," "Ste Anne Bout Lisle," "Ste Genevieve," respectively, and with MS. signatures, etc.).

895. LOYAL ASSOCIATION. *Quebec*

Heading: ASSOCIATION. [royal arms] ASSOCIATION / [3 rules] / <Text, signatures, etc.> /

Colophon: QUEBEC: PRINTED AT THE NEW PRINTING OFFICE. /

Broadside: printed in 2 parallel col. English and French, on two sheets pasted together (head to foot); type-page: 41.5 (upper sheet) + 22.5 (lower sheet) × 36.5 cm. *Printed at Quebec, by Wm. Voldenvelden, 1794.*

Contents: On the upper sheet, heading as above, and preamble: "It is with infinite concern, we, whose names are hereunto subscribed, have perceived the efforts practised by the enemies of our Parent state, to disseminate the seeds of discontent [in Lower Canada] . . . designing and wicked men by every Art are endeavouring to seduce the easy and credulous minds of our fellow subjects; . . . foreign emissaries, or seditious characters, are concealed among us, . . . by such arts . . . the merciless hand of desolating power has attained the supreme authority in France . . . subjects have murdered a lawful and acknowledged Sovereign . . . have persecuted and destroyed the ministers of the established Roman Catholic Church . . . and profaned the Holy Altars of God [etc.]."

Declaration: "That We the Inhabitants of the city and district of Quebec are firmly attached to our present Government ... That we hold in the utmost abhorrence, the seditious attempts lately made by wicked and designing men, in circulating false and inflammatory writings ... That we will ... use our utmost endeavours to counteract the efforts of seditious men [etc.]."

Signatures of Thomas Dunn, Francis Baby and 156 others, all printed from type; also the note: "Since this paper issued from the Press, the Citizens of this city come daily to join and sign the Association. Quebec, Monday, 30th June, 1794."

Contents on lower sheet, pasted to the *Declaration* above: minutes, dated: "City of Quebec, June 30, 1794." The minutes record a meeting on the 28th instant to organize an association "for the purposes of supporting the Laws, Constitution and Government of ... Lower Canada"; also the text of an *Address* to Gov. Dorchester begging his sanction of the association; and Dorchester's *Answer*, both dated: "Quebec 30th June, 1794." Below this, at foot of the lower sheet, appears the colophon quoted above.

This association, denominated in contemporary records as the "Loyal Association," appears to have been a "paper" organization, promoted by the administration in towns, villages, and parishes of Lower Canada, by publication of the Quebec declaration of June 30, 1794. Adherents were attracted by the example of local militia as signatories and by guidance of most of the Catholic clergy. The "members" of the association seem to have owed no dues or duties other than support of the government's campaign against French revolutionary agents in Lower Canada. A strong committee, of which Thomas Dunn, executive and legislative councillor, was chairman, directed activities in Quebec, militia and other officers of the crown gathered signatures in smaller communities. The declaration of June 30, was probably prepared by Attorney-General James Monk, who, as attorney-general of Nova Scotia, had seen, he reported, "during the Rebellion of 1775 ... the salutory effects of Associations and renewed Oaths of allegiance ... to check the progress of disaffection and draw forth a power to resist every open attempt against the execution of Law and resistence to His Majesty's government. [The Quebec Association was designed] to embrace all men by at least an open declaration, that obedience to, and aiding every possible exertion for the support of, the Laws and Government, was the duty of every good Subject. And thus silence the Traiterous voice of sedition and divest the prejudiced mind from passing upon those Trials that must happen, upon the criminals in custody, and which prior to such an event, I do not think could safely have proceeded." Monk continued his report of July 12, 1794, describing his measures to discover persons "tampered with by consuls' agents of the usurped power in France," who were distributing the pamphlet "*Les Françaises libres à leurs Frères les Canadiens,*" his efforts to suppress disaffection and disorder in Montreal, insurrection at Charlesbourg, and his arrest of the alleged leaders. He reported to Gov. Dorchester again, Oct. 2, 1794, that the "Association has extended to almost every part of the Province and has embraced the warm, or at least the apparent, approbation of at least two thirds of His Majesty's subjects ... has operated as a test to mark out refractory or disloyal subjects. Arrests have been made ... of persons who have held seditious and traiterous discourses, and others who have excited a disobedience to the Militia Laws." Monk continued, pointing out how the Association—and the arrests—had increased the number of French Canadians who reported for the annual militia review of July, 1794; noting the convictions already effected in his prosecutions for high treason and those he anticipated in the November court session.

Attorney-General Monk's reports were enclosed in Gov. Dorchester's despatches to Secretary of State Dundas, from Quebec, July 12, Oct. 5, 1794 (transcribed in Can.P.A., "Q" 68: 199 *et seq.*, and in *ibid.*, 69, pt. 1: 110 *et seq.*); they were also sent by Monk directly to Dundas with copies of the broadside declarations (transcribed in Can.P.A., "Q" 69, pt. 2: 326-57).

The stress laid upon the Association as an instrument of policy during war, and the function of the broadsides with their MSS. addenda, as sources of information, account for the location of extant copies. These copies (with a single exception) are filed with 18th-century records in official custody.

Copies located: CaOOA (in Can.P.A., "S" 45); GBLP (3 cop. in C.O. 42/99: 621, also 625; and in C.O. 42/100: 741, respectively); Ketcheson (with MS. notes, including "Association Quebec 30th June, 1794—generally adopted throughout Canada and sighed by upwards of Fifteen Hundred in Quebec & as many in Montreal").

896. LOYAL ASSOCIATION. *Quebec*

MESSIEURS <Text, signed:> Votre très humble serviteur, Th.D. [i.e. Thomas Dunn] Chairman, Québec le [blank] Juillet, 1794.

Broadside, about 500 words in French only. *Probably printed at Quebec, by Wm. Vondenvelden, 1794.*

Text begins: "Le Comité d'Association s'adresse avec confiance à des caractères tels que les votres. . . . En transmet tant pour votre information générale des copies imprimées de l'Association et de nos procédés, le Comité ne présume pas désirer que précisement le meme Association soit adoptée partout [etc.]."

This is a circular letter prepared to accompany copies of the Declaration of June 30, and minutes of proceedings, of the Quebec Association (No. 895) distributed in the country districts. It states that the form used in Quebec need not be used by other groups, but gives instructions for the inscribing of signatures and marks of declarants. It gives also a résumé of the objects and advantages of the Association.

Declarations with signatures from places outside Quebec were published in the *Quebec gazette*, July 17, 1794 *et seq.*

Copy located: GBLP (in C.O. 42/100: 743, enclosed in Attorney-General Monk's report to Secretary of State Dundas, July 5, 1794. It bears the MS. inscription: "Circular, through the whole province; By proper aids").

897. LOYAL ASSOCIATION. *Quebec*

ASSOCIATION. / [rule] / To the Loyal Inhabitants of the City and district of Quebec. / <Text> / By order of the Committee, / THOMAS DUNN, Chairman. / Quebec, 1st July, 1794. /

Broadside: 23 lines; type-page: 23 × 17.5 cm.

Text: The committee appointed for conducting the business of the Association give notice that two of its members will attend at the committee room of the House of Assembly in the Bishop's Palace till July 10, to receive "the signatures of such persons as have not already joined the Association" or to take "the names of those who do not write but wish to join it." The Committee charges members to point out "to all ranks of people with whom they may have occasion to mix either in town or country . . . the salutary effects . . . in forming such Associations in every part of the Country."

This notice appeared with the text of the declaration of June 30, and a long list of Quebec signatories in the *Quebec gazette*, July 10, 1794, *et seq.*

Copies located: GBLP (in C.O. 42/100: 752); Ketcheson.

898. NEW BRUNSWICK. HOUSE OF ASSEMBLY

JOURNAL / OF THE / VOTES and PROCEEDINGS / OF THE / HOUSE OF ASSEMBLY / OF THE / PROVINCE of NEW-BRUNSWICK: / From TUESDAY the 4th to THURSDAY the 27th of FE-/BRUARY, 1794. / [ornamental rule] / [royal arms] / [ornamental rule] / BROOK-VILLE: / Printed by CHRISTOPHER SOWER, Printer to the / KING'S MOST EXCELLENT MAJESTY. 1794. / [title within a frame of flower pieces]

fo. A-L²; 1 p. l., [343]-84 p., 1 fold. table; type-page: 23 × 13.5 cm. Paged in continuation of No. 843. One leaf of sig. L is folded around sig. A-K to form t.-p.

Contents: p. l. recto, t.-p.; verso, blank; p. [343]-84, Journal of the second session of the second assembly; fold. table, correctly inserted between p. 364-65, is ". . . Account of Merchandize imported into the Port of Saint John . . . [Feb. 15, 1793-Feb. 4, 1794] subject to a Duty at the Treasury Office."

Two hundred copies of the *Journal* and three hundred copies of the *Acts* (No. 899) of this session were ordered by the House to be printed, to be distributed by the government as in previous years. It was further resolved, as in each session since 1789, that the printer's bill be paid in the recess by the governor, the House making good the sum in its supply bill next session.—N.B. As. *Journal*, Feb. 25, 1794.

The works were long printing, for Lieut.-Gov. Carleton transmitted the *Acts* to the secretary of state, only on July 2, saying that the *Journals* were not yet received from the printer and would be sent later. Sower's bill "for printing the Acts of Assembly and Journals of last Session—£60.13.4." was duly passed by governor-in-council, Sept. 5, 1794.—Can.P.A., N.B.Ex.co. *Minutes.*

Copies located: CaN (t.-p. wanting); CaNU; CaOOA; RPJ.

899. NEW BRUNSWICK. LAWS, STATUTES, *etc.*

[Act For the better Regulating the Militia in this Province.
Printed at Saint John, N.B., by John Ryan? 1794.]

It is not certain whether John Ryan or Christopher Sower printed this Act. The latter's account for printing the *Acts* and *Journals* of the 1794 session does not include this item, nor does Ryan's account for sundry printing for government specify this item.

A measure to raise militia for local defence, recommended by Lieut.-Gov. Carleton in his speech opening the Legislature, Feb. 4, 1794, was prepared by Solicitor-General Ward Chipman and a committee of the Assembly. It was passed with an order that "two hundred copies of the Bill be immediately printed and distributed as . . . the Lieutenant governor shall . . . direct."—N.B. As. *Journal*, Feb. 26, 1794.

A year previously, Feb. 8, 1793, Secretary of State Dundas had instructed Carleton to raise a regiment of six hundred men for local defence in order to release the British troops stationed in the province for service elsewhere in the anticipated war with France. Recruiting for the King's New Brunswick Regiment began in Apr., 1793, but only 271 enlistments were made by October. The militia act, passed in February, required every able-bodied man of sixteen to sixty years to enroll in some company and to supply himself with arms. Civil and military officers and members of the legislature were exempted from enrolment, clergy and physicians were excused from carrying arms at muster. This act continued in force till 1802. Enlistment in the King's New Brunswick Regiment increased to 450 by July, 1794. It garrisoned Fredericton, Saint John, and other posts held by British troops who were sent to Barbadoes. *See* J. Hannay: *History of New Brunswick* (2 v., Saint John, N.B., 1909), I: 241; *also* J. Howe: *The King's New Brunswick Regiment 1793-1802,* in N.B. hist. soc. *Coll.* 1: 13-62, 1894.

Copy located: None.

900. NEW BRUNSWICK. LAWS, STATUTES, *etc.*

ACTS / OF THE / GENERAL ASSEMBLY / OF / His MAJESTY'S PROVINCE / OF / NEW-BRUNSWICK, / PASSED IN THE YEAR 1794. / [ornamental rule] / [royal arms] / [ornamental rule] / BROOKVILLE: / Printed by CHRISTOPHER SOWER, Printer to the / KING'S MOST EXCELLENT MAJESTY. 1794. / [title within a frame of flower pieces]

fo. [*[1], **[2]], A-F[2]; 3 p. l., 294-316 p.; type-page: 23 × 13.4 cm. Even numbers on recto, odd numbers on verso; paged in continuation of No. 844.

Contents: p. l. 1 recto, t.-p.; verso, blank; p. l. 2 recto, half title; verso, blank; p. l. 3 recto, Titles of the acts; verso, blank; p. 294-316, 34 Geo. III c. I-IX acts passed in the second session of the second assembly; verso of p. 316, blank.

An edition of 300 copies was printed for distribution by the government. *See* No. 898 *note.*

Copies located: Baxter; CaNsWA; CaOOA; DLC; GBLP (in C.O. 188/5: 381-441); MH; NNB.

901. NOVA SCOTIA. HOUSE OF ASSEMBLY

[rule] / JOURNAL / AND / PROCEEDINGS / OF THE / HOUSE of ASSEMBLY. / [rule] /

fo. sig. S-2H[2]; 1 p. l., 71-127 p.; type-page: 25 × 15 cm. paged in continuation of No. 845. *Printed at Halifax, N.S., by Anthony Henry, 1794.*

Contents: p. l. recto, t.-p.; verso, Proclamation; p. 71-127, Journal of the second session of the seventh assembly, June 6-July 9, 1794; verso of p. 127, blank.

Copies located: CaNs (p. 93-96, 123 to end, wanting); CaNsHA; CaOT; GBLP (in C.O. 217/66: 141-70); MH.

902. NOVA SCOTIA. LAWS, STATUTES, *etc.*

Running title: [rule] / 1794. Anno Tricessimo Quarto Regis, GEORGII III. CAP. I[-VI]. / [rule] /

Caption title: At the GENERAL ASSEMBLY of the Province / of Nova-Scotia, . . . / [5 lines] / being the Second Session of the Seventh / General Assembly, convened in the said Pro-/vince. / [rule] /

fo. sig. 3L-3M²; 359-365 p.; type-page: 25 × 15 cm. paged in continuation of No. 846. *Printed at Halifax, N.S., by Anthony Henry, 1794.*

Contents: p. 359-365, Cap. I-VI, perpetual acts passed in the session, June 6-July 9, 1794; verso of p. 365, blank.

Copies located: CaO; DLC; MH (2 cop.).

903. NOVA SCOTIA. LAWS, STATUTES, *etc.*

Running title: [rule] / 1794. Anno Tricessimo Quarto Regis, GEORGII III. CAP. I[-XI]. / [rule] /

Caption title: At the GENERAL ASSEMBLY of the Province / of Nova-Scotia, . . . / [5 lines] / being the Second Session of the Seventh / General Assembly, convened in the said Pro-/vince. / [rule] /

fo. sig. 4A-4H²; 389-419 p.; type-page: 25.5 × 15 cm. paged in continuation of No. 847. *Printed at Halifax, N.S., by Anthony Henry, 1794.*

Contents: p. 389-419, Cap. I-XI, temporary acts passed in the session, June 6-July 9, 1794; verso of p. 419, blank.

Copies located: CaO; MH; NNB.

904. NOVA SCOTIA. LAWS, STATUTES, *etc.*

[An Act in addition to, and Amendment of, an Act passed in the Thirty-first year of His present Majesty's Reign, entitled "An Act to raise a Revenue . . . also in Addition to, and Amendment of an Act passed in the thirty-third year of His present Majesty's Reign to amend and render more productive the Act aforesaid.]

Broadside, *Printed at Halifax, N.S., by Anthony Henry, 1794,* as recorded:

"Aug. 13, 1794. To printing the Poll-tax Law separate [on full face, extra.] —£1.10."—Henry's *Account [to Government] for Stationery &c. June-Aug. 1794* in P.A.N.S., *Miscellaneous Assembly papers,* 1795, also *ibid.,* 1796.

By 31 Geo. III c. 12, An act to raise a revenue for the purpose of paying off all debts as are now due by the Province etc., a poll tax, also called the Capitation tax, of 2*s.* 6*d.* to 10*s.* was levied on farmers, professional, and salaried persons. Its scope was extended by 33 Geo. III c. 2. It remained an extremely unpopular tax and a law difficult of enforcement. In 1794, 34 Geo. III c. 8 provided new regulations for assessors, collectors, and the manner of remitting returns to the Excise Office at Halifax; it provided also new penalties for non-observance.

Copy located: None.

905. NOVA SCOTIA. LIEUTENANT-GOVERNOR, 1792-1808 (*Wentworth*)

[A Proclamation By His Excellency, John Wentworth, Lieutenant Governor of Nova Scotia <Text> Halifax, 24th March, 1794.]

Broadside, *Printed at Halifax, N.S., by Anthony Henry, 1794*, as recorded:

"[1794] To printing proclamations Broadside, for a general fast, on account of the Wars—£1.10.

To 8 Quires demy for printing [ditto] 10/6.

[Total: £2.0.6.]."—Henry's *Account for extra printing [for government] 1792-94*, in P.A.N.S., *Miscellaneous Assembly papers*, 1794.

Text: "Whereas a solemn fast has lately been observed throughout His Majesty's Dominions in Europe on account of the War . . . with France, [I proclaim] . . . a like public fast and Humiliation throughout this province . . . Friday the 25th day of April [1794, etc., the Bishop of Nova Scotia being directed to prepare a prayer for the occasion]."

The proclamation was also published in the *Royal gazette*, Halifax, N.S., Mar. 25-Apr. 22, 1795, whence this entry was taken.

Copy located: None.

906. QUEBEC BENEVOLENT SOCIETY

RULES AND REGULATIONS / OF THE / QUEBEC BENEVOLENT SOCIETY, / ESTABLISHED THE FIRST WEDNESDAY IN MAY, / M.DCC.LXXXIX. / [rule] / [printer's ornament] / [rule] / [double rule] / QUEBEC: / PRINTED BY JOHN NEILSON, M.DCC.XCIV. / [rule] /

French t.-p.:

REGLES ET REGLEMENS / DE LA / SOCIETE' BIENVEILLANTE / DE QUEBEC, / ETABLIE LE PREMIER MECREDI [sic] DE MAI, / M.DCC.LXXXIX. / [rule] / [ornament] / [rule] / [double rule] / A QUEBEC: / DE L'IMPRIMERIE DE JOHN NEILSON, / M.DCC.XCIV. / [rule] /

12mo. A-C[6], D[4]; 43 p.; type-page: 13 × 7 cm. Text in English and French on opposite pages.

Contents: p. [1], English t.-p.; p. [2], blank; p. [3], French t.-p.; p. [4]-37, Rules (i.e., p. [4-5], preamble; p. [6]-37, rules no. 1-20); p. 38-39, List of members, Feb. 5, 1794; p. 38-43, Certificate forms; verso of p. 43, blank.

This is another edition of No. 853, revised and reprinted from another setting of type throughout.

The preamble states that "in view of the local situation of this country, the incidents of distress it was exposed to, and no legal provision being made for the same, a plan was proposed [at a meeting at the Merchants' Coffee House, Quebec, Apr. 25, 1789] to form a society in imitation of those useful ones of the mother country and to establish a fund for the mutual support of members in sickness, blindness, lameness and the infirmities of age, [etc.]." Rules were drawn up in 1789 (*see* No. 616), of which, on June 5, 1793, a revision was resolved. The revised *Rules* were printed for members' consideration in Aug., 1793 (*see* No. 853) then amended and published with a list of numbers' names and benefit certificate forms, 1794, to be purchased by all members at 1*s*. 6*d*. the copy.

In the *Rules* of 1794, the original admission fee was doubled to £2 6*s*. 8*d*., checks on frauds and abuses were increased, and the limit on number of members raised to 54. The temper of the times is reflected in a new rule that any member convicted of felony, perjury, treason, or misprision of treason, should be excluded from the Society. In its five years, the Society had acquired six French members and now published its *Rules* in English and French. Its former printer, Wm. Moore, a charter member, had ceased business, and its work was now printed at the shop of young John Neilson, who became a member in 1800, and who recorded this printing:

"1794, Mar. 1. [Debit] Quebec Benevolent Society for printing their Rules & Regulations (in August last) making 2 Sheets Demy on English Type, 60 copies—£4.10.

Reprinting the same with alterations, 150 copies, £3.10. [Total:] £8."

—Can.P.A., *Neilson papers*, v. 71.

Copies located: CaQM; CaQMS (mutilated and all before p. [5] wanting); CtY.

907. QUEBEC GAZETTE. CARRIER'S ADDRESS

VERSES / Of the Printer's Boy / WHO CARRIES THE QUEBEC GAZETTE / To the Customers. / [rule] / JANUARY 1st, 1795. /

French side:

CHANSON, / Du Garçon qui porte la / GAZETTE DE QUEBEC / AUX PRATIQUES. / [rule] / Le Ier JANVIER, 1795. / [rule] / Sur un Air très-connu. / [*Quebec, J. Neilson, 1794.*]

Broadside: type-page: 33 × 28 cm. English verse on left, 62 lines; French on right, 77 lines in 2 col. Each address has a strong popular appeal to its own language group in Canada, the English on a democratic theme, celebrating the common man, after the style set by Robert Burns; the French exuding loyalty to Establishment, and distrust of liberty, equality, and fraternity.

English side:

"...
Since you no Horace are, 'tis clear,
'Tis fit you in your shape appear;
And, to the world, behave as civil,
As can do a poor printer's devil.
Is it for you, you scurvy knave,
With a *sous* your soul to save,
The great or rich to dare attack,
And bring them all upon your back?
You! you poor dog, have an opinion!
As soon they judge you a civilian.
You who, on foot, like pedlars stroll
Nor once, at ease, in carriage roll.
You're nobody—to no one known,
To you what favour can be shewn?
Where's your credentials, from below?
...
Or where did you the right receive,
By reason or by rhime to live?
Plead you the right of hands and head?
Poor fool, they stand you in little stead.
[etc.]."

French side:

"...
La Liberté
Cause en nos jours bien du tapage
La Liberté
Avec Sa Soeur l'Egalité
Font un effroyable ravage
Et font gémir par leur carnage
L'humanité.

" Distinguons bien
Entre liberté et licence
Distinguons bien
L'une a les Loix pour son soutien
L'autre met tout en décadence
Sachons faire la differencè
Du mal au bien.

" Soumis aux loix
Ici, dans un sens politique
Soumis aux loix,
Le sujet jouit de tous ses droits
Du Gouvernement Britanique
Admirons la sage fabrique
Les justes loix.
[etc.]."

Copy located: CaO (bound in *Quebec gazette* at end of 1794).

908. QUEBEC THEATRE

[Playbill]

Broadside: *Printed at Quebec, by John Neilson, 1794,* as recorded:

"1794, Mar. 28. Printed for Theatre 100 Playbills on folio pott—10/."
—Can.P.A., *Neilson papers*, v. 71.

No information appears on the title of the play. This is the first playbill recorded in the Brown-Neilson books since 1788. From 1788-93, however, Wm. Moore, an active thespian, operated a printing press in Quebec, and probably printed the theatre's playbills.

Copy located: None.

909. ST. JOHN, ISLAND OF. LIEUTENANT-GOVERNOR, 1786-1804 (*Fanning*)

[Proclamation appointing a Public Fast day, Saturday 10th May, 1794, "to be observed throughout this Island as a day of public Fasting and Humiliation to implore the Pardon, Protection and Interposition of Almighty God to avert those dreadful evils which the Levelling Atheistic System of France and the Calamities of War threaten."]

Broadside: *Printed? at Charlottetown, Island of St. John, by Wm. A. Rind, 1794.*

The proclamation (as above) was read in Council and ordered to be issued, Apr. 27, 1794.—Can.P.A., P.E.I., "B" 1794. It is not clear, however, whether it was issued as a *printed* broadside in the Island of St. John, as it was in the other provinces, or not.

Copy located: None.

910. ST. JOHN, ISLAND OF. LIEUTENANT-GOVERNOR, 1786-1804 (*Fanning*)

[Notification. <Text, concerning enlistment of a militia corps, signed:> Edmund Fanning, Charlotte Town, Island of S^t. John, May 12, 1794.]

Broadside: paper-page: 40.5 × 30 cm. *Printed at Charlottetown, Island of St. John, by Wm. A. Rind, 1794.*

The text begins: "The Undersigned Edmund Fanning, Colonel of the King's (late) American Regiment of Foot . . . has the happiness to inform his Majesty's Loyal and dutiful Subjects . . . [of] the King's Commands . . . for raising . . . a corps not exceeding two hundred men . . . for the service of this Island [etc.]." The notice continues, stating that the militia corps is being raised for a "defensive war against the leaders of a Convention in France, . . . usurping Powers . . . and inculcating principles fatally ruinous to the Lives, Fortunes and Liberties of . . . fellow-subjects, utterly subversive to all loyal government and, if unresisted, justly alarming to the . . . constitutional government of every other Nation." To persons enlisting in the militia corps, the government offers a bounty of two guineas, quarters, the usual pay, and "accoutrements becoming a gentleman Volunteer Soldier in the Service of his King." To this Fanning adds his own offer of one hundred acres granted from his private lands, free but for quit rent, to every man enlisting before Nov. 1., 1794.

Title and text as above is taken from MS. transcript in Can.P.A., "M" 406D, p. 171-74, of the only printed copy located.

Copy located: GBLP (in C.O. 226/14, copy enclosed in Fanning's letter to Secretary of State Dundas, dated: "Charlotte Town 22^d May, 1794").

911. TASCHEREAU, GABRIEL ELZEAR, 1745-1809

[Paper for repairing Highways & Bridges]

fo. 2 p. Text probably in English and French on opposite pages. *Printed at Quebec, by John Neilson, 1794,* as recorded:

> "1794, May 17. [Debit] Gabriel Elzeard [sic] Taschereau, 100 Copies of a paper for repairing Highways & Bridges, making 2 pages on pott folio English type. 1 on a sheet.—£1.7.6."—Can.P.A., *Neilson papers*, v. 71.

Following a resolution in the House of Assembly, Dec. 7, 1793, "that the state of High Roads and Bridges in this Province requires the attention of the Legislature," a committee (Mathew MacNider, English merchant in Quebec, chairman) reported a bill on Mar. 5, 1794, for better making, amending, and repairing high roads, etc. Consideration of the bill was effectually stalled on May 14 by Taschereau (L.C. As. *Journal*, 1793-94). The latter, a seigneur representing the County of Dorchester, was appointed grand voyer (overseer of roads) for the district of Quebec in 1794, and himself introduced a highway and bridges bill in the 1795 session, which became 36 Geo. III c. 9.

The *Paper* printed by Neilson was apparently connected with Taschereau's efforts to postpone MacNider's bill.

Copy located: None.

912. THAYER, JOHN, 1758-1815

RELATION / DE LA / CONVERSION / DE / MR. THAYER, / Ministre Protestant, / ECRITE PAR LUI-MEME. / [printer's ornament] / A QUEBEC: / CHEZ LOUIS GERMAIN, N° 5, [sic] / Imprimé à la Nouvelle Imprimerie. /

8vo. A-H^{4}; 63 p.; type-page: 11.5 × 6.8 cm.

Contents: p. [1], t.-p.; p. [2], blank; p. [3]-29, Relation; p. [30]-63, "Lettre ou l'on rapporte ce que Mr. Thayer a fait de plus remarkable depuis son depart de Rome pour Paris, jusqu'à son embarquement pour Boston, et depuis son arrivée dans cette ville, jusqu'à present. [dated:] A Paris, ce 28 Septembre, 1790"; verso of p. 63, blank.

Lettre, p. 30-63, was apparently written by F. C. Nagot, the superior of Le Petit Séminaire de Saint Sulpice, Paris, where Thayer studied. This letter replaces in this edition Thayer's letter to his brother and the "Letter from a Young Lady," which usually appeared with his *Relation.*

This edition was printed probably by Wm. Vondenvelden after June, 1794, when the new printing office opened, for Louis Germain Jr., no. 5, rue de la Fabrique. It was not advertised in Vondenvelden's newspaper, *The Times,* which ran from Aug., 1794 to July, 1795. And the further circumstance that all copies seen were printed on paper with watermarks dated 1794, suggests that this edition was printed at least a year later. *See,* however, P. Merritt: *Bibliographical notes on "Account of the conversion of . . . Thayer,"* in Colonial Society of Massachusetts, *Publications,* 25: 129-40, 1924; *also* Sabin, no. 95248, where it is suggested by Ægidius Fauteux, that this edition was current in Montreal in 1791.

Written in English, this work was published in 18 pamphlet editions between 1787 and 1800 in English, French, Spanish, Portuguese, German, and Latin. Of the four French editions, one is known to have been printed in Quebec. Thayer, a native of Boston, educated at Yale, was a free lance Congregationalist minister in Boston, then an American army chaplain. He joined the Catholic church on May 25, 1783 and, trained by the Sulpicians in Paris, became a priest of great popularity in the United States, England, and Ireland.

Copies located: CaOT; CaQ; CaQM; CaQMS; CaQQL (p. 3-6, wanting).

913. THE TIMES, *Quebec*

A Specimen of / one half sheet of the Weekly / paper, intended / to be published / under the name / OF / THE TIMES. / [rule] / [in centre: royal arms] /

French side: Essay d'une dé-/mie feuille du / papier hebdo-/madaire, pro-/posé d'être pub-/lié sous le nom / DE / LE COURS DU TEMS. /

Colophon: QUEBEC: PRINTED BY WM. VONDENVELDEN at the NEW PRINTING- / OFFICE, Mountain-street. /

French side: QUÉBEC: IMPRIME' par GUILM. VONDENVELDEN, à la NOUVELLE IM-/ PRIMERIE, rue la Montagne. /

4to. 4 p. printed in 2 col. English and French; type-page: 25 × 19 cm.

Contents: p. [1]-2, the printer-editors' address to readers; p. 2-3, shipping and other brief news items; p. 4, advertisements (by the printer, Vondenvelden, and by John Jones, auctioneer).

The address to readers (unsigned) states: "The arrival of our Press and its attendant compleat apparatus enables us to open THE NEW-PRINTING-OFFICE and to commence Typographical labors. Anxious to accelerate our publication, as announced in our preparatory address of December last, we now present to the Publick this specimen and prospectus of our intended weekly paper under the designation of THE TIMES, the first sheet of which will make its appearance so soon as a sufficient number of Subscribers will put it in our power to carry our plan into effect [etc.].

". . . free from the presumption of deeming our task as editors, an easy one we are sensible of the difficulties we have to encounter . . . [Our aims are] to give pleasure and satisfaction to every individual . . . to make this paper the vehicle of moral instruction, a miscellany of pleasing subjects [etc.]."

The newspaper thus proposed began regular publication on Aug. 4, 1794, and appeared weekly for one year.

The New Printing-Office thus announced was advertised at the same time as "now completely fitted up at the house of Mr. Rollette, nearly the middle of the hill from Upper to the Lower-town [where] all kinds of hand and funeral bills, blanks of all sorts . . . will be executed on reasonable terms with accuracy neatness and despatch [etc.]." It had as original joint proprietors John Jones (? the auctioneer and broker) and William Vondenvelden, the printer. Vondenvelden became sole owner in May, 1795, and operated the press till early in 1798. Then Roger Lelievre and Pierre-Edouard Desbarats acquired the New Printing-Office, which had moved several times, and Desbarats continued the business till well into the 19th century.

Copy located: CaOOA (in *The Times* file).

914. THE TIMES, *Quebec.* CARRIER'S ADDRESS

The PRINTER'S BOY of the / TIMES. / To the SUBSCRIBERS. / [rule] / [*Quebec, Wm. Vondenvelden, 1794.*]

Broadside: type-page: 25 × 19 cm. in ornamental rule frame. 7 stanzas (64 lines) printed in 2 col. with footnotes dated at end: "QUEBEC, 1st JANUARY, 1795." They are lightsome verses on the Liberty-Equality-Fraternity theme, beginning:

"Citizens, Male and female all,
I dare not call you great and small;
For 'tis decreed, all must, you know,
In bulk and height, both *equal* grow.
[etc.]."

Copy located: CaO (bound in *Quebec gazette* at end of 1794).

915. UPPER CANADA. EXECUTIVE COUNCIL

Executive Council Chamber, / Of the Province of Upper Canada, / November 6, 1794. / Present in Council his Excellency JOHN GRAVES SIMCOE, / Esquire, / Lieutenant Governor and Commander in Chief of the said Province, and Colonel commanding / his Majesty's Forces &c.&c.&c. / [double rule] / [royal arms]

WHEREAS the existing state of the Province renders / the continuation of the Boards established expressly for the pur-/poses of facilitating the settling of such lands as his Majesty, in / his royal Beneficence has been pleased to grant to the Loyalists and redu-/ced troops, inexpedient and unnecessary, It is hereby resolved that the / authority heretofore granted to such Boards, shall, from and after the sixth / day of November, one thousand and seven hundred and ninety-four, cease and determine. / [etc.]"

Broadside: 55 lines (including rules); type-page: 22.5 × 15 cm. *Printed at Newark, U.C., probably by Gideon Tiffany, 1794.*

Signed by John Small, clerk of the Council, this order-in-council provides for the lieutenant-governor-in-council to take over the duties of the land boards. Appended to the end of the text is a list of the fees payable to various officials for services connected with the granting of land.

Copies located: CaOT (3 cop.); GBLP (in C.O. 42/319: 225).

916. UPPER CANADA. EXECUTIVE COUNCIL

Executive Council Chamber, / Of the Province of Upper Canada, / November 6, 1794. / Present in Council his Excellency JOHN GRAVES SIMCOE, Esquire, / Lieutenant Governor and Commander in Chief of the said Province, and Colonel commanding / his Majesty's Forces, &c.&c.&c. [double rule] /

WHEREAS the existing state of the Province renders the / continuation of the Boards established expressly for the purposes of fa-/cilitating the settling of such lands as his Majesty, in his Royal Benefi- / cence has been pleased to grant to the Loyalists and reduced troops, inexpedient / and unnecessary, It is hereby resolved, that the authority heretofore granted to / such Boards, shall, from and after the sixth day of November, one thousand seven / hundred and ninety-four, cease and determine. / [etc.]

Broadside: 55 lines (including rules); type-page: 22 × 16 cm. *Printed at Newark, U.C., probably by Gideon Tiffany, 1794.*

Signed: "J. Small, C.C." this is another edition of No. 915, with slight changes in text, typography, and additional note at end: "N.B. This list includes fees to all persons concerned in granting lands, except to the Provincial Land Officers of the crown."

Copy located: CaOT.

917. UPPER CANADA. LIEUTENANT-GOVERNOR, 1791-1799 (*Simcoe*)

J.G.S. / Proclamation. / [rule] / UPPER CANADA. / [royal arms] GEORGE the Third by the Grace of God of Great Britain / France and Ireland King . . . To / all whom these presents may come Greeting; WHEREAS . . . / [10 lines citing authority 31 Geo. III c. 1] / And whereas divers complaints have been made to me that many persons . . . / [6 lines] / [have] carried Rum and other strong liquors from Detroit . . . / . . . / . . . into the Miamis Country, and sold and distributed the / same amongst the Indians. Now I do strictly charge and command all persons / . . . / . . . to refrain / from such unlawful transactions in future: . . . / [7 lines] / . . . In witness whereof I have caused the great Seal of the / Province to be hereunto affixed this 1st day of November in the Thirty-fifth / year of his Majesty's Reign at Navy Hall in the Province foresaid. / J. G. SIMCOE. / Wm. JARVIS, Secretary. /

Broadside: 43 lines; type-page: 23 × 12.5 cm. *Printed at Newark, U.C., probably by Gideon Tiffany, 1794.*

Copy located: CaOOA (in *Askin papers*, v. 31).

918. UPPER CANADA. LIEUTENANT-GOVERNOR, 1791-1799 (*Simcoe*)

J.G.S. / Proclamation. / [rule] / HAÜT CANADA. / GEORGE trôis pai la grace de Dieu Roi de la grande Brïtagne [sic], France / de d'Irelande, . . . A Tous ceux qui les pre-/sentes verront, Salut: Vu-que . . . / [9 lines citing authority 31 Geo. III c. 1] / Et Vu-que divers plaintes m'ont etioent faites que plusieurs personnes . . . / [5 lines] / ont . . . / . . . / . . . porté de l'eau de vie et autres liqueures fortes du Detroit, / . . . / . . . dans le pays des Miamis, et parmi les Sauvages les ont vendü / et distribue." On Donc J'Ordonne et commande etroitement à toutes person-/nes, . . . de se retinir de / telles transactions à l'avenir . . . / [etc. 9 lines] / En Temoig-/nage de quoi J'ai fais apposer le grand sceau de Province aux presentes ce premier / jour de Novembrê en la Trente cinquieme Annêe du Régne de sa Majesté a / Navy Hall en la Province sous dite. / J. G. SIMCOE. /Wm. JARVIS. Sec./

Broadside: 44 lines; type-page: 23 × 12.2 cm. *Printed at Newark, U.C., probably by Gideon Tiffany, 1794.*

Tiffany succeeded Louis Roy as government printer in Upper Canada in the fall of 1794. This proclamation has the appearance of the former's rather than the latter's work. Set solid, like a page of book-work, ill composed and poorly printed, it shows an inexperienced hand, particularly one unpractised in the style of official publications.

Copy located: CaOOA (in "Proclamations" portfolio in the Library).

919. YOUNG, ARTHUR, 1741-1820

L'EXEMPLE DE LA FRANCE / AVIS A LA / GRANDE BRETAGNE. / "Tous principes politiques vrais dans la speculation sont faux dans la pra-/tique. Cette verité, quoique surprenante, n'en est pas moins certaine. La / raison en est que ces principes politiques sont appuïés sur cette supposition, / que les hommes agissent conformément à la raison. / Or il est absolument / faux que les hommes aient coutume de se conduire par la raison; par con-/sequent tout ce qu'on établit sur une pareille supposition tombe de soi-meme, / ainsi que l'expérience le prouve," / SOAME JENYNS. / [rule] / SECONDE EDITION. / PAR / ARTHUR YOUNG, ECUÏER, F.R.S. / [printer's ornament] / [double rule] / QUEBEC: / IMPRIME' PAR JEAN NEILSON, N° 3, RUE DE LA MONTAGNE. / M.DCC.XCIV. /

8vo. A-O^4, P-R^2, S^4, T^1, U^2, X^4, Y^2; 149 p.; type-page: 16.3 × 10 cm.

Contents: p. [1], t.-p.; p. [2], [Notice:] "Ouvrage qu'on se propose de républier comme Supplement à la Gazette de Québec, et fortement récommandé à la sérieuse considération de tout Canadien qui estime la sureté de ses biens, le bonheur de sa famille, la vraie liberté, et les intérêts permanens de sa patrie"; p. [3]-134, L'exemple de la France; p. [135]-48, Supplement; p. 148-49, Fautes à corriger; verso of p. 149, blank.

Written by the noted English agriculturalist and author of *Travels during the years 1787 . . . 1789 . . . [in] France,* this work is a discourse for landed gentry and husbandmen on the hazards implicit in an economy tolerant of republican principles. It includes a plan for the organization of national militia and is said to have been heartily approved by the English Whig administration, also by Edmund Burke. It was published in at least four editions, and an abridgement, in England, 1793-94. A French translation from the second English edition was issued in Brussels, 1793, from which the Quebec production was probably reprinted.

This publication was recorded by the Printer:

"1794, Oct. 11. [Debit] Governor General's Office for printing 700 Copies of a Pamphlet entitled L'Exemple de la France, avis à la Grande Bretagne, published along with the Gazette, making 9 sheets and ¾ [sic] on Demy paper, Pica type @ £2.10 [per] sheet for the 1st hundred and 12/6 [per] sheet for every additional hundred—£60.18.9. Deduct from the Common rate £20 [Balance:] £40.18.9."—Can.P.A., *Neilson papers,* v. 54.

Published in French only, at government expense, and issued with the *Gazette,* it was intended, perhaps as "Avis" to French Canadians. (It also appeared, in English, running serially in the *Royal gazette,* Halifax, N.S., Feb. 4-May 13, 1794.)

Copies located: CaQM; CaQMS; CaQQL; DLC.

920. ALMANACS. LOWER CANADA

CALENDAR, for the Leap-year 1796, for QUEBEC, in 306$^{\text{d.}}$ 30$^{\text{m.}}$ Longitude and 46$^{\text{d.}}$ 55$^{\text{m.}}$ Latitude. / CALENDRIER pour l'Année Bissextile 1796, pour QUEBEC, par les 306$^{\text{d.}}$ 30$^{\text{m.}}$ de Longitude, et 46$^{\text{d.}}$ 55$^{\text{m.}}$ de Latitude. / [rule] /

Colophon: QUEBEC: PRINTED AT THE NEW PRINTING-OFFICE, Mountain-Street.—QUEBEC: IMPRIMÉ A LA NOUVELLE IMPRIMERIE, Rue la Montagne. /

Broadside: type-page: 60 × 45 cm. in ornamental rule frame. *Printed at Quebec, by Wm. Vondenvelden, 1795.*

Contents: Les signes (du zodiaque), fêtes mobiles, les quatre tems, commencement des quatres saisons, nombres, phases de la lune, (in French only); eclipses (in English and French); monthly calendar in 12 tables, for each month is given the sun's place in the zodiac, moon's phases, day of week and month, fêtes, remembrance days (English), sun's rising & setting; table of Court days (in English & French); members of House of Assembly; table of days of year "shewing on what day of month they severally fall . . . convenient in Accompt Houses and Tradesmen's shops"; tide table for Quebec; table of interest at 6 per cent; weight of gold coins by ordinance of Mar. 29, 1777 (all in English & French).

This *Calendar*, or sheet almanac, had been issued by Wm. Vondenvelden for the first time, the previous year. It has rather more English matter than the Brown-Neilson *Calendrier . . . pour Québec*, which had been appearing regularly since 1765.

Copy located: CaO (bound in *Quebec gazette*, at end of 1795).

921. ALMANACS. LOWER CANADA

[Calendrier pour l'année 1796 pour Québec. *Québec, chez Jean Neilson, 1795.*]

Broadside. This sheet almanac was sold at Neilson's printing office from Oct. 27, 1795, at 5*s.* the dozen (4*s.* to the dealer in Montreal), 7½*d.* the copy. It was advertised as "just published" in the *Quebec gazette*, Oct. 29, 1795, *et seq.*

Copy located: None.

922. ALMANACS. LOWER CANADA

THE / QUEBEC / ALMANACK / FOR / The Year 1795. / [double rule] / 46D. 55M. N.LAT.—71D. 12M. W.LONG. / [double rule] / [ornament] / [double rule] / [Latin quotation, indecipherable] / [double rule] / QUEBEC: / Printed by JOHN NEILSON, / N° 3 MOUNTAIN STREET. / [title within ornamental rule frame]

French t.-p.:

ALMANAC / DE / QUEBEC, / POUR / L'ANNEE 1795. / [double rule] / 46D. 55M. N.LAT.—71D. 12M. W.LONG. / [double rule] / [printer's ornament] / [double rule] / [Latin quotation, indecipherable] / [double rule] / A QUEBEC: / CHEZ JEAN NEILSON, / N° 3 RUE LA MONTAGNE. / [title within ornamental rule frame]

12mo. A-K^6; 115, [2] p., front., fold. table; type-page: 10.8 × 6 cm.

Contents: p. [1], English t.-p.; verso, blank; p. [3], French t.-p.; p. [4-33], Epochs, eclipses, tide table, calendar; p. 34-35, Currency rule, interest table; p. 37-48, Excerpts from laws on the division of the province, land granting, counties and boundaries; court terms; fold. table: court sittings; p. [49]-115, Civil and military register, clergy, etc.; p. [1 (verso of p. 115)-2], at end, Index; p. [2], verso, blank; probably also 1 *l.* at end blank, or folded around sig. A-L to form a preliminary leaf bearing frontispiece. The frontispiece is an engraving of landscape and figures with the title: "La Vie Pastorale: Pastoral Life."

This almanac follows closely the model set by Samuel Neilson in the *Quebec almanack for 1792*. It was advertised as in the press, Dec. 11, 1794, and published Jan. 15, 1795, at 2*s*. the copy.

Copies located: CaOOA (photostat copy); CaQMS; CaQQA (p. [1-2], 97 to end, front. and fold. table, wanting).

923. ALMANACS. NOVA SCOTIA

[An Almanack for the Year 1796; . . . Calculated for the Meridian of Halifax . . . By Theophrastus. *Halifax, N.S., Printed by John Howe & Robert M'Kinstry, 1795.*]

This almanac was advertised: "Just published and to be sold by Howe and M'Kinstry, An Almanack for the Year, 1796 [etc.] Price 5/ per dozen. 7½d single."
—*Royal gazette,* Halifax, N.S., Nov. 24, 1795.

Copy located: None.

924. ALMANACS. NOVA SCOTIA

THE / NOVA-SCOTIA CALENDER / OR AN / ALMANACK, / FOR THE YEAR . . . / 1796. / [4 lines] / WHEREIN IS CONTAINED / The ECLIPSES [etc. 7 lines in col. 1] / MOON'S APOGEE [etc. 6 lines in col. 2] / The View of HALIFAX, was taken from FOSTER'S, on the Eastern side of / the Harbour. / Calculated for the Meridian of HALIFAX . . . / [3 lines] / [rule] / BY METONICUS. / [rule] / Whether Amid the Gloom of Night I stray, / [verse, 3 lines, by:] / GAY. / [rule] / HALIFAX: / Printed and sold by ANTHONY HENRY, at his Printing-Office, in Sack-/ville-Street, Corner of Grafton-Street. / [title and each page within single rule frame]

12mo. [A-D,[4] E[2]]; [36] p. (incl. illus.); type-page: 15.7 × 10 cm.

Contents: p. [1], View of Halifax; p. [2], blank; p. [3], t.-p.; p. [4-5], Vulgar notes, etc., Zodiac, eclipses; p. [6], Ephemeris; p. [7-18], Calendar; p. [19-22], Currency tables for all North America, clergy in Nova Scotia; [p. 23-36] Nova Scotia administration, legislature, judges, justices, courts, sheriffs, postal rates, fire company, etc.; naval and army officers, ships stationed in Nova Scotia; militia; distances, [etc.].

This almanac was advertised (with notes of errata in the calculations) for sale at 5*s*. per dozen, 7½*d*. the copy, in the *Royal gazette*, Halifax, N.S., and in the *Halifax journal*, from Nov. 24, 1795.

Copies located: CSmH; CaNsHA (p. 1-2, 33-34, wanting); CaNsWA (badly worn).

925. BOUCHER-BELLEVILLE, JEAN BAPTISTE, 1763-1839

RECUEIL / DE / CANTIQUES, / à l'usage des Missions, des Retraites / ET DES / CATECHISMES. / [rule] / Enfans! louez le Seigneur. Ps. 112. / [rule] / A la Prairie de la Madeleine. / [printer's ornament] / [rule] / A QUEBEC: / Chez JOHN NEILSON, No. 3, Rue la Montagne. / M.DCC.DCV. /

16mo. A-M^8, N^4, O^3; v, 195, [5] p.; type-page: 11.5 × 6.5 cm. Odd numbers on verso, even numbers on recto, in text. It seems reasonable that the book was made with the final section a full half sheet: O^4, giving a final blank leaf at end—of which all evidence has disappeared in copies located.

Contents: p. [i], t.-p.; p. [ii], blank; p. [iii]-v, Introduction; p. [1]-98, Pt. 1, Cantiques; p. [99]-195, Pt. 2, Cantiques; p. 195 at foot: Permission for use, ". . . donné à Québec, ce 26 Mars, 1795. Jean François Evêque de Québec"; p. [1-5] at end, Table alphabetique; p. [5] verso, blank.

The introduction states that this collection of devotional songs was made with the retreats immediately preceding children's first communion in the editor's mind. Catechisms used for the year preceding this rite are included, to teach children its significance. The collection, however, is suited to general use for retreats in colleges and missions throughout the diocese. The songs, selected from other printed and MS. collections, were occasionally altered for the purpose in hand. "Que n'est-il possible, de substituer des Cantiques pieux et édifians à ces chansons indecentes qui corrompent les coeurs, et répandent l'infection du vice. . . ." The first part comprises canticles for retreats, missions, first communion, and a few on themes of piety; the second part contains canticles on the mysteries and principal feasts of the year. In each part the songs are grouped by subject, numbered, etc., e.g. "Cantiques pour la Ste. Communion [no. 1-12]. Cantique première, Invitation aux Enfans qui doivent communier. Sur l'air *Dans cette étable.*" No music is given. The first work of its kind prepared in Canada—of a genre in long and constant use, however, for each generation of Catholic Canadians—the *Receuil* shows the skill and devotion of the parish priest. The first edition recorded as 1785-86 in Gagnon: *Essai de bibliographie canadienne,* 2: no. 1766, and repeated in John Wright: *The early prayer books of America* (St. Paul, Minn., 1896), 25, is a typographical error, no doubt, for its printer, John Neilson, was not printing at that date,

The printer's records give no details on the size or cost of the edition. But from publication day, Apr. 13, 1795 (*Quebec gazette,* Apr. 9, *et seq.*), they show a steady sale at 2*s.* the copy, 6*s.* for bound copies; also, on Apr. 23, 1795:

"[Debit] Profit and Loss, To 6 Cantiques sent as a present to the Seminary @ 2/ = 12/.

Ditto, 2 Ditto, bound @ 6/ = 12/ [Total] £1.4."

—Can.P.A., *Neilson papers,* v. 54.

Boucher-Belleville, born and educated at Quebec, was ordained and appointed vicar of Saint Ours in 1787. From 1792 till his death he was curé at Laprairie, an old settlement on the south shore of the River St. Lawrence near Montreal.

Copies located: CaQM; CaQQL.

926. BROWN, ANDREW *d.* 1834

THE / PERILS OF THE TIME, / AND THE / PURPOSES FOR WHICH THEY ARE APPOINTED. / [rule] / A / SERMON, / PREACHED / On the last Sabbath of the Year 1794, / AND / PUBLISHED AT THE REQUEST OF THE HEARERS. / [double rule] / BY ANDREW BROWN, D.D. / MINISTER OF THE PROTESTANT DISSENTING CONGREGATION OF / HALIFAX. / [double rule] / [double rule] / HALIFAX: / PRINTED BY HOWE AND M'KINSTRY, CORNER OF GEORGE AND / BARRINGTON STREETS, OPPOSITE THE PARADE. / M DCC XCV. /

8vo. A-E[4]; 1 p. l., ii, [5]-40 p.; type-page: 16.5 × 8.7 cm.

Contents: p. l. recto, t.-p.; verso, blank; p. [i]-ii, Dedication; p. [5], Letter from elders and committee, requesting Brown's permission to print sermon, dated at Halifax, Dec. 31, 1794; p. [6], blank; p. [7]-40, Sermon, II Timothy, iii, 1: This know also, that in the last days perilous times shall come.

Delivered to the Congregationalists and Presbyterians of St. Matthew's church (formerly Mather's meeting house) in Halifax, the sermon is dedicated to Thomas Andrew Strange, chief justice and president of council in Nova Scotia. Its object is "to expose the evils of anarchy and to concur with divine Providence in maintaining the great cause of religion, government and order." Superior in style and structure, the sermon "firstly" describes vividly the perils of the times: the political confusion and overthrow of the monarchical idea in France; republicanism based on specious theories of international implications is spreading elsewhere, and must be exterminated in France, or Church and King will fall in civil war in every monarchy. "Secondly," the preacher explains the divine purpose in these perils: punishment of impiety, irreligion and immorality, in which France with her Gallican theology of mystical doctrine and superstition, her deism and sceptical philosophies, France, the worst offender, is the first punished. The theory of equality is shown confounded by inequality in the order of nature, which God will see restored. "Thirdly," the pastor points to local evidence of divine approbation: Nova Scotia, free of political cabals, is shielded from the plague infesting American ports; Quebec is given an increased harvest to replace American supplies formerly imported into Nova Scotia. With the further, and temporal, protection of the British fleet, the Maritimes are safe indeed. So let all citizens join in praise of God.

This sermon is probably the most eloquent if not the most logical defence of the *status quo* in state and church printed in the 18th century in Canada. Unlike the Anglican Bishop Inglis, Brown, as he stated, rarely allowed "public transactions to give a colouring to religious instruction." But the political situation was critical, and Brown, though pastor to a dissenting congregation, had been ordained in Establishment—the Church of Scotland.

Copies located: CaNsHD (2 cop.); CaNsWA (2 cop.); MBAt (2 cop.); MH.

927. CATHOLIC CHURCH. LITURGY AND RITUAL

HEURES / ROMAINES / En gros Caractère, / CONTENANT / Les Offices de la Sainte Vierge / et des Morts pour l'usage des / Congréganistes; / Les Vêpres, Hymnes, Proses et / Antiennes de l'Eglise; /

Les prières du Matin et du Soir; / l'Entretien durant la Messe; la mé-/thode pour se bien confesser et com-/munier, et autres prières dévotes: / Le tout précédé du Calendrier, d'une / Table des jours d'abstinence, des jeûnes, / des Fêtes et Solemnités en usage dans / le Diocèse de Québec. / [printer's ornament] / A QUEBEC / Chez JEAN NEILSON, N° 3, Rue de la Montagne, / 1795. /

12mo. A-Ii[6], [Kk][2]; 7 p. l. [2]-371, [4] p.; type-page: 13.8 × 7 cm.; p. 122 mis-paged: 1 2; 260: 460; 309: 319. Even numbers on recto, odd numbers on verso.

Contents: p. l. 1 recto, t.-p.; verso, blank; p. l. 2 recto-7 recto, Fêtes; p. l. 7 verso, Elevation de notre coeur (a prayer); p. [2]-371, Heures romaines; [4] p. at end, Table [contents].

Though this work bears imprint of 1795, no record of its publication or sale appears during that year. It was advertised: "Soon will be ready for sale, Heures Romaines [etc.] on demy 12mo. neatly bound, 3/6 retail, 36/ per dozen."—*Quebec gazette*, July 28, 1796; then: "For Sale at the Printing Office, Heures Romaines [etc.]."—*ibid.*, Aug. 11, 1796, *et seq.*

Neilson's binding bears his label on the lining paper with advertisement in French and English: ". . . Books in general elegantly or neatly bound in the English, French and Italian Manner. From 1/ to 20/ price. At the Printing Office, Mountain street, Quebec."

Copies located: CaOT (in original binding by Neilson); CaQQL (well worn; pages discoloured and mutilated, p. l. 1-3, p. 60-71, 204-205, [1-4] wanting).

928. CATHOLIC CHURCH. LITURGY AND RITUAL

LA / JOURNÉE / DU CHRÉTIEN, / SANCTIFIÉE / PAR LA PRIERE / ET / LA MÉDITATION. / Nouvelle Édition augmentée. / [ornament] / A QUÉBEC, / Chez LOUIS GERMAIN fils / Rue de la Fabrique. / [double rule] / IMPRIMÉE A LA NOUVELLE IMPRIMERIE. / M.DCC. XCV.

12mo. A[3], B-P[6], Q[5]; 3 p. l., 176 p., 1 *l.*; type-page: 12.3 × 6.9 cm. *Printed at Quebec, by Wm. Vondenvelden for Louis Germain, Jr.*

Contents: p. l. 1 recto, t.-p.; verso, blank; p. l. 2 recto, Préface; verso-p. l. 3 recto, Table (contents); verso of p. l. 3, blank; p. [1]-86, Prières; p. 86-96, Reglement de vie; p. 97-147, Pensées chretiennes par le R. P. Bouhours, de la Campagnie de Jesus; p. 148-157, Les vespres; p. 158-76, Pseaulmes, etc.; 1 *l.* at end recto, Approbation; verso, blank.

The *Approbation* states: "Québec, 25me Aout, 1795. L'Expérience de bien des années prouve si manifestement l'utilité de la *Journée du Chrétien*, que je n'hésite point, au nom de Nos Seigneurs Eveques d'approuver et de louer beaucoup la Nouvelle édition qui se fait de cet excellent Livre. [signed:] Gravé, Vic. gen."

Copy located: CaO (p. 25-28, 33-38, 47-48, wanting).

929. COCKREL, RICHARD, 1773?-1829

THOUGHTS / ON THE / Education of Youth. / [double rule] / By RICHARD COCKREL, / TEACHER OF THE MATHEMATICS, AT NEWARK,

/ UPPER CANADA. / [double rule] / NEWARK: / Printed by G. TIFFANY, and sold at his / Book-Store.—M,DCC,XCV. /

12mo. A-C^4, D^1; 25 p.; type-page: 13.1 × 7.5 cm.

Contents: p. [1], t.-p.; p. [2], blank; p. [3]-25, Thoughts, etc.; verso of p. 25, blank.

This work gives a view into the state of society in the new province as well as standards of education. The young author sets forth the qualifications of a school master, of a good school, and the need of both in Upper Canada. The importance of education in society requires learning and character in the teacher. He should himself know his subjects and be a teacher by profession, not a jack of all trades. He should grade scholars carefully, then teach six as well as one, drawing instruction from familiar experience. Children should learn spelling from the literature of daily life, the newspaper, not from the bible—which has a place, but not in the school. Arithmetic should be learned from household problems, not by rote from a book—though the author lists, p. 18-19, the mathematical works "most esteemed in England." The school room should be quiet and orderly; children taught manners and standards of life at home as well as in school, and their holidays should be free of school tasks.

Cockrel recommends that a school house be built at Newark by public subscription, and that school and general reading books be imported to supply their woeful lack. Teachers should be licensed by the government in Upper Canada, on examination of their professional qualifications "as in the United States," and their pay increased. It averages at present, he states, but 12*s.* a scholar each quarter. It would be better to allow two or three dollars more a year and induce a worthy school master to settle in the province. The three recent teachers, the author observes, have fled the country for bad conduct: "one for robbing a gentleman of some dollars, another for * * * *—and a third for embezzling a certain quantity of wheat."

Cockrel himself settled at Newark about this time and opened a school, giving day and evening classes. He resigned at the end of 1796, however, and had a series of short-term successors (*Upper Canada gazette,* Dec. 30, 1796, *et seq.*). Cockrel moved to Ancaster where he opened a school, teaching English, mathematics, and classics, his wife assisting him and giving "private lessons in mantua making." His school achieved a reputation second only to that of John Strachan's at Cornwall. Cockrel was also a licensed surveyor, and later he published a newspaper, *The Spectator*, at St. David's in 1816, then the *Upper Canada Phoenix* at Dundas two years later. He remained in the Niagara Peninsula all his life and died at Ancaster, July 7, 1829.

This pamphlet was reproduced (not in facsimile) with introductory note, in Bibliographical Society of Canada: Reprint series, no. 1, 1949.

Copy located: DLC.

930. CULL, H., *Potash maker, Quebec*

DES CENDRES, / Le prix ordinaire de douze sols par minot comble serra donné pour de bonnes Cendres ... H. Cull. Manufacture de Potasse, Fauxbourg de St. Roc, Québec, le 29me Novembre, 1795.

Broadside: 15 lines; type-page: 14 × 9 cm.

Copy located: CaQQL.

931. FRIENDLY FIRE-CLUB, *Shelburne, N.S.*

RULES AND REGULATIONS / OF THE / FRIENDLY FIRE-CLUB, / Instituted at SHELBURNE A.D. 1784. / As Revised A.D. 1795. / [rule] / [row of commas] / SHELBURNE. / PRINTED BY JAMES HUMPHREYS, M,DCC, XCV. /

12mo., 9 p., 1 *l.*; type-page: 16.5 × 9 cm.

Contents: p. [1], t.-p.; p. [2], blank; p. [3]-9, Rules; verso of p. 9, blank; 1 *l.* at end, blank.

The club was a privately organized mutual benefit fire brigade, similar to the Quebec Amicable Society. The rules set forth the constitution, conduct of meetings, directions for attending fires, and an elaborate system of fines. The members, limited to forty in number, and admitted only by a unanimous ballot, met quarterly (each man paying his own reckoning for refreshment). But their serious duties were to maintain equipment and assist at fires: Every member should have "Two Bags sufficient to contain three Bushels each, with proper strings for closing same & Two Buckets, all marked with the owner's name . . . a Hat with a broad black brim, the crown painted white and having F.F.C. marked as large as the front of the Crown will admit. All these to be kept in constant readiness [penalty 20*s.* fine]. . . . Upon every alarm of Fire each member shall repair instantly with his bags and buckets, having his fire-hat on, to the houses of such members of the Society as he shall apprehend to be most in danger, and endeavour to the utmost to save their houses, and to preserve their effects . . . to prevent embezzlement of the same—And who ever shall be willfully missing . . . shall pay a fine of forty shillings. In order to prevent the admission of improper persons when the effects of any of the members in danger are removing, one or more shall stand as Centinels at the door . . . there shall be a watch word agreed upon . . . and none are to be admitted [to the burning house] who cannot give it. Any member who cannot give the watchword on such occasion shall pay a fine of two shillings [etc.]."

The *Rules and Regulations* were issued to members at 5*s.* the copy. Each member was required to bring his copy to all meetings (penalty 1*s.* fine)—apparently for emendation. Both copies located, bound in original marbled paper covers, with 6 to 10 blank leaves, contained members' MS. notes of additional rules, fellow members' names and addresses, etc.

Copies located: CaNsHD; CaNsWA.

932. GLENIE, JAMES, 1750?-1817

[PAMPHLET]

? *Printed at Saint John, N.B., by John Ryan, 1795.*

This publication is mentioned in a letter from Captain Daniel Lyman, Halifax, Oct. 5, 1795, to Edward Winslow, surrogate-general in New Brunswick, ". . . I have read Glenie's damned and blasted pamphlet. What plausibility mixed with falsehood, appropriating to himself every political virtue, tho' only guided and instigated by the most infernal motives . . . Sir John [Wentworth, lieutenant-governor of Nova Scotia] said he would write you. I see he had one of Glenie's pamphlets, which, he said, was sent by a Mr. Reid, but I believe at Glenie's instigation. His Excellency [Wentworth] condemns it in toto."—*Winslow papers, A.D. 1776-1826*, ed. by W. O. Raymond (Saint John, N.B., 1901), 421.

Glenie, whom Lyman termed "a known and most notorious violent Democrat Jacobin" (*ibid.*, 420), was a Scotsman, an officer in the Royal Engineers, who settled in New Brunswick, engaging in timber trade. He was member of Assembly for Sunbury from 1791 till 1805 when he returned to England. Well-educated and radical in his political attitudes, Glenie was conspicuous on committees and in debate in the Assembly, for his hostility to the views of the lieutenant-governor-in-council and American loyalists. "He attempted to gather the various discontents into an organized body of opposition to the governing oligarchy . . . but he lacked the dignity and stability essential to a real leader."—Marion E. Gilroy: *The loyalist experiment in New Brunswick*, unpublished M.A. thesis, University of Toronto, 1933, 91-98.

This pamphlet *may* have concerned the provincial election held in Aug., 1795, the first under the new elections act (No. 954). It was fiercely contested by popular and "official party" candidates, following a session which left the administration at deadlock with the Assembly on appropriations. In that same session Glenie's Declaratory Bill, "declaratory of what acts of Parliament are binding in this province" had been passed in Assembly, 15 to 10, and refused even a reading in Council as smacking of that Declaration of the American congress at Philadelphia in 1775 (*see* James Hannay: *History of New Brunswick*, 2 v., Saint John, N.B., 1909, 1:213, 245 *et seq.*).

Copy located: None.

933. GREAT BRITAIN. LAWS, STATUTES, *etc.*

[The Prize Act]

Printed at Halifax, N.S., by John Howe & Wm. Minns, 1795, or possibly published in London, imported and sold by Howe and Minns, this item was advertised:

"Just published and to be sold by the Printers—Price 5 Shillings—The Prize Act. Directions to the officers of His Majesty's Army and Navy for capture of vessells and other enemy property by sea or land, Mode of distribution . . . Complete directions for persons concerned in adjudication in H.M. Court of Vice Admiralty [etc.]. To this Act is subjoined His Majesty's Proclamation fixing the proportion of prize money [etc.]."—*Weekly chronicle*, Halifax, N.S., May 30, 1795.

The same advertisement appeared in the *Weekly chronicle* (Minns's paper) intermittently till Feb. 18, 1797, at least; also in the *Halifax journal* (printed by Minns's brother-in-law, John Howe) Jan. 14, 1796 (preceding issues not located).

Copy located: None.

934. GREAT BRITAIN. TREATIES

A / TREATY / OF / Amity, Commerce / AND / Navigation, / BETWEEN / His Britannic Majesty / AND THE / United States of America. / By their PRESIDENT, with the advice and consent / of their Senate. / [double rule] / NEW-YORK PRINTED. / NEWARK:—Re-printed by G. TIFFANY, / M,DCC,XCV. / (Price TWO SEILLINGS [sic], New-York currency.) /

12mo. A-D^4, E^1; 33 p.; type-page: 14.2 × 7.7 cm.

Contents: p. [1], t.-p.; p. [2], blank; p. [3]-30, Treaty; p. 30-31, Conditional ratification on the part of the United States, June 24, 1795; p. 31-33, A letter concerning vessels of European belligerents in American waters, signed by Thomas Jefferson, dated Philadelphia, Sept. 5, 1793, and addressed to Geo. Hammond; verso of p. 33, blank.

This is the final text of the Jay Treaty, as signed at London, Nov. 19, 1794, and ratified by the United States, but without British ratification and addenda. Among other matters it provided for the cession by Great Britain of the western border posts, for regulations of commerce, communications, boundaries, etc., between the United States and Canada.

Various interests in each of the British North American provinces were vitally concerned in some aspect of the treaty. The acuteness of their concern is evidenced by its publication in at least four of the six printing centres in Canada during 1795-96, in addition, of course, to its appearance in the newspapers. No other 18th century work was so widely published in Canada.

This edition, published at Newark, Upper Canada, was advertised "A few copies of The Treaty for sale at this Office, agreeable to a New York publication."

—*Upper Canada gazette*, Aug. 19, 1795.

The work is badly printed on poor paper. One copy seen (in Library of Congress) is on a thin cloudy paper, the other copy (in Toronto Public Library) is on the coarse blue-gray stock commonly used at the time as cover paper, and is badly out of register on p. 33.

The printer, Gideon Tiffany, born at Keene, N.H., Jan. 28, 1773, came to Upper Canada about 1793, settling with his parents in the Niagara Peninsula. He succeeded Louis Roy as government printer towards the end of 1794, and was joined shortly after by his brother Sylvester, a printer from Lansingburgh, N.Y. The Tiffanys soon lost favour with the administration—partly because of American connections and a practice of importing paper from Albany. Gideon was superseded as editor of the *Upper Canada gazette* by a loyalist, Titus G. Simons in 1797, and as government printer by Wm. Waters in 1798 (see *The first journalists in Upper Canada*, by W. S. Wallace, in *Canadian historical review*, 26: 372-81, Dec., 1945).

A facsim. illus. of t.-p. is in Toronto Public Library, *Bibliography of Canadiana*, 165. *See also* Evans no. 29748; Sabin no. 96578.

Copies located: CaOT (t.-p. mutilated); DLC (t.-p. mutilated).

935. GREAT BRITAIN. TREATIES

<Authentic.> / [ornamental rule] / TREATY / OF / Amity, Commerce & Navigation, / BETWEEN / HIS BRITANNIC MAJESTY, / AND THE / UNITED STATES OF AMERICA. / BY THEIR PRESIDENT, WITH THE ADVICE AND / CONSENT OF THEIR SENATE. / [ornamental rule] / PHILADELPHIA: PRINTED, JUNE 30, 1795. / [double rule] / ST. JOHN: RE-PRINTED by JOHN RYAN, N° 58, Prince William-Street. / 1795. /

38 p.; type-page: 16.8 × 9.3 cm. The format is eccentric: in the only copy seen, the paper was apparently folded in fours, showing chain lines horizontal but no water

mark, and lacking signatures. p. 23-24 was interchanged with p. 33-34. The type-page is noted to have proportions customary in 8vo format.

Contents: p. [1], t.-p.; p. [2], Letter, dated Philadelphia, June 29, 1795, accompanying "genuine copy" of treaty, signed by S. T. Mason, to Benjamin Franklin Bache, editor of the *Aurora;* p. [3]-33, Treaty; p. 33-34, Conditional ratification on the part of the United States, June 24, 1795; p. 34-37, A letter concerning European belligerents in American waters, dated Philadelphia, Sept. 5, 1793, signed by Thomas Jefferson, and addressed to Geo. Hammond; p. 37-38, Mr. Burr's defeated motion in amendment.

This edition and No. 936 were reprinted from the notorious Mason-Bache "scoop." Before the treaty was published officially by the United States government, Senator Mason of Virginia sent a copy to Bache, republican journalist, who printed it in substance in the *Aurora*, Philadelphia, June 29, 1795, and in full as a pamphlet, July 1, 1795 (Evans no. 29743). This edition contains the text of the treaty in full, lacking the British ratification, and addenda. The Treaty was also "reprinted from the Philadelphia *Aurora*, via Boston, July 7, 1795," in the *Royal gazette*, Halifax, N.S., July 21, 1795, which reprinted in succeeding issues, several American essays upon the Treaty.

Copy located: CaOOA.

936. GREAT BRITAIN. TREATIES

TREATY / OF / Amity, Commerce and Navigation, / BETWEEN / HIS BRITANNIC MAJESTY, / AND THE / UNITED STATES OF AMERICA. / BY THEIR PRESIDENT, WITH THE ADVICE AND / CONSENT OF THEIR SENATE. / [rule] / MONTREAL, / PRINTED BY E. EDWARDS, / N°. 10 ST. VINCENT STREET. / 1795. /

12mo. 44 p.; type-page: 13 × 8 cm.

Contents: p. [1], t.-p.; p. [2], Letter, dated Philadelphia, June 29, 1795, from S. T. Mason to B. F. Bache, accompanying a "genuine copy" of the Jay treaty for the *Aurora;* p. 3-33, Treaty; p. 34-44, United States ratification, etc. *See* No. 935 *note*.

Edwards also printed this text of the *Treaty* from another setting of type, and with French translation, in his *Montreal gazette*, seriatim, Aug. 3-17, 1795.*

Copies located: CaQMS; CaQQL.

937. LOWER CANADA. ADJUTANT GENERAL'S OFFICE

Rules and Articles / FOR THE BETTER / GOVERNMENT / OF THE MILITIA / of the Province of / LOWER-CANADA, / when embodied for Service. / [rule] / [royal arms] / [rule] / Published by The GOVERNNOR'S / Command / [rule] / QUEBEC: / Printed at the NEW PRINTING-OFFICE / Mountain Street. A.D. M.DCC.XCV. / [title within double rule frame]

*The Jay treaty with American ratification was also published this year at Quebec by Wm. Vondenvelden, as *The Times* Extra, no. 52, Friday, July 24, 1795; and by John Neilson in the *Quebec gazette*, July 30, 1795, p. [1-4]. Vondenvelden published the definitive edition the following year (No. 986).

French t.-p.:

Regles et Articles / POUR LE MEILLEUR / GOUVERNEMENT / DE LA MILICE / de la Province du / BAS-CANADA / lorsqu'elle sera incorporêe pour le / Service. / [rule] / [royal arms] / [rule] / Publie' par ordre DU GOUVER-/NEUR. / [rule] / QUEBEC, / Imprime' à la NOUV. IMPRIMERIE R. / de la Montagne A.D. M.DCC.XCV. / [title within double rule frame]

12mo. A-O[4]; 109, [2] p.; type-page: 12 × 7.5 cm. t.-p., text and index in English and French on opposite pages.

Contents: p. [1], blank; p. [2], English t.-p.; p. [3], French t.-p.; p. [4]-109, Rules; p. [1 (verso of p. 109) -2] at end, Index; verso of p. [2], blank.

Printed by Wm. Vondenvelden, this work was advertised in his paper; "Just published and for sale at this Office, Rules and Articles for the better government of the Militia of the Province of Lower Canada, when embodied for Service. Price 1/6, neatly stitched." *The Times,* Quebec, June 1, 1795.

The sheets of this edition were reissued in 1812. (*See* Toronto Public Library, *Bibliography of Canadiana,* no. 684) with t.-p. and some sheets of a genuine 1812 edition; (*see* Gagnon: *Essai de bibliographie canadienne,* 1: no. 3098.)

Copies located: CaQM; CaQMS (3 cop.).

938. LOWER CANADA. EXECUTIVE COUNCIL

EXECUTIVE COUNCIL OFFICE, / QUEBEC, 17th January, 1795. / [rule] / WHEREAS divers persons have hitherto petitioned . . . / . . . for Grants . . . / of the vacant Lands of the Crown, . . . / [etc.] . . . PUBLIC NOTICE is therefore now given . . . [etc., signed:] / By Order of His Excellency the Governor in Council. / J. WILLIAMS, C. Ex. C. /

French side:

BUREAU DU CONSEIL EXECUTIF. / QUEBEC, LE 17 JANVIER, 1795. / [rule] / DIVERSES personnes aiant autrefois Pétitionné . . . / . . . pour des Concessions . . . / des Terres vacantes de la Couronne . . . / [etc.] . . . notice / Public est à ces causes, actuellement donné . . . [etc., signé:] / Par Ordre de Son Excellence le Gouverneur en Conseil. / (Signé) J. WILLIAMS, C.Ex.C. / Pour Vraie Traduction conforme à l'original, / J. F. CUGNET, S. & T.F. /

Double broadside: English on left, 31 lines, type-page: 15 × 14.5 cm. French on right: 34 lines, type-page: 16.7 × 14.5 cm. *Printed at Quebec, by John Neilson, 1795,* as recorded:

> "1795, Jan. 20. [Debit] Executive Council 500 Proclamations respecting the granting of Lands. on 4to Post, French and English—£3."
>
> —Can.P.A., *Neilson papers,* v. 54.

Contents: Notice to persons claiming lands on survey warrants or on order-in-council, to send in particulars of the principal grantee and associates, according to the orders-in-council of Oct. 10 and Oct. 20, 1794 (*see* No. 878-879), by Aug. 1, 1795, or forfeit claim to land.

This order-in-council was passed and ordered "published in both languages in the *Quebec gazette* . . . for six successive Weeks [Jan. 29, 1795, *et seq.*]. And also that 500 Copies be struck off by way of Hand-Bills."—Can.P.A., L.C. *Land* C, pt. III, Jan. 17, 1795.

Copies located: CaOOA (in portfolio: *Miscellaneous newspaper clippings, 1812-1837*); CaQMS; GBLP (in C.O. 42/109: 722-23).

939. LOWER CANADA. GOVERNOR, 1791-1796 (*Dorchester*)

[By His Excellency the Right Honorable Guy Lord Dorchester Captain General and Governoı in Chief in . . . Lower Canada &c.&c.&c. A Proclamation. <Text> Given . . . at Quebec, 9th September 1795 Dorchester. By His Excellency's Command, Geo: Pownall Sec. God Save the King.

French side:

Par Son Excellence le Tres Honorable Guy Lord Dorchester Capitaine Générale et Gouverneur en Chef de la Province du Bas-Canada, &c.&c.&c. Proclamation <Text> Donné . . . at Quebec, le 9me Septembre 1795 Dorchester. Par ordre de Son Excellence, Geo: Pownall, Sec. Pour vraie Traduction, X. Lanaudiere, A.S. & T.F. Vive le Roi.]

Double broadside: Text in English on left, and French on right. *Printed at Quebec, by John Neilson, 1795*, as recorded:

> "1795, Sept. 23. [Debit] Council Office For printing in English and French 100 Proclamations for Embargo, on a Sheet of folio Crown, & distributing the same at Three Rivers, Berthier and Montreal—£1.10."
>
> —Can.P.A., *Neilson papers*, v. 54.

Text: "Whereas it hath been represented to me by divers Memorials and Petitions . . . setting forth that, on account of the great demand for Wheat and Flour, and the high prices given for the same, the Farmers had been induced to dispose of the greatest part of their stock on hand, to Agents buying up the same, for the purpose of Exportation, whereby the price of Bread had considerably increased; and that from the appearance of the Harvest, in many parts of the Country, it was likely to be less productive this Year than usual, whereby much inconvenience and distress might possibly ensue . . . And Whereas the consideration of such Memorials and Petitions was referred to a Committee of the Executive Council [who reported that much grain had been exported, that the present crop would be sufficient for immediate future needs but that much of it had been bargained for export] . . . And Whereas the Provincial Parliament stands prorogued to the fifteenth day of October next . . . I do order . . . that an Embargo be laid [on all vessels carrying Wheat, Pease, oats, Barley, Indian corn, Flour and Biscu t from Sept. 10 to Dec. 10, 1795, excepting flour purchased by the government for use of troops in Nova Scotia] . . . Officers of His Majesty's Customs hereof are to take notice and govern themselves accordingly."

This is one of several restrictions laid upon food supplies in 1795. A proclamation of May 18, limiting export to Great Britain to prevent the enemy securing Canadian grain, another proclamation of July 6, against forestallers, etc., raising prices in Quebec, and the proclamation of Sept. 9 (as above) are reprinted in Can.P.A., *Report, 1921.*

Copy located: GBLP (in C.O. 42/104: 258-59).

940. LOWER CANADA. HOUSE OF ASSEMBLY

JOURNAL / OF THE / HOUSE OF ASSEMBLY, / OF / LOWER-CANADA. / From the 5th January, to the 7th May 1795, both days inclusive. / IN THE THIRTY-FIFTH YEAR OF THE REIGN OF / KING GEORGE THE THIRD. / [royal arms] / [double rule] / QUEBEC: / PRINTED BY ORDER OF THE HOUSE OF ASSEMBLY, AND SOLD BY / JOHN NEILSON. / —M.DCC. XCV.— /

French t.-p.:

JOURNAL / DE LA / CHAMBRE D'ASSEMBLÉE, / DU / BAS-CANADA. / Du 5me Janvier, au 7me Mai 1795, inclusivement. / DANS LA TRENTE-CINQUIEME ANNÉE DU REGNE DE / SA MAJESTÉ GEORGE TROIS. / [royal arms] / [double rule] / QUEBEC: / IMPRIMÉ PAR ORDRE DE LA CHAMBRE D'ASSEMBLÉE, / ET A VENDRE PAR JOHN NEILSON. / M.DCC. XCV. /

4to. A-2R^4; 2 p. l. [i] 312 p., 1 *l.*; type-page: 18 × 12.3 cm. Two leaves of sig. A are folded around sig. A-2R to form p. 312 and leaf at end. Odd numbers on verso, even on recto. Text in English and French on opposite pages; fold. l attached to outer edge of p. 58-59, has table of receiver-general's accounts.

Contents: p. l. 1 recto, English t.-p.; verso, blank; p. l. 2 recto, French t.-p.; verso, English half-title; recto of p. [1], French half-title; p. [1]-312, Journal, of the third session of the first assembly, Jan. 5-May 7, 1795; verso of p. 312, blank; 1 *l.* at end recto, Faults to correct, Fautes à corriger; verso, blank.

The House ordered that 100 copies of its *Journal* be printed in English and French for the use of members, and that none but the printer so licensed print the same.—L.C. As. *Journal*, Mar. 30, 1795.

The production of this work was recorded by the printer:

"1795, June 29, For printing the Journals of the Third Session on Crown paper and Pica type, being 6 pages less than the former session.—£125."

—Can.P.A., *Neilson papers*, v. 54.

"Aug. 19. House of Assembly [owes for] sewing and cutting 100 Copies of the Journals of 3$^{d.}$ Session @ 3^{d}—£1.5."—*ibid.*

According to the Neilson price schedule (crown with pica, £2.2*s.* per sheet for the first hundred, 10*s.* each additional hundred) this record suggests that the edition comprised 300 copies. The House took 100 and the printer sold single copies at 15*s.* from July 22, 1795.

An index was issued with caption title: "Index to the third volume of the Journal"; collation: 4to. A-E^4; [40] p.; text in English, p. [1-19] and French, p. [20-40]. Though undated, it was apparently printed considerably later than the *Journal*, for it is on paper with the date 1801 in the water-mark. A copy of the *Index* is occasionally found bound with the *Journal*.

Copies located: CaO; CaOOA; CaOT; CaQM; CaQMA; CaQMM; CaQQL; CaQQLH; CtY; DLC; GBLP (in C.O. 42/103); MHi; N; NN; RPJ (includes *Index* but lacks p. 312 and errata leaf); WHi.

941. LOWER CANADA. HOUSE OF ASSEMBLY

[Petition from sundry Justices of the Peace for the District of Quebec, dated: Quebec, 15th December, 1795.

French title:

Une Requête signée d'un nombre de Juges à Paix du District de Québec.]

? Broadside. *Printed at Quebec, by John Neilson, 1795,* as recorded:

"1795, Dec. 30. Printed for House of Assembly, 60 copies Petition from the Magistrates &c.—10 ."—Can.P.A., *Neilson papers,* v. 54.

The petition sets forth the difficulties of local government: the magistrates' inability to repair streets, etc., to publish police regulations, or to execute laws and regulations, owing to their lack of funds, equipment, and certain legal authority. It prays the House to grant relief and remedy. The petition presented by Mr. Young, Dec. 15, was referred to a committee appointed Dec. 30, 1795, which reported on May 6, 1796, that "it may be expedient for the House to pass a bill granting more efficient powers to the magistrates of Quebec, Montreal and Three Rivers to establish and execute such regulations as they deem necessary." The text of the petition (about 1,500 words) is printed in L.C. As. *Journal,* May 15, 1795, from which the description above is taken.

Copy located: None.

942. LOWER CANADA. LAWS, STATUTES, *etc.*

ORDINANCES / MADE AND PASSED / BY THE / GOVERNOR / AND / LEGISLATIVE COUNCIL / OF THE PROVINCE / OF / QUEBEC. / AND NOW IN FORCE IN THE PROVINCE OF / LOWER-CANADA. / [rule] / [royal arms] / [rule] / QUEBEC: / PRINTED UNDER THE AUTHORITY AND BY COMMAND OF HIS EXCELLENCY THE GOVERNOR; / AS THE ACT OF THE PROVINCIAL PARLIAMENT DIRECTS. / By WILLIAM VONDENVELDEN, Printer at the NEW PRINTING-OFFICE, / Mountain-street, Anno Domino [sic], M.DCC.XCV. /

French t.-p.:

ORDONNANCES / FAITES ET PASSÉES / PAR LE / GOUVERNEUR / ET LE / CONSEIL LÉGISLATIF / DE LA PROVINCE / DE / QUÉBEC. / ACTUELLEMENT EN FORCE DANS LA PROVINCE DU / BAS-CANADA. / [rule] / [royal arms] / [rule] / A QUÉBEC: / IMPRIMÉ SOUS L'AUTORITÉ DU GOUVERNEMENT ET PAR ORDRE DE SON EXCELLENCE LE / GOUVERNEUR, ET CONFORMEMENT A L'ACTE DU PARLEMENT PROVINCIAL. / Par GUILLAUME VONDENVELDEN, Imprimeur à la NOUVELLE-IMPRIMERIE, / Rue de la Montagne, Anno Domini M.DCC.XCV. /

4to. A-Dd^4, Ee^2, Ff^4; 2 p. l., 214, [8] p.; type-page: 23.5 × 17.5 cm. Even numbers on recto, odd numbers on verso; p. 176 unnumbered. Text and contents table in English and French on opposite pages.

Contents: p. l. 1, recto, English t.-p.; verso, blank; p. l. 2 recto, French t.-p.; verso, blank; recto of p. 1, blank; p. 1-214, Ordinances; p. [1 (verso of p. 214) -8] at end, Table of contents; verso of p. [8], blank.

The *Ordinances* comprise the provincial statutes, 17 Geo. III c. 1 to 32 Geo. III c. 3, passed 1777-92. Full text of those in force is given, and title with note of expiration, repeal, or disallowance, of those not in force. Proclamations, regulations, etc., connected with the ordinances, and published in previous editions (*see* No. 268, 343, 495, 530) do not appear here. This is the first revision published since 1767. The contents were revised again and published in 1825. *See* Toronto Public Library, *Bibliography of Canadiana*, no. 642-643.

This work is frequently found, and was apparently reissued, as a part of *A Collection of acts . . . 1800* (No. 1169). It does not *appear* to have been reprinted for that publication (as some of the parts indubitably were). Most of the copies of *Ordinances* located are on paper with the date 1794 in the water mark. They were probably printed late in the year 1795, as the printer's bill is included in the government's accounts for Oct. 11, 1795-Apr., 1796:

> "[To] Vondenvelden for printing 600 copies of the Ordinances of the late Legislative Council now in force &c. allowed—stg. £150.8.3."
>
> —Can.P.A., L.C. *State* B, May 14, 1796.

Copies located: CaNsWA (2 cop.); CaO (2 cop.); CaOOA; CaOT; CaOTL; CaQM; CaQMJ; CaQMM (3 cop.); CaQQA; CaQQB; CaQQL; DLC (2 cop.); Ketcheson; M; MH (2 cop.); MiD-B (2 cop.); MiU; N; NN; NNB; PHi; RPJ; WHi; Witton.

943. LOWER CANADA. LAWS, STATUTES, *etc.*

THE / PROVINCIAL STATUTES / OF / LOWER-CANADA, / ENACTED BY THE KING's MOST EXCELLENT MAJESTY, BY AND WITH THE ADVICE / AND CONSENT OF THE LEGISLATIVE COUNCIL AND ASSEMBLY OF THE / SAID PROVINCE, CONSTITUTED AND ASSEMBLED BY VIRTUE OF / AND UNDER THE AUTHORITY OF AN ACT OF THE PARLIAMENT / OF GREAT BRITAIN, PASSED IN THE THIRTY-FIRST YEAR / OF THE REIGN OF OUR SOVEREIGN LORD GEORGE / THE THIRD BY THE GRACE OF GOD, OF GREAT / BRITAIN, FRANCE AND IRELAND KING, / DEFENDER OF THE FAITH, &c. / [rule] / VOLUME THE FIRST. / [rule] / [royal arms] / [double rule] / QUEBEC: / PRINTED UNDER THE AUTHORITY AND BY COMMAND OF HIS EXCELLENCY THE / GOVERNOR; AS THE ACT OF THE PROVINCIAL PARLIAMENT DIRECTS. / BY WILLIAM VONDENVELDEN, Printer at the New Printing-Office, / Mountain-street, Anno Domini, M.DCC.XCV. /

French t.-p.:

LES / STATUTS PROVINCIAUX / DU / BAS-CANADA. / STATUÉS PAR LA TRÈS EXCELLENTE MAJESTÉ DU ROI, PAR ET DE L'AVIS ET CONSEN-/TEMENT DU CONSEIL LÉGISLATIF ET ASSEMBLÉE DE LA DITE PROVINCE, / CONSTITUÉS ET ASSEMBLÉS EN VERTU DE ET

SOUS L'AUTORITÉ D'UN / ACTE DU PARLEMENT DE LA GRANDE BRETAGNE, PASSÉ DANS / LA TRENTE-ET-UNIÉME ANNÉE DU RÈGNE DE NOTRE / SOUVERAIN SEIGNEUR GEORGE TROIS, PAR LA / GRACE DE DIEU, ROI DE LA GRANDE BRETA-/GNE, DE FRANCE ET D'IRLANDE DÉ-/FENSEUR DE LA FOI, &c. / [rule] / PREMIER VOLUME. / [rule] / [royal arms] / [double rule] / QUEBEC: / IMPRIMÉ SOUS L'AUTORITÉ DU GOUVERNEMENT ET PAR ORDRE DE SON EXCELLENCE / LE GOUVERNEUR, ET CONFORMEMENT A L'ACTE DU PARLEMENT PROVINCIAL. / Par GUILLAUME VONDENVELDEN, Imprimeur à la Nouvelle Imprimerie. / Rue de la Montagne, Anno Domini M.DCC.XCV. /

4to. [*][4], A-Z[4], Aa[2], Bb-Rr[4], 4 p. l., 307 (or 308 [i e. 306]), [6] p.; type-page 23.5 × 17.3 cm. Odd numbers on verso, even numbers on recto. Text in English and French on opposite pages.

Through error in imposition of sig. Dd (p. 204-11) the text appears in the following forms:

Variant A (307 p.): p. 204 (bearing French text of p. 203) is omitted; sig. Dd appears: p. 207, 208, blank, 206, 211, 212, 209, 210; after p. 203 to end of text, odd numbers on recto, even numbers on verso.

Variant B (307 p.): 1 *l.* inserted before sig. Dd, recto paged: 204, verso blank; sig. Dd: blank, 206, 207, 208, 209, 210, 211, 212; after p. 204 to end of text, odd numbers on recto, even numbers on verso.

Variant C (308 [i.e. 306] p.): sig. Dd appears in correct order, text complete, odd numbers on verso, even numbers on recto throughout; p. 220-221 are omitted in numbering and the hiatus is not supplied, the text ending on p. 308 [i.e. 306].

Contents: p. l. 1 recto, English t.-p.; verso, blank; p. l. 2 recto, French t.-p.; verso, blank; p. l. 3 recto, English half-title; verso, blank; p. l. 4 recto, French half-title; verso, blank; recto of p. [1] blank; p. [1]-18, 33 Geo. III c. 1-8; p. [19], blank; p. [20], English half-title; p. [21], blank; p. [22], French half-title; p. [23-24], blank; p. [25]-110, 34 Geo. III c. 1-6; p. [111], blank; p. [112], English half-title; p. [113], blank; p. [114], French half-title; p. [115-116], blank; p. [117]-186, 35 Geo. III c. 1-11; p. [187], blank; p. [188], English half-title; p. [189], blank; p. [190], French half-title; p. [191-92], blank; p. [193]-307 (or 308), 36 Geo. III c. 1-12; verso of p. 307 (or 308)—recto of p. [1] at end, blank; p. [1-6] at end, Table of contents; verso of p. [6], blank.

This is the first volume in the serial publication of the provincial statutes of Lower Canada. The laws of 1792-93 and 1794 had been published previously in fo. (No. 837, 888). The laws of the first four sessions were published together (as above) in the format and general typographic style followed by the king's law printer thereafter. After 1795 each session's laws were printed and issued separately at the end of the session. The separate issues are described individually under their year of issue in this bibliography. Each successive Assembly's laws were published as a volume with a general t.-p., bearing appropriate volume number and an imprint dated for the first session in the volume, also with a table of the contents.

In 1794 the publication of provincial laws was put upon a new basis. The ordinance passed in 1777 declaring "that the printing and publishing of any ordinance in the *Quebec gazette* shall be deemed sufficient publication thereof" was superseded by 34 Geo. III c. 1. This act declared in force all laws passed in the previous session (1792-93), enacted that "all laws passed . . . under the present constitution shall be printed with all convenient speed after they have received the Assent of His Majesty's Representative, by such printer or printers as the Governor . . . shall employ for that purpose. And as it is expedient, that there should be further and more ample means of the Public having information of the laws.. . . it is also enacted . . . that as soon after the end of each session as can conveniently be effected, copies of the laws passed therein, so printed in both languages, shall be transmitted . . . to the Governor . . . members of the Legislature and . . . Executive Council, to the Judges, Clerks of the courts, Sheriffs, Coroners, Justices of the Peace, Field Officers and Captains of militia in each Parish . . . at the public expence." The printer "employed for that purpose" was Wm. Vondenvelden, a surveyor and translator, who opened a printing office in Quebec in the spring of 1794. From that date the laws were regularly printed at the New Printing Office and Vondenvelden was formally commissioned law printer to the government, Aug. 27, 1795. He worked on the terms of the Neilson price schedule and printed the laws on crown quarto, pica type, apparently in editions of 600-700 copies. His bill for "printing Acts of the Legislature—stg. £212.6.8." appears in the government's accounts for Apr.-Oct., 1795, and another "for printing Ordinances of government—£24.17.3," a year later. They refer, presumably, to the laws of the first three and of the fourth sessions, respectively.

This volume was reprinted in 1830 in a revised edition with title as above (288 p. 4to) and with titles only for the statutes no longer in force. Sections of this edition are occasionally found bound with complementary sections of the 1795 edition.

Copies located: Most law libraries and most reference libraries with Canadian collections have the series of Lower Canada statutes beginning with this volume, e.g.:

Variant A: CaOOA; NNB.

Variant B: CaOLU (p. [193]-307 only); CaOT (2 cop.); CaOTL; CaQM (Gagnon copy); CaQMA; CaQMM (2 cop.); CaQQL; MH; MHi (p. 206-307 only); MiD-B; MiU (p. [2-5] at end wanting); N; NN (unbound); NNB; WHi.

Variant C: CU; DLC; NN; RPJ.

Variant not noted: CaNsWA (2 cop.)*; CaOTL (p. [112]-186 only); CaOTU; CaQ*; CaQM*; CaQMM; CaQQ*; CaQQB; CtY*; MB.

944. LOWER CANADA. LAWS, STATUTES, *etc.*

THE / PROVINCIAL STATUTES / OF / LOWER-CANADA. / ENACTED by the KING'S most Excellent MAJESTY, by and with / the Advice and Consent of the Legislative Council and Assembly of the / said Province, constituted and assembled by virtue of and under the Au-/thority of an Act of the Parliament of GREAT BRITAIN, passed in / the thirty-first year of the Reign of our Sovereign Lord GEORGE the / Third, by the Grace of GOD, of Great Britain, France and Ireland KING, / De-fender of the faith, &c. / [rule] / [royal arms] / [rule] / QUEBEC: / PRINTED UNDER THE AUTHORITY AND BY COMMAND OF HIS EXCEL-

*Copy contains statutes of sessions 1-3, in 1795 edition, session 4 (paged: [188]-288) in 1830 reprint.

LENCY THE / GOVERNOR; AS THE ACT OF THE PROVINCIAL PARLIAMENT DIRECTS. / BY WILLIAM VONDENVELDEN, Printer at the New Printing-Office, / Mountain-street, Anno Domini. M.DCC.XCV. /

French t.-p.:

LES / STATUTS PROVINCIAUX / DU / BAS-CANADA. / STATUÉS par la Très Excellente MAJESTE' du ROI, par et de l'avis et / consentement du Conseil Législatif et Assemblée de la dite Province, con-/ stitués et assemblés en vertu de et sous l'autorité d'un ACTE du Parle-/ ment de la Grande Bretagne, passé dans la Trente-et-uniéme Année du / Règne de notre Souverain Seigneur GEORGE TROIS, par la Grace de / DIEU, ROI de la Grande Bretagne, de France et d'Irlande, Défenseur de / la Foi, &c. / [rule] / [royal arms] / [rule] / QUEBEC: / IMPRIME' SOUS L'AUTORITE' DU GOUVERNEMENT ET PAR ORDRE DE SON EXCEL-/LENCE LE GOUVERNEUR, ET CONFORMEMENT A L'ACTE DU PARLEMENT PROVINCIAL, / Par GUILLIAUME [sic] VONDENVELDEN, Imprimeur à la Nouvelle Imprimerie, / Rue de la Montagne, Anno Domini M.DCC.XCV. /

4to. [*][4], A-I[4]; 4 p. l. [5]-75 p.; type-page: 23 × 17.3 cm. Two leaves of sig. I are folded to precede sig. [*], forming English and French t.-p.; p. 8 mispaged: 7 in some copies. Text in English and French on opposite pages. In the English t.-p. in the imprint, the word "DIRECTS" has the roman numeral "I" in place of upper case alphabetical letter, "I."

Contents: p. l. 1 recto, English t.-p.; verso, blank; p. l. 2 recto, French t.-p.; verso, blank; p. l. 3 recto, English half-title; verso, blank; p. l. 4 recto, French half-title; verso, blank; p. [5], blank; p. [6]-75, 35 Geo. III c. I-XI, passed in the third session of the first Assembly, Jan. 5-May 7, 1795; verso of p. 75, blank.

This is a separate issue (with t.-p., signatures, and pagination printed from a different setting of type, text printed from the same setting of type) of the collected sessions laws published in No. 943, p. [112]-86.

Copies located: CaOLU; CaOOA; MiU; MiU-C; PHi; RPJ.

945. LOWER CANADA. LAWS, STATUTES, *etc.*

[A Provincial Statute of Lower-Canada Enacted by The King's most Excellent Majesty, by and with the advice and consent of the Legislative Council and Assembly of the said Province, constituted and assembled by virtue of and under the authority of an act of the Parliament of Great Britain passed in the thirty-first year of the reign of our Sovereign Lord George the Third by the Grace of God, of the United Kingdom of Great Britain and Ireland King, Defender of the Faith. (royal arms) Quebec. Printed under the authority and by command of his Excellency the Governor: as the Act of the Provincial Parliament directs. By William Vondenvelden, Printer at the New Printing-office, Mountain street. Anno Domini. MDCCXCV.]

4to. 17 p.; Text in English and French on opposite pages.

Contents: p. [1], English t.-p.; p. [2], blank; p. [3], French t.-p.; p. [4], blank; p. [5], blank; p. [6]-17, An act to establish the form of registers of baptisms, marriages, and burials [etc.]; verso of p. 17, blank. This is probably a separate issue (with different t.-p. and pagination) of 35 Geo. III c. 4, in *The Provincial Statutes* (Quebec, 1795), I: 131-42 (No. 943).

Copy recorded but not located: C. R. Brown: *Bibliography of Quebec or Lower Canada laws*, 18, from which title and description above is taken.

946. LOWER CANADA. LEGISLATIVE COUNCIL

PLAN / OF / A BILL, / For altering the Criminal law, / SENT BY THE / LEGISLATIVE COUNCIL, / TO THE ASSEMBLY, / MONDAY, 16th February, 1795. / [rule] / printer's ornament] / [rule] / [double rule] / QUEBEC:—PRINTED AT THE NEW PRINTING-OFFICE, / M.DCC.XCV. /

4to. A-C², [D]¹; 13 p.; type-page: 13.5 × 10 cm.

Contents: p. [1], t.-p.; p. [2], Order to print: "House of Assembly, Quebec, Monday 16th February 1795. Ordered that one hundred Copies of the Bill be printed in French and English . . . and that two copies in each language be sent by the Clerk of the House to each member in town, . . . attest. Sam. Phillips, clk."; p. [3]-13, An act to alter and amend the criminal law in certain cases and to provide more effectual Remedies against the commission of certain offences; verso of p. 13, blank.

The bill concerns grand and petit larceny, the theft, killing, and maiming of cattle, incendiarism, assault, etc. It was apparently drawn up and passed in the Legislative Council but dropped in the House of Assembly.

Copy located: CaQQL.

947. LOWER CANADA. LEGISLATIVE COUNCIL

French edition of No. 946. Probably 4to, about 13 p. *Printed at Quebec, by Wm. Vondenvelden*, 1795, and containing:

"Acte qui change et amende la Loi Criminelle dans certains cas, et qui établit des punitions plus efficaces pour ceux qui commettent des crimes et des offenses."—caption title from first reading and order to print, in L.C. As. *Journal*, Feb. 16, 1795.

Copy located: None.

948. LOWER CANADA. LEGISLATIVE COUNCIL

A BILL / OFFERED BY MR. CHIEF JUSTICE MONK, OF MONTREAL, / ON MONDAY 23d NOVEMBER, 1795. / TO THE / LEGISLATIVE COUNCIL, / Intituled "An Act for more effectually securing to Creditors the / "Estate and Effects of Persons in Trade failing therein and / "for the equal distribution of such Effects and Estate." / [double rule] / [royal arms] / QUEBEC: / PRINTED AT THE NEW PRINTING OFFICE, MOUNTAIN-STREET, / Anno Domini, M.DCC.XCV. /

French t.-p.:

BILL / PRESENTE' PAR MONSIEUR LE JUGE EN CHEF MONK DE MON-/TREAL, LUNDI LE 23 NOVEMBRE, 1795. / AU / CONSEIL LEGISLATIF / Intitulé "Acte qui assure plus efficacement aux Créanciers les / "Biens et Effets des Gens en Commerce faisant faillite, et pour / "l'égale distribution de tels Effets et Biens." / [double rule] / royal arms] / [rule] / QUEBEC, / IMPRIME' A LA NOUVELLE IMPRIMERIE, RUE LA MONTAGNE. / Anno Domini, M.DCC.XCV. /

4to. [*]^2, A-I^4; 2 p. l., 70 p.; type-page: 14 × 12 cm. Odd numbers on verso, even numbers on recto. Text in English and French on opposite pages.

Contents: p. l. 1 recto, English t.-p.; verso, Order to print, from the Legislative Council, Dec. 9, 1795, signed by Wm. Smith, C.L.C.; p. l. 2 recto, French t.-p., verso, Order to print (in French); recto of p. 1, blank; p. 1-70, Bill; verso of p. 70, blank.

The bill, read in Council for the first time Dec. 9, 1795, was ordered to be printed in both languages and 100 copies distributed for the use of members of the House. It does not appear to have been passed into law.

Copies located: CaQMS; CaQQL.

949. MARIE ANTOINETTE, *Queen consort of Louis XVI, King of France*, 1755-1793

[Portrait of the late Queen of France.]

Probably a wood engraving, *printed at Quebec, by John Neilson, 1795*, according to the printer's advertisement: "For sale at the Printing office a Portrait of the late Queen of France, copied from an original drawing lately brought from Paris and reckoned a very striking likeness."—*Quebec gazette*, Jan. 29, 1795.

Copy located: None.

950. METHODIST CHURCH. NOVA SCOTIA. CONFERENCE

[Minutes of a conference held at Windsor, N.S., 1795.]

4 p. *Printed at Halifax, N.S., by John Howe? 1795.*

Methodist societies in Nova Scotia, which appeared with the settlement of emigrants from Yorkshire in 1772, and increased after the American Revolution, numbered some 753 members by 1795. Their preachers or missionaries appointed from Wesleyans in England or by an American Methodist conference, held a provincial conference at Halifax, Oct. 10, 1786, and apparently annually thereafter.

"The Conference of 1795 was held at Windsor . . . [with] William Black as Presiding Elder . . . The Minutes of 1795 were printed in the form of a four-page tract. The ministers are urged to 'regularly appoint' and 'scrupulously attend' Quarterly meetings, at each of which a collection is to be taken up . . . 'If the Presiding Elder' it is said, 'cannot possibly be present and there be no Elder nor Deacon in the Circuit, let the neighbouring Elder or Deacon attend, and diligently enquire into the temporal and spiritual state of the society' [etc.]." The *Minutes* are synopsized, apparently from an unlocated copy of the printed tract, by T. Watson Smith in *History of the Methodist church . . . of eastern British America* (2 v., Halifax, N.S., 1877-90), 1: 307-09.

Copy located: None.

951. MONTREAL GAZETTE

[Prospectus announcing the Montreal Gazette to be published by Louis Roy.]

?Broadside: *Probably printed at Quebec, by Louis Roy, 1795.* The paper for this publication was supplied by John Neilson, as recorded:

"1795, July 9 [Debit] Louis Roy 6 Quires Demy for his Prospectus announcing his Gazette @ 1/3—£0.7.6."—Can.P.A., *Neilson papers*, v. 54.

The printing was probably done by Roy himself on his own recently acquired press in Neilson's office, where he was employed in July, 1795, and where he purchased the press. It may, indeed, have been done from the types of the *Quebec gazette*, where the *Prospectus* appeared:

"At this time when the conduct and wisdom of the Parliament of Great Britain . . . has granted to us a Constitution whose advantages have not escaped the notice of the most enlightened Politicians and celebrated Writers . . . now that the system of government in this Colony promises every encouragement in Arts and Literature . . . the Subscriber late printer in Upper Canada . . . having purchased a printing office proposes to publish a periodical paper—the *Montreal Gazette*

"Conditions: (1) to be published every Monday in English and French on good paper, folio Crown and with good type.

"(2) Each number shall contain news of Europe and the United States.

"(3) Also Essays, poems, literary productions and articles of intelligence will be inserted.

"(4) Every advertisement of not more than 10 lines in one language—5/ for the first insertion, 1/ thereafter; in 2 languages 7/6; 2/6.

"(5) Subscription, $3 per year. Mr. Saro at Montreal, Mr. Sills at Three Rivers, Louis Aimé at Berthier, and the Printing Office at Quebec will take Subscriptions [etc.]" Dated from Quebec, July 8, 1795, the *Prospectus* states that Roy is moving to Montreal at once with all necessary equipment."—*Quebec gazette*, July 9, 1795.

This prospectus announces the *Montreal gazette*, published in Montreal by Louis, then by his brother, Joseph-Marie, Roy, 1795-97.

Copy located: None.

952. NEW BRUNSWICK. HOUSE OF ASSEMBLY

JOURNAL / OF THE / VOTES and PROCEEDINGS / OF THE / HOUSE OF ASSEMBLY / OF THE / PROVINCE of NEW-BRUNSWICK: / From TUESDAY the 3d of FEBRUARY, to THURSDAY the / 5th of MARCH, 1795. / [ornamental rule] / [royal arms] / [ornamental rule] / FREDERICTON: / Printed by CHRISTOPHER SOWER, Printer to the / KING'S MOST EXCELLENT MAJESTY. 1795. / [title within a frame of flower pieces]

fo. A-Q^2; 1 p. l., [387]-448 p., fold table; type-page: 23 × 13.5 cm. Paged in continuation of No. 898. One leaf of sig. Q is folded around sig. A-P to form t.-p.

Contents: p. l. recto, t.-p.; verso, blank; p. [387]-448, Journal of the third session of the second assembly; fold. table, correctly inserted between p. 406-407, is "... Account of Merchandise imported into the Port of Saint John ... [Feb. 5, 1794-Jan. 31, 1795], subject to a duty at the Treasury Office."

Two hundred copies of the *Journal* and three hundred copies of the *Acts* of this session were ordered by the House to be printed, distributed, and paid for, as in the preceding years. Sower's bills of £39 18*s*. 8*d*. for the *Journals* and £30 13*s*. 8*d*. for the *Acts* (No. 953) and the *Elections Act* (No. 954) were apparently paid by the governor in 1795 and included in the Assembly's supply bill next session. From 1796 till 1799, however, no supply bill was enacted, the Council regularly refusing the Assembly's bill, which included provision for a salary to members of the House. So the printer's bill for 1795-98 remained on the books till Feb., 1799.

Though this and the following publications bear the imprint of Fredericton, there is no evidence to indicate that Sower actually moved his printing office there, as in the session of 1792. It appears rather that they were printed in Saint John. *See* No. 954 *note*.

Copies located: CaN (t.-p. wanting); CaNU (fold. table wanting); CaNsWA; CaOOA; RPJ.

953. NEW BRUNSWICK. LAWS, STATUTES, *etc.*

ACTS / OF THE / GENERAL ASSEMBLY / OF / His MAJESTY'S PROVINCE / OF / NEW-BRUNSWICK, / PASSED IN THE YEAR 1795. / [rule] / [royal arms] / [rule] / FREDERICTON: / Printed by CHRISTOPHER SOWER, Printer to the / KING'S MOST EXCELLENT MAJESTY. 1795. /

fo. A-F^2; 3 p. l., 324-44 p.; type-page: 23 × 13.4 cm. Even numbers on recto, odd numbers on verso; paged in continuation of No. 899. One leaf of sig. F is folded around sig. A-E to form a p. l.

Contents: p. l. 1 recto, t.-p.; verso, blank; p. l. 2 recto, half-title; verso, blank; p. l. 3 recto, Titles of the acts; verso, blank; p. 324-44, 35 Geo. III c. I-VII acts passed in the third session of the second assembly; verso of p. 344, blank.

An edition of 300 copies was printed probably at Saint John or Brookville (*see* No. 954 *note*).

Copies located: Baxter; DLC; MH; NNB.

954. NEW BRUNSWICK. LAWS, STATUTES, *etc.*

ANNO REGNI / GEORGII III. / REGIS / Magnæ Britanniæ, Franciæ & Hiberniæ, / TRICESMO PRIMO. / At the General Assembly of the Province of New-Brunswick begun and / holden at the City of Saint John, on the Third day of January, / Anno Domini 1786, in the Twenty-sixth Year of the Reign of / our Sovereign Lord GEORGE the Third, by the Grace of GOD, of / Great-Britain, France and Ireland, KING Defender of the Faith, &c. / And from thence continued by several prorogations to TUESDAY the / FIRST day of FEBRUARY 1791, at FREDERICTON; being the / FIFTH Session of the FIRST GENERAL

ASSEMBLY of NEW-/BRUNSWICK. / [rule] / [royal arms] / [rule] / FREDERICTON: / Printed by CHRISTOPHER SOWER, Printer to the KING'S / MOST EXCELLENT MAJESTY, 1795. /

fo. A-C[2]; 12 p. type-page: 23 × 13.5 cm. One leaf of sig. C is folded behind sig. A-B to form t.-p.

Contents: p. [1], t.-p.; p. [2], blank; p. [3]-12. An act for regulating elections of representatives in general Assembly and for limiting the duration of assemblies in this province. Note at end of text: "N.B. This act was 'confirmed, finally enacted and ratified' by an Order of His Majesty in Council, dated at the Court of St. James's the 3d of June, 1795."

This act, 31 Geo. III c. 17, was the first law regulating elections effective in New Brunswick. In the first Assembly 1786 (for the election of which Lieut.-Gov. Carleton had given franchise to all males of full age resident in the province three months) a bill for regulation of elections had been passed with a suspending clause. It remained inoperative, for royal assent was refused in Aug., 1790. Another bill was passed in the session of 1791, and transmitted to London. After at least two anxious inquiries from New Brunswick (—N.B. *Carleton* June 6, 1793, Mar. 12, 1795) it was passed by king-in-council, June 3, 1795.

This act conferred voting power upon persons possessed of freehold worth £25 (£5 higher than the 1786 bill—the principal change) and upon freemen of the city of Saint John owning personal property worth £25. Candidates were required to have freehold of £200 in their electoral district. The Assembly term was limited to seven years unless dissolved sooner. The act set forth other qualifications of candidates, forms of oaths, and routine of elections—including a fifteen-day polling period—twenty-three clauses in all.

Though it bears the imprint of Fredericton, the seat of government since 1786, this work was probably printed at Brookville, near Saint John, where Sower had a farm home and printing-house, or in Saint John, where he also had an office. For the provincial accounts of 1795 include: "To James Sutter for bringing 100 Copies of the Act for regulating elections from St. John to Fredericton—10/"; also, "To Christopher Sower for printing the Acts passed in last session also an Act for regulating elections—£30.13.8."—N.B. As. *Journal*, Feb. 27, 1796.

According to the charge for *Acts* of other sessions, Sower's charge for printing the elections act was about £10.

Copies located: MH; NNB; RPJ.

955. NEW BRUNSWICK. TREASURY OFFICE

(No. I) A GENERAL ACCOUNT of MERCHANDIZE imported into the Port of SAINT JOHN, (NEW-BRUN-/SWICK), from the 5th day of February 1794, to the 31st of January 1795, both days included, subject to Duty at / the TREASURY OFFICE. <Text> Saint John, New-Brunswick, 31st January, 1795. / A. DE PEYSTER, / P. Treasurer. /

Broadside: type-page: 26.5 × 23.5 cm. paper page: 35.5 × 30.5 cm. Probably *printed at Saint John or Brookville, N.B., by Christopher Sower, 1795.*

The treasurer's account of imports (duties on which were the principal source of provincial revenue) was usually published on a broadside, folded and inserted in the House of Assembly's *Journal* of the year. It was apparently issued separately also, in some years at least.

Abraham de Peyster came to New Brunswick in 1783, a loyalist from New York. A grantee of Parr Town (Saint John), he lived there and at Fredericton, became sheriff of Sunbury County in 1785, and was provincial treasurer from 1792 till his death Feb. 19, 1798, aged 46 years.

Copy located: GBLP (in C.O. 188/6: 193 enclosed in Lieut.-Gov. Carleton's despatch, no. 13, from Fredericton, Oct. 19, 1795.).

956. NOVA SCOTIA. HOUSE OF ASSEMBLY

[rule] / JOURNAL / AND / PROCEEDINGS / OF THE / HOUSE OF ASSEMBLY. / [rule] /

fo. sig. 2I-2N^2, 2M-2R^2, [$*$]^1; 1 p. l., p. 131-73; paged in continuation of No. 901. *Printed at Halifax, N.S., by Anthony Henry, 1795.*

Contents: p. l. recto, t.-p.; verso, Proclamation; p. 131-73, Journal of the third session of the seventh assembly, Mar. 12-Apr. 13, 1795; verso of p. 173, blank.

Copies located: CaNs; GBLP (in C.O. 217/67: 34-56); MH.

957. NOVA SCOTIA. LAWS, STATUTES, *etc.*

Running title: [rule] / 1795. Anno Tricessimo Quinto Regis GEORGII III. CAP. I[-V]. / [rule] /

Caption title: At the GENERAL ASSEMBLY of the Province / of Nova-Scotia, . . . / [5 lines] / being the Third Session of the Seventh / General Assembly, convened in the said Pro-/vince. / [rule] /

fo. 3N-3P^2; p. 367-377; type-page: 25 × 15 cm. paged in continuation of No. 902. *Printed at Halifax, N.S., by Anthony Henry, 1795.*

Contents: p. 367-377, Cap. I-V perpetual acts passed in the session, Mar. 12-Apr. 13, 1795; verso of p. 377, blank.

Copies located: CaO; DLC; MH (2 cop.).

958. NOVA SCOTIA. LAWS, STATUTES, *etc.*

Running title: [rule] / 1795. Anno Tricessimo Quinto Regis, GEORGII III. CAP. I[-V]. / [rule] /

Caption title: At the GENERAL ASSEMBLY of the Province / of Nova-Scotia, . . . / [5 lines] / being the Third Session of the Seventh / General Assembly, convened in the said Pro-/vince. / [rule] /

fo. sig. 4I-4P^2, [$*$]^1; p. 421-449; type-page: 24.5 × 15 cm. paged in continuation of No. 903. *Printed at Halifax, N.S., by Anthony Henry, 1795.*

Contents: p. 421-449, Cap. I-V temporary acts passed in the session, Mar. 12-Apr. 13, 1795; verso of p. 449, blank.

Copies located: CaO; MH.

959. NOVA SCOTIA. LAWS, STATUTES, *etc.*

[Anno tricesimo quinto Georgii III, Cap. VI. An Act to amend, and reduce into one Act, the several Laws now in being, relating to a Militia in this Province.]

4to. *Printed at Halifax, N.S., by Anthony Henry, 1795*, as recorded:

"To printing 200 Militia Laws in quarto books, covering and sewing—£15."
—Henry's *Account* [*to Government*] *for Stationery &c. Mar.-Apr. 1795*, in P.A.N.S., *Miscellaneous Assembly papers*, 1796.

This act, passed about Apr. 13, and published in the *Royal gazette*, Halifax, N.S., Apr. 21, 1795, superseded 32 Geo. II c. VI, passed in the first provincial legislature, 1758, and its amendments, to 34 Geo. III c. XI, 1794. It provided for the enrolment of all males aged sixteen to sixty years, and the organization of militia companies on a war-time basis. Passed as a temporary act to remain in force till July 1, 1796, it was renewed with occasional amendment, annually thereafter, and was reprinted in *The Statutes at large, passed in . . . Nova Scotia from . . . 1758-1804*, compiled by R. J. Uniacke (Halifax, N.S., 1805), from which this entry was taken.

Copy located: None.

960. PRIMERS, LOWER CANADA. *French*

[ALPHABET FRANCOIS]

Probably printed at Quebec by John Neilson, 1795, according to the printer's advertisement: "Recemment publié et à Vendre à l'Imprimerie, une nouvelle Edition des Alphabets François et Latins."—*Quebec gazette*, Feb. 26, 1795, *et seq.*

Copy located: None.

961. PRIMERS, LOWER CANADA. *Latin*

[ALPHABET LATIN]

Probably printed at Quebec by John Neilson, 1795, according to the printer's advertisement, cited in No. 960 *note*.

962. QUEBEC GAZETTE. CARRIER'S ADDRESS

The Printer's Boy / Wishes his Customers a happy NEW-YEAR. / [rule] / Cum Re Modoque. /

French side:

ETRENNES / DU GARCON qui porte la / GAZETTE DE QUEBEC / AUX PRATIQUES. / [rule] / Le Ier. JANVIER, 1796. / [*Quebec, J. Neilson, 1795.*]

Broadside: type-page: 28 × 28 cm. in ornamental rule frame. English verse on left, 10 stanzas of 4 lines each; French on right, 3 stanzas in 28 lines. The former begins somewhat sadly:

"Happiness where art thou found?
Where is thy blessed abode?
Thou'rt sought by all, the World around,
Few to thee find the Road."

The French verses entitled: "Description des Democrates, Le Democrate Réformé, Vraies Richesses," ridicule democracy:

"Aristote n'a pas trouvé notre vrai nom
Orgeuil et petitesse ensemble
Voilà le Democrate ce me semble
Est-ce donc la ce qu'on nomme Raison?"

Copy located: CaO (bound in *Quebec gazette*, at end of 1795).

963. ROYAL GAZETTE, *Halifax, N.S.*, CARRIER'S ADDRESS

THE / News-Carrier's / ADDRESS / To the CUSTOMERS / OF THE / Royal Gazette, / [*Halifax, N.S., Anthony Henry, 1795.*]

Broadside: 51 lines within elaborate ornamental frame; type-page: 32 × 18 cm. Verse in 4 stanzas of 6-17 lines:

"Twelve months my weekly course I've run,
And rose before the early sun.
. . .
May carnage, bloodshed, guillotining cease,
And Ninety-six produce a lasting peace.
. . .
That heav'n our country long may bless,
With Liberty and Happiness.
. . .
I'll now conclude and cheerful sing
God save great George our noble King."

Copy located: CaNsHA (bound in *Miscellaneous newspapers, 1795-1796*).

964. ST. JOHN, ISLAND OF. HOUSE OF ASSEMBLY

JOURNAL / OF THE HOUSE OF ASSEMBLY / OF HIS MAJESTY'S / ISLAND OF SAINT JOHN. / ANNO TRICESSIMO QUINTO / REGIS GEORGII III. / [rule] / FOURTH SESSION OF THE SIXTH GENERAL ASSEMBLY. / [rule] / [rule] / [royal arms] / [double rule] / CHARLOTTE TOWN, ISLAND OF SAINT JOHN: / [rule] / PRINTED BY WILLIAM ALEXANDER RIND, / PRINTER TO THE KING'S MOST EXCELLENT MAJESTY. / [double rule] / 1795. /

4to. Sig. [$*^1$, 1]-5^2; 21 p.; type-page: 21.5 × 15.4 cm.

Contents: p. [1], t.-p.; p. [2], blank; p. [3]-21, Journal, Feb. 16-Mar. 4, 1795, the first meeting of the House since Nov., 1792; verso of p. 21, blank.

Copies located: CaP (copy uncut, unbound, with original stitching as issued); GBLP (in C.O. 226/15: 51-71).

965. ST. JOHN, ISLAND OF. LAWS, STATUTES, *etc.*

Caption title: AT the GENERAL ASSEMBLY of his Majesty's Island of Saint John, . . . being the fourth Session of the Sixth General Assembly.

4to. Sig. [1]-4²; 15 p.; type-page: 21 × 17 cm. *Printed at Charlotte-town, Island of St. John, by Wm. A. Rind, 1795.* This item, like No. 964, may have been issued with an additional quarter-sheet preceding the first section and containing title-page, for Rind customarily issued each session's laws and journal of Assembly with its own title page. If so, the title leaf has become detached (as it easily could do) from the only copy located.

Contents: p. [1]-15, 35 Geo. III c. I-XII, Acts passed during the session, Feb. 16-Mar. 4, 1795. 35 Geo. III c. XI, the Appropriation Act, includes provision for "William Alexander Rind, Printer to the Government, from 1st Jan. 1795 to 1st Jan. 1796—£40"; verso of p. 15, blank.

Copy located: NNHi (t.-p. wanting?).

966. UPPER CANADA. EXECUTIVE COUNCIL

[Order in Council, July 21, 1795. *Probably printed at Niagara, U.C., by Gideon Tiffany, 1795.*]

This was another edition of the order-in-council of Nov. 6, 1794. It contained, apparently, the text as it appeared in No. 916. But the schedule of fees at the end of the text was altered. These fees were revised in Council on July 21, 1795, on instructions from the Home government, to conform with those which obtained in Nova Scotia and Lower Canada, and were ordered published: "Resolved that the Proclamation of November the 6th 1794 be reprinted and the fees now established be added thereto instead of those which had been formerly adopted."—Can.P.A., "Q" 281: pt. 2, p. 449. The various schedules of fees, are reprinted and discussed in Paterson: *Land settlement in Upper Canada*, 52-53.

Copy located: None.

967. UPPER CANADA. LAWS, STATUTES, *etc.*

LAWS, / OF / His Majesty's PROVINCE of / UPPER-CANADA, / IN / NORTH AMERICA; / COMPRISING / ALL THE ACTS OF THE HONORABLE THE LEGISLATURE, / OF THE PROVINCE AFORESAID, / Enacted at their First, Second, Third and Fourth Sessions, / 1792, 1793, 1794 and 1795. / [rule] / [royal arms] / [rule] / NIAGARA: / PRINTED BY GIDEON TIFFANY—PRINTER TO HIS MOST EXCELLENT MAJESTY. / [rule] / 1795. /

4to. A-X²; 88 p.; type-page: 23.1-25.2 × 17 cm.

Contents: p. [1], t.-p.; p. [2], blank; p. [3]-11, 32 Geo. III c. I-VIII; p. 11-51, 33 Geo. III c. I-XIII; p. 51-77, 34 Geo. III c. I-XII; p. [78]-88, 35 Geo. III c. I-V.

This is the second printing of the laws passed in the first and second sessions, and the first printing of those of the third (June 2-July 4, 1794) and fourth (July 6-Aug. 10, 1795) sessions. Though it bears the imprint of 1795 the work was actually published in the spring of 1796. The delay was due, as Tiffany complained, to the clerk of council's neglect to furnish copy of the Acts, and/or as Lieut.-Gov. Simcoe wrote Gov. Dorchester from Newark, May 8, 1796, "The indisposition of the Printer of this Province has retarded the printing of the Provincial Statutes of the last session till the present moment . . . I have now the honour to enclose to your Lordship three printed copies of the Acts of the several sessions [etc.]."—J. G. Simcoe: *Correspondence,* 4: 259.

These laws with t.-p. as above, were also issued later with the laws of the fifth session and an index to the whole (No. 1022).

Niagara, formerly called Newark (now Niagara-on-the-Lake), a small settlement on Lake Ontario at the mouth of the Niagara River, was the first seat of government, and the only printing centre in the province from 1793 till 1798.

Copies located: CaOOA; CaOTL (bound with No. 1022); DLC; MH (p. [1]-4, 85-88 wanting and supplied in photostat).

968. UPPER CANADA. LIEUTENANT-GOVERNOR, 1791-1799 (*Simcoe*)

A PROCLAMATION, / To such as are desirous to settle on the lands of the crown in the Province of / UPPER CANADA; / BY HIS EXCELLENCY / John Graves Simcoe, Esquire; / Lieutenant Governor and Commander in Chief of the said Province, and Colonel / Commanding His Majesty's Forces &c.&c.&c. / [royal arms] <Text> / Given under my hand and seal, in the city of Quebec, the seventh day of February, in the thirty-/second year of his majesty's reign, and in the year of our Lord, one thousand, seven hundred / and ninety-two. / John Graves Simcoe. / BY HIS EXCELLENCY'S COMMAND, / THOMAS TALBOT, Acting Secretary. / Re-printed at Newark, by G. TIFFANY, 1795. / [imprint in ornamental frame.]

Broadside: 69 lines; type-page: 29 × 16 cm. This is another edition of No. 815, with some variation in the typographic style (e.g. in use of upper and lower case), with an imprint added, but with no change in the purport or wording of the proclamation.

Copies located: CaOOA (3 cop., in *Proclamations* portfolio in the Library); CaOT (2 cop.); CaOTU; GBLP (in C.O. 42/320: 613).

Copy recorded but not located: Hodgins, no. 55.

969. UPPER CANADA. LIEUTENANT-GOVERNOR, 1791-1799 (*Simcoe*)

[Proclamation Pour telles Personnes qui désirent s'établir sur les Terres de la Couronne dans la Province du Haut-Canada, Par Son Excellence John Graves Simcoe, Ecuyer, Lieutenant-Gouverneur et Commandant en Chef de la dite Province, et Colonel Commandant les Forces de Sa Majesté &c.&c.&c. <Text: preamble and terms 1-10> Donné sous mon seing et sceau dans la ville de Québec, le septième jour de Février . . . mil sept quatre-vingt-douze (Signé) John Graves Simcoe. Par Ordre de Son Excellence, P.A. De Bonne, A. S. & T. F. *Reprinted at Newark, by G. Tiffany, 1795.*]

Broadside, about 78 lines. This is another edition of No. 816, with some variation in typographic style, with imprint added but no change in the purport or wording of the proclamation.

Title is taken from MS. transcript, in Can.P.A. "Q" 278: 82-87, of the only copy located.

Copy located: GBLP (in C.O. 42/320: 615).

970. UPPER CANADA. LIEUTENANT-GOVERNOR, 1791-1799 (*Simcoe*)

[Proclamation. George the Third, by the Grace of God, of Great-Britain, France and Ireland, King, . . . to all His Majesty's Subjects, Greeting <Text> Given 21 Aug. 1795 . . . WM. JARVIS, Secretary]

Broadside: ***probably printed at Newark, U.C., by Gideon Tiffany, 1795.***

Text: "Whereas the Loyalists who adhered to the unity of Empire, and others . . . received Tickets or certificates of occupation . . . as testimonials of the claims of such persons to receive grants of land . . . And Whereas deeds are now to be made out to perfect titles of such lands . . . Now Know Ye that I . . . with the advice . . . of the Executive Council of this Province do hereby direct . . . [claimants in Western, Midland, and Eastern Districts to deposit their certificates with Clerks of the peace for transmission to the Attorney general, and claimants in the Home District, with the Attorney general—within six months]."

This proclamation is reprinted in Ontario Archives, *Report, 1906*, from which this entry is taken.

Copy recorded but not located: Hodgins, no. 59.

971. [WALTER, JOHN]

[Catalogue of books to be sold at auction, Quebec, April 29, 1795. ? *Printed at Quebec, by Wm. Vondenvelden, 1795.*]

"By Auction will be sold on . . . 29th April [1795] and the following days at No. 2 Peter Street, Lower Town. Valuable household furniture, books & other articles, property of Mr. John Walter, Merchant, upon his departure for England . . . [list of furniture, etc.] Catalogues of his valuable Library will be delivered prior to the days of the Sale. Books and plate will be sold in the Evenings.—John Jones, auctioneer and broker."—The *Times*, Quebec, Apr. 6, 1795.

The owner of this library was probably the author of No. 680 and No. 866.

Copy located: None.

972. WATSON, RICHARD, *bp. of Llandaff*, 1737-1816

EXTRAIT D'UN DISCOURS / PRONONCE' PAR LE TRES HONORABLE / RICHARD WATSON, / EVEQUE DE LANDAFF. / [double rule] / [printer's ornament] / [double rule] / [double rule] / QURBEC [sic]:—IMPRIME' A LA NOUVELLE IMPRIMERIE, / M.DCC XCV. / [double rule] /

[*-2x⁴, 3*¹]; XVII p.; type-page: 12 × 7.6 cm.

Contents: p. [I], t.-p.; p. [II] blank; p. [III]-XVII, Extrait d'un discours, signed: "R. Landaff, Londres, 25 Janvier, 1793;" verso of p. XVII, blank.

An extract from one of the bishop's numerous sermons on contemporary affairs, probably translated for publication in French Canada. This is a closely reasoned statement of the English liberal attitude towards the revolution in France—approving its initial purpose, the removal of arbitrary power and curtailment of privilege, but disapproving the development of republican government, destruction of the nobility and the church, and condemning the bloodshed and disorder of revolutionary method. The extract lauds the principle of equality as equal rights under the law, and demonstrates how such rights are implicit in the government of a constitutional monarchy.

The author, termed "Professor of Chemistry at Cambridge and afterwards Bishop of Llandaff, an eminent and learned Prelate," was (from the titles of his works listed in Robt. Watt's *Bibliotheca Britannica*) a prolific and versatile writer. He is known chiefly for his *Apology for the Bible in a series of letters addressed to T. Paine* (London, 1796).

Copies located: CaOOA; CaQMJ; CaQMS (2 cop.); NN; RPJ. Another copy from the collection of Miss Maria Monk, Montreal, was offered for sale by G. Ducharme, Montreal, June, 1937.

973. ALMANACS. LOWER CANADA

[Calendrier pour l'année 1797, pour Québec. *Québec, chez Jean Neilson.*]

Broadside. This almanac was advertised: "Just published . . . the Quebec Calendar for 1797, containing the Eclipses, Table of weights and value of coins as regulated by Act of the Provincial Parliament, May 7, 1796. Court terms [etc.], the Sovereigns of Europe—Price 7½d. retail, 5/ per dozen."—*Quebec gazette,* Oct. 13, 1796, *et seq.*

Copy located: None. A copy recorded (for sale by G. Ducharme, Montreal, Catalogue no. 28, item no. 2280, Mar., 1928) was not located.

974. ALMANACS. LOWER CANADA

CALENDRIER pour l'Année 1797, pour QUEBEC, par les 306$^{d.}$ 30$^{m.}$ de Longitude, et 46$^{d.}$ 55$^{m.}$ de Latitude. / [rule] /

Colophon: QUEBEC: IMPRIME' A LA NOUVELLE IMPRIMERIE, Rue de Palais, /

Broadside: type-page: 59 × 45 cm. in ornamental rule frame; *printed by Wm. Vondenvelden, 1796.*

Contents: Les signes du zodiaque, calendrier; Tableau des comtés de cette province, les paroisses y comprises avec leurs limites et représentans respectifs; Table des jours, les cours de justice; Table de reduction, (all in French only); Abstract of 37 Geo. III c. V regulating weight and rate of monies; Table of linear measure, etc.; Tide table (all in English and French).

Copy located: CaO (bound in *Quebec gazette,* at end of 1796).

975. ALMANACS. LOWER CANADA

THE / QUEBEC / ALMANACK / FOR / The Year 1796. / [double rule] / 46 D. 55 M. N.LAT.—71 D. 12 M. W.LONG. / [double rule] / [printer's ornament] / [double rule] / In se, sua per vestigia, volvitur annus. / [double rule] / QUEBEC: / Printed by JOHN NEILSON, / N° 3, MOUNTAIN STREET. / [title within ornamental frame.]

French t.-p.:

ALMANAC / DE / QUEBEC, / POUR / L'ANNEE 1796. / [double rule] / 46D. 55M. N.LAT.—71D. 12M. W.LONG. / [double rule] / printer's ornament] / [double rule] / Fugaces labunter Anni. / [double rule] / A QUEBEC: / [rule] / CHEZ JEAN NEILSON, / N° 3 RUE LA MONTAGNE / [title within ornamental frame]

12mo. A-[K][6], L[2]; 120, [4] p., front., 2 fold. tables; type-page: 10.8 × 6 cm.

Contents: p. [1], English t.-p.; p. [2], blank; p. [3], French t.-p.; p. [4]-35, Epochs, eclipses, tide table, calendar, feasts, p. 36-37, Interest tables; p. 38-56, Excerpts from laws on division of the province, 1791, land granting, counties and boundaries; courts; p. 57-96, Civil and military register; p. 97-120, Ecclesiastical state, clergy, etc.; p. [1-4] at end, Index; fold. tables: "Table of the court terms," "Table of duties," follow p. 56, and p. 120 respectively. The frontispiece, an engraving 10 × 7 cm., numbered: 2, entitled "Etat du premier Chasseur et Guerrier—State of Hunting and War," is signed: "J. G. Hochstetter, Sculpt."

This almanac follows closely the model set by Samuel Neilson in *The Quebec almanack for 1792*. It was published on Jan. 22, 1796, and sold at 2*s*. the copy, 4*s*. bound; 20*s*. the dozen.

Copies located: CSmH; CaOOA; CaQ (front. and [4] p. at end wanting); CaQM; CaQMC; CaQMS; CaQQAr; CaQQL (front. wanting); MHi.

976. ALMANACS. NOVA SCOTIA

AN / ALMANACK, / FOR THE / YEAR . . . 1797; / . . . / CALCULATED FOR THE MERIDIAN OF / HALIFAX, . . . / CONTAINING / The ECLIPSES [etc. 8 lines] / SITTINGS of the COURTS [etc. 8 lines] / . . . / [rule] / BY THEOPHRASTUS. / [rule] / HALIFAX: / Printed and sold by JOHN HOWE, at his Printing-Office, Corner / of GEORGE and BARRINGTON-STREETS, oposite [sic] the PARADE. / [title within double rule frame]

12mo. A-D[4]; [32] p.; type-page: 15 × 8.3 cm.

Contents: p. [1], t.-p.; p. [2], Zodiac; p. [3], Ephemeris; p. [4], Directions to farmers; p. [5-16], Calendar; p. [17-23], Nova Scotia provincial officials, courts, etc., clergy; p. [24], Masonic lodges in Nova Scotia; p. [25-30], Naval, army officers, militia; p. [31-32], Distances, etc., buoys.

"Directions to farmers," p. [4], has the text as it appeared in *An Almanack for 1791*, but with added detail here.

Advertisement quoted in No. 978 *note*.

Copy located: CaNsHA.

977. ALMANACS. NOVA SCOTIA

[Der Neuschottländische Calender Auf das Jahr Christi 1797. *Halifax, N.S., gedruckt bey Anthon. Henrich, 1796.*]

Henry's advertisement for *The Nova-Scotia Calender* (see next entry) suggests that its German edition, published 1788-91 as *Der Neuschottländische Calender,* continued to appear.

Copy located: None.

978. ALMANACS. NOVA SCOTIA

[The Nova-Scotia Calender, or an Almanack for the Year 1797. *Halifax, N.S., Anthony Henry,* 1796.]

This almanac was advertised: "Just published and to be sold by Anthony Henry, the Nova-Scotia Calender . . . for 1797 . . . 5/ per dozen, 7½d single. Also the German Almanack for 1797 [No. 977]. Just published and to be sold by John Howe, An Almanack for . . . 1797 [No. 976] . . . 5/ per doz. 7½d single."

—*Royal gazette,* Halifax, N.S., Nov. 22, 1796.

Copy located: None.

979. ALMANACS. UPPER CANADA

[Upper Canada Calendar, for the year 1797.]

Proposed printing at Newark by Gideon Tiffany, 1796, was advertised: "Now Preparing and will be in press in a few days, The Upper Canada Calendar for the year 1797, being a Pocket Almanack, containing besides astronomical calculations, lists of Legislative, Executive and military officers, times & places of holding courts, etc. The first work of its kind ever attempted in this province. The Publisher solicits articles [etc., dated Nov. 16, 1796]."

—*Upper Canada gazette,* Nov. 23, 1796, *et seq.*

This almanac was not published as proposed, however, as Tiffany advertised later: "The printer returns his thanks to the gentlemen who have furnished him with returns of the times and places of holding courts, and of the officers of the Queen's rangers, designed for the callendar [sic], and is sorry to add that these are the only assistance he has received towards prosecuting his design, and that the want of time and opportunity to collect all the matters necessary to the work, of himself, is compelled notwithstanding the forwardness of the common parts, unwillingly to relinquish the valuable design, until he shall have had time himself to collect the material— The calendar page of each month will be published in the gazette."

—*Upper Canada gazette,* Feb. 22, 1797.

980. BONNEFONS, AMABLE, 1600-1653

[Le Petit Livre de Vie, qui apprend à bien vivre et à bien prier Dieu. ? *Printed at Quebec, by Wm. Vondenvelden, 1796.*]

This was a standard devotional work used by Catholics in French Canada and constantly advertised in its newspapers. The first Canadian-printed edition appeared in 1777, and a 1796 edition is recorded by Dionne: *Inventaire*, 1: 41. This may be an error for the 1798 edition which is *not* recorded by Dionne.

The editions of 1798 to 1815 (or later) include the *Approbation* of Bishop Hubert (*d.* Oct. 17, 1797) dated: "Québec, 1er Aout, 1796"—which suggests that the publication was projected at least in that year. The title appeared frequently in the list of books for sale by John Neilson, printer of the *Quebec gazette*, but there is no evidence in his office records that he printed an edition in 1796.

Copy located: None.

981. BOUCHER-BELLEVILLE, JEAN BAPTISTE, 1763-1839

[RECUEIL DE CANTIQUES]

As the main t.-p. is wanting in the only copy located of this work, the t.-p. to its second volume is given in full:

RECUEIL / DE / CANTIQUES, / à L'USAGE / Des MISSIONS, des RETRAITES / ET DES / CATECHISMES. / TOME SECOND, / Ou Troisième Partie. / CONTENANT / LES SUPPLEMENTS DE LA SECONDE EDITION / AUX DEUX PREMIERES PARTIES. / AVEC QUELQUES EXTRAITS DU POEME DE LA / RELIGION, &c. / [rule] / Ils chantoient comme un cantique nouveau de-/vant le Trône.—Apocalypse. C.14, V.3. / [rule] / [double rule] / [double rule] / A QUEBEC: / CHEZ JOHN NEILSON, IMPRIMEUR ET LI-/BRAIRE, N° 3 RUE LA MONTAGNE. /—1796.— /

12mo. A-G^{12}, H^{4}; Aa-Ee^{12}, Ff^{5}; 3 pt. in 2 v. v. 1: 1 p. l., ii, 172 p.; v. 2: 1 p. l., 120, [7] p.; type-page: 13 × 6.7 cm. It seems reasonable that in the making of the book the final section was a full half sheet, giving the sig. Ff^{6}, and a final blank? leaf at the end or used to form a t.-p.—of which all evidence has disappeared.

Contents: v. 1: p. l. recto, t.-p.; verso, blank?; p. i-ii, Preface; p. [1]-87, Partie I, cantiques; p. 88-172, Partie II, cantiques; v. 2: p. l. recto, Partie III, t.-p. (as above); verso, blank; p. [1]-59, Supplement to Partie I; p. 59-110, Supplement to Partie II; p. 111-120 Extraits du poëme de la religion, de Mr. Racine le jeune; p. [1-7] at end, Table alphabetique; verso of p. [7], blank.

This is the second edition of No. 925, corrected and enlarged by the editor. The preface states the purpose, scope, and sources of the *Cantiques*, as in the first edition. Partie I-II contain the *Cantiques* printed the previous year with corrections; Partie III is new material, supplementary to Partie I-II respectively. Abbé Boucher-Belleville wrote Neilson from Laprairie, May 16, 1796: "Si la première edition du recueil des Cantiques &c. est entierement epuissé et que vous soyer résolu d'en donner une seconde, je pourrai sur votre reponse, preparer pour le fin de l'été un Supplement assez considérable et corriger quelques fautes qui se sont glissées dans la 1re. [etc.]"; and again on June 17, 1796: "Since being an Englishman you have written to me a French letter, I can as well, being a Frenchman write you an English one . . . [states he will prepare another edition of *Cantiques*]. There will be a constant demand for this work, as it is prepared for young people who come every year to the Catechisms or Schools. The price must be kept low." So, says he (Boucher) cannot add prayers for the mass or vespers, but suggests that these, with psalms, hymns, and anthems for the whole year, could form a separate volume—this suggestion materialized in 1800 (*see* No. 1167). In the same letter Boucher suggested that the new *Cantiques* be printed at the end, as a "third part" which could be issued separately to owners of the first edition. The abbé wrote Neilson again on Aug. 16, 1796, sending copy for the printer.—Can.P.A., *Neilson papers*, 1: 24, *et seq.*

Though this work bears the imprint of 1796, it appears to have been published in June, 1797, when the record of its constant sale begins in Neilson's accounts (v. 54). Large consignments were sent to the author, also to Neilson's agents in Montreal, etc., at £1 4*s*. the dozen, "common" or stitched, probably in blue paper; £1 6*s*. a dozen "in red backs"; and small lots at £1 16*s*. the dozen, "bound and lettered." Single copies were sold retail at 2*s*. 6*d*.

This edition was marred by numerous errors, apparently, for the author wrote to Neilson, from Laprairie, Nov. 11, 1797: ". . . trente ou quarante fautes grossieres qui se sont glissées dans votre impression me font rougir de honte, quand je ouvre le livre; et c'est la ce qui se trouve appellé une edition *corrigée!* heureusement qu'on n'y trouve pas le nom de l'editeur; il faudra bien que M. L'Imprimeur porte tout le fardeau. . . ."—Can.P.A., *Neilson papers*, 1: 110.

Copy located: CaQM (t.-p. wanting).

982. CATHOLIC CHURCH. CATECHISMS

CATECHISME / A / L'USAGE / DU DIOCESE / DE QUEBEC. / [rule] / Imprimé par l'Ordre de Monseigneur JEAN / OLIVIER BRIAND, / Evêque de Québec. / [rule] / Se Vend chez Mr. L. GERMAIN, N° 5, Rue de la Fabrique. / [rule] / [ornament] / [rule] / QUATRIEME EDITION. / [rule] / A QUEBEC. / IMPRIME' A LA NOUVELLE IMPRIMERIE, / Rue du Palais, M.DCC.XCVI. / [ornamental rule frame]

12mo. A-G^4, H^3; 1 p. l., [2]-60, [1] p.; type-page: 15.5 × 8.2 cm. (Collation probably A-H^4; l. H4 (probably blank) wanting in the only—well worn—copy located). In pagination, even numbers on recto, odd numbers on verso.

Contents: p. l. recto, t.-p.; verso, blank; p. [2-5], Mandement, signed: "Québec, 7 Mars, 1777, J. Ol. Evêque de Québec"; p. [6], Avertissement; p. [7], Introduction; p. [8]-60, Le Petit Catéchisme; [1] p. (verso of p. 60), Table (contents).

Printed by Wm. Vondenvelden, at the New Printing-Office, for Louis Germain, son of the Louis Germain for whom Brown & Gilmore had printed the first Quebec edition of the *Catéchisme . . . de Sens*, 1765. This "quatrième édition" is at least the fifth edition (each printed from a new setting of type) of the preliminary matter and text of the *Catéchisme . . . de Québec*, first published in 1777.

Copy located: CaQMS (bound in original figured wall-paper covers now soiled and torn).

983. CATHOLIC CHURCH. LITURGY AND RITUAL

[NEUVAINE A L'HONNEUR DE SAINT FRANCOIS XAVIER. *Printed at Quebec, 1796?*]

A new edition of this work was projected, if not published in Quebec or Montreal, in 1796. No copy has been located, but subsequent editions, e.g., that published at

Montreal in 1811 (copy in Laval University Library) and at Saint Philippe, 1825 (*see* Toronto Public Library, *Bibliography of Canadiana* no. 1369), bear the *Approbation* of a 1796 edition:

"Québec, 29 Oct. 1796. L'experience de bien des années preuve si manifestement l'utilité de la Neuvaine de Saint François Xavier, que je n'hésite point, au Nom de Nos Seigneurs Evêques d'approuver et à louer beaucoup la Nouvelle Edition qui se fait de si excellent livre. [signed:] Gravé, Vic.-gen."

Henri-François Gravé de la Rive, 1730-1802, served as vicar-general of Quebec from 1787? till 1797.

Copy located: None.

984. CATHOLIC CHURCH. LITURGY AND RITUAL

[Les Vêpres Hymnes et Antiennes de l'Eglise, *Quebec, 1796*]

This title, recorded by Dionne: *Inventaire,* 1: no. 45, probably refers to a section of *Heures Romaines . . . 1795* (No. 927) which was advertised thus:

"Soon will be ready for sale at the Printing Office.

"Heures Romaines en gros caractères, contenant Les Offices de la Sainte Vierge. . . .

"Les Vêpres, Hymnes et Antiennes de l'Eglise &c.&c.&c. on Demy, 12mo neatly bound, price 3/6 by retail; and 36/ per dozen."

—*Quebec gazette,* July 28, 1796.

There is no evidence in the records of Neilson the printer, however, that *Les Vêpres Hymnes* was issued separately.

985. CHURCH OF ENGLAND. LITURGY AND RITUAL

[Form of Prayer for a Fast Day, appointed for Wednesday, July 6th, 1796.]

Printed at Saint John, N.B., by John Ryan, 1796, as recorded:

"Proclamation &c. for a solemn fast, appointed for Wednesday 6th day of July next. Ordered that 200 copies of the form of prayer, appointed for this occasion, be printed, to be distributed as the Rev. Mr. Pidgeon may direct."—Can.P.A., N.B. Ex. co. *Minutes,* May 17, 1796.

"1796, May 26. To printing 200 Copies of a Form of prayer for fast day 61s. [per] c.—£6."—John Ryans's *Account* [*to government*] *for printing &c. June 1795-June 1796,* in N.B. As. *Papers,* 1796.

"The Rev. Mr. Pidgeon" was George Pidgeon, 1760-1818, who, born and educated in Ireland, was ordained in Nova Scotia in 1793, and from 1795 till 1814 served the Church of England at Fredericton, N.B. He or Bishop Inglis probably arranged this *Form of Prayer.*

Copy located: None.

986. GREAT BRITAIN. TREATIES, *etc.*

TREATY / OF / Amity, Commerce, and Navigation, / BETWEEN / HIS BRITANNICK MAJESTY / AND THE / UNITED STATES of AMERICA, / Signed at London, the 19th of November, 1794. / [rule] / Published by Authority. / [rule] / [royal arms] / QUEBEC: / PRINTED BY COMMAND OF HIS EXCELLENCY THE GOVERNOR; AS THE ACT OF / THE PROVINCIAL PARLIAMENT DIRECTS. / BY WILLIAM VONDENVELDEN, Printer at the New Printing-Office, / Poor-street, Anno Domini, M.DCC. XCVI. /

French t.-p.:

TRAITÉ / d'Amitié, de Commerce, et de Navigation, / ENTRE / SA MAJESTÉ BRITANNIQUE / ET LES / ETATS UNIS de l'AMÉRIQUE, / Signé à Londres, le 19me Novembre, 1794. / [rule] / Publié par Autorité. / [rule] / [royal arms] / QUEBEC: / IMPRIME' PAR ORDRE DE SON EXCELLENCE LE GOUVERNEUR, ET CONFORME-/MENT A L'ACTE DU PARLEMENT PROVINCIAL. / Par GUILLAUME VONDENVELDEN, Imprimeur à la Nouvelle Imprimerie. / Rue des Pauvres, Anno Domini, M.DCC. XCVI. /

4to. A-F[4]; 45 p., 1 *l.*; type-page: 23 × 16.7 cm. Text in English and French on opposite pages. This work is frequently found in 39 p. without the *Explanatory article*.

Contents: p. [1], English t.-p.; p. [2], blank; p. [3], French t.-p.; p. [4], blank; p. [5], blank; p. [6]-39, Treaty, British and American ratifications and powers; p. [40-41], blank; p. [42]-45, Explanatory article, re-affirming rights of free intercourse and commerce as in article 3, signed by P. Bond and Timothy Pickering; verso of p. 45, blank; 1 *l.*, blank.

This is the definitive text of the Jay Treaty with the United States ratification, also the British ratification, dated Oct. 28, 1795. The Quebec edition was probably reprinted from a copy of the edition printed in London by Edward Johnson 1795 (33 p. 4to). despatched by Portland to Gov. Dorchester and laid before the Council at Quebec, May 17, 1796.

Vondenvelden's edition was reprinted without change, even of imprint, or else copies of the original 1796 edition were reissued, to form part of the miscellaneous group of documents issued as *A Collection of Acts* in 1800 (*see* No. 1169). The *Explanatory article* is sometimes found without the treaty, unpaged, and with typography and paper obviously later than that used in 1796.

Copies located: (in 39 p. without *Explanatory article* and usually on the paper water marked 1794, commonly used in 1796): CaNsWA; CaOOA; CaQ; Gordonsmith.

Copies located: (in 45 p. with *Explanatory article*, and some *certainly* printed in 1796): CaO (2 cop.); CaOT (2 cop.); CaOTL; CaQM; CaQMJ; Ketcheson; CaQMM (3 cop.); CaQQB (2 cop.); CaQQL (2 cop.); DLC (2 cop.); M; MH (2 cop.); MiD-B; MiU; MiU-C; N; NN; NNB; RPJ; WHi.

Copies located: (Explanatory article only): CaOTO; MWA.

987. HUBERT, AUGUSTE DAVID, 1751-1792

SERMON / SUR LA / CONVERSION; / PRONONCE' PAR / FEU MESSIRE A.D. HUBERT, / CURE' DE QUEBEC, / L'ANNE'E AVANT SA MORT, / LE 9me DIMANCHE / APRES LA PENTECOTE. / A QUEBEC: / IMPRIME' A LA NOUVELLE IM-/PRIMERIE, Rue du Palais, l'An / de notre Seigneur, M,DCC,DCVI. /

12mo. A-B^{12}, C^{6}; 2 p. l., 56 p.; type-page: 10 × 7 cm. *Printed by Wm. Vondenvelden.*

Contents: p. l. 1 recto, t.-p.; verso, blank; p. l. 2 recto, Preface, verso, blank; p. [1]-56, Sermon ". . . Si cognovisses et tu et quidem in hâc die tuâ quæ ad pacem tibi; nunc autem abscondita sunt ab oculis tuis."

The sermon is in French. The preface (unsigned) states: "Ce discours traitant un sujet religieux des plus importans au Christianiasme, avec cette simplicité et clarté qui distinguoient les sermons du digne pasteur qui l'a composé, il ne pourra être reçu que favorablement par les ames vraiment dévotes; d'autant plus que cette petite piece est remplie de vérités qui opéront sans faute le salut de tout lecteur sur lequel elles feront une heureuse et profonde impression."

The sermon was delivered by Hubert in 1791, according to the date inserted in MS. following the word "Pentecote" on the t.-p. of the Filteau-Hamel copy in the Bibliothèque Saint-Sulpice. The author was drowned near Quebec in 1792 (*see* No. 752).

Copies located: CaQM (a fragment of 2 *l.* containing t.-p. and preface only); CaQMS (2 cop., p. 55-56 wanting in Joubert-Boileau copy).

988. L'HOMOND, CHARLES FRANCOIS, 1727-1794

ELEMENS / DE LA / GRAMMAIRE LATINE, / A L'USAGE DES COLLEGES, / Par Mr. L'hommond, Professeur-émérite en / l'Université de Paris. / [double rule] / SYNTAXE. / [double rule] / [double rule] / [ornament] / [double rule] / A MONTREAL, / Chez LOUIS ROY, Imprimeur du Collège. / M.DCC.XCVI. /

12mo. A-B^{8}, C^{4}, [$*$]^{2}; 1 p. l., 41 p.; type-page: 14 × 8.5 cm. The paper of sig. [$*$] differs in shade and texture from that of sig. A-C. One leaf of [$*$] is folded around A-C to form t.-p.

Contents: p. l. recto, t.-p.; verso, blank; p. 1-41, Grammaire latine, Seconde partie; verso of p. 41, blank.

The first part of this popular text-book appeared the following year (No. 1044); the third part is described below.

Louis Roy, who had been an apprentice in Wm. Brown's printing office at Quebec, 1786-89, and printer for the government at Newark, Upper Canada, 1793-94, operated a press in Montreal from July-Aug., 1795 to ?Sept., 1796. These school books, prepared for the Sulpicians' Collège de Montréal, are all (besides a newspaper) known to bear his Montreal imprint.

Copy located: CaQMS. Another (Hart) copy known but not located (*see* No. 1044 *note*).

989. L'HOMOND, CHARLES FRANCOIS, 1727-1794

ELEMENS / DE LA / GRAMMAIRE LATINE, / A L'USAGE DES COLLEGES, / Par Mr. Lhommond, Professeur-émérite en / l'Université de Paris. / [double rule] / METHODE / [double rule] / [double rule] / [ornament] / [double rule] / A MONTREAL, / Chez LOUIS ROY, Imprimeur du Collège. / MDCCXCVI. /

12mo. A-D^{8}, [*]^{1}; 65 p.; type-page: 14 × 8.5 cm.

Contents: p. [1], t.-p.; p. [2], blank; p. [3]-65, Grammaire latine, troisième partie; verso of p. 65, blank.

This was published in sequel to No. 988.

Copy located: CaQMS. Another (Hart) copy known but not located (*see* No. 1044 *note*).

990. LOWER CANADA. ADJUTANT GENERAL'S OFFICE

[double rule] / ORDONNANCE / Pour loger les troupes, dans certaines occasions, chez les / habitans des campagnes, et qui pourvoit aux trans-/ports des effets du gouvernement. / [caption title]

fo. [4] p.; type-page: 31 × 19 cm. Text in French only. *Probably printed at Quebec at the New Printing Office, by Wm. Vondenvelden, 1796.*

Contents: p. [1-3], Ordonnance du 23 Avril 1787, Ordres du quartier général, 2 mai 1787-25 juillet 1796; p. [4], Table de tarif.

This publication complements No. 991. The text was also published, with parts in English, in *Rules and articles for the better government of the militia*, 1812. *See* No. 937 *note at end.*

Copy located: CaQMS.

991. LOWER CANADA. ADJUTANT GENERAL'S OFFICE

Régles et Articles / POUR MIEUX GOUVERNER / TOUTES LES FORCES / DE SA / MAJESTE' / Depuis le 24$^{me.}$ Jour de Mars, 1794. / [rule] / Publié par ordre de Son Excellence. / [rule] / QUEBEC: / IMPRIME' à la NOUVELLE IMPRIMERIE, / M.DCC. XCVI. /

12mo. A-M^{4}; 92 p., 2 *l.*; type-page: 13.7 × 8.5 cm. Text in French only.

Contents: p. [1], t.-p.; p. [2], blank; p. 3-92, Règles; *l.* 1 at end, recto, blank; verso, Index; *l.* 2 blank.

Copies located: CaOOA; CaQMS (2 cop.); CaQQL (in original gray paper covers complete with blank *l.*).

992. LOWER CANADA. EXECUTIVE COUNCIL

ORDER / OF THE / GOVERNOR IN COUNCIL, / OF THE / 7th July 1796, / FOR THE / Regulation of Commerce, / BETWEEN THIS PROVINCE / AND THE / United States of America. / [double rule] / QUEBEC: / By JOHN NEILSON, No. 3 Mountain Street. / —1796.— /

8vo. A-B[4]; p. l., 11 p., 1 *l.*; type-page: 17.1 × 10.2 cm.

Contents: p. l. recto, t.-p.; verso, blank; p. [1]-11, Order of the governor-in-council, signed at end by Herman Witsius Ryland, C. Ex. C.; verso of p. 11, blank; 1 *l.* (not seen, probably blank).

This is the first monograph edition of a notable order-in-council. It is a reprint of the text published (in English only) in the *Quebec gazette extraordinary*, Saturday, July 9, 1796. p. 1-11 was printed from the *Gazette* types with the type-page adjusted to a pamphlet, and issued with a specially set t.-p. The French text was also published a little later. The reprints are recorded:

"1796, July 9. [Debit] Lieutenant governor's Secretary's Office. To 50 copies of the American commercial Regulations [in English] @ 6d.—£1.5.

July 14. [Debit] Lieutenant governor's Secretary's Office per H. W. Ryland, 50 Copies of the American commercial Regulations in E[nglish] @ 6d. —£1.5.

50 Copies of do. in F[rench]—£1.5."

—Can.P.A., *Neilson papers*, v. 54.

They were advertised in the next regular issue of the *Gazette:*

"For Sale at the Printing Office, Quebec, Mr. Samuel Sill's Three Rivers, Mr. François Sarrault's, Montreal, [Neilson's agents] the Order of the Governor in Council . . . on 8vo. Demy stitched in blue paper. Price 6d."

—*Quebec gazette*, July 14, 1796.

This order-in-council gave effect to the clauses of the Jay Treaty providing for free intercourse between the United States and provinces of British North America. It repealed the Quebec-Lower Canada ordinances regulating trade, declared the pro vince open to trade from the United States, and the right of United States citizens equally with British subjects, in Lower Canada, to import unprohibited goods on payment of the usual duties, St. Johns, L.C., being the sole port of entry. It includes the regulations concerning the entry and declaration of goods at the Port of St. Johns, the schedule of fees to be taken by the Chief officer of customs there, but not the schedule of duties or of prohibited goods.

Copies located: CaQMS; GBLP (2 cop., in C.O. 42/12: 791-803; C.O. 42/108: 127-139 respectively); MHi (uncut, in original blue-gray paper covers).

993. LOWER CANADA. EXECUTIVE COUNCIL

[ORDRE DU GOUVERNEUR EN CONSEIL, Du 7me JUILLET, 1796, POUR LE REGLEMENT DU COMMERCE ENTRE CETTE PROVINCE ET LES ETATS UNIS DE L'AMERIQUE]

First French edition of the order-in-council described above. *Printed at Quebec by John Neilson, 1796.* The text was probably reprinted from the types of the *Quebec gazette supplement*, July 14, 1796, and issued with a t.-p. in 8vo Demy like No. 992. In the *Gazette supplement*, the French text occupies slightly more space (total type measure: 184 × 10.2 cm.) than the English in *Gazette extra* of July 9, 1796. So this pamphlet probably comprised 12 or 13 p. of text. Fifty copies of the French edition were sold to the government at 6*d.* the copy, on July 14, 1796 (*see* No. 992 *note*).

Copy located: None.

994. LOWER CANADA. EXECUTIVE COUNCIL

ORDER / OF THE / Governor in Council, / Of the 7th. July 1796, / FOR THE / REGULATION OF COMMERCE, / BETWEEN THIS / PROVINCE / AND THE / United States of America. / [rule] / [royal arms] / [rule] / QUEBEC: / PRINTED BY COMMAND OF HIS EXCELLENCY THE GOVERNOR; / BY WILLIAM VONDENVELDEN, Printer at the New Printing-Office, / Poor-street, Upper-Town Anno Domini, M.DCC. XCVI. /

French t.-p.:

ORDRE / DU / GOUVERNEUR en Conseil, / Du 7me Juillet, 1796, / POUR LE / REGLEMENT DU COMMERCE / ENTRE CETTE / PROVINCE / ET LES / Etats Unis de l'Amerique. / [rule] / royal arms] / [rule] / QUEBEC: / IMPRIME' PAR ORDRE DE SON EXCELLENCE LE GOUVERNEUR; / Par GUILLAUME VONDENVELDEN, Imprimeur à la Nouvelle Imprimerie. / Haute-Ville Rue des Pauvres, Anno Domini, M.DCC. XCVI. /

4to. A-C[4]; 2 p. l.; 16 p., 1 *l.*; type-page: 22.5 × 5-23 × 17.3 cm. Text in English and French on opposite pages.

Contents: p. l. 1 recto, English t.-p.; verso, blank; p. l. 2 recto, French t.-p.; verso, blank; recto of p. [1], blank; p. [1]-16, Order of the governor-in-council dated at head, Quebec, July 7, 1796, and signed at end by Herman Witsius Ryland, C. Ex. C.; verso of p. 16, blank; 1 *l.* at end, blank.

Another edition of No. 992-993. This edition was reprinted (with the 1796 imprint unchanged) in 1800. *See* No. 1179.

Copies of this (16 p.) edition are found, as issued, separately; also, apparently as issued later, in *A Collection of acts . . . 1800* (No. 1169) and in *A Collection of acts . . . 1824,* also bound with *Ordinances . . . 1795* (No. 942) or with *Provincial statutes.*

Copies located: CaNsWA; CaO (Munroe-Macnider-Sulte copy); CaOOA; CaOT (2 cop.); CaQM; CaQMM (2 cop.); CaQMS; CaQQA; CaQQB (2 cop.); CaQQL (2 cop.: "Ex. A"—crisp, uncut copy, stitched in sheets as issued—"Ex. C"); DLC (2 cop.); Ketcheson; M; MH; MHi (uncut, unopened, bound in original gray paper covers); MiD-B; MiU; NN; NNB; WHi.

LOWER CANADA. EXECUTIVE COUNCIL

Order of the Governor-in-Council of the 7th July 1796, . . . *Quebec: Printed . . . by William Vondenvelden . . . MDCCXCVI* [*i.e. by P.-E. Desbarats, 1800?*] 4to. 19 p. *See* No. 1179.

995. LOWER CANADA. EXECUTIVE COUNCIL

PROVINCE OF / LOWER CANADA. } / To Wit. / AT His Majesty's Executive Council of and for / the said Province of Lower Canada, held at / the Castle of Saint Lewis, in the City of Quebec, / in the said

Province, on Sunday the Thirtieth day of / October, in the Thirty-seventh Year of His Majes-/ty's Reign, and in the Year of Our Lord one thou-/sand seven hundred and ninety-six. / PRESENT. / His EXCELLENCY the LIEUTENANT GOVERNOR in Council. / <Text signed:> HERMAN WITSIUS RYLAND. /

French side:

PROVINCE DU / BAS-CANADA. } / Savoir. / Au Conseil Exécutif de Sa Majesté pour la dite Pro-/vince du Bas Canada, tenu au Château Saint / Loüis, dans la Cité de Québec dans la dite Province, / Dimanche le Trentième jour d'Octobre dans la Tren-/te Septième Année du Regne de Sa Majesté et dans / l'An de Notre Seigneur Mil Sept Cent Quatre-vingt / Seize. / PRESENT. SON EXCELLENCE LE LIEUTENANT GOUVERNEUR EN / CONSEIL. / <Text, signed:>: / HERMAN WITSIUS RYLAND. / Traduit par ordre de Son Excellence, / X. LANAUDIERE, S. & T.F. /

Double broadside: English on left, 36 lines, type-page: 26.5 × 19.5 cm. French on right, 40 lines, type-page: 28.3 × 19 cm. *Printed at Quebec, by John Neilson, 1796,* as recorded:

"1796, Nov. 5. [Debit] Executive Council Office. To Printing 500 Copies of an Order to the Governor commanding Aliens to depart this Province. E & F. 1 on a Sheet Crown, E[nglish] type.—£2.19."

—Can.P.A., *Neilson papers*, v. 54.

Contents: This excerpt from Council minutes is an order-in-council passed on authority of *An Act for establishing regulations respecting aliens &c.*, 34 Geo. III c. 5, clause 10. The text states:

"Whereas . . . divers Aliens and other evil disposed Persons have lately manifested seditious and wicked attempts to alienate the affections of his Majesty's Loyal Subjects, by false Representations of the cause and conduct of the Persons at present exercising the supreme authority in France, and particularly certain Frenchmen . . . acting in concert with Persons in foreign Dominions . . . Enemies of the Peace and happiness of the Inhabitants of this Province, and of all Religion, Government and social Order; [etc.]." It concludes ordering all subjects of France who arrived in Lower Canada since May 1, 1794, to depart within twenty days under penalties set forth in 34 Geo. III c. 5.

The proclamation against aliens (No. 1003) as well as this order-in-council, ordering aliens out of the province were ordered to "be published for three successive weeks in the Quebec Gazette and Montreal Paper in both languages. Also that 500 copies of each be printed in both languages, to be affixed against the Church Doors and other parts of the Towns and Suburbs of Quebec, Montreal and Three Rivers and the other parishes of the Province."

—Can.P.A., L.C. *State* B, Oct. 30, 1796.

Order-in-council and proclamation are reprinted in Can.P.A., *Report, 1921.*

Copies located: CaOOA (2 cop. filed in portfolio *Miscellaneous newspaper clippings, 1812-1837*); GBLP (in C.O. 42/108: 162-63).

996. LOWER CANADA. HOUSE OF ASSEMBLY

JOURNAL / OF THE / HOUSE OF ASSEMBLY, / OF / LOWER-CANADA. / From the 20th November 1795, to the 7th May 1796, both days / inclusive. / IN THE THIRTY-SIXTH YEAR OF THE REIGN OF / KING GEORGE THE THIRD. / [royal arms] / [double rule] / QUEBEC: / PRINTED BY ORDER OF THE HOUSE OF ASSEMBLY, AND SOLD BY / JOHN NEILSON. / M.DCC.XCVI. /

French t.-p.:

JOURNAL / DE LA / CHAMBRE D'ASSEMBLEE / DU / BAS-CANADA. / Du 20me Novembre 1795, au 7me Mai 1796, inclusivement. / DANS LA TRENTE SIXIEME ANNE'E DU REGNE DE / SA MAJESTE GEORGE TROIS. / [royal arms] / [double rule] / QUEBEC: / IMPRIME PAR ORDRE DE LA CHAMBRE D'ASSEMBLEE, ET A VENDRE / PAR JOHN NEILSON. / M.DCC.XCVI. /

4to. A^2, B-$2S^4$; 2 p. l., 318 p.; type-page: 18.3 × 12.3 cm. Odd numbers on verso, even numbers on recto. Text in English and French on opposite pages. Some copies at least are printed upon paper apparently folded in 8vo., the chain lines running vertically and a counter mark, the date 1794, occasionally visible in the lower outer corner.

Contents: p. l. 1 recto, English t.-p.; verso, blank; p. l. 2 recto, French t.-p.; verso, blank; recto of p. [1] blank; p. [1]-318, Journal of the fourth session of the first assembly, Nov. 20, 1795-May 7, 1796; verso of p. 318, blank.

The House ordered that 100 copies of its *Journal* be printed in English and French for the use of members and that none but the printer so licensed print the same.
—L.C. As. *Journal*, Dec. 9, 1795.

The printer recorded this work:

"1796, Apr. 30. [Debit] House of Assembly . . . for printing Journals of the 4th Session.—£125.

May 10. Cutting 100 copies of the Journals @ 3d. ea.—£1.5.

Binding 1 copy of the Journals—6/.

June 30. To 12 copies Journals 4th Sess. for use of the Gov[r] @ 10/—£6."
—Can.P.A., *Neilson papers*, v. 54.

An *Index* was issued later ([41] p. 4to.; p. [1-20] English, p. [21-41] French, p. [41] verso, blank). Without printer's name or date it was printed upon paper with the date 1807 in the water mark. It is only occasionally found with copies of the *Journal*.

Copies located: CaO (2 cop.); CaOOA; CaOT; CaQM; CaQMA; CaQMM; CaQQL; CaQQLH; CtY; DLC; GBLP (in C.O. 42/106); ICN; MHi; N; NN (with index); RPJ (with index); WHi.

997. LOWER CANADA. HOUSE OF ASSEMBLY

RULES / AND / REGULATIONS / OF THE / HOUSE OF ASSEMBLY, / LOWER-CANADA. / [printer's ornament] / [double rule] / QUEBEC: / PRINTED BY JOHN NEILSON, / M.DCC.XCVI. /

French t.-p.:

REGLES / ET / REGLEMENTS / DE LA / CHAMBRE D'ASSEMBLE'E, / DU / BAS CANADA. / [printer's ornament] / [double rule] / QUEBEC: / DE L'IMPRIMERIE DE JEAN NEILSON. / M.DCC.XCVI. /

12mo. A-H^6, [I]^1; 1 p. l., [i], 92, [2] p.; type-page: 13 × 7 cm. Odd numbers on verso, even numbers on recto; text in English and French on opposite pages.

Contents: p. l. recto, t.-p.; verso, blank; p. [i] (recto of p. [1]), French t.-p.; p. [1]-92, Rules; verso of p. 92, blank; [2] p. at end, Index.

This is the second edition of the *Rules* of the House, a new printing of the rules published in 1793, apparently without amendment. Without preliminary discussion "On the motion of Mr. Lees, seconded by Mr. de Salaberry, [it was] Ordered that 100 copies of the Rules and Regulations of this House be printed under the inspection of the Clerk for the use of the House."—L.C. As. *Journal*, May 4, 1796.

The printer recorded the work succinctly: "1796, May 10. To be done for the House of Assembly . . . Printing the Rules—£10." He also recorded the sale of single copies, following May 10, at 2*s*. the copy.—Can.P.A., *Neilson papers*, v. 54.

Copies located: CaQMS (2 cop.); CaQQL.

998. LOWER CANADA. LAWS, STATUTES, *etc.*

[The Provincial Statutes of Lower Canada. *Quebec, printed by William Vondenvelden, 1796.*]

4to. Probably about 120 p., a separate issue of the laws passed in the fourth session of the first Assembly, Nov. 20, 1795-May 7, 1796, 36 Geo. III c. 1-12. It was also published in a collected issue, No. 943 p. [188]-307 (or 308). This separate issue was probably similar to those of other sessions, e.g. No. 944.

Vondenvelden charged for "Printing Ordinances for government [600 copies?] —£24.17.3."—in *Provincial Accounts, Apr.-Oct. 1796*, in Can.P.A., L.C. *State* B, Jan. 3, 1797.

Copy located: None.

999. LOWER CANADA. LAWS, STATUTES, *etc.*

AN / ABSTRACT / OF THE MOST MATERIAL PARTS / OF AN ACT OF THE / Provincial Parliament / OF / LOWER-CANADA, / Passed in the thirty-sixth year of the reign of his / present Majesty GEORGE the III. KING of / Great-Britain, &c. Intituled, "An Act for ma- / "king, repairing and altering the Highways and / "Bridges within this Province, and for other pur-/"poses." so far as the same is relative to the / Cities and Parishes of Quebec and Montreal. / [rule] / [royal arms] / [rule] / QUEBEC: / PRINTED BY WILLIAM VONDENVELDEN, Printer / at the New Printing-Office. / Palace Street, Upper-Town, Anno Domini, M.DCC.XCVI. /

French t.-p.:

EXTRAIT / DES POINTS LES PLUS ESSENTIELS / D'UN ACTE DE / Parliament Provincial / DU / BAS-CANADA, / Passé dans la trente-sixiéme année du Règne de / sa présente Majesté GEORGE III. ROI de la / Grande-Bretagne. &c. Intitulé, "Acte pour faire, / "réparer et changer les Grande Chemins et Ponts / "dans cette Province, et pour d'autres effets." en autant qu'il a rapport aux Citiés et Paroisses de / Québec et Montréal. / [rule] / [royal arms] / [rule] / QUEBEC: / IMPRIME' PAR GUILLAUME VONDENVELDEN, Im-/primeur à la Nouvelle Imprimerie. / Haute-Ville, Rue du Palais, Anno Domini, M.DCC.XCVI. /

8vo. A-F[4]; 2 p. l. [i], 42 p.; type-page: 16 × 10.5 cm. Odd numbers on verso, even numbers on recto; text in English and French on opposite pages.

Contents: p. l. 1 recto, t.-p.; verso, blank; p. l. 2 recto, French t.-p.; verso, blank; p. [1] (recto of p. [1]), blank; p. [1]-42, Abstract of 36 Geo. III c. 9, certified at end: "I do hereby certify that the foregoing Abstract was made by me, in obedience to the 77th Section of the Provincial Statute, 36 Geo. III c. 9. [signed] J. Sewell, His Majesty's Attorney General of and for the Province of Lower-Canada"; verso of p. 42, blank.

This abstract contains those sections and parts of sections of 36 Geo. III c. 9, which related to roads and bridges within the "municipal" areas and under the jurisdiction of the justices of the peace in Quebec and Montreal. 36 Geo. III c. 9 was a comprehensive act in 83 sections introduced by Gabriel Elzéar Taschereau, grand voyer of the district of Quebec. Repealing previous enactments, it regulated road and bridge construction and maintenance in the towns (as abstracted in this work) and the rural districts (as abstracted in No. 1000). It remained long the basic road act in Lower Canada, despite the immediate difficulty of enforcement and its general unpopularity.

Chief Justice Osgoode commented repeatedly upon it, to John King, under-secretary of state, in London, e.g., writing from Quebec, Aug. 27, 1796:

"Yesterday the new Act respecting paving was attempted to be put in Execution [in Quebec] those who had not commuted were summoned to labour, great Dissatisfaction was expressed and several who had compounded exhorted the others to refuse working, after a short time they began to take the Wheels from the Carts employed, gave three Chears [sic] and went off. Five of the Ring leaders were secured and sent to Gaol notwithstanding the Menaces of 500 Women."

And again Osgoode to King, Quebec, Oct. 13, 1796:

". . . the most disorderly Race is in the Neighbourhood of Montreal, which is partly owing to their Vicinity to the Vermontese and perhaps more from their having almost generally been engaged as Voyageurs in Expeditions to the North West where they become more uncivilized & unruly than the savages themselves. Some very truculent scenes have taken place on carrying the Road Bill into execution. The Magistrates were induced to a Compromise with the mob till the Answer to a Petition to the Governor should be received praying him to convene the Legislature forthwith for the purpose of repealing the Bill. The prevailing Opinion is that the Magistrates have not been sufficiently firm [etc.]."

—Can.P.A., "C.O. 42", v. 22, p. 50, 54.

The elaborate machinery for the administration of 36 Geo. III c. 9 and popular opposition to its enforcement in a part of the county of Dorchester (for which Taschereau, who introduced the bill and who administered it as grand voyer in Quebec district, was member of Assembly) is described by J. E. Roy in *Histoire de la seigneurie de Lauzon* (3 v., Levis, 1900), 3: 272-79.

The original documents of the administration of this act (among others) are calendared by Pierre-Georges Roy in *Inventaire des procès-verbaux des grands voyers conservés aux archives de la province de Québec* (6 v., Beauceville, Que., 1923-32).

Copies located: CaO; CaQM; CaQQL.

1000. LOWER CANADA. LAWS, STATUTES, *etc.*

AN / ABSTRACT / of the most material parts of an / ACT OF THE / Provincial Parliament of / LOWER-CANADA, / Passed in the thirty-sixth year of the reign of his / Present Majesty GEORGE the III. KING of Great / Britain, &c. / Intituled, "an Act for making, repairing and / "altering the Highways and Bridges within / "this Province, and for other purposes." So / far as the same is relative to the Districts / of Quebec, Montreal and Three-Rivers. / [rule] / [royal arms] / [rule] / QUEBEC: / PRINTED by WILLIAM VONDENVELDEN, Printer / at the New Printing-Office. / Palace Street, Upper-Town, Anno Domini, MDCC. XCVI. /

French t.-p.:

EXTRAIT / Des parties les plus essentielles d'un / ACTE DU / Parlement Provincial du / BAS-CANADA, / Passé dans la trente-sixiéme année du Règne de / sa présente Majesté GEORGE III. ROI de la / Grande-Bretagne, &c. / Intitulé, "Acte pour faire, réparer et changer / "les Grands Chemins et Ponts dans cette / "Province, et pour d'autres effets." en tant / qu'il se rapporte aux Districts de Qué-/bec, de Montréal et des Trois Riviéres. / [rule] / [royal arms] / [rule] / QUEBEC: / IMPRIME' PAR GUILLAUME VONDENVELDEN, Im-/primeur à la Nouvelle Imprimerie. / Haute-Ville, Rue du Palais, Anno Domini, M.DCC. XCVI. /

8vo. A-E^4, [F]^2; 2 p. l., [1], 36 p., 1 *l.*; type-page: 16 × 10.2 cm. Odd numbers on verso, even numbers on recto; text in English and French on opposite pages.

Contents: p. l. 1 recto, t.-p.; verso, blank; p. l. 2 recto, French t.-p.; verso, blank; [1] (recto of p. [1]), blank; p. [1]-36, Abstract; verso of p. 36, blank; 1 *l.* at end, blank.

This *Abstract*, complementing No. 999, contains those sections and parts of sections of 36 Geo. III c. 9 which relate to the construction and maintenance of roads and bridges in the *districts* (as distinct from the *towns*) of Quebec, Montreal, and Three Rivers. These districts included all the then organized area of the province, had each a grand voyer, also local surveyors and overseers of roads who administered the act in the district.

The date of this publication is sometimes recorded as 1795, owing to faulty impression of the imprint date (the final figure "I" is out of alignment and more or less faintly inked, on the English t.-p. of copies seen). *See* Gagnon: *Essai de bibliographie canadienne;* 2: no. 1816.

Copies located: CaQ; CaQM; CaQMJ; CaQMS (2 cop.); CaQQL.

1001. LOWER CANADA. LAWS, STATUTES, *etc.*

[A table of the weight and rates of Gold coin as regulated by Act of the Provincial Parliament passed 7th May, 1796. *Printed at Quebec, by John Neilson, 1796.*]

Advertised: "A Table of the weight and rates of Gold Coin as regulated by Act of the Provincial Parliament passed 7th May, 1796, neatly printed on cards and for sale at the Printing Office [Price 3*d*.]."—*Quebec gazette,* Aug. 4, 1796, *et seq.*

The table, published regularly in *The Quebec almanac* set forth the weight and rates specified in the terms of 36 Geo. III c. 5, "An act for better regulating the weight and rates at which certain coins shall pass current in this province, for preventing the falsifying counterfeiting or impairing the same [etc.]."

Copy located: None.

1002. LOWER CANADA. LIEUTENANT-GOVERNOR, 1796-1797 (*Prescott*)

[royal arms] / BY HIS EXCELLENCY / ROBERT PRESCOTT, ESQUIRE, / Lieutenant-Governor [etc., 6 lines] / A PROCLAMATION, / <Text> / Given . . . / . . . [at] Quebec, . . . / . . . / . . . [12 July 1796] / ROBT. PRESCOTT. / . . . / . . . / . . . /

French on right:

[royal arms] / PAR SON EXCELLENCE / ROBERT PRESCOTT, ECUYER, / Lieutenant Gouverneur [etc. 6 lines] / PROCLAMATION. / <Text> / Donné . . . / [à] Québec [12 Juillet 1796] . . . / . . . / . . . / ROBT. PRESCOTT. / [etc. 5 lines]

Double broadside: English on left, 30 lines, type-page: 27.6 × 14.5 cm.; French on right, 32 lines, type-page: 27.8 × 14.5 cm. *Printed at Quebec, by John Neilson, 1796,* as recorded:

"1796, July 13, [Debit] Provincial Secretary's Office, To 100 proclamations notifying that the Government has Devolved on General Prescott 1 on a Sheet—£1.2.6."—Can.P.A., *Neilson papers,* v. 54.

Text: "Whereas His Most Gracious Majesty has been pleased to grant His Royal Leave of Absence to . . . Lord Dorchester [etc. Prescott, now in command of the province, orders present officers of the Crown to continue in their offices]."

French text: "Ayant plus à sa très gracieuse Majesté d'accorder Congé royal d'absence à . . . Lord Dorchester [etc.]."

Prescott, who served in America in the Seven Years' War and in the American Revolutionary War, was appointed lieutenant-governor of Lower Canada, Jan. 1,

1796. He administered the province from July 12, as proclaimed here, and Dec. 15, 1796 was appointed governor-in-chief succeeding Dorchester. He was active in that office (which he assumed Apr. 27, 1797) till he left the country July 29, 1799, and remained governor *in absentia* till 1807.

This proclamation is reprinted in Can.P.A., *Report, 1921*.

Copy located: CaOOA (in *Proclamations* portfolio in the Library).

1003. LOWER CANADA. LIEUTENANT-GOVERNOR, 1796-1797 (*Prescott*)

[By His Excellency Robert Prescott, Esquire, Lieutenant Governor and Commander in Chief of . . . Lower Canada, . . . A Proclamation <Text> Given under my Hand and Seal at Arms at . . . Quebec 30th October, 1796 Robt. Prescott. By His Excellency's Command, Geo: Pownall, Secy. God Save the King.

French side:

Robert Prescott, Ecuier, Lieutenant Gouverneur et Commandant en Chef . . . du Bas Canada, . . . Proclamation. <Text> Donné sous mon Seing et le Sceau de mes Armes . . . Québec . . . 30me Octobre, 1796. Robert Prescott, Par ordre de Son Excellence, Geo: Pownall, Sec. Traduit . . . X. Lanaudiere, S. & T.F. Vive le Roi.]

Double broadside: Text in English and French. *Printed at Quebec, by John Neilson, 1796*, as recorded:

> "1796, Nov. 5. [Debit] Provincial Secretary's Office. To printing 500 Copies of a Proclamation commanding Magistrates, Cap[ts] of Militia &c. to apprehend persons charged with Treason &c. 1 on a Sheet Crown, E[nglish] type—£2.19.
> Pasting up 100 of ditto in Quebec—10/."
>
> —Can.P.A., *Neilson papers*, v. 54.

Text: "Whereas divers evil disposed Persons, have lately manifested seditious and wicked Attempts, to alienate the Affections of His Majesty's Loyal Subjects [etc.]."

French text: "Vu que diverses personnes mal intentionées ont depuis peu manifesté des tentatives séditieuses et méchantes pour aliener l'affection des Loyaux Sujets de Sa Majesté [etc.]."

This proclamation has the same text as Gov. Dorchester's of Nov. 26, 1793. Prescott's proclamation was issued with an order-in-council of the same date (*see* No. 995). Both are reprinted in Can.P.A., *Report, 1921*, from which this entry is taken.

Copy located: GBLP (in C.O. 42/108: 158-59).

1004. MASSON, ALEXANDRE

[Coutûme de Paris, mise en un nouvel ordre avec des notes et conferences pour en faciliter l'intelligence, par Mr. Alexandre Masson, avocat du Parlement.]

Proposed printing (in weekly parts of 36 p. 18mo.) *at Montreal, by Louis Roy, 1796*, was advertised:

"Prospectus pour l'Impression de la Coutûme de Paris, mise en nouvel ordre avec notes et conférences pour en faciliter l'intelligence—par M. Alexandre Masson, Avocat du Parlement. L'utilite d'un pareil ouvrage doit frapper toutes les personnes instruites qui connoissent combien l'étude des loix du pays est malheureusement négligée dans cette Province, et que l'on doit particulierement attribuer cette négligence au manque d'ouvrages méthodiques sur ces matières interessantes . . . Conditions. I, Cet ouvrage sera imprimé sur de beau papier et bon caractère, dans le format d'un in-18 pour être plus portatif; et sera livré chaque semaine aux souscripteurs par cahier de trente-six pages jusqu'à ce que le volume soit complet. II, Le prix de la souscription sera de 5/ pour l'ouvrage entier, et la livraison des numéros dépendera de l'encouragement que reçevra l'imprimeur qui commencera la première, dès que la souscription sera suffisante pour lui rembourser les frais [etc.]."

—*Montreal gazette* (Louis Roy), Sept. 19, 1796.

The Custom of Paris (the customary laws and usages long accepted, then enacted in 1510 by the Prêvoté et Vicomté de Paris, and revised in 1580) was established in 1663 as law in Canada. It remained an integral part of the civil law of French Canada under French and English régimes (*see* No. 176). Most of its sections ultimately found place in the *Civil Code of Lower Canada* prepared in 1857 and still in force.

The *Coûtume de Paris* with Masson's commentary, one of many, was (first?) published in Paris in 1703, 12mo. 324 p. (copy in the Bibliothèque nationale). There is no evidence that this work was printed in Montreal in 1796, however, either by Louis Roy, who abandoned his printing shop soon after the advertisement appeared (in the last number of his paper located), or by his brother Joseph-Marie Roy, who carried on the business with John Bennett till Aug., 1797.

Copy located: None.

1005. NEW BRUNSWICK. HOUSE OF ASSEMBLY

JOURNAL / OF THE / VOTES and PROCEEDINGS / OF THE / HOUSE OF ASSEMBLY / OF THE / PROVINCE of NEW-BRUNSWICK: / From TUESDAY the 9th of FEBRUARY, to SATURDAY / the 12th of MARCH, 1796. / [ornamental rule] / [royal arms] / [ornamental rule] / FREDERICTON: / Printed by CHRISTOPHER SOWER, Printer to the / KING'S MOST EXCELLENT MAJESTY, 1796. / [title within a frame of flower pieces.]

fo. A-T^2, V^1; 1 p. l., p. [451]-525 [i.e. 526], fold. table; type-page: 23 × 13.5 cm. paged in continuation of No. 952. p. 482-484 mispaged: 481-483, 484 omitted in numbering; p. 504 is misnumbered: 503, and pagination thereafter diminished by 1.

Contents: p. l. recto, t.-p.; verso, blank; p. [451-52], Proclamations; p. [453]-525, Journal of the first session of the third assembly. Fold. table correctly inserted between p. 474-75, is ". . . An Account of Merchandize imported into the Port of Saint John . . . and of Transient and Auctioneers Accounts subject to a Duty at the Treasury Office from 1st February, 1795, to 9th of February, 1796, inclusive."

Two hundred copies of the *Journal* of this session were ordered by the House, Mar. 7, 1796, to be printed, for which Sower presented the bill:

"1796—To printing 200 Copies of the Journal of Votes . . . of Assembly consisting of 20½ Sheets @ 46/ a Sheet—£47.3.
To folding & Stitching the Same @ 1d.—16/8
[Total:] 47.19.8. Voted on account £30. Balance due £17.19.8. [paid in 1799]."

—N.B. As. *Papers*, 1798.

Copies located: CaN (p. 508-509, 512-13 mut., p. 510-511, 514-15 wanting); CaNS (p. 524-25 wanting); CaNU; CaNsWA; CaOOA; RPJ.

1006. NEW BRUNSWICK. LAWS, STATUTES, *etc.*

ACTS / OF THE / GENERAL ASSEMBLY / OF / HIS MAJESTY'S PROVINCE / OF / NEW-BRUNSWICK, / PASSED IN THE YEAR 1796. / [ornamental rule] / [royal arms] / [ornamental rule] / FREDERICTON: / Printed by CHRISTOPHER SOWER, Printer to the / KING'S MOST EXCELLENT MAJESTY, 1796. / [title within frame of flower pieces]

fo. [*][2], A-E[2]; 3 p. l., 352-69 p.; type-page: 22.5 × 13.4 cm. Even numbers on recto, odd numbers on verso; paged in continuation of No. 953; one leaf of sig. E is folded around sig. A-D to form a p. l.

Contents: p. l. 1 recto, t.-p.; verso, blank; p. l. 2 recto, half title; verso, blank; p. l. 3 recto, Titles of the acts; verso, blank; p. 352-69, 36 Geo. III c. I-VII, acts passed in the first session of the third assembly.

The acts of this session were published, not as in previous years or like the *Journal* above, by order of the House, but by order of the lieutenant-governor, who submitted the printer's bill of £15 9*s*. for 300 copies to the House. The Assembly's distinction between its desire to print its *Journal* and its duty to print the *Acts*, was probably a gesture of defiance to the executive branch of the legislature which had repudiated the supply bill including provision of salary for members of the House.

Copies located: CaNSA; DLC; MH; NNB.

1007. NEW BRUNSWICK. LIEUTENANT-GOVERNOR, 1786-1817 (*Carleton*)

[Sundry proclamations. ? *Printed at Saint John, N.B., by John Ryan, 1796.*]

Lieut.-Gov. Carleton's message to the House of Assembly, Jan. 27, 1797, includes reference to an account due John Ryan "for printing sundry proclamations and other public papers—£9.11.9."—N.B. As. *Journal.* The printing, presumably done during the previous year, is not specified, nor do the Executive Council minutes (where orders to print are usually recorded) or other official papers include details to indicate whether the "sundry proclamations" etc., were published separately or in the columns of Ryan's paper, the *Saint John gazette.*

Copy located: None.

1008. NOVA SCOTIA. HOUSE OF ASSEMBLY

[rule] / JOURNAL / AND / PROCEEDINGS / OF THE / HOUSE of ASSEMBLY. / [rule] /

fo. sig. 2S-4[i.e. 3]H²; 1 p. l., 175-231 p.; type-page: 25 × 15 cm. paged in continuation of No. 956. Sig. 3H appears as 4H, and this sequence is continued in *Journals* for succeeding years. *Printed at Halifax, N.S., by Anthony Henry, 1796.*

Contents: p. l. recto, t.-p.; verso, proclamation; p. 175-231, Journal of the fourth session of the seventh assembly, Mar. 3-Apr. 11, 1796; verso of p. 231, blank.

Copies located: CaNs; CaOT (p. 209-12 wanting); GBLP (in C.O. 217/68: 65-94); MH.

1009. NOVA SCOTIA. LAWS, STATUTES, *etc.*

Running title: [rule] / 1796. Anno Tricessimo Sexto Regis, GEORGII III. CAP. I[-VII]. / [rule] /

Caption title: At the GENERAL ASSEMBLY of the Province / of Nova-Scotia, . . . / [5 lines] / being the Fourth Session of the Seventh General Assembly, convened in the said Pro-/vince. / [rule] /

fo. sig. 3Q-3S²; 379-389p.; paged in continuation of No. 957. *Printed at Halifax, N.S., by Anthony Henry, 1796.*

Contents: p. 379-389, Cap. I-VII, perpetual acts passed in the session, Mar. 3-Apr. 11, 1796; verso of p. 389, blank.

Copies located: DLC; MH (2 cop.).

1010. NOVA SCOTIA. LAWS, STATUTES, *etc.*

Running title: [rule] / 1796. Anno Tricessimo Sexto Regis, GEORGII III. CAP. I[-XI]. / [rule] /

Caption title: At the GENERAL ASSEMBLY of the Province / of Nova-Scotia, . . . / [5 lines] / being the Fourth Session of the Seventh / General Assembly, convened in the said Pro-/vince. / [rule] /

fo. sig. 4Q-4Y², 4Z¹; 451-484 p.; type-page: 25 × 15 cm. paged in continuation of No. 958. *Printed at Halifax, N.S., by Anthony Henry, 1796.*

Contents: p. 451-484, Cap. I-IX, temporary acts passed in the session, Mar. 3-Apr. 11, 1796.

Copies located: CaO; MH.

1011. NOVA SCOTIA. LIEUTENANT-GOVERNOR, 1792-1808 (*Wentworth*)

[Proclamation for apprehending deserters]

Broadside? *Printed at Halifax, N.S., by Anthony Henry, 1796,* as recorded:

"To printing folio proclamations by order of the Lieutenant governor, for apprehending deserters throughout this province, delivered to Sheriff Hutchinson—£3.10."—This is the first item in Henry's *Account for extra printing [for government] 1796-1797*, in P.A.N.S., *Miscellaneous Assembly papers*, 1797.

This is the first item in Henry's *Account for extra printing [for government] 1796-1797*, in P.A.N.S., *Miscellaneous Assembly papers*, 1797.

Copy located: None.

1012. QUEBEC, *City.* SEMINAIRE DE QUEBEC

THESES / DE / MATHEMATIQUES. / [rule] / [text in 2 col. of 56-64 lines respectively] / Ces Theses seront soutenues au Séminaire de Québec, Vendredi 3 Juin depuis 10 heures jusqu'à 2 après midi. / Par M.M. { THOMAS MAGUIRE, Ecclesiastique, / LOUIS BARDY, / J. AMABLE BERTHELOT, / THOMAS TASCHEREAU, } étudians en Physique. / Sous Mr. J. RAIMBAULT, Prètre professeur de Mathématiques. / [rule] / <De L'IMPRIMERIE de J. NEILSON, N° 3 Rue la Montagne.> /

Broadside: 76 lines; type-page: 39.5 × 29.5 cm.

Though the imprint bears no date, this work was probably printed in 1796, as a programme for a public examination on June 3, which fell upon a Friday in that year. The theses include propositions in "Calcul, Arithmetique, Algebrique, Analogique, Analytique, Des logarithmes; Géometrie speculative; Géometrie practique; Trigometrie."

Copies located: CaQMS; CaQQL (this copy, dated 1796 in MS. and bound (no. 5) in a volume labelled *Séminaire de Québec, Theses 1775-1815*, was probably preserved by the Séminaire itself, for the archives and library of that institution are part of Laval University Library).

1013. QUEBEC BENEVOLENT SOCIETY

RULES AND REGULATIONS / OF THE / QUEBEC BENEVOLENT SOCIETY, / ESTABLISHED THE FIRST WEDNESDAY IN / MAY, M.DCC.-LXXXIX. / [rule] / [ornament] / [rule] / [ornamental rule] / QUEBEC: / PRINTED AT THE NEW PRINTING-OFFICE, / M.DCC.XCI. [sic] /

French t.-p.:

REGLES ET REGLEMENS / DE LA / SOCIETE' BIENVEILLANTE / DE QUEBEC, / ETABLIE LE PREMIER MERCREDI DE MAI, / M.DCC.-LXXXIX. / [rule] / [ornament] / [rule] / [ornamental rule] / A QUEBEC: / IMPRIME' A LA NOUVELLE IMPRIMERIE, / M.DCC.XCVI. /

12mo. A-C^6, D^6 (in only copy located); 45 p.; type-page: 13 × 7.2 cm. Text in English and French on opposite pages. *Printed by Wm. Vondenvelden, 1796.*

A cancel leaf pasted over verso of p. 37, is paged 38; dated Quebec, Sept. 10, 1796, it contains names of members. Another cancel leaf pasted over recto of p. 40, is paged 41; it contains names of members, also "Forme du Certificat," etc.

Contents: p. [1], t.-p.; p. [2], blank; p. [3], French t.-p.; p. [4]-45, Rules, etc.; verso of p. 45, blank.

Copy located: CaQMS.

1014. QUEBEC GAZETTE. CARRIER'S ADDRESS

VERSES / Of the Printer's Boy who carries the / QUEBEC GAZETTE / To the Customers. / [rule] / JANUARY 1st, 1797. /

French side:

ETRENNES / DU GARÇON qui porte la / GAZETTE DE QUEBEC / AUX PRATIQUES. / [rule] / LE Ier. JANVIER, 1797. / [*Quebec, J. Neilson, 1796*]

Broadside: type-page: 33.5 × 29.5 in ornamental rule frame. English verse on left, 88 lines in 2 col., French on right, 88 lines. The English is a series of squibs on French campaigns in Europe and on the French agents' (Genet and Adet), activities in Canada:

"Lo! a New Year! and, strange to tell!
I find you, Sirs, alive and well,
Regaling on bak'd, boild and roast
And briskly pushing round the toast . . .

You, who by this time, in minc'd meat,
By *Sans Culottes* ought to be eat;
Those fierce *Anthropophagi* sent,
With hungry maw and dire intent
To swallow this devoted land—
Such first was Genet's dread command;
All without mercy to cut up,
And on our blood and marrow sup,
For this invincible *Bompard*,
Denounc'd against us dreadful war . . ."

The French side is in the conventional vein:

"Toujours de mes devoirs fidele observateur
Je viens en humble Serviteur . . ."

Copy located: CaO (bound in *Quebec gazette*, at end of 1796).

1015. QUEBEC LIBRARY

CATALOGUE / OF / ENGLISH AND FRENCH / BOOKS / IN THE / Quebec Library, / At the BISHOP'S PALACE, / Where the RULES may be seen. / [ornamental rule] / QUEBEC: / Printed at the New Printing-Office, 1796. /

8vo. A-D[4]; 32 p.; type-page: 17 × 10.5 cm.

Contents: p. [1], t.-p.; p. [2], blank; p. 3-17, English books; p. 18, Latin and Greek books; p. [19], blank; p. 20-32, French books.

The *Catalogue* lists 1,341 English works and 1,822 French works, under the headings: Religion; Law and government; Science, Arts and Literature; History, Memoirs and Travel; Poetry, Drama and Fiction; Miscellaneous; also 23 Latin and Greek works. *See* Fauteux: *Les bibliothèques canadiennes*, in *Révue canadienne*, mars, 1916.

Copy located: CaQMS.

1016. QUEBEC THEATRE

[Play bill, etc.]

Broadsides: *Printed at Quebec, by John Neilson, 1796,* as recorded:

"1796, Feb. 8. [Debit] Love & Beatty, To printing 150 Demy handbills for a play on Thursday evening, the 11th inst.—11/3.

Feb. 12. [Debit] Love & Beatty, To printing 200 small handbills fools^{P}: putting off their performance to 15th inst.—10/.

Feb. 22, [Debit] Love & Beatty, To printing 200 Demy Handbills for the Benefit of Mr. Love @ 7/6—15/."

Love and Beatty's performance was probably that advertised in the *Quebec gazette,* Feb. 11, 1796: "Theatre—The Public are informed that the performance of Lethe, The Highland Reel, and Sultan, are unavoidable postponed till tomorrow, when they most assuredly will be performed." Other entries in the *Gazette* and in Neilson's MS. account book, v. 54, indicate that Love and Beatty presented a number of performances, Jan.-Feb., 1796, "for the benefit of the Poor," "for the benefit of Mr. Love," "for the benefit of Beatty."

Their performances do not *appear* to have been connected with those also advertised in the *Gazette* about this time by the "Canadian theatre." The latter seems to have been a dramatic society in which John Neilson the printer had some interest: it is termed "le nouveau theatre Canadien érigé le 12 novembre 1795."

—Can.P.A., *Neilson papers,* 1: 76.

Copy located: None.

1017. ROYAL ORDER OF BLUE AND ORANGE

[LIST OF MEMBERS OF ROYAL ORDER OF BLUE AND ORANGE]

4to. about 16 p. *Printed at Quebec, by John Neilson, 1796,* as recorded:

"1796, Jan. 8. [Debit] Capt. S. Dales, 4th Regt. To printing 200 Copies of list of members of Royal order of Blue & Orange, 2 sheets 4to folio post, English type—£4.7.6.

Furnishing 1 Ream paper for ditto—£1.10.

Feb. 17. [Debit] Captain Saml Dales, 17 Quires folio post for waste paper for 200 copies of the list of the members of the Blue & Orange—£1.15.9.

4 Quires marble French for covering d^{o}—16/

Stitching covering & gilding d^{o} @ 2^{d} each—£1.13.4.

[Total: £9 12*s.* 7*d.*]."—Can.P.A., *Neilson papers,* v. 54.

Copy located: None.

1018. ST. JOHN, ISLAND OF. HOUSE OF ASSEMBLY

*[Journal of the House of Assembly of His Majesty's Island of Saint John. Anno tricessimo sexto Regis Georgii III. Fifth session of the Sixth General Assembly. *Charlotte Town, Island of Saint John. Printed by William Alexander Rind, . . . 1796.*]

4to. 18 p.

Contents: Journal, Feb. 2-13, 1796.

Copy located: GBLP (in C.O. 226/15: 193-210).

*Title and description from notes taken by a correspondent in the Public Record Office, London, from the only copy located.

1019. ST. JOHN, ISLAND OF. LAWS, STATUTES, *etc.*

ACTS / PASSED / AT THE GENERAL ASSEMBLY / OF HIS MAJESTY'S / ISLAND OF SAINT JOHN, / ANNO TRICESSIMO SEXTO / REGIS GEORGII III. / [rule] / FIFTH SESSION OF THE SIXTH GENERAL ASSEMBLY. / [rule] / [rule] / [royal arms] / [double rule] / CHARLOTTE TOWN, ISLAND OF SAINT JOHN: / [rule] / PRINTED BY WILLIAM ALEXANDER RIND, / PRINTER TO THE KING'S MOST EXCELLENT MAJESTY. / [double rule] / 1796. /

4to. Sig. [1-3]^2; 11 p.; type-page: 21.5 × 14 cm. One leaf of sig. [3] is folded around sig. [1]-2 to form t.-p.

Contents: p. [1], t.-p.; p. [2], blank; p. [3]-11, 36 Geo. III c. I-VII, Acts passed Feb. 2-13, 1796; verso of p. 11, blank.

Copies located: GBLP (2 cop. in C.O. 226/15: 215-25; and C.O. 216/16: 449-59 (respectively); NNHi.

1020. SAINT JOHN, N.B., *City.* ORDINANCES

[By-laws of the corporation revised]

? fo. about 36 p. *Printed at Saint John, N.B., by John Ryan, 1796.* This publication is recorded in the City Council *Minutes:*

"1795, May 12. Ordered that the Mayor [Ludlow] be requested to be of a committee with the Recorder [Ward Chipman] and Mr. Jarvis [alderman] to revise the laws now in being, and suggest such alterations, amendments and additions as they shall think proper."

On Dec. 12, the laws, as amended and revised, were produced, read, and ordered to remain in the clerk's office will Dec. 15, for inspection by members of the Council.

Dec. 19. "Read proposals from Mr. Sower and Mr. Ryan for printing the Laws of the Common Council . . . Ordered that Mr. Ryan be employed to print the Laws of the City on the Terms this day given in, and the Mayor is requested to join with the [sic] in Superintending the printing of the same, viz: £5 [per] sheet."

On the same day the recorder was ordered to obtain confirmation by the lieutenant-governor-in-council of all the laws except those regulating fisheries and pilotage, and on Dec. 24, the clerk ordered to furnish copy therefor.

"1796, Apr. 11. The Committee for printing the Laws report that the Printing of the Laws amounts to upwards of £44. Ordered that a copy of the same Laws be deliver'd to each of the Members of the Common Council and to the Clerk gratis."

—Saint John, N.B., Common Council *Minutes*, v. 2.

The work is also recorded by the provincial administration:

"1796, Apr. 1. Whereas by Royal charter . . . the Common Council of the City of St. John are authorized . . . to make laws, statutes . . . which . . . remain in force for twelve months . . . and no longer unless they be . . . confirmed by the Governor and Council [etc., the laws no. I-XX are allowed and confirmed excepting no. XIV, on anchorage rates; [their titles are listed, but text not given]."

—Can.P.A., N.B. Ex. co. *Minutes.*

Copy located: None.

1021. SAY, THOMAS, 1709-1796

[A Particular Account of Mr. Thomas Say, of Philadelphia, while in a Trance, for eight hours giving a strange Revelation of what he both saw and heard, during that time. To which is added. A Remarkable vision by the Revd. Isaac Watts, D.D.]

Probably printed at Saint John, N.B., by John Ryan, 1796, this work was advertised: "Just published and to be sold at this Office (Price 9d.) A Particular Account [etc., as above]."—*Saint John gazette,* Nov. 4, 1796 (previous numbers not seen)-July 21, 1797.

It was published in Philadelphia, 1774 (23 p., 12mo, Evans, no. 13598) and repeatedly thereafter. A Saint John, N.B., edition may have been reprinted from *A short compilation of the extraordinary life and writings of Thomas Say in which is . . . the uncommon vision which he had as a young man* (Philadelphia, 1796). *See* Evans, no. 31161. Or, Ryan may have imported a stock of the Philadelphia edition, which he advertised as above and sold in Saint John.

Say's *Account* describes his early life of sinful frivolity, his efforts to know God, and his mystic experiences communing with the deity, especially in the years 1726 and 1740. Say, bred a harness-maker, later became an apothecary and healer, a substantial and respected citizen of Philadelphia—known, no doubt, to American loyalists who moved to New Brunswick in 1783-84.

Copy located: None.

1022. UPPER CANADA. LAWS, STATUTES, *etc.*

Caption title: [double rule] / LAWS / OF HIS MAJESTY'S PROVINCE OF / UPPER-CANADA: / [rule] / PASSED IN THE FIFTH SESSION OF THE PROVINCIAL PARLIAMENT OF UPPER-/CANADA, MET AT NEWARK, ON THE SIXTEENTH DAY OF MAY, IN THE / THIRTY-SIXTH YEAR OF THE REIGN OF OUR SOVEREIGN LORD, GEORGE THE / THIRD, AND PROROGUED ON THE THIRD DAY OF JUNE, FOLLOWING. / [rule] /

4to Y-Z², [*]¹; [89]-96, [2] p.; type-page: 26 × 18.5 cm. Paged in continuation of No. 967. *Printed at Niagara [Newark], U.C., by Gideon Tiffany, 1796.*

Contents: p [89]-96, 36 Geo. III c. I-VII; [2] p. at end, Titles of the laws passed by the province of Upper Canada, 1792-96.

Published between Oct. 26, and Nov. 9, 1796, this work was issued separately, also with No. 967, which is included in the contents list. It was advertised as "Just published" on Nov. 9, 1796, also: "A few copies of the Laws of Upper Canada, comprising five Sessions for sale at the Printing Office [of Gideon Tiffany] Price 5th Session, 2/6; Volume complete, 15/4."—*Upper Canada gazette,* Nov. 30, 1796, *et seq.*

It was probably printed in a small edition soon exhausted, for D. W. Smith, speaker of the House, wrote from York, Oct. 12, 1798, to J. A. Panet, speaker of the House of Assembly of Lower Canada: ". . . When I transmitted our laws to you those of the Fifth Session of the first Parliament were out of print, I therefore now enclose a few sets. Our Journals have not yet been printed, nor the Statutes of the last Session

of Parliament [June-July, 1798] when they are they shall be transmitted to you."
—U.C. As. *Journal,* June 13, 1799, in Ontario Archives, *Report, 1909,* 101.

These remarks suggest that the *Laws* of 1796 were reprinted in 1798, possibly by Gideon or Sylvester Tiffany, to whom the House voted on July 5, 1798: "£10 still due to Mr. Tiffany, for printing the Journals [i.e. Laws?] of the 5th Session of the last Parliament for the use of the Province."—*ibid.*, 91.

Though the House regularly included in its estimates a sum for printing (usually 50 copies) of the journals of the session, and the Committee appointed to revise the journals for publication regularly reported, yet the journals do not appear to have been printed in the 18th century In fact the *Journal* for 1801 is the earliest of which there is certain evidence of publication

Copy located: CaOTL; photostat in MH.

1023. UPPER CANADA. LIEUTENANT-GOVERNOR, 1791-1799 (*Simcoe*)

Upper-Canada. / BY HIS EXCELLENCY JOHN G. SIMCOE, ESQ. / LIEUTENANT GOVERNOR AND MAJOR GENERAL OF / HIS MAJESTY'S FORCES, &c.&c.&c. / PROCLAMATION. / [double rule] / [royal arms] <Text> / Given under my hand and seal at arms, at the government house at York, this sixth day of A-/pril, in the year of our Lord, one thousand seven hundred and ninety-six, and in the thirty-sixth / year of his Majesty's reign. / JOHN GRAVES SIMCOE. / GOD SAVE THE KING! / By his Excellency's Command, / E. B. LITTLEHALES. /

Broadside: 40 lines; type-page: 23.1 × 14.8 cm. *Probably printed at Niagara, U.C., by Gideon Tiffany, 1796.*

Text: "Whereas it appears by the minutes of the Council of the late Province of Quebec, dated Monday the ninth day of November 1789, to have been the desire of his Excellency Lord Dorchester the Governor-General 'To put a *mark of honor* upon the families who had adhered to the Unity of the Empire and joined the Royal Standard in America, before the treaty of separation in . . . 1783,'[etc.]" In pursuance of the Quebec order-in-Council for land boards to maintain a registry of loyalists (*see* No. 615) and in the absence of such registries in Upper Canada, Simcoe directs loyalists claiming confirmation of land grants to take oath of their adherence to the unity of Empire in the American Revolution, before local magistrates in the next michaelmas quarter-sessions, or forfeit their right to fee-free grants.

This proclamation is reprinted in Ontario Archives, *Report, 1905, ibid., 1906,* also in Simcoe: *Correspondence,* v. 4.

Copies located: CaOT; GBLP (2 cop., in C.O. 42/320: 633, 787).

1024. UPPER CANADA. LIEUTENANT-GOVERNOR, 1791-1799 (*Simcoe*)

SPEECH / OF / HIS EXCELLENCY / John Graves Simcoe, Esquire, / LIEUTENANT GOVERNOR / of the Province of Upper-Canada, &c. &c.&c. / UPON OPENING THE FIFTH SESSION OF THE / Provincial

Parliament; / WITH / The respective Addresses of both Houses thereupon / —LIKEWISE— / HIS EXCELLENCY'S ANSWERS. / [rule] / [royal arms] / [rule] / BY AUTHORITY. / [rule] / NIAGARA: PRINTED BY G. TIFFANY, / PRINTER TO THE KING'S MOST EXCELLENT MAJESTY. / [rule] / 1796. /

12mo. [*]^4; 8 p.; type-page: 14.6 × 9.6 cm.? the only copy seen was cropped, bleeding.

Contents: p. [1], t.-p.; p. [2], blank; p. [3]-4, Speech of Simcoe, May 16, 1796; p. 5-6, Address of the legislative council in answer to Simcoe's speech, May 17, 1796, and Simcoe's reply thereto; p. 7-8, Address of the Assembly in answer to Simcoe's speech, May 17, 1796, and Simcoe's reply thereto.

This was the last session of the Legislature held in the old capital, Niagara (formerly called Newark), U.C.

Copies located: DLC (cropped); GBLP (in C.O. 42/320: 547-54).

1025. UPPER CANADA. LIEUTENANT-GOVERNOR, 1791-1799 (*Simcoe*)

[Proclamation. By His Excellency John Graves Simcoe, Esq. Lieutenant Governor and Major-General of His Majesty's Forces, &c. &c.&c. in Upper Canada. <Text> Given . . . at the Government House at Navy-Hall, [Niagara] the twenty-fifth day of May . . . one thousand seven hundred and ninety-six . . . J.G.S. By Command of His Excellency in Council. John Small, c.c.]

Broadside. *Probably printed at Niagara, U.C., by Gideon Tiffany, 1796.*

Text: "Whereas in pursuance of His Majesty's gracious intention respecting the granting and settling of the waste lands of the Crown," etc., states that since persons to whom lands were granted under terms of Simcoe's proclamation of Feb. 7, 1792, have failed to observe those terms and have offered their lands for sale exacting illegal charges therefor, the Executive Council resolved, May 25, 1796, (1) that lands held by order-in-council be forfeited in townships of Osgood, Wolford, Montague, Russel, Kitley, Loughborough, Huntingdon, Rawdon, Murray, Clarke, Whitby, and Windham; (2) that appeal against forfeiture must be made by June 1, 1797; (3) that occupants of lands in these townships should apply for title deeds within six months.

This proclamation is reprinted in Ontario Archives, *Report, 1905, ibid., 1906,* also in Simcoe: *Correspondence,* v. 4, from which this entry is taken.

Copy recorded but not located: Hodgins, no. 62.

1026. UPPER CANADA. LIEUTENANT-GOVERNOR, 1791-1799 (*Simcoe*)

SPEECH / OF HIS EXCELLENCY / John Graves Simcoe, Esquire, / LIEUTENANT GOVERNOR / of the Province of Upper-Canada, &c.&c. &c. / Upon proroguing the Fifth Session of the Provincial Parliament of Upper-Canada. / [rule] /

Broadside: 40 lines; type-page: 29 × 15.2 cm. *Probably printed at Niagara, U.C., by Gideon Tiffany, 1796.*

Delivered at Niagara, June 3, 1796, this was Simcoe's farewell speech to the Legislature, for he left Upper Canada in July, sailed from Quebec in Sept., and became governor of Saint Domingo in Dec., 1796. The speech was also published in the *Quebec gazette*, July 28, 1796.

Copies located: CaOT; GBLP (2 cop. in C.O. 42/320: 555, 557).

1027. UPPER CANADA. LIEUTENANT-GOVERNOR, 1791-1799 (*Simcoe*)

PROCLAMATION / [rule] / BY HIS EXCELLENCY / JOHN G. SIMCOE, ESQUIRE, / Lieutenant-Governor, and Major-General of his Majesty's / Forces, &c.&c.&c. / To such as are desirous of settling on the Lands of the Crown, in the / Province of Upper-Canada. / <Text> / GIVEN under my hand and seal, in the town of York, the / first day July, in the year of our Lord one thousand seven / hundred and ninety-six. / By his excellency's command, / J. SMALL, C.E.C. /

Broadside: 46 lines; type-page: 38.5 × 17 cm. *Probably printed at Niagara, U.C., by Gideon Tiffany, 1796.*

Text: "Whereas, by a proclamation bearing date at Quebec, the seventh day of February, 1792, [etc., revision of article 8 is announced and cited:] in addition to the fees established by the government on all grants of land, the respective petitioners will, in future, on receipt of their patents, be charged with the expences of survey in proportion to the extent of their patents [etc.]."

This proclamation is reprinted in Ontario Archives, *Report, 1905, ibid., 1906.*

Copy located: CaOT. *Copy recorded but not located:* Hodgins, no. 63.

1028. UPPER CANADA. LIEUTENANT-GOVERNOR, 1791-1799 (*Simcoe*)

[Proclamation. John Graves Simcoe. George the Third by the Grace of God of Great-Britain, France, and Ireland, King. Defender of the Faith, &c.&c.,&c. To all our loving Subjects,—Greeting: <Text> In testimony whereof We have caused the Great Seal of our Province to be hereunto affixed.—Witness our trusty and well beloved John Graves Simcoe, Esq. . . . York, this Twentieth Day of July, in the Thirty-sixth year of our Reign. J.G.S. Wm. Jarvis, Secretary.]

Broadside. *Probably printed at Niagara, U.C., by Gideon Tiffany, 1796.*

Text: "Whereas, by our Proclamation bearing date the first of July, we thought fit by and with the advice of our Executive Council . . . to issue our Royal Proclamation dissolving our Provincial Parliament . . . Now Know Ye, that [elections announced and held, the provincial parliament is convoked at York, Aug. 15, 1796] of which all concerned will take notice and not fail."

Thus convoking the legislature to the new provincial capital, York (now Toronto), was one of Simcoe's last official acts. For he left York for England on the following day.—*Mrs.* Elizabeth P. Simcoe: *The diary of Mrs. John Graves Simcoe* (Toronto 1911; rev. ed., 1934). This legislature actually met at York, June 1, 1797.

This proclamation is reprinted in Ontario Archives, *Report, 1906*, from which this entry is taken.

Copy recorded but not located: Hodgins no. 64.

1029. UPPER CANADA. SURVEYOR-GENERAL'S OFFICE

[Notice to land claimants, dated July 29, 1796, that claims must be presented before August 20 "or they cannot be attended to", signed, D. W. Smith, Acting Surveyor general.]

? Broadside: *Probably printed at Niagara, U.C., by Gideon Tiffany, 1796.*

Copy recorded but not located: Hodgins, no. 65.

1030. ALMANACS. LOWER CANADA

ALMANAC / DE / QUEBEC / POUR / L'ANNEE 1798. / [rule] / QUEBEC: / IMPRIMÉ A LA NOUVELLE IMPRIME-/RIE, RUE DU PALAIS. /

The only copy located is apparently incomplete. It comprises 11 unsigned *l.*, 24 *l.* signed: D-G[6], 24mo. Its pagination appears to be: [1-22], [37]-86, [2] p., 2 fold. tables, type-page: 9 × 5.4 cm. Text in French.

Contents: p. [1], t.-p.; p. [2], blank; p. [3-10], Epoques, etc., p. [11-22], Calendrier; fold. table showing court sittings; p. [37]-62, Liste civile (includes Lower Canada administrative officers, legislature, courts, lawyers, justices, departments of government, customs officers, notaries, doctors, surveyors, pilots, constables, army and militia officers, Indian interpreters); p. 63-73, Etat ecclésiastique (Catholic, Church of England clergy); p. 73-80, Bureau de la poste (rates, schedules, routes and names of post-masters); p. 81-86, Table des droits, etc. (duties on imports, fees to customs officers); [2] p. at end, Index. Fold. table between p. 38-39, Tableau de comtés, les paroisses, etc.

This almanac was issued apparently only for the year 1798, by Wm. Vondenvelden, or by P.-E. Desbarats who took over Vondenvelden's printing business about this time. It is handsomely produced for an initial effort in almanac work. It is smaller in size, on thinner paper, smaller types, and finer in appearance than Neilson's *Quebec almanac*'s of the period. Though the contents are comprehensive and detailed, they include nothing unrecorded by Neilson.

Copy located: CaQQA (incomplete).

1031. ALMANACS. LOWER CANADA

CALENDRIER pour l'Année 1798, pour Montreal, par les $304^{d.}$ $20^{m.}$ de Longitude, & $45^{d.}$ $35^{m.}$ de Latitude. / [rule] /

Colophon: [double rule] / A MONTREAL, Chez E. EDWARDS, Rue Notre Dame. /

Broadside: type-page: 51.5 × 40 cm.

Contents: Comput ecclésiastique, fêtes mobiles, quatre-tems, quatre saisons, eclipses; Calendrier (12 tables); At foot of sheet: "Membres de la Chambre d'Assemblée, Commissaires de la paix . . . de Montréal, liste des personnes appointées, connetables dans la Cour de Quartier de sessions d'Octobre, 1797, . . . Montréal."

Copy located: CaO (bound in *Montreal gazette*, 1798).

1032. ALMANACS. LOWER CANADA

CALENDRIER pour l'Année 1798 pour Québec, par les 306$^{d.}$ 30$^{m.}$ de Longitude, et 46$^{d.}$ 55$^{m.}$ de Latitude. / [ornamental rule] /

Colophon: A QUEBEC: chez JEAN NEILSON, Imprimeur & Libraire, N° 3 Rue la Montagne. /

Broadside: type-page: 54.5 × 40.5 cm.

Contents: Calendrier; Poids et taux de la monnaie d'or, tels que reglés par l'Acte, 7 Mai 1796; Termes des cours de justice (in French only); Time of attendance at public offices, departure of mails (in English and French).

This sheet almanac was sold at Neilson's printing office from Oct. 11, 1797, at 5*s.* the dozen.

Copy located: CaO (bound in *Quebec gazette* at end of 1797).

1033. ALMANACS. LOWER CANADA

THE / QUEBEC ALMANAC / FOR / THE YEAR 1797. / N:LAT: 46d: 55m:--W: LONG: 71d: 12m. / [rule] / QUEBEC: / PRINTED BY JOHN NEILSON, / MOUNTAIN STREET. /

French t.-p.:

ALMANAC / DE / QUEBEC, / POUR L'ANNEE 1797. / [ornament] / QUEBEC: / DE L'IMPRIMERIE DE J: NEILSON, / RUE LA MONTAGNE. /

12mo. A-P^6, [*]^2; 1 p. l. 178, [4] p., fold. table; type-page: 10.8 × 6 cm. One leaf of sig. [*] at end is folded around sig. A-I to form p. l.

Contents: p. l., blank; p. [1], English t.-p.; p. [2], blank; p. [3], French t.-p.; p. [4]-35, Epochs, tide table, calendar, feasts; p. 36-84, Chronique historique, 1792-1795; p. 85-120, Regulations on post office, county boundaries, etc., land grants, roads and bridges, courts, import duties; p. [121]-140, Civil list; p. [141]-167, Military register, etc.; p. 168-78, Ecclesiastical state, clergy, schools, fire society, etc.; p. [1-4] at end, Index. Fold. table: "Termes des cours de justice" inserted between p. 116-17.

This almanac follows closely the model set by Samuel Neilson in *The Quebec almanac for 1792.* This year, however, John Neilson introduced some new features: "Chronique historique," a chronology of events mainly in Lower Canada, 1792-95, also excerpts from the recent statutes on roads and bridges.

Copies were sold from Jan. 12, 1797, at 2*s.* 6*d.* the copy, £1 4*s.* the dozen.

Copies located: CaNsWA (p. [1-4] at end, wanting); CaO; CaOOA; CaOT; CaQ; CaQM; CaQMC; CaQMS; CaQQA; CaQQAr; CaQQL (p. [1-4] at end, wanting).

1034. ALMANACS. LOWER CANADA

THE / QUEBEC ALMANAC / FOR / THE YEAR 1798. / N:LAT: 46d. 55m:--W. LONG. 71 d: 12 m. / [double rule] / QUEBEC: / PRINTED BY JOHN NEILSON, / MOUNTAIN STREET. /

French t.-p.:

ALMANAC / DE / QUEBEC, / POUR / L'ANNE'E 1798. / [double rule] / QUEBEC: / DE L'IMPRIMERIE DE J: NEILSON, / RUE LA MONTAGNE. /

12mo. A-L[6], [*][2]; 132, [4] p., fold. table; type-page: 10.8 × 6 cm.

Contents: p. [1], English t.-p.; p. [2], blank; p. [3], French t.-p.; p. [4-35], Epochs, etc., calendar; p. 36-73, Provincial regulations on coin weight and values, postal rates, routes, etc., boundary of Upper and Lower Canada, regulations on land granting, roads and bridges; list of counties and parishes, court terms, import duties; ordinance of Apr. 23, 1777, for preventing people leaving the province without a pass; p. [74], blank; p. 75-94, Civil list; p. [95]-119, Military register; p. 120-32, Ecclesiastical state, clergy, schools, etc.; p. [1-4] at end, Contents table. Fold. table; "Termes des Cours de justice" inserted between p. 68-69.

Copies were sold from Dec. 11, 1797, and advertised: "Just published and for sale at this [Printing] Office, Price 2/ Retail, 20/ per dozen, stitched in red leather. And 3/ bound, [etc.]."—*Quebec gazette*, Dec. 21, 1797.

Copies located: CaNsWA; CaOOA (fold. table and p. 97 to end wanting; has also complete copy in photostat); CaQ; CaQMM; CaQMS; CaQQAr; CaQQL; DLC.

1035. ALMANACS. NOVA SCOTIA

AN / ALMANACK / FOR THE / Year . . . 1798; / . . . / CALCULATED FOR THE MERIDIAN OF / HALIFAX, . . . / . . . / CONTAINING / The ECLIPSES [etc. 8 lines in col. 1.] / SITTINGS of the COURTS [etc. 8 lines in col. 2.] / . . . / [rule] / BY THEOPHRASTUS. / [rule] / HALIFAX: / Printed and sold by JOHN HOWE, at his Printing-Office, / in GEORGE-STREET, near the PARADE. /

12mo. [32] p.; type-page: 15 × 8.2 cm.

Contents: p. [1], t.-p.; p. [2], Ephemeris; p. [3], Zodiac; p. [4], Directions to farmers; p. [5-16], Calendar; p. [17-22], Nova Scotia provincial officials, courts; p. [23-24], Masonic lodges in Nova Scotia, clergy; p. [25-30], Naval and army officers stationed in Nova Scotia, militia; p. [31-32], Distances from Halifax, etc.

Copy located: CaNsHA.

1036. ALMANACS. NOVA SCOTIA

THE / NOVA-SCOTIA CALENDER, / OR AN / ALMANACK, / FOR THE / Year . . . 1798. / [4 lines] / WHEREIN IS CONTAINED, / The ECLIPSES . . . / [4 lines] / Calculated for the Meridian of HALIFAX . . . / [3 lines] / [rule] / By METONICUS. / [rule] / [verse, 6 lines, from] / DRY-

DEN'S VIRGIL. / [double rule] / HALIFAX: / Printed and sold by A. HENRY, at his Printing-Office, in Sack-/ville-Street, Corner of Grafton-Street. / [title and each page within ornamental frame]

12mo. [36] p.; type-page: 13.5 × 8.5 cm.

Contents: p. [1], t.-p.; p. [2], Directions to farmers; p. [3], Vulgar notes; p. [4-5], Ephemeris; p. [6], Eclipses; p. [7-18], Calendar; p. [19-25], Province of Nova Scotia, administration, legislature, judges, justices, freemasons, courts, clergy, etc.; p. [26-34], naval, army, militia officers in Nova Scotia, post offices, etc.; p. [35-36], Distances, errata.

This almanic was advertised: "Just published and for Sale by Anthony Henry, Price 5/ per dozen, 7½d single, The Nova-Scotia Calender, or an Almanack, for the Year 1798 [etc.]."—*Royal gazette*, Halifax, N.S., Nov. 21, 1797.

Copy located: DLC. Another copy (not located) recorded in Charles F. Heartman: Sale Cat. no. 105, Sept. 10, 1920, item no. 6.

1037. CARY, THOMAS, 1751-1823

[Catalogue of a circulating library]

Broadside or leaflet. *Printed at Quebec, by John Neilson, 1797*, as recorded:

"1797, Sept. 15. [Debit] Mr. Cary printing 300 Catalogues—£4.13.4.
Printing 1000 [ditto] Mr. Cary's Circulating Library—10/
[Total: £5 3*s.* 4*d.*]—Can.P.A., *Neilson papers*, v. 66 [*Sales for credit 1796-98*].

Cary, author of *Abram's plains* (No. 585) opened a library at Quebec in 1787, as he advertised:

"Mr. Cary has just opened at No. 3, in St. Louis Street a circulating library adapted to every description of readers, where books are let to be read by the year [!] half year, quarter, month, or single volume. Catalogues with Conditions are to be seen at the Library.

"As the utility of this undertaking must be obvious to all and as the best recommendation to the patronage of an enlightened and discerning community is the being useful, the Public is looked up to, with confidence, for encouragement and support. Persons having French books for sale—bring them to the Library."

—*Quebec gazette*, Sept. 14, 1797.

Cary described the "Conditions" in his next advertisement:

"The Circulating library is daily increasing. Books will be sent to any part of the Province from whence they can be returned in a fortnight, the Reader paying carriage and being answerable for the books. Not more than four will be sent at once, two to be returned when read and two will be sent in their place, by which a constant supply can be kept up. The charge is 20/ per annum; 12/ for six months; 7/ for three months, paid in advance. The remaining conditions are to be seen in the Catalogue to be had at the Library, price 7½d. No change in conditions to Quebec subscribers. [The Proprietor] expects American papers by Burlington [Vermont] and intends taking all the provincial papers. Any persons having European papers, please lend them to Cary's library, They will be paid for if wanted. All the papers are laid on a table in a commodious well-warmed room on the second floor at the Library open from ten until three oclock. As this will be attended with additional expence, the Subscriber would be wanting in justice to a liberal community not to confide in the continuation of its patronage for the requisite support: signed, M. Cary. Letters to be addressed to Thomas Cary postpaid for the sale of books and stationery."—*Quebec gazette,* Jan. 4, 1798.

The Library prospered through Cary's life time, for it appears (with two others) in T. H. Gleason: *The Quebec directory for 1822,* as "A Circulating Library containing a respectable number of books, the property of Thomas Cary, corner Garden street near the Ursuline Convent [in Parloir street]. The Collection is chaste and the terms reasonable."

It was continued by Cary's son and namesake whose *Catalogue, 1830* lists 4,515 English and 799 French titles. The catalogue of 1797, however, must have been more modest.

Copy located: None.

1038. CATHOLIC CHURCH. LITURGY AND RITUAL

LA / JOURNÉE / DU CHRÉTIEN, / SANCTIFIÉE / PAR LA PRIERE / ET / LA MÉDITATION / Seconde Edition augmentée. / [printer's ornament] / A QUEBEC, / Chez LOUIS GERMAIN. / Rue de la Fabrique. / [double rule] / IMPRIME'E A LA NOUVELLE IMPRIME-/ RIE. M.DCC.XCVII. /

This edition, like No. 928, was printed by Wm. Voldenvelden, at the new printing office, Quebec, and "published" like many other devotional works of the period by Louis Langlois dit Germain, a merchant. Germain, Senior, who died probably early in 1798, had a shop at no. 10 rue de la Fabrique. His son, with the same name, also had a shop, at no. 5 rue de la Fabrique.

As the only copy located is highly defective, the following collation and contents are *suggested:*

18mo. $[A]^5$, $B\text{-}?^9$ $[*\text{-}3*]^9$, $F\text{-}K^9$ $[*]_1$, $L\text{-}M^9$, N^4; 1 *l.*, [viii] 276 p., 1 *l.*; type-page: 9.5 × 5.5 cm. 3 extra signatures (making 6 in all) seem to occur between B and F, and another between K and L. p. 232-33 are numbered at inner margin; p. 263 mispaged: 293.

Contents: 1 *l.* blank; p. [i], t.-p.; p. [ii], blank; p. [iii]-iv, Preface; p. [v]-vii, Table (contents); p. [viii], blank; p. [1]-97?, Prières; p. 98-113?, Practique de dévotion; p. 114-33, Prières diverses; p. 134-49, Réglement de la vie; p. 149-225, Pensées chrêtiennes pour les jours du mois: p. 225-227, Les commandemens; p. 228-243, Les vêpres, etc.; p. 243-253, Pseaulmes; p. 253-64, Les litanies, etc.; p. 264-72, Petit office; p. 272-76, Réponse de la messe; 1 *l.* at end, recto: Approbation; verso, blank.

Approbation: "Québec. 7me Avril 1797. L'experience de bien des années prouve si manifestement l'utilité de la Journée du Chrétien, que je n'hesite point, au nom de Nos Seigneurs Evêques d'approuver et de louer beaucoup la Nouvelle édition qui se fait cet excellent livre.—Gravé, Vic. Gen."

This edition is recorded in Dionne: *Inventaire,* 1: no. 49; and in Gagnon: *Essai de bibliographie canadienne,* 1: no. 1924; probably from the copy located below.

Copy located: CaQM (this copy with original calf binding intact, stitching broken, paper discoloured throughout, lacks p. 3-128, 143-48, 153-54, 159-62. p. l. bears MS. inscription: "Madéline Yaté, 1799 [etc.]").

1039. CHURCH OF ENGLAND. LITURGY AND RITUAL

[A Form of Prayer to be used in all Churches in Nova Scotia on Wednesday June 21, 1797. Appointed for a General Fast.]

Printed at Halifax, N.S., by Anthony Henry, 1797, as recorded:

"To 500 Prayers to be read in churches [for a general fast in 1797].—£5."—Henry's *Account for extra printing [for government] 1796-97,* in P.A.N.S., *Miscellaneous Assembly papers,* 1797.

Bishop Inglis wrote Lieut.-Gov. Wentworth, Halifax, Apr. 24, 1797, stating that he saw by the last English packet that His Majesty had issued a proclamation on Feb. 1, appointing a fast day on Mar. 8, and requested Wentworth to appoint by proclamation a day of general humiliation in Nova Scotia. "There never was a time when it was more necessary to supplicate the aid of Heaven . . . I shall take care to prepare a suitable Form of Prayer [etc.]." He suggested that the day be upwards of five weeks following the proclamation, as in His Majesty's proclamation.—Can.P.A., *Inglis papers,* v. 2.

Wentworth, accordingly, appointed June 21, 1797, a fast day (*see* No. 1064).

Bishop Inglis wrote similarly to Lieut.-Gov. Fanning of the Island of St. John, and probably to Carleton of New Brunswick, also part of Inglis's diocese. The former (and probably the latter too) proclaimed, on May 21, 1797, a fast day in his province on June 21, but no evidence had been found to indicate another locally printed edition of the Form of prayer, or even printed publication of the Proclamation at Charlottetown, or Saint John.

Copy located: None.

1040. GREAT BRITAIN. LAWS, STATUTES, *etc.*

ANNO REGNI / GEORGII III, / REGIS / MAGNÆ BRITANNIÆ, FRANCIÆ ET HIBERNIÆ / DECIMO QUARTO. / At the Parliament begun and holden at Westminster, the Tenth Day / of May, Anno Domini 1768, in the Eighth Year of the Reign of our / Sovereign Lord GEORGE the Third, by the Grace of GOD, of Great / Britain, France and Ireland King, Defender of the Faith, &c. / And from thence continued, by several Prorogations to the Thirteenth Day of Ja-/ nuary, 1774; being the Seventh Session of the Thirteenth Parliament of Great Britain. / [rule] / [royal arms] / [rule] / QUEBEC: / PRINTED BY WILLIAM VONDENVELDEN, / LAW PRINTER TO THE KING'S MOST EXCELLENT MAJESTY. / M.DCC.XCVII. /

French t.-p.:

ANNO REGNI / GEORGII III, / REGIS / MAGNÆ BRITANNIÆ FRANCIÆ ET HIBERNIÆ / DECIMO QUARTO. / Au Parlement commencé et tenu à Westminster, le dixiéme jour de Mai, / l'an de notre Seigneur 1768, et dans la huitième année du Règne de / notre Souverain Seigneur GEORGE Trois, par la grace de DIEU, Roi / de la Grande Bretagne, de France et d'Irlande, Défenseur de la Foi, &c. / Et depuis ce tems continué, par plusieurs Prorogations jusqu'au treizième jour de / Janvier 1774; étant la septième Session du treizième Parlement de la Grande Bretagne. / [rule] / [royal arms] / [rule] /A QUEBEC: / IMPRIME' PAR GUILLAUME VONDENVELDEN, / IMPRIMEUR DE LOI [sic] DE SA TRES EXCELLENT MAJESTE LE ROI. / M.DCC. XCVII. /

4to. [A^2, B]-H^4; 59 p.; type-page: 21.5 × 17 cm. One leaf of sig. D is folded around sig. E-H, to form p. 59. Text in English and French on opposite pages.

Contents: p. [1], English t.-p.; p. [2], blank; p. [3], French t.-p.; p. [4], blank; p. [5], blank; p. 6-15, 14 Geo. III c. 83, An act for making more effectual provision for the government of the province of Quebec in North America; p. 16-21, 14 Geo. III c. 88, An act to establish a fund towards further defraying the charges of the administration of justice and support of the civil government within the province of Quebec in America; p. [22], blank; p. [23]:

ANNO REGNI / GEORGII III, / REGIS / MAGNÆ BRITANNIÆ, FRANCIÆ ET HIBERNIÆ / TRICESIMO PRIMO. / At the Parliament begun and holden at Westminster, the Twenty-fifth Day / of November, Anno Domini 1790, in the Thirty-first Year of the Reign / of our Sovereign Lord GEORGE the Third, by the Grace of GOD, / of Great Britain, France and Ireland King, Defender of the Faith, &c. / being the First Session of the Seventeenth Parliament of Great Britain. / [rule] / [royal arms] / [rule] / QUEBEC: / PRINTED BY WILLIAM VONDENVELDEN, / LAW PRINTER TO THE KING'S MOST EXCELLENT MAJESTY. / M.DCC. XCVII. /

p. [24], blank; p. [25], French t.-p.:

ANNO REGNI / GEORGII III, / REGIS / MAGNÆ BRITANNIÆ FRANCIÆ ET HIBERNIÆ / TRICESIMO PRIMO. / Au Parlement commencé et tenu à Westminster, le Vingt-cinquième jour / de Novembre, l'an de notre Seigneur 1790, et dans la Trente-unième / année du Règne de notre Souverain Seigneur GEORGE Trois, par la / grace de DIEU, Roi de la Grande Bretagne, de France et d'Irlande, Dé-/fenseur de la Foi, &c. étant la première Session du dix-septième Parle-/ment de la Grande Bretagne / [rule] / [royal arms] / [rule] / A QUEBEC: / IMPRIME' PAR GUILLAUME VONDENVELDEN, / IMPRIMEUR DE LOIX [sic] DE SA TRES EXCELLENTE MAJESTE' LE ROI. / M.DCC. XCVII. /

p. [26-27], blank; p. 28-59, 31 Geo. III c. 3, An act to repeal certain parts of an act passed in the fourteenth year of His Majesty's reign intituled An act for making more effectual provision for the government of the province of Quebec, in North America; and to make further provision for the said province; verso of p. 59, blank.

The so-called Quebec Act and Quebec Revenue Act, 1774, and the so-called Constitutional or Canada Act, 1791—the British statutes fundamental to Canadian government—comprise this publication. The work was reprinted from another setting of type with title-page (including the imprint) and content unchanged, probably by P.-E. Desbarats shortly after the year 1818 (*see* No. 1041).

The genuine 1797 edition is to be distinguished from the reprint in its typography: the rotund letters and even colour of its old face type are easily distinguished from the modern face (in title pages and marginal matter) of the reprint, with its seemingly tall, narrow letters of contrasting light and heavy lines—the heavy vertical lines strongly accented as in types from British founders between 1815 and 1840 (*see* D. B. Updike: *Printing types, their history, forms, and use,* 2 v., Cambridge, Mass., 1937, v. 2, chap. 20).

The line endings on the title pages and signatures A and H in the genuine 1797 edition, are changed in the reprint (cf. titles and collation of No. 1040 and No. 1041). Several catchwords were changed when the pages were reset, e.g., p. 17 and 29 have catchwords "Province" and "ront" respectively, in the genuine 1797 edition; "Pour" and "sentes" respectively in the reprint. Several typographical errors were made in resetting, e.g. on the first English t.-p. MAGNÆ (in the original) appears as MACNÆ in the reprint; on p. 8, the headline date 1774 (in the original) appears as 1744 in the reprint; p. 18-21, the headline . . . c. 88 (in the original), appears as . . . c. 83, in the reprint.

The genuine 1797 edition is to be distinguished from the reprint by its *paper* also. All the copies seen in old face type are printed on laid paper, cream or gray in tone, with 1794 in the watermark. Other works from Vondenvelden's shop in 1797 and 1798 were printed on similar paper. All the copies seen with modern face type in title pages and marginal matter are printed on a thin crisp laid paper clearly watermarked 1818.

Copies of either printing are found complete as a unit, or complete in two parts, with another document inserted between the Quebec acts and the Constitutional act, or sometimes either part alone, incomplete. Copies of either printing in any form are found bound most frequently in *A collection of the acts . . . 1800*, or its 1824 edition (*see* No. 1169) bound occasionally with No. 942, or with No. 943. Copies appear occasionally bound individually or stitched in their original blue-gray printer's paper covers.

Copies located of the genuine 1797 edition (in case of doubt a query is prefixed to location symbol): CSmH; CaO (2 cop.); CaOOA (copy complete, also pt. 1 only); CaOT; CaOTL; CaQM; CaQMJ (copy complete, also pt. 2 only); CaQMM (4 cop.); CaQQA; CaQQB; CaQQL ("Ex.A" stitched in original gray paper covers); CtY; DLC (2 cop.); ?Ketcheson; ?M (pt. 1 only); MH (2 cop.); MiD-B (2 cop.); N; NN (p. 59 in photostat); NNB; RPJ (copy complete, also pt. 2 only); WHi; ?Witton.

1041. GREAT BRITAIN. LAWS, STATUTES, *etc.*

ANNO REGNI / GEORGII III, / REGIS / MACNÆ [sic] BRITANNIÆ FRANCIÆ ET HIBERNIÆ, / DECIMO QUARTO. / At the Parliament begun and holden at Westminster, the / Tenth Day of May, Anno Domini 1768, in the Eighth / Year of the Reign of our Sovereign Lord GEORGE / the Third, by the Grace of GOD, of Great Britain, / France and Ireland King, Defender of the Faith, &c. / And from thence continued, . . . January, / 1774; . . . Britain. / [rule] / [royal arms] / [rule] / QUEBEC: / PRINTED BY WILLIAM VONDENVELDEN, LAW PRINTER TO THE KING'S MOST EXCELLENT MAJESTY. / M.DCC. XCVII. /

French t.-p.:

ANNO REGNI / GEORGII III, / REGIS / MAGNÆ BRITANNIÆ FRANCIÆ ET HIBERNIÆ, / DECIMO QUARTO. / Au Parlement commencé et tenu à Westminster, le dix-/ième jour de Mai, l'an de Notre Seigneur 1768, et / dans la huitième année du Régne de notre Souverain / Seigneur GEORGE Trois, par la grace de DIEU, Roi / de la Grande Bretagne, de France et d'Irlande, Dé/fenseur de la Foi, &c. / Et depuis ce tems . . . jour de / Janvier 1774; . . . Bretagne. / [rule] / [royal arms] / [rule] / A QUEBEC: / IMPRIME' PAR GUILLAUME VONDENVELDEN, / IMPRIMEUR DE LOI [sic] DE SA TRES EXCELLENTE MAJESTE' LE ROI. / M.DCC.XCVII. /

4to. [A]-G[4], H[2]; 59 p.; type-page: 21.5 × 17 cm. Text in English and French on opposite pages.

Probably printed at Quebec, by Pierre-Edouard Desbarats shortly after 1818. This is another edition of No. 1040, printed from different types but with titles and content unchanged, excepting for minor discrepancies noted in No. 1040 *note*.

Contents: Same as No. 1040.

p. [23] t.-p.: ANNO REGNI / GEORGII III, / REGIS / MAGNÆ BRITANNIÆ FRANCIÆ ET HIBERNIÆ, / TRICESIMO PRIMO. / At the Parliament begun and holden at Westminster, the / . . . in / . . . Sovereign / . . . of / . . . of / . . . Seven- / . . . Britain. / [rule] / [royal arms] / [rule] / QUEBEC: / PRINTED BY WILLIAM VONDENVELDEN, / LAW PRINTER TO THE KING'S MOST EXCELLENT MAJESTY. / M.DCC.XCVII. /

p. [25], French t.-p.: ANNO REGNI / GEORGII III, / REGIS / MAGNÆ BRITANNIÆ FRANCIÆ ET HIBERNIÆ, / TRICESIMO PRIMO. / Au Parlement commencé et tenu à Westminster, le / . . . notre / . . . du / . . . Trois, / . . . de / . . . etant la / . . . de la / Grande Bretagne. / [rule] / [royal arms] / [rule] / A QUEBEC: / IMPRIME' PAR GUILLAUME VONDENVELDEN, / IMPRIMEUR DE LOIX [sic] DE SA TRES EXCELLENTE MAJESTE' LE ROI. / M.DCC.XCVII. /

Copies located of 19th-century reprint: CaOT (2 cop.); CaOTO; CaQQL (2 cop.: "Ex B" stitched in original gray paper covers, "Ex C" bound in *A Collection of acts . . . 1824*); DLC; MWA; MiD-B; ? MiU; NN; NNB (copy complete, also pt. 1 only).

1042. HISTOIRE ABREGEE . . . DE LA SAINTE VIERGE

HISTOIRE ABREGEE / DES / EVENEMENS EXTRAORDINAIRES / ET / MIRACLEUX / ARRIVES A JERUSALEM A LA MORT, / OU / DORMITION, / DE LA / SAINTE VIERGE, / SUIVANT LA TRADITION APOSTCLIQUE. / OU / On DEVOILE la MAUVAISE FOY de QUELQUES / AUTEURS MODERNES. / Qui pour en flêtrir la gloire, l'ont dite morte a

Ephese. / [double rule] / Question de pieté interessante. / [double rule] / Par M***, PRESTRE, Français. / [double rule] / 1797. /

8vo. [A]-C[4], [D][2]; 28 p.; type-page: 16.5 × 8.7 cm. One leaf of sig. D is folded around sig. [A]-C to form t.-p.

Contents: p. [1], t.-p.; p. [2], blank; p. [3]-28, Histoire.

Said (by Gagnon in *Essai de bibliographie canadienne,* 1: no. 1673) probably to have been printed at Quebec, this publication, though extremely eccentric in appearance, is difficult to localize. The old face type and paper (with the standardized watermark: a fleur de lys and counter mark: IV, (*see* W. A. Churchill: *Watermarks in paper . . . in the XVII and XVIII centuries* [*etc.*], Amsterdam, 1935, 22) were used by both Neilson and Vondenvelden at Quebec, as by many late 18th-century printers supplied from English sources. Typographical errors abound. The spelling is very faulty, accents are commonly omitted. The text itself, though French, is frequently a literal translation of English idiom—the work of a tyro throughout.

Histoire abregée shows that the misfortunes befallen France upon the withdrawal of mediation of Jesus Christ and the Sacred Mother are the inevitable sequel to the French philosophers' treatment of religion. It (*Histoire abregée*) reveals the errors and obscurities implicit in their rational examination of belief. It exposes Baillet [Adrien Baillet, 1649-1706, author of *Les vies des saints*, Paris, 1701) and the Jansenist author of "the Dictionary" (i.e. *L'Encyclopedie*, Paris, 1752 *et seq.*) who state that the Virgin died at Ephesus—and do so, less to instruct than to cast doubt in the minds of the faithful. The author of *Histoire abregée* proves that the Blessed Virgin died, not at Ephesus but at Jerusalem, and, in the final paragraph of the *Histoire*, dedicates his vindication of Her glory to the Virgin herself.

Copy located: CaQM (Gagnon's copy).

1043. LAFORCE, P.

[Song.]

?Broadside. *Printed at Quebec, by John Neilson, 1797,* as recorded:

"1797, June 22, [Debit] P. Laforce, Jr. To printing 400 Songs—£1."
—Can.P.A., *Neilson papers*, v. 54.

Copy located: None.

1044. L'HOMOND, CHARLES FRANCOIS, 1727-1794

ELEMENTS / DE LA / GRAMMAIRE LATINE. / [double rule] / A MONTREAL: / Chez ROY & BENNETT Imprimeurs No. 58, / Rue Notre-Dame. / [rule] 1797 [rule] /

12mo. A-I[4]; 1 p. l., 67, [1] p., 1 *l.*; type-page: 14 × 8.5 cm.

Contents: p. l. recto, t.-p ; verso, blank; p. 1-67, Elements, [1] p. at end (verso of p. 67), Fautes principaux à corriger; 1 *l.*, blank.

This is part 1 of L'Homond's *Elements,* treating of the parts of speech, noun, adjective, verb, etc., with declension and conjugation tables. Parts 2-3, on syntax and method, were printed in the same office the previous year (No. 989). The three publications together formed the first Canadian-printed edition of L'Homond's Latin grammar. Abbé L'Homond was a teacher of great skill, who spent most of his life instructing the boys of Collège du Cardinal-Lemoine in religion and classics. His *Elements de la grammaire latine,* which first appeared about 1780, remained the standard text commonly used in classical colleges and schools, and published in many editions, revised, enlarged, and abridged, in French Canada as in France, through the 19th century.

The 1796-97 edition was sponsored by the Séminaire de Saint Sulpice for the Collège de Montréal, and was adopted by the Séminaire des Missions Etrangères for use in the Collège de Québec. To the latter on Aug. 17, 1797, Bennett sent thirty copies, for which he charged 3*s.* in boards and 3*s.* 6*d.* half bound. The work was advertised:

"A vendre à l'Imprimerie [de J. Neilson, Québec], Les Elements de la Grammaire latine par M[r] l'Homond. Imprimé pour l'usage et sous la direction du Collège de Montréal et maintenant usités dans le Seminaire de Québec. Prix 4/ proprement reliés."—*Quebec gazette,* Dec. 28, 1797.

After the publication of parts 2-3, and while part 1 was in preparation, Louis Roy abandoned his printing office in Montreal and the work was carried on by his brother Joseph-Marie Roy, who formed a partnership with John Bennett. Bennett, who had been John Neilson's foreman at the *Quebec gazette* office, arrived in Montreal Apr. 13, 1797, and on Aug. 17 he wrote Neilson that the Latin grammar was just finished and that his partnership with Roy was dissolved.—Can.P.A., *Neilson papers,* I: 56-89. So L'Homond's *Elements* is probably the only book published with the Roy-Bennett imprint. Bennett's revelation of the lack of equipment and organization in Roy's printing house accounts for the shoddy appearance of this work. He found everything in the office in the greatest confusion, he wrote John Neilson, Apr. 17, 1797, "a great quantity of pye, . . . no furniture, scabbards or Rules and what is worse, not a single quire of paper . . . not even so much as a mallet or shooting stick are to be seen, in fact if we are to get on with the work (of which there is considerable) we must have the 'Devil's Luck and our own too.' "

Copy located: CaQMS: complete copy in one volume containing [pt. 1] Elements (No. 1044), pt. 2 Syntaxe (No. 988) and pt. 3, Methode (No. 989)—in original full calf binding.

Another copy not located, formerly owned by Gerald E. Hart, author of *The Fall of New France,* etc., is described: "Elemens . . . 3 Parts, with titles to Syntax and Method. The first title page is missing together with the first page up to 5, otherwise perfect though first pages are thumbed on the edges. 12° original paper cover." —No. 2170 in *Catalogue of the library . . . of Gerald E. Hart . . . to be sold April 15th to 19th 1890,* by Libbie, Boston.

1045. LOWER CANADA. COURT OF QUARTER SESSIONS of the PEACE (*Montreal district*)

[Le Tarif pour regler le prix du Pain.]

Broadside: 79 lines; type-page: 24 × 21.5 cm. ? *Printed at Quebec, by J. Neilson, 1797.*

Caption at head: "C'est avec un vrai plaisir que nous mettons devant le Public le Tarif suivant pour regler le Prix du Pain (qui a été dressé par P. Foretier, Ecuier de Montréal) étant persuadés que les Magistrats de Quebec seront flattés de faire usage d'une Table . . ."

The text, regulations for the price, weight, etc., of bread, is signed "Pierre Foretier, J.P. A Montreal 27e Janvier, 1797." Appended is the note: "Ce tarif a été mis en force, au Quartier général de sessions tenu à Montréal, du 21 au 30 Avril, 1797."

Copy located: CaQQL.

1046. LOWER CANADA. EXECUTIVE COUNCIL

[rule] / PROVINCE OF / LOWER-CANADA. / TO WIT. / At His Majesty's Executive Council, of and for the said / Province of Lower Canada, held in the Castle of Saint / Lewis, in the City of Quebec, in the said Province on / Tuesday the Twenty second day of August, in the thirty / seventh year of His Majesty's Reign and in the year of our Lord, one thousand seven hundred and ninety seven. / PRESENT. / HIS EXCELLENCY THE GOVERNOR IN COUNCIL. / <Text, signed:> Herman Witsius Ryland.

Broadside: 91 lines, 2 col. English and French; type-page: 61.2 × 21.5 cm. *Probably printed at Quebec, by Wm. Vondenvelden, 1797.*

Text is order-in-council for further regulating the inland navigation from the United States by the port of St. Johns, L.C. Amending that of July 7, 1796 (*see* No. 992) it authorizes and specifies the fees to be levied by the collector of customs at St. Johns, upon owners of vessels, carts, etc., and merchandise *going to* the United States. It is a schedule, not of duties, but of the official's charges for preparing the reports required by the government upon the vehicles and content. A draft of the regulations, prepared by Attorney-General Sewell, was laid before the Council, passed and ordered to be published in two languages for three weeks in the *Quebec gazette* and the *Montreal gazette*, and 500 copies to be printed for distribution.—Can.P.A., "S" *Int. Corres.* Aug. 22, 1797.

Copy located: NNB.

1047. LOWER CANADA. EXECUTIVE COUNCIL

Caption title: Order of the Governor in Council, / [rule] / For further regulating the Inland Navigation from / the United States by the Port of St. Johns. /

4to. 4 *l.* without signature or pagination; type-page: 21 × 15 cm. Text in English and French on opposite pages.

Contents: l. 1 recto, blank; *l.* 1 verso-*l.* 3 recto, Order of the governor-in-council, dated from Quebec, Aug. 22, 1797, and signed by Herman Witsius Ryland; p. [6], blank; 1 *l.* at end, blank.

This is another edition of No. 1046. It was *printed at Quebec possibly by P.-E. Desbarats about 1800,* for copies are commonly found bound (apparently as issued) in his *Collection of the acts . . . 1800.* Printed from old face types and (the copies seen) on paper, laid or woven, without visible watermark, it has the appearance of the law printer's work at the turn of the century.

Copies located: CaO; CaOT; CaOTL; CaQM; CaQMJ; CaQMM (2 cop.); CaQQA; CaQQB; CaQQL (2 cop., one bound with No. 943; the other, unsewn, the sheet folded as issued); DLC; ?Ketcheson; M; MH (2 cop.); MiD-B; MiU; N; NN; RPJ; WHi.

1048. LOWER CANADA. GOVERNOR, 1797-1807 (*Prescott*)

[royal arms] / BY HIS EXCELLENCY / ROBERT PRESCOTT, ESQUIRE, / Captain General [etc. 7 lines] / [rule] / A PROCLAMATION. / <Text> / Given . . . / . . . Quebec, . . . / . . . / . . . [22 Aug. 1797] / ROBT. PRESCOTT. / By His EXCELLENCY'S COMMAND, / GEO: POWNALL, Secry. / God Save the KING. / (PRINTED BY JOHN NEILSON.) /

French side: [royal arms] / PAR SON EXCELLENCE / ROBERT PRESCOTT, ECUYER, / Capitaine Général [etc. 7 lines] / [rule] / PROCLAMATION. / <Text> / Donné . . . / . . . [à Québec, le 22 Août, 1797] / . . . / . . . / ROB$^{t.}$ PRESCOTT. / [5 lines] / (DE L'IMPRIMERIE DE J: NEILSON.) /

Double broadside: English on left, 46 lines, type-page: 36.5 × 16 cm. French on right, 50 lines, type-page: 36.7 × 16 cm.

Neilson recorded the printing:

"1797, Aug. 26. [Debit] Provincal Secretary's Office To printing 500 Proclamations 1 on a Sh^{t} Crown English type—£3.18.

—Can.P.A., *Neilson papers*, v. 54.

Text: "Whereas divers Persons, without sufficient authority, have possessed themselves of several Tracts and Parcels of His Majesty's ungranted Lands [etc., Prescott orders such persons quietly to remove from the lands and enjoins] all . . . Civil Officers . . . to transmit to the Clerk of the Executive Council . . . the names of all [such] Persons."

French text: "Vu que divers Personnes, sans aucune autorité suffisante, se sont emparées de plusieurs Pieces et Portions de Terre de Sa Majesté non concédées [etc.]."

A Committee of the whole Council was ordered July 31, 1797, to prepare a report on "some Regular plan and system for placing Church and Crown lands upon such a footing as shall best secure them from individual enroachments and shall soonest render them profitable." They reported, Aug. 15, that "tho' they apprehended they shall find considerable difficulty in suggesting any effectual system for the purpose required, yet in the mean time, as they have reason to believe that great encroachments have already been made on the Church and Crown lands, and that the same are likely to increase, they conceive it necessary that a proclamation should immediately issue [etc.]." Attorney-General Sewell drew up the proclamation. It was issued by Gov. Prescott and ordered published in the two languages for three successive weeks in the Quebec and Montreal gazettes and 500 copies printed for distribution.—Can.P.A., L.C. *Land* D, pt. 1, p. 127-29.

This proclamation, apparently directed against "pitchers" or squatters, especially recent arrivals from the United States, affected also bona fide settlers who held lands on survey warrants or Council orders, to whom, by neglect or otherwise, final title deeds had never been issued.

This was the first publication deriving from the Council committee on the land question—which rapidly developed into one of the most contentious issues in the struggle between the Council and Prescott, resulting in the latter's recall to England in 1799.

The Proclamation is reprinted in Can.P.A., *Report, 1921.*

Copy located: CaOOA (in *Proclamations* portfolio in the Library).

1049. LOWER CANADA. HOUSE OF ASSEMBLY

[A Bill for taking down and removing such part of the old wall and fortifications now surrounding the City of Montreal, as shall not be deemed necessary for military or other purposes; and for otherwise improving the said City of Montreal.]

? fo. 32 p. *Printed at Quebec, by John Neilson, 1797,* as recorded:

"1797, Aug. 26. [Debit] House of Assembly. To printing 300 Copies of the Bill for taking down the fortifications of Montreal, &c. making 8 Sheets Pott (say) Foolscap, English type.—£18.16.

Folding & stitching Ditto @ 1^{d} each—£1.5."

—Can.P.A., *Neilson papers,* v. 54.

In another record of the same publication "Pott" is scored out.—*ibid.,* v. 66.

On May 2, 1797, the last day of the session, "Mr. Attorney-general [Jonathan Sewell, member for the borough of William Henry (now Sorel), 1796-1808] presented a Bill for taking down and removing such part of the old wall and fortifications now surrounding the City of Montreal, as shall not be deemed necessary for military or other purposes; and for otherwise improving the said City of Montreal . . . Ordered that 300 copies of the said Bill be printed in English and French . . . and that four copies . . . be sent . . . to each member."—L.C. As. *Journal.* This bill was apparently dropped.

Copy located: None.

1050. LOWER CANADA. HOUSE OF ASSEMBLY

JOURNAL / OF THE / HOUSE OF ASSEMBLY, / OF / LOWER-CANADA. / From the 24th January to the 2d May, 1797, both days inclusive. / IN THE THIRTY SEVENTH YEAR OF THE REIGN OF / KING GEORGE THE THIRD. / Being the First Session of the Second Provincial Parliament / of this Province. / [royal arms] / [double rule] / QUEBEC: / PRINTED BY ORDER OF THE HOUSE OF ASSEMBLY, / AND SOLD BY JOHN NEILSON. / —M.DCC.XCVII.— /

French t.-p.:

JOURNAL / DE LA / CHAMBRE D'ASSEMBLE'E, / DU / BAS-CANADA. / Depuis le 24e. Janvier jusqu'au 2e. Mai, 1797, inclusivement. / DANS LA TRENTE SEPTIEME ANNE'E DU REGNE DE / SA MAJESTÉ GEORGE TROIS. / Etant la premiere Session du Second Parlement Provincial / de cette Province. / [royal arms] / [double rule] / QUEBEC: / IMPRIME' PAR ORDRE DE LA CHAMBRE D'ASSEMBLE'E, / ET A VENDRE PAR JOHN NEILSON. / M.DCC.XCVII. /

4to., A-2E^4; 9 p. l., [1], 206 p., 3 *l.*; type-page: 18 × 12.3 cm. Odd numbers on verso, even numbers on recto. Text in English and French on opposite pages.

Mint copies of the *Journal* for the years 1797-1800, in the New York State Library, show the first and last signatures complete, making blank leaves before and after the text, the first and last of which are pasted to the blue, printer's paper covers in which the *Journal* was issued.

Contents: p. l. 1-2, blank; p. l. 3 recto, English t.-p.; verso, blank; p. l. 4 recto, French t.-p.; verso, blank; p. l. 5 recto, blank; p. l. 5 verso-recto of p. [1], Proclamations, etc.; p. [1]-206, Journal; verso of p. 206, blank; 3 *l.* at end, blank.

The House ordered that 100 copies of its *Journal* be printed in English and French for the use of members and that none but the printer so licensed print the same.—L.C. As. *Journal*, Apr. 28, 1797.

The printer recorded this work:

"1797, Aug. 26. [Debit] House of Assembly To printing at the rate of £125 for 318 pages being the mean rate of the 3 former sessions—100 Copies Journals of the first session of the second Assembly charged @ 150 pages, with condition that if they should make more or less the parties should mutually reimburse each other.—£62.10.

D° Cutting 100 Copies Journals—£1.5.

D° Binding 1 Copy Journals—6/.

Aug. 27. To Printing 50 pages of the Journals more than chgd for in Acc^t for Printing the Same @ £125 for 300 pages—£20.16.8."

—Can.P.A., *Neilson papers*, v. 54.

The *Journal* of the House of Assembly was advertised for sale at the printing office of John Neilson, for the four sessions of the first Assembly (1792-96), 4 v. for 45*s.*; for the first session of the second Assembly (1797) for 7*s.* 6*d.* —*Quebec gazette*, Aug. 3, 1797.

An *Index* was issued later ([31] p. 4to; p. [1-15] English; p. [16] blank; p. [17-31], French; verso of p. [31], blank). Though without printer's name or date, it was issued considerably later, being printed on paper with the date 1807 in the watermark. The *Index* is only occasionally found with copies of the *Journal.*

Copies located: CaNsWA; CaO; CaOOA; CaOT; CaOTU; CaQM; CaQMA; CaQMM; CaQQL; CaQQLH; CtY; DLC; GBLP (in C.O. 42/109); ICJ; ICN; MH; N (mint copy, uncut, unopened, sewn in original blue paper covers with blank leaves of sig. A and 2E complete); NN (with index); RPJ (with index); WHi.

1051. LOWER CANADA. LAWS, STATUTES, *etc.*

THE / PROVINCIAL STATUTES / OF / LOWER-CANADA, / ENACTED BY THE KING'S MOST EXCELLENT MAJESTY, BY AND WITH THE ADVICE / AND CONSENT OF THE LEGISLATIVE COUNCIL AND ASSEMBLY OF THE / SAID PROVINCE, CONSTITUTED AND ASSEMBLED BY VIRTUE OF / AND UNDER THE AUTHORITY OF AN ACT OF THE PARLIAMENT / OF GREAT BRITAIN, PASSED IN THE THIRTY-FIRST

YEAR / OF THE REIGN OF OUR SOVEREIGN LORD GEORGE / THE THIRD, BY THE GRACE OF GOD, OF GREAT / BRITAIN, FRANCE AND IRELAND KING, / DEFENDER OF THE FAITH, &c. / [rule] / VOLUME THE SECOND. / [rule] / [royal arms] / [double rule] / QUEBEC: / PRINTED UNDER THE AUTHORITY AND BY COMMAND OF HIS EXCELLENCY THE / GOVERNOR; AS THE ACT OF THE PROVINCIAL PARLIAMENT DIRECTS. / BY WILLIAM VONDENVELDEN, Printer at the New Printing-Office, / Palace-street, Anno Domini, M.DCC.XCVII. /

French t.-p.:

LES / STATUTS PROVINCIAUX / DU / BAS-CANADA / STATUÉS PAR LA TRÈS EXCELLENTE MAJESTÉ DU ROI, PAR ET DE L'AVIS ET CONSEN-/TEMENT DU CONSEIL LEGISLATIF ET ASSEMBLÉE DE LA DITE PROVINCE, / CONSTITUÉS ET ASSEMBLÉS EN VERTU DE ET SOUS L'AUTORITÉ D'UN / ACTE DU PARLEMENT DE LA GRANDE BRETAGNE, PASSÉ DANS / LA TRENT-ET-UNIÉME ANNEÉ DU RÈGNE DE NOTRE / SOUVERAIN SEIGNEUR GEORGE TROIS, PAR LA / GRACE DE DIEU, ROI DE LA GRANDE BRETA-/GNE, DE FRANCE ET D'IRLANDE, DÉ-/FENSEUR DE LA FOI, &c. / [rule] / SECOND VOLUME. / [rule] / [royal arms] / [double rule] / QUÉBEC: / IMPRIME' SOUS L'AUTORITE' DU GOUVERNEMENT ET PAR ORDRE DE SON EXCELLENCE / LE GOUVERNEUR, ET CONFORMEMENT A L'ACTE DU PARLEMENT PROVINCIAL. / PAR GUILLAUME VONDENVELDEN, Imprimeur à la Nouvelle Imprimerie. / Rue du Palais Anno Domini M.DCC.XCVII. /

4to. [A^2, B]-D^4, E^3, [*-**]^4, [F]-M^4, N^2, *^{4}, P-[2C]^4; 4 p. l., 195 p., 5 *l.*; type-page: 22 × 17 cm. Text in English and French on opposite pages.

Contents: p. l. 1 recto, English t.-p.; verso, blank; p. l. 2 recto, French t.-p.; verso, blank; p. l. 3 recto, English half-title; verso, blank; p. l. 4 recto, French half-title; verso, blank; p. [1], blank; p. [2]-25, 37 Geo. III c. 1-6; p. [26], blank; p. [27], English half-title; p. [28], blank; p. [29], French half-title; p. [30-31], blank; p. [32]-41, 38 Geo. III c. 1-5; p. [42], blank; p. [43], English half-title; p. [44], blank; p. [45], French half-title; p. [46-47], blank; p. [48]-141, 39 Geo. III c. 1-10; p. [142], blank; p. [143], English t.-p.; p. [144], blank; p. [145], French t.-p.; p. [146-47], blank; p. [148]-165, 40 Geo. III c. 1; p. [166], blank; p. [167], English half-title; p. [168], blank; p. [169], French half-title; p. [170-71], blank; p. [172]-95, 40 Geo. III c. 2-8; verso of p. 195, blank; *l.* 1, blank; recto of *l.* 2, blank; *l.* 2 verso-*l.* 4 recto, Table of contents in English and French; verso of *l.* 4, blank; *l.* 5, blank.

40 Geo. III c. 1, Elections Act, 1800, was published separately with its own t.-p. (No. 1181) and reissued with the other provincial statutes of that session (As. 2, sess. 4, 1800). The English and French half-titles which usually precede chapter 1 of each sessions' laws, here precede chapter 2.

While the imprint bears the name of William Vondenvelden, and the date 1797, the laws of the second and succeeding sessions (p. [27] to end) were actually printed (in 1798, 1799, and 1800 respectively) by Roger Lelievre and Pierre-Edouard Desbarats, who were commissioned law printers to the government, May 14, 1798, succeeding Vondenvelden who resigned his commission and left the printing business. For the separate issues of the four sessions' laws, *see* No. 1052, 1095, 1131, 1182.

This volume was reprinted: *The Provincial Statutes of Lower-Canada . . . Volume 2. Quebec: Printed by William Vondenvelden . . . MDCCXCVII. and reprinted by P. E. Desbarats, . . . 1828.* This is a revised edition with titles only of statutes no longer in force. Sections of this edition are occasionally found bound with complementary sections of the 1797-1800 edition.

Copies located: Most law libraries and most reference libraries with a Canadian collection have this volume as part of their file of Lower Canada Statutes, e.g. CU; CaNsWA; CaO (in this copy the original sessions laws of 1799 p. [48]-141 are replaced by the revised edition of 1828, p. [48]-91); CaOLU; CaOOA; CaOT (p. [143-166], 40 Geo. III c. 1, wanting); CaOTL (2 cop.); CaQ*; CaQM (2 cop.); CaQMA; CaQMM (2 cop.); CaQQA; CaQQB; CaQQL; CtY; DLC*; Gordonsmith; MH; MiU; N; NN (2 cop., one*); NNB; RPJ; WHi.

1052. LOWER CANADA. LAWS, STATUTES, *etc.*

THE / PROVINCIAL STATUTES / OF / LOWER-CANADA, / [10 lines]/ VOLUME THE SECOND. / . . . / . . . / . . . / QUEBEC: / PRINTED . . . / . . . / BY WILLIAM VONDENVELDEN, Printer at the New Printing-Office, / . . . M.DCC.XCVII. /

4to [A², B]-D⁴, E³, 4 p. l., [2]-25 p.; type-page: 22 × 17 cm.

Contents: p. l. 1 recto, English t.-p.; verso, blank; p. l. 2 recto, French t.-p.; verso, blank; p. l. 3 recto, English half-title; verso, blank; p. l. 4, French half-title; verso, blank; p. [1], blank; p. [2]-25, Statutes, verso of p. 25, blank.

This is a separate issue of the title-pages, half-titles, and text of the laws of the first session of the second Assembly, 37 Geo. III c. 1-6, as published in No. 1051. It is the last session's laws printed by Vondenvelden, who charged the government for "printing and stitching Acts of First session of Second Provincial Parliament [600 copies?]—£24.17.10."—*Provincial Accounts, Oct. 1796-Apr. 1797* in Can.P.A., L.C. *State* B, May 25, 1797.

Copies located: CaOOA; CaOTA; CaQQL; GBLP (in C.O. 44/6 1797); NN. All copies located (except NN are stitched, apparently as issued, in blue-gray printer's paper covers.

1053. LOWER CANADA. LAWS, STATUTES, *etc.*

[Abstract from the Ordinance for regulating the the Fisheries.]

? Broadside. *Printed at Quebec, by John Neilson, 1797,* as recorded:

"1797, May 5. [Debit] P. Stuart Es. To Printing 25 Copies of an Abstract from the Ordinance for regulating the Fisheries—5/."

Can.P.A., *Neilson papers,* v. 54.

This is probably an abstract from the Quebec provincial statute, 28 Geo. III c. 6, "An Act or Ordinance for regulating the fisheries in the River St. Lawrence, in the

*These copies were issued apparently without separate t.-p. for 40 Geo. III c. 1, and with half-titles to laws of fourth session preceding the text of that chapter.

Bays of Gaspé and Chaleurs, on the Island of Bonaventure, and the opposite shore of Percé." It concerns fishing areas, flakes, curing grounds, etc.; permits British subjects to take, cure, and dry fish, using the shores, woods, etc., and prohibits molestation of bait, nets, seines, flakes, etc. The *Abstract* was probably prepared as a notice by Peter Stuart, a merchant in Quebec with interests along the lower St. Lawrence.

Copy located: None.

1054. McLANE, DAVID, ca. 1767?-1797

LE / PROCES DE DAVID M'LANE / POUR HAUTE TRAHISON, / DEVANT / UNE COUR SPECIALE D'OYER ET TERMINER / A QUEBEC, / LE 7me JUILLET, 1797. / [rule] / QUEBEC: / IMPRIME' ET A VENDRE CHEZ J: NEILSON. / 1797. /

8vo. A-B[4], C[3]; 22 p.; type-page: 17.3 × 10.3 cm.

Contents: p. [1], t.-p.; p. [2], blank; p. [3]-21, Le Proces; p. 21-22, an account of the execution.

This is a French translation of No. 1055, reprinted from the types of the *Quebec gazette* where the text appeared serially, July 27-Aug. 17, 1797. Of the French edition, Neilson recorded considerable sale (though less than of the English) during Sept., 1797, in Can.P.A., *Neilson papers*, v. 54, 66.

The pamphlet, including its t.-p., was reprinted: *Sommaire Procès de David Mc-Lane reproduction avec notes* in *Les Soirées canadiennes*, 2: [353]-400, Dec., 1862.

Copies located: CaOOA; CaQM; CaQMJ (p. 5-6 wanting); CaQMM; CaQQL (stitched in original blue paper covers apparently as issued); MH; NN.

1055. McLANE, DAVID, *ca.* 1767?-1797

THE / TRIAL OF DAVID M'LANE / FOR HIGH TREASON, / BEFORE / A SPECIAL COURT OF OYER AND TERMINER / AT QUEBEC, / ON THE 7th JULY 1797. / [rule] / QUEBEC: / PRINTED AND SOLD BY J: NEILSON. / 1797. /

8vo. A-B[4], C[3]; 21 p.; type-page: 17 × 10.3 cm.

Contents: t.-p.; p. [2], blank; p. [3]-20, The trial of David McLane, etc.; p. 20-21, An account of the execution of McLane; verso of p. 21, blank.

This is a summary of proceedings and evidence apparently supplied to the printer by the attorney-general, Sewell. Appended is an eye-witness's description of the execution. It was published serially in the *Quebec gazette*, July 13-Aug. 3, 1797, then printed from the same types and published in pamphlet form as advertised:

"Soon will be published in French and English The Trial of David M'Lane [etc.] stitched in blue paper. Price 6/ per dozen, 7½d. retail. English ready Saturday [Aug. 5]."—*Quebec gazette,* Aug. 3, 1797.

During August, Neilson recorded a large sale of single copies in Quebec and a dozen lots sent to his agents in Montreal, Three Rivers, and Berthier, in Can.P.A., *Neilson Papers*, v. 54, 66 (*see* No. 1056 *notes*).

Copies located: CaQQL; CtY.

1056. McLANE, DAVID, *ca.* 1767?-1797

THE / TRIAL / OF / DAVID McLANE / FOR / High Treason, / AT THE / CITY OF QUEBEC, IN THE PROVINCE OF LOWER-CANADA. / ON / Friday, the Seventh day of July, A.D. 1797: / [rule] / TAKEN IN SHORT-HAND, AT THE TRIAL. / [rule] / QUEBEC: / PRINTED BY W. VONDENVELDEN, / LAW PRINTER TO THE KrNG'S [sic] MOST EXCELLENT MAJESTY, / 1797. /

8vo. A-Q[4]; 127 p.; type-page: 19.5 × 11.5 cm.; p. 126-27 appear to have been printed from same types as p. 20-21 of the edition above.

Contents: p. [1], t.-p.; p. [2], blank; p. [3]-126, Trial; p. 126-27, An account of the execution; verso of p. 127, blank.

McLane, or McLean, was said to have been a native of Great Britain and a citizen of the United States, resident in Rhode Island. A small trader or pedlar moving around the border district of the United States and Lower Canada. he was alleged by an informer to have been promoting a plot designed by Adet (representative of the French Directorate to the United States) to arm French Canadians and seize the garrison and officers of government at Quebec. McLane was arrested on May 10, tried, convicted, and sentenced to be hanged, drawn, and quartered on July 21, 1797. The zealous prosecution—in a community already excited and disturbed by the international enmities in Europe and by political dissentions and intrigues in Quebec and London—the bloody and apparently bungled execution of this simple if blundering stranger, at once made the case a *cause célèbre.*

Vondenvelden's edition of *The Trial* containing full *verbatim* record of evidence and proceedings, was published five weeks after the execution in an edition of 2,000 copies. It was prepared on order of the government through Attorney-General Sewell, the government taking one hundred copies at 5*s.* each, and giving the rights on the remainder to the printer. In 1798 Vondenvelden memorialized the government, claiming £210 12*s.*; the cost of printing, for, he stated, the latter had furnished John Neilson with a summary account of trial proceedings "divested only of its formal and tedious parts," and this, published in the *Quebec gazette* and sold at the same time as a pamphlet, prevented the sale of Vondenvelden's edition. Sewell replied that "it was thought indispensibly necessary that the conduct of the Government, the evidence against the Prisoner, his guilt and Punishment, and the designs formed against the peace and welfare of the province should be made public as speedily and extensively as possibly." Vondenvelden defended himself against the counter charge of unnecessary delay in printing, but he does not appear to have been compensated for his loss. He had, in the meantime (by May, 1798), resigned his commission as law printer to the government and in June, 1799, was appointed surveyor of streets in the city of Quebec.—Can.P.A., "S" *Int. corresp.* 1798, v. 51, p. 87 *et seq.*

The text of Vondenvelden's edition was reprinted in Thos. B. Howell: *Complete collection of state trials* (33v., London, 1809-26), v. 26, col. 721-828.

The case was noticed widely in the newspapers of the day—probably from exchange copies of the *Quebec gazette.* The Canadian journals, however, included no editorial comment. At least one American pamphlet was published: *The trial, condemnation and horrid execution of David M'Lean, formerly of Pennsylvania . . .* (Windham [Conn.], 1797, 12 p. 12mo., copy in Harvard College Library). Some of the gossip of the day is repeated in G. T. Landmann: *Adventures and recollections* (2 v., London, 1852), I: 318-26.

The case received considerable comment later, notably in *An account of the trial, conviction and execution of David M'Lane, of Providence, Rhode Island, at Quebec in 1797 for the alleged crime of high treason,* by J.R.B[artlett], published in Providence *Evening bulletin supplement,* Apr. 26, 1873, also in *Providence journal,* Apr. 28, 1873.

Notes showing some French-Canadian opinion appear in *Les Soirées canadiennes,* 2: [353]-400, Dec., 1862.

Copies located: CaNsHA; CaNsWA; CaOT; CaQ; CaQM; CaQMM (2 cop.); CaQMS (2 cop.); CaQQL; Gordonsmith; MBAt (p. 71-72 wanting); MH; NN; RPJ (enclosed in this copy are two A.L.S. from E.B.O'Callaghan, a Canadian *patriote* of 1837, later state historian of New York, to John Bartlett, librarian of John Carter Brown Library. The letters, dated Mar. 31 and Apr. 12, 1871, urge Bartlett to vindicate McLane's memory and supply information collected by Louis Joseph Papineau, leader of the Lower Canada rebellion of 1837, calculated to prove that McLane's execution was a judicial murder, arranged by provincial officials to forward their interests in London. Also enclosed is a page of the Providence *Evening bulletin sup.* Apr. 26, 1873, containing Bartlett's *Account of the trial . . . David M'Lane* [etc.])

1057. NEW BRUNSWICK. HOUSE OF ASSEMBLY

JOURNAL / OF THE / VOTES and PROCEEDINGS / OF THE / HOUSE OF ASSEMBLY / OF THE / PROVINCE of NEW-BRUNSWICK: / From TUESDAY the 17th JANUARY, to SATURDAY the 18th / of FEBRUARY, 1797. / [ornamental rule] / [royal arms] / [ornamental rule] / ST. JOHN: / PRINTED by CHRISTOPHER SOWER, Printer to the / KING'S MOST EXCELLENT MAJESTY, 1797. / [title within a frame of flower pieces.]

fo. A-Q²; 1 p. l., [528]-581 p.; type-page: 23.5 × 13.7 cm. Even numbers on recto, odd numbers on verso; paged in continuation of No. 1005. One leaf of sig. O forms t.-p.

Contents: p. l. recto, t.-p.; verso, blank; p. 528-581, Journal of the second session of the third assembly.

The *Journal* was printed probably in an edition of 200 copies, and at a rate of charge similar to that of 1796, for Sower's bill to the Assembly amounted to £33 8*d*.

Copies located: CaN; CaNU; CaNSA (p. 572-79 wanting); CaOOA; RPJ (p. 580-81 wanting).

1058. NEW BRUNSWICK. LAWS, STATUTES, *etc.*

ACTS / OF THE / GENERAL ASSEMBLY / OF / HIS MAJESTY'S PROVINCE / OF / NEW-BRUNSWICK, / PASSED IN THE YEAR 1797. / [rule] / [royal arms] / [rule] / FREDERICTON: / Printed by CHRISTOPHER SOWER, Printer to the / KING'S MOST EXCELLENT MAJESTY, 1797. / [title within a frame]

fo. [*¹, **²], A-C²; 3 p. l., 376-86 p.; type-page: 23 × 13.7 cm. Even numbers on recto, odd numbers on verso, paged in continuation of No. 1006.

Contents: p. l. 1 recto, t.-p.; verso, blank; p. l. 2 recto, half-title; verso, blank; p. l. 3, recto, Titles of the acts; verso, blank; p. 376-86, 37 Geo. III c. I-VI acts passed in the second session of the third assembly; p. 386 of verso, blank.

Like the *Acts* of 1796, these were printed on order of the lieutenant-governor, in an edition of 300 copies—for which the printer charged £15 9*s*.

Copies located: GBLP (in 188/8: 171-87); MH; NNB.

1059. NOVA SCOTIA. COMMISSION ON SHUBENACCADIE CANAL

TO HIS EXCELLENCY / SIR JOHN WENTWORTH, BARONET. / And the Honourable Commissioners appointed to examine into the practicability and / expence of opening an Inland Navigable Communication between the Harbour of / HALIFAX and the BASON of MINAS, in the Province of NOVA-SCOTIA. /

2 *l.* in fo., with text on recto and verso of *l.* 1, *l.* 2 blank; type-page: 29 × 19.5 cm. ? *Printed at Halifax, N.S., by Anthony Henry, 1797.* This is another edition of No. 1060, printed from larger types, in more handsome format, with wording of text unchanged.

Contents: l. 1, Report of the surveyors (appointed by the commissioners according to a resolution of the House of Assembly, July 7, 1797), signed at end: "Isaac Hildrith, Theophilus Chamberlain, Halifax, 15th November, 1797"; *l.* 2, blank.

On July 7, 1797, it was "Resolved [by the House that] a sum not exceeding £250 be drawn by warrant to enable Hon. S. S. Blowers, Chas. Morris, Thos. Barclay, . . . to procure a fit person to make a survey of the water and ground between River Shubenaccadie and the Harbour of Halifax and report on the practicability and expence of cutting a navigable canal from the Bason of Minas to Halifax."—P.A.N.S., *Miscellaneous Assembly papers*, 1797. In this resolution, the Council (of which Blowers was a member) concurred the following day.

The report summarizes a survey of levels between Halifax harbour and tide water flowing up the Shubenaccadie River from the Basin of Minas and the Bay of Fundy. It includes an estimate of the necessary locks, dams, etc., with blank spaces left for costs thereof; and mentions "the Plan herewith connected" of those works.

Copies located: CaNsHA (filed in N.S. Assembly papers, v. 6, *Petitions, reports, resolutions, 1797-1799*. In this copy, rates and total sums of cost of construction are inserted in MS. in blank spaces. Attached is a printed *Key* to a plan, but no plan. Endorsed in MS.: "Report of the Survey of the Dartmouth and Shubenaccadie Lakes and Rivers, Novem^{r} 1797. Issue sparingly, cautious. Canals . . . Governor to establish Corporation"); GBLP (filed in M.P.M. 99 removed from B.T. 6/59. To this copy is attached a MS. plan of the proposed navigation).

1060. NOVA SCOTIA. COMMISSION ON SHUBENACCADIE CANAL

TO HIS EXCELLENCY / SIR JOHN WENTWORTH, Baronet. / And the Honorable Commissioners appointed to examine into the Practicability and Expense of / opening an INLAND NAVIGABLE COMMUNICATION between the HARBOUR of HALIFAX and the / BASIN of MINAS, in the Province of NOVA-SCOTIA. / <Text, signed:> ISAAC

HILDRITH, / THEOPHILUS CHAMBERLAIN. / HALIFAX, 15th November, 1797. /

Broadside: 74 lines; type-page: 40 × 23.5 cm. ? *Printed at Halifax, N.S., probably by Anthony Henry*, 1797. This is another edition of No. 1059, printed from smaller types, with wording of text unchanged.
Copy located: CaNsHD.

1061. NOVA SCOTIA. HOUSE OF ASSEMBLY

[rule] / JOURNAL / AND / PROCEEDINGS / OF THE / HOUSE of ASSEMBLY. / [rule] /

fo. sig. 4I-4S², 4S² [sic]; 1 p. l., 235-275 p.; paged in continuation of No. 1008. *Printed at Halifax, N.S., by Anthony Henry, 1797.*
Contents: p. l. recto, t.-p.; verso, Proclamation; p. 235-75, Journal of the fifth session of the seventh assembly, June 6-July 10, 1797; verso of p. 275, blank.
Copies located: CaNs; CaNsHA; GBLP (in C.O. 217/73: 77-98; another copy, p. 261-74 only, in C.O. 217/69: 300-303d); MH.

1062. NOVA SCOTIA. LAWS, STATUTES, *etc.*

Running title: [rule] / 1797. Anno Tricessimo Septimo Regis, GEORGII III. Cap. I[-V]. / [rules] /
Caption title: At the GENERAL ASSEMBLY of the / Province of NOVA-SCOTIA, . . . / [5 lines] / . . . being the Fifth Session of / the Seventh GENERAL ASSEMBLY, / convened in the said Province. / [rules] /

fo. sig. 3T², 3S¹ [sic]; 391-396 p.; paged in continuation of No. 1009. *Printed at Halifax, N.S., by Anthony Henry, 1797.*
Contents: p. 391-396, Cap. I-V perpetual acts passed in the session, June 6-July 10. 1797.
Copies located: DLC; GBLP (in C.O. 219/19); MH.

1063. NOVA SCOTIA. LAWS, STATUTES, *etc.*

Running title: [rule] / 1797. Anno Tricessimo Septimo Regis, GEORGII III. CAP. I[-V]. / [rule] /
Caption title: At the GENERAL ASSEMBLY of the / Province of NOVA-SCOTIA, . . . / [5 lines] / . . . being the Fifth Session of / the Seventh GENERAL ASSEMBLY, / convened in the said Province. / [rule] /

fo. sig. 5A-5C²; 485-496 p.; type-page: 25 × 15 cm. paged in continuation of No. 1010. *Printed at Halifax, N.S., by Anthony Henry, 1797.*
Contents: p. 485-496, Cap. I-V, temporary acts passed in the session, June 6-July 10, 1797.
Copies located: CaO; GBLP (C.O. 219/19; p. 485-88 wanting); MH.

1064. NOVA SCOTIA. LIEUTENANT-GOVERNOR, 1792-1808 (*Wentworth*)

[A Proclamation by His Excellency Sir John Wentworth . . . Lieutenant-Governor . . . of Nova Scotia <Text> Halifax, May 1, 1797.]

Broadside? *Printed at Halifax, N.S., by Anthony Henry, 1797, as recorded:* "To 500 Proclamations for a general Fast in 1797—£4."—Henry's *Account for extra printing [for government] 1796-97,* in P.A.N.S., *Miscellaneous Assembly papers,* 1797.

Text: "Whereas it is fitting and proper, agreeable to the laudable example set us in His Majesty's European Dominions . . . I have therefore thought fit . . . to appoint Wednesday the twenty-first day of June [1797] as a day of public fasting and Humiliation . . . imploring blessing and assistance in the present war, and for restoring peace and prosperity to His Majesty and all his Dominions [etc., the bishop of Nova Scotia is to prepare a form of prayer]."

The Proclamation was printed also in the *Royal gazette,* Halifax, N.S., May 2. 1797, from which this entry is taken. *See also* No. 1039.

Copy located: None.

1065. QUEBEC GAZETTE. CARRIER'S ADDRESS

QUEBEC, 1st JANUARY, 1798. / VERSES of the Boy who carries the QUEBEC / GAZETTE to the SUBSCRIBERS. / [double rule] /

French side:

QUEBEE [sic] Ier JANVIER, 1798 / [rule] / ETRENNES du GARÇON qui porte la GAZETTE de QUEBEC, / AUX PRATIQUES. / [rule] / Chanson sur l'air que mon épouse s'amuse. / [*Quebec, J. Neilson, 1797.*]

Broadside: type-page: 26.5 × 24 cm. English verse on left, 72 lines; French verse on right, 72 lines in 2 col. The English side, a routine *Address,* begins:

"Again his annual glass old Time
Anew has turn'd and I must rhime.
[Etc.]"

The French side lauds life under a British king:

"Que dans Paris on s'applique
A la réforme des Lois
Que le peuple au lieu de Rois
Admette une République;
Qu'est qu'ça m' fait à moi
Si je vis dans l'Amérique
Qu'est qu'ça m'fait à moi
Si je vis sous un bon Roi
[Etc.]."

Copy located: CaO (bound in *Quebec gazette* at end of 1797).

1066. ST. JOHN, ISLAND OF. HOUSE OF ASSEMBLY

*[Journal of the House of Assembly of His Majesty's Island of Saint John. Anno tricessimo septimo Regis Georgii III. Sixth Session of the Sixth General Assembly. *Charlotte Town, Island of Saint John, Printed by William Alexander Rind* . . . 1797.]

4to. 19p.

Contents: Journal, July 11-22, 1797.

This was the last *Journal* printed for several years (probably till 1805), for Rind left the Island before the next session and he had no immediate successor.

Copies located: GBLP (2 cop. in C.O. 226/15: 327-45; *ibid.*, 507-25).

1067. ST. JOHN, ISLAND OF. LAWS, STATUTES, *etc.*

ACTS / PASSED / AT THE GENERAL ASSEMBLY / OF HIS MAJESTY'S / ISLAND OF SAINT JOHN, / NNO [sic] TRICESSIMO SEPTIMO / REGIS GEORGII III. / [rule] / SIXTH SESSION OF THE SIXTH GENERAL ASSEMBLY. / [rule] / [rule] / [royal arms] / [double rule] / HARLOTTE [sic] TOWN, ISLAND OF SAINT JOHN: / [rule] / PRINTED BY WILLIAM ALEXANDER RIND, / PRINTER TO THE KING'S MOST EXCELLENT MAJESTY. / [double rule] / 1797.

4to. Sig. [*][1], 1-2[2]; 9 p.

Contents: p. [1], t.-p.; p. [2], blank; p. [3]-9, 37 Geo. III c. I-II, acts passed July 11-22, 1797; verso of p. 9, blank.

This was the last session's laws printed for several years. The House met but once again in the 18th century, Nov. 20-26, 1798, and the province was then without a printer. Lieut.-Gov. Fanning, transmitting to the Duke of Portland, Oct. 12, 1798, a complete set of the *Acts* to that date, and commenting upon the difficulty of obtaining them, stated: ". . . The Printer having lately left the Island with his Family to the United States of America . . . I fear it will be with some delay at least in the future, that I shall be able to procure and transmit printed copies of such Acts [etc.]"—Can P.A., P.E.I. "A".

Copies located: GBLP (in C.O. 226/16: 465-73); NNHi.

1068. SAINT JOHN, N.B., *City.* ORDINANCES

[Law for regulating the Pilotage of Vessels into and out of the Harbour of Saint John; The Ballast law and Amendment? to the Fishery law.]

? Broadside: *Printed at Saint John, N.B., by John Ryan, 1797.* This publication was ordered by the City Council:

> "1796, Dec. 28. Read and passed a Law for regulating the Pilotage of Vessels into and out of the Harbour of Saint John. The Ballast Law and [blank space for "Amendment"?] to the Fishery Law to be printed."
>
> —Saint John, N.B., *Minutes.*

*Title and description from notes taken by a correspondent in the Public Record Office, London, from the only copies located.

Probably printed in broadside by Ryan, who did most of the municipal government's work, these laws do not appear in his newspaper, the *Saint John gazette*, during Jan., 1797 (subsequent issues could not be located).

The laws regulating fisheries and pilotage were specifically excluded (perhaps as being temporary measures, subject to frequent amendment) from the revised edition of by-laws published by the Council in the spring of 1796.

Copy located: None.

1069. SOREL, NICHOLAS

Caption title: [ornamental rule] / A NARRATIVE / OF / FACTS. / *Colophon*, p. [19]: QUEBEC—PRINTED BY JOHN NEILSON—1797. /

8vo. A-B^4, C^2; 19 p.; type-page: 16 × 10.3 cm.

Contents: p. 1-19, Narrative, signed at end: "Nichs. Sorel, Lieut. King's own Infantry. Quebec, 9th March, 1797"; verso of p. 19, blank.

This is the *Apologia* of a young profligate prepared to vindicate his "honour." It comprises (p. 1-10) an explanation of his financial misfortunes since his departure from England in Aug., 1795—the consequence apparently of some previous scrape. Sorel describes his progress to New York and Quebec, the neglect of his mother to meet his bills drawn on London and backed by fellow-officers in Quebec, his ostracism from Quebec society, the sufferings of himself, his young wife, and infant, etc. Appended (p. 11-19) are supporting documents.

Neilson recorded this work:

"1797, Apr. 8. [Debit] Lieut. Sorel, King's Own R. To printing 222 copies of a Pamphlet intituled "a narrative of facts", on demy paper, long primer type 1¼ Sheet.—£4.14.7½.

To folding & stitching ditto in blue cover—10/4

[Total:] £5.5."—Can.P.A., *Neilson papers*, v. 54.

Copy located: Ketcheson (a fine, clean copy in 18th-century marbled paper covers. The text is signed in MS. at end: "Nich^s. Sorel, Lieu^t Kings Own Inf^y.," also: "Thos Montgomery Quebec, May the 25th").

1070. UPPER CANADA. ADMINISTRATOR, 1796-1799 (*Russell*)

THE / SPEECH / OF HIS HONOR / PETER RUSSELL, ESQUIRE, / President of the Province of / UPPER-CANADA, / AT THE / Opening of the First Session of / The Second Parliament, JUNE 6, 1797. / AND THE / ADDRESSES / Of the two Houses of LEGISLATURE. /

8vo. 8 p.; type-page: 14.2 × 11.1 cm. *Probably printed at Niagara, U.C., by Gideon Tiffany, 1797.*

Contents: p. [1], t.-p.; p. [2], blank; p. [3]-5, Pres. Russell's speech to the Legislative Council and House of Assembly, York, June 6, 1797; p. 5-6, Address of the Legislative Council in answer, signed John Elmsley, speaker, June 7, 1797; p. 7, The president's answer; p. 7-8, Address of the Commons House of Assembly in answer to the president's speech, signed D. W. Smith, Speaker, June 7; p. 8, The president's answer.

In his speech Russell recommends the Council and Assembly to prepare regulations for trade with the United States and lays before them a copy of the *Treaty of*

Amity, etc., also the Lower Canada order-in-council of July 7, 1796, regulating trade by the Port of St. Johns. He also lays before them a provisional agreement of the commissioners of Upper and Lower Canada for apportionment of revenues, Jan. 28, 1797. The House of Assembly he recommends to find remedies for defalcation of revenues from tavern licences, etc. To both Council and Assembly he conveys a message from His Majesty on war with Spain and recommends measures against aliens, also amendments to the militia laws. The *Answers* are all brief acknowledgements.

Copy located: GBLP (in C.O. 42/321: 209-216, enclosed in Russell's despatch dated June 30, 1797).

1071. UPPER CANADA. EXECUTIVE COUNCIL

Caption title: [ornamental rule] / TO HIS HONOR PETER RUSSELL, ESQUIRE, PRESIDENT / OF THE PROVINCE OF UPPER-CANADA. /

8vo. [*]^4; [7] p.; type-page: 14.6 × 9.6 cm. *Probably printed at Niagara, U.C., between July 3 and Aug. 12, 1797, by Gideon Tiffany or by Titus Geer Simons,* who succeeded Tiffany at the *Upper Canada gazette* printing office, between July 5 and Sept. 20, 1797.

Contents: p. [1-7], Report of the Executive Council, undated and signed at end: "By order of the Board, John Small, C.E.C."; verso of p. [7], blank.

The report recommends that appropriations for township grants be rescinded, and the land thrown open to other applicants, that all grants be limited to 200 acres, etc., and that surveying and locating on new tracts proceed. It was passed by the Council in its capacity of land board, at York, July 3, 1797, and "printed copy confirmed" by the Council in its executive capacity, Aug. 12, 1797. Russell, president of council and administrator of the province, in the absence of Lieut.-Gov. Simcoe presided at both meetings.—Can.P.A., U.C. *State* B, p. 71.

Copies located: CaOOA (this copy, filed in the *Askin papers*, v. 31, uncut and unsewn as issued, bears MS. subscription in a contemporary hand, at end of text: "York 3^{d} July 1797. Read & approved in Council. Peter Russell, President &c.&c. J.S. [i.e. John Small, Clerk of Executive Council]"; CaOT (this copy bears MS. note in contemporary hand: "This was Printed in the y^{r} 1798 and given as Answer of the E. Council to the Grantees of townships, as the reason for not giving them Patents"); DLC; GBLP (in C.O. 42/322, this copy endorsed: "July 1797 confirmed in Council," was enclosed in Russell's despatch of Feb. 20, 1798, to the Duke of Portland).

1072. UPPER CANADA. LAWS, STATUTES, *etc.*

LAWS / OF / His Majesty's Province / OF / UPPER-CANADA, / IN / NORTH-AMERICA, / ENACTED IN THE FIRST SESSION OF THE SECOND PARLIAMENT, / IN THE YEAR OF OUR LORD ONE THOUSAND SEVEN HUN-/DRED AND NINETY-SEVEN, AND OF HIS MAJESTY'S / REIGN THE THIRTY-SEVENTH. / [rule] / R. [royal arms] G. [sic] / [rule] / WEST-NIAGARA: / PRINTED BY TITUS G. SIMONS, PRINTER TO THE KING'S MOST EXCELLENT MAJESTY. / MDCCXCVII. /

4to. A-B^2, D-H^2; 27 p.; type-page: 22 × 16 cm. The royal initials on t.-p. are corrected (in type in DLC copy) to read: "G. [royal arms] R." Chap. [XVII] is misnumbered: XVI. Unlike No. 1073, this item was printed in 4to format (chain lines horizontal with the page, and watermark: 179 [?] in lower outer corners appear distinctly in the rather soft, blue-flecked paper of the copies seen).

Contents: p. [1], t.-p.; p. [2], blank; p. [3]-27, 37 Geo.III c. I-XVI [i.e. XVII], laws passed in the first session of the second provincial parliament, York, June 1-July 3, 1797; verso of p. 27, blank. Chap. XVII [i.e. XVIII], the Marriage Act, passed in this session was reserved for royal assent and published later (No. 1149).

This was the first session of the legislature held at York (renamed Toronto in 1834), whither the offices of government moved during 1797, and the printer, the following year from the old capital, Newark, later called Niagara, or West Niagara.

Copies located: CaOTL; DLC; GBLP (in C.O. 44/40, 1797).

1073. UPPER CANADA. LAWS, STATUTES, *etc.*

LAWS / Of His Majesty's Province of / UPPER--CANADA, / IN / NORTH--AMERICA, / ENACTED IN THE FIRST SESSION OF THE SECOND PAPLIAMENT [sic] / IN THE YEAR OF OUR LORD ONE THOUSAND SEVEN HUND-/RED AND NINETY-SEVEN, AND OF HIS MAJESTY'S / REIGN THE THIRTY-SEVENTH. / The Honorable PETER RUSSELL, Esquire, PRESIDENT. / [rule] / G. [royal arms] R. / [rule] / WEST-NIAGARA: / PRINTED BY TITUS G. SMONS [sic] PRINTER TO THE KING's MOST EXCELLENT MAJESTY. / MDCCXCVII. /

fo. [A]-B^2, D-H^2; 27 p.; type-page: 22.2 × 16.2 cm.

Contents: p. [1], t.-p.; p. [2], blank; p. [3]-27, 37 Geo. III c. I-XVI [i.e. XVII], laws passed in the first session of the second provincial parliament, York, June 1-July 3, 1797; verso of p. 27, blank.

Chap. [XVII] An act for the better division of the County of Prince-Edward into townships, is misnumbered XVI.

This is another issue, or a somewhat corrected copy, of the item preceding. The only copy of this "issue" located was printed on paper folded in fo. (chain lines vertical with the page) and with t.-p. reset, showing the addition of President Russell's name, typographical errors in lines 6 and 15, and slightly different arrangement of lines. The text appears to have been printed from the same setting of type as No. 1072.

Copy located: CaOOA.

1074. ALMANACS. LOWER CANADA

[Calendrier pour l'Année 1799, pour Montréal. *A Montréal, Chez E. Edwards, 1798.*]

Broadside, advertised: "For Sale, The Sheet Almanack for 1799, Corrected and Improved by a Gentleman of this City, The Rising and Setting of the Sun, calculated for the Latitude of Montreal, Printing Office [of Edward Edwards] December 10, 1798."

The French section of the same advertisement included additional information: "Calendrier pour l'Année 1799, pour Montréal . . . Continuant une Table des Fastes Chronologiques du Canada . . . l'entrée du Soleil dans les differens signes du Zodiaque & les Lunaisons y sont aussi adaptées à la long. de Montréal; on y trouvera de plus les differentes couleurs des ornemens d'Eglise pour chaque jour, designées par les lettres initiales de ces couleurs."—*Montreal gazette*, Dec. 10, 1798.

Copy located: None.

1075. ALMANACS. LOWER CANADA

[Calendrier pour l'année 1799, pour Québec. *A Québec, chez Jean Neilson, 1798.*]

Broadside. This almanac was advertised: "Just published, Le Calendrier de Quebec pour l'année 1799, containing [calendar, eclipses, zodiac, etc., also] A Chronological Table of the Principal events which have taken place in Canada since the Discovery; Table of the sittings of the Courts; Table for the intelligence of the French dates [i.e. Calendar of the Republic]; and a Table of the extent, population and sovereigns of the different states of Europe. Price 5/ per dozen, 7½d. retail." —*Quebec gazette*, Nov. 1, 1798, *et seq.* This sheet almanac was published also on fine paper at 1*s.* the copy.

Copy located (but not examined): Chateau de Ramezay, Montreal, as recorded in its *Catalogue*, 1912, 68.

1076. ALMANACS. LOWER CANADA

CALENDRIER pour l'Année 1799, pour QUEBEC, par les 306$^{d.}$ 30^{m} de Longitude, et 46$^{d.}$ 55$^{m.}$ de Latitude. / [rule] /

Colophon: QUEBEC: Imprimé à la Nouvelle-Imprimerie, Rue des Jardins. /

Broadside: type-page: 57.5 × 43 cm. in single rule frame. *Printed by R. Lelievre & P.-E. Desbarats.*

Contents: Les signes, etc.; Monthly calendar, etc.; also Tableau des comptés; Tide table (as in No. 920).

Copy located: CaO (bound in *Quebec gazette*, at end of 1798).

1077. ALMANACS. LOWER CANADA

ETRENNES / MIGNONES / POUR L'ANNÉE / 1799. / Quisquis es, ô faveas, nostrisque / laboribus adsis! / [rule] / [printer's ornament] / [rule] / QUEBEC: / IMPRIMEES à LA NOUVELLE IM-/PRIMERIE, Rue des Jardins. /

12mo. A-D^{6}, [E]^{4}; 56 p.; type-page: 9.2 × 5 cm. *Printed by R. Lelievre & P.-E. Desbarats, 1798.*

Contents: p. [1], t.-p.; p. [2], blank; p. 3-6, Periodes du calendrier, cycle, des astres; p. 7-8, Vents; p. [9-20], Calendrier; p. [21]-25, Bons mots; p. 25-27, Epoques historiques; p. 27-33, Poesie; p. 34-51, Le jeu de Whisk [sic]; p. 52-56, Lettre à Mm. Historiens, etc., signed: "L'Année 1800."

This is a Quebec edition of an almanac in a style popular with the French of France. It follows the European model closely and includes no Canadian information. The winds listed are those which blow upon the Mediterranean. In the calendar, fête days are different and more numerous than those observed in Quebec. The bons mots, verses, and essays are light, more epigrammatic and sentimental than corresponding matter in almanacs of Canadian origin. *Le Jeu de Whisk* is the most substantial part of *Etrennes*, setting forth in careful detail, the method of play, rules, score-keeping, etc., of whist, including also "Les Loix de Jeu tel qu'il est joué à Bath."

Etrennes mignones did not appear again, however, in Quebec in the years succeeding this experiment in almanac publication.

John Neilson bought three dozen *Etrennes* from P.-E. Desbarats, at 10*s*. the dozen on Jan. 16, 1799 and advertised copies for sale in his *Quebec gazette,* Jan. 17, 1799.

Copies located: CaQM; CaQMS (2 cop.); CaQQL.

1078. ALMANACS. LOWER CANADA

[Indian Almanack for 1798? *Quebec, J. Neilson, 1798.*]

A small pamphlet *printed at Quebec, by John Neilson, 1798,* as recorded:

"1798, Feb. 27. [Debit] Peter Stewart to printing 200 Copies Indian Almks. —23/4.

Cutting and covering do.—5/.

[Total:] £1.8.4."—Can.P.A., *Neilson papers,* v. 54.

This almanac was prepared possibly for Peter Stewart, a merchant in Quebec, who had considerable land and trading interests below Quebec, and was possibly in Montagnais or a related Algonkian dialect, for use among native hunters and fishers of the district.

Copy located: None.

1079. ALMANACS. LOWER CANADA

THE / QUEBEC ALMANAC / FOR / THE YEAR 1799. / N:LAT: 46d: 55m:--W:LONG: 69d: 46m: / [rule] / QUEBEC: / PRINTED BY JOHN NEILSON, / MOUNTAIN STREET. /

French t.-p.:

ALMANACH / DE QUÉBEC, / POUR L'ANNÉE 1799. / Par les 306° 30′ long. et 46° 55′ lat. / [rule] / QUEBEC: / DE L'IMPRIMERIE DE J: NEILSON, / RUE LA MONTAGNE. /

12mo. A-L[6]; 126, [6] p. front., 2 fold. tables; type-page: 10.8 × 6 cm.; p. [3-4] at end, pasted together.

Contents: p. [1], English t.-p.; p. [2], blank; p. [3], French t.-p.; p. [4]-35, Epochs, eclipses, tide table, calendar, feasts; p. 36-40, Coin, currency, interest tables; p. 41-45, Postal and travellers rates and distances; p. 46-68, Extracts from laws, regulations, etc. on boundaries, roads, courts; p. [69]-88, Civil list, etc.; p. 89-113, Military register; p. 114-126, Etat ecclésiastique, etc.; p. [1-6] at end, Contents table. Fold. table of "Days of the year" beginning March, and of "Termes des cours de justice," are inserted after p. 36 and 62, respectively.

The engraved frontispiece entitled "Origine de la Societé: Rise of Society" depicts in the background a stone image and worshippers, in the foreground, a man and woman sowing grain. The numeral 4 appears in the upper right hand corner.

This almanac was advertised as "Just published and for sale at 2/ the copy retail and 20/ the dozen, stitched in blue paper, 3/ the copy bound," in Neilson's paper, the *Quebec gazette,* Jan. 3, 1799, *et seq.*

Copies located: CaNsWA (front. wanting); CaOOA; CaOT (front. wanting); CaQ; CaQM; CaQMC; CaQMS; CaQN; CaQQA; CaQQAr; CaQQL (front. wanting).

1080. ALMANACS. NOVA SCOTIA

AN / ALMANACK, / FOR THE / Year ... 1799; / ... / CALCULATED FOR THE MERIDIAN OF / HALIFAX, ... / ... / CONTAINING / The Eclipses [etc. 9 lines in col. 1] / Sittings of the Courts, [etc. 7 lines in col. 2] / ... / [rule] / BY THEOPHRASTUS. / [rule] / HALIFAX: / Printed and Sold by JOHN HOWE, at his Printing-/Office, in GEORGE-STREET, near the Parade. / [title within double rule frame]

12mo. [32] p.; type-page: 14.8 × 8.5 cm.

Contents: p. [1], t.-p.; p. [2], Directions to farmers; p. [3], Zodiac; p. [4], Ephemeris; p. [5-16], Calendar; p. [17-21], Nova Scotia provincial officials, courts; p. [23-24], Masonic lodges, clergy; [25-30], Naval, army officers, militia in Nova Scotia; p. [31-32], Distances, etc.

Copy located: CaNsHA.

1081. ALMANACS. NOVA SCOTIA

THE / NOVA-SCOTIA CALENDER, / OR AN / ALMANACK, / For the Year ... 1799. / [4 lines] / WHEREIN IS CONTAINED, / The ECLIPSES ... / [5 lines] / Calculated for the Meridian of HALIFAX ... / [3 lines] / [rule] / By METONICUS. / [rule] / [verse, 5 lines, by:] / MILTON / [double rule] / HALIFAX: Printed and Sold by A. HENRY, at his Printing-/Office, in Sackville-Street, Corner of Grafton-Street. / [title within ornamental frame]

12mo. [32] p.; type-page: 13.5 × 8.5 cm.

Contents: p. [1], t.-p.; p. [2], Directions to farmers; p. [3], Vulgar notes; p. [4], Zodiac; p. [5-16], Calendar; p. [17], Ephemeris, also Errata for *The Nova-Scotia Calender . . . 1798;* p. [18], Royal family; p. [19-20], Table of kings of England, currency; p. [21-27], Nova Scotia administration, legislature, judges, justices, courts, etc.; p. [27-30], Naval and army officers, militia, in Nova Scotia; p. [31-32], Coin tables, distances, etc.

"Directions for farmers" on p. [2] is the same as the "Directions for farmers" in John Howe's *Almanack for . . . 1790,* and subsequent years.

This almanac was advertised: "Just published and for sale by Anthony Henry, The Nova-Scotia Calender . . . for . . . 1799 [etc.]"

—*Royal gazette,* Halifax, N.S., Nov. 20, 1798.

Copies located: CaNsHA; CaOOA (2 cop., p. [31-32] wanting in one copy).

1082. AVIS AU CANADA . . . PAR UN CANADIEN

AVIS / AU / CANADA, / A L'OCCASION DE LA CRISE IMPORTANTE AC-/TUELLE, CONTENANT / Une rélation fidéle d'un nombre de cruautés / inouies, commises depuis la révolution / Françoise, par les personnes qui / exercent actuellement les pou-/voirs de gouvernement / en France et par / leurs adherents. / PAR / UN CANADIEN. / [rule] / Il est essentiel à la cause de la justice et l'humanité d'avertir ici, que /

ce recit mélancolique n'est pas l'effet d'une malice factieuse, mais qu'il con-/tient des faits qui n'admettent aucun doute, comme étant tirés des PRO-/CEDURES d'ETAT de la FRANCE, et recueillis de dépositions for-/melles, faites sous SERMENT, soit par des témoins oculaires ou par les / complices indirects des crimes qu'ils attestent. / [rule] / QUEBEC: / IMPRIME A LA NOUVELLE IMPRIMERIE, Rue des Jardins, / 1798. /

12mo. A,C,E,G², B,D,F,H-I⁴; 1 p. l., ii-iii, 49 p. 1 *l.*; type-page: 14 × 8 cm.

Contents: p. l. recto, t.-p.; verso, blank; p. ii-iii, Au lecteur; p. 1-31, Avis au Canada; p. [32], blank; p. [33]-49, "Abrégé d'un détail de la conduite perfide et inhumaine des officiers et soldats François, envers les paysans de la Suabe, pendant l'invasion en Allemagne, en 1796"; verso of p. 49, blank; 1 *l.*, blank.

Though anonymous, this work was patently compiled by a French Canadian, and published in the interest of the English administration and/or of the Catholic church in Lower Canada. In "Au lecteur" the compiler states it is to be a concise and specific account of the enormities and horrors of the French Revolution, prepared to show the inhabitants of Canada proof of the horrible effects of anarchy and impiety, the overthrow of law and religion. All the material in the brochure, he states, is drawn from different published sources, all written by Frenchmen, and all but one published in Paris.

Avis contains seventy-four circumstantial accounts of arrest, execution, etc., of identified individuals, or of revolutionary operations in specified districts of France. These are extracted from: (1), source not stated; (2-7), *Histoire du clergé françois*, par l'abbé Barruel; (8-11), *Extraits d'une rélation des cruautés commises à Lion;* (12-45), *Extraits des precédures les Committés Revolutionaires à Nantes, et du représentant Carrier;* (46-50), Faits tirés de differens ouvrages . . . ; (51-66), Extraits des *Bandits Demasqués* . . . par le General Danican; 67-74, various sources.

Similar propaganda was reprinted from English sources in Canadian newspapers of the day, e.g., in the *Royal gazette,* Halifax, N.S., June 5, 1798, "A warning to Britons against French Perfidy. Some account of the cruelties committed by the French [etc.]."

Avis was *probably printed by R. Lelievre & P.-E. Desbarats, towards the end of the year 1798.* These printers succeeded Vondenvelden at the Nouvelle Imprimerie during or before May, 1798, and moved their shop from rue du Palais to rue des Jardins during or before September of that year.

Copies located: CaOOA; CaQM; CaQMS (2 cop.); CaQQL.

1083. BONNEFONS, AMABLE, 1600-1653

LE PETIT / LIVRE DE VIE; / QUE APPREND / A BIEN VIVRE / ET / A BIEN PRIER DIEU, / CONTENANT plusieurs Offices, Litanies, Exerci/ces de dévotion; les sacrées Paroles de Jesus-/Christ, des Saints et les moyens de bien profiter / des maladies, ou autres peines de cette vie. / Avec des Méditations pour tous les jours / de la Semaine. / [rule] / NOUVELLE EDITION. / Corrigée & augmentée de la Dévotion des Elus. / Par le P. AMABLE BONNEFONS, de la Comp. de

Jesus / [printer's ornament] / A QUEBEC: / IMPRIME' A LA NOUVELLE IMPRIMERIE. / Et à Vendre chez F. Huot, Rue de la Fabrique. / [rule] / 1798.—AVEC APPROBATION. / [title within a single rule frame]

12mo. A-T[6], [*][2], U-2V[6]; xvi, 498 p., 3 *l.*; type-page: 10.2 × 6.1 cm.; p. 193 mispaged: 192; 259: 159; 494: 594. In the imprint the word IMPRIMERIE has for its last I the arabic numeral 1.

Contents: p. [i], t.-p.; p. [ii], blank; p. [iii-iv], Table, etc.; p. v-xvi, Calendar; p. [1]-498, Instructions, etc.; *l.* 1, recto, blank; *l.* 1 verso-*l.* 2 recto, Table; *l.* 2 verso, blank; *l.* 3 recto, Approbation, dated: "Québec, Ier Août, 1796," and signed: "J. François, Evêque de Québec," i.e. Jean François Hubert, 1739-1797, who was succeeded as bishop of Quebec, by Pierre Denaut in 1797. Verso of *l.* 3, blank.

The dates of *Approbation* and imprint suggest that this work was begun or at least projected in 1796, by Wm. Vondenvelden, then continued and published by his successors at the New Printing Office, Roger Lelievre & Pierre-Edouard Desbarats. In the two copies examined, several different paper stocks were used, in some of which the watermarks show dates 1794 or 1796. This and the lengthy text, requiring an extraordinarily large quantity of type for a young colonial printing house, suggest that *Le Petit livre* was a standing job at la Nouvelle Imprimerie, composed a few forms at a time, and printed at intervals, the type distributed after each printing and used again.

Copies located: CaOT (p. 47-48 mutilated; p. 135-36, 335-36 wanting); CaQQL (p. 47-62 mutilated).

It is interesting to note that both copies located are bound in old dark red morocco with gilt tooling worn blind—similar doubtless to that recorded by Neilson, whose printing house included a binding department: "1798, Dec. 17 [Debit] Roger Lelievre binding 2 vols. livre de vie in morocco gilt @ 6/6—13/."—Can.P.A., *Neilson papers*, v. 54.

1084. CATHOLIC CHURCH. CATECHISMS

CATECHISME / A / L'USAGE / DU / DIOCESE / DE / QUEBEC. / [rule] / Imprimé par l'Ordre de Monseigneur JEAN / OLIVIER BRIAND, Evêque de Quebec. / [rule] / Se vend chez F. HUOT, N° 9. Rue de la Fabrique. / [rule] / [printer's ornament] / [rule] / CINQUIEME EDITION. / [rule] / A QUEBEC. / IMPRIME' A LA NOUVELLE IMPRIMERIE / Rue du Palais, MDCCXCVIII. / [title within double rule frame]

12mo. A-E[6] [+?]; 4 p. l., 52 [+?] p.; type-page: 14.5 × 8.3 cm.

Contents: p. l. 1 recto, t.-p.; verso, blank; p. l. 2 recto-3 verso, Mandement, 7 Mars 1777, signed: "J.Ol. Evêque de Québec"; p. l. 4 recto, Avertissement; verso, Introduction; p. [1]-52 [+?], Premier partie, Petit catéchisme.

The only copy located lacked pages following p. 52, containing (from comparison with No. 699-700) about 17 lines of text and contents table of *Le petit catéchisme*. Whether the publication included also *Le grand catéchisme* is not evident.

Copy located: CaQQL (unbound, original stitching, outer leaves soiled; all after p. 52, wanting).

1085. CHURCH OF ENGLAND. LITURGY AND RITUAL

[A Form of Prayer To be used in all Churches in Nova Scotia, on Thursday, May 31, 1798, Appointed for a General Fast.]

Prepared by Bishop Inglis and *printed at Halifax, N.S., by Anthony Henry, 1798,* in an edition of 800 copies (*see* No. 1100 *note*).

Copy located: None.

1086. CLERY, JEAN BAPTISTE CANT HANET, 1759-1809

JOURNAL / DE CE QUI S'EST PASSE' / A LA TOUR DU TEMPLE, / PENDANT LA CAPTIVITE' / DE' LOUIS XVI, / ROI DE FRANCE. / [rule] / Animus meminisse horret [4 dots] VIRG. / Par M. CLERY, Valet de Chambre du Roi. / [rule] / A QUEBEC: / CHEZ JOHN NEILSON, IMPRIMEUR-LIBRAIRE. / [rule] / 1798. /

8vo. A-I[4]; 1 p. l., 66 p., 2 *l.*; type-page: 17.8 × 10.3 cm. Printed on fine paper, the type of the text leaded, making 43 lines to the page.

Contents: p. l. recto, t.-p.; verso, blank; p. [1]-66, Journal; *l.* 1 recto, blank; verso, Nota (editorial comment on documents following); *l.* 2 recto, text of two brief letters, signed (1): "M.A., M R Louis, E.M." (2): "M A," (farewell messages from Louis XVI to Marie Antoinette and the Dauphin); verso of *l.* 2, blank.

Journal is a retrospective account of episodes in the life of Louis XVI, between the time of his arrest and his execution, written by his devoted valet. It depicts the noble sensibility of Louis's character, the heroic self-discipline of royalist prisoners, their physical and spiritual sufferings and tragic death.

This work had immediate and long sustained popular appeal. It was published in several editions, French, English, and also Italian, in London from 1798, and frequently there and elsewhere through the 19th century. From the beginning it was circulated widely and printed several times in Canada. The English text was published serially (without documents at the end) in the *Saint John gazette,* May 24-July 12, 1799. Two French editions were published in Quebec, the first of which Neilson produced in two issues: on fine paper (as described above) and in cheaper format (No. 1087). They were advertised:

"Just published in the French language and for sale at the Printing Office, A Journal of occurrences at the Temple [etc.] Price 2/6 fine copies, 1/3 on coarse paper; 25/ per dozen fine copies, 12/ per dozen on coarse paper. The London edition of May '98 was sold at 6/ sterling."—*Quebec gazette,* Nov. 29, 1798, *et seq.*

For other Quebec editions *see* No. 1119, *also* Dionne: *Inventaire,* 1: no. 106; 3: no. 65.

Copies located: CaO; CaOT; CaQM; CaQMM; CaQQL; Ketcheson. All copies located (except CaQQL) are bound in original marble paper covers with cover label "Journal . . . roi de France. his virtues Will plead like angels' trumpet tongues . . . Shak."

1087. CLERY, JEAN BAPTISTE CANT HANET, 1759-1809

JOURNAL / DE CE QUI S'EST PASSE' / A LA TOUR DU TEMPLE, / PENDANT LA CAPTIVITE' / DE LOUIS XVI, / ROI DE FRANCE. / [rule] / Animus meminisse horret. [4 dots] VIRG. / Par M. CLERY, Valet de

Chambre du Roi. / [rule] / A QUEBEC: / CHEZ JOHN NEILSON, IMPRIMEUR-LIBRAIRE. / [rule] / 1798. /

8vo. A-G[4], [H][2]; 1 p. l., 54 p. 2 *l.*; type-page: 17.8 × 10.3 cm.

Contents: p. l. recto, t.-p.; verso, blank; p. [1]-54, Journal; *l.* 1 recto, blank; verso, Nota; *l.* 2 recto [Letters]; verso, blank.

Another issue of No. 1086, printed from the same type, on coarse paper, with t.-p. unchanged, but the text set solid (51 lines to the page). This is the publication advertised by Neilson in the *Quebec gazette* to sell at 1*s.* 3*d.* the copy, 12*s.* the dozen.

Copies located: CaQM; CaQMM (2 cop.); CaQMS; CaQQL; Ketcheson, RPJ.

1088. DENAUT, PIERRE, *bp. of Quebec*, 1743-1806

Marginal title: MANDEMENT de / Monseigneur l'Evêque de / Québec, pour des actions / de Graces Publiques. /

Caption: PIERRE DENAUT, par la Miséricorde de / DIEU et la grace du St. Siège Apostolique, Evêque de / Québec &c.&c. A tous les Curés, Vicaires, Missi-onnaires, et à tous les Fideles de ce Diocèse, Salut et / Bénédiction en Notre Seigneur. /

2 *l.* in fo. with text on recto and verso of *l.* 1, *l.* 2 blank; type-page: 26 × 16 cm.

Probably printed at Quebec, by R. Lelievre & P.-E. Desbarats, 1798.

Contents: l. 1, Mandement, signed at end: "Donné à Longueuil . . . [Dec. 22, 1798] (Signé) P. Evêque de Québec, Par Monseigneur, (Signé) Chaboillez Ptre. Secr. Bon Pour Copie"; *l.* 2, blank.

The *Mandement* conveys the Bishop's orders for the consecration of Jan. 10, 1799, to thanksgiving for Nelson's vistory over the French fleet in the Mediterranean, Aug. 1-2, 1798. It reinforces for the Catholic inhabitants of the province the governor's proclamation of the same date (No. 1093).

Reprinted in Têtu and Gagnon: *Mandements de Québec,* 2: 515-17.

Copies located: CaO; CaOOA (filed in Can.P.A., "S" 51, *Int. Corresp.* L.C., 1798); CaQQL.

1089. [HUMBERT, PIERRE HUBERT], 1687?-1779

INSTRUCTIONS / CHRÉTIENNES / POUR / LES JEUNES GENS / Utiles à toutes sortes de Personnes, / mêlées de plusieurs traits d'his-toi-/res et d'exemples édifians. / [rule] / Imprimé sur la QUATORZIEME EDITION / D'AVIGNON, revue et corrigée. / [rule] / QUEBEC, / CHEZ J: NEILSON IMPRIMEUR-LIBRAIRE, / RUE LA MONTAGNE. / 1798. /

12mo. A-T[12] U[6]; xvi, 448 [4] p.; type-page: 13 × 6.6 cm.

Contents: p. [i], t.-p.; p..[ii], Chretien, Souviens-toi; p. iii-iv, Avertissement; p. v-xvi, Exercise spirituel; p. [1]-439, Instructions; p. [440], blank; p. 441-48, Vêpres; p. [1-3] at end, Table (contents); p. [4], fautes à corriger.

The *Avertissement,* without indication of its origin or date, sets forth the necessity of religious instruction for young people.

A *Recommendation* slip (pasted upon binder's fly leaf) was issued with this edition: "Nous recommendons aux fidèles de ce Diocèse, l'usage du livre intitulé 'Instructions Chrétiennes pour les jeunes gens' . . . J.O.Plessis, Vic.Gen. 6 Avril, 1799."

This publication apparently started printing in 1798 and, like other lengthy devotional works, was issued the following year. It was advertised: "Actuellement à vendre à l'Imprimerie, Instructions Chrétiennes . . . Quatorze editions sont déja un assez bel eloge de ce livre, et ceux qui le liront ne seront pas surpris qui ait tant de fortune. Il renferme une morale sainte et solide sous un stile simple et sans artifice. Des Personnes éclairées assurent qu'en aucune langue il n'a été fait un ouvrage ausse convenable à la jeunesse et aux habitants des campagnes. On a rendu un service signale à cette Province en l'enrichessant d'une Production qui a pour but de former les jeunes gens à la Religion et à la vertu. Quebec 18me Avril, 1799."—*Quebec gazette*, Apr. 18, 1799. Subsequent advertisements include the price: "Prix 3/, 33/ par la douzaine, très proprement reliés."

Copies located: CaO; CaQQL; Gordonsmith.

1090. LIVIUS, PETER, 1727?-1795

[Catalogue of Library of late Chief Justice Livius to be sold at auction, May 18-19, 1798, at Freemasons Hall, by Burns & Woolsey, Auctioneers.]

Printed at Quebec, by R. Lelievre & P.-E. Desbarats at the New Printing Office, or else by John Neilson, 1798, though not recorded in the latter's account books; the publication is mentioned in the following advertisement:

"The extensive and valuable library of Chief Justice Livius, of which Printed Catalogues have been recently distributed [is] to be sold by Burns & Woolsey, Friday and Saturday [May] the 18th and 19th, at Freemason's Hall, at the same time will be sold some excellent Madeira wine in casks and bottles, Port and Cape ditto [etc.]."

Peter Livius, who had held office of chief justice of Quebec, 1777-86, lived a very short time in Canada, 1775-78, and died in England, July 23, 1795. He was long remembered for his quarrels with Gov. Carleton.

Copy located: None.

1091. LOWER CANADA. EXECUTIVE COUNCIL

EXTRACT / FROM THE / MINUTES OF COUNCIL, / Containing His His Majesty's late regulations relati-/ve tc the waste lands of the Crown, with His Ex/cellency, the Governor General's order of refe-/ rence respecting the same, to a Committee of the / whole Council, of the Province of Lower-Cana/da, the said Committee's report thereon, and His / Excellency's speech in reply. / [double rule] / [printer's ornament] / [double rule] / QUEBEC: / PRINTED AT THE NEW-PRINTING OFFICE, / PALACE STREET, 1798. / [title within a double rule frame]

8vo. A-F^4, G^2; 1 p. l., iv, 45 p; type-page: 16 × 9.5 cm.

Contents: p. l. recto, t.-p.; verso, Authority for publication of extracts from Minutes of Executive Council; p. [i]-iv, Introduction, signed by William Berczy; p. [1]-11, Order of reference, June 11, 1798; p. 12-18, Report of the Committee of the whole Council, June 20, 1798; p. 19-45, Extract from the Minutes of Council, July 9, 1798; verso of p. 45, blank.

The *Introduction* reviews the government's policy since 1792 in granting land to encourage settlement and repudiates the application of the proclamation of Aug. 22, 1797, to bona fide settlers. Gov. Prescott's *Order of reference* presents to the Council, in its capacity as land board, the recent, but undated, directions from the secretary of state, Portland, for disposal of crown lands. It reviews the provincial government's policy and regulations on township grants, fees, occupation without patent, and the proposed public sale of crown lands. The Council's *Report* affirms its purpose "to prohibit and repel every attempt to acquire lands by the robust title of occupancy," condemns Portland's directions one by one, as encouraging encroachments by that "lawless and obstructive Race who dwell upon the borders of this Province." In *Extract* of July 9, Prescott refutes the Council's objections and refers the directions back for reconsideration.

Though composed (excepting Berczy's *Introduction*) entirely of excerpts from official records, this and the following work were not official publications. Of them (or of similar publications in the newpapers) Chief Justice Osgoode, chairman of the Council committee, wrote to John King, from Quebec, May 2, 1799: ". . . What do you think of the madness and imbecility of G [i.e. Samuel Gale?] in resorting to the Press? Berczy was made the stalking Horse. The materials were supplied from the Council Office even before any of the Council was apprized of part of them."—Osgoode's private and confidential letters to King (who was undersecretary to the Duke of Portland, then secretary of state for war and colonies). These letters contain much information on conflicting personalities and viewpoints in Quebec land granting, 1792-1800.—in Can.P.A., "C.O. 42" v. 22.

Samuel Gale, *d.* 1826, a British army officer who settled a township grant in Quebec, subsequently represented protestants against the Council's policy before the Privy Council, presenting . . . *The Memorial and petition of the undersigned Attorney for . . . applicants for grant of various tracts . . . of waste lands . . . in Lower Canada* (12 p., 1 *l.*, London, H. Revell, [1800]). Copy in Can.P.A., "S" 55 *Int. Corresp.* 1800.

Wm. von Moll Berczy, 1748-1813, was head of a colony of Germans recently settled near York, Upper Canada, who tried from 1795 till 1801 to obtain title deeds to lands in Markham township, U.C. (*see* H. J. Morgan: *Sketches of celebrated Canadians*, Quebec, 1862, 110-13).

Printed by Roger Lelievre & P.-E. Desbarats, who succeeded Vondenvelden at the New Printing Office in May, 1798, this (and the following work) was advertised:

"Just published and for sale at the New Printing Office Extracts from the Minutes of Council of the 11th June & of the 20th September 1798, on the Waste Lands of the Crown. Price, 4/ for the two, or 2/ for the former and 2/6 for the latter."—*Quebec gazette*, Oct. 25, 1798, *et seq.*

Copies located: CaOOA; CaOT (2 cop.); CaOTU (Introd. wanting); CaQM; CaQMJ; CaQMS (3 cop.); CaQQL; GBLP (2 cop. in C.O. 42/111: 209-60; *ibid.*, 653-703); DLC; Ketcheson; MiU-C (2 cop. with interlinear MS. notes, in Melville papers); NN; NNHi (copy not seen); Witton.

1092. LOWER CANADA. EXECUTIVE COUNCIL

EXTRACT / OF THE / MINUTES OF COUNCIL, / of the 20th September, 1798. / ON THE / WASTE LANDS of the CROWN, / BEING A CONTINUATION, / OF THE / EXTRACT, / of the 11th of June last. / [double rule] / QUEBEC: / PRINTED AT THE NEW PRINTING-OFFICE, / Palace Street, 1798. /

8vo. [*][1] H-S[4], 1 p. l., 47-133, [1] p.; type-page: 15 × 9 cm. *Printed by R. Lelievre and P.-E. Desbarats.*

Contents: p. l. recto, t.-p.; verso, blank; p. [47]-133, Extract, signed at end: "A true extract, Thomas Cary, A.C. Ex. C."; [1] p. at end (verso of p. 133), Errata.

The *Extract* contains: (1) Gov. Prescott's opening speech to Council as land board: and his repudiation of responsibility for publication of *Extracts* of June 11, etc., (No. 1091) on the grounds that he deprecated recording such matters in the *Minutes*, not that he withheld the *Extracts* from publication; (2) the Council's *Report* confirming that of June 20, with further evidence and precedent to support close restriction of land grants, and a request that it be forwarded to the secretary of state; (3) Prescott's refutation of the Council's arguments. To the *Extracts*, Acting Secretary Thomas Cary appended, p. 132-33, his personal apology to the councillors for offensive passages written into the records in his official capacity.

Following the receipt by the Home Government of despatches and memorials on the land question, Prescott was ordered, Apr. 10, 1799, to return to England, "to restore harmony to the executive part of the government."

Copies located: CaQMS (3 cop.); CaQQL; GBLP (2 cop. in C.O. 42/111: 311-400; *ibid.*, 729-807); DLC (2 cop.); MiU-C (2 cop. with interlinear ms. notes, in Melville papers); NNHi (copy not seen); Witton.

1093. LOWER CANADA. GOVERNOR, 1797-1807 (*Prescott*]

[royal arms] / PROCLAMATION. / [*English text on left:*] ROBT. PRESCOTT, GOVR. / GEORGE THE THIRD by the Grace of GOD of Great Britain, / France and Ireland, KING, . . . / To all our loving and Faithful Subjects in our Province of Lower / Canada; GREETING. FORASMUCH as it has pleased Almighty / GOD lately to bless Our Arms with an unexampled and most important VICTORY / over the Fleet and Forces of the Persons who now exercise the Supreme Au- / thority in France, KNOW YE, that we . . . / [etc. 5 lines] / . . . [appoint] a General Thanksgiving to / Almighty GOD . . . / . . . on Thursday the / Tenth of January next. And we do strictly charge and command that the said / public day of Thanksgiving be religiously observed by all Our loving and faithful / Subjects in . . . Lower Canada . . . / . . . / . . . IN TESTIMONY whereof these our Let- / ters WE have caused to be made Patent and the Great Seal of Our said Province to be / hereunto affixed.—WITNESS . . . ROBERT PRESCOTT, . . . / . . . / . . . Quebec, . . . / . . . / [22 Dec. 1798.] . . . / R.P. / GEO: POWNALL, Secy. / GOD SAVE THE KING. /

[*French text on right:*] ROBT. PRESCOTT, Gouvr. / GEORGE TROIS [etc., 26 lines, signed:] R.P. / Traduit par Ordre de son Excellence, / X. LANAUDIERE, S. & T.F. / VIVE LE ROI. /

Broadside: overall type-measure: 33.2 × 17 cm., with a heading across the middle of the sheet, text in two type pages of 24 × 15.5 cm., English on left (30 lines) French on right (31 lines). *Printed at Quebec, by John Neilson, ?1798,* as recorded:

"1799, Jan. 5. [Debit] Provincial Secretary, printing 500 proclamations for thanksgiving on 10th Jany 99 one on a sheet of Crown. English type —£3.18."—Can.P.A., *Neilson papers*, v. 54.

On Dec. 22, 1798, this proclamation was ordered "published in the *Quebec gazette* and Montreal paper; and five hundred copies printed, to be affixed against the Church and other conspicuous parts of the towns of Quebec, Montreal, Three Rivers and the different parishes of the Province."—Can.P.A., L.C. State B. It appeared in the *Gazette*, Dec. 27, 1798–Jan. 3, 1799, and from the necessity of delivering the broadside to distant points by winter express, the printing was probably completed earlier than Neilson recorded it.

This proclamation has an unusual appearance, with its striking heading and narrow type-pages of large type in leaded lines—a departure from the double broadside layout hitherto used by the government printer in Quebec. The highly formal style of the letters patent, issued in the king's name by his local representative, was uncommon in French Canada—though Simcoe had occasionally used this form in Upper Canada. Altogether it is an impressive document, giving due importance to its charge—the celebration of the battle of the Nile, that long-hoped blow dealt to French power, nearly five months before the news reached Canada.

Copies located: CaOOA (2 cop. in *Proclamations* portfolio in the Library).

1094. LOWER CANADA. HOUSE OF ASSEMBLY

JOURNAL / OF THE / HOUSE OF ASSEMBLY, / OF / LOWER-CANADA. / From the 20th February to the 11th May, 1798, both days inclusive. / IN THE THIRTY-EIGHTH YEAR OF THE REIGN OF / KING GEORGE THE THIRD. / Being the Second Session of the Second Provincial Parliament / of this Province. / [royal arms] / [double rule] / QUEBEC: / PRINTED BY ORDER OF THE HOUSE OF ASSEMBLY, / AND SOLD BY JOHN NEILSON. / M.DCC.XCVIII. /

French t.-p.:

JOURNAL / DE LA / CHAMBRE D'ASSEMBLÉE / DU / BAS-CANADA. / Depuis le 20e. Février jusqu'au 11e. Mai, 1798, inclusivement. / DANS LA TRENTE HUITIEME ANNÉE DU REGNE DE / SA MAJESTÉ GEORGE TROIS. / Etant la Seconde Session du Second Parlement Provincial / de cette Province. / [royal arms] / [double rule] / QUEBEC: / IMPRIME' PAR ORDRE DE LA CHAMBRE D'ASSEMBLE'E / ET A VENDRE PAR JOHN NEILSON. / M.DCC.XCVIII. /

4to. A-2E^{4}; 7 p. l., 204 p., 2 *l.*; type-page: 18 × 12.3 cm. Odd numbers on verso, even numbers on recto; text in English and French on opposite pages.

Contents: p. l. 1-2 blank; p. l. 3 recto, English t.-p.; verso, blank; p. l. 4 recto, French t.-p.; verso, blank; p. l. 5 recto, blank; p. l. 5 verso-recto of p. [1], Proclamations, etc.; p. [1]-204, Journal; verso of p. 204, blank; 2 *l.* at end, blank.

The House ordered that 100 copies of its *Journal* be printed in English and French for the use of members, and that none but the printer so licensed print the same. —L.C. As. *Journal*, Mar. 23, 1798.

The printer recorded this work:

"1798, June 30 [Debit] House of Assembly [for] Printing 100 Copies Journals 1798 charged @ 150 pages at the rate of £125 for 300 pages—£62.10.

House of Assembly Dr. to Printing 63 pages of the Journal of 1798 more than charged for in the acc[t] for printing the same @ £125. for 300 pages. as per agreement with the clerk—£26.5.

Binding 2 copies Journals in Calf—12/.

Folding, stitching & cutting 100 Copies d° @ 3[d]—£1.5."

—Can.P.A., *Neilson papers*, v. 54.

An *Index* was issued probably much later ([27] p., 4to., p. [1-13] English; p. [14-27] French). Without printer's name or date, this *Index* has not (like the indices to *Journals* for preceding and succeeding years) even a date in the watermark of its paper. The latter (a fine wove) is, however, quite different from the stock used for the *Journal* (laid paper watermarked 1796). The *Index* is only occasionally found with copies of the *Journal*.

Copies located: CaO (2 cop.); CaOOA; CaOT; CaQM; CaQMA; CaQMM; CaQQL; CaQQLH; CtY; DLC; GBLP (in C.O. 42/110); ICJ; ICN; MH; N (mint copy, uncut, unopened, sewn in original blue paper covers with blank leaves of sig. A and 2E complete); NN; RPJ (with index); WHi.

1095. LOWER CANADA. LAWS, STATUTES, *etc.*

Half-title: THE / PROVINCIAL STATUTES / OF / LOWER-CANADA, / Anno Regni GEORGII III. REGIS, MAGNÆ BRITANNIÆ, FRANCIÆ ET HIBERNIÆ TRICESIMO OCTAVO. / HIS EXCELLENCY / ROBERT PRESCOTT, ESQ. GOVERNOR. / Being the SECOND Session of the / SECOND Provincial Parliament of LOWER-CANADA. /

French half-title:

LES / STATUTS PROVINCIAUX / DU / BAS-CANADA. / Anno Regni GEORGII III. REGIS, / MAGNÆ BRITANNIÆ, FRANCIÆ ET HIBERNIÆ TRICESIMO OCTAVO. / SON EXCELLENCE / ROBERT PRESCOTT, ECUYER, GOUVERNEUR. / Etant la SECONDE Session du / SECOND Parlement Provincial du BAS-CANADA. /

4to [*-2*]^4; [27]-41 p.; type-page: 22 × 17 cm. Text in English and French on opposite pages. Two leaves of sig. [2*] are folded around sig. [*] to form half-title pages. *Printed at Quebec, by R. Lelievre & P.-E. Desbarats, 1798.*

Contents: p. [27], English half-title; p. [28], blank; p. [29], French half-title; p. [30], blank; p. [31], blank; p. [32]-41, Statutes 38 Geo. III c. 1-5 (assented to, May 11, 1798); verso of p. 41, blank.

This is a separate issue of the sessions laws of 1798 as they appear in No. 1051 with half-titles, text, signatures, and pagination unchanged.

Copies located: MiU-C (in blue-gray printer's paper covers, uncut as issued); NN.

1096. NEW BRUNSWICK. LAWS, STATUTES, *etc.*

ACTS / OF THE / GENERAL ASSEMBLY / OF / HIS MAJESTY'S PROVINCE / OF / NEW-BRUNSWICK, / PASSED IN THE YEAR 1798. / [rule] / [royal arms] / [rule] / FREDERICTON: / Printed by CHRISTOPHER SOWER, Printer to the / KING'S MOST EXCELLENT MAJESTY. / [title within a frame] fo. [$*^1$, 2_*-3_*^2]; 3 p. l., 394-96 p.; type-page: 23.5 × 13.7 cm. Even numbers on recto, odd numbers on verso; paged in continuation of No. 1058.

Contents: p. l. 1 recto, t.-p.; verso, blank; p. l. 2 recto, half-title; verso, blank; p. l. 3 recto, Titles of the acts; verso, blank; p. 394-96, 38 Geo. III c. I-II, acts passed in the third session of the third assembly, Jan. 16-Feb. 9, 1798.; verso of p. 396, blank.

Though undated in imprint the work was printed in 1798, as Sower's bill, "for printing the acts of last session—£9," sent by Lieut.-Gov. Carleton to the Assembly, Jan. 23, 1799, suggests. Though the place of publication was Fredericton, the seat of government, the printing was probably done at Sower's printing office in Britain Street, at Saint John.

This was Sower's last session's work, for he left New Brunswick in the spring of 1799 and died on July 3, in Baltimore. It was the only publication from the session of 1798, for the *Journal* of the House of Assembly was not printed (probably owing to the financial deadlock between Assembly and Council) until 1801. Sower addressed a letter to the Assembly committee for superintending the printing of the *Journal*, etc., on Jan. 15, 1798, stating:

"I send you enclosed my accounts for printing the Journals . . . for 1796 and 1797 . . . I beg leave to remind you that . . . I have not received any payment of monies voted to me since those of the year 1794 and to assure you that I actually [owe] interest for some of those very materials with which I have printed the Journals and Laws [etc.]."—N.B. As. *Papers, 1798*.

Copies located: GBLP (in C.O. 188/9: 457-62); MH; NNB.

1097. NOVA SCOTIA. HOUSE OF ASSEMBLY

[A Bill to encourage the making a navigable Canal from the Harbour of Halifax, to the Bason [sic] of Minas.]

? *Printed at Halifax, N.S., by Anthony Henry, 1798*, by order of the House.

On June 21, 1798, Charles Morris, provincial surveyor, offered to the House, the petition of Wm. Forsyth, Andrew Belcher, Richard Kidston, and others, showing that a navigable communication from Halifax through the Dartmouth and Shubenaccadie lakes and the Shubenaccadie river to Minas Basin would promote commerce and agriculture. "In consequence of a survey made and levels taken of land and water . . . by Order of this House (*see* No. 1059] such a navigation seems practicable, and may be accomplished at little more expence than that in the Report of the Surveyors." The petitioners state that they and others are willing to subscribe a considerable sum and will complete the work if the Legislature will grant encouragement and reasonable aid. They pray that an act be passed in the present session (1798) authorizing them to proceed and granting them the right to levy reasonable toll for the space of [blank] years. At the same time Morris? presented a "Bill to encourage the making a navigable canal from the Harbour of Halifax to the Bason of Minas." The bill was read, tabled, and ordered printed for the use of the Assembly and Council. On June 28, the House in committee recommended that the lieutenant-governor be asked to grant a charter to the petitioners and that the House afford aid and encouragement, but that the bill be deferred to its next session.

—Can.P.A., N.S. "D".

The bill does not appear to have been passed at that time. In 1824, however, other bills were enacted for the incorporation and organization of a Shubenaccadie canal company—without reference to the earlier project.

Copy located: None.

1098. NOVA SCOTIA. HOUSE OF ASSEMBLY

[rule] / JOURNAL / AND / PROCEEDINGS / OF THE / HOUSE of ASSEMBLY. / [rule] /

fo. sig. 4K-4R², 4S¹; 1 p. l., p. 279-309; type-page: 27 × 14.5 cm. paged in continuation of No. 1061. *Printed at Halifax, N.S., by Anthony Henry, 1798.*

Contents: p. l. recto, t.-p.; verso, Proclamation; p. 279-309, Journal of the sixth session of the seventh assembly, June 8-July 7, 1798; verso of p. 309, blank.

Copies located: CaNs; CaNsHA; CaP; GBLP (in C.O. 217/73: 130-46; another copy, p. 279-82, June 8-14 only, enclosed in Sir J. Wentworth's dispatch of June 23, 1798, filed in C.O. 217/69: 141-43d); NN.

1099. NOVA SCOTIA. LAWS, STATUTES, *etc.**

Running title: [rule] / 1798. Anno Tricessimo Octova [sic] Regis, GEORGII III. CAP. I[-VI]. / [rule] /

Caption title: At the GENERAL ASSEMBLY of the / Province of NOVA-SCOTIA, . . . / [5 lines] / . . . being the Fifth [sic] Session of / the Seventh GENERAL ASSEMBLY, / convened in the said Province. / [rule]

fo. sig. 5D-5G², 5H¹; p. 497-514; type-page: 26 × 15 cm. paged in continuation of No. 1063; p. [507] mispaged: 407. *Printed at Halifax, N.S., by Anthony Henry, 1798.*

Contents: p. 497-514, Cap. I-VI, temporary acts passed in the sixth session of the seventh assembly, June 8-July 7, 1798.

Copies located: CaO; GBLP (in C.O. 219/19).

1100. NOVA SCOTIA. LIEUTENANT-GOVERNOR, 1792-1808 (*Wentworth*)

[A Proclamation by His Excellency Sir John Wentworth . . . Lieutenant governor . . . of Nova Scotia <Text> Halifax, April 21, 1798.]

Broadside. *Printed at Halifax, N.S., by Anthony Henry, 1798,* as recorded:

"1798, Apr. 29. Printing Proclamation for a general fast and continuing [in the *Royal gazette,* May 1, *et seq.*]—£1.10.

200 Proclamations in full face &c.—£3.

800 Prayers for a general fast—£8.6."

—Henry's *Account for extra printing* [*for government*] *in P.A.N.S., Miscellaneous Assembly papers,* 1798.

Text: ". . . [I appoint a day of] Public fast and humiliation to be observed throughout this Province on Thursday the 31st Day of May [1798] for the safety and prosperity . . . that the wicked devices of [the King's] Enemies may be confounded and peace restored," etc., states that the bishop of Nova Scotia is to prepare a form of prayer."†—*Royal gazette,* Halifax, N.S., May 1, 1798.

Copy located: None.

*No Perpetual Acts were passed in this session.

†Fast days were similarly appointed for June ?, 1799 and June 27, 1800, but no broadside proclamation thereof has been recorded.

1101. QUEBEC GAZETTE. CARRIER'S ADDRESS

VERSES / of the Boy who carries the / QUEBEC GAZETTE to the SUBSCRIBERS. / [rule] / Ist. JANUARY, 1799. /

French side:

ETRENNES / du Garçon qui porte la / GAZETTE de QUEBEC, / aux PRATIQUES. / [rule] / Ier JANVIER, 1799. / Chanson—sur l'air: Eh! mais, oui-da, &c. /

Broadside: type-page: 30 × 23 cm. in ornamental double rule frame. English verse on left, 42 lines; French on right, 42 lines. The English verse reviews the *Gazette's* journalistic achievements of the year:

"...
When the red Signal from the flagstaff's heighth,
Proclaims a sail or two within our sight,
With eager steps to gain the news I run,
Swift as the light, unwearied as the Sun:
When glorious DUNCAN beat our hauty [sic] foe
The whole account I knew you long'd to know,
And when BRAVE NELSON gain'd immortal name
With speed I ran to circulate his Fame
And tell his deeds to all who aid our cause
Protect our freedom and support our Laws.
[Etc.]."

The French side is a conventional New Year greeting:

"Aujourd'hui sans racune
L'on va se visiter,
Et suivant la coutume
Maints baiser se donner,
Eh! mais, oui-da!
Comment trouver du mal à ça?
[Etc.]."

Copy located: CaO (bound in *Quebec gazette* at end of 1798).

1102. RICKETTS, J. B.

[Handbill announcing performances of Rickett's Circus at Montreal, March 29, 1798.]

Broadside: *Printed at Montreal, by Edward Edwards, 1798*, as noted in the following advertisement of "Surprising Performances of Horsemanship, and Manly feats of Strength and Activity by Mr. Ricketts and Comy.... On Thursday next the 29th of March, Mr. Ricketts will for that evening only, through [sic] a Summerset over thirty Mens heads; this surprising Feat was never performed by anyone but himself. Mr. Ricketts and horse will fly through a Blazing Sun—with a number of other astonishing performances which will be announced in the hand bills."

—*Montreal gazette*, Mar. 26, 1798.

Similar advertisements appeared regularly for weeks in Montreal, then in Quebec, newspapers towards the end of the century.

Copy located: None.

1103. TUNSTALL, JAMES MARMADUKE, 1760-1840

A / SERMON, / Preached on St. John's Day, / BEFORE THE LODGES / No. 4, 8, and 12, / ANCIENT YORK MASONS: / IN CHRIST'S CHURCH, / MONTREAL. / [double rule] / BY THE REV. JAMES TUNSTALL. / [double rule] / MONTREAL: / PRINTED BY E. EDWARDS. / [double rule] / 1798.

8vo. [*]^8; 3 p. l., 9 p.; type-page: 15.3 × 8.6 cm.

Contents: p. l. 1, blank; p. l. 2 recto, t.-p.; verso, blank; p. l. 3 recto, Resolution to thank Rev. Brother Tunstall, signed: "Gwyn Radford, Secr'y of St. Paul's Lodge No. 12, February 13th, 1798"; verso, blank; p. [1]-9, Sermon; text: Genesis, 13 chap. 18 ver. And Abram said unto Lot, let there be no strife between me and thee, for we be Brethren.; verso of p. 9, blank.

The sermon treats of the principles of masonry universally acknowledged, its foundation in the Christian religion, and its headquarters in England, of the history of the York masons from 926 A.D. to 1702 when, on the decline of Sir Christopher Wren, grand master—"novel forms of doctrine crept into the institution in lieu of those which were sanctioned by the most venerable antiquity." The preacher exhorts freemasons to repel accusations of misrule and anarchy, to support constitution, king, and church, and to win back "the modern brethren of our Order."

The relations of "Ancients" and "Moderns" are indicated in the records of their lodges, synopsized in John H. Graham: *Outlines of the history of freemasonry in the province of Quebec* (Montreal, 1892), chap. 4-5.

Tunstall, educated at Oxford and ordained in the Church of England, came to Canada in 1787 under the auspices of the Society for the Propagation of the Gospel. He served as itinerant preacher in Quebec, then in 1789 he was appointed by the provincial government to the charge in Montreal.

Copy located: CaOT.

1104. UPPER CANADA. ADMINISTRATOR, 1796-1799 (*Russell*)

PROCLAMATION. / PETER RUSSELL, Esq; President, administering the Government of the / Province of UPPER CANADA, &c.&c. / <Text and Schedule> / [ornamental rule] / YORK: Printed by WM. WATERS and T. G. SIMONS, Printers to the KING'S most Excellent Majesty. /

Broadside: 39 lines; type-page: 47 × 37 cm.

Text: "Whereas it appears by letters lately received from his Grace the Duke of Portland, one of his Majesty's Principal Secretaries of State, to be his Majesty's Royal Will and Pleasure, that in order to raise a Fund for the Public Service of the Province, all future Grants of Land (those only excepted for which his Majesty's Governments were actually pledged previous to the receipt of those Letters) be subject to a Fee of Six Pence, Halifax currency, per Acre, exclusive of the usual Expences of Survey:—

"Be it therefore known, That [etc., all grants of land made after Dec. 22, 1797, shall be subject to fee of sixpence per acre excepting grants to U.E.loyalists, three pence per acre. York, Oct. 31, 1798] Peter Russell. By the President's Command, John Small, Clerk of the Executive Council. [Appended:] Schedule of the Charges for Survey, ordered to be taken by the Surveyor-General, to enable him to defray the Expences of the Surveys which he shall receive Warrants for [etc.]."

This broadside is reprinted in Ontario Archives, *Report, 1905*.

Copy located: CaOT (acquired with papers of Sir D. W. Smith, surveyor-general of Upper Canada). Another copy, *not located:* Hodgins, no. 66.

1105. UPPER CANADA. ADMINISTRATOR, 1796-1799 (*Russell*)

[royal arms] / PROCLAMATION. / [rule] / PETER RUSSELL, esq. President, administering / the government of Upper-Canada. / <Text> / GIVEN under my hand and seal at arms, / in council at York, this fifteenth day of December, in the thirty- / ninth year of his Majesty's reign, and in the year of our Lord one / thousand seven hundred and ninety-eight. / PETER RUSSELL. / By Command of the President in Council, / John Small, C.E.C. / [rule] / YORK: Printed by WILLIAM WATERS and TITUS G. SIMONS. /

Broadside: 42 lines; type-page: 35+? × 20 cm.

Text: "Whereas by letters received from his Grace the Duke of Portland, one of his Majesty's principal secretaries of state, since the issuing the proclamation of the thirty-first of October last, it appears that, in consequence of a Representation made by the Executive Government of this Province, to his Majesty's Ministers, on the Exemption of the U.E.Loyalists and their Children from every expence attending the grants of land made, or to be made to them, his Majesty has been graciously pleased to signify his Royal Pleasure that the First Loyalists, and their Sons and Daughters shall continue to receive his Majesty's Bounty of Two Hundred Acres Each as heretofore, free from any axpence [sic] whatever. And that it is to be understood, that this Mark of the Royal Munificence is expressly confined to Loyalists only, who were actually resident in the province on, or before the Twenty-eighth of July Last [etc.].

"Be it therefore known that [etc., loyalists enrolled in U.E. lists previous to Dec. 15, 1798, are to be exempted from terms of proclamation of Oct. 31, 1798, and may continue to receive grants of 200 acres without payment of fees except the standing fees]."

This broadside is reprinted in Ontario Archives, *Report, 1905*.

Copies located: CaOOA (in *Proclamations* portfolio in the Library); CaOT (acquired with the papers of Sir D. W. Smith, surveyor-general of Upper Canada. This copy is cropped at foot and lacks imprint). Another copy, *not located:* Hodgins, no. 67.

1106. UPPER CANADA. EXECUTIVE COUNCIL

Council-Office, Dec. 29, 1798. / YONGE- / STREET. / [rule] / <Text> [signed:] JOHN SMALL, C.E.C. /

Broadside: 31 lines; type-page: 40.5 × 20 cm. *Probably printed at York, U.C., by Wm. Waters and T. G. Simons, 1798 or 1799.*

Text: "Notice is hereby given to all persons settled, or about to settle on Yonge-Street, and whose locations have not yet been confirmed by order of the President in council, that before such locations can be confirmed it will be expected that the following Conditions be complied with: [etc. In one year the settler must (1) erect a house 16 by 20 feet; (2) clear and fence five acres of land; (3) open the Yonge-street road fronting one acre]."

Yonge Street, named for Sir George Yonge, 1731-1812, English official, was the road laid under Lieut.-Gov. Simcoe's direction, north from the harbour of York; it is now the main north-south thoroughfare in the city of Toronto and continues north through the province of Ontario as king's highway no. 11.

Copy located: CaOT (acquired with the papers of Sir D. W. Smith, surveyor-general of Upper Canada).

1107. VONDENVELDEN, WILLIAM, *d.* 1809, and CHARLAND, LOUIS, 1772?-1813

[The Canadian Topographer.]

Proposed printing was advertised:

"By Subscription will be published, Dedicated . . . to His Excellency Robert Prescott, Esq. Governor-General, &c. A Topographical Chart of . . . Lower Canada, To be engraved by an able Artist and impressed on Paper of the best quality; laid down by a Scale of eight miles to one English Inch; exhibiting the Grants made by the French Crown and the Townships lately surveyed . . . by order of Government [It is to be] compiled from the best Materials and the latest Surveys, viz. from the Southwestern boundary of the Province down to the Counties of Quebec and Dorchester by Samuel Gale Esq. and Mr. Jean Baptiste Duberger and from the said Counties downwards by [Wm. Vondenvelden and Louis Charland].

"With this Chart will be delivered the CANADIAN TOPOGRAPHER in 8vo Printed on good paper and with new types, containing the descriptive part of the original French grants as recorded in the Secretary's Office . . . and other interesting information relating to the geography of this Country; preceded by a List of the subscribers.

"Price £2:12:0. The Charts in three sheets; and the book stitched, etc. [Money is not required in advance but Subscribers please signify, as one of the promotors will go to London to superintend the execution of the work. signed:] Wm. Vondenvelden, Louis Charland . . . Quebec, 4th July, 1798."—*Quebec gazette*, July 5, 1798, and *Montreal gazette*, July 31, 1798.

This was probably the announcement of the work which appeared later as: *Topographical map of the Province of Lower Canada* [*etc.*] (London, W. Faden, 1803); and *Extraits des titres des anciennes concessions de terre . . . compilé par William Vondenvelden . . . et Louis Charland* (Quebec, P.-E. Desbarats, 1803). *See* Toronto Public Library, *Bibliography of Canadiana*, no. 768.

Vondenvelden and Charland were surveyors in the service of the provincial government. The former held the post of assistant surveyor-general, also, from 1795-98, that of law printer to the government.

1108. ALMANACS. LOWER CANADA

CALENDRIER pour l'Année 1800, pour QUEBEC, par les 306$^{d.}$ 30$^{m.}$ de Longitude, et 46$^{d.}$ 55$^{m.}$ de Latitude. / [rule] /

Colophon: QUEBEC: Imprimé à la Nouvelle Imprimerie. /

Broadside: type-page: 57.5 × 43.5 cm. in single rule frame. *Printed by R. Lelievre and P.-E. Desbarats, 1799.*

Contents: Les signes, monthly calendar tables, etc.; Tableau des comtés, Tide tables, as in No. 920.

Copy located: CaO (bound in *Quebec gazette*, at end of 1799).

1109. ALMANACS. LOWER CANADA

[Calendrier pour l'Année 1800 pour Québec, *Quebec, chez Jean Neilson, 1799.*]

Broadside. This almanac was advertised in the *Quebec gazette*, Dec. 26, 1799, as recently published, price 7½*d*., 5*s*. per dozen, 37*s*. 6*d*. per hundred. "Calendrier de Québec pour l'année 1800," containing the signs, the ecclesiastical calendar, commencement of the seasons, zodiac, moon's phases, festivals of the Church of England and of the Catholic Church, the rising and setting of the sun, tables of English measure, court terms, tide tables for the harbour of Quebec, the value of gold and silver coins.

Copy located: None.

1110. ALMANACS. LOWER CANADA

[An English Calendar for the Year 1800. *Quebec, John Neilson 1799.*]

Broadside. This almanac was advertised in a postscript to the advertisement of *Calendrier de Québec . . . 1800* (No. 1109):

"[Recently published] . . . Also, An English Calendar for the year, 1800. Price 5$^{d.}$, 4/ per dozen, 27/ per hundred."—*Quebec gazette*, Dec. 26, 1799.

It was probably a sheet almanac, an English version of the information in *Calendrier*. The latter had been issued almost every year since 1765, but this was the first publication noted of an English edition from the Brown-Neilson printing office. Its price is noticeably cheaper than that of the French edition.

Copy located: None.

1111. ALMANACS. NOVA SCOTIA

AN / ALMANACK / FOR THE / Year . . . 1800; / . . . / CALCULATED FOR THE MERIDIAN OF / HALIFAX . . . / . . . / CONTAINING / THE ECLIPSES [etc. 8 lines in col. 1] / SITTINGS of the COURTS / [etc. 8 lines in col. 2] / . . . / [rule] / BY THEOPHRASTUS. / [rule] / HALIFAX. / Printed and Sold by JOHN HOWE, at his Printing-Office, / in GEORGE-STREET, near the PARADE. / [title within double rule frame]

12mo. A^6, B^4, C^6; [32] p.; type-page: 14.2 × 8.3 cm.

Contents: p. [1], t.-p.; p. [2], Ship signals; p. [3], Eclipses, Directions to farmers; p. [4], Zodiac; p. [5-16], Calendar; p. [17-23], Naval, army officers, militia in Nova Scotia; p. [24-28], Nova Scotia provincial officials, courts, etc.; p. [29-30], Masonic lodges, clergy; p. [31-32], Distances from Halifax, etc.

"Ship signals," p. [2], gave an interpretation of the signals to be raised on Halifax citadel to warn inhabitants of vessels approaching the harbour—a defence measure against French marauders.

Copy located: CaNsHA.

1112. ALMANACS. NOVA SCOTIA

THE / NOVA-SCOTIA CALENDER / OR AN / ALMANACK; / For the Year . . . / 1800 / . . . / . . . / . . . / . . . / WHEREIN IS CONTAINED, / The ECLIPSES [etc. 6 lines in col. 1] / Moon's apogee [etc. 6 lines in col. 2] / Calculated for the Meridian of / HALIFAX . . . / [3 lines] / [rule] / BY METONICUS. / [rule] / "Amidst the hurry of tumultuous war, / "The Stars, the Gods, the Heav'ns, were still his care, / Nor did his skill to fix the rolling Year, / "Inferior to Eudoxu's art appear." / "LUCAN." / [rule] / HALIFAX: / Printed and Sold by A. HENRY, at his Printing-Office, in Sackville- / Street, corner of Grafton-Street. / [title and each page within ornamental frame.]

12mo. [A-C]^6; [36] p.; type-page: 13.5 × 8.5 cm.

Contents: p. [1], t.-p.; p. [2], Directions to farmers; p. [3], Vulgar notes; p. [4-6], Eclipses, etc.; p. [7-18], Calendar; p. [19-24], Nova Scotia administration, legislature, courts, judges, justices, collectors of customs, road commissioners, etc.; p. [25-34], holidays, fire companies, court sittings, naval and army officers, militia, masonic lodges; p. [35-36], Distances from Halifax to Annapolis, Pictou, Truro, Ft. Cumberland, etc.

"Directions to farmers" p. [27], is the same as in No. 1081.

Copies located: CaNsWA (p. 5-6 wanting); CaOOA; MWA (p. 13-16 wanting).

1113. ALMANACS. UPPER CANADA

[The Upper Canada Almanack for the Year 1800, *printed at Niagara, U.C., by Sylvester Tiffany.*]

This almanac was advertised: "Now in the Press and will soon appear, the Upper Canada Almanack for the Year 1800, calculated for the meridian of Niagara and will contain many things particular to our situation [etc.]."—*Canada Constellation*, Nov. 30, 1799, *et seq.* Also: "Just published and for sale at this Office The Upper Canada Almanack for the year 1800. They will be immediately distributed to the different stores thro' this part of the province."—*ibid.*, Jan. 4, 1800.

This is the first almanac known to have been printed in Upper Canada (though Waters & Simons had advertised "copies of this years Almanacks [?imported] for sale at the Printing Office."—*Upper Canada gazette*, June 15, 1799). *The Upper Canada Almanack* was published annually for a time, but the edition for 1802 is the earliest of which a copy is known to be extant (in Montreal Civic Library, *see* Gagnon: *Essai de bibliographie canadienne*, 1: no. 3539; also in Toronto Public Library, *see* its *Bibliography of Canadiana*, no. 761).

1114. [BERRY, SIR EDWARD], 1768-1831

A NARRATIVE / OF THE PROCEEDINGS OF / HIS MAJESTY'S SQUADRON / UNDER THE COMMAND OF / REAR-ADMIRAL SIR H. NELSON K.B. / From its sailing from Gibraltar to the conclusion of / The GLORIOUS VICTORY of the NILE. / Drawn from the Minutes / By AN OFFICER OF RANK IN THE SQUADRON. / To which is added, Lord

Nelson's official dispatches, and an intercepted letter from / Rear Admiral Genteaume, giving an account of the engagement. / [printer's ornament] / QUEBEC / REPUBLISHED BY JOHN NEILSON, MOUNTAIN STREET. / 1799. /

8vo A-H[4], 2 p.l.; 58 p., 1 *l.*; type-page : 15 x 8.5 cm.

Contents: p. l. 1 recto, half-title: "A Narrative of the Glorious Victory of the Nile. 1798"; verso, blank; p. l. 2 recto, t.-p.; verso, blank; p. 1-32, A narrative; p. 33-36, Despatches, dated from the Nile, Aug. 7, 1798, reprinted from the *London gazette extra*, Oct. 2, 1798; p. 37-45, Letter from Genteaume to Bruix, minister of marine and colonies, Alexandria, Aug. 23; p. 46-58, French, Dutch, and Spanish ships taken or destroyed by the English, 1793-98; 1 *l.* at end, blank.

This edition was advertised: "Just published and for sale at the Printing Office, Price 1/6, 15/ per dozen, A Narrative of the Proceedings of His Majesty's Squadron [etc.]. Undoubtedly drawn up by Capt. Berry, now Sir E. Berry. . . . No certain account of the proceedings of the squadron under Rear admiral Nelson previous to the Battle of the Nile has been made public except that contained in this Narrative. The justly admired despatches of our noble Admiral are here in a form easier to be preserved than in a . . . newspaper, and the list of the enemy's vessels taken or destroyed in the war set forth in an impressive manner the unexampled glory of our Mother Country. To every lover of that Country the present publication cannot fail to be acceptable."—*Quebec gazette*, Mày 9, 1799.

First published in London, 1798, reprinted and circulated widely in Europe and America, this pamphlet supplemented the official reports of the battle in the *London gazette* of Oct. 2, 1798, and the many unofficial accounts in other papers; these were reprinted in Canadian newspapers (at Halifax, then at Saint John, Quebec, Montreal, and York) from the last week of Nov., 1798. Berry's *Narrative* was also reprinted seriatim in the *Royal gazette*, Halifax, N.S., Apr. 9, 1799, *et seq.*

Berry, a brilliant young officer, was captain of Nelson's flagship and a hot participant in the Battle of the Nile. He bore the Admiral's despatches on the victory to London, received a knighthood for his services and subsequently pursued a distinguished career throughout the Napoleonic wars. His *Narrative* is reprinted with supporting documents in Horatio Nelson, *The Despatches and letters of . . . Nelson*, with notes by Sir Nicholas Harris Nicolas (7 v., London, 1845-46), 3: 48-91.

Facsim. illus. of t.-p. of this Quebec edition appears in Gagnon: *Essai de bibliographie canadienne*, 1: no. 115.

Copies located: CaQM; CaQMM; CaQMS; CaQQL (2 cop.); Ketcheson.

1115. BYLES, MATHER, 1734-1814

The VICTORY ascribed to GOD. / A / SERMON, / DELIVERED DECEMBER 2d, 1798. / ON THE LATE / SIGNAL SUCCESSES, / GRANTED TO / HIS MAJESTY'S ARMS. / [double rule] / By MATHER BYLES, D.D. / RECTOR OF ST. JOHN, AND CHAPLAIN / TO THE GARRISON OF NEW- / BRUNSWICK. / [double rule] / SAINT JOHN : / PRINTED BY J. RYAN, AT HIS PRINTING-OFFICE, N°. 58, / PRINCE WILLIAM-STREET. /

4to. 19 p.; type-page: 16.7 × 11 cm. Probably published in 1799, for the work was advertised: "Just published and for sale at J. Ryan's Printing Office, Price 3/6.

A Sermon delivered on the 2d December, 1798 [etc.]."—*Saint John gazette*, Jan. 11, 1799, *et seq.*

Contents: p. [1], t.-p.; p. [2], Dedication to the congregation of Trinity church; p. [3]-19, Sermon, text: Psalm XCVIII: 1, O Sing unto the Lord a new Song, for He hath done marvellous things, His right Hand and His holy Arm hath gotten him the Victory; verso of p. 19, blank.

The sermon sets forth two propositions: (1) God always wins the battle; (2) God chooses the victor and bestows the victory. These are supported by descriptions of numerous battles in the Scriptures and of Nelson's victory on the Nile. Even as Satan the first rebel against authority despised government, insulted the king, renounced God—and was vanquished, so the French, rebelling in the same spirit, are punished by God. His chosen champion is the English nation. Byles speaks impressively in the language of the King James version, but his further development of this theme is restrained, he states, only by the season (Trinity Church at that time had no stove).

Byles, son of the "Famous Mather Byles" and grandson of Cotton Mather, was born in Boston and graduated from Harvard College in 1751. He received a master's degree from Harvard, 1754, and from Yale, 1757. Bred and ordained a Congregationalist, Byles turned Episcopalian in 1768, and became rector of Christ Church, Boston. In 1770 Oxford University conferred upon him the degree of Doctor of Divinity. Six years later, a conspicuous loyalist, he removed to Nova Scotia. Appointed chaplain to the garrison at Halifax, he failed, however, to please Bishop Inglis, who wrote, deprecating Byle's appointment to a rectorship, ". . . his chaplaincy is a perfect Sinecure . . . [he] is said to be a good preacher and he certainly is not indifferent in abilities. But . . . he has given offence to most of the leading people here by some satirical poems which he has written, or at least they were ascribed to him." Thus handicapped in Halifax, Byles moved to New Brunswick about 1786, worked as a draughtsman in the surveyor-general's office at 7*s*. a day. In 1789 he succeeded Bissett as rector of Trinity in Saint John, and as provincial chaplain.

Cf. Long: *Nova Scotia authors*, who lists this work but apparently saw no copy; also MacFarlane: *New Brunswick bibliography*, 16-17; and Sabin, no. 9718n.

Copy located: CaOOA.

1116. CATHOLIC CHURCH. PRAYER BOOK. *French*

FORMULAIRE / DE PRIERES, / A L'USAGE / DES PENSIONNAIRES / DES RELIGIEUSES URSULINES; / NOUVELLE EDITION, / Revue, corrigée & augmentée de l'Office de la / Ste. Vierge, en Latin & François, sans ren- / voi; & des Prières pour offrir son intention / en communiant les Fêtes principales de l'an- / née. / [rule] / AVEC APPROBATION. / [rule] / [double rule] / QUEBEC: / IMPRIME'E à LA NOUVELLE IMPRIMERIE, / RUE DES JARDINS. / 1799. /

12mo. A-2T[6]; 4 p. l., 486 [i.e. 488], [7] p.; type-page: 14.3 × 7.2 cm.; p. 211 mispaged: 111, 232: 132; 279-280 repeated in numbering; 415 mispaged: 4; 483-484 mispaged: 482-483; 484 omitted in numbering. *Printed by R. Lelievre & P.-E. Desbarats.*

Contents: p. l. 1 recto, t.-p.; verso, Approbation; p. l. 2-4 recto, Fêtes, etc.; p. l. 4 verso, Méditation; p. [1]-486, Formulaire, etc.; p. [1-7] at end, Table (contents); verso of p. [7], blank.

Approbation reads: "Nous recommandons aux Maîtresses d'Ecole d'inspirer en toute occasion à leurs écolières le goût du Formulaire de Prières, livre très propres à nourrir la piété surtout dans les personnes de leur sexe. [signé:] J. O. Plessis, Vicr. Génl. Quebec, 22e. Août, 1799."

This publication was advertised: "Recemment publié à la Nouvelle Imprimerie, Le Formulaire . . . nouvelle édition . . . avec Approbation. Il se vend en gros et en détail à l'Imprimeur, Rue de la Montagne [i.e. John Neilson]. Prix relié, 54/ par douzaine, 5/ l'éxemplaire. Un Rabais de 3/ par douz. est accordé à ceux qui acheteront 8 douz. et audessus."—*Quebec gazette*, Feb 7, 1800.

Copies located: CaOT; CaQMJ; CaQQL; Ketcheson; NN.

1117. CHANSON . . . DU 10 JANVIER, 1799

Chanson pour la fête du 10 Janvier, 1799—Trois Rivières. Air: Moi, Je pense comme Gregoire.

Broadside. Apparently composed in Lower Canada, 1799, in celebration of the battle of the Nile,* this handbill has the appearance of publication about a century later. It is printed on wove paper, with considerable non-rag content, highly discoloured. By sight and touch it seems conspicuously different from the paper of works actually printed in Canada in the 18th century.

The *Chanson*, in five stanzas, begins:

"Le fameux Buonaparté
En Egypte est arrivé
Mais qu'y pourra-t-il donc faire?
Triste pays pour un Corsaire
Puis qu'il n'offre aucun butin;
Puis à la fin
Ses troupes mourront de faim
Moi, je pense comme Gregoire,
J'aime mieux boire (bis)."

and ends:

"Anglois, peuple valeureux,
Pour vous quels succès heureux!
Le tableau de votre histoire
N'offrit jamais tant de gloire
Que sous ce meilleur des rois;
Qui George Trois
Sur tous nos coeurs a des droits,
A ses vertus et sa victoire
Il nous faut boire (bis)."

Copy located: CaQQL.

*Louis Labadie, schoolmaster at Trois Rivières, sent similar *Chansons* in MS. to John Neilson, printer of the *Quebec gazette*, from time to time. His "Chanson 7 Janvier . . . sur la glorieuse victoire Remportée par l'Amiral Duncan," and "Ode sur la Fête du 10 Janvier 1799. Air: De la Bataille de Fontenoy" are preserved in Can. P.A. *Neilson papers*, I: 122, 143.

1118. CHURCH OF ENGLAND. LITURGY AND RITUAL

A FORM OF / PRAYER, / WITH / THANKSGIVING, / To be used on THURSDAY the 10th January, 1799, being the / day appointed for a / General Thanksgiving to / ALMIGHTY GOD, / For the late unexampled and most important VICTORY obtain- / ed by His Majesty's arms over the Fleet and Forces of the / Enemy. / [rule] / QUEBEC: / PRINTED AT THE NEW PRINTING OFFICE, GARDEN STREET, /

4to. 6 p., 1 *l.*; type-page: 18 × 14 cm. *Printed by R. Lelievre & P.-E. Desbarats, 1799* and advertised: "For sale at the New Printing Office, A Form of prayer [etc.] Quebec, Jan. 2, 1799."—*Quebec gazette*, Jan. 3, 1799.

Contents: p. [1], t.-p.; p. [2], blank; p. [3], half-title; p. [4]-6, A form of prayer; 1 *l.*, blank. The half-title includes instruction: ". . . The minister of every church shall give notice to his Parishioners publicly in the Church, at Morning Prayer, the Sunday before, for the due observation of the said day, by there and then reading His Majesty's Proclamation."

This *Form of prayer* was prepared by Bishop Mountain for use in the Church of England diocese of Quebec. It is reprinted in his *Sermon* of Jan. 10, 1799 (No. 1135). That day was appointed, as Gov. Prescott wrote the Duke of Portland, from Quebec, Jan. 8, 1799: "Receiving thru the American States Authentic Intelligence [of Nelson's victory at the Nile in Aug., 1798, I decided to appoint a day of thanksgiving to afford] a real Joy to the well-affected and . . . to impress on the minds of the Disaffected, such ideas of the Power and Supremacy of Great Britain, as might check their inclination in favour of the Enemy." Bishop Mountain and the Catholic coadjutor bishop, Plessis, agreed, Prescott wrote, so he called the Council and passed a proclamation. He enclosed Bishop Mountain's *Form of Prayer* and Bishop Denaut's (MS.) *Mandement* to the Catholic clergy.—Can.P.A. "Q", 82: 55.

Bishop Denaut's *Mandement* is printed in Têtu and Gagnon: *Mandements de Québec*, 2: 515-17. The sermons preached in Quebec were also published (No. 1135, 1140, 1142).

Copies located: CaOOA; GBLP (in C.O. 42/112: 125-32).

1119. CLERY, JEAN BAPTISTE CANT HANET, 1759-1809

JOURNAL / DE CE QUI S'EST PASSÉ / A LA TOUR DU TEMPLE, / PENDANT LA CAPTIVITE' / DE LOUIS XVI, / ROI DE FRANCE. / [rule] / Animus meminisse horret [5 dots] VIRG. / PAR M. CLERY, Valet de Chambre du Roi. / [rule] / QUEBEC: / IMPRIME' A LA NOUVELLE IMPRIMERIE. / [rule] / 1799. /

8vo. [*]^2, A-R^2; 1 p. l. 67, [2] p.; type-page: 17 × 10 cm.

Contents: p. l. recto, t.-p.; verso, blank; p. [1]-67, Journal; at end: p. [1] (verso of p. 67), Nota; p. [2] text of messages sent by Louis XVI to Marie Antoinette and the Dauphin; verso of p. [2], blank.

Printed by R. Lelievre & P.-E. Desbarats, from a new setting of type, with text unchanged, this is another edition of No. 1086.

Copies located: CaQ; CaQM; CaQMS (2 cop.); DLC; NN (p. [2] at end wanting); RPJ.

1120. [COBBETT, WILLIAM], 1762-1835

DEMOCRATIC PRINCIPLES / ILLUSTRATED / BY / EXAMPLE. / [rule] / BY PETER PORCUPINE. / [rule] / PART THE FIRST. / [rule] / Sixteenth Edition. / QUEBEC: / PRINTED AT THE NEW-PRINTING-OFFICE, / GARDEN STREET. / [rule] / 1799. / (Price 6d. Twelve for 5s. 6d. or 45s. per Hundred.) /

12mo. $[*]^8, *^4, B^4$; 2 p. l., [i], 25 p., 1 *l.*; type-page: 13.5 × 7.8 cm. Odd numbers on verso, even numbers on recto.

Contents: p. l. recto, t.-p.; verso, blank; p. l. 2 recto-verso, Address to the reader; p. [i] (recto of p. [1]), "the following facts are faithfully extracted from Authentic Documents . . ."; p. [1]-25, Democratic principles; 1 *l.* at end, blank.

This work was advertised (in English only) for P.-E. Desbarats, the printer: "Just published and for sale at the New Printing Office, Democratic Principles . . . by Peter Porcupine. Price 6d. 12 for 5/6; 45/ per hundred. Quebec, March 12, 1799."—*Quebec gazette*, Mar. 14, 1799.

It is a reprint of section 2 only, of Cobbett's *A bone to gnaw for the Democrats*, part 2. This section (the second of three published together at Philadelphia in Mar., 1795, Evans, no. 28434-5) is an account of the siege of Lyons and the slaughter of the Lyonese, by the army of the National Convention of France in 1793. Though this is the only 18th-century Canadian imprint of Cobbett discovered, his writings were frequently advertised by booksellers in Canada—where his nostalgic anglophilism and his antipathy to French revolutionaries were assured of attention from most of those who read newspapers and books of the day. Indeed, it is said that his political sympathizers in Canada later compensated Cobbett for the losses from the libel suit of Dr. Benjamin Rush, which ruinously concluded his American career (Cobbett's *Political register*, Apr. 10, 1830, quoted by E. I. Carlyle: *William Cobbett*, London, 1904, 72).

The text of this item has been reprinted frequently, e.g., as a section of *A bone to gnaw for the Democrats*, pt. 2, in *Porcupine's Works* (12 v., London, 1801), 2: 114-32; also with title: *A bone to gnaw for the democrats*, in *Selections from Cobbett's political works* (6 v., London, [1835]), 1: 37-45.

It is an interesting coincidence that Cobbett had lived in Canada, 1785-91, stationed with his regiment in Nova Scotia.

Copy located: CaQMS.

1121. DENAUT, PIERRE, *bp. of Quebec*, 1743-1806

CIRCULAIRE à Messrs les ARCHI-PRETES / LONGUEIL, 28 Novembre, 1799. / <Text> / P. Evêque de Québec. / Pour vraie copie.

fo. 2 *l.* text in 30 lines (type-page: 19.5 × 14.5 cm.) on recto of *l.* 1; *l.* 1 verso-*l.* 2, blank. *Probably printed at Quebec, by John Neilson, 1799.*

Text: "Monsieur, Depuis près de deux années, le Père commun des fidèles, Pie VI, est dans les fers. Des impiés ont osé porter leurs mains sacrilèges sur l'oint du Seigneur [etc.]."

This is a circular letter from Bishop Denaut to parish priests, ordering prayers, etc., for Pope Pius VI, in exile. The pope, a member of the league against Napoleon, had been taken prisoner when the French occupied Rome in Feb., 1798. He was removed to Florence, thence, in July, 1799, to the citadel at Valence, where his death occurred Aug. 29, 1799—of which news had not yet reached Quebec apparently.

This circular is reprinted in Têtu and Gagnon: *Mandements de Québec*, 2: 518-19.

Copies located: CaO; CaQQL.

1122. DICKSON, STEPHEN, *b.* 1761?

[Catalogue of Mr. Dickson's books, to be sold at auction by Burns and Woolsey, Quebec, April 19-20, 1799.]

Printed at Quebec, by John Neilson, 1799, as recorded:

"1799, Apr. 16. [Debit] Burns & Woolsey, printing 100 Catalogues of Mr. Dickson's Books.—17/6."—Can.P.A., *Neilson papers*, v. 54.

The sale was advertised: "By Auction will be sold . . . on the 19th & 20th Instants at Burns & Woolsey's Auction Room, 3 Pipes and 1 Hogshead London Particular Madeira . . . a very extensive Assortment of Dry Goods & Groceries and a large Collection of valuable Books, the property of a gentleman gone to England, Catalogues of which will be timely distributed. Clear Samples of the Liquors may be tasted at the Brokers . . . Quebec 9th April, 1799."—*Quebec gazette*, Apr. 11, 1799.

This may be a list of books belonging to Stephen Dickson, who, though he remained in Quebec but six months, and apparently lived in a small way, may yet have abandoned here, the library from which he proposed to endow a college to be established in Quebec (*see* No. 1123).

Copy located: None.

1123. DICKSON, STEPHEN, *b.* 1761?

CONSIDERATIONS / ON THE ESTABLISHMENT OF A / College IN Quebec / For the instruction of YOUTH in / LITERATURE & PHILOSOPHY. / BY / STEPHEN DICKSON / Honorary Doct. of Med. of the Univ. of Dublin / Fell. Roy. Soc. Scot. Antiq. Edin. Phys. & Med. / Fr. & Amer. Acad. Sci. Coll. Phys. Dub. &c. / lately state Physician of Ireland & Professor of / the practice of Physic in the University of Dublin. / [rule] / [rule] / [rule] / QUEBEC: / PRINTED AT THE NEW PRINTING / OFFICE, GARDEN-STREET. / 1799. /

?12mo. 14 p.; type-page: 12.8 × 6.6 cm.; p. 3 has sig: A2; p. 5: B.

Contents: p. [1], t.-p.; p. [2], blank; p. 3-14, Considerations, etc.

The author, apparently oblivious of the abortive Dorchester-Smith plan for a non-sectarian college, which had precipitated bitter controversies throughout the colony in 1790-91 (*see* No. 669) here presents a similar scheme. In the introduction he exhorts Canadians to establish a college to diffuse culture and knowledge of useful arts; then sketches a plan for its organization, with the king as patron; as visitors: the governor and bishop of Quebec (whether Church of England and/or Catholic is not specified); also trustees, a principal and professors. He outlines courses in the learned languages, history and civil policy, taste, moral philosophy, mathematical and natural philosophy, natural history, and chemistry; then later, divinity, law, and medicine. He describes the current modes of instruction by tutorial and public lecture and the equipment necessary for each course in each discipline. Dickson suggests financing this enterprise by funds from private subscribers, from the confiscated Jesuit estates in Quebec, and from government grant. He offers his own "humble but zealous exertions" in preparing a natural history collection and a meteorological observatory, in contributing instruments and scarce books and in giving courses of instruction.

The author seems to have been the Stephen Dickson who graduated from the University of Dublin (B.A., 1781; M.B. and M.D., 1793) and who was professor of the practice of medicine in that university's school of physics, 1792-98. He was active in academic and medical societies in Ireland and Scotland and author of several works on scientific subjects (Dublin University: *Alumni Dublinenses*, edited by G. D. Burtchaell and T. U. Sadleir, Dublin, 1935; also, Sir Charles A. Cameron: *History of the Royal college of surgeons in Ireland*, Dublin, 1886). He was apparently implicated in the Irish rebellion of 1798, and like many of his compatriots came to America in consequence.

The author of this pamphlet arrived in Quebec from New York about Oct. 24, 1798, and remained till about Mar. 5, 1799, under close surveillance of Authority. Gov. Prescott wrote: ". . . from Circumstances that have taken place in Ireland, from his not having announced himself (other than merely by his Christian and Surname) until some weeks after his Arrival, and from the retired manner in which he lives compared with what might be expected of a man in that station of Life—added to the Extraordinary Circumstances of a man in such eligible Situation in his own Country to seek his Fortune among strangers, I am induced to suspect that he may be actuated from motives different from any that he may be expected to avow. I am using necessary means to discover his real views and motives . . . should he prepare to depart I will not let him go without being previously examined [etc.]."

". . . He has within a few days past [of Jan. 7, 1799] published some Considerations respecting the Establishment of a College in this province, a copy of which I have the Honor to enclose herewith; It does not appear to me that this Country is yet Ripe for such an Establishment; nor Can I avoid considering it exceedingly Strange that a Man should leave the eligible Situation he appears to have held in his own Country upon so wild a Scheme [etc.]."—Prescott's despatches to the Duke of Portland, from Quebec, Dec. 12, 1798, Jan. 7, Mar. 5, 1799, in Can.P.A., "Q" 82: 32-68, 246.

Dickson, aware that he was regarded with suspicion, obtained an introduction to the Chateau, composed and published an impressive eulogy of its incumbents (*see* No. 1124), then, his ingenuousness neither established nor disproved, departed for Boston en route to England.

Chief Justice Osgoode wrote John King, undersecretary of state, from Quebec, Aug. 7, 1799: ". . . Doctor Dickson, the noted Irish partisan of whom such honourable mention is made in the Report of the Secret Committ^e of both Houses in Ireland . . . came here under every Circumstance of Suspicion . . . but his Merit and Talents brought him forward, and in return for Three Dinners a week at the Chateau he wrote a Poem called The Union of Science and Taste [sic], and talked of Prescott's reflecting 'Lustre on the Throne'. He took care to be off Scampato! alla fuga! before any intelligence respecting him could be received from Home. Genl. Hunter regretted he had not stayed a little longer."—Can.P.A., "C.O. 42", v. 22, p. 147.

Copy located: GBLP (in C.O. 42/112: 55-68, endorsed: "In Genl Prescott's [despatch] N°. 95, 7 Jan. 1799").

1124. DICKSON, STEPHEN, *b.* 1761?

THE UNION / OF / TASTE AND SCIENCE / A POEM: / TO WHICH ARE SUBJOINED A FEW ELUCIDATING NOTES / BY STEPHEN DICKSON Esqr. / QUEBEC / PRINTED BY JOHN NEILSON, N° 3 MOUNTAIN STREET / 1799 /

4to. [A-F]^2 1 p. l., 17, [3] p.; type-page: 20.7 × 12.7 cm.

Contents: p. l. recto, t.-p.; verso, blank; p. 1-17, The union; verso of p. 17, blank; p. [1-3] at end, Notes; verso of p. [3], blank.

A handsome production, printed in large (great primer?) type, with a brilliant impression on fine heavy wove paper. The poem, 298 lines of rhyming pentameters in four to ten line stanzas, has a simple theme—laudation of the governor—developed in an elaborate allegorical framework. It depicts the birth, development, and attainments of the man, Science, and the maiden, Taste, who become united in Europe, then sundered by war and reunited ultimately in Quebec in the persons of Gov. and Mrs. Prescott. The outlines of the narrative are filled in with classical allusions, pastoral descriptions, episodes of horror, patriotism, praise of the British constitution, and of the glory of Nelson. The poem begins:

"When Nature first at Heaven's almighty word
Smiling from chaos sprang with sweet accord
Through every nerve a secret influence stole
And Genius triumph'd o'er her inmost soul.
From her, untortur'd by maternal throes
Their eldest-born, immortal Science, rose.
. . . [the feats of Science through the ages are described]
Taste—a lovely nymph of tender years
Daughter of Beauty by a reverend sire,
. . . She oft has risen at earliest dawn
And sauntered on the dew bespangled lawn
Greeting the orient sun's inspiring beams
That tune the grove and animate the streams."

The influence of Taste is shown in nature, art, and literature, her marriage with Science, who, however, goes to war, and Taste, bereft, becomes disillusioned till Memory reminds her of:

" . . . the sequester'd scene
Where Canada enjoys her lov'd vice-Queen
. . . the wife, the mother and the friend
Learned Elegance and Love with Dignity to blend."

also:

"The veteran warrior, o'er whose laurel'd brow
The olive loves to shoot its foliage now . . .

Long may the honour'd union bless the land
Of Taste and Science! wide may they impart
The influence that refines and cheers the heart,
Yet nerves the soul t'establish as to feel
The public glory and the public weal!
And long may Canada exulting own
Prescotts reflecting lustre to the throne."

In *Notes*, the author states: "From the nature of the foregoing poëm, some allusions necessarily arose which may not be generally obvious. To elucidate these the author has subjoined a few notes for . . . his fair readers. The learned philosopher . . . should pass them by without spleen, as he does the toy-shop, or the perfume warehouse."

Copies located: CaQM; CaQMS (p. 15 to end wanting); CaQQL; Ketcheson.

1125. GRAHAM, HUGH, 1758-1829

[Two sermons entitled the Relation and relative duties of the pastor and people, delivered at the admission of the Reverend John Waddel to the Charge of the United Congregations of Truro and Onslow, by the Reverend Hugh Graham of Cornwallis. *Halifax, N.S., Printed by Anthony Henry, 1799.*]

12mo. 54 p. This work was advertised:

"In the press and speedily will be published, Two Sermons . . . Cornwallis. Printed by Anthony Henry and Sold by Wm. Kidston, Merchant, Halifax."

—*Royal gazette*, Halifax, N.S., Geb. 26, 1799.

It was advertised again as "Just published, Two Sermons [etc.]."—*ibid.* Apr. 23, 1799. It is described: "[On Nov. 16, 1798, Graham] presided at the induction of Mr. John Waddell to the collegiate charge of Truro and afterwards published the sermon and addresses he delivered on the occasion as well as the discourse he preached on the Sabbath following. This publication which now lies before us and which was printed at Halifax in 1799, proves him to have been [very eloquent indeed, etc.]." —James Robertson: *History of the mission of the Secession church to Nova Scotia and Prince Edward Island from its commencement in 1765* (Edinburgh, 1847), 37.

Graham, born in West Calder, Edinburgh county, Scotland, and educated at the University of Edinburgh, was licensed to preach by the presbytery of Edinburgh, 1781. He came to Nova Scotia in June, 1785, under the auspices of the Associate synod [Burgher] of the Secession church. He took charge of the Presbyterian congregation at Cornwallis till 1800, then at Stewiacke till his death. Though of the so-called Burgher group in the Secession church, Graham seems to have been on good terms with the "Anti-Burghers" stationed in Nova Scotia, e.g. Waddell, and that doughty controversialist, James M'Gregor, also with the Presbyterians of the Church of Scotland itself.

This work is recorded by Morgan in *Bibliotheca canadensis* as *Sermon and addresses delivered at the induction of the Rev. John Waddell* [*etc.*], also as *The relation and relative duties of pastor and people* [*etc.*]. *See also* Sabin, no. 28208, and R. J. Long *Nova Scotia authors.*

Copy located: None.

1126. [HUMBERT, PIERRE HUBERT], 1687-1779

INSTRUCTIONS / CHRÉTIENNES / POUR LES JEUNES GENS; / Utiles à toutes sortes de personnes; mêlées / de plusieurs traits d'histoires et d'ex- / amples édifians. / [rule] / Imprimé sur la 14e édition d'Avignon révue et corrigée. / [double rule] / Deuxieme Edition, / avec corrections. / [double rule] / QUEBEC: / CHEZ JOHN NEILSON, IMPRIMEUR-LIBRAIRE / n° 3 rue la Montagne 1799. /

12mo. A-2M[6], 2 N[4]; xvi, 405 [i.e. 406] p., 3 *l.*; type-page: 13.3 × 6.8 cm.; p. 320 mispaged: 319, numbering thereafter diminished by 1, with even numbers on recto.

Contents: p. [i], t.-p.; p. [ii], blank; p. iii-iv, Avertissement, Québec, 2e Décembre, 1799; p. v-xvi, Exercice spirituel; p. [1]-397, Instructions chretiennes; p. 398-405, Vêpres de dimanches; *l.* 1-2 recto, Table (contents); verso of *l.* 2, blank; *l.* 3 recto, Recommendation; verso, blank.

Recommendation: "Nous recommendons aux Fidèles de ce Diocèse l'usage de cette seconde édition des Instructions Chrétiennes pour les Jeunes-Gens; le prompt debit de la première ayant demontré combien la lecture leur en étoit avantageuse. [signé:] J. O. Plessis, Vic. Gén. Québec, 26 Octobre, 1800."

Like the first Quebec edition, this was issued in the year following the imprint date, as the bishop's *Recommendation* and the printer's advertisement indicate:

"On vient de publier à l'Imprimerie, l'Instructions chretiennes . . . 2e édition. Prix relié en mouton 3/; 33/ par la douzaine; relié en bougran pour les écoles 2/9; 30/ par la douzaine; Papiers fines reliés en veau 4/. Quebec, 16 Decembre, 1800."

—*Quebec gazette*, Dec. 18, 1800.

Copy located: CaOT (p. 265-268 wanting).

1127. [L'HOMOND, CHARLES FRANCOIS], 1727-1794

ELEMENS / DE LA / LANGUE LATINE, / A L'USSAGE [sic] DU / SEMINAIRE DES MISSIONS ETRANGERES DE QUEBEC. / [double rule] / Imprimé sous la direction de M.M. du Seminaire. / [double rule] / [printer's ornament] / QUEBEC: / [double rule] / CHEZ JOHN NEILSON, IMPRIMEUR-LIBRAIRE, / RUE LA MONTAGNE: 1799. /

8vo. pt. 1: A-E[4], F[2], G-Y[4]; 172 p.; pt. 2-3: A-Q[4]; 226 [i.e. 126] p., 1 *l.*; type-page: 15.5 × 9 cm.; pt. 3, p. 121-126 mispaged: 221-226.

Contents: pt. 1: p. [1], t.-p.; p. [2], blank; p. [3]-172, Elemens; pt. 2: p. 1-49, Syntaxe; p. [50], blank; pt. 3: p. 51-226 (i.e. 126), Methode; 1 *l.* blank.

This like No. 1128 is another edition of the latin grammar by L'Homond published in Montreal, 1796-97. This differs from No. 1128 in its title and first part only, pt. 1 in this (Neilson's) edition having the same order and arrangement of sections as in No. 1128, but with added detail and examples in each section. Pt. 2-3 was printed with the same text and from the same types as the Nouvelle Imprimerie publication. In the copies seen, it was printed throughout (excepting sig. P in pt. 1 on laid paper) on a soft coarse wove paper, showing an open mesh and the water mark 98. It is aptly described: "Joli volume, dont la typographie ne laisse rien à désirer."—Gagnon, *Essai de bibliographie canadienne*, 1: no. 1254.

It was apparently issued pt. 1 separately, also pt. 1-3 complete, near the end of the year. It was advertised:

"A Vendre à l'Imprimerie [i.e. Neilson's] Elements de la langue latine à l'usage du Séminaire des Missions étrangeres de Quebec. Imprimé sous l'inspection de M. M. du Séminaire. prix 5/. Quebec, 4 Dec. 1799."

—*Quebec gazette*, Dec. 5, 1799.

Copies located (*issued complete*): CaQM (well worn, in old, seemingly original, calf binding); CaQQL (clean and unused, bound in original golden linen-covered boards).

Copies located (*separate issue of pt. 1*): CaO; CaQMS. Both copies on original binding of brown ?canvas-covered boards).

1128. [L'HOMOND, CHARLES FRANCOIS], 1727-1794

ELEMENTS / DE LA / GRAMMAIRE LATINE. / [rule] / QUEBEC: / IMPRIMES A LA NOUVELLE IMPRIMERIE, / Rue des Jardins,—1799. /

pt. 1: 12mo. A-I[4], K[2]; 1 p. l., 76 [i.e. 74] p., 63-64 omitted in numbering; p. 68 mispaged: 8; 69: 99; pt. 2-3: 8vo. A-Q[4]; 226 [i.e. 126] p., 1 *l.;* p. 121-126 mispaged: 221-226; type-page: 15.5 × 9 cm.

Contents: pt. 1: p. l. recto, t.-p.; verso, blank; p. 1-76, Elements; pt. 2: p. 1-49, Syntaxe; p. [50], blank; pt. 3: p. 51-226 [i.e. 126], Methode; 1 *l.*, blank.

This is another edition of L'Homond's latin grammar. It differs from No. 1127, in its title and first part. Here, part 1 is printed from different setting of type, with the text somewhat simpler and lacking the illustrative detail and examples contained in Neilson's publication for the Seminary. Parts 2-3 are printed on inferior paper but from the same types as those of No. 1127. This work has the unattractive appearance of most early school books. The title-page lacks style—it looks like a bastard title really—the imprint added as an afterthought. The type is comparatively large—pica with brevier—and correctly set, but the pages, unleaded, with much italic, columnar matter, rules, etc., and frequently off register, repel the eye. The paper in the first part (laid paper with chain lines horizontal to the fold) is gray in tone and coarse in texture, with a rough absorbent surface blotching the ink.

The Nouvelle Imprimerie passed, in 1798, from Wm. Vondenvelden to Roger Lelievre & Pierre-Edouard Desbarats, both of whom formerly had worked for Neilson—with whom the new firm maintained close connections. Like No. 1127, this edition seems to have been issued pt. 1-3 complete, also pt. 1 separately.

Copies located (complete): CaO; CaQM; CaQQL ("Ex. A")—the last two copies in original binding, sheepskin with gray boards. Another copy not located, formerly owned by J. L. Hubert Neilson, Quebec, sold by Dora Hood, Toronto, *Catalogue no. 3*, Spring 1930, item no. 394 "in original boards and in excellent condition, $4.00." See also *ibid.*, no. 175.

Copy located (separate issue of pt. 1): CaQMJ (in original gray boards).

1129. LOWER CANADA. GRAND VOYER (*Quebec district*)

Caption title: Province du BAS-CANADA. / District de QUEBEC. } / GABRIEL ELEZEAR TASCHEREAU, Ecuyer . . . / . . . Grand Voyer du District de Quebec &c.&c. / A L'Inspecteur et aux Sous Voyers de la Paroisse de [blank] dans le Comté de [blank] /

fo. [3] p.; type-page: 26.5 × 20.5 cm. Text in French only. *Printed at Quebec by ?R. Lelievre & P.-E. Desbarats, 1799.*

Contents: p. [1-3], Ordres I-XXIV, donné à l'office de Grand Voyer à Quebec, 15 Avril, 1799; p. [3] at end: Observations; verso of p. [3], blank.

This is a renewal of orders of May 1, 1797, and Apr. 1, 1798, conformably to provincial statute, 36 Geo. III c. 9.

Copy located: CaQMS (blanks in title filled with place-names in MS.; Ordres signed in MS.: "G. E. Taschereau, g.v.").

1130. LOWER CANADA. HOUSE OF ASSEMBLY

JOURNAL / OF THE / HOUSE OF ASSEMBLY / OF / LOWER-CANADA. / From the 28th March to the 3d June, 1799, both days inclusive. / IN THE THIRTY-NINTH YEAR OF THE REIGN OF / KING GEORGE THE THIRD. / Being the Third Session of the Second Provincial Parliament of this / Province. / [royal arms] / [double rule] / QUEBEC: / PRINTED BY ORDER OF THE HOUSE OF ASSEMBLY, / AND SOLD BY JOHN NEILSON. / M.DCC.XCIX. /

French t.-p.:

JOURNAL / DE LA / CHAMBRE D'ASSEMBLE'E / DU / BAS-CANADA. / Depuis le 28e. Mars jusqu'au 3e Juin, 1799, inclusivement. / DANS LA TRENTE NEUVIEME ANNE'E DU REGNE DE / SA MAJESTÉ GEORGE TROIS. / Etant la Troisieme Session du Second Parlement Pro- / vincial de cette Province. / [royal arms] / [double rule] / QUEBEC: / IMPRIME' PAR ORDRE DE LA CHAMBRE D'ASSEMBLÉE, / ET A VENDRE PAR JOHN NEILSON. / M.DCC.XCIX. /

4to. [$_*^4$, A]-2K^4; 2 p. l., 263 p., 2 *l.;* type-page: 17.5 × 12.3 cm. Text in English and French on opposite pages.

Contents: p. l. 1-2, blank; p. [1], English t.-p.; p. [2]— blank; p. [3], French t.-p.; p. [4-5], blank; p. [6-11], Proclamations, etc.; p. [12]-263, Journal; verso of p. 263, blank; 2 *l.* at end, blank.

The House ordered that 100 copies of its *Journals* be printed in English and French for the use of members and that none but the printer so licensed print the same.—L.C. As. *Journal,* May 21, 1799.

The printer recorded this work:

"1799, May 27, [Debit] House of Assembly To printing the Journals of 1799, calculated to make 275 pages when printed and with the condition that the surplus or deficit shall be accounted for by the respective parties at the rate of the customary charge, viz. £125 for 300 pages.—£114.11.8."

—Can.P.A., *Neilson papers,* v. 54.

An *Index* was issued later (4to. A-D^4; [32] p., text in English p. [1-16], and French p. [17-32]). Though undated it was apparently printed later than the *Journal.* probably after the year 1800, but before 1820, and is only occasionally found with copies of the *Journal.*

Copies located: CaO; CaOOA; CaOT; CaQM; CaQMA; CaQMM; CaQQL; CaQQLH; CtY; DLC; GBLP (in C.O. 45/29); ICJ; ICN; MH; N (mint copy, uncut, unopened, sewn in original blue paper covers with blank leaves at both ends, complete); NN; RPJ (with index); WHi.

1131. LOWER CANADA. LAWS, STATUTES, *etc.*

Half-title: THE / PROVINCIAL STATUTES / OF / LOWER-CANADA, / Anno Regni GEORGII III. REGIS. / MAGNÆ BRITANNIÆ FRANCIÆ ET HIBERNIÆ TRICESIMO NONO. / HIS EXCELLENCY / ROBERT PRESCOTT ESQ; GOVERNOR. / Being the THIRD Session of the / SECOND Provincial Parliament of LOWER-CANADA. /

French half-title:

LES / STATUTS PROVINCIAUX / DU / BAS-CANADA. / Anno Regni GEORGII III. REGIS / MAGNÆ BRITANNIÆ FRANCIÆ ET HIBERNIÆ TRICESIMO NONO. / SON EXCELLENCE / ROBERT PRESCOTT ECUYER, GOUVERNEUR. / Etant la TROISIEME Session du / SECOND Parlement du BAS-CANADA. /

4to. [F]-M^4, $*^4$, P-S^4; [43]-141 p. type-page: 22 × 17 cm. Text in English and French on opposite pages. *Printed at Quebec by R. Lelievre & P.-E. Desbarats, 1799.*

Contents: p. [43], English half-title; p. [44], blank; p. [45], French half-title; p. [46-47], blank; p. [48]-141, Statutes 39 Geo. III c. 1-10, assented to, June 3, 1799. Like No. 1095 this was also issued as a part of *The provincial statutes*, v. 2 (No. 1051). The item "Printing 712 copies of the laws of the 3rd Session of the 2d Parliament [no specific charge given]" appears in Lelievre & Desbarats' bill to the government in the Public accounts for Apr.-Oct., 1799.—L.C. *State* C, Dec. 22, 1799.

Copy located: NN.

1132. LOWER CANADA. MILITARY SECRETARY'S OFFICE

[Notice to claimants of lots at William Henry] CASTLE OF ST. LOUIS, QUEBEC, 15th JANUARY, 1799. /

fo. [4] p.; type-page: 34 × 21 cm. type lines run lengthwise of page.

Contents: p. [1], Notice, Jan. 15, 1799, signed: "James Green, Mily. Sec.," that certain persons holding lots at William Henry (Sorel) on occupation certificates are to be given regular title, other claimants to said lots must represent their claim within six months; appended, p. [1-4] is a list of lot holders, lots, etc.

This leaflet was *printed at Quebec, by John Neilson,* as recorded:

"1799, Feb. 28. [Debit] Military Secretary's Office. Printing and distributing with the Gazettes 3 weeks, 1500 copies 1 Sheet Crown, L. Primer type, concerning Lots at Wm Henry.—£9.10.10."

—Can.P.A., *Neilson papers*, v. 54.

Copies located: CaO (bound in *Quebec gazette*, Jan. 31, 1799); CaOOA (bound in *Quebec gazette*, Feb. 14, 1799).

1133. LOWER CANADA. SUPERINTENDENT OF POST HOUSES

TABLE of MEASURED DISTANCES and POST FARES between QUEBEC and MONTREAL, under the ACT passed the 3d June, 1799.

Broadside: type-page: 33 × 15 cm. *Printed at Quebec, by John Neilson, 1799,* as recorded:

"[To] John Neilson for printing Table of Distances & Fares to be taken from Travellers, under Act of Provincial Parliament, by Order of Supt. of Post Houses—£3.16.6 Stg."—Provincial Accounts, Apr.-Oct. 1799, in Can.P.A., L.C. *State* C, Feb. 11, 1800.

This schedule of fares was prepared according to the rates established by 39 Geo. III c. 8, "An Act for granting further encouragement and a more ample allowance to the Maitres and Aides de Poste in this province." It was usually published in *The Quebec almanac*, and sometimes the schedule, printed broadside for use in post houses, etc., was issued also as a folded plate in the almanac.

Copies located: CaQQL (folded apparently as issued in *Quebec almanac for 1801*); DLC (prices inserted in MS. in New York currency).

1134. MONTREAL

[Views of Montreal: Two engraved prints]

Proposed publication was advertised: "By Subscription. Two engravings in Aqua Tinta comprehending the East and North west views of Montreal, the first essay of a Youth of 16 years of age and principally self-taught genius. The Drawings are to be sent to London in the fall and the plates executed by best artist that can be found.

"Subscription—one guinea, each View, to be paid on delivery of the print; List of Subscribers to be given with the print. dated: Montreal, Aug. 30, 1799."

—*Quebec gazette*, Sept. 5, 1799.

No further information on this work has been found, nor copy located.

1135. MOUNTAIN, JACOB, *bp. of Quebec*, 1749-1825

A / SERMON / PREACHED AT QUEBEC, / ON THURSDAY, JANUARY 10th, 1799; / BEING THE DAY APPOINTED / FOR A / GENERAL THANKSGIVING. / By JACOB, LORD BISHOP of QUEBEC. / TOGETHER WITH THE FORM OF PRAYER DRAWN UP UPON / THE OCCASION. / [double rule] / Published by Request. / [double rule] / QUEBEC: / PRINTED BY JOHN NEILSON, MOUNTAIN STREET. / 1799. /

8vo. [*][4], A-E[4], [F][2]; 2 p. l., xi, 35 p.; type-page: 15 × 8.5 cm. Sig. [F] is folded to form p. 35 and p. l., Errata slip is inserted to face p. l. 1.

Contents: p. l. 1 recto, half-title; verso, blank; p. l. 2 recto, t.-p.; verso, blank; p. i-ii, Request "To . . . the Lord Bishop of Quebec" to print sermon, signed by 31 gentlemen, Quebec, Jan. 11, 1799; p. iii-v, Bishop Mountain's reply, Quebec, Jan. 14, 1799; p. [vi], blank; p. vii-xi, A form of prayer; verso of p. xi, blank; p. 1-35, Sermon, text: Rom. c. 8, v. 31. If God be for us, who can be against us; verso of p. 35, blank.

The *Form of prayer* was also published previously by Lelievre & Desbarats (*see* No. 1118).

The *Sermon* demonstrates how God, the governor of nations, chastised the corrupt in ancient times: Judah, Israel, Assyria, Greece, Rome, and now, France; and how Great Britain is God's arm of chastisement. Though not without sin—notably a cold neglect of Christian doctrine and duty—Britain has just laws, purely administered, protects the freedom of individuals, encourages arts and commerce, and maintains an excellent army and navy. It is her glorious distinction to become the instrument of "banishing from men that spurious Philosophy which has deprived them at once of the benefits of Divine instruction and human Experience; and delivered them over to the darkness of Skepticism, and the wild Speculations of conjectural policy, which has dissolved all the bonds of order and society and under the specious names of Fraternity, Equality and Liberty, let loose all the plagues of tyranny and oppression, of assassination and plunder, of debauchery and atheism [etc.]." The lord bishop closed a thunderous denunciation of revolution by exhorting his hearers to distinguish themselves for their attachment to country, constitution, king, religion, and God.

Born in England, educated at Cambridge, Mountain entered the established church and received several ecclesiastical preferments through the friendly interest of Wm. Pitt. In 1793 he was appointed (the first) protestant bishop of Quebec—with the title lord bishop. His papers have been published: *Jacob Mountain, first lord bishop of Quebec: a summary of his correspondence and of papers related thereto . . . 1793-1799*, edited by A. R. Kelley, in Quebec, Provincial Archives: ***Rapport, 1942-43***, Quebec, 1943, 177-260.

Published Feb. 1, 1799, this *Sermon* was sold at 1*s.* 6*d.* the copy.

Copies located: CSmH (2 cop. uncut, with original stitching as issued); CaOOA; CaQM; CaQMM (mint copy); CaQMS; CaQQL; GBLP (in C.O. 42/112: 169-221); MB; MBA; MWA; NNHi; RPJ.

NEW BRUNSWICK. HOUSE OF ASSEMBLY

"The Journal of Assembly of the last [1798] and the present [1799] Session [were ordered] to be printed [in 200 copies] and Mr. Attorney General [Bliss], Mr. Younghusband and Mr. Gilbert [appointed] to be a committee to contract for and superintend the printing of the same."—N.B. As. *Journal*, Feb. 6, 1799.

These journals were actually printed, however, by John Ryan in 1801 (copies in CaN; CaNU; CaOOA (1798 only); and RPJ).

1136. NEW BRUNSWICK. LAWS, STATUTES, *etc.*

ACTS / OF THE / GENERAL ASSEMBLY / OF / HIS MAJESTY'S PROVINCE / OF / NEW-BRUNSWICK, / PASSED IN THE YEAR 1799. / [rule] / [royal arms] / [rule] / ST. JOHN: / Printed by JOHN RYAN, No. 58, Prince William-Street, / PRINTER to the KING'S MOST EXCELLENT MAJESTY. / [rule] / 1799. /

fo. [$*^1$, $**^2$], A-G^2; 3 p. l. [389]-416 p.; type-page: 23.7 × 14.3 cm. paged in continuation of No. 1096 apparently, p. [398] mispaged: [389] and the error continued in subsequent numbering.

Contents: p. l. 1 recto, t.-p.; verso, blank; p. l. 2 recto, half-title; verso, blank; p. l. 3 recto, Titles of the acts; verso, blank; p. [389]-416, 39 Geo. III c. I-XI, acts passed in the fourth session of the third assembly, Jan. 15-Feb. 8, 1799.

This work was printed in an edition of 300 copies, for which the printer charged £32 5*s.*—N.B. As. *Journal*, Feb. 5, 1801.

It was the first session's laws printed by Ryan since 1788, and the first with his imprint as king's printer; the next appeared in 1801, no session being held in 1800.

Copies located: CaOOA (p. 393-94, 401-402, mutilated); MH.

1137. NOVA SCOTIA. HOUSE OF ASSEMBLY

Journal and Proceedings of the House of Assembly.

Note: title not transcribed from copy.

fo. 5T-5 [i.e. 6] M²; 1 p. l., p. 313-82, paged in continuation of No. 1098; sig. [6A] appears as 2A; [6F-M] as 5F-M. *Printed at Halifax, N.S., by Anthony Henry, 1799.*

Contents: p. l. recto, t.-p.; verso, Proclamation; p. 313-82, Journal of the seventh assembly, June 7-July 31, 1799.

Copies located: CaNs; GBLP (in C.O. 217/73: 230-65d).

1138. NOVA SCOTIA. LAWS, STATUTES, *etc.*

[1799. Anno Tricessimo Nono Regis Georgii III Cap. I-XI. At the General Assembly of the Province of Nova Scotia, etc.]

Probably printed at Halifax, N.S., by Anthony Henry, 1799. Perpetual acts passed in the seventh session of the seventh assembly, June 7-July 31, 1799.

These acts appear, in full or by title, in *The statutes at large, passed in . . . Nova Scotia from . . . 1758 to . . . 1804, . . . [revised] by Richard John Uniacke* (Halifax, N.S., 1805). There is a possibility, indeed, that unlike this session's temporary acts, they were not printed in 1799, in view of the revised edition, already projected.

Copy located: None.

1139. NOVA SCOTIA. LAWS, STATUTES, *etc.*

Running title: [rule] / 1799. Anno Tricessimo Nono Regis, GEORGII III. CAP. I[-V]. / [rule] /

Caption title: At the GENERAL ASSEMBLY of the / Province of NOVA-SCOTIA, . . . / [5 lines] / . . . being the Seventh Session / of the Seventh GENERAL ASSEM- / BLY, convened in the said Province. / [rule] /

fo. sig. 5I-5N², 5M² [sic]; p. 515-538; type-page: 25 × 15 cm. paged in continuation of No. 1099. *Printed at Halifax, N.S., by Anthony Henry, 1799.*

Contents: p. 515-538, Cap. I-V temporary acts passed in the session June 7-July 31, 1799.

Copies located: CaO; DLC; GBLP (2 cop. in C.O. 219/19, p. 535-38 wanting in one copy).

1140. PLESSIS, JOSEPH OCTAVE, *bp. of Quebec*, 1763-1825

DISCOURS / A L'OCCASION / DE LA VICTOIRE REMPORTE'E / PAR LES / FORCES NAVALES DE SA MAJESTE' BRITANNIQUE / DANS LA MEDITERRANNE'E LE 1 et 2 AOUT 1798, / SUR / La Flotte Francoise. / PRONONCE' DANS L'EGLISE CATHEDRALE DE QUEBEC / LE 10 JANVIER 1799. / [rule] / Par Messire J. O. PLESSIS / Curé de Québec Coadjuteur-élu et Vicaire Général du Diocèse. / [rule] / PRRCEDE' [sic] DU MANDEMENT DE MGR. L'ILLUSTRISSIME ET REVEREN- / DISME P. EVEQUE DE QUEBEC. / [ornament] / A QUE-

BEC: / IMPRIME' AU PROFIT DES PAUVRES DE LA PAROISSE / ET SE VEND à L'IMPRIMERIE. /

Printed by John Neilson, 1799, who recorded the work:

"1799, Jan. 26. To printing 497 Copies Discours de M. Plessis, 2 sheets demy English type at £2.5 for the first and 12/6 for every additional hundred [per] Sheet—£9.10.

Folding & Stitching D° @ 1d.—£2.1.5.

[Total:] £11.17.5.

Creditor for Poor by 497 Copies *Discours de M. Plessis* to be sold on commission at 10 per centem at 1/ each—£24.17."

—Can.P.A., *Neilson papers,* v. 54.

8vo. A-D[4]; 3 p. l., 24 p., 1 *l.;* type-page: 15 × 8.7 cm. Last two leaves of sig. D are folded around A1-D2, to form half-title, and blank leaf at end.

Contents: p. l. 1 recto, half-title; verso, blank; p. l. 2 recto, t.-p.; verso, blank; p. l. 3 recto-verso, Mandement, by Bishop Pierre Denaut, Dec. 22, 1798; p. [1]-24, Sermon (text: Dextera tua, Domine, percussit inimicum. Votre main droite, Seigneur, a frappé l'ennemi.—Exod. 15); 1 *l.* at end, blank.

The sermon shows "firstly that this victory humbles and confounds France, secondly that it adds lustre to the glory of England, . . . and thirdly that it guarantees specially the happiness of this province." Under the last head, Plessis summarizes the advantages of living under British administration in Lower Canada over that of the former French régime, contrasting the lot of habitant and small tradesmen of the 1750's with that of their descendants of the 1790's. He touches upon free exercise of religion, popular participation in government, absence of heavy taxation, regulation of food supplies, adoption of English criminal code, and retention of *Coûtume de Paris,* and finally the government's respect for Catholic institutions and its sanction of the episcopal succession in Quebec.

Plessis, born in Montreal, was educated there and at the Séminaire de Québec. He entered orders, was consecrated priest in 1786 and succeeded Rev. Auguste-David Hubert as curé of Quebec in 1792. In Sept., 1797 he was chosen as coadjutor by Bishop Denaut, whom he duly succeeded as bishop of Quebec in 1806. Plessis became one of the most distinguished prelates and efficient administrators of the Catholic church in Canada. He achieved official recognition by the British government, for the Catholic church in Canada, and a seat in the Legislative Council of Lower Canada for its head. He was created the first archbishop and reorganized his vast diocese from Prince Edward Island to Upper Canada. His papers in the Archevêché de Québec are calendared by Abbé Ivanhoë Caron: *Inventaire de la correspondance de Mgr. Joseph-Octave Plessis, archévêque de Québec, 1797-1825,* in Quebec, Provincial Archives: *Rapport, 1927-28,* 213-316; *Rapport, 1928-29,* 89-208.

This work was reprinted: *Discours à l'occasion de la victoire . . . le 1 et 2 août, 1798 . . . prononcé . . . par Messire J. O. Plessis* [*etc.*] "Reimprimé par Dussault et Proulx, de Québec à 150 exemplaires sous les soins du Lt. Col. Mills, un gendre de Sir. H.-G. Joly, gouverneur de la Colombie Anglaise," 25 p. 8vo.—Gagnon: *Essai de bibliographie canadienne,* 2: no. 1624. Also: *Thanksgiving sermon . . . January 10th, 1799, by Monseigneur Plessis . . . Translated from the French by Sir Henri Joly de Lotbinière, K.C.M.G. Dussault & Proulx, Quebec, 1906,* 40 p. 8vo.—Toronto Public Library, *Bibliography of Canadiana,* no. 732.

Copies located: CaNsWA; CaO (2 cop.); CaOOA; CaOT; CaQ; CaQM; CaQMJ; CaQMM (2 cop.); CaQMS (3 cop.); CaQQL; GBLP (in C.O. 42/112: 255-84); RPJ.

1141. QUEBEC GAZETTE. CARRIER'S ADDRESS

VERSES / From the News-boy to his Customers. / [double rule] / 1st. JANUARY, 1800. / [double rule] / [? *Quebec, J. Neilson, 1799.*]

Broadside: type-page: 18 × 7 cm. Text in English only, 7 stanzas of 4 lines each. This carrier's address does not resemble those of the *Quebec gazette* in previous or succeeding years. But it is difficult to know where else it could have originated, or if it had originally a French side too. It has a sad little verse like the *Gazette's* address for 1796.

"Care enough—enough of Sorrow
Every mortal man has known:
Whilst we think upon to-morrow,
What we call'd to-day is flown.
[Etc.]."

Copy located: CaOA (bound in *Quebec gazette* at end of 1799).

1142. SPARK, ALEXANDER, 1762-1819

A / SERMON, / PREACHED / IN THE PRESBYTERIAN CHAPEL AT QUEBEC, /ON / THURSDAY, THE 10th JANUARY 1799, / BEING / THE DAY APPOINTED FOR A / GENERAL THANKSGIVING. / [double rule] / By The REV^{D}. ALEX^{R}. SPARK. / [double rule] / TO WHICH IS ADDED A FORM OF THANKSGIVING USED / ON THE OCCASION. / [rule] / QUEBEC: / PRINTED BY JOHN NEILSON, MOUNTAIN STREET. / 1799. /

8vo. A-D^{4}; 2 p. l., ii, 25 p.; type-page: 14.5 × 8.6 cm.

Contents: p. l. 1, recto, half-title; verso, blank; p. l. 2, recto, t.-p.; verso, blank; p. i-ii, Introduction; p. 1-22, Sermon, text: Genesis, 20: 11. "Abraham said, because I thought, surely the fear of God is not in this place; and they will slay me for my wife's sake"; p. 23-25, Form of thanksgiving; verso of p. 25, blank.

From the text, Spark derives the general proposition that a nation without religion has no public faith nor any steady principle of virtue. He shows in detail, evidences of the French revolutionists' repudiation of Christianity, deduces therefrom the immorality of their body politic and its menace to society, and concludes: "As we now have the satisfaction of seeing the arms of our Country repel the attacks and frustrate the ambitious projects of that apostate power, which hath erected the standard of Impiety and Atheism . . . So may we soon expect to find that power humbled [etc.]."

Like Bishop Mountain in the Church of England and Coadjutor Bishop Plessis to Catholics, Spark in the Church of Scotland, celebrates the battle of the Nile as the triumph of Christianity over atheism. His sermon, more temperate in style and more logical in structure than Mountain's, does not, like the latter, identify religion and the Church, nor the Church and the state, nor the ideal state with the British government.

This work was printed for the author and sold by the printer, on a percentage basis:

"1799, Feb. 22. [Debit] Alexander Spark, Printing 400 Sermons, making 2 Sheets demy paper Eng. Type—£8.5.

Folding & stitching d° @ 1^d —£1.13.4.
[Total:] £9.18.4.
Feb. 25, Cr.[edit] Alexander Spark By 400 Copies Sermon @ 1/3 on Commission at 10 per C^t —£25."

—Can.P.A., *Neilson papers*, v. 54.

Copies located: CSmH; CaNsWA; CaOOA; CaQQL; GBLP (in C.O. 42/112: 223-253); MWA.

1143. TOOSEY, ?PHILIP, *d.* 1797

[Catalogue of Mr. Toosey's books, to be sold at auction by Burns and Woolsey, March 1, 1799.]

Broadside. *Printed at Quebec, by John Neilson, 1799,* as recorded:
"1799, Feb. 25. [Debit] Burns & Woolsey, Printing 100 Catalogues Mr. Toosey's Books, 1 Sheet Crown Long Primer type—£1.17.6."

—Can.P.A., *Neilson papers*, v. 54.

The sale was advertised: "By Auction to be sold . . . Friday, February 15, [1799] at Stoneham Lodge, residence of the late Mr. Toosey, . . . [farming utensils, stock, furniture, also] On Friday March 1, [1799] at Burns & Woolsey's Auction Room [Quebec] will be sold such articles of Mr. Toosey as are in Town . . . [coach, clothing, etc., and] a number of valuable books, catalogues of which will be distributed previous to the Sale."—*Quebec gazette*, Jan. 24, 1799.

This was apparently the estate of Rev. Philip Toosey, for whom a sale (which did not include books) had been held in 1792. *See* No. 814.

Copy located: None.

1144. UPPER CANADA. EXECUTIVE COUNCIL

YORK, / COUNCIL-OFFICE, / JULY 3d, 1799. / [rule] / NOTICE is hereby gi- / ven, that the Town- / ships of Dereham and Nor- / wich, in the Western District / of this Province will be sold / in Blocks of four thousand / acres each, on the first of No- / vember next. Further parti- / culars will, in due time, be / published in the Upper-Ca- / nada Gazette. / John Small, C.E.C / [rule] / YORK: printed by W. WATERS & T. G. SIMONS. /

Broadside: 18 lines; type-page: 21.3 × 14 cm.

It was ordered in Council, July 3, 1799, that this "Advertisement be printed on Hand Bills and be also inserted in some of the New York, New Jersey and Pennsylvania newspapers."—Can.P.A., U.C. *State* B, p. 389.

Copy located: CaOT.

1145. UPPER CANADA. EXECUTIVE COUNCIL

YORK, / COUNCIL-OFFICE, / JULY 8, 1799. / WHEREAS many persons have settled upon Lands in different parts / of this Province, without having obtained any Authority, Licence, or Title so to do, such intrusion is injuri- / ous to the Right of the Crown, [etc., Orders, signed:] JOHN SMALL, / Clerk of the Executive Council. / [ornamental rule] / YORK, Upper Canada: Printed by WM. WATERS and T. G. SIMONS, Printers to the KING'S Most Excellent Majesty. /

Broadside: 42 lines; type-page: 46.5 × 36.5 cm.

The text contains orders (1) for ejection of unauthorized pitchers (or squatters); (2) for registration of claims to lands occupied with permission given at the time of the first settlement of the Home District; (3) for obtaining "regular assignment" of Lands held on "certificate" only (*see* Toronto Public Library, *Bibliography of Canadiana*, no. 740).

Copies located: CaOT (2 cop.).

1146. UPPER CANADA. EXECUTIVE COUNCIL

UPPER--CANADA. / [rule] / COUNCIL-OFFICE, / Sept. 24, '99. / [rule] / NOTICE is hereby given, / that the Townships of DEREHAM & NOR- / WICH, in the Western District of this pro- / vince, are to be sold in Lots of three thousand acres each, / exclusive of the Crown and Clergy reserves. There are / sixteen blocks in each township, numbered from one to six- / teen. The lands are of excellent quality, and lie between the River La Tranche and Lake Erie. / [etc., conditions and terms of purchase, signed:] JOHN SMALL, C.E.C. / [rule] / YORK: Printed by WM. WATERS & TITUS G. SIMONS, printers to the King's most excellent Majesty. /

Broadside: 31 lines; type-page: 26. × 15.5 cm.

Copies located: CaOT (2 cop.).

1147. UPPER CANADA. EXECUTIVE COUNCIL

Council-Chamber, Oct. 29, '99. / THE BOARD having rea- / son to believe, that very frequent FRAUDS have / been committed, by persons who are ENTITLED to land FREE of EXPENCE, having asked for, and received the / same two, or three times over: / ORDERED [etc., text, signed:] JOHN SMALL, C.E.C. / [ornamental rule] / YORK: Printed by WATERS & SIMONS, printers to the King's most excellent Majesty. /

Broadside: 22 lines; type-page: 23 × 15.5 cm.

Text: "Ordered that hereafter no petition be received [by the land board] from any person claiming [fee-free grant of land] as a U.E. [loyalist] or child of a U.E.; unless the same be signed by the petitioner in presence of a magistrate, and be accompanied by an affadavit by the petitioner," stating that he is twenty-one years of age or (if female) married and has not previously received land from the Crown in Upper Canada.

Copies located: CaOT (2 cop.).

1148. UPPER CANADA. HOUSE OF ASSEMBLY

[A Bill intituled An Act to amend and improve the Communication by Land and Water between the Lakes of Ontario and Erie.]

Printed at Niagara, U.C., by Sylvester Tiffany, 1799. This publication is recorded in the Accounts for 1799, in U.C. As. *Journal*, July 1, 1800:

> "[Credit] To Sylvester Tiffany, Printer, for printing a Bill intituled An Act to improve the communication by land and water between the lakes of Ontario and Erie pursuant to the Order of [June 25, 1799] last Session —£4.10."

Tiffany was not paid, however, for the Council refused to honour the Assembly's printing commitments, and this account appeared again July 3, 1801: ". . . Printing the Niagara Postage [i.e. Road] Bill—£4.10."

The bill, introduced in the Assembly, June 15, 1799, was based upon the petition of Robert Hamilton, George Forsyth, and Thomas Clark, praying for "the authority of Parliament [of Upper Canada] to enable them to make some necessary and extensive improvements on His Majesty's Highway leading from Queenstown to Lake Erie and to construct a Canal with locks to facilitate the passage of boats at the rapids of this latter place, and for authorizing them to collect a toll on the merchandise, peltries and stores benefitted in passing through these works, as an indemnification for the expenses of the original construction, and a fund for keeping the same constantly in repair." The Bill was amended in committee, tabled for three months, and on June 25, 1799, "ordered [to] be in the meantime printed, and . . . fifty copies . . . distributed among Members of this House for the information and opinion of their constituents upon the advantages thereof." In the following session petitions against the bill as "monopolous and oppressive" were read, June 12-14, 1800, and the bill dropped.—U.C. As. *Journal*, in Ontario Archives, *Report, 1909.* The project was revived in 1816, however, and the canal, begun by a joint stock company in 1824, was opened five years later as the Welland Canal. *See* Ernest A. Cruikshank: *The Centenary of the Welland canal*, in Welland county historical society *Publications*, no. 1, 35 p., Welland, 1924.

Tiffany advertised this work: "Just published. Price 1/6. N. York currency. The Bill to improve the Communication between Lakes Ontario and Erie by land and water."—*Canada constellation*, Niagara, U.C., Nov. 15, 1799.

Copy located: None.

1149. UPPER CANADA. LAWS, STATUTES, *etc.*

Running title: LAWS OF THE PROVINCE OF UPPER CANADA, / [rule] / CHAP. XVII [sic].

Caption title: An act to extend the provisions of an act passed in the second session of the first provincial parliament of Upper Canada entitled "An act to confirm and make valid certain marriages . . ."

4to. [*][2]; 29-31 p. type-page: 22 × 16 cm. Paged in continuation of No. 1072. *Probably printed at York, U.C., by Wm. Waters and T. G. Simons, 1799.*

Contents: p. 29-31, 37 Geo. III c. XVII, i.e. XVIII, "An act . . . marriages"; p. 31 verso, blank. Note at foot of p. 21: "The Royal Assent to this Bill was signified by Proclamation on the twenty-ninth day of December in the thirty-ninth year of

His Majesty's Reign and in the year of our Lord one thousand seven hundred and eighty-eight [i.e. 1798]."

This act, the eighteenth and last passed in the first session of the second provincial parliament, June 1-July 3, 1797, was reserved for royal assent and published for the first time in 1799. In later revised editions of the statutes it appears as 38 Geo. III c. IV. It authorized the celebration of marriage in Upper Canada by Church of Scotland, Lutheran, and Calvinist ministers. This rite had been legally solemnized hitherto by Church of England clergymen only—the privilege was extended later to ministers of other denominations.

Copy located: CaOTL.

1150. UPPER CANADA. LAWS, STATUTES, *etc.*

LAWS / OF / HIS MAJESTY'S PROVINCE / OF UPPER-CANADA, / IN / NORTH AMERICA, / ENACTED IN THE SECOND SESSION OF THE SECOND PARLIAMENT, IN THE / YEAR OF OUR LORD ONE THOUSAND SEVEN HUNDRED / AND NINETY-EIGHT, AND OF HIS MAJESTY'S / REIGN THE THIRTY-EIGHTH. / [rule] / HIS HONOR PETER RUSSELL, Esq; PRESIDENT. / [rule] / [royal arms] / [rule] / YORK, UPPER CANADA: / PRINTED BY WM. WATERS AND T. G. SIMONS, PRINTERS TO THE KING'S MOST EXCELLENT MAJESTY, 1799. /

4to. A^4; 7 p.; type-page: 22.3 × 16.6 cm.

Contents: p. [1], t.-p.; p. [2], blank; p. [3]-7, 38 Geo. III c. 1-3, acts passed in the second session of the second legislature, York, June 5-July 5, 1798; verso of p. 7, blank. Three additional acts passed in this session, were reserved for royal assent and published later, No. 1198.

This publication was advertised: "A few copies of the Laws of Second Session of the Second Parliament for sale at this [i.e. Waters & Simons'] Office. Also some excellent Honey, by the pound or larger quantity."—*Upper Canada gazette,* York, U.C., June 1, 1799, *et seq.*

Copies located: CaOTL; GBLP (in C.O. 42/324, 1798).

1151. UPPER CANADA. LAWS, STATUTES, *etc.*

LAWS / OF / HIS MAJESTY'S PROVINCE / OF / UPPER-CANADA, / IN / NORTH AMERICA, /ENACTED IN THE THIRD SESSION OF THE SECOND PROVINCIAL PARLIAMENT, / IN THE YEAR OF OUR LORD ONE THOUSAND SEVEN HUNDRED / AND NINETY-NINE AND OF HIS MAJESTY'S / REIGN THE THIRTY-NINTH. / [rule] / HIS HONOR PETER RUSSELL, ESQ. PRESIDENT. / [rule] / [royal arms] / [rule] / YORK, UPPER CANADA: / PRINTED BY WM. WATERS AND T. G. SIMONS, PRINTERS TO THE KING'S MOST EXCELLENT MAJESTY, 1799. /

4to. A-C^2; 11 p.; type-page: 22 × 16.5 cm.

Contents: p. [1], t.-p.; p. [2], blank; p. [3]-11, 39 Geo. III c. I-V, acts passed at York, June 2-29, 1799; verso of p. 11, blank.

Though possibly published in 1799, this work was advertised (for the first time?): "A few copies of the laws of the Second and Third Sessions of the Second Provincial

Parliament of Upper Canada, for sale at this Office."—*Upper Canada gazette*, Apr. 5, 1800.

Copies located: CaOTA (a mint copy uncut and unopened); CaOTL.

1152. UPPER CANADA GAZETTE, EXTRA

Upper Canada Gazette Extraordinary. . . . Saturday, January 12, 1799. /

Broadside: 110 lines, heading as above, and text (109 lines) printed in 4 col.; type-page: 40.5 × 24.7 cm. *Printed at York, U.C., by Wm. Waters & T. G. Simons, 1799.*

The text comprises accounts, dated London, Oct. 5-6, 1798, and New York, Nov. 31, 1798, of the Battle of the Nile, and includes excerpts from Nelson's despatches, dated Aug. 9, 1798. The accounts are reprinted from the *London gazette* and the *New-York mercantile advertiser*.

Copy located: CaOT.

1153. VIETS, ROGER, 1738-1811

A / SERMON, / PREACHED AT / SISSABOO, / NOW CALLED / WEYMOUTH, / IN / NOVA-SCOTIA, / On the 15th October, 1797. / [rule] / BY ROGER VIETS, / RECTOR OF DIGBY, AND MISSIONARY FROM / THE VENERABLE SOCIETY FOR THE / PROPAGATION OF THE GOSPEL / IN FOREIGN PARTS. / [rule] / SAINT JOHN: / PRINTED BY JOHN RYAN, FOR THE AUTHOR. / —1799.— /

8vo. [A]-B[4]; 15 p.; type-page: 16.8 × 9.2 cm.

Contents: p. [1], t.-p.; p. [2], Dedication "to the worthy Inhabitants of Sissaboo or Weymouth [etc.]"; p. [3]-15, Sermon, II Corinthians, 5, 20: We are Ambassadors for Christ, as though God did beseech you by us: We pray you in Christ's stead, be ye reconciled to God.; verso of p. 15, blank.

This pamphlet was published—as the imprint 1799 indicates—in the second year following the delivery of the sermon on Sunday, Oct. 15, 1797.

In theme and style the sermon has a touch of evangelism uncommon in work by clergymen of the Church Established in Nova Scotia. The author's mission field included those parts of the province where the gospel of the fiery New Light preacher, Henry Alline, had left a deep and lasting impression upon religious life. And this sermon was evidently prepared to bring non-churchmen into the Church. Viets exhorts all to come to Christ, to prepare themselves for eternity through observance of Church of England prayers and fasts—the form and significance of which he describes—and through private communion with God. He stresses the precedence of spiritual preoccupations over temporal affairs, and unlike most preachers of the period in Canada, he omits mention of loyalty, patriotism, and public events. He even refers but obliquely to iconoclasm in France—enjoining his hearers to avoid baneful contagion, to shun rationalists, who by word and evil deeds deny God, and heap up wrath to come. He closes with a final exhortation to embrace salvation and avoid eternity of torment in everlasting burnings. Viets, loyalist and Anglican though he was, had been bred a Connecticut Congregationalist and this sermon shows a *via media* between two ways of religious life in colonial America.

Copy located: CaNsWA.

1154. ALMANACS. LOWER CANADA

CALENDRIER pour l'Année 1801, pour QUEBEC, par les 306$^{d.}$30$^{m.}$ de Longitude, et 46$^{d.}$55$^{m.}$ de Latitude. / [rule] /

Colophon: QUEBEC: Imprimé à la Nouvelle Imprimerie. /

Broadside: type-page: 59.5 × 45.5 cm., including calendar tables within ornamental rule frame, 47 × 45.5 cm. *Printed by P.-E. Desbarats, 1800.*

Contents: Les signes, calendrier, tableaux des comptés, tide tables, etc., as in No. 920.

Copy located: CaO (bound in *Quebec gazette*, at end of 1800).

1155. ALMANACS. LOWER CANADA

[Calendrier pour l'année 1801 pour Québec, *Québec, chez Jean Neilson.*]

Broadside. This almanac was advertised: "Publié et à vendre Le Calendrier de Québec . . . 1801, contenant les Notes communes ci-après et plusieurs Tables utiles. Prix 7½d. 5/ par douzaine."—*Quebec gazette*, Dec. 18, 1800. There is no indication that the *Calendrier* was published also in an English edition, as in the previous year.

Copy located: None.

1156. ALMANACS. LOWER CANADA

THE / QUEBEC ALMANAC / FOR / THE YEAR 1800. / N:LAT: 46d: 55m:--W.LONG: 69d:46m. / [double rule] / QUEBEC: / PRINTED BY JOHN NEILSON, / MOUNTAIN STREET. /

French t.-p.:

ALMANACH / DE QUEBEC, / POUR L'ANNEE 1800. / Par les 306° 30′ long. et 46° 55′ lat. / [double rule] / QUEBEC: / DE L'IMPRIMERIE DE J:NEILSON, / RUE LA MONTAGNE. /

18mo. A-C^{18}, D^{9}, E^{5}; 130, [5] p., 2 fold. tables; type-page: 10.8 × 6 cm.

Contents: p. [1], English t.-p.; p. [2], blank; p. [3], French t.-p.; p. [4]-35, Epochs, eclipses, tide tables, calendar, etc.; p. 36-37, Why 1800 is not a leap year; p. 38-49, De la météorologie; p. 50-79, Provincial regulations and information as in preceding years' almanacs; p. [80], blank; p. [81]-102, Civil list, etc.; p. 103-117, Militia; p. 118-30, Ecclesiastical state, etc.; p. [1-5] at end, Contents table; verso of p. [5], blank. Fold. tables: "Table of distances and post fares between Quebec and Montreal," and "Termes des cours de justice," are inserted after p. 54 and 62 respectively.

This almanac was advertised as just published and for sale at 2*s*. the copy, 20*s*. the dozen in the *Quebec gazette*, Jan. 23, 1800.

Copies located: CaOOA (p. [5] at end wanting and supplied in MS.); CaQ; CaQMC; CaQMS; CaQQAr; CaQQL.

1157. ALMANACS. LOWER CANADA

THE / QUEBEC ALMANAC / FOR / THE YEAR 1801. / N:LAT: 46d: 55m:--W:LONG: 69d: 46m: / [double rule] / QUEBEC: / PRINTED BY JOHN NEILSON, / MOUNTAIN STREET. /

French t.-p.:

ALMANACH / DE QUÉBEC, / POUR L'ANNÉE 1801. / Par les 306° 30′ long. et 46° 55′ lat. / [double rule] / QUEBEC: / DE L'IMPRIMERIE DE J: NEILSON, / RUE LA MONTAGNE. /

12mo. A-E[12], F[9]; 132, [6] p., 2 fold. tables; type-page: 10.8 × 6 cm.

Contents: p. [1], English t.-p.; p. [2], blank; p. [3], French t.-p.; p. [4-33], Epochs, eclipses, tide table, calendar, etc.; p. 34-41, Liste généalogique des maisons de l'Europe; p. 42-66, Tide, money and other tables, provincial regulations and information as in *The Quebec almanac* for 1798 and 1799; p. 67-88, Civil list; p. [89-90], blank; p. [91]-116, Military register, etc.; p. 117-32, Ecclesiastical state, etc.; [p. 1-6] at end, Contents table. Fold. tables, "Termes des cours de justice," "Table of measured distances and post fares between Quebec and Montreal, under the act passed the 3d June, 1799," are inserted after p. 54 and 132, respectively.

This almanac was advertised: "Just printed and may be had on Monday next [Dec. 29, 1800] the Quebec Almanac for the year 1801, [etc.]."

—*Quebec gazette,* Dec. 25, 1800.

Copies located: CaOOA; CaQ; CaQM; CaQMC; CaQMS; CaQN; CaQQA; CaQQAr; CaQQL.

1158. ALMANACS. NOVA-SCOTIA

AN / ALMANACK / FOR THE / Year . . . 1801; / . . . / CALCULATED FOR THE MERIDIAN OF / HALIFAX . . . / . . . / CONTAINING / THE ECLIPSES [etc. 8 lines in col. 1] / SITTINGS of the COURTS [etc. 8 lines in col. 2] / . . . / [rule] / By THEOPHRASTUS. / [rule] / HALIFAX, / Printed and Sold by JOHN HOWE, at his Printing-Office / in George Street, near the Parade. / [title and each page within double rule frame]

12mo. A[4], B-C[6]; [32] p.; type-page: 14.3 × 8 cm.

Contents: p. [1], t.-p.; p. [2], Ship signals; p. [3], Eclipses; p. [4], Ephemeris; p. [5-16], Calendar; p. [17-22], Nova Scotia provincial officials, courts; p. [23-24], Masonic lodges in Nova Scotia; p. [25], Clergy; p. [26-30], Naval, army and militia officers in Nova Scotia; p. [31-32], Distances from Halifax, etc.

Copies located: CaNs; CaNsHA (2 incomplete cop., one cop. lacks p. [1-2, 7-8]; the other lacks p. [17-20, 25-30]); CaOOA.

1159. ALMANACS. NOVA SCOTIA

[The Nova-Scotia Calender, or An Almanack; for the year . . . 1801 . . . *Halifax, N.S., Printed by Anthony Henry.*]

The following advertisement appeared in Henry's newspaper: "Just published and for sale at this Office, An Almanack for the Year 1801, also The German Almanack."—*Royal gazette, Halifax, N.S.,* Dec. 9, 1800. It refers apparently to the *Nova-Scotia Calender or An Almanack* which Henry had published regularly about this time of year, since 1768, and its German edition, *Der Neuschottländische Calender,* published 1788-91 and perhaps subsequently also. If so, the advertisement marked the end of the series, for Anthony Henry died after a short illness on Dec. 1, 1800.

Copy located: None.

1160. ALMANACS. UPPER CANADA

[The Upper-Canada Pocket Almanac for the Year 1801, *printed at Niagara, U.C., by Sylvester Tiffany.*]

50 p. This almanac was advertised:

"For Sale, The Upper-Canada Pocket Almanac for the year 1801, containing zodiac, eclipses, vulgar notes, calendar; Register of civil officers, &c.&c. &c., towns, counties and districts; Military and naval departments; Miscellanies:—The Probability of human life, Anecdotes, tales, Informations &c. Distances. In some parts the information is imperfect being all the Publisher could obtain. [The almanac is] enlarged to 50 pages this year . . . sold at 2 / retail [etc.]."—*Niagara herald,* Jan. 24, 1801 (earliest issue seen).

Copy located: None.

1161. BAPTIST ASSOCIATION OF NOVA SCOTIA

[Articles of faith and practice. ? *Printed at Halifax, N.S., 1800?*]

A resolution to print "our church articles of faith and practice" was included in the Minutes of the fourth conference at Lower Granville, N.S., June 23-24, 1800, of the Baptist Association of Nova Scotia,—Saunders: *infra,* p. 89, but no further evidence of publication has appeared.

The Association was formed at a meeting of Baptist and Congregationalist ministers at Cornwallis, N.S., July 12, 1797, and the plan or constitution prepared by Edward Manning was adopted at the 1800 meeting. The latter was printed in Silas T. Rand: *Historical sketch of the Nova Scotia Baptist association, read at Wolfville on Monday, June 25, 1849, being the fiftieth anniversary* (31 p., Charlottetown, P.E.I., 1849), 8-11.

Edward Manning, 1766?-1851, came as a child from Ireland to Falmouth, N.S. Here in 1776 he heard the New Light preacher, Henry Alline, and grew up himself to become a founder of the Baptist church which developed from Alline's work in Nova Scotia. *See* Edward Manning Saunders: *History of the Baptists of the Maritime provinces* (520 p., Halifax, N.S., 1902), 84 *et seq.* Manning's MS. papers are in the library of Acadia University, Wolfville, N.S.

Copy located: None.

1162. BONNEFONS, AMABLE, 1600-1653

LE PETIT / LIVRE DE VIE / qui apprend à bien vivre / ET A BIEN PRIER DIEU. / Contient plusieurs Offices, Litanies, In- / dulgences, Exercises de dévotion; les / sacres paroles de Jésus-Christ, de ses Saints / & de Gerson; et le moyen de / bien profiter des maladies, ou autres / peines de cette vie. / [rule] / Avec les Méditations pour tous les jours de / la Semaine, & un Calendrier Sacré. / Nouvelle Edition, corrigée et augmen- / tée de la Dévotion des Elus. / Par le R.P. AMABLE DE BONNEFONS, / de la Compagnie de Jesus. / [printer's ornament] / QUEBEC: / Imprimé à la Nouvelle Imprimerie. / [rule] / 1800 / [rule] / AVEC APPROBATION. /

A-2L⁸, 2M⁴; 546, [5] p.; type-page: 8.5 × 4.7 cm.; 5 woodcut illustrations 5 × 4.4 cm.; p. 261 mispaged: 161; 514-515: 314-315.

Contents: p. [1], t.-p.; p. [2-3], Fêtes mobiles; p. 4-13, Calendrier; p. [14], blank; p. [15]-546, Instructions chrétiennes, etc. at end: p. [1], blank; p. [2-4], Table (contents); p. [5], Approbation, dated and signed: "Quebec, 1er Août, 1796. Jean François [Hubert], Ev. de Québec"; verso of p. [5], blank.

Copy located: CaQQL (in old red morocco binding). Another copy not located, but recorded in J. B. Learmont sale, pt. 2, New York, Apr. 16-19, 1917, Anderson Galleries catalogue no. 1297, item no. 1613, ". . . old calf, 2 leaves damaged [etc.]."

1163. BOUCHER-BELLEVILLE, JEAN BAPTISTE, 1763-1839

[Recueil de Cantiques, à l'usage des Missions, des Retraites, et des Catéchismes. Troisième édition. *A Québec: chez John Neilson, 1800.*]

A third edition of this work was prepared in 1800 by John Neilson, who printed the first edition in 1795, the second in 1796, and the fourth in 1804.

A third edition of *Recueil des Cantiques* was suggested by the author who wrote to John Neilson from Laprairie, Feb. 15, 1800: ". . . Je serai à votre service pour en préparer une nouvelle [édition] où je ferai entrer le supplement dans le corps de l'ouvrage, où je propose aussi de faire quelques additions et retranchements et surtout de faire disparaître les Fautes qui se sont glissées dans la dernière [etc.]." On Mar. 1, Boucher suggested the further addition of "les prières pour la messe," and on May 12, 1800, he wrote Neilson that he had sent copy for the printer. The work was published about a year later. For Boucher wrote Neilson ". . . J'ai reçu hier au soir 1er May [1801] vos deux Douz. Cantiques dont je vous remercie de nouveau. L'édition est très jolie, et il n'y a que peu de fautes. Le papier, le format, tout en est beau [vous allez dire] tout est beau [excepté les vers.] Vous êtes un malin [etc.]."

—Can.P.A., *Neilson papers,* I: 170, 174, 275.

The third edition was probably similar in size to No. 981, containing the same material rearranged and corrected, with a few additions. Bishop Denaut's approbation to the third edition was reprinted in the fourth edition (copies seen at CaQM and CaQQL): "Nous approuvons la troisième édition du Recueil des Cantiques . . . donné à Longueil le 7me mai 1800. P. Evêque de Québec."

Though issued early in 1801, this work began printing in 1800, and probably bore that imprint.

Copy located: None.

1164. CASOT, JEAN JOSEPH, 1728-1800

[Portrait. *Printed at Quebec, by John Neilson, 1800.*]

This ?engraving was advertised: "A few first impressions of a portrait of Rev. Pere Casot. Price 1/6. Also a few proof impressions of the same Portrait, Price 5/ [for sale by John Neilson].—*Quebec gazette,* Nov. 20, 1800.

Father Casot, a Jesuit, came to Quebec in 1756, and remaining after the English conquest and suppression of the order in Canada, he died, Mar. 18, 1800, the last of la Compagnie de Jésus en la Nouvelle France.

Copy located: None.

1165. CATHOLIC CHURCH

[An Abridgement of Christian doctrine. ? *Printed at Quebec, by John Neilson, 1800.*]

This work was advertised: "Just published and for sale at the Printing Office [of John Neilson], An abridgement of Christian doctrine (according to the tenets of the Church of Rome) Published for the use of the Diocese of Quebec. Price 7½d. each, stitched in marble cover."—*Quebec gazette,* Nov. 20, 1800.

Copy located: None.

1166. CATHOLIC CHURCH. LITURGY AND RITUAL

GRADUEL / ROMAIN / A L'USAGE / DU DIOCESE DE QUEBEC. / A QUEBEC. /

12mo. [*][4], A-R[12], S[8], a-i[12]; viii, 424, ccxvi p.; type-page: 14.4 × 7.2 cm. Square note music throughout. p. 15 appears as 1; 52: 2; 64: 4; 68: 8; 169: 1 9; 201: 101; 205: 20; 214: 114; xxij: xxj; lxxviij: xxviij; c: cx; cvij: cvi; cxiij: cxlij; cl: c; clxiv: civx.

Contents: p. [i], t.-p.; p. [ii], blank; p. [iii]-viii, Table (contents); p. 1-424, Messes des dimanches et fêtes; p. j-cvi [i.e. cvii], Le commun des saints, etc.; p. cvi [i.e. cvii]-clxiv, Kyrie, etc.; cxliv-cl, Messe Royale du Mr. H. Dumont; cl-clvij, Messe Baptise de M.J. Bapt. de Lully; clvij-clxxij, Messe de M. l'Abbé Bonaud; clxxij-clxxxviij, Messe dite la Recollette; clxxxix-cc, Messe trompette dite de Bordeaux; ccj-ccvij . . . Gloria patri, etc.; ccviij-ccxvj, Litanies majeurs [etc.].

This *Graduel* has a curtailed imprint: "A Quebec," but it is without date of printing or name of printer, without bishop's Approbation or any other indication of the time or place of publication. Its typography has the appearance of early 19th rather than 18th-century work in Canada. Both music and letter-press are printed from well-worn types. It may have been printed abroad for issue in Quebec, with space left at foot of t.-p. for name of local printer or "publisher."

The only copy seen, bound in old worn calf is inscribed on the t.-p.: "Léon Vohl," also in a later hand: "C. Vohl, 1857." This copy was purchased by the Toronto Public Library from the estate of Gerald E. Hart, 1890, and bears on a fly-lead a MS. note in Hart's hand: "Gagnon's copy [of No. 1167] bears the imprint, J. Neilson, 1800. I believe this copy preceded it." Hart's opinion is controverted by Neilson's statement in his preface that his edition was the first attempt of its kind in Canada.

Copy located: CaOT.

1167. CATHOLIC CHURCH. LITURGY AND RITUAL

LE / GRADUEL / ROMAIN / A L'USAGE DU / DIOCESE DE QUEBEC. / [double rule] / [printer's ornament] / [double rule] / A QUEBEC: / CHEZ JOHN NEILSON, IMPRIMEUR-LIBRAIRE: / No. 3, RUE LA MONTAGNE, 1800. /

12mo. a[6], A-2F[6], 2F*-2F7*[6], 2G-3C[6], 3D[2]; 6 p. l., 431, ccxlv [i.e. ccxliv] p.; type-page: 15.7 × 8.4 cm.; p. ccxliv mispaged: ccxlv. Square note music throughout.

Contents: p. l. 1 recto, t.-p.; verso, blank; p. l. 2 recto-3 recto, Preface; p. l. 3 recto-verso, Errata; p.l. 4 recto-6 verso, Table (contents); p. 1-431, Graduel; verso of p. 431, blank; p. j-ccxlv, Commun des saints, etc.

This *Graduel* differs slightly in content and order from No. 1166, and is printed apparently throughout from another setting of type.

The preface states: "... nous presentons au Public une édition de Livres de Chant portatifs imprimé à Québec, et conformés à l'édition des grands livres de Lyon, la plus correcte et la plus recente qu'on l'on connoisse. C'est le premier essai de ce genre qui ait été fait en Canada ... On va mettre immédiatement sous presse le Vesperal ou Antiphonaire et le Processional. Ce dernier qui est le supplement du Vesperal et du Graduel, sera imprimé le premier, parce qu'il renferme des choses essentiales [etc.]."

Proposals to print the *Graduel* and *Vesperal* (when four hundred copies had been subscribed) had been made by Neilson nearly three years earlier: "Annonce—Plusieurs personnes de differentes paroisses ayant paru de désirer se procurer le Graduel et le Vesperal Romain portatifs, l'Imprimeur informe le public, et particulariment MM les Curés et autres ecclesiastiques qu'il est disposé à entreprendre l'impression et publication des dits graduel et Antiphonaire Romain en 8vo. sur le modèle de l'édition de Vannes, en ajoutant à l'un et à l'autre les offices propres au Diocèse de Québec ... Les deux volumes bien reliés, se vendront ensemble pour la modique prix d'Une demi-guinée [etc.]."—*Quebec gazette*, Nov. 23, 1797, *et seq.*

After publication this work was advertised: "Recemment publié et à vendre à l'Imprimerie, N° 3 Rue de la Montagne, Le Graduel Romain ... Prix relié, papier ordinaire 7/6 ... papier velin 10/ [etc.]."—*Quebec gazette*, Sept. 18, 1800.

Its companion volumes were also published: *Le Processional Romain* in 1801 and *Le Vesperal Romain*, 1802 (Dionne 1: 63, 68).

Copies located: CaQM; CaQMJ; CaQQL; Ketcheson; NN; RPJ.

1168. CATHOLIC CHURCH. LITURGY AND RITUAL

THE / SINCERE CATHOLICK'S / COMPANION. / [double rule] / SECOND EDITION / printed according to the edition of 1778. / [double rule] / QUEBEC: / Printed by JOHN NEILSON, Mountain street. / 1800. /

18mo. A-B^{6}, C-G^{12}, H^{6}; 68, 83 p., 2 *l.*; type-page: 11 × 5.6 cm.

Contents: p. [1], t.-p.; p. [2], blank; p. [3-9], Holy days, Quebec [etc.]; p. [10], blank; p. [11]-68, Prayers [etc.]; p. [1], half-title: An abstract of the Douay catechism; p. [2], the ABC; p. [3]-83, the Douay catechism; verso of p. 83, blank; [at end:] *l.* 1 recto, Approbation dated and signed: "Quebec, 17th Nov. 1800, J. Plessis, Vic. gen."; verso, blank; *l.* 2, blank.

This work was announced: "In press and soon will be published, The Sincere Catholic's Companion Second edition, printed according to the edition of 1778, to which is affixed An Abstract of the Douay Catechism. Price 1/8 each."—*Quebec gazette*, Nov. 20, 1800. It was advertised (for the first time) as "Just published" —*ibid.*, Feb. 26, 1801.

Copy located: CaQQL.

1169. A COLLECTION OF THE ACTS ... RELATIVE TO CANADA

A Collection / OF THE / ACTS PASSED IN THE PARLIAMENT / OF / GREAT BRITAIN / AND OF / OTHER PUBLIC ACTS / RELATIVE TO /

CANADA. / [royal arms] / QUEBEC: / PRINTED BY P.E.DESBARATS, / LAW-PRINTER TO THE KING'S MOST EXCELLENT MAJESTY. / [rule] / 1800. /

This is a miscellaneous group of documents comprising remainder sheets of official publications printed in Quebec, 1795-1800, and issued with a common t.-p. Different copies have slightly different order and combinations of documents. In some cases, the remainder sheets apparently having been exhausted, the document has been reprinted verbatim, including the original t.-p. on paper obviously made later than the date of imprint.

This collection, first issued in 1800, was also issued from time to time later, with the same 1800 title-page, or with an 1824 t.-p. or an 1834 t.-p. These later issues include also later documents, 1801-39. The volume occasionally appears with binder's title: "Public Acts, vol. O." or "Lower Canada Statutes, vol. O" in a file of Canada, or Lower Canada, sessions laws.

Those pieces in the *Collection* known to have been printed before 1801 are described in this Bibliography under the year of their printing or their apparent printing. For the later documents *see* C. R. Brown, *Bibliography of Quebec or Lower Canada law*, 16-17, also G. Ducharme, Montreal: Catalogue no. 33, Mar., 1929, item no. 14557. The earlier publications most commonly found in the *Collection* are: Capitulations —No. 1174. 14 Geo. III c. 83, 88, and 31 Geo. III c. 31—No. 1040. Ordinances [1777-92] . . . now in force—No. 942. Proclamation . . . of the 31st Geo. III [c. 31] —No. 1184. A Treaty of amity—No. 986. Order in council of the 7th July, 1796— No. 994, also No. 1179. Order in council for further regulating the Inland Navigation [Aug. 22, 1797]—No. 1046.

Copies located: Most public and private libraries of Canadian or legal publications include one or more copies of *A Collection of the Acts* [etc.]. Few of the copies contain precisely the same combination of documents. But the following collections are among those whose copies include some 18th-century Canadian-printed work. CSmH; CaO; CaOOA; CaOT; CaOTL; CaOTO; CaQM; CaQMJ; CaQMM; DLC; Ketcheson; M; MH; MWA; MiD-B; MiU; N; NNB; RPJ; WHi; Witton.

1170. DENAUT, PIERRE, *bp. of Quebec*, 1743-1806

PIERRE DENAUT, / par la Miséricorde de / Dieu, & la grace du St. Siège Apostolique / Evêque de Québec, &c.&c.&c. à tous les / Curés, Vicaires, Missionaires, et à tous les / fidèles de ce Diocèse, Salut & Bénédiction en / Notre Seigneur. /

fo. [3] p.; type-page: 26 × 14.5 cm. *?Printed at Quebec, by John Neilson, 1800.*

Contents: p. [1-3], A circular letter, ending: "Donné à Longueuil" signed in MS.: "9 mai 1800. P. Evêque de Québec. J. J. Lartique D^{cr} Sec^{r}"; verso of p. [3], blank.

The letter gives notice of, and instructions for, the bishop's visitation throughout the diocese, with blanks in the printed text for details of places and times to be inserted in MS. The schedule of his itinerary (but *not* the text of this letter) is given in Têtu and Gagnon: *Mandements de Québec*, 2: 519-20.

Copy located: CaQQL.

1171. DENAUT, PIERRE, *bp. of Quebec*, 1743-1806

Marginal title: Mandement de Mon- / seigneur l'Evêque de / Québec pour un Te / Deum &c. /

Caption title: PIERRE DENAUT PAR LA MISERICORDE / DE DIEU ET LA GRACE DU S.SIEGE APOS- / TOLIQUE, EVEQUE DE QUEBEC &c. &c. A / tous les Prêtres, Curés, Vicaires, Missionaires / et à tous les Fidèles de notre Diocèse Salut et / Bénédiction. /

4to. 2 *l.* with text on recto and verso of *l.* 1, *l.* 2, blank. type-page: 20 × 17 cm. ?*Printed at Quebec, by John Neilson, 1800.*

Contents: l. 1, Mandement, ending: "Donné à Québec . . . 7 Juillet 1800. J. O. Plessis Vic. Gén. . . . Par Monseigneur. Tho. Maguire P[tre] Sec: Collationé à la minute restée aux Archives de l'Evêché. [signed in MS.] Tho. Maguire p[tre] sec." *l.* 2, blank.

The *Mandement* announces the death at Valence, Italy, Aug. 29, 1799, of Pope Pius VI, the proclamation, Mar. 14, 1800, of Cardinal Chiaramonti, Bishop of Imola, as Pope Pius VII. It orders Te Deum to be sung in all parishes on the first Sunday after receipt of this mandement. The text is reprinted in Têtu and Gagnon: *Mandements de Québec,* 2: 521-22.

Apparently printed in 1800, this leaflet has a "later-in-the-nineteenth-century" appearance. The paper (wove) shows unusual discolouration around the edges, though the text type, Caslon old face, in rather poor impression, is familiar in the productions of all Canadian presses of the early period, and the open caps in the head line, P I E R R E D E N A U T, had been introduced in Canada by Neilson before the turn of the century.

Copies located: CaO; CaQQL.

1172A. DISSERTATION ON . . . THE BOOK OF REVELATION

Advertised: "Proposals for printing by Subscription, A dissertation on the thirteenth and seventeenth Chapters of the Book of Revelation, proving that Jacobism is the Eighth head of the Beast and Voltaire the number of the Beast. Price one shilling. Those who subscribe for six will have a 7th gratis. Subscriptions received at this office [i.e. the printing-office of John Ryan, king's printer, Saint John, N.B.] and by the Rev. Mr. Pidgeon at Fredericton, the Rev. Mr. Viets at Digby, the Rev. Mr. Bailey at Annapolis, the Rev. Mr. Wiswall at Wilmot, and the Rev. Mr. Stansur [sic] at Halifax."—*Royal gazette,* Saint John, N.B., Oct. 14-Nov. 18, 1800, also Jan. 6, 1801, *et seq.*

This anonymous work was actually published by Ryan in 1802. *See* Gagnon: *Essai de bibliographie canadienne,* 2: no. 13.

1172B. DODSLEY, ROBERT, 1703-1764

[SELECT FABLES OF AESOP AND OTHER FABULISTS. *Printed at Montreal, by Edward Edwards, 1800?*]

This publication is recorded by G. Ducharme, Montreal, in his sale catalogue no. 29, May, 1928, *Canadiana, Americana, &c. à vendre,* item no. 5347: "Dodsley, (R). Select fable [sic] of Aesop and other fabulists in 3 books. Mtl. 1800. 96 p. (wants more than that) $2.00." Mr. Ducharme told the writer that this item was correctly described. The purchaser could not be traced, however, nor the copy located. If printed in Montreal in 1800, it was by Edward Edwards, who had the only printing-office there at that time.

Another? edition was published: *Select fables of Æsop and other fabulists, in three books, by R. Dodsley . . . Montreal, printed and sold by J. Brown, . . . 1810,* 106 p., 12mo. This edition is also recorded by Ducharme, *ibid.*, no. 5348, and by Gagnon: *Essai de bibliographie canadienne,* 1: no. 1154, whose copy is now in CaQM.

This popular collection of fables edited by Dodsley, the poet-dramatist and book-seller, was first printed at Birmingham, England, by John Baskerville, 1761, and occasionally by others, later.

Copy located: None.

1173. DURAND, LAURENS, 1629-1708

CANTIQUES / DE / MARSEILLES / Accommodés à des Airs vulgaires, / PAR M. LAURENT DURANT / Prêtre du Diocèse de Toulon. / Implemini Spiritu Sancto, loquentes vobismetipsis in / Psalmis & Hymnis & Canticis spiritualibus, cantantes, / & psallentes in cordibus vestris Domino. Ephes. ch. 5 / v. 18 & 19. / [printer's ornament] / QUEBEC, / Imprimé à la Nouvelle Imprimerie / 1800. /

16mo. A-Bb[8], Cc[4]; 422 [2] p.; type-page: 13 × 7.6 cm.

Contents: p. [1], t.-p.; p. [2], blank; p. 3-422, Cantiques; p. [1-2] at end, Table (contents).

Copies located: CaO; CaQQL (2 cop. both well worn, one lacking p. 255-58, 317-18; the other lacking t.-p. and several other p.); Ketcheson (fine clean copy in original calf binding, complete with end papers intact).

1174. GREAT BRITAIN. TREATIES

[rule] / Capitulations and Extracts of Treaties / Relating to Canada; / With His Majesty's Proclamation of 1763, establishing the Government of / Quebec. / [rule] / Capitulations et Extraits des Traités / concernant le Canada; / Avec la Proclamation de Sa Majesté, de 1763, qui établit le Gouvernement / de Québec. / [rule] /

4to. [A]-E[4], [F]i; 41 p.; type-page: 23 × 14.4 cm. Text in English and French on opposite pages. p. 4 mispaged: 3; 5: 4; 3 being repeated, 5 omitted, in numbering. The t.-p. has the style of a half-title.

Contents: p. [1], t.-p.; p. 2-4, Sept. 18, 1759. Articles of capitulation demanded by Mr. de Ramsay; p. 6-25, Sept. 8, 1760, Articles of Capitulation between Major-General Amherst and the Marquis de Vaudreuil; p. 24-27, the Fourth article of the definitive treaty of peace between Great Britain and France, concluded Feb. 10, 1763, containing the Cession of Canada; p. 26-35, By the King, a Proclamation Oct. 7, 1763; p. 34-41, Articles of the definitive treaty concluded at Paris, between his Britannic Majesty and the U.S.A., Sept. 3, 1783; verso of p. 41, blank.

Printed at Quebec, by P.-E. Desbarats, 1800, this work was advertised: "Just published and in a form to admit of being bound up with the Laws, Price 3/9. And for Sale at the New Printing Office [by Desbarats] and at the Printing Office [by John Neilson] 3 Mountain Street—The Capitulation of Quebec and Montreal [etc.] . . . Quebec, New Printing Office, 1 May, 1800."—*Quebec gazette,* May 1, 1800.

It was reprinted in whole or part during or before 1825, from another setting of type, with arrangement and wording of title, imprint, and text unchanged. The genuine 1800 edition is to be distinguished from the reprint by its paper—a coarse-mesh wove with the watermark: "COBB'S / Patent / 1798 /" clearly visible in most sections of most copies examind. The later printing is on various paper stocks, that most common in copies seen, being a laid paper watermarked 1818; another stock seen, e.g., in one copy in CaO, is a fine wove, watermarked 1809. The typography produces a general dissimilarity in the appearance of the two editions, the earlier has the lighter, more even colour of old face type, the later many characteristics of modern face. Also, numerous slight changes were made in resetting the text: e.g. in the genuine 1800 edition, p. 27, line 6, the word "pais" becomes "païs" when reset; p. 27, line 7, "cede" becomes "céde"; p. 28, line 36, "St. Marys" becomes "St. Mary's"; p. 29, line 15, "Troisiemement" becomes "Troisièmement"; p. 29, line 21, "Quatriemement" becomes "Quatrièmement"; etc.

Some copies examined are composed of sheets from both editions—e.g. one copy in CaOT, CaOTO, and NN has signature [A]-C, E-[F] of the earlier, and signature D (p. 25-32) of the later edition. This or other combinations may occur in other copies located below.

Capitulations is usually found bound as the first (occasionally as a later) piece in *A collection of the acts . . . 1800* (*see* No. 1169) or in *A Collection of acts . . . 1824* (*see* Toronto Public Library, *Bibliography of Canadiana*, no. 1315). Copies of the earlier printing appear in the former; copies of the earlier or the later, or sheets from both editions, in the latter publication.

Copies located: CSmH; CaO; CaOOA; CaOT (composite copy); CaOTL; CaOTO (composite copy); CaQM; CaQMJ; CaQMM (2 cop.); CaQQB; CaQQL (2 cop., one printed on superior paper and bound, apparently as issued, in blue printer's paper cover); DLC; Ketcheson; M; MH (2 cop.); MWA; MiD-B (2 cop.); MiU; N; NN (composite copy, p. 41 wanting); NNB (2 cop.); RPJ; WHi; Witton.

1175. KENT AND STRATHERN, EDWARD AUGUSTUS, *Duke of*, 1767-1820

By General His Royal Highness EDWARD, Duke of Kent and Strathern, Earl of Dublin, Knight of / the Most Noble Order of the Garter, [etc.] . . . / and Commander in Chief of the Forces serving in British North-America. / [rule] / <Text>

Broadside: type-page: 48 × 39 cm. type: small pica set solid. ?*Printed at Halifax, N.S., by Anthony Henry, 1800.*

Text: "It having been found expedient to revise the Allowances of Rations, Fuel, and Candles, established by Barrack Regulations, which have hitherto been in force throughout British North-America, and more particularly to specify the same, the Commissary and Storekeeper-General is hereby directed to cause the following General Schedule of the several Allowances of Rations, Fuel and Candles, To be distributed to his Deputies, and Assistants, from which no deviation is on any account to be admitted." Appended is *Schedule* and *Remarks*, printed in 3 col., and signed: "Approved, Edward. By Order of His Royal Highness the Commander in Chief, James Willoughby Gordon, Military Secretary. Head Quarters, Halifax, March 25, 1800."

The Duke of Kent, fourth son of King George III and Queen Charlotte, and later, father of the future Queen Victoria, was stationed in Canada at intervals between 1791 and 1802, and was commander-in-chief of forces in British North America from May 17, 1799. He is said to have been unpopular with the troops for his exacting requirements in details of military etiquette and discipline and for his stringent enforcement of petty regulations—of which the present publication appears as example.

Copy located: CaOOA (in *Miscellaneous newspaper clippings 1812-1837* portfolio).

1176. KING, WILLIAM COLSELL, 1772?-1843?

[A Provincial fast sermon, preached at Windsor and Falmouth, on Friday, the 27th day of June, 1800, by the Reverend Doctor King.]

Printed at Halifax, N.S., by Anthony Henry, 1800 this work was advertised:

"A new publication. A provincial fast sermon preached at Windsor and Falmouth, on Friday the 27th day of June, 1800, by the Reverend Doctor King. It contains A Dedication to the illustrious members of the University of Aberdeen, together with a particular account of New-Light Principles and the State of Politics in most Nations; It will be out this week, and sold by Messrs. A. Kidston, A. Morrison, and A. Henry, Halifax, by Dr. Dennison in Horton, and by the Author at Windsor. Price 1/3."—*Royal gazette*, Halifax, N.S., July 29, 1800. Also advertised: "Just published [etc.]," *ibid.*, Aug. 5, 1800.

William Colsell King, M.A., Oxon., about whom curiously little seems to be known, was stationed as a missionary under the Society for the Propagation of the Gospel, at Douglas and Rawdon (a charge near Windsor, N.S.) 1797-1808, and at Windsor itself, 1813-43 (C. F. Pascoe: *Two hundred years of the S.P.G.*). In the interval, Jan., 1808-1814, he was headmaster of the Academy, or Grammar School, attached to King's College, Windsor, and was rector of Windsor parish from 1814-41, as a tablet to his memory records (H. Y. Hind: *Sketch of the old parish burying ground, Windsor, Nova Scotia*, Windsor, N.S., 1889, 16, 74).

The author of this sermon was probably that William King who matriculated at Oxford, Apr. 22, 1788, aged 16 years, and graduated B.A. 1792, M.A. 1794.—J. Foster: *Alumni Oxonienses* (8v., Oxford, 1888-92).

Copy located: None.

1177. L'HOMOND, CHARLES FRANCOIS, 1727-1794

ÉLÉMENS / DE LA / GRAMMAIRE FRANCAISE,/ PAR M. L'HOMOND. / Professeur-Emérité en l'Université de Paris. / [rule] / PREMIERE EDITION DE QUEBEC. / [rule] / [printer's ornament] / A QUEBEC: / Chez J. NEILSON, Imprimeur-Libraire, / rue la Montagne, n° 3. / [rule] / M.DCCC. /

12mo. A^8, C-G^8, H^4, I^2; 106 p., 1 *l.;* 2 fold. *l.* (opp. p. 48, 52).

Contents: p. [1], t.-p.; p. [2], blank; p. [3]-4, Preface; p. [5]-106, Elémens, 1 *l.* at end, blank.

Though "conçue comme une préparation à l'étude de la grammaire latine" (Larousse), L'Homond's *Grammaire française* became a standard school text in Europe and America for a century. It was first published in Paris, 1780, and subsequently in hundreds of reprinted, revised, enlarged, and abridged editions, in France —also in Quebec, 1800, 1810, 1819, etc. The early Quebec editions have L'Homond's preface (to the original, or an early, Paris edition, for the author refers to his *twenty* years' teaching experience), but no evidence of Canadian editorship—though a few slight changes of text appear in 1819. European French apparently remained the Canadian standard of instruction.

It was advertised: "Recemment imprimés et seront mis au vente Samedi prochaine [Oct. 25, 1800] à l'Imprimerie [de J. Neilson] Elémens de la grammaire française . . . M. Lhomond est un de ces hommes de lettres illustres qui ont bien voulu consacrer leurs talents à la Composition de Livres elémentaires; il a composé l'ouvrage actuel après s'être appliqué vingt années à la tache penible de l'instruction publique et des personnes les plus éclairées le regardent comme très digne de son experience et de ses talents."—*Quebec gazette*, Oct. 23, 1800.

Copies located: CaQM; CaQQL. Both are fresh copies in original boards covered with golden linen, the Laval copy with a slip cover also.

1178. LOWER CANADA. ELECTIONS. 1800

To the Free and Independent Electors of the Lower Town of Quebec. <Text> Robert Lester. Quebec 28 June 1800.

Copy located: CaQMS.

1179. LOWER CANADA. EXECUTIVE COUNCIL

ORDER / OF THE / Governor in Council. / Of the 7th. July 1796, / FOR THE / REGULATION OF COMMERCE, / BETWEEN THIS / PROVINCE / AND THE / United States of America. / [rule] / [royal arms] / [rule] / QUEBEC: / PRINTED BY COMMAND OF HIS EXCELLENCY THE GOVERNOR; / BY WILLIAM VONDENVELDEN, Printer at the New Printing-Office, / Poor-street, Upper-Town Anno Domini, M.DCC.XCVI. /

French t.-p.:

ORDRE / DU / Gouverneur en Conseil. / Du 7me Juillet, 1796, / POUR LE / REGLEMENT DU COMMERCE / ENTRE CETTE / PROVINCE / ET LES / Etats Unis de l'Amerique. / [rule] / [royal arms] / [rule] / QUEBEC: / IMPRIME' PAR ORDRE DE SON EXCELLENCE LE GOUVERNEUR; / Par GUILLAUME VONDENVELDEN, Imprimeur à la Nouvelle Imprimerie, / Haute-Ville Rue des Pauvres, Anno Domini, M,DCC,XCVI. /

4to. B-[D]^4; 2 p. l., 19 p.; type-page: 21.2-23.2 × 17.5 cm. 2 leaves of sig. [D] are folded around sig. B-C to form t.-p.'s. Text in English and French on opposite pages. This work was actually *printed at Quebec, by P.-E. Desbarats, 1800 or later.*

Contents: p. l. 1 recto, English t.-p.; verso, blank; p. l. 2 recto, French t.-p.; verso, blank; p. [1], blank; p. [2]-19, Odder [sic] of the Governor in council, dated at head: Quebec, July 7, 1796, and signed at end: "Herman Witsius Ryland, C.Ex.C."; verso of p. 19, blank.

This is another edition of No. 994 printed from another setting of type with wording of t.-p. and text unchanged. It is to be distinguished from No. 994 by its pagination: odd numbers on recto, text beginning on p. [2] and ending on p. 19; by its English t.-p. with period, not comma, after "Council" line 3; by its French t.-p. with two commas, not periods, within imprint date; by its English caption, p. [2] with "ODDER" not "ORDER"; and by its paper.

In the copies located all or most of this work is printed on wove paper without watermark. In some copies, however, sig. [D] is laid paper watermarked: 1800. Most of the copies located are bound (some at least as issued) as a component in *A Collection of the Acts . . . 1800* or *A Collection of the Acts . . . 1824* (*see* No. 1169). This edition, therefore, appears to have been printed during or after the year 1800, a reprint prepared to supplement the remainder of No. 994, issued in the *Collection*. The *Collection* was published by Pierre-Edward Desbarats, who succeeded Vondenvelden at the New Printing Office in 1798, and who, therefore, actually printed this reprint.

Copies located: CaOOA; CaOT; CaOTL; CaOTO; CaQMJ; CaQMM (2 cop.); CaQQL ("Ex.B"); Ketcheson; MH (2 cop.); MWA; N; NN; NNB 2 cop.); RPJ.

1180. LOWER CANADA. HOUSE OF ASSEMBLY

JOURNAL / OF THE / HOUSE OF ASSEMBLY / OF / LOWER-CANADA. /From the 5th March to the 29th May 1800, both days inclusive. / IN THE FORTIETH YEAR OF THE REIGN OF / KING GEORGE THE THIRD. / Being the Fourth Session of the Second Provincial Parliament of / this Province. / [royal arms] / [double rule] / QUEBEC: PRINTED BY ORDER OF THE HOUSE OF ASSEMBLY,/AND SOLD BY JOHN NEILSON. / M.DCCC. /

French t.-p.:

JOURNAL / DE LA / CHAMBRE D'ASSEMBLÉE / DU / BAS-CANADA. / Depuis le 5e Mars jusqu'au 29e Mai 1800, inclusivement. / DANS LA QUARANTIEME ANNE'E DU REGNE DE / SA MAJESTÉ GEORGE TROIS. / Etant la Quatrieme Session du Second Parlement Provincial de / cette Province. / [royal arms] / [double rule] / QUEBEC: / IMPRIME' PAR ORDRE DE LA CHAMBRE D'ASSEMBLE'E, / ET A VENDRE PAR JOHN NEILSON. / M.DCCC. /

4to. $[*]^4$, A-2O^4, 2P-2Q^2; 2 p. l., 305 p., 1 *l.*; type-page: 17.5 × 12.3 cm. Text in English and French on opposite pages.

Contents: 2 p. l., blank; p. [1], English t.-p.; p. [2], blank; p.[3], French t.-p.; p. [4-5], blank; p. [6-11], Proclamations, etc.; p. [12]-305, Journal; verso of p. 305, blank; 1 *l.*, blank.

The House ordered that 100 copies of its *Journals* be printed in English and French for the use of members, and that none but the printer so licensed print the same.—*Journal*, Mar. 18, 1800. It was probably produced on terms similar to those for the journals of preceding years, viz. the House contributing about £125, the printer having privilege of public sale.

This *Journal* was advertised: "Just published and for sale at the Printing Office [of John Neilson] the Journal for the fourth session of the second Assembly. Price 10/ sewed. Also, Complete sets of former Journals [i.e. from first session of first Assembly, 1792-93] up to the present time. Price £3.17.6. August 25, 1800."

—*Quebec gazette*, Aug. 18, 1800.

An *Index* was issued later (4to. A-B[4], a-b[4]; [32] p.; text in English p. [1-14], p. [15-16], blank; and French p. [17-32]). Like indices to journals of preceding years, this was apparently printed some time after the *Journal*, and before 1820. It is only occasionally found with copies of the *Journal*.

Copies located: CaO; CaOOA; CaOT; CaQM; CaQMA; CaQMM; CaQQL; CaQQLH; CtY; DLC; GBLP (in C.O. 45/30); ICN; MH; N; NN; RPJ (with index); WHi.

1181. LOWER CANADA. LAWS, STATUTES, *etc.*

A PROVINCIAL STATUTE / OF / LOWER-CANADA, / ENACTED by the KING'S most excellent MAJESTY, by and with / the Advice and Consent of the Legislative Council and Assembly of the / said Province, constituted and assembled by virtue of and under the / Authority of an Act of the Parliament of GREAT BRITAIN, passed / in the thirty-first year of the Reign of our Sovereign Lord GEORGE / the Third, by the Grace of GOD of Great Britain, France and Ireland, / KING, Defender of the Faith, &c. / [royal arms] / QUEBEC: / PRINTED UNDER THE AUTHORITY AND BY COMMAND OF HIS EXCELLENCY THE LIEUTENANT / GOVERNOR; AS THE ACT OF THE PROVINCIAL PARLIAMENT DIRECTS. / BY P.E. DESBARATS, / LAW PRINTER TO THE KING'S MOST EXCELLENT MAJESTY. / [rule] / Anno Domini, M.DCCC. /

French t.-p.:

STATUT PROVINCIAL / DU / BAS-CANADA. / STATUÉ par la Très Excellente MAJESTÉ du ROI, par et de l'Avis / et Consentement du Conseil Législatif et Assemblée de la dite Province, / constitués et assemblés en vertu et sous l'autorité d'un ACTE du Par- / lement de la Grande Bretagne, passé dans la Trente-et-unieme année du / Règne de notre Souverain Seigneur GEORGE TROIS, par la Grace / de DIEU, ROI de la Grande Bretagne, de France et d'Irlande, Défenseur / de la Foi, &c. / [royal arms] / QUEBEC: / IMPRIMÉ SOUS L'AUTORITÉ DU GOUVERNEMENT ET PAR ORDRE DE SON EXCELLENCE LE LIEU- / TENANT GOUVERNEUR, ET CONFORMEMENT A L'ACTE DU PARLEMENT PROVINCIAL, / PAR P. E. DESBARATS, / IMPRIMEUR DE LOIX DE SA TRES EXCELLENTE MAJESTÉ. / [rule] / Anno Domini M.DCCC. /

4to. [T]-X[4]; [143]-165 p.; type-page: 22.5 × 17.5 cm. Text in English and French on opposite pages. Paged in continuation of *The Provincial Statutes* of 1799. All copies seen bear this continuous pagination.

Contents: p. [143], English t.-p.; p. [144], blank; p. [145], French t.-p.; p. [146], blank; p. [147], blank; p. [148]-165, 40 Geo. III c. 1, An act to provide returning officers for knights, citizens and burgesses to serve in Assembly, and regulating elections to be held for that purpose (May 29, 1800).

This publication (40 Geo. III c. 1) was issued separately as advertised: "In press and will be ready for sale at the New Printing Office, on Saturday next [i.e. June 7, 1800] Price 2/6. 'An Act to provide Returning Officers [etc.]'."—*Quebec gazette*, June 5, 1800. Also advertised: "Just published [etc.]."—*ibid.*, June 12, 1800. It was also issued later (either with or without its own t.-p.) with *The Provincial statutes* of 1800 (*see* No. 1051) and is usually so found.

Copies located (bound, though not of necessity as issued, with *The provincial statutes of Lower-Canada*, vol. 2): CU; CaNsWA; CaO; CaOOA; CaOTL (2 cop.); CaQM; CaQMB; CaQMM; CaQQA; CaQQL; CtY; Gordonsmith; MH; MiU; N; NN; NNB; RPJ; WHi.

1182. LOWER CANADA. LAWS, STATUTES, *etc.*

Half-title: THE / PROVINCIAL STATUTES / OF / LOWER-CANADA. / Anno Regni GEORGII III. Regis. / MAGNÆ BRITANNIÆ, FRANCIÆ ET HIBERNIÆ, QUADRAGESIMO. / HIS EXCELLENCY / ROBERT SHORE MILNES, ESQUIRE, LIEUTENANT GOVERNOR, / Being the FOURTH Session of the / SECOND Provincial Parliament of LOWER-CANADA. /

French half-title: LES / STATUTS PROVINCIAUX / DU / BAS-CANADA. / Anno Regni GEORGII III. REGIS / MAGNÆ BRITANNIÆ, FRANCIÆ ET HIBERNIÆ QUADRAGESIMO. / SON EXCELLENCE / ROBERT SHORE MILNES, ECUYER, LIEUTENANT GOUVERNEUR, / Etant la QUATRIEME Session du / SECOND Parlement Provincial du BAS-CANADA. /

4to. [Y]-2A^4, 2B^3; [167]-195 p.; type-page: 22.5 × 17.5 cm. Text in English and French on opposite pages. Paged in continuation of No. 1181. *Printed at Quebec by P.-E. Desbarats, 1800.*

Contents: p. [167], English half-title; p. [168], blank; p. [169], French half-title; p. [170-71], blank; p. [172]-95, 40 Geo. III c. 2-8. This was also issued as a part of *The provincial statutes*, v. 2 (No. 1051).

Copy located: NN.

1183. LOWER CANADA. LAWS, STATUTES, *etc.*

[Extract from the Road Act]

Double broadside: text in English and French. *Printed at Quebec, by John Neilson, 1800*, as recorded:

"1800, Oct. 24. [Debit] J. F. Perrault, Clk. of Court, Printing 100 copies of an Extract from the Road Act, 1 on a Sheet folio foolscap, Eng. & French dble—Pica type. [price not given]."—Can.P.A., *Neilson papers*, v. 55.

This is probably an extract from 36 Geo. III c. 9 (*see* No. 999), which was amended by 39 Geo. III c. 5. Joseph François Perrault was clerk of the Court of Quarter Sessions of the Peace which supervised road work in the town of Quebec.

Copy located: None.

1184. LOWER CANADA. LIEUTENANT-GOVERNOR, 1791-1795 (*Clarke*)

Caption title: PROCLAMATION, / Declaring when the Act of the 3$^{1st.}$ / GEO:III. shall have effect in / the Provinces of UPPER and / LOWER-CANADA. / [rule] /

French caption: PROCLAMATION, / Qui declare le temps ou l'Acte de la / 3$^{1me.}$ de GEO:III. aura eflet [sic] dans / les Provinces du HAUT et du / BAS-CANADA. / [rule] /

4to. A-B^4; 16 p.; type-page: 21-22.5 × 15 cm. Text in English and French on opposite pages. Odd numbers on verso, even numbers on recto. In this edition the caption title on p. 16 reads: "Proclamation qui déclare l'emanation des ordres pour la conservation [i.e. convocation] du premier parlement [etc.]."

Contents: recto of p. [1], blank; p. [1]-4, Proclamation declaring when the act of the 31 Geo. III shall have effect in the provinces of Upper and Lower Canada, dated Quebec, Nov. 18, 1791; p. 3-14, Proclamation, dividing the province of Lower Canada into counties, cities, and towns and fixing the number of representatives of each, dated Quebec, May 7, 1792; p. 15-16, Proclamation, declaring the issuing out writs for calling together the first provincial parliament of the province of Lower Canada, dated Quebec, May 14, 1792; verso of p. 16, blank. Each proclamation is signed: "A. C." i.e. Alured Clarke, lieutenant-governor of Lower Canada, commanding the province in the absence of Lord Dorchester also: "Hugh Finlay, Acting Secretary."

These proclamations gave effect to the Constitutional Act and instituted measures preliminary to the election of the legislature established by that act.

The printer and place and date of publication of this work has not been definitely ascertained. It was probably printed at Quebec, 1792-1800, by the government printer—Samuel Neilson till Jan. 12, 1793, then John Neilson; or by the law printer, Wm. Vondenvelden, 1795-98, to accompany his quarto edition of the statutes, 1795, *et seq.* or by his successor, P.-E. Desbarats, between 1797 and 1800. The last, indeed, seems likely, for one copy in the Public Archives of Canada is printed on paper dated in its watermark 1800. It is usually found in a miscellaneous group of laws, No. 1169.

This work was reprinted (from another setting of type) on paper dated in its watermark 1806. The reprint resembles closely the edition described here, but in the reprint the *French caption* is corrected to read . . . effet . . .; p. [16] is mispaged: 17; and in the caption title on p. 17 [i.e., p. 16] the word "conservation" is corrected to read: "convocation"; also the paper is "wove," not "laid" as that used in the earlier printing.

Copies located: CaO (2 cop.); CaOOA (in *Proclamations* portfolio in the Library); CaOTL; CaQM; CaQMJ; CaQQA; CaQQB; CtY; DLC; Gordonsmith; Ketcheson; MH; MiU; N; NN; RPJ; (2 cop.); Witton.

Reprint edition, copies located: CSmH; CaO; CaOOA; CaOT; (2 cop.); CaOTO; CaQMM; CaQQB; CaQQL; DLC; Gordonsmith; MWA; MiD-B (3 cop.); NNB (2 cop.); WHi; Witton.

1185. LOWER CANADA. LIEUTENANT-GOVERNOR, 1797-1808 (*Milnes*)

The following SIGNALS will be made on the Sig- / nal Staff when Vessels are coming into the Harbour / of Quebec / <Text> / 3d. June, 1800. /

Broadside: type-page: 27.5 × 16 cm. The text contains a code of signals to notify inhabitants of the approach of ships of various types, including potential enemy vessels. A similar *Code of signals . . . May 28th, 1800,* for the port of Saint John, N.B., was issued by Lieut.-Gov. Carleton, and published in the *Royal gazette,* Saint John, N.B., June 3, 1800. The code of signals for the port of Halifax appears in *An Almanack for . . . 1801* (No. 1158).

Copy located: CaQMS.

1186. MONTREAL, *City.* COLLEGE DE MONTREAL

EXERCISES / Qui se seront au College de Montréal le Mardi 12, et le Mercredi 13 d'Août 1800; et commenceront / le matin à 9 heures, et le soir à 1 heure. / [rule] / THESES DE MATHEMATIQUES ET PHYSIQUE. /

Broadside: text printed in 2 col.; type-page: 33.5 × 21 cm. *Probably printed at Montreal, by Edward Edwards, 1800.*

The Collège de Montréal, similar to the classical colleges of Europe and corresponding in a way to the modern North American high school and junior college, was a school for boys, maintained in Montreal since 1773 by "les Messieurs" of the Séminaire de St. Sulpice (*see* No. 229). This publication marked the end of the school year, 1799-1800.

Copy located: CaQMS.

1187. MONTREAL GAZETTE. CARRIER'S ADDRESS

ETRENNES / du Garçon qui porte la Gazette de / MONTREAL, aux Pratiques. / [rule] / 1er Janvier, 1801. / CHANSON: sur l'air: Des Fraises. / [*Montreal, E.Edwards, 1800.*]

Broadside: 35 lines within ornamental frame: 25 × 17 cm. The verse is a conventional New Year's greeting:

"Voici l'aimable saison,
Ou chacun se tourmente,
Pour former à sa façon,
Des voeux qui repondent à son
Attente, Attente, Attente.
[Etc.]."

Copy located: CaQQL (filed with *Montreal gazette,* 1803).

1188. NEILSON, JOHN, 1776-1848

[Catalogue of Books for Sale, 3 Mountain St. Quebec, 1800.]

Leaflet of 2 or 4 pages. *Printed at Quebec, by John Neilson, 1800.*

Neilson recorded this *Catalogue* in his advertisement: "Imported from London in the Brickwood, and will be ready for sale tomorrow at the Printing Office, 3 Mountain Street, for Cash only—A small assortment of new and valuable French and English books, of which Catalogues may be had at the Office."—*Quebec gazette*, Nov. 20, 1800.

This seems to be the publication of which a copy was listed by Dora Hood, Toronto, in her *Catalogue no. 4*, Autumn, 1930 (which included works from the collection of Col. J. Hubert Neilson, a grandson of the printer), item no. 316. Mrs. Hood recalls the item as a leaflet of 2 or 4 pages, sold for 75 cents.

Copy known but not located: J. Hubert Neilson copy *supra*.

1189. NOVA SCOTIA. HOUSE OF ASSEMBLY

[Bill for providing and establishing of English schools throughout the Province of Nova Scotia. *Halifax, N.S., printed by Anthony Henry? 1800.*]

A "Bill for providing and establishing of English Schools throughout the Province of Nova Scotia" was presented to the House of Assembly by William Cotnam Tonge, member for the county of Halifax, Apr. 7, 1800, read twice and referred to committee the following day. On Apr. 29, the bill was reported from the committee with "Several alterations and amendments," read and deferred to next session with the order "that the Bill be printed and that the Clerk furnish the Several Members with copies for their Perusal and Information during the recess of the House." It was deferred in the following session on Tonge's motion, July 15, 1801. And again in the next session, Apr. 1, 1802, "the Bill for establishing public schools throughout the Province" was postponed, dropping from sight thereafter.—N.S. As. *Journal*, 1800, *et seq.*

Another bill providing for free public schools supported by local taxes and a provincial government grant and governed by locally elected trustees was passed in 1811 (*see* Patrick W. Thibeau: *Education in Nova Scotia before 1811*, 121 p., Ph.D. dissertation to Catholic University of America, Washington, D.C., 1922, chap. 8. Thibeau does not mention Tonge's *Bill*, however).

Copy located: None.

1190. NOVA SCOTIA. HOUSE OF ASSEMBLY

Journal and Proceedings of the House of Assembly.

Note: title above not transcribed from copy.

fo. A-2C^2, 2D^1; 1 p. l., 108 p. *Printed at Halifax, N.S., by Anthony Henry, 1800.*

Contents: p. l. recto, t.-p.; verso, Proclamation; p. 1-108, Journal of the first session of the eighth assembly, Feb. 20-May 2, 1800.

Copies located: CaNs; CaNsHA (p. 43-66 wanting and supplied in typescript); GBLP (in C.O. 217/74: 173-282).

1191. NOVA SCOTIA. LAWS, STATUTES, *etc.*

[1800. Anno Quadragesimo Regis Georgii III Cap. I-VII. At the General Assembly of the Province of Nova Scotia, etc.]

Probably printed at Halifax, N.S., by Anthony Henry, 1800. Perpetual acts passed in the first session of the eighth assembly, Feb. 20-May 2, 1800

These acts appear in full or by title, in *The Statutes at large passed in . . . Nova-Scotia from 1758 to . . . 1804, . . .* [revised] by *Richard John Uniacke* (Halifax, N.S., 1805). There is a possibility, indeed, that unlike this session's temporary acts they were not printed in 1800, in view of the revised edition, already projected.

Copy located: None.

1192. NOVA SCOTIA. LAWS, STATUTES, *etc.*

Running title: [rule] / 1800. Anno Quadragesimo Regis, GEORGII III. CAP. I[-XII]. / [rule] /

Caption title: At the GENERAL ASSEMBLY of the / Province of NOVA-SCOTIA, . . . / [5 lines] / . . . being the First Session of the Eighth GENERAL ASSEMBLY, / convened in the said Province. /

fo. sig. 5N-5T²; p. 539-565; type-page: 25 × 15 cm. paged in continuation of No. 1138. *Printed at Halifax, N.S., by Anthony Henry, 1800.*

Contents: p. 539-565, Cap. I-XII temporary acts passed in the session, Feb. 20-May 2, 1800; verso of p. 565, blank.

Copies located: CaO; DLC (p. 549-565 wanting).

1193. PLESSIS, JOSEPH OCTAVE, *bp. of Quebec,* 1763-1825

Circulaire à Messieurs les Curés du District de / Québec. /

4to. 2 *l.*; type-page: 15.5 × 15 cm. *Probably printed at Quebec, by John Neilson, 1800.*

Contents: l. 1 recto, Circulaire, signed: "J. O. Plessis, Vic. gén. Quebéc, 18 Juin, 1800. Bon pour Copie [signed in MS.] Tho. Maguire, Ptre Sec."; verso, blank; *l.* 2, blank.

This circular letter states that the lieutenant-governor requested the bishop (Denaut) of Quebec to keep him informed on the wheat supply. Accordingly Plessis (then vicar general) asks the curés to report to him where wheat still remains in their parishes.

This *Circulaire* is reprinted in Têtu and Gagnon: *Mandements de Québec,* 2: 520.

Copies located: CaO; CaQQL (blank *l.* wanting).

1194. PRIMERS. QUEBEC

GRAND / ALPHABET, / Divisé par SYLLABLES / POUR INSTRUIRE / Avec grande facilité les Enfans à / épeler, lire et chanter à l'Eglise. / Contenant ce qui se chante à la Ste. / Messe, à Vêpres et à Complies. / [double rule] / [printer's ornament] / [double rule] / A QUEBEC, / Imprimé à la NOUVELLE IMPRIMƎRIE [sic], Rue des / Jardins. 1800. /

16mo. A-D⁸, E²; 1 p. l., 65 p.; type-page: 9.5-9.8 × 7.5 cm. t.-p. and section titles in French, text in latin. *Printed by P.-E. Desbarats.*

Contents: p. l., t.-p.; verso, blank; p. [1]-2, Alphabet; p. 3-4, Syllables; p. 5-14, Pater noster, etc.; p. 14-20, Les reponses à la sainte messe; p. 20-38, Les sept pseaumes; p. 38-41, Kyrie eleison, etc.; p. 42-65, Heures canoniales; verso of p. 65, blank. From p. 5-38, all words are divided into syllables, with an em space between words and syllables.

The contents of this elementary school book are given in some detail, for it is the earliest example seen by the writer, of the many editions of "Alphabets" advertised, sold, and apparently printed in Quebec during the latter part of the 18th century.

Copies located: CaQ (p. 65 wanting); CaQM; CaQQL.

1195. QUEBEC GAZETTE. CARRIER'S ADDRESS

ADDRESS / Of the Boy who carries the Quebec / Gazette. / [double rule] / JANUARY 1st. 1801. /

French side:

ETRENNES / DU / GARÇON QUI PORTE LA GAZETTE DE QUÉBEC / AUX PRACTIQUES. / [double rule] / 1er JANVIER, 1801. / Sur l'Air: Avec les Jeux dans le Vilage [sic]. / [*Quebec, J. Neilson, 1800.*]

Broadside: type-page: 29.5 × 33 cm. English verse on left, 42 lines; French on right, 64 lines in 2 col. Both sides bear conventional greetings and praise of the Press.

Copy located: CaO (bound in *Quebec gazette* at end of 1800).

1196. STANSER, ROBERT, *d.* 1829

A / SERMON, / Preached before the Honorable House of Assembly, / OF THE / PROVINCE of NOVA-SCOTIA, / IN THE PARISH CHURCH of ST. PAUL in HALIFAX, / On SUNDAY, MARCH 16th, 1800, / By ROBERT STANSER, L.L.B. / Rector of the Parish of St. PAUL, / And Chaplain to His Majesty's COUNCIL, / AND THE / HOUSE OF ASSEMBLY. / [rule] / HALIFAX: / Printed by A. HENRY, Printer to the King's Most Excellent Majesty. /

4to. A^4; 8 p.; type-page: 16.5 × 10.3 cm. Though without imprint date, this work was printed between Mar. 17 and Dec. 1, 1800, when the printer died.

Contents: p. [1], t.-p.; p. [2], Note: "In the House of Assembly, 17th March, 1800, Ordered that the thanks of this House be given to the Reverend M[r] Stanser, Rector of St. Paul's, & chaplain to the House, for the sermon by him preached before this House yesterday, and that M[r] Stanser, be requested to furnish this House with a Copy of the Sermon for the purpose of printing the same"; p. 3-8, Sermon, text: Deut. chap. 4, v. 7-8, "For what nation is there so great, who hath God so nigh unto them as the Lord our God is in all things that we call upon Him for? And what Nation is there so great, who hath statutes & judgements so righteous!"

The *Sermon* sets forth, with much quoting of Scriptures, the blessings of God on the British Empire, and of the British government on its subjects: ". . . At Home we find that a Spirit of unanimity and brotherly love has pervaded all ranks . . . from the King in his palace to the Peasant in his cottage. . . . [We have] many local blessings . . . civil and religious differences are not known amongst us, the one being prevented by the mild administration of just and salutary Laws, the other by the toleration of that religious liberty which permits each individual to worship his Creator [in his own] manner."

Stanser came to Nova Scotia in Sept., 1791, as Bishop Inglis remarked after meeting him, "a very genteel young man." He served as rector of St. Paul's, Halifax till 1815, and was bishop of Nova Scotia *in absentia*, 1816-24.

Copy located: GBLP (in C.O. 217/74: 463-70).

1197. UPPER CANADA. ELECTIONS, 1800

TO THE / FREE, AND INDEPENDENT / ELECTORS / of the Counties of / Durham, Simcoe, and the East Rid- / ing of the County of York. / Gentlemen, / [text, signed:] Wm. Jarvis. / York, 14 July, 1800. / [ornamental frame]

Broadside: 36 lines; type-page: 30.3 × 16.6 cm. *Probably printed at York, U.C., by Wm. Waters & T. G. Simons, 1800.*

The text contains Jarvis's solicitation of votes as candidate to represent the county of Durham, etc. in the House of Assembly of Upper Canada. The election was held in Aug., 1800. Jarvis, however, was not returned.

One of the several loyalist members of a Connecticut family who settled in New Brunswick and Upper Canada after the American Revolution, William Jarvis, 1756-1817, held the office of provincial secretary in the latter province from its organization in 1791 till his death. Some of his papers are in the Toronto Public Library.

Copy located: CaOTU has photostat of the original broadside, said to be in possession of Stewart Jarvis, Esq., Toronto.

1198. UPPER CANADA. LAWS, STATUTES, *etc.*

Caption title: [double rule] / LAWS / Passed in the Second Session of the Second Provincial Parliament, which were / reserved for, and received / HIS MAJESTY'S ASSENT. / [rule] /

4to. A-B^2, C^1; 9 p.; type-page: 22.5 × 16.5 cm. *Printed at York, U.C., by Wm. Waters & T. G. Simons, 1800.*

Contents: p. [1]-9, Chap. [I]-III. Each chapter bears the note: "The Royal Assent to this Act was promulgated by Proclamation, bearing date January 1, . . . 1800 [etc.]"; verso of p. 9, blank. *See also* No. 1200.

These acts, passed (with 38 Geo. III c. I-III) at York, June 5-July 5, 1798, were reserved for royal assent and published for the first time in 1800. They appear in later revised editions of the statutes as 38 Geo. III c. V-VII.

This publication was advertised as "Now in the press and shortly will be completed" in the *Upper Canada gazette*, Apr. 5, 1800, and as "Now completed and ready for sale [etc.]."—*ibid.*, May 3, 1800.

Copy located: CaOTL.

1199. UPPER CANADA. LAWS, STATUTES, *etc.*

LAWS / OF HIS / MAJESTY'S PROVINCE / OF / UPPER-CANADA, / IN / NORTH AMERICA, / ENACTED IN THE FOURTH SESSION OF THE SECOND PROVINCIAL PARLIAMENT, / IN THE YEAR OF OUR LORD ONE THOUSAND EIGHT HUNDRED, AND OF HIS MAJESTY'S REIGN

THE FORTIETH. / [rule] / HIS EXCELLENCY PETER HUNTER, ESQUIRE, LIEUTENANT GOVERNOR. / [rule] / [royal arms] / [rule] / YORK: Printed by WM. WATERS and T.G.SIMONS, Printers to the King's most excellent Majesty, 1800. /

4to. A-C²; 12 p.; type-page: 22.2 × 16.5 cm. sig. B, p. 5-8, is printed on blue cover paper.

Contents: p. [1], t.-p.; p. [2], blank; p. [3]-12, 40 Geo. III c. I-VI, acts passed at York, U.C., June 2-July 4, 1800.

This session's laws were published more promptly than those of previous sessions, for Lieut.-Gov. Hunter transmitted a copy to the secretary of state on Aug. 20, 1800, and the publication was advertised (with those of preceding sessions): "A few copies of the laws passed in the Second, Third and Fourth Sessions of the Second Parliament . . . for Sale at this Office."—*Upper Canada gazette,* Sept. 20, 1800.

Copies located: CaOTA; GBLP (in C.O. 42/325, 1800).

1200. UPPER CANADA. LIEUTENANT-GOVERNOR, 1799-1805 (*Hunter*)

[Proclamation announcing the Royal assent to the Reserved Bills. *Printed at York, U.C., by Wm. Waters and T.G.Simons, 1800.*]

Ordered printed by the Executive Council, Feb. 10, 1800: ". . . moved . . . That two hundred and fifty copies of this Proclamation, announcing the Royal assent to the Reserved Bills, be immediately printed, and that the Secretary do [forward them to the proper persons by the Winter Express]."—Can.P.A., U.C. *State* C.

The proclamation, bearing date Jan. 1, 1800, had been prepared at York, forwarded for the signature of Lieut.-Gov. Peter Hunter, who, also commander-in-chief in Canada, was at Quebec; then it was returned to York for publication. It announced the home government's decision on acts passed with a suspending clause in the legislature of Upper Canada in 1798. By order-in-council, London, Feb. 1, 1799, "An act for the more uniform laying on of assessments" was disallowed, and assent given to "An act for the better division of this province," "An act to amend [34 Geo. III c. 2] An Act to establish a Superior court of civil and criminal jurisdiction [etc.]," and "An act to alter the method of performing statute duty on the highways and roads [etc.]."—Can.P.A., "Q" 278 A, p. 174-75. These acts were published in No. 1198.

This proclamation is recorded (but no text given) in Ontario Archives, *Report, 1906,* 199-200.

Copy located: None.

1201. UPPER CANADA. LIEUTENANT-GOVERNOR, 1799-1805 (*Hunter*)

[Circular Letter notifying Members of Assembly that the ensuing Session of the Provincial Parliament will be holden at York, June 2, 1800.]

Broadside? *Printed at York, U.C., by Wm. Waters & T. G. Simons, 1800.*

The publication of this circular is known from a reference in the following notice: "Office of the Commons House of Parliament, Feb. 10, 1800. His Excellency the

Lieutenant Governor has been pleased to direct official information to be given that the ensuing session of the Provincial Parliament will be holden . . . at York, on the second day of June next. In the apprehension of the miscarriage of the circular letters, this additional notification is given [etc.] A. M'Donell, Assembly Clerk."—*Upper Canada gazette*, Feb. 22, 1800.

This item is included in the record of early Canadian printing, not for its intrinsic importance, but as a sample of printed publications frequently issued and soon destroyed—short routine announcements of the opening, prorogation, dissolution, and frequent postponements of sessions of Assembly.

Copy located: None.

1202. CATHOLIC CHURCH. CATECHISMS. *French*

[Catéchisme à l'usage du diocèse de Québec.]

12mo. A-B^{12}, C^{6}, D-G^{12}, H-L^{6}; [62, 141] p.; type-page: 14.4 × 8.4 cm.

Contents: p. [1] (wanting in only copy located), probably t.-p.; p. [2], probably blank; p. [3]-6, Mandement, dated and signed: "Donné à Québec . . . le 7 Mars, 1777, J. Ol. Evêque de Québec"; p. [7], Advertissement; p. [8], Introduction; p. 9-61, Petit catéchisme; p. [62], Table (contents of *Petit catéchisme*); p. 1-139, Le grand catéchisme à l'usage du diocèse de Québec; p. 139-[141], Table (contents of *Le grand catéchisme*); verso of p. [141], blank.

Another edition of No. 255, this work was probably printed in Quebec in the late 18th or early 19th century. The paper and typography have the appearance of late 18th-century productions in Quebec or Montreal, the type being mainly well worn old face. The word "Catéchisme" in the caption title Le Grand Catéchisme (p. 1), however, is shaded modern face double English caps, similar to that used by John Neilson for the line with the King's name in the title page of the *Journal of . . . Assembly of Lower Canada*, 1799 and 1800.

Copy located: CaOT (t.-p. wanting).

1203. GREAT BRITAIN. POST OFFICE

RATES OF POSTAGE / AS ESTABLISHED BY AN ACT / PASSED IN THE FIFTH YEAR OF THE REIGN OF / His Majesty King George, III. / [rule] / [double rule frame]

Broadside: 20 lines; type-page: 22.3 × 17.5 cm.

From its general appearance, this piece may have been printed at Halifax, N.S., by Anthony Henry about 1790. But these *Rates of postage* broadsides were probably published repeatedly at Halifax, Quebec, and Saint John, N.B., for they remained in force from 1765 till 1851. Dear in the British Isles, these rates (a single sheet letter cost from 4*d*. for 60 miles to 2*s*. for a thousand miles) were a hardship in 18th-century Canada where distances between settlements were great and cash was scarce. The postal rates and schedules from point to point, also lists of local postmasters and riders were published each year in the almanacs of the various provinces. The post office in British North America was directed under the imperial act of 1710 (9 Anne c. 10) by the postmaster general in London, with deputy postmasters in Quebec, Halifax, and Saint John. *See* Wm. Smith: *The early post office in Nova Scotia, 1755-1867*, in N.S. hist. soc. *Coll.* 1918 (19: 53-73); and Wm. Smith: *History of the post office in British North America* (Cambridge, Eng., 1920).

Copy located: White.

1204. PRIERES DE LA CONGREGATION

Prieres / de la / Congregation. /

16 p.; paper-page: 12 × 8.75 cm. *Obviously* printed at Montreal before 1800, this work was *probably* printed by Fleury Mesplet, between 1776 and Jan., 1794, for the Séminaire de Saint Sulpice. The only copy known has been described by the late Ægidius Fauteux, librarian of Bibliothèque de Saint Sulpice, then of Bibliothèque Civique, Montreal, in his *Mesplet*, no. 69, from which the following notes are translated:

"This little book which bears no printer's name, was certainly printed at Montreal, for it was prepared for the parish of Montreal . . . and has, p. 15, a special prayer entitled 'Election de Saint Joseph pour prefet perpétuel de la Congregation à Ville-Marie en l'oratoire de la Congregation sous la titre de l'Assomption de la Três Sainte Vierge, le 29 Mars 1694. . . .'

"It was printed before 1800 for the cover lining bears the ms. inscription: 'Ad usum congregationis Colegii Marianapolitanensis . . . 1800'. The type resembles that regularly used by Mesplet and there is reason to believe that this booklet came from his press. It is true that [Edward] Edwards, in taking over Mesplet's shop, also acquired his types in 1795. But no French printing is known to have issued from Edwards' shop excepting the bilingual *Montreal gazette*. And it seems hardly probable that the Seminaire de Saint Sulpice would have given such an order to any but Mesplet."

Copy located: CaQMC.

NEWSPAPERS*

*Files of most of these newspapers have been photographed by the Canadian Library Association. Microfilm copies may be purchased through the office of the Association's executive secretary, 46 Elgin St. Ottawa

Newspapers

New Brunswick
The Royal gazette and the New Brunswick advertiser, 1785-19th century 595
The Saint John gazette and weekly advertiser, 1783-19th century 597
Nova Scotia
The Halifax gazette, 1752-1766 599
The Nova-Scotia gazette, 1766-1770 601
The Nova Scotia chronicle, 1769-1770 602
The Nova-Scotia gazette and the weekly chronicle, 1770-1800 604
The Halifax journal, 1780?-1800 610
The Nova-Scotia packet and general advertiser, 1785-1787 612
The Port-Roseway gazetteer and the Shelburne advertiser, 1784-1785 614
The Royal American gazette, 1783?-1786? 616
The Weekly chronicle, 1786-19th century 617
Die Welt, 1788-1789 619
Quebec
Courier de Québec ou Heraut françois, 1788 620
Gazette de commerce et litteraire, 1778-1779 622
The Montreal gazette, 1785-20th century 623
Montreal gazette, 1795-1797 628
The Quebec gazette, 1764-19th century 629
The Quebec herald and universal miscellany, 1788-1793 639
The Times, 1794-1795 643
St. John Island
The Royal American gazette and weekly intelligencer, 1787?-1790 646
The Royal gazette, 1791-1792 648
Upper Canada
The Canada constellation, 1799-1800 649
Upper Canada gazette, 1793-19th century 650

Magazines

The Nova-Scotia magazine, 1789-1792 653
The Quebec magazine, 1792-1794 656

THE ROYAL GAZETTE AND THE NEW BRUNSWICK ADVERTISER. *Printed at Saint John, N.B., by Christopher Sower, then others, 1785–19th century.*

The *Royal gazette and the New Brunswick advertiser*, a weekly, was established at Saint John, Oct. 11, 1785, by Christopher Sower III, king's printer and deputy postmaster of New Brunswick, who continued it till Mar. 19, 1799. With no. 671, Mar. 26, 1799, John Ryan, formerly printer of the *Saint John gazette*, took over the *Royal gazette*, becoming king's printer on Sower's resignation from that office. Sower's *Vale* (seen in the issue of Apr. 23, 1799) was dated Saint John, Mar. 25, 1799; appended is Ryan's *Ave*: "Mr. John Ryan as King's Printer having become editor of the *Royal gazette*, thanks the public for its patronage and will try to merit its favours. dated: Mar. 26, 1799." Ryan continued the *Royal gazette* till, like Sower, he left the province and it passed to his wife's brother, Jacob S. Mott, in 1807.

On its establishment, the *Royal gazette* was "Printed by Christopher Sower, Printer to the King's Most Excellent Majesty, at his Printing-Office [and post office] in Dock Street, two doors below Mrs. Leonard's [coffee house]." The offices were removed to King and Germain Streets where the *Gazette* was printed from May 8, 1787, till 1792. Then for a time it was printed at Brookville, Sower's farm, twelve miles from Saint John, on the Hammond River, though probably issued from the office in Germain, and later in Britain Street, but some numbers at least in the period 1792-99, bear no place of publication. It was probably printed in the Saint John office again from about 1797. It was published on Tuesdays. The subscription was 10*s*. a year.

Printed on a demy or medium folio sheet of superior quality, in 4 pages (of 4 or 3 col.) to each number, excepting during an occasional emergency when quality deteriorated and size diminished, Sower's newspaper was of handsome appearance, laid out and printed by a skilled and conscientious craftsman in "a proper manner" as he stated in his first number:

> "Having the honour to be appointed by His Majesty printer in this province, I have spared no pains and no expence to enter upon the Office in a proper manner. I have imported a set of the very best types, entirely new and cast by the most celebrated Letter founders [probably the Caslon Co., London]. The workmen are the best procurable. . . No care or pains shall be wanting to make it truly respectable. The Authenticity of articles of intelligence will be attended to as much as possible. . . Letters and essays are solicited, such as are calculated to promote loyalty to our Sovereign, peace and harmony amongst ourselves, improvement or cultivation of the arts, sciences, manufactures or commerce, promotion of fisheries, agriculture &c. or affording amusement. Neither disrespect to Government, nor abuse or ridicule of fellow subjects will be permitted in this paper."

A considerable part of the *Royal gazette* was occupied with publications of the New Brunswick, Nova Scotia, and Quebec governments, and with notices and unclaimed letter lists of Postmaster Sower. This official matter and advertisements, repeated from week to week, occupying sometimes twelve of its sixteen columns, limited the space for local contributions and made the *Royal gazette* a formal and monotonous journal. Sower was more conscious of the "official" character of his newspaper than others who enjoyed king's printerships in the Canadian provinces. Though he published no editorial opinions in his local column on the third page, an authoritarian attitude is revealed in his publication of letters and essays, consistently in defence of officialdom and occasionally vilifying its critics, also in the communications which appeared occasionally over his own signature as king's printer, postmaster, or city councillor. It was no mere coincidence that contributions "affording amusement" were the last that Sower "solicited." His paper was humourless, his choice and presentation of material notably lacking the human interest and lively journalistic sense of his rival John Ryan. His official positions gave Sower some priority in publishing the activities of the local government and in receiving news from outside. The news items, reprinted from Quebec, Nova Scotian, American, and European papers were extensive, but their appearance was sometimes retarded by lack of space, or by Sower's lack of initiative. He would announce, for example, "Last evening sundry Newspapers were handed to the Printer from different States containing further particulars of the approaching millenium in Massachusetts; but too late to extract anything for this day's paper."—*Royal gazette*, Oct. 17, 1786.

Ryan, assuming editorship in 1797, changed the aspect and character of the *Royal gazette*, increasing the news matter and diminishing its style. He enlarged the page, crowding it with large text types—Sower had favoured small pica, bold headings and generous margins. Sower's sedate pronouncements were succeeded by: "☛ GREAT NEWS FROM EUROPE." Towards the end of the century the controversial give-and-take between the *Royal gazette* and the *Saint John gazette* disappeared. The old issues, if not the factions, were passing. Ryan's appointment to the former placed both papers in control of one family, his king's printership restraining, no doubt, his encouragement of government's critics.

Copies located:

CaNS	v. 1	(no. 4)	Nov. 1, 1785
	v. 2	(no. 142)	June 17, 1788
	v. 4	(no. 213)	Oct. 27, 1789
	v. 8	(no. 412)	Mar. 25, 1794
	v. 14	(no. 643, 646)	Sept. 11, Oct. 2, 1798
	v. 15	(694-763)	Sept. 3, 1799-Dec. 30, 1800
	Sup. with	(no. 700, 711, 727)	Oct. 15, 1799, Jan. 7, Apr. 22, 1800
	Mutilated:		Nov. 1, 1785, Oct. 27, 1789, Sept. 23, 1800
	Misnumbered:		
	v. 14	(no. 711-12 misnumbered 710-11; 713-16 " 711-14.	
CaNSA	v. 1 [sic]	(no. 105)	Oct. 2, 1787 (mutilated)
	v. 4	(no. 232)	Mar. 9, 1790
	v. 13	(no. 597)	Oct. 24, 1797
	v. 14	(no. 655)	Dec. 4, 1798
	v. 15	(no. 675, 791)	Apr. 23, Aug. 13, 1799

CaNU	v. 1	(no. 1-2	Oct. 11-18, 1785
	v. 1	7- 50	Nov. 22, 1785-Sept. 19, 1786
		53-59, 62-90	Oct. 10-Nov. 21, Dec. 12, 1786-June 19, 1787
		93-97, 99	July 10-Aug. 7, Aug. 21, 1787
		101-103	Sept. 4-18, 1787
		106-116)	Oct. 9-Dec. 18, 1787
	v. 14	(no. 672-674, 677-678	Apr. 2-16, May 7-14, 1799
		681-686	June 4-July 9, 1799
		688-696	July 23-Sept. 17, 1799
		703, 709	Nov. 5, Dec. 17, 1799
		714 [i.e. 716]-763)	Feb. 4-Dec. 30, 1800
	and	Extra	May 25, 1787
		Sup.	Apr. 22, 1800
		Mut.	Nov. 22, 1785, July 4, 1786
			July 17, Sept. 4, 1787, Oct. 7, 1800
		Misnumbered:	no. 716 appears as 714
			v. 14 " " 15 occasionally
			v. 15 " " 14 "
MWA	v. 15	(no. 662)	Jan. 22, 1799

THE SAINT JOHN GAZETTE AND WEEKLY ADVERTISER.

Printed at Saint John, N.B., by Wm. Lewis & John Ryan, then others, 1783-19th century.

This weekly newspaper was originally called the *Royal St. John's gazette, and Nova Scotia Intelligencer,* and was established at Saint John (also called Carleton, Parr Town, or St. John's, till incorporated as Saint John, May, 1785) Dec. 18, 1783, judging from the earliest issue seen, v. 1, no. 7, Thursday, Jan. 29, 1784; it was printed by William Lewis and John Ryan. Lewis left the partnership Apr. 1, 1786, and the paper was continued by Ryan till Mar. 22, 1799, when he succeeded Christopher Sower as king's printer in New Brunswick and publisher of the *Royal gazette.* Jacob S. Mott bought the *Saint John gazette* from Ryan, his brother-in-law, and printed it from Mar. 29, 1799 (v. 13, no. 1, total no. 670) till it was discontinued in 1806?, when Mott took over the *Royal gazette* and succeeded Ryan as king's printer (commission dated Mar. 5, 1808). The earliest issue seen bears the heading:

<Vol. I THE ROYAL NUMB. VII.> / S$^{T.}$ JOHN$^{'S}$ GAZETTE, / and NOVA-SCOTIA INTELLIGENCER: / [rule] / THURSDAY, JANUARY 29, 1784. / [rule] /

and *colophon*:

Carleton: Printed by Lewis and Ryan, Printers to his Majesty's Loyal Settlement of St. John's River, Nova-Scotia, at the Printing and Post Office, No. 3, King Street, where all manner of Printing Work is performed with Accuracy and Dispatch.*$_*$*Advertisements not exceeding twenty Lines will be inserted for one Dollar, and others more lengthy in proportion.

The title was changed to drop the words "Royal" and "Nova-Scotia," probably when the western part of Nova Scotia was organized as a separate province, New

Brunswick, in 1784, and the *Royal gazette* established by its king's printer in 1785. In the later issues seen, 1789 *et seq.*, the heading reads: *The Saint John Gazette and Weekly Advertiser, Saint John: Published Every Friday by John Ryan at his Printing-office, N° 58, Prince William Street.*

Published on Thursday till 1787 then (excepting for an interval in 1789 when it appeared on Wednesday) on Friday, this paper was printed on a small folio sheet (later enlarged), four pages of three or four columns in each issue, occasionally increased to eight pages, or, by a supplement of two pages. Towards the end of the century more and more advertising and news matter was compressed into the pages, but even so, Ryan used less of the smaller type, brevier or small pica, and more pica, than other Canadian newspaper printers of the period.

Few official publications of the provincial government appeared in the *Saint John gazette*, but the proceedings, ordinances, advertisements, etc., of the Common [City] Council were published there, Ryan being unofficially "municipal" printer. No editorials appeared, but a column on the third page headed "St. John [and date of issue]" contained a condensed bulletin of foreign and local news with an occasional expression of Ryan's commendation or regret, or the caption: "Good News *if* True." Here, too, appeared a record of the local events of the preceding week, and of marriages, deaths, and shipping. Apparently a keen journalist, he occasionally "featured" in the regular or an Extra number, important news just received from abroad, "scooping" the king's printer, a fact which he would point out with some complacency.

Though Ryan expressed no editorial opinion, he appears to have had a policy and his paper, particularly while Lewis was still co-owner, was characterized by occasional anonymous communications criticizing the provincial administration and discussing political issues. On Mar. 4, 1784, appeared the notice:

> "The editors of the *St. John Gazette* beg leave once more to inform their correspondents that pieces tending to scurrility or faction will not be attended to, nor have any countenance in this paper. The office is already teaming [sic] with such NEQUID, MINIS. Essays conveying liberality of sentiment will always be cheerfully received and published."—quoted (from a copy not located) in *Early printers and old newspapers in New Brunswick*, in Saint John, N.B., Free Public Library: Jack Collection.

In the same issue appeared a blistering letter in criticism of the government's relief and land granting practices. This led to Lewis and Ryan's arrest and indictment before Grand Jury at Maugerville, Mar. 10, 1784. They were arrested again apparently for publications during the first municipal elections, Nov., 1785,* and tried for libel in the Supreme Court at Saint John, May 2, 1786. Each partner was fined £20 and costs and ordered to provide surety of £100 for good behaviour for six months. Lewis returned to the United States after this experience and Ryan published a less contentious, though still independent *Gazette.*

He got into difficulty again, however, for "intermeddling with the proceedings of the House [of Assembly]" by printing (in the *Saint John gazette*, Feb. 10, 1797)

---

*Feelings ran high between candidates supported by "Lower Cove" settlers and those backed by provincial officials. Lewis & Ryan's *Saint John gazette* was described at this time by King's Printer Sower's *Royal gazette* as "a certain paper devoted to the purposes of wretched faction . . . filled with despicable publications calculated to favour the most dishonourable and pernicious news."

letters to the House from Wm. Knox, provincial agent in London. But Ryan, who was apparently with the Assembly in its current quarrel with the administration, was found (by a Committee of the House) to have been without evil intention. He was acquitted without censure, Jan. 31, 1798. When Ryan became king's printer and publisher of the *Royal gazette* the following year, his brother-in-law, Jacob S. Mott, continued the *Saint John gazette* as an independent though not necessarily "opposition" journal.

Copies located:

CaNS	v.1	(no. 39)	Sept. 9, 1784
	v. 11	(no. 546-554	Nov. 4-Dec. 30, 1796
		555-565)	Jan. 6-Mar. 17, 1797
	v. 11-12	(no. 569-600	Apr. 14-Nov. 17, 1797
	v. 12	602-606)	Dec. 1-29, 1797
	v. 12-13	(no. 607-634	Jan. 5-July 13, 1798
	v. 13	636-641	July 27-Aug. 31, 1798
		644-645	Sept. 21-28, 1798
		647-648	Oct. 12-19, 1798
		450 [i.e. 650]-658)	Nov. 2-Dec. 28, 1798
	v. 13-14	(no. 659-691)	Jan. 4-Aug. 23, 1799
	v. 15	(no. 753 n.s. no. 84)	Oct. 31, 1800
	and	Extra June 17, 1797	
		Sup. with Mar. 1, 1799	
		Mut: Feb. 3, Oct. 20, Nov. 3, 1797; Jan. 11, Feb. 15-Mar. 1, May 10, 1799.	
CaNSA	v. 1	(no. 7, 11)	Jan. 29, Feb. 26, 1784
	v. 3	(no. 155)	May 1, 1789
	v. 5	(no. 221, 226	Aug. 6, Sept. 10, 1790
		250)	Feb. 25, 1791
	v. 14	(no. 683 n.s. no. 14)	June 28, 1799 (Mut.—4 of its 8 pages wanting)
CaNU	v. 2	(no. 74-76, 78,	Oct. 12-26, Nov. 9, 1787
		80-83)	Nov. 23-Dec. 14, 1787
CaNsHA	v. 14	(no. 690)	Aug. 16, 1799
CaO	v. 1	(no. 7)	Jan. 29, 1784
MWA	v. 1	(no. 30-31, 41)	July 8-15, Sept. 23, 1784

The following Extra numbers are known to have been published but no copies have been located: 1798, Nov. 28 or Dec. 5 (reports on the Battle of the Nile); 1799, Aug. 14.

THE HALIFAX GAZETTE. *Printed at Halifax, N.S., by John Bushell, then by Anthony Henry, 1752-1766.*

The *Halifax gazette* was established by John Bushell, who issued the first number Mar. 23, 1752. It had been projected, apparently, and a prospectus issued, by Bushell's former partner, Bartholomew Green, in 1751 (*see* No. 1). The paper was printed by Bushell till his death in Jan., 1761, though edited and supervised by the provincial secretary, Richard Bulkeley, from 1758. The latest issue of Bushell's printing which has been located, is no. 343, Dec. 9, 1758. It was continued by Bushell's assistant and successor in the printing office, Anthony Henry, who produced his first number in Feb., 1761, judging from his earliest issue located, no. 129, July 28, 1763. Henry continued till some time between Mar. 6, 1766 (no. 245) and Aug., 1766, when the *Halifax gazette* had ceased publication. From Oct. 31, 1765, the issues were double-dated, i.e., they bore the day date of the beginning and end of the publication week. This paper bore the heading:

> [ornament: ship in sail] / NOVA-SCOTIA. No. / THE / HALIFAX GAZETTE. / [double rule] / [small cut of man with rifle stepping out of woods towards settlement in a clearing] / [rule] / [date] /

The colophon read: "Halifax: Printed by John Bushell at the Printing-Office in Grafton-Street, where advertisements are taken in." To this was added, Apr. 13, 1753: "and all persons may be supplied with this paper at 12 Shillings a Year." Each number was a half sheet of foolscap printed in 2 col. on both sides, later enlarged (by Henry?) to a full sheet—4 pages. It was issued on Mondays for the first four issues, then on Saturdays, till some time between Dec. 9, 1758 and July 28, 1763, when it had changed to Thursday. From the first, the *Halifax gazette* contained principally excerpts "from the British Prints" on European politics and government, "Plantation News" from American and West Indian colonies, shipping notices of Boston and Halifax. About a quarter of its space contained matter relating to Nova Scotia, e.g., proclamations, sessions laws, a few business cards, and occasionally advertisements for runaway Negroes, stolen goods, and straying wives.

The *Gazette* showed little change (in the broken files located) until the Stamp Act came into effect. The first issue thereafter, Oct. 31-Nov. 7, 1765, was 4 pages (a full folio sheet bearing the stamp) with the heading:

> "The Halifax Gazette or the Weekly Advertiser, containing the freshest Intelligence Foreign and Domestic. Halifax (in Nova Scotia) printed and sold by A. Henry at his Printing Office in Sackvile [sic] Street where all persons may be supplied with this paper at 18 Shillings a year, untill the Publisher has 150 Subscribers, when it will be no more than Twelve Shillings. Advertisements are taken in and inserted as Cheap as the Stamp Act will allow."

One-quarter to one-half the space of each issue till Feb. 27-Mar. 6, 1766, was occupied with accounts, reprinted from Boston, New York, and Philadelphia papers, of colonial resistance to the Stamp Act, and with an occasional innuendo suggesting the Nova Scotians' distaste for the Stamp. From Nov. 28-Dec. 5 till Feb. 27-Mar. 6, each number had mourning border and rules. On several of the surviving copies, some derisive cut was added, or substituted for the revenue stamp, e.g., a skull and cross-bones (in black, on an unstamped half sheet, Dec. 12-19, 1765, a death's head (in red on an unstamped, also on a stamped, half sheet, Dec. 19-26, 1765). The most elaborate was a wood-cut about an inch square depicting the devil with pitch fork directed towards the stamp, which is framed in the legend: "Behold me the Scorn and contempt of AMERICA pitching down to Destruction Devils clear the Way for B——s and STAMPS." This is said to have been the work of Isaiah Thomas (later patriot printer and historian of American printing) who worked in Henry's office from Oct., 1765 till Mar., 1766. As the located copies of issues in this period are those sent to New England subscribers or preserved by Thomas himself, it is not certain that the *Gazette* was circulated in Nova Scotia with these embellishments. Its reprinted accounts of the Act in New England, etc., and remarks upon local enforcement, however, certainly gave offense to the administration. The government's printing was withheld from Henry, and given to a new-comer apparently brought from England for the purpose. Thomas left the province in Mar., 1766, and Henry discontinued the *Halifax gazette* some time before Fletcher began issuing the *Nova-Scotia gazette*, in the following August. *See also:* J. B. Brebner: *The neutral Yankees of Nova Scotia* (New York, 1937), p. 157-63; W. B. Kerr: *The Stamp Act in Nova Scotia*, in *New England quarterly*, 6: 522-66, 1933; A. M. Schlesinger: *The colonial newspaper and the Stamp Act*, *ibid.*, 8: 63-83, 1935; J. J. Stewart: *Early journalism in Nova Scotia*, in N.S. Hist. soc. *Coll.* 6: 91-122, 1888; Isaiah Thomas: *History of printing in America* (2 v., Albany, N.Y, 1874) 2: 180.

Copies located: A modern facsimile reprint of no. 1, Mar. 23, 1752, is commonly found in large public libraries and in private collections of Canadiana.

CaOOA	no. 129	July 28, 1763
MHi	no. 1-11, 15	Mar. 23-May 30, June 27, 1752
	17-19, 23-30	July 11-25, Aug. 22-Oct. 21, 1752
	33-42,	Nov. 11, 1752-Jan. 13, 1753
	44-53, 55-76	Jan. 27-Mar. 31, Apr. 14-Sept. 8, 1753
	79-80, 82-85,	Sept. 29-Oct. 6, Oct. 20-Nov. 10, 1753
	88-116,	Dec. 1, 1753-July 6, 1754
	118-123,	July 20-Aug. 24, 1754
	128-131,	Sept. 28-Oct. 19, 1754
	135, 137,	Nov. 16, Nov. 30, 1754
	175,	Aug. 23, 1755
	343,	Dec. 9, 1758
	n.s., no. 189-190,	Dec. 13-20, 1764
	242.	Feb. 6-13, 1766
MWA	no. 5-6, 10,	Apr. 18-25, May 23, 1752
	148, 150	Feb. 15, Mar. 1, 1755
	228, 223, 225-226	Aug. 29, Oct. 3, 17-24, 1765
	228-232	Oct. 31-Nov. 7 (double-dated)—Nov. 28-Dec. 5, 1765
	234-236	Dec. 12-19—Dec. 26-Jan. 2, 1766
	237-245	Jan. 2-9—Feb. 27-Mar. 6, 1766

THE NOVA-SCOTIA GAZETTE. *Printed at Halifax, N.S., by Robert Fletcher, 1766-1770.*

The *Nova-Scotia gazette* was established at Halifax by Robert Fletcher, Aug. 14 or 15, 1766 (v. 1, no. 1) and printed by him till Aug. 30, 1770 (v. 5, no. 213). It was a single sheet in folio, 4 pages, printed 3 col. to the page, and issued weekly on Thursdays. It bore the heading: "The Nova-Scotia Gazette, Halifax: Printed by R. Fletcher at the Printing Office on the Parade, where all sorts of blank warrants . . . are printed and sold," and a footnote: "Subscriptions . . . 12 Shillings a year or three pence a paper. Advertisements of moderate Length are inserted at three shillings each." From Sept. 1, 1768, the price was reduced to 8*s*. a year, 2*d*. a paper.

Fletcher came to Nova Scotia from England in the summer of 1766, probably on the invitation or encouragement of the provincial government, for he immediately superseded Anthony Henry as government printer. Fletcher brought a new printing-house, a stock of books, stationery, and patent medicines, and set up shop. His newspaper had a fine appearance and was singularly free from typographic error and misnumbering (only v. 4, no. [161] was misprinted no. 171). Its content was principally Nova Scotia sessions laws and other official publications, with news and essays on innocuous topics reprinted from English sources, and lengthy advertisements of Fletcher's own wares for sale. It included little current or local news, or colonial opinion. The printer, a new-comer probably unfamiliar with Nova Scotian and New England affairs, with few colonial connections, was less enterprising as a publisher than as a shopkeeper. And he produced a paper of decidedly less interest than the former *Halifax gazette* or, the later, *Nova Scotia chronicle*, published by that well-established Haligonian, Anthony Henry. Fletcher received little support but from the government, and he abandoned the printing side of his business after four years. His paper was taken over by Henry and combined with the *Nova Scotia chronicle*, to form the *Nova-Scotia gazette and the weekly chronicle*.

Copies located:

MHi	v. 2	(no. 68,	Nov. 26, 1767
		84-87,	Mar. 17-31, 1768
		89-90,	Apr. 14-21, 1768
		104-105,	July 28-Aug. 4, 1768
		109-111)	Sept. 1-15, 1768
	v. 4	(no. 199, [201])	May 24, June 7 (mut.), 1770
NN	v. 4	(no. 160-165,	Aug. 24-Sept. 28, 1769
		169-174,	Oct. 26-Nov. 30, 1769
		177-185,	Dec. 21, 1769-Feb. 15, 1770
		189, 191-193)	Mar. 15, Mar. 29-Apr. 12, 1770
	v. 4-5	(no. 195-211, 213)	Apr. 26-Aug. 16, Aug. 30, 1770

Sup. with Apr. 12, 1770
Mut.: Aug. 24, 1769; Mar. 15, May 3-17, June 28, Aug. 30, 1770

THE NOVA SCOTIA CHRONICLE AND WEEKLY ADVERTISER. *Printed at Halifax, N.S., by Anthony Henry, 1769-1770.*

The *Nova Scotia chronicle* was established at Halifax by Anthony Henry, Jan. 3, 1769 (v. 1, no. 1), and printed and published by him weekly on Tuesdays till Aug. 28, 1770 (v. 2, no. 38). This paper bore the heading:

> ([Year, volume and issue number]) / THE / NOVA SCOTIA G II [sic] [royal arms] R CHRONICLE, / And WEEKLY ADVERTISER, / [double rule] / Containing the freshest Advices, both Foreign and Domestic; / with a Variety of other Matter, useful, instructive and entertaining. / [double rule] / [date, issue no. and vol. no.] / [double rule] /

and *colophon:*

HALIFAX: Printed by Anthony Henry, at his PRINTING-OFFICE, in George-Street, where / Subscriptions at EIGHT SHILLINGS, per Annum, ADVERTISEMENTS, ARTICLES and LETTERS of / INTELLIGENCE, are gratefully received. All Manner of Printing performed at the most reasonable Rate. /

From Feb. 21, 1769, the paper was printed "at his Printing-Office in Sackville-Street" which remained Henry's address till his death. Each issue was a single sheet in quarto, 8 pages, printed 3 col. to the page. The pages were numbered continuously within each volume, as were the issues. In v. 2, no. 1-10 bear also the whole numbers 53-62. This paper, like Henry's other productions, shows considerable typographical error, e.g. in numbering of issues; in v. 1, 45 is omitted, no. [45-51] numbered: 46-52, followed by no. 0. In v. 2, 26 is repeated and 27-29, 31, omitted. Most issues are double-dated, showing the first and last (or publication) day covered by that issue.

Henry's former newspaper had been discontinued in 1766, when the indispensable patronage of government was transferred to Robert Fletcher and his *Nova-Scotia gazette*. It became apparent, however, that Fletcher's advantage in official favour was offset by his lack of journalistic enterprise. So two-and-a-half years later, Henry launched the *Nova Scotia chronicle*, the first Canadian newspaper completely dependent upon support of the general public. He introduced the first number with an address thanking the public for encouragement and begging the favour that "gentlemen of experience and knowledge (of whom there are many in this colony) would lay before the Public, their Experiments and Discoveries, as well in Husbandry, as in other Arts and Sciences, by the Channel of this paper. Every piece of History, Politicks, Agriculture, Poetry and the freshest news both Foreign and Domestic, that . . . can be properly comprised in the Chronicle, shall find a place in it." Henry continued, advising readers not to expect news of the "Different Quarters of the World" immediately, as winter having set in, British and foreign intelligence was cut off, but entertaining and instructive articles would be published and advertisements inserted at a reasonable rate. A year's issues of the *Chronicle*, the printer added optimistically, would be bound for 2*s*. 6*d*.

During its course the *Nova Scotia chronicle and weekly advertiser* contained few advertisements. Latterly only about one-tenth of its space was so occupied, the longest and most consistent advertisement being that of Henry's rival, Robert Fletcher. No official government publications appeared. But the journal of the Assembly, in session Oct. 10-Nov. 10, 1769, was printed seriatim in the *Chronicle*, Oct. 31-Nov. 21, 1769, the text apparently supplied to the printer unofficially, and quite contrary to precedent, by a correspondent who signed himself "Constant Reader." Most of the space was filled with essays and articles stating the case for the colonies, or the cause of John Wilkes, against Lord North's government. They were reprinted from Boston, Philadelphia, and London papers, without comment by Henry or by his contributors. The *Nova Scotia chronicle* was almost a party organ, so consistently and exclusively did it represent the Whig attitude. It included also numerous letters, verses, and light essays of local origin on "entertaining" themes, e.g. "On the Manners of Whist Players." Foreign and shipping news appeared in season, also —a new feature in Canadian newspapers—weekly tables showing the time of tides, the sun's rising and setting for the ensuing week, and meteorological observations on weather, temperature, and winds for the preceding week—a by-product, no doubt, of Henry's *Nova-Scotia calender or an almanack*, inaugurated in 1768.

Till Wm. Moore's *Herald* appeared in Quebec twenty years later, also independent of government patronage, Henry's *Chronicle* in its brief span, was the liveliest journal of opinion produced in Canada. Its twenty-month run, with little income from advertisements and none from government, and with subscriptions at 8*s*. a year, is proof of its popular character, or possibly some private support. This evidently discouraged Fletcher, for, whatever the reason, he stopped printing and his newspaper business was transferred to Henry. The latter merged Fletcher's *Nova-Scotia gazette* with his own *Nova Scotia chronicle* and produced the *Nova-Scotia gazette and the weekly chronicle* after the end of Aug., 1770.

Copies located:

CaNs	v. 1	(no. 3-5,	Jan. 10-17—24-31, 1769
		25,	June 13-20, 1769
		29-0 [i.e. 52])	July 11-18—Dec. 19-26, 1769
			Mut. July 11-18, Sept. 19-26, Dec. 19-26, 1769
	Cop. 2, v. 1	(no. 48)	Nov. 14-21, 1769 (mut.)
CaNsHD	v. 1	(no. 1-0 [i.e. 52])	Jan. 3—Dec. 19-26, 1769
	v. 2	(no. 1-38)	Jan. 2—Aug. 21-28, 1770
		Sup. with	Apr. 17-24, July 24-31, 1770
			Mut. May 1-8—15-22, 1770
	Cop. 2, v. 1	(no. 1-16, 22,	Jan. 3—Apr. 11-18, May 23-30, 1769
		24-51, 0 [i.e. 52])	June 6-13—Dec. 5-12, Dec. 19-26, 1769
			Mut. Feb. 28–Mar. 7, May 23-30, June 6-13, 1769
MHi	v. 1	(no. 51)	Dec. 5-12, 1769
	v. 2	(no. 17 + Sup.	Apr. 17-24, 1770
		20, 22-23)	May 8-15, May 22-29—May 29-June 5, 1770
			Mut. May 22-29, 1770

THE NOVA-SCOTIA GAZETTE AND THE WEEKLY CHRONICLE. *Printed at Halifax, N.S., by Anthony Henry, 1770-1800.*

The *Nova-Scotia gazette and the weekly chronicle* was the third newspaper printed at Halifax by Anthony Henry. It represented a merger of the semi-official *Nova-Scotia gazette*, printed by Robert Fletcher, 1766-70, and Henry's second paper, the *Nova Scotia chronicle*, 1769-70. It was published weekly on Tuesdays from v. 1 (no. 1) Sept. 4, 1770, or thereabouts (the earliest issue located being no. 24, Feb. 12, 1771), to v. 19 (no. 1199) Mar. 31, 1789; then, with title the *Royal gazette and Nova-Scotia advertiser*, from v. 1 (no. 1) Apr. 7, 1789, to v. 13 (no. 673) published Dec. 30, 1800, four weeks after Henry's death. At first this paper bore the heading:

> VOL. [no]>THE< NUMBER [no.] / Nova-Scotia [royal arms] GAZETTE: / AND THE / WEEKLY CHRONICLE / [double rule] / TUESDAY [date] / [double rule] /

and *colophon:*

> "Halifax Printed by Anthony Henry at his Printing Office in Sackville-Street, where Subscriptions are at ten Shillings per annum. Advertisements and letters of intelligence are gratefully received."

The subscription rose during the war. "On account of the extraordinary high price of every necessary of life as well as of stock and materials for three years past [the printer] is under the disagreeable necessity of raising the price to 15/ . . . which he hopes will not be thought hard of."—*Nova-Scotia gazette*, July 20, 1779. Later the imprint was transferred from colophon to mast-head, and on May 13, 1788, changed to read: "Halifax, Printed by Anthony Henry, Printer to the Government of His Majesty's Province of Nova-Scotia." Henry was appointed king's printer by royal commission, dated [London] June 11, 1788, and from Dec. 2, 1788, his imprint read: "Halifax, Printed by Anthony Henry, Printer to the King's Most Excellent Majesty at the Printing Office in Sackville-Street [etc.]." On Apr. 7, 1789 he changed the title to: "*The Royal gazette and Nova-Scotia Advertiser*" beginning a new numbering series as noted above.

The *Nova-Scotia gazette and weekly chronicle* combined the essential features of its two components. Like Fletcher's *Nova-Scotia gazette*, it was the medium of lawful publication of proclamations, laws, and public notices. Like Henry's *Nova Scotia chronicle* it contained—besides local news, advertisements, and correspondence—numerous extracts from American papers on colonial affairs and relations with Great Britain, and proceedings of colonial legislatures. After the Revolution broke out, political discussions became more restricted in the *Nova-Scotia gazette*. Though not king's printer till 1788, Henry was in effect a government printer, with a salary and a flexible agreement for printing official publications. Especially after loyalist printers came to the province, he became more careful in excluding matters offensive to the administration—notably in his refusal to print reports from the Continental Congress (*see* No. 246). With Halifax a British military and naval base, and Nova Scotia an asylum for refugees and loyalists, local news, advertisements, and correspondence increased proportionately. From 1789, the content of Henry's paper became more official, and less "opinionative" than it had been in earlier years, also than the content of other newspapers, by then established in Halifax. During the war with France, with Halifax a naval base and Prince Edward in residence, business booming and society bustling, the *Royal gazette* was crowded with foreign news and official notices of provincial, military, and naval authorities, also with advertisements of local merchants, taverns and theatrical companies, tagged "By Permission" or "By Authority."

Typographically Henry's third newspaper was much superior to its predecessors. He obtained new equipment about the time it started, more skill in his office, and a wider knowledge of colonial printing style—probably from his increasing exchanges with other newspapers. His early eccentricity in the use of ornament and heavy type disappeared. Succeeding to Robert Fletcher's well-printed *Nova-Scotia gazette*, and later with several American printers in the province, and John Howe's *Halifax journal*, a challenging weekly model, Henry improved layout, spacing, and press work, and enlarged his sheet. The *Nova-Scotia gazette* (from Apr., 1789, the *Royal gazette*) became a newspaper of high legibility and pleasing dignity—if not one of originality or distinction.

Henry died on Dec. 1, 1800. On Tuesday, Dec. 2, his paper appeared with the outer pages as usual, but the inner pages set with mourning rules, and including the notice: "Last evening departed this life after a short illness Mr. Anthony Henry, aged 66. Printer to the King's Most Excellent Majesty, and for forty years publisher of this Gazette [etc.]." Henry had published the semi-official *Halifax gazette*, 1761-66, and the semi-official *Nova-Scotia* (or *Royal*) *gazette*, 1770-1800. In the interval,

1766-70, the semi-official paper was published by Robert Fletcher as the *Nova-Scotia gazette,* while an independent paper was issued by Henry (the *Nova Scotia chronicle*), 1769-70 only.

The *Royal gazette* continued, "printed at the Office of the late Anthony Henry [etc.]," till Dec. 30, 1800, when his widow announced:

> "Mrs. Henry finding that her state of health and advanced age will not permit her any longer to carry on the printing business, or conduct the publishing of The Royal Gazette, begs leave gratefully to acknowledge the generous support and liberal encouragement her late Husband experienced thro' a series of years, not only from the public at large but from the principal officers and Departments of government . . . Messrs Gay and Merlin have purchased all the material of the printing office and this Gazette will in future be published by them. She [Mrs. Henry] is satisfied with their abilities and recommends them to the countenance and patronage of the Public."
>
> —*Royal gazette,* Halifax, N.S., Dec. 30, 1800.

The *Royal gazette,* however, ceased with the issue of Dec. 30, 1800, for John Howe, appointed king's printer immediately, absorbed its official character into his *Halifax journal,* and produced the *Nova-Scotia royal gazette* from Jan. 3, 1801. Gay and Merlin started another paper, the *Nova Scotia gazette and weekly chronicle* in 1801.

Henry's *Nova-Scotia gazette and weekly chronicle* (and his *Royal gazette*) was a 4-page folio, printed 3 (later 4) col. to the page, with occasional 2-page supplements. The pages were unnumbered. The issues were numbered, with some errors and omissions in one continuous sequence under each title. The volume number changed annually about Sept., 1770-82, then at the turn of the calendar year till 1789. Subsequently it changed irregularly at 8 to 17 month intervals with occasional misprintings, e.g., 12 was omitted entirely in the *Royal gazette* series, v. 11 ending with Feb. 18, 1800, v. 13 beginning Feb. 25, 1800.

Errors noted in numbering of issues are as follows:

In the *Nova-Scotia gazette* series:

In v. 3 no. 147-149 repeated (on July 13-27, 1773).
v. 5 no. [213] Oct. 18, 1774, appears as no. 123, numbers thereafter run 124-150, 251-259, 251 and thenceforward in continuous sequence.
v. 9 no. [530-539] Feb. 16-June 29, 1779, misnumbered: 260-279; no. 280 (or [550]) misnumbered: 680, and issues thereafter in sequence.
v. 9 no. [736] July 11, 1780, misnumbered: 734.
v. 11 no. 806-808 omitted in numbering.
v. 12 no. 857-859 omitted in numbering.
v. 13 appears as v. 12 from no. 883-906, Apr. 8-Sept. 16, 1783.
v. 14 no. 946-947 omitted in numbering.
v. 18 no. [1043] Mar. 4, 1788, misnumbered: 1042.

In the *Royal gazette* series:

In v. 1 no. 5 omitted in numbering (or else assigned to an unrecorded Extra between Apr. 28 and May 5, 1789.
v. 4 no. 173, 184 omitted in numbering.
v. 5 no. [220-223] May 21-June 11, 1793, misnumbered: 211-213.
v. 6 no. 298 repeated on Jan. 6, 1795.

v. 7 no. 326-328, 332-334, 370-399, 414, 417, omitted in numbering.
v. 9 no. 473, 476-477, 480-499, 518 omitted in numbering.
v. 10 no. 566-568 omitted in numbering.
v. 11 no. 603 repeated on Aug. 30, 1799.
v. 13 no. 637-638 repeated on Apr. 22-29, 1800.

Copies located:

CaNS		Extra	Mar. 23, 1781
CaNSA	v. 10	(no. 702)	Nov. 23, 1779
	v. 12	(no. 814)	Jan. 1, 1782
CaNs	v. 5	(no. 207-130	Sept. 6-Dec. 6, 1774
		132-146,	Dec. 20, 1774-Mar. 28, 1775
		148-253,	Apr. 11-July 18, 1775
		255-257)	Aug. 1-15, 1775
	v. 5-[6]	(no. 260-268,	Aug. 29-Oct. 24, 1775
		270)	Nov. 7, 1775
	v. 9	(no. 525-527,	Jan. 12-26, 1779
		260-275,	Feb. 16-June 1, 1779
		277-688)	June 15-Aug. 31, 1779
	v. 10	(no. 690-714,	Sept. 14, 1779-Feb. 15, 1780
		716-724,	Feb. 29-Apr. 18, 1780
		726-734	May 2-June 27, 1780
		734-740, 742,	July 11-Aug. 8, Aug. 22, 1780
	[v. 11]	744-745,	Sept. 5-12, 1780
		747-748)	Sept. 26-Oct. 3, 1780
	v. 11	(no. 751, 754-756,	Oct. 24, Nov. 14-28, 1780
		758-760)	Dec. 12-26, 1780
		Sup. with no. 212, 269	Oct. 11, 1774, Oct. 31, 1775
		680, 732	July 6, 1779, June 13, 1780
		Another copy	
	v. 9	(no. 688)	Aug. 31, 1779
CaNsHA	v. 3	(no. 106-111,	Sept. 8-Oct. 13, 1772
		113-115,	Oct. 27-Nov. 10, 1772
		117-119,	Nov. 24-Dec. 8, 1772
		121-144)	Dec. 22, 1772-June 1, 1773
	v. 3-4	(no. 147-159,	June 22-Oct. 5, 1773
		161-169,	Oct. 19-Dec. 14, 1773
		171-174	Dec. 28, 1773-Jan. 18, 1774
		176-180	Feb. 1-Mar. 1, 1774
		182-192	Mar. 15-May 24, 1774
		194-200	June 7-July 19, 1774
		202-206)	Aug. 2-30, 1774
	and	Extra	Apr. 24, 1789
		Sup. with	Apr. 27, 1773; May 17-24, 1774

continued as the *Royal gazette:*

CaNsHA con.	v. 1-3	(no. 41-145)	Jan. 5, 1790–Dec. 27, 1791, (a broken file in the Akins collection).

also	v. 2	(no. 74)	Aug. 17, 1790
	v. 3	(no. 141)	Nov. 29, 1791
	v. 4	(no. 165)	May 15, 1792
	v. 5	(no. 210, 215,	Mar. 12, Apr. 16, 1793
		259)	Apr. 1, 1794
	v. 6	(no. 313)	Apr. 21, 1795
	v. 7	(no. 356-357	Jan. 5-12, 1796
		360-365	Feb. 2-Mar. 8, 1796
		367-406	Mar. 22-May 24, 1796
		408-417)	June 7-Aug. 2
	v. 7-8	(no. 420-427	Aug. 23-Oct. 4
		429-434,	Oct. 18-Nov. 22,
		436-439)	Dec. 6-27, 1796
	v. 9	(no. 511)	Dec. 5, 1797
	v. 10	(no. 550)	Aug. 14, 1798
	v. 11	(no. 583, 597	Mar. 12, June 18, 1799
		606, 609,	Aug. 27, Sept. 17, 1799
		613, 618)	Oct. 15, Nov. 19, 1799
	v. 13	(no. 644)	June 10, 1800
		Mut.	Apr. 19, 1796; Dec. 5, 1797; Aug. 14, 1798; Mar. 12, June 18, 1799
CaNsHD	*Nova-Scotia gazette*		
	v. 3	(no. 105-113,	Sept. 1-Oct. 27, 1772
		115, 117-119	Nov. 10, Nov. 24-Dec. 8, 1772
		121-140)	Dec. 22, 1772-May 4, 1773
	v. 3-4	(no. 142-174	May 18, 1773-Jan. 18, 1774
		176-192,	Feb. 1-May 24, 1774
		194-206)	June 7-Aug. 30, 1774
	v. 6	(no. 290)	Mar. 26, 1776
	v. 11-12	(no. 761-800,	Jan. 2-Oct. 2, 1781
		802, 804-805,	Oct. 16, Oct. 30-Nov. 6, 1781
		809-811,	Nov. 27-Dec. 11, 1781
		814, 817-827,	Jan. 1, Jan. 22-Apr. 2, 1782
		829-830,	Apr. 16-23, 1782
		833-834, 836	May 7-14, May 28, 1782
		839-840,	June 18-25, 1782
		842, 844-847)	July 9, July 23-Aug. 13, 1782
	v. 12-13	(no. 849-860,	Aug. 27-Oct. 29, 1782
		862-867,	Nov. 12-Dec. 17, 1782
		869-872	Dec. 31, 1782-Jan. 21, 1783
		874, 876-899,	Feb. 4, Feb. 18-July 29, 1783
		902-906,	Aug. 19-Sept. 16, 1783
		908-914, 916	Sept. 30-Nov. 11, Nov. 25, 1783
		918-921)	Dec. 9-30, 1783
	v. 14	(no. 925-936,	Jan. 20-Apr. 6, 1784
		938, 940-941)	Apr. 20, May 4-11, 1784
	v. 14-15	(no. 943-991,	May 25, 1784-Apr. 5, 1785
		993-1022)	Apr. 19-Nov. 8, 1785
	v. 15-16	(no. 1024-1030)	Nov. 22, 1785-Jan. 3, 1786
	v. 16-19	(no. 1032-1199)	Jan. 16, 1786-Mar. 31, 1789

continued as *The Royal Gazette*

CaNsHD con.	v. 1	(no. 1-40)	Apr. 7-Dec. 29, 1789
	v. 3-4	(no. 146-199)	Jan. 3-Dec. 25, 1792
	v. 4-7	(no. 201-354, 357-403)	Jan. 8, 1793-Dec. 22, 1795 Jan. 12-May 3, 1796
	v. 7-9	(no. 405-511)	May 17, 1796-Dec. 5, 1797
	v. 9-13	(no. 517-673)	Jan. 2, 1798-Dec. 30, 1800

Sup. with *Nova-Scotia gazette,* Mar. 20, June 12, Aug. 13, Oct. 30, 1781;
Apr. 16, 1782; Dec. 16, 1783;
Mar. 30, May 25, June 1, 1784;

Sup. with *Royal gazette,* [Mar. 27], May 15, July 3-17, 1792;
Mar. 19, Apr. 16, June 4, July 16, 1793;
Mar. 18, 1794; June 6, 1797; July 30, 1799

Another cop. *Nova-Scotia gazette,* v. 17 (no. 1092) Mar. 13, 1787

Another cop. *Royal gazette,* v. 6 (no. 313) Apr. 21, 1795

Mut. (*Nova Scotia gazette*) Sept. 1, 1772; June 15, 1773; Mar. 26, 1776;
May 1-15, Nov. 6, 1781; June 24, 1783;
Jan. 20, 1784; Feb. 1, May 10, 1785;
Jan. 27, 1789.

Mut. (*Royal gazette*) Jan. 3, 1792; Jan. 7, 1794;
Nov. 8, Dec. 27, 1796; Jan. 2, 1798;
Nov. 25, 1800.

MH entitled *The Royal gazette*

	v. 10	(no. 538, 540)	May 22, June 5, 1798

MHi entitled *The Nova-Scotia gazette and Weekly chronicle*

	v. 1	(no. 24, 36)	Feb. 12, May 7, 1771
	v. 2	(no. 98)	July 14, 1772
	v. 3	(no. 124-126, 132-134)	Jan. 12-26, 1773 Mar. 9-23, 1773
	v. 6	(no. 262, 298, 304)	Sept. 12, 1775 May 28, July 9, 1776
	v. 7	(no. 313-314)	Sept. 10-17, 1776
	v. 9	(no. 511)	Oct. 6, 1778
	v. 13	(no. 920)	Dec. 23, 1783
	v. 14	(no. 925, 927-929)	Jan. 20, 1784 Feb. 3-17, 1784
	v. 16	(no. 1030-1057, 1059-1060)	Jan. 3-July 11, 1786 July 25-Aug. 1, 1786

	v. 16-17	(no. 1062-1093,	Aug. 15, 1786-Mar. 20, 1787
		1096, 1098-1104	Apr. 10, Apr. 24-June 5, 1787
		1106-1113)	June 19-Aug. 7, 1787
	v. 17-18	(no. 1116-1138)	Aug. 28, 1787-Jan. 29, 1788
	v. 18-19	(no. 1140-1199)	Feb. 12, 1788-Mar. 31, 1789
	continued as *The Royal gazette*		
MHi	v. 1	(no. 1, 3-48,	Apr. 7, Apr. 21, 1789-Feb. 23, 1790
con.		50-52	Mar. 9-23, 1790
	v. 2	(no. 56-83)	Apr. 13-Oct. 19, 1790
	v. 2-3	(no. 85-113)	Nov. 2, 1790-May 17, 1791
	v. 3-4	(no. 115-183)	May 31, 1791-Sept. 11, 1792
	v. 4-6	(no. 186-298)	Sept. 25, 1792-Dec. 30, 1794
	and	Extra	Sept. 16, 1790, Apr. 13, 1793
	Sup. with	*Nova-Scotia Gazette*	Mar. 31, 1789;
	with	*Royal gazette*	June 23, 1789; Apr. 20, 1790; Aug. 16, 1791; May 15-22, June 5-[12?], July 3-17, 1792; Mar. 19, Apr. 16, July 16, 1793; June 10, 1794.
	Mut.	(*Nova-Scotia gazette*)	Feb. 10-17, 1784; May 2, 1786; Nov. 4, 1788;
		(*Royal gazette*)	Dec. 7, 1790; Apr. 9, 1793
NN	entitled *The Royal gazette*		
	v. 8	(no. 458)	May 9, 1797
	v. 9	(no. 472, 474)	Aug. 15, Aug. 22, 1797
	v. 10	(no. 545)	July 10, 1798

THE HALIFAX JOURNAL. *Printed at Halifax, N.S., by John Howe, 1780?-1800.*

The *Halifax journal* was established at Halifax, N.S., as a weekly newspaper by John Howe. According to Isaiah Thomas's *History of printing in America* (2 v., Albany, N.Y., 1874), 1: 177 *note,* James Munro was a partner, but no evidence of Munro's connection appears in the paper. The first number was published Dec. 28, 1780, judging from the earliest number located (no. 28) July 5, 1781. The last number located (no. 1038) was published Dec. 19, 1799, but the *Halifax journal* probably continued till Dec., 1800. This paper bore the heading:

THE / HALIFAX JOURNAL. / Printed by JOHN HOWE, at his Printing-Office in BARRINGTON-STREET, nearly opposite the PARADE

Latterly, the word "nearly" was dropped. In the years 1793-95, the *Halifax journal*'s imprint probably read: "Printed by Howe & McKinstry [etc.]" for Howe had one McKinstry as his partner in this period, and his other publications bore the imprint of the firm. Each issue was a 4-page folio, printed 3 col. to the page. The issues were numbered in one continuous series (with discrepancies noted below). The volume number changed with the first issue of each calendar year after 1780. Publication day was Thursday in the earliest issue located, changing to Friday sometime between the issues of July 1 and Nov. 2, 1781, and to Thursday again sometime between Nov. 11, 1785 and Nov. 16, 1786, after which it remained Thursday.

The *Halifax journal* had about half of its space occupied with foreign news or essays reprinted mainly from European publications, a short section headed Halifax, and date of issue, containing shipping and other local news. It included less official matter (proclamations, laws, notices of the provincial government) than the *Nova-Scotia gazette*, and more advertisements. These were remarkably well composed, illustrated with small cuts and, unlike the practice of most early Canadian papers, changed frequently in layout and location on the page. Howe, trained in the Draper printing office in Boston, set a new standard of newspaper printing in Eastern Canada.

John Howe was commissioned king's printer in Nova Scotia by Lieut.-Gov. Wentworth, Halifax, Dec. 4, 1800.* From Jan. 1, 1801 (or thereabouts, judging from no. 12, dated March 19, 1801), he published the *Nova-Scotia royal gazette*, a general newspaper with the government's official publications. His son, John Howe Junior, established another *Halifax journal* in 1810.

Copies located:

CaNS	v. 9	(no. 457)	Sept. 17, 1789
CaNsHA	v. 10	(no. 495-497, 515)	July 22-Aug. 5, Dec. 9, 1790
	v. 17	(no. 775-778	Jan. 7-28, 1796
		†780-738, 740	Feb. 11-May 5, 19, 1796
		743-745,	June 9-23, 1796
		747-756	July 7-Sept. 8, 1796
		758-768, 770, 772)	Sept. 22-Dec. 1, 15, 29, 1796
	v. 18	(no. 626 [sic]-628, 630)	Oct. 26-Nov. 9, 23, 1797
	v. 19	(no. 940 [sic], 941, 943	Jan. 18, Feb. 1, 15, 1798
		951, 953	Apr. 19, May 3, 1798
		958-959	June 7-14, 1798
		966, 968, 973	Aug. 2, 16, Sept. 20, 1798
		676 [i.e. 976]-977	Oct. 11-18, 1798
		984)	Nov. 29, 1798
	v. 20	(no. 999-1000)	May 14-21, 1799
		1004	Apr. 18, 1799
		1008-1009	May 23-30, 1799
		1011-1027	June 13-Oct. 3, 1799
		1030-1035	Oct. 24-Nov. 28, 1799
		1037-1038	Dec. 12-19, 1799
Cop. 2,	v. 20	(no. 999-1000)	May 14-21, 1799
		Mut.	July 22, 1790; Dec. 29, 1796
			Nov. 9, 23, 1797; June 14, 1798
MH	v. 10	(no. 488)	Apr. 1, 1790
	v. 12	(no. 583, 585)	Mar. 29, Apr. 12, 1792
	v. 19	(no. 060 [i.e. 960])	June 21, 1798

*His predecessor, Anthony Henry, who died Dec. 1, 1800, had received a royal commission from London, as had Christopher Sower, first king's printer of New Brunswick.

†Following (no. 782) Feb. 25, 1796, issues of Mar. 3 *et seq*. are numbered 729 *et seq*.

MHi	v. 1	(no. 44)	Nov. 2, 1781
	v. 3	(no. 150)	Nov. 14, 1783
	v. 4	(no. 208)	Dec. 24, 1784
	v. 5	(no. 210-211,	Jan. 7-14, 1785
		215-218,	Feb. 11-Mar. 4, 1785
		254)	Nov. 11, 1785
	v. 6	(no. 306-308,	Nov. 16-23, 1786
		310)	Dec. 7, 1786
	v. 7	(no. 319-320	Feb. 8-15, 1787
		322, 324-326)	Mar. 1, 15-29, 1787
	v. 11	(no. 560-561)	Oct. 21-27, 1791
	v. 12	(no. 584, 590	Apr. 5, May 17, 1792
		594)	June 14, 1792 (mut.)
MWA	v. 3	(no. 143)	Sept. 26, 1783
	v. 5	(no. 252)	Oct. 28, 1785
	v. 12	(no. 605)	Aug. 30, 1792
NNHi	v. 1	(no. 28)	July 5, 1781 (mut.)

NOVA-SCOTIA PACKET AND GENERAL ADVERTISER.

Printed at Shelburne, N.S., by James Humphreys, 1785-1787 or later.

The *Nova-Scotia packet and general advertiser* was established as a weekly on or before May 5, 1785, judging from the earliest number located (no. 53, May 4, 1786), and from the printer's statement, 1787 (Apr. 19) that "the next number of this Packet [no. 104, Apr. 26, 1787] completes the Second Year of its Publication." It was published till Feb. 19, 1789 (for this issue is mentioned in the *Nova-Scotia gazette*, Mar. 17, 1789) and possibly till about 1796, as suggested by J. J. Stewart in *Early journalism in Nova Scotia*. This paper was announced:

> "On Wednesday, the second day of February will be published, by the Subscriber, at his Printing-office, in Water-Street, next Door below Valentine Nutter's Esq. The first Number of The Nova-Scotia Packet, and General Advertiser; To be continued every Wednesday, at Twelve Shillings per Year; Six Shillings to be paid at the Time of Subscribing and Six Shillings at the End of the Year. Subscriptions, Advertisements &c. are now receiving at his Office.—where he hopes for the Encouragement of the Public, not doubting but by the constant Attention to their Interests and Amusements, to render his Paper worthy of their Attention and Approbation. [signed:] James Humphreys. Subscriptions from any Part of the Province will be thankfully received, and constantly attended to. All kinds of Printing Work done in the neatest Manner and on as low Terms as possible at said Office."—*Royal American gazette*, Shelburne, N.S., Jan. 24, 1785.

The paper bore the heading (in copies located):

> THURSDAY, [date] THE No. [no] / NOVA-SCOTIA [ornament: Galleon in full sail] PACKET: / And General Advertiser. / [rule] / SHELBURNE: Printed by JAMES HUMPHREYS, at his Office the Corner of George and Water Streets. / [rule] /

It was probably issued at first on Wednesday, 4 p. in fo., but size and publication day were altered with no. 53, May 4, 1786, which appears 4 p. in 4to. printed 3 col. to the page, and includes the announcement:

"The Printer would have been happy to have continued publishing this Packet in its folio form, but the income of it for the past year not being equal to the expense of conducting it, he is constrained for the present to contract its size, determined as soon as the increase of business shall enable him, to restore it to its original form [etc. he thanks subscribers and advertisers who pay promptly, and observes] to the many that are anxious daily, by every means in their power to promote the welfare of Shelburne, that perhaps there is nothing can so much tend to the advantage of it abroad, as a decent, well-conducted Newspaper; and that the more a printer is enabled by encouragement at home, with subscriptions and advertisements, to conduct it with spirit, the more he will be enabled to circulate it abroad, and render it of real service. With this view, he has ever hitherto furnished Strangers and others going abroad, with a number of papers they were pleased to take gratis, and shall still continue this practice. For the immediate convenience of the Town, it will be published on Thursdays."

The *Nova-Scotia packet* was the third newspaper established at Shelburne, while there still seemed a prospect of the town becoming a British-American metropolis. As Humphreys's notice of May 4, 1786, suggests, the paper was devoted to local interests. While a certain amount of foreign news appeared, it contained principally advertisements and announcements of merchants, settlers, social, and municipal bodies of Shelburne, weekly weather forecasts, and shipping news for that port, advertisements and reprints of British and American publications relating to loyalists. Provincial laws, public notices, and news were reprinted from Halifax, Saint John, and Quebec papers. The local contributions of light verse and moral essays which usually appeared in early Canadian newspapers, were notably absent from the *Packet*. Humphreys himself advertised a miscellaneous stock of fabrics, household and farming utensils, books, and printed blanks, for sale. He was a prominent citizen of Shelburne, latterly holding office of justice of the peace, and member of the provincial assembly. How long he continued the *Packet* after Feb., 1789, is not known, but he left the dwindling community between June, 1796 and Apr., 1797, to settle again in his native city, Philadelphia.

The *Nova-Scotia packet* bore no volume numbers, the issues were numbered in one continuous sequence. They appeared regularly, unpaged, in 4 pages, occasionally increased to 8 pages or augmented by a 2-page supplement in copies located, as recorded below.

A facsim. illus. of the first page of the *Nova-Scotia packet*, July 27, 1787, appears in D. C. McMurtrie's *The Royalist printers of Shelburne, Nova Scotia* in *American book collector*, Jan., 1933.

Copies located:

CaNs	no. 62-63, 65,	July 6-13, July 27, 1786
	no. 67-86,	Aug. 10–Dec. 21, 1786
	no. 88-90,	Jan. 4-18, 1787
	Sup. with	July 20, Aug. 31, Sept. 28, 1786

The following issues have 8 p.: July 6, 27, Aug. 10, Oct. 5, 1786

Mut. July 13, 27, Aug. 10-17, Sept. 7-14, 28, Oct. 19, Nov. 23, 1786: Jan. 11-18, 1787

GBLBM	no. 57, 59,	June 1, 15, 1786
	no. 65-66	July 27–Aug. 3, 1786
	Sup. with	Aug. 3, 1786
	The following issue has 8 p.:	July 27, 1786
MHi	no. 53-114	May 4, 1786–July 5, 1787
	no. 116-133;	July 19–Nov. 15, 1787
	no. 138	Dec. 20, 1787
	Cop. 2, no. 73	Sept. 21, 1786, sup. only
	Sup. with	June 22, July 20, Aug. 31, Sept. 21, 1786 Apr. 12, 26, 1787
	The following issues have 8 p.:	May 18, July 6, 27, Aug. 10, Oct. 5, 1786.
	Mut.	May 4, Nov. 23, 1786; Dec. 20, 1787
MWA	no. 75,	Oct. 5, 1786 (mut.)

THE PORT-ROSEWAY GAZETTEER AND THE SHELBURNE ADVERTISER. *Printed at Shelburne, N.S., by James Robertson, Junior, and T. & J. Swords, 1784-1785, or later.*

The *Port-Roseway gazetteer and the Shelburne advertiser* was established as a weekly at Shelburne, N.S., Nov. 4, 1784, judging from the earliest number located (no. 11, Jan. 13, 1785). It was published there by James Robertson, Junior, and Thomas and James Swords till some time between July 21, 1785 (no. 38, the latest number located), and Sept., 1787, when the Robertson press had left Shelburne. The earlier issues were printed in folio, 4 p. (about 18 × 12 inches) to the issue, 4 col. to the page, and bore the heading:

<VOL. I> THE <NUMBER [no.]> / PORT-ROSEWAY GAZETTEER AND, THE / SHELBURNE ADVERTISER. / [rule] / SHELBURNE: Printed by J. ROBERTSON, junior, T. and J. SWORDS, at the Printing-Office in King-Street / [rule] / THURSDAY [date] / [double rule] /.

With the issue of May 12 (or May 5) 1785, the size was decreased to 4to., 4 p. (about 12 × 10 inches) to the issue (though occasionally extended to 8 p.), printed 3 col. to the page. At the same time the heading was rearranged:

VOL. I THE NUMBER [no.] / PORT-ROSEWAY [ornament: G. R. in festoons crowned] GAZETTEER; / AND, THE / SHELBURNE ADVERTISER. / [rule] / [date] / SHELBURNE: Printed by J. ROBERTSON, junior, T. and J. SWORDS, at the Printing-Office, in King-Street. / [double rule] /

All the issues located are numbered in one sequence as part of volume 1 and paged continuously. The paper derives its title from the former name of the place, Port Roseway (an anglicization of Razoir, an out-port in the French régime) having been renamed Shelburne, Aug. 2, 1783. It is on the south shore of Nova Scotia, about 150 miles below Halifax and about 70 miles from Yarmouth.

Unlike the *Royal American gazette*, and, later, the *Nova-Scotia packet*, the *Port-Roseway gazetteer* contained few advertisements and little news, local or foreign. It included, occasionally, notices or enactments of municipal or provincial authorities, but its content was principally descriptive essays, letters of opinion, tales and verse, extracted from American papers or English periodicals. The publishers were apparently interested in similar material of local origin, for one of the few numbers located includes one of the few original political-economic essays published in the province during the 18th century, the anonymous *Address to the public* (No. 445). Impartiality was duly observed in the insertion of these productions, as James Robertson, senior, promised for the *Royal American gazette*, for the editors' political predilections are by no means discernible from their selection of extracts from foreign papers or of local contributions.

The *Port-Roseway gazetteer* was printed in the same office and from the same fonts of type as the *Royal American gazette*. And while distinct from the older paper in title, numbering, and *apparently* in ownership, it served as a second weekly edition issued on Thursdays, of the *Gazette*, issued on Mondays. Some of the repetitive matter, e.g. advertisements, was printed from the same setting of type in both papers. In other matters they complement each other, reprinting different items from the same exchange paper, the *Gazette*, reprinting official publications and news, the *Gazetteer*, the more "literary" items. Often, too, the same event was recorded quite differently (more fully, or more briefly) in the two papers. Two publications a week stimulated local contributors, who answered in "Thursday's paper," correspondence which had appeared in "Monday's paper," as they termed it, and vice versa.

James Robertson, Junior, whose name appears at the mast-head of the *Gazetteer*, was a son of Alexander, the younger brother and partner of James Robertson, senior, who printed the *Gazette*. The *Gazetteer* was started about the time of Alexander's death, possibly in some reorganization of the family business following that event. Thomas and James Swords were brothers, American loyalists like the Robertsons. They came to Halifax in 1776, then to Shelburne about 1783, and returned to the United States, where they had established their own printing office in New York, by July 5, 1790. Their erstwhile partner, James Robertson, Junior, remained in Shelburne (as the parish christening records of his offspring show) till 1795 at least. But their paper, the *Port-Roseway gazetteer*, probably ceased publication when (or before) James Robertson, senior, moved his printing office to the Island of Saint John in 1786 or 1787.

Facsim. illus. of no. 11, Jan. 13, 1785, appears in D. C. McMurtrie: *The Royalist printers of Shelburne, Nova Scotia*, in *American book collector*, Jan., 1933.

Note: The issue of June 9, 1785, ends with p. 128, that of July 21 is paged [169]-176; suggesting (1) that extra numbers were issued in the interval; or (2) that the intervening regular numbers were all eight-page issues; or (3) that pages were misnumbered.

Copies located:

CaNs	v. 1	(no. 15-17,	Feb. 10-24, 1785
		25-26,	Apr. 21-28, 1785
		28-30,	May 12-26, 1785
		32,	June 9, 1785
		38)	July 21, 1785 (8-page issue)
		Mut.	Feb. 10, July 21, 1785
MBAt	v. 1	(no. 18)	Mar. 3, 1785
NN	v. 1	(no. 11)	Jan. 13, 1785

THE ROYAL AMERICAN GAZETTE. *Printed at Shelburne, N.S., by James and Alexander Robertson, 1783?-1786?*

The *Royal American gazette* was established in New York, Jan. 16, 1777, and published there semi-weekly by James Robertson, then by Alexander Robertson with, at intervals, his elder brother James and/or Nathaniel Mills and John Hicks, till 1783. The last issue known to have been published in New York is v. 9, no. 604, July 31, 1783. (*See* Clarence S. Brigham: *History and bibliography of American newspapers 1690-1820*, New York, 1946.) The Robertsons, loyalists, moved to Shelburne before Nov. 10, 1783 (when James presented a memorial to the Nova Scotia House of Assembly on behalf of inhabitants of Shelburne—P.A.N.S. *Misc. doc. of N.S., 1783-87*, v. 220, doc. 20) and resumed publication of their newspaper there. Judging from the last New York issue known, and the earliest Shelburne issue located (v. 10, no. 647, June 28, 1784), the *Royal American gazette* began appearing in Shelburne as v. 9, no. 605 or thereabouts, on Sept. 8, 1783 or thereabouts. Alexander Robertson died Nov. 8, 1784 (or a little earlier) and James Robertson continued the paper. Publication was suspended in Aug., 1785 (?with v. 11, no. 706, Aug. 22, 1785), the latest number located being v. 11, no. 704, Aug. 8, 1785, then resumed in May, 1786 (with vol. 11, no. 707, May 8, 1786), the earliest number located being v. 11, no. 710, May 29, 1786. The paper was continued by James Robertson in Shelburne till sometime between July 31, 1786 (the date of the latest Shelburne issue located) and Sept. 15, 1787, when he began printing it at Charlottetown, Island of St. John.

The earliest located Shelburne issue of the *Royal American gazette* bore the heading:

> [date, volume and issue no.] THE ROYAL / AMERICAN [royal arms] GAZETTE. / [rule] / SHELBURNE: Printed by ALEXANDER ROBERTSON, at his OFFICE, in KING-STREET, Corner of WATER-STREET. /

In 1784-85 it was printed on 4 p. in fo., 4 col. to the page; from May, 1786, in 4to. 4 p., occasionally increased to 8 p., and issued on Mondays throughout. The issue of Dec. 13, 1784 (at least) has each page framed in thick black rules, probably mourning Alexander Robertson.

The *Gazette's* reappearance after the end of the suspension interval, Aug., 1785-May, 1786 was announced by Robertson in a windy address:

> "Shelburne, April 24, 1786. To the Public. James Robertson, encouraged by the advice of his friends, proposes to re-assume the publication of the *Royal American Gazette*, upon Monday the eighth of May next, providing a sufficient number of subscriptions are obtained to defray the expense."
>
> "It would be absurd in the Printer to trouble the Public with a long and flattering address, as he has been known for several years, concerned in the publication of as impartial vehicles of intelligence as were ever emitted by any of his Profession. He therefore imagines it will suffice to mention that Candour and impartiality will be duly observed in the insertion of any performance which merits a place in the Gazette. Nor shall his party prejudice ever make him forget the duty he owes to the community.
>
> "Conditions. 1, Printed on 4 pages, large demy 4to. every Monday morning. 2, Essays calculated for innocent amusement, will be thankfully received and inserted gratis. 3, Price 12 Shillings a year, half on receipt of the 1st issue, the rest at the end of the year. 4, Advertisements will be inserted in a conspicuous

manner, up to 20 lines, 5 shillings, 1 shilling for each reinsertion. Subscriptions received and printing done on the shortest notice at the Office, in King-Street."

—*Nova-Scotia Packet*, Shelburne, N.S., May 4, 1786.

The *Royal American gazette* contained principally local advertising and foreign news reprinted from European papers. It included also a certain amount of local correspondence, especially after the establishment of the *Port Roseway gazetteer*, the two papers providing means of spontaneous rebuttal in the petty but bitter dissensions which flourished in the new settlement of Shelburne.

See J. P. Edwards: *The Shelburne that was and is not*, in *Dalhousie rev.* 2: 179-97, July, 1922; also *Vicissitudes of a loyalist city, ibid.* 2: 313-28, Oct., 1922. *See also* D. C. McMurtrie: *The Royalist printers of Shelburne, Nova Scotia* in *American book collector*, 2: 359-61; 3: 40-44, Dec., 1932-Jan., 1933 (includes facsim. illus. of the *Royal American gazette*, Dec. 13, 1784).

Copies located:

CaNs	v. 11	(no. 676-678	Jan. 24-Feb. 7, 1785
		680,	Feb. 21, 1785
		686-689,	Apr. 4-25, 1785
		691, 694-698,	May 9, May 30-June 27, 1785
		703-704)	Aug. 1-8, 1785
		Mut.	Jan. 31, 1785
GBLBM	v. 11	(no. 710-711	May 29-June 5, 1786
		713-714	June 19-26, 1786
		716-719)	July 10-31, 1786 (8-page issues)
MWA	v. 10	(no. 647)	June 28, 1784
NN	v. 10	(no. 670)	Dec. 13, 1784
	v. 11	(no. 676)	Jan. 24, 1785
White	v. 10	(no. 671)	Dec. 20, 1784 (mut.)
	v. 11	(no. 673)	Jan. 3, 1785 (mut.)

THE WEEKLY CHRONICLE. *Printed at Halifax, N.S., by William Minns, 1786–19th century.*

The *Weekly chronicle* was established at Halifax, N.S., Apr. 29, 1786, or thereabouts, judging from the earliest number located, v. 2, no. 91, Jan. 19, 1788. The first number appeared Saturday, May 28, 1786, according to J. J. Stewart: *Early journalism in Nova Scotia*, but this date fell on a Sunday. It was continued by its founder, Wm. Minns, till his death, 1827. The paper bore the heading:

> THE WEEKLY CHRONICLE. / Vol. [no.] Saturday, [date] No. [no.] HALIFAX: Printed by WILLIAM MINNS, at the CORNER of GEORGE and BARRINGTON STREET opposite the Parade. /

This imprint was changed between 1796 and 1798 to "Corner of George and Granville Street near the Parade."

In the 18th century the *Weekly Chronicle* was a large folio sheet making 4 pages about 18 × 12 inches, printed 3 col. to the page. The issues were numbered in one continuous series, the volume numbers changing with the calendar year. The subscription (probably 10*s*.) was raised to 12*s*. 6*d*. in Halifax, 15*s*. in the country, from Jan. 1, 1799, according to notice in the issue of Nov. 3, 1798.

From 1786 Halifax had three weekly newspapers, the *Nova-Scotia gazette*, published on Tuesdays by Anthony Henry, now an old resident and government printer, the *Halifax journal*, on Thursdays, by John Howe, American loyalist emigré, and the *Weekly chronicle*, on Saturdays, by Minns. The last named had come to Halifax as a lad, with his brother-in-law, John Howe, and had learned his trade in the latter's shop. No acrimonious rivalry appears to have existed among the printers, nor did conflicting principles inform their papers. They all contain a certain amount of complementary correspondence from contributors, but show no sustained controversy on local or other issues. The *Chronicle*, published on Saturdays, had more extensive and more detailed local news than the others, less trade-advertisement than the *Journal*, and less official matter and legal notices than the *Gazette*. Like the others it shows more interest in American and European than in Canadian affairs; e.g., on Mar. 26, 1796, Minns noted: "The Post from Annapolis brought mails from Canada and New Brunswick. No news from Quebec papers. The New Brunswick papers are filled with proceedings of the Assembly in altercation with the Council, as these are lengthy and merely local we print no extracts." And again on Apr. 9, 1796: "London papers have just arrived (via Boston) with news to Feb. 13th. It is unfortunate after waiting this long and impatiently for European intelligence that the first we have been able to obtain is through the medium of a paper so notoriously engaged in opposition as the [London] Morning Chronicle."

Minn's paper had a plainer, more monotonous appearance than the others, lacking the royal arms which appeared in both their headings, lacking also the variety and skill of Howe's composition. It was remarkably free of error, however. The only misnumbering noted in the files located, is in v. 12, where no. 634-635 (of July [21-]28, 1798) is repeated on the issued of Aug. 4-11, and this sequence continued.

Copies located:

CaNs	v. 12	(no. [614?]	Mar. 3, 1798
		631-633	June 30-July 14, 1798
		635-641, 643	July 28-Sept. 22, Oct. 6, 1798
		645-648	Oct. 20-Nov. 10, 1798
		650-653)	Nov. 24-Dec. 15, 1798
	v. 13	(no. 662-681	Feb. 16-June 29, 1799
		683-688	July 13-Aug. 17, 1799
		690-694,	Aug. 31-Sept. 28, 1799
		696)	Oct. 12, 1799
Another copy	v. 12	(no. 643)	Oct. 6, 1798
	v. 13	(no. 668, 677)	Mar. 30, June 1, 1799
		Mut.	Mar. 3, July 14, 28, Aug. 25, Sept. 15-22, Dec. 1, 1798; Mar. 2, 16, Apr. 6-13, May 4-11, June 15-29, July 27-Aug. 3, Sept. 21-28, Oct. 12, 1799
CaNsHA	v. 2	(no. 91)	Jan. 19, 1788
	v. 9	(no. 484)	Sept. 12, 1795
	v. 10	(no. 500-501	Jan. 2-9, 1796
		503-510, 512	Jan. 23-Mar. 12, 26, 1796
		514-515	Apr. 9-16, 1796

		517-520	Apr. 30-May 21, 1796
		522-524	June 4-18, 1796
		526-543	July 2-Oct. 29, 1796
		545-551)	Nov. 5-Dec. 17, 1796
	v. 13	(no. 665, 670,	Mar. 9, Apr. 13, 1799
		682-683, 685	July 6-13, 27, 1799
		687)	Aug. 10, 1799
		Mut.	Sept. 12, 1795; Mar. 26, July 16, Aug. 7, Dec. 3-17, 1796; Mar. 9, Apr. 13, 1799
CaNsWA	v. 11	(no. 561, 599)	Feb. 18, Nov. 11, 1797
MH	v. 10	(no. 543)	Oct. 29, 1796
	v. 12	(no. 631)	June 30, 1798
MHi	v. 9	(no. 470)	May 31, 1795

DIE WELT UND DIE NEUSCHOTTLÆNDISCHE CORRESPONDENZ. *Projected at Halifax, N.S., by Anthony Henry, 1788-1789.*

Die Welt und die Neuschottlændische Correspondenz was projected as a weekly, to be published by Anthony Henry at Halifax on Fridays beginning Jan. 4, 1788. It was announced in English and German (roman letter): "The Printer intends to publish a German Almanack for 1788 . . . also a German newspaper at the beginning of January 1788. Subscribers are requested to send in their names on or before the 25th of December next."—*Nova-Scotia gazette,* Aug. 14, 1787.

The German Almanack (in black letter) was duly published on Dec. 5, 1787, (No. 503) with a foreword which set forth Henry's aspiration to fulfil a pious duty to his mother tongue by publishing a newspaper of which all real Germans, including those in the United States, even the younger generation, need not be ashamed. It would contain news of remarkable events from the four corners of the world and particularly of affairs in Nova Scotia itself. Some subscriptions had been received and many more were expected.

". . . So will ich meinen mœglichsten Fleisz anwenden, durch diese Druckerey unsere Muttersprache im Gange zu erhaben, deren sich auch gewisz kein alter redlicher Deutscher, sowohl in dieser Landschaft, als auch in den Vereinigten Nordamerikanischen Staaten, schæmen wird; obgleich viele von der Jugend, aus einer wunderlichen Einbildung einen Eckel davor bezeugen. Zu diesem Ende will ich woechentlich, Freytags, eine deutsche Zeitung, unter dem Titel: *Die Welt, und die Neuschottlændische Correspondenz* herausgeben, und derselben, nach Anleitung dieses Titels, alle merkwuerdige Begebenheiten der 4 Welttheile, so mir durch fremde Englische Zeitungen zu Ohren kommen, ueberhaupt, als auch insbesondere die intereszantesten Sachen dieser Provinz, einverleiben. Die erste wird den 4ten Jenner [i.e. Januar] dieses 1788sten Jahrs ausgegeben werden. Ich habe bereits eine Anzahl Subscribenten; und ich schmeichle nur, nach und nach noch mehrere derselben zu bekommen; wann sie erst ueberzeugt werden, dasz ich mein Versprechen erfuelle.—Anth. Henrich."—*Die Neuschottlændische Calender . . . 1788,* p. [2].

Subscribers to the German newspaper were solicited by Henry in the *Nova-Scotia gazette,* Nov. 27-Dec. 18, 1787, after which no reference to his project appeared.

Henry Stirner, a German printer who worked in Henry's shop between 1783 and 1789, recalled (in 1814) that a German paper entitled the *Halifax gazette* [sic] was printed there for about two years, 1787-89, on types which Stirner himself procured for Henry from Justus Fox of Germantown, Pennsylvania. This paper had three (increasing to five) hundred subscribers [!] Stirner's interlocutor vouched for his veracity (Wm. McCulloch: *Additions to Thomas's History of printing*, in American antiquarian soc. *Proceedings, 1921*, v. 31: 247; *vide* p. 176 *et seq.*) These reminiscences probably exaggerated the facts, however, as they certainly exalted Stirner's activities in Henry's office.

Some circumstances were conducive to the publication of *Die Welt:* Henry had in his printing office news matter prepared for the *Nova-Scotia gazette*, skill to translate and type to print it, in German. The German population, mainly in Lunenburg County and in Dutch Village near Halifax, was small however (between two and three thousand). *Die Welt* probably had few subscribers, and appeared in few (if any) issues. No copy has been located.

COURIER DE QUEBEC OU HERAUT FRANCOIS, *printed at Quebec by Wm. Moore, 1788.*

The *Courier de Québec* was announced in a prospectus dated Jan. 1, 1788 (*see* No. 551) which stated that the paper would be published weekly on Mondays, beginning the following June. It would be compiled and corrected by Mr. James Tanswell, a schoolmaster in Quebec, printed on good paper in 4to., 4 p. each issue in French only, and would contain the occurrences of the province, moral and instructive essays, anecdotes, and advertisements. A title page and contents table would be issued free to subscribers at the end of the year; subscription, a half guinea or 40 francs a year, single copies 10 sous [5*d*.]. Advertisement rates were given and contributions solicited. The first number actually appeared on Nov. 24, 1788, at the same time as the *Quebec herald* (in English only). The paper bore the heading:

> COURIER DE QUEBEC: / ou / Heraut [ornaments] François. / Nombre [no.] TOM. I / [rule] / [date], 1788 / [rule].

and colophon:

> IMPRIMÉ par GUILLAUME MOORE, sous la seule inspection & direction de MONSIEUR / TANSWELL Maitre de l'Academie de QUEBEC, qui recevra avec reconnaissance de toutes parts (le / port de lettres etant pagé) & inserera soigneusement & fidelement dans cette GAZETTE des ADVERTISEMENS, / ARTICLES D'INTELLIGENCE, EVENEMENS REMARQUABLES, ACCIDENS, NAISSANCES, MARRIAGES, / MORTS, &c. &c. &c. /

An editorial introduction repeated the terms of the prospectus, revising the price of advertisements to: 15 lines, 3*s*. 6*d*. for the first week, 5*s*. 3*d*. for 2 weeks, or 7*s*. a month; every 5 lines additional, 2 sous in proportion. Editorial principles were set forth by Tanswell:

"Adresse de l'Editeur aux Canadiens—C'est avec une entière satisfaction que je m'adresse à un peuple, qui est aujourd'hui le plus heureux qu'il y ait dans l'Univers, & qui, j'ose le dire, est le plus digne de l'être. Un peuple qui par un noble caractère de l'Esprit, des Moeurs pures, une conduite sage, vertueuse & chrétienne, & sur tout par son attachement & sa Fidélité au Gouvernement, s'et [sic] attiré sans doute, les avantages & les prospèrités dont il jouit. [etc. Then follows equally fulsome tribute to Governor, Lieutenant Governor, clergy, seigneurs, and magistrates.] "Exciter à la vertu par les exemples des grands hommes, allumer les désirs d'être utile à nos semblables, prévenir contre les Ecueils de la vie . . . voilà le but que je me propose dans la publication de cette gazette Françoise ou Courrier de Québec. . . .

"L'Editeur n'épargnera rien & fera toutes les dépenses nécessaires pour procurer toutes les Intelligences, afin de satisfaire la curiosité et de contenter les différens gouts de ses Souscripteurs. Et pour parvenir à ce point il prie très instamment tous ses amis, de vouloir bien lui fournir de tems en tems de tels articles d'Intelligence, qui pourront rendre cette Feuille plus intéressante, instructive et amusante. Lesquels il aura soin d'insérer et s'engage en même tems de garder inviolablement le secret, si on l'exige.

"Ceux qui voudroient les lui faire tenir incognito, trouveront une Boete attachée à la porte de son Académie à l'Evêché: pourvû néanmoins, que dans ces articles, il n'y ait rien de contraire aux bonnes moeurs, ni qui intéresse à la moindre chose l'honneur et la réputation de qui que soit, non pl......e le Gouvernement et la Religion.

"On souscrira à Québec chez Mons. Moore, l'Imprimeur et chez Mons. Tanswell, L'Editeur; à Montréal chez Mons. David David's; aux Trois-Rivières chez Mons. Sills; à St. Jean, chez M. Gill; à Nouveau Johnstown chez M. Jackson Hoyle; à Kingston chez M. Clark, à Niagara chez M. Edwards, au Detroit chez M. Hand, à l'Imprimerie de M. How à Halifax, et l'Imprimerie de M. Robertson à L'Isle de St. Jean."

The *Courier* was similar in appearance to the *Quebec herald*, printed 3 col. to the page, with 4 p. in 4to. to the issue (paged continuously), instead of the *Herald*'s 8 pages. In No. 3 of the *Courier*, the royal arms type ornament in the mast head was replaced by another ornament, roughly cut in a design similar to the Triton ornament in the *Herald*'s mast head. The *Courier* never achieved the *Herald*'s lively character, however. The three numbers published contain few original contributions from Quebecois. About one-quarter of each issue comprised local news and advertisements, the remainder was official publications and excerpts from English and American newspapers translated into French. The editor advertised his school, and the printer, his establishment of a domestic service employment bureau, also his need of a French-writing apprentice. There was little evidence of local interest in the *Courier*, despite Tanswell's ingratiating *Adresse*, and it ceased without warning. Moore announced on the day that the fourth number should have appeared that he was "sorry to acquaint the Public that he is under the necessity of discontinuing the Courier, there not being subscribers sufficient to pay for the paper."—*Quebec herald*, Dec. 15, 1788, *et seq.*

In the same number of the *Herald*, however, Moore again announced that a French gazette for the use of Canadians "will be published every Monday," and he solicited subscriptions. On Apr. 20, 1789, he advertised that the "subscription for *Le Courier de Québec* increases fast . . . there are about 100 already subscribed and immediately on its near approach to another [hundred] it will commence publication." This was probably the paper for which an undated prospectus was issued, proposing the weekly publication on *Thursdays* of *Le Courier de Québec ou Heraut François* (*see* No. 590). But there is no evidence that this Thursday paper ever appeared. Of the Monday *Courier* only one copy of each issue has been located, no. 2-3, being double-dated.

Copies located:

CaOOA	v. 1	(no. 2-3)	Nov. 24-Dec. 1—Dec. 1-8, 1788
CaQQL	v. 1	Prospectus	Jan. 1, 1788 *See* No. 551
		(no. 1)	Nov. 24, 1788
		Prospectus	?1789 *See* No. 590

GAZETTE DU COMMERCE ET LITTERAIRE. *Printed at Montreal by F. Mesplet, 1778-1779.*

The *Gazette du commerce et litteraire* announced in a prospectus (*see* No. 286-287), was established at Montreal, June 3, 1778 (v. 1, no. 1), by Fleury Mesplet, in the name of the firm, Mesplet and C[harles]. Berger. It was printed thus by Mesplet till Aug. 19, 1778, (no. 12). After this issue, Berger having cancelled the partnership, Mesplet continued to print the *Gazette* in his own name, from Sept. 2, 1778 (v. 1, no. 13-14) till June 2, 1779 (v. 2, no. 22) when it ceased publication. This paper bore the heading:

GAZETTE / DU COMMERCE / ET LITTERAIRE, / Pour la Ville & District de MONTREAL. /

and *colophon:*

MONTREAL Chez F. MESPLET & C. BERGER, Imprimeurs & Libraires—/.

From Sept. 2, 1778, the title read: "Gazette littéraire, Pour la Ville & District de Montréal" and the *colophon:* "Montreal, chez F. Mesplet, Imprimeur et Libraire."

This paper, issued weekly on Wednesdays, was entirely in French, each issue a half sheet quarto, making 4 pages about 9 × 7½ inches—excepting the issues of v. 1, no. 12 (Aug. 19, 1778) one page; no. 13-14 together (Sept. 2, 1778) four pages; and v. 2, no. 19, 21 (May 12, 26, 1779) each five pages—printed 2 col. to the page. The issues were numbered and paged continuously within each volume—v. 1: 92 p.; v. 2: [2], 118 p.

The price of the *Gazette*, as the prospectus stated, was 2½ Spanish dollars (or 12*s.*) a year, 10 sols (5*d.*) a copy. Advertisements $1.00 (or 5*s.*) to subscribers for three insertions, $1.50 to non-subscribers.

This was the first newspaper established in Montreal. It contained few advertisements (besides lists of Mesplet's books and stationery, etc., for sale), few, if any, government publications, and little local or foreign news. Most of the space was occupied with essays, verses, and correspondence, of an anecdotal, literary, or philosophic, nature—for the first few months on trivial topics. Despite the precautionary policy stated in the prospectus, however, the printer ran foul of authority, apparently for some previous misdemeanour. In August he and his editor-assistant were ordered to cease printing and to leave the province by Sept. 15, 1778. This order was suspended, however, Aug. 24 (*see* No. 291), and Mesplet resumed publication of the *Gazette*, Sept. 2, on condition that he print nothing not previously inspected and approved by authority (Can.P.A., "B" v. 62: 103; v. 80: 2-3).

Closely associated with Mesplet in the production of the *Gazette littéraire* was Valentin Jautard, a lawyer in Montreal, who served as editor, or at least as principal contributor, over the pseudonym "le Spectateur Tranquille." From Oct., 1778, he published a series of essays in defence of Voltairianism—regularly answered by "Le Canadian curieux." Later, in Mar., 1779, Jautard introduced another controversy, over local legal affairs, in which Pierre Du Calvet figured as a protagonist, and Simon

Sanguinet, a bitter antagonist. This correspondence developed into virulent abuse and defense of local judges, and apparently had wider implications than cases then before the courts. It provoked civil and military authorities, as the previous Voltairian essays had done the church (Can.P.A., "B" 66: 102). Mesplet and Jautard were arrested, and the *Gazette littéraire* ceased publication on June 2, 1779. Mesplet, in jail at Quebec till Sept., 1782, only resumed newspaper publication in 1785, then launching an entirely different journal, the *Montreal gazette*.

The contents of Mesplet's *Gazette* are analysed by Mgr. Camille Roy in *Nos origines littéraires* (354 p., Quebec, 1909, p. 62-81). He shows it to have been the vehicle of an evanescent literary movement, and to reveal two distinct currents of thought—the European-French and the French-Canadian, scepticism and nationalism—which informed French-Canadian culture thereafter.

See also Fauteux: *Mesplet:* p. 171-73; and McLachlan: *Mesplet:* 207-12.

Copies located:

CaQMM		Prospectus	*See* No. 286 and 287
	v. 1	(no. 1-31)	June 3-Dec. 30, 1778
	v. 2	(no. 1-22)	Jan. 6-June 2, 1779
CaQMS	v. 1	(no. 1-31)	June 3-Dec. 30, 1778
	v. 2	(no. 1-22)	Jan. 6-June 2, 1779
CaQQL	v. 1	(no. 1-31)	June 3-Dec. 30, 1778
	v. 2	(no. 1-22)	Jan. 6-June 2, 1779
Gordonsmith	v. 2	(no. 5)	Feb. 3, 1779
MWA	v. 1	(no. 2, 13-14)	June 10, Sept. 2, 1778
Witton	v. 2	(no. 9-15, 17-18)	Mar. 3-Apr. 14, 1779 Apr. 28-May 5, 1779 (p. 67-70 only)

THE MONTREAL GAZETTE. *Printed at Montreal by Fleury Mesplet, Edward Edwards, then others, 1785–20th century.*

The *Montreal gazette*, announced in a preliminary number or prospectus (*see* No. 460), was established at Montreal by Fleury Mesplet, printed by him from Aug. 25, 1785 (v. 1, no. 1) till Jan. 16, 1794 (v. 9, no. 3), possible later (Mesplet died Jan. 28, 1794). It was continued for his widow, Marie-Anne Tison Mesplet, from v. 9, no. 6, Feb. 6, 1794 (possibly earlier) to v. 9, no. 7, Feb. 13, 1794, then apparently ceased to appear for a time.* Publication of the *Montreal gazette* was resumed Aug. 3, 1795 (n.s. v. 1, no. 1) by Edward Edwards, who continued to produce it till his

*Mesplet's stock and furniture were inventoried Feb. 17-20, for sale by auction, Feb. 24-27, 1794—McLachlan, *Mesplet:* 220. Subsequently the *Gazette* is said to have "passed into the hands of Thomas Turner, and there is extant a copy issued by him from an office on the corner of Notre Dame and St. Jean Baptiste St. in 1796 [sic]. The next volume that we have was printed by E. Edwards from 135 St. Paul Street."—Geo. F. Wright: *Journalism*, chap. 6, in *The storied province of Quebec*, ed. by Wm. Wood (5 v., Toronto, 1931), I: 585.

death in 1810. It was continued by James Brown, printer, and the pioneer paper maker of Canada, till 1825; then by Thomas Andrew Turner, and a series of successors till the present day. The latest issue located within the period of this study (the 18th century) is no. 232, Dec. 30, 1799. The first issue bore the heading:

> [*left col:*] 1785 / THE / MONTREAL / GAZETTE. / [rule] / THURSDAY, AUGUST 25 / [rule] /
> [*right col:*] Numb. I. / GAZETE / DE / MONTREAL. / [rule] / JEUDI, 25 AOUT. / [rule] /
> *Colophon:* MONTREAL, Printed by F. MESPLET.—A MONTREAL, chez F. MESPLET. /

With v. 5, no. 8, Feb. 25, 1790, Mesplet added the royal arms to his heading, and in large or small, this ornament appeared at the masthead thereafter. On May 6, 1788, the printing office was removed from rue Capital "près le marché" to "the house of Mr. Tabeau Senior between those of Mr. Vallé and Mr. Langley, in Notre Dame street," and the address "Notre Dame Street" (from Apr. 25, 1793, "N° 40, Notre Dame Street") appeared in the colophon. After Mesplet's death the colophon read: "Montreal: for Mary-Ann Mesplet, N° 40, Notre-Dame Street—Montreal: pour Marie-Anne Mesplet, N° 40, rue Notre Dame." From Aug. 3, 1795—Sept. 12, 1796 the paper was "Printed by E. Edwards, N° 10, St. Vincent-Street"; from Oct. 31, 1796 (or earlier): "Printed by E. Edwards, N° 135, St. Paul's Street."

The *Montreal gazette* was published weekly on Thursdays, 1785-94, then weekly on Mondays, 1795 *et seq.*, 4 pages in folio, printed 2 col. to the page, English and French. No. XVI [i.e. XIV], Nov. 24, 1785, however, was issued with 3 pages blank, the first page bearing the usual *Gazette* heading, and a notice to subscribers from the printer, apologizing for the non-appearance of the newspaper due to "un derangement dans mes affairs que je crois vous connoissez tous."* Mesplet resumed publication the following week. The regular issues were occasionally augmented by a 2-page supplement. Sometimes advertisements for which there was no space, were printed on handbills and circulated with the *Gazette*. Extras published between the regular weekly issues, were numbered in the regular series. From 1785 to 1794 the issues were numbered anew (by Mesplet) within each volume, and the volume numbers changed with the calendar year. (Through 1786, however, v. 1 was repeated, and following years numbered in sequence). Edwards introduced a new series in 1795, numbering the issues continuously and changing the volume number at the end of a publishing year till July 23, 1798 (no. 156) after which the volume number was dropped.

Mesplet's *Montreal gazette* contained no such disputatious essays as had brought disaster to his *Gazette littéraire* (though his former contentious "editor", Valentin Jautard, continued to work with *Mesplet* for a time at least, as translator). It published foreign and American news, rather meagre and late, for Mesplet's newspaper exchanges were apparently limited and his translation facilities poor—for which he frequently apologized. He reprinted considerable material from Quebec papers, both the *Quebec gazette* and the *Herald*, particularly on provincial affairs. Indeed, correspondence and memorials on social and political questions, originating in Montreal, were frequently published there only *after* they had appeared in the

---

*On Nov. 21, 1785, Mesplet's stock and furniture were sold at auction for debt. After the sale he secured use of the presses on lease from the purchaser, Sheriff Edward Wm. Gray.—McLachlan, *Mesplet:* 216.

Quebec papers. After a few years, however, when his editorial "character" had become more secure, Mesplet published numerous letters on burning topics of the day —education, the judicature, militia, etc. Provincial and municipal publications appeared, laws, notices and regulations, sometimes reprinted from the *Quebec gazette*, but latterly printed on order of Authority "in the Montreal paper." A most interesting feature of the *Montreal gazette* is the large number of business and professional cards, the advertisements and notices of local organizations, showing developments in the commercial, social, and cultural life of the future metropolis of Canada.

Edward Edwards continued the *Montreal gazette* with little change in appearance or content, though with consistent use of smaller types he greatly increased the latter. Edwards announced:

> "The Subscriber having purchased the Printing Office which belonged to the late Mr. Mesplet and since his death has carried on the Printing business, purposes immediately to revive the *Montreal gazette* lately printed by the deceased . . . it is to be published in English and French every Monday on folio crown. The subscription is to be three dollars a year . . . He will conduct it on so extensive a plan as to deserve the encouragement of the Public and is with great respect their Obliged Humble Servant. Edw. Edwards."—*Quebec gazette*, July 16, 1795.

Edwards, who had been in the stationery business in Montreal since 1781, and was also postmaster, lacked Mesplet's journalistic instinct and literary flair. But he had wider sources of information and less difficulty with French-English translation. The poet's corner and correspondence columns contracted, but the foreign news increased noticeably, as did the amount of advertising matter and of official publication.

A calendar of the *Montreal gazette*, 1778-1841 [i.e. of *Gazette litteraire*, 1778-79, and *Montreal gazette*, 1785-1841] has been prepared by Professor A. R. M. Lower. Typescript copies of this unpublished work are in the University of Toronto History Department, and in the Public Archives, Ottawa. An account of the origin and history of the *Gazette* was published as *One and a half centuries of public service*, an article in the *Montreal gazette*, June 2, 1928.

Irregularities in numbering of issues have been noted as follows:

In v. 5, 14 is omitted or else assigned to an unlocated Extra issued between Apr. 1-8, 1790

In v. 6, 29 is repeated, appearing in issues of July 7 and 14, 1791

In v. 6, 42 is omitted or else assigned to an unlocated Extra issued between Oct. 6-13, 1791

In v. 8, 17 is repeated, appearing on issues of Apr. 28 and May 2, 1793

In v. 8, 51 is omitted, or else assigned to an unlocated Extra issued between Dec. 19-26, 1793.

Copies located:

CaO	[n.s.] v. 3	(no. 127-142,	Jan. 1-Apr. 16, 1798
		145-148,	May 7-28, 1798
		150-167,	June 11-Oct. 8, 1798
		169-180)	Oct. 22-Dec. 31, 1798
		incl. *Sup.* to Feb. 5, Dec. 31; *Postscript* to July 16 and *Extra* (no. 177) Dec. 11, 1798	
CaOT	v. 1	(no. 1-19)	Aug. 25-Dec. 29, 1785
	v. 1 [sic]	(no. 1-10)	Jan. 5-Mar. 9, 1786

	v. 2	(no. 1-52)	Jan. 4-Dec. 27, 1787
	v. 3	(no. 1-20,	Jan. 3-May 15, 1788
		22-45,	May 29-Nov. 6, 1788
		48-52)	Nov. 27-Dec. 25, 1788
	v. 4	(no. 1-53)	Jan. 1-Dec. 31, 1789
	v. 5	(no. 1-53)	Jan. 7-Dec. 30, 1790
	v. 6	(no. 1-54)	Jan. 6-Dec. 29, 1791 (incl. Extra no. 6, 23, Feb. 7, May 27)
	v. 7	(no. 4-20,	Jan. 19-May 10, 1792
		22, 24-25,	May 24, June 7-14, 1792
		27-53)	June 28-Dec. 27, 1792
	v. 8	(no. 1-4,	Jan. 3-24, 1793
		6-10, 12,	Feb. 7-Mar. 7, Mar. 21, 1793
		14, 16-20,	Apr. 4, Apr. 18-May 23, 1793
		25, 27-30	June 27, July 11-Aug. 1, 1793
		32-47	Aug. 15-Nov. 28, 1793
		49-52	Dec. 12-31, 1793
	v. 9	(no. 1-3,	Jan. 2-16, 1794
		6-7)	Feb. 6-13, 1794
	[n.s.] v. 1	(no. 1, 3,	Aug. 3, Aug. 17, 1795
		8-9,	Sept. 21-28, 1795
		17-23,	Nov. 23, 1795–Jan. 4, 1796
		25, 27-31,	Jan. 18, Feb. 1-29, 1796
		32-33,	Mar. 7-14, 1796
		36-41,	Apr. 4-May 9, 1796
		43-48)	May 23-June 27, 1796
	[n.s.] v. 1-2	(no. 51-59,	July 18-Sept. 12, 1796
		66)	Oct. 31, 1796
	[n.s.] **v. 3**	(no. 107-111,	Aug. 14-Sept. 11, 1797
		113-116,	Sept. 25-Oct. 16, 1797
		120-123, 125,	Nov. 13-Dec. 4, 18, 1797
		127)	Jan. 1, 1798
		incl. sup. with	Jan. 26, 1786; Jan. 18, 1787; Sept. 11, 1788; Feb. 5, 1789; Jan. 7, May 13 (2 cop.), May 27, Sept. 30, Dec. 9, 1790; Feb. 24, Mar. 10, May 26, June 2, Dec. 15, 1791; Feb. 7, Feb. 28, May 2, 1793; Apr. 25, 1796; Sept. 4, 1797
		mut.	Nov. 3, 1785, Aug. 23, Oct. 11, 1787
CaQMF	[n.s.] **v. 1**	(no. 7-12,	Sept. 14-Oct. 19, 1795
		14-17,	Nov. 2-23, 1795
		19-28,	Dec. 7, 1795–Feb. 8, 1796
		30-31,	Feb. 22-29, 1796
		incl. sup. with	Jan. 11, 1796
CaQMM	**v. 3**	(no. 23-27,	June 5-July 3, 1788
		49-52)	Dec. 4-Dec. 25, 1788
	v. 4	(no. 1-40,	Jan. 1-Oct. 1, 1789
		42-47)	Oct. 15-Nov. 19, 1789

	v. 6	(no. 4)	Jan. 27, 1791
		incl. sup. with	Feb. 5, 1789
		mut.	Dec. 4, 1788
CaQMS	v. 2	(no. 27, 45,	July 5, Nov. 8, 1787
		47-49,	Nov. 22-Dec. 6, 1787
		51-52)	Dec. 20-27, 1787
	v. 4	(no. 1-53)	Jan. 1-Dec. 31, 1789
	[n.s.] v. 1	(no. 2-35,	Aug. 10, 1795-Mar. 28, 1796
		37-44)	Apr. 11-May 30, 1796
	[n.s.] v. 1-2	(no. 46-64)	June 13-Oct. 17, 1796
	[n.s.] v. 2-3	(no. 67-112,	Nov. 7, 1796-Sept. 18, 1797
		114-116,	Oct. 2-16, 1797
		118-126,	Oct. 30-Dec. 25, 1797
		181-198,	Jan. 7-May 6, 1799
		200-206,	May 20-July 1, 1799
		208, 210-214,	July 15, July 29-Aug. 26, 1799
		216-222,	Sept. 9-Oct. 21, 1799
		224-232)	Nov. 4-Dec. 30, 1799
		incl. sup. with	Dec. 23, 1799
CaQQL	Prospectus		*See* No. 460
	v. 1	(no. 1-2,	Aug. 25-Sept. 1, 1785
		8-13,	Oct. 13-Nov. 17, 1785
		15-19)	Dec. 1-29, 1785
	v. 1[sic]	(no. 1-52)	Jan. 5-Dec. 28, 1786
	v. 2	(no. 2-3,	Jan. 11-18, 1787
		5-7, 9-13,	Feb. 1-15, Mar. 1-29, 1787
		15-29,	Apr. 12-July 19, 1787
		31-52)	Aug. 2-Dec. 27, 1787
	v. 3	(no. 1-19,	Jan. 3-May 8, 1788
		21-52)	May 22-Dec. 25, 1788
	v. 4	(no. 1, 3,	Jan. 1, Jan. 15, 1789
		5-8, 10-13,	Jan. 29-Feb. 19, Mar. 5-26, 1789
		15-27,	Apr. 9-July 2, 1789
		29-45,	July 16-Nov. 5, 1789
		47-53)	Nov. 19-Dec. 31, 1789
	v. 5	(no. 1-18,	Jan. 7-Apr. 29, 1790
		20-34,	May 13-Aug. 19, 1790
		36-44,	Sept. 2-Oct. 28, 1790
		46-50,	Nov. 11-Dec. 9, 1790
		52-53)	Dec. 23-30, 1790
	v. 6	(no. 1-8,	Jan. 6-Feb. 17, 1791 (incl. Extra, no. 6, Feb. 7)
		10-17, 19, 21,	Mar. 3-Apr. 21, May 5, May 19, 1791
		23-30, 32,	May 27 (Extra)-July 21, Aug. 4, 1791
		34-54)	Aug. 18-Dec. 29, 1791
	[n.s.] v. 3	(no. 128-136,	Jan. 8-Mar. 5, 1798
		138-154,	Mar. 19-July 9, 1798
		156-157,	July 23-30, 1798

	159-169, 175, 213)	Aug. 13-Oct. 22, Dec. 3, 1798 Aug. 19, 1799
	incl. sup. with	Feb. 5, 1798
Gordonsmith v. 8	(no. 15)	Apr. 11, 1793
Ketcheson	odd numbers	

MONTREAL GAZETTE. *Printed at Montreal by Louis Roy >J. M. Roy, 1795-1797.*

Announced in a prospectus (*see* No. 951) the *Montreal gazette* was established at Montreal by Louis Roy, Aug. 17, 1795, or thereabouts, judging from the earliest issue located, no. 2, Aug. 24, 1795. It was printed by the founder, Louis Roy, till Sept. 19, 1796 (the latest issue located) or a little later, then by his brother Joseph-Marie Roy who was *probably* one of "the proprietors" of the paper issued with Louis's imprint. Louis left Montreal some time in 1796-97 and Joseph-Marie was *certainly* with, or succeeding, his brother at the printing office by Jan., 1797. But the only issue of his paper located is v. 3, no. 12, Oct. 30, 1797. This *Montreal gazette* was not continued beyond 1797, however, for J.-M. Roy's notice that he had abandoned the printing business, dated Jan. 1, 1798, was published in the other (Edwards's) *Montreal gazette* of that date. And John Bennett, who took over the Roy office for a short time, published no newspaper.

This paper bore the heading:

[left col.:] MONTREAL / GAZETTE / [double rule] / MONDAY, 24 AUGUST, 1795. / [double rule] / VOL. I. Printed by LOUIS ROY. / [centre: royal arms] / [rule] /
[right col:] GAZETTE / DE / MONTREAL. / [double rule] / LUNDI, 24 AOUT, 1795. / [double rule] / Imprimée chez LOUIS ROY, NOM. 2 / [double rule] /

It was published weekly on Mondays, 4 pages in folio, printed 2 col. to the page, English and French. With uniformly small type and few ornaments, the pages presented a crowded but neat appearance. Roy, a printer of some skill, had produced the *Upper Canada gazette*, q.v., in creditable style, and though he started his Montreal adventure with secondhand equipment and ran his shop on a shoe-string, his *Montreal gazette*, despite its shoddy paper and worn types, showed his craftsmanship. The content of his paper compared favourably with that of the other *Montreal gazette*, which Edward Edwards began printing about the same time. Roy's journal secured more advertising—about one-quarter of his space was so occupied. He published notice that advertisements and notices sent to his printing office by 12 o'clock Sunday would appear in Monday's paper. Edwards's advertising space increased noticeably after Roy abandoned the printing business. Both papers published the same official matter: provincial government and court proceedings, municipal regulations, etc. The two *Montreal gazette*'s were genuine rivals, and in a short time considerable partisan correspondence developed between them, the contributors criticizing in one journal the contents of the other. Roy was stronger on local affairs; he would give a quarter column to the death of a Montrealer, noticed by his rival in a few lines. Edwards gave more space to foreign news, having, as postmaster, some advantage in this respect, as Roy's notice suggests:

"We are sorry to be under the disagreeable necessity of informing our Customers that the refusal of Mr. Edwards (Post Master for this City) to deliver yesterday the Newspapers received at his office by the last Burlington post [i.e. papers from the United States via Burlington, Vermont] to the Proprietors prevent us from laying before our Readers an account of the latest European Intelligence received on this side of the Atlantic."

—[Roy's] *Montreal gazette*, Sept. 19, 1796.

Copies located:

CaOT	v. 1	(no. 2, 4, 9,	Aug. 24, Sept. 7, Oct. 12, 1795
		14, 16-17, 19	Nov. 16, Nov. 30-Dec. 7, Dec. 21, 1795
		26-27, 29	Feb. 8-15, Feb. 29, 1796
		31, 33-34,	Mar. 14, Mar. 28-Apr. 4, 1796
		37-38	Apr. 25-May 2, 1796
		40-42,	May 16-30, 1796
		44-45,	June 13-20, 1796
		49-50)	July 18-25, 1796
	v. 2	(no. 1-2,	Aug. 15-22, 1796
		4, 6)	Sept. 5, 19, 1796
		incl. sup. with	Feb. 8, 29, June 13, 1796
CaQMS	v. 3	(no. 12)	Oct. 30, 1797

THE QUEBEC GAZETTE. *Printed at Quebec by Brown & Gilmore, then by Wm. Brown, by S. Neilson, by J. Neilson, and by others, 1764–19th century.*

This paper bore the heading, unchanged through the 18th century except in number and date line:

[*on left:*] THE / QUEBEC / GAZETTE. / [rule] / THURSDAY, JUNE 21, 1764. / [double rule] /
[*in centre:* ROYAL ARMS] /
[*on right:*] NOMB. I. / LA / GAZETTE / DE / QUEBEC. / [rule] / JEUDY, / le 21 JUIN, 1764. / [double rule] /

The *Quebec gazette* was established at Quebec by William Brown and Thomas Gilmore, June 21, 1764 (no. 1), and published by them (though Brown was the dominant partner) till Gilmore's death in Feb., 1773. It was continued by Brown to no. 1231, Mar. 19, 1789, three days before his own death on Mar. 22, 1789; then from no. 1232, Mar. 26, 1789 to no. 1436, Jan 10, 1793 by Brown's nephew, Samuel Neilson, who died on Jan. 12, 1793. From no. 1437, Jan. 17 to no. 1466, Aug. 15, 1793, it was "printed for John Neilson," Samuel's young brother, under supervision of Rev. Alexander Spark. From Aug. 22, 1793 it was "printed by John Neilson," till the end of the period of this survey (no. 1861, Dec. 25, 1800) and thereafter by Neilson and others till 1874. *See* E. Gerin: *La gazette de Québec* (65 p., Quebec, 1864).

The *Quebec gazette* was published weekly from June 21, 1764 (no. 1) till Oct. 31, 1765 (no. 72); then from May 29, 1766 (no. 73) till Nov. 30, 1775 (no. 568). No. 569-570 were issued Mar. 14-21, 1776, and the paper resumed publication with no. 571, Aug. 8, 1776, appearing regularly till after no. 1861, Dec. 25, 1800, the end of the period of this survey. It bore no volume number and the issues were numbered in one continuous sequence. It was published on Thursdays, June 21, 1764—July 3, 1766, on Mondays, July 7, 1766—Mar. 23, 1767, and thereafter (from Mar. 26) on Thursdays. Extra numbers, with extraordinary news or announcements, were published occasionally between the weekly issues, and they were numbered in the regular sequence. The weekly issues were 4 pages in folio (excepting Oct. 20, 1768, Dec. 21, 1769, Mar. 1, Nov. 1, 1770, Oct. 3, 1771, Mar. 14, 1776, 2 p.; Mar. 21, 1776, broadside). They were printed in 2 col., English and French, later 3 or 4 col. as the size of sheet increased. Most of the matter inserted was printed in both languages, and when official publications were lengthy and business advertisements numerous, the weekly issue was increased by supplements of 2 to 4 (occasionally to 10) pages. Sometimes the supplement (or the regular number) was occupied mainly or entirely by proclamations, provincial ordinances, or municipal regulations, and was also issued separately with or without the *Gazette* heading and any other matter which filled in the pages. These supplements are a feature peculiar to the *Quebec gazette* in their size and frequency, especially in the years 1765-66, 1771, 1787 *et seq*. During the last decade of the century nearly every issue included a supplement.

Announced in Brown and Gilmore's [Proposals] (No. 56) the *Quebec gazette* duly appeared with its *raison d'être* stated in the first issue:

> "The Printers to the Publick—As every kind of knowledge is not only useful and instructive to individuals, but a benefit to the community, there is great reason to hope, that a NEWSPAPER, properly conducted and written with ACCURACY, FREEDOM, and IMPARTIALITY, cannot fail of meeting with universal encouragement; especially as it is allowed by all, that such a paper is at present much wanted in this colony. . . .
>
> "Our design . . . is to publish in English and French under title THE QUEBEC GAZETTE, . . . foreign affairs, political transactions . . . of the several powers of Europe, occurrences of the Mother Country, also events, debates, etc., of amusement and interest to people . . . [and] Material occurrences of the American Colonies and West-Indian Islands . . . [derived] from extensive correspondence already established. [When] the rigour of winter prevents the arrival of ships and news, the Printers will present originals in prose and verse, philosophy, politicks and history. . . .
>
> "Our intentions to please the Whole, without offence to any individual, will be better evinced by our practice than by writing volumes on this subject. This one thing we beg to be believed that PARTY PREJUDICE, or PRIVATE SCANDAL, will never find a place in this PAPER."

[also in French]

The colophon read: "Printed by Brown & Gilmore, at the Printing-Office in St. Lewis's-Street, in the Upper-Town, two Doors above the [Governor's] Secretary's-Office, where Subscriptions for this Paper are taken in. Advertisements of a moderate length (in one language) inserted for Five Shillings the first Week and One Shilling each week after; if in both languages Eight Shillings the first Week and Two Shillings each Week after; and all kinds of printing done in the neatest Manner with Care and Expedition." [also in French]

The subscription (not stated here) was $3.00 a year (increased to $4.00 on May 1, 1800, with an extra half-dollar, or 2*s*. 6*d*., courrier charge for out-of-town delivery from July 1, 1779). The advertising rates were increased, Jan. 3, 1765, to 6*s*. the first week, 1*s*. each week after, in one language, 9*s*. and 3*s*. in both languages. Later they were revised: ten lines or less, 7*s*. 6*d*. for the first, 2*s*. 6*d*. for each subsequent week with insertion in both languages; 5*s.*, 1*s.* 3*d.*, in one language only; more than ten lines at the same rate.

The *Quebec gazette* was printed in St. Lewis's Street till May 30, 1765. Then it was "Printed by Brown & Gilmore at the Printing Office in Parlour Street in the Upper Town, a little above the Bishop's Palace" till Jan. 27, 1774. The partnership of Brown & Gilmore being dissolved on Jan. 28, about a year after Gilmore's death, from Feb. 3, 1774, the paper was "Printed by Wm. Brown near the Bishop's Palace," or, as it presently appeared: "Behind the Cathedral Church." On May 1, 1780, Brown's shop was "remov'd to the Lower House about the middle of the Hill between Upper and Lower Town" and thereafter the *Quebec gazette* was printed in Mountain Street. The printing office was gutted by fire, Dec. 25, 1789, but the *Quebec gazette* continued publication as usual, being printed "with Mr. Moore's assistance" (i.e. at the *Herald* printing office?) until damages were repaired.

For Brown and Gilmore, born in Great Britain and trained in Philadelphia, bilingual publication created special difficulties. They frequently advertised for an apprentice, "an ingenious Boy about 14 years old who can be well recommended. If he can read and write and should be able to make himself understood in both French and English he will be the more acceptable [etc.]."—*Quebec gazette*, July 5, 1764, *et seq.* Advertisements were solicited early "as Intelligence, some Times arrives only the Evening before our Gazette comes out . . . we have it first to translate and afterwards to compose double [i.e. in English and French]. We hope our Customers will make allowance if we fall something short [by holding news till next week] of those who publish only in one Language, as every Paragraph with us requires at least triple the Time; and for this reason we beg Advertisements be sent in as soon as possible."—*ibid.*, May 29, 1766.

The Stamp Act aggravated their early difficulties, as they stated, announcing a rise in subscription of one half dollar per annum—"Though it may seem high for a *Gazette* of this size, we hope that Gentlemen will think otherwise, when they consider we are now obliged to buy our Paper of one Person only, and at Thirty-Six Shillings per Ream, which stood us formerly but Eight Shillings. We must pay for a Translation £60 per Annum by which means, together with many other Expences we incur by publication in two Languages, our Gazette costs us at least £100 more than any other [paper] on the Continent of the same size." The suggestion of publishing the paper, in two separate sections, one half sheet [2 p.] in English and one half sheet [2 p.] in French, the printers dismissed, as no saving in cost, and as a real hardship ultimately. For the one bilingual paper instructs the new subjects [i.e. French Canadians] in the English language, and by regulation under the Stamp Act, anything published in any language other than English must pay double—from which Grenada and Quebec are exempt for 5 years only.—*ibid.*, Sup. Oct. 17, 1765. On Oct. 31, 1765, the printers acquainted "the Publick, that . . . by Means of the small Number of Subscribers which they have at present, *occasioned by the Stamp-Act*, [they] are obliged to discontinue publishing the GAZETTE from this DAY!! . . . All kinds of Printing will be carried on at the PRINTING-OFFICE (during the Winter Season) with Care and Expedition-→There is no Stamp-Duty on Hand-Bills."—*ibid.*, Oct. 31, 1765.

On May 29, 1766, Brown and Gilmore resumed publication with:

NOMB. 73 "THE RESURRECTION / OF THE / QUEBEC GAZETTE / [royal arms] / LA RESURRECTION / DE LA / GAZETTE DE / QUEBEC". / It contained a lengthy editorial on the "impositions of the grievous stamp" (*see* No. 78) and a restatement of the printers' policy outlined in their first number, adding: "A Report having been . . . industriously propagated, that our Gazette was under the Inspection of the [Governor's] Secretary . . . we think it necessary to declare, that ever since the Establishment of Civil Government [Aug. 10, 1764] our Paper has been, and ever shall be, as free of Inspection or Restrictions of any Person whatsoever, as it is of the late Stamp. . . . We profess'd at our first setting out, our avow'd Resolution against making our Publication the Conveyance a private Scandal, or the Tool and Stimulator to Political Faction; we trust that from Principle we should keep to this, though Regard to our own safety did not oblige us to it. . . . It is a Happiness peculiar to the Subjects of the British Empire only, to have the Liberty of thinking for themselves on all Subjects, to speak what they think, and to publish such thoughts as may seem innoxious to Individuals, and undisturbing to the Publick."

The provincial government exercised some supervision over the *Quebec gazette*, however, if not then, later, as the revolutionary movement developed in the American colonies. Pierre DuCalvet complained (in *Gazette litteraire*, Montreal, April 6, 1779) that Brown had submitted DuCalvet's advertisements to a government official, who refused him permission to print them. Also Brown, petitioning the Governor-in-Council for an increase in salary, stated "That for some time past he [the petitioner] has been restrain'd from printing but by Order or Permission of Government, which is attended with some trouble, impediment &c."—Can.P.A., Que. "S" *Leg. co. papers*, Apr. 7, 1777. Also, Lieut.-Gov. Cramahé writing from Quebec, Oct. 1, 1778, to Gov. Haldimand at Sorel: ". . . Our Printer has some Penchant to the popular cause, and when he gets a cup too much, which is not seldom, his zeal increases. I have cautioned him two or three times since your Departure, and shall, untill you can find a proper Person to inspect his Press, desire him to lay before me whatever he intends to publish."—Can.P.A., "B" 95: 53.*

Activities in the American colonies were front page news, but the *Quebec gazette* was strongly loyalist before and during the Revolution. Its outbreak was reported thus: "A Circumstantial Account of an Attack that happened on the 19th of April, 1775, on His Majesty's Troops by a Number of the People of the Province of Massachusetts-Bay [the account over a page long in English and French ends:] Thus this unfortunate Affair has happened through the Rashness and Imprudence of a few People, who began Firing on the Troops at Lexington."—*Quebec gazette,* June 22, 1775.

For the next several years the *Quebec gazette* was an unofficial government gazette. Proclamations and notices appeared with increased cogency. The local contributions, also the printers' selection of news and essays for reprinting from British and American prints, were obviously inspired by a government striving to keep French Canada, British. During the invasion of the province and the siege of the city, Brown continued to issue the paper till Nov. 31, 1775, when he announced: "The Printer finding it impossible to continue the publication of this Gazette, begs Leave to return to the Publick his most sincere thanks for their encouragement hitherto, to wish them better times, and to assure them of his readiness again to serve them as soon as it may be in his power."

The paper appeared again on Mar. 14, 1776 (2 p.) and Mar. 21, 1776 (broadside) with American documents on the failure of the attack on Quebec, "published by [Governor Carleton's] Authority." Then it resumed regular publication Aug. 8, 1776

*Cramahé continued, speaking of government's publication in "this day's [Thursday, Oct. 1, 1778] Gazette." The context suggests that "Our Printer" refers to Wm. Brown in Quebec, not to Fleury Mesplet in Montreal as McLachlan infers (*Mesplet:* p. 208).

(no. 571), with the heading: "THE RESURRECTION N° II. OF THE QUEBEC GAZETTE [royal arms] LA RESURRECTION No II. . . . DE LA GAZETTE DE QUEBEC."—and with a congratulatory address "To the Publick." In this, Brown stated that his paper "has so far justly merited the Title of THE MOST INNOCENT GAZETTE IN THE BRITISH DOMINIONS, and as there is little likelihood of its loosing [sic] Claim to so laudible an Attribute, he [the printer] flatters himself it will meet with such further Encouragement as will enable him to continue its Publication, which he has determined to prosecute if 200 Subscribers at the usual Price of three Spanish dollars per annum can be procured by the Middle of September next—When it is consider'd that Numbers of the Most Turbulent Weekly Productions are constantly supported by more than ten Times that Number, it cannot be thought extravagant to expect the Most Peaceable might be patroniz'd, in so extensive and populous a Providence as this, by so moderate a Number, the Completion whereof will not only evince that Innocence and Good Order are yet encouraged in one Corner of the World, notwithstanding the lamentable Curruption [sic] of the Times, but also confer an additional Obligation on . . . the Printer."—*Quebec gazette*, Aug. 8, 1776.

It remained a "Most Innocent Gazette," and probably a most profitable one—despite Brown's frequent notices dunning subscribers, of which he had 250-300, about half of whom were outside Quebec. Most of its content was paid for by advertisers, or by authority. Due and legal promulgation of laws, etc., (was according to Ordinance of Oct. 3, 1764) by printing in the *Gazette;* provincial ordinances, proclamations and announcements emanating from the governor's or Council's office, Brown inserted in return for his salary as government printer. This was £55, increased in 1769 to £100, a year. But much "Extra printing" was done for these and other offices, for which Brown made extra charge (especially after his petition of 1777) at the regular advertising rate. His successors charged government 80 per cent of that rate. Regulations and notices of the justices of the peace, who were the municipal authority, were regularly published in the *Gazette,* even those of Montreal specifically ordered official publication in the *Quebec gazette.* Brown's successors received no salary from the government, but continued to print official publications, on a schedule established by Samuel Neilson, Oct. 10, 1789, and revised by John Neilson in 1795. This schedule remained the standard of charge for government printing in Lower and Upper Canada for many years.

From 1789 the proportion of non-official matter—news, essays, and local contributions—increased. Especially before the passage of the Canada, or Constitutional, Act in London, 1791, both English and French interests in Quebec, published memorials and correspondence in the local newspapers.

Samuel Neilson, who became printer of the *Gazette* in Mar., 1789, was a young man of vigorous intellect, with a keen interest in contemporary affairs. From 1789 through 1792, he practically doubled the space devoted to news, commentary, and documents reprinted from European sources, particularly on events in France. He also published documents and lengthy essays of local origin on political issues in Canada. During each of these years half or more (in 1791 *every* one) of the regular issues of the *Gazette* included a supplement of 2 to 6 pages. Neilson stated:

> "As the printer has uniformly made it his study to furnish as extensive, free, and impartial, account of the most interesting events in every part of the world, and having thereby incurred a considerable and unproductive expence, he hopes the subscribers will . . . second his future endeavours by their alacrity in paying the Subscriptions, . . . without which he is sorry to remark that the public mind will be deprived of a great share in that information which it is in the interest of every free people to maintain and to extend thro' every class of society."
>
> —*Quebec gazette*, May 3, 1792.

Neilson's subscribers had increased to 475 by 1792, of which half were in Quebec and vicinity, about 18 on the Halifax road, and the remainder on the Montreal road. His editorial policy was continued, though less vigorously, by Rev. Alexander Spark—who "supervised" the *Gazette* just before and after Neilson's death, (from tuberculosis, Jan., 1793) from Sept., 1792 till Sept., 1794—then by Samuel's younger brother, John Neilson.

Liberty, Equality, and Fraternity occupied considerable space in the *Gazette* for a time, and news and comment on the progress of revolution in France were reprinted at length from sympathetic sources until the execution of the King. The blow to Establishment, royal and ecclesiastical, shocked British and French Canada alike. Then the outbreak of war between Britain and France altered the printer's attitude, and the aspect of events presented in the *Gazette*, especially when the Lower Canada government instituted repressive measures against potential enemies in America.

From 1794 (by 34 Geo. III c. 1) the sessions laws passed under the new constitution were published serially in book form by a specially appointed King's law printer.*—Though the laws, proclamations, and notices, continued to appear in the *Quebec gazette*, its official function became relatively less important.

It is noteworthy that the *Quebec gazette* contained few references, either by printer or correspondent, to the contents of other newspapers published in Quebec itself, or in Montreal. Little inter-paper controversy appeared in its columns, though occasionally news items were reprinted from other Canadian papers, particularly from those in Nova Scotia, and later in Upper Canada. The Brown>Neilson business, however, included a large retail bookselling and stationery trade, and the *Gazette's* advertisements of its own and other printers' books and pamphlets are one of the best sources of information on early Canadian publications; so, too, are its extensive lists of imported works, an excellent gauge of the reading interests of the community it served.

*Copies located:***

CaNsWA	no. 1437-1526	Jan. 17, 1793-Sept. 25, 1794
	1508 Extra;	May 29, 1794
	1521 Extra:	Aug. 23, 1794
	1576,	Aug. 27, 1795
	1649, 1673-1674	Jan. 5, June 15-22, 1797
CaO	no. 73-157,	May 29, 1766-Dec. 31, 1767
	210-261,	Jan. 5-Dec. 28, 1769
	516,	Dec. 1, 1774
	518-567,	Dec. 15, 1774-Nov. 23, 1775
	570,	Mar. 21, 1776
	571-665,	Aug. 8, 1776-May 28, 1778
	667-683	June 11-Oct. 1, 1778
	685-812,	Oct. 1, 1778-Mar. 29, 1781

*This was not Neilson but Wm. Vondenvelden, 1795-98, then Lelievre & Desbarats.

**A modern facsimile reprint of no. 1 (June 21, 1764) is commonly found in large public libraries and private collections of Canadiana. The reprint may be readily distinguished from the original edition by its paper—which is wove, not laid, and which is tending now to discolour and crumble at the edges.

814-878,	Apr. 12, 1781-June 20, 1782
880-1087,	July 4, 1782-June 15, 1786
1089-1579,	June 29, 1786-Sept. 10, 1795
1581-1630,	Sept. 24, 1795-Aug. 25, 1796
1632-1861.	Sept. 8, 1796-Dec. 25, 1800
and Postscripts	Sept. 8, Nov. 10, 1798
Another copy of no. 1702-1755	Jan. 4-Dec. 27, 1798 intercollated with the *Montreal gazette*, 1798

This file contains nearly all the numerous Supplements in the CaOOA file, also a few Supplements and the *Postscripts* of 1798, and extra no. 1461, *not* in the CaOOA file. It is remarkable for the inclusion, in many volumes, of copies of private and official publications, of *Carrier's addresses* and *Calendriers*, broadsides or leaflets, published separately, also distributed, in part at least, with the *Quebec gazette* of the week. Such pieces are described (and their location indicated) under their year of printing.

CaO has also a folio volume (about 150 p.) containing MS. notes of the contents of the *Quebec gazette*, 1764-74; also another volume (69 p. fo.) a MS. abstract of the *Quebec gazette*, issue by issue, 1772-78. Both volumes are written in French, in an old but unidentified hand.

CaOOA	[Prospectus]	*See* No. 56
	no. 1-72	June 21, 1764-Oct. 31, 1765
	73-417,	May 29, 1766-Dec. 31, 1772
	418-468,	Jan. 7-Dec. 30, 1773 wanting, and supplied in photostat.
	469-568,	Jan. 6, 1774-Nov. 30, 1775.
	569-570	Mar. 14-21, 1776
	571-1485,	Aug. 8, 1776-Dec. 26, 1793
	1487-1560	Jan. 9, 1794-May 14, 1795
	1562-1861	May 21, 1795-Dec. 25, 1800

Another copy of the following numbers or parts thereof, containing recently passed ordinances, etc.:—

no. 452,	Sept. 9, 1773
1124	Mar. 1, 1787
1132-1134	Apr. 26-May 10, 1787
1383, 1391	Jan. 5, Mar. 1, 1792

This file, preserved by the printers in the *Quebec gazette* office (passing later from the Neilson family to the Public Archives of Canada) is practically complete. It includes most of the numerous supplements (excepting in the year 1773, supplied in photostat from a less complete file). Occasional numbers have small mutilations but the missing sections are usually supplied in mss. Printers' MS. memoranda, mainly on repeated matter and charges, frequently appear in the margins.

Another copy of no. 1	June 21, 1752 in the Fairchild papers.
Another copy of no. 1118-1219	Jan. 3-Dec. 25, 1788

CaOT	no. 159-209,	Jan. 14-Dec. 29, 1768
	1540-1648,	Jan. 1, 1795-Dec. 29, 1796
	1810-1852,	Jan. 2-Oct. 23, 1800
	1854-1861.	Nov. 6-Dec. 25, 1800

CaQMA	no. 1124, 1132,	Mar. 1,* Apr. 26,* 1787
	1134,	May 10, 1787*
	1183-1184,	Apr. 17-24, 1788
	1186-1187,	May 8-15, 1788
	1190, 1198,	June 5, July 31, 1788
	1199,	Aug. 7, 1788
	1235-1236,	Apr. 13*-16*, 1789
	1239-1240,	May 7*-14,* 1789
	1308,	Aug. 26, 1790
	1351	June 16, 1791

This is a collection of *Quebec gazette* regular and extra numbers or supplements, containing recently passed ordinances, proclamations, regulations, etc.; also separate issues of the ordinances (marked*) printed from *Gazette* types, similar to No. 531, etc.

CaQMM	no. 800-824,	Jan. 4-June 21, 1781
	826-827,	July 5-12, 1781
	830-886,	Aug. 2, 1781-Aug. 15, 1782
	888-905,	Aug. 29-Dec. 26, 1782
	1116-1167,	Jan. 4-Dec. 27, 1787
	1274-1285,	Jan. 7-Mar. 25, 1790
	1287-1289,	Apr. 8-22, 1790
	1292, 1294-1313,	May 13, May 27-Sept. 30, 1799
	1315-1433	Oct. 14, 1790-Dec. 20, 1792

In this file the issues are fairly complete, though occasionally lacking 2 pages or supplement, and occasionally represented by the supplement only. Small mutilations occur in the pages, especially those of 1790-92. This file includes no numbers or supplements not in CaOOA or CaO.

CaQQL	no. 1-157,	June 21, 1764-Dec. 31, 1767
	210-261,	Jan. 5-Dec. 28, 1769
	418-468,	Jan. 7-Dec. 30, 1773
	521-568,	Jan. 5-Nov. 30, 1775
	570, 571-582,	Mar. 21, Aug. 8-Oct. 24, 1776
	584-596,	Nov. 7, 1776-Jan. 30, 1777
	598-609,	Feb. 13-May 1, 1777
	611-614,	May 15-June 5, 1777
	616-620,	June 19-July 17, 1777
	622-648,	July 31, 1777-Jan. 29, 1778
	650-663,	Feb. 12-May 14, 1778
	665-705,	May 28, 1778-Mar. 4, 1779
	707-717,	Mar. 18-May 27, 1779
	719-743,	June 10-Nov. 25, 1779
	745-765,	Dec. 9, 1779-Apr. 27, 1780

	770-1132,	June 1, 1780-Apr. 26, 1787
	1134-1199,	May 10, 1787-Aug. 7, 1788
	1201-1289,	Aug. 21, 1788-Apr. 22, 1790
	1291-1378,	May 6, 1790-Dec. 1, 1791
	1380-1574,	Dec. 15, 1791-Aug. 13, 1795
	1576-1776,	Aug. 27, 1795-May 23, 1799
	1778-1861,	June 3 (Extra), 1799-Dec. 25, 1800

This file, practically complete within the years represented, and the file of CaQQLH complement each other. Together they form a *Quebec gazette* series in Quebec city second only to that in Ottawa.

CaQQLH	no. 2, 4-15,	June 28, July 12-Sept. 27, 1764
	17-46,	Oct. 11, 1764-May 2, 1765
	48-71,	May 16-Oct. 24, 1765
	73, 75,	May 29, June 12, 1766
	77-143,	June 26, 1766-Sept. 24, 1767
	145-164,	Oct. 8, 1767-Feb. 18, 1768
	166-168,	Mar. 3-17, 1768
	170-176,	Mar. 31-May 12, 1768
	178-184,	May 26-July 7, 1768
	186-191,	July 21-Aug. 25, 1768
	193-271,	Sept. 8, 1768-Mar. 8, 1770
	273-291,	Mar. 22-July 26, 1770
	293-299,	Aug. 9-Sept. 20, 1770
	301-334,	Oct. 4, 1770-May 30, 1771
	336-361,	June 13-Dec. 5, 1771
	365-409,	Jan. 2-Nov. 5, 1772
	411-439,	Nov. 19, 1772-June 10, 1773
	441-453,	June 24-Sept. 16, 1773
	455-489,	Sept. 30, 1773-May 26, 1774
	491-494,	June 9-30, 1774
	496-510,	July 14-Oct. 20, 1774
	512-514,	Nov. 3-17, 1774
	516-523,	Dec. 1, 1774-Jan. 19, 1775
	525-531,	Feb. 2-Mar, 16, 1775
	533-563,	Mar. 30-Oct. 26, 1775
	565-567,	Nov. 9-23, 1775
	571-587,	Aug. 8-Nov. 28, 1776
	589-591,	Dec. 12-26, 1776
	697-719,	Jan. 7-June 10, 1779
	721-737,	June 24-Oct. 14, 1779
	739-745,	Oct. 28-Dec. 9, 1779
	747-799,	Dec. 23, 1779-Dec. 28, 1780
	958-968,	Jan. 1-Mar. 11, 1784
	970-1002,	Mar. 25-Nov. 4, 1784
	1004-1009,	Nov. 18-Dec. 23, 1784
	1011-1059,	Jan. 6-Dec. 8, 1785
	1061-1132,	Dec. 22, 1785-Apr. 26, 1787
	1134-1331,	May 10, 1787-Feb. 3, 1791
	1333-1377,	Feb. 10-Nov. 24, 1791

	1380-1403,	Dec. 15, 1791-May 31, 1792
	1405-1538,	June 14, 1792-Dec. 18, 1794
	1588, 1594,	Nov. 12 (Sup. only), Dec. 24, 1795 (Sup. only)
	1540-1595,	Jan. 1-Dec. 31, 1795 (in photostat from CaOOA)
	1596,	Jan. 7, 1796 (Sup. only)
	1649-1676,	Jan. 5-July 6, 1797
	1680-1745,	Aug. 3, 1797-Oct. 18, 1798
	1747-1821,	Nov. 1, 1798-Mar. 20, 1800
	1823-1825,	Apr. 3-17, 1800
	1827-1861.	May 1-Dec. 25, 1800

This file, the property of the Literary and Historical Society of Quebec, is stored in the vault of the Provincial Archives of Quebec. It has few mutilations but occasionally lacks 2 pages or supplement in some issues. It includes no numbers or supplements *not* in CaOOA or CaO.

DLC *See* p. 659

Ketcheson "odd numbers before 1792, 1792-1793 complete."

MH	no. 1560,	May 14, 1795
	1562-1564, 1566,	May 21-June 4, June 18, 1795
	1570, 1581,	July 16, Sept. 24, 1795
	1610-1611,	Apr. 14-21, 1796
	1618-1619,	June 9-16, 1796
	1625-1629,	July 21-Aug. 18, 1796
	1631-1641,	Sept. 1-Nov. 10, 1796
	1645-1651,	Dec. 8, 1796-Jan. 19, 1797
	1655-1660, 1662,	Feb. 9 (Sup. only)-Mar. 16, Mar. 30, 1797
	1699-1700.	Dec. 14-21, 1797

The forty-three issues in this broken file are complete, excepting Apr. 14, 1796, Nov. 10, 1796, which lack supplement; Feb. 9, 1797, which lacks main number; and June 9, July 28, Sept. 8, 1796, which are slightly mutilated.

MHi	no. 41,	Mar. 28, 1765
	124,	May 14, 1767
	159, 163-164,	Jan. 14, Feb. 11-18, 1768
	1183.	Apr. 17, 1788
MiU-C	no. 80-81,	July 14-21, 1766 (slightly mut.)
	106,	Jan. 12, 1767
	[107],	[Jan. 19], 1767 (p. [1-2] wanting)
	149,	Nov. 5, 1767 (slightly mut.)
	155-156.	Dec. 17-24, 1767
MWA	no. 1543,	Jan. 15, 1795
	[1596]-1648,	Jan. 7-Dec. 29, 1796

	1669, 1691,	May 18, Oct. 19, 1797
	1750,	Nov. 22, 1798
	1798,	Oct. 10, 1799
	1799,	Oct. 17, 1799 (Sup. only)

These issues are complete with supplements as published, excepting July 7, 1796, which lacks supplement, and Oct. 17, 1799, which lacks main number.

NN	no. 1116-1160,	Jan. 4-Nov. 8, 1787
	1273-1297,	Dec. 31, 1789-June 17, 1790
	1299-1318,	July 1-Nov. 4, 1790
	1320-1326.	Nov. 18-Dec. 30, 1790
PHi	no. 332,	May 16, 1771

THE QUEBEC HERALD AND UNIVERSAL MISCELLANY.

Printed at Quebec by William Moore, 1788-93.

The *Quebec herald and universal miscellany* was announced by a specimen (No. 566) in May, 1788, and a prospectus (No. 558) Oct. 25, 1788. It was edited, printed, and published by William Moore, weekly on Mondays, from Nov. 24, 1788 probably till Feb. 11, 1793. At first it bore the heading:

QUEBEC / HERALD / AND / Universal Miscellany. / NUMBER I. [ornament] VOLUME, I. / [rule] / "Quid verum atque decens, curo et rogo, et omnis in hoc sum: condo, & compono." HOR. / [rule] / Monday, NOVEMBER 24th. 1788. / [rule] /

With v. 1, no. 2, Dec. 1, 1788, the title at the mast head was shortened to *Herald and universal miscellany,* though the title page to v. 1, issued Nov. 23, 1789, bore the original title as above. With v. 2, no. 1, the title was further changed to *Herald miscellany and advertiser.* The colophon states the place of printing simply as "The Herald Printing Office." This was "Apartments" in a house owned by one Dorion in Mountain street opposite Freemasons' Hall, till May, 1790 when it was moved to no. 24 Mountain street, a house then occupied by Moore (who had married on Mar. 11, 1790).

The *Herald* was a sheet in quarto, 8 pages to the issue (printed 3 col. to the page) occasionally increased to 9 pages or enlarged (excepting in 1789-91 when the Thursday edition was published) by a postscript of 2 or 4 pages. The issues were numbered in one continuous series (the latest located being no. 270, July 23, 1792; they were also numbered in volumes of 52 issues, from v. 1 no. 1 to [v. 5, no. 13]. The contents of each volume, usually including postscripts and index, were paged continuously and a title page and index issued after the 52nd number. An "Advertisement to the Public" conveying Moore's thanks for "approbation and encouragement" was issued on a separate leaf with t.-p. to v. 1. The only volume collated complete is v. 1: 2 p. l., 452 p. Each issue after v. 1, no. 1, was "double-dated" to show the first and last (or publication) day of the week covered. The t.-p. to v. 1 read:

THE / QUEBEC HERALD / AND / Universal Miscellany: / From the 24th. of NOVEMBER 1788, to the 16th of / NOVEMBER, 1789. / [rule] / VOLUME I. / [rule] / "Quid verum atque decens caro et rogo, et omnis in hoc sum: condo, / & compono." / HOR. / [rule] / [royal arms] / [rule] / QUEBEC: / PRINTED BY WILLIAM MOORE. /

The *Herald* was printed, as Moore stated in his prospectus of Oct. 25, 1788: ". . . with intire new type cast by Mr. Caslon, on demy paper . . . each number to contain . . . with 8 pages printed matter in English consisting of the most interesting intelligence from Europe, Asia and America &c., the important debates of parliament, ingenious essays, humourous anecdotes, poetry, the occurrences of the Province and advertisements. In the first number a philosophic history of the province will be given and 2 pages in each number will continue this till it is complete, then the most useful works published in English will appear in the same manner . . . The Subscription is one guinea for the first year, to be paid on delivery of the first number . . . Advertisements of 15 lines, 3/6 for 1 week; 2 weeks 5/3; a month 7/, every 5 lines above 15, in proportion. [etc. The printer invites advertisements and contributions of copy.] He presumes it will not be held unimportant by the heads of families, to declare that where he cannot improve the morals of the rising generation, he will not viciate them by the promulgation of anything offensive to delicacy, or virtue; it will be his invariable rule to paint virtue in such lively colours to put vice out of countenance. A letter box will be placed at the door, but it is hoped that nothing will be put in, but what tends to convey to the liberal and enlightened mind, information and rational amusement. To what aims to sacrifice the reputation of private individuals, whose manners are unoffending, or wantonly stabs the characters of those who are candidates for popular applause, no place will be given in the Herald."

The "philosophic history of the province" mentioned in the prospectus, duly appeared as excerpts from Abbé Raynal's *A philosophic and political history* [*etc.*]. Other "useful works" were reprinted, and official notices and announcements were published occasionally, but such "routine" material occupied relatively less space in Moore's paper than in any other Canadian journal of the century—in marked contrast with the *Quebec gazette*. The *Herald* is remarkable for its local news, its essays and correspondence on political and social matters in the province, and for the frequent expression of the printer's own opinions. His random comments upon local happenings or characters—even occasional speculation on the estate of the deceased in obituary notices—elicited correspondence in reproof or correction which is now a useful source of information. Himself an amateur actor, musician, and versifier, and a member of most of the social and benefit organizations in Quebec, Moore published formal notices and informal accounts of a wide range of social activities. Also he maintained a lively banter with his cronies in his own correspondence columns, and published their light effusions even those at his own expense, e.g.

"*Extempore on Seeing the Printer of the Herald inclined to Drink.*
Physicians they say once a week do allow,
A P****** for his health to get drunk—as a sow,
That is right quoth old *****, but the day they dont say,
So for fear I should miss it—I'm drunk every day."
—[*Quebec*] *Herald*, Jan. 5, 1789.

He printed, too, a mass of correspondence on the "occurrences of the province," e.g. on the controversy between Bishop Hubert and his coadjutor bishop, Bailly de Messein, on the squabble between soldiers and civilians over militia duty, on constitutional questions in Canada and England—the numerous petitions, counter-petitions, and commentary thereon, produced by English and French, merchants, clerics, gentry, and bureaucrats, preceding the passage of the Constitutional Act.

Though Moore, with a couple of his contributors, was charged with libel by Col. Henry Caldwell in a militia fracas (*see* No. 680) he does not appear to have been restricted in publication by authority. He hinted at restraints occasionally, as on Mar. 9, 1789: "It being the Editor's intention to furnish the Public with valuable and interesting Parliamentary discussions [from England] such extracts as may be of general utility and not abstruse will constantly appear in the Herald. How far the Printer may be suppressed he cannot say. But . . . he has been disappointed in the receipt of sundry publications he should have had [etc.]." On Nov. 23, 1789, his second volume opened with an embryo editorial on the Liberty of the press: ". . . Of all the liberties of which we boast under a mild government, that of a free press is the most we prize, because it is the basis of all others; it is the great defender of our rights, and the support of our liberty and property. It has therefore been justly observed that 'the Liberty of the press . . . should be touched with a trembling hand'." Moore does not dwell upon the relations of the press and its potential oppressor, but suggests that it is because this liberty is enjoyed by the press of England and America, their newspapers are of high character, and are impartial, allowing all persons to express their sentiments with decency on public subjects, whatever their talents or opinions. To its adherence to this policy is due the encouragement which the *Herald* received of its contributors, subscribers, and advertisers. . . .

Whether they paid him or not, Moore's correspondents and advertisers supplied him with more copy than his 8-page weekly could publish. On Sept. 21, 1789, in his [Notice to] *The friends of the Printer* (No. 618) he announced the publication of a second weekly number of the *Herald*, to appear on Thursdays, beginning Nov. 26, 1789. It had the same title, format, size, subscription, and advertising rates, as the Monday paper, but it was published in an independent series, with its own volume, issue and page, numbering, and its own title-page and index at the end of the first year. With the issue of May 12-19, 1791, however, the Thursday edition ceased without warning, and in the next Monday's *Herald*, Moore announced that "as the Half year expired on Thursday last [the Printer] purposed to issue a title page and index on Monday next and continue the Monday paper only." Collation of the Thursday edition:—v. 1: 1 p. l. (t.-p.), 419 p. (p. [417]-419 = Index), [2] p. (unpaged *Postscript* to v. 1. no. 95, Sept. 23-30, 1790). v. 2: 1 p. l. (t.-p.), 210 p. (p. 209-210 Index).

The "Monday paper" appeared for nearly two years longer, the issue of Feb. 11, 1795, being the latest recorded (though no copy located). This issue was cited in the *Quebec gazette*, Feb. 21, 1793, and in the *Montreal gazette*, of Mar. 7, 1793, which also published "A letter intended for the Herald . . . as Mr. Moore has discontinued his Herald." John Neilson's MS. *Journal* notes on Mar. 1, 1793, "Samuel Holland owes the Estate of Wm. Moore for one quarter's Subscription to the Herald, ended No. 13, volume 5—5/10"—suggesting that with the *Herald*, the *Herald* printing office ceased also, if not indeed, the printer too. At any rate nothing further is recorded of William Moore.

Copies located, Monday edition:

CaOOA	v. 1	(no. 1-52)	Nov. 24, 1788—Nov. 9-16, 1789
		Postscript with	
		(no. 4-5,	Dec. 8-15—15-22, 1788
		9-10,	Jan. 12-19—19-26, 1789
		14, 18,	Feb. 16-23, Mar. 16-23, 1789
		21-23, 31,	Apr. 6-13—20-27, June 15-22, 1789
		34 [i.e. 36], 45)	July 20-27, Sept. 21-28, 1789

	and	[Extra]	*See* No. 591
		t.-p. and Index	
CaQM	v. 1	(no. 1-19,	Nov. 24, 1788—Mar. 23-30, 1789
		21-52,	Apr. 6-13—Nov. 9-16, 1789
		Postscript with	
		no. 4-5,	Dec. 8-15—15-22, 1788
		9-10,	Jan. 12-19—19-26, 1789
		18, 22)	Mar. 16-23, Apr. 13-20, 1789
	t.-p.; "Advertisement to the Public," undated and signed: William Moore (1 *l.*); and index		
	v. 2	(no. 1-37,	Nov. 16-23, 1789—July 26-Aug. 2, 1790
		39-51	Aug. 9-16—Nov. 1-8, 1790
	Mutilated and defective (v. 1)		Nov. 24-Dec. 1, 1788
			Feb. 2-9—16-23, 1789
			Mar. 9-16—16-23, 1789
			Apr. 6-13 Postscript, Apr. 13-20, Apr. 20-27 Postscript, June 15-22—22-29, 1789
			July 20-27, Sept. 14-21—21-28, 1789
			Oct. 12-19, Oct. 26-Nov. 2, Nov. 9-16, 1789
	Mutilated and defective (v. 2)		Mar. 8-15, May 17-24, June 14-21, June 28-July 5, July 26-Aug. 2, Aug. 9-16, 1790
CaQMJ	v. 2	(no. 2-6)	Nov. 23-30—Dec. 21-28, 1789
	defective		Nov. 23-30, 1789
CaQQL	v. 2	(no. 1-28,	Nov. 16-23, 1789—May 24-31, 1790
		50)	Oct. 25-Nov. 1, 1790
	v. 3	(no. 2-25,	Nov. 22-29, 1790—May 2-9, 1791
		27-37,	May 16-23—July 25-Aug. 1, 1791
		39-52)	Aug. 8-15—Nov. 7-14, 1791
	including Postscript with		
	v. 3	(no. 28, 36,	May 23-30, [2] p. July 18-25, 1791
		41, 46)	Aug. 22-29, Sept. 26-Oct. 3, 1791
	and	t.-p. & index	
	v. 4	(no. 1-3,	Nov. 14-21—Nov. 28-Dec. 5, 1791
		5-18,	Dec. 12-19, 1791—Mar. 12-19, 1792
		20-23,	Mar. 26-Apr. 2—Apr. 16-23, 1792
		25-28,	Apr. 30-May 7—May 21-28, 1792
		30-36)	June 4-11—July 16-23, 1792
	including Postscript to (no. 15)		Feb. 20-27, 1792
Ketcheson:	odd numbers to v. 4 (no. 46)		Sept. 24-Oct. 6, 1792
Morin	v. 1	(no. 2-7,	Nov. 24-Dec. 1, 1788—Dec. 28, 1788-Jan. 5, 1789
		9-52)	Jan. 12-19—Nov. 9-16, 1789

	including Postscripts		same as CaOOA
	and	Index	
	v. 2	(no. 1-2,	Nov. 16-23—23-30, 1789
		4-22,	Dec. 7-14, 1789—Apr. 12-19, 1790
		25-52)	May 3-10—Nov. 8-15, 1790
	and	t.-p., index	
	v. 3	(no. 1-22,	Nov. 17-22, 1790—Apr. 11-18, 1791
		24-33)	Apr. 25-May 2—June 27-July 4, 1791
		Postscript (only) to	
		(no. 36)	July 18-25, 1791
	defective v. 1	(no. 20)	Mar. 30-Apr. 6, 1789
	v. 3	(no. 20)	Mar. 28-Apr. 4, 1791

Copies located Thursday edition:

CaQQL	v. 1	(no. 1-52)	Nov. 19-26, 1789—Nov. 11-18, 1790
	including Postscript to		
	v. 1	(no. 45)	Sept. 23-30, 1790 [2] p.
	and	t.-p. & index	
	v. 2	(no. 7-21,	Dec. 30, 1790-Jan. 6, 1791—Apr. 7-14, 1791
		23-26)	Apr. 21-28—May 12-19, 1791
MWA	v. 1	(no. 2)	Nov. 26-Dec. 3, 1789
Morin	v. 1	(no. 1-52)	Nov. 19-26, 1789—Nov. 11-18, 1790
	including Postscripts to no. 45		Sept. 23-30, 1790 [2] p.
	and t.-p. and index		
	v. 2	(no. 1-26)	Nov. 18-25, 1790—May 12-19, 1791
	and t.-p. & index		
	defective v. 2	(no. 8)	Jan. 6-13, 1791

THE TIMES: LE COURS DU TEMS. *Printed at Quebec by Wm. Vondenvelden, 1794-95.*

The *Times* was announced by a "preparatory address" in Dec., 1793 (No. 859) and by a specimen-prospectus, June 23, 1794 (No. 913). It appeared in a specimen issue dated June 25, 1794, unnumbered and unpaged, then an extra July 29, 1794 (broadside); then weekly from Aug. 4, 1794 (no. 1) till July 27, 1795 (no. 52 sup.) when it ceased publication.

It bore the heading:

N°. I / THE [Royal arms] LE / TIMES. / [rule] / COURS DU TEMS. / [ornamental rule] / MONDAY, AUGUST 4, 1794. / [rule] / LUNDI, 4 AOUST, 1794 / [ornamental rule] /

The preliminary issues of June 23-25, 1794, had colophon: "Quebec: Printed by Wm. Vondenvelden at the New Printing-Office, Mountain-Street. Quebec: Imprimé par Guilm. Vondenvelden, à la Nouvelle Imprimerie, rue la Montagne." But with the first regular number, Aug. 4, the printer's name disappeared; that of the press remained alone till the paper ceased publication.

The *Times* was evidently printed by Vondenvelden, edited and published, and the printing-office owned, jointly by Vondenvelden and one John Jones. The former had worked as French translator at the Brown>Neilson printing-office intermittently since 1783. John Jones possibly had only a financial and/or editorial interest in the *Times* for there is no evidence to suggest that he was a printer. An auctioneer-broker, named John Jones, flourished at this time in Quebec, advertising in the *Quebec gazette* also in the *Times.* He it was, no doubt, who occasionally advanced sums of money to the John Neilson printing-office as recorded in its account books. "John Jones the School master" also appears in newspaper advertisements, subscription lists, etc., in Quebec in the 1790's. But it is not clear what John Jones was associated in the production of the *Times.* He withdrew presently in any case, according to the notice in which his name appears for the only time in connection with the New Printing-Office and the *Times:*

> "The Subscriber informs the public that he has relinquished and ceded to Mr. W$^{\text{m.}}$ Vondenvelden, all concern, interest and share whatsoever in the New Printing-Office; and that the said W$^{\text{m.}}$ Vondenvelden is the sole proprietor thereof, as well as sole printer and editor of the weekly paper called The Times, Quebec, 14th May 1795 [signed:] John Jones.
>
> "The Subscriber, having by notarial deed of cession become sole proprietor of the press and apparatus known by name of the New Printing Office, informs those concerned that . . . all the debts due by and to the said Office are to be discharged by and paid to the said Subscriber. He embraces this opportunity to solicit a continuance of the patronage and very liberal encouragement received by the former joint Editors in their typographical pursuits, who will ever entertain the warmest sense of gratitude for the support with which has favoured their enterprize [sic].
>
> "With the utmost diffidence the Subscriber now declares himself the Editor of the TIMES, which he shall endeavour . . . to improve by pursuing his aim to render that paper entertaining and instructive. [signed:] William Vondenvelden."
>
> —The *Times*, May 18, 1795.

Vondenvelden continued to produce the paper for two months when he announced:

> "The Subscriber having compleated the issuing of The Times for twelve months and not finding the subscribers requisite for conducting that paper to the satisfaction of his readers and with credit to himself, is under the necessity of closing that weekly publication. He assures the Subscribers that he is impressed with Sentiments of the most lively gratitude for the very liberal support, which they have given him in making the experiment [signed:] William Vondenvelden. Monday, 27th July, 1795." —*The Times*, Quebec, July 27, 1795.

As the prospectus of June 23, 1794 indicated, the *Times* was projected as an organ of political news and opinion, "Open to all parties and influenced by none," the editors inviting contributions on "literature, politicks, commerce, agriculture, or any other science, and communications of domestic and foreign intelligence, especially 'animadversion and discussion of public measures,' which must bear the signature of the writer and if not marked with respect and decorum must ever be inadmissible." They undertook to provide regular information on the public procedure of the two houses of the legislature to the most obscure parts of the province, and to sister colonies their paper should "offer hints and suggestions to the Legislative body for bills under discussion as well as laws in actual operation. . . . It may be expected that when we usher this [paper] into the world with a publick confession of our political faith. . . . We therefore aver that, with the Right-Honourable and Honourables of the Province, with the Legislature, Executive, representative, and administrative, bodies we . . . concur in an enthusiastic veneration for the glorious constitution . . . of the British government. The press is free, freedom is triumphant without licentiousness, personal liberty and property of all are preserved. Prince, Peer, and People, all enjoy inviolable their respective prerogatives, rights privileges and immunities. On the other hand we abhor Regal despotism, Aristocratical tyranny, and Democratic domination."

Despite the request for contributions upon local affairs, the *Times* hardly became a medium of opinion. Themselves uncritical of *status quo* in Lower Canada, the editors exercised a careful censorship, constantly refusing publication, and rebuking froward correspondents, as being "too free with a person in no manner deserving to be ridiculed," or "as loose as a slattern's Pettycoat." Though more catholic, perhaps, than the *Gazette*, the *Times* did not reveal the diverse interests and strong attitudes expressed in the columns of the *Herald*, nor was it more successful in publishing news of government. During the session of the Legislature, the *Times* printed a full account of opening ceremonies and the first day's routine business, but only a brief weekly diary of subsequent proceedings. Though correspondents requested full and immediate report of Assembly and Council proceedings, neither appeared in current newspapers. The *Times* did print what the administration allowed or ordered, especially the text, abstract, and proclamation, of laws, though the *Gazette* had long been the recognized medium of "due and legal publication by government." Vondenvelden was actually commissioned law printer to the government, Aug. 27, 1795, a month after his newspaper ceased.

Like all Canadian papers of the period, the *Times* filled considerable space reprinting excerpts from other newspapers, magazines, and books. It had more foreign and less British material than the *Herald*, also more advertisements. After the first few numbers, about a quarter of its space was occupied by local advertising matter. Vondenvelden himself advertised repeatedly from May 12, 1795, for "An apprentice of good Morals and well-educated, aged 13-16." In the early issues he published a list of subscribers to the *Times*, showing 150 in Quebec, 53 in Montreal, 6 in Three Rivers, 5 in William Henry [Sorel], and 14 "in the Country"—a total of 228.

The *Times* was published on Mondays, each number comprising 8 p. in 4to, with occasional supplements of 2 or 4 p., printed in English and French in parallel columns. The issues were numbered 1-52, and paged continuously (with supplements and extras) in a single sequence (p. 1-449, [1]). Following no. 13, Oct. 27, 1794 appeared no. 14, *Extraordinary to the Times*, undated but paged [105]-108, containing news from London of Aug. 19, on the execution of Robespierre. It was issued apparently on Thursday, Oct. 30, 1794 (the proof, uncorrected, sent hastily to Montreal, then corrected and published in Quebec) and reissued with a regular no. 14, Nov. 3, 1794, which was paged [109]-116. With no. 21, Dec. 29, 1794, the printers issued copies of the *Abstract of the Judicature Bill* (*see* No. 890) free to their subscribers. No. 52 was an *Extraordinary* issue, published on Friday, July 24, 1795, containing the text of the Jay treaty, also news and advertisements. On the following Monday, July 27, 1795, the regular publication day, no. 52 *Supplement* appeared with the announcement that the *Times* had ceased publication.

Copies located:

CaOOA Prospectus and Specimen June 23, 1794 (No. 913)

	Specimen issue	June 25, 1794, [2] p.
	no. 1-7;	Aug. 4-Sept. 15, 1794
	10-34;	Oct. 6, 1794-Mar. 23, 1795
	36-52 and Sup.	Apr. 6-July 24, and Sept. 27, 1795
	Extra no. 14	[Oct. 30, 1794]
	Extra	[Feb? 1795] broadside containing despatch dated: Albany, Feb. 2, 1795
	Extra no. 52	July 24, 1795
	Sup. with Jan. 12-19, Mar 2,	May 11, June 8-15, July 6-27, 1795
CaOTL	Extra	July 29, 1794 broadside.

THE ROYAL AMERICAN GAZETTE AND WEEKLY INTELLIGENCER. *Printed at Charlottetown, Island of St. John, by James Robertson, 1787-?1790.*

The *Royal American gazette* was established at Charlottetown, Island of St. John, by James Robertson, Sept. 15, 1787 (v. 1, no. 1) and printed by him till some time between March 6, 1788 (the latest issue located), and the spring of 1790, when he left the Island. This paper bore the heading:

> SATURDAY SEPTEMBER 15, 1787. THE <NUMBER I.—VOLUME I.> / ROYAL AMERICAN GAZETTE, / AND / WEEKLY INTELLIGENCER OF THE ISLAND OF SAINT JOHN. / [rule] / CHARLOTTE-TOWN: Printed by JAMES ROBERTSON / [rule] /

Robertson, an American loyalist, had produced several newspapers in the American colonies, including a *Royal American Gazette*, started in New York, 1777 (*see* Clarence S. Brigham: *History and bibliography of American newspapers*, New York, 1946) and resumed in Shelburne, N.S., 1783. In the first number he introduced his paper in Charlottetown:

> "To the Public—A Long Desertation upon the Importance of a PRINTING-OFFICE would be futile, as its Utility is perfectly understood; and, it will be readily granted, that the Cultivation of this Island, for want of such an Establishment, has been much retarded.
>
> "Interested Men in the neighbouring Provinces, gave such an unfavourable Representation of this, that the baneful Effects have been severely felt, not only by the Inhabitants, who had not the Means to contradict the injurious Reports, but by a vast Number of Loyalists, who, putting implicit Confidence in an almost general though uncandid Description of this Island, have settled upon sterile Lands, the Production of which can never compensate for the Expence of Cultivation. . . . Had the real Value of this Soil, at the Termination of the late War, been universally known, the numerous Accession of Inhabitants, which constitute the Riches of a Country, would have accelerated the Zenith of this.
>
> "Impressed with an Idea that former Prejudices are not unconquerable, and that, like a well toned Instrument, every Part of this Community will act in Unison, the Editor has ventured to issue this Specimen of THE ROYAL GAZETTE, which for a Series of Years has been favourably received by the Public . . . If it is fortunate enough to meet the Approbation of the respectable In-

habitants of this Island, no Exertions shall be wanting to render it useful and Entertaining.

"CONDITIONS.

I. It will be published every Saturday and Delivered at the Printing-Office, where Subscriptions, at Twelve Shillings per Annum, will be thankfully received.

II. One Half of the Subscription Money to be paid on subscribing, and the Residue at the Expiration of the Year.

III. The Ingenuous Productions of literary Gentlemen who wish to communicate Improvements upon Agriculture or any Sience [sic], or whose Study is to amuse and instruct, will be gratefully received and inserted gratis.

IV. Advertisements not exceeding Fifteen Lines will be inserted in Five Shillings the First Time, and Two Shillings for each Reinsertion—Those of a greater Length will be charged in Proportion.

V. If a sufficient Number of Subscriptions are obtained, before Saturday the 29th Instant, to defray the Expence, the GAZETTE will be published, and continued agreeable to the first Condition; but, if not, the Money will then be returned.

"From the Situation of this Island it is evident that the Inhabitants will receive earlier Intelligence from Europe, the West-Indies, &c. than those of the Capital of His Majesty's North-American Dominions; and during the Time this Coast is inaccessible, some of the important Debates in the British Senate, which, from their Length, cannot be inserted as received, Extracts from the Magazines and other late European Publications, together with domestic Occurrences and Essays, will be a never failing Source of literary Amusement.

"In populous Towns the Veichles [sic] of Intelligence are crowded with Advertisements which amply defray the Expence of each Impression; and, though the Paper is large, seldom more than one Page, often less, contribute to the Entertainment of the Reader. It is obvious that the Publisher can, at present, reap but a small Emolument from Advertisements, he therefore hopes that the Inhabitants, as the Price is small, will not class Two or Three under one Signature and thereby defeat the Intention (through an ill-timed Parsimony) of gratifying themselves and fellow Subjects with a Weekly Production which ALL are anxious to see established."—*Royal American gazette*, Charlottetown, Sept. 15, 1787.

This paper was a quarto half sheet, 4 pages the issue, printed 3 col. to the page. In the copies seen a large proportion of the space was occupied with official matter, proclamations of the lieutenant-governor, etc. The local news was concerned principally with government affairs. Few advertisements appeared excepting the printer's own, and bits of belated foreign news filled in odd spaces. The issue of Oct. 6, 1787, contained a notice, dated Sept. 27, 1787, that "the Lieutenant governor has appointed the printer, J. Robertson, deputy postmaster, and the Post Office will be in the same house as the Printing Office."

Copies located:

GBLP	v. 1	(no. 2)	Sept. 29, 1787 (in C.O. 226/11: 331-34)
			Nov. 19, 1787 (in C.O. 226/11: 347-50)
			Mar. 6, 1788 (3 cop., in C.O. 226/11: 67-70; *ibid:* 191-94; B.T. 6/56: 809-812.
MWA	v. 1	(no. 1-3)	Sept. 15-Oct. 6, 1787.

THE ROYAL GAZETTE. *Printed at Charlottetown, Island of Saint John, by Wm. A. Rind, 1791-1792.*

The *Royal gazette and miscellany of the Island of Saint John.* a fortnightly, was established at Charlottetown, by Wm. A. Rind, about July 15, 1791, judging from the earliest issue seen, v. 1, no. 2, July 29, 1791. It was continued by Rind, appearing somewhat irregularly till the latter part of 1792; v. 1, no. 26 being the latest issue seen, though references to further issues as late as Dec., 1792, are known.*

It was well printed in good clear type, 3 col. to the page, 4 pages about 10 by 8 inches, 4to, to each issue. It contained the Island's official publications and advertisements; little local news or general advertising, except note of ships in port, births and marriages. Reprints appeared from Halifax newspapers and magazines, mainly Nova Scotia official publications and material on agricultural practices, also reprints from London papers, of British and some other foreign news. A running account of "Proceedings in France" appeared from issue to issue, also essays and addresses on the French Revolution, all obviously reprinted from sources outside the Island. In each issue from Jan. 14 through Feb. 25, 1792, Rind published a month of the New Year's calendar, indicating in his introduction the community's limitations, "In another Country an Almanack is generally an Article of great Emolument to the Printer, and reputed Advantage to the Public—in this, it has not met with such Encouragement from the Community as to make it an object worthy of Publication in the usual Way." Rind apparently found that his newspaper also found little encouragement and abandoned it after a couple of years' run. Twenty-five issues have been located in the possession of J. T. Robison, Esq., Charlottetown, P.E.I.

Copies located:

Robison	v. 2	(no. 2-26)	July 29, 1791-July 30, 1792

---

*The widow of Attorney-General Callbeck in her memorial to Lord Dundas, Feb. 24, 1794, refers to her complaint "of an Article in the Gazette of St. John's the 17th of October, 1792."—Can.P.A., P.E.I. "A".

Judge A. B. Warburton, author of *A history of Prince Edward Island,* wrote from Charlottetown, July 9, 1909, to David Russell Jack, ". . . The only number of this paper [The Royal gazette and Miscellany of the Island of St. John] that I have seen, was Volume II, Number XXIX, dated Wednesday, Sept. 26, 1792 . . . It was (vol. 2, no. 29) an 8 page 2 column paper about nine inches long [etc.]." P. R. Bowers, also, a journalist and sometime queen's printer in Prince Edward Island wrote from St. John's, Newfoundland, June 6, 1911, to Jack ". . . I find that the Royal Gazette mentioned . . . was printed by William A. Rind, and the date of issue I have, vol. 1, no. 3, is Friday, Dec. 20th, 1792. It was a sheet of four pages, 12 columns; each page 9 × 12 inches [etc.]."

These letters, also a MS., *The press in Prince Edward Island,* by Wm. L. Cotton, editor of the *Charlottetown examiner,* are in David Russell Jack's MS. *Historical data relating to the press in the Maritime Provinces,* in the Jack papers in the Free Public Library, Saint John, N.B.

THE CANADA CONSTELLATION. *Printed at Niagara, U.C., by S. and G. Tiffany, 1799-1800.*

The *Canada constellation* was established at Niagara, U.C., by Silvester and Gideon Tiffany, July 20, 1799, judging from their introduction of that date, in the copy of Aug. 2, 1799 (no. 3), the earliest located. It was printed by the brothers Tiffany till Jan. 18, 1800, in which issue Silvester announced his withdrawal. The paper was apparently continued by Gideon till July, 1800, for Silvester stated later: ". . . The Constellation . . . existed one year . . . it expired some months since."

—*Niagara herald*, Jan. 29, 1801.

This paper bore the heading:

[Double rule] / THE CANADA CONSTELLATION. / [double rule] / NIAGARA, (UPPER-CANADA)—PUBLISHED WEEKLY BY S. & G. TIFFANY, OPPOSITE THE LION TAVERN. / [double rule] / NUMBER 3 FRIDAY, AUGUST 2d, 1799. 4 DOLS. PER YEAR / [double rule] /

4 pages in folio, printed 4 col. to the page (about 15″ × 10″) this paper was published weekly on Friday till Nov. 15, 1799, then according to notice during the winter on Saturday. The printers introduced their paper:

"To the Public. On commencing a new publication much is expected in the address of the publishers . . . We will not flatter with promises of being useful or entertaining

". . . To please All we cannot hope; prejudice, the natural and baneful effect of weak heads or evil hearts, too often proves a bar to that happiness; and it is under the watchfulness of a few of this description we embark on the present undertaking, regarding their ravings as unworthy of our notice. To the unprejudiced only shall we direct our attention;—of these are our Patrons, lovers and promoters of useful knowledge and who wish to see man not debased below, but on a level with man, his capacities enlarged, and his abilities to serve his God, his King and country strengthened.

"It is a truth long acknowledged that no men hold situations more influential of the minds and conduct of men, than do printers; political principles are sucked from, nursed and directed by, the press, and when they are just, the community is in unity and prosperity; but when vicious, every evil ensues; and it is lamentable that many printers produce the latter or no effect; and to which of these classes we belong, Time will unfold. [etc.] [signed:] S. &. G. Tiffany, Newark, July 20th, 1799."—*Canada constellation,* Aug. 2, 1799.

In the same notice the printers state that the *Canada constellation* is a substitute for a paper projected by them the previous year, and that it will be published at $1.00 a quarter payable in advance, in its present size or larger, as subscribers and payments allow. The latter were desultory, as appears from the printers' frequent appeals for "timely relief" by a quarter's advance, or by payment in peas, oats, or wheat.

The *Canada constellation* was established, according to a previous announcement by the printers, "to disseminate political knowledge thro' this Province" (P. Russell: *Correspondence*, 2: 111). They published a digest of news on contemporary affairs in a column headed "British America"; also reprinted news, essays, anecdotes from English and American papers, and published numerous legal and other notices of interest in the Niagara peninsula. The copies seen of this paper, contained little of a controversial nature, but its printers, with their American affinities, were not regarded with favour by the provincial administration. With no government business and a short list of poor subscribers, the *Constellation* inevitably died, as Silvester Tiffany said, "of starvation . . . [leaving] a rich legacy of advice to its parents and nurses,"—which legacy he utilized to produce its successor the *Niagara herald* in 1801. (*See* W. S. Wallace: *The first journalists in Upper Canada*, in *Can. hist. rev.* 26: 272-81, Dec., 1945.)

Copies located:

CaOTL	no. 3-12,	Aug. 2-Oct. 4, 1799
	17-27,	Nov. 8, 1799-Jan. 18, 1800

UPPER CANADA GAZETTE, OR AMERICAN ORACLE.
Printed at Newark, U.C., by Louis Roy, then others, 1793–19th century.

The *Upper Canada gazette* was established at Newark, U.C., by Louis Roy, under government auspices, and printed from Apr. 18, 1793 (v. 1, no. 1) till the fall of 1794. The latest issue located, printed by Roy, is an unnumbered [Extra] Supplement, Aug. 29, 1794. The *Gazette* was continued by Gideon Tiffany, whose earliest issue located is v. 2, no. 2, Dec. 10, 1794. Through the early years this paper appeared irregularly; it was suspended entirely between Aug. 10 and Oct. 5, 1796, because of illness in the printer's family, and by Oct. 26, 1796 (v. 3, no. 1) Tiffany stated "the total of [my] numbers complete but one year, or 52 papers." His last issue located is v. 3, no. 27 (total no. 141) July 5, 1797. After this, the *Gazette* was continued by Titus Geer Simons (with Silvester Tiffany, though the latter's name does not appear on the paper) from Sept. 20, 1797 (no. [142], misprinted: 152). Silvester Tiffany left the printing office, May 1, 1798, and Simons continued the paper, soon acquiring a senior partner. From July 6, 1798 till July 18, 1801, the *Upper Canada gazette* was printed by William Waters and T. G. Simons, then by a succession of printers till 1845. (*See* W. S. Wallace: *The periodical literature of Upper Canada*, in *Can. hist. rev.* 13: 4-22, 181-83. 1931 (p. 11-12).

This paper bore the heading:

[double rule] / NUMBER I. G. [royal arms] R. VOLUME I. / [double rule] / UPPER CANADA GAZETTE, / OR / AMERICAN ORACLE. / [ornamental rule] / THURSDAY, APRIL 18, 1793. / [ornamental rule] /

and Colophon: [ornamental rule] / UPPER CANADA: PRINTED BY LOUIS ROY. / [ornamental rule] /

The paper retained the same title under its successive printers. The imprint was transferred from colophon to masthead by G. Tiffany. The name Newark (now Niagara-on-the-Lake, a settlement on Lake Ontario at the mouth of the Niagara River) was changed in the colophon to Niagara between the issues of June 10 and Aug. 19, 1795, then to West Niagara, Feb. 15 (or Feb. 8), 1797. The press was moved to the new capital, York (now Toronto), in Sept., 1798, and from Oct. 4 the *Gazette* was printed there.

The *Upper Canada gazette* began with a rather handsome appearance in the 18th-century style. It was printed on good paper from new types, 4 pages folio, 2 col. to the page (about 36 × 23 cm. page size). Roy had been well trained in the *Quebec gazette* office, and he got his paper there and from government supplies. His successors (both Gideon Tiffany and T. G. Simons lacked experience and assistance, repeatedly advertising for apprentices) produced a *Gazette* inferior in both typography and material. The paper was sometimes coarse, straw-coloured, and speckled with fibres (probably smuggled by Tiffany from a little mill at Albany, N.Y.). The size was reduced to 4to in 1796, occasionally to small folio and possibly to a half sheet in Feb., 1797. The *Gazette* was published on Thursdays by Roy, on Wednesdays by Tiffany, also Simons, who sometimes published at ten-day intervals from Wednesday to Saturday, latterly publishing regularly on Saturdays.

The numbering, like the time of publication, was irregular. At first the issues bore part-numbers and were numbered anew in each volume. A whole number began with no. 111, Dec., 1796 (v. 3, no. 7), and thereafter the part numbers were sometimes dropped, e.g. Sept., 1797-Nov., 1799. A continuous pagination began with p. 1861 on Apr. 5, 1800 (v. 8, no. 466) and continued to p. 2112, July 18, 1801 (v. 11, no. 531) the end of Waters and Simons's publication. In volume numbering 5 was omitted between v. 4, no. 179, June 30, 1798 and v. 6, no. 180, July 6 [i.e. 7], 1798. v. 7 runs Nov. 2-23, 1799 (no. 244-247); v. 8 runs Nov. 30, 1799—Apr. 19, 1800 (no. 448-467); v. 9, Apr. 26—June 28, 1800 (no. 468-478); and v. 10 began Aug. 30 (or earlier).

v. 6, no. 202, was published Jan. 12, 1799, but suppressed by the government, for "the Secretary had without authority inserted a list of Persons whose names were ordered to be struck off the E[mpire loyalist] list; [but] some copies of that Gazette got into circulation."—*U.C. gazette*, Feb. 2, 1799.

Printing was introduced into Upper Canada, and the *Upper Canada gazette* established, on the impetus of Lieut.-Gov. Simcoe, at the beginning of his administration, for the express purpose of promulgating governmental decrees in the new province. The newspaper was not an official gazette in the 18th century, but its printer used government-owned equipment, received a salary for official work, and was more dependent on the provincial administration for other work in that province, than in any other excepting the Island of St. John. The first printer, Louis Roy, gave due prominence to official publications, in style and position, printing also bits of foreign and local news and announcements on the inner pages. Gideon Tiffany, aged 21, New England bred, featured foreign news via the United States, also essays on moral and social topics, ascribed to contributors with pseudonyms; he printed bits of local information and advertisements and usually ran the government's publications in the last place. This independent attitude was corrected by the administration in appointing Tiffany's successor, as appears:

> "Resolved that the following proposals be made to Messrs. Waters and Simons as Joint printers, but if Mr. Waters shall decline to act in partnership with Mr. Simons that they be made to Mr. Simons as sole printer—Viz[t]
>
> "1st. that the King's printer do print in the Town of York at his own expence a weekly paper to be called the Upper Canada Gazette or American Oracle, of which he shall present one Copy to the Lieut. Governor or Person administering the Government, and deliver another to this Secretary, and a third to the Clerk of the Council.
>
> "2d. That he print on the first page all proclamations and also whatever issues from the Lieut. Governor's Office.
>
> "3d. That for this duty he receive a salary of ninety pounds Halifax per annum, and an allowance of forty pounds per annum for house rent.
>
> "4th. That he be paid by the respective officers of government for such matters as issue from their respective offices at the Quebec [i.e. John Neilson's] price.

"As an additional encouragement, the Chief Justice will employ him as long as he conducts himself with propriety to print the Acts of Parliament and the Journals of the Upper House. The influence of the government will also be exerted to procure for him the printing of the Journals of the Lower House. He will also be allowed to make such use as he shall be able of the mutilated set of Type now belonging to Government, but when he wants others, he must purchase them at his own expence."—U.C. Ex. Council *Minutes*, Apr. 25, 1798, printed in P. Russell: *Correspondence*, 2: 144.

Simons introduced himself:

"The Editor having been appointed to succeed the late printer most respectfully presents the public his first number of the GAZETTE, and humbly solicits their patronage. . . . The GAZETTE had hitherto labored under the greatest possible disadvantages, from the want of a regular receipt of intelligence; but it is with pleasure he assures the public, that a mail is established to run to the United States' garrison of Niagara, . . . which opens a correspondence with every part of the United States and the provinces of Nova Scotia, New Brunswick &c. . . . [The Editor] shall endeavour to convince the canded [sic] patrons that his intention is faultless while his youth and inexperience may commit an error. [West Niagara, Sept. 20, 1797]"—*U.C. gazette*, Sept. 20, 1797.

Simons had an embryonic editorial column which, from May 5, 1798, he headed "The Oracle." A similar column appeared in most 18-century Canadian newspapers, usually on the third page, with place and date of issue for a heading, and containing the printer's own announcement of local happenings or notable foreign events, but rarely his commentary. Waters and Simons gave, as well, oracular messages to the public justifying their conduct of the paper and occasionally touching upon local affairs in nascent editorial vein, e.g.,

"It is astonishing that the postmasters in this Province do not exert themselves to establish a post between this town [York] and Niagara . . . but we flatter ourselves that when His Excellency shall have arrived, that he will remedy the great inconveniency which the inhabitants of this town labor under for the want of a post to Niagara."—*U.C. gazette*, Dec. 21, 1799.

After the establishment of the *Niagara herald*, the *Upper Canada gazette*, as champion of Upper Canada government and religion, engaged in a journalistic duel with the Tiffanys. The latter had strong critics among the official hierarchy of the province, and these (with Waters and Simons, stung by Tiffany's taunts of government patronage), published vituperation hardly equalled in early Canadian newspapers.

". . . I give you rank of scavenger—and from the perverseness of a swinish disposition, I anticipate nothing but to see you constantly groveling amongst the filth, your natural element. Upper Canada . . . reluctantly tolerates the editor of the *Herald*, that same Upper Canada, which unfortunately for it, is an asylum to exiles and aliens, to atheists and prawling democrats [etc.]."

—*U.C. gazette*, Jan. 31, 1801.

Copies located:

CaOT	v. 6	(no. 192,	Nov. 3, 1798
		194-196,	Nov. 17-Dec. 1, 1798
		199-200,	Dec. 22-29, 1798
		202-205,	Jan. 12-Feb. 5, 1799
		207-209,	Feb. 16-Mar. 2, 1799

		211, 214-217,	Mar. 16, Apr. 6-27, 1799
		220, 222)	May 18, June 1, 1799
	and	Extra	Jan. 12, 1799
		mut.	Dec. 28, 1798, Jan. 12, 1799.
CaOTL	v. 1	(no. 1-5,	Apr. 18-May 16, 1793
		7-9,	May 30-June 13, 1793
		12-17,	July 4-Aug. 8, 1793
		42-43, 45)	July 10-17, July 31, 1794
	v. 2	(no. 2,	Dec. 10, 1794
		28, 37)	June 10, Aug. 19, 1795
	v. 2-3	(no. 50-52, no. 1-6 continued as	Oct. 5-Nov. 30, 1796
		Total no. 111-115,	Dec. 7, 1796-Jan. 4, 1797
		117-132,	Jan. 18-May 3, 1797
		134-136,	May 17-31, 1797
		138, 140-156	June 14, June 28-Dec. 30, 1797
	v. 4	(no. 158-161)	Jan. 13-Feb. 3, 1798
	v. 4-8	(no. 163-451	Feb. 17, 1798-Dec. 21, 1799
		453-454,	Jan. 4-11, 1800
		456-464)	Jan. 25-Mar. 22, 1800
	v. 8-9	(no. 466-472,	Apr. 5-May 17, 1800
		474-478)	May 31-June 28, 1800
	v. 10	(no. 486-489,	Aug. 30-Sept. 20, 1800
		490, 492-493,	Oct. 4, Oct. 18-25, 1800
		495-502)	Nov. 8-Dec. 27, 1800
		Sup.	Dec. 21, 1799, Feb. 8, 1800
	and	[Extra]	Aug. 29, 1794
			Jan. 12, 1799
		Defective	Most of the following issues contain 2 pages only, and some may have been published complete thus: July 10, 17, 31, 1794; Oct. 5-19, Nov. 16, 1796; Jan. 18-Feb. 22, Mar. 8, Apr. 12, 1797; May 17, Sept. 6, Nov. 15, 1800.

THE NOVA-SCOTIA MAGAZINE. *Printed at Halifax, N.S., by John Howe, 1789-1792.*

The *Nova-Scotia magazine,* edited at first by Rev. Wm. Cochran, was printed and published monthly at Halifax by John Howe, from July, 1789 (v. 1, no. 1) till Mar., 1792 (v. 5, no. 3). Cochran resigned as editor with the issue of June, 1790 (v. 2, no. 6), and Howe took over the editorship himself. In addition to monthly parts, a title page and index were issued after the last number of each volume (excepting v. 5). The t.-p. to v. 1 reads:

THE / NOVA-SCOTIA MAGAZINE / AND / COMPREHENSIVE REVIEW / OF / LITERATURE, POLITICS, AND NEWS. / VOLUME I. / For July . . . / . . . December, / 1789. / ORIENTIA TEMPORA NOTIS /

INSTRUIT EXEMPLIS. HOR. / SCRIBENTEM JUVAT / IPSE FAVOR, MINUITQUE LABOREM. OVID. / HALIFAX: / PRINTED FOR THE EDITOR, BY JOHN HOWE. / M.DCC.LXXXIX. /

In the second and later volumes the title was extended: "The Nova-Scotia Magazine and comprehensive review of Literature, Politics and News. Being a Collection of the most valuable Articles which appear in the Periodical Publications of Great Britain Ireland and America; with various pieces in prose and verse never before published [etc.]." Each number comprised 80 pages (July, 1789-Dec., 1790), then 64 pages (Jan., 1791-Mar., 1792), in 8vo; printed in 2 col. and paged continuously within each volume, viz:

v. 1 (no. 1-6) July-Dec., 1789: viii, 480, [5] p.;
v. 2 (no. 1-6) Jan.-June, 1790: iv, 487 [1], iv p.;
v. 3 (no. 1-6) July-Dec., 1790: 4, 476, iv p.;
v. 4 (no. 1-12) Jan.-Dec., 1791: iv, 760, 4 p.;
v. 5 (no. 1-3) Jan.-Mar., 1792: 191 [1] p.
No t.-p. or index was published for v. 5.

This magazine was announced in a prospectus, published in the newspapers of the day, which fairly describes its scope:

> Halifax, May 25 1789. Proposals for publishing a monthly work by the title the Nova-Scotia Magazine and History of Literature . . . A repository . . . for literary productions of ingenious men on subjects that particularly concern the country where we live, and which we can never expect to find discussed in English prints. . . The proposed magazine will include:
>
> (1) Miscellaneous papers in prose selected from Annual registers, Philosophical transactions and various magazines of Great Britain and Ireland to which will be added extracts and translations from rare and curious books.
>
> (2) Political transactions, state papers, parliamentary speeches, a summary of proceedings in the House of Commons and a more particular account of debates in the House of Assembly of Nova Scotia.
>
> (3) An Account of the new books: the substance of the *Monthly Review* with some observations on books and pamphlets as appear among ourselves [i.e. Nova Scotia publications].
>
> (4) Political pieces, selected, translated and original.
>
> (5) A Chronicle of remarkable events of the world: promotions, deaths and marriages in the British dominions.
>
> (6) Each number about 80 pages 8vo. close letter press with a copious index at the end of each year. 12 numbers to make one good volume. Subscription $1 per quarter 2/ per number. If successful the magazine will be enlarged for 12 numbers to make 2 volumes. Subscriptions received at Halifax: Mr. Cochran at the Bishop of Nova Scotia's; also by Mr. Howe, Printer; St. John: by Mr. Sower.—*Royal gazette*, Saint John, N.B., Mar. 9, 1790.

William Cochran, the editor (*see* No. 828) was principal of the Academy at Windsor and became president of King's College in 1790. In his issue for June, 1790 (published July 24), he addressed a letter "To the Public," dated Windsor, July 15, 1790. In this he reviewed with satisfaction the policy and development of the *Nova-Scotia magazine* through its first twelve numbers; and announced his resignation as editor, owing to his remoteness from the printing office in Halifax, and to other duties. In the next number, July, 1790, John Howe announced that he would carry on the publication without alteration in the original plan, excepting that, unless articles on politics were very important, they would give place to more amusing and instructive miscellanies. He complained that few original contributions were received.

The magazine, in fact, contained little of local origin. Its *Chronicle*, modelled after the *Chronicle* in the *Annual Register* (London, 1761—), included a "Domestic Affairs" section. Here appeared, from time to time, the lieutenant-governor's speeches opening the House of Assembly (but no records of debates), reports upon the Windsor Academy and College, the Church, the Agricultural Society and other semi-official organizations, a few obituary and marriage notices—the meagre chronicle of local affairs in a small community where such matters were common knowledge, and their publication rather a gesture of respect than a means of disseminating information.

The initial success of the *Nova-Scotia magazine* soon declined. Size and price were reduced in Jan., 1791, and in Mar., 1792, Howe abandoned the enterprise in disgust. He announced on the last page of that issue that the magazine ceases publication with this number as the number of subscribers is so small and for the want of punctuality in their payment of subscriptions. "When the late Editor [Cochran] relinquished the undertaking, it was the desire of the printer to continue publication . . . the original number of subscribers was reduced, so size and price were likewise reduced to meet the general wish and keep alive the Magazine, 'till either a greater taste for science should prevail, or those who wished to encourage it should have the ability to contribute more than their wishes. These Expectations failing, the printer has only to return his grateful thanks to those gentlemen who have uniformly afforded him their patronage and support."

Copies located:

CaNs	v. 2	(no. 1-6)	Jan.-June, 1790
CaNsHA	v. 1	(no. 2-6)	Aug.-Dec., 1789
	v. 2	(no. 1-6)	Jan.-June, 1790*† (2 cop. one*)
	v. 4	(no. 3-5, 8, 10-11)	Mar.*-May, Aug.,* Oct.-Nov., 1791
	v. 5	(no. 2)	Feb., 1792
CaNsHD	v. 1	(no. 1-6)	July-Dec., 1789†
	v. 2	(no. 1-6)	Jan.-June, 1790†*
	v. 3	(no. 1-6)	July-Dec., 1790†
	v. 4	(no. 1-12)	Jan.-Dec., 1791
CaO	File not seen.		
CaOOA	v. 1	(no. 1-6)	July-Dec., 1789*
CaOT	v. 1	(no. 1-6)	July-Dec., 1789*
	v. 2	(no. 1-6)	Jan.-June, 1790
	v. 3	(no. 1-6)	July-Dec., 1790
CaQM	v. 2	(no. 2-6)	Feb.-June, 1790 (fragments only)
CtY	v. 1	(no. 1-6)	July-Dec., 1789
DLC	v. 1	(no. 1-6)	July-Dec., 1789
ICN	v. 1	(no. 1-6)	July-Dec., 1789

MB	v. 2	(no. 1-6)	Jan.-June, 1790*
MBAt	v. 1	(no. 1-6)	July-Dec., 1789
MH	v. 1	(no. 4-6)	Oct.-Dec., 1789
MHi	v. 1	(no. 1)	July, 1789*
	v. 2	(no. 1)	Jan., 1790*
MWA	v. 4	(no. 7-12)	July-Dec., 1791
	v. 5	(no. 1-3)	Jan.-Mar., 1792
NN	v. 1	(no. 1-3, 5-6)	July-Sept., Nov.-Dec., 1789
	v. 2	(no. 4-6)	Apr.-June, 1790
WHi	v. 1	(no. 1-6)	July-Dec., 1789
	v. 3	(no. 1-6)	July-Dec., 1790

Note: * = incomplete
† = two copies.

THE QUEBEC MAGAZINE. *Printed at Quebec by Samuel Neilson (and successor), 1792-1794.*

The *Quebec magazine* was printed monthly at Quebec by Samuel Neilson, from Aug., 1792 till his death in Jan., 1793, then in the same office for (later, by) his younger brother, John, till May, 1794, after which it ceased to appear. It was edited by Rev. Alexander Spark, Presbyterian clergyman in Quebec, who received the sum of £59 10*s*. for his work from Sept. 1, 1792 till June 1, 1794. In addition to the monthly parts a title-page and index was issued after the last number of each volume. The t.-p. reads:

> THE / QUEBEC MAGAZINE, / OR USEFUL AND ENTERTAINING REPOSITORY OF / SCIENCE, MORALS, HISTORY, POLITICS, &c. / PARTICULARLY ADAPTED FOR THE USE OF BRITISH AMERICA. / [rule] / BY A SOCIETY OF GENTLEMEN IN QUEBEC. / [double rule] / [double rule] / LE / MAGAZIN DE QUEBEC, / OU RECEUIL UTILE ET AMUSANT DE / LITERATURE, HISTOIRE, POLITIQUE, &c. &c. / PARTICULIEREMENT ADAPTE' A L'USAGE DE L'AMERIQUE BRITANNIQUE. / [rule] / PAR UNE SOCIETE' DE GENS DE LETTRES. / [double rule] / VOL. I.—August 1792, to February 1793. / [double rule] / printer's ornament] / [double rule] / A QUEBEC: chez Samuel Neilson, Imprimeur et Libraire. / [double rule] / M.DCC.XCII. / [printer's ornament] /

The issues were paged continuously within each volume. A complete set comprises:

v. 1 (no. 1-6) Aug., 1792-Jan., 1793: 3 p. l., 389 [i.e. 398], [4] p., 2 fold. pl.
v. 2 (no. 1-6) Feb.-July, 1793: 2 p. l., 386, [3] p., 3 pl.
v. 3 (no. 1-6) Aug., 1793-Jan., 1794: 1 p. l., 392, [2] p., 2 pl. (1 fold., 1 port.)
v. 4 (no. 1-4) Feb.-May, 1794

t.-p. to v. 2 reads [as above] . . . vol. II. From February to August, 1793; t.-p. to v. 3 reads [as above] . . . vol. III. From August, 1793 to February, 1794. t.-p. to v. 4 was probably never issued.

The *Quebec magazine* was announced by *Proposals* (*see* No. 800) and by notices in Quebec and Montreal newspapers:

"New Magazine—With the encouragement of the Public soon will be undertaken a new periodical publication entitled The Quebec Magazine, Or, an useful and entertaining Repository of Science, Morals, History, Politics, &c. particularly adapted for the use of British America, By a Society of Gentlemen at Quebec." Conditions:—

(1) To be printed on good paper with an elegant new type . . . articles of intelligence in English and French, also occasionally original essays in either language.

(2) One number to be published monthly, 64 p. in 8vo. stitched in blue paper, and forwarded to all parts of the British Empire or elsewhere.

(3) Price 15 pence per number, $3 per annum. No money demanded till the end of the year.

(4) With N° I will be given an elegant new engraving of a view of the city of Quebec from the opposite side of the St. Lawrence. Others will be added occasionally.

"Care has been taken to commission all the most celebrated productions of the Press" from Great Britain, France, and the United States of America. The publishers have reason to expect also that many persons of genius and education in this country will lend aid.

"Proposals containing a fuller account of the plan to be had at Samuel Neilson's, Quebec; Mr. Edwards, Montreal; Mr. Peter Clarke's, Kingston; Mr. Geo. Leith's, Detroit; Mr. Howe's, Halifax; Mr. Sower's, St John's, New Brunswick."

—*Quebec gazette*, Mar. 22, 1792.

Publication was delayed till Sept. 13, 1793, awaiting new types "purposely commissioned" for the magazine. No. 2 appeared on Oct. 15, and at the same time No. 1 was announced as out of print, those who still wanted copies were invited to send in their names for a second impression.

The introduction to the first number states:

". . . Upon the whole, we think that few periods of History have ever appeared more favourable or inviting to an undertaking of this kind than the present time —more fertile in subjects fit for the animadversion of the Statesman or Philosopher—or more productive of incidents worthy of being recorded. By the Spirit of Enquiry (which in no age was ever more awake) new discoveries in History and antiquities, and improvements in Philosophy, are to be expected almost every day. The political World is also pregnant with great events. And whether . . . Mankind shall hereafter . . . deem the present age auspicious or the contrary these events themselves are . . . highly interesting . . . and will probably afford an important Lesson to Mankind for many ages to come. The warmth with which many at present enter into the subject of Politics we mean entirely to avoid; and we would recommend our correspondents to do the same. . . . Formerly . . . An Alexander or a Caesar gave laws to the world at the point of the Sword . . . and said to them this shall be your Constitution. . . . At present the Philosophers have taken up the subject on the side of the many. . . . The Sword of the Mouth is opposed to the sword of steel and the World awaits the result of the Contest."

Each issue had a table of contents and on verso a monthly barometer and thermometer for Quebec. Then followed papers alternately in English and French, reprinted from European or American periodicals and contemporary classics. These treated of philosophical, political, or scientific topics, the last particularly on agricultural methods or experiments. Here, too, appeared occasionally original essays on agricultural matters in Canada, on questions arising from the new constitution, also provincial government documents, bits of light verse or entertaining prose.

A second section, "The Monthly Chronicle," usually of some twenty pages in English and French vis-à-vis, reviewed events in European countries (about two months since) and in the United States (about one month or less).

A third section, "The Provincial Register," concerned affairs in Lower and Upper Canada. It, too, was printed in English and French on opposite pages, and enlarged as the *Magazine* developed. This provided a useful survey of local events, covering proceedings of government, prices current, shipping news, births and deaths (numbers, later names, given).

The illustrations are engravings, executed in Quebec, some unsigned, some the work of J. G. Hochstetter. A few depict local scenes, and one is a portrait of the late Judge Adam Mabane.

After the number for May, 1794, no further publication was announced. Then appeared notice that "Owing to the necessity of employing all hands in the Printing Office on Acts of the Legislature and Journals of the House of Assembly, the Printer postpones for two or three months the Quebec Magazine and will resume publication as soon as possible."—*Quebec gazette*, July 31, 1794. There is no evidence that the magazine was ever resumed.

Copies located:

CaNsWA	v. 1	(no. 2-6)	Sept., 1792-Jan., 1793
CaO	v. 1	(no. 1-6)	Aug., 1792-Jan., 1793
	v. 2	(no. 1-6)	Feb.,-July, 1793
	v. 3	(no. 1-6)	Aug., 1793-Jan., 1794
CaOOA	v. 1	(no. 4, 6)	Nov., 1792, Jan., 1793
CaQM	v. 1	(no. 1-6)	Aug., 1792-Jan., 1793
	v. 2	(no. 1-6)	Feb.-July, 1793
	v. 3	(no. 1-6)	Aug., 1793-Jan., 1794
CaQMS	v. 1	(no. 1-6)	Aug., 1792-Jan., 1793
	v. 2	(no. 1-6)	Feb.-July, 1793
	v. 3	(no. 1-6)	Aug., 1793-Jan., 1794
	v. 4	(no. 1-4)	Feb.-May, 1794
CaQQL	v. 1	(no. 1-6)	Aug., 1792-Jan., 1793
	v. 2	(no. 1-6)	Feb.-July, 1793
	v. 3	(no. 1-6)	Aug., 1793-Jan., 1794
	v. 4	(no. 1)	Feb., 1794
Gordonsmith	v. 1	(no. 6)	Jan., 1793
Ketcheson	"odd numbers, also Neilson's MS. notes on costs of production, subscribers, etc."		

ADDENDUM

THE QUEBEC GAZETTE

DLC	no. 73,	May 29, 1766
	75-156,	June 12, 1766-Dec. 24, 1767
	1345-1372,	May 5-Oct. 20, 1791
	1374, 1376-1434,	Nov. 3, Nov. 17, 1791-Dec. 27, 1792
	1454, 1457, 1459,	May 16, 1793, June 6, 20, 1793
	1463-1464,	July 25-Aug. 1, 1793
	1467, 1470-1474,	Aug. 22, Sept. 12-Oct. 10, 1793
	1476-1484,	Oct. 24, 1793-Dec. 19, 1793
	1486-1511,	Jan. 2-June 19, 1794
	1513-1514,	July 3-10, 1794
	1516-1533,	July 24-Nov. 13, 1794
	1536-1538,	Dec. 4-18, 1794
	1540, 1545-1550,	Jan. 1, Jan. 29-Mar. 5, 1795
	1552-1560,	Mar. 19, 1795-May 14, 1795
	1562-1572,	May 21, 1795-July 30, 1795
	1588-1594,	Nov. 12, 1795-Dec. 24, 1795
	1598, 1600-1605,	Jan. 21, Feb. 4-Mar. 10, 1796
	1607-1628,	Mar. 24-Aug. 11, 1796
	1630-1646, 1648,	Aug. 25-Dec. 15, 29, 1796
	1649-1652,	Jan. 5-26, 1797
	1654-1661,	Feb. 2-Mar. 23, 1797
	1663-1668,	Apr. 6-May 11, 1797
	1673, 1675-1682,	June 15, June 29-Aug. 17, 1797
	1684, 1687,	Aug. 31, Sept. 21, 1797
	1689, 1691-1694,	Oct. 5, Oct. 19-Nov. 9, 1797
	1697-1701,	Nov. 30-Dec. 28, 1797
	1702, 1704-1712,	Jan. 4, Jan. 11-Mar. 8, 1798
	1714-1719,	Mar. 22-Apr. 26, 1798
	1721-1726,	May 10-June 14, 1798
	1728-1732,	June 28-July 26, 1798
	1734-1737,	Aug. 9-30, 1798
	1739 Extra,	Sept. 8, 1798
	1742-1749, 1751,	Sept. 27-Nov. 15, 29, 1798
	1756-1759,	Jan. 3-24, 1799
	1784-1785,	July 11-18, 1799
	Defective	Dec. 8, 1791, June 15, 1797

PRINTING OFFICES IN CANADA 1751-1800

Halifax, Nova Scotia

BARTHOLOMEW GREEN, 1751

Bartholomew Green was born in 1699 in Cambridge, Mass., and learned printing in Boston in the shop of his father of the same name, of whom Isaiah Thomas remarked "He was the most distinguished printer of that period in this country and did more business than any of the profession." In 1725, Bartholomew Jr. printed over his own imprint half a dozen small works for Boston booksellers and continued printing in Boston, for a while in some association with his brother-in-law, Richard Draper (who succeeded to Bartholomew Sr.'s business on the latter's death in 1732), for some years in partnership with John Bushell and Bezoune Allen. In August 1751 he moved his printing office to Halifax, N.S., took a lot on Grafton Street and proceeded to set up the first printing shop in what is now Canada. Green died however, about October 1751 and it is not known whether he printed anything at all after his arrival in Nova Scotia. Green had two sons trained to the printing trade, but they do not seem to have been associated with him in the business at Halifax, which shortly was developed by John Bushell.

JOHN BUSHELL, 1752-1761

John Bushell, a Bostonian, printed in association or partnership with Bartholomew Green from 1742 till 1749, then over his own imprint. He followed Green to Halifax after the latter's death and operated the printing office Green was establishing there, from early in 1752. He produced the *Halifax gazette* from March 23, 1752, and other government work in good style, also no doubt job printing for tradesmen which has not survived; but his output was certainly limited in quantity and variety. His son and daughter learned the printing trade, the former however was apprenticed, not in his father's shop, but to Daniel Fowle at Portsmouth, New Hampshire. Bushell died in January 1761, and his work was carried on by Anthony Henry.

ANTHONY HENRY, 1761-1800

Anthony Henry was born of German parents near Montbeliard in Alsace in 1734. When he came to America is not known but he had had some training as a printer, and had recently been a bandsman in one of the regiments investing Louisburg when he appeared in Halifax in 1758. As Bushell, who operated the only printing office, was deteriorating, Henry became attached to his shop either on Bushell's initiative or that of Richard Bulkeley, the provincial secretary, probably in line with the policy after the fall of Louisburg of rehabilitating the soldiers into civilian occupations in Halifax. On September 23, 1760, Henry was given a partnership in the business, which he took over completely on Bushell's death, four months later. The business was principally government printing and stationery. In the early years Henry billed the government for all work, and "about £50" was allowed in the annual estimates as "allowance for printing." In 1773, the basic work, the printing of the sessions laws, the Assembly *Journal*, Proclamations, and certain *Gazette* insertions was established on a salary basis, at £60 a year, increased in 1778 or 79 to £80, and in 1790 to £100. Initially, Henry was handicapped in his business by limited craft experience, a foreign background, worn types, and lack of capital. However, he was the only printer in Halifax. The Government purchased type for him in London on his promissory note. Richard Bulkeley assumed editorial supervision of the *Halifax Gazette* in 1758, and as time went on Henry gained experience and experienced help in his shop. Isaiah Thomas was his assistant in the period of the enforcement of the Stamp Act, and the independent attitude of the paper at that time resulted in Henry's loss of government patronage and the introduction of a rival printer. However, Henry's successful conduct of a genuinely popular newspaper, the *Nova Scotia Chronicle*, and possibly other factors, put his rival out of business. Henry became government printer again in 1770, was commissioned King's printer in 1788, and ran a prosperous business until his death, December 1, 1800. His publications included the long-lived *Nova-Scotia Calender* and the short-lived *Neuschöttlandische Calender*, sermons of both dissenters and established churchmen, Nova Scotia statutes, as well as nearly four decades of the provincial government's regular publications. Henry's business was carried on briefly by his widow, then transferred to Gay & Merlin. His adopted son, Anthony Henry Holland, was also a printer in Halifax in the early nineteenth century.

ROBERT FLETCHER, 1766-1770

Robert Fletcher came to Halifax, N.S., from London in the summer of 1766, with equipment to establish a book and stationery business and a printing-office. He probably came with some encouragement from the provincial administration, because government patronage was transferred from Anthony Henry to Fletcher. The latter printed the *Nova-Scotia Gazette* and all government work for three years in a highly competent style. Then he abandoned the printing side of his business to Henry and sold his press and types to John Boyle of Boston. Fletcher remained in Halifax as a merchant, however, expanding his book and stationery business to general merchandise.

JOHN HOWE, 1780-nineteenth century

John Howe was born in Boston October 14, 1754. He was trained to the printing trade in the shop of Richard Draper, and came to Halifax in 1776 (or 1780?) as a loyalist with Richard's widow, Margaret Draper's printing-office. When Mrs. Draper went on to England shortly, Howe purchased her equipment. He started his own printing business about 1780 (*see* J. J. Stewart's *Early journalism in Nova Scotia*). Howe published non-official works, the *Halifax Journal*, the short-lived *Nova-Scotia Magazine*, various pamphlets and sermons for the Freemasons, Methodists, and other groups until in 1801 he became King's printer.

WILLIAM MINNS, 1786-nineteenth century

William Minns was born about 1762, son of a medical doctor in Salem, Mass. He came to Halifax as a lad with his brother-in-law, John Howe, and learned printing in Howe's shop, 1781-85, then started in business for himself, publishing the *Weekly Chronicle* (*see* J. J. Stewart *op. cit.*). Minns died in Halifax in 1827.

QUEBEC, QUEBEC

BROWN & GILMORE, 1764-73
WILLIAM BROWN, 1773-89

William Brown was born in Scotland in 1738, came to America about 1753, and learned printing in the shop of William Dunlap of Philadelphia. He formed a partnership there with Thomas Gilmore in 1763, then went to England and purchased press and types. In 1764 the two young men established the first printing office in Quebec. Gilmore died in Feb. 1773 and Brown continued the business till his death in March, 1789. His was the most important printing office in eighteenth-century Canada both in the amount and variety of its production and as a source of supplies and personnel for other printers. Brown published a newspaper, the *Quebec Gazette*, almost continuously from June 1764, also sheet and later pamphlet almanacs. Most of his other printing—laws, legislative journals, proclamations, devotional and school books, playbills, sermons, etc., and a great deal of small job work—was done on contract for government, institutions, or individuals, to whom he sold also office supplies, patent medicines, and the like. Though Brown was never commissioned King's printer, he early got his basic government work on a salary basis, albeit with persisting acrimonious disputes over payments for additional work. Brown is the subject of a memoir by F. J. Audet, *William Brown . . . sa vie et ses oeuvres*, 1932. *See also* W. S. Wallace, *Dictionary of Canadian Biography*, 1945.

WILLIAM MOORE, 1788-93

William Moore seems to have come to Quebec about 1787 as an actor, or a printer (he appears as both in Wm. Brown's account books from January 1787). He gave entertainments, theatricals, and lectures for a time and began his own printing business with an English and a French newspaper, the *Quebec Herald* and *Courier de Québec*, in November 1788. He printed a few small works including a directory prepared by his father-in-law, William MacKay, and an almanac. But his printing ceased abruptly in March 1793, a few accounts are credited or debited to "William Moore's estate," and nothing further is known of him.

SAMUEL NEILSON, 1789-93

Samuel Neilson was born in Balmaghie, Kirkcudbrightshire, Scotland, in 1771. He learned printing in Quebec in the shop of his maternal uncle, William Brown, whom he succeeded in March 1789. In the remainder of his brief life Neilson greatly extended the scope of this prosperous business. He abandoned the annual salary so necessary to his uncle in early years, and substituted a price schedule* on which government as well as other work was done. The *Quebec Gazette* and *Quebec Almanac* were expanded, the *Quebec Magazine* was launched. The first (albeit slight) volume of poetry appeared and a few publications on current local problems. That these were not necessarily the printer's own publishing venture seems irrelevant, for Neilson apparently made the printing-office more influential in Quebec in three years than his uncle throughout his lifetime. Samuel Neilson died of tuberculosis on January 12, 1793. *See also* W. S. Wallace, *Dictionary of Canadian Biography*, 1945. His business passed to his brother John.

*Plate XII.

JOHN NEILSON, 1793-nineteenth century

John Neilson was born on July 17, 1776, in Balmaghie, Kirkcudbrightshire, Scotland. He came to Quebec in 1790, learned printing in the Brown-Neilson shop and inherited the business on his brother Samuel's death in 1793. Rev. Alexander Spark superintended the publication of the *Quebec Magazine* and of the *Quebec Gazette* till young Neilson's majority. Though the *Quebec Magazine* was abandoned, John Neilson continued printing on the traditional lines of the firm excepting that law printing was transferred to another shop in which Neilson had an interest. Gifted like his elder brother, he achieved a long and rather brilliant career in publishing, journalism, and public affairs. He is the subject of a memoir by F. J. Audet, *John Neilson, 1776-1848*. *See also* W. S. Wallace, *Dictionary of Canadian Biography*, 1945.

WILLIAM VONDENVELDEN, 1794-98

William Vondenvelden appeared in Quebec in 1782, worked as a translator for Wm. Brown the printer, and as a surveyor for the government. He opened the New Printing Office in 1795, published a newspaper, the Quebec *Times*, and a few other publications including an European-style almanac. As "law printer" to the Government, he inaugurated the quarto editions of the Lower Canada statutes which appeared regularly for nearly fifty years. Vondenvelden sold his printing business in 1798 to Desbarats & Lelievre. He was elected in 1800 to the provincial Assembly as member for Gaspé where he had long been deputy surveyor. He died in 1809. *See also* W. S. Wallace, *Dictionary of Canadian Biography*, 1945.

LELIEVRE & DESBARATS, 1798-99
PIERRE EDOUARD DESBARATS, 1799-nineteenth century

Pierre Edouard Desbarats with Roger Lelievre, both former employees in the Neilson printing office, purchased the New Printing Office from Wm. Vondenvelden on May 23, 1798, and were commissioned as provincial law printers on May 14, 1798. Lelievre transferred his interest to Desbarats on November 16, 1799, and on May 19, 1800, John Neilson entered into a partnership with Desbarats retroactive to October 23, 1799, though his name did not appear in the firm's name. Thus was launched a notable printing and publishing business operated by successive generations of the Desbarats family through the nineteenth century.

MONTREAL, QUEBEC

FLEURY MESPLET, 1776-94

Fleury Mesplet was born in France. about 1735. He learned printing there, migrated to London, then to Philadelphia in 1774. He moved to Montreal with a printing office in 1776, establishing the first French press in Canada and the only one west of Quebec. He published a newspaper, *La Gazette Litteraire*, and later the *Montreal Gazette*, also an almanac and numerous school books and Roman Catholic devotional works. Unlike many early Canadian printers, he had little government work, in fact during his first few years he was highly suspect to government because of his American antecedents. Mesplet died on January 22, 1794. He has been the subject of several monographs: by R. W. MacLachlan, Aegidius Fauteux, and Victor Morin (*see* Authorities cited at end of this volume).

EDWARD EDWARDS, 1795-nineteenth century
LOUIS ROY, 1795-96
JOSEPH-MARIE ROY, 1796-97
JOHN BENNETT, 1798

SAINT JOHN, NEW BRUNSWICK

WILLIAM LEWIS & JOHN RYAN, 1783-86

William Lewis was said (by C. R. Hildeburn in his *Sketches of printers of colonial New York*, N.Y., 1895, p. 169-70) to have been a native of Kent, England. He was an apprentice in James and Alexander Robertson's printing office in Albany in 1776, was arrested with Alexander, released, then rearrested when loyalist material continued to come from the hidden Robertson press. Lewis was printing in New York intermittently during 1779-83, then went to Saint John, apparently taking printing equipment with him. With John Ryan as a partner, he produced the *Royal St. John's Gazette* from December 1783 until the partnership was dissolved in 1786 and Lewis returned to the United States.

JOHN RYAN, 1786-nineteenth century

John Ryan was born in Newport, R.I., October 7, 1761, and began to learn printing in 1776 under John Howe when the latter went to Newport with the Draper printing office after the British evacuation of Boston. On evacuation of Newport, Ryan is said to have accompanied Howe to New York and to Halifax, N.S. In 1783 he proceeded to Parrtown (later Saint John, N.B.) and formed a partnership with William Lewis. They began to print a newspaper, the *Royal St. John's Gazette*, in December 1783, evidently on Lewis's press, for Ryan petitioned in the following February for permission to bring his own (or his father-in-law's?) press and types from New York. The young printers soon became involved in the quarrels which marked the loyalist influx to Saint John. In March 1784 they were in a libel case for printing an article criticizing the governor's land-granting policy. In the bitter election contests of 1785 they were arrested on another libel charge, and fined. After this experience Lewis sold out his interest in the business to Ryan. Some years later (February 1797) Ryan was again in trouble, this time for printing Assembly documents in his newspaper, for which he was simply reprimanded. On the whole, his relations with government were good and he received considerable municipal and provincial work, including, some years, the printing of sessions laws and Assembly *Journal*. When his competitor, Christopher Sower, gave up business in New Brunswick, Ryan, on his recommendation, became King's printer, took over Sower's *Royal Gazette* and transferred his own (by now) *St. John Gazette* to his brother-in-law, Jacob S. Mott. Ryan continued printing in Saint John till 1807, when (after an exploratory trip the previous year) he removed to Newfoundland and operated that colony's first printing office in St. John's till his death in 1847. Two of Ryan's sons, Michael and Lewis, became printers but predeceased their father.

CHRISTOPHER SOWER, 1785-99

Christopher Sower, the third of that name, was born on January 27, 1754 in Germantown, Pa., and was bred to the printing trade in the distinguished (German-language) family business. He became head of the firm in 1774, and by 1777 was taking an active part on the royalist side of the American Revolution (see *Dictionary of American Biography*). His property confiscated, he came (by way of England where he pressed claims for indemnification of his losses) to Saint John, N.B. in 1785, with a commission as King's printer. No salary was attached to the office and government work was assigned to both Sower and John Ryan, sometimes with competitive bidding. Sower, however, did hold the salaried office of postmaster, a London appointment, which he retained *in absentia* under some criticism after he moved his residence and printing office twelve miles from Saint John to his extensive and fertile farm, Brookville, on the Hammond River in 1792. While he had warm friends in high places, notably Brook Watson, Sower seems to have been rather stiff and irascible in his own community, involved more than occasionally in business and political squabbles. He held at times minor municipal offices but for brief periods only, and he was defeated as candidate for the Assembly in the provincial election of 1795. He was, however, an outstanding craftsman among early Canadian printers, his rather heavy, formal style an advantage in the official publications, his characteristic productions. He also published an almanac for a few years, and a weekly newspaper, *The Royal Gazette and New-Brunswick Advertiser* from October 1785 till March 1799. Early in 1799 in ill-health, he transferred his newspaper to John Ryan, resigned his offices as King's printer and postmaster, and in June travelled to Baltimore to complete arrangements for joining his brother Samuel's type-founding business. There he died of apoplexy on July 2. His son, Brook Watson Sower, later became a printer in Baltimore.

JACOB S. MOTT, 1799-nineteenth century

Jacob S. Mott was born about 1772, son of John Mott, a printer resident on Long Island, N.Y. who brought his family to Saint John, N.B., in 1783. The Motts returned shortly to New York, however, Mrs. Mott declaring that she would "never live in such a god-forsaken place as Parrtown". Jacob learned the printing trade in New York and came again with his family to Saint John in 1798. He took over the *St. John Gazette* from his sister's husband, John Ryan, in 1799, and operated a printing business (becoming King's printer in 1808) till his death, January 17, 1814. Jacob Mott's son Gabriel also became a printer, carried on his father's business for a time, worked briefly for his uncle, John Ryan, in Newfoundland, then returned to the United States.

Shelburne, Nova Scotia

JAMES & ALEXANDER ROBERTSON, 1783-84

James Robertson was born in Edinburgh in 1740, learned the printing trade from his father, and came to Boston about 1764. With his brother Alexander as partner, James set up a printing office in New York and began publishing the *New York Chronicle* in 1768. On the encouragement of Sir William Johnson, the brothers moved to Albany, where they established the town's first press; in 1773 they also opened a printing office in Norwich, Conn. As the Revolution developed, the Robertsons, royalists, withdrew from Norwich in 1776, but continued for a time at Albany, where Alexander, a cripple, was jailed, and the press, in the woods thirteen miles from town, was operated in the British interest.

James escaped to New York where he started printing again with hired equipment, launching the *Royal American Gazette* in January 1777. After Alexander's release on prisoners' exchange, he carried on the work in New York, and James printed in various towns during their British occupation (see *Dictionary of American Biography*). At the end of the war the brothers memorialized the British government for losses sustained as loyalists amounting to £650. 8*s*., and moved to Shelburne, N.S., in 1783. Here the *Royal American Gazette* was resumed by Alexander Robertson and, after his death in 1784, carried on (with some interruption) by James. The latter was active in local affairs, held office as justice of the peace, and did the local official printing, in part for his taxes. The business outlook was poor as the new loyalist settlement included several refugee printers, and Robertson moved to Charlottetown, Island of St. John (Prince Edward Island) in or before September 1787, on the governor's invitation. Here he resumed publication of the *Royal American Gazette*, and by the end of 1789 his shop had completed, in one massive volume, the first printing of the laws of the island colony. Robertson was given a sheriff's office for a year and a small salary (£60) as King's printer, but it was apparent, as Governor Fanning stated, "that it is absolutely impossible for him to support himself and his family on the profits of his Press in this Island." Robertson went to Quebec in the spring of 1789, thence to Britain. He is said (by Isaiah Thomas) to have set up a printing and book-selling business in Edinburgh, which he was still operating in 1810. His printing office in Charlottetown was carried on by William A. Rind.

Alexander Robertson was born about 1742, the son of an Edinburgh printer. He migrated to America and, usually in partnership with his elder brother James (q.v.), operated a printing business in New York, Albany, Norwich, Conn., and in Shelburne, N.S. In New York, from January 1778, he produced the *Royal American Gazette* and resumed its publication in Shelburne until his death in November 1784. His son, James, Jr., was also a printer in Shelburne.

JAMES ROBERTSON, SR., 1784-86

JAMES ROBERTSON, JR., & T. & J. SWORDS, 1784-86?

James Robertson, Jr., was the son of Alexander Robertson, 1742-84. He probably learned the printing trade in the family shop, and came to Shelburne when loyalists were evacuated from New York in April 1783. With Thomas and James Swords, young Robertson produced the *Port Roseway Gazetteer* in the family printing-office in Shelburne for a year or so, the little journal serving in effect as a second weekly issue of the senior Robertsons' *Royal American Gazette.* After the removal of James, Sr. and his press to Charlottetown in the summer of 1786, James, Jr.'s printing probably ceased. He is said (by J. J. Stewart) to have gone later to Scotland where, like his uncle and namesake, he was engaged in the printing and book-selling business in Edinburgh in 1810.

Thomas and James Swords, brothers and printers in New York, probably came to Nova Scotia as loyalists in 1783. Each received a grant of 250 acres in a tract on the Roseway River near Shelburne in 1785. Their association with James Robertson, Jr., in production of the *Port Roseway Gazetteer* is their only known activity in printing there. Their sojourn was probably brief for in 1790 they were again operating as printers in New York.

JAMES HUMPHREYS, 1785-96

James Humphreys was born in Philadelphia on January 15, 1748, the son of a conveyancer, and was educated towards a legal career. He learned the printing trade however, in the shop of William Bradford the younger, set up his own business in 1770, and in January 1775 began publication of the *Philadelphia Ledger.* (See *Dictionary of American Biography.*) A loyalist, he came to Shelburne, N.S., probably in 1784 via England, where he had secured equipment for a new printing office. Early in 1785 he began publishing the *Nova-Scotia Packet.* He was active in local government affairs and in the Anglican St. Patrick's Church, where his three children born in Shelburne were baptized. He was county treasurer in 1792, and in 1793 was elected to the provincial Assembly as one of the two members for the county of Shelburne. In June 1796 he was commissioned a justice of the peace for the county of Shelburne. Besides the newspaper, which ran but a few years, Humphreys printed a small amount of work for local offices, and after about five years in Shelburne apparently abandoned printing or (more likely) depended rather on a general merchant's business for his livelihood. He is said to have suffered heavily from depredation of French privateers, and in the spring of 1797 he removed from Shelburne to Philadelphia. There he again established a printing business which he carried on till his death on Feb. 10, 1810.

Charlottetown, Island of St. John

JAMES ROBERTSON, SR., 1787-90
WILLIAM ALEXANDER RIND, 1790-98

William Alexander Rind was born and educated in Virginia, the son of William and Clementina Rind. His father, printer of the *Virginia Gazette,* having died in 1773 and his mother the following year, young William and his brother John received their schooling at the expense of the Williamsburg Lodge of Freemasons, and his father's press in Williamsburg was operated "for the benefit of Clementina Rind's children" by John Pinkney. William Rind came to the Island of St. John in 1788, according to his statement in the *Washington Federalist,* February 19, 1802. He worked as a journeyman in the printing office of James Robertson, Sr., and when Robertson left the Island in the following spring, Rind completed the printing of the basic volume of the colony's laws. As King's printer he received an annual salary of £40 for the regular printing of sessions laws and Assembly *Journal,* and produced a few other small pieces for the governor. Almost his only other publication probably was the *Royal Gazette and Miscellany of the Island of St. John.* Rind married on August 24, 1790, Elizabeth Bagnall, daughter of Samuel Bagnall, a loyalist from Philadelphia, who settled in Charlottetown in 1787. Four children born to the Rinds are recorded in the MS baptismal records of St. Paul's Church, Charlottetown, 1791-97. On November 9, 1797, a grant of twelve acres of "wilderness land" in the royalty of Charlottetown was made to Rind, and that is the last record we have of his presence on the Island. In October 1798 Lieutenant-Governor Fanning wrote the Colonial Office in London that "the Printer having lately left the Island with his Family for the United States of America . . . I fear it will be with some delay at least in the future that I shall be able to procure and transmit printed copies of the Acts." Before he left, however, Rind is said to have taught printing to his nephew, James Douglas Bagnall, who in 1805, aged 20 years, was King's printer on the Island. Rind began publication at Richmond, of the *Virginia Federalist*, May 25, 1799, succeeded the following year, by the *Washington Federalist*, at Georgetown, D.C., which he carried on for some years.

NEWARK, NIAGARA, OR WEST NIAGARA, UPPER CANADA

LOUIS ROY, 1793-94

See W. S. Wallace, *Dictionary of Canadian Biography*, 1945.

GIDEON & SILVESTER TIFFANY, 1794-1802 (worked sometimes separately, together, or with Simons)

See W. S. Wallace, *Dictionary of Canadian Biography*, 1945; also his "The first journalists in Upper Canada" in *Canadian Historical Review*, 26: 372-81, Dec. 1945.

TITUS GEER SIMONS, 1797-98

See W. S. Wallace, *Dictionary of Canadian Biography*, 1945.

TITUS GEER SIMONS & WM. WATERS, July-October 1798

YORK, UPPER CANADA

WM. WATERS & TITUS GEER SIMONS, 1798-1801

AUTHORITIES

Manuscripts

CANADA. PUBLIC ARCHIVES: "B" series. Transcripts of the Haldimand papers in the British Museum. (Brit. Mus. Add. MSS. 21661-21892). Correspondence and a mass of miscellaneous papers, 1760-90, collected by Frederick Haldimand, governor of Quebec, 1777-86. Calendared in Can. P.A., *Report 1884* [*-89*].

CANADA. PUBLIC ARCHIVES. BROWN & GILMORE MSS., *see* Can. P.A., *Neilson papers.*

CANADA. PUBLIC ARCHIVES. CLAUS PAPERS: A miscellaneous collection in several volumes which includes the correspondence, memoranda, etc., of Daniel Claus, deputy superintendent of Indians in Canada, 1760-87. Cited: Can. P.A., *Claus papers.*

CANADA. PUBLIC ARCHIVES: "CO 42" series. Transcripts of original papers in the Public record office, London (CO 42 series) comprising correspondence between provincial officials of Quebec, Lower Canada, and the Board of Trade 1763-1821. 23vols. calendared in Can. P.A., *Report 1921.*

CANADA. PUBLIC ARCHIVES. DARTMOUTH PAPERS: Correspondence, etc., of the Earl of Dartmouth, secretary of state for colonies, 1772-5. The Archives has transcripts, also the original papers (subsequently donated). The latter are described in Great Britain. Hist. MSS. Commission. *Eleventh report.* Appendix pt. 5. London, 1887; and cited in this work: Can. P.A., *Dartmouth.*

CANADA. PUBLIC ARCHIVES. FINLAY PAPERS: Memoranda by Hugh Finlay, deputy postmaster general for Canada, on matters considered by Legislative Council of Quebec, 1773-93.

CANADA. PUBLIC ARCHIVES. INGLIS PAPERS: Transcripts of journals, correspondence, etc., 1775-1848, of Charles Inglis and John Inglis, first and third bishop of Nova Scotia, respectively; 8 vols., calendared in Can. P.A., *Report 1912.* (App. M.)—*1913* (App. I).

CANADA. PUBLIC ARCHIVES. LOWER CANADA. LEGISLATIVE COUNCIL. MINUTES: Records similar to and in continuation of those of the Quebec Council, q.v., are cited similarly: Can. P.A., L.C. Leg. Co. *Minutes*, Can. P.A., L.C. *State*, Can. P.A., L.C. *Land.*

CANADA. PUBLIC ARCHIVES. NEILSON PAPERS: Some 175 volumes and portfolios of accounts, correspondence, memoranda, etc., conserved by John Neilson, printer and radical politician in Lower Canada. Neilson conducted the printing and stationery business established at Quebec in 1764 by his uncle, Wm. Brown, and controlled by members of the family till 1849. His papers include the records of the firm. Most of those of the eighteenth century are bound in volumes labelled: *Brown & Gilmore Memorial A*, 1763-74, *Brown & Gilmore Account book*, 1763-74 and *Neilson papers*, v. 42-84. The records include day books or journals, also ledgers, cash, account, and waste books, though the various types of record are not available for every year, and for a few short periods no record whatever appears. As the Brown & Gilmore-Neilson firm had the oldest printing office west of Halifax and supplied most of the others with printers, stationery, and advice, the Neilson papers are obviously the single most important source of information on early printing and publishing in Canada. The later papers, 1801-47, are calendared in Can. P.A., *Report 1913-1918*. Neilson papers are cited in this work: Can. P.A., Brown & Gilmore: *Memorial A;* Can. P.A., Brown & Gilmore: *Account book*, 1763-74; Can. P.A., *Neilson papers*.

CANADA. PUBLIC ARCHIVES. NEW BRUNSWICK EXECUTIVE COUNCIL MINUTES: The Minutes (original drafts on separate folio sheets now filed in portfolios) cover the period Feb. 15, 1785-1857. The Council papers, i.e. petitions, accounts, etc., mentioned in the Minutes are not included. The Archives has these papers for the period 1816-56 filed separately; the only earlier papers seen are those stored in the Legislative Library at Fredericton (*see* NEW BRUNSWICK. EXECUTIVE COUNCIL, below). The Archives has also the lieutenant-governors' correspondence (original in-letters, 1784-1865, and drafts of out-letters 1784-1861) also the lieutenant-governors' commissions and instructions (originals) formerly in the provincial secretary's office, Fredericton. The Minutes are cited in this work: Can. P.A., N.B. Ex. co. *Minutes*.

CANADA. PUBLIC ARCHIVES. NEW BRUNSWICK STATE PAPERS: Transcribed from various original papers in the Public Record Office, British Museum, and Lambeth Palace, London. (*See* Parker's *Guide* for description of the various series in this group.) Correspondence between Lieut.-Gov. Carleton and the Colonial Office, 1784-1800, included in series A, is cited in this work: Can. P.A., N.B. "A".

CANADA. PUBLIC ARCHIVES. NOVA SCOTIA STATE PAPERS: Transcripts of original papers in the Public Record Office, British Museum and Lambeth Palace, London. "A" series calendared in Can. P.A., *Report 1894*, comprises correspondence between provincial officials and the home government. It includes the transcribed text of Canadian printed pieces enclosed in letters from Halifax to London; the printed originals filed in the Public Record Office, etc., are in some cases the only copies located; "B" series: Executive Council journals; "C" series: Legislative Council journals; "D" series: House of Assembly journals. Cited: Can. P.A., N.S. "A"; Can. P.A., N.S. "B"; Can. P.A., N.S. "C"; Can. P.A., N.S. "D".

CANADA. PUBLIC ARCHIVES. PRINCE EDWARD ISLAND STATE PAPERS: Transcripts of papers in the Public Record Office, British Museum and Lambeth Palace, etc. London, beginning 1763. (For description of series, see Parker's *Guide*.) The transcripts used in this work are: "A" series, Correspondence; "B" series, Minutes of Executive Council (1763-1801, calendared in Can. P.A., *Report 1895*); "C" series, Journals of Legislative Council; "D" series, Journals of Assembly. Cited: Can. P.A., P.E.I. "A", *etc*. *See also:* St. John Island.

CANADA. PUBLIC ARCHIVES: "Q" series. Transcripts of original papers in the Public Record Office, London (CO 42 series); comprising correspondence between the provincial officials of Quebec, Lower Canada, and Upper Canada, and the home government, 1760-1841; calendared in Can. P.A., *Report 1890* [-*1902*].

CANADA. PUBLIC ARCHIVES. QUEBEC. LEGISLATIVE COUNCIL MINUTES: Original minutes, also transcripts for use, now arranged according to functions of Council: vol. A-C includes minutes of Council in its executive and legislative capacity 1764-75; vol. D-F legislative only, 1775-91 (cited in this work: Can. P.A., Que. Leg. Co. *Minutes* A-F); State book or Privy council, vol. D-I, minutes of Council in its executive capacity, 1775-91; (cited: Can. P.A., Que. *State*-D-I). Land book vol. A-B comprises records of Council as Land board, 1787-91, published in Ontario Archives *Report for 1938* (and cited in this work: Can. P.A., Que. *Land* A-B). These minutes include records and texts of *some* publications ordered printed, also of payments to printers (original ms. petitions and accounts submitted by printers also a few printed texts are filed in "S" series).

CANADA. PUBLIC ARCHIVES: "S" series. "Sundries", several hundred portfolios, cartons and volumes, 1760-1841, containing original papers submitted to the Council of Quebec, later Lower Canada, also memoranda by the secretary, etc., now arranged by date or subject matter and labelled "Internal Correspondence," "Public Accounts," etc. These papers include printers' petitions, bills, etc., also a few printed broadsides and leaflets. Cited in this work: Can. P.A., *"S" Int. corres.;* Can. P.A., *"S" Pub. accts.*, etc.

CANADA. PUBLIC ARCHIVES: UPPER CANADA. EXECUTIVE COUNCIL. MINUTES: Original minutes similar in subject matter and arrangement to Quebec Legislative council minutes, q.v. (cited: Can. P.A., U.C. Ex. co. *Minutes;* Can. P.A., U.C. *Land;* Can. P.A., U.C. *State*).

NEW BRUNSWICK. EXECUTIVE COUNCIL PAPERS: Several bundles of original documents apparently connected with the Council, including some of its minutes, a few petitions for land grants (most land papers are well preserved in the Crown Lands Office, Fredericton), for payments of accounts, also vouchers, receipts, memoranda of contingent expenses. These papers, in no discernible arrangement, some of them discoloured and partially decomposed by damp, are stored in the vault of the Legislative Library, Fredericton. (*See also* Can. P.A., N.B. Ex. co.) Cited: N.B. Ex. co. *Papers*.

NEW BRUNSWICK. ASSEMBLY PAPERS: Original documents of each session, beginning 1786, comprising the journal, bills, petitions, and miscellaneous. The latter group includes the lieutenant-governors' speeches, replies thereto, Council communications, distribution lists for government publications, estimates, treasurer's report; also accounts, letters, etc., submitted to the Assembly. These mss. are tied in several hundred bundles and stored in the Legislative library, Fredericton. For the early period they are bundled year by year (parts of "Miscellaneous" occasionally missing; 1791 missing altogether) later, by year and subject matter. Some papers are discoloured and partially decomposed by damp. A typewritten contents list of the bundles 1786-1835 is in the library. These papers include petitions, proposals, accounts, etc., from the principal printers in New Brunswick, as well as records of printing ordered, and of accounts paid by the Assembly. Cited: N.B. As. *Papers.*

NEW BRUNSWICK. THOMAS CARLETON'S LETTER BOOKS: Drafts of letters from Lieut.-Gov. Carleton to the colonial secretary in London and to the governor-in-chief at Quebec, Lord Dorchester, Carleton's brother. 7v. 1784-1810; in the Legislative library, Fredericton. Cited: N.B. *Carleton.*

NEW BRUNSWICK. WINSLOW PAPERS: Letters to, and memoranda of Edward Winslow, secretary to the British commander-in-chief in North America, executive councillor and surrogate general in New Brunswick. These papers, mainly 1770-1810, mounted and bound in 10v. (also others not available for use) are in New Brunswick Archives, Saint John, N.B. Cited: N.B., *Winslow* papers. Some (less than half) of these papers are printed in W. O. Raymond: *Winslow papers, A.D. 1776-1826* (Saint John, N.B. 1901).

NOVA SCOTIA. PUBLIC ARCHIVES. MSS. SERIES: Original and transcribed documents collected according to a resolution of the House of Assembly of April 30, 1857, by T. B. Akins, and described in Nova Scotia Public Record Commission: *Catalogue or list of manuscript documents* (Halifax, 1886). Of this series the following volumes of original papers were particularly useful in the present work: v. 169, Commission book, 1781-[92]; v. 172, Commission book, 1787-1809; v. 286-87, Legislative council papers, 1760-1809; v. 301-302, Assembly papers, 1758-1800. The documents, 535 v., described in the *Catalogue* are now part of an extensive collection of mss., printed books, newspapers, maps and prints, etc., in the Public Archives of Nova Scotia, Halifax, N.S. Cited: P.A.N.S., v. 169 [etc.]

ST. JOHN, Island of (renamed 1797: PRINCE EDWARD ISLAND): Few early original records of the government appear to survive in Canada. A volume of 18th-century MSS. comprising the *Assembly Journal*, Mar. 21, 1785-Nov. 17, 1792, is in the Legislative and Public Library, Charlottetown; unbound MSS. containing the *Assembly Journal*, Feb. 16-Mar. 4, 1795 (also 1825 et seq.) is in the Province Building, Charlottetown. Cited: St. John Is., As. *Journal.* (*See also* Can. P. A., Prince Edward Island.)

SAINT JOHN, N.B. COMMON COUNCIL: Minute book, v. 2, May 30, 1790-May 16, 1800, in Common clerk's office, City Hall, Saint John, N.B. Original MS. minutes of the Council of the city of Saint John, the only Canadian municipality incorporated in the eighteenth century. v.1, 1785-90, and v.3, 1800-1812, could not be located, but the file thereafter appears complete. Cited: Saint John, N.B. *Minutes.*

SAINT JOHN, N.B. FREE PUBLIC LIBRARY. JACK COLLECTION: This collection contains several hundred printed books and pamphlets relating to the history of the Maritime provinces, also the papers of David Russell Jack, 1864-1913, editor of *Acadiensis*, and of his uncle, Isaac Allen Jack, 1843-1903. These include correspondence, notes, etc., from private sources and clippings on local history and genealogy. Especially useful were the volumes labelled: *Early printers and old newspapers in New Brunswick and their times* (about 300 p.) and *Historical data relating to the press in the Maritime provinces.* Cited in this work: Saint John, N.B., *Jack papers.*

SHELBURNE, N.S. GENERAL QUARTER SESSIONS OF THE PEACE. Records, Mar. 30, 1784-1800, *et seq.* in the Municipal clerk's office, Shelburne, N.S. Cited: Shelburne, N.S., Quarter sessions *Records.*

UPPER CANADA. EXECUTIVE COUNCIL. MINUTES: Land Book, State Book. *See* CANADA. PUBLIC ARCHIVES: UPPER CANADA, *etc.*

UPPER CANADA. PETER RUSSELL ACCOUNT BOOK, 1793-1808. A folio ledger of about 300 p. in the Provincial Archives of Ontario, Toronto, containing rough notes of personal and public accounts, including some for the period when Russell was receiver general of Upper Canada.

Printed Works

ACADIENSIS, a quarterly devoted to the interests of the Maritime provinces of Canada; ed. by D. R. Jack. v. 1, no. 1 (Jan., 1901)-v. 8, no. 4 (Oct., 1908). Saint John, N.B., 1901-1908.

AKINS, THOMAS BEAMISH, *ed.:* Selections from the public documents of the province of Nova Scotia. p. l., ii, 755 p. 8vo. Halifax, N.S., 1869.

AUDET, FRANCIS J.: John Neilson, 1776-1848. (in Roy. Soc. of Can. *Trans.* 1928, ser. 3, v. 22, sec. 1, p. 81-97).

AUDET, FRANCIS J.: William Brown (1737-1789); premier imprimeur journaliste et libraire de Québec. Sa vie et ses oeuvres. (in Roy. Soc. of Can. *Trans.* 1932, ser. 3, v. 26, sec. 2, p. 97-112).

BROWN, CHARLES RAYNOR: Bibliography of Quebec or Lower Canada laws, 1764-1841. 22 p. (reprinted from *Law library journal,* v. 19, no. 4, Jan., 1927). Toronto, the Author, Carswell Co., 1927.

*CANADA. DEPT. OF MILITIA: A history of the organization, development and services of the military and naval forces of Canada from . . . 1763 to the present time, with illustrative documents, 3 v. (1763-1784). Ottawa, King's printer, 1919?

*CANADA. PUBLIC ARCHIVES:

†Report . . . for the year 1904. Ottawa, 1905. Appendix I: Text of documents on War of 1775-76, p. 343-90.

*Publications of the Federal Government are issued also in a French edition, of the same content, and of format and pagination approximately the same, as the English edition. In modern reprints of eighteenth-century bi-lingual publications, the old French text is issued separately in the modern *Rapport* . . . unless otherwise noted.

†The *Reports* (including appendices) of the Public Archives 1887-1926, are also published in Canada. Parliament. Sessional papers 1887-1926.

Report . . . for the year 1905. *See* SHORTT and DOUGHTY.

Report . . . for the year 1913. Ottawa, 1914. Appendix E. Ordinances made for the province of Quebec . . . since the establishment of the civil government, Quebec: Printed by Brown & Gilmore . . . MDCCLXVII, p. 45-86.

Report . . . for the years 1914 and 1915. Ottawa, 1916. Appendix C: Ordinances made for the province of Quebec . . . from 1768 until 1791, 255 p.

——— Appendix D: Catalogue of pamphlets, journals and reports in the Public Archives of Canada 1611-1867, 471 p. illus. (facsim.). For later enlarged ed. without illus., *see* CASEY.

Report . . . for the year 1918. Ottawa, 1919. Appendix B: Ordinances and proclamations of the Règne militaire. xvii, 208 p. (French originals and English translation)

——— Appendix C: Proclamations issued by the Governor in chief from the establishment of civil government on August 10, 1764, until the partition of the province of Quebec into the province of Upper and Lower Canada, on December 26, 1791. ii, 71 p.

Report . . . for the year 1921. Ottawa, 1922. Appendix B: Proclamations of the Governor of Lower Canada, 1792-1815. viii, 206 p. (1792-1800; p. 1-65).

——— Appendix F: Statutes of Upper Canada, 1792-1793. i, 40 p.

CANADIAN HISTORICAL REVIEW. Toronto, Univ. of Toronto Press, quarterly Mar. 1920—in progress. (Continuation of *Review of historical publications*).

CARSWELL Co. Ltd., *Toronto:* Check list of the statutes of the Dominion of Canada, the provinces, the earlier legislatures and Newfoundland. caption title 52 p. 8vo. Toronto, Carswell Co., [1908?] rev. & enl.: *Check list of Canadian and Newfoundland statutes*, 1937, 2 p. l. 59 p. 8vo. privately printed. Toronto, Carswell Co. 1937.

CASEY, MAGDALEN: Catalogue of pamphlets in the Public Archives of Canada, 1493-1931. (Can. P.A. *Pub.* no. 13). 2v. Ottawa, King's printer, 1931. For earlier smaller edition with many facsim. illus., *see* CAN. P.A. *Report for 1914-15.*

COTTON, W. L.: Chapters in our Island story. 102 p. Charlottetown, P.E.I., Irwin print. co., 1927.

DIONNE, NARCISSE EUTROPE: Inventaire chronologique des livres, brochures, journaux et revues. (pub. in Roy. Soc. of Canada *Trans.* ser. 2, v. 10-12, 14, 1904-06, 1908. 4v. Quebec, 1905-09; sup. 1912).

DOUGHTY, *SIR* ARTHUR G., and McARTHUR, DUNCAN A., *eds.:* Documents relating to the constitutional history of Canada, 1791-1818. (Can. Parl. Sess. paper no. 29c, 1914). xiii, 576 p. fold. pl., map. Ottawa, King's printer, 1914.

EAKINS, W. G.: Bibliography of Canadian statute law. (in *Law library journal*, v. 1, no. 3, Oct. 1908, p. 61-75; also *Law library journal*, v. 2, no. 4, Jan. 1910, p. 65-75).

EVANS, CHARLES: American bibliography; a chronological dictionary of all books, pamphlets and periodical publications printed in the United States . . . 1639 . . . 1820. Chicago, the Author, 1903-1934. (1639-1799, v. 1-12).

FARIBAULT, GEORGES BARTHÉLEMI, *ed.*: Catalogue d'ouvrages sur l'histoire de l'Amérique. Quebec, W. Cowan, 1837. 2 p. l., 207 p.

FAUTEUX, ÆGIDIUS: Les bibliothèques canadiennes; étude historique. 45 p. (reprinted from *Revue canadienne*, n.s., v. 17, fév.-mars, 1916, p. 97-114, 193-217).

FAUTEUX, ÆGIDIUS: Fleury Mesplet: une étude sur les commencements de l'imprimerie dans la ville de Montréal. (in Bibliographical society of America *Papers*, 1934, v. 28, pt. 2, p. 164-193).

FAUTEUX, ÆGIDIUS: The introduction of printing into Canada, a brief history. xii, 178 p. illus. (facsim.) Montreal, Rolland paper co., 1930.

GAGNON, PHILÉAS: . . . Essai de bibliographie canadienne; inventaire d'une bibliothèque comprenant imprimés, manuscrits, estampes, etc., relatifs à l'histoire du Canada . . . 2 v., facsim. Québec, 1895: v. 2, Montreal, 1913. (Gagnon's collection as catalogued in the *Essai*, with a few additional pieces, is in the Montreal Civic Library).

GERIN, ELZÉAR: La gazette de Québec. 65 p. Québec, J. N. Duquet et cie., 1864.

GOSSELIN, AUGUSTE HONORÉ: L'église du Canada après la conquête. 2 v. Québec. Impr. Laflamme, 1916-17.

GOSSELIN, AUGUSTE HONORÉ: . . . L'église du Canada depuis Monseigneur de Laval jusqu'à la conquête. 3 v. Québec, Laflamme & Proulx, 1911-14.

JACK, DAVID RUSSELL: Acadian magazines. (in Roy. Soc. of Can. *Trans.* ser. 2, v. 9, sec. 2, p. 173-203, 1903).

JACK, DAVID RUSSELL: Early journalism in New Brunswick. (in *Acadiensis*, 8: 260-65).

KENNEDY, WILLIAM PAUL McCLURE, *ed.:* Statutes, treaties and documents of the Canadian constitution, 1713-1929. Second ed. rev. and enl. xxviii, 752 p. Toronto, Oxford univ. press, 1930.

LITERARY AND HISTORICAL SOCIETY OF QUEBEC: Manuscripts relating to the early history of Canada. Ser. 1-9, 9 v. in 8. Quebec, Wm. Cowan & fils, 1840-1906.

LITERARY AND HISTORICAL SOCIETY OF QUEBEC: Transactions. 14 v. illus., pl. maps. Quebec, 1829-1900. (Index . . . 1829-1891, in *Trans.* 1891, n.s., v. 8, pt. 20, p. i-xlix).
Index to the archival publications of the . . . Society, 1824-1924. 215 p. Quebec, L'evenement press, 1923.

LONG, ROBERT J.: Nova Scotia authors and their work; a bibliography of the province. 312, 4 p. East Orange, N.J., the Author, 1918. (Said to have been printed in 7? copies. *Copies located:* CaNsB; CaNsHD; CaNsWA (with addenda); CaOTU; MH (typescript).

MACFARLANE, WILLIAM GODSOE: New Brunswick bibliography; the books and writers of the province. 2 p. l., 98 p. Saint John, N.B., Sun print. co., 1895.

MACLACHLAN, ROBERT WALLACE: Fleury Mesplet, the first printer at Montreal. (in Roy. Soc. of Can. *Trans.*, ser. 2, v. 12, Sec. 2, p. 197-309, 1906.

MACLACHLAN, ROBERT WALLACE: Some unpublished documents relating to Fleury Mesplet. (in Roy. Soc. of Can. *Trans.*, ser. 3, v. 14, Sec. 2, p. 85-95, 1920.

MORGAN, HENRY JAMES: Bibliotheca canadensis; or, a manual of Canadian literature. xii, 411 p. Ottawa, G. E. Desbarats, 1867.

MORIN, VICTOR. Fleury Mesplet. Montreal, the Author, 1939.

NEW BRUNSWICK HISTORICAL SOCIETY: Collections. Saint John, N.B., the Society, 1894- (in progress).

NOVA SCOTIA, PUBLIC RECORD COMMISSION. Catalogue or list of manuscript documents, arranged, bound and catalogued under the direction of the Commissioner of public records [i.e. T. B. Akins] together with list of books of entry consisting of minutes of His Majesty's council, letters, registers of crown grants of lands, commissions, orders of government, etc., etc., from . . . 1710 to . . . 1867, preserved in the Government offices at Halifax, N.S. [etc.] 42 p. Halifax, N.S., Queen's printer, 1886.

NOVA SCOTIA HISTORICAL SOCIETY: Collections. Halifax, N.S., the Society, 1879- (in progress).

ONTARIO. BUREAU OF ARCHIVES: Third report . . . 1905. cxxxix 546 p. il. port. facsim. Toronto, 1906. Section B, Notes on land tenure in Canada to A.D. 1800, p. xliv-cxxxix; Section C, Documents, etc. 548 p.

Fourth report . . . 1906. xxxiv, 476 p. il. pl. ports. Toronto, 1907. Catalogue of *Upper Canada gazette*, 1793-1836, p. xii-xxxii; Proclamations of governors and lieutenant-governors of Quebec and Upper Canada, 1760-1841, p. 1-474.

Sixth report . . . 1909. xi, 484 p. 1 l. (errata). Toronto, 1910. Contains Journals of the Legislative assembly of Upper Canada . . . 1792, 1793, 1794 (partly) 1798, 1799, 1800, 1801, 1802, 1803, 1804; Journals, 1805-1824 continued in *Report . . . 1911*, [*-1914*].

Seventh report . . . 1910. xv, 514 p. Toronto, 1911. Contains Journals of the Legislative council of Upper Canada 1792-1794, 1798-1808, 1810-1812, 1814, 1819.

ONTARIO. DEPT. OF ARCHIVES:

Seventeenth report . . . 1928. 242 p. Toronto, 1929. Grants of crown lands in Upper Canada, 1787-1791. (printed from transcripts in the Ontario archives of Can. P.A. Que. *Land A-B.*)

Eighteenth report . . . 1929. viii, 206 p. Toronto, 1930. Grants of crown lands, etc., in Upper Canada, 1792-1796, p. 1-206; printed from U.C. Ex. Co., *Minutes.*

Nineteenth report . . . 1930. xi, 222 p. Toronto, 1931. Grants of crown lands, etc., in Upper Canada, 1796-1797, p. 1-222; printed from U.C. Ex. Co., *Minutes.*

Twentieth report . . . 1931. ix, 222 p. Toronto, 1932. Grants of crown lands in Upper Canada, 1796-1798; printed from U.C. *Land Book C-D;* grants, 1799-1800 "to be published"—Preface.

PARKER, DAVID: A guide to the documents in the Manuscript room at the Public Archives of Canada. Vol. 1. (Can. P.A., *Pub.* no. 10) 318 p. Ottawa, Govt. printing bureau, 1914. (only v. 1 pub.)

PASCOE, CHARLES FREDERICK: Two hundred years of the S.P.G., an historical account of the Society for the propagation of the gospel in foreign parts 1701-1900. (Based on a digest of the Society's records). xlii, 1429 p. front. illus. fold. pl., ports. London, the Society, 1901.

PATERSON, GILBERT CLARENCE: Land settlement in Upper Canada 1783-1840, by George C. Patterson [sic] M.A. (in Ontario, Dept. of archives. *Report . . . 1920,* Toronto, 1921. p. 1-278, il. pl. ports. maps, facsims.)

PILLING, JAMES CONSTANTINE: . . . Bibliography of the Algonquian languages. (U.S. Bur. of Am. Ethnology. Bul. no. 13.) x, 614 p. 97 facsim. on 81 pl. Washington, D.C., U.S. Govt. print. off., 1891.

PILLING, JAMES CONSTANTINE: . . . Bibliography of the Iroquoian languages. (Smithsonian Institution. Bureau of American ethnology. Bul. no. 6.) vi, 208 p. incl. 4 facsim., 5 facsim. Washington, D.C., U.S. Govt. print. off. 1888.

QUEBEC, PROVINCE. Provincial Archives. Rapport . . . 1920-21 [etc.] Québec, 1921—This valuable annual publication contains principally the texts of documents of the French régime in Canada. The volumes for 1927-28 *et seq.* however, include calendars of the papers of bishops of Quebec during the English régime, cited specifically in this work.

REVIEW OF HISTORICAL PUBLICATIONS relating to Canada. 22 v. Toronto, Univ. of Toronto press, 1897-1919. (continued as *Canadian Historical review*).

ROY, PIERRE GEORGES: Les premiers manuels scolaires canadiens. in *Bul. des recherches historiques,* 52: 231-303, Oct. 1946.

ROYAL SOCIETY OF CANADA: Transactions and Proceedings, Montreal [etc.], 1883-(in progress). Transactions or Mémoires in the annual volumes comprise four (later five) sections: English, French literature, Mathematical, Geological and Biological sciences; papers are published in English or French.

RUSSELL, PETER: The correspondence of the Honourable Peter Russell with allied documents relating to his administration of the government of Upper Canada [1796-99] . . . edited for the Ontario historical society, by Brig.-Gen. E. A. Cruikshank and A. F. Hunter. 3 v. Toronto, the Society, 1932-36.

SABIN, JOSEPH, *et al.*: Bibliotheca americana. A dictionary of books relating to America from its discovery to the present time. 29 v. N.Y., Bibliographical society of America, 1868-1936.

SHORTT, ADAM, *ed.:* Documents relating to Canadian currency, exchange and finance during the French period. (Can. P.A., Board of historical publications.) 2v. xci, 577 p.; 4 p.l., 578-1127 p. Ottawa, King's printer, 1925.

SHORTT, ADAM, and DOUGHTY, *SIR* ARTHUR G., *eds.:* Documents relating to the constitutional history of Canada 1759-1791, rev. ed. by the Historical documents publication board. (Can. Sess. paper no. 18, 1907 [revised]). 2 pt. v. 1: xvi, 581, fold. map.; v. 2: 2 p.l. p. 583-1084. Ottawa, King's printer, 1918. Cited as Shortt and Doughty: *Constitutional documents . . . 1759-1791.*

SHORTT, ADAM, JOHNSTON, V. K., and LANCTOT, G., *eds.:* Documents relating to currency, exchange and finance in Nova Scotia with prefatory documents 1675-1758. (Can. P.A., Board of historical publications.) li, 495 p. Ottawa, King's printer, 1933.

SIMCOE, JOHN GRAVES: The correspondence of Lieut. General John Graves Simcoe with allied documents relating to his administration of the government of Upper Canada [1789-96] coll. and ed. by Brigadier General E. A. Cruikshank for the Ontario Historical Society. 5 v., il. pl. ports. maps, etc. Toronto, 1923-31.

STEWART, JOHN JAMES: Early journalism in Nova Scotia [1751-1827]. (in N.S. hist. soc. *Col.* v. 6: 91-122, 1888).

TÊTU, HENRI, and GAGNON, C. O., *eds.:* Mandements, lettres pastorales, et circulaires des évêques de Québec. 8 v. Québec, Cote & cie., 1887-93.

TÊTU, HORACE: Historique des journaux de Québec. Nouv. éd., rev., augm. et annotée. 107 p. Québec, 1889.

TÊTU, HORACE: Journaux et revues de Montréal par ordre chronologique. Québec, 1881.

TORONTO. PUBLIC LIBRARY: A bibliography of Canadiana, being items in the Public Library of Toronto, Canada, relating to the early history and development of Canada 1834-1867; ed. by Frances M. Staton and Marie Tremaine. 828 p. illus. (facsim.) Toronto, 1934.

VERREAU, H. A. J.B.: Invasion du Canada, collection de mémoires recueillis et annotés. xix, 394 p. Montréal, Sénécal, 1873.

WALLACE, W. S.: The dictionary of Canadian biography. 2nd ed. 2v. Toronto, 1945.

WALLACE, W. S.: The encyclopedia of Canada. 6v. Toronto, 1948.

INDEX

Index includes listings by author, title, topic, also type (almanacs, devotional books, etc.) of publication. Listings by title are italicized, and in all listings titles are represented by key words only. Government publications are listed under name of province, etc., concerned, proclamations also under that of official.

L.C. = Lower Canada
N.B. = New Brunswick
N.S. = Nova Scotia
Que. = Quebec
U.C. = Upper Canada

Bold face numbers refer to numbered items, or, if preceded by p., refer to page.

A

A-B-C's, *see* Primers
A son excellence Guy Carleton, 1778. **291**
Abram's Plains, a poem, 1789. **585**
Abrégé . . . de la versification française, 1778. **300**
Abstract . . . Douay catechism, 1778. **280**
Abstract . . . judicature bill, 1794. **890**
Abstract . . proceeding in . . . Commons, 1792. **812**
Abstract . . . regulations . . . aliens, 1794. **887**
Acadians' lands. N.S. applications, 1759. **16**
  N.S. Proposals for settling, 1758. **13**
  N.S. Quieting possessions, 1759. **18**
Account . . . battle . . . Montreal, 1775. **193**
Account . . . religion . . . in Nisqueunia, 1781. **347**
Actes des apôtres, 1791. **682**
Address . . . Nova Scotia . . . Assembly, 1775. **205**
Address . . . proclamation . . . piety, 1787. **513**
Address . . . state . . . Nova-Scotia, 1785. **445**
Address to husbandmen, 1791. **683**
Adresse aux canadiens, 1775. **194**
Advertisement, *see also* Auction sales, Entertainment, Quebec Theatre.
  Birnie & Jones: Bread, hair powder, 1792. **753**
  Brown: Dentist, 1792. **754**
  Cleaning clothing, 1791. **684**
  Cull: Des cendres, potasse, 1795. **930**
  Dunière: Facteur de grains, 1792. **757**
  Johnston & Purss: Spruce beer, 1783. **400**
  Latham: Inoculation, 1768-86. **136n**
  Nathans & Hart: Price current, 1752. **3**
  Schieffelin: Earthen, china, glass ware, 1793. **851**
  Ward: Scouring business, 1789. **622**
Advice to a new married lady, 1790. **643**
Æsop, Select fables of, 1800. **1172B**
Agricultural Society in Canada. **573n**
  Circular abandon, 1791. **685-86**
  Circular hemp seed, 1791. **685, 687**
  Culture du chanvre, 1791. **685, 687**
  Method grain smut, 1792. **745**
  Moyens . . . du bled noir, 1792. **744**
  Papers & letters, 1790. **623**
  Projet, 1789. **573**
  Quebec: Hemp seed, 1791. **721n**
Agricultural Society of N.B. Plan, 1790. **624**
Agricultural Society of N.S., *see* Society for promoting agriculture in N.S.
Agriculture. Hubert: Lettre, 1789. **592**
  On history culture potato, 1791. **720n**
  Quebec: Seed to poor, 1789. **604, 608**
Akitami, 1770. **147**
Aliens. L.C. Act, 1794. **886-87**
  L.C. Order, 1796. **995**
  L.C. Proclamation, 1796. **1003**
Alline, H. **348n**
  Anti-traditionist, 1783. **386**
  Scott: Brief view, 1784. **442n**
  Sermon Liverpool, Nov. 19, 1782. **364**
  Sermon Liverpool, Nov. 21, 1782. **365**
  Sermon 19 Feb. 1783. **387**
  Two mites, 1781. **348**
Almanacs, **695n.** *See also* Sheet almanacs
  Almanac de Québec (Vondenvelden) 1798. **1030**
  Almanac St. John (Sower?) 1791. **625**
  Almanach curieux (Mesplet) 1778, **248.**—1779, 1778, **270.**—1781, **331.**—1782, **351.**—1783, **367.**—1784, **389.**—1786, **449**
  Almanach de Québec (Brown) 1780, **332.**—1781 (*not pub.*), **352n.**—1782, **352.**—1783, **368.**—1784, **390.**—1785, **412.**—1786, **448.**—1787, **473.**—1788, **505.**—1789, **544.**—1790 (*not pub.*), **578A.**—(pub. by Neilson) 1791, **630.**—continued as *Quebec almanack*.
  Almanach encyclopédique (Mesplet) 1777. **225**
  Almanack Halifax (Howe) 1790, **575.**—1791, **627.**—1792, **689.**—1794, **823.**—1795, **870.**—1796, **923.**—1797, **976.**—

1798, **1035.** —1799, **1080.** —1800, **1111.**—1801, **1158.**
Astronomical diary Halifax (Howe) 1782. **349**
Astronomical diary St. John (Sower) 1786, **446.**—1788, **502.**—1790, **574**
British American almanack St. John (Ryan) 1790, **626.**—1792, **688**
British American register (Henry) 1781. **330**
British gentleman's pocket almanack (Moore) 1790, **578B.**—1791, **631**
British lady's diary (Moore) 1790. **579**
Etrennes mignones (Desbarats) 1799. **1077**
Indian almanack 1798. **1078**
Moore's pocket almanack 1789, **548.** —1792, **694**
Neuschottländische Calender (Henry) 1788, **503.**—1789, **542.**—1790, **576.** —1791, **628.** —1792, **690.** —1793, **749.**—1794, **824.**—1797, **977**
Nova-Scotia calender (Henry) 1769, **119.**—1770, **127.**—1771, **143.**—1772, **156.**—1773, **163.**—1774, **169.**—1775, **184.**—1776, **195.**—1777, **224.**—1778, **247.**—1780, **302.**—1782, **350.**—1783, **366.**—1784, **388.**—1785, **411.**—1786, **447.**—1787, **472.**—1788, **504.**—1789, **543.**—1790, **577.**—1791, **629.**—1792, **691.**—1792, 2d. ed. **750.**—1793, **751.** —1794, **825.**—1795, **871.**—1796, **924.** 1797, **978.**—1798, **1036.**—1799, **1081.** —1800, **1112.**—1801, **1159**
Quebec almanack (Neilson) 1792, **695.** —1793(*not pub.*), **748.**—1794, **869.**—1795, **922.**—1796, **975.**—1797, **1033.** 1798, 1797, **1034.**—1799, 1798, **1079.** 1800, **1156.**—1801, **1157;** *see also*—Almanach de Québec
Upper Canada almanac (Tiffany) 1797 (*not pub.*), **979.**—1800, **1113.**—1801, **1160**
Almanacs, German, **503n**
Alphabets, *see* Primers
American Revolution. Articles prélim. de la paix, 1783. **399**
Cessation of arms, 1783. **398**
U.S. Extracts from papers, 1776. **246**
Amicable Society for extinguishing fires, Quebec. **371n**
List members, 1782. **371**
Rules & regulations, 1782. **372**
Ancient French archives, 1791. **734**
Annapolis-Royal, 1788. **571**
Anti-traditionist, 1783. **386**
Archives. Quebec: Ancient French, 1791. **734**
Au public (de Salaberry), 1792. **779**
Au roi . . . placet, 1791. **720**
Auction sales. Bowman: Catalogue books, 1787. **509**
Burns & Woolsey: Books wines, 1792. **755**
Dickson: Books, 1799. **1122**
Fargues: Books & furniture, 1780. **336**
Livius: Books, 1798. **1090**
Mabane & Gray: Libraries, 1792. **787**
Melvin & Wills: Books medicine wine, 1789. **597**
Furs, 1781. **356**
Phillips & Lane: Books, 1787. **526**
Saint John: Land, 1788. **568**
Sketchley & Freeman: Books, 1782. **384**
Books & jewellery, 1784. **443**
Toosey: Books, 1799. **1143**
Furniture stock hay, 1792. **814**
Vialar: Books, 1781. **363**
Walter: Books, 1795. **971**
Auguste (ship). **288n**
Aux canadiens, 1792. **763**
Aux citoyens et habitants, 1785. **453**
Aux electeurs de . . . Québec, 1792. **773**
Aux electeurs du Bas Canada, 1792. **777**
Aux libres electeurs . . . Hampshire, 1792. **775**
Aux libres electeurs . . . Québec, 1792. **766**
Avis au Canada, 1798. **1082**
Avis aux canadiens, 1792. **764**
Avis important aux electeurs, 1792. **765**

B

Baby, F. Lease king's posts, 1786. **497**
Badelard, P. L. F. **455n**
Direction mal de la baie, 1785. **454-55**
Baillargé, P. F. Elégie, 1792. **752**
Bailly de Messein, C. F. **214n; 635n**
Copy letter on education, 1790. **635**
Baptist Association. Articles, 1800. **1161**
Barclay, D. Walter: Answer, 1793. **866**
Bargeas, J. **103n**
Latin alphabets, 1767. **115n**
Barkly, G. Representations to publick, 1764. **36**
Bastille septentrionale, 1791. **739**
Batchellor, R. Reward, 1792. **789**
Bédard, T. L. **196n; 696n**
Lanaudière: To Bédard, 1791. **708**
Observ. on tenures, 1791. **696**
Thèses de mathématique, 1775. **196**
Belcher, *Chief Justice*. Proclamation Geo. III, 1761. **27**
Temporary acts N.S., 1767. **114n**
Belcher, *Mrs.* Abigail. Wood: Sermon on, 1771. **162**
Benevolent Societies, *see* Societies.
Bennett, J. *printer*. **1044n**
Montreal gazette, ***p.* 622**
Berczy, W. **1091n**
Berger, C. Gazette du com. et lit. **p. 622**
Berry, Sir E. **1114n**
Narrative, 1799. **1114**

Berthelot d'Artigny, M. A. Conversation election, 1792. **761**
Bill securing to creditors, 1795. **948**
Birnie & Jones. Bread tobacco, 1792. **753**
Bisset, G. **508n**
Brotherly unity sermon, 1787. **508**
Black market. N.S.: Price provisions, 1776. **236, 240n**
Quebec: Forestalling, 1779. **322, 324.** —1782, **382**
Blackwood, J., & co. Election circular, 1792. **762**
Blue & Orange, *see* Royal order of Blue & Orange.
Boissonault, J. Exercise rhetorique, 1792. **796**
Bonnefons, A. Petit livre de vie 1777, **251.** —1796? **980.** —1798, **1083.** —1800, **1162**
Book catalogues, **799n**
Bowman: Books, 1787. **509**
Burns & Woolsey: Auction, 1792. **755**
Cary: Circulating library, 1797. **1037**
Dickson: Sale, 1799. **1122**
Farques: Sale, 1780. **336**
Inglis: Charge, 1790. **641n**
Livius: Library to be sold, 1798. **1090**
Mabane & Gray: Libraries, 1792. **787**
Melvin & Wills: Auction, 1789. **597**
Neilson: Sale, 1800. **1188**
Phillips & Lane: 1787. **526**
Quebec Library: Catalogue 1783, **406.** —1785 ed., **466.**—1790 additions: **672.**—1792 ed. **799.**—1796 ed. **1015**
Sketchley & Freeman: Sale, 1782, **384.** —1784, **443**
Toosey: Auction, 1799. **1143**
Vialar: Auction, 1781. **363**
Walter: Auction, 1795. **971**
Botany. Wright: Catalogue seeds, 1767. **118**
Boucher-Belleville, J. B. **925n; 981n**
Recueil de cantiques 1795, **925.**—1796 ed. **981.**—1800 ed. **1163**
Bouchette, J. B. **327n**
Boutelier, G. F., & J. Trials murder, 1791. **697**
Bowman, J. **455n**
Catalogue books, 1787. **509**
Poem on Miss Wilcocks, 1784. **444**
Bread
L.C. Tarif, 1797. **1045**
N.S. Assize, 1776. **240n**
Brenton, J. **570n**
N.S. Petition & impeachment, 1790. **646**
Briand, *Bp.*: Lettre circulaire, 1777. **252**
Mandates, 1769. **133**
Mandement, 1777. **257n**
Britannica's intercession for John Wilkes, 1769. **134**
Brookville printing, **843n**
Brotherly love . . . sermon, 1780. **337**
Brown, A. **698n**
Discourse N. Br. Soc. 1791. **698**
Perils of the time, 1795. **926**
Sermon seafaring life, 1793. **826**
Brown, J. *dentist.* **754n**
Directions dentist, 1792. **754**
Brown, Wm. *printer.* **p. xiii; 663**
Printing charge, **197n; 531n**
Quebec gazette, **p. 629-33**
Bruyas, *Father.* Mohawk primer, 1777. **265n**
Brumoy, P. **229n**
Jonathas et David, 1776. **229**
Buchan, W. Domestic medicine, 1786. **476**
Bulkeley, R. Address N.S. 1785. **445n**
Halifax gazette, **p. 600**
Burgoyne, J. Manifesto, 1777. **253-54**
Burke, E. **651n**
Burn, R. Extract Burn's Justice, 1787. **528**
Juge à paix, 1789. **583**
Souscription, 1788. **549**
Burns, R. Poems (prospectus) 1789. **584**
Burns & Woolsey, *see also* Auction sales. Catalogue 1792. **755**
Bushell, J. *printer.* **p. 661**
Halifax gazette, **p. 599-600**
Halifax gaz. proposals, 1751-52. **1**
Byles, M. **1115n**
Victory, sermon, 1799. **1115**

C

Calcott, W. Candid disquisition Freemasons, 1784. **414**
Caldwell, H. **680n; p. 641**
Mohawk song, 1780. **334**
Calendar. N.S.: Alteration, 1752. **4**
Calendars, *see* Almanacs; Sheet almanacs
Campbell, *Gov. of N.S.* Proc. coal mines, 1767. **107-108**
Canada Co., *see* St. John's River Society
Canada constellation, **p. 649-50**
Canada paper money, 1766. **79-80; 91-92**
Canadian theatre. **1016n**
Canadian topographer, 1798. **1107**
Canadien: Avis au Canada, 1798. **1082**
Canadian curieux, *pseud.* **p. 622**
Canadiens, Adresse aux, 1775. **194**
Canals. N.S. Bill Shubenaccadie, 1798. **1097**
N.S. Report, 1797. **1059-60**
U.C. Bill L. Erie-Ontario, 1799. **1148**
Cantiques de l'ame dévoté, 1776. **232**
Cantiques de Marseilles, 1800. **1173**
Cape Breton. **858n**
Capitulations & . . . treaties, 1800. **1174**

Capsa, Bishop of, *see* Bailly de Messein, C. F.
Carleton, *Gov. of N.B.* Proclamations on:
Continuing officers, 1784. **423**
Illicit trade, 1784. **424**
Regulations for farms, 1785. **461**
Register land grants, 1784. **425**
Carleton, *Lt.-Gov. of Que.*, *see* Dorchester, *Gov.*
Carrier's addresses, *see under* Montreal gazette; Quebec gazette; Royal gazette, Halifax; Times, Quebec.
Cartel . . . exchange . . . deserters, 1752. **5**
Carters, Regulations for, 1780. **341**
Cary, T. **585n; 1092n**
Abram's plains, 1789. **585**
Catalogue library, 1797. **1037**
Cary's circulating library. **1037n**
Casot, J. J. **1164n**
Portrait, 1800. **1164**
Catalogue . . . household furniture, 1792. **814**
Catéchisme de Québec 1777, **255.**—1782 ed. **373A.**—1791 ed. **699-700.**—1796 ed. **982.**—1798 ed. **1084.**—undated: **1202;** *see also* Petit catéchisme.
Catéchisme . . . de Sens 1765, **59.**—1766 ed. **76**
Catholic Church, *see also* Briand, Denaud, Esglis, Hubert, Plessis, Pontbriand, *Bp.*
Abridgement christian doctrine, 1800. **1165**
Abstract Douay catechism, 1778. **280**
Bishop's mandates, 1769. **133**
Catéchisme de Québec 1777, **255.**—1782 ed. **373A.**—1791 ed. **699-700.**—1796 ed. **982.**—1798 ed. **1084.**—undated: **1202**
Catéchisme de Sens 1765, **59.**—1766 ed. **76**
Dévotion aux anges, 1783. **394**
Formulaire de prières 1777, **258.**—1799 ed. **1116**
Gradual romain, 1800. **1166-67**
Heures de vie, 1769. **135**
Heures romaines, 1795. **927**
Journée du chrétien 1795, **928.**—1797 ed. **1038**
La Marche: Lettre, 1793. **833**
La Poterie: Requête, 1789. **596**
Missa, 1777. **256**
Neuvaine 1772, **165.**—1778 ed. **283.**—1796 ed. **983**
Office semaine sainte, 1778. **282**
Officium, 1777. **257**
Petit catéchisme 1782, **373B.**—1791 ed. **701**
Pseautier, 1774 **186.**—1782 ed. **374.**—1785 ed. **456**
Sincere Catholick's companion 1778, **281.**—1800 ed. **1168**
Vêpres hymnes, 1796. **984**
Cawthorne, J. Considerations . . . state . . . trade, 1766. **77**
Census. Hubert: Lettre circulaire, 1789. 593
Que.: Rôle des paroissiens, 1790. **668**
Chanson pour la fête, 1799. **1117**
Charge . . . clergy of N.S. . . . 1788, 1789. **594**
Charge . . . clergy of N.S. . . . 1791, 1792. **759**
Charges . . . free . . . masons, 1786. **480**
Charland, L. Canadian topographer, 1798. **1107**
Chipman, *Mrs.* Jane, Sermon on, 1775. **212**
Church of England, *see also* Inglis, Mountain, *Bp.*
Address from clergy N.B., 1792. **756**
Address of clergy N.S., 1788. **550**
Form of prayer & thanksgiving, 1789. **586-88**
Form of prayer for fast, 1793. **827**
Form of prayer for fast, 1794. **872**
Form of prayer for fast, 1796. **985**
Form of prayer for fast, 1797. **1039**
Form of prayer for fast, 1798. **1085**
Form of prayer for victory, 1797. **1118**
Order for prayer Mohawk, 1780. **335**
Prayers for legislature, 1793. **848**
Scott: Appointment to Sorel, 1782. **383**
Church of Scotland. Catechism, 1790. **636**
Churches. Quebec: Build & repair, 1791. **726, 729, 730**
Clarke, *Lt.-Gov.* L.C. Proclamations on:
Continuing officers, 1791. **735**
Constitutional act: **704-705n; 1184**
Counties & election 1792, **786; 1184**
Privateers, 1793. **841**
Settle lands, 1792. **784-85**
Claus, D. **335n**
La Brosse: Nehiro-iriniui, 1767. **105n**
Order for prayer Mohawk, 1780. **335**
Primer Mohawk, 1781. **355**
Clery, J. Journal Louis XVI 1798, **1086-87.**—1798 ed. **1119**
Coal. N.S.: Proc. mines, 1767. **107-108**
Cobbett, W. **1120n**
Democratic principles, 1799. **1120**
Cochran, W. **828n**
Nova-Scotia magazine, **p. 653-54**
Sermon Falmouth, 1793. **828**
Cock, D. **557n**
Cockburn, J. Court martial, 1783. **395**
Cockrel, R. **929n**
Thoughts on education, 1795. **929**
Collection . . . acts . . . Canada, 1800. **1169**
Collection . . . poems (prospectus) 1789. **589**
Collection papers . . . Oliver . . . sheriff, 1791. **717**
Collège de Montréal. **115n; 116n**
Jonathas et David, 1776. **229**

L'Homond: Grammaire latine, 1796. **988-89**
Thèses de mathématique, 1800. **1186**
Collège des Jésuites. **65n**
Colman, G. Jealous wife, 1770. **145**
Comingoe, B. R. **155n**
Comité canadien. **415n**
Objections aux demandes, 1784. **434**
St. Ours: Au public, 1784. **441**
Très-humble adresse, 1784. **435**
Commentaire sur Delanaudière, 1792. **770**
Commissioners of the peace, Quebec. **216; 241-42**
Confessions.
Cope & Heney: Two letters, 1786. **477**
Fitzgerald & Clark: Last words, 1790. **637**
Mahir: Confession, 1785. **459**
Tool & Wallace: Dying speech, 1782. **385**
Confrèrie de l'adoration. Reglement, 1776. **230-31**
Confrèrie de la Ste. Famille. Solide dévotion, 1787. **510**
Considerations . . . college . . . Quebec, 1799. **1123**
Constitution, Scheme of, 1791. **682**
Constitutional act, 1791. **704-705; 786n; 1040-41; 1184n**
Lymburner: Paper, 1791. **709**
Lymburner: Papier, 1791. **710**
Que.: Proc. 1791. **704-705n;** 1800 ed. **1184**
Solon: New constitution, 1792. **813**
Constitutional club. **p. 360** *footnote.*
Dialogue, 1792. **767**
Dumas: Speech, 1792. **768**
Lanaudière: Discours, 1792. **772A**
Solon: New constitution, 1792. **813**
Consultation of 2 lawyers, 1778. **289**
Conversation . . . election, 1792. **761**
Cope, J. B. N.S.: Treaty Indians, 1752. **9**
Copes, F., & T. Heney. Two letters, 1786. **477**
Copy . . . letter . . . Bishop of Capsa . . . on education, 1790. **635**
Coquart, *Father* C. G. **147n**
Courier de Québec. **p. 620-22**
Prospectus, 1788. **551**
Prospectus, 1789. **590**
Court martial, J. Cockburn, 1783. **395**
Courts of justice, *see also* Justices of the peace.
Boutelier: Trials murder, 1791. **697**
L.C.: Causes in appeal, 1792. **782**
Judicature act, 1794. **880, 889-90**
Judicature bill, 1793. **838-40**
King's bench, 1792. **783**
McLane: Procès, 1797. **1054**
Trial, 1797. **1055-56**
N.S.: Impeachment judges, 1790. **646**
Que.: Act practice law (draft), 1789. **603**
Decrees military court, 1764. **48**
Draught of act adm. justice, 1787. **436**
Grands et petits jurés, 1767. **117**
Law in civil causes, 1791. **723; 728**
Ordinance court King's bench, 1787. **531**
Ordinance regulating, 1770. **152**
Projet d'acte adm. justice, 1787. **537**
Regulate & estab. 1764. **49-55**
Three Rivers, 1790. **656**
Sterns & Taylor: Impeachment of judges, 1788. **570**
Sterns & Taylor: Reply to judges, 1789. **621**
Taylor: For public information, 1790. **679**
Ursulines v. Lemaitre Duème, 1779. **311-12**
Walter: Defence, 1790. **680**
Watson & Rashleigh v. Du Calvet, 1778-79. **284-85; 313**
Coutûme de Paris, 1796. **1004**
Cow-pox. Hubert: Discours, 1783. **390n**
Cramahé, *Lt.-Gov. of Que*. Proclamation on:
Embargo, 1775. **221-23**
Strangers to register, 1775. **220**
Creditors. L.C. bill securing, 1795. **948**
Creepers, Handbill forbidding, 1787. **519**
Cugnet, F. J. **197n**
Extraits des édits, 1775. **200**
Traité de la loi des fiefs, 1775. **197**
Traité de la police, 1775. **199**
Traité des ancienes loix, 1775. **198**
Cull, H. Des cendres, 1795. **930**
Currency.
L.C.: Weight & rates gold coin, 1796. **1001**
Que.: Canada paper money, 1766. **79-80; 91-92**
Ordinance regulating, 1764. **46-47**
St. John I.: Paper money, 1792. **802**

D

Davison, A. & G. King's posts, 1786. **497**
Day, J. Essay Nova-Scotia, 1774. **187n**
DeBonne, P. A. **873n**
A mes compatriotes, 1784. **415**
Aux canadiens, 1792. **763**
Avis aux canadiens, 1792. **764**
Avis important, 1792. **765**
Précis d'un acte, 1794. **873**
Probus: Aux electeurs, 1792. **777n**
Debtors. N.S.: Relief, 1752. **6**
Declaration of Independence, U.S. cf. **246n**
Defence . . . prosecution . . . libel . . . Caldwell, 1790. **680**
Delanaudière, C. L., *see* Lanaudière, C. L. de

Delaroche, P. **177n**
Doctrinal commentary, 1783. **396**
Gospel of Christ, 1773. **177**; 1787 ed. **511**
Delisle, D. C. **512n**
Sermon mort de Frobisher, 1787. **512**
DeLisle de la Cailleterie. Administration de fabrique, 1777. **259**
Democratic principles, 1799. **1120**
Denaut, *Bp.* A tous les vicaires, 1800. **1170**
Circulaire 28 Nov. 1799. **1121**
Mandement graces publiques, 1798. **1088**
Mandement (Pius VII) 1800. **1171**
Dentist. Brown: Directions, 1792. **754**
DePeyster, A., *see* Peyster, A. de.
Dermott, L. Ahiman rezon, 1786. **480**
Deschamps, I. **570n**
Impeachment, 1790. **646**
Perpetual acts N.S., 1784. **428n**
Deschenaux, L. Aux libres electeurs, 1792. **766**
Deserters. N.S. Cartel exchange, 1752. **5**
N.S. Proclamation 1793, **851**; 1796, **1011**
Destruction of feudal monster, 1791. **702**
Dévotion aux S.S. anges gardiens, 1783. **394**
Devotional books
Bonnefons: Petit livre 1777, **251.**—1798 ed. **1083.**—1800 ed. **1162**
Boucher-Belleville: Recueil de cantiques 1795, **925.**—1796 ed. **981.**—1800 ed. **1163**
Catholic Church: Abridgement of christian doctrine, 1800. **1165**
Abstract Douay catechism 1778, **280.**—1800, **1168n**
Catéchisme de Québec 1777, **255.**—1782 ed. **373A.**—1791 ed. **699-700.**—1796 ed. **982.**—1798 ed. **1084.**—undated, **1202**
Catéchisme de Sens 1765, **59.**—1766 ed. **76**
Dévotion aux anges gardiens, 1783. **394**
Formulaire de prières 1777, **258.**—1799 ed. **1116**
Gradual romain, 1800. **1166-67**
Heures de vie, 1769. **135**
Heures romaines, 1795. **927**
Journée du chrétien 1795, **928.**—1797 ed. **1038**
Missa, 1777. **256**
Neuvaine 1772, **165.**—1778 ed. **283.**—1796 ed. **983**
Office semaine sainte, 1778. **282**
Officium, 1777. **257**
Petit catéchisme, 1782. **373B.** —1791 ed. **701**
Pseautier 1774, **186.**—1782 ed. **374.**—1785 ed. **456**
Sincere Catholick's companion 1778, **281.**—1800 ed. **1168**
Vêpres hymnes, 1796. **984**
Church of England: Form of prayer & thanksgiving, 1789. **586-88**
Form of prayer for fast, 1793. **827**
Form of prayer for fast, 1794. **872**
Form of prayer for fast, 1796. **985**
Form of prayer for fast, 1797. **1039**
Form of prayer for fast, 1798. **1085**
Form of prayer for victory, 1799. **1118**
Order for prayer Mohawk, 1780. **335**
Church of Scotland: Shorter catechism, 1790. **636**
Claus: Primer Mohawk, 1781. **355**
Confrèrie de l'adoration: Reglement, 1776. **230-31**
Confrèrie de la Ste. Famille, 1787. **510**
Delaroche: Doctrinal commentary, 1783. **396**
Delaroche: Gospel of Christ 1773. **177.**—2d. ed. 1787, **511**
Doyle: Universal prayer, 1770. **146**
DuMonceau: Exercise, 1777. **260**
Durand: Cantiques 1776, **232.**—1800 ed. **1173**
Grand alphabet, 1800. **1194**
Histoire abregée Ste. Vierge, 1797. **1042**
Humbert: Instructions chrétiennes 1798, **1089.**—1799 ed. **1126**
Hymn St. Paul's Halifax, 1788. **555**
Iontri8aiestsk8a (Mohawk) 1777. **265**
LaBrosse: *Nehiro-iriniui* Montagnais, 1767. **105**
Prières de la congregation, *n.d.* **1204**
Scott: Brief view, 1784. **442**
Thayer: Relation, 1794. **912**
Dialogue between Andre & Brigite, 1794. **874**
Dialogue sur l'interêt du jour, 1792. **767**
Dickson, S. **1123n**
Catalogue books, 1799. **1122**
Establishment college, 1799. **1123**
Union taste & science, 1799. **1124**
Direction pour la guerison du mal de la baie, 1785. **454-55**
Directory for . . . Quebec 1790, **650.**—1791 ed. **718**
Discours . . . Lanaudière, 1792. **772A**
Discours . . . victoire, 1799. **1140**
Discourse . . . North British Soc., 1791. **698**
Diseases, *see* Cow pox; Mal de la baie St. Paul; Yellow fever
Disney, D. Trial, 1767. **103**
Dissertation on Revelation, 1800. **1172A**
Dodsley, R. Select fables Æsop, 1800. **1172B**
Domestic medicine, 1786. **476**
Donegane, *rope-dancer.* Handbill, 1788. **552**

Dorchester, *Gov. of Que. & L.C.*
Alphabet for, 1788. **561**
Aveu seigniories, 1777. **266**
Memorial to, on tenures, 1791. **719**
Proclamation on: Barracks & fuel for troops, 1786. **493**
Commissioners of the peace, 1775. **216**
Continuing officers, 1766. **97-98**
Culture of hemp, 1791. **721**
Embargo cattle & grain, 1777. **267**
Embargo on wheat, 1795. **939**
Free import & export, 1787. **529**
Habitants enlist, 1775. **218**
Judicature act, 1794. **880**
Martial law, 1775. **217**
Noncombattants & deserters, 1776. **244**
Noncombattants quit town, 1775. **219**
Outrages on Indians, 1766. **99**
Sedition, 1793. **834**
Winter roads, cleared, 1776. **245**
Wounded rebels, 1776. **243**
Doty, J. **478n**
Advice on piety & vice, 1787. **513**
Sermon, 1786. **478**
Douay catechism 1778, **280.**—1800, **1168n**
Doyle, W. **146n**
Universal prayer, 1770. **146**
Drama, *see also* Quebec Theatre
Brumoy: Jonathas et David, 1776. **229**
Jealous wife, 1770. **145**
Monde demasqué, 1775. **214**
Draught of an act . . . administration of justice . . . Que., 1787. **536**
DuCalvet, P. **284n**
Défenses, 1778. **284**
Dupliques, 1778. **285**
Mémoire, 1779. **313**
Dumas, A. Explanation of constitution, 1792. **813n**
Speech, 1792. **768**
DuMonceau, A. Exercise S. Antoine, 1777. **260**
Duport, *Judge.* Temporary acts N.S., 1767. **114n**
Dunière, L. Services facteur de grains, 1792. **757**
Durand, L. Cantiques 1776, **232.**—1800 ed. **1173**
Dutch Reformed Church. Religion in Nisqueunia, 1781. **347**
Seccombe: Sermon 1770. **155**
Dying speech . . . Tool & Wallace, 1782. **385**

E

L'écu de six francs, 1784. **416**
Education, *see also* Primers
Bailly de Messein: Letter, 1790. **635**
Cockrel: Thoughts on, 1795. **929**
Collège de Montréal: Thèses, 1800. **1186**
Dickson: College in Quebec, 1799. **1123**
L'Homond: Grammaire française, 1800. **1177**
Grammaire latine 1797, **1044.**—1799 ed. **1128**
Grammaire latine methode, 1796. **989**
Grammaire latine syntaxe, 1796. **988**
Langue latine, 1799. **1127**
N.S.: Bill for schools, 1800. **1189**
Quebec: Report on means, 1790. **669**
Sanguinet: Bequest university, 1791. **737n**
Séminaire de Québec: Exercise rhetorique, 1792. **796**
Palmare 1773, **183.**—1775, **215**
Quod felix (palmare), 1770. **151**
Thèses de mathématique 1775, **196.**—1790, **651.**—1792, **797.**—1796, **1012**
Edwards, E. *printer.* Montreal gazette, **p. 623, 628-29**
84th Regiment of Foot. MacLean: Land to volunteers, 1779. **314-15**
Quebec: Land to veterans, 1790. **664**
Elégie, 1792. **752**
Elégie sur le funeste évênement, 1792. **810**
Elemens de la grammaire française, 1800. **1177**
Elemens de la grammaire latine, methode, 1796. **989**
Elemens de la grammaire latine, syntaxe, 1796. **988**
Elemens de la langue latine, 1799. **1127**
Elements de la grammaire latine, 1797. **1044**
Elements de la grammaire latine, 1799. **1128**
Embargo. L.C.: Wheat, 1795. **939**
N.S.: Ships with provisions, 1757. **12**
Que.: Cattle & grain, 1777. **267**
Wheat, flower & biscuit, 1778. **297**
Wheat; forestalling, 1779. **322**
Eminaud, F. Boutelier: Trials murder, 1791. **697**
Engravings, *see* Illustrations
Entertainment, *see also* Quebec Theatre
Donegane: Feats of activity, 1788. 552
Mensforth: Automate, 1792. **788**
Partridge: Feats of horsemanship, 1787. **525**
Rickets: Circus, 1798. **1102**
Esglis, *Bp.* **457n**
Circulaire (mal de la baie) 1786. **479, 496**
Lettre circulaire, 1785. **457**
Essay on . . . state . . . Nova-Scotia, 1774. **187**

Etrennes du garçon, see *Montreal gazette*. Carrier's address; *Quebec gazette*. Carrier's address
Etrennes mignones pour 1799, 1798. **1077**
Exemple de la France, avis, 1794. **919**
Exercise sur la rhetorique, 1792. **796**
Exercise très-devot, 1777. **260**
Exercises . . . Collège de Montréal, 1800. **1186**
Explanations . . . manual exercise . . . Foot, 1759. **15**
Extract . . . minutes . . . Council . . . waste lands, 1798. **1091-92**
Extrait d'un discours, 1795. **972**
Extraits des édits, 1775. **200**

F

Falconer, T. St. John's R. soc. 1766. **101**
False imprints. Pontbriand: Mandement, 1759. **21-22**
  Restif de la Bretonne: Lucile, 1768. **126A**
  Young freemason's assistant, 1765. **60**
Fanning, *Gov. of St. John I.* **569n**
  Address of Assembly to, 1790. **673**
    of citizens to, 1792. **803-806**
  Proclamation: Import. bread, 1789. **620**
    Notification militia corps, 1794. **910**
    Public fast day May 10, 1794. **909**
  Reply to Assembly, 1790. **678**
  Speech to Assembly, 1790. **677**
Fargues, P. Catalogue books, 1780. **336**
Ferries, Rates for, 1766. **86A**
Ferries, Regulations for 1766, **86B.**—1780, **341**
Fillis, J. **801n**
  Ritchie: Discourse on, 1792. **801**
Finlay, H. **153n**
  Election circular, 1792. **769**
  Song, 1783. **397**
Fire societies, *see* Amicable society, Quebec; Friendly fire club, Shelburne
Fisheries. L.C.: Abstract ordinance, 1797. **1053**
  Quebec: Bill, 1789. **609n**
  Saint John: Law, 1797. **1068**
Fitzgerald, W. M., & J. Clark. Last words, 1790. **637**
Fletcher, R. *printer*. **p. 662;** Nova Scotia gazette, **p. 601-602**
For public information, 1790. **679**
Form of prayer . . . 10th May 1793. **827**
Form of prayer . . . 10th Jan. 1799. **1118**
Formulaire de prières . . . Ursulines, 1799. **1116**
Formule . . . rôle des paroissiens, 1790. **668**
Fort-Midway, *see* Port Medway
Food conservation, *see also* Black market; Embargo.
  Quebec: Grain, cattle, provisions 1781, **360.**—1782, **379.**—1783, **404**
Food shortage. St. John I.: Import. bread, 1789. **620**
France. Actes des apôtres, 1791. **682**
  Avis au Canada, 1798. **1082**
  Clery: Journal de Louis XVI, 1798, **1086-87.**—1799 ed. **1119**
  Destruction feudal monster, 1791. **702**
  L'écu de six francs, 1784. **416**
  Histoire abregée Ste. Vierge, 1797. **1042**
  Hubert: Circulaire, 1793. **831**
  Inglis: Steadfastness, 1793. **832**
  La Roche du Maine: Paris, 1784. **420**
  L.C.: Proclamation privateers, 1793. **841**
  Marie Antoinette, 1795. **949**
  Mort du roi, 1793. **842**
  New constitution, 1792. **758**
  N.S.: Proclamation privateers, 1793. **849**
  Quebec gazette, **p. 634**
  Watson: Extrait d'un discours, 1795. **972**
  Young: Exemple de la France, 1794. **919**
Fraser, M. **737n**
Fraternal societies, *see* Freemasons; Royal order of blue & orange
Fredericton printing, **790n; 952n; 954n**
Freemasons: Account N.S., 1786. **480n**
  Bisset: Sermon, 1787. **508**
  Calcott: Candid disquisition, 1784. **414**
  Charges & regulations, 1786. **480**
  Elements, or Pocket companion, 1786. **481**
  Henry: Brotherly love, 1780. **337**
  Spark: Oration, 1787. **541**
  Tunstall: Sermon, 1798. **1103**
  Viets: Sermon Digby, 1793. **865**
  Weeks: Sermon, 1785. **471**
  Young freemason's assistant, 1765. **60**
Frères et compatriotes, 1784. **417**
Friendly fire club, Shelburne, N.S. **931n**
  Rules 1784, **418.**—1795, **931**
Frobisher, B. **512n**
  Delisle: Sermon, 1787. **512**
Fur trade. Instructions pour voyageurs, 1779. **321**
  Melvin & Wills: Catalogue furs, 1781. **356**
  Quebec: Inland navigation & trade, 1791. **722; 728**

G

Gale, S. **1091n**
Gay & Merlin, *printers*. Nova Scotia gazette, **p. 606**
Gazette du commerce et litteraire, **p. 622-23; 291n**
  Prospectus, 1778. **286-87**
General Haldimand, (ship). **356n**
General orders for the militia, 1790. **652**

George III. Form of prayer for, 1789. **586-88**
H.M. recovery, 1789. **591**
N.S.: Proclaiming H.M., 1761. **27**
Gilmore, T. *printer.* **p. 663;** Quebec gazette, **p. 629-31**
Glenie, J. **932n**
Pamphlet, 1795. **932**
Goragh asharegowa, 1779. **325**
Gospel of Christ preached to the poor 1773, **177.**—2d. ed. 1787, **511**
Government printer, *see* King's printer
Graduel romain . . . de Québec, 1800. **1166-67**
Graham, H. **1125n**
Two sermons, 1799. **1125**
Grant, W. **722n**
Commentaire, 1792. **770**
Gravé de la Rive, H. F. **983n**
Gray, A. Catalogue library, 1792. **787**
Great Britain.
Adjutant-General. Manual exercise 1759, **15.**—1787, **514.**—1788, **553**
Rules formations, 1793. **829**
Commission . . . losses of loyalists. Notice Montreal, 1788. **554**
Laws. Abstracts, 1765. **61-62**
Commission losses loyalists, 1785. **458**
Constitutional act, 1791, **704-705; 786n; 1040-41; 1184n**
Encourage settlers, 1791. **703**
Extraits, 1765. **62**
Forestalling, regrating, 1779. **324n**
Prize act, 1795. **933**
Quebec act 1774: **188;** 1791: **706;** 1797: **1040-41**
Shipping & navigation, 1786. **482**
Stamp act 1766. **78**
Statutes on timber, 1784. **419**
Parliament. H.M. recovery, 1789. **591**
Post Office. General instructions, 1790? **638**
Rates of postage, n.d. **1203**
Proclamation. Cessation of arms, 1783. **398**
Proc. Oct. 7, 1763, 1800. **1174n**
Suppress rebellion, 1776. **234**
Treaties. Amity & commerce (Jay) 1795, **934-36.**—1796, **986**
Articles prélim. de la paix, 1783. **399**
Canada paper money, 1766. **79-80**
Capitulations & extracts, **1174**
Green, Bartholomew, *printer.* **1**
Green, Benjamin. **301n**
Green, *Mrs.* M. Seccombe: Sermon on, 1778. **301**
Green, W. British American almanac, 1791. **688**

H

Haldimand, *Gov. of Quebec.*
Declaration to Ohio settlers, 1780. **342**
Proclamation: Embargo wheat 1778. **297**
Embargo wheat, forestalling, 1779. **322**
Fealty & hommage seigneurs, 1778. **298**
Forestallers ordinance, 1782. **380**
Forestalling, regrating, 1779. **324**
Grain, cattle provisions 1781, **360.**—1782, **379.**—1783, **404**
Instructions militia, 1779. **323**
Speech to Oneidas, 1779. **325**
Halifax, N.S. Coroner. Inquisition, 1752. **2**
Justices of peace. Handbills, 1776. **240**
St. Paul's church. Hymn, 1788. **555**
View of harbour, 1775. **195n**
Halifax gazette, **p. 599-601**
Proposals, 1751-52. **1**
Halifax journal, **p. 610-612**
Halifax marine society, **483n; 826n**
Brown: Sermon, 1793. **826**
Laws, 1786. **483**
Hand-bill for enlisting sailors, 1775. **201**
Hart, *see* Nathans & Hart
Hay, J. Answers to libel, 1764. **37**
Hemp. Circular, 1791. **685, 687**
Quebec: Notice of seed, 1791. **721**
Heney, T. Two letters, 1786. **477**
Henry, A. **p. 661-2;** death, **1159n**
Halifax gazette, **p. 600-601**
Nova Scotia chronicle, **p. 602-604**
Nova-Scotia gazette, **p. 604-605**
Royal gazette, **p. 605**
Welt, **p. 619**
Henry, *Mrs.* A., **p. 606; p. 662**
Henry, G. **337n**
Brotherly love sermon, 1780. **337**
Hesse, District. Deeds & writings, 1789. **603-605, 608**
Heures romaines, 1795. **927**
Histoire abregée de la Sainte Vierge, 1797. **1042**
Hochstetter, J.G. *engraver.* D.A. Hubert, 1793. **830**
Etat primitif, 1794. **869n**
Printing press, 1791. **695n**
Quebec magazine, **p. 657**
Hope, *Lt.-Gov. of Que.* Circulaire (mal de la baie) 1786. **496**
Proclamations on: Continuing officers, 1785. **465**
Ordres du quartier general, 1787. **538**
Trade with Indians, 1786. **497**
Hopkins, S. Pot ashes, 1791. **727, 731**
Hopson, *Gov. of N.S.* Proclamations on:
Alteration calendar, 1752. **4**
Cartel exchange deserters, 1752. **5**
Militia, 1753. **7**
Treaty with Indians, 1753. **9**
Howe, J. *printer.* **p. 662; 366n**
Halifax journal, **p. 610-611**

Nova-Scotia magazine, **p. 653-55**
Nova-Scotia royal gazette, **p. 606**
Hubert, A. D. **752n**
Baillargé: Elégie, 1792. **752**
Discours (cow-pox), 1783. **390n**
Sarreau: Elégie, 1792. **810**
Suite de l'elégie, 1792. **811**
Sermon conversion, 1796. **987**
Portrait, 1793. **830**
Hubert, *Bp.* Circulaire (France) 1793. **831**
Lettre circulaire (census) 1789. **593**
Lettre circulaire (liquor licences) 1787. **515**
Lettre circulaire (map) 1790. **639**
Lettre circulaire (militia) 1790. **640**
Lettre circulaire (seed grain) 1789. **592**
Mandement du 28 Oct. 1794. **875**
Mandement jour de fêtes, 1791. **707**
Mandement jurisdiction des prêtres, 1788. **556**
Quebec: Report education, 1790. **669n**
Humbert, P. H. Instructions chrétiennes 1798, **1089.**—1799 ed. **1126**
Humble adresse des anciens et nouveaux sujets, 1790. **653**
Humble petition . . . impeachment . . . Deschamps . . . Brenton, 1790. **646**
Humphreys, J. *printer.* **p. 668**
Nova-Scotia packet, **p. 612-13**
Hunter, *Lt.-Gov. of U.C.* Proclamations on:
Royal assent to reserved bills, 1800. **1200**
Session of parliament, 1800. **1201**

I

Illustrations, *see also* Maps
Bonnefons: Petit livre, 1777. **251n**
Casot: Portrait, 1800. **1164**
Hochstetter: D. A. Hubert, 1793. **830;** Etat primitif 1794, **869n;** printing press, 1791. **695n**
Marie Antoinette, 1795. **949**
Montreal, 1799. **1134**
Neuschottländische Calender 1788. **503n**
Nova-Scotia calender 1776. **195n**
Quebec almanac, 1794. **869n**: 1799. **1079n**
Quebec magazine, **p. 658**
Vue de la guillotine, 1793. **842**
Indians.
Almanack or Calendar (Montagnais) 1769-72, **129-32.**—1773-78, **171-76.** —1779-85, **273-79.**—1779-86, **304-310.**—1798, **1078**
Catalogue Tadousak, 1767. **104**
C. of E.: Order for prayer Mohawk, 1780. **335**
Haldimand: Speech to Oneidas, 1779. **325**
Kalendrier perpétuel 1766. **75**
Mohawk primer, 1777. **265**
Mohawk song & dance, 1780. **334**
Nehiro-iriniui Montagnais prayer book, 1767. **105**
N.S.: Price on Indians (Micmac), 1756. **10**
Treaty Mickmack Indians, 1753. **9**
Primer (Abnaki) 1770. **147**
Primer (Montagnais) 1767. **106**
Quebec: Proclamation outrages on, 1766. **99**
Sale of rum, 1791. **722; 728**
U.C.: Proc. sale of rum, 1794. **917-18**
Inglis, *Bp.* **555n; 641n; 1039n**
Address from clergy & answer, 1792. **756**
Address of clergy & answer, 1788. **550**
Charge to clergy June 1788. **594**
Charge to clergy Aug. 1789. **641**
Charge to clergy June 1791. **759**
Injunctions to clergy Quebec, 1789. **595**
Prayers for legislature, 1793. **848**
Questions to clergy, 1794. **876**
Sermon Apr. 25, 1794 general fast. **877**
Sermon before Assembly Nov. 25, 1787. **516**
Steadfastness in religion (sermon) 1793. **832**
Inoculation. Latham's advertisement, 1768-86. **136n**
Instructions chrétiennes, 1798. **1089;** 1799 ed. **1126**

J

Jarvis, Wm. To electors, 1800. **1197**
Jarvis, *Mrs.* Wm., letter on printer. **860n**
Jautard, V. Gazette du com. et lit. **p. 622**
Jay treaty 1795, **934-36.**—1796 ed. **986; 992n**
Jealous wife a comedy, 1770. **145**
Johnston, J. Presentments of grand jury, 1765. **66**
Representations de la séance, 1765. **67**
Johnston & Purss. Directions for brewing spruce, 1783. **400**
Jonathas et David, 1776. **229**
Jones, J. Times, **p. 644**
Jones, R. Remarks on molbay disease, 1786. **484**
Remarques maladie de la baie, 1787. **517**
Jordan, J. St. John's R. Society, 1766. **101**
Journal . . . de Louis XVI, 1798, **1086-87.** —1799 ed. **1119**
Journal du voyage de M. Saint-Luc, 1778. **288**
Journée du chrétien 1795, **928.**—1797 ed. **1038**
Jouve. Concert, 1792. **760**

Juge à paix . . . Québec, 1789. **583**
Justices of the peace, **68n; 240n;** *see also* Quebec. Quarter sessions; Shelburne, N.S. Quarter sessions
Burn: Juge à paix, 1789. **549, 583**
L.C.: Petition to Assembly, 1795. **941**
Quebec: Act to regulate police, 1789. **607**
Appointment, 1764. **44-45**
Police, 1791. **724, 728**

K

Kent, *Duke of*, **1175n**
Order on rations, 1800. **1175**
King, W. C. **1176n**
Sermon, 1800. **1176**
King's, or government, printer, **p. xiii**
Brown, W. **p. 633**
Desbarats & Lelievre, **1051n**
Henry, A. **p. 605**
Howe, J. **p. 611**
Rind, W. A. **p. 668**
Robertson, J. *Sr.* **p. 667**
Ryan, W. A. **p. 599**
Sower, C. **559n; p. 595**
Vondenvelden, W. **943n; 1051n**
Waters & Simons, **p. 651**

L

Labadie, L. **p. 547** *footnote*
Labrador, a poem, 1790. **643**
LaBrosse, J. B. de. **75n; 105n**
Akitami (Abnaki primer) 1770. **147**
Bishop's mandates, 1769. **133n**
Catalogue Indians, 1767. **104**
Indian almanack 1779-85, 1778. **273-79**
Indian calendar 1769-72, 1769. **129-32**
Indian calendar 1773-78, 1773. **171-76**
Indian calendar 1779-86? 1779. **304-310**
Indian kalendar, 1768. **122**
Nehiro-iriniui (prayer book) 1767. **105**
Primer Montagnais, 1767. **106**
LaCorne. Journal du voyage, 1778. **288**
Laforce, P. Song, 1797. **1043**
La Marche, J. F. de. Lettre aux ecclésiastiques, 1793. **833**
Lanaudière, C. L. T. de Chanson, 1792. **771**
Consultation, 1778. **289**
Discours, 1792. **772A**
Grant: Commentaire, 1792. **770**
Handbill Deschenaux, 1792. **772B**
Speech, 1792. **772C**
To M. Bédard, 1791. **708**
Land grants & sales
Auction Bass River N.S., 1788. **568**
Address to refugees R. St. John, 1784. **426**
L.C.: Claims on survey warrant, 1775. **938**
Extract on waste lands, 1798. **1091-92**
Notice lots at Wm. Henry, 1799. **1132**
Procedure for warrants, 1794. **878-79**
Proclamation settle lands, 1792. **784-85**
Proc. squatters, 1797. **1048**
MacLean: To volunteers, 1779. **314-15**
Melville: Accurate history, 1784. **421**
N.B.: Register, 1784. **425**
Regulations, 1785. **461**
N.S.: Acadians' lands, 1758. **13**
Free application, 1759. **16**
Possession Acadians' lands, 1759. **18**
Que.: Locations in Lunenburg, 1790. **665**
Loyalists' sons & daughters, 1789. **615**
Ordres du quartier general, 1787. **538**
Refugee loyalists, 1784. **439**
Rules land-office dept. 1789. **613-14**
Rules land office, 1790. **663-64**
St. John's R. Soc.: Descrip. townships, 1768. **126B**
Descrip. townships, 1783. **410**
Grants, 1766. **101**
U.C.: Dereham & Norwich, 1799. **1144, 1146**
Expences of survey, 1796. **1027**
Fees on, 1798. **1104**
Forfeiture, 1796. **1025**
Frauds in fee-free grants, 1799. **1147**
Land boards, fees schedule 1794, **915-16.**—1795, **966**
Loyalists' fee-free, 1798. **1105**
Loyalists' tickets, 1795. **970**
Notice to claimants, 1796. **1029**
Pitchers, 1799. **1145**
Proc. settle lands 1792, **815-16.**—1795 ed. **968-69**
Register claims, 1793. **860**
Township grants, 1797. **1071**
Yonge St. settlers, 1798. **1106**
Land tenures
Address to husbandmen, 1791. **683**
Bédard: Observations, 1791. **696**
Lanaudière: To Bédard, 1791. **708**
Memorial of seigniors, 1791. **719**
Que.: Ancient Fr. archives, 1791. **734**
Aveu seigniories, 1777. **266**
Extract proceedings, 1790. **667**
Placet des sujets, 1791. **720**
Languet de Gergy, J. J. Catéchisme de Sens 1765, **59.**—1766 ed. **76**
La Poterie. Requête, 1789. **596**
LaRoche du Maine, J. P. L. de. Paris en miniature, 1784. **420**

Latham, J. Regiments for children, 1769. **136**
Lawrence, *Gov. of N.S.* Proclamations on:
Acadians' lands, 1758. **13**
Land applications free, 1759. **16**
Price on Indians, 1756. **10**
Soldiers to work, 1758. **14**
Laws, *see under* Great Britain, Lower Canada, New Brunswick, Nova Scotia, Quebec, Saint John, N.B., St. John Island, Upper Canada; *also* Quebec. Quarter sessions; Shelburne, N.S. Quarter sessions
Laws, "due publication" of, 1765, **71-72.** —1794, **943n**
Lebrun de Duplessis, J. B. **642n**
Mémoire, 1790. **642**
Lees, J. Aux electeurs, 1792. **773**
Legge, *Gov. of N.S.* Proclamation on:
Asylum to refugees, 1775. **203**
Loyal regiment volunteers, 1776. **235**
Price provisions, 1776. **236**
Strangers & spies, 1775. **204**
Lemaistre, F. Rules for barracks, 1786. **493**
Lemaitre Duème, F. Duplique, 1779. **311**
Réponses, 1779. **312**
Lester, R. To electors Quebec, 1800. **1178**
Létourneaux, M. New map of Canada, 1790. **630n**
Letters & papers on agriculture, 1791. **740**
Lettre circulaire à M. les cures, 1787. **515**
Lettre de M. l'Evêque de Léon, 1793. **833**
Lewis, Wm. *printer.* **p. 665**
Saint John gazette, **p. 597-98**
L'Homond, C. F. Elémens de la grammaire française, 1800. **1177**
Elemens de la grammaire latine methode, 1796. **989**
Elemens de la grammaire latine syntaxe, 1796. **988**
Elemens de la langue latine, 1799. **1127**
Elements de la grammaire latine, 1797. **1044**
Elements de la grammaire latine, 1799. **1128**
Libel. Barkly-Hay dispute, 1764-65. **36-37**
Lewis & Ryan, *printers.* **p. 598**
Mills & Hicks, *printers.* **246n**
Walter, J.: Defence, 1790. **680**
Libraries, *see* Book catalogues; Cary's circulating library; Quebec library
Liquor licences, 1776. **242**
Hubert: Lettre circulaire, 1787. **515**
Livius, P. Catalogue library, 1798. **1090**
Livre pour apprendre . . . français, 1778. **290**
Lord's day observance, 1766. **87-88**
Lottery for prison Montreal, 1783. **402**
Louis XVI, Journal de, 1798, **1086-87.**—1799 ed. **1119**
Lower Canada, *see also* Quebec (for publications prior to the establishment of Lower Canada by the Constitutional Act and related documents in the latter part of 1791)
Adjutant-general. Ordonnance pour loger les troupes, 1796. **990**
Règles pour les forces, 1796. **991**
Rules & articles militia, 1795. **937**
Elections, 1792. **p. 357-63**
Proclamation 1792, **786.**—1800 ed. **1184**
Elections, 1800. Act. **1181**
Handbill, 1800. **1178**
Executive Council. Extract waste lands, 1798. **1091**
Inland navigation fees, 1797. **1046-47**
Land claims, 1795. **938**
Order aliens, 1796. **995**
Order 7 July 1796 commerce 1796, **992; 994.**—1800 ed. **1179**
Ordre 7me Juillet 1796. **993**
Survey warrants procedure, 1794. **878-79**
Grand voyer. Ordres, 1799. **1129**
House of Assembly. Bill Montreal fortifications, 1797. **1049**
Journal 1793, **835.**—1793-94, **881.**—1795, **940.**—1795-96, **996.**—1797, **1050.**—1798, **1094.**—1799, **1130.** —1800, **1180**
Journal index: **835n; 940n; 996n; 1050n; 1094n; 1130n; 1180n**
Petition justices peace, 1795. **941**
Rules 1793, **836.**—1796 ed. **997**
Sergeant-at-arms. Paper, 1794. **882**
Sewell: Abstract of proceeding, 1792. **812**
Taschereau: Highways & bridges, 1794. **911**
Laws. Abstract fisheries, 1797. **1053**
Abstract highways & bridges, 1796. **999-1000**
Aliens, 1794. **886-87**
Bill for Militia act, 1794. **883**
Causes in appeal court, 1792. **782**
Collection acts rel. to Canada, 1800. **1169**
Constitutional act, 1791. **704-705; 786n; 1040-41; 1184n**
Court King's bench, 1792. **783**
DeBonne: Précis (Militia act) 1794. **873**
Elections act, 1800. **1181**
Extract road act, 1800. **1183**
Judicature act, 1794. **889**
Abstract, 1794. **890**
Proclamation, 1794. **880**

Laws (fo. ed.) 1793, **837.**—1794, **888-89**. *See also* Prov. statutes
Loger les troupes, 1796. **990**
Militia act, 1794. **884-85**
Ordinances (rev. ed. 1777-92) 1795. **942**
Pilotage R. St. Lawrence, 1794. **891,** cf. **657**
Plan Judicature bill, 1793. **838-40**
Provincial statute baptisms, marriages, burials, 1795. **945**
Prov. statutes (4to. ed. 1792-96) 1795, **943.**—1797-1800, 1797. **1051**
Prov. statutes (separate issue) 1795, **944.**—1795-96, 1796, **998.**—1797, **1052.**—1798, **1095.**—1799, **1131.** —1800, **1182**
Weight & rates gold coin, 1796. **1001**
Legislative Council. Bill criminal law, 1795. **946-47**
Bill persons failing in trade, 1795. **948**
Military Secretary. Notice lots at Wm. Henry, 1799. **1132**
Post houses. Table distances & fares, 1799. **1133**
Proclamations. Declaring Constitutional act 1791, **705; 704n.**—1800 ed. **1184**
Divide province into counties, & election 1792, **786.**—1800 ed. **1184**
Embargo on wheat, 1795. **939**
Judicature act, 1794. **880**
Prescott, Lt.-Gov., 1796. **1002**
Privateers, 1793. **841**
Sedition, 1793. **834**
Settle lands in L.C., 1792. **784-85**
Signals harbour Quebec, 1800. **1185**
Squatters on crown lands, 1797. **1048**
Treason, 1796. **1003**
Victory over France, 1798. **1093**
Quarter Sessions of the Peace. Tarif prix du pain, 1797. **1045**
"Lower Canada statutes vol. 0" **1169n**
Loyal association. **895n**
Circular, 1794. **896**
Declaration, 1794. **892-95**
Notice, 1794. **897**
Loyalists. Address from agents St. John R., 1784. **426**
Commission on losses, 1788. **554**
Commissioners on claims, 1785. **458**
Melville: Accurate history settlement, 1784. **421**
Notice, land & provisions, 1784. **439**
N.S.: Asylum, 1775. **203**
Que.: Registry & land grants, 1789. **615**
U.C.: Fees on land grants, 1798. **1104-1105**
Frauds in fee-free grants, 1799. **1147**
Land tickets, 1795. **970**
Oath of adherence, 1796. **1023**
Lucile, ou les progrès de la vertu, 1768. **126A**
Lyman, D. **932n**
Lymburner, A. **709n**
Hand-bills election, 1792. **774**
Paper read at H. of Commons, 1791. **709**
Papier lu à la barre, 1791. **710**

M

Mabane, A., & A. Gray. Catalogue libraries, 1792. **787**
Macdonell, A. Pot ashes, 1791. **727; 731**
MacGregor, J. **557n**
Letter to free black girl, 1788. **557**
MacKay, H. Sergeant-at-arms, **882n**
Directory Quebec 1790, **650.**—1791 ed. **718**
McLane, D. **1056n**
Procès pour haute trahison, 1797. **1054**
Trial for treason, 1797. **1055-56**
MacLean, A. To volunteers & loyalists, 1779. **314-15**
MacNider, M. Aux libres electeurs, 1792. **775**
Mahir, E. Confession, 1785. **459**
Maîtres de poste, *s.e* Post houses
Mal de la baie St. Paul. **455n**
Badelard: Direction, 1785. **454-55**
Esglis: Circulaire, 1786. **479; 496n**
Esglis: Lettre circulaire, 1785. **457**
Hope: Circulaire, 1786. **496**
Jones: Remarks, 1786. **484**
Jones: Remarques, 1787. **517**
Mandements, Lettres circulaires, etc., *see* Briand, Denaud, Esglis, Hubert, Plessis, Pontbriand, *Bp.*
Manners & customs in British America, 1791. **711**
Manning, E. **1161n**
Manual exercise 1787, **514.**—1788 ed. **553**
Maps. Hubert: Lettre circulaire, 1790. **639**
New map of Canada, 1790. **630n**
Que.: Order-in-council for map, 1790. **660**
Vondenvelden & Charland. Topographical chart L.C. **1107n**
Marie Antoinette portrait, 1795. **949**
Martial law proclaimed, 1775. **217**
Mascall, E. J. Duties drawbacks, 1787. **518**
Masons, *see* Freemasons
Masson, A. Coutûme de Paris, 1796. **1004**
Mathews, R. Notice to loyalists, 1784. **439**
McKinstry, *printer*. **870; 923**
Halifax journal, **p. 610**
McMurray, W. Two poems, 1790. **643**

Medicine, *see also* Cow pox; Dentist; Mal de la baie St. Paul; Yellow fever
Buchan: Domestic medicine, 1786. **476**
Latham: Regiments for children, 1769. **136**
Melville, D. History loyalists, 1784. **421**
Melvin & Wills, *see also* Auction sales.
Catalogue books, medicine, 1789. **597**
Catalogue furs, 1781. **356**
Mémoire en réponse. à . . Me Panet, 1779. **313**
Mémoire . . . testament de . . . Sanguinet, 1791. **737**
Mensforth. Aux curieux, 1792. **788**
Mesplet, F. **p. 664**
Gazette du com. et lit. **p. 622-23**
Memorial to Congress, 1783. **401**
Memorial to Congress, 1784. **422**
Montreal citizens: Petition, 1778. **291**
Montreal gazette, **p. 623-24**
Mesplet, *Mme.* **p. 624**
Messieurs et citoyens (de Salaberry), 1792. **780**
Method . . . preserving grain . . . smut, 1792. **745**
Methodist church. Minutes conference. 1795. **950**
Wesley: Short history, 1786. **501**
Metonicus, **349n**
Mezière, P. Addition aux répliques, 1779. **312n**
Micmac Indians, *see* Indians
Militia
Debonne: Precis d'un acte, 1794. **873**
Gr. Britain: Manual exercise 1759, **15**. —1787 ed. **514**.—1788 ed. **553**
Rules formations, 1793. **829**
Hubert: Lettre circulaire, 1790. **640**
Kent: Rations, 1800. **1175**
Lower Canada: Act 1794. **884-85**
Bill 1794. **883**
Loger les troupes, 1796. **990**
Règles, 1796. **991**
Rules & articles, 1795. **937**
MacLean: To volunteers, 1779. **314-15**
New Brunswick: Act, 1794. **899**
Nova Scotia: Act 1753, **8**.—1795. **959**
Proclamation, 1752. **7**
Tax, 1775. **202**
Nova Scotia Volunteers, 1776. **235**
Quebec: Act, 1789. **606**
Bill, 1791. **733**
Billeting troops, 1766. **87-88**
Circulaire invasion, 1778. **296**
Firewood for H.M. forces, 1765. **73-74**
General orders, 1790. **652**
Habitants enlist, 1775. **218**
Instructions 1779. **323**
Non-combatants quit town, 1775. **219**
Ordinance 1779, **326n**.—1787, **532**
Ordinances, 1790. **662**
Ordres du quartier general, 1787. **538**
Rules for barracks & fuel, 1786. **493**
St. John Island: Militia corps, 1794. **910**
Sills: Bastille septentrionale, 1791. **739**
Mills & Hicks, *printers*, **246n**
Milnes, *Lt.-Gov. of L.C.* Proclamation on: Signals harbour Quebec, 1800. **1185**
Minchin, P. Trading & fishing Mingan, 1786. **485**
Mingan trading & fishing rights, 1786. **485**
Minns, W. *printer*. **p. 662**
Weekly chronicle, **p. 617**
Missa in festo, 1777. **256**
Mowhawk song & dance, 1780. **334**
Monckton, *Lt. Gov. of N.S.* Proclamation. Embargo on ships, 1757. **12**
Monde demasqué, comedie, 1775. **214**
Mongolfier, E., Proposes publications, 1777. **255n**
Monk, Sir J. L.C. Bill securing estates to creditors, 1795. **948**
Montreal. Citizens' petition on Mesplet, 1778. **291**
Lottery to build prison, 1783. **402**
L.C. Bill on fortifications, 1797. **1049**
Oeuvres de fabrique, 1777. **259**
Tableau des rues 1789. **598**
View 1799. **1134**
Montreal, Account battle of, 1775. **193**
Montreal gazette (Mesplet-Edwards), **p. 623-27**
Carrier's address: Etrennes du garçon 1801. **1187**
Prospectus, 1785. **460**
Montreal gazette (Roy), **p. 628-29**
Prospectus, 1795. **951**
Moore, Wm., *printer*. **p. 663; 481n; 499n; 566n**
Announcement printing office, 1788. **558**
Collection poems prospectus, 1789. **589**
Courier de Québec, 1789. **551; 590; p. 620-21**
Quebec herald, **p. 639-41**
Morris, C. St. John R. Soc.: Descrip. townships, 1768. **126B**
Mort tragique du roi de France, 1793. **842**
Mott, J. S., *printer*. **p. 666**
Saint John gazette, **p. 597**
Mountain, *Bp.* **1135n**
Sermon, 1799. **1135**
Moyens de se preserver du bled noir, 1792. **744**
Munro, J. *printer*. **p. 610**
Murray, *Gov. of Quebec*. Proclamation on Assault Thos. Walker, 1764. **43**
Appoint. justices of peace, 1764. **44-5**
Canada paper money, 1766. **91-92**
Disallowance ordinances, 1766. **87-88**

Enregistering deeds, 1766. **89-90**
Repeal of Stamp act; Declaratory act, 1766. **93-94**
Music, *see also* Entertainment
Jouve: Concert, 1792. **760**
Mutual benefit societies, *see* Halifax marine society; Quebec benevolent society; *also* other organizations under: Societies

N

Napier, *Capt.* **201n**
Hand-bill for sailors, 1775. **201**
Narrative . . . Nelson . . . Nile, 1799. **1114**
Narrative of facts, 1797. **1069**
Nathans & Hart. Price current 1752. **3**
Necessity of . . . paper money, 1792. **802**
Neilson, J., *printer*. **p.664; p. 629, 634, 838n**
Neilson, S., *printer*. **p. 663;** plate XII
Quebec gazette, **p. 629, 633-34**
Quebec magazine, **p. 656**
Nelson, *Lord*, *see also* Nile, Battle of
Berry: Narrative, 1799. **1114**
Neuvaine à . . . S. François Xavier 1772, **165.**—1778 ed. **283.**—1796, **983**
New Brunswick (for documents prior to its establishment as a separate province in 1784, *see* Nova Scotia)
Address of clergy, 1792. **756**
Address to loyal refugees, 1784. **426**
Customs office. Reward theft smuggled goods, 1792. **789**
Executive Council. Handbill fobidding creepers, 1787. **519**
Glenie: Pamphlet, 1795. **932**
House of Assembly. Journal, 1786, **486.**—1787, **520.**—1788, **559.**—1789, **644.**—1791, **712.**—1792, **790.**—1793, **843.**—1794, **898.**—1795, **952.**—1796, **1005.**—1797, **1057.**—1798-99, **p. 559**
Laws. Acts of 1786, **487.**—1787, **521.** —1788, **560.**—1789, **645.**—1791, **713.** —1792, **791.**—1793, **844.**—1794, **900.** —1795, **953.**—1796, **1006.**—1797, **1058.**—1798, **1096.**—1799, **1136**
Elections & franchise, 1795. **954**
Militia, 1794. **899**
Proclamations. **1007n**
Carleton governor, 1784. **423**
Illicit trade, 1784. **424**
Register land grants, 1784. **425**
Regulations for farms, 1785. **461**
Treasury. Gen. acct. merchandize, 1795. **955**
Goods imported, 1792. **792**
New constitution explained, 1792. **813**
New constitution of France, 1792. **758**
New lights, *see* Alline, H.
New Printing Office, *see* Nouvelle Imprimerie
New-Year's verses of the printer's lad, see *Quebec gazette*. Carrier's address
Newspapers, **p. 593-652,** *see also* (in index) Courier de Québec; Gazette du commerce et litteraire; Halifax gazette; Halifax journal; Montreal gazette (Mesplet-Edwards); Montreal gazette (Roy); Quebec gazette; Quebec herald; Royal gazette, Halifax; Times, Quebec; Upper Canada gazette
Niagara. **967n**
Niagara postage (road) bill, 1799. **1148n**
Nile, Battle of
Berry: Narrative, 1799. **1114**
Byles: Sermon, 1799. **1115**
Chanson pour la fête, 1799. **1117**
C. of Eng.: Form of prayer, 1799. **1118**
Denaut: Mandement, 1798. **1088**
L.C. Proc. thanksgiving, 1798. **1093**
Mountain: Sermon, 1799. **1135**
Plessis: Discours, 1799. **1140**
Spark: Sermon, 1799. **1142**
U.C. gazette Extra, 1799. **1152**
North British Society. Brown: Discourse, 1791. **698**
North West Passage. Rogers: Petition, 1780. **346**
Nouvelle Imprimerie, **913n; 1128n;** *see also* Desbarats, P.-E.; Vondenvelden, W.
Nova Scotia, present state 1785. **445**
Nova Scotia, H.M. timber, 1784. **419**
Nova Scotia (including till 1784 the region which then became New Brunswick)
Advertisement clear roads 1764. **42**
Com. on Shubenaccadie canal. Report, 1797. **1059-1060**
Executive Council. Resolutions establish Assembly, 1757. **11**
House of Assembly. Address for reform, 1775. **205**
Bill canal Halifax-Minas, 1798. **1097**
Bill for schools, 1800. **1189**
Journal 1759. **17.**—1759-60, **23.**—1760, **24.**—1761, **28.**—1762, **31.**—Apr.-July 1763, **32.**—Oct.-Nov. 1763, **33.**—Mar.-Apr. 1764, **38.**—Oct.-Nov. 1764, **39.**—1765, **63.**—June-Aug. 1766, **81.**—Oct.-Nov. 1766, **82.**—July-Aug. 1767, **109.** —Oct. 1767, **110.**—1768, **123.**—1768-69, **137.**—1769, **138.**—1770, **148.**—1771, **158.**—1772, **166.**—Apr. 1773, **178.**—Oct.-Nov. 1773, **179.**—1774, **189.**—June-July 1775, **206.**—Oct.-Nov. 1775, **207.**—1776, **237.**—1777, **261.**—1778, **292.**—1779, **316.**—1780, **338.**—1781, **357.**—1782, **375.**—1783, **403.**—1784, **427.**—1785, **462.**—1786, **488.**—1787, **522.**—

1789, **599.**—1790, **647.**—1791, **714.**—1792, **793.**—1793, **845.**—1794, **901.**—1795, **956.**—1796, **1008.**—1797, **1061.**—1798, **1098.** 1799, **1137.**—1800, **1190**
Petition & impeachment, 1790. **646**
Resolutions to establish, 1757. **11**
Justices of peace. Handbills, 1776. **240**
Laws, *see also* Shelburne, N.S. Quarter sessions.
Frauds in selling flour, 1789. **602**
Militia, 1753, **8.**—1795, **959**
Militia tax, 1775. **202**
Perpetual acts rev. ed. 1767, **111.**—1784, **428**
Poll tax, 1794. **904**
Possession Acadians' lands, 1759. **18**
Relief of debtors, 1752. **6**
Sessions laws, 1758-59, **19.**—1759, **20.**—1759-60, **25.**—1760, **26.**—1761, **29.**—1762, **30.**—Apr.-July 1763, **34.**—Oct.-Nov. 1763, **35.**—Mar.-Apr. 1764, **40.**—Oct.-Nov. 1764, **41.**—1765, **64.**—June-Aug. 1766, **83.**—Oct.-Nov. 1766, **84**
Sessions laws *perpetual*, July-Aug. 1767, **112.**—Oct. 1767, **113.**—1768, **124.**—1768-69, **139.**—1769, **141.**—1770, **149.**—1771, **159.**—1772, **167.**—Oct.-Nov. 1773, **181.**—1774, **190.**—June-July 1775, **208.**—Oct.-Nov. 1775, **210.**—1776, **238.**—1777, **262.**—1778, **293.**—1779, **317.**—1780, **339.**—1781, **358.**—1782, **376.**—1783, **430.**—1784, **432.**—1785, **489.**—1786, **491.**—1787, **523.**—1789, **600.**—1790, **648.**—1791, **715.**—1792, **794.**—1793, **846.**—1794, **902.**—1795, **957.**—1796, **1009.**—1797, **1062.**—1799, **1138.**—1800, **1191**
Sessions laws *temporary*, 1768, **125.**—1768-69, **140.**—1769, **142.**—1770, **150.**—1771, **160.**—1772, **168.**—Apr. 1773, **180.**—Oct.-Nov. 1773, **182.**—1774, **191.**—June-July 1775, **209.**—Oct.-Nov. 1775, **211.**—1776, **239.**—1777, **263.**—1778, **294.**—1779, **318.**—1780, **340.**—1781, **359.**—1782, **377.**—1783, **431.**—1784, **433.**—1785, **490.**—1786, **492.**—1787, **524.**—1789, **601.**—1790, **649.**—1791, **716.**—1792, **795.**—1793, **847.**—1794, **903.**—1795, **958.**—1796, **1010.**—1797, **1063.**—1798, **1099.**—1799, **1139.**—1800, **1192**
Temporary acts rev. ed. 1767, **114.**—1783, **429**
Proclamations. Acadians' lands 1758, **13.**—1759, **16; 18**
Alteration calendar 1752. **4**
Asylum to refugees, 1775. **203**
Cartel for exchange deserters, 1752. **5**
Coal mines, 1767. **107-108**
Contagious distempers, 1793. **852**
Deserters 1793, **851.**—1796, **1011**
Embargo on ships, 1757. **12**
Fast day Mar. 1, 1793. **850**
Fast day Apr. 25, 1794. **905**
Fast day, 1798. **1100**
General fast, 1797. **1064**
George III king, 1761. **27**
Land applications free, 1759. **16**
Loyal Regiment Volunteers, 1776. **235**
Militia, 1753. **7**
Prayers for legislature, 1793. **848**
Price provisions, 1776. **236**
Privateers, 1793. **849**
Registration of strangers, 1775. **204**
Reward on Indian scalps, 1756. **10**
Soldiers to work, 1758. **14**
Treaty with Indians, 1753. **9**
Nova-Scotia, Essay on, 1774. **187**
Nova-Scotia calender, see under Almanacs
Nova Scotia chronicle, **p. 602-604**
Nova-Scotia gazette, **p. 601-602**
Nova-Scotia gazette & weekly chronicle, **p. 604-610**
Nova-Scotia magazine, **p. 653-56**
Nova-Scotia packet, **p. 612-13**

O

Objections aux demandes . . . 30 Nov. 1784. **434**
Observations . . . change tenures, 1791. **696**
Ode for 31 Dec. 1776. **233**
Office de la semaine sainte, 1778. **282**
Officium in honorem D.N.J.C. 1777. **257**
Ohio settlers, Declaration to, 1780. **342**
Oliver, W. S. **717n**
Dismission sheriff, 1791. **717**
Oneida Indians, Rebel interest, 1779. **325**
Order . . . 7th July, 1796 . . . commerce 1796, **992; 994.**—1800 ed. **1179**
Order for morning & evening prayer . . . Mohawk, 1780. **335**
Ordinances made for . . . Quebec, 1767. **116**
Ordinances made & passed . . . Quebec 1777, **268.**—1780, **343.**—1782-86, **495.**—1787, **530.**—1777-92, **942**
Ordinances, *see under* Quebec. Laws, ordinances, etc., for those not issued as bound vol. with title-page.
Osgoode, W. **999n;**—on Dickson, **1123n**

P

Palmare, *see* Séminaire de Québec
Panet, P. L. To electors, 1792. **776**
Panet, P. M. Réponse aux dupliques, 1778. **295**
Paper read . . . by Mr. Lymburner, 1791. **709**

Papers & letters on agriculture, 1790. **623**
Papier lu . . . par Mr. Lymburner, 1791. **710**
Paris en miniature, 1784. **420**
Parlement of Paris, Consultation, 1778. **289**
Partridge, J. Horsemanship, 1787. **525**
Perils of the time, 1795. **926**
Perpetual acts . . . Nova Scotia 1767, **111**.—1783, **428**
Perrault, J. F. Burn: Juge, 1789. **583**
  Testament de Sanguinet, 1791. **737**
Peters, S. **550n**
Petit catéchisme, 1782. **373B**
Petit livre de vie 1798, **1083**.—1800 ed. **1162**
Petitions. Anciens et nouveaux sujets au Roi 1785, **453**.—1790, **653**
  Au Roi placet, habitans de Québec, 1791. **720**
  Citoyens et habitants au Roi, 1784. **435**
  Mesplet to U.S. Congress 1783, **401**.—1784, **422**
  Montreal citizens on Mesplet, 1778. **291**
  Nova Scotia Assembly for reform, 1775. **205**
  Nova Scotia Assembly on judges, 1790. **646**
  Objections aux demandes, 1784. **434**
  Quebec citizens on tenure, 1791. **719**
Peyster, A. de. **955n**
Phelps, B. **212n**
  Death Mrs. Chipman, 1775. **212**
Phillips & Lane, *see also* Auction sales.
  Catalogue of books, 1787. **526**
Philomath, E. W. **452n**
Pidgeon, G. **985n**
Pius VI, *Pope*. Denaut: Circulaire, 1799. **1121**
Pius VII, *Pope*. Denaut: Mandement, 1800. **1171**
Plan d'un bill . . . 8me Avril, 1793. **839**
Plan . . . lottery . . . Montreal, 1783. **402**
Plan of bill . . . altering courts, 1793. **840**
Plan of bill . . . criminal law, 1795. **946**
Plan of bill . . . 10th Mar. 1793. **838**
Play-bills, *see* Quebec Theatre
Pleasure . . . brotherly unity, 1787. **508**
Plessis, *Bp.* **1140n**
  Circulaire, 1800. **1193**
  Discours, 1799. **1140**
Poetry, *see also* Carrier's address under *Quebec gazette*, *Royal gazette*, Halifax; *Times*, Quebec; *also* Prospectuses
  Baillargé: Elégie, 1792. **752**
  Cary: Abram's Plains, 1789. **585**
  Chanson pour la fête, 1799. **1117**
  Dickson: Taste & science, 1799. **1124**
  Finlay: Song, 1783. **397**
  Laforce: Song, 1797. **1043**
  McMurray: Two poems, 1790. **643**
  Ode for 31 Dec. 1776. **233**
  Poem on Miss Willcocks, 1784. **444**
  Restaut: Règles versification, 1778. **300**
  Sarreau: Elégies, 1792. **810**
  Sarreau: Suite de l'elégie, 1792. **811**
  Viets: Annapolis Royal, 1788. **571**
Police, *see also* Quebec. Quarter sessions; Nova Scotia. Justices; Shelburne, N.S. Quarter sessions
  Quebec: Act to regulate, 1791. **724; 728**
    Réglemens, 1790. **654**
    Regulations for, 1780. **341**
Political societies, *see* Constitutional club; Loyal association
Poll tax, Nova Scotia, 1794. **904**
Pontbriand, *Bp.* Mandements, 1759. **21-22**
Porcupine, P. *pseud.* Democratic principles, 1799. **1120**
Port Medway. Alline: Sermon, 1783. 387
Port Roseway, *see* Shelburne, N.S.
Port-Roseway gazetteer, **p. 614-16**
Post houses. L.C.: Distances & fares, 1799. **1133**
  Que.: Maîtres de poste, 1780. **344**
    Ordres et instructions, 1770. **153-54**
Post office. Gen. instructions, 1790? **638**
  Rates of postage, *n.d.* **1203**
Potash. Cull: Des cendres, 1795. **930**
  Hopkins & Macdonell, 1791. **727; 731**
Prayer books, *see* Devotional books
Précis ou abrégé d'un acte. 1794. **873**
Presbyterian church, *see* Church of Scotland
Prescott, *Gov. of L.C.* **1002n**
  Dickson: Taste & science, 1799. **1124**
  On Battle of Nile, **1118n**
  On waste lands of crown, **1091n; 1092n**
  Proclamation officers, 1796. **1002**
    Squatters on crown lands, 1797. **1048**
    Treason, 1796. **1003**
    Victory over France, 1798. **1093**
Presentments of grand jury, 1765. **66-67**
Press into H.M. ships, 1779. **327-28**
Price current Nathans & Hart, 1752. **3**
Price provisions Halifax, 1776. **236, 240n**
Prières de la congregation, n.d. **1204**
Primers. **65n**
  Abeghjikmnop (Montagnais) 1767. **106**
  Alphabet 1765, **65**.—1771, **161**.—1775, **213**.—1777, **264**.—1785, **463**
  Alphabet en française, 1774. **192**
  Alphabet, for Lord Dorchester, 1788. **561**
  Alphabet françois, 1795. **960**
  Alphabet in French, 1788. **562**

Alphabet in Latin, 1788. **563**
Alphabet latin, 1795. **961**
Claus: P. for Mohawk children, 1781. **355**
French alphabet, 1779. **319**
Grand alphabet, 1782. **378.**—1800, **1194**
Iontri8aiestsk8a (Mohawk) 1777. **265**
LaBrosse: Akitami (Abnaki) 1770. **147**
Latin alphabet 1766, **85.**—1767, **115.** —1779, **320**
Livre pour apprendre, 1778. **290**
Printed blanks, **2; 153-54; 321; 1129**
Privateers. L.C.: Proclamation, 1793. **841**
N.S.: Proclamation, 1793. **849**
Prize act, 1795. **933**
Probus, *pseud.* Aux electeurs, 1792. **777**
DeBonne: Aux canadiens, 1792. **763n**
To electors, 1792. **778**
Procès de David M'Lane, 1797. **1054**
Proclamation Oct. 7, 1763, 1800. **1174n**
Projet d'acte . . . pour la meilleure administration de la justice . . . Québec, 1787. **537**
Prospectuses (*works not published)
Agricultural Society, 1788. **573**
*Buchan: Domestic medicine, 1786. **476**
Burn: Juges à paix, 1788. **549**
*Burns: Poems, 1789. **584**
*Cawthorne: Considerations on state of trade, 1766. **77**
*Collection of original poems, 1789. **589**
Courier de Québec, 1788, **551.**—Thursday ed. 1789. **590**
*Delaroche: Doctrinal commentary, 1783. **396**
Dissertation on Revelation, 1800. **1172A**
*Freemason's pocket companion, 1786. **481**
Gazette du commerce, 1778. **286-87**
Halifax gazette, 1751-52. **1**
*Manners & customs Br. Am., 1791. **711**
*Mascall: Duties & drawbacks, 1787. **518**
*Masson: Coutûme de Paris, 1796. **1004**
*Melville: Accurate history settlement loyalists, 1784. **421**
Montreal gazette (Mesplet), 1785. **460**
Montreal gazette (Roy), 1795. **951**
Moore: Almanacs &c. 1788. **558**
Quebec gazette, 1763-64. **56**
Quebec herald, 1788. **566.**—Thursday ed. 1789, **618**
Quebec magazine, 1792. **800**
Tanswell: Grammar*, 1791. **741
Times: Preparatory address, 1793. **859**
Times: Specimen, 1794. **913**
*Upper Canada almanac, 1797. **979**
*Views Montreal, 1799. **1134**
*Vondenvelden: Can. surveyor, 1785. **470**
Vondenvelden & Charland: Can. topographer, 1798. **1107**
*Zimmermann: Political survey, 1791. **743**
Pseautier de David, 1774, **186.**—1782, **374.**—1785, **456**
Publication of Laws, L.C. 1794, **943n**
Quebec 1765. **71-72**
Upper Canada 1792. **817**

Q

Quebec (province), *see also* Lower Canada, Upper Canada, for publications subsequent to the division of Quebec into two provinces in 1791
Adjutant-general. Circulaire invasion, 1778. **296**
General orders militia, 1790. **652**
Citizens. Aux citoyens et habitants, 1785. **453**
Humble adresse, 1790. 653
Lymburner: Paper, 1791. **709**
Lymburner: Papier, 1791. **710**
Memorial on tenures, 1791. **719**
Objections aux démandes, 1784. **434**
Placet lodes et ventes, 1791. **720**
Très-humble adresse, 1784. **435**
Customs office. Duties on wines, 1765. **69**
Executive Council. List fees, 1765. **70**
Governor, *see* Proclamations
Laws, ordinances, bills, etc., *see also* Quebec. Quarter sessions, for municipal regulations.
Abstracts statutes Gr. Britain, 1765. **61-62**
Administration of justice, 1770. **152**
Age of majority, 1782. **381**
Bill advocates' licence, 1791. **732**
Build & repair churches, 1791. **726**
Communication 1789. **611**
Courts, 1790. **656**
Fisheries R. St. Lawrence, 1789. **609n**
Grist mills, 1790. **666**
Habeas corpus ordinance, 1784. **438**
Inland commerce 1790, **655.**—1791, **727**
Inland navigation 1789, **609.**—1791, **728**
Inland navigation & trade to W. country, 1791. **722**
Maîtres de poste, 1791. **725**
Militia, 1791. **733**
Police, 1791. **724**

Practice law in civil causes, 1791. **723**
Prohibit small stills, 1789. **611**
Seamen merchant service, 1789. **610**
Toll R. St. Charles, 1789. **610**
Build & repair churches, 1791. **729-30**
Civil causes, 1791. **728**
Court king's bench, 1787. **531**
Courts of judicature, 1764. **49-55**
Cugnet: Extraits des édits, 1775. **200**
Traité de la loi fiefs, 1775. **197**
Traité de la police, 1775. **199**
Traité des anciennes loix, 1775. **198**
Currency, 1764. **46-47**
Decrees court ratified, 1764. **48**
Disallowance forestallers, 1782. **380**
Disallowance of ordinances, 1766. **87-88**
Draught of act adm. justice, 1787. **536**
Firewood for H.M. forces, 1765. **73-74**
Grand et petit jurés, 1767. **117**
Hopkins & Macdonell pot & pearl ashes, 1791. **731**
Inland commerce 1788, **564.**—1790, **658.**—1791, **729**
Loan of seed to poor, 1789. **604; 608**
Maîtres de poste 1780, **344.**—1791, **729**
Map of province, 1790. **660**
Militia 1779, **326.**—1787, **532.**—1789, **606**
Mesurage du bois de chauffage, 1765. **71**
Ordinances (coll. ed.) 1767. **116**
Ordinances, 1777. **268**
Ordinances, 1780. **343**
Ordinances I-III, 1781. **361**
Ordinances I-IV, 1782. **382**
Ordinances (1782-86) 1786. **495**
Ordinances I-IV, 1783. **405**
Ordinances I-III, 1784. **437-38**
Ordinances I-III, 1786. **494**
Ordinances, 1787. **530**
Ordinances IV-VI, 1787. **534**
Ordinances VII-XII, 1787. **535**
Ordinances V-IX, 1790. **659**
Ordinances I-III, 1791. **728**
Ordinances (rev. ed. 1777-92) 1795. **942**
Ordinances militia, 1790. **662**
Ordinances pilots & navigation, 1790. **661**
Pilotage & port of Quebec, 1790. **657**
Police 1789, **607.**—1791, **728**
Practice of law, 1789. **603; 606**
Projet d'un acte justice, 1787. **537**
Publication of laws, 1765. **71-72**
Quartering troops, 1787. **533**
Quebec act & Quebec revenue act 1774, **188.**—1791, **706.**—1797, **1040-41**
Repair highways, 1766. **95-96**
Strengthen deeds Dist. Hesse, 1789. **605, 608**
Legislative Council. Ancient French archives, 1791. **734**
Extract high roads & bridges, 1789. **612**
Extract on tenures, 1790. **667**
Fines, 1790. **670**
Locations in Lunenburg, 1790. **665**
Registry of loyalists & land grants, 1789. **615**
Report on education, 1790. **669**
Rôle des paroissiens, 1790. **668**
Rules land office, 1790. **663-64**
Rules land-office dept., 1789. **613-14**
Military court. Decrees ratified, 1764. **48**
Military Secretary. Notice to loyalists, lands & provisions, 1784. **439**
Navy. Volunteers, 1779. **327-28**
Proclamation on
Appoint. justices of peace, 1764. **44-45**
Assault of Thos. Walker, 1764. **43**
Aveu seigniories, 1777. **266**
Barracks & fuel for troops, 1786. **493**
Canada paper money, 1766. **91-92**
Carleton lt.-gov. 1766. **97-98**
Circulaire (mal de la baie) 1786. **496**
Clarke lt.-gov. 1791. **735**
Commissioners of the peace 1775. **216**
Culture of hemp, 1791. **721**
Declaration to Ohio settlers, 1780. **342**
Disallowance of ordinances, 1766. **87-88**
Embargo cattle & grain, 1777. **267**
Embargo on shipping, 1775. **221-23**
Embargo on wheat, 1778. **297**
Embargo on wheat, forestalling, 1779. **322**
Enregistering deeds, 1766. **89-90**
Fealty & hommage, seigneurs, 1778. **298**
Forestallers' ordinance disallowed, 1782. **380**
Forestalling, regrating, 1779. **324**
Free import & export U.S. 1787. **529**
Grain, cattle provisions 1781, **360.**—1782, **379.**—1783, **404**
Habitants enlist, 1775. **218**
Haldimand's speech to Oneidas 1779. **325**
Hope, Lt. gov. 1785. **464**
Instructions for militia, 1779. **323**
Martial law, 1775. **217**

Non-combattants & deserters, 1776. **244**
Non-combattants to quit town 1775. **219**
Ordres du quartier general, 1787. **538**
Outrages on Indians, 1766. **99**
Repeal of Stamp act; Declaratory act, 1766. **93-94**
Strangers to register, 1775. **220**
Suppress rebellion, 1776. **234**
Trade with Indians, 1786. **497**
Winter roads cleared, 1776. **245**
Wounded rebels, 1776. **243**
Quarter sessions of the peace. A la premier cour de séance Oct. 1764. **67**
Extract Burn's Justice, 1787. **528**
Fares & rates carriage wood, 1765. **68**
First court Oct. 1764. **66**
Order liquor licence, 1776. **242**
Order to strangers entering province, 1776. **241**
Orders firewood, goats &c. 1787. **527**
Prohibitions liquor Sunday, 1784. **436**
Rates for ferries, 1766. **86A**
Réglemens de police, 1790. **654**
Regulations carters police, 1780. **341**
Regulations ferries, 1766. **86B**
Supt. of post houses. Regulations for post riders, 1770. **153-54**
Quebec act 1774, **188.**—1791, **706.**—1797, **1040-41**
Quebec Benevolent Society, **616n**
Rules 1789, **616.**—1793, **853.**—1795, **906.**—1796, **1013**
Quebec Co., *see* St. John's River Society
Quebec gazette, **p. 629-39**. Prospectus, 1763-64. **54**
Carrier's address. Address of boy who carries Gazette, 1800. **1195**
Etrennes du garçon 1778, **269.**—1779, **299.**—1780, **329.**—1787, **498.**—1788, **539.**—1789, **565.**—1790, **617**
New-Year's verses of the printer's boy, 1781, **345.**—1782, **362.**—1785, **440.**—1786, **465**
Printer's boy wishes customers happy New Year 1795, **962**
Verses from the news-boy, 1799. **1141**
Verses of the boy who carries the Gazette, 1798, **1065.**—1799, **1101**
Verses of the printer's boy 1791, **671.**—1792, **736.**—1793, **798.**—1794, **854.**—1795, **907.**—1797, **1014**
Quebec gazette reprints: Act loan of seed to poor, 1789. **604, 608**
Act practice of law, 1789. **606**
Act strengthen deeds Dist. Hesse, 1789. **605, 608**
Act to regulate police, 1789. **607**
Ordinance 1, 1788. **564**
Ordinance causes in appeal, 1792. **782**
Ordinances I-XII, 1787. **531-35**
Proclamation commissioners of the peace, 1775. **216**
Proclamation May 24, 1792. **786**
Quebec herald, **p. 639-43**
Prospectus, 1789. **618**
Specimen, 1788. **566**
Quebec library. **408n; 799n**
Additions, 1790. **672**
Catalogue 1783, **406.**—1785, **466.**—1792, **799.**—1796, **1015**
Rules & laws, 1783. **407-408**
Quebec magazine, **p. 656-58**
Proposals, 1792. **800**
Quebec revenue act 1774, **188.**—1791, **706.**—1797, **1040-41**
Quebec, Séminaire de, *see* Séminaire de Québec
Quebec, Siege of. Non-combattants & deserters, 1776. **244**
Non-combattants quit town, 1775. **219**
Ode for 31 Dec. 1776. **233**
Strangers to register, 1775. **220**
Wounded rebels, 1776. **243**
Quebec (town). Directory 1790, **650.**—1791, **718**
Quebec Theatre. Playbills 1783, **409.**—1786, **499.**—1787, **540.**—1788, **567.**—1794, **908.**—1796, **1016**
Quebeck, to the publick, 1763-64. **56**

R

Raimbault, J. Thèses de math. 1796. **1012**
Rates of postage, n.d. **1203**
Ready reckoner, 1790., **681.**—1791, **742**
Recollect House meeting Montreal, Nov. 30, 1784. **415n; 434-35; 441n**
Recueil de cantiques 1795, **925.**—1796, **981.**—1800, **1163**
Reflexions sur le Canaiden gemissant, 1766. **100**
Reform committee, **417n; 453n**
Aux citoyens de Québec, 1785. **453**
Humble adresse, 1790. **653**
Lymburner: Paper, 1791. **709**
Lymburner: Papier, 1791. **710**
Petition, 1784. **434n**
Règles et articles pour mieux gouverner toutes les forces, 1796. **991**
Relation . . . conversion . . . Mr. Thayer, 1794. **912**
Religion, *see* Catholic church; Church of England; Church of Scotland; Devotional books; Dutch Reformed church; Methodist church; Sermons
Religious societies, *see* Confrérie de la bonne mort; Confrérie de la Sainte Famille

Remarks on . . . molbay disease, 1786. **484**
Remarques sur la maladie contagieuse, 1787. **517**
Ricketts, J. B. Circus, 1798. **1102**
Rind, W. A., *printer*, **p. xiii, p 668-9**
  Royal gazette, **p. 648**
Ritchie, D. Discourse on Fillis, 1792. **801**
Roads. L.C.: Abstract highways & bridges, 1796. **999-1000**
  L.C.: Extract road act, 1800. **1183**
    Ordres, 1799. **1129**
  Nova Scotia: Adv. to clear, 1764. **42**
  Quebec: Extract report, 1789. **612**
    Repair highways, 1766. **95-96**
    Winter roads cleared, 1776. **245**
  Taschereau : Repair highways & bridges, 1794. **911**
Robert. Thèses de mathématique, 1792. **797**
Robertson, A., *printer*, **p. 667**
  Royal Am. gazette, **p. 616**
Robertson, J. *Jr.*, *printer*, **p. 667**
  Port-Roseway gazetteer, **p. 614-15**
Robertson, James *Sr.*, *printer*, **p. 666-7; 619n**
  Royal Am. gazette, Shelburne, **p. 616**
  Roy. Am. gazette, Charlottetown, **p. 646-47**
Roch de St. Ours, Paul. **536n**
Rogers, R. **346n**
  Petition N.W. Passage, 1780. **346**
Rollins, Carl P. **60n**
Roy, J. J. **822n**
Roy, J.-M., *printer*, **p. 1044n**
  Montreal gazette, **p. 628-29**
Roy, L., *printer*, **p. 669; 988n; 1044n**
  Montreal gazette, **p. 628**
  Prospectus Montreal gazette, 1795. **951**
  Upper Canada gazette, **p. 650-51**
Royal American gazette, Charlottetown, **p. 646-47**
Royal American gazette, Shelburne, **p. 616-17**
Royal gazette, Charlottetown, **p. 648**
Royal gazette, Halifax, **p. 605-610**
Royal gazette, Halifax. Carrier's address, 1795. **963**
Royal gazette & N.B. advertiser, Saint John, **p. 595-97**
Royal Highland Emigrants, *see* 84th Regiment of Foot
Royal Order of Blue & Orange. List members, 1796. **1017**
Rules & articles for . . . militia, 1795. **937**
Rules . . . Quebec benevolent society 1793, **853.**—1794, **906.**—1796, **1013**
Russell, P. *Administrator of U.C.*
  Loyalists fee-free grants, 1798. **1105**
  Proc. Fees on land grants, 1798. **1104**
  Speech to parliament, 1797. **1070**
Ryan, J., *printer*, **p. 665; 520n**
  Royal gazette, **p. 596**
  Saint John gazette, **p. 597-99**

S

Sailors. Napier: Enlisting, 1775. **201**
  Quebec: Bill desertion, 1789. **610**
    Volunteers & press, 1779. **327-28**
Saint John, N.B. **467n**
  Auction of land, 1788. **568**
  Charter, 1785. **467**
  Laws: Anchorage money, 1792. **809**
    Fishery, 1793. **855**
    Infectious distempers, 1793. **856**
    Pilotage ballast fishery, 1797. **1068**
    Revised, 1796. **1020**
  Oliver: Dismission sheriff, 1791. **717**
Saint John gazette, **p. 597-99**
St. John, Island of (Prince Edward I.)
  Citizens: Paper money, 1792. **802**
    To H. E. Fanning, 1792. **803-805**
  Grand jury: Address Fanning, 1792. **806**
  House of Assembly: Address, 1790. **673**
    Journal 1788, **569.**—1790, **674-75.**—1792, **807.**—1795, **964.**—1796, **1018.**—1797, **1066**
    Lt. Gov. Fanning to As. 1790. **677-78**
  Laws. Acts rev. 1773-88, 1789. **619**
    Acts (sessions laws) 1790, **676.**—1791, **738.**—1792, **808.**—1795, **965.**—1796, **1019.**—1797, **1067**
  Proclamation import bread, 1789. **620**
    Militia corps, 1794. **910**
    Public fast May 10, 1794. **909**
St. John's River Society, **101n**
  Descrip. harbour, river & townships, 1768. **126B**
  Descrip. townships, 1783. **410**
  Tenor of grants, 1766. **101**
St. Lawrence River pilotage, 1790. **657.**—1794, **891**
Saint Luc de LaCorne, *see* LaCorne
St. Ours. Au public, défenses, 1784. **441**
Salaberry, I. de. Election circulars 1792. **779-80**
Sally (schooner). **789n**
Sanguinet, S. Testament, 1791. **737n**
Sans Bruit Farm. Toosey: Catalogue auction, 1792. **814**
Sarreau, F. Elégie, 1792. **810**
  Suite de l'elégie, 1792. **811**
Say, T. Particular account, 1796. **1021**
Scaliger, J., *see* Astronomical diary (Sower)
Scheme of constitution, 1791. **682n**
Schieffelin, J. Earthen & china ware, 1793. **857**
Schoolbred & Barclay, **866n**

Scott, J. **442n**
  Brief view of . . . Alline, 1784. **442**
Scott, T. C. H. **383n**
  Appointment clergyman Sorel, 1782. **383**
Seccombe, J. **155n**
  Sermon death Mrs. Green, 1778. **301**
  Sermon Ordination Comingoe, 1770. **155**
Sedition, *see also* Treason.
  L.C.: Proclamation 1793. **834**
Seeds. Wright's catalogue, 1767. **118**
Séminaire des missions étrangères.
  L'Homond: Elemens, 1799. **1127**
Séminaire de Québec, **151n**
  Exercise rhetorique, 1792. **796**
  List scholars, 1773. **183**
  Memorial on tenures, 1791. **719n**
  Monde demasqué, 1775. **214**
  Palmare, 1775. **215**
  Quod felix (palmare), 1770. **151**
  Thèses de mathématique, 1775, **196.**—1790, **651.**—1792, **797.**—1796, **1012**
Séminaire de St. Sulpice, *see also* Montgolfier, E.
  Reglement de la Confrerie, 1776. **230-31**
Sermons. Adresse aux canadiens, 1775. **194**
  Alline: Anti-traditionist, 1783. **386**
    Sermon 19 Feb. 1783. **387**
    Thanksgiving Liverpool, 1782. **365**
    To young men Liverpool, 1782. **364**
    Two mites, 1781. **348**
  Bisset: Brotherly unity, 1787. **508**
  Brown: Discourse, 1791. **698**
    Perils of the time, **1795**. **926**
    Seafaring life, 1793. **826**
  Byles: Victory, 1799. **1115**
  Cochran: Sermon Falmouth, 1793. **828**
  Delisle: Mort de Frobisher, 1787. **512**
  Doty: Address piety & vice, 1787. **513**
    Christ's Church Sorel, 1786. **478**
  Graham: Two sermons, 1799. **1125**
  Henry: Brotherly love, 1780. **337**
  Hubert: Conversion, 1796. **987**
  Inglis: Charge 1789, 1790. **641**
    Sermon Apr. 25, 1794. **877**
    Sermon Nov. 25, 1787. **516**
    Steadfastness, 1793. **832**
  King: Fast sermon, 1800. **1176**
  Mountain: Thanksgiving, 1799. **1135**
  Phelps: Death Mrs. Chipman, 1775. **212**
  Plessis: Discours, 1799. **1140**
  Ritchie: Discourse Fillis, 1792. **801**
  Seccombe: Death Mrs. Green, 1778. **301**
    Ordination Comingoe, 1770. **155**
  Spark: Oration Freemasons, 1787. **541**
    Thanksgiving, 1799. **1142**
  Stackhouse: Two sermons, 1793. **858**
  Stanser: Sermon to House Assembly, 1800. **1196**
  Tunstall: Before masons, 1798. **1103**
  Viets: Preached at Sissaboo, 1799. **1153**
    To freemasons, 1793. **865**
  Watson: Extrait, 1795. **972**
  Weeks: Freemasons, 1785. **471**
  Wesley: Death Fletcher, 1786. **500**
  Wood: Death Mrs. Belcher, 1771. **162**
Settlers, Act to encourage, 1791. **703**
Sewell, J. **812n**
  Abstract of proceeding, 1792. **812**
Sheet almanacs.
  Almanac de cabinet Québec (Brown) 1765, **57.**—1766, **58.**—1767, **102.**—1768, **120.**—1769, **121**
  Calendrier de cabinet Québec (Brown) 1770, **128.**—1771, **144.**—1772, **157.**—1773, **164.**—1774, **170.**—1775, **185.**—1776, **226.**—1777, **227.**—1778, **249.**—1779, **272.**—1780, **303.**—1781, **333.**—1782, **353.**—1783, **369.**—1784, **392.**—1785, **413.**—1786, **450.**—1787, **474.**—1788, **506.**—1789, **546.**—(continued by Neilson) 1790, **580.**—1791, **632.**—1792, **692.**—1793, **747.**—1794, **821.**—1795, **868.**—1796, **921.**—1797, **973.**—1798, **1032.**—1799, **1075.**—1800, **1109.**—1801, **1155**
  Calendrier Montréal (Edwards) 1798, **1031.**—1799, **1074**
  Calendrier Montréal (Mesplet) 1777, **228.**—1778, **250.**—1779, **271.**—1782, **354.**—1783, **370.**—1784, **393.**—1786, **451.**—1787, **475.**—1788, **507.**—1789, **545.**—1790, **581.**—1791, **633.**—1792, **693.**—1793, **746.**—1794, **820**
  Calendrier perpétuel (Mesplet) 1783, **391**
  Calendrier Québec (Nouvelle Imprimerie) 1795, **867.**—1796, **920.**—1797, **974.**—1799, **1076.**—1800, **1108.**—1801, **1154**
  English calender Quebec (Neilson) 1800, **1110**
  Indian almanack 1779-85, **273-79**
  Indian calendar 1769-72, **129-32.**—1773-78, **171-76.**—1799-86, **304-310**
  Indian calendar 1793, **822**
  Indian kalendar 1768, **122**
  Kalendrier à l'usage des sauvages 1766, **75**
  Moore's English sheet almanac 1789, **547.**—1790, **582.**—1791, **634**
  Perpetual chronological tables (Mesplet) 1785, **452**
Shelburne, N.S. **468n**; *see also* Friendly fire club
  Quarter sessions of the peace. Frauds selling flour, 1789. **602**
    Markets, 1785. **469**
    Negro dances & frolicks, 1785. **468**

Shipping. Gr. Britain. Act for increase, 1786. **482**
L.C.: Ordinances pilotage, 1794. **891**
Quebec: Embargo, 1775. **221-23**
Pilotage & port, 1790. **657**
Pilots & navigation, 1790. **661**
Saint John: Law anchorage money, 1792. **809**
Pilotage, ballast, 1797. **1068**
Shubenaccadie Canal. N.S. Bill, 1798. **1097**
Commission report, 1797. **1059-60**
Sills, J. Bastille septentrionale, 1791. **739**
Simcoe, *Lt.-Gov. of U.C.*, **p. 379** *footnote*
Proclamations: Continuing officers, 1792. **817**
Convocation parl. 1796. **1028**
Lands forfeit, 1796. **1025**
Land grant fees, 1796. **1027**
Loyalists' land tickets, 1795. **970**
Loyalists' oath, 1796. **1023**
Postpone legislature, 1793. **864**
Publication laws, 1792. **817**
Sale rum to Indians, 1794. **917-18**
Settle lands 1792, **815**; 1795 ed. **968**
Terres de la couronne 1792, **816**; 1795 3d. **969**
U.C. counties & representatives, 1792. **818-19**
Speech opening parl., 1796. **1024**
Speech proroguing parl. 1796. **1026**
Speech to legislature, 1793. **863**
Simonin, M. Almanac de cabinet 1765. **57**
Simons, T. G., *printer*. **p. 669**
Upper Canada gazette, **p. 650-52**
Sincere Catholick's companion 1778, **281**; 1800 ed. **1168**
Sketchley & Freeman, *see also* Auction sales.
Catalogue books, 1784. **443**
Catalogue books sale, 1782. **384**
Slavery. MacGregor: Letter, 1788. **557**
Smith, Wm. Election circular, 1792. **781**
Smith, Wm., *Chief Justice of Que.* Draught of act administration justice, 1787. **536**
Projet d'acte justice, 1787. **537**
Quebec: Report education, 1790. **669**
Smuggling. **424; 789n**
Societies, *see* Agricultural society in Canada; Agricultural society of New Brunswick; Amicable society; Canadian theatre; Confrerie de la bonne mort; Confrerie de la Sainte Famille; Constitutional club; Freemasons; Friendly fire club; Halifax marine society; North British society; Quebec benevolent society; Royal order of blue & orange; Society for promoting agriculture in Nova Scotia; *see also* Loyal association
Society for promoting agriculture in Nova Scotia. **740n**
Letters & papers, 1791. **740**
Society for the propagation of the gospel. **478n**
Solide dévotion . . . Ste. Famille, 1787. **510**
Solon, *pseud.* New constitution, 1792. **813**
Sorel. Doty: Sermon Christ's Church, 1786. **478**
Scott clergyman at, 1782. **383**
Sorel, N. Narrative facts, 1797. **1069**
Sower, C., *printer*. **p. 665-6; 520n**
Astronomical diary, 1786. **446n**
Brockville printing, **843n**
Fredericton printing, **790n**
last work of, **1096n**
on king's printer's duties, **559n**
Royal gazette, **p. 595**
Spark, A. Oration Freemason's Hall Hall, 1787. **541**
Quebec gazette, **p. 634**
Quebec magazine, **p. 656**
Sermon Jan. 10, 1799. **1142**
Spectateur tranquille, *pseud.* **p. 622**
Spruce beer. Directions, 1783. **400**
Spry, W. Remonstrance, 1783. **410**
Stackhouse, T. Two sermons, 1793. **858**
Stamp Act, 1766. **78**
Halifax gazette, **p. 600**
Quebec gazette, **p. 631**
Repeal, 1766. **93-94**
Stanser, R. **1196n**
Sermon St. Paul's Halifax, 1800. **1196**
Steadfastness in religion, 1793. **832**
Sterns, J., & W. Taylor. Impeachment of judges, 1788. **570**
Reply to judges Nova Scotia, 1789. **621**
Stewart, J. Trials Boutelier murder, 1791. **697**
Stewart, P. **1053n; 1078n**
Stirner, H. **p. 620**
Stuart, P. **1053n; 1078n**
Suite de l'elégie du naufrage, 1792. **811**
Sunday schools, **555n; 594n**
Suppressed publications. U.S. Resolution independence, 1776. **246**
Surveying. Vondenvelden: Proposals, 1785. **470**
Swords, T., & J. Port-Roseway gazetteer. **p. 614-15**

T

Table of net duties . . . & drawbacks, 1787. **518**
Tableau des rues et faubourgs Montreal, 1789. **598**
Tanswell, J. Courier de Québec, 1788. **551n; p. 620-21**
Grammar & syntax, 1791. **741**

Taschereau, G. E. **999n**
Ordres, 1799. **1129**
Repair highways & bridges, 1794. **911**
Taxes. N.S.: Militia 1775. **202**
N.S.: Poll tax, 1794. **904**
Quebec: Duties on wines, 1765. **69**
Taylor, T. For public information, 1790. **679**
Taylor, Wm. Impeachment of judges, 1788. **570**
Reply to judges Nova Scotia, 1789. **621**
Temporary acts . . . Nova Scotia 1767, **114.**—1783, **429.** *See also* Nova Scotia. Laws. Sessions laws temporary
Thayer, J. Relation de la conversion, 1794. **912**
Theatre, *see* Drama; Entertainment; Canadian theatre; Quebec theatre
Theophrastus, **575n**
Thèses de mathématique 1775, **196.**—1790, **651.**—1792, **797.**—1796, **1012**
Thomas, I. **p. 600**
Thoughts on education, 1795. **929**
Tiffany, G., *printer*, **p. 669; 934n**
Canada constellation, **p. 649-51**
on almanac, **979n**
on printing delay, **967n**
Upper Canada gazette, **p. 650-51**
Tiffany, S. Canada constellation, **p. 649-50**
Timber, Statutes on preservation of, 1784. **419**
Times, Quebec. **p. 643-46**
Carrier's address, 1795. **914**
Preparatory address, 1793. **859**
Specimen, 1794. **913**
To . . . electors . . . L. Canada, 1792. **778**
To . . . electors . . . Quebec, 1792. **776**
To . . . electors . . . York, 1800. **1197**
To . . . free electors . . . Quebec, 1800. **1178**
Tool, J., & R. Wallace. Dying speech, 1782. **385**
Toosey, P. **814n**
Catalogue books, 1799. **1143**
Catalogue furniture, 1792. **814**
Toronto, *see* York
Trade & commerce, *see also* Advertisement; Auction sales; Fur trade; Shipping
L.C.: Bill person failing in trade, 1795. **948**
Inland navigation, fees 1797. **1046-47**
Order 7 July 1796, **992-94;** 1800 ed. **1179**
N.B.: General acct. goods imported 1792, **792.**—1795, **955**
Quebec: Directory 1790, **650n.**—1791, **718**
Free import & export U.S., 1787. **529**
Grist mills, 1790. **666**
Pot & pearl ashes, 1791. **727, 731**
Vermont trade, 1790. **655, 658**
Traité abregé des ancienes loix, 1775. **198**
Traité de la loi des fiefs, 1775. **197**
Traité de la police, 1775. **199**
Translation . . . speech to . . . Oneida, 1779. **325**
Transportation, *see also* Roads; Shipping
Distances & post fares, 1799. **1133**
N.S.: Shubenaccadie canal bill, 1798. **1097**
Shubenaccadie com. report, 1797. **1059-60**
Quebec: Bill on post, 1789. **611**
Ferries, 1766. **86A-B**
Ferries, carters, 1780. **341**
Inland navigation 1789, **609.**—1791, **722; 728**
Maîtres de poste 1770, **153-54.**—1780, **344.**—1791, **725; 729**
Rates carriage wood, 1765. **68**
U.C.: Communication Ontario-Erie, 1799. **1148**
Treason, *see also* Sedition.
L.C.: Proclamation, 1796. **1003**
McLane: Procès, 1797. **1054**
Trial, 1797. **1055-56**
Treaties. Articles prélim. 1783. **399**
Capitulations & extracts. **1174**
Cessation of arms, 1783. **398**
Jay treaty 1795, **934-36.**—1796, **986**
Nova Scotia Indians, 1753. **9**
Très-humble adresse . . . au Roi, 1784. **435**
Trial of David M'Lane, 1797. **1055-56**
Trials . . . Boutelier . . . murder, 1791. **697**
Tunstall, J. M. **1103n**
Sermon before masons, 1798. **1103**
Two mites on . . . divinity, 1781. **348**
Two sermons . . . for Cape Breton, 1793. **858**

U

Union of taste & science, 1799. **1124**
U.S. Congress. Mesplet: Memorial 1783, **401.**—1784, **422**
Continental Congress. Resolution independence, 1776. **246**
University, Sanguinet bequest, 1792. **737n**
Upper Canada, *see also* Quebec for publications relating to this region before it was made a separate province in 1791
Elections, 1800. **1197**
Executive Council. Dereham & Norwich land sale, 1799. **1144, 1146**
Land boards & fees, 1794. **915-16**
Land boards & fees, 1795. **966**
Land claims, 1793. **860**
Land free of expence, 1799. **1147**
Pitchers, 1799. **1145**
Township grants, 1797. **1071**
Yonge St. settlers, 1798. **1106**
House of Assembly. Bill communication Ontario-Erie, 1799. **1148**
Laws. Acts 1793. **861-62**

Laws 1792-95, **967.**—1796, **1022.**—1797, **1072-73.**—1798, **1150, 1198.**—1799, **1151.**—1800, **1199**
Marriage act, 1799. **1149**
Quebec: Practice of law new districts 1789, **603, 606**
Quebec: Strengthen deeds Dist. Hesse, 1789. **605, 608**
Legislature. Speech of lt.-gov. & address of both houses 1793, **863.**—1796, **1024, 1026.**—1797, **1070**
Proclamations. Circular on session of parl., 1800. **1201**
Convocation of parl. 1796. **1028**
Counties & representatives, 1792. **818-19**
Fees on land grants, 1798. **1104**
Land grant fees, 1796. **1027**
Lands forfeit, 1796. **1025**
Loyalists' fee-free grants, 1798. **1105**
Loyalists' land tickets, 1795. **970**
Loyalists' oath, 1796. **1023**
Postpone legislature, 1793. **864**
Publication laws, 1792. **817**
Royal assent to bills, 1800. **1200**
Sale of rum to Indians, 1794. **917-18**
Settle lands of crown 1792, **815;** 1795 ed. **968**
Simcoe Lt.-Gov. 1792. **817**
Terres de la couronne 1792, **816;** 1795 ed. **969**
Surveyor-General. Notice to land claimants, 1796. **1029**
Upper Canada gazette, **p. 650-53**
Battle of Nile, 1799. **1152**
Ursulines. Catholic church: Formulaire de prières 1777, **258.**—1799, **1116**
Ursulines v. Lemaitre Duème, 1779. **311-12**

V

Vialar, A. Catalogue books, 1781. **363**
Viets, R. **571n; 865n**
Annapolis Royal, 1788. **571**
Sermon, 1793. **865**
Sermon at Sissaboo, 1799. **1153**
Vondenvelden, W., *printer*, **p. 664; 470n; 943n**
Proposals Can. surveyor, 1785. **470**
Times, **p. 643-44**
Vondenvelden, W., & L. Charland. Canadian topographer, 1798. **1107**
Voyageurs. Instructions, 1779. **321**

W

Waddell, J. Graham: Two sermons, 1799. **1125**
Walker, Thos. Quebec: Adv. assault, 1764. **43**
Quebec: Ordinance on investigation, 1767. **117**
Trial of Disney, 1767. **103**
Wall calendars, *see* Sheet almanacs
Wallace, R. Dying speech, 1782. **385**
Walter, J. Answer to Barclay, 1793. **866**
Catalogue books, 1795. **971**
Defence, 1790. **680**
Ward, *Mrs.* Scouring business, 1789. **622**
Waters, W., *printer*, **p. 669**
Upper Canada gazette, **p. 650-52**
Watson, R. Extrait d'un discours, 1795. **972**
Watson & Rashleigh v. DuCalvet 1778-79, **284-85; 295; 313**
Weekly chronicle Halifax, **p. 617-619**
Weeks, J. W. **471n**
Charges Freemasons, 1786. **480**
Sermon. Halifax freemasons, 1785. **471**
Welt u. Neuschottlaendische Correspondenz, **p. 619-20**
Wentworth, *Lt.-Gov. of N.S.*
Preservation H.M. timber, 1784. **419**
Proclamations: Contagious distempers, 1793. **852**
Deserters 1793, **851.**—1796, **1011**
Fast day Mar. 1, 1793, **850.**—Apr. 25, 1794, **905.**—May 1, 1797, **1064.**—Apr. 21, 1798, **1100**
Prayers for legislature, 1793. **848**
Privateers, 1793. **849**
Wesley, J. **348n**
Sermon on Fletcher, 1786. **500**
Short history Methodists, 1786. **501**
Wheat, *see also* Embargo
Agric. soc. Bled noir, 1792. **744**
Grain from smut, 1792. **745**
Dunière: Services facteur, 1792. **757**
Plessis: Circulaire, 1800. **1193**
Wilkes, John, Britannia's intercession for, 1769. **134**
Willcocks, *Miss*. Poem on, 1784. **444**
Williams, E. Ready reckoner 1790, **681.**—1791, **742**
Windsor Academy, Windsor, N.S. **516n; 572n; 594n**
Account of opening, 1788. **572**
Wood, T. Sermon death Mrs. Belcher, 1771. **162**
Woodcuts, *see* Illustrations
Woolsey, J., *mercantile agent*, Quebec, **107n**
Wright, J. Catalogue of seeds, 1767. **118**

Y

Yellow fever. Nova Scotia: Proclamation, 1793. **852**
Saint John: Ordinance, 1793. **856**
Yonge St., York. U.C.: Conditions of settlement, 1798. **1106**
York, U.C. **1072n**
U.C.: Yonge St. settlers, 1798. **1106**
Young, A. Exemple de France, 1794. **919**
Young freemason's assistant, 1765. **60**

Z

Zimmermann, E. A. W. Political survey, 1791. **743**